A Review of the Events of 1973

The 1974 World Book Year Book

The Annual Supplement to The World Book Encyclopedia

Field Enterprises Educational Corporation

Chicago   London   Paris   Rome   Stuttgart   Sydney   Tokyo   Toronto

Staff

Editorial Director
William H. Nault

Editorial Staff
Executive Editor
Wayne Wille

Managing Editor
Paul C. Tullier

Chief Copy Editor
Joseph P. Spohn

Senior Editors
Ed Nelson, Kathryn Sederberg,
Darlene R. Stille, Foster P.
Stockwell, Lillian Zahrt

Assistant Copy Editor
Helen Howell Dixon

Senior Index Editor
Pamela Williams

Editorial Assistants
Cynthia Hillman, Irene Laura

Executive Editor,
The World Book Encyclopedia
A. Richard Harmet

Art Staff
Executive Art Director
Gordon J. Kwiatkowski

Senior Art Director
Clifford L. Birklund

Art Director
for Year Book
Robert Schemmel

Senior Artist
Gumé Nuñez

Artists
Roberta Dimmer,
Norton Rock, Wilma Stevens

Cartographic Designer
Leon Bishop

Photography Director
Fred C. Eckhardt, Jr.

Assistant Photography Director
Ann Eriksen

Senior Photographs Editors
Marilyn Gartman,
John S. Marshall

Art Production Director
Barbara J. McDonald

Art Quality Control
Alfred J. Mozdzen

Research and Services
Director of Educational Services
John Sternig

Director of Editorial Services
Carl A. Tamminen

Head, Editorial Research
Jo Ann McDonald

Head, Cartographic Services
Joseph J. Stack

Cartographer
H. George Stoll

Cartographic Designer
Mary Jo Schrader

Cartographic Researcher
Amelia R. Gintautas

Manufacturing Staff
Executive Director
Philip B. Hall

Production Manager
Jerry R. Higdon

Manager, Research
and Development
Henry Koval

Manager, Pre-Press
John Babrick

Assistant Manager, Pre-Press
Marguerite DuMais

Year Book Board of Editors

Harrison Brown, Alistair Cooke, Lawrence A. Cremin, John Holmes, James Murray, Sylvia Porter, James Reston

World Book Advisory Board

Phillip Bacon, Professor and Chairman, Department of Geography, University of Houston; Jean Sutherland Boggs, Director, The National Gallery of Canada; George B. Brain, Dean, College of Education, Washington State University; Marcus A. Foster, Superintendent of Schools, Oakland, California; John H. Glenn, Jr., Adviser to the National Aeronautics and Space Administration; William E. McManus, Director of Catholic Education, Archdiocese of Chicago; Robert K. Merton, Giddings Professor of Sociology, Columbia University; A. Harry Passow, Jacob H. Schiff Professor of Education and Chairman, Department of Curriculum and Teaching, Teachers College, Columbia University; John Rowell, Director, School Libraries Programs, School of Library Science, Case Western Reserve University; William M. Smith, Dean of Social Sciences and Professor of Psychology, Dartmouth College.

Printed in the United States of America
ISBN 0-7166-0474-4
Library of Congress Catalog Card Number: 62-4818

Preface

With this edition of the YEAR BOOK, we introduce an authoritative new voice and a permanent new feature to our readers. Each will add a new dimension to our coverage of world events.

The voice is that of a new member of the Board of Editors—John Holmes, a noted scholar and statesman who is director-general of the Canadian Institute of International Affairs in Toronto. Mr. Holmes has served with several organizations dealing with international affairs

Presidents Grant and Nixon: a hundred years apart, but were the problems they faced all that different?

and, in addition, has held posts with Canada's diplomatic corps in Great Britain, Russia, and the United Nations. He has held his post with the institute since 1960. Through his wide-ranging expertise, as reflected in his Focus on The World essays, our readers will be presented with penetrating in-depth analyses of the international scene.

The new feature we are introducing is entitled "A Year in Perspective." You will find this new section between the Special Reports and the Year on File section. Unlike other sections of the book, Perspective will not look at the events of the year just past, but instead will look back 100 years. In so doing, it will attempt to bring the world of a hundred years ago a little closer to our times (the problems faced by President Richard M. Nixon during 1973 were not too different from those confronting President Ulysses S. Grant in 1873). Hopefully, Perspective will bring a certain reassurance that world events in our own troubled times are neither unparalleled in history nor hopelessly insolvable. Corruption in government, racial prejudice, and war were widespread in 1973. But so they were in 1873, too. And, as Perspective will show, the world survived.   WAYNE WILLE

Contents

A chronology of some of the most important events of 1973 appears on pages 8 through 14. A preview of 1974 is given on pages 607 and 608.

Contributors

Abrams, Edward, Ph.D.; Director of Technical Development, Chemetron Corporation. [CHEMICAL INDUSTRY]

Alexiou, Arthur G., M.S., E.E.; Program Director, Office of Sea Grant Programs. National Science Foundation. [OCEAN]

Anderson, Joseph P., M.S., LL.D.; Consultant, National Association of Social Workers. [POVERTY; Social Organizations]

Arnold, Rus; Photojournalism Editor, *Writer's Digest.* [PHOTOGRAPHY]

Augelli, John P., Ph.D.; Professor of Geography, University of Kansas. [Consultant, Mexico Trans-Vision®]

Banovetz, James M., Ph.D.; Professor of Political Science and Director, Center for Governmental Studies, Northern Illinois University. [CITY; City Articles; HOUSING]

Barabba, Vincent P., B.S., M.B.A.; Acting Director, Bureau of the Census. [CENSUS, U.S.]

Bautz, Laura P., Ph.D.; Assistant Professor of Astronomy, Northwestern University. [ASTRONOMY]

Bazell, Robert J., B.A., C. Phil.; News Writer, *New York Post.* [SCIENCE AND RESEARCH]

Beaumont, Lynn; Travel and Public Relations Consultant. [FAIRS AND EXPOSITIONS; TRAVEL]

Beckwith, David C., J.D.; Correspondent, *Time* Magazine. [COURTS AND LAWS; CRIME; PRISON; SUPREME COURT]

Benson, Barbara N., A.B., M.S.; Instructor, Biology, Cedar Crest College. [BOTANY; ZOOLOGY]

Berkwitt, George J., B.S.J.; Senior Editor, *Dun's Review* Magazine. [MANUFACTURING]

Bornstein, Leon, B.A., M.A.; Labor Economist, U.S. Dept. of Labor. [LABOR]

Boyum, Joy Gould, Ph.D.; Associate Professor of English, New York University. [MOTION PICTURES]

Bradley, Van Allen, B.J.; former Literary Editor,*Chicago Daily News.*[LITERATURE]

Bradsher, Henry S., A.B., B.J.; Correspondent, *Washington Star-News.* [KOREA, NORTH; KOREA, SOUTH; PHILIPPINES]

Brown, Kenneth; European Journalist. [EUROPE; Western Europe Articles]

Brown, Madison B., M.D.; Acting President, American Hospital Association. [HOSPITAL]

Bushinsky, Jay, B.A., M.S.Ed., M.S.J.; Correspondent, *Chicago Daily News.* [MIDDLE EAST (Close-Up)]

Cain, Charles C., III, B.A.; Automotive Writer, Associated Press. [AUTOMOBILE]

Carroll, Paul, M.A.; Professor of English, University of Illinois at Chicago Circle. [POETRY]

Collins, William G., B.S., M.A.; Research Meteorologist, National Meteorological Center. [WEATHER]

Commager, Henry Steele, Ph.D.; Professor of History, Amherst College; Lecturer; Author. [DEATHS OF NOTABLE PERSONS (Close-Up)]

Cook, Robert C.; former Population Consultant, National Parks Association. [POPULATION, WORLD]

Cromie, William J., B.S.; President, Universal Science News, Inc. [ASTRONAUTS; SPACE EXPLORATION]

Csida, June Bundy; former Radio-TV Editor, *Billboard* Magazine. [RADIO; TELEVISION]

Cuscaden, Rob; Author; Architecture Critic, *Chicago Sun-Times.* [ARCHITECTURE; ARCHITECTURE (Close-Up)]

Cviic, Chris, B.A., B.Sc.; Editorial Staff, *The Economist.* [Eastern Europe Articles]

Dale, Edwin L., Jr., B.A.; Reporter, *The New York Times,* Washington Bureau. [INTERNATIONAL TRADE AND FINANCE]

Davies, Richard P., B.S.; Medical Writer. [HEALTH AND DISEASE; MEDICINE; MENTAL HEALTH]

DeFrank, Thomas M., B.A., M.A.; Correspondent, *Newsweek.* [ARMED FORCES OF THE WORLD; NATIONAL DEFENSE]

Delaune, Lynn de Grummond, M.A.; Assistant Professor, College of William and Mary; Author. [LITERATURE FOR CHILDREN]

Derickson, Ralph Wayne; Public Information Associate, Council of State Governments. [STATE GOVERNMENT]

Dewald, William G., Ph.D.; Professor of Economics, Ohio State University. [Finance Articles]

Dixon, Gloria Ricks, B.A.; Director of Public Relations, Magazine Publishers Association. [MAGAZINE]

Donoghue, J. Larry, B.S., M.S.; President, Ralph H. Burke, Inc., Airport Consultants. [WORLD BOOK SUPPLEMENT: AIRPORT]

Eaton, William J., B.S.J., M.S.J.; Washington Correspondent, *Chicago Daily News.* [WATERGATE]

Evans, Earl A., Jr., Ph.D.; Professor and Chairman, Department of Biochemistry, University of Chicago. [BIOCHEMISTRY; BIOLOGY]

Farr, David M.L., D.Phil.; Professor of History, Carleton University, Ottawa. [CANADA; MICHENER, ROLAND; TRUDEAU, PIERRE ELLIOTT]

Farrell, Warren T., Ph.D.; Professor of Government, American University. [Special Report: GROWING UP MALE IN AMERICA]

Feather, Leonard; Author, *The Encyclopedia of Jazz in the Sixties.* [MUSIC, POPULAR; RECORDINGS]

Flynn, Betty, B.A.; UN Correspondent, *Chicago Daily News.* [UNITED NATIONS]

French, Charles E., Ph.D.; Head, Agricultural Economics Department, Purdue University. [AGRICULTURE]

Gayn, Mark, B.S.; Asia Bureau Chief, *The Toronto Star;* Author. [BANGLADESH; CHINA; INDIA; PAKISTAN]

Goldner, Nancy, B.A.; Critic, *Dance News* and *Christian Science Monitor.* [DANCING]

Goldstein, Jane, B.A.; U.S. Representative, International Racing Bureau. [HORSE RACING]

Goy, Robert W., Ph.D.; Director, Wisconsin Regional Primate Research Center. [PSYCHOLOGY]

Grasso, Thomas X., M.A.; Associate Professor and Chairman, Department of Geosciences, Monroe Community College. [GEOLOGY]

Graubart, Judah L., B.A.; Columnist, *Jewish Post and Opinion* (Chicago). [JEWS]

Griffin, Alice, Ph.D.; Professor of English, Lehman College, City University of New York. [THEATER; Special Report: THE THEATER IS ALIVE, WELL, AND LIVING ALL OVER]

Havighurst, Robert J., Ph.D.; Professor of Education and Human Development, University of Chicago. [OLD AGE]

Hayes, Helen; Actress; President, American National Theatre. [Special Report: THE THEATER IS ALIVE, WELL, AND LIVING ALL OVER]

Healey, Gerald B.; Midwest Editor, *Editor & Publisher* Magazine. [NEWSPAPERS]

Heath, Jacquelyn; Northwestern University. [Biographies; CELEBRATIONS]

Hechinger, Fred M., B.A.; member, Editorial Board, *The New York Times.* [EDUCATION]

Hernández, Deluvina, B.A., M.S.; Research Assistant, Department of Sociology, University of California, Los Angeles. [WORLD BOOK SUPPLEMENT: MEXICAN AMERICANS]

Howe, Gordie; Right Wing, Houston Aeros; former Right Wing, Detroit Red Wings. [WORLD BOOK SUPPLEMENT: HOCKEY]

Jacobi, Peter P., B.S.J., M.S.J.; Professor and Associate Dean, Medill School of Journalism, Northwestern University. [MUSIC, CLASSICAL]

Jessup, Mary E., B.A.; former News Editor, *Civil Engineering* Magazine. [DRUGS; Engineering Articles; PETROLEUM AND GAS]

Joseph, Lou, B.A.; Assistant Director, Bureau of Public Information, American Dental Association. [DENTISTRY]

Kind, Joshua B., Ph.D.; Associate Professor of Art History, Northern Illinois University; Author; *Rouault*; Midwest Correspondent, *Art News*. [VISUAL ARTS]

Kingman, Merle, B.A.; Senior Editor, *Advertising Age*. [ADVERTISING]

Koenig, Louis W., Ph.D., L.H.D.; Professor of Government, New York University; Author: *The Life and Times of William Jennings Bryan*. [CIVIL RIGHTS]

Lach, Alma, Diplome de Cordon Bleu; Author, *Cooking à la Cordon Bleu; Hows and Whys of French Cooking*. [FOOD]

Levy, Emanuel, B.A.; Editor, *Insurance Advocate*. [INSURANCE]

Lewis, Ralph H., M.A.; Chief, Branch of Museum Operations, National Park Service. [MUSEUMS]

Litsky, Frank, B.S.; Assistant Sports Editor, *The New York Times*. [Sports Articles]

Livingston, Kathryn Zahony, B.A.; Feature Editor, *Town and Country*. [FASHION]

Maki, John M., Ph.D.; Professor of Political Science Dept., University of Massachusetts. [JAPAN]

Malia, Thomas M., Ph.B.; Executive Editor, *Telecommunications Reports*. [COMMUNICATIONS; TELEPHONE]

Marty, Martin E., Ph.D.; Professor, University of Chicago. [PROTESTANT; RELIGION]

Maxon, John, M.A., Ph.D.; Director of Fine Arts, The Art Institute of Chicago. [VISUAL ARTS (Close-Up)]

McGaffin, William, B.A., B.Sc.; Washington Correspondent, *Chicago Daily News*. [Political and Government Articles]

Mickelson, Sig, B.A., M.A.; Professor of Journalism, Northwestern University. [WORLD BOOK SUPPLEMENT: TELEVISION]

Miller, J. D. B., M.Ec.; Professor of International Relations, Research School of Pacific Studies, Australian National University. [AUSTRALIA]

Morton, Elizabeth H., LL.D.; former Editor in Chief, Canadian Library Association. [CANADIAN LIBRARY ASSOCIATION; CANADIAN LITERATURE]

Mullen, Frances A., Ph.D.; Consultant on Education of the Handicapped. [CHILD WELFARE]

Nelson, Larry L., Ph.D.; Executive Vice-President, Snyder Associates, Inc. [AGRICULTURE]

Newman, Andrew L., M.A.; Deputy Director of Information, U.S. Department of the Interior. [CONSERVATION; ENVIRONMENT; FISHING; FOREST AND FOREST PRODUCTS; HUNTING; INDIAN, AMERICAN]

O'Connor, James J., E.E.; Editor in Chief, *Power* Magazine. [ENERGY; Special Report: HOW CAN WE SOLVE THE ENERGY CRISIS?]

Offenheiser, Marilyn J., B.S.; Editor, *Electronics* Magazine. [ELECTRONICS]

O'Leary, Theodore M., B.A.; Special Correspondent, *Sports Illustrated* Magazine. [BRIDGE, CONTRACT; CHESS; COIN COLLECTING; GAMES, MODELS, AND TOYS; HOBBIES; PET; STAMP COLLECTING]

Plog, Fred, Ph.D.; Associate Professor of Anthropology, State University of New York, Binghamton. [ANTHROPOLOGY; ARCHAEOLOGY]

Quirk, Robert E., Ph.D.; Professor of History, University of Indiana. [Consultant, Mexico Trans-Vision®; Special Report: MEXICO: THE SURGING SPIRIT OF NATIONALISM]

Rabb, George B., Ph.D.; Associate Director, Research and Education, Chicago Zoological Park. [ZOOS AND AQUARIUMS]

Reedy, George E.; Dean, College of Journalism, Marquette University. [Special Report: THE RISE AND FALTER OF THE FREE PRESS]

Remsberg, Bonnie, B.S.; Free-Lance Writer. [Special Report: BLUE-COLLAR BLUES, WHITE-COLLAR WOES]

Remsberg, Charles, M.S.J.; Free-Lance Writer. [Special Report: BLUE-COLLAR BLUES, WHITE-COLLAR WOES]

Roberts, John Storm, M.A.; Editor in Chief, *Africa Report*. [Africa Articles]

Rogers, Morris E., B.S.; former Chicago Area Editor, *Drovers Journal*. [INTERNATIONAL LIVE STOCK EXPOSITION]

Rowen, Joseph R., A.B.; Vice-President, National Retail Merchants Association. [RETAILING]

Rowse, Arthur E., I.A., M.B.A.; President, Consumer News, Inc. [CONSUMER AFFAIRS]

Schaefle, Kenneth E., M.B.A.; President, The Communication Center, Inc. [AVIATION; RAILROAD; SHIPS AND SHIPPING; TRANSIT; TRANSPORTATION; TRUCK AND TRUCKING]

Schmemann, The Reverend Alexander, S.T.D., D.D., LL.D., Th.D.; Dean, St. Vladimir's Orthodox Theological Seminary, New York. [EASTERN ORTHODOX CHURCHES]

Schubert, Helen C., B.S.; Home Furnishings Writer. [INTERIOR DESIGN]

Scott, George, B.A.; Author; Journalist; Broadcaster; Staff Member, *The Economist*. [CYPRUS; GREAT BRITAIN; IRELAND; NORTHERN IRELAND]

Shaw, Robert J., B.S.B.A.; former Editor, *Library Technology Reports*, American Library Association. [LIBRARY]

Shearer, Warren W., Ph.D.; former Chairman, Department of Economics, Wabash College. [ECONOMICS]

Sheerin, John B., C.S.P., A.B., M.A., LL.D., J.D.; Editor Emeritus, *New Catholic World*. [ROMAN CATHOLIC CHURCH]

Snider, Arthur J.; Medical Writer, *Chicago Daily News*. [Special Report: THE FITNESS CRAZE]

Soper, Mary Webster, B.A.; Editor, *Noticias* Magazine. [LATIN AMERICA; Latin America Articles]

Spencer, William, Ph.D.; Professor of History, Florida State University; Author, *Land and People of Algeria*. [MIDDLE EAST; Middle East Articles; North Africa Articles]

Stalker, John N., Ph.D.; Professor of History, University of Hawaii. [ASIA; Asia Articles]

Steffek, Edwin F., B.S.; Editor, *Horticulture* Magazine. [GARDENING]

Swanson, Curtis E., B.A.; Manager, Public Relations, American Library Association. [AMERICAN LIBRARY ASSOCIATION]

Thompson, Carol L., M.A.; Editor, *Current History* Magazine. [U.S. Government Articles]

Tofany, Vincent L., President, National Safety Council. [SAFETY]

von Smolinski, Alfred W., Ph.D.; Assistant Professor of Chemistry, University of Illinois at the Medical Center. [CHEMISTRY]

White, Thomas O., Ph.D.; Physicist, Oxford University, Oxford, England. [PHYSICS]

Zettl, Herbert, Ph.D.; Professor of Broadcast Communication Arts, California State University, San Francisco. [WORLD BOOK SUPPLEMENT: TELEVISION]

Contributors not listed on these pages are members of the WORLD BOOK YEAR BOOK editorial staff.

Chronology 1973

January

Sun	Mon	Tue	Wed	Thu	Fri	Sat
	1	2	3	4	5	6
7	8	9	10	11	12	13
14	15	16	17	18	19	20
21	22	23	24	25	26	27
28	29	30	31			

1   **Denmark, Great Britain, and Ireland** formally join the European Community (Common Market).

2   **Rafael Hernández Colón** is sworn in as Puerto Rico's fourth elected governor.

3   **The Congress of the United States** reconvenes for its 93rd session.

6   **At a joint session of Congress,** President Richard M. Nixon is officially declared winner of the 1972 presidential election by a 520-17 electoral vote.

7   **President Ferdinand E. Marcos** returns the Philippines to martial law, renews restrictions on free speech, and postpones a constitutional referendum scheduled for January 15.

8   **Secret peace talks on Indochina** are resumed by Henry A. Kissinger of the United States and Le Duc Tho of North Vietnam.

11   **President Nixon terminates** mandatory wage and price controls except for food, health care, and construction.

     The trial of seven defendants involved in the June, 1972, break-in and alleged bugging of Democratic Party national headquarters at the Watergate complex in Washington, D.C., begins; Judge John J. Sirica of the U.S. District Court in Washington is the presiding judge.

15   **President Nixon cites progress** in peace talks, and orders a halt to all U.S. offensive action against North Vietnam.

     An unprecedented meeting between Pope Paul VI and Israeli Prime Minister Golda Meir is held in Rome; discussions include peace efforts in the Middle East and the status of Jerusalem.

17   **President Marcos assumes** indefinite rule of the Philippines under a new Constitution whose ratification he proclaims.

18   **Finland's parliament** approves a law prolonging President Urho Kekkonen's current term, due to expire March 1, 1974, for four more years, without a new election.

20   **President Nixon is inaugurated** for his second four-year term in office.

22   **Lyndon B. Johnson,** 36th President of the United States, dies after being stricken by a heart attack at his ranch in Johnson City, Tex.

27   **A cease-fire accord** ending the Vietnam conflict is signed in Paris; agreement calls for withdrawal of U.S. troops from South Vietnam, release of U.S. prisoners held in North Vietnam, and a four-nation commission to supervise the truce.

Jan. 20

Jan. 27

Feb. 27

February

Sun	Mon	Tue	Wed	Thu	Fri	Sat
				1	2	3
4	5	6	7	8	9	10
11	12	13	14	15	16	17
18	19	20	21	22	23	24
25	26	27	28			

2   **President Nixon sends** Congress his State of the Union message; he breaks precedent by announcing it is only the first part of a segmented series of messages to be sent to the Congress during the first weeks of 1973.

5   **Japan and China** agree to re-establish diplomatic relations and exchange ambassadors for the first time in 35 years.

7   **The U.S. Senate,** by a 70-0 vote, adopts a resolution establishing a seven-member select committee to probe the Watergate bugging case and other purported acts of political sabotage in the 1972 presidential election campaign.

9-11   **The first convention** of the National Women's Political Caucus is held in Houston.

11   **The all-male electorate** of Liechtenstein, by a 2,128 to 1,675 vote, rejects a proposal giving women the right to vote; Liechtenstein is the only European nation to deny the franchise to women.

     The Inter-American Judicial Committee of the Organization of American States, meeting in Brazil, endorses several Latin American countries' decision to extend their territorial waters.

12-13   **The first 116** of the 456 U.S. military men held prisoner in North Vietnam are released in Hanoi.

21   **Prime Minister Souvanna Phouma** and the Communist Pathet Lao sign an agreement aimed at ending the 20-year war in Laos.

24   **The distribution in Uganda** of businesses formerly owned by noncitizen Asians is declared completed.

25 **Albert Bernard Bongo,** the only presidential candidate, wins Gabon's national elections.

27 **About 200 armed supporters** of the American Indian Movement seize the hamlet of Wounded Knee on the Oglala Sioux Reservation in South Dakota and resist efforts to evict them.
Governor General Sir Paul Hasluck opens the 28th Australian Parliament.
South Korea's governing Democratic Republican Party wins 73 of 146 National Assembly seats in a legislative election; the government is assured of a majority in the 219-member body.

28 **The Fianna Fáil Party,** which has ruled Ireland for 16 years, is defeated by a coalition of the Fine Gael and Labour parties in general elections.
President Mathieu Kerekou of Dahomey announces a military coup d'état has been foiled.

March

Sun	Mon	Tue	Wed	Thu	Fri	Sat
				1	2	3
4	5	6	7	8	9	10
11	12	13	14	15	16	17
18	19	20	21	22	23	24
25	26	27	28	29	30	31

2 **Representatives of 80 countries** meet in Washington, D.C., and agree to a treaty banning commercial trade in 375 species of endangered wildlife.

5 **Thirty-two new Roman Catholic** cardinals are installed in Vatican ceremonies; one, Luis Aponte Martinez, archbishop of San Juan, is the first Puerto Rican cardinal.

7 **Prime Minister Sheik** Mujibur Rahman's ruling Awami League wins 292 of the 300 National Assembly seats in the first parliamentary elections held in Bangladesh.

8 **Northern Ireland Protestants** vote overwhelmingly to remain part of the United Kingdom rather than join the Irish Republic; the referendum was boycotted by Roman Catholics.
The Paraguayan Congress, in special session, confirms President Alfredo Stroessner's re-election to a fifth five-year term.

11 **Ex-President Juan Perón's** Justicialista Liberation Front sweeps the first round of national elections in Argentina; Perón's candidate, Hector J. Cámpora, wins 49 per cent of the vote.

12 **The U.S.-Russian strategic arms** limitation talks, in recess since December, 1972, resume in Geneva, Switzerland.

13 **Syrian voters,** in a two-day referendum, approve their first permanent Constitution since 1961.

21 **Australia adopts** legislation permitting all 18-year-olds and British subjects to vote in federal elections and to run for office.

22 **Washington becomes** the 30th state to ratify the Equal Rights Amendment.
General Suharto of Indonesia is re-elected unopposed to a second five-year term as president.
Ludvik Svoboda is re-elected to a second five-year term as president of Czechoslovakia.

24 **President Anwar al-Sadat** of Egypt assumes the prime ministership following the forced resignation of Aziz Sidky from that position.

26 **Greek students end** an eight-week strike and return to classes at the University of Athens.

28 **South Vietnam's President** Nguyen Van Thieu

Mar. 8

Apr. 7

formally inaugurates his Democratic Party at its first national convention in Saigon; it is one of three that met the requirements of a new regulation restricting the number of parties.

30 **Hector J. Cámpora** is declared president-elect of Argentina for a four-year term.

April

Sun	Mon	Tue	Wed	Thu	Fri	Sat
1	2	3	4	5	6	7
8	9	10	11	12	13	14
15	16	17	18	19	20	21
22	23	24	25	26	27	28
29	30					

2-3 **President Nixon confers** with South Vietnamese President Nguyen Van Thieu in Washington, D.C., to discuss the continuance of U.S. economic assistance to South Vietnam after hostilities end.

5 **The nomination** of L. Patrick Gray III to the directorship of the Federal Bureau of Investigation is withdrawn by President Nixon.

May 17

June 1

June 22

May

Sun	Mon	Tue	Wed	Thu	Fri	Sat
		1	2	3	4	5
6	7	8	9	10	11	12
13	14	15	16	17	18	19
20	21	22	23	24	25	26
27	28	29	30	31		

26   **Ahmad al-Lawzi,** prime minister of Jordan since 1971, resigns his post; King Hussein I replaces him with Zayd Rifai, the monarch's closest friend.

29   **Thomas Bradley,** defeating incumbent Sam Yorty, is elected mayor of Los Angeles and becomes the city's first black mayor.

June

Sun	Mon	Tue	Wed	Thu	Fri	Sat
					1	2
3	4	5	6	7	8	9
10	11	12	13	14	15	16
17	18	19	20	21	22	23
24	25	26	27	28	29	30

1   **British Honduras,** a British colony, is officially renamed Belize following approval by the territory's House of Representatives in March, 1973.
The Greek Council of Ministers, by decree, deposes King Constantine II and proclaims a "presidential parliamentary republic"; Prime Minister George Papadopoulos is named provisional president.

6   **The Swedish Riksdag** (parliament) approves a new Constitution that would abolish most of the monarch's residual powers.

8   **General Francisco Franco** relinquishes his post as president of the Cabinet (premier) to his closest aide, Admiral Luis Carrero Blanco.

13   **A new Vietnam accord** aimed at strengthening the Jan. 27, 1973, cease-fire agreement in South Vietnam is signed in Paris by representatives of the signers of the original pact.

15   **A protocol is signed** by the French government and Ahmed Abdullah, president of the executive council of the Comoro Islands, a French territory off the southeast coast of Africa, instituting a Comoro independence plan.

16   **Russia's Communist Party** General Secretary Leonid I. Brezhnev arrives in Washington, D.C., for summit talks with President Nixon.

18   **Brazilian President** Emílio G. Médici announces he will be succeeded by retired General Ernesto Geisel; the succession is subject to ratification on Jan. 15, 1974, by an electoral college including 66 senators, 310 deputies, and 126 state assemblymen.

20   **A nationwide strike** in Chile involving thousands of professionals, teachers, and students erupts in five major provinces; strikers march in support of the 63-day stoppage of El Teniente copper mine and to protest the government's labor policies.

22   **Three U.S. astronauts** return safely to earth at 9:50 A.M., E.D.S.T., after having spent 28 days living, working, and performing scientific experiments aboard *Skylab 1.*
President Nixon and Russian Communist Party General Secretary Leonid I. Brezhnev sign an agreement designed to avert a nuclear war between the two superpowers or between one of them and any other country.

25-26   **Heavy fighting erupts** around Phnom Penh, capital of Khmer, with U.S. forces providing heavy air support to Khmer's forces fighting off Communist rebel attacks.

27   **Uruguay's President** Juan María Bordaberry Arocena yields to pressure from the armed forces and dissolves Congress, ending 40 years of Uruguayan constitutional rule.

29   **Troops loyal** to President Salvador Allende Gossens crush the first bid to overthrow an elected Chilean government in 42 years.

July

Sun	Mon	Tue	Wed	Thu	Fri	Sat
1	2	3	4	5	6	7
8	9	10	11	12	13	14
15	16	17	18	19	20	21
22	23	24	25	26	27	28
29	30	31				

1   **Mexico's ruling** Revolutionary Institutional Party wins an overwhelming majority in elections held for 194 federal deputies, 7 state governors, and 87 mayors.
Iraq announces it has thwarted a plot to overthrow President Ahmad Hasan al-Bakr.

2   **Striking workers** at the El Teniente mine in Chile agree to end a 75-day walkout that cost the nation an estimated $70 million.

3   **The 35-nation Conference** on Security and Cooperation in Europe opens in Helsinki, Finland; discussions on the agenda include security and economic affairs.

5   **Rwandan President** Grégoire Kayibanda is overthrown in a bloodless coup led by Defense Minister Juvenal Habyarimana.
Queen Elizabeth II and Prince Philip end an 11-day tour of Canada during which they visited more than 20 towns and cities in Ontario, Prince Edward Island, Saskatchewan, and Alberta.

July 10

July 30

8   **Italy's President** Giovanni Leone swears in a new center-left Cabinet headed by Mariano Rumor; the new government becomes Italy's 35th since World War II.

10   **Three centuries** of British colonial rule end as the Bahamas becomes an independent nation and the 33rd member of the British Commonwealth.

13   **Argentina's President** Hector J. Cámpora resigns to enable Juan Perón to regain the presidency through new elections.

17   **King Mohammed Zahir Shah** of Afghanistan is deposed in a coup d'état led by Lieutenant General Mohammad Daud.

21   **France defies** an interim injunction by the International Court of Justice at The Hague and conducts the first nuclear test of its current series in the South Pacific.

24-26   **Premiers of Canada's** four western provinces meet with Prime Minister Pierre Elliott Trudeau in Calgary at a Western Economic Opportunities Conference to discuss western Canada's needs in agriculture, minerals, and finance.

27-28   **In a nationwide plebiscite,** Philippine voters overwhelmingly approve a proposition permitting President Ferdinand E. Marcos to remain in office beyond the expiration of his current term on Dec. 31, 1973.

28   *Skylab 2* crew of three U.S. astronauts takes off at 7:11 A.M., E.D.S.T. from Cape Kennedy, Fla., bound for the U.S. orbiting laboratory; they enter the *Skylab* on the same day.

30   **President Nixon** meets with Australian Prime Minister Edward Gough Whitlam in Washington, D.C.

Aug. 15

Sept. 11

August

Sun	Mon	Tue	Wed	Thu	Fri	Sat
			1	2	3	4
5	6	7	8	9	10	11
12	13	14	15	16	17	18
19	20	21	22	23	24	25
26	27	28	29	30	31	

2-10   **Leaders of 32 Commonwealth** nations meet in Ottawa, Canada, to discuss topics of mutual concern, including nuclear testing and the effects of Britain's entry into the Common Market on their economies.

3   **Public transportation** in Santiago, Chile, is suspended when 60,000 bus, truck, taxi, and jitney owners join private truckers in a crippling strike.

5   **The 10th World Youth Festival** held in East Berlin over an 11-day period ends; about 20,000 delegates, mostly from European Communist countries, and 50,000 East Germans attended.

6   **Vice-President Spiro T. Agnew** acknowledges he is being investigated for possible law violation.

9   **The Soviet Union launches** *Mars 7* from Baikonur; it is the latest of four unmanned space probes launched by the Russians in 1973 to obtain "fuller data about the planet Mars and the dynamics of physical processes which occur in space."

14   **Under a new Pakistani** Constitution that comes into force, Zulfikar Ali Bhutto resigns his presidency and becomes prime minister; Chaudhry Fazal Elahi succeeds Bhutto as president.

15   **U.S. combat involvement** in Indochina officially ends as U.S. planes halt all bombing in Khmer.

19   **George Papadopoulos,** head of the Greek regime, is sworn in as the country's first president; he will serve an eight-year term.

20   **Loyal Laotian troops** crush an attempt to overthrow Prime Minister Souvanna Phouma. A "possible conspiracy" to assassinate President Nixon during a visit to New Orleans is reported by the U.S. Secret Service.

27   **Canadian Prime Minister** Pierre Elliott Trudeau recalls Parliament for a special session to legislate an end to a national railroad strike that began August 24 and that involves about 100,000 rail workers.

28   **India and Pakistan** sign an agreement in New Delhi providing for the release of 790,000 Pakistani prisoners of war held by India.

29   **Egypt and Libya** announce they will merge as a "unified state" but no specific date is given.

September

Sun	Mon	Tue	Wed	Thu	Fri	Sat
						1
2	3	4	5	6	7	8
9	10	11	12	13	14	15
16	17	18	19	20	21	22
23	24	25	26	27	28	29
30						

1   **Libya announces** nationalization of 51 per cent of all foreign-owned operations in the country.

2   **Canadian railroads resume** operations

after an act of Parliament approves the previous day's orders to 56,000 nonoperating employees to end their nine-day strike.

6   **Switzerland announces** the creation of a commission to revise the nation's 125-year-old Constitution.

11   **The Chilean armed forces** and national police overthrow the Popular Front government of President Salvador Allende Gossens; the ousted president reportedly commits suicide.

12-15   **Riots in India** protesting food shortages and price rises break out in three regions: Mysore, Manipur, and Maddur.

13   **The military junta** that deposed Chile's President Salvador Allende Gossens swears in a new Cabinet.

14   **Laotian government representatives** and members of the Pathet Lao, whose forces have been engaged in a 20-year civil war, sign an accord providing for a coalition regime.

18   **The Bahamas is admitted** to the United Nations at the convening of the 28th General Assembly; also admitted are East and West Germany.

19   **Crown Prince Carl Gustaf** of Sweden is formally installed as King Carl XVI Gustaf.

23   **Ex-President Juan D. Perón** and his wife, Maria Estela (Isabel) Martinez Perón, are elected president and vice-president, respectively, of Argentina.

24   **The U.S. Senate Select Committee** on Presidential Campaign Activities, chaired by Senator Sam J. Ervin, Jr. (D., N.C.) begins the second phase of its probe.

25   **Three U.S. astronauts,** sent into orbit on July 28, return to earth from *Skylab 2;* their 59-day 11-hour 9-minute mission constitutes the longest manned space flight to date.

28   **Vice-President Spiro T. Agnew** files suit in federal district court in Baltimore, Md., in an attempt to halt the grand jury investigation of possible criminal violations by him.

Oct. 2   Oct. 10

Oct. 6

October

Sun	Mon	Tue	Wed	Thu	Fri	Sat
		1	2	3	4	5	6
7	8	9	10	11	12	13
14	15	16	17	18	19	20
21	22	23	24	25	26	27
28	29	30	31			

2   **President Nixon orders** mandatory allocation of propane and distillate fuel supplies as part of a plan to avert an energy crisis in the United States.

5   **Northern Ireland's** Protestant and Roman Catholic leaders meet for the first time in two years to seek a viable government in the strife-torn country.

6   **War erupts** in Middle East as Egyptian forces cross the Suez Canal and engage Israeli troops in combat; Syria simultaneously launches an attack on the Golan Heights.

10   **Spiro T. Agnew,** Vice-President of the United States, resigns, pleading "no contest" to one count of income tax evasion.

12   **President Nixon names** Congressman Gerald R. Ford (R., Mich.), Republican leader of the House of Representatives, as his choice to become Vice-President.

14   **Demonstrating students** in Thailand, demanding return to constitutional rule, topple regime of Thai Prime Minister Thanom Kittikachorn; Sanya Thammasak is named as his successor.

16   **Norway's new minority** Labor government, headed by Trygve M. Bratteli, is sworn into office.

20   **President Nixon orders** special Watergate prosecutor Archibald Cox discharged; Attorney General Elliot L. Richardson resigns; Solicitor General Robert H. Bork is named acting attorney general.

21   **An embargo** by Arab oil-producing states on all petroleum exports bound for the United States becomes total when Kuwait, Bahrain, Qatar, and Dubai announce they have cut off shipments of their supplies.

25   **U.S. military forces** at key bases in the United States and abroad are placed on "precautionary alert"; the move follows developments in the Middle East.

27   **First contingent** of a 7,000-man United Nations peacekeeping force that will act as a buffer between Israeli and Egyptian forces in the Sinai arrives in Egypt.

31   **The United States ends** its worldwide military alert.

November

Sun	Mon	Tue	Wed	Thu	Fri	Sat
				1	2	3
4	5	6	7	8	9	10
11	12	13	14	15	16	17
18	19	20	21	22	23	24
25	26	27	28	29	30	

1   **President Nixon announces** he will appoint Senator William B. Saxbe (R., Ohio) to succeed Elliot L. Richardson as attorney general of the United States.

2   **Delegates from 71 countries** meeting in London approve an international convention to curb pollution by ships.

3   **U.S. launches** 1,100-lb. scientific probe *Mariner 10* from Cape Canaveral on a journey pointed toward planet Mercury.

12   **Egypt and Israel sign** a cease-fire accord, bringing Middle East war to a halt.

Nov. 12

Nov. 14

Dec. 6

13   **The Icelandic Parliament** approves an interim agreement with Great Britain ending territorial fishing dispute between the two nations.

14   **Princess Anne,** fourth in line of succession to the British throne, is married in Westminster Abbey to Captain Mark Phillips, a commoner.

16   *Skylab 3*'s three-man crew is launched from Cape Canaveral for rendezvous with the U.S. orbiting *Skylab* space laboratory; it marks 1,900th launching of U.S. spacecraft from the Florida launching center.

21   **Northern Ireland** political leaders reach a compromise and agree to the creation of an 11-member executive body that will share power between Protestants and Roman Catholic communities in Ulster.

25   **President George Papadopoulos** of Greece is ousted in a military coup d'état; he is replaced by Lieutenant General Phaidon Gizikis, a leader of the coup.

December

Sun	Mon	Tue	Wed	Thu	Fri	Sat
						1
2	3	4	5	6	7	8
9	10	11	12	13	14	15
16	17	18	19	20	21	22
23	24	25	26	27	28	29
30	31					

5   **Prime Minister Anker Jørgensen** submits his resignation to Denmark's Queen Margrethe II after suffering major setback in the parliamentary elections held the preceding day.

6   **Gerald R. Ford,** minority leader of the House since 1965, is sworn in as the 40th Vice-President of the United States.
President Kenneth D. Kaunda, the only candidate, is re-elected for a third term in Zambia's first presidential and general elections since becoming a one-party state.

9   **Protestant and Roman Catholic** leaders of Northern Ireland, meeting in London, agree to form the first Protestant-Catholic coalition in Northern Ireland's history.

10   **Nobel prizes** for 1973 are awarded in Stockholm, Sweden, and Oslo, Norway.

14   **Common Market** heads of state assemble in Copenhagen to talk over U.S. Secretary of State Henry Kissinger's proposal for North American, European, and Japanese cooperation to solve the growing energy shortage.

16   **Thailand's King** Phumiphon Aduldet dissolves the 299-seat National Assembly; preparations begin for the convening of a national governmental convention to choose another assembly and to ratify a new Constitution.

18   **Syria announces** it will not attend the Middle East peace conference scheduled to open in Geneva within a few days.

20   **President Luis Carrero Blanco,** who was governing Spain in the name of aging chief of state Francisco Franco, is assassinated in Madrid.

22   **The first session** of the 93rd Congress adjourns.

26   **Two U.S. astronauts,** commander Gerald Carr and pilot William Pogue, aboard *Skylab 3,* walk in space for a record 7 hours and photograph comet Kohoutek.
Russia's manned spacecraft, *Soyuz 13,* returns to earth after an 8-day, 128-orbit mission.
President Lon Nol names Foreign Minister Long Boret as the new prime minister of Khmer.

Section One

The Year
In Focus

THE YEAR BOOK Board of Editors analyzes some significant developments of 1973 and considers their impact on contemporary affairs. The Related Articles list following each report directs the reader to THE YEAR BOOK's additional coverage of related subjects.

Focus on The World

John Holmes

While 1973 was not a year of peace, it was, on the whole, a good year for détente—even though it ended in panicky fear of a whole new breed of tensions

It was the year of détente—or rather of the testing of détente. The 1973 Nobel Peace Prize honored the contribution of negotiators to peace. Although Le Duc Tho of North Vietnam declined, the prize was appropriately accepted by its co-winner, the new U.S. secretary of state, Henry A. Kissinger, whose remarkable success in contracting truces for Indochina and the Middle East dominated the international scene. The great powers, weary and frightened of confrontation, were ready for armistice. But détente was still far from entente. The Cold War could not just be wished away. Perverse conflicts of interest had to be faced after the agreement to agree had been reached.

It was not a year of peace. Détente is only a beginning, a relaxation of tension. It makes possible the setting of limits within which contention can be more safely carried on. The fighting in Vietnam subsided only gradually, and the truce violations remained beyond the power of the four-nation supervisory commission to control. It was not until autumn that a kind of peace came to Laos and a kind of military stalemate to Khmer (Cambodia). But the United States withdrew its forces from Vietnam, ended its military involvement in Khmer, and reduced its troops in Thailand. The Nixon doctrine of withdrawal from exposed commitments was being implemented. Vietnam moved out of the headlines, and the Indochinese settled into the search and struggle for their own compromises or their own victories.

The settlement in Laos was reportedly reached in the Russian Embassy in Vientiane under pressure from the Soviet and American ambassadors. The most notable feature of the year was this persistence of the Russians and Americans in concocting and imposing agreement on their clients. The Arab-Israeli truce followed meetings of Russia's Communist Party leader Leonid I. Brezhnev and Kissinger with each other and with the contending parties. When any of the truces threatened to become unstuck, each power sought to support and thereby control its protégé, but they resisted the temptation to go for victory. The military confrontation of protectors and protected nevertheless remained dangerous.

But the propaganda war was muted. The Russians notably refrained from exploiting President Richard M. Nixon's distress over the Watergate affair, and Brezhnev came to the United States in June in a jovial mood, minimizing differences and stressing common interests. For its part, the Nixon Administration opposed efforts in Congress to tie economic agreements with Moscow to a change of Russian policies on emigration. Widespread concern in Western countries over the persecution of dissident intellectuals in Russia threatened to stall indefinitely the Conference on Security and Cooperation in Europe, which finally got underway during the summer.

John Holmes

On the economic, as distinct from the military, side, there was a promise of movement forward from simple equilibrium. Brezhnev's prime motive for détente seemed to be a felt need for advanced technology, wheat, foreign trade, and exchange. In the United States, he made a series of deals over agriculture, oceanography, transportation, and atomic energy. The managerial men on both sides were asserting themselves. The United States Export-Import Bank put up a $200-million loan to Russia for industrial equipment, and both Occidental Petroleum Corporation and General Electric Company were involved in industrial arrangements with the Russians. Particularly significant were negotiations, involving Japan as well, for the development of Siberian natural gas. The need for technology and resources was making strange bedfellows. The Chinese likewise wanted American technology—and it was announced in July that the Chase Manhattan Bank, no less, would henceforth represent the Bank of China. It was still only the tentative testing, under pressure of necessity, of détente in economic affairs. Whether interdependence would make war among old antagonists impossible or render their relations more critical remained to be seen.

The need for world trade made strange bedfellows

Peaceful coexistence still meant competitive coexistence in military capability. For the time being, the superpowers concentrated on bringing their strength up to the levels provided in the interim agreement on the limitation of offensive missiles reached in 1972. The Russians continued to expand their navy and were reported to have challenged the United States nuclear lead by testing the missile bundles called MIRV's (Multiple Independent Re-entry Vehicles). Nevertheless, the powers—except China and France—were locked into negotiation over arms control. The Strategic Arms Limitation Talks (between the United States and Russia) and the broad-based Geneva disarmament negotiations went doggedly on. Work began at last on considering mutual force reductions in Europe. Progress toward disarmament was not spectacular in 1973, but the negotiations had moved from the dramatic but easy agreement to negotiate to the hard calculations of great risk and had settled in for a long haul. Meanwhile, pressure to lessen the arms burden increased in all countries, partly as a consequence of détente and partly because of the rising priority of economic over military considerations. For many countries, Japan for example, national security looked more like an economic than a military problem.

Although it was superpower diplomacy that attracted attention during 1973, the authority of the United Nations (UN) was revived. A historic step toward universality and coexistence was the admission to UN membership of both East and West Germany. And, although the Russians and Americans were fulfilling their special responsibilities as great powers under the UN Charter by conjuring a cease-fire for the Middle East, it was the independent initiative of the nonpermanent members of the Security Council that made agreement possible on all sides and gave universal sanction. The Chinese rejected it but, in

Kissinger in China

accordance with the spirit of the charter, refrained from using their veto. At the same time, the General Assembly was asserting more boldly the will of an increasing majority in support of forceful pressure against the white-dominated regimes of southern Africa. Even European countries were getting harsher with Portugal and offering cautious support to the African guerrillas.

The increasing militancy and confidence of the nonaligned countries was notable in their massive conference in Algiers in September. The concept of nonalignment was confused by the curious new alignments of the United States, Russia, and China. So the delegates, largely from Africa, Asia, and Latin America, asked themselves whether they were bound together by nonalignment or, as the Chinese told them, by their need to stand together against the industrialized powers. A message from Brezhnev saying the division was still between the Socialist and non-Socialist worlds was not well received. President Muammar Muhammad al-Qadhaafi of Libya stridently accused Cuba's Premier Fidel Castro of being aligned—with Russia. Denunciations of Western "imperialism" were accompanied by offers of cooperation on equitable terms. In spite of the disparate emotions, loyalties, and vested interests, a new consciousness of power was evident on a few basic issues. The common front against Israel was widened, with some consequences for the balance of forces in the Middle East. Above all, however, it was the newly summoned will to use the power of oil which exhilarated the nations of the nonaligned third world, even though that power remained in the hands of a few.

The assertion of power by terrorism continued, but resistance was growing. Attempts continued in various UN bodies to control it, but they were stymied by the fear in the third world that no distinction would be made between the terror they, too, deplored and the legitimate violence of the anticolonial struggle. However, concern over air piracy did bring Communist and Western governments together in the search for international measures. Cuba reached agreements against hijacking with five other Western Hemisphere countries, including the United States and Canada. A fear of uncontrollable subversion tends to unite established governments, whether conservative or revolutionary, and thereby encourages détente.

Neither the aligned nor the nonaligned wanted to stand in the way of East-West settlements, but there were widespread misgivings about "superpower hegemony," or political domination. Instinctively, sources of balancing power were developed. The West Europeans felt disregarded. The nations of the European Community (Common Market) started off the year with the expectation of increasing influence, as they welcomed Great Britain, Denmark, and Ireland into the community. Their difficulty, however, in agreeing on common positions on either economic or political issues weakened their hand. Inflation, monetary crises, and fuel shortages accentuated their differences. The proposal from Kissinger in the spring for a new "Atlantic Charter" and a visit from President Nixon got a weak response. The Europeans

New alignments confused the concept of nonalignment

UN troops in Mideast

did not feel sufficiently united to divert their attention to transatlantic community building. The Middle East crisis strained the old alliance by revealing serious divergence of interest and attitude between the community and the United States, and within the community as well. It was not a year when an entity called "Europe" was able to challenge effectively the diplomacy of the superpowers.

The Asian powers also tempered a will to détente with concern to assert their voice and interests. Japanese Prime Minister Kakuei Tanaka went to Europe to establish links, embassies were exchanged between Peking and Tokyo, and an unsuccessful effort was made to agree on a peace treaty with Russia. Kissinger was careful to pay more attention to Japan.

In South Asia, tension eased as India, Pakistan, and Bangladesh reached agreements in August on the repatriation of prisoners and internees. India was no longer active, however, in the peacemaking elsewhere and was even excluded from the new international supervisory commission in Vietnam.

China denounced, but did not interfere with, the peacemaking of the Russians and Americans. Premier Chou En-lai quietly strengthened his country's position by entertaining heads of government and other professional visitors from the West, whose reports back home were building for China a more favorable image than that of Russia. Quasi-diplomatic missions were exchanged with Washington, contradictory positions on world issues were politely acknowledged, and the détente cordiale persisted. Relations with Russia, however, were worse than ever. To his Western visitors, Chou sounded like an old Cold Warrior, urging North Atlantic Treaty Organization intransigence and the solidarity of Europe, and warning against Soviet machinations. While rejecting on principle the role of a great military power, China nevertheless maintained its powerful army, became the world's third-ranking naval power, and continued nuclear testing. Détente without risk was the motto in the East as well as in the West. French President Georges Pompidou, Kissinger, and others made clear in Peking, however, that they were not to be diverted from the search for détente with Moscow.

The stubborn determination of Moscow and Washington to get along was evident also in the distance they kept from the turbulence in Latin America. On the whole, it was a year of reaction. Forces of "law and order" took over in Uruguay and Chile. When Juan D. Perón became president of Argentina, he sought to control the leftist elements among his supporters; neither right nor left professed pro-American sentiments. There was talk again of a United States approach to Castro, in line with the Kissinger policy of coexistence with old antagonists, but Castro showed no public interest. The overthrow of the Salvador Allende Gossens regime in Chile tempted the world back into Cold War patterns; U.S. complicity was, of course, charged, but not very effectively proved. The ruling group that replaced Allende was not warmly welcomed by Americans, and Washington

Tanaka in Russia

Asia's powers also wanted to voice their own interests

was reserved. The Russians had supported Allende and they broke off relations with the new government, but the foreign "Communists" who had been accused of interference in Chilean affairs were largely other Latin Americans. The violence in Chile may well have advanced the tempo of confrontation in South America, but the forces engaged seemed increasingly indigenous.

The great powers were challenged by new patterns of alignments. Such countries as South Korea, Iran, and Brazil were emerging as economic powers to be reckoned with in the future. The Persian Gulf states, with their oil politics, decisively confronted the great industrial powers. African states, under the leadership of their great power, Nigeria, began tougher collective bargaining with the European Community. Australia and New Zealand, under forceful new Labor Party governments, brought a fresh voice into international diplomacy and vigorously challenged France over its nuclear tests in the Pacific. The Commonwealth of Nations displayed renewed vitality at the Ottawa Conference of Prime Ministers in August. A vigorous coalition to oppose the United States and the other great maritime powers at the important negotiations on the law of the sea in 1974 was being organized by Canada, Australia, and a number of African and Latin American countries. The Southeast Asia Treaty Organization was in disarray, but the sturdier security alliances held firm. American troops were not withdrawn from Europe, in spite of increasing pressure in Congress; that was one link with America the European Community still valued. The Japanese, though seeking greater flexibility in foreign policy, continued to reject either neutrality or independent military and nuclear power. Détente, for the present, was based not on the abolition of military alliances, but on building confidence from the assurance of reliable, though less provocative, provisions for security.

By the end of the year, attention was shifting from the liquidation of old conflicts to what looks like the major challenge of the future: the pressure of growing populations on diminishing resources. Crisis has been predicted for several years, but it became alarmingly real in 1973 when a threatened fuel shortage from natural causes was aggravated by war in the Middle East. It came after a year of drought in India and Africa, tensions in Europe and North America over migrant labor, currency fluctuations, and worldwide inflation—all of which provided evidence that there was not enough food, clothing, housing, and breathing space to meet rising demands. So what had on the whole been a good year for détente ended in panicky fear of a whole new breed of tensions.

New patterns of alignment challenged the great powers

Related Articles

For further information on international relations in 1973, see the articles on the various nations in Section Four, and also the following:

Africa	International Trade	Middle East
Asia	and Finance	Pacific Islands
Europe	Latin America	United Nations

Commonwealth conference

Focus on The Nation

James Reston

In many ways, 1973 was a tragic year, but it may be seen eventually as the year that compelled some fundamental, long-overdue reforms in American life

Nations, like families or football teams, have their bad years. Nobody knows quite how it happens, but some combination of sickness, overconfidence, poor leadership, and bad luck brings them down, and this is the way it was with the United States in 1973.

The year started with the triumphant inauguration of President Richard M. Nixon for a second term in the White House, and it ended with insistent public demands for his resignation or impeachment. Within a year of winning the presidency by the largest popular majority in the history of the republic, he had dropped to the lowest rating in the presidential popularity polls in more than 20 years.

Between these two extremes, 1973 was a year of acute internal political tension, dominated by charges that men close to the President had helped secure his re-election by improper and illegal means, and that, in his handling of the crisis, Mr. Nixon had squandered much of his support and weakened his capacity to govern.

This was one view of the American political scene at the beginning of 1974. But in the longer perspectives of history, 1973 was much more than that, and maybe even because of the scandals, crimes, and blunders, 1973 may be seen eventually as the year that compelled fundamental and long-overdue reforms in American life.

Essentially, it was a year of changing political relationships. It was the first year in more than a decade when no American troops were engaged in military action overseas, thus marking a new policy of limiting the nation's commitments abroad. It was the first year in more than a quarter of a century when American men were no longer subject to compulsory military service. It was a year of reappraisal of the United States relations with Russia, China, Japan, the Middle East, and the countries of the European Community (Common Market). And, dominating all else, it was a year of turmoil over the very nature of the presidency itself.

Probably few Americans celebrated the end of 1973 on New Year's Eve without a sense of relief. Somehow, the misdeeds of a few powerful individuals seemed to overwhelm the positive actions of the people as a whole. Yet, this was not a "lost year," as many observers seemed to feel, for the corrective impulses of the nation and its enduring institutions held up very well.

The basic question underlying all the turmoil was whether Mr. Nixon had created what historian Arthur M. Schlesinger, Jr., called an "imperial presidency," overreaching the authority granted to him by the Constitution, impinging on the rights of the Congress, eroding the influence of the Cabinet, and centralizing undue power in a secretive White House staff beyond the questioning of the press or even of the Congress.

James Reston

This general question of presidential power had been argued for more than 200 years. But President Nixon insisted on specific powers that produced constitutional controversy even before his Administration was involved in criminal charges arising from the election of 1972.

For example, he insisted on personal authority not to expend funds that had been voted by both houses of Congress if, in his personal opinion, expending those funds would add to the inflation or otherwise be against the interests of the country – as he defined those interests. Also, he insisted on a degree of secrecy unknown to past Presidents, claiming "executive privilege" against disclosing any information he personally felt touched on questions of "national security." Thus, there was a constitutional crisis before there was a moral and legal crisis over the elections scandals of 1972.

It was against this background of presidential claims of secrecy and executive privilege that the specific charges of illegal action were raised about the men appointed by the President. These charges included burglary of the opposition party's headquarters, illegal wiretapping and electronic surveillance, forgery of documents to distort the record of the late President John F. Kennedy, destruction of evidence, obstruction of justice, bribery, tampering with witnesses, and conspiracy to cover up the truth by trying to involve the Federal Bureau of Investigation, the Central Intelligence Agency, the Internal Revenue Service, and the Securities and Exchange Commission in illegal action.

For most of 1973, the nation was startled and preoccupied by these charges and by speculation about whether President Nixon knew about the conspiracies or tried to cover them up. In any event, two of his former Cabinet officers – John N. Mitchell and Maurice H. Stans – were indicted, and leading members of his White House staff and re-election committee were forced to resign. And most of the year was given over to public discussion of whether the President had lost the trust of the public and whether he should resign, be impeached, or be cleared. All of this was a fundamental change from the President's confident start at the beginning of the year.

There was a general feeling at the start of 1973 that a new chapter in the history of the United States was beginning. Between the election of November, 1972, and the end of January, 1973, the only two living former Presidents – Harry S. Truman and Lyndon B. Johnson – had died. The last of the American prisoners and fighters in Vietnam had come home, and President Nixon was talking about "a generation of peace" without unemployment or inflation.

As he described it, the four years between his election and the 200th anniversary of the Declaration of Independence on July 4, 1976, were to be years of reform. Abroad, he would continue to work for accommodation with Russia and China, peace in the Middle East, and reappraisal of the United States relations with Japan and the emerging but not yet unified Common Market.

At home, he interpreted his spectacular election victory as a

President Nixon

mandate to fight crime and inflation, to modernize the armed services of the nation without military conscription, to strengthen the state and local governments by giving them more control over the federal money spent in their districts, and to work for a new era of responsibility and even morality.

Mr. Nixon had substantial support in the country for these general reforms at the beginning of 1973. There was a feeling in the nation that the United States had taken on too many burdens for maintaining peace all over the world. Therefore, his policy of pulling back a bit and helping only those peoples who helped themselves was popular.

Likewise, since the majority of the American people were living fairly well, there was also a feeling that the time had come to reform the system of welfare payments to the poor, and to oppose those members of Congress who supported a federal dole for their own political reasons.

The President had sensed the mood of the majority fairly well. They didn't want to police the world, pay more taxes to finance higher welfare payments or welfare corruption, or pay higher prices for the inflation. They were against demonstrations in the streets, campus revolts, and the permissive life styles of the young radicals.

So the President began his second term with popular support, a divided and weak Democratic Party, and enough votes—even in a Congress dominated by the Democrats—to impound congressionally approved funds, to increase the military budget, and to insist on "law and order."

Then the Watergate scandals of the 1972 presidential election began to come out. And the mind of the country and the mind of the President, both of which had been looking forward to new beginnings and new policies for a rapidly changing world, were suddenly turned back to the past.

An Administration that had been elected to restore "law and order" was suddenly confronted with damaging evidence that officials chosen by the President to run his White House, his staff, and his Cabinet and to assure his re-election had broken the law and created America's worst political disorder of this century.

In this sense, 1973 was a tragic year. But America has always hesitated to correct itself when the going was good. Usually, it has made its progress through adversity. It was satisfied to be a British colony as long as the British were reasonable, but it agreed to fight reluctantly for its independence when the spectacular demands and stupidity of the British government became intolerable.

Slavery was abolished in America, and the union preserved, not by the foresight and common sense of the people and their leaders, but only by the tragedy and violence of the Civil War.

The United States did not modify its free enterprise system or adjust to the industrial and scientific revolution until the system collapsed during the worldwide economic Great Depression of the early 1930s, which led to mass unemployment and commercial bankruptcy.

America has hesitated to correct itself when the going has been good

Watergate bug

25

The balance
of political
power has been
tipped to the
White House

This may not be the best way to make progress, but it seems to be the American way. It took two world wars to make the American people realize that the policy of political isolation was not in America's interest, but was in fact destroying the civilization of the West. It took 10 years of the Vietnam War, run primarily by the personal will of Presidents Kennedy, Johnson, and Nixon, to force the Congress to insist on its constitutional rights. Finally, it took the violent controversy over the political scandals of the 1972 presidential election to compel a re-examination of the rules of American politics.

Thoughtful men and women had been worried about the dangers of excessive presidential power since the beginning of the republic. Six weeks before George Washington's first inauguration, Thomas Jefferson wrote to James Madison: "The tyranny of the legislature is really the danger most to be feared and will continue to be so for many years to come. The tyranny of the executive power will come in its turn, but at a more distant period."

Early in the 20th century, Theodore Roosevelt believed that only a strong President could break the power of big business over the general welfare of the people. Later, Woodrow Wilson and Franklin D. Roosevelt insisted that presidential power was the main hope of both freedom and equality.

But with the invention of the atom bomb and the intercontinental ballistic missile, the balance of power shifted dramatically to the White House—and with good reason. For in a world in which such weapons were in the hands of potential enemies, the republic could be destroyed before the members of Congress could ever be gathered on Capitol Hill to consider a vote to "declare war."

These two inventions—the atom bomb and the intercontinental missile—plus the development of nationwide network television, with a television studio available in the White House to be used whenever the President chose to use it, obviously tipped the balance of political power to the White House. And it was only in 1973—after the misuse of presidential power in the Vietnam War and the misuse of political power and secrecy in the 1972 presidential election—that public opinion forced the Congress to insist on basic reforms.

In this sense, 1973 was a very special year. It was "bad" but it was not "lost," for—unlike most moderate years with their mixture of good and bad—it was just outrageous enough to affront the decency and common sense of the people and stir them to insist on remedies.

Accordingly, a movement was started, but by no means completed, in 1973 to write new laws that would:
- Put much more rigid controls on the amount of money that individuals could contribute to presidential and congressional candidates.
- Place much heavier penalties on anybody violating the new campaign-financing laws.
- Make provision for public financing of presidential and perhaps even congressional election campaigns.
- Provide free television time for major presidential candidates.

Sign of the times

The political crises of 1973 did more than encourage new laws to control campaign financing. They demonstrated that bad tactics could bring good politicians down, that political dirty tricks hurt the party in power more than the opposition, that corporate political funds were not good but bad for business, that loyalty to the President was not as important as loyalty to the Constitution, and that good and honorable ends do not justify improper or illegal means.

In short, 1973 was an odd year in America, a controversial but corrective year. It destroyed a lot of old bad habits and illusions. We thought we were self-sufficient, that gas to run our automobiles and oil to heat our houses would always be cheap and plentiful; that we could outproduce, outbid, and outsell anybody in the export markets of the world; that we had better products, better weapons, and more power than anybody else; and that our dollar was sounder than any other currency in the world.

But after the disappointments of 1973, we knew better, and this may be all to the good. Going into 1974, America had a better and more accurate estimate of its leaders and its powers. In many ways, 1973 was a tragic year, but at least it brought the nation back to reality.

Related Articles

For further information on United States affairs in 1973, see also Section One, Focus on The Economy; Section Two, The Rise and Falter of the Free Press; and the following articles in Section Four:

Agnew, Spiro T.	Economics	Republican Party
Agriculture	Elections	Richardson, Elliot L.
Baker, Howard	Ellsberg, Daniel	Sirica, John
Civil Rights	Ervin, Samuel J., Jr.	State Government
Congress of the	Ford, Gerald R.	Supreme Court of the
United States	Labor	United States
Courts and Laws	National Defense	Taxation
Cox, Archibald	Nixon, Richard M.	U.S. Government
Democratic Party	President of the U.S.	Watergate

Focus on The Economy

Sylvia Porter

For the United States, 1973 was a year of joyless boom—and for the entire world, it became obvious that inflation is the number-one economic problem

The year 1973 will take its place in United States economic history as the year of joyless boom. That it was a boom year is beyond dispute. Profits recorded the biggest upsurge in history. Total employment, personal dollar incomes, retail sales, factory production, new car sales—all climbed to the highest levels ever. The rate of unemployment in late fall dipped to 4.5 per cent, the lowest in 3½ years. The U.S. economy's output of goods and services (gross national product) zoomed above $1.3 trillion, up an enormous 11 per cent in one year.

In fact, by midyear the economy was running flat out—straining at its full capacity in terms of machines, manpower, and money. It could and it did go farther, of course, just as a race horse running at its top speed can and does go farther. But it could not accelerate its pace, and, on the contrary, it had to (and it did) slow perceptibly as the year neared its end.

Equally undeniable, though, 1973 was a year of queasy prosperity, of despondent affluence. Inflation cursed us from the start. The overall rise in the U.S. cost of living approximated an oppressive 8.5 per cent, triple the rate President Richard M. Nixon had forecast when the year began and giving this era's inflation the unenviable distinction of being the worst and most prolonged in the nation's history. Interest rates were pushed up to crisis levels as the Federal Reserve System severely tightened the credit screws in a belated effort to curb the price upsurge. The U.S. dollar, once the strongest currency in the world, was officially devalued for the second time within 14 months and then unofficially slashed even more under relentless selling pressure in the international money markets. The stock market hit its high at the start of the year, then went into a tailspin that made Wall Street a disaster area in the midst of apparent economic prosperity. Finally, when signs began to appear in late 1973 that the worst might be behind us, the energy crisis broke wide open. Prices of all types of fuels skyrocketed and again sent the cost of living soaring.

No one within the Nixon Administration (or outside of it, for that matter), foresaw when 1973 opened that food prices would take off in one of the most astounding spirals in U.S. history. As an indication of how wrong the forecasts were—on food prices particularly—George P. Shultz, secretary of the treasury and the Administration's economic czar, pledged in February that "prices of raw agricultural products at the end of 1973 will be no higher than at the beginning of 1973." Herbert Stein, chairman of the President's Council of Economic Advisers, publicly boasted that "the American anti-inflation policy had become the marvel of the world. Largely because of this change, the rest of the world is willing to hold increasing amounts of dollars."

Instead of stability, wholesale farm prices rose at an annual rate of

Sylvia Porter

29

65 per cent during the first half of 1973. By midyear, consumer prices across the board were jumping at an annual rate of 26 per cent. The world was not merely unwilling to hold increasing amounts of dollars; it was feverishly dumping billions of the dollars it already held.

What went wrong? Why? There are, I submit, at least seven basic reasons why:

■ From the very beginning, the White House failed utterly to grasp the awesome power of 1973's worldwide economic boom superimposed on our own boom—and the subsequent explosive demands for our foodstuffs, goods, and services. We were in an unprecedented global expansion. All over the world, people were eating more and better food. Hundreds of millions of customers were clamoring for our production in Europe, Japan, Russia, China, and other lands. The boom marked a watershed in world history and must rank among the most fundamental, historic developments of our age. Mr. Nixon encouraged the boom and perhaps he fully appreciated it—but by no stretch of the imagination did the economic policies he proposed for our country match the challenge.

■ The Administration shockingly underestimated the impact of its foreign sales of foodstuffs on food prices at home—most notably the sale of wheat to Russia. As a result, President Nixon did not simultaneously fight for an overhaul of our agricultural policies to bolster our production of foodstuffs and offset the inflationary impact of the foreign sales. Not until August 10 did the President sign into law the new farm program designed to stimulate full production. And it must be noted that the White House did not recommend the program; Mr. Nixon simply accepted it as a "constructive" compromise. Other Administration officials admitted later, though, that the White House's failure to concentrate on increasing food supplies (as Treasury Secretary Shultz's shockingly overconfident prediction implied it would) was a crucial error.

■ Bad weather, droughts, and crop failures interfered with food production all over the world. And long before the Arab oil embargo, shortages of fuel and transportation facilities adversely affected farm and food prices as well as many other vital prices. Nature itself helped to restrict the supply of vital raw materials at a time of exploding demand—and this excess demand pressing against inadequate supplies was the basic cause for the demand-pull inflations blotching the booms everywhere.

■ The successive devaluations of the dollar to the point where it became one of the most undervalued currencies in the world vastly stimulated U.S. exports—a trend devoutly to be wished, for it helped put our balance of trade back in the black. But the ironic fact was that agricultural exports led the list of increases over 1972. The dollar devaluations may have been essential shock medicine to the world—but they scarcely helped the squeezed American consumer.

■ Despite earnest and well-publicized goals of limiting inflationary spending, the White House and Congress continued to follow pro-inflationary, not anti-inflationary, fiscal policies. The federal budget

A worldwide boom, on top of the U.S. boom in 1973, was awesome

Wheat for Russia

started to approach balance for a short time only because extra taxes were collected on inflated prices and profits. There was no anti-inflationary tax rate hike, nor even a request for one; no really rough limit on government spending; no curbs on excessive installment buying. Fiscal policy was exceedingly inflationary all through 1972.

■ Only the Federal Reserve began fighting the price spiral with a tight monetary policy, and that was not until the spring and summer of 1973—when inflation already was at a galloping rate. What's more, the historically high interest rates added to the cost of living and doing business. The prime rate granted only to the top business risks of the nation reached a hard-to-believe 10 per cent. Rates to all other business borrowers scaled up from there to 11 or 12 per cent and more a year. The discount rate—the foundation interest rate that banks pay when they have to borrow funds from the Federal Reserve to lend in turn to us—touched the historic peak of 7½ per cent. This classic anti-inflation weapon was in itself a contributing factor to inflation in 1973. Higher mortgage rates on home mortgages or stiffer interest rates on personal or business loans are as much a part of living costs as higher prices on a pound of steak (and they last a lot longer, too).

■ On top of all this came the Middle East war, the Arab oil boycott, and spiraling prices for all forms of energy. Once again, the White House was caught utterly unprepared. When asked what energy cutbacks would mean, for instance, Herbert Stein replied, "I'm ashamed to say I can't answer the question." As late as mid-November, other officials confessed they were "just starting" to calculate the economic consequences of energy shortages. "Belatedly," however, they jacked up their estimates for inflation and they reduced their estimates for economic output in 1974.

An objective reading of these seven factors surely not only explains why the forecasts were so wrong, but also underlines why the boom was so unhappy. Meanwhile, throughout the first half of the year, the U.S. dollar sank to new lows day after day—reflecting a deepening distrust both at home and abroad of the economy behind the dollar as well as the White House's capacity to strengthen the U.S. currency.

The rush by speculators, international businessmen, bankers, and oil-wealthy Middle East sheiks to get rid of dollars reached the proportions of a frightening stampede in early 1973. And as the dollar's value sank in terms of foreign currencies, Americans felt it directly in the soaring costs of imported products and travel abroad—adding still more to inflation's evil impact.

While the attack became monstrously exaggerated, it originally had a very sound basis in the fact that during the entire post-World War II period, we spent far more abroad than we earned abroad—on loans and on gifts, on foreign investments and foreign travel, on war in Vietnam, and on other war-connected activities. Our balance of payments went deeply into the red in the early 1950s, and we flooded the world with billions of surplus dollars.

Then, in 1971, for the first time in the 1900s, our trade balance fell

Then, on top of everything else, came the Middle East war in October

George P. Shultz

into the red, too. In 1972, we imported almost $7 billion more in merchandise than we exported. Huge totals of dollars now hung "undigested" over the world's markets. Indeed, it appeared that the United States had lost all control over its economy, its currency, and its destiny.

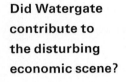

Did Watergate contribute to the disturbing economic scene?

Under the circumstances, it is not in the least surprising that individual investors ignored the business expansion and the most sparkling corporate earnings reports ever, and deserted the stock market in massive numbers. In 1973, the number of shareholders in the United States actually went into a decline—the first drop since the depression 1930s, a full generation ago. The upswing in ownership of stocks in our country began in the 1940s, speeded up in the 1950s and 1960s, reached a dramatic average of 2 million additional shareholders each year between 1965 and 1970, and hit an all-time high of 32.5 million individuals in 1972. Then came the chilling reversal in 1973.

How much did the Watergate affair contribute to the disturbing economic scenario of a superheated economic boom, a galloping rate of inflation, a dollar under speculative attack, a sick stock market, and—at year-end—deepening danger of real recession in 1974? You'll never be able to prove precisely how much, and comments blaming all of 1973's sad economic-financial developments on the scandals were nonsense. But the psychology of this political crisis undeniably became a factor. Also:

■ Major economic policy decisions at the White House level were greatly modified or shelved. Preoccupation with Watergate played a direct part in this weakening of leadership.

■ As a result of this lack of anti-inflation leadership from the White House, the Federal Reserve assumed an extraordinary share of the burden of the inflation fight. It clamped down even more on credit than it had planned and encouraged interest rates to rise even higher —and both policies added to the slump in stock prices and the threat of business downturn.

Watching stocks fall

■ Out in the real world, consumers and businessmen spent at an unsustainable rate for goods, services, plants, and equipment. But in the stock market, prices faded—more in reflection of dwindling buying than heavy selling. It's ridiculous to blame the stock market's prolonged slump on Watergate. That decline began long, long before Watergate entered the American language. But the individual investor's confidence was further undercut by dismay over Watergate—and there's no doubt that this helped declines feed on declines.

■ The renewed attack on the dollar and the upsurge in the price of gold in world markets to an early 1973 high of $127 an ounce must be attributed in major part to Watergate. Here, the tie was clear, and the danger of political upheaval in the United States obviously ran over into the economic sphere. There was no economic-monetary reason in the spring for another attack on the dollar. Our trade balance was improving, not worsening; our dollar had been devalued twice in a short span; our inflation was bad, but not nearly as bad as in

other leading nations. The attack reflected a crisis of confidence arising out of Watergate and fear the President wouldn't be able to lead.
■ Finally, a preoccupied Administration allowed the 1972-1973 business boom to become so superheated and unsustainable that it could not last—and with energy shortages forcing slowdowns in Europe and Japan, the United States could be in for much worse than a lower rate of growth in 1974.

At best, the 1974 outlook is for a leveling off—with only a moderate impact on jobs, paychecks, and profits. At worst, an actual downturn, the second recession of the Nixon tenure, could be ahead.

As the year ended, one bright note was a comeback in the U.S. dollar. A spectacular swing in U.S. trade shaped up—this time a swing in our favor—as the official and unofficial devaluations of the dollar made the United States a bargain country for foreigners to buy in, travel in, invest in. As our sales of goods and services abroad accelerated, the pace of rise in foreign sales of goods in the United States decelerated. In 1973, we started to price ourselves back into the world's markets, while other lands started to price themselves out.

But the year-end energy shortages and the price spiral in all forms of fuel arrested other possibly favorable trends. In fact, it was even more painfully obvious at 1973's end than at 1973's start that inflation is the number-one economic problem of our country.

The world now recognizes that the inflations eroding purchasing power in all nations in the 1970s are as disastrous as the deflations creating armies of jobless were in the 1930s. The world knows that inflation is the global enemy that must now be tackled on a global basis. All of us are infecting each other with the disease, exporting it and importing it. Yet, when the Arab oil boycott hit Europe in October, the nations of the European Community couldn't even agree on a policy to share their energy supplies—much less on a policy to seek with the United States and Japan for some international answer to the international evil of inflation.

How far down must we dig for inflation's causes in international trade jealousies, quotas, and walls? In currency relationships and money flows? In sovereignty? Must we create a global central bank to help regulate us? Must we strive for new heights of cooperation? I ask these questions, certain that in them we will find some of the answers.

But at no 1973 forum of finance ministers—in Washington or Paris, in London or Nairobi—were these questions even asked, much less the answers debated.

Inflation is a global foe that must be met globally

Finance ministers in Nairobi

Related Articles

For further information on the 1973 year in economics, see the following articles in Section Four:

Agriculture	International Trade	Manufacturing
Banks and Banking	and Finance	Money
Economics	Labor	Stocks and Bonds

Focus on Science

Harrison Brown

There is evidence that a major change in the world's climate is taking place, and it may well have a very profound effect on food supplies in Asia and Africa

On the southern fringe of Africa's Sahara Desert is a desolate region called the Sahel. This is a broad belt of arid land that extends nearly 2,000 miles from west to east, and in it about 25 million people —most of them farmers or herdsmen—coax a meager living from the soil. Rainfall there is normally sparse, averaging in "good" times some 4 to 12 inches a year and concentrated entirely between May and October. But in 1973, the region was in the fifth year of the most serious drought in living memory. In large areas of six nations— Chad, Mali, Mauritania, Niger, Senegal, and Upper Volta—wells had dried up, crops had failed, pastures had disappeared, millions of cattle and other domestic animals had perished, and countless thousands of human beings had died.

The full scope of the disaster in the Sahel was not fully appreciated until it had already reached substantial proportions, and though many nations provided generous aid, it was belated. Hundreds of thousands of tons of grains were provided by the United States, Canada, countries of the European Community, and even China, which had recently had a serious shortage itself. Yet, impressive though these shipments were, they barely sufficed to avert the worst.

The effects of the drought in the Sahel were felt far to the south, partly as the result of mass migrations of people and cattle and partly as the result of the diminished flow of rivers. The water supply to Lake Chad fell by two-thirds from 1971 to 1972, with the result that Nigeria now has a land frontier with Chad for the first time in history. Flows of water to the Kainji Dam lake in Nigeria, to the Volta Dam lake in Ghana, and to the Kossou Dam lake in Ivory Coast have appreciably lessened, with drastic consequences for electricity supplies.

Disasters resulting from drought have not been confined to the Sahel, however. Ethiopia is in the third year of a drought in which perhaps as many as 100,000 people have already died and which threatens the livelihood of approximately 2 million people. Sudan, south of Egypt, has also been hard hit.

To what can these disasters, and others like them, be attributed? Are they simply random pranks of nature that hit people who live in marginal areas particularly hard but which are temporary? Or is there something more deep-seated and pervasive involved in what is happening? Could it be, for example, that the Sahara is actually moving southward?

Some scientists say no, observing that modern public health techniques in the drought-stricken areas have led to increased population and to more intensive cropping. Increased numbers of livestock have led to overgrazing, and the movements of the cattle, camels, sheep, and goats have loosened the soil. All of this has accelerated soil ero-

Harrison Brown

sion. The original open woodland of thorn bush has been destroyed and replaced partly by grass steppe and partly by man-made desert. It is these man-made deserts that are advancing, not the natural desert, these scientists believe.

Important as such effects might be, some other scientists say that they are only contributing factors and that the primary cause of the disasters is a changing world climate. British meteorologist Derek Winstanley has analyzed the rainfall pattern of the Mediterranean area and the Middle East, and that of the Sahel band that stretches from the Atlantic Ocean to India. He sees the decline of rainfall in the African Sahel since about 1960 as part of a much larger pattern of shifting climatic zones. Most notably, North Africa is getting wetter, the Sahel is getting drier, and the Sahara is moving southward at the rate of several miles each year. Fluctuations are superimposed upon this long-term trend, and Winstanley says that the Sahel is now at the low point of such a fluctuation. Thus, although the drought might be temporarily eased, he believes that the long-term trend will inexorably re-establish itself.

The Sahel is part of the monsoon belt, where torrential rains from May to October have historically made up for the rest of the year's drought. In 1972, these rains failed extensively from Africa to Sri Lanka, India, and Bangladesh. If Winstanley is correct, they will fail with increasing frequency in the future.

Professor Reid Bryson, director of the Institute of Environmental Studies at the University of Wisconsin, believes that the Sahelian drought can be linked directly to changes in the world distribution of temperature. Since 1945, average surface temperatures in the Northern Hemisphere have declined by about 0.3°C. (somewhat over 0.5°F.) —enough, according to Bryson, to account for the observed southward movement of the deserts.

But why should the world distribution of temperature be changing? Bryson suggests that the increasing carbon dioxide content of the atmosphere generated by the burning of fossil fuels—petroleum, coal, and natural gas—coupled with increased particulate matter in the atmosphere generated by human activity such as industry and farming, might well be responsible. If this view turns out to be correct, the rains of the monsoon belt are destined to disappear, not to return in the foreseeable future. On the other hand, Winstanley suggests that present trends are part of a "natural" cycle with a period of 200 years. On that basis, the current southward drift of climate is destined to reverse around the year 2030.

Unfortunately, our understanding of weather and climate and the ways in which the many factors that influence them operate is pitifully small. Major efforts are now being made to simulate the global weather picture, using elaborate mathematical models and large computers. But much work must be done before such a complicated phenomenon as the southward drift of climate can really be understood. Nevertheless, the meager evidence at hand suggests that we are

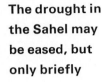

The drought in the Sahel may be eased, but only briefly

Reid Bryson

dealing with a major climatic change that may well have a profound effect upon the food supplies in much of Africa and Asia during the next few decades.

It is also important for scientists to study in detail the present cooling trend in the Northern Hemisphere and its causes in order to determine how much longer it is likely to last. Continued cooling can give rise to changing precipitation patterns and to a substantially altered agricultural environment that could have serious effects upon crops in Europe and North America. Will this situation reverse itself in a few decades? Or is it possible, as some scientists have suggested, that we are entering another glacial period? Here, again, our ignorance is vast, and there is much research to be done.

Famine, which usually has been brought on by the vagaries of weather, or by plant diseases or pests, has been a basic constraint upon human life since man first became dependent upon agriculture. Droughts have decimated populations in entire regions, and settlements that have not been stricken have seldom been able to give much help. Even if they had surpluses to share, which they usually did not, the means for transporting food to the heart of a stricken area simply did not exist.

With the onset of the Industrial Revolution, this situation changed dramatically. Once railroads and highways were built, food could readily be transported from areas of food surplus to areas of food deficiency. Indeed, as the railroad network was extended in India during the 1900s, the incidence and severity of famine in that country diminished. And today, though roads in the Sahel are poor, massive airlifts of food have at least postponed the ultimate disaster there.

But if modern transportation is to be an effective tool in lessening the effects of crop failure, there must be—somewhere in the world— a food surplus that can be shipped. Unfortunately, we are rapidly reaching the point where surpluses for shipment on a reasonably predictable basis may no longer be available.

In 1972, worldwide production of cereal grains amounted to 1.2-billion tons. That was enough to provide every person on earth with about 700 pounds. But the distribution of this food was by no means uniform. In the less developed areas of the world, the average person received only about 400 pounds of grains. In the United States and Canada, by contrast, the average person consumed nearly five times as much—about a ton of grains.

This does not mean that the average North American actually eats five times as much cereal as does an average Indian. Rather, the North American likes meat, eggs, and dairy products—and to obtain them, he feeds huge quantities of cereals to cattle and to chickens. Indeed, of the 1 ton of cereals he uses, he himself consumes only 150 pounds directly, and feeds the remainder to animals, who use up most of the food's energy value merely in moving about and staying warm. By contrast, very little cereal is fed to animals in the less developed countries; the people themselves eat most of the available grains.

We are rapidly reaching the point of no food surplus

Grain for drought area

In all countries, as people's incomes go up, so do their grain requirements, simply because they can then afford the luxury of eating more meat, eggs, and dairy products. In the United States, for example, per capita beef consumption climbed from 55 pounds in 1940 to 115 pounds in 1972. In Europe, Russia, and Japan, dietary habits are changing equally remarkably as incomes rise.

At present, the average annual increase in world cereal production is about 30 million tons. Of this amount, about 22 million tons is required merely to keep pace with the increase in world population, which is growing at the rate of about 2 per cent a year. Most of the remaining 8 million tons is used to produce more meat, milk, and eggs for the increasingly affluent people in the industrialized nations.

It is very doubtful that the population of the world will stop growing much before the time when 6.5 billion persons inhabit our tiny globe. If every one of these billions of people were to live on a modern American diet, the world's annual cereal requirements would reach 6.5 billion tons—or five times the present production. For a variety of reasons, it is most unlikely that such a level will ever be reached. Indeed, it is likely that a variety of adverse effects and constraints, perhaps climatic change among them, will hinder agricultural expansion long before that level of population is reached.

Of the 1.2 billion tons of cereal currently being produced each year, some 92 million tons—or nearly 8 per cent—are shipped from areas of surplus to areas where insufficient grain is grown to satisfy needs. Since World War II, the pattern of world trade in cereals has changed profoundly, with the needs of the importing nations rising rapidly and with North America and, to a much lesser extent, Australia remaining as the only net exporters. Between 1950 and 1972, exports of cereals from North America rose from 23 million tons to 84 million tons, with the customers including Asia, Russia and Eastern Europe, Western Europe, and, to a smaller extent, Africa and Latin America.

Reserves of cereals for export take two forms. First, about 100 million tons of cereals (or about 8 per cent of the world's annual requirements) are stored and can be drawn upon. Second, for the last decade or so, about 14 per cent of the cropland in the United States has been intentionally idled, and it could be put back into production fairly quickly.

In recent years, the need to draw upon our reserves of grain and to bring idle cropland back into use has occurred with increasing frequency. A world food crisis in 1966 and 1967 and a corn blight in the United States in 1971 produced major fluctuations. Food scarcities in 1973 in Russia, China, Bangladesh, and other areas—including the Sahel—resulted in a further decline in world grain reserves, and now all but a small fraction of our idle cropland is being brought back into production.

Fortunately, at a time when the food situation has been going badly in so many parts of the world, the United States and Canadian abilities to help meet the needs have remained high. But those abilities are

The world's population may reach 6.5 billion

Our tiny globe

lessening, in part because world needs (including America's) are increasing faster than man's ability to meet them.

About every 20 years, there is a prolonged drought in the United States. There was one in the 1930s that resulted in the famous Dust Bowl. Another occurred in the 1950s. If the cycle repeats itself, there will be another in the 1970s. If this were to coincide with an intensification of the drought situation in the monsoon belt, and if there were also low crop yields in Russia, China, and other areas, mankind would indeed be in serious trouble, and mass starvation would be widespread. Were this to happen, we in America would not starve, nor would we even go hungry, but there would be tremendous economic dislocations. Agricultural products are essential exports if we are to pay for our growing importations of raw materials, including petroleum.

We must work to unravel the intricacies of climatic change

We must recognize, however, that in the long run, North America cannot make up for more than a tiny fraction of the world food deficit. Major steps must be taken to solve the problem, including increasing the scientific level of agriculture in the poor countries, stabilizing their populations, and encouraging their economic and social development. In the meantime, we should do everything we can to unravel the intricacies of climatic change so that we can understand what the agricultural environment of the world is likely to be in the years and decades ahead, and prepare ourselves for new and difficult situations.

Related Articles

For further information on science and technology in 1973, see Section Two, How Can We Solve the Energy Crisis?; and the articles on the various sciences in Section Four.

Focus on Education

Lawrence A. Cremin

**Three important reports that were produced during
1973 pictured the American high school as a troubled
institution largely victimized by its own success**

During much of the 20th century, the report on a significant
domain of public policy by some prestigious individual or commission
has been a favorite mechanism by which the American people have
focused attention on important social problems and attempted to
work out reasonable solutions. In the realm of education, one thinks
immediately of the "Flexner Report" of 1910, which literally recon-
ceived American medical education, or the "Harvard Report" of 1945,
which dramatically redefined the meaning of general education in a
free society on the eve of an unprecedented expansion in American college enrollments, or the "Coleman Report" of 1966, which profoundly
altered the American meaning of equal educational opportunity.

Each year, dozens of such reports pass across the desks of educational policymakers in schools, universities, and government agencies.
Most of them go unnoticed and unread. A few attract scattered attention and lead to important reforms in a handful of localities. And now
and then one seems to catch the public eye, setting off a national
debate and generating profound changes across the country.

The year 1973 brought three reports on the American high school
that appeared to promise profound change. The first was prepared by
a panel of the President's Science Advisory Committee (PSAC), under
the chairmanship of James S. Coleman (the same Coleman who wrote
the 1966 report on equal educational opportunity). The second was
prepared by the National Commission on the Reform of Secondary
Education, under the chairmanship of B. Frank Brown, the former
principal of Melbourne (Fla.) High School. And the third was prepared by a panel of the United States Office of Education (USOE),
under the chairmanship of John Henry Martin, the former superintendent of schools in Mount Vernon, N.Y. All three of the committees
included scholars, government officials, and practicing educators; one
of the three, the National Commission, included high school students
as well. There was some overlap in membership—Professor Coleman,
for example, was a member of both the USOE panel and the PSAC
panel—but on the whole the three committees worked independently
and undertook their own investigations. And hence the striking
similarity in the diagnoses they came up with and the recommendations they advanced lent additional weight to their analyses.

What were the diagnoses? Essentially, they pictured the high school
as a troubled institution largely victimized by its own success. Starting
out a century ago as an élite institution designed to train a small
proportion of adolescent youth along traditional academic lines, it
had steadily evolved into a popular institution enrolling over 90 per
cent of all Americans between the ages of 14 and 18 and attempting
to perform for them a prodigious array of services. In the process,

Lawrence A. Cremin

however, several unfortunate consequences had come to pass. Young people had been effectively isolated during most of their waking hours from other segments of society, notably adults. They had been organized into rigidly defined age groups (freshmen, sophomores, juniors, seniors) and locked into tight and inflexible academic programs. And all too often, owing to more general patterns of discrimination in housing and employment, they had ended up segregated as well according to race, religion, or national origin. As the USOE panel put it, the schools had "decoupled the generations."

The processes by which youths become adults were weakened and disjointed

As a result, the diagnoses maintained, the ordinary processes by which young people become adults—behavioral scientists refer to them as the processes of socialization—had been weakened, confused, and disjointed. And the symptoms were seen as everywhere apparent— in the relentless decline of academic achievement in inner-city schools, in the growing irregularity of attendance at most schools, and in the rising incidence of theft, vandalism, personal assault, and general alienation at all schools. The National Commission referred to the high schools as "beleaguered institutions," generally deteriorating and, in the largest cities at least, "on the verge of complete collapse." The PSAC panel pictured the high schools as on the one hand "monopolizing" the formal education of adolescents but on the other hand "inherently ill-suited" to perform many of the tasks essential to the creation of adults. And the USOE panel flatly asserted that the high schools had become "aging vats" and "custodial shelters" designed to protect young people from the hard realities of the world at precisely the same time as a growing number of them were simply "too mature to live all day under the routine controls of a large high school."

Given these diagnoses, what did the reports prescribe? In general, they urged an "opening up" of the school system in the interest of "recoupling the generations." The PSAC panel was the most far-reaching in its recommendations. It proposed that high schools be made smaller and more specialized, that students be permitted to attend more than one specialized high school, simultaneously or one after another, and that the schools themselves experiment with ways of serving as "agents" for their students in arranging for appropriate education outside of school (in businesses, for example, or in child-care centers or in museums). The panel proposed, additionally, that a whole series of work-study arrangements be developed so that young people could continue part-time study along with part-time work, or, alternatively, go back and forth between full-time study and full-time work. (It also proposed the legal modifications that would permit young people to do so, such as changing the minimum-age and minimum-wage laws so that employers might be encouraged to hire younger workers.) The panel proposed, further, that special government credit vouchers be devised, equivalent in value to the cost of a four-year college education, and given to young people at the age of, say, 16, so that responsibility for their education from that time forward would be in their own hands. And the panel proposed,

Suburban high school

finally, that a wide range of residential and nonresidential youth facilities and public-service programs (such as the Peace Corps, VISTA, or the Neighborhood Youth Corps) be created, under governmental sponsorship and on an experimental basis, that would allow formal education and community service to go forward hand-in-hand.

The National Commission and the USOE panel advanced similar proposals. They then added a number of recommendations that went far beyond, such as the wide use of broadcast commercial television and cable television for educational purposes, a national program of credit by examination, the abolition of corporal punishment in schools, and the development of codes of student rights and obligations (including the right of privacy with respect to student records).

On at least one major issue that cut across many of these recommendations, the three committees divided conspicuously. The National Commission stated outright that if the high school were to be anything other than a custodial institution, the state ought not to compel adolescents to attend it, and then went on to urge that the school-leaving age be dropped to 14. "The nation does not need laws that force adolescents to go to school," the commission asserted. "It needs schools and school-related programs that make adolescents wish to come." True, the commission also proposed that the right to free public education be extended to include two years beyond high school for all Americans. But it was the proposal to reduce the compulsory schooling requirement that was newsworthy and bound to provoke controversy. After all, it was only 50 years since another generation of reformers had fought valiantly and successfully to assure that every American would be able to attend school until the age of 16, no matter how much he or his family wanted the earnings that might come from full-time work.

Neither the PSAC panel nor the USOE panel went so far as to recommend a cutback in compulsory schooling, though the more general recommendation of the PSAC panel that laws relating to the protection of youth be reviewed with an eye to present-day needs and realities certainly made room for such a possibility. And doubtless many of the more general proposals put forward in all three reports would, if set in motion, dramatically transform the operational meaning of compulsory school attendance.

How accurate were these diagnoses and how appropriate were the remedies? Certainly there was no denying the pervasiveness of the symptoms. While one could point to any number of inner-city high schools—such as the John Dewey High School in New York City or the Parkway School in Philadelphia or the Robert Lindblom Technical High School in Chicago—that were centers of academic excellence and of high student and faculty morale, the overall academic achievement of inner-city schools was indeed declining and their overall disciplinary problems were indeed mounting. In fact, problems of school security had become sufficiently acute during 1973 for Representative Jonathan B. Bingham (D., N.Y.) to introduce a Safe Schools

In one report, it was urged that states drop school-leaving age to only 14

Lindblom Tech

Act into the Congress that would make federal funds available for un-armed security officers to patrol school corridors in districts across the country. But security problems were merely the highly visible tip of a much larger iceberg; for the signs of student alienation and unrest were everywhere, in wealthy suburban districts as well as in impoverished urban districts and among adolescents from well-to-do households as well as adolescents from disadvantaged households.

Some of this alienation could scarcely be blamed on the school, originating as it did in a larger society relentlessly taught by television, incessantly mobile, and increasingly polarized along racial, ethnic, and religious lines. But some of it was almost surely related to the social organization of the school itself. One 1973 study, for example, reported in preliminary form by Francis A. J. Ianni, Hope J. Leichter, and Hervé Varenne of Teachers College, Columbia University, and based on data from three quite different and widely separated institutions (a consolidated rural high school, a large inner-city high school, and a suburban high school), found a remarkably similar pattern of adult-youth segregation in all three schools. The pattern was apparent not only in conflicting sets of social and moral values (teachers and students differed profoundly on what constituted appropriate dress), but also in certain agreed-upon stand-offs in the day-by-day life of the school (particular washrooms were considered "off limits" to teachers and became the scene of various student activities considered illegitimate by teachers but legitimate by the students who engaged in them). In many significant realms of school activity, the "decoupling of the generations" was a substantial fact.

Yet, the "decoupling of the generations" has always been, in some measure, a fact of school life. What made it seem so significant in 1973? As is often the case when facts become diagnoses, certain theories played a crucial role. Students of socialization had been pointing out for almost a decade that Americans during the 20th century had assigned to their schools a growing number of tasks that in other societies were carried out by families, religious institutions, and farms and factories. These were tasks involving preparation for adulthood, and the schools were simply not managing them effectively. The argument was stated most eloquently, perhaps, by Urie Bronfenbrenner of Cornell University in a 1970 book entitled *Two Worlds of Childhood: U.S. and U.S.S.R.* Using comparative data on child-rearing in Russia and the United States, Bronfenbrenner cataloged the many situations in which adults and children interact freely in Russian families, neighborhood centers, schools, youth groups, farms, shops, factories, and government bureaus, with certain common civic and moral goals held constantly before both the adults and the children. He then pointed to the relative paucity of such interactions in the United States, where television watching and peer group activities have tended to replace adult-child associations. "As we read the evidence," Bronfenbrenner concluded, "both from our own research and that of others, we cannot escape the conclusion

Some signs of student unrest were surely related to the school itself

Bronfenbrenner's book

that, if the current trend persists, if the institutions of our society continue to remove parents and other adults, and older youth from active participation in the lives of children, and if the resulting vacuum is filled by the age-segregated peer group, we can anticipate increased alienation, indifference, antagonism, and violence on the part of the younger generation in all segments of our society—middle-class children as well as the disadvantaged."

Bronfenbrenner's recommendations for reversing what he called "the disruptive trends in the process of socialization in American society" all went in the direction of increasing opportunities for children to associate with adults in real situations—outside of school as well as inside—in which children undertake genuine responsibility for genuinely worth-while tasks. And by way of example, he and David Goslin of the Russell Sage Foundation arranged for a group of 12-year-olds to spend a few days actively participating in the work of the *Detroit Free Press*, a leading Midwestern newspaper. The employees of the *Free Press* actually began the experiment with serious misgivings —after all, they had a newspaper to get out—but they ended it with a warmly positive feeling about what the young people had contributed. For Bronfenbrenner and Goslin, the experiment eloquently demonstrated the potential of "recoupling the generations."

It was this line of theory that provided the intellectual context for the 1973 reports on the high school. And to many, the theory indicated some valuable leads to reform. However shrill the criticisms of American schooling in 1973, however poignant the special problems of inner-city institutions, American schools at large were teaching academic subject matter quite as effectively as they ever had, and to a steadily increasing segment of American youth—a 1973 study by Herbert H. Hyman of Wesleyan University confirmed once again this fact that had been repeatedly demonstrated since World War II. And yet there could be no denying that the schools were also attempting to accomplish many other tasks on behalf of the society that they appeared to be doing less effectively. It was in this latter realm that the reports of 1973 had made their most significant contribution. For while the continued reform of schooling itself would doubtless be one major outcome of the reports—indeed, many of the recommended changes were already in evidence in schools across the country—an even more important outcome might be the reform of education outside the school. And that reform was surely overdue, given the revolutionary changes that had occurred in American education during the second third of the 20th century.

The reform of education outside the school might be one result

Related Articles

For further information on education in 1973, see the following articles in Section Four:

Focus on The Arts

Alistair Cooke

The long road tour for plays to "Barnes-proof" them, the buying up of art works, and some good that came out of Watergate—all made 1973 a memorable year

There is a peculiar Broadway folk custom that is unknown, I believe, to any other theater capital. It is also unknown to the vast population of ordinary citizens, whom the theater people, in their clannish way, call "civilians." It is known as "the death watch," and it begins almost as soon as the curtain falls on any Broadway first night that involves a sizable investment of cash. Friends of the cast, stage-struck socialites, publicity people, and other hangers-on retire to a large private dining room of a fashionable restaurant in New York City to get the drinks flowing and to await the arrival of the stars, who —with their battle makeup on or off—march in like monarchs deferring gracefully to whoops of applause from their "people." There is an air of coziness so frantic as to be suspicious. And for good reason, for the uninvolved guest will notice that the food is only nervously pecked at by the stars in the intervals of waving, "visiting," and flashing radiant smiles at their idolaters. They are all waiting for the early edition of *The New York Times*, which will contain in its pages a review of the opening-night performance written by the *Times*'s daily theater critic, Clive Barnes. Resourceful public relations men can shorten the waiting ordeal by employing a runner to get galley proofs of the review from the newspaper even before it is off the press.

At some awful point between midnight and 2 A.M., the runner arrives, and the *Times*'s review is handed to someone sufficiently above the battle to be able to read it aloud without breaking into tears or hoarse shouts of triumph. It takes no more than a couple of minutes for the play's producer, the director, the backers, and the actors to know whether they have a hit or a bomb on their hands, whether they are about to reap a fortune or fold on Saturday night. Such is the unprecedented power of one man—akin to that of the emperor at a circus in ancient Rome—to turn his thumb up or down on every production of a Broadway season.

The fear and loathing of Barnes in the industry is understandable, but it is infantile at worst and unfair at best. Anyone who exhibits a talent in public—by way of a book, a picture, a concert, a television appearance, or whatever—is, in the act, inviting a public opinion. In law, there is the concept of "fair comment," by which critics and others have the right to state their honest and nonmalicious opinions about the public acts of public figures. Critics are as essential to an open society as a free press is to self-government.

Barnes's excessive power is a misfortune, but it is none of his doing. It is the fault of the society in which he practices his trade, the fault—if you like—of the audience, the newspaper industry, the labor unions, or whoever makes it impossible to maintain more than one influential morning newspaper in New York City. London has eight morning

Alistair Cooke

papers and a range of critical opinion divergent enough to scatter or dampen the power of the big guns. Accordingly, it takes an attack as concentrated as an artillery barrage to mow down any single play. The critics, the Londoners like to say, appeal to people who are interested in criticism, but they seldom have much influence on the ability of a production to survive. Consequently, any London season has a healthy crop of interesting, if unspectacular, plays that divert a small audience, run for several months, and make a small profit. More and more on Broadway, we have only smash hits and disasters.

In 1973, the producers and the increasingly reluctant backers, the people who put up the money, did something to assuage this harrowing ordeal. For decades, they have been accustomed to insure themselves against the ruin of a Broadway investment by the device known as an out-of-town tryout. According to the producer's guess of his play's probable longevity in New York City, he opens it in Boston or Detroit or Toronto or New Haven, Conn., for a week or a month. If he is deeply unsure of his Broadway reception, he is likely to launch the show in one of these cities and then doctor it up during a tour of the others. The night he opens on Broadway, the die is cast, and it is cast – as we have painfully demonstrated – by nobody but Clive Barnes.

Every Broadway theater has a minimum "break-even" box-office take. For example, a musical just mounted in New York City must take in $80,000 a week to make a profit over the long run. This figure has been partly insured by an advance sale of tickets to charities that buy up blocks of seats for a run of performances. When this charity investment is considerable, the producer hastens to publicize it ("Half a Million Advance Sale for *Yes, Yes, Blanchette!*"). But there have been musicals with an advance of over a million dollars that closed on the second night. For the advance is spread over many months, and even if the aforementioned musical is sure of reaping $40,000 a week from charity benefits, it must still take in another $40,000 at the box office to survive in the black.

In short, any Broadway production is both a hazard and a luxury. In 1973, several producers decided to by-pass the Broadway agony altogether. In February, a well-rigged Broadway show – *Lorelei*, starring Carol Channing – opened, improbably enough, in Oklahoma City. From there, it went on to a dozen other cities from coast to coast, and at the end of the year it was playing to large houses in Los Angeles. The plan was to unveil this $500,000 capital investment on Broadway in January, 1974, by which time it will have handsomely recovered its investors' money, so that it could close in a week and still leave its backers happy.

The travels of *Lorelei* constitute not so much a protracted tryout as the innovation of a long and independent road tour. One producer has concluded, after several trying experiences on Broadway, that "the long road tour is a way to be Barnes-proof." He opened his revival of the 1927 musical *Good News* in the middle of December in Boston, from where it will embark on a road tour ad infinitum. He may well wind

Gone with the Wind

up with a fat profit on a "Broadway" show that never appeared on Broadway. Similarly, regional audiences have already reimbursed another producer with a mammoth staging of *Gone with the Wind*, which is not even meant to be seen in New York. And although Angela Lansbury became, as they say, the toast of London in a revival of *Gypsy*, she will be seen on Broadway, if at all, only after six months on the Barnes-proof circuit.

Undoubtedly, these audacious producers have met and conquered the most dire of Broadway's problems. But in so doing, they have exposed the root weakness of Broadway as a national theater capital: its evidently chronic incapacity to sustain on a paying basis—as London, Paris, and Tokyo do—a classical repertory and a seasonal range of interesting new playwrights, as well as the hit shows and the profitable trash.

Two amazing ads appeared in newspapers' arts sections

The most experienced private collector of art objects I know strolls into a gallery or a furniture shop and after glancing with simulated indifference at something he actually lusts after, he drifts off hinting that if the price could be dramatically sliced, "I might be interested." This is the first hand of a poker game that usually ends with my friend acquiring the object of his desire at a price rather better than the agent's customary 30 per cent off. It seems, though, that this inscrutable Western technique is unknown to Oriental customers. At any rate, on the first Sunday in November, two extraordinary advertisements appeared in the arts sections of newspapers in New York City, Chicago, Dallas, and Los Angeles. They were placed by two Japanese investment groups, who proclaimed in bold type: "Unlimited Cash Available" and "Highest Possible Prices Paid." It is not the normal Western way of sidling up to a bargain. What the Japanese tycoons were after was all the available work of a score of impressionist and postimpressionist and modern painters.

It is by now a facetious cliché that, as the Europeans peevishly complain, "the Japanese are the new postwar Americans" who—like Americans in the 1920s and 1930s—irritate the natives by inflating the going price of everything from restaurant meals to works of art. In the United States, the Japanese have been briskly buying up rafts of country clubs, hotels, conglomerates, and even investment houses. They have now descended—like our first generation of robber barons in the late 1800s—on those beautiful baubles known as works of art, without which the new-rich feel uncomfortably anonymous.

Of course, the latest tycoon—from the time of the first Queen Elizabeth to the second—has always wanted to annex the work of the most fashionable painters, sculptors, and furniture designers as status symbols. But in our time, there has been nothing like the decade of the 1960s for re-evaluating works of art as stock-exchange collateral. The Germans were the first to get on their feet, and they inflated alarmingly the prices of French and English furniture, and, more recently, Chinese jade and Indian sculpture. For 20 years or more, the impressionists and postimpressionists have been the favorite safe investments.

Ad for art

Renoir, Monet, Manet, Degas, even Miro, Chagall, and Soutine have remained unflaggingly chic as their original revolutionary impact has softened. But I suspect that their stock value will soon be in doubt, and perhaps the Japanese are more naïve than we think. It takes only one decisive change of fashion to send the prices tumbling for artists we had assumed to be immortal. Who would have thought that in our time the Pre-Raphaelites and the academic Victorians would come charging back into style, even into frantic demand? Yet George Frederick Watts's mournful lady sitting on top of a globe (and cryptically called *Hope*), which fetched only $750 at auction 40 years ago, was sold in 1970 for close to $1 million.

Australia made a dramatic move on the artistic stock exchange

A waggish neophyte collector, none other than Allen Funt of television's "Candid Camera" series, started only six years ago a risky experiment designed to expose the vanity of the art market–and incidentally to make a small fortune out of it. He saw a painting by Sir Lawrence Alma-Tadema, Queen Victoria's favorite artist, and on the expert assurance that he was looking at "the worst painter of the 19th century," he began to buy up Alma-Tademas. Hardly for a song, because the incredible resurrection of the Victorians was already well underway. But his first purchase happened to be Alma-Tadema's last painting, and Funt bought it for $8,000. In November, 1973, he sold his entire collection–35 paintings, for $570,000.

The Japanese, I am told, are now moving into English silver and porcelain, which have consequently almost doubled their prices in the past three years. But this could be the last of the Japanese raids for some time to come. The Arab boycott that resulted from the October war between Israel and the Arab states has caused an enormous cut in the Japanese supply of oil, with damaging effects on the nation's economy that, at this writing, can only be guessed at.

How far the Australians are affected by the Arab-Israeli vendetta is, at the moment, obscure. But before it all happened, it was the Australians who made the most dramatic invasion of the artistic stock exchange. And it came not from tycoons but from the Australian government, which, on behalf of the taxpayer, set a new record for a modern work by purchasing a Jackson Pollock canvas–*Blue Poles*, one of the masterpieces of 20th century art–for $2 million. The costliest painting ever to enter Australia, it will hang in the Australian National Gallery, on which construction began in 1973. Had it not been for the loyalty or mulishness of Pablo Picasso's widow, the Australians would have dropped an unequaled blockbuster on the international art exchange. For Picasso's famous *Guernica* they offered, and the widow rejected, $16 million.

Art at auction

The year 1973 will also be remembered, I hope, for the strengthening of the Public Broadcasting Service by a curious and unintended consequence of a public scandal. When the Senate Select Committee looking into the Watergate affair was riding high in the spring ("every Senator," as one politician put it, "running for President in prime time"), the White House became alarmed at the television monopoly its accusers seemed to be setting up with their long, live coverage of the hearings. The White House began to protest that it was being denied, in the official phrase, "equal communication" in a medium over which, in fact, the President has an instant monopoly anytime he wishes. In the late fall, President Richard M. Nixon began to redress this fancied imbalance with his frequent appearances on the networks during his campaign known as Operation Candor. What was little noticed, between the first protest and the President's acting on it, was the fate of a congressional authorization to provide the base of public television's budget. The President had vetoed a two-year funding bill for the Corporation for Public Broadcasting (CPB) in June, 1972. When he did so, he indicated that his action had been influenced by the "public and legislative" debate about the bill. During this debate, the corporation's increasing tendency to focus on public affairs, rather than more straightforward educational matters, had drawn considerable criticism. But then came the Watergate hearings, on commercial television by day and on public television by night. And as more and more of the cloak-and-dagger epic began to unfold, as more and more White House aides confessed, or were fired, or indicted, the White House found it prudent to demonstrate that it had nothing to fear from the very popular "gavel to gavel" replays of the hearings in prime time by the stations of the Public Broadcasting Service.

Public TV is now more safely funded than it has ever been

To have tried to kill the service's budget at that point would have looked like a White House effort to plug freedom of information at its source. So, on August 6, Mr. Nixon signed legislation authorizing $55-million for the CPB for fiscal 1974, with another $65 million assured for fiscal 1975. True, the legislation requires the CPB to raise $10-million in matching funds from nonfederal sources. And true, the nation's 237 public broadcasting stations are required to keep logs of any of their programs on which public issues are aired. But the appropriation went through, and the noncommercial network of publicly supported stations is now more safely funded than ever before. It is a consolation to reflect that the ill wind of Watergate blew all of us some good.

Related Articles

For further information on the arts in 1973, see the following articles in Section Four:

Watergate hearing

Focus on Sports
Jim Murray

In 1973, sports swapped its helmet for a Homburg, and even the bench-sitters were paid the kind of money only the biggest businessmen used to make

Spell it $port$. List it on the Big Board. Cover it with a ticker. Admit the gentleman from the *Wall Street Journal* to the press box. Never mind the score, give us the gross. Instead of industrials, rails, and utilities for closing stock averages, give us athletics. Never mind the bid-and-asked on 7-Up stock, just give us the bid-and-asked on 7-foot basketball centers. Who needs a scorekeeper? Give us a bookkeeper. Who wants to write off an oil field when he can write off an outfield? The financial pages of daily papers are usually on the back of the sports pages. They should merge.

In 1973, $port$ swapped its helmet for a Homburg. It's gone from Main Street to Wall Street. It's a whole new moneyed class in our society. There was a time when the country went into shock at the news that a mere athlete earned more than the President. Never mind that it was Babe Ruth, who stood alone on the landscape of his profession and that the President was Herbert Hoover who, you might say, did too, at the time. (Ruth's crack that "I had a better year than he did" was—alas!—all too true. But even though it was Babe Ruth, that did little to allay the unconscionable priorities involved.)

Well, in 1973, a single basketball player was paid three times more—and, as it happens, not to play—than the President of the United States. And nobody even looked up. Wilt Chamberlain got $600,000 in unmarked bills for *coaching* the San Diego Conquistadors, which is not to be confused with settling the Middle East crisis. No one called for impeachment, though Wilt had a worse year than Hoover did.

Remember when the papers published the pictures of the 10 highest salaried men in the United States? I think they stopped it because it had a bad effect on guys in soup lines to read that movie moguls or automakers were paying themselves $762,409.12 a year with stock options. But there weren't any *basketball* players in there, for cryin' out loud. There was Alfred P. Sloan of General Motors, and Thomas J. Watson of IBM, and Louis B. Mayer of MGM. Ballplayers got paid just enough to buy a new hunting dog. The Four Horsemen got a couple of hundred dollars a game. Not apiece—for all *four* of them.

Of all the athletes of the so-called "Golden Era of Sports," the 1920s, only Jack Dempsey and Gene Tunney really gave any indication of the capital explosion that was to come in childhood games played by men. They split $2 million, and it would be 40 years before any two pugilists—Muhammad Ali and Joe Frazier—excited the same kind of hang-the-price-I've-got-to-see-it feeling again.

But it's not the once-in-a-lifetime superstars or super events. *Scrubs* make more money than Presidents today. Callow youths have bank presidents and federal judges and high-priced lawyers fighting over them and lavishing sums on them that once would have bought rail-

Jim Murray

roads—for dribbling a basketball. Guys go from one-o-cat sandlots to Park Avenue, Bel Air, Shaker Heights.

Wilt Chamberlain, no less, built the biggest, most expensive house that has been built in this country since, probably, the heyday of Palm Beach and Newport, R.I. An outsize million-dollar pad on the biggest hill in Los Angeles. Citizen Kane should come walking out of it, not some articulated egret of a man whose contribution to society is the 2-inch dunk. The interior-decorating bill alone would have been beyond the budgetary reach of a basketball player a decade ago.

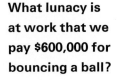

What lunacy is at work that we pay $600,000 for bouncing a ball?

How in the world did we evolve into a society paying people $600,000 to run around in their underwear for 48 minutes a night, bouncing a ball up and down on a hardwood court or picking it off a glass backboard? What lunacy is at work here? Whatever would Horatio Alger think? How can you write a story of a poor but honest boy who, by dint of pluck, grit, sand, and determination rose to be 7 feet 1 inch tall?

It wouldn't be so eye-opening if it were confined to basketball, where even the bench-sitters turn green from money instead of from envy of the Chamberlains. But pick a sport. *Any* sport.

Baseball? Richard Anthony Allen is a moderately skilled outfielder-first baseman with the Chicago White Sox. He's not precisely a "superstar" because "superstars" never get shopped around and traded in the prime of their careers. Franchise owners would find a way to accommodate Dracula if he could bat .400. Richard has a lifetime batting average of .299, which is no threat at all to Ty Cobb's .367 or Rogers Hornsby's .358. Richard could catch them only if he batted .480 a year from here on out. At age 31, even then he'd have to last longer than he probably will. No one ever compared him to Joe DiMaggio in the field, and he's a cool 426 home runs behind Babe Ruth. He's 2,071 lifetime hits behind Cobb.

Never mind. Richard Anthony Allen, semicastoff who has played with three National League teams and one American League club (to date), is the highest-salaried player in all the long annals of baseball—$675,000 for three years. No candy bars will be named after him. He will never be a statue in centerfield. He is not otherwise a serious candidate for the Hall of Fame, though he may go there as a historic figure—the *first* $200,000-a-year ballplayer.

Joe Namath at work

Football? In 1965, the New York Jets, a have-not team in a have-not league (the old AFL) bought a gimpy-legged, fast-living quarterback for $400,000 (for three years), and the deal changed the face of football. Joe Willie Namath could do only one thing in a game and do it well: pass. It was enough. And Joe Willie is still the highest-paid in the NFL—the league *he* merged—at $275,000 a year, even though he misses more games than the waterboy. With a new league forming, the World Football League, the possibility exists that a Joe Willie Namath of the future may be able to hold out for Rhode Island and parts of Massachusetts, including the offshore islands.

Hockey? Hockey may be the most amazing of all. In 1965, hockey was a six-team "league," as private as a key club, as clannish as Scotland. The "National Hockey League" was about as "national" as the Grand Banks of Labrador. It didn't grow, it fissioned. It had been running a nice little private grift where there were about two new openings a year on the ice for recruits and playing to 100 per cent capacity in most arenas. Games were almost incestuous, players were swapped around so freely. But it wasn't getting in on the burgeoning television budgets, so the czars of the league moved. They went from 6 to 12 franchises overnight. They knew the players—performing for peon pay compared to other sports—would get restless. But they couldn't leave that money lying around.

The new hockey league paid to get players with marquee value

Contracts were upgraded but still manageable—until the World Hockey Association (WHA) came into the picture. Like the AFL, the WHA went after marquee value. Unlike football, hockey doesn't have instant celebrities coming out of colleges. *It* had to settle for established stars. You don't get a publicized commodity like O. J. Simpson out of an ice pond in Edmonton.

Bobby Hull was the first to jump. Miffed when the Boston Bruins' Bobby Orr signed a million-dollar five-year contract, he demanded one dollar more from the Chicago Black Hawks. When they demurred, he jumped to Winnipeg in the WHA for $1 million just to sign and $1.75 million spread out over 10 years.

Gordie Howe may be the oldest "recruit" ever wooed by new owners. After 25 years at Detroit, Gordie, at 45, signed for four years at $1 million with Houston. Houston also signed his two sons.

The Bruins' Derek Sanderson, who earned $13,000 in 1971 in Boston, jumped to the WHA (Philadelphia) for $2.65 million. He scored just three goals—and Philadelphia settled with him for $1 million. His pay came to $333,333.33 per goal.

This table illustrates the dollar explosion that was raining $100 bills down on the athletes as 1973 faded into the record books:

	Football	Baseball	Hockey	Basketball
Minimum salary	$ 12,000	$ 15,000	$ 15,000	$ 17,500
Average salary	$ 29,000	$ 31,000	$ 45,000	$ 90,000-$100,000
High salary	$275,000	$225,000	$200,000	$600,000
Number of players	1,000	600	304	204
Players earning over $100,000	12	42	45	60

The image of the athlete as a Cro-Magnon cretin with the instincts of a goat, the appetites of a sybarite, the judgment of a moth, and an IQ that would barely enable him to feed himself dies hard. To be sure, the guys selling electric toothpick franchises, the real estate hucksters with the property quite literally on the water—the whole fraternity of fast-buck barkers—are on their trail. A Jerry Lucas goes broke, a prizefighter ends up shining shoes, and everybody says, "Uh-huh! You see, they can't add." The presumption is, it's a good thing somebody is keeping score for them in a game.

Bobby Hull and million

But, when you make a million-two for two years' work, who needs the fast-buck operator? Bank interest is all right on *that* kind of money. Pensions are not peonage, either. A hockey player gets $2,738 a month after 20 years. Baseball players get $2,400 a month after age 65 for 20 years' service. Leo Durocher even stopped dyeing his hair and 'fessed up for that kind of money. He went "from 58 to 65 in one year," San Diego Padres president Buzzie Bavasi commented. Football players get $465 a month at age 55 if they've played 5 years.

Sports is a Big Rock Candy Mountain. Even without mentioning Jack Nicklaus and golf and Bobby Riggs and tennis, it is possible to see the new economic élite makes its fortunes in cleats. And all this without pay-TV, which may bring the *billion*-dollar contract within the grasp of 7-foot centers or Slobbovian field goal kickers. In the light of this, it's well to consider the dire future the late columnist W. O. McGeehan predicted for televised sports in January, 1925:

"Science seems to be working out the doom of professional sports. A dispatch from Washington says that Mr. C. Francis Jenkins has perfected an apparatus by which persons may see moving objects miles away by radio.

"Dipping only casually into the future, one can see the time when . . . persons possessing these machines will be able to sit in their homes or offices and watch a World Series or a heavyweight championship fight without contributing to the gate receipts.

"It sounds very ominous for the promoters of professional sports. It has been made . . . obvious . . . sports cannot exist without customers.

"How long could Mr. Charles A. Stoneham maintain the Polo Grounds without customers? How long could Colonel Jacob Ruppert support the Yankee Stadium and Mr. Babe Ruth if there were no gate receipts?

"It means the unemployment of practically all our professional athletes, from Mr. Jack Dempsey and Mr. Babe Ruth down to the preliminary prizefighters and semipro baseball players.

"Mr. Babe Ruth, deprived of his professional standing, and his salary of $50,000 a year, would be forced to depend entirely on literature for his livelihood, and literary work at best is a precarious existence . . . The Government should consider the far-reaching possibilities and its effects on posterity."

Obviously, in his wildest imaginings, Mr. McGeehan could never even *dream* of Howard Cosell.

Related Articles

For further information on sports in 1973, see Sports and the articles on individual sports in Section Four.

Someday, pay-TV might bring the billion-dollar sports contract

TV at the game

Section Two

Special Reports

Seven articles give special treatment to subjects
of current importance and lasting interest.

Mexico: The Surging Spirit Of Nationalism

By Robert E. Quirk

**A revolutionary fervor for reform has helped
to create a growing sense of national unity**

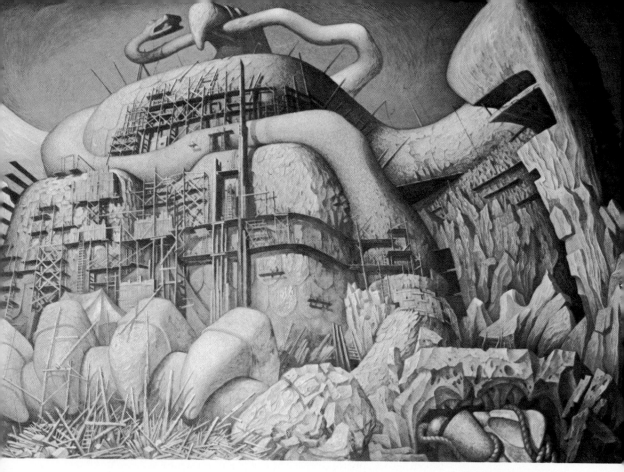

Mexico, mural by Jorge
Gonzalez Camarena (1950).

Mexico's identity as a
nation incorporates many
diverse elements. They
are symbolized here as
a Spanish conquistador
and an Aztec chief (both
left foreground), the fires
of revolution, and the
intertwined figures of
an eagle and a serpent,
symbols of Mexico's past.

Each year, on the 15th of September, at precisely 11 P. M., the president of Mexico steps out onto the central balcony of the National Palace in Mexico City. Below, in Constitution Plaza (known as the Zócalo), thousands of Mexicans have been gathering for hours. They have come to hear the president read the *Grito de Dolores* (Cry of Dolores)—the call to arms sounded by Mexico's hero priest Miguel Hidalgo y Costilla on Sept. 15, 1810, in the town of Dolores (now Dolores Hidalgo). "Mexicanos, viva México," cries the president, and at those concluding words, the Liberty Bell above the main entrance begins to ring. High above the palace, fireworks explode.

The re-enactment of that night in 1810 when Hidalgo sparked Mexico's War of Independence against Spain has a twofold significance today. It is a graphic reminder of the nation's revolutionary past. It is also a nationwide ritual that celebrates the nation's successful struggle to achieve a sense of unity through the successful creation of a dynamic Mexico for Mexicans.

For centuries, national unity was lacking in Mexico. Most Mexicans lived in poverty and in rural isolation, separated from the educated city population by economic, social, and even language barriers. There was little sense of nationalism or even national purpose. Poor communications and high production costs hindered economic development. Nor did the revolution bring any marked social change to Mexico during the 19th century. One ruling class merely replaced another. Feuding political factions kept the country in turmoil. Conservatives favored a strongly centralized government; liberals believed in a federal system that gave more powers to the states and deliberately weakened the national government. Some Mexicans were monarchists who used the occasion of foreign intervention to set up an empire. This rivalry, made worse by stubbornness on all sides, helped doom the country to half a century of civil war.

An even more formidable obstacle to national unity—from a psychological standpoint—was the proximity of the United States. Sebastián Lerdo de Tejada, a Mexican president during the 1870s, is said to have lamented: "Poor Mexico! So far from God and so close to the United States!" And for good or for bad, Mexico's history since independence has been closely linked with the destiny of its neighbor to the north. The contacts between the two peoples during the 1800s gave rise to attitudes and stereotypes that determined Mexico's self-image for more than a century.

One reason was obvious—war between the two countries. The westward expansion of the United States in the 19th century had posed an obvious threat to the Mexicans. They claimed the vast area comprising present-day Texas, New Mexico, Arizona, Utah, Nevada, Colorado, and California as part of their Spanish heritage, but they maintained spotty control over it. As ever-increasing numbers of American pioneers moved onto Mexico's lands, the friendship initially inspired by the common cause of independence turned to suspicion and finally enmity. Inevitably, war came in 1846. By 1848, Mexico had been forced to give up half of its national territory to the victorious troops of the United States.

The defeat left Mexico with bitter memories, and though the United States paid $15 million in compensation for the conquered territories, Mexicans preserved their feelings of hostility and frustration in histories and popular literature. Herein, however, lay a paradox: While most Mexicans condemned the invasions, many at the same time admired the political institutions of the United States. They adopted the American principles of federalism in their Constitution of 1857 and chose a system of government with executive, legislative, and judicial branches, and with checks and balances similar to those provided in the U.S. Constitution. And, like the American Founding Fathers, such as Thomas Jefferson, Mexico's 19th-century liberals drew inspiration from the philosophical ideals of the French Enlightenment. They believed that reason, not passion and superstition, should guide the nation.

These Mexicans imitated outsiders. Not wanting to be Spanish, rejecting the culture of the native Indian population, Mexico's liberals hoped, through education, to make their nation Anglo-American in

The author:
Robert E. Quirk is a professor of history at Indiana University. He is the author of *The Mexican Revolution, 1914-1915* and *Mexico.* He was managing editor of the *Hispanic American Historical Review* from 1965 to 1970.

The Revolution Against the Porfirio Díaz Dictatorship (detail), mural by David Alfaro Siqueiros (1957-1967)

The Revolution of 1910 marked the beginning of Mexico's march toward unity. It was directed against the tyrannical rule of Porfirio Díaz, here shown surrounded by fawning military leaders and businessmen.

politics and business, and French in culture. Mexicans wrote novels, composed salon music, painted pictures, and built their city houses according to the prevailing fashions in Paris. They turned their backs on their own past.

As Mexico borrowed the customs of non-Spanish foreigners, the Americans, by contrast, grew in confidence and self-esteem. They professed to admire those virtues they found in their own Protestant forebears and in the hardy pioneers of the West—honesty, hard work, thrift, and punctuality. Nationalism is relative; it requires a yardstick. And Americans began to measure themselves against the Mexicans they had met in the Southwest and had defeated in battle during the Texas War for Independence and the 1846 conflict. The Mexicans were Roman Catholics and closer to the Middle Ages than to the modern world, the Americans felt. To the Americans, they seemed easygoing, unenterprising, and wasteful. The growing American racial consciousness and feelings of superiority can best be seen in the "portraits" depicted in the dime novels, the popular adventure literature of the day. These pictured the Mexican on the frontier as a "greaser" who should be distrusted by the brave, honorable, American pioneer. And these juvenile prejudices were reinforced when educated Americans came under the influence of Social Darwinism, a new theory based on the survival of the fittest. These followers of biologist

Charles Darwin and philosopher Herbert Spencer held that some human "races," notably those of mixed blood, were inferior and must inevitably lose out in nature's "struggle for survival" to those who were "fitter" and more modern and scientific in their outlook. By the end of the 19th century, educators, businessmen, and statesmen in the United States, convinced of the superiority of their own culture, tended to see Mexico as a second-class country that could be saved only by the "civilizing" influences of American political leaders and foreign investors.

Mexicans responded by creating their own stereotypes of the Americans. Conservative newspapers rejected American values. Roman Catholic priests and bishops in Mexico pointed to the dangers of Protestant missionary activity from the United States. Wandering balladeers sang in towns and villages of "gringo" treachery and cowardice. The American invaders, they said, were "soft"; unlike the tough Mexican soldiers who ate tortillas and beans, the Americans required ham and cakes.

But Social Darwinism made a strong impact in Mexico, too. By 1910, many Mexican leaders had come to believe that their people might, indeed, be inferior. They concluded that they must reject ever more resolutely their Spanish and Indian past, that if they hoped to survive the savage competition among the world's nations they must act like Anglo-Saxons. The dictatorial regime of Porfirio Díaz (1876-1880; 1884-1911) stressed the new doctrine of "scientificism," a philosophy of French Positivism. It called for the scientific allocation of skills and resources to put the nation on a sound economic, political, and social footing. The program, however, was to be administered only by the ruling classes, the "fittest" of the Mexicans. The Díaz government welcomed foreign capital with large land grants and lucrative mineral and petroleum concessions. As one critic of the government summed up his frustrations, Mexico became the "mother of foreigners and the stepmother of the Mexicans."

This was the situation when a rebellion led by Francisco I. Madero broke out against the Díaz regime in November, 1910, and the aged dictator was forced into exile. The Revolution (always spelled in Mexico with a capital R) was basically nationalistic. It was also an exceedingly complex movement lasting for more than half a century and involving many diverse revolutions: It was a political revolt against dictatorship and a religious revolt against a conservative church. It repudiated the Social Darwinists and opposed foreign influences in the arts and literature, insisting on the value of Mexico's native, Indian culture. Leaders of the Revolution called for Mexicanization of foreign oil properties and mining ventures. They insisted on land reform

The Trench, fresco by José Clemente Orozco (1926).

The crucifixlike design formed by the torsos of three revolutionaries dramatizes Mexico's fight to remove political and social inequities.

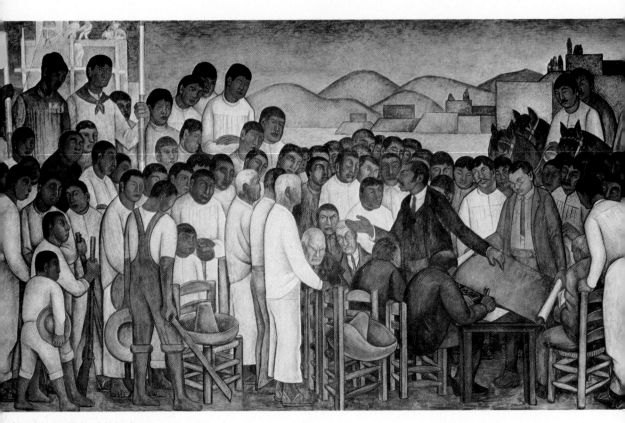

Distribution of the Land,
fresco by Diego Rivera (1926).

A revolutionary program
of land reform, under
which large privately
held tracts were broken
up and distributed
to Mexican peasants
as communal holdings,
sparked a much-needed
sense of participation
in the nation's destiny.

through the division of vast, privately held estates among the people.

Madero hoped to go back to the liberalism of the pre-Díaz era and, at the same time, prevent violent social upheaval that would, he feared, destroy lives and private property. He believed that social improvement should come slowly and within the law. But in declaring his revolt, Madero had uncaged a wild beast, and the more radical revolutionaries turned in fury upon the supporters of the Díaz government. They attacked landowners, businessmen, the Roman Catholic Church, and foreign capital. Madero, a weak president, lost control of his Revolution and died in 1913, the victim of assassins' bullets. For the next seven years, Mexicans fought out the issues raised by the revolutionaries of 1910, and not until Álvaro Obregón took over the presidency in 1920 did peace return.

Beginning with Álvaro Obregón's term of office (1920-1924), dynamic young Mexican revolutionaries heralded the creation of a new but ever-old Mexico, as they preached with missionary fervor the ideals of patriots such as Emiliano Zapata, leader of the Revolution in Morelos. They called for an expanded educational system. They found their ideals dramatically expressed in the novels of Mariano Azuela and Martín Luis Guzmán, in the music of Carlos Chávez, and in the mural paintings of Diego Rivera, David Siqueiros, and José

Text continued on page 66

The *Year Book* Trans-Vision®:
Toward Mexicanism

The Trans-Vision® unit on the following pages illustrates some of the factors contributing to the growth of Mexican nationalism discussed in the Special Report by Robert E. Quirk. Professor Quirk assisted in the preparation of this unit, as did John P. Augelli, Dean of International Programs at the University of Kansas.

At the time of the Mexican Revolution of 1910, about 1 per cent of the Mexican people owned most of the agricultural land. But as part of the continuing revolution, agrarian reform–which reached its peak between 1934 and 1940–has brought land to the landless peasants and helped give them a sense of belonging to the Mexican nation. The Trans-Vision® overlays demonstrate how Mexico's cultivated cropland has been successfully redistributed, chiefly by means of *ejidos* (communal landholdings worked by individual farmers). The diagram on this page shows on the local level the nationwide reforms presented on the overlays. It illustrates how two *haciendas* (large privately owned estates) became ejidos in an area where land distribution has had a major impact. Today, ejidos comprise about half of Mexico's total cropland.

The unit also dramatizes the growth of a transportation network that now reaches into all corners of the republic–aiding the circulation of people, goods, and ideas, and helping tie Mexico's dissimilar regions into a national whole. Finally, the unit shows the tremendous increase in city populations, a trend that has loosened old ties to places of origin and contributed to the feeling of Mexicanism.

Land Reform in Action: from Haciendas to Ejidos

Cultivated land (haciendas)   Redistributed land (ejidos)

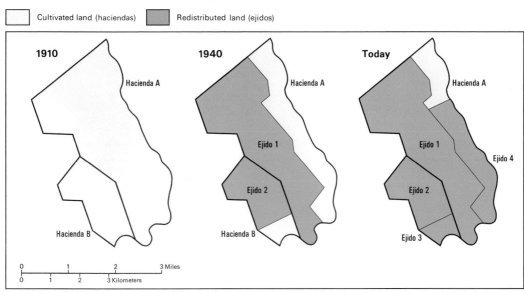

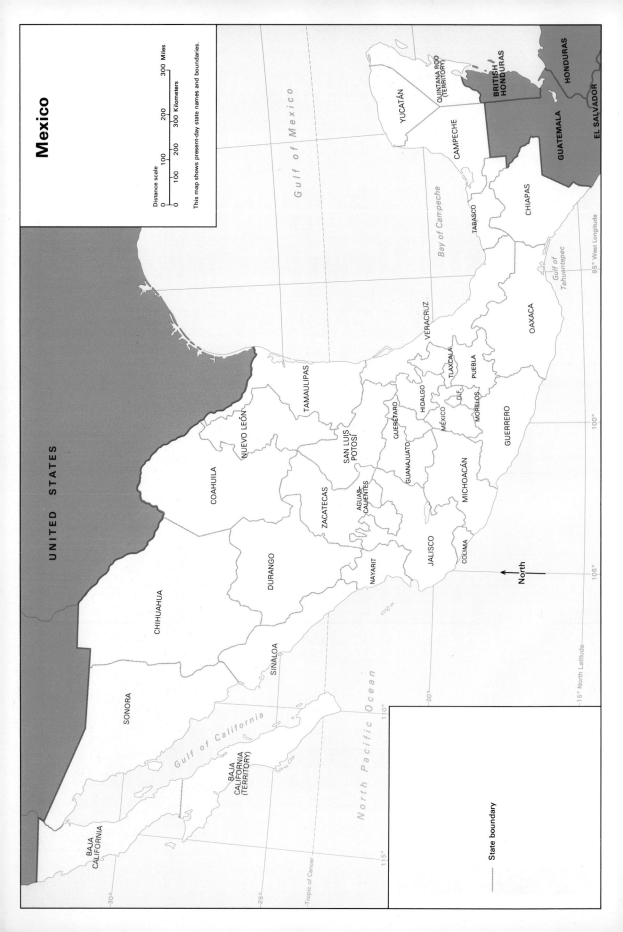

Mexico

Distance scale

0   100   200   300 Miles

0   100   200   300 Kilometers

This map shows present-day state names and boundaries.

UNITED STATES

Gulf of Mexico

Bay of Campeche

Gulf of Tehuantepec

North Pacific Ocean

Gulf of California

BAJA CALIFORNIA

BAJA CALIFORNIA (TERRITORY)

SONORA

CHIHUAHUA

SINALOA

DURANGO

COAHUILA

NUEVO LEÓN

TAMAULIPAS

NAYARIT

ZACATECAS

SAN LUIS POTOSÍ

AGUAS-CALIENTES

JALISCO

COLIMA

GUANAJUATO

QUERÉTARO

HIDALGO

MÉXICO

D.F.

TLAXCALA

PUEBLA

MORELOS

MICHOACÁN

GUERRERO

VERACRUZ

OAXACA

TABASCO

CHIAPAS

CAMPECHE

YUCATÁN

QUINTANA ROO (TERRITORY)

BRITISH HONDURAS

GUATEMALA

HONDURAS

EL SALVADOR

95° West Longitude

100°

105°

110°

115°

15° North Latitude

20°

25°

30°

Tropic of Cancer

North

————— State boundary

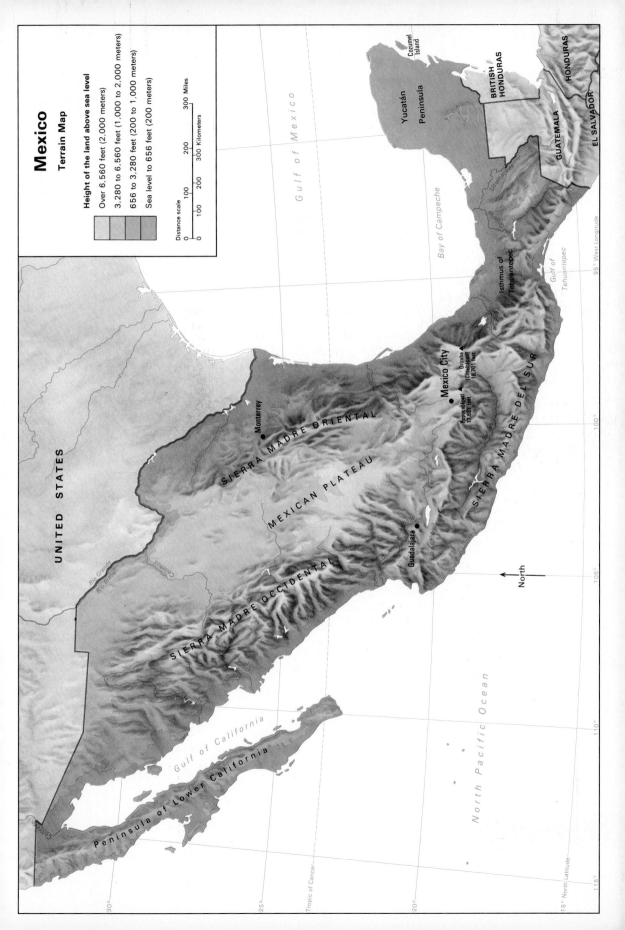

Mexico

Terrain Map

Height of the land above sea level

Over 6,560 feet (2,000 meters)

3,280 to 6,560 feet (1,000 to 2,000 meters)

656 to 3,280 feet (200 to 1,000 meters)

Sea level to 656 feet (200 meters)

Distance scale

0   100   200   300 Miles

0   100   200   300 Kilometers

UNITED STATES

Gulf of Mexico

Bay of Campeche

Yucatán Peninsula

Cozumel Island

BRITISH HONDURAS

GUATEMALA

HONDURAS

EL SALVADOR

Isthmus of Tehuantepec

Gulf of Tehuantepec

Monterrey

SIERRA MADRE ORIENTAL

MEXICAN PLATEAU

Mexico City

Popocatepetl 17,887 feet

Orizaba (Chitlatepetl) 18,701 feet

SIERRA MADRE DEL SUR

Guadalajara

SIERRA MADRE OCCIDENTAL

Rio Grande
Rio Bravo

Conchos

North

North Pacific Ocean

Gulf of California

Peninsula of Lower California

Tropic of Cancer

15° North Latitude

95° West Longitude

100°

105°

110°

115°

30°

25°

20°

Clemente Orozco. Prominent Mexicans named their children after preconquest Aztec chiefs, instead of Christian saints. Indian folk art—pottery, weaving, and lacquer trays—was collected and displayed with pride. Revolutionary Mexico proposed to identify the nation with the ancient glories of the Aztec, Maya, and Toltec civilizations.

Inevitably, the Revolution involved the United States. The U.S. ambassador to Mexico in 1911 admired Díaz and worked against the new Madero government. When Victoriano Huerta overthrew Madero in 1913, U.S. President Woodrow Wilson declined to recognize the new regime. In his dealings with a succession of revolutionary factions in Mexico, he refused to accept the Mexican leaders as his equals. By treating them like schoolchildren, he said, he would teach the Mexicans to elect "good men." To bring about the defeat of Huerta, he sent U.S. soldiers and marines into Veracruz. To punish Francisco (Pancho) Villa, a Mexican rebel leader, for an attack on U.S. territory, he ordered General John J. Pershing to invade northern Mexico in 1916. But the new head of Mexico's revolutionary government, Venustiano Carranza, would not agree to the presence of American troops in his country, even to help defeat Huerta and Villa. Wilson was forced to back down. In his contest with the obstinate Carranza, President Wilson met his match.

Carranza, by standing up for his country's sovereign rights, compelled the U.S. government to begin changing its manner of dealing with Mexico, to recognize that Mexico was not a client state that could be manipulated by Washington. The stubbornness of Carranza and his successors bore fruit in the 1930s, when President Franklin D. Roosevelt, as part of his new Latin American policy, officially recognized that Mexico and the United States were indeed "Good Neighbors," and that there would be no more U.S. interference in Mexican domestic or foreign affairs.

Although the well-intentioned leaders of both nations could sign international treaties of friendship, deep-seated attitudes and century-old prejudices on each side were less easily altered. And in Mexico, by the end of the 1920s, the reforming spirit and the revolutionary enthusiasm that had characterized the Obregón years began to wane, as successful revolutionaries became rich, conservative, and corrupt. Many Mexicans expressed doubts that their politicians could ever fulfill the ideals of the 1910 Revolution or that their country, under a succession of corrupt presidents, could really deal with the United States on equal terms.

It was during this period of widespread disillusionment that Samuel Ramos wrote his *Profile of Man and Culture in Mexico* (1934). Ramos, a professor of philosophy at the National University, used Freudian

Night of the Rich, fresco by Diego Rivera (1929).

Exploitation by profit-hungry foreigners was resented by Mexicans. To eliminate it, Mexico began nationalizing its industries in 1938.

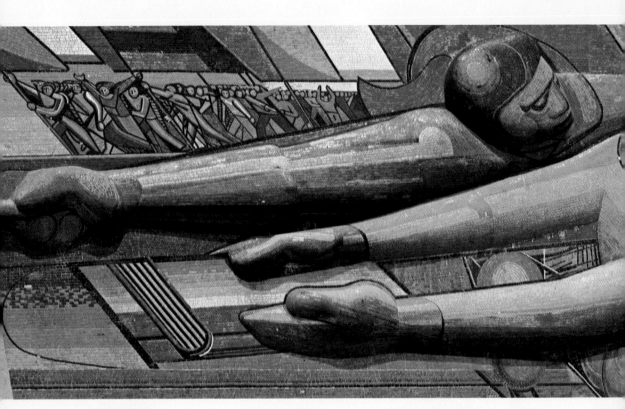

The People to the University, the University to the People, sculpture painting by David Alfaro Siqueiros (1955).

A student with outflung arms, background, urges a group of learned men to impart their knowledge of science and the arts to Mexico's youth. The view that full dissemination of knowledge would shape the nation's future was a tenet of the Revolution.

psychology to explain what he saw to be Mexico's chief shortcomings. His people had preferred since independence to copy the ways of foreigners, he wrote, because they had an "inferiority complex." This complex made them distrustful, suspicious, and touchy when dealing with outsiders. Ramos insisted, however, that Mexicans were not really inferior, as the Social Darwinists had said. He maintained that they only felt so, that the long-range solution to the problem lay in the field of education. He had great faith, he wrote, in the nation's youth.

Ramos' essay had no immediate impact in the literary field. But it is significant that the Lázaro Cárdenas administration (1934-1940) marked the beginning of a new outlook both for Mexico as a nation and for the Mexicans as an integrated entity. The Obregón years had been largely a period of proposing, not planning. Now the government took positive action. The spirit of nationalism once more began to rise. Under Cárdenas, genuine land reform became a reality. The government broke up large estates into small farms and distributed them among the peasants. It also formed moderate-sized communal farms called ejidos. With the ejidos, Mexicans tried to revive the ancient Indian values of cooperative farming and at the same time to give the peasants a sense of dignity and national purpose. It was also hoped that pride of landownership would encourage a greater sense of participation in the nation's affairs. Offering new labor legislation, Cárdenas proposed to improve the lives and working conditions of factory

employees. He nationalized Mexico's extensive railway system, which, under foreign control, had served primarily the interests of outsiders. To promote national unity, he encouraged parades and patriotic demonstrations. His nationalization of the petroleum industry in 1938 (with compensation to the American and British owners) proved to be a most powerful stimulant to national self-esteem.

In 1940, Cárdenas chose a conservative general, Manuel Ávila Camacho, as his successor. To some, this seemed a betrayal of the Revolution. But Cárdenas believed that Mexico could not move to the left without bloodshed, that further social reform and national unity must await economic progress. This was the chief goal of Ávila Camacho, and it has remained the goal of all presidents of Mexico since 1940. Because Mexico lacked the resources to finance the needed industrialization, the capital could come only from abroad. Once more the Mexican governments turned to foreign investors, mostly from the United States.

Critics complained that the ideals Villa and Zapata fought for in the early days of the Revolution had been betrayed. They had a point. Ávila Camacho and his successors continued to pay lip service to the 1917 Constitution, which called for government control over education, farms, oil properties, and the Roman Catholic Church. They extolled the virtues of agrarian reform and social change through revolution, and praised the growing number of ejidos. But each new

The Story of Mexican Labor and Commerce (detail), mural by Raúl Anguiano (1956).

The vitality of Mexico's growth as a nation came from a carefully planned intermeshing of such divergent elements as transportation, natural resources, and efficient business practices—all symbolically presided over here by Mercury, the Roman god of commerce.

government stressed industrial and business activities instead of social programs. Like Cárdenas, the presidents felt that Mexico could ill afford the loss of life, the destruction of property, and the suppression of civil liberties that had accompanied Communist revolutions in Russia and China. They were convinced that Mexico would progress only if the government and businessmen worked hand in hand.

The great economic successes that were achieved, however, posed a dilemma for Mexico's intellectuals. Few doubted that Mexicans needed more factories, more food and clothing, better housing, improved health and sanitation, and expanded transportation and communication systems. Yet how could they achieve these goals without sacrificing values that were uniquely Mexican? Plainly, modernization seemed to be synonymous with "Americanization." Industrial and business efficiency required that Mexican factory employees work on complicated machines and in shifts, that businessmen and shopkeepers practice cost accounting, that they give up their leisurely midday dinners and afternoon siestas, and that small owner-operated shops give way to supermarkets and huge department stores. More and more Mexicans drove American cars, traveled the highways in air-conditioned buses, listened to American popular music on their transistor radios, watched American programs on their television sets, consumed such American foods as hamburgers, hot dogs, and cola drinks, cooked on gas ranges, wore American-style clothes, and slept on innerspring mattresses. The chief result of Mexico's economic progress was that the Mexican people, in the cities and towns, at least, did come to live like Americans. In this sense, the aims of the 19th-century liberals, repudiated by most revolutionaries after 1910, were being achieved – and under the leadership of presidents who maintained in their public speeches that they, too, were "revolutionaries."

During the 1950s, as the national shift in emphasis became apparent, Mexico's intellectuals concerned themselves with the problems brought on by the new life styles. Each change meant a further rejection of the past, of Spanish traditions, and of the Indian values proclaimed by the 1910 Revolution. If American ways were really more desirable, were they then "better"? Were Mexican customs "inferior"? Poet Octavio Paz addressed himself to these questions in *The Labyrinth of Solitude* (1950), one of the most influential publications in Mexican history.

Paz spent two years in the United States studying in California on a Guggenheim fellowship. His firsthand experience of Anglo-American attitudes toward his countrymen is reflected in his book. Using Ramos' 1934 essay as his point of departure, he admitted that Mexicans might "feel" inferior as a result of the overwhelming power of the United States and the domination of American culture. But, he added, the mere fact that the two countries had always been so different in the past did not prove that the Americans were superior. Rather, he found the culture of the United States too "materialistic." The Mexicans, because they had a more "spiritual" outlook, were actually superior to the Anglo-Americans. Mexican ways were to be preferred, not rejected.

The publication of Paz's book touched off a torrentlike flow of essays, histories, poems, and novels, as other Mexican intellectuals began to examine all aspects of the Mexican "soul." Leopoldo Zea Aguilar, a philosopher, edited a series of studies by leading writers under the general title, *México y lo Mexicano* (Mexico and That Which Is Mexican). By and large, they agreed that American "cultural imperialism" should be resisted, and that the politicians had ceased to be genuine revolutionaries. None was more critical of the United States or of Mexico's political leaders than the novelist Carlos Fuentes, author of *The Death of Artemio Cruz* (1962), in which the dying man remembers the disillusionment and opportunism that arose in the aftermath of the idealism of the Revolution.

The criticisms failed, however, to hold back the flood tide of industrial progress. With the aid of American (and some West European and Japanese) investments, and guided by sophisticated public serv-

ants, Mexico in the 1950s and 1960s achieved an economic development that was unique among the developing countries. By the end of the 1960s, the country's gross national product was increasing each year at a rate of 6 to 7 per cent. Today, Mexico stands tall before the world. Its citizens are slowly but surely being transformed from a heterogeneous mixture of Spanish, Indian, and foreign cultures into a homogeneous entity. A nationwide response to the call of "Mexico for Mexicans" has helped make Mexico one of the most stable and economically sound republics in the Western Hemisphere. Vast areas of nonproductive soil have been transformed into fertile farmland – thanks to dams and modern irrigation methods, new agricultural fertilization techniques, and new varieties of seeds that have brought interested observers from all over the world. The land itself, 90 per cent of

The City of Mexico,
tempera over masonite,
by Juan O'Gorman (1949).

Mexico's colonial past,
symbolized by an ancient
Spanish map, contrasts
sharply with the nation's
vigorous development
of the present. A working
man, trowel and blueprint
in hand, builds toward
the world of the future.

which was once controlled by a mere handful of landlords before the Revolution, has today been subdivided and parceled out among hundreds of thousands of Mexicans. Networks of paved roads and superhighways facilitate the interchange of goods. A concurrent growth in radio and television networks has helped tie the nation together.

Educational facilities, from preschool to university, continue to grow. Industry not only thrives, but it has replaced agriculture as the nation's chief source of income. Once considered "backward" by foreigners and Mexicans alike, Mexico today is without doubt the most dynamic country in Latin America and a leader among the developing countries of the world. Oil production has increased dramatically. Factories of all sorts have sprung up, from great automobile assembly lines to lace-manufacturing plants. Steel and concrete production fa-

cilities have been expanded. Farm and ranch output is on the rise, as
are the exports of cotton, citrus fruits, coffee, tomatoes, strawberries,
and cattle.

The lessons taught by the intellectuals were not lost, however, on
the political leaders. They proved to be every bit as nationalistic as
Carranza. They welcomed American capital, as had Porfirio Díaz
before the Revolution, but they expressed their determination to take
from American culture and American technology only that which
would most benefit the Mexican people. The government assumed a
leading role in determining the directions economic progress should
take. If some presidents used the opportunities provided by industrial
growth to enrich themselves and their associates, all the governments
since the 1940s have kept a steady hand on the tiller. Mexico has
steered an economic course that is somewhat revolutionary and thoroughly nationalistic in scope.

Today, Mexico's friends and critics agree that their country has
brought about an "economic miracle." The peso is a rock of monetary
stability. Although Mexico has had trade deficits with the United
States and the Western European countries, the national budget balances each year because of the hundreds of millions of dollars earned
by the tourist industry. American tourists alone were expected to
spend about $700 million in Mexico in 1973.

Yet this spectacular growth has brought new difficulties and intensified old ones. With better health and sanitation measures and new
drugs to cure diseases, Mexico's population is increasing about 3.5 per
cent a year, one of the highest rates in the world. Cities grow larger,
and new ones spring up almost overnight, creating grave problems of
housing, roadbuilding, water and electricity supplies, and police and
fire protection. Industrial growth has brought air and water pollution.
Universities and technical schools are threatening to burst at the
seams as increasing numbers of young Mexicans seek the advantages
of higher education.

Unemployment remains a serious problem. About 3.5 million Mexicans were unemployed in 1973, and another 5 million were at best
only marginally employed part of the year. It has been estimated that
no more than half of the potential working population is productive,
and employment opportunities increase by only about 3 per cent per
year. To close the gap, it is estimated that the republic will have to
create 500,000 new jobs over the next 10 years. So heavy have been
the pressures that a birth-control program, once opposed by both
church and government, has been inaugurated to help slow the rate of
population growth.

Major questions have arisen as to the effectiveness of the land-reform program. With the distribution of almost all available land,
Mexico has nearly completed the first stage of its agrarian reform. But
the second stage, that of raising productivity and living standards
among those farmers who grow barely enough to feed their own fami-

lies, has proved more difficult. In 1966, the government decided to give this its top priority. It acknowledged that land reform, the nation's most sacred of revolutionary tenets, had not created a farming system capable of feeding the burgeoning population. Accordingly, the government has begun making fundamental changes in its land-distribution program. The first changes involve the granting of individual titles rather than communal control in the hopes that such a move will spur farm output.

There still remains, too, the psychological barrier between the United States and Mexico, despite efforts by both nations to eradicate it. Some old disputes have been settled, notably one involving boundary problems caused by the shifting of the Rio Grande. This had been a cause of friction from 1864, when the Rio Grande changed its course, until it was settled in 1963. There have been other adjustments. In 1971, the United States and Mexico concluded a treaty that would help prevent the despoliation of Mexican archaeological, historical, and cultural treasures by U.S. collectors. On Aug. 30, 1973, the United States announced it had agreed to build a desalting plant that would improve the quality of water flowing from the Colorado River into Mexico. But other problems remained—flood control on the Rio Grande, illegal immigration of Mexican workers into the United States, and the smuggling of narcotics and dangerous drugs, as well as unresolved economic issues. The United States, to protect American farmers, restricted the import of tomatoes and other Mexican-grown agricultural products. The Mexicans, in turn, placed new and more severe restrictions on foreign firms operating in Mexico.

Mexico, like many countries in the world today, has experienced terrorism and violence. Guerrilla bands have carried out kidnapings, hijacked planes, and robbed banks. Student riots have led to bloodshed. In 1968, as the country prepared for the Olympic Games, students at the National University in Mexico City went out on strike to protest the government's failure to solve the social problems. Before the strike ended, perhaps as many as 300 Mexicans had lost their lives.

It is true that these disturbances reflect an impatience among Mexico's young people for quick solutions to the country's social, political, and economic problems. But in a larger sense, they also reflect those very same nationalistic concerns that led Hidalgo to utter his call to arms more than 160 years ago. Significantly, many of the students participating in the strikes—and even those who did not—wore tiny replicas of Hidalgo's Liberty Bell pinned to their shirt fronts. In a symbolic way, they were reaffirming the revolutionary desire for reform that was inaugurated in 1810 and restated in 1910. That same spirit of nationalism and desire for reform was emphasized again in 1973 when President Luis Echeverría Alvárez, standing on the balcony of the National Palace, ended his reading of the Grito de Dolores with Hidalgo's rallying cry of "Mexicanos, viva México."

See also Section Five, MEXICAN AMERICANS.

How Can We Solve the Energy Crisis?

By James J. O'Connor

The Arabs' use of oil as a diplomatic weapon has worsened already severe fuel problems, and second looks are being taken at alternative energy sources

When "Closed" signs sprouted on U.S. service stations during the summer of 1973, motorists merely shrugged and drove on to the next gas pump. Some of them grumped briefly if they had to wait in line or were limited to 10 gallons, but few regarded the situation as more than a momentary inconvenience.

But then war flared in the Middle East in October, reducing fuel imports, and Americans were suddenly faced with a chilling reality—a serious fuel shortage, with prospects for colder homes, lowered speed limits, cuts in airline flights, and reduced store hours. "We are heading toward the most acute shortage of energy since World War II," President Richard M. Nixon declared in a nationwide radio and television address on November 7.

The shortage was not confined to the United States, however. For example, motorists in Lebanon could drive their cars only on given days; the Netherlands and some other European countries banned

Sunday driving and lowered speed limits; prices were raised on all petroleum products in Greece; all gasoline stations in Luxembourg were closed on Saturdays and Sundays; and the government assumed control of petroleum supplies and production in Belgium. Japan, which depends entirely on oil imports, banned the use of crude oil in steam power plants, and India boosted gasoline prices 90 per cent to discourage consumption. In Great Britain, a national state of emergency was declared. The crisis was considered just as severe in the United States, where barely 6 per cent of the world's population uses over 33 per cent of the world's energy. "Our problems are serious," warned John G. McLean, chairman of the Continental Oil Company. And he added ominously, "They will get worse."

To underscore this concern, utility companies and energy suppliers began an unprecedented advertising campaign in mid-1973 urging Americans to use less of their products. Turn off unused lights, drive slower to conserve gasoline, lower furnace thermostats 2 degrees to save fuel, they implored.

In October, President Nixon announced the first peacetime allocation of heating oil and propane, a fuel used to dry grain and heat rural homes. John A. Love, director of the U.S. Energy Office, said allocations would "ensure that no home or hospital goes without adequate heat and no farm is without adequate propane." Then, on November 7, the President called for a series of voluntary controls, such as increased use of car pools and lower thermostat settings, as well as legislation to exempt certain industries from environmental regulations, so they can burn fuels that may cause some pollution. The possibility of a World War II type of gas rationing was later raised by Love.

On November 25, President Nixon outlined his plan for dealing with the energy crisis. This included a 15 per cent cutback in home heating oil, a 25 per cent cut to stores and other commercial customers, and a 10 per cent cut to industrial users. The President also said he would lower highway speed limits throughout the nation to 50 miles an hour for cars and 55 miles an hour for trucks and buses. And he called for a reduction in airline flights and a ban on all outdoor Christmas lights, even those used to decorate homes.

Mr. Nixon said that the measures would reduce to about 7 per cent an estimated 17 per cent shortage of oil, and that "additional actions will be necessary." He then closed on an optimistic note. "As we look to the future, we can do so confident that the energy crisis will be resolved—not only for our time, but for all time." Others were not so confident. The stock market promptly dropped sharply and many top energy officials said the Nixon plan was short-sighted and inadequate. Even before the President's address, government agencies, fuel oil distributors, homeowners, businesses in many parts of the country had begun preparations to cope with the expected shortages.

All of this came as a shock to a nation accustomed to unlimited supplies of coal, oil, and gas. For the first time, Americans could not

The author:
James J. O'Connor is editor in chief of *Power* magazine and a regular contributor of energy articles to THE WORLD BOOK YEAR BOOK.

take fuel for granted. The insatiable U.S. appetite for energy, which had grown rapidly over the years to maintain an ever-improving standard of living, finally reached its breaking point. The nation now uses far more energy than it can possibly produce, within the framework of our pre-crisis environmental and social restrictions. Requirements for electric power alone have more than doubled each decade. The United States still sits on ample supplies of coal and oil, but the cost of recovering and refining them, in the face of rigid environmental standards, has made greater exploitation of U.S. deposits ever more difficult. The United States has had to buy oil from other nations to make up its energy deficit, and this has forced changes in both its way of life and its foreign policies.

The Arab countries of the Middle East and North Africa control about 68 per cent of the world's present oil production, and many industrialized nations depend heavily on this source to fuel their economies. The Arab countries supply about 30 per cent of Western Europe's oil, about 90 per cent of Japan's, and 5 per cent of U.S. needs. And it is likely that these nations will become even more dependent on Arab oil in the next 5 or 10 years.

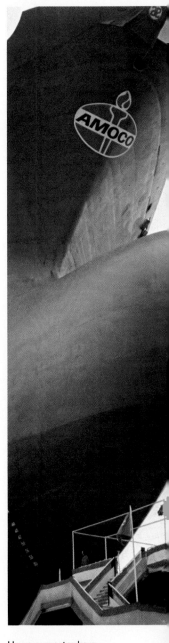

Outside the United States, per capita use is relatively low, but it is growing more rapidly there than it is in the United States. According to the most recent data, Russia and Eastern Europe account for 22 per cent of the world's energy consumption, though they have just 8 per cent of the world's people. Western Europe—with about 10 per cent of the population—uses 20 per cent of the energy. Together, these areas—along with the United States—hold 24 per cent of the world's 3.8-billion people, but account for 75 per cent of all the energy consumed. The situation in the rest of the world is almost exactly reversed. There, a total of 76 per cent of the world's people use only about 25 per cent of the energy consumed.

And, paradoxically, it is this last group—comprised mainly of the developing countries—that may finally threaten to deplete the world's remaining energy. As these nations become more industrialized and their standard of living increases, their need for more and more fuel every year will strain to the utmost the world's existing supplies.

Fortunately, the world has a rich stock of known fossil reserves that have not yet been tapped. There are 456 billion tons of coal still to be mined—200 times the amount used by the world in 1970. Proven oil reserves hold about 68 billion tons, which is 32 times the 1970 consumption. There are 55 trillion cubic yards of proven natural gas reserves, 39 times the world's 1970 consumption. And none of these figures includes the much greater reserves that geologists believe are underground, but that have not yet been proven.

So it would appear that the world can continue to rely on—and expand—its production of the heavily used fossil fuels. The reserves are there, waiting to be tapped. But serious difficulties must be overcome, and the situation in the United States is fairly typical of that faced by

Huge supertankers, such as this 230,000-ton vessel, can carry much crude oil across the sea. But the U.S. does not have enough deepwater ports to unload these enormous carriers.

other industrialized nations. Years of sheer neglect in planning, a failure to consider the problem of environmental pollution caused by energy production, and complex international situations—such as who owns the rights to oil under the ocean floor—have all helped to create the U.S. energy crisis. Added to this is the long-held hope we have harbored that nuclear energy would quickly solve all our energy needs, which has given us a false sense of security.

Consider the case of oil. In 1965, the United States consumed nearly 12 million barrels of oil a day. Of that amount, it produced 9 million barrels and imported 2.5 million barrels. In 1972, the United States consumed more than 16 million barrels a day. It produced over 11-million barrels of this amount, imported about 4.5 million, and dipped into its reserves for the remainder. By 1985, the U.S. demand will probably exceed 25 million barrels a day, and there will be no surplus to dip into.

Prior to the 1973 energy crisis, experts foresaw the United States as relying in the future on the power sources shown in the chart, *below*. But the crisis may lead to some changes, with, for example, much greater reliance on coal and less on petroleum.

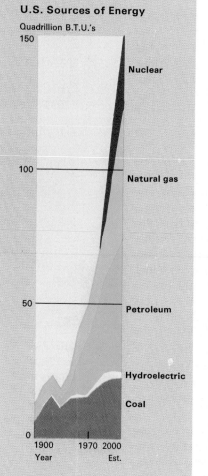

U.S. Sources of Energy

Quadrillion B.T.U.'s

150

Nuclear

100

Natural gas

50

Petroleum

Hydroelectric

Coal

0

1900   1970 2000
Year   Est.

United States refineries are now running at over 90 per cent of capacity–near their practical limit. Thus, the policy statement by President Nixon, on April 18, 1973, in which he said the Administration would discourage imports while encouraging domestic exploration, may do little to alleviate the fuel crisis. Unless refinery capacity is increased, there will still be a shortage of gasoline and other refined oil products no matter how many new deposits are finally discovered and tapped for their oil. And the simple truth is that new refineries are not being built.

Attempts to build several new refineries on the Atlantic Coast have been blocked by environmental groups and by what oilmen say are inadequate market prices that do not produce the profits needed to finance construction. Some new facilities have been stopped for as long as 10 years by the legal action of environmentalists, who fear the possibility of pollution. Oilmen estimate that seven new refineries will

Energy comes to us by such diverse means as, *left to right below,* nuclear power plants, high-tension electric power lines, and Persian Gulf oil pipelines.

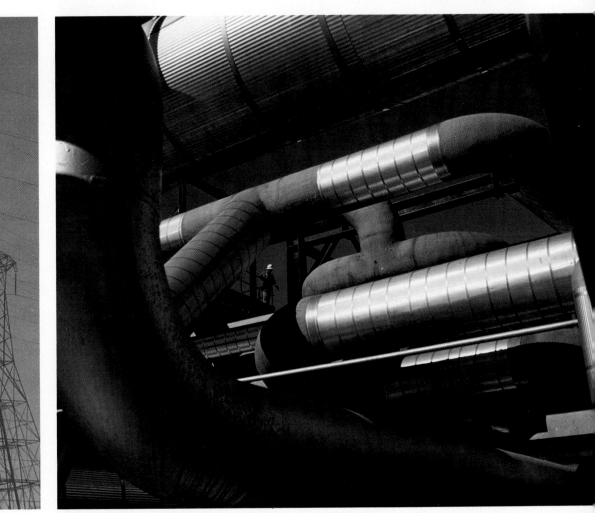

be needed on the Atlantic Coast alone by 1975, and they will not be there—even if construction could begin immediately. It takes more than three years just to locate an adequate site for a refinery, plus two or three more years of actual construction. Similarly, the building of a pipeline to carry oil from Alaska was long delayed.

In addition to these domestic problems, there are thorny international political problems other than the question of ownership of the oil under the ocean. The Arab countries of the Middle East are beginning to use their enormous reserves of oil as a bargaining tool with the West in their continuing struggle against Israel. On May 15, 1973, four of the countries—Algeria, Iraq, Kuwait, and Libya—temporarily halted oil shipments to the United States and other Western nations

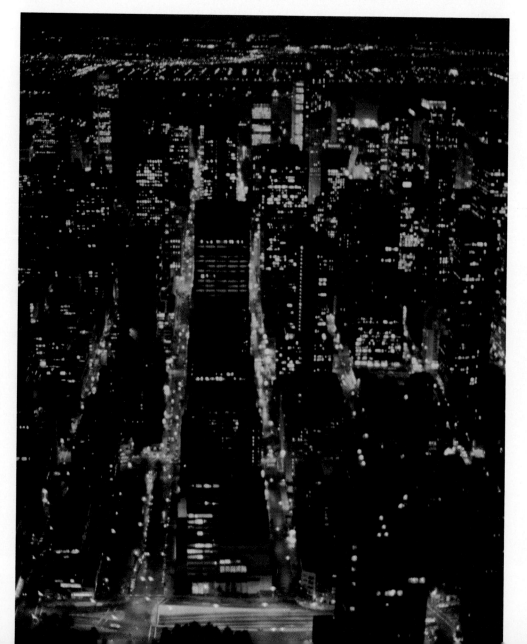

in protest against Western support of Israel. Then, after the war between Israel and the Arab countries began on October 6, the Arab suppliers began another boycott of oil shipments to the United States and other nations. The implications for the future are clear. Any nation dependent to any extent on oil from the Arab countries will have to take the political factor into account. It is no longer a question merely of oil production, but also one of oil politics.

Poor planning has also hampered natural gas production in the United States. Restrictions placed on the price of wellhead gas—the gas as it comes from the ground—have posed the main difficulty. These price controls were imposed by the Federal Power Commission as far back as 1954, when the United States had a surplus of domestic gas and gas prices were low. The controls kept gas prices well below those of other fuels. As a result, about 36 per cent of the total power generated in the United States has come from natural gas.

But the same price controls that made natural gas so attractive to the user discouraged the producers from looking for enough new wells to keep up with the demand. They didn't have the money needed to finance search efforts, especially when they saw their production costs rising steadily. There was a time when drillers had to probe only about a mile into the earth at a cost of $100,000 to open a natural gas well.

U.S. Energy Consumers

Industry 32%
Utilities 25%
Transportation 24%
Private homes 14%
Other businesses 5%

In order to span the energy gap, Americans may have to turn off some city lights and limit the use of cars.

Today, they must sink their wells from 4 to 5 miles deep, at a cost of at least $1 million a mile.

As a result of all this, both natural gas and oil exploration has declined steadily in the United States. The number of new wells dropped from 58,000 in 1956 to 27,000 in 1971. Combine a skyrocketing demand for oil and gas with a supply that could not keep pace, and the shortages of today were inevitable. Imports of both liquefied and pipeline natural gas would help, but they would not completely satisfy the demand. Higher wellhead prices might stimulate gas-field explorations, but the higher costs to consumers could at the same time discourage further gas purchases.

Coal, the most traditional fossil fuel, has always fueled more than 50 per cent of the U.S. power-generating capacity. And, while the Middle East may have the corner on oil, the United States sits on 16 per cent of the world's coal resources—more than 3 trillion tons. Almost half of this is considered economically recoverable, using existing technology. Even at the present rate of consumption, coal from the U.S. fields and from other parts of the world could still supply U.S. energy requirements for 500 years or more. Because it is so plentiful, President Nixon said in his November 7 speech that industries and utilities that burn coal will be prohibited from converting to oil. Further, utilities with oil-fueled power plants will be encouraged—and in some cases, required—to convert to coal. But one basic problem will remain for the future—how to burn coal cleanly. Industry must eliminate the offensive products of coal combustion, the particulates and sulfur dioxide that pollute the environment. The particles of soot and fly ash can now be controlled, but the sulfur problem is difficult to deal with. Coal cannot yet be desulfurized in its natural state, so industry is trying to remove sulfur from emissions in the smokestack with filter systems and electrostatic precipitators.

The engineers of the American Gas Association and many other observers are optimistic about the possibility of turning coal into a gas or a liquid and eliminating the sulfur dioxide before this is burned as a fuel. Research is promising, and some power producers predict that the coal-powered electric generating station of the future will be a chemical complex, producing a variety of chemicals from coal. The gas produced in this process would then be burned to create electric power. The conversion of coal into gas, or gasification, is an old idea. But industry is not yet able to do it economically and efficiently.

In a sense, what we really have today is just as much of an "environmental and economic crisis" as an "energy crisis." There is a real concern over whether the continually increasing costs of making energy usable will become a major handicap to social and economic betterment. If there had been no mass outcry about environmental pollution, no price controls on natural gas, no low-cost foreign oil, and no prospects that nuclear energy could supply our power, there would be no U.S. energy crisis today. The United States would simply have

There are vast supplies of oil under the oceans, but they are difficult to tap because of problems in anchoring the drilling rigs. There also are questions as to which countries own the oil.

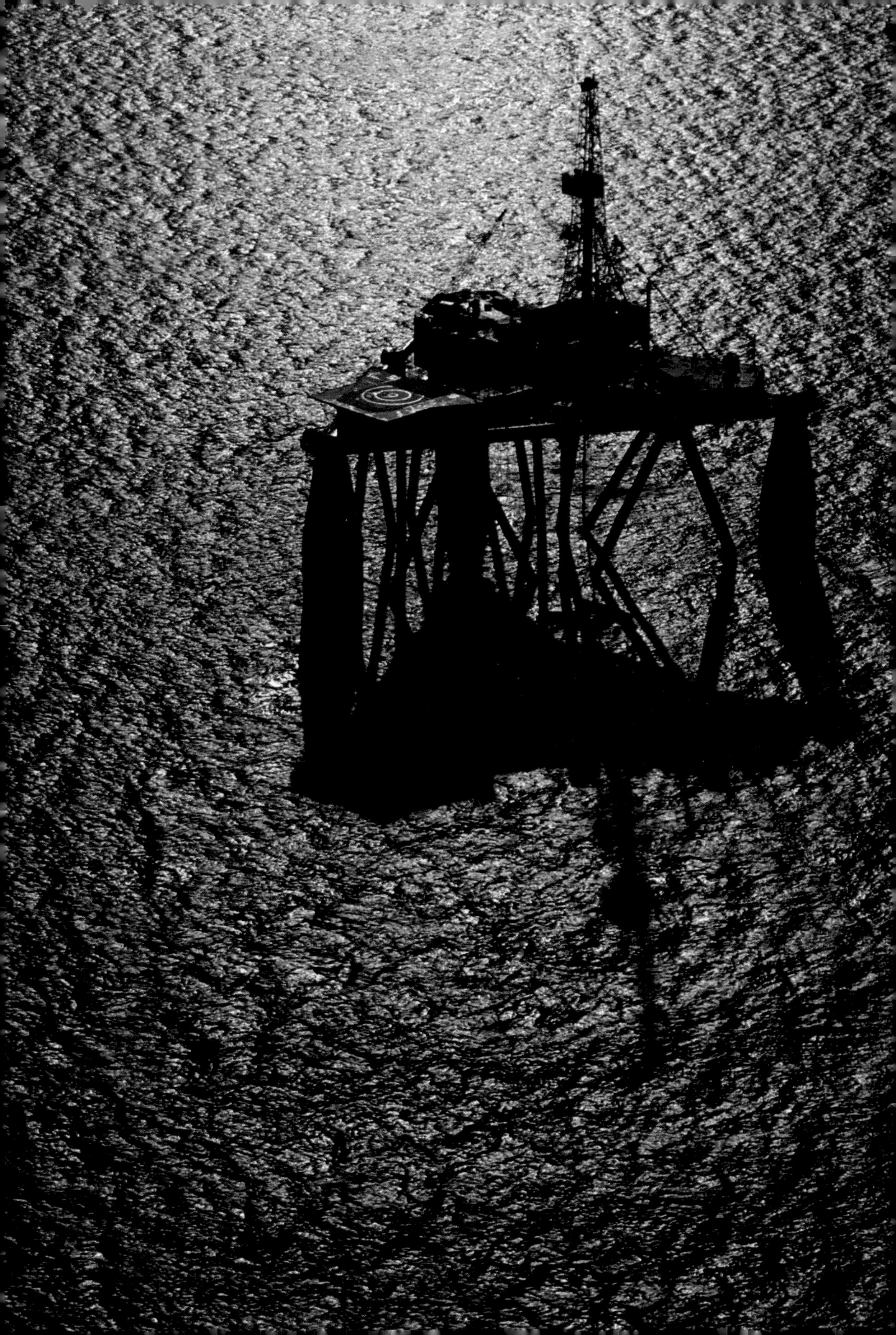

used its own coal, oil, and gas without depending on other countries or nuclear energy to bail it out.

But the crisis is real. It is "the greatest issue facing the American people during the next decade," according to Secretary of the Interior Rogers C. B. Morton. Morton points out that we will depend heavily upon fossil fuels for the remainder of this century. But what about other sources of energy? If we cannot rely on oil, gas, and coal as much as in the past to meet future needs, where can we turn?

The foremost alternative–despite its delayed promise–is nuclear energy, which has virtually unlimited fuel supplies. Nuclear power plants are expensive to build and require elaborate cooling systems, yet there are now 35 nuclear power units generating power in the United States and 69 throughout the world (excluding Russia, for

The Four Corners power plant, located where Utah, Colorado, New Mexico, and Arizona meet, is fueled by coal taken from the extensive strip mines in the area.

Fossil fuel reserves exist throughout the world, as shown in the chart, *below right.* Such fuels are the backbone of our energy supply. *Above,* a natural-gas refinery lights the sky; *below,* oil-distribution pipes.

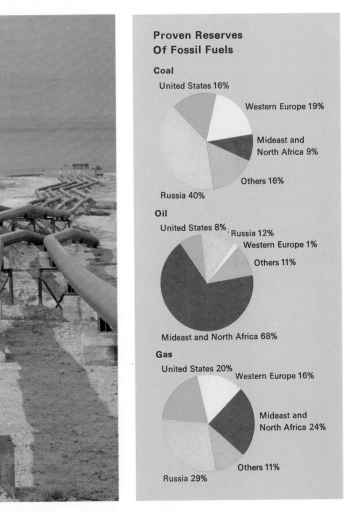

Proven Reserves Of Fossil Fuels

Coal

United States 16%

Western Europe 19%

Mideast and North Africa 9%

Others 16%

Russia 40%

Oil

United States 8%

Russia 12%

Western Europe 1%

Others 11%

Mideast and North Africa 68%

Gas

United States 20%

Western Europe 16%

Mideast and North Africa 24%

Others 11%

Russia 29%

which we have no figures). Not the least among their attractions is their cleanliness of operation. They produce no soot or chemicals to foul the air. However, this latter point is disputed by some who object to radioactivity in the waste materials that the power plants discharge in the air. Their opposition came to a head with the famous 1971 Calvert Cliffs decision in a suit seeking to halt construction of the Calvert Cliffs nuclear power plant on Chesapeake Bay in Maryland. The U.S. Court of Appeals for the District of Columbia ruled that the U.S. Atomic Energy Commission (AEC) violated the Environmental Policy Act of 1970 by considering radiation hazards primarily and not stressing such other hazards as thermal pollution when it granted plant permits. The AEC then ordered a review of operating licenses and construction permits for more than 100 nuclear power units in 21 states. That brought nuclear construction virtually to a halt. In his "energy crisis" speech of November 7, however, President Nixon said the AEC will speed up the licensing and construction of nuclear power plants. This promising energy source undoubtedly will play a major role in the future, even though it has little chance of meeting the United States most urgent energy needs in the next decade.

Most of the nuclear plants in the United States are light-water reactors, which use uranium isotopes (U-235) as fuel. The U-235, enriched with the more common U-238 isotope, is packaged in zirconium-encased fuel elements, which are supported in a manner that permits water to flow near them and be heated. The water boils and

Strip mining in the Southwest, *opposite page,*
an oil-drilling rig in a Louisiana lake, *left,* and a
rig on Alaska's North Slope, *above,* typify the
extremes resorted to in the search for more fuel.

the steam that is produced passes to a steam turbine, is condensed, and
recycled as in a fossil-fueled power plant.

Recently, the emphasis has shifted from light-water reactors to
breeder reactors, which President Nixon described in June, 1971, as
"our best hope today for meeting the nation's growing demand for
economical, clean energy." Breeder reactors, although they use the
same uranium fuel as light-water reactors and much the same cooling
system, differ in that they produce new fuel as they consume the
energy from the uranium ore. In some cases, through a process of
capturing the radioactive neutrons from fission, they may even produce more fuel than they consume. Although still not developed commercially, breeder reactors are expected to use about 75 per cent of the
energy available from uranium ore as compared with less than 2 per
cent in light-water reactors. They will also have a thermal efficiency of
40 per cent—that is, they will use 40 per cent of the energy they produce—compared with 33 per cent in the light-water units.

Another energy source, the harnessing of water power, or hydroelectric generation, is a natural favorite, but few hydroelectric sites
remain to be exploited in the United States. In addition, hydroelectric
power is usually produced far from where it is needed, so there is a
problem in sending it economically over long distances. In other countries, such as Russia, China, and Australia, a number of new hydroelectric power plants have been opened and are producing significant
amounts of electric power. One of the most interesting is the vast
Snowy Mountains Scheme in southeastern Australia, which began
operating in 1972. This network of dams, reservoirs, and tunnels cov-

Americans have grown used to a steady supply
of fuel. Indeed, until the 1973 crisis, experts
saw the already extravagant use of energy
in the United States soaring even higher, *right*.

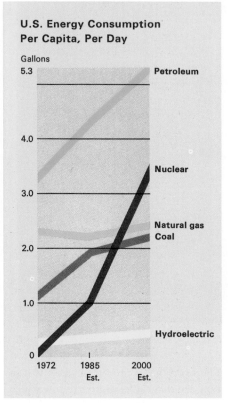

**U.S. Energy Consumption
Per Capita, Per Day**

Gallons

5.3 — Petroleum

4.0 — Nuclear

3.0 —

Natural gas
Coal

2.0 —

1.0 —

Hydroelectric

0

| 1972 | 1985 Est. | 2000 Est. |

ers about 2,000 square miles of rugged mountain terrain and diverts
water from the east slopes to the west slopes of the Great Dividing
Range. A series of power stations generate 3.74 million kilowatts of
electricity for the cities of Canberra, Melbourne, and Sydney.

Two final sources of energy that should be considered are geothermal power and solar power, though neither produces a significant
amount of usable energy at this time. However, geothermal energy—
both hot water and steam piped from underground supplies—has recently been getting renewed consideration, both in generation of electric power and in industrial and residential heating.

A study sponsored by the National Science Foundation in 1972
endorsed the suggestion that geothermal sources could supply 20 per
cent of U.S. electric power needs by 1985. To do this, the country
would need at least 26,000 productive geothermal wells.

The U.S. petroleum industry completes about 27,000 oil wells annually. But the track record on drilling successful geothermal wells is
poor. Of 30 geothermal drilling ventures reported on at the 1970
United Nations Geothermal Symposium, only four had a successful
yield. These were the geyser field near San Francisco, and those at
Lakeview, Klamath Falls, and Burns, in Oregon. The California gey-
sers north of San Francisco have increased their output of electricity

about 200 per cent since 1960, while geothermal water from the Oregon wells heats houses and greenhouses.

The practicality and economics of geothermal energy–at least on a modest scale–have also been demonstrated in Italy and New Zealand. A spin-off benefit comes from the chemicals and minerals extracted from the geothermal water or steam. The Waraikei installation in New Zealand yields close to 300 megawatts of electricity, and the Lardarello wells in central Italy supply over 300 megawatts. Reykjavík, Iceland, uses water from deep geothermal springs for heating homes and growing vegetables indoors. Geothermal energy, then, is potentially capable of supporting industries and communities that need electric power, heat, drinkable water, and minerals extracted from the effluent of the geothermal springs.

Solar energy stands out as a significant, inexhaustible source of energy when you consider that the earth receives power from the sun at a constant rate of about 1 horsepower per square yard, at least wherever and whenever clouds do not obscure the sunlight. Some regions, such as the Middle East, get more than the average amount of sunlight because they are near the equator and relatively cloud-free. Although technology and cost factors have so far prevented the use of solar energy on anything but a small scale, interest in it is growing. The U.S. National Science Foundation, for example, spent nothing on solar research in 1970. But it spent $3.8 million in 1973, and it will increase its budget for solar research to $12.2 million in 1974. Ecologists concerned about the polluting effects of the oil and electrical industries are interested in the sun as a clean, safe, and quiet energy source. The Arthur D. Little research firm in Cambridge, Mass., which has studied the subject, says that, "If solar energy provided 1 per cent of the nation's energy needs by 1983, this would conserve approximately 100 million barrels of oil per year."

With all these options, it is safe to say that the United States will not run out of energy for the next 50 years. But that is not a very long period of time. Thus, there was urgency in President Nixon's words on November 7 when he said that the time has come to meet "not only the current crisis, but also the long-range challenge that we face."

The current crisis will affect the life of every American as we learn to use less fuel. The long-range challenge is far greater:

"Our failure to act now on our long-term energy problems could seriously endanger the capacity of our farms and of our factories to employ Americans at record-breaking rates," said President Nixon. "Nearly 86 million people are now at work in this country to provide the highest standard of living we or any other nation has ever known. It could reduce the capacity of our farmers to provide the food we need; it could jeopardize our entire transportation system; it could seriously weaken the ability of America to continue to give the leadership which only we can provide to keep the peace that we have won at such great cost of thousands of our finest young Americans."

Growing Up
Male in America

By Warren T. Farrell

**The traditional view of what it means to be a
man—at work or play, in prestige or salary—may
give men less freedom of choice than women have**

A girl can be a tomboy—but we never hear of a "janegirl." A woman can wear a pants suit, but can a man be seen in a dress? A woman can light up a Marlboro, but can a man smoke an Eve? Some women can put "Dr." on their résumés to help them obtain a job, but would any man dare to include on his résumé, "In 1973, I took care of children"? In theory, of course, a man is free to do any of these things. But in reality, everything a boy or man learns about "what a man should be" tells him that he must never, under any circumstances, act like a woman.

Last year I actually asked a group of male corporate executives how they would feel about a man who presented a résumé saying, "From 1972 to 1974 I took care of children." You can imagine their mocking responses. Yet these same men say they want to spend more time with their children. They speak of "the importance and creativity of my wife's role as a mother and manager of our home." But when it comes to caring for their children full time and without pay, these fathers are nowhere to be seen.

Today, people often interpret women's liberation as women rejecting their traditional role and "coming up" to a man's work and status,

Young boys grow up in the company of women at home and in school. When their fathers come home from work, they often encourage their sons to prove their strength in such sports as wrestling.

The author:
Warren T. Farrell teaches sexual politics in the department of government at American University, and he is the author of *Beyond Masculinity,* scheduled for publication in 1974.

such as that of an executive. We seldom hear of men's liberation, though, and when we do, it is not usually in terms of men coming up to women's status. Many men, however, have begun to feel that they are just as trapped as women in a system that determines their behavior and limits their choices. For example, one problem of the American male is not the woman's problem of being underpaid on the job, but the fact that he lacks the psychological freedom *not* to make money —a freedom millions of women but only a few men possess.

The need of many men to have a title next to their name when they are introduced at a party, or to have a new car when they drive up to the party, is now being questioned. Some men are making the connection between this need to prove their masculinity through job and prestige striving and the fact that men have more heart attacks, ulcers, and migraine headaches, commit 70 per cent of the suicides, and die almost eight years sooner than women in the United States. Many studies have also shown that masculine expectations tend to encourage men to commit 88 per cent of all crimes—83 per cent of the murders and 86 per cent of the sex offenses, not including rape.

Men are also becoming aware that negative images of women also affect men since it is just these images—and the fear of expressing the "feminine" traits of their own personality, which all men have—that help prevent men from doing what they want to do if that makes them appear like less of a man. Such negative images are seen every night in television commercials that portray women as being preoccupied with

A father's work in the home involves fixing things, while a mother prepares the meals and does the housework. These separate roles may eventually discourage a boy from trying such tasks as cooking because they are not "manly."

whiter washes and cleaner floors while the male announcer's voice puts the final seal of approval on the product. Fear of being thought "feminine" can drive men to prove their masculinity—not only by developing muscles, but also by trying to prove themselves in all aspects of the man's role.

A boy learns to prove himself a man through the examples in his own home. On the surface, it appears that a boy learns only that the role of a man should be *different* from that of a woman. Eventually, though, he sees that his father's work is paid for, has a title, and requires training. It is a career or a trade. His mother's work in the home is not paid for, has no title, and requires no formal training. It is "just housework." If his mother does work outside the home, it is usually only a job, not a career. The boy is thus told indirectly that his mother's job is not as important as his father's career, because when they both come home his mother still does far more of the shopping, cooking, and cleaning than his father. If their outside work were equally important, would they not share the housework?

A boy shares moments of fun with his father, but his mother usually has the main job of restricting him. His father may lay down a broad restriction when he is really bad, but his mother—because she is usually at home and spends more time with him—must restrict him on a minute-to-minute basis, exert the petty discipline, the little cautions. This only enhances his image of his father's authority.

A boy does see his father work around the house, but he fixes things or does things that the boy's mother apparently cannot do. His father's work has a special quality, a mystique. And so does his relaxation. Many a boy sees his father watching football on television, while his mother is serving the beer and potato chips. In these ways he absorbs a subtle contempt for the woman's role in the home that reinforces the contempt for women shown in television commercials and in other places, including the classroom.

A 1972 analysis of 134 elementary school readers, for example, found hundreds of quotations in which girls say such things about themselves as, "Even I know that, and I'm just a stupid girl," and boys say, "Girls' advice isn't worth two cents; yours isn't worth a penny." Even classics such as "Jack and the Beanstalk" portray Jack's

School football games dramatize the traditional view of men as the performers, with women standing behind them in a supporting role.

mother as a contemptible and helpless woman who appeals to Jack's bravery by nagging *him* to chop down the beanstalk even though she is physically much bigger. Jack is pressured into proving himself a man rather than appearing as "helpless" as his mother.

A boy's fear of appearing like a woman also develops as he looks at newspapers and magazines and sees men featured almost exclusively, especially on the front page—male astronauts, male Cabinet members, supreme court justices, and senators. He is being told indirectly that this is his role, that the higher he achieves in these male roles, the more of a man he is. The same pictures tell him he will never be a "real" man by concentrating on washing dishes or being a good father or good husband. The fear of being caught in a woman's role sets in. It is little surprise that psychologist Daniel G. Brown of the U.S. Public Health Service finds that by the age of 5, about half the girls prefer the father's role while only a fourth of the boys prefer the mother's role.

All of the images of male and female roles make a boy aware that he will gain more respect if he acts as a "real boy" instead of just being

All-male shop classes and all-female home economics classes convince boys that they may work with machine tools, but not with needle and thread.

Advertisers exploit the masculine mystique by implying that a man can be as distant, cool, and strong as the image in the ad — if he will just use the product.

himself. What must a boy do to prove to himself, other boys, and "the girls" that he is masculine? First, he cannot admit that he is wrong, or that he is enthusiastic, especially about something as tame as school-work. So a boy's hand that eagerly shoots up to ask a question in kindergarten is seldom seen by the time he reaches ninth grade. It is not a boy's role to ask a question, unless he already has some idea of the answer; and it certainly is not masculine to ask a question with enthusiasm. A boy must always maintain a certain distance, a cool-ness, an indifference.

Although he may be unaware of it, his contempt for girls leads him to not treat girls' remarks too seriously, particularly if another boy is present. He may listen to girls, but only for the purpose of gathering enough information to create his own story designed to impress them in return. When he speaks, he speaks somewhat condescendingly. As a boy gets older, the condescension continues; he must feel he has con-trol of "his woman"; he must see himself as being more concerned with practical results than with ideals; he must convince himself he can make decisions quickly; he must be on top, earn more, and always be proving himself better than other persons, especially girls.

Proving his masculinity even hurts a boy's grades in school. Psychologist Roberta Oetzel's studies of sex typing made at Stanford University show that the higher a boy's "masculinity" score, the lower his academic average tends to be. Psychologists Jerome Kagan of Harvard University and Howard A. Moss of the National Institute of Mental Health, Bethesda, Md., find that the one common element between high-achieving boys and high-achieving girls is that the boys do not act typically "masculine" and the girls do not act typically "feminine." For example, psychological tests and interviews with parents revealed that high-achieving boys are less outwardly aggressive or competitive than low-achieving boys. The passive feminine role hurts high achievement because it stymies daring and exploration; the active masculine role for a young boy stymies the seriousness of purpose and self-discipline necessary for high achievement.

In school, the pressures for men to do one thing and women another are everywhere. Usually the secretaries and most of the teachers are women, while all the administrators are men. The higher the grade level, the higher the status and the more likely a man is teaching it; the highest status goes to the top administrator, the superintendent—who is a man in all except 8 of 90,000 school systems in the United States. A

A common morning sight in many cities and towns is a wife delivering her husband—the family provider—to the train he takes to go to work.

Because the masculine role requires a man to be the leader and the decision maker, he must propose a date — and then pay the bill.

boy who has thoughts of becoming a teacher soon sees that "No *man* becomes a kindergarten teacher."

It may sound innocent enough to have separate gym classes for boys and girls, separate home economics and shop classes, all-boy athletic teams, and all-girl cheerleading squads. However, just as separate facilities for blacks and whites often produce inequities, the separation of boys and girls is not as innocent as it sounds. It forces boys to take part in athletics lest they appear to be sissies, and it forces boys in shop classes to feel they must make things that go on the lathe but not in the oven. "Like it or not, in the past the educational system has tended to point girls to certain types of careers and boys toward others," says John C. Pittenger, Pennsylvania's secretary of education. "On balance, I think it's accurate to say that education hasn't been fair to anybody—not to boys or girls, or their mothers and fathers, or to teachers and administrators."

Another way that separation may hurt both boys and girls was revealed in a conversation I had with Marge Donahue and her husband Phil, host of a nationwide television show, about their children's interest in ice skating. The outlet for their 9-year-old son became a boys' hockey team; since there was no such team for girls, their 7-year-old daughter took up figure skating. Within a few months, the son had expensive knee and shoulder guards, a hockey stick, and a colorful uniform, and his team was receiving newspaper publicity. The games took place in a stadium with lights keeping track of the score and loudspeakers announcing the achievements of the boys. The fathers reserved every Tuesday evening to sit together in the stands, cheer enthusiastically for their sons, and go out with them afterward to "talk like men" about the game.

The Donahue's daughter went to figure-skating practice where no one watched and no one cheered, except occasionally Marge. She became jealous of the attention her brother received, but could not pin down an injustice. Both children were doing what was appropriate—presumably "what they wanted." When Marge noticed the jealousy and asked if she would like to join a girls' hockey team, her daughter answered, "Can I play hockey, too—me, a girl?" When Marge said she would try to start a team, her daughter jumped with happiness.

While on the surface it appears that only the Donahue's daughter was being wronged—by the lack of attention—the son was in danger of being hurt in a more subtle way by being the *focus* of attention. Every time the announcer broadcasts another boy's achievement, the pressure for him to perform increases. With scoreboard lights flashing and father shouting, a boy has much more than his self-evaluation at stake. The rewards after the game are sweet for the achiever, but bitter for the nonachiever. There is no overt punishment, just the punishment of being left out. The boy who did not even make the team is completely left out. The town does not finance his recreation, and his parents and friends do not watch him; and he feels he has disappointed them as a man. He must prove himself in another way.

"Well," say most fathers, "this is all in fun, and besides, any real boy learns to take the downs with the ups." In some ways, boys do. They soon learn to "take it like a man" by learning to become well defended; sarcasms, witticisms, and put-downs become the mode of communicating with their "friends." Underneath, though, many boys do not learn to "take it." They grow up with an ego so fragile that only a woman who will spend her life supporting it can be tolerated.

The separation of boys and girls can also be observed at school dances. The boys line up near one wall, the girls near another. The separation is a way of hinting that the boys must ask the girls to dance; they must put their egos on the line. If a boy and girl go home together after the dance, it is he who usually proposes it directly—she is forced into having to suggest it indirectly, reinforcing the boy's image of girls as coy, manipulating, and indirect. Meanwhile, he must maintain a façade of courage—a deep, smooth voice, a body carried with assurance, a certain swagger, a distance without being too distant, a confidence that defies refusal. But on the inside he may be shaking, his heart running amuck.

His role as decision-maker starts even before the dance, should he decide he would like to take a girl (note that *he* usually decides). Not only must he decide to ask a girl, but he must also make decisions as to which girl, and how to get the car.

Always being forced to take the initiative encourages boys to look at sex in an aggressive way. Each boy does this by telling stories of his conquests with as much convincing self-confidence as he can. Since he knows his own stories are exaggerations, but does not know whether the other boys are exaggerating, his self-confidence *decreases*. He decides to become more aggressive the next time he takes a girl out, and once again builds up a strong façade on the outside while inadvertently developing a more fragile ego on the inside.

The boy goes to the next dance or party with a new determination to be seen with a girl who will make him look good in the eyes of "the guys." He spends time with her, invests money in her, and, perhaps, eventually "marks her as his territory." But, while he chose her originally on the basis of her attractiveness, he becomes more interested in whether they get along well together and enjoy similar activities as he spends more time with her. Since his original choice was mostly physical, it is only a coincidence if he happened to choose someone who is mentally compatible. Thus he is caught in "the sex object trap."

The sex object trap has broader implications when it happens a few times in succession. The girl assumes a passive role when she knows the boy will "come on strong"–making the boy always seem to have sex on his mind; the girl tries to develop a deeper emotional relationship– sometimes to justify the physical one, sometimes for its own sake. The boy resents finding himself "tied down" in what started out only as a physical interest. The resentment contributes to a break in the relationship, his sexual interests wander, and he prepares to repeat the sex object trap by once again "eyeing" girls whose major appeal to him is physical. Each step increases a boy's contempt for women without his realizing his own role in creating the situation.

One of the most pervasive of masculine traps, specialization, may occur later in life. A survey by psychologist Herbert Greenberg of Princeton, N.J., of all types of jobs in 4,000 business firms revealed in 1973 that 80 per cent of the workers were dissatisfied. One of the major reasons for job dissatisfaction is job specialization, according to a 1972 Department of Health, Education, and Welfare study, "Work in America." Typically, a man who likes math in high school studies it in college, becomes an accountant, then a Certified Public Accountant and perhaps a partner in an accounting firm. Somewhere along the way, though, he may have wanted to be a travel agent for a while, dabble in real estate, or just spend a few years doing something else. But once he has become a specialist, he feels he cannot try other careers because he has made too great an investment in his present

The gap between
men and women in the
living room after dinner
symbolizes their differing
interests in life—a division
that usually results
from the division of labor.

career. The greater the investment, the more reluctant he is to try something new. He has built up a pension, vacation time, a group of colleagues, and a reputation; if he is a teacher, his tenure serves as a further inducement not to think about change.

These inducements are, in a way, "male bribes." But a man is not free to ignore these bribes if no one is sharing the responsibility for earning the income. Frequently, a thoughtful young man who gets a few years into his job says, "I'd like to object to that policy, but I have a wife and family to support." It is only when his wife is helping to support the family that he can risk questioning on his job, because then if he loses his job he will not leave his family destitute. A man who assumes the burden of sole breadwinner finds himself postponing questioning "until I am in a better position to be effective." The problem, though, is that there is always a "more effective" level. The result is the organization man who finds himself confronted with a tragedy.

During the 1973 congressional hearings into the scandals of the Watergate Affair, numerous witnesses attested to this phenomenon.

The pressure on men not to question is only one price of the male bribes. A second is the need always to maintain an external appearance of strength. Politics and business strongly encourage this show of external strength. But while in business one must prove oneself only to a handful of "superiors," in politics one must constantly prove oneself to the entire electorate. Even one slip in this masculine role can severely damage or ruin a career. Michigan Governor George W. Romney's admission of being brainwashed by White House briefings on the Vietnam War during the 1968 presidential primary campaign led to a torrent of criticism declaring that a man who could be brainwashed was "unfit for the presidency." The public's reaction was not, "Here is a man big enough to admit it in the middle of a political campaign." Within two weeks he was forced to withdraw.

In the 1972 presidential primary, Senator Edmund S. Muskie (D., Me.) learned the price of admitting weakness when he broke into tears while countering a slur on his wife. The tears resulted in speculation about his emotional stability rather than admiration for honestly expressing his emotions. *The New York Times* said Muskie "showed himself here, in the view of many politicians, to be a man who tires easily and tends toward emotional outbursts under pressure."

Senator Thomas F. Eagleton (D., Mo.) was the victim of some of the worst punishment Americans deal out to those who break a rule of masculinity. When Eagleton admitted in 1972 that he had undergone electric shock treatments more than six years prior to his candidacy for Vice-President, despite no subsequent evidence of depression, it became such an issue that he was forced to become the first vice-presidential candidate in the history of the United States to resign. If Eagleton had never admitted weakness, if he had refused to acknowledge that he had a problem and might profit from psychiatric help, he probably would not have had to resign. While Eagleton, Muskie, and Romney were all victims of the masculine mystique, the real victims were the American people, because they lost the type of honest leadership that is strong enough to appear "weak." This encourages a leadership that will keep information from the people and succeed at all odds, creating both credibility gaps and Watergate scandals.

Today, men in their 30s and 40s as well as men in their teens and 20s are questioning this mystique. Often a middle-aged man sees that his drive to make it to the top of a corporation will level off at vice-president rather than chairman of the board. By then he realizes that the vice-presidency is not everything he once thought it was. Frequently, his children have grown up and he wishes he knew them better; for all the work he has done, he finds himself alienated from his wife. She is interested in the home and children, countering loneliness with activities that serve to fill in the time she spends waiting for him. He, in turn, is interested in his job and sports. It is disappointing for a man who has sweated for those he loves to discover he has lost contact with those for whom he thought he was working, that his need to control his emotions at work has caused him to lose contact with the emotions needed to love at home. For some men, enough of these factors add up to make them question their whole value system, to want to break out of their trap.

When a man begins to question the masculine mystique, he may get involved in a "consciousness-raising" group—a group of men who sit in a circle and talk to raise their awareness (consciousness) of whether they are playing roles, such as earning the most money, merely to conform to the images they have of themselves as men. In most cases, the man concludes that in order for him to broaden his role as a man, the woman he is living with must broaden hers—that it is impossible for him to be free of the total responsibility for breadwinning unless she shares it; that it is impossible for her to be free of the total responsibility for housework and child care unless he shares that.

These men are also trying to understand how success can be defined in ways other than higher salaries and positions—how a man who makes himself into a status or money striver gets caught in the trap of being a "security object," existing merely for the security of his wife and children. Instead, they find that a man can define his own success by broadening his interests, even if it means changing careers or taking a job with less status and salary. A school principal, for example, may know that he is really a better teacher than administrator, that he likes people more than paperwork; but he fears going back to teaching because he might lose prestige and income. A woman usually is not as psychologically tied to having to prove herself as a principal. Part of men's liberation is having the strength to adopt the best of traditional female values without worrying about being less of a man.

Getting beyond masculinity, then, is achieving new freedoms—freedom beyond proving oneself, beyond worrying about appearances—on the playing field, or in the office; in earned degrees or in job titles; in clothes, status, or swagger. It is getting beyond condescension and contempt toward women, needing to be in control and to have an answer to all problems at all times, beyond specializing, needing to become the expert, being the sole breadwinner, the victim of male bribes—ultimately a security object. It is learning how to listen to others rather than dominate a conversation, to be personal as well as intellectual, to be vulnerable rather than construct false façades of infallibility, to feel and show emotions rather than be emotionally constipated, to be dependent as well as independent, to value internal, human rewards as well as external rewards. It is recognizing the trap involved in treating women as sex objects while at the same time not becoming a success object. It is being willing to spend hours asking, "How do each of these areas apply to me?" rather than declaring, "I know that already," or, "I don't fall into that stereotype." Going beyond masculinity, then, is getting in touch with one's humanity.

The Fitness Craze

By Arthur J. Snider

There are skeptics, but surveys indicate that a good exercise program can improve your overall health

At dawn and twilight, sweat-suited physical-fitness buffs can be seen running for their lives along tree-lined streets and roads, and in parks and playgrounds. Others grunt through pushups on the bedroom floor, pedal bicycles, suffer the shock of medicine balls smacking into fleshy abdomens, and flail their arms in a desperate effort to redeem years of physical neglect.

The fitness kick is on, as any hospital emergency room can testify. More people are injuring more parts of themselves in more sports than ever before. Pulled calf muscles, puffed ankles, painful tennis elbows, stiff necks, and sore backs and shoulders are increasingly common complaints in almost every doctor's waiting room. "They come into the office, restless for the necessary repairs that will return them to the fray, like so many racing drivers bringing their battered machines in for a pit stop," reports University of Pennsylvania orthopedic surgeon James E. Nixon.

Bicycling has become an activity bordering on a national craze. The Bicycle Institute of America estimates that 80 million Americans now ride bicycles at least once a year. For the first time since 1897, Americans are purchasing more bicycles than automobiles, and 60 per cent

The author:
Arthur J. Snider,
science editor of the
Chicago Daily News,
received an American
Medical Association
award for medical
journalism in 1971.

Exercise producing big
muscles may not bring
true physical fitness.
Daily living depends on
healthy circulatory and
respiratory systems,
not on big biceps.

of the bikes are sold to adults. The President's Council on Physical Fitness and Sports released a survey in May, 1973, showing that 60-million American adults engage in sports for exercise (as opposed to recreation). More than 18 million ride bicycles, 14 million swim, 14-million do calisthenics, 7.2 million play tennis, and 6.5 million jog.

Asked why they engaged in these sports, exercisers invariably cited a concern about health. Nearly half explained, "It's good for my heart" or "I can breathe better," and 26 per cent said they "felt better." Another 26 per cent, mostly women, confessed they wanted to lose weight and flatten their stomachs. Unspoken but implicit was the desire of many of the exercisers to relieve tensions naturally rather than by gulping pills.

Some business and industrial leaders say exercise is an exhilarating experience in self-discipline. Frederick R. Meyer, senior vice-president of the Tyler Corporation in Dallas, encourages running on the part of his executives in the belief that it will help them bring more self-discipline to the job. The Zenith Corporation in Chicago gives its executives health club memberships and requires them to work out three times a week on treadmills, bicycles, and rowing machines. "We have a lot invested in these men," explains John Post, the company's medical director. "There is a lot of pressure in business and we want to make sure that when one of them is on the run, he'll be able to get to the finish line."

The passion for vim and vigor has not engulfed everyone, however. There are still many who subscribe to the put-down attributed to educator Robert M. Hutchins: "Whenever I feel like exercise, I lie down until the feeling passes."

Nor does every physician advocate exercise as a key to health. Peter Steincrohn, a Florida cardiologist, contends that exercise is necessary only for growing children, young adults, and those recovering from injury or illness. "Middle-aged nerves and muscles require relaxation, not exercise," he advises. "Raising the pulse rate through exercise is a foolish expenditure of heartbeats." Another skeptic, Frank P. Foster of the Lahey Clinic in Boston, says athletics and physical-fitness programs are "in danger of becoming a patriotic enigma wrapped in tradition, misinformation, and foggy thinking. Many people who never exercise live to a ripe old age." Even the American Medical Association (AMA) says not everyone needs exercise; an active person may require little, if any, additional exercise to maintain fitness.

Nevertheless, mounting evidence tends to support the belief that physical activity prevents, or at least postpones, the onset of heart attacks, which account for 600,000 deaths each year in the United States. Much data has been gathered by comparing people who work in sedentary jobs with those in more physically active occupations.

The first survey to attract wide attention compared 31,000 bus drivers and conductors who worked on the double-deck red buses and trolleys in London. Jeremy N. Morris, a doctor, and his associates found in 1956 that heart attacks caused 30 per cent fewer deaths among the conductors, who ran up and down the stairs collecting fares, than among the drivers, who sat at the steering wheel all day. They later confirmed this data in a similar study on 110,000 sedentary postal clerks and walking mail carriers. In their most recent study of 17,000 civil servants, reported in 1973, the British scientists showed that vigorous leisure-time work promoted heart health. The work included digging in a garden, shoveling snow, sawing, cycling, and taking brisk walks of at least 30 minutes on hilly terrain.

A University of Minnesota research team determined in 1962 that the age-adjusted mortality rate for heart disease is 5.7 per 1,000 persons for sedentary railroad clerks, 3.9 for moderately active switchmen, and 2.8 for the section men who perform more hard labor. Similar comparisons in San Francisco showed that heart disease killed about 30 per cent fewer longshoremen than office workers.

A study made in Canada showed that business executives, lawyers, judges, and physicians had 5.7 times as many coronary deaths as

Many businesses urge employees to exercise regularly to improve their physical fitness and self-discipline.

farmers, miners, and laborers. And a 1967 Harvard University study of 500 pairs of middle-aged brothers born in Ireland also showed that exercise was the most important factor in holding down the incidence of heart disease. In each case studied, one brother immigrated to the Boston area while the other remained in Ireland. Those who stayed in Ireland remained in farming while their Boston brothers became city dwellers, most of them with sedentary jobs. The Irish farmers got more exercise, since their farms are not highly mechanized and most of them still walk or ride bicycles to town. Most of the Boston group owned cars and rode to work on public transportation.

Even though studies show it, scientists still do not know exactly how exercise protects the heart. Factors other than inactivity, such as high cholesterol levels, high blood pressure, smoking, obesity, heredity, and diet, are established contributors to heart disease. One view is that the coronary vessels dilate and form new branches when exercise forces the heart to demand more oxygen. This allows the blood to flow rapidly to the parts of the body that most need it. Another view is that exercise forces the heart to perform more efficiently. The heart then needs less oxygen for the same level of exertion and produces a larger volume of blood with each contraction.

Studies have shown that muscle fibers become larger and redder with exercise and contain more myoglobin, a protein that stores oxygen for future use. The liver more readily releases glucose, which

provides energy to the body, and better metabolizes the unwanted acids produced during exercise, while the kidneys excrete the metabolic acids more rapidly. Over a long period of regular exercise, the blood volume is increased, as are the amounts of hemoglobin and the number of red blood cells, which means that the oxygen-carrying capacity of the blood increases.

Cardiologist Paul Dudley White, a staunch advocate of exercise, who died in 1973 at the age of 87, said activity promotes leg muscle tone, thereby improving the return of blood from the lower portions of the body to the heart, and enables the heart to work better. Exercise also may lower blood pressure and cholesterol levels, and make the lungs operate more efficiently.

Physical activity is standard therapy today, not only for those seeking to ward off a heart attack, but also for convalescing heart patients. Herbert Gillard, a Houston dentist, provides striking testimony on how exercise helps recondition a damaged heart. Gillard suffered three heart attacks when he was in his early 40s, and his physician said he would have to give up dentistry and reduce his physical activity.

"At first, I could scarcely walk a block," he recalls. "But I slowly built it up to a mile, then more." Later, with his physician's permission, he enrolled in an exercise program at the Houston YMCA. It was based on a program developed by Professor Thomas K. Cureton of the University of Illinois, a noted authority on physical fitness. The

program involved jogging half a mile followed by 20 minutes of moderate calisthenics.

"In the beginning, I couldn't jog three laps around the gym, a seventh of a mile," Gillard recounts. "But by the time of my next examination, the doctor was astonished by the improvement in my electrocardiogram." Within a year, Gillard could jog a mile without stopping. He moved up from the Cureton "low gear" program to the "intermediate" program of jogging 2 miles in 17 minutes, then doing 30 minutes of calisthenics.

Today, more than 10 years after his first coronary attack, the 55-year-old Gillard is working full time as a dentist and jogs 5 miles every day. One of his proudest possessions is a commendatory letter from former U.S. Air Force Major Kenneth H. Cooper, whose 1968 best seller on physical fitness, *Aerobics*, started millions on a fitness kick. After he exercised at the Cooper Clinic in Dallas on a stationary bicycle and treadmill, Gillard's heart action and blood pressure scores were described by Cooper as "excellent for even a man under 30. In view of your cardiac history, I am amazed at this response."

Despite all this interest in physical fitness, and the millions of man-hours spent exercising every day, misconceptions still exist in many people's minds. One such idea is that exercise causes you to eat more, so you automatically gain weight. Not necessarily, says the AMA. A surplus of 100 calories a day—an apple or a potato—will produce 10 pounds of fat in a year, but these 100 calories can be used up by walking only 20 minutes a day. Only 12 minutes of fast bicycle riding will burn up 101 calories; 30 minutes of running will offset a club sandwich; and 6 minutes of swimming, a glass of orange juice.

Fears of overstraining a normal heart with exercise are also unfounded. Many young athletes develop enlarged hearts because the muscle fibers thicken. But this so-called athlete's heart is advantageous, not harmful, according to Allan J. Ryan, University of Wisconsin physician and former president of the American College of Sports Medicine. The enlarged heart pumps more slowly and efficiently.

It is the "loafer's heart," not the athlete's heart, that is likely to be in trouble. The loafer's heart has a capacity geared only to the sedentary life that produced it, and it may not be able to meet the challenge of unusual stress, such as running upstairs or shoveling snow.

James Counsilman, coach of the Indiana University swimming team and developer of such Olympic swimming stars as Mark Spitz, Gary Hall, and John Kinsella, drives his charges to the point of exhaustion, until their hearts are pounding at a peak. But no physician has found any adverse effects on their cardiovascular systems.

The physiological adjustments the human body makes to exercise are astonishing. Even in anticipation of exercise, the autonomic nervous system, which controls the body's internal organs, begins to gear

Physical fitness experts caution that last-minute efforts cannot make up for years of physical inactivity and bad eating habits.

up. It releases adrenal hormones into the blood stream, quickens the pulse rate, contracts the heart muscle more forcibly, and deepens the breathing. With the start of exercise, there is an immediate jump in lung ventilation. An adult, who normally gets along on about three-tenths of a quart of oxygen a minute at rest, requires 10 times that much during great physical exertion. The heart, which pumps about 5.8 quarts of blood per minute at rest, increases its blood output to nearly five times that amount during strenuous exercise.

But even when the body machinery is working at full speed, it cannot supply the 50-fold increase in oxygen that is demanded by the muscles. This demand is met by changing the pattern of blood flow. At rest, muscles get only about 20 per cent of the total oxygen intake, and the remainder goes to the brain and other organs. But at full physical exertion, almost all the oxygen goes to the muscles, as shown in the illustration on page 117.

The body has one other adaptive mechanism that physiologists admire. It can live beyond its capacity to transport oxygen to the active muscles, and pay back this "oxygen debt" after exercise. The fast pulse and heavy breathing that follow heavy exercise is the body's way of repaying the oxygen debt.

Physical fitness experts, however, caution anyone who has been inactive for several years not to begin running, even a short distance, until he makes certain he has a normal heart. And the flabby fellow who attempts three fast sets of tennis under a blazing sun is tempting disaster. Cooper recommends that persons up to 30 years of age have a complete physical examination within the year preceding any decision to take up tennis or jogging. The examination should be within the preceding three months for those from 30 to 60, and for those over 60, immediately before the fitness program begins.

Exercise should always start with a warm-up. Former astronaut James A. Lovell, chairman of the President's Council on Physical Fitness and Sports, recommends about 5 or 10 minutes of warm-up—twisting, turning, stretching, and bending—to loosen the muscles and prepare the heart and lungs for greater exertion. Ten minutes of gradually increasing exercise will speed the pulse rate from a resting level of about 70 beats a minute to about 120, and smooth out the extra heartbeats that many experience at the start of strenuous exercise.

Mornings are probably the best time to exercise. Cooper finds that the drop-out rate among morning exercisers is only about 15 per cent, compared to as high as 70 per cent for those who wait until the afternoon or evening for their workouts. On the other hand, those whose daily jobs involve mental stress may find that exercising immediately after work refreshes them. Margaret M. Kenrick, director of physical medicine at Georgetown University medical school in Washington, D.C., walks and runs on a treadmill for 15 minutes every night before going home. "I won't leave here without going on that treadmill five days a week," she says, "and I've been on it as late as 9 o'clock. But I

Fitness leaders urge
a physical examination
by a doctor before
beginning a strenuous
exercise program.

feel fine afterward, ready to do something in the evening rather than go home bushed to just sit in front of the television set."

Evidence suggests that workouts five days a week are desirable in achieving fitness, but then it can be maintained with as few as three workouts a week. Cooper rates activities by measuring the amount of energy the body must use to perform them. He has translated these measurements into points so that you can pick and choose exercises to reach the desired goal of 30 points a week for men and 24 for women. Cureton measures the adequacy of exercise by calories used up. He says that sedentary adults need to use up from 300 to 500 calories daily to significantly improve their respiratory and cardiovascular fitness.

The pulse rate provides the best measurement of the intensity of exercise. Most authorities agree that exercising at 70 to 80 per cent of your maximum capacity will achieve a reasonable level of fitness. That percentage can be reached in about five minutes of vigorous exertion. For example, the pulse of a well-conditioned young person will accelerate to 200 beats a minute at peak performance. But 70 per cent of that, or a pulse rate of 140 to 160, is sufficient. A 45-year-old man with a maximum rate of 170 will benefit from 20 to 30 minutes of sustained exertion that keeps his pulse at 120 beats. Maximum pulse rates decrease with age from about 200 at age 25 to 150 at age 65.

Your ability to recover quickly is a good indication of whether the exercise is too strenuous. If you are breathless and your heart is still pounding noticeably 10 minutes later, and if weakness or fatigue persists after two hours, then the exercise has been too severe. Stop exercising if you become faint or unusually short of breath, or if you experience chest pains. Exercise that produces heart and lung fitness is more beneficial for most sedentary Americans than that which produces big muscles and eliminates swimsuit bulge. Daily living depends on the condition of the circulatory and respiratory systems, not on the size or shape of the biceps.

Running, jogging, swimming, and cycling are considered the best exercises for such fitness, but just plain walking should not be minimized. "Brisk walking is high on my list," says Cooper. He lists running, swimming, cycling, walking, running in place, and either handball, basketball, or squash in his order of productivity. Rapid walking uses up about 300 calories an hour, freshens the senses, and promotes the feeling of well-being. When walking does not place sufficient stress on the body, jogging is recommended.

"Jogging may be varied from being slightly more strenuous than walking on the level to an extremely vigorous exercise," says Waldo E. Harris of the University of Oregon medical school. "A gradually increasing stress can be placed on the body. The amount of exercise can be varied by the total distance covered, the percentage of walking, and the pace of running. Unless medical reasons forbid, it is a form of exercise that can be performed by almost anyone, regardless of age or level of physical fitness. It requires no special skills, no expensive equipment, no special arrangements, and no special time."

Senator William Proxmire (D., Wis.), who runs and jogs the 4.7 miles between his home and the Senate Office Building, says it beats the nerve-wracking, bumper-to-bumper, horn-blowing, lane-switching ride that most motorists suffer in commuting to their jobs in Washington, D.C. "A runner who can do 5 miles in 45 minutes is in better physical condition than 90 per cent of the National Football League players," he contends. "It also enables you to eat 500 to 600 calories more a day without gaining an ounce."

The President's Council on Physical Fitness and Sports offers five jogging guidelines:
- Run in an upright position, avoiding the tendency to lean. Keep the back as straight as you can while still remaining comfortable, and keep the head up. Don't look at your feet.
- Hold your arms slightly away from your body, with the elbows bent so that the forearms are roughly parallel to the ground. Occasionally shake and relax the arms and shoulders to help reduce any tightness that sometimes develops while jogging. Take several deep breaths periodically and blow them out completely.
- It is best to land on the heel of your foot and rock forward so that you drive off the ball of your foot for your next step. If this proves difficult, try a more flat-footed style of walking.
- Keep your steps short. The length of stride should vary with your rate of speed.

During exercise, the body diverts blood to the muscles from all organs but the brain. The numbers show the blood flow in milliliters per minute.

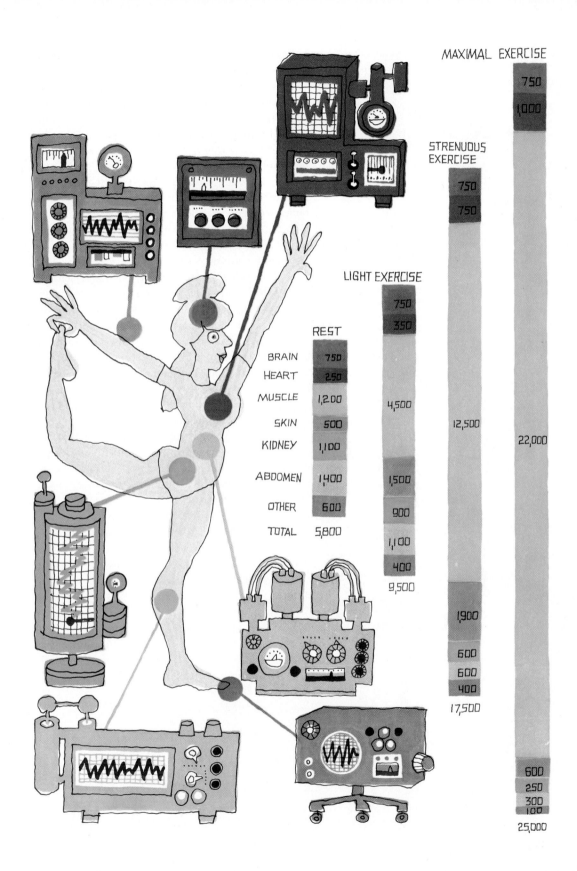

MAXIMAL EXERCISE

750
1,000

22,000

600
250
300
100

25,000

STRENUOUS
EXERCISE

750
750

12,500

1,900

600
600
400

17,500

LIGHT EXERCISE

750
350

4,500

1,500

900

1,100

400

9,500

	REST
BRAIN	750
HEART	250
MUSCLE	1,200
SKIN	500
KIDNEY	1,100
ABDOMEN	1,400
OTHER	600
TOTAL	5,800

210

These drawings show the number of calories you use up each hour that you engage in one of the activities shown here.

216

270

270

300

300

■ Breathe deeply with your mouth open. Do not hold your breath.

Heart specialist White favored bicycling. He said it provides cardiovascular stress along with the opportunity to rediscover America beyond the highways. Interest in bicycling has grown so much that about 200,000 miles of bikeways are projected for the United States by 1975.

The bicycling craze is almost matched by the zeal for tennis. About 5,000 new tennis courts are being constructed each year in the United States, including hundreds of indoor centers for year-round use. An hour of sustained tennis burns up about 425 calories.

Golf, another popular sport, does not yield the same calorie burn-up. "It can be a fine way to spoil a good walk," says Herman Hellerstein, Case Western Reserve University rehabilitation expert. "Swinging a club takes 15 seconds. For 18 holes, the total expenditure of energy takes 20 minutes. In the 5,000 to 6,000 yards a golfer covers, he would have to walk at 3 to 4 miles an hour to derive any benefit." A golfer who walks between shots expends up to 250 calories an hour.

Swimming is regarded as one of the best all-around conditioners, burning about 5 calories per minute. Snow-skiing burns almost 600 calories an hour, but water-skiing, only 480. Bowling, probably America's favorite participation sport, is not vigorous enough to give more than mild exercise to the heart and lungs. A bowler uses only 4.5 calories each time he rolls the ball.

One of the poorest heart conditioners, apparently, is isometric exercise. Billed as an instant conditioner, isometrics promise fitness without the fuss of sweaty exercise. The system pits muscle against muscle without moving the body part involved – for example, pushing hands against a wall, or palm against palm. But isometrics do little to improve overall health. And some cardiologists caution that they can send the blood pressure zooming to levels that are dangerous. Health authorities also criticize passive or effortless exercise equipment, such as vibrating belts, electric bicycles, belts, girdles, and perspiration-inducing garments, which health salons promise will shake off, sweat off, or shift fat.

John Boyer, medical director of the Exercise Physiology Laboratory at the University of California in San Diego, says, "Health clubs traditionally concentrate on building muscular strength through calisthenics such as pushups and weight training. But muscular strength is not fitness. Our living is not dependent on our biceps. It is dependent on the condition of our heart and lungs."

However, some medically supervised exercise salons operate on sound principles developed mainly by physicians and physiologists concerned with cardiovascular health. In general, they prescribe exercise much as a doctor prescribes medicine – developing a systematic "dosage" of sports and calisthenics based on scientific tests that have been analyzed by a cardiologist.

Only time will tell whether the renewed interest in jogging, tennis, bicycling, and other sports and exercise is more than just a passing fad. After all, it may fade as did the Davy Crockett craze and the crew haircut. Hopefully, the mass interest in exercise will have real staying power and, instead of giving way to some new fad, show up in improved health statistics.

The Theater Is Alive, Well, and Living All Over

By Helen Hayes

As told to Alice Griffin

America's first lady of the theater tells how the "fabulous invalid" continues to fool doomsayers

The theater, like all of us, has had its ups and downs over the nearly 70 years I have known it. When it was down, some gloomy Jeremiah always said, "The theater is dying." But none of us actors really believed it in our hearts, because we were in the unique position of hearing the sound of total applause as it came rolling in from the audience night after night. It was a very reassuring sound, especially when the voices of doom were at their loudest.

Even as a child actor, I associated managers with worried looks. The first of a long line of worried managers I would meet was Fred Burger of the Columbia Players in my hometown of Washington, D.C. I began acting for him in 1905, at the age of 5, in *The Prince Chap*. Even after curtain calls that included not only applause, but also stamping of feet, he would glumly remind the grown-up members of the cast that he had spotted a number of empty seats.

I grew up in what was known later as the golden age of theater. Theater was *the* entertainment medium for all the people. There were no motion pictures and no television. Instead, the world of make-believe in the United States was found on the stages of some 5,000 theaters in 3,500 towns. Men, women, and children walked or rode trolleys or buses (sometimes a special fare included the theater ticket) to spend a few hours thrilling to melodramas, Shakespeare, operettas, or dramatizations of popular novels.

Besides such resident companies as the Columbia Players, there

were touring troupes making one-night stands in towns throughout the United States. I embarked on my first tour at the age of 10. The year was 1910–one thing about being born at the turn of the century is that no one ever forgets your age, or lets you forget it–and the show was *Old Dutch*. As an operetta, I think it was the only failure Victor Herbert ever wrote. For the tour, my mother had a special fur coat made for me because the trains were always drafty.

I hate to admit that the same coat still fit me when I toured the Western and Southern states in *Pollyanna* seven years later. I had always hoped I would grow into a tall, elegant, beautiful actress, but by then it was apparent that I not only would have quite ordinary looks, but also would be the shortest actress on the American stage. The role of Pollyanna, based on the heroine in the novel about the "glad girl," was particularly obnoxious. She was idiotically cheerful in the face of all adversity. One of my lines was, "I'm glad my legs are broken–glad, glad, GLAD!"

A recession after World War I, rising prices, and the high cost of touring practically put an end to the road. However, on the brighter side, plays such as *Pollyanna* spurred the growth during the war years of little theaters, founded by people who were fed up with some of the pap that the commercial theater was offering. The little theaters were part of a movement here and abroad–the playwright August Strindberg was an early spokesman for it in Europe–to create more good theater. The American little theater movement is said to have begun in 1900 with the Hull House Players in Chicago.

Reacting against the huge commercial theaters in which actors and audience were far apart, the founders of the little theaters made them just that in size. Maurice Browne's Little Theatre of Chicago had 91 seats. The Washington Square Players in New York City, later to become the Theatre Guild, called their tiny theater the Bandbox. It set the pattern for the later off-Broadway playhouses, none of which had more than 300 seats.

Encouraging new, serious playwrights was another credo of the little theater movement. In 1916, the Wharf Theatre in Provincetown, Mass., gave Eugene O'Neill the first opportunity to see his work performed. As the Provincetown Players, this group later moved to Greenwich Village in New York City. I went to all the openings of O'Neill's plays there. We sat on the hard seats, never noticing any discomfort, knowing something tremendous was happening in the theater, as we saw such plays as *The Emperor Jones*, *The Moon of the Caribbees*, and *Beyond the Horizon*. In recent years, the Wharf Theatre has reopened, and it is again staging works by new playwrights and sponsoring sessions where writers and critics can analyze these works.

After World War I, the little theaters broadened their outlooks and their aims. Originally, members had staged plays to express themselves as a group. After the war, they saw theater as part of the cultural life of a community and began to produce plays for audiences rather

The authors:
Helen Hayes has starred on stage, screen, and television and has won two Academy Awards during her distinguished career. Alice Griffin, a professor of English at Lehman College, City University of New York, contributes theater articles to THE WORLD BOOK YEAR BOOK.

than for themselves. This was the real birth of community theater as we know it today.

New Orleans, which had five theaters in 1835, was without a permanent theater group in 1919 when Le Petit Théâtre du Vieux Carré (The Little Theater of the Old Quarter) opened in the city's French Quarter. The founding group had been meeting for five years before that in members' homes. (It is a delightful little theater, still operating, and I enjoyed seeing Friedrich Dürrenmatt's *The Visit* there in 1963.) The Erie Playhouse in Pennsylvania started in a similar way in 1917, when a few theater-minded people began to meet to read plays on Sunday afternoons. The organization developed into a professional, year-round theater. In most of these theaters, a small professional staff was augmented by volunteer workers, as demonstrated by the Portland Civic Theatre in Oregon, organized in 1926.

The 1920s were exciting years for theater. On Broadway, plays by O'Neill, Maxwell Anderson, Robert Sherwood, and Elmer Rice demonstrated that theater in America could be an art as well as an entertainment. Through the Theatre Guild, many of George Bernard Shaw's plays had their premières on Broadway. And in 1925, I played Cleopatra in Shaw's *Caesar and Cleopatra* to open the guild's new Guild Theatre. (That theater is now the ANTA Theater, run by the American National Theater and Academy, on 52nd Street.) By 1928, there were over 60 theaters in New York City. The American theater really seemed established, thriving, and permanent. But then came 1929.

The Great Depression, which destroyed so many hopes and so many fortunes, almost wiped out the theater in the 1930s. Broadway shows closed, the road nearly disappeared again, and community theaters fell on hard times. No wonder the theater became known as "the fabulous invalid." A threat to the fabulous invalid's recovery was the advent of the talkies, motion pictures with sound. Most people during the depression found it easier to pay 15 cents for entertainment and escape in a movie house that resembled the Alhambra than to pay 55 cents for a balcony seat in a legitimate theater.

Motion pictures took over not only the theater's audiences, but also its stars. I was among those lured to Hollywood, and was fortunate to find a good part in my first film, *The Sin of Madelon Claudet,* in 1931. It won me an Oscar, and I thought at the time that this was surely one of the high points of my life. I know now that if I hadn't won it, my life would have been the same. I confess that when I won my second Oscar, awarded in 1971 for *Airport,* I learned about it by watching the Academy Awards show on television with the girls in the dormitory at Catholic University in Washington, D.C. I was staying at the dormitory during rehearsals of the college production of O'Neill's *Long Day's Journey into Night.*

Threatened by both the depression and the movies, why didn't the fabulous invalid give a final gasp and expire? Why was the applause, though sparse, still heard through the louder voices of doom?

Helen Hayes's career has spanned nearly 70 years, from her stage debut in 1905 as Prince Charles in *The Prince Chap* to a starring role in "The Snoop Sisters," an NBC television series that went on the air in 1973.

Broadway continues to represent the epitome of American theater, with productions that range from the musical *Irene* to the black drama *The River Niger.*

I think it must be because the theater is not merely an art; it is a truly *living* art. The playwright communicates through living people, the actors, to other living, breathing people, the audience. Movies and television may be enjoyable, they may even attain occasional artistry, but they are not the same as theater. Their transmission is mechanical, not human. A staged play is a creative effort among playwright, producer, director, and actors. But television and moviemakers are pressured to turn out so many products (in cans) that all too often they sacrifice humanity and creativity in the process. Theater as an imitation and representation of life is possibly the oldest of all the arts; a need for and response to theater is part of the human condition.

As far as theater in the United States is concerned, the very size of the country and the diversity and resourcefulness of the people are an impetus, not a deterrent, to theatrical growth. We can see this from the little theater and community theater movements, both born in times of stress. The exciting thing is that the people who wanted theater went ahead and created it. They got together, read plays, built a stage, and invited audiences in. Along the way, they became aware of their role as a cultural force in the community, and they learned the value of good management.

Today, we can look with amazement and delight at all the different kinds of theater buildings and stages throughout the country. Many of them have facilities that put Broadway to shame, and a good many cost more than a million dollars. But during the depression, theater-minded people made do with what was at hand—hard times taught them to be realists. In Toledo, Ohio, a group of professional and college actors met in 1933, determined to restore legitimate theater to their city. They staged Henrik Ibsen's *A Doll's House* at the First Congregational Church. Then they leased an abandoned brick church, took up their tools, and remodeled it into a theater.

In the same year, the Fort Wayne (Ind.) Civic Theatre took over the Majestic. Touring companies had long since deserted it, but it had been a proud and attractive playhouse when it opened in 1904. I remember it from my touring days. The idea that all art renews itself was perhaps symbolized by the way the Fort Wayne Civic Players put into their plays the old props they found in a back room. Earlier, David Warfield, Helen Modjeska, and Sarah Bernhardt had used the same props.

Then there was the Works Progress Administration (WPA) and its Federal Theater Project, organized in 1935. It was the first time the U.S. government subsidized drama, though several theaters, notably the Raleigh Little Theatre in North Carolina, had benefited from WPA construction aid. Under Hallie Flanagan, who had been director of the Vassar Experimental Theater in Poughkeepsie, N.Y., the theater project gave work to 10,000 people in 1,000 productions in 40 towns. During its four-year life span, the Federal Theater Project encouraged young writers, developed a black theater ensemble, and explored new production techniques, such as the documentary drama called the Living Newspaper. Living Newspaper, developed by Elmer Rice, was a form of drama in which newspaper headlines were used as the basis for a series of short sketches. Among its productions were *Ethiopia* (1936), *Power* (1937), and *One Third of a Nation* (1938). Congressional objection to some of the project's outspoken productions eventually led in 1939 to refusal to support it any longer.

The depression failed to stop at least one other community theater founder. In 1932, when shows were closing right and left on Broadway, Robert Porterfield took 22 lean and hungry actors and headed for the rolling farmland of Virginia. When they got to Abingdon, they set up the Barter Theatre, where audiences starved for drama could swap produce for the 35-cent admission. Even in its first season, Barter was successful, ending with $4.30 in cash, a barrel of homemade jellies and jams, and a collective total of 305 pounds in weight gained by the cast. Playwrights' royalties were paid with Virginia hams. The only playwright to object was George Bernard Shaw, who returned his ham with a reminder that he was a vegetarian.

Today, Barter still operates in Abingdon and sends out troupes to tour the state from the same theater building–built in 1830–that once housed stock companies on one-night stands. Most patrons pay cash for their $4 tickets, but recently a group of 16 farmworkers gained admittance by bartering two small pigs. In 1947, the theater group was kind enough to honor me with its Barter Award as "best performer of the year." The award consists of a Virginia ham, a platter to serve it from, and an acre of land.

The plaque that hangs under the Barter marquee seems to sum up the aim and the ideals of many community theaters: "The Barter Theatre pledges itself to combat the evils that would destroy the culture and enlightenment of the world by giving the best of its strength and devotion to the cause of truth, beauty, and the spiritual nourishment of the human soul." Surely such devotion to an ideal, rather than to a profit-and-loss sheet, is at the heart of the success of the regional theater movement.

Of course, budgets have to balance, too. In this respect, a subscription audience, which pays in advance to attend a series of plays, can provide a working budget to make the difference between life and death for a theater. Subscription has been the magic formula that has rescued the fabulous invalid more than once. The Theatre Guild, in a cooperative program with its American Theatre Society, led the way in using subscriptions on a large scale to save the road for touring shows before and after their appearance on Broadway.

One of my happiest tours for the guild was in 1940 as Viola in Shakespeare's *Twelfth Night*. Acting in Shakespeare and reading his works has been one of the joys of my career. This great playwright never ceases to astonish me with his knowledge of the human heart and his glorious expression of what he sees there. I hail the practice of using live productions of Shakespeare to teach his works to schoolchildren, just as I deplore stuffy teaching that presents him to students only through dry texts.

Since the founding of the Oregon Shakespeare Festival at Ashland in 1935, the growth and development of Shakespeare festivals has been encouraging. University drama departments have contributed by staging such festivals as the ones at Ashland and at Shakespeare Under the Stars in Boulder, Colo. Universities also have trained young actors to play in these and other festivals, such as the New York Shakespeare Festival. When I participated in the American Shakespeare Festival in Stratford, Conn., in 1962, I was impressed with the large number of actors who had been drawn from university theaters.

Theater activity slowed, but did not die, during World War II. Among the theaters successfully started during the war years was the Sacramento Civic Repertory Theater in California, which toured its first productions to nearby Army camps and hospitals in 1942. As well as producing its own plays and operating a theater school, this community organization also books touring shows into its theater.

Theater thrives on the West Coast with such groups as the American Conservatory Theatre (ACT) in San Francisco. The actors rotate in a standard repertory program. William Ball directed ACT's production of *Cyrano de Bergerac*.

The Academy Theatre in Atlanta, *above left,* is often controversial and always involved. Such experimental plays as *Ubu the King, top,* and *Tango Palace, above right,* offer theatergoers some unusual challenges.

One of the features of postwar years has been the tremendous growth of children's theater, which both entertains young audiences and introduces them early to the theater-going habit. I remember that when I was acting in such plays as *Victoria Regina* (1935-1938), *Harriet* (1943-1945), and *Mrs. McThing* (1952), we presented special matinées for children. They were about the most exhilarating audiences I've ever played to—very exacting in following the story and very vocal in shouting out advice to me.

Winifred Ward, a pioneer worker in children's theater, founded the Children's Theatre Conference, a national organization of children's theater groups, in 1944. She summed up the importance of such theater when she said, "No art can become a vital, moving force in a country unless the children grow up in it, unless it is part of their lives from the time they are very young."

Today, more than 100 colleges and 500 community and touring

Shakespeare's plays have become so popular that the Stratford Festival Theatre in Canada was forced to add a third stage, in an old barn, in 1971. In the theater's warehouse, the founder, Tom Patterson, sits amidst a 20-year collection of costumes and props.

groups stage plays for children, with a total audience estimated at more than 7 million young people. On the stage of the historic Dock Street Theatre in Charleston, S.C., for example, the Footlighters bring to life fairy tales and modern stories for young audiences. Then they troupe these plays to schools in the surrounding areas. Theaters in other parts of the country do the same thing.

The Goodman Memorial Theatre in Chicago operates one of the oldest children's theaters in the United States. Some members of its early audiences now have not only children of their own, but also grandchildren. The year 1976, an anniversary for the United States, also marks the golden anniversary season at the Goodman Children's Theatre. It is interesting to speculate on the influence this one children's theater has had in making Chicago the good theater town it is.

Today, we accept the idea of college training for actors, technicians, directors, managers, and designers as a matter of course. But such training didn't become widespread until after World War II. In 1914, it was a revolutionary move when the Carnegie Institute of Technology in Pittsburgh became the first American institution of higher learning to offer a four-year course in theater arts leading to an academic degree. Other universities encouraged the writing of plays, especially on folk and regional themes. Maxwell Anderson did his early writing at the University of North Dakota, where he helped to organize the dramatic society and wrote, directed, and acted in the senior class play in 1911. Paul Green's outdoor pageants at historical sites are one outgrowth of the interest in regional themes at the University of North Carolina.

Behind-the-scenes activity includes scenery design and construction, as at Northwestern University, *above and below;* makeup, as at the University of Chicago, *below;* and the handling of ticket sales, as at the Trinity Square Repertory Company in Providence, R.I., *bottom.*

Many groups use dramatic outdoor settings to take their productions to the people. They perform in such locations as New York City's Central Park, *top,* a bank plaza in Chicago's Loop, *left,* a mountainside in Tennessee, *above,* or a Miami park, *center above.*

Not only have regional theaters—including both college and community theaters—kept the older classics alive, but they also have led the way in reviving American plays of the past and in training actors in the styles of our own earlier stage. In 1968, the Association of Producing Artists Repertory Company, a group of young actors headquartered in New York City who are interested in reviving the classics, invited me to tour with them in a 1924 comedy by George Kelly called *The Show-Off*. Acting with these young players, I was impressed with the way they caught the style of the 1920s, period style for them. To act in period style is to observe all the details of movement, speech, and dress as they were at the time in which the play is set. The simple act of sitting down is an example. In the 1920s, debs and flappers didn't just flop down or even sit back in a chair. They perched on the edge, ready to spring up vivaciously on invitation or impulse.

Today, there are some 1,900 U.S. colleges where a young man or woman can study theater. Over 200 universities offer degrees in theater, and 1,600 more give courses in drama and produce plays. When a university theater works with a professional theater, the student profits by putting his training to practical use. The Tyrone Guthrie Theatre in Minneapolis draws its interns from students in the University of Minnesota Drama Department. Tulane University in New Orleans cooperates in a similar way with Le Petit Théâtre du Vieux Carré.

The college theater also prepares its students for the profession by inviting theater specialists to the campus—directors, technicians, critics, playwrights, and, of course, actors. I taught a class for a quarter at the Chicago Circle campus of the University of Illinois in 1969 and still hear from some of my former students who are now working at community theaters in the area.

At New Orleans' Le Petit Théâtre du Vieux Carré, patrons at a matinée performance relax in an outdoor courtyard during intermission. The stage is beyond the open doors.

In 1971, I accepted an invitation to appear at the new Hartke Theatre at Catholic University in Washington, D.C. The theater is named in honor of the drama department's founder, Father Gilbert V. Hartke. Beginning in 1937, this worker of stage miracles used platforms, halls, and an Army surplus Quonset hut to mount his outstanding productions. Now the department operates the year around, and gives professional employment to its graduates at the Olney summer theater in Maryland and in a touring organization, Players, Inc. The Players have covered not only the United States innumerable times, but Europe as well.

When asked what part I wished to play at the Hartke, I thought of the mother in O'Neill's *Long Day's Journey into Night*. I had played Nora Melody in O'Neill's *A Touch of the Poet* on Broadway, but the role of Mary Tyrone in *Long Day's Journey* is far more demanding, physically and emotionally.

A respiratory illness during rehearsals postponed our opening for a week. That didn't help my customary first-night jitters when that occasion arrived. I was waiting to go on and trying to remember my first line, when I noticed that Peggy Cosgrave, the student who was playing the maid Cathleen, was even more nervous than I was. Whether or not I would ever recall my first line, or any line after that, it was more important at that moment to encourage Peggy, and I did. I made my entrance and found my lines, or they found me.

That play was my last stage performance. The respiratory weakness, which has plagued me since I was in *Victoria Regina* in 1935, is aggravated by theater dust, and my doctor has given me strict orders to stay off the stage. Of course, that can't keep me from acting, except that now I appear only in movies and on TV. But it's not the same. I miss the excitement of the live stage.

The question young people ask me most often is whether they should choose acting as a career. It seems to me that unless one is absolutely sure that theater is what he or she wants and is prepared to devote years of hard work, self-discipline, and self-denial to that career, he should choose another field. For those willing to make the sacrifices, there is a wide choice of theater training available at drama schools and colleges. The hardest part of all comes after graduation. One must have the courage and resilience to pursue one's aim, even if it means starting with the lowest, most remotely connected job. But opportunities exist, or can be made to exist, for those who persevere. There may be only 10 plays on Broadway at the time I write this, but there are 5,000 other theaters staging plays throughout the country.

And acting isn't the only career in the theater for a man or a woman. A hundred people might work on the production of a play that has only two actors in the cast. On opening night, the curtain goes up on the combined creative efforts of the men and women who have worked as stage director, stage manager, lighting and sound technicians, scenery designers, and costume designers, not to mention the people who paint and move the scenery, sew the costumes, apply the makeup and wigs, dress the actors, and supply and care for the proper-

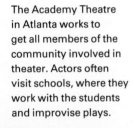

The Academy Theatre in Atlanta works to get all members of the community involved in theater. Actors often visit schools, where they work with the students and improvise plays.

Theater holds a special magic for children. After a performance, an actor may chat with his young audience, as at Chicago's Goodman Theatre, *left.* Many companies, such as the Court Theatre at the University of Chicago, offer opportunities for children to act, *above.*

A young actor applies makeup for his role in *Wind in the Willows,* a Goodman Children's Theatre production.

Dinner theater is one of the fastest-growing areas of theater. At such places as Candlelight Dinner Playhouse in a suburb of Chicago, customers enjoy dinner, then stay right at their tables for a musical or light comedy.

ties. Then there is the administrative staff, concerned with the business side of the theater–the house manager and his assistants who are responsible for the theater building itself, the company manager who handles the production budget, the box-office treasurers, the ticket and subscription staff, and the public relations person who publicizes the production. Overseeing both the creative and administrative sides is the producing organization, which fills all these jobs and provides the budget for the production.

Theater is one field where being a woman is a help rather than a handicap. I have always felt that women get all the best parts. And a number of women have written memorably for the stage, including Lillian Hellman and two greatly gifted younger women whose early deaths were a great loss, Lorraine Hansberry and Carson McCullers.

Nor is it surprising that women have pioneered new theaters. Encouraging new writers was the original aim of both Nina Vance, who founded the Alley Theatre in Houston in 1947, and the late Margo Jones, who in 1948 founded the theater in Dallas that now bears her name. Even in the tough, early days when their theaters had not yet won the followings they now enjoy, both of these women chose to gamble on new works rather than play it safe with old Broadway hits.

In 1950, Zelda Fichandler and other theater lovers deplored the closing of the last remaining legitimate theater in Washington, D.C. The National closed when it refused to amend its policy of segregation at the request of Actors Equity, the stage actors' union. But Zelda Fichandler took positive action. Taking over a former burlesque house in an unsavory neighborhood, she opened her professional, nonsegregated Arena Stage. Arena has grown from humble beginnings into a Washington institution. It, too, encourages new playwrights. Audiences may be disappointed sometimes, but at other times they are rewarded with a work such as Howard Sackler's *The Great White Hope*, which went from Arena to Broadway in 1969. Jane Alexander, a member of the original Arena cast, won a Tony award for her Broadway performance in *The Great White Hope*. The Tony awards, Broadway's equivalent of the Oscar, are named for Antoinette Perry, a former American actress, theater manager, and producer, and are given for excellence in acting and other theater arts.

Those who shed tears over the passing of the old stock companies should remember that production standards are much higher today at such repertory companies as the Arena and the Tyrone Guthrie Theatre. I first saw Zoe Caldwell, another Tony winner, on the Guthrie stage in Molière's *The Miser* in 1963.

California has been a good theater state since the gold rush days, when the first civic building erected in many towns was a playhouse. The San Francisco Actors Workshop originated at San Francisco State College. Members performed plays in the loft of a judo academy and in a warehouse that had been converted to a church. They moved into one of the city's oldest theaters, the Marines' Memorial, in 1956. Their productions of modern and older classics attracted so much attention that their 1956 production of Samuel Beckett's *Waiting for Godot* was chosen to represent the United States in a drama festival abroad. San Francisco also houses the American Conservatory Theatre (ACT), founded in 1965. Among other things, ACT specializes in saving recent worthwhile plays from oblivion. Some critics liked their production of Edward Albee's *Tiny Alice* better than the one on Broadway. In Los Angeles, the Mark Taper Forum also has achieved success by reviving old American plays as well as the classics.

With all the stage activity and diversity of theaters that have developed since the turn of the century, it's a wonder anyone ever doubts whether theater will survive. Answering the doubters are the community, college, and children's theaters, drama festivals, theaters in lofts and parking lots, lunchtime theaters, theater for therapy, theater in industry, in nightclubs, department stores, bars, restaurants, under the stars and underground, as well as on rooftops. *Variety*, the show business weekly newspaper, noted that road receipts for the 1972-1973 theater season exceeded those of Broadway for the first time in history. The total road gross was $55,532,992, topping the $50-million mark for the first time. The Broadway total was $44,898,579.

When I think back to the state of theater as it was when I joined it in its so-called golden age, and remember all it has gone through since then to arrive at its present flourishing condition, I believe I am entitled to be optimistic about its future. I think I can say that the applause has drowned out the voices of doom.

Blue-Collar Blues, White-Collar Woes

By Charles and Bonnie Remsberg

Everybody would like to get more pay for less work, but the reactions of some workers indicate that the problem of job dissatisfaction has far deeper roots

It's hard to explain how I have the energy to work so much. I just have a constant drive," says a young man with two jobs. "Nobody's happier than me." But a thoughtful former clergyman says, "I think any boss can expect me to be a good worker–and a hard worker. He cannot expect me to be a work addict."

Debates about work and our relationship to it grow ever louder. Since 1971, a variety of surveys have shown that up to 40 per cent of U.S. workers are unhappy with their jobs despite improved pay and other benefits. A controversial report issued by the U.S. Department of Health, Education, and Welfare (HEW) in December, 1972, paints an even darker picture.

It says only 24 per cent of the blue-collar workers and 43 per cent of the white-collar group said they would choose the same job again, and more and more middle-management executives seek a mid-career change to other work. "Vulnerability to the [job] 'blues' is endemic to the whole of [today's] work force," concludes a study by the University of Michigan's Institute for Social Research. It has little to do with professional status or income–or even geography. The same problem is reported in Canada, Europe, South America, and the Orient.

But despite the surveys, not all authorities agree that job unrest is so epidemic. Some charge that the statistics are twisted to support the theories of intellectual academicians who don't really understand the average worker and his views. The critics say these researchers are trying to create an issue where none exists. The danger, they warn, is that workers who are told that their jobs are boring and unfulfilling will begin to believe it. The whole problem of worker discontent "would go away if sociologists and reporters would quit writing about it," asserts one U.S. Department of Labor official.

Even experts who agree that discontent *is* widespread often disagree about its causes. Some argue that the blame lies with modern workers themselves–that they have grown lazy and deserted the traditional work ethic. Others blame the nature of today's jobs. More than ever before, they hold, work is dehumanized.

The discontent, many experts say, shows up in many ways–reduced productivity, more "wildcat" strikes, dramatic increases in company pilferage, rising absenteeism and turnover rates, and poor quality of work. Alcoholism, drug abuse, impotence, and other psychological problems are also present. Monday and Friday absenteeism at some automobile assembly plants approaches 20 per cent. In some companies, an estimated 15 per cent of the workers have become addicted to drugs; in others, workers turn to heavy drinking "to get through the day." Frustrated employees of some firms have damaged products with dye, slashed them with razor blades, or smashed them with hammers. Management consultant Roy W. Walters of Glen Rock, N.J., says work forces today rarely operate at more than half their potential productivity, despite all of their new equipment.

Says Professor Richard E. Walton of the Harvard Business School: "The current [job] alienation is not merely a phase that will pass in due time. It is a basic, long-term, and mounting problem."

For more than 12 of the 22 years she has worked at the Kellogg Company cereal plant in Battle Creek, Mich., Alyce Parker has manned a "reclaim belt" in one of the large, hot, oven rooms where 9 to 10-million boxes of breakfast food are processed each day. A slim, intense divorcée with two grown daughters and two grandchildren, she is paid $4.90 an hour to flick out any foreign objects and poor-quality flakes and kernels she spots in the river of dry cereal flowing endlessly past her on a conveyor belt. One daughter works in the plant's personnel department; her mother, now retired, cleaned rest rooms at Kellogg's for 20 years. Alyce Parker talks about her work:

People tell me I don't look 48, but I feel it. I'm nervous, and I need to get off the belt. I am so bored. The lady I work with, she's done this for 27 years. She has a huge indentation in her arm from leaning on that belt for 27 years. She's so easily satisfied; she told me she's happy peeling onions. But I feel desperate. Sometimes I feel like the walls are comin' in on me.

All I do is just go to work and come home. I dread it every day. Some days I even hate myself. When that heat hits me in the face as soon as I get in, I automatically get depressed. I always start on the Raisin-Bran belt if it's run-

The authors:
Charles and Bonnie Remsberg, husband and wife, are a writing team specializing in social issues.

ning. The other lady starts on rice. We trade belts every half-hour. That's the thrill of the day.

In 1968, after I was there 17 years—well, the company was scared to death because of all the fires and rioting in Detroit, and they called all the blacks into the office, one at a time. They wanted us to think the company cared about us. I was told it was just to check my record. You know, they didn't think I'd have sense enough to figure it out, and they said, "Is this the way you spell your name?" I said, "After 17 years, you ask!" I resented it, really, because he talked to me like I was so stupid.

I would love to quit, but with all the seniority I have, it would be kind of silly. I've asked myself, "What else can I do?" I'm not getting any younger, so I might as well stay.

I'm tired of the belt. I feel worse than I would if I worked hard all day. I feel so tired when I come home I just take a shower and pass out on the couch. I've gotten to the place where this left side aches, you know, and it's very uncomfortable for me. If I cross my leg, it gets numb. I'm not growing old very gracefully.

Labor-relations experts dispute whether a fatter paycheck or a program of job enrichment is the most important avenue to labor peace.

In March, 1972, the predominantly young workers (average age 24) at a new General Motors (GM) Vega assembly plant in Lordstown, Ohio, launched a 22-day strike that many observers consider a classic example of contemporary work dissatisfaction. The plant boasted the world's fastest, most automated assembly line, capable of turning out 100 finished cars an hour. But shifts were filled with what *The New York Times* called "empty, repetitive. . .duties as nursemaids to [an assembly] line." For example, one man's day consisted of installing four bolts on every passing bumper. In the year before the strike, absenteeism nearly doubled. Some cars were deliberately damaged by sabotage. Production rarely reached full capacity. Workers filed thousands of grievances. The young local union president told reporters: "The attitude that a guy goes to work and slaves to get his $4 an hour is passé. The guys don't want to feel like a part of the machines."

The villain behind some of today's unrest appears to be Frederick Taylor, a turn-of-the-century engineer who theorized that workers prefer to be "used" efficiently. He pioneered time and motion study, and industry soon split complex jobs into many simple ones that could be repeated hundreds of times a day by "specialized" employees.

This "efficiency" cut down training time and increased productivity. But it also meant sacrificing the satisfaction of carrying a job through to the end. It meant that machinery is designed with little concern for—or consultation with—the workers who operate it. And it meant that the mechanistic approach to workers, developed with the Industrial Revolution, is still with us.

But mechanization alone does not always cause job dissatisfaction. Some surveys among production-line workers reveal that only about 20 per cent object strongly to simplified repetition. Moreover, fewer than 2 per cent of American employees man true assembly lines, where mechanization is most obvious. Being *treated* as machines—both on and off production lines—seems to cause the deepest job alienation.

"People tell me I don't look 48, but I feel it," says
Alyce Parker. "I'm nervous, and I need to get off the
belt. Sometimes I feel like the walls are comin' in.
I'm not getting any younger, so I might as well stay."

More than half the employees of most U.S. organizations are said to be of "the younger generation"; one-third of organized labor's members are in their 20s. And workers' average educational level is expected to continue shooting up dramatically at least until 1980. "Being trapped eight hours a day on a dull job is a helpless, hopeless feeling," says consultant Walters. Especially the younger, better-educated workers rebel against it; they want to feel achievement and personal growth from their work, he says. They want recognition.

Judy Wise, a vivacious, 32-year-old brunette, quit a $16,000-a-year "glamour" job researching, producing, and occasionally reading editorials on the air for station WMAQ-TV in Chicago. She has been a social worker and a campaign staffer for several Democratic politicians and, at this writing, is waiting to start work as head of a consulting firm's branch office. She lives in a chic neighborhood on Chicago's North Side in an old house filled with modern furnishings. Judy Wise remarks thoughtfully:

When I wake up consistently dreading getting up, then I quit my job because I know something is wrong. I quit TV because I was bored doing research and tired of being someone's assistant. I enjoyed being on the air, but I realized that was an ego kick and certainly not intellectually satisfying. I cannot be bored. Unless I was starving, I just wouldn't have enough self-discipline for that. I won't stay in a job that's boring just because it might get me somewhere in five years. Because it also might not. I need constant stimulation, constant challenge. But I have to have flexibility and free time for myself, too. I don't want my job to be my life. I want my job to be a part of my life.

I'm in a women's group and work was our subject one week. Careers were terribly important to most of the women, but they weren't going to sacrifice everything else. The men we knew worked so much more. We decided that was one area where we did not want to emulate them; we were healthier.

I intentionally went several months once without working. I was really tired of work, and I wanted to see how I would function. I traveled and really had a lovely time. Then all of a sudden, about the sixth or seventh month, something went "Bong-bong—I gotta get back to work," and within a week I was working again. I don't work to make money. I need to work for me, for the fulfillment, the stimulation. When the work gets boring, I come home crabby and tired. I just want to sleep. I don't enjoy any other part of my life if I don't like my work.

"I have to have some flexibility and time for myself," says Judy Wise. "I don't want my job to be my life. I want my job to be a part of my life."

With job alienation getting more and more attention, thousands of firms are trying innovations to stir new enthusiasm for work. Generally, they reflect the theory of a Netherlands industrial psychologist, H. G. van Beek. It is more effective, he says, to *give* people responsibility than to point out repeatedly that they should *feel* responsible.

One of the most dramatic new programs began three years ago with the opening of a General Foods factory in Topeka, Kans., where 300 tons of Gaines dog food are produced daily. Instead of the usual rigid job classifications, the plant's 72 blue-collar employees are divided into two groups: A processing team unloads and mixes raw materials and controls production; a packaging team packs, stores, and ships. Each worker is encouraged to learn *all* his team's jobs—and, eventually, the other team's, too. He can rotate to any position in the plant, from operating a fork-lift truck to conducting complex laboratory tests. The more jobs he can do, the more he is paid, regardless of seniority. The inevitable factory drudge work, such as janitorial chores, is split up and parceled out as a fraction of each person's day. No longer does it make up someone's full-time job.

Job assignments and rotations are decided collectively in workers' team meetings rather than by management. The workers themselves screen and hire new employees, and they also counsel or dismiss those who fail to meet team standards. They revise production methods to solve problems, decide on some equipment purchases, and answer consumer complaints.

Production runs as much as 40 per cent higher per man-day than in comparable plants organized along conventional lines. Absenteeism and turnover are significantly below industry averages; theft and vandalism are virtually nonexistent; and quality rejects ran *80 per cent lower* during the first 18 months than in old General Foods plants. Says 34-year-old Jim Weaver: "It's the only job I ever had where I felt I was part of the company. We're the foundation of what it's going to be in the future—the Topeka system." Other experiments that have drawn some enthusiastic responses include:

- Gliding time. This system, originated in West Germany in the late 1960s, lets employees vary starting and quitting times each day. Computer workers in a Los Angeles insurance headquarters, for instance, can show up any time between 6:30 and 10A.M. and leave after working 7¾ hours. Some other firms allow early starting and late stopping, with extra free time at midday. A few let workers "bank" extra hours for future time off or go "in debt" to the company for additional time when they work a light schedule. The employee gets a greater sense of controlling his life.
- Compressed workweeks. Employees at an estimated 4,000 U.S. firms have cut their workweeks from five to four or even three days by working shifts of from 10 to 13 hours a day. They get more leisure and they reduce both commuting cost and aggravation.
- Production teams. Long assembly lines are being broken up and simple, repetitive tasks eliminated at many plants. At a Netherlands television plant, autonomous, seven-member teams do jobs once spread among more than 100 production-line workers. With more responsibilities, the seven produce a TV set ready for sale in less assembly time, increasing company profits. And workers, seeing their impact on the finished product, rarely phone in "sick."
- Job democracy. In another West German innovation, employee representatives sit on company boards of directors. The European Community has proposed such participation throughout Europe.

■ Praise. More and more firms train management personnel to commend employees in creative ways for jobs well done. For example, a North Carolina women's-wear manufacturer hired a disk jockey to play records over a plant loudspeaker and name employees who did outstanding work.

From 8:30 in the morning until midnight, at least five days a week, hard-driving, athletic-looking Jerry Engyel, 31, is on the job. On two jobs, actually. Until 3 in the afternoon, he works in the parts department at a Buick dealership for $2.20 an hour, then puts in a full shift operating a sand-slinger machine at the Inland Steel Company in East Chicago, Ind., for $30 a night plus incentive pay. With his wife, who works as a bank secretary, and their grade-school-age son, he lives in a ranch-style house in a subdivision 10 minutes from either job. The back yard and basement are well outfitted with recreation equipment: an aboveground swimming pool, barbecue pit, table tennis setup, and wet bar. Jerry Engyel inventories his time:

During the week, my time is filled mostly with working and sleeping. I spend five minutes driving between the two jobs; I go out for a good lunch for 45 minutes at Buick and grab a sandwich from a catering wagon at the mill; I change clothes between jobs; I spend a few minutes on the bus that runs between the parking lot and the shop where I work at the mill; I take a shower after my shift, and that's about it.

When I get home, my wife and son are asleep. I may grab a bite to eat by myself or read the paper. I just sit for so long and then, like it's automatic, I go to bed, usually by 10 to 1. I may get interested in a movie on TV and stay with it, but I try not to. I fight myself on that all week. By 8 or so I'm up again; I have a cup of coffee and I'm gone.

I put in a fair amount of overtime. I maybe work 25 Saturdays a year at the mill; sometimes I just stay on after my Friday-night shift and work from midnight to 8.

I don't envy guys with just one job; that I never do. I wonder how they can do it sometimes. I'd go out of my mind. I think my schedule does me a lot of good because I'm not under too much stress from one particular thing. That is what's wrong with a lot of people; they're under so much tension from just one particular job that they have no break, no place else. They can't relax like I can. I can go to Buick and if I have a problem there, well, I won't take it to the mill with me and vice versa. And I don't bring any problems home.

If I'm not working on the weekend, I play golf or bowl or hunt or just spend time with my family around the house. If the weather comes up bad then, it depresses me. My wife says something and I jump down her throat. I'm unbearable, like a tiger. That's my main fault.

Normally, though, the recreation I'm interested in I can do and enjoy in two days. If a person does too much, the fun wears off, so I kind of ration my recreation time so I don't have too much of it. If I didn't have the second job, I'd start thinking, "What'll I do today? How am I going to fill the time?" I'd probably play a lot of golf, but it wouldn't be as much of a challenge. I'd get fairly good at the game, and it would be nothing to go out and shoot 72 or 70.

Workers at an innovative Kansas dog-food plant hold meetings, *top,* at which they discuss the day's work and offer their comments and criticisms. Each team member learns how to perform a variety of jobs, from weighing bags on the production line, *above,* to monitoring complex control-room panels, *right.*

Now it's a big challenge. I got so good at bowling, I had a 195 average. That's when I really started on golf. Next winter, I'm going to take up skiing.

If the union contracts continue to go the way they're going, retirement age will probably be 50 for my generation. That's so far off, who knows what I'll do? I haven't made plans. It's the furthest thing from my mind. I worry about today and let tomorrow take care of itself. And right now, nobody's happier than me.

Two powerful forces, management personnel and union officials, often strongly oppose change, despite the apparent success of some job-enrichment programs. Some labor leaders are now talking of making "alternatives to the assembly line" a bargaining issue, but both management and union representatives most often seem to agree philosophically with Henry Ford II. He remarked that "the average worker wants a job in which he does not have to think." Talk of "deadly monotony on the job," says one union staff member, is merely "an intellectual, middle-class concept," not a workers' concern.

Some union leaders complain that the first goal of work innovation is efficiency, a "speed-up." That, they say, eliminates jobs. General Foods's Topeka facility, for instance, requires at least 25 per cent fewer employees than a conventional factory with a similar output. Some unions also believe work experiments threaten to destroy some of their hardest-won gains: wage scales, job specialty classifications, shorter

Production-line workers at the Kansas plant may repair equipment, *above,* or conduct important water tests, *right.* This procedure avoids specialization — and boosts production.

workdays, and seniority systems. Job enrichment sometimes brings workers to identify more closely with management. This and their new sense of self-sufficiency have led some to reject union affiliation—and reinforced organized labor's belief that such programs are anti-union strategies. So far, the major enrichment experiments have been conducted in plants where employees are not organized.

Management executives, for their part, tend to be wary of work systems that deviate "from uniform practices in quality control, accounting, engineering, or personnel," says Harvard's Professor Walton. They "resent radical change, presuming that it implies they have been doing their jobs poorly." Many fear losing control of their organizations, and some feel that the costs of production disruptions, such as worker retraining, will increase the cost of their product. American business is, above all, conservative. One plant manager illustrated this by keeping highly successful work experiments secret from his company's top management for 10 years. He feared they would be arbitrarily scuttled as "too unorthodox."

Some representatives of labor, management, and the academic community insist that the "fad" of work innovation will pass when industry realizes most workers want enriched pocketbooks, not enriched jobs. The behaviorists advocating work experimentation accept the Hierarchy of Needs theory of psychologist Abraham Maslow. It holds that, once survival is assured, workers raise their sights to social needs, ego needs, and finally to "self-actualization," a stage now reached by many workers. But skeptics cite surveys showing that workers put better pay, job security, and fringe benefits well ahead of job enrichment. "I can't get it through some thick skulls," says David Sirota, who heads a New York City management consultant firm specializing in behavioral sciences, "that people may want both—they would like to finish a day's work and feel that they have accomplished something and still get paid for it."

Soft-spoken and slightly stooped at 44, Arden Sundheim has spent 13 years as a public-school teacher. He now earns $16,000 a year for teaching eighth-grade mathematics and coordinating the math curriculum at Fairview School in Skokie, Ill. He lives with his wife and three children in a modest apartment and for seven years has worked part time in a Sears, Roebuck and Company appliance service center. Says Arden Sundheim:

There are bad hours, bad days, bad weeks, even bad years at school. Teachers gripe just like assembly-line workers, and the better things get it seems the more they complain. I can't say I'm unhappy to see 3:30 come around and I don't like Monday mornings, but I don't have to force myself out of bed. But I don't dread going to work. I suppose it's my personality that lets me be happy with a job like teaching. I'm kind of a "ride-along" person. I have a certain amount of resignation in my character, and I lack the drive and aggressiveness for real money-making.

There's a lot of satisfaction. Occasionally you have rapport with a student,

Night shift on the "sand slinger" at an Inland Steel Company foundry, *above,* begins after a day as garage parts man, *left.* But, "Nobody's happier than me," says a very contented Jerry Engyel.

and sometimes they come back and seem happy to see you and remember odd little incidents you've forgotten. One of the sad aspects is that there are a lot of "assembly-line" teachers. They're quite dissatisfied with teaching as a whole and almost look with disdain on others who put a tremendous amount of effort into it.

They blame teaching for interrupting their trips to the dry cleaner. "What am I going to fix my husband for dinner?"—that's their whole day. Actually, if you're going to do a decent job, there's an awful lot of paperwork to take home in preparation for tomorrow.

But doing a job well doesn't seem to count as much as it once did. On my moonlighting job, I hear of repairmen just kicking an appliance together just to hold it until they get out of a customer's home. They just don't seem to care.

When I was going to college, I used to work for my father driving a truck during the summer, spreading limestone on a farm field as fertilizer. You'd get in as many loads as you could just for the satisfaction of a job well done. It was the Old World type of craftsmanship satisfaction.

I've turned down being an administrator at school. I got torn apart for a few days trying to find reasons to present to other people why I didn't think I'd be tremendously successful at it. I would be just average, and not being really good at it would bother me. There's a special satisfaction in knowing that whatever job you're doing, you're doing well. Even when I replace an electric outlet in a wall, I

"Doing a job well doesn't seem to count as much as it once did," laments high school mathematics teacher Arden Sundheim.

can stand there and reflect on it for a couple of minutes and think, "There's a job well done. You know, I did that."

By and large, I've found that same satisfaction in teaching. But there's a general feeling developing that most students don't learn as much math as they used to. It's getting harder and harder to get them to put the effort in, and when they encounter difficulties, they lay the blame on others for not forcing them to learn. How I'll feel about my job 5 or 10 years from now, if this problem gets worse, I just don't know.

What lies behind most of today's work problems, contends Jim L. Windle, a professor of industrial supervision at Purdue University, is not the nature of jobs themselves but a "don't-give-a-damn" attitude that he sees sweeping the nation. He lists some problems: "New products fall apart like cheap junk; waiters act like they're doing you a favor by waiting on you; you wait hours in a physician's office as if your time was worth nothing; airlines misdirect thousands of pieces of luggage; and dry cleaners not only fail to get your clothes clean, they lose them."

These factors are not based in the workplace, Windle says. They are probably tied in with the growing disintegration of the family, where pride in excellence was once instilled. "Someone is going to have to show me that employers can replace, through tinkering with the jobs, the missing link–that is, self-respect."

Consultant Walters argues that the Protestant Ethic, which emphasized industriousness, among other virtues, is rapidly being replaced by the Leisure Ethic. "People identify more with leisure than with work," he says, particularly if it is work they consider meaningless.

In some quarters, the negative attitude toward work has widened. Its breadth can be estimated by the counterattack it is stimulating. For example, a summer camp for boys 12 to 14–called the Work Attitude Institute–has been founded in California. Parents who consider their boys lazy can send them to the institute. Its advertising says the youngsters will "learn to work. . .to hammer, saw, dig ditches, and sweat and get a little pay for it."

The kind of product or service he helps to turn out may have a subtle influence on a person's attitude toward his job. In probing job dissatisfaction, writer Robert Sherrill noted that the most compliant worker, if he is helping to manufacture ersatz food or some product he cannot respect, "must realize that it wouldn't really matter if his factory closed down forever. So why should he care about his work?" Sheldon Samuels, an official of the Industrial Union Department at AFL-CIO headquarters in Washington, D.C., remarks that the consumer movement with its drive to upgrade merchandise "is going to do more for workers' morale than anything else could do."

In his 39 years, Richard Dunn, a loquacious man with a quick wit and a thoughtful taste for introspection, has worked as a Presbyterian

Richard Dunn moved his family to the Catskills for a better life, but not vocational gain, and "it became clear that I'd broken a societal rule."

minister, television host and floor director, mental health counselor, industrial policeman, sales manager for a natural-foods company, bread-truck driver, camp groundskeeper, and college psychology instructor–among other things. In 1972, he moved his wife and two children from the urban "rat race" to an isolated religious community in the Catskill Mountains to help men and women overcome drug and alcohol addictions. The Dunns live in a house nestled in the wooded hills near the hamlet of Hankins, N.Y. Richard Dunn reflects on his attitude about work:

When we moved to the Catskills, it was not to go to a job as such and it became clear to me from people's reactions that I'd broken a societal rule which says a man can take his family at any time to any place, no matter what, if it involves vocational advancement. The whole society smiles on such a man and pronounces him good. But when you decide you want to make a move for nonvocational reasons, like just trying to improve the quality of your life, then you're regarded as a little peculiar.

I think that's because Americans have bought the notion that one's identity, as a person, comes exclusively from what he does for a living. It doesn't matter what's become of your family or your relationships or your dreams; if you're good at your vocation, that seems to be the big payoff.

I think there are two jobs that everybody has got to have, male or female. The first is "householder," and that means you do whatever is expected of you by your wife, husband, or children to maintain a home—you provide an income, you're responsible and show up every day, you care for the sick in the family, you prepare the meals, you pay the bills, and so on. It's a contract between humans, and I think that a man and a woman have to do that work with great diligence and commitment but knowing philosophically that it has no ultimate value. It doesn't matter. What seems to me to matter is the second job: your Work with a capital W, those private pursuits which seem more ultimate. To me, it's being useful to people. That's what will move me across the country, and that's what I'll get up in the middle of the night to attend to.

My work with a small w, the vocation I chose as a "householder," has one function only: to enable me to provide in the ways in which I have agreed to provide. There are only two requirements for this work—that it pay a living wage and that it not be dishonest or hurtful. When you try to make your work be what your life is all about, which should be your Work, it just loads up your vocation with way more baggage than it can carry.

We simply expect too much of work, of vocation, and then deeply resent it if vocation doesn't deliver all the goodies we want. Let's face it: Every company has only one president, and why should I feel like a failure if it isn't me. I'm not sure that's sane. I'm certainly not sure it's wise.

I think there is rampant, today, work addiction that gets confused with being a good worker. I think any boss can expect me to be a good worker—and a hard worker. He cannot expect me to be a work addict.

When I try to say of my vocation, "It's got to carry the basic meaning of my life, and based on how I do my vocation, I will be pronounced successful or a failure," then I think I become a work addict. Addictions are destructive. Ten years from now I don't know what I'll be doing vocationally, and I don't much care. What I plan to be in terms of my Work with a capital W is very clear to me. I want to be involved in some kind of community situation in which people are helped to wake up and be made whole. I want to have enough going in my life so that, when I'm 65 and my vocation is stripped away, I don't go absolutely berserk and wind up making potholders out of sheer desperation.

The debate over job dissatisfaction shows no signs of winding down. Many experts believe the issue simply reflects widening dissatisfaction with aspects of modern life. As more and more of us begin to examine the quality of our lives, this concern is likely to mount. As a seamen's union official says, "It happened in the schools, it's happening in the Army. Why did they ever think the same thing wouldn't happen in the factories?"

See also Section Four, Labor.

The Rise and Falter of the Free Press

By George E. Reedy

A noted journalist wonders if freedom of the press can survive today's trend toward regulation

To the beleaguered American press, the Watergate affair in 1973 brought welcome relief from attacks that have been mounting in intensity during recent years. First, there was heavy criticism of the press by politicians. This was followed by government attempts to suppress publication of the Pentagon Papers, an analysis of the Vietnam War, on the basis of national security. Then courts began demanding that reporters reveal their secret sources of information to aid in prosecutions. And a congressional committee even tried to review film from which a television documentary was produced to determine whether the program presented a fair and unbiased view.

This unrelenting pressure on the news media was accompanied by a decline in the public's respect for and trust in the free press, and the relief brought about by the Watergate revelations may only be temporary. In the case of Watergate, the press won a major victory because its contention that something was amiss in the White House turned out to be true. But this did not resolve the deeper problems of the press. The major question facing the press today is: Can a free press survive in a society that tends increasingly to regulate all forms of human activity?

"Can a free press survive in a society that tends increasingly to regulate all forms of human activity?"

alan E. Cober '73

The question can never be settled by a victory—or even a series of victories—on the part of the press itself. The ultimate answer lies in the direction in which U.S. society is moving. And if it ceases to be a free society, there will be no free press.

It may come as a surprise to some, but the free press is not an old and respected institution based on long-standing traditions. Instead, it is a relatively new experiment. It has existed for little more than 200 years. Even today, it is established in only a few parts of the world.

There was, of course, a press before there was a free press, because mass society requires some form of mass communication. In the ancient Roman world, for example, public announcements were posted in the forum so that scribes could make copies for provincial subscribers. After Johannes Gutenberg invented movable type in the mid-1400s, occasional leaflets announcing events began to circulate. In the early 1600s, a few appeared on a regular basis, beginning in Germany and spreading to the rest of Europe and England.

These publications bore little resemblance to today's newspapers. They were crude, expensive, and carried few news items. But the really vital distinction between them and modern journals is that they were controlled by the government. Under no circumstances could they print anything offensive to the religious or secular authorities. However, it is unlikely that these early publishers even regarded a free press as desirable. Such an institution had never existed before and was probably inconceivable to them.

Every known society had operated on the basis of an official truth, interpreted and enforced by rulers who had a "divine right" to make ultimate decisions. Men and women who knew "the truth" were not going to permit the dissemination of falsehood. This seemed to be a perfectly natural order of things to most human beings. Official truth was even accepted in the Greek city-state of Athens, the most tolerant of the ancient societies. There, in 399 B.C., the philosopher Socrates was sentenced to drink the poisonous hemlock because his ideas ran counter to the thinking of the time and were corrupting the young.

Dissent arose frequently in these early societies, but it was not based on an idealistic desire to discuss freely a variety of ideas and viewpoints. This kind of freedom was something that no one understood. Instead, dissent took the form of an opposing truth that went to war with the established doctrine until one side or the other was crushed.

During the A.D. 300s, Christianity found itself confronted by Manicheism, a religious movement based on the Persian doctrine of an eternal battle between the forces of light and darkness (good and evil). The Christian church stamped it out and ruthlessly exterminated the heretics. But at no time did either side in this quarrel between two opposing truths consider the possibility of throwing their arguments open to public debate in which the losers would not face annihilation.

To the people of these early societies, the most serious of all crimes was heresy. Men and women convicted of heresy were condemned to a

The author:
George E. Reedy reported on Congress for United Press International, and served as press secretary to President Lyndon B. Johnson in 1964 and 1965. He is now dean of the Marquette University College of Journalism.

Illustrations by
Alan E. Cober

painful death—usually by fire—which presumably was only a foretaste of the eternal torments ahead. Few people questioned the necessity for such savagery. The only issue that disturbed their minds was the proper identification of the heretic. In such an intellectual climate, it is doubtful that a free press could even have found readers. People were not concerned with the elements of an argument. They sought, instead, to purify what they already regarded as the truth.

The application of official truth was not limited to religion. Rulers governed by divine right, and, therefore, their decisions in secular matters were as binding as though they came from God Himself. A king might be challenged and even overthrown, but the challenger was careful to do so in the name of his own divine right, which, for some reason, was superior to that of the king he was trying to depose.

It was not until what is known as the Age of Reason, or the Enlightenment, in the 1600s and 1700s that significant numbers of thinkers began to question the validity of any "revealed" truth. The beginnings were tentative. The French philosopher René Descartes (1596-1650) questioned his own existence and formed the famous answer: "I think, therefore I am." English philosopher John Locke (1632-1704) believed that citizens have a right to choose their leaders and that the purpose of government is to protect the rights of individuals. Scottish philosopher David Hume (1711-1776), an agnostic, believed that all knowledge is limited by experience, and that no one can know absolute truth. In less than 200 years, there was a complete revolution in the intellectual climate of England and France and a profound change in attitudes toward the proper role of government.

The struggle for freedom of the press also began during this time. The thinkers had provided not only an impetus, but also a market for a free press, and British and French publishers chafed under the restrictions of licensing and of special stamp taxes that forced them to buy and affix government stamps to their publications before they could be distributed.

For nearly 300 years after the first English press was established in 1476, publishing was considered a prerogative of the English Crown. Printing was permitted at first only under a royal patent. Then, in 1534, Henry VIII decreed that all books had to be licensed before they were printed and distributed. And the official licenser reviewed and censored all publications.

There were other devices to restrain the fledgling newspapers. A protest against the government could be construed as seditious libel, punishable by fines and imprisonment. Even if the accusations against the government were true, the publisher could not use this as a defense. Truth was no defense against seditious libel. The only question considered was whether the material had actually been printed. Furthermore, Parliament considered the publication of any of its debates illegal. The spirit of the British government was expressed by Roger L'Estrange, the official licenser of the press, when he wrote in 1663:

". . .a Publick Mercury should never have my vote; because I think it makes the Multitude too Familiar with the Actions, and Counsels of their Superiors; too Pragmaticall and Censorious, and gives them, not only an Itch, but a kind of Colourable Right and License, to be meddling with Government. . . ."

The English government, however, was swimming against the times. England was no longer a "tight little island" whose people could be contained and controlled. British sailors were roaming the seven seas, returning not only with goods but with new ideas; British colonizers were bursting into the New World, where the English monarch's authority seemed not only distant but also irrelevant.

One by one, the barriers to a free press fell. First, licensing disappeared in 1695. Then, in 1769, a jury acquitted an English publisher accused of seditious libel; in 1771, London newspapers won the right to report parliamentary proceedings. The stamp taxes persisted until the mid-1800s, but by then they were merely an economic burden. The prevailing environment of freedom had become far too strong for the press to be regulated by law.

The colonists in America followed closely the events taking place in Great Britain. They imported presses from England and clipped and reprinted articles from English newspapers. Colonial publishers felt a direct kinship with their counterparts at home. In Britain, the press won its battle well before the end of the 1700s, and the American Colonies that broke from England to become the United States followed right along in the mainstream of British thought.

In this context, the guarantee of press freedom written into the U.S. Constitution cannot be regarded as a mere gift of a benevolent group of men to a nation they had created. The Founding Fathers of the United States were reacting to the spirit of their times. They disagreed over many issues, but they were remarkably unanimous in their attitude toward safeguards for the protection of individual liberties. Nowhere is this feeling more clear than in the language of the Bill of Rights, which rings like the words of an Old Testament prophet: "Congress shall make no law. . . ."

Such a remarkably sophisticated group of men must have been aware of the dangers inherent in the sections on individual rights. They must have known that due process of law would enable many lawbreakers to escape just punishment and that the free-speech provisions would provide sheltered platforms for demagogues and insurrectionists. The Founding Fathers surely realized that freedom of the press meant freedom for gross irresponsibility as well as for providing balanced information to the public.

The example of the press was already before them, and the newspapers of the day were certainly not among the glories of American journalism. They were fiercely partisan, usually lacked solid news, and most of them were openly controlled by political leaders. For example, the *Gazette of the United States* was dominated by Alexander Hamilton,

The BOSTON Evening-Post.

"Religious establishment prohibited,
Freedom of speech, of the press,
and right to petition."

"The birth of the free
press was basically just
a part of the birth of
free social institutions."

and the *National Gazette* took its lead from Thomas Jefferson. The warfare between these journals was so bitter that President George Washington felt compelled to request Hamilton and Jefferson, who were also members of his Cabinet, to moderate their language, which he believed was tearing the nation apart.

Hamilton, a Federalist, was the apostle of centralized government, while Jefferson was the original advocate of states' rights. Hamilton's paper described Jefferson as "the instituter and patron of a certain Gazette ... the object and tendency of which are to vilify and depreciate the government of the United States, to misrepresent and traduce the administration of it. ..." Jefferson, on the other hand, accused the Hamiltonian faction of "galloping fast into monarchy."

Nevertheless, the delegates to the constitutional convention had determined that there would be no official arbiter for public debate and that one of the early amendments to the Constitution would prohibit the enactment of any law abridging the freedom of the press. That provision was included in the First Amendment–possibly an indication of the importance they attached to it: "Congress shall make no law respecting an establishment of religion, or prohibiting the free exercise thereof; or abridging the freedom of speech, or of the press; or the right of the people peaceably to assemble, and to petition the Government for a redress of grievances."

Some of the Founding Fathers later had second thoughts about the blessings of unlimited freedom of the press. In 1798, Congress passed the Alien and Sedition Acts, prohibiting "false, scandalous and malicious writing or writings against the government of the United States." The sedition law did not silence editorial attacks on the government, however, and it was allowed to lapse in 1801.

In view of the temper of the times, it is doubtful that any law could have curbed the press. American society was not sufficiently structured to foster instruments of repression. There was virtually no federal army and no federal police force, and what law existed could easily be escaped by resolute Americans willing to move west.

When this background is taken into consideration, the current attacks on the U.S. press must be considered in a far wider dimension than the industry of journalism itself, which is much fairer and less biased in its coverage of the news than ever before in history. The birth of the free press was basically just a part of the birth of free social institutions. And so we must ask: Do the increasing efforts to regulate the free press indicate a decline in the strength of all free institutions? Is a new intellectual climate emerging that is leading our society back to a form of official "truth"?

In the early 1960s, few people would have taken such an issue seriously. The U.S. press had behind it nearly two centuries of steady growth in terms of wealth and influence. If anything, the press was too untouchable. People took for granted its essential right to freedom and assumed that it was a socially useful institution. Generally speaking,

political leaders thought it suicidal to take on newspapers and television. They paid lip service to free journalism in public even though they may have raged against the press in private.

This atmosphere tended to promote sanctity but not understanding. As one who was involved in both press and government during the mid-1960s, I could not avoid feeling that the public commitment to a free press was ritualistic, with very few interpreters available who could explain the ritual.

The early signs of the impending storm were misinterpreted and too easily dismissed. News correspondents covering the 1964 Republican National Convention were shocked by the delegates' hostility. But they rationalized the situation, explaining that the convention had been taken over by a minority group of right-wing extremists who did not represent mainstream American thought. The landslide victory of the Democratic Party in the national elections that year seemed to prove the point.

Then, Governor George C. Wallace of Alabama began drawing extraordinary responses from crowds with attacks on the press. Again, the journalists dismissed Governor Wallace and his following merely as disgruntled outsiders who were envious of the progress that was being made by mainstream America.

The attacks by former Vice-President Spiro T. Agnew in 1969 and 1970, however, could not be brushed aside so carelessly. Vice-Presidents are not notorious for speaking against the wishes of their Administrations, and it was assumed that Agnew's campaign against the press had the blessings of President Richard M. Nixon. The White House did nothing to dispel the assumption.

To Agnew, the press was a motley collection of "effete intellectual snobs" determined to undermine the President because he lacked the graces of an Eastern "élite." Typewriter journalists, in his view, were constantly seeking unfavorable news items, and television commentators were masters of eyebrow wiggling that could completely demolish a presidential speech by mockery.

It would be pointless to analyze the Agnew charges and the press responses. The significance lies in the fact that, for the first time in U.S. history, the White House had provided a launching pad for a concerted campaign against the press. Previous Presidents had indulged themselves in outbursts against the press. But they had all been isolated instances of men blowing off steam against conditions they regarded as intolerable. This was a far cry from the series of carefully drafted speeches by a man who was certainly not going to displease his chief. It was the unmistakable voice of federal power.

The exercise of this power began to be felt during 1971 and 1972 on three issues: the Pentagon Papers, the Columbia Broadcasting System (CBS) documentary *The Selling of the Pentagon*, and Supreme Court of the United States decisions in the so-called shield law cases, involving journalists' right to protect confidential sources.

In the 1971 Pentagon Papers case, *The New York Times* and other newspapers printed a group of top-secret documents on the Vietnam War. The government won a court injunction halting publication of the documents for a few days. However, the Supreme Court finally ruled against the government, and the newspapers resumed publication. But it was an empty victory for the press.

The Nixon Administration argued that the government has an "inherent right" to protect itself, overriding such constitutional barriers as the First Amendment. And a majority of the Supreme Court justices accepted this concept. The newspapers won the Pentagon Papers case only because the court ruled that the government did not prove that publication of the papers was a sufficient threat to national security. It was not much of a victory for the press when the inherent-right principle is taken into account.

In the case of the CBS documentary *The Selling of the Pentagon*, a committee of the House of Representatives tried to subpoena unused film clips from the television network. They wanted to determine whether the final editing of the film presentation had been fair and balanced. The House voted down the committee's request.

The House committee's action illustrated that willingness to interfere with the press was not confined to the Nixon Administration. The committee was controlled by the Democratic Party, so the attitude toward the press crossed partisan lines. Clearly, an official willingness to regulate the press, as long as the regulation was in the name of high motives, had come into being.

In the shield law cases, the Supreme Court ruled that journalists could not refuse to disclose their source of information before judicial tribunals. The press protested in vain that this would dry up sources of information and deprive the public of needed facts.

Most newspaper investigative stories, such as those about Watergate, begin with tips from anonymous sources who will talk only if they are assured that their names will not be made public. Without such sources, it would be extremely difficult to report anything about the government other than the official version of events. The same situation holds true for articles about dissident groups whose members fear police retaliation. To restrain the press from using such sources is to deprive the public of important information. This argument did not impress the court, and, in 1972 alone, four reporters were sent to jail when they refused to break the confidence of their informants.

There is no reason to believe that these cases indicated a master plan to destroy the freedom of the press. They were disconnected acts performed by officials in different levels and branches of government who were trying to carry out their obligations as they saw them. A much more ominous threat was contained in a series of memoranda written by White House staff members, suggesting that government agencies, such as the Internal Revenue Service, be used against unfriendly reporters.

"The liberties of the press cannot be curtailed without curtailing the liberties of the people."

But, not considering the White House memoranda, those three cases represented the most massive application of governmental power upon U.S. journalism in our history. The intellectual climate of the country had reached a point where governmental leaders felt they no longer had to keep a "hands-off" policy toward the press. The fact that in two of the instances the efforts failed is irrelevant. In previous decades, the efforts would not even have been made. It is not yet clear how far these efforts to regulate the press might be backed by the public, but every opinion poll indicated a heavy drop in press credibility up to the time of the Watergate affair.

The Watergate revelations of 1973 were a tremendous boon to the press simply because the government was wrong, the journalists were right, and nothing succeeds like success. Unfortunately, the journalistic triumph did not really change the conditions under which federal officials were willing to use police powers against the press. The Nixon Administration had simply become too distracted by its own internal troubles to pursue the matter.

The situation leads to some disturbing reflections. The Founding Fathers assumed that there could be no official truth in political disputes. But the House committee was seeking to make a finding of fairness and balance from an official position. The Constitution states that no governmental influence may be exercised in the affairs of the press. But the Supreme Court decisions on the shield laws certainly had the effect of drying up sources of newspaper information. The men who wrote the Constitution proceeded on the assumption that individual citizens must be protected from government. But the Pentagon Papers prosecution assumed that the government must be protected from individual citizens.

Any government will act to protect itself when it feels endangered. This, however, is different than stating that the government has an inherent constitutional right to override individual liberties in doing so. Even more important, the inherent-right concept avoids the deeper issue of whether the government has the authority to withhold from its own people the facts upon which life or death policies should be based. It is easy for most Americans to accept the premise that some information should be withheld from the public in the interests of national security. When this premise is viewed in another way, however, a troublesome question arises: Do the political leaders in a democracy have the right to make decisions without explaining to their constituents why they made them?

This goes to the heart of the whole issue of the free press. If we assume that the basis of a democracy is the right of the people to determine, through a majority, the policies under which they are governed and to change those policies when they believe change to be prudent, certain requirements must be met. The voters must have a way to gather facts, to communicate with each other, and to hear all views and opinions. The major means of communication is the press.

"The free press may turn out to be just another experiment in the history of humanity -- an experiment that was abandoned after a brief trial because people decided that they preferred government control to freedom as long as the control was in terms of fairness and social justice rather than divine right.

snap

Alan E. Cober

Because the extent of democracy depends on the extent of uncensored communication, the liberties of the press cannot be curtailed without curtailing the liberties of the people.

A free press, of course, is troublesome to public administrators; complex government programs are difficult to carry out when each move is subjected to public debate. This has led to a notion in government circles that once the people have elected their leaders, criticism should cease so programs can be worked out in peace. Furthermore, since World War II, there has been an increasing tendency on the part of governmental leaders to accept the premise that the government has the right to withhold vital information from the people.

The crucial question is whether there has been an increasing tendency on the part of the public to accept that premise. If so, the days of the free press are numbered and the numbers do not run very high. What is at stake here is not what men and women think about public affairs, but how social and historical conditions affect the way in which they do their thinking.

It is obvious that social and historical conditions have undergone sweeping changes since the era in which the free press was born. The Founding Fathers lived in an age of intense individualism, and they had a philosophical abhorrence of federal regulation. To them, government was an institution that had to be tolerated but from which citizens must be protected.

The early Americans did not become overly excited about law and order; they lived in a land of abundant opportunity where no one was worried about running out of resources. Nor did they develop paranoid fears of an overnight social collapse; theirs was an age when land travel depended on the stagecoach and sea travel on the vagaries of the wind. Calls for a "no-nonsense" dictator usually arise when resources are limited and must be shared or when people expect catastrophe to hit them with the speed of a supersonic missile.

The Founding Fathers lived in a leisurely world. The major form of energy was muscle, and a person of wit and determination could make a fortune with very little backing. Small wonder, then, that they had a distaste for governmental interference in individual conduct.

That abhorrence cannot be said to exist in the mass society of today. At least two generations have been raised on the philosophy that governmental regulation is the preferred answer to most social problems. The attitude is so deeply ingrained that regulation is no longer regarded as a serious issue for debate.

Regulation has been accepted so readily because, in its modern form, it is not truly oppressive. On the contrary, most of it has come about in pursuit of noble goals and to protect the ordinary citizen from predators in a mass society. The radio and television industries have been placed under the Federal Communications Commission (FCC) to ensure that the public will benefit from the use of public channels. The food and drug industries have been placed under the Food and

Drug Administration to safeguard the health of consumers. The hiring of workers is subject to the jurisdiction of the Equal Employment Opportunity Commission to prevent discrimination against racial, religious, and ethnic minorities and against women.

Thus far, the printed press has fought off challenges to its freedoms. But radio and television newscasting must conform to the "fairness doctrine" of the Federal Communications Act. This has rarely been applied directly, but the threat is ever present, and sharp reminders of its existence have recently come from the government.

The very nature of the fairness-doctrine threat illustrates the revolution in thinking that has taken place in the Western world. The publishers struggling for freedom in the 1700s were trying to rid themselves of regulation based on the idea of divine right, an official truth that was coming into disrepute. But, if regulation of the press comes today, it will be based on a new official truth—social justice and fairness, two qualities held in high esteem.

It is, of course, entirely possible that the Watergate revelations in the wake of the disastrous Vietnam War will breed a sophisticated skepticism about the quality of governmental regulation. The government already has suffered a tremendous loss of public confidence. This, however, may only be a loss of confidence in leaders rather than in government itself. For it is interesting that the inflation of 1973 brought an immediate demand for federal price controls. The people might not trust their government, but they want it to step in and help them whenever they are hurt.

The future of press freedom in the United States really hinges on the development of the American intellectual climate. When the free press was born, freedom was regarded as an absolute. It was not just a social value that could be compared to other social values. It was the first consideration to which all other social needs were adapted.

The question today is whether the intellectual climate of our times will sustain such an attitude. There are many signs that it will not. The law states, however vaguely, that television and radio presentations must be fair and balanced—with the determination of fairness and balance presumably left to the members of the FCC. The chief justice of the United States has said that the inherent right of the government to defend itself can take precedence over the right of the press to freedom. A House committee has asserted, although unsuccessfully, its right to subpoena material from the electronic press in order to make a judgment about fairness and objectivity.

Perhaps these are the actions of only a few leaders who are out of step with the dominant thinking of our era. But if they represent deeper forces in our society, the free press may turn out to be just another experiment in the history of humanity—an experiment that was abandoned after a brief trial because people decided that they preferred government control to freedom, as long as the control was in terms of fairness and social justice rather than divine right.

Section Three

A Year
In Perspective

THE YEAR BOOK casts a backward glance at
the furors, fancies, and follies of yesteryear. The
coincidences of history so revealed offer substantial
proof that, although the physical world continually
changes, human nature—in all its inventiveness,
amiability, and even perversity—remains fairly
constant, for better or worse, throughout the years.

A Time
Of Turmoil

By Paul C. Tullier

Political chicanery, militant minorities, and public morality made provocative headline news

It was a disturbing year politically; it was a distressing one economically; it was a hectic one from any standpoint. To most Americans, it was a year unlike any other in their history.

On the political front, the President of the United States was sworn in to a second term of office. He was a man whose policies, domestic and foreign, had been debated repeatedly—often heatedly—throughout his first term. People either loved him or they didn't. Middle-of-the-road reactions were rare. Yet, the President had won re-election by a greater majority than he had received four years earlier. His principal opponent had captured only three Electoral College votes, and he himself had even carried a large part of the "solid South."

Early in the first year of his second term, the President faced a number of dilemmas. Financial scandals rocked the Administration. Many of the President's closest associates were tarred by the brush of scandal. Even the man who had been Vice-President during his first term was accused of having accepted bribes from contractors seeking government work. The ugliest word in the political lexicon—impeachment—was in the air.

Crime in high places was cause enough for distress. Even more distressing to a President who professed an abhorrence of lawlessness was the rising crime rate in New York, Chicago, San Francisco, and New Orleans. Prostitution and gambling flourished. Gangs skulked through the streets, not only by night, but also in broad daylight.

Civil rights agitation was another presidential headache, involving not only the nation's black minority but the Indian population as well. The blacks insisted that they were as firmly shackled and as deprived of their citizenship privileges as if they had never been freed by the

The decorum evident at Ulysses S. Grant's second inauguration as President of the United States belied the many undercurrents of political chicanery undermining his Administration.

Emancipation Proclamation. No less indignant were America's red men who literally took to the warpath in the Dakotas in midyear.

The ire of the blacks and the belligerence of the Indians were as nothing compared to the militant attitude of many American women who believed that they were entitled to enjoy the same prerogatives as men. Women's groups dedicated to the cause of "women's freedom" were springing up all over the country. Some American men reacted with sneers, a comparative few with encouragement.

Obscenity troubled many Americans during the year. The United States, they said, was fast forgetting the Christian virtues on which it had been founded; because of this, "nudity" was being flaunted in the nation's theaters even as an underground press was churning out what the moralists called "unspeakable" literature.

All of this unrest—chicanery in government, proliferating crime, women's rights, loose morals—was, in the eyes of many, simply the aftermath of a terrible war, one of the most bitterly divisive—and costly—engagements in United States history. The slaughter had ceased; prisoners of war had been exchanged. But loose ends, such as the granting of amnesties to those considered traitors to the United States, had still to be tidied up.

There were other troubles on the domestic front. Inflation was rampant. The price of food and clothing had soared. The U.S. dollar fell to a new low on foreign exchanges. But these were mere pinpricks compared to the controversies that raged abroad. In Northern Ireland, Protestants and Roman Catholics fought openly and at times savagely for political dominance. In Belgium, a seemingly insurmountable language barrier separated the Flemish-speaking Flemings from the French-speaking Walloons. Each group insisted that its language become the official one.

The author:
Paul C. Tullier is Managing Editor of THE WORLD BOOK YEAR BOOK.

170

In other European countries, governments faced problems far more crippling than linguistic discord. France's various political groups—including a Royalist faction—were each intent on imposing their own ideologies on the nation's administrative structure. As a result, the government often found itself functioning in limbo. In Italy also, the government was hard put to maintain its authority. In Spain, the population wavered between desire for a monarchy and desire for an elective administration. Russia was under a government that ruthlessly used censorship to suppress opposition; to circumvent the censors, the nation's creative writers resorted to secret presses and the underground distribution of manuscripts.

Asia, Latin America, and Africa were no less roiled by dissensions than Europe. A war sputtered and crackled in Indochina, with Hanoi as the flash point. China, that xenophobic giant, viewed with suspicion any dealings with the West. Latin American countries resounded to gunfire as governments toppled in country after country.

In Africa, a most pressing issue was that of white superiority. The issue was particularly acute in South Africa, where the whites were exploiting—some said ruthlessly—not only the natives but also the natural resources. In one of the Canadian provinces, there were rumblings of discontent among die-hard "separatists." Even the prime minister of the federal government was held in contempt; calls for his resignation were legion.

These were but a few of the crises bedeviling the world when the President of the United States began his second term. Members of a cult devoted to numerology professed to find a certain significance in the fact that there were seven letters in the President's first name and five in his last one. Here, however, interpretations diverged; one school maintained that the number, the arrangements, and the "vibrations" of the letters presaged a brilliant four-year term; another group insisted that they foreshadowed trouble galore. One thing is certain—put together, the 12 letters did not spell Richard Nixon. Nor were the issues part of a social, political, and economic ambiance peculiar to today. The name of the President was Ulysses Grant. The major political scandal involving government officials was not the Watergate affair—and the political and financial skulduggery that it revealed—but the Credit Mobilier debacle and the political rot it unveiled. The Vice-President who was confronted with the possibility of impeachment was not President Nixon's Spiro T. Agnew but President Grant's outgoing Vice-President Schuyler Colfax. The disruptive, bitterly divisive conflict whose effects were still being felt was the Civil War, not the war in Vietnam. The American "traitors" around whom the question of amnesty revolved were not those U.S. youths who had avoided the Vietnamese conflict by seeking refuge in Canada and elsewhere, but 38 former champions of the Confederacy—including its president, Jefferson T. Davis. The year was 1873, not 1973.

Of such are the coincidences of history, occurrences so frequent and

Rioting between Irish Protestants and Catholics disrupts an Orange Day parade in Belfast. Home rule was the key issue that embroiled the two groups in violence.

Belva Ann Bennett Lockwood, a fighter for women's rights, not only won equal pay for female government employees, but also pushed through a law allowing women to practice before the U.S. Supreme Court.

so marvelously interlocked that a scholar, delving into the past, often suspects that history is predestined to repeat itself. Thus, the talk of "separatism" simmering in Canada's Nova Scotia in 1873 had its echo in Quebec in 1973. The calls for Prime Minister Pierre Elliott Trudeau's resignation in 1973 were bitter but far less so than those that actually forced the resignation of Canada's first prime minister, John A. Macdonald, a hundred years before. The harsh, repressive policies of Russia's Czar Alexander II in 1873 found a counterpart in those enforced by the Communist regime of Leonid I. Brezhnev in 1973. The religious disputes in Northern Ireland, the language issues in Belgium, and the troubled political conditions in France, Italy, and Spain in 1873, were all distressing those countries in 1973.

The same was true on the other continents: In Asia, war flared in Indochina as the French sought to establish themselves in Hanoi. In Latin America, the fall of the Allende government in Chile in 1973 echoed what happened in Paraguay and Costa Rica exactly a hundred years before. The internecine warfare between the Watusi and the Bahutu in Burundi in 1973 was but a brutal reflection of a similar intertribal conflict between the Ashantis and the Pygmies in 1873. Today's oppressive apartheid policies in South Africa are similar to those that were in effect in 1873.

There were other such historical coincidences tying 1873 to 1973, particularly in areas involving human nature, with all its urges, its aesthetic needs, its inventiveness, and its wide range of tastes. The advocates of women's rights in 1973 were jubilant when Dixy Lee Ray became the first female to head the U.S. Atomic Energy Commission. But the suffragettes of 1873 were no less joyful when, on March 3, Belva Ann Bennett Lockwood of Washington, D.C., became the first woman lawyer admitted to practice before the U.S. Supreme Court.

Pornography was a grave concern in 1973. But so had it been a hundred years before. The immediate provocation then, as today, was the theater, which loomed large as a purveyor of sinful images. It had all started in 1866 at Niblo's Garden in New York City, where America's first musical comedy, a flamboyant spectacle entitled *The Black Crook*, had its première. It featured 100 girls in costumes considered daring. They had scandalized the staid and proper. Yet *The Black Crook* ran for 16 months with box-office receipts totaling over $1 million. Sin appeared to pay; imitators soon followed. In 1873, the toast of a newly introduced burlesque circuit was Lydia Thompson and her bevy of beefy blondes. Featured in the act was Pauline Markham playing a strapping Venus in flesh-colored tights. It was a sight to behold – or *not* to behold according to Anthony J. Comstock, a formidable, frock-coated, beaver-hatted, moral crusader. His New York Society for the Suppression of Vice, founded in 1873, was the outraged citizen's way of stifling temptation. (That same year, Canada's citizens – outraged by criminals roaming the forestlands – organized a police force known today as the Royal Canadian Mounted Police.)

The average American, however, still preferred wholesome family-style entertainment. To capture this market, the ever-alert Phineas T. Barnum in 1873 opened his Hippodrome in New York City. Emblazoned across its façade was a sign that, unwittingly, gave the language a phrase to remember long after Barnum had departed this world—"The Greatest Show on Earth." A motion picture with that title would still enthrall "Late, Late Show" television audiences in 1973.

If one preferred classical music as a stimulant, 1873 was a vintage year. Johannes Brahms's *A German Requiem* was given its first performance in the United States. On November 26 of that same year, Giuseppe Verdi's electrifying opera *Aïda* had its U.S. debut at the New York Academy of Music. In New Orleans, the French Opera House—which had purchased the original *Aïda* sets for *its* performances of that work—continued to offer in its repertory such stellar attractions as Gaetano Donizetti's *L'Elisir d'amour* (The Elixir of Love) and *Fille de Regiment* (Daughter of the Regiment), both of which operas had been given their American premières at that institution and both of which were featured at New York City's Metropolitan Opera House in 1973. Popular songs published in 1873 included Hart Pease Danks's "Silver Threads Among the Gold" and Johann Strauss's "Weiner Blut."

Periodicals had begun to proliferate in 1873. *Harper's Illustrated Weekly* (the *Life* magazine of its day) was almost *de rigueur* in every American parlor. Hitherto, *Demorest's* had taken the palm for high-fashion news, but in 1873 a competitor was born: *The Delineator* would soon set the pace for the discerning. Ebenezer Butterick began publication of his *Home Companion* in Cleveland; Butterick's paper patterns for women's apparel were already a force—as they would be a hundred years later. Nor was youth forgotten in the outpouring; under the editorship of Mary Elizabeth Mapes Dodge, *St. Nicholas Magazine* for

New York's Hippodrome was showman Phineas T. Barnum's contribution to American culture. It was built to house his newly formed circus—The Greatest Show on Earth. North-West Mounted Police, wearing white cork helmets, were organized to impose law and order in Canada.

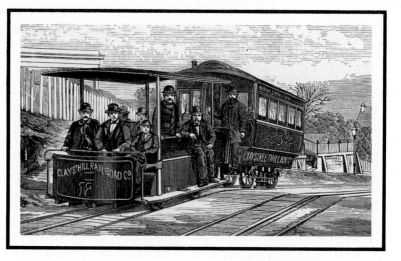

The world's first commercial typewriter revolutionized office work. Barbed wire, a fencing material that was inspired by thorned shrubs, spelled doom for the Wild West. And an ingenious invention —the cable car—was the forerunner of today's rapid transit systems.

youngsters made its bow in 1873. That same concern for youth remained constant through the years. In 1973, *Cricket* and *Ebony, Jr.* made their respective bows before an audience of juveniles.

And if music, theater, and periodicals palled, there were the everyday fads to be depended on for diversion. One of these was the new sport invented in 1873 by Major Walter C. Wingfield of Great Britain. He called it Sphairistiké; it was known a hundred years later to millions of players as lawn tennis. But the biggest fad in 1873 was, of all things, walking. In every city in the country, walking contests were the *in* thing, even as daily jogging would hold people's attention in 1973. In 1873, the epitome of all walkers was Edward Payson Weston. Known as the Great American Walker, Weston on May 15 shank's-mared 100 miles in 22 hours in New York City's Empire City Rink.

Fun and games were only two sides of the many-faceted prism that was life a hundred years ago. On another plane were the movers and shakers, men of action whose pursuits would not only radically change their times but leave their indelible marks on the 1970s as well.

One of these was Andrew S. Hallidie, an engineer, whose revolutionary new cable car began operating on Clay Street in San Francisco in 1873. It was a breakthrough in rapid transit, even as the ever-pioneering San Francisco Bay Area Rapid Transit (BART) system would be the rapid-transit innovation a hundred years later. In Berkshire County, Massachusetts, the 25,081-foot Hoosac railway tunnel was completed in November, 1873, at the then staggering cost of about $14 million. It marked the first American use of the power drill and of nitroglycerine for blasting. The year 1873 also marked the first birthday of an adding machine that printed totals and subtotals. An invention of Edmund D. Barbour, it was not only a lineal descendant of the ancient abacus but the forefather of the hand-sized electronic calculators that would flood the country in 1973. Celluloid, the first artificial plastics material, went into commercial production in 1873.

Petroleum, too, was in "full" production; it literally bubbled from the earth. Demand, however, except from those few who considered it medicinal or useful for lighting, was outpaced by supply; the price of crude petroleum plummeted to 75 cents a barrel. In truth, no one in 1873 knew what to do with it all. In 1973, no one could do without it.

The Remington Company—makers of firearms—also was manufacturing sewing machines. Then, in March, 1873, Philo Remington signed a contract with Carlos Glidden, C. L. Sholes, and S. W. Soulé giving him the right to manufacture a new machine to which they owned the patents. It was called a typewriter.

Other inventive men were at work in 1873. One was Joseph F. Glidden of DeKalb, Ill., who, in that year, designed the first barbed wire. One of invention's all-time greats, it was fated to end the open range and make possible the settlement of the U.S. frontier by small farmers, thus literally changing the face of America. Another was James Clerk Maxwell, a British mathematician and physicist. In 1873, Maxwell published his *Treatise on Electricity and Magnetism,* which is now recognized as the foundation of the present-day electromagnetic theory of light. The subsequent proving-out of this theory by Heinrich R. Hertz eventually led to today's radio, television, and radar.

No less inventive, although on a less exalted plane, were the fashion experts of the day. Because of them, women in 1873 were wearing the newfangled bustle; it had just succeeded the hoop. Most men deplored it. Hair styles also followed the dictates of fashion. Women wore their hair parted in the middle and gathered in a bun at the nape of the neck; men wore their hair at collar length and kept it in place with a concoction called Macassar Oil. No parlor settee was complete with-

The collapse of Jay Cooke & Company, a major U.S. banking firm, touched off a serious financial panic. Frantic investors rushed from the New York Stock Exchange to withdraw their money from nearby banks before they closed.

out an antimacassar, a tidy or doily that protected the back of the chair against the oily back of the (male) head. Beards were also popular, though some, à la Napoleon III, were considered far out.

The acme of social success in 1873 for both wearers of bustles and users of Macassar Oil was a visit to Saratoga Springs, N.Y. Those in the know spent a large part of their time on the spacious verandas of the Union Hotel drinking tea rather than sipping the "healthful" waters, which were not only highly carbonated but also highly cathartic. Those Saratoga vacationers who abhorred letter-writing could send their messages home via the first U.S. penny post card, which went on sale May 12, 1873. (A hundred years later, a commemorative issue that went on sale in Washington, D.C., cost *six* cents per card.) For those who enjoyed new taste sensations, there were Saratoga (potato) chips, a culinary triumph invented in 1873 by the head chef of the Union Hotel. That chip was destined to become a staple at picnics, barbecues, and cocktail parties a hundred years later.

Whether rocking comfortably on a posh veranda or de-rocking the stubbled fields of Colorado, which was awaiting admission as the 38th state of the Union, Americans in all walks of life felt the effects of what has since become known as the Panic of 1873. The failure of Jay Cooke and Company in September precipitated one of the greatest financial panics the United States had ever experienced. By December, more than 5,000 businesses had failed, with losses estimated at $228 million.

Those Americans seeking escape from their financially woebegone thoughts could do so through literature, an artistic field that bore a bumper crop in 1873. Best sellers from the year before were Louisa May Alcott's *Little Men* and Edward Eggleston's *The Hoosier Schoolmaster*. On the new year's list, there were Bret Harte's *M'Liss: An Idyll of Red Mountain* and Thomas Bailey Aldrich's *Marjorie Daw and Other People*. And then there was Mark Twain, who, together with a collaborator, had just published a satirical novel entitled *The Gilded Age*. It was a title that was to give its name to an era. All of the books would be in vogue a hundred years later—as collectors' items.

The best seller of them all, perhaps, was Jules Verne's *Around the World in Eighty Days*, a hardy perennial that, as a motion picture, would still be seen on television a hundred years later. Still popular, too, were his previous books: *From the Earth to the Moon* and *Around the Moon*, in both of which he envisioned man's journeying into outer space. Little did Verne or his readers know that by 1973 his science fiction would have become scientific fact. He might have been startled—but no more so than President Grant over Mr. Nixon's plight or Colfax over Agnew's.

"The Past is Imperfect," an anonymous historian with a grammatical bent wrote, "and the Present is Tense. But in both," he said, "the Future is Indicative." If one compares and considers the events of 1973 in the context of those that occurred in 1873, that anonymous historian may well have had a point.

The Year On File, 1973

Contributors to THE WORLD BOOK YEAR BOOK report on
the major developments of 1973 in their respective fields. The
names of these contributors appear at the end of the articles
they have written. A complete roster of contributors,
giving their professional affiliations and listing the articles
they have prepared, appears on pages 6 and 7.

Articles in this section are alphabetically arranged by subject
matter. In most cases, titles refer directly to articles in
THE WORLD BOOK ENCYCLOPEDIA. Numerous cross references
(in bold type) are a part of this alphabetical listing. Their
function is to guide the reader to a subject or to information that
may be a part of some other article, or that may appear under
an alternative title. *See* and *See also* cross references appear
within and at the end of articles and similarly direct the reader
to related information contained elsewhere in THE YEAR BOOK.

ADVERTISING

ADVERTISING. Despite some uncertainty at mid-year, 1973 was clearly a good year for advertising. Only a real bust in the second half could have put a crimp in the year, and no such debacle developed. Data prepared by the Media Research Department of McCann-Erickson showed advertising investment increased in the first half at an even higher rate than in record 1972. Ad spending was up 10 per cent, compared with an increase of 8 per cent in the first half of 1972. The ad total for the full year was projected at a record $25 billion, up from 1972's record $23.1-billion.

Compilations by *Advertising Age* showed the 100 leading national advertisers entered 1973 with total annual ad spending at $5.27 billion, up 7.5 per cent from $4.9 billion a year earlier. The top 10 U.S. advertising agencies all showed billing increases as they entered 1973, except the leader, J. Walter Thompson Company, which was off 1.5 per cent to $767 million.

Television led all media in revenue increases in the first six months, with advertisers spending about 14 per cent more on spot and network TV than they did a year earlier.

Cautious Note. Several agency chiefs expressed concern about the depressing effects of the Watergate scandal, inflation, and the skittish dollar. In July, Leonard S. Matthews, president of Leo Burnett Company, predicted a drop in Burnett's fourth-quarter billings after a significant increase in the first half. Leo Kelmenson, president of Kenyon & Eckhardt, conceded that his agency had a "better than expected" first half, but feared that the final half might be "disastrous." Edward B. Wilson, new advertising operations director of J. Walter Thompson, maintained that too much of the 60-day price-freeze pressure had landed on food companies, leaving them in a difficult profit squeeze that had adverse effects on their agencies.

But not all agency heads shared the cloudy view. Mary Wells Lawrence, chairman of Wells, Rich, Greene, declared, "I keep hearing about the million and one problems out there, but they don't seem to be touching us. Our business is booming."

Advertising Agencies. Despite agency apprehensions about the final quarter, the bright side of 1973 included not only the record amount of advertising, but also an improved profit situation. After hitting a 10-year low in 1971, when agency net profit sank to 2.87 per cent of gross income, the profit figure rose to 3.62 per cent in 1972, bolstered by some payroll trimming that was expected to maintain the profit improvement in 1973. The figures are from annual studies by the American Association of Advertising Agencies (AAAA).

To help protect agencies when a client defaults on bill payment, three advertising associations adopted a new standard contract that includes the option of a dual-responsibility clause in advertiser-agency-magazine transactions. The new dual-responsibility

The U.S. government enlisted Snoopy in October as the symbol for a massive public-service ad campaign promoting the conservation of energy.

clause makes the advertiser, as well as the agency, responsible for payment of media bills. It was adopted by the AAAA, the Magazine Publishers Association, and the American Business Press.

Meanwhile, agencies contended with the usual account shifts. Biggest of all was the transfer, by the Liggett & Myers cigarette division, of $15 million in billings from Thompson to Cunningham & Walsh and Norman, Craig & Kummel. Cunningham & Walsh acquired the L&M brand, while Adam, Eve, Chesterfield, and Lark went to Norman, Craig & Kummel. Second biggest shift was the $12 million in billing that Hertz Corporation consolidated at Ted Bates & Company when it dropped Carl Ally Incorporated and McCann-Erickson. But the volume of first-half account changes fell 15 per cent below that of 1972. An *Advertising Age* tabulation showed that about $226 million in billings, representing 112 major advertisers, had changed hands by June 30, compared with about $266 million redistributed by 108 companies in the first half of 1972.

In November, Young & Rubicam acquired Wunderman, Ricotta & Kline, bringing its total estimated billings to $423 million. Young & Rubicam said this would make it the largest agency in the United States, ahead of Thompson, which had $393-million in domestic billings in 1972.

One of the year's surprises was the emergence of the U.S. government as a major national advertiser.

After spending an estimated $65 million on advertising in 1972 (up from $42 million in 1971) to rank 22nd in the nation, the government was slated to spend $100 million in 1973.

Social Problems touched advertising in several ways. The energy shortage caused the curtailment of gasoline advertising, which was cut back by about $40 million, of which 80 per cent was from television. The energy pinch may affect $2 billion in ad budgets for various products during the next 15 years.

In September, the U.S. Congress banned television advertising of little cigars. A 30-day grace period was allowed for Consolidated Cigar Company to get commercials for its Dutch Treat brand off the air. Earlier in the year, R. J. Reynolds Industries and Lorillard voluntarily took commercials for their little cigars off the air.

Some other heavily advertised products fared better. Procter & Gamble launched Sure aerosol antiperspirant/deodorant during the summer with an introductory ad campaign expected to total $15 million. Mazda Motors of America planned to end the year with an advertising and promotion expenditure of as much as $18 million for the Mazda car. By fall, Gillette had spent $16 million to advertise its Trac II twin-blade shaving system during its first two years. This included a $2-million campaign for a Trac II twin-injector shaving system. Merle Kingman

AFGHANISTAN. The 40-year rule of King Mohammed Zahir Shah ended abruptly on July 17, 1973, when his brother-in-law, Lieutenant General Mohammad Daud, carried out a military coup. Prince Daud, who had been the prime minister from 1953 until he was dismissed in 1963, declared Afghanistan a republic while the king was in Italy for medical treatment. He pledged an end to the corruption and despotism that he said had hampered Afghan progress. Russia was the first of many countries that promptly recognized the new government.

Daud declared the old Constitution invalid and dissolved the parliament. He formed his first Cabinet on August 2 with himself as president, prime minister, defense minister, and minister of foreign affairs.

Daud pledged to continue the country's traditional nonalignment policy. He declared that Zahir's refusal to delegate authority or allow political parties had made the revolution necessary.

The end of a two-year drought produced some improvement in the economy. Cotton and wheat harvests were 50 per cent higher, and rice production increased 20 per cent. Foreign loans continued to be the main source of support for the fourth five-year plan, which started in January. Russia granted the largest, 100 million rubles (about $138 million). It was for a new oil refinery. William Spencer

See also Asia (Facts in Brief Table).

Arthur Schultz, center, of Foote, Cone & Belding, gets help in cutting the cake at a celebration honoring the agency's 100th anniversary in May.

AFRICA. Disaster struck several African countries in 1973. Thousands of people died in a famine; thousands more were killed in ethnic and racial violence. The Middle East war prompted shifting political alliances. Most black African nations severed diplomatic relations with Israel and demanded that Israeli troops be withdrawn from Arab territory.

There also were major economic changes. The French-speaking African nations loosened their ties to France, and regional economic alliances crumbled.

Drought and Famine. The devastating drought in western Africa began attracting worldwide attention in May and June. Six countries along the southern edge of the Sahara – Chad, Mali, Mauritania, Niger, Senegal, and Upper Volta – had been suffering from the drought for four and a half years. The drought had killed about 80 per cent of the livestock in Mali. Chad and Niger suffered the least of these six countries, but still lost about 33 per cent of their livestock.

Widespread famine resulted. In May, the United Nations (UN) Food and Agriculture Organization reported that 6 million persons were facing starvation. International organizations and individual countries sent more than 600,000 tons of food. The United States estimated in August that enough food had been distributed to prevent mass starvation.

The six affected African nations held a conference in September in Upper Volta and formulated a $1.5-billion plan for constructing irrigation projects and transportation systems. They requested aid for the projects and also asked for a 10-year moratorium on their international debts.

Ethiopia also suffered from famine in 1973. A UN report released in September stated that at least 50,000 persons had starved to death as a result of drought in northeastern Ethiopia. See ETHIOPIA; Section One, FOCUS ON SCIENCE.

Cholera also left a trail of death in Ethiopia and other parts of eastern, western, and northern Africa. The disease killed about 20,000 in Africa in 1972 and 1973, according to the World Health Organization. See HEALTH AND DISEASE.

OAU Anniversary. The Organization of African Unity (OAU) observed the 10th anniversary of its founding on May 24 and 25 at a summit meeting in Addis Ababa, Ethiopia. The head of Nigeria's military government, Yakubu Gowon, was elected OAU chairman for the year.

At the meeting, a major dispute about the Middle East broke out between delegates from Libya and Ethiopia. Ethiopia recognized Israel, and Libya was campaigning against Israel among the member OAU nations. A compromise OAU resolution called on member nations to take individual or joint action if Israel continued to hold territory taken from the Arabs in 1967.

French-Speaking Africa showed a new economic militancy in 1973. Although there was no actual breakdown in cooperation between France and its former African colonies, there were changes in the system long dominated by France. The 13 French-speaking African nations were unhappy with French cooperation agreements, and many of them demanded revisions.

The People's Republic of Congo began the movement on January 3, when President Marien N'Gouabi demanded that France negotiate new economic ties. On February 9, Cameroon's President Ahmadou Ahidjo also requested a revision in its cooperation agreement with France.

The Malagasy Republic and France agreed to dissolve their economic ties in April, and French military forces left Madagascar. The Malagasy Republic made plans to switch from the franc to a new currency. Mauritania also abandoned the franc for a new currency, the ouguiya, backed by Arab monetary guarantees. In July, President Felix Houphouet-Boigny of Ivory Coast announced a renegotiation of French agreements, and Senegal's President Léopold Sédar Senghor went to Paris in September for economic talks.

Political observers linked these changes with the virtual collapse of the Common Organization of Africa, Malagasy-Mauritius (OCAM). Cameroon and Chad withdrew from OCAM in July, and Malagasy pulled out in August. Cameroon favored smaller regional organizations. In turn, OCAM's collapse was linked to African negotiations with the European Community (Common Market). All OCAM members are Common Market associates.

A crucial meeting held in Lagos, Nigeria, in July may have spelled the eventual end of OCAM. At the meeting, African, Pacific, and Asian nations formulated a common position for negotiations with the Common Market (see NIGERIA). Nevertheless, the 10 remaining members of OCAM met in Senegal on August 9 and 10 and pledged continued economic cooperation.

Regional Economic Unions. In April, six French-speaking nations in western Africa – Ivory Coast, Mali, Mauritania, Niger, Senegal, and Upper Volta – formed the West African Economic Community. French-speaking Dahomey decided against full economic ties with the new organization, because most of its trade is with English-speaking Nigeria. Dahomey would not join any economic community that did not include Nigeria.

Dahomey, Nigeria, and Togo discussed forming their own economic union. Sierra Leone and Liberia also moved toward economic union, with the first stage of their plan to be completed by January, 1977.

Middle East Crisis. The Arab-Israeli war that flared in October almost totally ruptured relations between Israel and African nations. Most African nations broke diplomatic ties with Israel in 1973, including such former strong supporters as Zaire, Ethiopia, and Kenya. However, some countries, including Nigeria, implied that they would renew

International organizations and individual
nations rushed food supplies to West Africans
suffering from famine caused by a drought.

relations as soon as Israeli forces were withdrawn
from the west bank of the Suez Canal. One significant factor in the decline of Israeli-African relations
was Israel's close links with white-ruled South Africa.

Portuguese Africa. Violence continued through-
out the year in Portuguese-controlled Africa
(Mozambique, Angola, and Guinea-Bissau). On
September 24, the African Party for the Independ-
ence of Guinea-Bissau and the Cape Verde Islands
(PAIGC) declared independence for Guinea-Bissau.
PAIGC guerrillas control about two-thirds of the
country.

The new nation was recognized by most members
of the OAU, China, Russia, and other Eastern
European countries. However, it seemed probable
that one of Portugal's North Atlantic Treaty Organization allies in the UN Security Council would veto
Guinea-Bissau's admission to the UN.

The war between the Portuguese and the Mozambique Liberation Front (FRELIMO) continued in
1973, and nationalist guerrillas often used Mozambique as a base for attacks in Rhodesia. A journalist
who reported that the guerrillas entered from Mozambique rather than Zambia was jailed by Rhodesian authorities. See RHODESIA.

FRELIMO guerrillas reportedly did well in Tete and Manica e Sofala provinces. They continued to attack the Cabora Bassa Dam, being built on the Zambezi River. In April, Portugal announced it would add 10,000 troops to the 30,000 stationed in Mozambique. By June, FRELIMO claimed control of 70,000 square miles, containing 1.2 million persons.

Portuguese forces clashed with Malawi troops in May. Portugal had charged that Malawi was harboring FRELIMO guerrilla bases.

In March, the first elections were held to pick legislative assembly members in Angola, Mozambique, and Guinea-Bissau. These consultative bodies are made up of both elected and appointed members.

Although only persons holding Portuguese citizenship could vote – about 1 per cent of the population in Mozambique – the new Mozambique legislative assembly consisted of a nonwhite majority of elected and appointed members. Guinea-Bissau also had a nonwhite majority in its legislative assembly, but Angola's was dominated by white Portuguese.

Mozambique Massacre. Missionaries in Mozambique reported in July that Portuguese soldiers had brutally massacred up to 400 villagers in Tete province in December, 1972. The villagers were suspected of harboring guerrillas.

The UN Committee on Colonialism called for an on-site investigation. However, Portugal said it would not allow a UN team to investigate. Two Roman Catholic priests who first reported the massacre and other atrocities were charged with treason and ordered to leave Mozambique in August.

However, in September, a Portuguese investigation confirmed that the massacre had taken place. The investigators uncovered up to 80 bodies and heard 30 eyewitness accounts. Portugal fired the Tete military commander. See PORTUGAL.

Ethnic Strife between the Hutu (Bahutu) and the Tutsi (Watusi) again flared. Thousands of Hutu had been living in exile since the Tutsi massacred up to 100,000 Hutu in Burundi in 1972. In May, Hutu refugees entered Burundi from Rwanda and Tanzania and tried to overthrow the Tutsi minority government. About 50 persons were killed in the fighting.

There were reports in June that Tutsi had killed at least 10,000 Hutu in retaliation for the attempted coup. The Rwanda government, which is controlled by the Hutu, called for retaliation against the Tutsi.

Trouble between the Hutu and Tutsi broke out in Rwanda in February when about 70 persons were reported killed. The trouble apparently began when Hutu students attacked Tutsi students. Burundi accused Rwanda of "slaughtering" Tutsi tribesmen, and more than 600 Tutsis fled to Uganda. However, Rwanda denied that anyone had been killed or even injured during the unrest.

The fighting adversely affected Burundi's relations with Tanzania. Tanzania charged Burundi with bombing three of its villages in March. Burundi apologized for the raid in April. See TANZANIA.

White Southern Africa. Racial tensions continued to plague the white-minority regimes in Rhodesia and South Africa. African nationalist guerrillas stepped up their activity in Rhodesia, forcing the government to close off some rural areas. Again, Rhodesia failed to reach a settlement with Great Britain, which does not recognize the independence Rhodesia unilaterally declared in 1965.

In South Africa, political attention shifted from the guerrilla movements to black workers and the leaders of black homelands, or Bantustans. Thousands of black workers staged massive strikes, and Bantustan leaders warned of violence if blacks were not granted political rights. In Namibia (South West Africa), blacks rioted to protest continued South African rule in defiance of UN resolutions calling for Namibian independence. See NAMIBIA; SOUTH AFRICA.

A Major Quarrel between Guinea, Senegal, and Ivory Coast broke out on September 11. Guinea's President Ahmed Sékou Touré accused the other two nations of aiding an alleged attempt to overthrow his government. Touré called for the ouster of President Senghor of Senegal and President Houphouet-Boigny of Ivory Coast. Guinea claimed on September 7 that it captured 59 guerrillas trained in Ivory Coast and Senegal. Senegal broke diplomatic

President Idi Amin Dada of Uganda acknowledges the welcome of Emperor Haile Selassie upon his arrival in Ethiopia for a meeting in May.

Facts in Brief on African Political Units

Country	Population	Government	Monetary Unit*	Foreign Trade (million U.S. $) Exports	Foreign Trade (million U.S. $) Imports
Algeria	16,375,000	President Houari Boumediene	dinar (4.1 = $1)	730	1,162
Angola	5,997,000	Governor General Fernando Augusto Santos de Castro	escudo (23.1 = $1)	479	392
Botswana	726,000	President Sir Seretse Khama	rand (1 = $1.42)	46	85
Burundi	3,836,000	President & Prime Minister Michel Micombero	franc (78.8 = $1)	26	31
Cameroon	6,367,000	President Ahmadou Ahidjo	CFA franc (230.21 = $1)	218	299
Central African Republic	1,747,000	President Jean Bedel Bokassa	CFA franc (230.21 = $1)	34	35
Chad	4,068,000	President N'Garta Tombalbaye	CFA franc (230.21 = $1)	30	67
Congo	1,023,000	President Marien N'Gouabi; Prime Minister Henri Lopes	CFA franc (230.21 = $1)	42	79
Dahomey	2,972,000	President & Premier Mathieu Kerekou	CFA franc (230.21 = $1)	46	83
Egypt	36,754,000	President & Prime Minister Anwar al-Sadat	pound (1 = $2.56)	825	874
Equatorial Guinea	302,000	President Francisco Macias Nguema	peseta (58.16 = $1)	29	16
Ethiopia	26,636,000	Emperor Haile Selassie I; Prime Minister T. T. Aklilou Abte-Wold	dollar (2.1 = $1)	168	189
Gabon	520,000	President Albert Bernard Bongo	CFA franc (230.21 = $1)	187	97
Gambia	399,000	President Sir Dawda Kairaba Jawara	dalasi (1.61 = $1)	19	25
Ghana	9,679,000	National Redemption Council Chairman Ignatius Kutu Acheampong	new cedi (1.15 = $1)	322	434
Guinea	4,281,000	President Ahmed Sékou Touré; Prime Minister Lansana Béavogui	sily (20.5 = $1)	55	70
Ivory Coast	4,746,000	President Felix Houphouet-Boigny	CFA franc (230.21 = $1)	546	442
Kenya	12,816,000	President Jomo Kenyatta	shilling (6.9 = $1)	314	560
Lesotho	990,000	King Motlotlehi Moshoeshoe II; Prime Minister Leabua Jonathan	rand (1 = $1.42)	3	36
Liberia	1,731,000	President William R. Tolbert	dollar (1 = $1)	244	179
Libya	2,241,000	Revolutionary Command Council President Muammar Muhammad al-Qadhaafi; Prime Minister Abd al-Salam Jallud	pound (1 = $3.37)	2,938	1,043
Malagasy	7,393,000	President Gabriel Ramanantsoa	franc (230.21 = $1)	164	202
Malawi	4,914,000	President Hastings Kamuzu Banda	kwacha (1 = $1.29)	81	130
Mali	5,474,000	President & Prime Minister Moussa Traoré	franc (460.41 = $1)	38	60
Mauritania	1,281,000	President Moktar Ould Daddah	ouguiya (46.04 = $1)	90	57
Mauritius	870,000	Governor General Sir Abdul Raman Osman; Prime Minister Sir Seewoosagur Ramgoolam	rupee (5.16 = $1)	107	120
Morocco	16,561,000	King Hassan II; Prime Minister Ahmed Osman	dirham (4.19 = $1)	639	771
Mozambique	8,885,000	Governor General Manuel Pimentel dos Santos	escudo (23.1 = $1)	160	335
Niger	4,469,000	President Hamani Diori	CFA franc (230.21 = $1)	38	54
Nigeria	60,855,000	Federal Military Government Head Yakubu Gowon	naira (1 = $1.52)	2,144	1,511
Rhodesia	6,080,000	President Clifford Dupont; Prime Minister Ian D. Smith	dollar (1 = $1.68)	402	429
Rwanda	4,170,000	President Juvenal Habyarimana	franc (82.9 = $1)	19	35
Senegal	4,319,000	President Léopold Sédar Senghor; Prime Minister Abdou Diouf	CFA franc (230.21 = $1)	213	274
Sierra Leone	2,727,000	President Siaka P. Stevens; Prime Minister Sorie Ibrahim Koroma	leone (1 = $1.24)	117	121
Somalia	3,066,000	Supreme Revolutionary Council President Mohamed Siad Barre	shilling (6.23 = $1)	43	76
South Africa, Republic of	24,211,000	President Jacobus Johannes Fouché; Prime Minister Balthazar Johannes Vorster	rand (1 = $1.42)	2,602	3,648
Sudan	17,476,000	President Sayed Gaafar Mohamed Nimeiri	pound (1 = $2.87)	357	353
Swaziland	455,000	King Sobhuza II; Prime Minister Makhosini Dlamini	rand (1 = $1.42)	71	61
Tanzania	14,714,000	President Julius K. Nyerere; Prime Minister Rashidi Kawawa	shilling (6.9 = $1)	284	364
Togo	2,177,000	President Etienne Eyadema	CFA franc (230.21 = $1)	49	84
Tunisia	5,586,000	President Habib Bourguiba; Prime Minister Hedi Nouira	dinar (1 = $2.30)	311	460
Uganda	10,970,000	President Idi Amin Dada	shilling (6.9 = $1)	260	113
Upper Volta	5,844,000	President Sangoulé Lamizana; Prime Minister Gerard Kango Ouedraogo	CFA franc (230.21 = $1)	20	59
Zaire	25,430,000	President Mobutu Sese Seko	zaire (1 = $2.00)	690	643
Zambia	4,658,000	President Kenneth David Kaunda; Prime Minister Mainza Chona	kwacha (1 = $1.55)	758	565

*Exchange rates as of Nov. 1, 1973

183

relations with Guinea on September 18. OAU Chairman Gowon of Nigeria tried to heal this rift between radical Guinea and its two conservative neighbors. He finally persuaded Senegal to withdraw its appeal to the OAU.

Coups and Unrest. Senegal experienced a revival of student unrest in 1973. University students were arrested in January, and in March, students burned nine school buildings. President Senghor accused French Communists of encouraging the student demonstrations.

The student rioting worsened in May after an imprisoned student was found hanged in his cell. He had been serving a three-year sentence for subversion. The Senegalese government claimed the youth had committed suicide. But his father claimed he had been murdered.

Liberia charged a former government official and two army officers with plotting to assassinate President William R. Tolbert in January. They were tried in May and sentenced to death in June.

Authorities in Dahomey arrested 15 persons in February and charged them with plotting to overthrow the government. President Mathieu Kerekou said that a foreign government was also involved in the plot.

This sparked anti-French demonstrations, and rioters stoned the French Embassy, but Kerekou said that France was not the foreign power behind the subversive conspiracy.

Ivory Coast in June charged seven army officers with plotting to overthrow the government and assassinate all military and political leaders. The plotters were also charged with ritually murdering five fishermen to ensure the plot's success.

In Congo (Brazzaville), 30 persons, including former Prime Minister Pascal Lissouba, were arrested in February in connection with a plot against the government of President N'Gouabi. Four of the accused were condemned to death in April, and others were given prison sentences. Lissouba was acquitted.

In Rwanda, President Grégoire Kayibanda's government was overthrown by army officers in a bloodless coup on July 5. Major General Juvenal Habyarimana, the defense minister and leader of the coup, became president. Habyarimana said he moved against Kayibanda to avoid further violence between Hutu and Tutsi and to prevent regional disputes. Presidents Habyarimana and Kayibanda are Hutus.

The African Authenticity Movement spread from Zaire to other countries. Chad began an authenticity campaign as President Tombalbaye changed his first name from François to N'Garta, and Chad's capital, Fort-Lamy, was renamed Ndjamena.

Equatorial Guinea renamed Santa Isabel, its capital, Malabo. Gambia changed the name of its capital from Bathurst to Banjul.   John Storm Roberts

AGNEW, SPIRO THEODORE, resigned as Vice-President of the United States on Oct. 10, 1973. That same day, he pleaded "no contest" to a charge of federal income tax evasion in U.S. District Court in Baltimore. Judge Walter E. Hoffman sentenced him to three years of unsupervised probation and fined him $10,000.

In return for Agnew's resignation and no-contest plea to the tax-evasion charge, the government agreed not to prosecute him for alleged acts of extortion and bribery. The alleged crimes covered a 10-year period and involved at least $87,500. The agreement was reached after weeks of secret negotiations between Agnew's lawyers and U.S. Department of Justice officials.

United States Attorney General Elliot L. Richardson asked Judge Hoffman not to send Agnew to prison "out of compassion for the man, out of respect for the office he has held, and out of appreciation for the fact that by his resignation he has spared the nation the prolonged agony that would have attended upon his trial."

Congressman Gerald R. Ford (R., Mich.), minority leader in the House of Representatives, was chosen by President Richard M. Nixon on October 12 to succeed Agnew. Congress confirmed Ford as Vice-President on December 6, and he was sworn in the same day. See FORD, GERALD R.

Fall from Power. When Agnew was sworn in for his second term as Vice-President in January, he was generally regarded as the leading contender for the 1976 Republican presidential nomination. He remained in a strong, untainted position even after the Watergate scandal began to embarrass the White House. On August 1, however, Agnew was informed by the Justice Department that he was under investigation for possible violation of bribery, extortion, conspiracy, and tax laws.

On August 6, Agnew publicly acknowledged that he was under investigation, but claimed, "I am innocent of any wrongdoing." In a press conference on August 8, he denounced reports that he had received kickbacks from Maryland consulting engineers in return for state contracts as "damned lies." For the next two months, he continued to declare his innocence.

In September, there were news reports that the Justice Department would bring evidence against Agnew before a grand jury. On September 25, Agnew asked House Speaker Carl B. Albert (D., Okla.) to have the U.S. House of Representatives investigate him.

In asking for a congressional investigation, which could lead to his impeachment, Agnew apparently hoped to head off criminal proceedings in the courts. He cited as a precedent a similar request by Vice-President John C. Calhoun in 1826.

Calhoun had been accused of profiting from a Department of War contract while serving as secretary of war. A House Select Committee investigated the charge, at Calhoun's request, and concluded that he was not guilty.

Agnew did not mention, when he recalled the Calhoun precedent, that Calhoun was not under investigation at that time by criminal authorities. Albert declined to order an investigation because Agnew's case was in the courts.

Agnew vowed that he would not resign, even if he was indicted. He accused the Justice Department of attempting to "destroy" his career by allowing news leaks designed to influence the outcome of possible grand jury proceedings. And on October 3, Judge Hoffman granted him the power to subpoena newspapermen and government prosecutors so that he might try to uncover the source of the leaks.

But Agnew finally decided to drop the fight. He said it "would be against the national interest" to continue it and that a prolonged fight would have "a brutalizing effect" on his family. In pleading no contest, Agnew acknowledged that he had evaded payment of $13,551.47 in federal income taxes in 1967.

Kickback Scheme. In a 40-page exposition of evidence, the government alleged that shortly after his election as executive of Baltimore County in 1962, Agnew began and directed a complex scheme to extort thousands of dollars from consulting engineers in Maryland. In return, he allegedly granted them profitable government contracts.

Allegedly, Agnew continued to operate the kickback scheme from 1962 through his two years as governor of Maryland and during his first four years as Vice-President. According to the government report, he received cash payments in his vice-presidential office up to the end of December, 1972.

Agnew, however, denied that he was guilty. He said that accepting "contributions" while governor of Maryland was "part of a long-established pattern" of political fund-raising in the state. In his final televised address to the nation on October 15, he stated, "I have never . . . enriched myself in betrayal of my public trust."

The Investigation began in the fall of 1972, after the Internal Revenue Service found inconsistencies in some tax returns of Maryland officials. A special grand jury was formed in December, 1972, to investigate corruption. The inquiry broadened, and Agnew became a definite target in mid-1973.

Two consulting engineers, Jerome B. Wolff and Lester Matz; I. H. Hammerman II, a wealthy Baltimore investment banker; and Alan I. Green, head of the engineering firm of Green Associates, Inc., cooperated with federal prosecutors in the Agnew case.

According to the government evidence, when Agnew was governor of Maryland he used Hammerman and Wolff as his agents in the scheme to obtain kickbacks from engineers. The government document stated: "With each step up the political ladder, Agnew told his associates that while his salary was

Spiro T. Agnew faces reporters after resigning as Vice-President and pleading "no contest" to tax-evasion charges in Baltimore on October 10.

rising [to $25,000 as Maryland governor and $62,500 as Vice-President] so were his social demands and other factors demanding additional income."

The government document added that under Agnew's auspices, the Green firm received state contracts involving fees totaling $4 million. "From 1967 to 1972, Green paid Agnew $50,000, with many of the payments being delivered to Agnew's vice-presidential office in the Executive Office Building in Washington or to Agnew's apartment at the Sheraton Park Hotel," according to the statement.

The document contained similar details about payments made by Matz. It stated that shortly after Agnew became Vice-President, Matz visited him in his vice-presidential office and gave him an envelope containing $10,000 in cash. When Matz returned to his office in Baltimore later that day, he told his partner that he was shaken by his actions "because he had just made a payoff to the Vice-President of the United States."

On October 31, Agnew paid his $10,000 fine. However, his defense costs were reportedly more than $200,000. Chicago insurance millionaire W. Clement Stone had set up a legal defense fund to help cover legal costs, but withdrew his support after Agnew resigned. In November, singer Frank Sinatra began raising funds to help Agnew.   William McGaffin

See also PRESIDENT OF THE UNITED STATES; REPUBLICAN PARTY.

AGRICULTURE. While large areas in Africa and Asia struggled with crop failures, shortages, drought, and disasters, American agriculture was showered with affluence and attention in 1973. Net farm income in the United States rose to a record $25.5 billion, 29 per cent above that of 1972, which was 30 per cent above 1971.

World harvests began to look more encouraging toward the end of 1973 than had been expected. They were particularly critical because of dangerously low reserves in many countries. Estimates made in November by the Food and Agriculture Organization (FAO) indicated that world agricultural production would increase by from 3 to 4 per cent over 1972.

A major factor was the dramatic increase in the official estimate of the grain harvest in Russia. This was put at more than 215 million tons, about 30 per cent more than 1972's 168 million tons.

That 1972 harvest forced purchases of about 30-million tons from Australia, Canada, France, Sweden, and the United States. Mainly because of these purchases, world wheat reserves fell to the lowest level in 20 years, and the price of wheat trebled. With other agricultural products in short supply, a chain reaction drove food prices up all over the world

Late data for the developing countries indicated an encouraging 3 to 4 per cent increase in agricultural production. The best results were reported in the Far East, where a 6 to 8 per cent increase was estimated with some rice crops yet to be harvested. Unofficial data indicated that China's crop production increased from 2 to 3 per cent. Latin American output was up 3 to 4 per cent, but production in Africa and the Middle East was down an estimated 3 or 4 per cent.

Greater Affluence was hailed as a proud accomplishment in American agricultural circles. But American consumers did not see it that way. Thousands were highly critical of what they regarded as unbelievably high prices, and many formed shopping cooperatives in an effort to get some semblance of the quantity and quality of food their families were accustomed to.

Agricultural leaders said the higher prices were the result of greater farm exports, and they claimed that these exports had greatly helped the nation. Secretary of Agriculture Earl L. Butz spoke for his constituency on July 23. Defending the much-criticized Russian and Chinese wheat deals before a U.S. Senate subcommittee, he said, "We have achieved a détente with the Russians and rapprochement with the People's Republic of China. . . . I am quite willing to accept, for American agriculture, a major share of the credit for these history-making developments. Food has been a valuable tool in our strategy of peace – a lever that more than any other

"Soybean pit" at Chicago Board of Trade was empty on June 21 after skyrocketing prices forced a suspension of trading in soybean futures.

single factor has brought back into the world economy some 1.1 billion people. . . . We are still in a very serious payments deficit with other countries, and this is important to every American. In *some* sector of our economy we have to export if we are to continue to import the foreign goods that our consumers demand. Our agriculture is a sector that is able to export in world competition against all comers, and we need to nurture and expand our farm exports. . . ."

Placing the Blame. Yet, the shadow of high food prices hung over agriculture's new prosperity and public image. People moved quickly from asking, "Why high food prices?" to, "Who caused high food prices?" Everyone got into the act. For example, *Science*, the journal of the American Association for the Advancement of Science, surprised many of its readers with an unlikely editorial titled "Rising Food Prices: Who's Responsible?" Agriculture was not alone as a suspect. The list included food retailers and processors, consumers, environmentalists, Congress, labor unions, politicians, farm-policy makers, international diplomats, and others. A survey in May, 1973, by Pennsylvania State University found an interesting diversity of suspects:

Who to Blame?	Consumers Naming This Group (Usually along with other groups)
Farmers	8%
Grocery stores	14%
Food manufacturers	25%
Consumers	15%
Labor unions	45%
Others	16%
Don't know	17%

Energy and Environment. The energy crisis hit agriculture hard because of its high-energy technology, particularly in grain drying and the manufacture of fertilizer. The pressure on agriculture by environmentalists relaxed some as other energy-hungry groups asked for a more rational environmental policy. Agriculture gained some new respect from both groups as farm products proved to be important items to be traded for oil.

Agricultural Exports rose to a record $12.9 billion for fiscal 1973, up more than 60 per cent from fiscal 1972. The sharp rise in exports more than offset the 21 per cent increase in U.S. agricultural imports, and boosted the agricultural trade surplus to $5.6-billion. Farm exports proved a major factor in helping to create a positive national trade balance for the first time since 1971.

Exports continued to grow at an increasing rate in 1973. Wheat recorded the largest increase–133 per cent in total value–and exports of corn increased 107 per cent. Cattle hides and soybean shipments also increased substantially. United States Department of Agriculture predictions set agricultural exports at a virtually unbelievable $19 billion for the fiscal year ending June 30, 1974. This would be the fifth straight increase since the $5.7 billion in fiscal 1969.

Agricultural Statistics, 1973

Output of Major U.S. Crops
(millions of bushels)

Crop	1962-66†	1972	1973*
Corn	3,862	5,553	5,678
Sorghums	595	822	971
Oats	912	695	702
Wheat	1,230	1,545	1,727
Soybeans	769	1,283	1,575
Rice (a)	742	851	952
Potatoes (b)	275	296	299
Cotton (c)	125	137	132
Tobacco (d)	2,126	1,749	1,788

†Average; *Preliminary
(a) 100,000 cwt.; (b) 1,000,000 cwt.;
(c) 100,000 bales; (d) 1,000,000 lbs.

U.S. Production of Animal Products
(millions of pounds)

	1957-59†	1972	1973*
Beef	13,704	22,413	21,400
Veal	1,240	458	384
Lamb and Mutton	711	543	500
Pork	10,957	13,626	13,000
Eggs (a)	5,475	5,791	5,560
Chicken	5,292	11,330	11,130
Turkey	1,382	2,424	2,425
Total Milk (b)	123.2	120.3	117.0

†Average; *Preliminary
(a) 1,000,000 dozens; (b) 100,000,000 lbs.

World Crop Production
(million units)

Crop	Units	1972	1973	%U.S.
Corn	Metric tons	284.1	(NA)	49.6[1]
Wheat	Metric tons	330.9	348.6	13.5
Rice	Metric tons	285.7	(NA)	1.3[1]
Barley	Metric tons	138.6	147.3	6.3
Oats	Metric tons	50.7	54.7	18.7
Rye	Metric tons	28.6	25.9	2.5
Soybeans	Metric tons	47.8	58.2	74.3
Cotton	Bales[2]	59.3	59.6	22.0
Coffee	Bags[3]	76.0	66.1	0.3

[1]Based on 1972 production
[2]480 pounds net
[3]132.276 pounds
NA Not available

Although higher prices accounted for most of the increase, other forces also played prominent roles. Limited world grain supplies, improved economic conditions around the world, expansion of trade with Russia and the People's Republic of China, a realignment of currencies, and the availability of U.S. supplies and the capability to move large quantities of grains and oilseeds into the international market were also factors.

Although U.S. agricultural trade was a very bright spot in 1973, two serious questions need be asked: Was it the poor weather in other parts of the world that was responsible, or was it a realignment of our trade relations because of devaluation, changed diplomatic relations, and related factors?

AGRICULTURE

Farm Prices, of course, made the big headlines in 1973. Many commodities reached record highs. For example, live hog prices climbed to an average of $56.50 per 100 pounds in August compared with $28 in August, 1972, and $18.50 in August, 1971. Cattle prices climbed to an average of $55.20 per 100 pounds in August compared with $35.60 in August, 1972. The index of prices received by farmers for meat animals set a record of 253 (1967=100) in August. Meat animal prices moderated somewhat, but in November they still stood about 28 per cent above a year earlier.

And price increases were not confined to meat animals. The food grains index was at an astounding 286 (1967=100) in August compared with 103 in August, 1972. The August feed grains index reached 215 compared with 98 in August, 1972. Soybean prices climbed to a record $8.99 average in August, corn to $2.68, and wheat to $4.45.

High price levels were attributable in most part to a very strong demand for farm products plus, in the case of meat animals, a somewhat shortened supply. Some of the extremely high prices were due mostly to market reactions to Economic Stabilization Program regulations relaxing ceilings on food prices. See Economics.

Farmers, too, paid higher prices. In October, the index of prices paid by farmers for production items

Cotton juice? No, just water from widespread rains that delayed harvests and prevented winter planting in parts of the United States.

was up 22 per cent. A large share of the increase was due to substantially higher feed prices, up over 60 per cent from a year earlier.

Crop Production took a dramatic jump as the all-crops production index reached 119 (1967=100), up from the previous record of 113 set in 1972. Oil crops, primarily soybeans, led the increase at 157 compared with 130 in 1972. Food and feed grains also showed gains. Tobacco registered a small gain in production, but still stood at only 91 per cent of 1967 levels. Sugar production dropped from a record of 139 in 1972 to 124 in 1973, largely because of a 12 per cent decline in sugar beet output.

Many individual crops established new production records. Soybeans were up a spectacular 23 per cent over 1972's record level.

The expanded crop production was almost entirely due to farmers planting more acres. Average yield per acre for most major crops was near or slightly below 1972 levels.

Livestock Production leveled off near the record high achieved in 1972. The index of all livestock production in the United States stayed at 1972's 144 (1950=100), but production of several major livestock types declined. Beef and veal production fell to 21.8 billion pounds, down 4.8 per cent. Output of pork, lamb and mutton, chicken, eggs, and milk also dropped.

The failure of farmers to expand livestock production in spite of higher prices for livestock products was attributed primarily to two interrelated factors – high feed prices, and high prices for grains. It was more profitable for farmers to sell grain directly than to feed it to animals.

Farm Income, bolstered by both increased crop production and higher prices for most farm commodities, reached an unprecedented level. It was estimated at $25.5 billion, compared to the previous record of $19.7 billion in 1972, and $16.9 billion in each of the three preceding years.

The increased income should further narrow the gap between the incomes of farm and nonfarm families. The 1972 disposable personal income per capita for the farm population was 82.7 per cent that of the nonfarm population. This was up from 75.9 per cent in 1971 and 54.5 per cent in 1960.

Farmers' net worth rose by 16 per cent to $361-billion on Jan. 1, 1974. This was the largest annual increase since the 15 per cent recorded in 1951. The sharp rise in net worth resulted from a $57-billion rise in farm assets compared to a rise of only $7-billion in liabilities.

Farm real estate prices increased a record 20 per cent from November, 1972, to November, 1973. Interest rates on farm loans in 1973 averaged well above those of 1972 for short-term credit and slightly higher for farm-mortgage debt. Farm interest payments for both long- and short-term debt in 1973 totaled about $4.8 billion, up 13 per cent from 1972.

All of the increase in the value of farmers' assets was due to higher prices. In terms of constant prices (1967 base), the total value of farm assets dropped to $274 billion from $274.2 billion on Jan. 1, 1972.

The Farm Labor Force stood at 4.99 million workers in October, 1973, up 5 per cent from a year earlier. The labor force consisted of 3.69 million family workers and 1.3 million hired workers. The number of family workers was up 4 per cent and hired workers up 9 per cent from Nov. 1, 1972.

Hired farm labor received higher wages in 1973 than ever before. On October 1, the average hourly rate for hired farmworkers was $1.80 per hour, up 15 cents per hour from 1972.

Total farm population resumed its long-term decline after a slight increase in 1972. Farm population was estimated at 9.5 million persons, 4.5 per cent of the total U.S. population.

New Technologies. Grains were being redesigned so thoroughly by plant breeders that the May-June issue of *The Furrow* magazine had a feature, "New Era of Supergrains." On September 28, John A. Hannah, administrator for the U.S. Agency for International Development (AID) announced that AID-funded Purdue University plant researchers had climaxed a seven-year, global search with a sorghum variety containing twice as much lysine (a component of high-quality protein) as average sorghum.

Hannah hailed the work as a "breakthrough of the first magnitude." He said, "When we recall that sorghum is the principal subsistence cereal for more than 300 million people–indeed the poorest people in the world's poorest countries–improving its protein quality will amount to a gift of life, especially for children."

Extensive work on how the weather affects agriculture continued. For example, basic research at the University of East Anglia in England advances a theory that we are now experiencing the most sustained shift in the world's climate since 1700. This would mean cooler, drier times. Applied work at Iowa State University shows remarkably predictive weather trends that influence Corn Belt crop prospects. Jet airstream and weather satellite research, particularly at Purdue University, is increasing long-range weather forecasts with substantial implications for agriculture production. See Section One, FOCUS ON SCIENCE.

New Legislation. The Agricultural and Consumer Protection Act, signed August 10, will provide several new farm policies for the next four years. The act introduced a new concept of target prices, redefined payment limitations, and placed increased emphasis on national acreage allotments. The new payment provisions will virtually eliminate government payments to farmers in 1974. In a sense, the program is a compromise designed to reduce government support of agriculture, but to keep a protective floor if such factors as export demand go sour. Payment limitations were lowered to a maximum of $20,000 annually per person, as compared to the $55,000 limit per program (feed grain, wheat, and cotton) in effect the last three years.

The national allotment replaces the concept of base acreage in the feed grain program, and domestic allotments (and marketing certificates) in the wheat program. National allotments will be announced annually. Program payments for feed grain or wheat programs will be determined by multiplying a farmer's acreage allotment times his established yield times the payment rate. Payment rate in both the feed grain and wheat programs is defined as the amount by which the target price exceeds the average price received by farmers during the first five months of the crop-marketing year, or the loan support rate, whichever is higher. Target prices for 1974 and 1975 corn and wheat crops are established at $1.38 and $2.05 per bushel, respectively. Loan support rates are boosted to higher minimum levels. For example, the minimum support rate will be $1.10 per bushel on corn, and it will be $1.37 per bushel for wheat.   Charles E. French and Larry L. Nelson

AIR FORCE, U.S. See NATIONAL DEFENSE.

AIR POLLUTION. See ENVIRONMENT.

AIRPORT. See AVIATION; Section Five, AIRPORT.

ALABAMA. See STATE GOVERNMENT.

ALASKA. See STATE GOVERNMENT.

ALBANIA continued to develop its modest trade and diplomatic links with non-Communist nations in 1973, but it resolutely kept aloof from the East-West talks on security, cooperation, and mutual force reduction that were held in Helsinki, Geneva, and Vienna. Albania was the only European nation to spurn the security conference.

However, it signed a road-haulage agreement with Austria in July and established diplomatic relations with Argentina in October. But it ignored a United States call for the resumption of diplomatic relations in April. The two nations have not had diplomatic relations since Italy occupied Albania in 1939.

Albania's alliance with the People's Republic of China remained firm, and China continued to provide technical aid and financing for Albania's major construction projects. A Chinese economic-technological delegation visited Albania in November, and Albania's army chief of staff visited Peking at the same time. Relations with the Eastern European nations in the Russian bloc remained tense, however, and the state-controlled Albanian press and radio continued to accuse Russian leaders of collusion with U.S. "imperialists." But in November, the Soviet-bloc press published a number of friendly commentaries on Albania, calling for an end to the "abnormal situation" that only "played into the hands of enemies of Socialism."

"Enemies" Purged. In June, the Albanian Communist Party launched a campaign against "bourgeois revisionists" and "other domestic enemies." It increased pressure against Roman Catholic priests and religious believers still living in Albania. A priest was executed in March, allegedly for spying for Italy and the Vatican. But the Vatican claimed that the man, Father Stephen Kurti, an inmate in a labor camp, was guilty only of baptizing a child. In July, the leadership of the writers' union was changed, and top leaders of the youth organization were dismissed for failing to protect Albanian youth against "liberalism."

Fadil Pacrami, chairman of the National Assembly since 1970, was dismissed in September for "antiparty" and "antinational" activity. He was replaced by Iljas Reka. Bilbil Klosi, secretary of the National Assembly Presidium since 1966, was fired for "incompetence," and replaced by Telo Mezini.

The government claimed that heavy industrial output increased by 12 per cent over 1972. It reported especially good growth in oil production and processing, coal and chrome-ore mining, and the production of fertilizers, caustic soda, and paints. Albanian farmers reported a good grain harvest, but the nation did not achieve its planned 23 per cent increase in agricultural production.   Chris Cviic

See also EUROPE (Facts in Brief Table).

ALBERTA. See CANADA.

ALGERIA concentrated on economic development and cultivating better links with its neighbors in 1973. When the fourth Arab-Israeli war began in October, Algeria sent jet fighters into action against Israel along the Suez Canal front. For details on the war and its aftermath, see MIDDLE EAST.

Support for other revolutionary movements, once a cardinal feature of Algerian foreign policy, was limited to allowing the establishment of offices in Algiers for two such movements. They were the Liberation Front for the Spanish Sahara and the anti-French Somali Coast Liberation Front. On October 10, Algerian United Nations delegates were among those who walked out of the General Assembly to protest a speech defending the military junta that seized control in Chile.

Foreign Investment. The absence of internal unrest and of Algerian adventurism in the affairs of other countries attracted foreign investments. After several years of complex negotiations, the national oil and gas monopoly, Sonatrach, agreed on April 6 to sell the El Paso Natural Gas Company about 1 billion cubic feet of Algerian natural gas daily over a 25-year period beginning in 1976. The agreement, which required the approval of official U.S. agencies, also provided $402 million in loans to finance the expansion of Algerian gas fields.

Aid Funds. In January, the Export-Import Bank of the United States approved funds for irrigation projects and for rehabilitating the nation's largest lead and zinc mine at El Obeid, west of Tlemcen. Sonatrach received $550 million in loans from Japanese, European, and United States banks for capital expansion under Algeria's 1973 public finance law governing development expenses. On June 18, the World Bank approved its first loans to Algeria since 1964—$18.5 million for road improvements and $6 million to expand Algerian technical education. Canada loaned $118 million for road modernization, and Poland $80 million for prefabricated industrial plants. President Houari Boumediene marked the eighth anniversary of his regime by dedicating a new oil refinery at Arzew on June 26.

The Land Reform program completed a census of private holdings to identify those deemed to be too large. Land taken from them will be given to the landless. Some communal lands already exist.

Algeria's central location in the African-Mediterranean world was emphasized with the completion on January 5 of an underwater communications cable from Algiers to Pisa, Italy, and the opening on January 20 of direct sea service to Senegal. A 225-mile section of the trans-Sahara "Road of African Unity" was formally opened to traffic in ceremonies on April 26.   William Spencer

See also AFRICA (Facts in Brief Table).

AMERICAN LEGION. See VETERANS.

Algeria hosted the fourth conference of nonaligned nations in September. Leaders of 76 countries in Asia, Africa, and Latin America met in Algiers.

AMERICAN LIBRARY ASSOCIATION (ALA).

The annual conference of the American Library Association – the first under the administration of the new executive director, Robert Wedgeworth – was held in Las Vegas, Nev., in June. Jean E. Lowrie, director of the Department of Librarianship, Western Michigan University, took office as president. Edward G. Holley is president-elect.

Among its diverse activities during the year, the ALA Council set up a new Office for Research and the Intellectual Freedom Round Table; acting in conjunction with the Association of Hospital and Institution Libraries and the Library Service to the Blind Round Table, it also made plans to form a new health and rehabilitative services division in 1974.

Congressional Approval. The ALA held a congressional luncheon meeting at the 1973 midwinter conference, and urged the representatives and senators attending to continue federal support of library and library-related programs, which the Nixon Administration wanted to cut out. In the wake of the efforts of interested citizens, Congress voted in June to continue the programs. An ALA petition to the Supreme Court of the United States for a rehearing of its decisions on obscenity, which turned over discretionary power in matters of censorship to local communities, was denied. But on December 10, the court decided to re-evaluate the matter.

Two ALA units shared the 1973 J. Morris Jones-World Book Encyclopedia-ALA Goals Award: The ALA Legislation Committee (for formation of a national legislative network for libraries) and the Association of College and Research Libraries, to revise *Standards for College Libraries* (1959).

The Year's Prizes. Jean George won the Newbery Medal for the most distinguished children's book, *Julie of the Wolves*. Blair Lent received the Caldecott Medal for the most outstanding illustrations in a children's book, *The Funny Little Woman*. William Morrow & Co., Inc., won the Mildred L. Batchelder Award for *Pulga*, by Siny R. van Iterson, named as the most outstanding book originally published in a foreign language. Olga Lendway won the Eunice Rockwell Oberly Award for *Bibliography of Corn* and *Bibliography of Wheat*. The Clarence Day Award was given to Sol and Mary Ann Malkin, publishers and editors of the *AB Bookman's Weekly*.

ALA Publications in 1973 included: *Famous American Playhouses*: Vol. 1, 1716-1899; and Vol. 2, 1900-1971 (two volumes in a projected seven-volume set); *Voices of Brooklyn*; *and Guide to the Development of Educational Media Selection Centers.* Curtis Swanson

See also CANADIAN LIBRARY ASSOCIATION (CLA); LIBRARY.

ANDORRA. See EUROPE.

ANGOLA. See AFRICA; PORTUGAL.

ANIMAL. See CONSERVATION; INTERNATIONAL LIVE STOCK EXPOSITION; PET; ZOOLOGY; ZOOS AND AQUARIUMS.

ANNE, PRINCESS (1950-   ), fourth in line to

the British throne, married a 24-year-old British Army officer, Mark Phillips, on Nov. 14, 1973, in Westminster Abbey. The couple met at the 1968 Olympic Games in Mexico City, where he competed in the equestrian events.

The only daughter of Queen Elizabeth II and Prince Philip, Anne Elizabeth Alice Louise Mountbatten-Windsor was born Aug. 15, 1950. Her brothers are Prince Charles, 26, heir to the throne; Prince Andrew, 13; and Prince Edward, 9. She attended Benenden School, an exclusive girls' school near Cranbrook, Kent. She began her public ceremonial duties on March 1, 1969, when she presented leeks, symbol of Wales, to the First Battalion of the Welsh Guards.

Princess Anne enjoys horseback riding, sailing, tennis, skiing, and dancing. A keen horsewoman since she was 3 years old, she has competed with distinction in several major shows. In September, 1971, she won the Raleigh Trophy riding her horse Doublet in competition against the best riders from eight nations.

Upon her marriage, Princess Anne's annual allowance was raised to $87,500. Phillips, an instructor at the Royal Military Academy, Sandhurst, earns $6,625 a year as an acting captain. The British taxpayers gave them a honeymoon cruise and a token-rent house as wedding presents.   Lillian Zahrt

ANTHROPOLOGY.

American Indian groups pressed their claims against U.S. anthropologists at various anthropological meetings in 1973. They argued that anthropologists have used Indian communities to gather data, but have focused on only the traditional customs in those communities rather than on the realities of the present. In so doing, the Indians argued, anthropologists fail to understand native American society, fail to make the public aware of the poverty and disease that is characteristic on most reservations, and fail to aid the Indians in combating the forces that produce poverty.

Frances L. K. Hsu of Northwestern University, Evanston, Ill., an American anthropologist of Chinese ancestry, suggested that U.S. anthropological theorizing about communities throughout the world reflects the predispositions of our own society. He noted a heavy materialist and individualist bias in these theories. This bias, Hsu believes, limits the usefulness of these theories in non-Western societies, where ties of friendship are much more important.

Developing Societies. Anthropologist John W. Cole of the University of Massachusetts studied domestic groups in two communities in the Italian Alps, St. Felix and Tret. He found that the domestic groups in the two communities are organized and exercise authority differently. In St. Felix, each domestic group has a single strong leader, and relations between the groups are characterized by mistrust and strict economic accounting. In Tret, decision making within each domestic group is shared, and relations between groups are friendlier and economic accounting less strict. Cole suggested that the two villages were much more alike in the recent past, and both are now being integrated into the Italian economy. The integration process, Cole says, has proceeded further in Tret than in St. Felix.

Eugene A. Hammel and Djordje Soc of the University of California, Berkeley, studied differences in lineage organization in eastern Yugoslavia. Lineage is a form of organization in which individuals tracing descent from a common ancestor share certain rights and obligations toward each other. Hammel and Soc measured differences in the organization from region to region by counting the number of households in each lineage.

Following standard anthropological practice, they sought to explain this variation by differences in the economic conditions and ideological heritage of the different regions. They found, however, that regional variations in fertility and in the time elapsed since the area was settled provided the best explanation for the variations in lineage. Thus, this study, like Cole's, suggests that greater understanding of change may be necessary to understand stability and similarities and differences in the organization of different communities. It also suggests that more detailed historical data will be needed by anthropologists in order to understand the effect of these factors on social organization.

Aggressiveness. Richard G. Sipes of the State University of New York, Buffalo, completed a study of combative sports in 1973 that tends to support the view that aggressiveness is learned, not inborn. Two theories have been offered to explain the presence of combative sports in many societies. The drive-discharge theory suggests that there is an innate aggressive drive in humans for which warfare and combative sports provide alternative release mechanisms. The cultural-pattern theory suggests that aggressive behavior, warfare, and combative sports are learned cultural behavior.

Sipes noted that while the cultural-pattern theory predicts that warfare and combative sports should occur together as part of an aggressive cultural pattern, the drive-discharge theory predicts that they should not. Since warfare and combative sports are alternative release mechanisms in drive discharge, only one need be present for the release of aggressive drives in a society. He then showed that the cross-cultural and historical data for the United States indicate that warfare and combative sports are positively correlated, thereby supporting the theory that aggressiveness is learned. Fred Plog

ARAB EMIRATES, UNITED. See UNITED ARAB EMIRATES.

ARAB REPUBLICS, FEDERATION OF. See EGYPT; LIBYA; SYRIA.

ARCHAEOLOGY. The date of man's entry into the New World generated new debate in 1973. Vance Haynes of Southern Methodist University studied the case of the Calico Site in southern California, which some archaeologists claim may be as much as 400,000 years old. This date exceeds by over 375,000 years the earliest date that most archaeologists accept for man's arrival in North America.

Haynes concluded that a date of 500,000 years ago is acceptable for the geological deposit in which the site occurs. He questioned, however, whether the chipped stones found at the site are *artifacts* (man-made). He said that they may be *geofacts*, objects that are chipped and flaked as a result of being banged against each other during natural geological processes. Of the thousands of pieces of chipped stone found at the site, only a few hundred have been identified as artifacts, and archaeologists disagree as to which are and which are not artifacts. Haynes argued that all of them could simply represent extreme cases of natural chipping.

At the same time, evidence for other earlier dates of entry into the New World continues to accumulate. W. N. Irving of the University of Toronto and C. R. Harrington of the National Museum of Canada, Ottawa, reported the discovery of a bone tool in the northern Yukon that was radiocarbon dated to 27,000 years ago. The bone tool came from a river deposit and was found with some other artifacts. Additional bone material taken from the site indicated that it was much warmer at that time.

Near Sarasota, Fla., underwater archaeologists found a human skeleton that is at least 10,000 years old. This is the earliest evidence of humans in the Southeastern United States.

Domestication. Archaeologists Reiner Protsch and Reiner Berger of the University of California, Los Angeles, re-examined the evidence for early animal domestication in Europe. Using improved techniques of radiocarbon dating, they found that cattle and pigs were first domesticated in Europe, while sheep and goats were first domesticated in the Middle East. Dogs were domesticated in both places at about the same time, while domesticated horses first appeared in the Ukraine. The evidence indicates that experimentation with domestication was widespread between 9,000 and 10,000 years ago.

The prehistory of domesticated cotton in the New World has yet to be determined. The prehistoric cotton found thus far has all been at an advanced stage of domestication. Because wild ancestors of cotton grow in both the Old and New Worlds, it is possible that domesticated cotton was brought across the ocean. Now, Stanley G. Stephens of North Carolina State University and Edward Mosely of Harvard University report that cotton obtained from sites on the coast of Peru that were occupied between 3,000 and 4,500 years ago shows a complete sequence of transition from wild to domesticated forms. Fully

Prehistoric Indian rock carvings, such as these in the Mojave Desert, are being destroyed or stolen, says carvings expert Ike Eastvold.

domesticated cotton from the Tehuacán Valley of Mexico is between 4,500 and 5,500 years old.

Mayan Organization. Recent studies offered new insights into the organization of the Mayan civilization, which existed in Guatemala and portions of Mexico from about A.D. 350 to 1540. N. Hammond of Cambridge University in England showed that obsidian found at sites in the southern area inhabited by the Maya came from two volcanic sources, El Cayal and Ixtepeque, which are about 60 miles from each other. Obsidian from these two sources was traded over hundreds of miles, but Hammond identified two distinct trade routes.

Joyce Marcus of Harvard University, using data on Mayan cosmology and translations of hieroglyphics, demonstrated that the Mayan myths of a quadripartite division in the universe and their village settlement pattern were much alike. In the southern Mayan area, there were four sociopolitical units, each with a regional capital that was the center of an important dynasty. Junior members of the dynasty ruled over lesser centers that lay in a hexagonal pattern around the capitals. These, in turn, were surrounded by still lesser centers with acropolises (fortified areas) and monuments, again in a fairly regular hexagonal pattern. A final set of local centers was surrounded by hamlets in which most of the people lived. Thus, each hamlet was tied to a capital through regional centers.   Fred Plog

ARCHITECTURE. The eagerly awaited results of the U.S.-Canadian competition for the design of Rainbow Center Plaza in Niagara Falls, N.Y., were announced in February, 1973. New York City architects Abraham W. Geller, Raimund Abraham, and Giuliamo Fiorenzoli won. The new plaza is part of the Niagara Falls City Council's master plan to redevelop an 82-acre site adjacent to the city's downtown area and stretching to the world-famous falls.

A large convention center, designed by Philip Johnson and John Burgee of New York City, anchors the far end of the redevelopment to a major street that leads directly to the falls. The center is under construction and will open in 1974. Along this linear core, Skidmore, Owings & Merrill has already completed a new office building.

Rainbow Center Plaza, the focal point of the master plan, will be built on a 5.1-acre site immediately in front of the center, and will be used as a center for all kinds of activities. Its prize-winning architects have imaginatively designed a two-level, three-dimensional plaza. The site is carved out in a sculptural fashion. A pedestrian bridge leads from the convention center to two central "islands" and continues to the major street. The architects gouged out the lower level to provide shelter from the wind for the plaza areas. The second level, most of which is open, has restaurants, shops, and an amphitheater that seats 3,000 persons.

Good Design. The federal government, the country's largest planner, builder, and landlord, sponsored the first Federal Design Assembly in United States history on April 2 and 3 in Washington, D.C. Under the auspices of the Federal Council on the Arts and the Humanities, with a $100,000 grant from the National Endowment for the Arts, the assembly's goal was to improve the quality of federally commissioned designs.

AIA Convention. The Women's Liberation Movement came to the attention of the American Institute of Architects (AIA) at its annual convention in San Francisco in May. The New York chapter introduced a resolution that the AIA conduct a study of the current status of women architects and present the results at the 1974 convention in Washington, D.C. There are some 36,000 registered architects in the United States, 1,500 of them women. The AIA's record is even more dismal—fewer than 300 of its 24,000 members are women.

The resolution caused a furor, but it passed, requiring the convention's only roll-call vote.

Notable New Buildings. Architect and developer John Portman of Atlanta has not received much critical acclaim for the series of hotels he has designed in Atlanta, Chicago, and San Francisco. But no one doubts the enormous appeal of his hanging, revolving bars and his glass-enclosed elevators that shoot up and down banner-clad *atria* (courtyards). His

Today's Giant

With the possible exception of a chap who has just parachuted in from the planet Mars, everyone must surely know by now that the Sears Tower in Chicago is the tallest structure in the world. It achieved that distinction on May 3, 1973, when it was officially topped out at 1,450 feet – with a mind-boggling 110 stories and almost 5 million square feet of office space.

The $200-million Sears Tower owes its physical presence to the pioneer mail-order firm of Sears, Roebuck and Company, whose corporate strength and ego dictated the structure's incredible size.

Sears Tower is a handsome building. Chief designer Bruce Graham has refused to indulge in certain bizarre mannerisms that many of his contemporaries are using to produce "different" or "interesting" high-rise office structures. Instead, he adhered to the philosophy of the late Mies van der Rohe, who once remarked, "There is no need to invent a new architecture every Monday morning."

Sears Tower is a Miesian type of building, a glass box with no-nonsense, sleek, dark glass and aluminum walls hung on a structural-steel frame. Actually, it is nine glass boxes bundled together. Architectural engineer Fazlur Khan evolved a series of nine 75-foot-square tubes cut off at various heights, forcibly calling to mind the ziggurat architecture of the 1920s. Two go to the 50th floor, two to the 66th, three to the 80th, and two to the 110th.

Khan's structural innovation makes the height of Sears Tower irrelevant and its claim to being the tallest meaningless and certainly temporary. Architectural engineering has advanced so much that there seems to be no limit to the height of our buildings. We will surely soon read about a proposed 150- or even 200-story building. The World Trade Center's twin 110-story towers in New York City held their claim of "world's tallest" (at 1,350 feet) for only a brief year before Sears Tower was crowned champion.

But what does all this mean? Is it just a mindless kind of design one-upmanship, a sort of architectural equivalent to "Can You Top This?" Does the tall building have a real purpose in our society? More important, what will its impact be on the men and women who must work and live in and near these behemoths?

These questions have no easy answers. Judgments must await experience, because we have never before had 110-story buildings looming in our midst.

Not that the critics of the tall building in general, or the Sears Tower in particular, are doing much waiting. Some of them say the building's scale is inhuman and inexcusable in today's crowded cities. Others predict that the structure will consume far more public services than it can pay for. In addition, they believe it will inevitably create congestion, and overload public and private transportation in its immediate area.

City planners and architects deny these charges. They claim that the very tall building is more environmentally correct in a city than a series of low-rise structures could ever be. Stacking several buildings on top of one another covers less ground and theoretically opens up more space for plazas and other landscaped amenities. The tall building is thus not only more efficient, but it also makes the city more livable.

We shall be hearing such pros and cons on the subject for some time to come. But then, human beings have always debated this question, simply because they have always had a love affair with the tall structure and its symbolic representation of private power and public strength.

More than 3,000 years ago, Pharaonic architecture reached its peak with the 481-foot-high Great Pyramid of Khufu in Giza, Egypt. The great cathedrals of the Middle Ages strained mightily toward the heavens. And the Eiffel Tower, built in Paris in 1889, astounded the world with its height of 984 feet, and reigned for many years as the world's tallest structure.

Today, Sears Tower wears the crown. And tomorrow? The Canadian National Railways will complete the CN Tower in Toronto in 1974. Basically a transmitting tower, the $21-million structure will be a formidable 1,805 feet high – a new record, of course, and a new "world's tallest." Until the next one. Rob Cuscaden

The Sears Tower

latest design is a 54-story, $150-million, 2,000-room extravaganza for Times Square in New York City. This hotel will have the same kind of elevators, but two atria.

It somehow required more than a decade to overcome design problems, but the AIA finally moved into its new Washington, D.C., headquarters in March, 1973. The architectural firm of Mitchell/Giurgola Associates of Philadelphia won a competition held in 1960, but the city's Fine Arts Commission did not like the winning design or its revisions. Mitchell/Giurgola Associates then resigned the commission. The Architects Collaborative of Cambridge eventually designed the building, a curved, rather bland expanse of marble wrapping around the back of the AIA's former headquarters, the finely proportioned and stately old Octagon House of 1800.

But no one has had troubles such as those of Sydney, Australia. An unknown, 38-year-old Danish architect, Jørn Utzon, won the city's international competition in 1956 for the Sydney Opera House. He designed a romantic structure with huge, saillike roofs of shell concrete. After years of construction problems and what Utzon termed governmental interference, the architect washed his hands of the whole affair and left for Denmark in a huff. Finally, the Opera House officially opened on October 2,

at a total cost of about $140 million, or $32 million more than the initial estimate.

The Herbert F. Johnson Museum of Art opened at Cornell University in midsummer. Johnson, as a 1922 graduate of Cornell, commissioned Frank Lloyd Wright to design his family's S. C. Johnson Company Administration Building in Racine, Wis. This time, Johnson asked a committee to find the "Frank Lloyd Wright of today." I. M. Pei was chosen, and his boldly articulated, assertive, marble structure will probably be as controversial as Wright's once was.

Exhibitions. Marcel Breuer, Hungarian-born architect, influential teacher at the Bauhaus school of design in Germany, and innovative designer of buildings throughout the world, was honored by an exhibition at the Metropolitan Museum of Art in New York City from November, 1972, to January, 1973.

A New Monthly architectural magazine created quite a stir in 1973. Peter Blake, former editor of *The Architectural Forum* and author of such well-known books as *God's Own Junkyard* (1965), launched his *Architecture Plus* in February. This lively "International Magazine of Architecture" has fine graphics and sparkling writing, and is unafraid of either strongly held opinions or a bit of humor. The June issue featured "Learning from Hamburgers: The Architecture of White Towers."   Rob Cuscaden

The Octagon, the American Institute of Architects new headquarters in Washington, D.C., was formally dedicated and opened on June 11, 1973.

ARGENTINA. Former President Juan Domingo Perón, who was overthrown by the military in 1955 after a decade in power, won the presidential election on Sept. 23, 1973. It was a remarkable political comeback in which Perón, as a candidate of the Justicialist Party, captured 61.81 per cent of the vote. He and his wife Maria Estela (Isabel) Perón, who had been elected vice-president, were sworn into office on October 12 to carry out the 3½-year balance of Hector José Cámpora's term. Perón promised to end terrorism and violence and to restore prosperity to the unsettled nation. See PERÓN, JUAN DOMINGO.

Earlier, the military government had barred Perón from entering Argentina until after a presidential election scheduled for March 11. The winner, Cámpora, was Perón's hand-picked nominee. Cámpora's inauguration on May 25 marked Argentina's return to civilian government after seven years of military rule.

Perón's Return. On June 20, Perón ended almost 18 years of exile and returned to Argentina. Violence among the more than 1 million people gathered to welcome him home left at least 30 dead and over 400 injured; the uncontrolled hatred between left wing and right wing Perónists was enough to guarantee confrontation, and the violence underlined the apparently irreconcilable differences among the followers of the former dictator. On July 13, President Cámpora resigned to clear the way for new elections and thus enable Perón to return to power. Many Argentines believed he was the only man for the grave hour in Argentina's history.

Violence Spreads. Throughout the year, extremists were on a kidnaping-killing binge, demanding—and at times getting—ransom sums of $1 million or more. Some businessmen, the potential victims of kidnaping and extortion attempts, began leaving the country. Guerrillas blew up buildings and robbed banks; under the cover of the political activism, common thieves had a field day. On April 30, the military government declared a state of emergency in the federal district and the five most populous provinces. The move followed the assassination of retired Rear Admiral Hermes José Quijada, former chairman of the joint chiefs of staff. On September 25, José Ignacio Rucci, secretary general of the General Confederation of Labor, was assassinated. He was Argentina's principal labor leader and a strong supporter of Perón. It was then that the government disclosed specific and widespread plans to crack down on Marxists and urban guerrillas, declaring that the country must "eradicate violence and subversion forever."

Soaring Inflation, fueled by a huge budget deficit, remained a greater threat to the country than the guerrilla warfare and kidnapings. Living costs in the first nine months rose 29.9 per cent; to control inflation, the government imposed price controls, but

After 17 years in exile, Juan Perón returned to Argentina and again became president. His wife Isabel was elected to the vice-presidency.

scarcities soon began to plague the housewife as well as the businessman. Money expanded at an alarming rate—by 33 per cent in the first six months—thus counteracting the price freeze. It was hoped that the gross domestic product would climb 5 per cent in 1973, but the hope seemed unachievable in the face of unemployment that totaled about 1 million persons at year's end.

New laws were put into effect, too, directing private banks to turn deposits over to the Central Bank. Banks were also forbidden from operating adjunct finance corporations. Thus, the Central Bank was given the power to designate to which sectors of the economy—even to which business—banks must give credit.

Normally a major grain exporter, Argentina had to import wheat in order to meet its own export commitments during the year. It also temporarily banned wheat shipments in order to meet domestic demand. January-to-July grain exports totaled 6,602,454 tons, exceeding those of the preceding year by 70.9 per cent. Earnings for the year were calculated at $900-million. While meat exports for the first six months fell to 355,000 tons from 398,000 a year before, higher world prices brought earnings to $421 million from $335.3 million. *Mary Webster Soper*

See also LATIN AMERICA (Facts in Brief Table).

ARIZONA. See STATE GOVERNMENT.

ARKANSAS. See STATE GOVERNMENT.

196

ARMED FORCES OF THE WORLD. Russia achieved a major armaments breakthrough in 1973 with the first successful flight tests of multiple independent re-entry vehicle (MIRV) warheads for its intercontinental ballistic missiles (ICBM's). The new warheads, expected to be operational by 1975, significantly narrowed the U.S. nuclear lead, and were seen by defense experts as a major escalation of the arms race.

Russia had 1,527 ICBM's and was building toward the limit of 1,618 agreed upon in the 1972 strategic arms limitation talks. Russia also had 140 bombers and 628 ballistic missiles on 66 submarines. The United States had 1,000 Minuteman and 54 Titan II ICBM's, and 41 Polaris and Poseidon missile submarines with a total of 656 missiles. The United States also had 450 B-52 and FB-111 bombers. Although Russia had more megatonnage in its warheads, the United States had a more than 2-to-1 lead in deliverable warheads.

In tactical air forces, the United States led with more than 5,700 aircraft. Russia had 4,500; China, 3,800. Russia had more than 3,000 jet interceptors and 10,000 surface-to-air missiles (SAM's). The United States had 585 interceptors and 500 SAM's.

New Weapons. The United States went ahead with plans to modernize its strategic systems. Converting 31 of the 41 Polaris submarines to fire the

longer-range, MIRV Poseidon missile was to be completed by 1975; 20 subs have already been converted. Half the 1,000 Minuteman ICBM's were to be converted to MIRV warheads by 1975; 350 missiles had already been converted by late 1973. The United States was also speeding up the Trident nuclear submarine program so that the Trident and its 4,000-mile missile would be operational by 1978.

Military observers believed the People's Republic of China has from 15 to 20 intermediate-range ballistic missiles (IRBM's). China also has produced a new, 3,500-mile IRBM, which may be ready for operational deployment. Observers also believed that China has tested a 6,000-mile, 3-megaton ICBM.

Sea Power. The U.S. Navy maintained a lead in the number of vessels, but Russia was catching up. Some Western intelligence experts believed the Russians had surpassed the U.S. fleet in overall strength. The U.S. Navy had 218 major surface warships – 14 attack carriers, 9 cruisers, 28 frigates, 29 missile destroyers, 71 other destroyers, and 67 escort ships – and 125 submarines.

The Russian Navy had 213 surface warships – its new *Kiev* attack carrier, 2 helicopter carriers, 30 cruisers, 11 surface-missile destroyers, 29 air-defense missile destroyers, 37 other destroyers, and 103 ocean escort ships – and 351 submarines.

Great Britain had 78 surface warships, including 1 attack carrier, 2 helicopter carriers, 2 assault ships, 2 cruisers, 9 missile destroyers, and 62 frigates. Britain also had 33 submarines, including 4 nuclear-powered missile submarines and 7 nuclear-powered attack submarines. France had 47 surface ships and 21 submarines. China had 6 destroyers, 20 escort ships, and 45 diesel-powered attack submarines, in addition to its single diesel-powered missile submarine.

Troop Strength. China had the largest army, with 2.5 million ground combat troops. Russia had 2.1 million troops; the United States, about 980,000, including Marines. China had 150 divisions; Russia, 164; the United States, 13.

Thirty-one Russian divisions were stationed in Warsaw Pact nations: 20 in East Germany, 2 in Poland, 4 in Hungary, and 5 in Czechoslovakia. Russia also had almost a million troops posted along its border with China. The East European Warsaw Pact nations had 53 divisions: 8 Bulgarian, 10 Czechoslovak, 6 East German, 15 Polish, 9 Romanian, and 5 Hungarian.

North Atlantic Treaty Organization defenses in Europe included 4⅓ U.S. divisions, 3 British divisions, 2 Belgian divisions, 1 Canadian battle group, 4 Danish brigades, 12 West German divisions, 12 Greek divisions, 7 Italian divisions, 1 Dutch mechanized brigade, 1 Norwegian infantry brigade, and 14 Turkish divisions. Thomas M. DeFrank

ARMY, UNITED STATES. See NATIONAL DEFENSE.

ART. See ARCHITECTURE; DANCING; LITERATURE; MUSIC, CLASSICAL; POETRY; VISUAL ARTS.

Comparative Military Manpower

	United States	Russia	China
Army	791,460	2,050,000	2,500,000
Air Force	681,731	900,000**	220,000
Navy	758,717*	475,000	180,000
Total	2,231,908	3,425,000	2,900,000

*Includes 192,064 Marines as of Sept. 30, 1973.

**Includes a strategic rocket force of 350,000.

The Strategic Balance in 1973

	United States	Russia
ICBM's	1,054	1,527
Polaris-type missile submarines	41	34
Polaris-type missiles	656	532
Other missile submarines	0	32
Other submarine missiles	0	96
Long-range bombers	450	140
Deliverable nuclear warheads	6,000*	2,500

*Includes triple warheads on 350 Minuteman III ICBM's and 320 missiles with 10 warheads each on Poseidon submarines.

ASIA. The importance of Asia in the world grew in 1973, and, contrary to the past, it was being asserted by Asians rather than non-Asians. Acknowledgment of Asia's importance also came from Russia and the United States. Their diplomats flew back and forth throughout the year in an effort to gain advantage with Asian countries.

The withdrawal of U.S. military forces from Vietnam, Laos, and Khmer (formerly Cambodia) produced a variety of consequences in both the large and small Asian countries. The truce in Vietnam was supervised by a control commission composed of Canada, Hungary, Indonesia, and Poland, though Canada later withdrew to be replaced by Iran. The growing hostility between China and Russia continued. Their fear of each other prompted actions by both countries that had grave consequences throughout Asia.

China's Role. China's steady emergence as the largest, most disciplined power in Asia dominated the year. The isolation of China for almost 20 years had ended. China's foreign policy, largely molded by Premier Chou En-lai, was aimed at consolidating its role as the major determining force in Asia and at strengthening its capacity to meet a Russian threat. The Russian-Chinese border is one of the largest open frontiers in the world. Russian Asia (Siberia and Mongolia) is sparsely populated but heavily armed

with the latest missiles and fully one-third of the huge Russian Army. The Russians were apparently obsessed with the fear that 850 million Chinese, with long-standing territorial claims to huge sections of Soviet Asia, might move to reclaim this land. The Chinese feared that Russia might make a pre-emptive nuclear strike against them.

China pursued two courses of action to counter this threat. On the military front, it demonstrated its own nuclear capacity with a major test blast on June 27 at Lop Nor, in Sinkiang Region on the border of Russia. It was a clear and unmistakable warning to the Russians. In addition, millions of Chinese workers began building extensive underground shelters in all the major cities. If war did come, the Chinese would be ready for it.

On the diplomatic front, Chinese gains were more subtle but nonetheless important. China encouraged the growing cordiality with the United States, which began after President Richard M. Nixon's visit to China in February, 1972. United States Secretary of State Henry A. Kissinger made numerous trips to Peking to cement U.S.-China relations, and the two governments found themselves in accord on several important questions. China, pleased with the U.S. military pullout in Southeast Asia, exerted pressure on the Communists in North Vietnam to accept the cease-fire agreement. There were also indications

The international conference on Vietnam met in Paris on February 26 to guarantee the January truce. It endorsed the truce agreement on March 2.

that China was not too eager to see Hanoi dominate Indochina, particularly in view of its Russian backing. China thus sided with the position taken by the United States.

The two nations also found it easy to reach an accommodation on Taiwan. China sought and got U.S. acknowledgment of its sovereignty over the island, as well as the withdrawal of U.S. air power from Taiwan. In turn, China did not press for an immediate take-over of Taiwan. Continued exchanges between the two nations and an upgrading of diplomatic representatives seemed to point to the growing desire of China to have the United States as a counterweight to Russia.

China also courted Japan carefully. Chinese missions went to Tokyo in August for talks with Prime Minister Kakuei Tanaka's government. The Chinese made it clear to Japan that they did not regard the U.S.-Japanese security treaty as anything but a defensive alliance against Russia. The Chinese went even further, continuing their open support of Pakistan, and lauded the U.S. military support of Iran. Both Pakistan and Iran are on Russia's southern border. China was guarded in its approach to the Communists of Southeast Asia, lest the troubles there spoil its new-found friendship with the United States and Japan.

Russia Woos India. Russia courted India, the second largest nation in Asia, as never before. India had demonstrated in convincing fashion in 1971 that it could easily defeat Pakistan, and the Russians were eager to solidify their relationship with India. They increased their arms credits and proposed a series of treaties, most of them related to economic development, that were completed by the end of 1973.

Russia tried but could not get a firm military commitment from India in case of war with China. India's internal problems were far too great to enable it to consider such grandiose military schemes. Its major problem was near-famine.

Hunger in India. For about two years, drought had crippled India's food production. By June, official food stocks were down to a bare 3 million tons, which could feed the people for only about three months. In an effort to bolster production and stop farmers from hoarding their crops while waiting for prices to rise on the open market, Prime Minister Indira Gandhi ordered a price increase for wheat.

The government itself was partially to blame for hoarding. It set unrealistically low purchase prices, and then tried to take over the wholesale grain trade. It was inadequately prepared and failed to accomplish this effectively. As a result, much of the trade went underground, while official markets were bare. The grain policies also inflated the prices of such coarse grains as millet and gram. This further encouraged wheat farmers to hold out for higher prices. The result was that in the drought-stricken state of Mahārāshtra, rations were cut from 13 kilograms (about 29 pounds) of cereal per month per person to 5 kilograms (about 11 pounds) and even this starvation diet was not always available.

India was forced to buy wheat on the world market. It bought 2 million tons from the United States and Canada and borrowed 2 million from Russia, hopefully enough to last until the next harvest. Much would depend on the weather. The monsoons came early to central India in 1973, but whether they brought enough rain to help the crops was still open to question. The crop failures, drought, military costs, and caring for the refugees from Bangladesh gave India plenty of problems to attend to at home without having to dabble in other Asian matters.

In foreign affairs, India continued its talks with China on re-establishing diplomatic relations. China, however, appeared in no hurry to embrace India and its problems, along with its Russian partner.

Japan's Balancing Act. Asia's other major power, Japan, balanced on two tightropes throughout the year. One strand stretched between Peking and Moscow, the other between the United States and Western Europe. Both China and Russia made overtures, and Japan bargained as best it could to get concessions from both. Japan wanted Russia to return four small islands north of Japan that Russia has occupied since the end of World War II in 1945. More important, Japan wanted some of the vast oil and natural gas supplies that are coming from Russian wells. Prime Minister Tanaka journeyed to Moscow in October to see what he could do, but got little more than generalities from the Russians.

He achieved better results with China. Japan completed a deal with China to finance a $300-million power plant, and other trade deals were planned. Various cultural exchanges were also arranged. China gave tacit backing to Japan's relations with the United States, even in defense matters, and the Chinese urged the Japanese to stand firm against the Russians.

Japan's relations with the United States and Western Europe revolved around basic economic issues that were reflected in trade imbalances. Part of the imbalance was caused by a disparity in currency valuations, and part by the vigor of the Japanese economy, with its intense export policies and huge surpluses. But the balancing act also involved the U.S. government's rather callous disregard of Japan's interests in Asia. Japan was deeply shocked that it was not informed ahead of time when the United States suddenly reversed its diplomatic relations with China in 1972. Bans on U.S. commodity exports to Japan also struck at the friendly relationship between the two countries, especially the ban on soybeans, a major Japanese import from the United States. Some of the tension was removed by concessions on both sides.

The devaluation of the dollar and a corresponding upward floating of the yen helped the trade im-

Facts in Brief on the Asian Countries

Country	Population	Government	Monetary Unit*	Foreign Trade (million U.S. $) Exports	Imports
Afghanistan	18,714,000	President & Prime Minister Mohammad Daud	afghani (63 = $1)	86	75
Australia	13,467,000	Governor General Sir Paul M.C. Hasluck; Prime Minister Edward Gough Whitlam	dollar (1 = $1.49)	6,456	5,140
Bangladesh	78,200,000	President Mohammad Ullah; Prime Minister Sheik Mujibur Rahman	taka (7.4 = $1)	36	38
Bhutan	912,000	King Jigme Singhi Wangchuk	Indian rupee	no statistics available	
Burma	30,088,000	Union Revolutionary Council Chairman & Prime Minister U Ne Win	kyat (4.9 = $1)	114	129
China	815,808,000	Communist Party Chairman Mao Tse-tung; Premier Chou En-lai	yuan (1.87 = $1)	2,300	2,100
India	587,502,000	President V. V. Giri; Prime Minister Indira Gandhi	rupee (7.3 = $1)	2,445	2,230
Indonesia	136,671,000	President Suharto	rupiah (415 = $1)	1,549	1,458
Iran	32,545,000	Shah Mohammed Reza Pahlavi; Prime Minister Amir Abbas Hoveyda	rial (68.17 = $1)	2,964	2,410
Japan	108,152,000	Emperor Hirohito; Prime Minister Kakuei Tanaka	yen (265.3 = $1)	28,655	23,481
Khmer (Cambodia)	7,507,000	President Lon Nol; Prime Minister In Tam	riel (165 = $1)	8	50
Korea (North)	15,514,000	President Kim Il-song; Prime Minister Kim Il	won (1.1 = $1)	156	230
Korea (South)	34,070,000	President Chung Hee Park; Prime Minister Kim Jong Pil	won (399 = $1)	1,633	2,522
Laos	3,253,000	King Savang Vatthana; Prime Minister Souvanna Phouma	kip (600 = $1)	6	114
Malaysia	11,477,000	Paramount Ruler Abdul Halim Muazzam; Prime Minister Abdul Razak	dollar (2.49 = $1)	1,721	1,643
Maldives	116,000	President Ibrahim Nasir; Prime Minister Ahmed Zaki	rupee (6.1 = $1)	no statistics available	
Mongolia	1,394,000	People's Revolutionary Party First Secretary & Premier Yumjaagiyn Tsedenbal	tugrik (3.2 = $1)	90	125
Nepal	11,911,000	King Birendra Bir Bikram Shah Deva; Prime Minister Nagendra Prasad Rijal	rupee (10.56 = $1)	29	39
New Zealand	2,983,000	Governor General Sir Denis Blundell; Prime Minister Norman E. Kirk	dollar (1 = $1.48)	1,766	1,531
Pakistan	66,600,000	President Chaudhry Fazal Elahi; Prime Minister Zulfikar Ali Bhutto	rupee (9.9 = $1)	697	681
Philippines	41,479,000	President Ferdinand E. Marcos	peso (6.78 = $1)	1,105	1,397
Russia	253,039,000	Communist Party General Secretary Leonid I. Brezhnev; Premier Aleksei N. Kosygin; Supreme Soviet Presidium Chairman Nikolai V. Podgorny	ruble (1 = $1.38)	15,361	16,047
Sikkim	210,000	Maharaja Palden Thondup Namgyal	Indian rupee	no statistics available	
Singapore	2,252,000	President Benjamin H. Sheares; Prime Minister Lee Kuan Yew	dollar (2.49 = $1)	2,181	3,383
Sri Lanka (Ceylon)	13,524,000	President William Gopallawa; Prime Minister Sirimavo Bandaranaike	rupee (6.1 = $1)	314	342
Taiwan	15,553,000	President Chiang Kai-shek; Vice-President C. K. Yen; Prime Minister Chiang Ching-kuo	new Taiwan dollar (38.1 = $1)	2,916	2,372
Thailand	28,275,000	King Phumiphon Aduldet; Prime Minister Sanya Thammasak	baht (21 = $1)	1,051	1,479
Vietnam (North)	23,187,000	President Ton Duc Thang; Premier Pham Van Dong	dong (2.4 = $1)	51	134
Vietnam (South)	20,316,000	President Nguyen Van Thieu; Vice-President Tran Van Huong; Prime Minister Tran Thien Khiem	piastre (500 = $1)	4	255

*Exchange rates as of Nov. 1, 1973

balance. In turn, the United States eased its ban on commodity exports to Japan. Japan sought and got assurances from Washington, D.C., that it would be consulted more frequently on future U.S. moves in Asia. Tanaka went to Europe in October to discuss increased trade with the European Community (Common Market). Japan also increased the size of its military forces, as it sought to establish itself more firmly as an Asian power.

Oil and Peace. For the rest of Asia, the year was one of instability, yet hope. The fragile cease-fire worked out in Vietnam, Khmer, and Laos did not bring peace; hostilities still flared. But the United States military intervention was ended, and this alone lessened the scope of the conflict. However, the end of major hostilities was not going to solve the problems of Asia. Most of these were economic, and stemmed from drought and inflationary world prices.

Asia, much like the rest of the world, was shaken by the October war in the Middle East and the resulting Arab oil boycott. Drastic oil shortages struck those countries that depend on Arab petroleum. India was also hit by shortages of kerosene, and all the Southeast Asian nations suffered from a shortage of fuel supplies for transport. Japan was hurt most by the oil boycott. Its industry depends heavily on energy from petroleum, and it imports about 90 per cent of its oil from the Middle East.

Because of its close ties with the United States, Japan had generally followed America's foreign policy lead in supporting Israel. But an already growing disenchantment with general U.S. policies crystallized quickly when the Arab states began to threaten Japan with an oil boycott if it continued to support Israel. Japan abruptly reversed its long-standing policy and withdrew its support of Israel. This action was a sharp reminder to the United States that Japan would consider its own interests first. There was, of course, little else Japan could do in the face of the oil crisis. And the general world energy crisis emphasized the importance to Japan of some kind of accommodation with Russia so that the vast resources of Siberia might be tapped.

Indonesia, on the other hand, viewed the oil crisis somewhat differently. It had increased its oil production to some 2 million barrels per day and profited handsomely from skyrocketing prices. The oil crisis also stimulated a rush of exploration for new sources of oil in Asia, spearheaded by Japan and the United States. South Vietnam, backed by the United States, laid claim to the 35 tiny Nansha islands, located midway between Vietnam and the Philippines. The islands, largely uninhabited, had been previously claimed by China. South Vietnam's claim, however, was not disputed by China, and preliminary drilling operations indicated a rich oil field might be uncovered there.

Political Changes in Asia reflected a growing awareness of the implications of the U.S. withdrawal

Carrying their possessions with them, members of a Khmer family flee from their home near Phnom Penh, scene of intensive fighting in 1973.

from Indochina. For the Philippines and North and South Korea it meant a tightening of political and military control. President Ferdinand E. Marcos of the Philippines dumped a constitutionally limited government in favor of martial law. In South Korea, President Chung Hee Park held a controlled plebiscite that ensured him of six more years in office. North and South Korea held talks during the year, but failed to make much headway toward unification.

Military regimes continued to dominate Burma and Indonesia, and the military leadership began to play a larger role in Sri Lanka's parliamentary government. Yet there was a major setback for the military forces in Thailand. Massive demonstrations by Thai students and workers toppled the military dictatorship there in October. King Phumiphon Aduldet actively intervened on the side of the students and workers. A caretaker civilian government was set up that promised the adoption of a constitution by June, 1974.

The princes of Laos finally agreed on a truce and a provisional government that would give some respite to their war-shattered nation. But Khmer and Vietnam were still consumed with civil war despite various cease-fire agreements. In December, South Vietnam reported a large-scale attack by Northern regulars, which may signal the start of full-scale hostilities in 1974. Few gave the beleaguered Lon Nol government much of a chance to survive in Khmer.

Rebel forces were reported on the outskirts of Phnom Penh in December. This time the U.S. military support was no longer there.

The ban on U.S. bombing in Khmer and Laos did not bar unarmed reconnaissance flights over the two countries. However, the planes involved were prohibited from calling for armed support if fired upon, an official of the Pentagon said in August. He also revealed that up to 400 fighter-bombers and 175 B-52s would remain on call in Thailand and Guam and aboard carriers.

Yet, Asia ended the year on a cautiously hopeful note. The potential for peace, orderly development, and growth was present. The absence of entanglements in the area by the big non-Asian powers meant that Asians would finally have a chance to settle their problems themselves. Much would depend on efforts to solve basic economic problems such as increasing food production and building sufficient reserve stocks to eliminate the specter of famine. Also they would need to find ways to adjust to the energy crisis, such as pushing oil exploration and development more vigorously. This was most important for Japan, and might mitigate its massive pollution problems. But if the guns could be kept silent, there was reason for guarded optimism.　　　　　　　　John N. Stalker

See also the various Asian country articles; Section One, FOCUS ON THE WORLD.

ASTRONAUTS doubled and then redoubled the length of U.S. space missions in 1973. They carried out the first repair work in space and proved man could live and work for months in a condition of weightlessness.

Charles Conrad, Jr.; Joseph P. Kerwin; and Paul J. Weitz were launched from Cape Kennedy on the first *Skylab* mission on May 25. They returned to earth on June 22, after a mission of 28 days, twice as long as the 14-day record established in 1965 on *Gemini 7* by Frank Borman and James Lovell, Jr. See SPACE EXPLORATION.

On July 28, a second team left the earth for a rendezvous with the *Skylab* station. Orbiting at an altitude of 270 miles, Alan L. Bean, Owen K. Garriott, and Jack R. Lousma spent more than 59 days 11 hours in space on this flight, more than doubling the time of the first *Skylab* crew.

Gerald P. Carr, Edward G. Gibson, and William R. Pogue, the third and last *Skylab* crew, lifted off on November 16 to spend as much as 84 days in space. The astronauts conducted a series of medical experiments that are expected to provide new data about the effects of long-term missions on human beings.

The National Aeronautics and Space Administration (NASA) announced the astronauts who will make the joint U.S.–Russian space mission, scheduled for 1975. The U.S. crew will be composed of Thomas P. Stafford, Donald K. Slayton, and Vance D. Brand.　　　　　　　　William J. Cromie

ASTRONOMY. The fourth bright comet in recent years appeared in the night sky in the latter months of 1973. Comet Kohoutek, named after its discoverer, Lubos Kohoutek of the Hamburg Observatory in West Germany, was found on March 7, 1973. At the time of discovery it was a faint, distant, ball of ice approaching the Sun from beyond the orbit of Jupiter. It steadily brightened as it approached the Sun on a parabolic orbit. However, it never became as bright as some astronomers hoped it would, and, though it could be seen with the naked eye, it was difficult to find in the sky. Material scattering from the head of the comet formed a long, characteristic tail that made the comet a spectacular object for telescopic viewing. By late November, it was visible an hour or so before dawn in the Northern Hemisphere. It swept past the Sun, about 13.2 million miles away at its closest point on December 28. It passed behind the Sun and moved into the evening sky in early 1974.

Although few amateur astronomers watched and photographed this extraordinary comet, it was observed by teams of scientists on the ground as well as by *Skylab* cameras and smaller orbiting observatories and satellites. The National Aeronautics and Space Administration (NASA) conducted extensive scientific observations of the comet. NASA photographed it with stereoscopic cameras from the Earth and with cameras on the *Mariner 10* spacecraft. This gave astronomers the first true picture of the shape of a comet, as distinct from its appearance as seen from one angle alone. *Mariner 10* was launched toward Venus and Mercury on Nov. 3, 1973.

Milky Way Map. An enormous survey of the northern sky, conducted at the Hat Creek Observatory of the University of California, Berkeley, has been converted into a computer-generated photograph of hydrogen gas in the neighborhood of the Sun. Hydrogen gas fills the space between the stars, and makes up 3 or 4 per cent of the total mass in the Milky Way. The gas is detected by its radio signal emission.

The map shows huge streamers of gas extending halfway across the sky that resemble the patterns of iron filings near a bar magnet. Additional tangled loops and filaments indicate a complicated structure and mixing of patterns. An especially noticeable feature is an empty area where the gas must have been swept away when a star exploded.

Solar Eclipse. The longest solar eclipse of the century passed over North Africa on June 30, 1973. It began in northern South America, crossed the Atlantic Ocean, and traversed Africa from Mauritania to Kenya. The Moon completely covered the Sun for up to seven minutes along the central line of the shadow, and the length of the total eclipse provided observers with an unusually good opportunity to measure the Sun's corona, the outer solar atmosphere most easily observed during total eclipses.

They observed some streamers from the Sun that extend out to six times the radius of the Sun.

People observed the eclipse from land sites in South America and Africa and from ships in the Atlantic Ocean. The supersonic French aircraft *Concorde* flew along the eclipse path in Africa at nearly the same speed as the Moon's shadow moved, and astronomers aboard the aircraft were able to observe 72 minutes of totality.

Kitt Peak's New Telescope. A reflecting telescope four meters (158 inches) in diameter was completed at Kitt Peak National Observatory near Tucson, Ariz. The first light was focused in the telescope in March, 1973. The instrument, named for former Kitt Peak director Nicholas U. Mayall, was dedicated on June 20. It is the world's second largest operating telescope. Early photographs taken with it indicate that the instrument forms excellent star and nebula images over a field about 50 minutes in diameter. Additional mirrors are being installed so it can take the spectra of stars, galaxies, and interstellar clouds, and measure the intensities of light from celestial objects.

A duplicate telescope is under construction on Cerro Tololo in the Chilean Andes for observing stars in the Southern Hemisphere skies. The two telescopes will observe the faintest, most distant objects in the universe and also will provide further information on nearby stars and galaxies.

Pluto's Rotation Axis. Pluto, the most distant planet in our solar system, is so small that no surface features can be seen. The rotation of the planet around its axis takes 6.4 Earth-days, as shown by small variations of brightness when different parts of the planet face the Earth. Astronomer Leif Anderson of Indiana University reported in 1973 that he found the brightness changes almost twice as vivid in 1972 as they had been in 1955. He said that this probably means that Pluto's axis is nearly in its orbital plane rather than highly inclined to the plane as is the case for the Earth. As Pluto moves in its orbit, the pole points farther away from the Earth each year.

The effect of having the pole in the orbital plane is to make a season at one of the poles last for about half the time that Pluto takes to revolve around the Sun. Thus, there would be roughly 124 Earth-years of summer with constant sunlight, followed by 124 Earth-years of winter with constant darkness.

Jupiter Close-Up. After traveling 620 million miles in 21 months, the unmanned U.S. space probe *Pioneer 10* passed the planet Jupiter at only 81,000 miles distance on December 3. The probe's infrared radiometer confirmed that the largest of Jupiter's 12 moons is coated with frozen water. Radioed data also included measurements of Jupiter's radiation belts, magnetic field, temperatures, and atmospheric composition. Jupiter's surface temperature was measured at $-215°$ to $-230°$ F., and helium was found in the planet's atmosphere.

***Skylab* Experiments.** The *Skylab* space station launched in May is the largest and most complex craft ever put into Earth orbit (see SPACE EXPLORATION). It is equipped to perform numerous astronomy experiments, and six instruments in its telescope mount have viewed various parts of the Sun's radiation. Five of these also observed X rays and ultraviolet light that do not penetrate the Earth's atmosphere. Other experiments were performed to study stars, the Sun, and interplanetary dust.

New Limits. Two previously unknown quasars were discovered in 1973, one in April by the Steward Observatory in Arizona and one in June by the Lick Observatory in California. Quasars are light sources that look like stars but have their light strongly shifted toward redder, or longer, wave lengths than originally emitted. Ten years after their discovery, quasars are still mysterious and exciting to astronomers. The principal controversy is whether the large red shifts mean that quasars are moving rapidly away from us or whether something else causes their large red shifts. If the red shift is due to their velocity and they are moving with the general expansion of the universe, then they are the most distant, most energetic objects ever found.

The red shifts of the new quasars are extremely large, 3.4 and 3.5. If shifts this large are produced by velocity, the quasars must be moving away from the Earth at about 90 per cent of the speed of light. Before the latest discovery, some scientists believed that we had found the most distant existing quasars, and had thus seen the edge of the universe. These new quasars boosted the search for more to extend the limits even farther.

X Rays. Galaxies cluster together in large groups, sometimes with thousands of star systems. Each one, such as the Milky Way, our Galaxy, forms huge agglomerations of matter. These aggregates are the largest known objects in the universe. Data from the *Uhuru* satellite shows that some rich clusters of galaxies emit energetic X rays in addition to the visible light and radio waves previously detected. The X rays come from hot gases filling the space between the galaxies. Galaxies stir up the gas by moving around in it or by ejecting hot material into it, thereby heating it to millions of degrees.

Some pairs of stars in our Galaxy also emit X rays. In each case, one star is visible and has a much fainter companion in orbit around it. The X rays come from the vicinity of the fainter star, and astronomers now think that this may be the result of matter falling into a black hole, or a neutron star. A black hole cannot be seen because it is so dense that light rays cannot escape from its surface. Its gravity, however, can pull matter toward it. As the material falls into the black hole, particles collide at high speeds, giving off X rays. Astronomers must search for black holes indirectly, since they are invisible.   Laura P. Bautz

ATOMIC ENERGY. See ENERGY.

AUSTRALIA

Rapid economic growth, low unemployment, and growing national reserves were major factors that contributed to a sense of national stability in 1973. Counteracting these, however, were a large budget deficit, rapidly rising wages, and increasing inflation – the result of high prices for imports and foodstuffs.

The Labor Party government, led by Prime Minister Edward Gough Whitlam, tried to deal with inflation by a 5 per cent revaluation of the Australian dollar on September 9. This followed an earlier revaluation of 7.05 per cent on Dec. 23, 1972. Other efforts included an unexpected cut of 25 per cent in tariffs on July 18, an increase in interest rates, and the creation of a Prices Justification Tribunal.

None of these measures, however, enabled the government to exercise direct control over incomes and prices. Constitutionally, power lay with the state governments, not all of which were prepared to transfer it to the federal government, though only a few exercised any actual control. Prime Minister Whitlam scheduled a referendum for December 8 on the issue of federal price controls. The Senate, where the government did not have a majority, widened the proposal to include incomes as well.

Whitlam immediately encountered opposition on the incomes question from some of the trade unions, and the referendum resulted in a setback for the Whitlam government. About 65 per cent of the electorate voted against giving the Labor Party government control over income; 55 per cent rejected federal price controls.

Other Economic Changes. The government's successive revaluations encouraged imports, but Australia had continued to amass large reserves overseas. For the financial year ending June 30, 1973, there was a trade surplus of 2.2 million Australian dollars (almost $3.3 million in U.S. currency), more than twice the record set in 1972. Exports were 27 per cent higher, with minerals, wool, wheat, and meat contributing strongly. While exports of minerals rose, production of home-produced petroleum increased, so that two-thirds of the country's needs were met from local sources.

Minerals and oil were two major growing points in the economy. Western Australia's proposals for industrial development in the remote Pilbara iron ore region were encouraged by the federal authorities. Plans were pursued for the development of offshore oil and gas, and for a national pipeline authority.

The monumental $140-million Sydney Opera House was officially opened on October 20 by Queen Elizabeth II in spectacular ceremonies.

The withdrawal in May of tax concessions and subsidies for minerals and oil had some effect on marginal companies but did not lessen expansion.

The budget, brought before Parliament by Treasurer Frank Crean on August 21, contained considerable increases in spending, especially on social services, education, and foreign aid, but no increase in direct taxes. Excise taxes on gasoline, alcoholic beverages, and tobacco were raised. Some expenditures were reduced, including bounties for dairy farmers.

Defense Policy was affected by the general détente in Asia and the winding down of Australia's effort in Vietnam. In spite of a small budget increase, previously planned developments were modified. Construction of certain Navy ships was deferred, and a Mirage Air Force squadron was disbanded. Manpower in the three services was reduced, along with the number of civilian employees. Following the Labor policy of not stationing troops permanently abroad, all troops in the ANZUK (Australia, New Zealand, and the United Kingdom) brigade in Singapore were to be withdrawn by March 1, 1974. Australia would continue to honor its obligations under the five-power agreement with Britain, New Zealand, Malaysia, and Singapore.

Foreign Policy also showed changes. The most publicized were in relations with the United States. Previous Australian governments had followed American policies closely. Prime Minister Whitlam told the National Press Club in Washington, D.C., in July, that he wanted "to move away from the narrow view that the ANZUK Treaty is the only significant factor in our relations with the United States and the equally narrow view that our relations with the United States are the only significant factor in Australia's foreign relations." In January, three ministers had publicly condemned U.S. President Richard M. Nixon's renewed bombing of North Vietnam, and Prime Minister Whitlam had protested privately to Mr. Nixon. It was known that sections of the Labor Party objected to U.S. military installations in Australia. Subsequently, the government announced it was satisfied with all the installations except one, about which it wished to negotiate a new agreement.

The government repeatedly emphasized its stand against racism and militarism. In the United Nations (UN) General Assembly, it voted more often with the third world majority, especially on questions involving Africa. It arranged diplomatic relations with East Germany and the People's Republic of China in January, withdrew Australian representation from Taiwan, and recognized North Vietnam on February 26. In January, it ratified the nuclear nonproliferation treaty, and on March 9 announced the ratification of a number of International Labor Organization conventions. It negotiated the first exchange of envoys with the Vatican in the same month. On December 1, Papua New Guinea became self-governing, ending direct rule by Australia. Defense and foreign affairs would continue to be administered by the Australian government pending complete independence.

French Nuclear Tests. The Whitlam government's only major dispute with another country involved French nuclear tests over Mururoa Atoll in the Pacific. Together with New Zealand and Fiji, Australia carried the tests issue to the International Court of Justice at The Hague in May, obtaining an interim ruling that France ignored.

In March and April, charges that Croatian separatists in Australia were terrorizing their fellow Yugoslav immigrants and training some people for terrorism in Yugoslavia created a furor. Attorney General Lionel K. Murphy indicated he was dissatisfied with the handling of the matter by the Australian Security Intelligence Organization (ASIO). When Yugoslav Prime Minister Djemal Bijedic visited Australia in March, intense security measures were in force to protect him. The discovery that the Yugoslav government had executed three naturalized Australians for terrorist activities added to the tension. At the end of the year, ASIO and the Yugoslav immigrants were being investigated.

The government's wish to end all traces of British authority in Australia was expressed by Prime Minister Whitlam on May 1. He discussed with Queen Elizabeth II and the British government such issues as the desirability of ending Australian legal appeals to the Privy Council, of changing the Royal Style and Titles to emphasize the queen's position as Queen of Australia, and of having the governor general approve diplomatic accreditations. The first of these objectives was opposed by the states; the second and third were duly achieved.

Social Reform was a basic aim of the government during the year. Apart from increasing pensions, it sought improvements in the educational system, medical and other social services, and improved conditions for aborigines and immigrants. The minister for social security, William G. Hayden, presented plans for a basic guaranteed income, school dental services, a single health insurance fund, and new arrangements for medical services. However, the Australian Medical Association opposed them. New efforts were made to deal with the complex problems of Australia's 140,000 aborigines (about 1 per cent of the population), especially in providing land rights. The government decided on May 28 to assume complete responsibility for the aborigines, but this led to disagreement with some of the states, especially Queensland. Perhaps the most far-reaching decision in the social field was the adoption in June of the Karmel Report on Australian schools. This involved accepting responsibility for bringing all Australian schools up to certain stated levels of efficiency through federal grants.

The Arts Development was symbolized by the opening of the new Adelaide Festival Theatre in June, the official opening of the Sydney Opera House by Queen Elizabeth II on October 20, and the award of the Nobel Prize for literature to Australian novelist Patrick White (see BUILDING AND CONSTRUCTION; NOBEL PRIZES). More than $Australian 1 million was provided by the federal government in grants to writers. Plans were underway for the construction of a building in Canberra to house the national art collection, and officials paid $U.S. 2 million in September for a Jackson Pollock painting, *Blue Poles*, to hang in it. A group of 51 paintings by the late Sir William Dobell were exhibited in the world's major art centers before being auctioned in Sydney on November 19. A competition for a new national anthem was, however, unsuccessful.

Social Change took several forms. The voting age was lowered from 21 to 18 in March. The divorce rate in 1972 was reported at 12.03 per 1,000 persons, the highest on record. A bill to make abortion easier in the Australian Capital Territory suffered a massive defeat in the federal Parliament in May.

In sports, the Melbourne Cup was won by Gala Supreme. Richmond beat Carlton to win the Victorian Football League Grand Final, and the Sydney Rugby League Grand Final was captured by Manly-Warringah.   J. D. B. Miller

See also ASIA (Facts in Brief Table).

Australian of the Year medallion was presented to swimmer Shane Gould, who won three gold medals at the Olympic Games in Munich in 1972.

AUSTRIA was deeply divided and perplexed by re-action to a September, 1973, decision to close transit facilities for Jews emigrating from Russia to Israel. Schönau Castle, on 400 heavily wooded acres 20 miles south of Vienna, had been the Russian Jews' first stopover.

Arab gunmen took four hostages – three Russian Jews and an Austrian border guard – from a Mos-cow-to-Vienna train and held them at the Vienna airport. On September 29, Chancellor Bruno Krei-sky announced Austria would close the facility in exchange for the hostages' lives. Israel, many persons in other countries, and political opponents in Austria criticized Kreisky harshly for yielding.

In November, a substitute facility was established at Wollersdorf. It was operated by the Red Cross instead of an Israeli organization.

The Economy. Inflation increased, with price hikes exceeding an annual rate of 8 per cent. Over the last decade, they had averaged about 5 per cent. A freeze on prices and wages, imposed in November, 1972, ended in May, 1973. Union demands for wage increases of up to 18 per cent and employers' calls for wider profit margins prevented the Socialist gov-ernment from holding the line. Building costs rose 22.4 per cent in the first part of 1973.

Chancellor Kreisky preferred to put up with the inflation rather than endanger Austria's full employ-ment. Out of Austria's total labor force of 2.5 million, only 7,000 workers were involved in strikes in 1972, and only 120,000 man-hours were lost.

Nevertheless, a big influx of foreign workers be-came a political issue in local elections. Their num-bers rose by 40,000 to a record 240,000 in mid-July. But there were also tens of thousands of "illegal workers," tourists working without labor permits. The trade unions pressed for a ceiling on foreigners of 9 per cent of the labor force.

The independent Institute for Economic Research reported no sign of the export boom cooling off despite two revaluations of the schilling in 1973. In the first six months, exports increased 15 per cent over the same period in 1972. Industrial output was growing at an annual rate of 7 per cent.

Worker Participation. The government decided to allow worker representatives to be seated on the supervisory board of Voest-Alpine AG, a state steel company formed on Jan. 1, 1973, by the merger of two of the largest steel firms. This led the Trade Union Federation to press for worker participation in the management of other companies. Many firms accepted the proposal in principle.

Border Tensions. Talks took place in Bratislava, Czechoslovakia, to try to settle differences with that neighboring country. A communiqué signed by the foreign ministers of the two countries on March 3 expressed their "decisive will" to deal with border incidents.   Kenneth Brown

See also EUROPE (Facts in Brief Table).

AUTOMOBILE. New-car sales in the United States hit an all-time high of 11.4 million in 1973, topping by 5 per cent the old record of 10.9 million set in 1972. The board chairmen of the three largest U.S. auto companies – Henry Ford II of Ford Motor Company, Lynn A. Townsend of Chrysler Corporation, and Richard C. Gerstenberg of General Motors Corpo-ration (GM) – agreed that new-car sales would drop to between 10 million and 10.3 million cars in 1974. The energy shortage was blamed for the drop.

Worldwide car sales reached an estimated 16.6-million cars in 1973 – more than a million above the 1972 level. But again, sales prospects for 1974 did not appear as bright. Sales of domestic and imported cars set records in the U.S. market, with about 1.6-million imports and 9.7 million domestic cars sold.

Late in 1973, market indicators suggested the United States industry would sell fewer domestic cars in 1974. At the end of November, GM had the largest inventory of unsold cars in its history for that time of year. As a result, 16 of the 24 GM assembly plants in North America were partly or totally closed for a week in December.

The most noticeable sales trend was the swing away from standard-sized cars in favor of intermedi-ate, compact, and subcompact models that get more mileage per gallon of gasoline. Auto industry spokes-men said customers' concern about a reduced gaso-

"Smoking is definitely hazardous to your health."

line supply was the big factor in the swing to the smaller, less high-powered types.

On December 10, the U.S. Senate passed legislation that would require auto manufacturers to produce cars by 1984 that will operate on less gasoline. House action on the broad, energy-conservation bill was expected early in 1974.

Struggling Imports. The German-built Volkswagen (VW) continued its dominance as the best-selling import in the U.S. market for 1973 as it sold 476,318 cars, about 9,000 fewer than in 1972. Toyota, Datsun, and Mazda – all Japanese built – held the next three spots in foreign-car sales.

United States production in 1973 set a record of about 9.7 million cars, compared with the 9.3 million in 1965. As production of 1973 model cars came to an end, U.S. automakers were busy reshuffling production schedules to get more small-car output. Shutdowns were scheduled at many assembly plants to "bring production in line with customer demand," as the auto companies phrased it.

Henry Ford said on December 14 that, while small cars accounted for 42 per cent of U.S. sales in 1973, the figure could rise to 50 per cent in 1974. He pointed out that demand for standard and medium-sized cars was down about 25 per cent in the first three months of the 1974 model run.

The imports had many problems, too. They had to cope with devaluation of the dollar, tough U.S. safety standards, and higher labor and materials costs.

The VW Beetle, for example, long priced under its American competitors, began the 1974 model year with a higher basic price tag – about $2,625. Among domestic cars, American Motors Corporation's (AMC) Gremlin checked in at $2,150; GM's Vega, $2,237; and Ford's Pinto, $2,292, in November, 1973. And in December, VW sales lost ground while other imports gained.

In France, Citroen announced it would close down for a week and a half at the end of the year to reorganize car production lines. The shut-down would reduce production by about 10,000 cars, and the new lines would produce more small cars and fewer large ones, Citroen said.

Government Controls. The federal Cost of Living Council (COL) on December 10 exempted the auto industry from wage and price controls. In return, Ford, GM, and AMC agreed that wholesale price increases for full-sized and intermediate models would be held to about $150, and there would be no further increases in 1974 prices. Chrysler refused to accept this understanding, but competition appeared to hold Chrysler prices in line with those of the rest of the industry. That effect had been predicted by John Dunlop, COL director. The COL decision also meant government approval of new three-year union contracts. See LABOR.

The 1974 Cars. There were few style changes in 1974 models. Instead, manufacturers concentrated on providing features required by law to improve safety and to control exhaust emissions.

The airbag, a "passive restraint" safety device to cushion car occupants in a crash, was not yet a legal requirement, although safety experts had long sought such a device. The first GM car equipped with an airbag rolled off an assembly line on November 29. The device was installed on an Oldsmobile Toronado as a $225, extra-cost option. See SAFETY.

The federal government said that all new cars must be able to withstand a 5-miles-per-hour front- or rear-end crash with no damage to the fuel tank, lighting system, door locks, or exhaust or cooling systems. Another addition to the 1974 cars was a federally ordered seat-belt interlock system. This system prevents the car from starting until the driver and front-seat passenger have seated themselves and buckled the three-point, lap-shoulder restraint system. Engineers continued their efforts to meet government emissions requirements. In several cases, company negotiators won delays in imposition of stricter limits.

Henry Ford was among the first auto executives to urge careful governmental consideration of any new vehicle requirements that would add weight to cars or reduce fuel efficiency. He said the 1974 Pinto is 350 pounds, or 15 per cent, heavier than the original 1971 version, mainly because of government safety and damageability standards. Ford said that, from 1967 to 1973 models, federal emission standards had led to a 13 per cent loss of fuel economy for the typical car. In late December, he urged a government slowdown in imposing new emissions requirements for the next two years.

Experimental Engines. The gasoline shortage led to increased experimentation with alternate power systems. They ranged from electricity to steam, but virtually all were discarded as being too expensive or too cumbersome. Chrysler continued its gas-turbine research, but Chrysler's president John Riccardo said on December 15 that the gas-turbine car was a good many years away from use on the highway.

Major attention went to the Wankel rotary engine, first developed in Germany, mainly because it is so small. It is about one-third the size of the conventional internal-combustion engine and has about one-sixth as many moving parts. Twenty-six auto firms around the world were testing the Wankel. Hurried production plans for Wankel-powered Chevrolet Vegas dimmed, however. GM planned to introduce them with the first 1975 models, but canceled the plan on December 24. It said the first models would probably be introduced later in the 1975 model year.

About 120,000 Japanese-built Mazdas, 81 per cent of them rotary-powered, were sold in the United States in 1973. Their manufacturer had built about 400,000 of the rotary engines for use in various parts of the world.   Charles C. Cain III

Driver Salt Walther survived this fiery crash on the first lap of the Indianapolis 500, but the race had to be postponed for two days.

AUTOMOBILE RACING. Jackie Stewart, a 34-year-old Scotsman, survived a close call with death, regained the world driving championship, and announced his retirement – all in 1973. Gordon Johncock, a 36-year-old driver from Franklin, Ind., who had declared bankruptcy, won the Indianapolis 500.

Stewart was world driving champion in 1969 and 1971, and finished second to Emerson Fittipaldi of Brazil in 1972. The 1973 championship series for the Formula One cars comprised 15 Grand Prix races.

Stewart narrowly escaped death when his brakes failed at 186 miles per hour in practice for the South African Grand Prix. He crashed into a protective bank, escaped injury, then won the race. Driving a British Tyrrell chassis with a 3-liter Cosworth-Ford engine, Stewart then won in Belgium, Monaco, the Netherlands, and West Germany, then retired from racing on October 14. He had won more Grand Prix races – 27 – than any other driver in history.

Fittipaldi won in Argentina, Brazil, and Spain, and Ronnie Peterson of Sweden in the United States (at Watkins Glen, N.Y.), France, Austria, and Italy. They drove Lotus-Fords. Driving similar McLaren-Fords, Peter Revson of New York City won in England and Canada, and Denis Hulme of New Zealand won in Sweden.

Indianapolis 500. The winning car in the Indianapolis 500, an STP Eagle-Offenhauser, earned $236,022 of the $1,006,105 purse. After most of the money had gone to the car owner, sponsor, and mechanic, $70,000 was left for Johncock. He had to turn over $17,500 to creditors, leaving him about $30,000 after taxes.

The race was ended by rain after 332½ miles on May 30. It started on May 28, but 400 feet past the start, David (Salt) Walther of Dayton, Ohio, became involved in a 12-car accident, and his car sailed through the air and burst into flame. He was severely burned. When the race was resumed two days later, David (Swede) Savage of Santa Ana, Calif., crashed. He died five weeks later.

David Hobbs of England, who was involved in the Walther accident, said, "I don't understand how the supposedly best 33 drivers in the world cannot drive down a straightaway without something like this happening." Hobbs's words were strikingly similar to those of Dan Gurney in 1966, when almost half of the Indianapolis field, including Gurney, was eliminated in a pile-up at the start. Gurney said then, "Wouldn't you think that a bunch of grown men, all supposedly experienced race drivers, could drive together down a simple stretch of straight road?"

Other Series. David Pearson, a 38-year-old driver from Spartanburg, S.C., was the star of the National Association for Stock Car Auto Racing (NASCAR) Grand National series. In a four-month span from March to July, he won 9 of the 10 races he entered, and he barely missed winning the other. In his 1971

Mercury, prepared by the Wood brothers of Stuart, Va., he won 11 of the 18 races he entered, and earned $213,966. Richard Petty of Randleman, N.C., won NASCAR's richest race, the $236,325 Daytona 500 on February 18 at Daytona Beach, Fla.

The Canadian-American Challenge Cup series of eight road races for big sports cars with unlimited engines produced another victory for Porsche. In 1972, George Follmer of Arcadia, Calif., won in a Porsche 917-10. Driving the same car in 1973, Follmer finished second to Mark Donohue of Newtown Square, Pa., in a turbocharged Porsche 917-30.

The Formula 5000 series of road races was dominated by Jody Scheckter, 23, of South Africa, who gained the championship in a Trojan chassis with a 305-cubic-inch Chevrolet V8 engine. Scheckter's devil-may-care driving style excited spectators.

The Trans-American series, formerly for such so-called "pony" cars as Mustangs and Javelins, was limited to touring and grand-touring cars. Peter Gregg of Jacksonville, Fla., won the seven-race series in a Porsche Carrera RS.

The French Matra factory dropped out of Grand Prix racing to concentrate on the world manufacturers championship and won that series title with a Matra-Simca 670. Roger McCluskey of Tucson, Ariz., was champion of the United States Auto Club's championship-car series, and Benny Parsons of Ellerbe, N.C., won the NASCAR title.   Frank Litsky

AVIATION encountered some unexpected turbulence in 1973 from sluggish traffic growth, rapidly rising costs, and uncertainty about the effects of the energy crisis on future operations. On the brighter side, the skyjacking problem was finally brought under control in the United States, commercial carriers had one of the best safety records in their history, air freight revenues topped $1 billion for the first time, and the Civil Aeronautics Board (CAB) took an active role in seeking to raise the profits of American carriers. Nevertheless, at year-end, the menacing cloud of the energy crisis hung threateningly over the future of worldwide aviation.

Scheduled Airlines Profits were estimated at $215 million for American lines, about the same as in 1972. The $215 million compared with earlier 1973 profit projections of $250 million. The two major reasons that profits fell short of original expectations were a slackening of traffic growth and sharply rising costs.

Domestic traffic increased about 7 per cent over 1972, significantly below a predicted rise of more than 10 per cent. Airline officials said they failed to attain anticipated traffic growth because of a decline in pleasure travel.

The failure of international traffic to meet growth expectations was even greater than the domestic decline. Travel by Americans to Europe fell into its biggest slump in more than a decade. Most early forecasts projected a rise in international air traffic of 13 to 15 per cent over 1972. The actual advance, however, was only about 4 per cent.

Travel agents and airline officials gave the following reasons for the decline in international travel:
- Uncertainty about fare levels during March and April.
- Cautious spending by many Americans because of inflation and an uncertain economy.
- Higher prices abroad, in terms of the U.S. dollar, because of dollar devaluation and inflation.
- Fears related to tensions in the Middle East.
- Higher air fares.

Air Freight revenues topped $1 billion for the first time. This was an increase of 9.3 per cent over 1972's $915 million. Total air freight traffic was estimated at 4.8 billion ton-miles, an increase of 14.5 per cent over 1972's 4.2 billion ton-miles. Domestic air freight increased 17.3 per cent, while international air freight carried by U.S. carriers rose 10.2 per cent.

Aviation officials cited two major reasons – bigger planes and containerization – for the impressive growth of air freight. The approximately 200 wide-bodied jets (747s, DC-10s, and L-1011s) put into airline service since early 1970 helped to double the industry's cargo capacity by mid-1973.

Containerization helped to open the door to new markets. By 1973, the airlines had developed standard containers for use in the underbellies of the wide-bodied jets and all-cargo freighters, as well as containers that could be used in any aircraft.

The Fuel Shortage. Reductions in air service over much of the United States began on November 1 as the airlines were affected by the federal government's mandatory fuel-allocation program. The first three stages of the program reduced the industry's fuel consumption from 10 to 15 per cent below planned levels within 70 days. Effective November 1, fuel was reduced to the same level as that in 1972, or from 5 to 10 per cent less than the airlines had expected to use. On December 1, allocation was reduced to a level 5 per cent below 1972 levels. On December 27, the Office of Energy Conservation said no further reductions in fuel allocations would be necessary and major domestic airlines would be able to have 95 per cent of their 1972 fuel levels in 1974. Regional carriers and air taxi services would receive 100 per cent of their 1972 levels.

Airline officials estimated that by early December, about 1,000 out of a total of 13,800 daily scheduled flights, or 7.2 per cent of all U.S. commercial flights, had been canceled as a result of reduced fuel allocations. They also estimated that by Feb. 1, 1974, the number of daily flights canceled would reach 2,600, or 18 per cent.

Consequently, Robert D. Timm, CAB chairman, announced on December 5 that his agency must become more deeply involved in scheduling flights in order to maintain adequate service. He supported

New Dallas-Fort Worth Airport, the world's largest, covers an area bigger than Manhattan Island and will handle peak loads well past the year 2000.

pending legislation that would give the CAB new authority to tell the nation's airlines, if it chose, which flights could be canceled because of fuel shortages.

As flights continued to be cut back, the airlines began laying off pilots and other personnel in December. By year-end, announced employment cuts totaled 14,400, or 9 per cent of the industry's work force.

TWA Strike. Trans World Airlines (TWA) cabin attendants ended a 45-day strike, longest in TWA history, on December 18 by ratifying a new contract that provides a 13.5 per cent pay increase, spread over three years. A 5.5 per cent increase was retroactive to Aug. 1, 1972, when the old contract expired. Wages and working conditions were the major issues, but union officials also challenged the airline mutual-aid pact, under which excess revenues earned by other airlines during the strike were paid to TWA.

Airports. The Dallas-Fort Worth Regional Airport, the largest and most expensive airport ever built, was dedicated on September 22. The $700-million airport is larger than Manhattan Island. It covers more than 27 square miles and is twice the size of any other airport. The airport features four large, half-loop terminals separated by a freeway, with access roads to allow passengers to park close to aircraft. It also has its own 13-mile transit system.

New Equipment. United States airlines spent about $1.8 billion in 1973 for new air and ground equipment. They had spent $1.5 billion for equipment in 1972. At the same time, a number of older jet aircraft were retired. About $1.6 billion of the 1973 total went for new aircraft, primarily wide-bodied jets.

Supersonic Transport (SST). It was a year of disappointment for makers of the British-French *Concorde* and Russia's TU-144. Pan American World Airways, TWA, Sabena, and El Al canceled their options to buy a total of 22 *Concordes* in February. These cancellations brought the total number of cancellations in 18 months to 32, leaving only 9 firm orders – 5 from British Overseas Airways Corporation and 4 from Air France.

A Russian TU-144 supersonic jetliner production model exploded and crashed on June 3 during an international air show at Le Bourget Airport near Paris. Six crewmen and seven area residents were killed.

Aviation experts speculated that the crash would delay the introduction of the TU-144 beyond the scheduled date of 1975 and would allow British and French authorities to delay their own 1975 deadline for the *Concorde*'s introduction. The delay would enable them to increase passenger capacity to more commercially attractive levels if they chose. Meanwhile, it was announced on June 22 that the total development costs of the *Concorde* had reached $2.7-billion.

AVIATION

Skyjackings. Five Arab terrorists attacked a Pan American World Airways jetliner at Rome's international airport on December 17 and set it afire with hand grenades. They killed 31 persons in the attack, then hijacked a West German jetliner and forced the pilot to fly them to Athens, Greece. They killed a hostage there, then flew on to Damascus, Syria. They surrendered in Kuwait and freed 12 hostages. The terrorists had unsuccessfully demanded the release of two Palestinian terrorists held in Greece.

Until that bloody attack, no U.S. airliner had been victimized in 1973. This dramatic change from recent years was the result of intensified efforts implemented during the year to eliminate hijackings.

Between 1931 and 1972, there had been 160 skyjackings in the United States. However, between 1968 and 1972, there were 147 attempts; 85 were successful—all to Cuba. The last successful skyjacking in the United States occurred on Nov. 10, 1972.

Three important steps were taken in 1973 to reduce skyjackings. Electronic inspection of all carry-on luggage and passengers started on January 5, armed security guards were posted at the nation's 531 commercial airports beginning on February 16, and the United States, Canada, and Cuba signed agreements in which they said they would not offer a haven to hijackers.   Kenneth E. Schaefle

See also Section Five, AIRPORT.

Crash of Russia's supersonic airplane, the TU-144, at the Paris Air Show in June may delay its passenger-service debut beyond 1975.

AWARDS AND PRIZES presented in 1973 included the following:

Arts Awards

American Institute of Architects. *Allied Professions Medal,* Hideo Sasaki, Watertown, Mass., for his work in landscape architecture and urban design. *Architecture Critics' Medal,* the late Robin Boyd, architect and author, Melbourne, Australia. *Fine Arts Medal,* Harry Bertoia, Italian-born sculptor, Bally, Pa. *Twenty-Five Year Award,* Taliesin West, built as a desert camp near Phoenix, Ariz., by Frank Lloyd Wright and his associates and students.

Capezio Dance Award. Isadora Bennett, former press representative, Joffrey Ballet.

National Academy of Design. *Benjamin Altman Prize for Figure Painting,* Isabel Bishop, New York City, for *Campus Students;* **Landscape Painting,** Ethel Magafan, Woodstock, N.Y., for *Meadows.*

National Academy of Recording Arts and Sciences. *Grammy Awards: Record of the Year,* "The First Time Ever I Saw Your Face" by Roberta Flack. *Song of the Year,* "The First Time Ever I Saw Your Face," written by Ewan MacColl. *Album of the Year, Pop,* "The Concert for Bangladesh" performed by George Harrison and many of his friends, including Ringo Starr. *Classical,* Mahler's *Symphony No. 8* with Georg Solti conducting the Chicago Symphony Orchestra. *Best Classical Performance, Orchestra,* Mahler's *Symphony No. 7* with Georg Solti conducting the Chicago Symphony Orchestra; *Soloist with Orchestra,* Arthur Rubinstein for Brahm's *Concerto No. 2* (with Eugene Ormandy conducting the Philadelphia Orchestra); *Soloist Without Orchestra,* Vladimir Horowitz for "Horowitz Plays Chopin." *Best Contemporary Vocal Performance, Female,* Helen Reddy for "I Am Woman"; *Male,* Harry Nilsson for "Without You"; *Duo,* Roberta Flack and Donny Hathaway for "Where Is the Love?" *Best Country Vocal Performance, Female,* Donna Fargo for "Happiest Girl in the Whole U.S.A."; *Male,* Charley Pride for "Charley Pride Sings Heart Songs." *Best Opera Recording,* Berlioz's *Benvenuto Cellini* with Colin Davis conducting the B.B.C. Orchestra. *Best Jazz Performance, Big Band,* Duke Ellington for "Togo Brava Suite"; *Group,* Freddie Hubbard for "First Light"; *Solo,* Gary Burton for "Alone at Last." *Best New Artists,* America.

National Academy of Television Arts and Sciences. *Emmy Awards: Best Actor and Actress in a Single Dramatic Performance,* Laurence Olivier in "Long Day's Journey into Night" and Cloris Leachman in "A Brand New Life." *Best Supporting Actor and Actress,* Scott Jacoby in "That Certain Summer" and Ellen Corby in "The Waltons." *Best Actor and Actress in a Dramatic Series,* Richard Thomas and Michael Learned in "The Waltons." *Best Actor and Actress in a Comedy Series,* Jack Klugman in "The Odd Couple" and Mary Tyler Moore in "The Mary Tyler Moore Show." *Best Supporting Actor and Actress in a Comedy Series,* Ted Knight and Valerie Harper in "The Mary Tyler Moore Show." *Best Producer, Director, and Choreographer of a Single Dramatic Program,* Bob Fosse, three Emmys, for "Singer Presents Liza with a Z." *Outstanding Single Program, Best Comedy Series,* "All in the Family." *Best Drama Series,* "The Waltons." *Best Single Drama,* "A War of Children." *Best Variety Show—Music,* "Singer Presents Liza with a Z." *Best Variety and Musical Series,* "The Julie Andrews Hour."

National Institute of Arts and Letters and American Academy of Arts and Letters. *Award of Merit Medal for Sculpture,* Reuben Nakian. *Arnold W. Brunner Memorial Prize in Architecture,* Robert Venturi. *Gold Medal, Architecture,* Louis J. Kahn; *Poetry,* John Crowe Ransom. *National Institute Awards. Art,* Rudolf Baranik, Leon Golub, and Philip Pearlstein, painters; Robert Grosvenor, Raoul Hague, Michio Ihara, and Clement Meadmore, sculptors. *Literature,* the late Marius Bewley, critic; Maeve Brennan, story writer; Irving Feldman, poet; Frances FitzGerald, journalist; Dorothy Hughes, poet; Philip Levine, poet; Daniel P. Mannix, novelist; Cynthia Ozick, novelist; Jonathan Schell, journalist; and Austin Warren, biographer. *Music,* John Heiss, Betsy Jolas, Barbara Kolb, and Curry Tison Street, composers. *Richard and Hinda Rosenthal Foundation Award for the Novel,* Thomas Rogers; *Painting,* Jim Sullivan.

Journalism Awards

American Newspaper Guild. *Heywood Broun Award,* Carl Bernstein and Bob Woodward, reporters, the *Washington Post,* for their series exposing the wide scope of political espionage involved in the bugging of Democratic National Headquarters at the Watergate complex during the 1972 election campaign.

Long Island University. *George Polk Memorial Awards: Book,* Stanford J. Ungar for *The Paper & The Papers,* an account of the struggle between newspapers and the U.S. federal government over the Pentagon Papers. *Foreign Reporting,* Jean Thoraval and Jean LeClerc du Sablon, Agence France-Presse, for articles on life in Hanoi, North Vietnam. *Magazine Reporting,* Frances FitzGerald, free-lance journalist, for "Annals of War: Vietnam," in *The New Yorker. Metropolitan Reporting,* Martin McLaughlin, Joseph Martin, and James Ryan, the *New York News,* for disclosures on the padding of city payrolls. *National Reporting,* Carl Bernstein and Bob Woodward, the *Washington Post,* for bringing the Watergate bugging story to public attention. *News Photography,* Huynh Cong (Nick) Ut, Associated Press, for a photo of a girl who had torn off her burning clothing after a napalm strike on Highway 1 in South Vietnam. *Television Reporting,* Jim McKay, American Broadcasting Company, for his report on the Arab terrorist kidnaping and murder of Israeli athletes at the Munich Olympic Games. *Special Award* for outstanding journalistic achievement, Lesley Oelsner, *The New York Times,* for a series of articles on New York State's criminal justice system.

National Cartoonists Society. *Reuben,* Pat Oliphant, editorial cartoonist, *Denver Post.*

Sigma Delta Chi, Professional Journalistic Society. *Newspaper Awards: General Reporting,* William F. Reed, Jr., and James M. Bolus, the *Louisville Courier-Journal,* for their investigation of the thoroughbred racing industry. *Editorial Writing,* John R. Harrison, president of *The Ledger,* Lakeland, Fla., for a 10-part series calling for competitive bidding and removal of patronage from engineering services funded by the state. *Foreign Correspondence,* Charlotte Saikowski, the *Christian Science Monitor,* for her "highly imaginative and insightful series of 'letters to President Nixon' on the eve of his Moscow trip." *Washington Correspondence,* Carl Bernstein and Bob Woodward, the *Washington Post,* for reporting on events connected with the bugging of the Democratic National Headquarters at the Watergate complex. *News Photography,* Huynh Cong (Nick) Ut, Associated Press, Saigon staff, for his photo of a naked Vietnamese girl fleeing the war. *Editorial Cartooning,* William H. (Bill) Mauldin, the *Chicago Sun-Times,* for cartoon entitled "U.S. Press," showing reporter in handcuffs reaching through the bars of a cell to type his article. *Public Service,* Sun Newspapers, Omaha, Nebr., for six-month investigation of Father Flanagan's Boys Town. *Magazine Awards: Reporting,* Thomas Thompson, *Life* magazine, for article about a father who killed his son because of

drug abuse. *Public Service, Philadelphia* magazine, for article by Mike Mallowe about unsanitary conditions in public restaurants. *Radio Awards: Reporting,* Val Hymes, WTOP Radio, Washington, D.C., for her coverage of the shooting of Governor George C. Wallace of Alabama. *Public Service,* WGAR Radio, Cleveland, for a six-week campaign to solve the problem of transportation for mentally retarded children. *Editorializing,* Frank Reynolds, American Broadcasting Company News, for his comments on the Christmas, 1972, bombing of North Vietnam. *Television Awards: Reporting,* Laurens Pierce, Columbia Broadcasting System (CBS) News, Atlanta, Ga., for his filming of the shooting of Governor Wallace. *Public Service,* WABC-TV, New York City, for "Willowbrook: The Last Great Disgrace," a program on the mentally retarded. *Editorializing,* WCKT-TV, Miami, for a series on fraudulent auto repairs. *Research in Journalism,* William J. Small, vice-president of CBS News, Washington, D.C., for his book, *Political Power and the Press. Distinguished Teaching in Journalism,* DeWitt C. Reddick, University of Texas.

Literature Awards

Academy of American Poets. *1973 Fellowship,* W. S. Merwin, American poet and translator, for "distinguished poetic achievement." *Lamont Poetry Selection Award,* Marilyn Hacker, former editor of *City,* a poetry magazine, and *Quark,* a fiction quarterly, for *Presentation Piece,* her first book of poems.

American Library Association. *Beta Phi Mu Award,* Lester Asheim, University of Chicago, for distinguished service to education for librarianship. *Caldecott Medal,* Blair Lent, illustrator of *The Funny Little Woman,* for the most distinguished picture book of 1972. *Francis Joseph Campbell Citation,* Marjorie Hooper of Louisville, Ky., for outstanding contributions to the advancement of library services for the blind. *Melvil Dewey Medal,* Virginia Lacy Jones of Atlanta, Ga., for creative professional achievement. *Joseph W. Lippincott Award,* Jesse Shera of Cleveland, for distinguished service in librarianship. *Newbery Medal,* Jean Craighead George for *Julie of the Wolves,* the most distinguished contribution to children's literature.

Columbia University. *Bancroft Prizes,* Frances Fitz-Gerald, free-lance journalist, for *Fire in the Lake: The Vietnamese and the Americans in Vietnam;* John L. Gaddis, associate professor of history, Ohio University, for *The U.S. and the Origins of the Cold War;* and Louis R. Harlan, professor of history and editor of the papers of Booker T. Washington, University of Maryland, for *Booker T. Washington.*

National Book Committee. *National Book Awards: Arts and Letters,* Arthur M. Wilson, retired Dartmouth professor, for *Diderot. Biography,* James Thomas Flexner, writer on historical subjects, for *George Washington: Anguish and Farewell (1793-1799). Children's Literature,* Ursula Le Guin, for *The Farthest Shore. Contemporary Affairs,* Frances FitzGerald, free-lance journalist, for *Fire in the Lake. Fiction,* John Barth, professor of English, State University of New York, Buffalo, for *Chimera;* and John Williams, professor of English, University of Denver, for *Augustus. History,* Robert M. Myers, who teaches English at the University of Maryland, for *The Children of Pride;* and Isaiah Trunk, research associate, YIVO Institute for Jewish Research, New York City, for *Judenrat. Philosophy and Religion,* Sidney E. Ahlstrom, for *A Religious History of the American People. Poetry,* A. R. Ammons, professor of English, Cornell University, for *Collected Poems: 1951-1971. Science,* George B. Schaller, associate of the Institute for Research in Animal Behavior of the New York Zoological Society and Rockefeller University, for

AWARDS AND PRIZES

The Serengeti Lion. Translation, Allen Mandelbaum, professor of English, City University of New York, for *The Aeneid of Virgil. National Medal for Literature,* Vladimir Nabokov, "for the excellence of his total contribution to the world of letters."

Poetry Society of America. *Alice Fay di Castagnola Award,* Mary Oliver and George Keithley, for works in progress. *Shelley Memorial Award,* Richard Wilbur, for excellence in his published work.

Yale University. *Bollingen Prize in Poetry,* James Merrill, Stonington, Conn., for "his wit and delight in language, his exceptional craft . . . and his sustained vitality shown in five volumes over the past half-dozen years."

Nobel Prizes. See NOBEL PRIZES.

Public Service Awards

Albert and Mary Lasker Foundation. *Public Service Award,* Senator Warren G. Magnuson (D., Wash.).

American Institute of Public Service Awards for distinguished public service, to Cesar Chavez, migratory farmworkers organizer, for his continuing "struggle for a full role for Mexican Americans in the society"; John W. Gardner, head of Common Cause, for the "zeal and imagination he brought to the creation of an effective national citizens' lobby"; Henry A. Kissinger, President Richard M. Nixon's assistant for national security affairs, for his "ranging and diligent pursuit of peace"; and Joseph A. Yablonski, son of the slain United Mine Workers leader and general counsel of the union, for his "courage in pursuing the goals of progressive union leadership."

Freedoms Foundation. *George Washington Award,* Donald Hurrebrink, Warren, Ohio, bandleader,

National Association for the Advancement of Colored People. *Spingarn Medal,* Wilson C. Riles, superintendent of public education, California.

Planned Parenthood—World Population Center. *Margaret Sanger Award,* Christopher Tietze, associate director of the Biomedical Division, Population Council, New York City, and Sarah Lewitt, research associate, Population Council.

Rockefeller Public Service Awards for "distinguished service to the government of the United States and the American people." *Administration,* Phillip S. Hughes, director, Office of Federal Elections, U.S. General Accounting Office. *Human Resource Development and Protection,* Martin Marc Cummings, director, National Library of Medicine, National Institutes of Health, Department of Health, Education, and Welfare. *Intergovernmental Operations,* David D. Newsom, assistant secretary of state for African affairs, U.S. Department of State. *Physical Source Development and Protection,* Vincent Ellis McKelvey, director, U.S. Geological Survey, Department of the Interior. *Professional Accomplishment and Leadership,* Ruth Margaret Davis, director, Institute for Computer Sciences and Technology, National Bureau of Standards, U.S. Department of Commerce.

United Nations Educational, Scientific, and Cultural Organization. *Kalinga Prize for the Popularization of Science,* Philip H. Abelson, editor of *Science* magazine and president of the Carnegie Institution of Washington; and Nigel Calder, British science writer and editor.

Pulitzer Prizes. See PULITZER PRIZES.

Science and Technology Awards

American Chemical Society. *Priestley Medal,* to Paul John Flory, J. G. Jackson-C. J. Wood Professor in Chemistry, Stanford University.

American Institute of Physics. *Dannie Heineman Prize for Mathematical Physics,* Kenneth G. Wilson, Cornell University.

American Physical Society. *Bonner Prize in Nuclear Physics,* Herman Feshbach, professor of physics and director of the Center for Theoretical Physics, Massachusetts Institute of Technology. *Buckley Solid State Physics Prize,* Gen Shirane, a senior physicist at Brookhaven National Laboratory, New York City. *Irving Langmuir Prize,* Peter M. Rentzepis, Bell Telephone Laboratories. *High Polymer Physics Prize,* H. Douglas Keith and Frank J. Padden, Jr., Bell Telephone Laboratories. *Ernest O. Lawrence Memorial Awards,* Louis Baker, Jr., a chemical engineer at Argonne National Laboratory, Chicago; Seymour Sack and Thomas E. Wainwright, physicists, Lawrence Livermore Laboratory, in California; James R. Weir, Jr., assistant section chief of the metals and ceramics division, Oak Ridge.(Tenn.) National Laboratory; and Sheldon Wolff, professor of cytogenetics, University of California, San Francisco.

Margaret Chase Smith and Mamie Eisenhower (far left) and Lenore Hershey (center, back row) presented *Ladies' Home Journal* Women of the Year awards to (left to right) Helen Hayes, Katharine Graham, Virginia Apgar, Shirley Chisholm, Nikki Giovanni, LaDonna Harris, Mary Lasker, and Ellen Straus.

Columbia University. *Louisa Gross Horwitz Prize,* for outstanding contributions to tissue culture research, to Renato Dulbecco, assistant director of research, Imperial Cancer Research Fund Laboratories, London; Harry Eagle, professor, Albert Einstein College of Medicine, New York City; and Theodore Puck, professor of biophysics and genetics, University of Colorado, Denver. *Vetlesen Prize,* for achievement in the earth sciences, to William A. Fowler, Institute Professor of Physics, California Institute of Technology.

Franklin Institute. *Franklin Medal,* Theodosius Grigorevich Dobzhansky, adjunct professor of genetics, University of California, Davis.

Geological Society of America. *Penrose Medal,* M. King Hubbert, research geophysicist, United States Geological Survey, and professor emeritus of geology and geophysics, Stanford University. *Arthur L. Day Medal,* David T. Griggs, professor of geophysics, University of California at Los Angeles.

International Academy of Astronautics. *Daniel and Florence Guggenheim International Astronautics Award,* Maxine A. Faget, director of engineering and development, Johnson Space Center.

Albert and Mary Lasker Foundation Awards. *Albert Lasker Award for Clinical Medical Research,* William B. Kouwenhoven, professor emeritus of engineering and lecturer in surgery, Johns Hopkins University; and Paul M. Zoll, a clinical professor of medicine, Harvard Medical School, for advances in correcting abnormal heart rhythms.

National Academy of Engineering. *Founders Medal,* Warren K. Lewis, professor emeritus and lecturer at Massachusetts Institute of Technology.

National Academy of Sciences (NAS). *Comstock Prize,* Robert H. Dicke, Cyrus Fogg Brackett Professor of Physics, Princeton University, for his development and use of high precision instruments, including tests of the general theory of relativity and the "big bang" theory of the origin of the universe. *J. Lawrence Smith Medal,* Clair C. Patterson, geochemist, California Institute of Technology, for his investigations of meteoric bodies. *NAS Award in Aeronautical Engineering,* Donald W. Douglas, Sr., founder of the Douglas Aircraft Company and honorary chairman of the board of directors, McDonnell Douglas Corporation, for his contributions to aviation. *NAS Award for Environmental Quality,* W. Thomas Edmondson, professor of zoology, University of Washington, for his studies of the pollution of Lake Washington near Seattle. *U.S. Steel Foundation Award in Molecular Biology,* Donald D. Brown, embryologist, Carnegie Institution of Washington, for his investigations into the structure, regulation, and evolution of genes in animals. *Benjamin Apthorp Gould Prize,* Kenneth I. Kellermann, radio astronomer, National Radio Astronomy Observatory, Charlottesville, Va., for his contributions to planetary radio astronomy and long baseline interferometry. *Mary Clark Thompson Gold Medal,* Hollis D. Hedberg, professor emeritus of geology, Princeton University, for his services to geology. *NAS Award in Applied Mathematics and Numerical Analysis,* Samuel Karlin, professor of mathematics, Stanford University and the Weizmann Institute of Science, Rehovot, Israel, for contributions to the theory of inventory, including mathematical methods for making optimum use of natural resources. *Jessie Stevenson Kovalenko Gold Medal,* Seymour S. Kety, director of Psychiatric Research Laboratories at Massachusetts General Hospital, Boston, and professor of psychiatry, Harvard Medical School, for research on the balance between biological and psychosocial factors affecting schizophrenia.

National Medal of Science, the U.S. government's highest award for distinguished achievement in science, mathematics, and engineering, to Daniel I. Arnon, professor and chairman, Department of Cell Physiology, University of California, Berkeley; Carl Djerassi, professor of chemistry, Stanford University; Harold E. Edgerton, professor emeritus of electrical engineering, Massachusetts Institute of Technology; William M. Ewing, chief, earth and planetary sciences division, Marine Biomedical Institute, University of Texas; Arie Jan Haagen-Smit, professor of biochemistry, California Institute of Technology; Vladimir Haensel, vice-president for science and technology, Universal Oil Products Company, Des Plaines, Ill.; Frederick Seitz, president, Rockefeller University; Earl W. Sutherland, Jr., professor of biochemistry, University of Miami; John W. Tukey, associate executive director, Research-Communications Principles Division, Bell Laboratories, and professor of statistics, Princeton University; Richard T. Whitcomb, aeronautical engineer, National Aeronautics and Space Administration, Langley Research Center, Hampton, Va.; and Robert R. Wilson, director, National Accelerator Laboratory, Batavia, Ill.

Theater and Motion Picture Awards

Academy of Motion Picture Arts and Sciences. *"Oscar" Awards: Best Picture,* The Godfather, Paramount Pictures. *Best Actor,* Marlon Brando in *The Godfather* (award refused by Brando). *Best Supporting Actor,* Joel Grey in *Cabaret. Best Actress,* Liza Minnelli in *Cabaret. Best Supporting Actress,* Eileen Heckart in *Butterflies Are Free. Best Director,* Bob Fosse for *Cabaret. Best Foreign Language Film,* The Discreet Charm of the Bourgeoisie, directed by Luis Buñuel. *Best Story* (based on original material), Jeremy Larner for *The Candidate. Best Documentary, Marjoe,* produced by Howard Smith and Sarah Kernochan. *Best Song,* "The Morning After," from *Poseidon Adventure.*

Antoinette Perry (Tony) Awards. *Drama: Best Play, That Championship Season* by Jason Miller. *Best Actor,* Alan Bates in *Butley. Best Actress,* Julie Harris in *The Last of Mrs. Lincoln. Best Director,* A. J. Antoon for *That Championship Season. Musical: Best Musical, A Little Night Music. Best Actor,* Ben Vereen in *Pippin. Best Actress,* Glynis Johns in *A Little Night Music. Best Director,* Bob Fosse for *Pippin. Best Choreographer,* Bob Fosse for *Pippin. Composer of the Best Music,* Stephen Sondheim for *A Little Night Music. Writer of the Best Lyrics,* Stephen Sondheim for *A Little Night Music.*

Cannes International Film Festival. *Grand Prix International, Scarecrow,* United States; and *The Hireling,* Great Britain. *Best Actor,* Giancarlo Giannini, *Film of Love and Anarchy. Best Actress,* Joanne Woodward, *The Effects of Gamma Rays on Man-in-the-Moon Marigolds. Outstanding Performances,* Gene Hackman and Al Pacino, *Scarecrow;* and Sarah Miles, *The Hireling.*

New York Drama Critics' Circle Awards. *Best Play of 1972–1973, The Changing Room,* written by David Storey. *Best American Play, The Hot L Baltimore,* written by Lanford Wilson. *Best Musical, A Little Night Music,* with book by Hugh Wheeler and music and lyrics by Stephen Sondheim.

New York Film Critics Awards: *Best Actor,* Laurence Olivier in *Sleuth; Actress,* Liv Ullmann in *Cries and Whispers. Best Supporting Actor,* Robert Duvall in *The Godfather; Actress,* Jeannie Berlin in *The Heartbreak Kid. Best Film,* Cries and Whispers. *Best Director,* Ingmar Bergman for *Cries and Whispers. Best Screenwriting,* Ingmar Bergman for *Cries and Whispers. Best Documentary,* The Sorrow and the Pity. Lillian Zahrt

See also Brando, Marlon; Canadian Literature; Chemistry; Fosse, Bob; Literature for Children; Minnelli, Liza.

BAHAMAS. On July 10, 1973, at 12:01 A.M., the Bahamas became an independent nation. Representatives of 52 countries attended independence ceremonies in Clifford Park in Nassau. At a second ceremony, Great Britain's Prince Charles, representing Queen Elizabeth II, presented to Bahamian Prime Minister Lynden O. Pindling constitutional documents symbolizing the end of 300 years of British colonial rule. The new nation was admitted to membership in the United Nations on September 18.

Prime Minister Pindling, in discussing the new nation's future plans, indicated that he expected tourism to remain the Bahamas' largest single source of foreign exchange. About 1.5 million tourists poured $285 million into the Bahamian economy in 1972, and the total for 1973 was expected to exceed that figure. The government also planned to encourage more banking organizations to establish offices in the Bahamas, a traditional tax haven.

Earlier in the year, the Pindling government signed an agreement with the United States to develop a $10-million livestock-production program on Andros Island. United States specialists would provide technical training in economics, animal husbandry, and soil science. The government also indicated it would try to diversify its economy by expanding the fishing industry.   Paul C. Tullier

See also LATIN AMERICA (Facts in Brief Table).

BAHRAIN took a major step toward democratic government when Amir Isa bin Salman Al Khalifa proclaimed the first national Constitution on June 2, 1973. The 108-article Constitution was prepared in six months by a Constituent Assembly. It guarantees equal rights for all Bahrainis, women's suffrage in future national elections, free and compulsory primary education, and free medical care.

The Constitution provides for a National Assembly of 30 elected members plus the royal Cabinet. Elections for the assembly were held December 7.

The economy continued to grow despite a 6.4 per cent decline in oil production. The budget of 32.5-million dinars ($80 million) showed a 16 per cent increase in expenditures. An atomized-aluminum powder plant with a 3,000-ton annual capacity opened May 1, as Bahrain sought to shift its economy away from total dependence on oil. In October, a low-sulfur fuel-oil plant opened in Awali.

Cooperation with other Persian Gulf states increased. In January, Bahrain and Qatar set up a joint shipping company. On June 19, an agreement with Kuwait established free transfers of capital and labor and eliminated customs barriers between the two states. Bahrain was one of the Arab states that either reduced or cut off oil supplies to countries that it deemed pro-Israel, as a result of the October Arab-Israeli war.   William Spencer

See also MIDDLE EAST (Facts in Brief Table).

BAKER, HOWARD HENRY, JR. (1925-   ), U.S. senator from Tennessee, served as vice-chairman of the Senate committee that conducted the Watergate investigation in 1973. The son of a Tennessee congressman and son-in-law of the late Senator Everett M. Dirksen of Illinois, he is one of the leading Republicans in Congress.

Baker seconded Richard M. Nixon's nomination to the presidency in 1968, and was mentioned as a possible 1972 vice-presidential candidate. In 1969, he challenged Senator Hugh D. Scott of Pennsylvania for the post of Senate minority leader. Although Baker lost, he gained stature in the defeat.

Baker was born in Huntsville, Tenn. His father, Howard H. Baker, served in the U.S. House of Representatives from 1951 until he died in 1964. His mother, Irene, then served the balance of his father's unexpired term.

Baker graduated from McCallie School in Chattanooga, Tenn., in 1943, and served as an officer in the U.S. Navy from 1943 to 1946. He studied at Tulane University and the University of the South, and received his law degree from the University of Tennessee Law College in 1949. He was elected to the U.S. Senate in 1966, and was re-elected in 1972.

He married Joy Dirksen in 1951. They have two children, Darek and Cynthia.   Foster Stockwell

See also WATERGATE.

BALLET. See DANCING.

Bahamas' Prime Minister Lynden O. Pindling beams proudly as Prince Charles of Great Britain proclaims independence for the former colony.

BALTIMORE. A federal grand jury, working with U.S. Attorney George Beall, exposed widespread political corruption in 1973. This investigation of corruption in Maryland politics led to the resignation of U.S. Vice-President Spiro T. Agnew in October and the indictment of Agnew's successor as chief executive of Baltimore County, N. Dale Anderson, in August. Agnew was allegedly involved in a kickback scheme, beginning when he was elected county executive in 1962. See AGNEW, SPIRO THEODORE.

On August 23, the grand jury indicted Anderson, a Democrat, on 39 counts of extortion, bribery, and conspiracy in connection with kickback payments he allegedly received from contractors doing business with the county. Anderson pleaded innocent. Anderson was also indicted by the grand jury on October 4 on charges of income tax evasion.

William E. Fornoff, a former Baltimore county official, was named as a co-conspirator but not as a defendant in the indictments. He had resigned in June after pleading guilty to a tax violation and charges related to a kickback scheme.

Political Favoritism. In September, Maryland Governor Marvin Mandel and Lieutenant Governor Blair Lee III were accused of political favoritism because of their efforts to secure a building permit for Alan I. Kay, a Washington, D.C., developer. The state secretary of health and mental hygiene had ordered a moratorium on building along a Baltimore watershed until better sewage-treatment facilities could be provided. Mandel and Lee allegedly intervened in an effort to secure a building permit for Kay after Kay contributed $2,500 to a testimonial dinner held in May for the two political leaders.

The U.S. Department of the Treasury reported in February that its Revenue Sharing Office would re-evaluate its distribution of funds to local governments because of complaints from several cities, including the Baltimore area. Revenue-sharing funds are allocated on the basis of a formula that includes the amount of local taxes collected. But local taxes for public education are not included in the computation. Local governments in the Baltimore area complained that the federal Revenue Sharing Office wrote off too much of their tax collections as education funding.

Cost of Living. Baltimore residents experienced a sharp increase of 6.5 per cent in their cost of living between June, 1972, and June, 1973. However, according to a U.S. Department of Labor report issued on June 15, Baltimore's cost of living ranked only 24th among the nation's 25 largest cities. An average family of four in Baltimore would require $11,327 a year to live in "moderate comfort."

Baltimore enjoyed an overall drop in its serious crime rate during the first quarter of 1973. The crime rate was down 14 per cent from the same period in 1972, according to figures compiled by the Federal Bureau of Investigation.   James M. Banovetz

BANGLADESH. At the Commonwealth of Nations meeting in Ottawa, Canada, in August, 1973, Prime Minister Sheik Mujibur Rahman showed a visitor a cable from home. It described a flood that had left a million people homeless.

"What can I do?" Mujibur asked. "In 1970, a cyclone killed half a million people. In 1971, the war cost us 3 million lives. In 1972, a drought. And now, floods."

This was not the only calamity in 1973. Once again, the young republic was short of food. A United Nations appeal on behalf of Bangladesh for 1.7 million tons of grain brought in pledges of less than half that amount.

Jute has always been the region's main money earner. But the yield in 1973 was 40 per cent below what it was before East Pakistan won its independence in December, 1971, and became Bangladesh. Industry as a whole was working at only 70 per cent of capacity.

Lawlessness was one of the by-products of the war and economic distress. In September, the government estimated nearly 5,000 persons had been murdered between January, 1972, and June, 1973. The government created a national militia in June.

Mujibur Rahman himself was the glue that held the state together. In the March election, his Awami (People's) League took 291 of the 300 seats in the Constituent Assembly to confirm his hold on power.

But his problems were harrowing. Prices on some essentials doubled during the year, in a country with an average per capita income of only $40 a year. The population also kept growing, by 3 per cent a year. And President Abu Sayeed Chowdhury resigned on December 24.

As 1973 began, 40,000 persons were being held as wartime collaborators. Most of them were set free during the year. Of the 700,000 or so Biharis, or non-Bengali Moslems, some 200,000 opted to go to Pakistan, which would accept only some of them. But the most sensitive issue was the proposed war crimes trial of 195 Pakistanis. Even though Pakistan had indicated it would recognize Bangladesh's independence, it vehemently opposed the trial.

Foreign Aid, which totaled $1.3 billion in Bangladesh's first 14 months, sustained the young state. The United States, which did its best in 1971 to prevent the birth of the republic, became its most generous friend by 1973. In the first 16 months, U.S. aid came to $318 million, with another $100 million expected before the year's end. India came close behind, with Russia a poor third.

Mujibur did not believe the picture was all dark. "We were told a year ago," he said, "that a few million would die of hunger. None did. Today, Bangladesh has a democratic Constitution. It is a free and independent country. Isn't that enough for the first two years?"   Mark Gayn

See also ASIA (Facts in Brief Table).

BANKS AND BANKING. Interest rates in the United States touched highs in 1973 unmatched since the Civil War. The prime rate that banks charge on loans to their best commercial customers rose from 6 per cent in January to an unprecedented 10 per cent in September, then backed and filled toward the end of the year. As Federal Reserve (Fed) open-market policy became more restrictive, the three-month treasury bill interest rate accelerated to a record 8.9 per cent in September before declining.

Savings Institutions. Savings and loan associations (SLA's), limited in the rates they could pay for savings capital, experienced a $3.3-million net outflow of funds in July, after midyear dividend credits. They lost another $1.1 billion in August, their third largest loss ever, as depositors transferred funds to such higher-paying investments as treasury bills. SLA's increased their borrowings from the Federal Home Loan Bank System by $2.4 billion in July and August, the largest two-month increase in history.

The situation was alleviated by an increase in the maximum interest rate on government-guaranteed mortgages from 7 to 7.75 per cent, and by substantial purchases of mortgages by the Federal National Mortgage Association. Mortgage rates on new homes rose to 8 per cent in August, but remained somewhat below their 1970 level. Housing starts, which began the year at a record 2,497,000 units, moved down much of the year. SLA's and other institutions were able to withstand these pressures on their assets in part because of large savings gains in 1972.

Commercial banks countered the tendency to withdraw funds by raising rates on large ($100,000 and up) certificates of deposit that were not subject to interest rate maximums. Effective July 1, banks were temporarily freed from interest restrictions on certificates of $1,000 or more with at least a four-year maturity. Maximum rates payable on savings were raised generally one-half percentage point at commercial banks and one-fourth percentage point at nonbank financial institutions. Ceilings were reinstated in October, with a maximum rate of 7.25 per cent at banks, and 7.5 per cent at SLA's. The passbook savings rate stood at 5 per cent at commercial banks and 5.25 per cent at SLA's and mutual savings banks at year-end.

Federal Reserve Policy in 1973 was aimed primarily at controlling credit conditions and thereby the expansion of credit and the money supply. In May and again in September, the Fed increased marginal reserve requirements on large certificates of deposit to a maximum of 11 per cent. The rate was cut by 3 percentage points in December. In July, the Fed required member banks to increase their reserves on demand deposits by one-half percentage point.

During the year, the Fed also steadily increased the discount rate, the interest rate that a commercial bank pays when it borrows from a Federal Reserve bank. Trailing behind market interest rates, the discount rate rose from 4.5 to 5 per cent in January, and then moved, mainly by half-point jumps, to a historic high of 7.5 per cent in August. Because treasury bill rates were much higher, the Fed had to ration credit to eager member-bank borrowers. Borrowings rose to over $2.5 billion at the end of August, a level unmatched since the post-World War I adjustment period. Most important, Fed open-market purchases pumped about $7 billion of new money into the economy during the first half of the year before the open-market policy was reversed.

Largest Bank Failure. James E. Smith, U.S. comptroller of the currency, declared the United States Bank of San Diego insolvent on October 18. It was the largest bank failure in U.S. history, but involved no loss to depositors. Crocker National Bank of San Francisco took over the liabilities and assets of the bank, except for $400 million in dubious loans made to companies controlled by C. Arnholt Smith, the defunct bank's principal stockholder.

Consumer Credit advanced briskly to $167 billion during the first half of 1973, a gain that was about equal to the 13 per cent growth in 1972. The delinquency rate on installment loans rose to more than 2 per cent, the highest level since during the 1953 recession.

Personal savings fell somewhat relative to income in 1973, partly because many taxpayers had with-

Up Goes the Prime Loan Rate

Predominant weekly rate

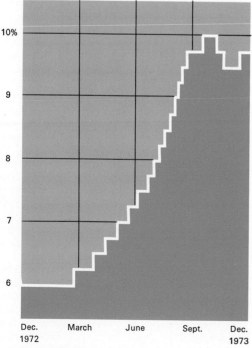

Source: Federal Reserve Board

held more than was necessary for 1972 taxes under new withholding schedules. Consequently, they enjoyed a surprise windfall when they filled out their tax forms after the first of the year and received refunds to spend.

Financial Reform. In August, President Richard M. Nixon proposed a major overhaul of the banking system. The proposal grew out of recommendations submitted in December, 1971, by his Commission on Financial Structure and Regulation. The most significant reforms would:

- Phase out interest ceilings on savings accounts.
- Allow SLA's to issue checking accounts.
- Broaden SLA lending powers to include consumer loans and corporate securities.
- Eliminate ceilings on mortgage rates.
- Remove tax advantages for SLA's, but substitute a new mortgage tax credit for banks and SLA's as an incentive for mortgage lending.

Washington observers expected it might take years to bring the controversial legislation to a final vote.

International Banking. International businesses and banks precipitated another run on the dollar in February, partly in response to preliminary reports of a large U.S. balance of payments deficit in the last quarter of 1972. Foreign central banks accumulated about 10 billion more dollars in February and March from banks and businesses trading dollars for foreign currencies. As a result, the dollar was devalued about 10 per cent. This, added to earlier devaluations that began Aug. 15, 1971, meant that the dollar had fallen about 20 per cent, on the average, relative to foreign currencies in a two-year period. When the latest currency convulsion was over, many experts thought the dollar had fallen so far that it was undervalued. By year-end, the dollar had begun to appreciate.

In the second quarter of 1973, the U.S. official balance of payments showed a surplus for the first time since 1969. In the third quarter of 1973, the official settlements balance of payments had a record $2.15-billion surplus. During the deficit years, official foreign holders had accumulated about $70 billion of short-term claims on the dollar. The U.S. balance of trade for the year was expected to shift to a surplus for the first time in a decade after posting an $873.3-million surplus in September, the largest monthly surplus since March, 1965.

H. Johannes Witteveen, former finance minister of the Netherlands, succeeded Pierre-Paul Schweitzer as managing director of the International Monetary Fund (IMF). Schweitzer retired on August 31. In September, the IMF met in Nairobi, Kenya, to negotiate a new international monetary system. However, little progress was made toward re-establishing an exchange rate parity system. The United States wanted more flexibility in whatever international monetary reserve was adopted. France, in particular, wanted a system that ended the dollar's role as a reserve currency.

Computers now perform banking functions that range from withdrawals to making loans in some 800 banks throughout the United States.

Gold and the Dollar. Effective November 14, the United States and six European countries ended a five-year pact that had barred them from selling gold on the free market. The agreement had created a two-tier gold market, with the free market price generally well above the official price at which government stocks of gold were valued. The free market price of gold rose as high as $125 a troy ounce in 1973. The official price was $38 an ounce until February, when it was raised to $42.22.

Arthur Burns, chairman of the U.S. Federal Reserve Board, announced the long-sought policy change on November 14. However, he said that Washington had not yet decided whether to sell any of the 275 million ounces of gold held by the U.S. government. The change was expected to eventually eliminate the two-tier gold market.

Other factors increased the attractiveness of private gold holdings. Commodities, including gold, became more desirable alternatives to monies whose values were eroded by inflation. Domestic inflation in the United States, though the highest in 20 years, was well below the inflation in most other countries. In addition, the dollar looked cheap to a lot of international investors and traders. Devaluation of the dollar over the preceding two years made U.S. goods and investments that much less expensive when compared with foreign alternatives.   William G. Dewald

BARBADOS. See WEST INDIES.

BASEBALL

BASEBALL. Normally, the victory of the Oakland A's in the World Series for the second straight year would have been the highlight of the baseball season. But in 1973, hardly a normal year, the A's shared attention with their free-wheeling owner, Charles O. Finley; the closest pennant race in history; the home-run hitting of Henry Aaron of the Atlanta Braves; the pitching of Nolan Ryan of the California Angels; and the American League's designated-hitter rule.

The A's were a solid team. They had good pitching, with three 20-game winners in Jim (Catfish) Hunter, Ken Holtzman, and Vida Blue. They had good hitting, notably by Reggie Jackson, who led the American League in home runs (32) and runs batted in (117) and became the American League's Most Valuable Player and World Series hero.

The A's won the American League's Western Division by six games for their third consecutive division title. They beat the Baltimore Orioles in five games for the American League pennant. Then they won the last two games of the World Series and beat the New York Mets, 4 games to 3.

The most memorable game of the series was the second. The Mets won it, 10-7, scoring four runs in the 12th inning after Mike Andrews, the A's substitute second baseman, made two errors. An angry Finley tried to put Andrews on the disabled list because of a sore shoulder, and he had Andrews sign a

This home run was Henry Aaron's last in 1973 and the 713th of his career. His first in 1974 will tie Babe Ruth's career record of 714.

statement agreeing to such a move. He hoped to replace Andrews with another player. The next day, Andrews said he had been pressured into signing.

Finley's Problems. Commissioner Bowie Kuhn refused to let Andrews be placed on the disabled list. He fined Finley $5,000 for coercing Andrews, $1,000 for ordering a public-address announcement before the first game in Oakland that the Mets had refused to let the A's activate another player, and $1,000 for ordering the lights turned on in Oakland during the second game when the A's were coming to bat. Lights can be turned on during a game only at the start of an inning. The commissioner also put Finley on probation. Finley defended his action in the Andrews case and said that he would sue Kuhn.

Dick Williams, the A's manager, apparently felt the same way about Finley's frequent advice. After the World Series, and with two years still left on a three-year contract, Williams quit. Finley at first said he would not stand in his way. Then, when it seemed Williams would become the New York Yankees manager, Finley demanded players in compensation. The Yankees signed Williams, but American League president Joe Cronin disapproved the Yankee contract, ruling that Williams was still Oakland property. The Yankees refused to meet Finley's demands and finally hired Bill Virdon as manager. Williams took a job in Florida, temporarily retiring from baseball. Ironically, Ralph Houk, who had resigned as Yankee manager, soon signed as pilot of the Detroit Tigers.

Miracle of the Mets. The miracle of the World Series was the presence of the Mets, whose .509 won-lost percentage was the lowest of any pennant winner in history. Slowed by injury after injury, the Mets were last in the National League's six-team Eastern Division on August 30. Then they won 20 of their last 28 games, and became division champions on October 1, the day after the regular season had been scheduled to end. They probably saved Manager Yogi Berra's job, too.

The Mets victory came in the closest race in major-league history. Five teams—New York, St. Louis, Pittsburgh, Montreal, and Chicago—were still in contention when the season entered its final week. And St. Louis and Pittsburgh still had a chance to tie for the division championship if the Mets lost both games of a scheduled double-header in Chicago on the last day of play. But the Mets won the first game.

The Cincinnati Reds, once 11 games behind the Los Angeles Dodgers, won the National League's Western Division title for the third time in four years. The Mets then beat the Reds in five games in the play-off.

In the third game of the play-offs, in New York, a fight between Pete Rose of the Reds and Bud Harrelson of the Mets erupted into a near free-for-all. When Rose went to left field, Met fans pelted him with flying objects. A whiskey bottle just missed Rose's head, and Reds manager Sparky Anderson ordered his

Final Standings in Major League Baseball

American League	W.	L.	Pct.	GB.
Eastern Division				
Baltimore	97	65	.599	
Boston	89	73	.549	8
Detroit	85	77	.525	12
New York	80	82	.494	17
Milwaukee	74	88	.457	23
Cleveland	71	91	.438	26
Western Division				
Oakland	94	68	.580	
Kansas City	88	74	.543	6
Minnesota	81	81	.500	13
California	79	83	.488	15
Chicago	77	85	.475	17
Texas	57	105	.352	37

Leading Batters

Batting Average—Rod Carew, Minnesota	.350
Home Runs—Reggie Jackson, Oakland	32
Runs Batted In—Reggie Jackson, Oakland	117
Hits—Rod Carew, Minnesota	203

Leading Pitchers

Games Won—Wilbur Wood, Chicago	24
Win Average—Jim Hunter, Oakland (21-5) (162 or more innings)	.808
Earned-Run Average—Jim Palmer, Baltimore (162 or more innings)	2.40
Strikeouts—Nolan Ryan, California	383

Awards

Most Valuable Player—Reggie Jackson, Oakland
Cy Young—Jim Palmer, Baltimore
Rookie of the Year—Al Bumbry, Baltimore
Manager of the Year—Earl Weaver, Baltimore

National League	W.	L.	Pct.	GB.
Eastern Division				
New York	82	79	.509	
St. Louis	81	81	.500	1½
Pittsburgh	80	82	.494	2½
Montreal	79	83	.488	3½
Chicago	77	84	.478	5
Philadelphia	71	91	.438	11½
Western Division				
Cincinnati	99	63	.611	
Los Angeles	95	66	.590	3½
San Francisco	88	74	.543	11
Houston	82	80	.506	17
Atlanta	76	85	.472	22½
San Diego	60	102	.370	39

Leading Batters

Batting Average—Pete Rose, Cincinnati	.338
Home Runs—Willie Stargell, Pittsburgh	44
Runs Batted In—Willie Stargell, Pittsburgh	119
Hits—Pete Rose, Cincinnati	230

Leading Pitchers

Games Won—Ron Bryant, San Francisco	24
Win Average—Ron Bryant, San Francisco (24-12) (162 or more innings)	.667
Earned-Run Average—Tom Seaver, New York (162 or more innings)	2.08
Strikeouts—Tom Seaver, New York	251

Awards

Most Valuable Player—Pete Rose, Cincinnati
Cy Young—Tom Seaver, New York
Rookie of the Year—Gary Matthews, San Francisco
Manager of the Year—Gene Mauch, Montreal

team off the field and into the dugout. The umpires warned the Mets that the game could be forfeited unless order was restored, and Berra and four players walked to left field and quieted the fans.

As the final game ended, thousands of youngsters swarmed onto the field, clawed chunks of fence and sod, dug craters in the infield, and tore away sections of the outfield fence. Women and children in ground-level boxes were evacuated through the dugouts. Cincinnati players grabbed bats to protect Rose.

Hammerin' Hank. Perhaps the most hallowed record in baseball is Babe Ruth's lifetime total of 714 home runs. Aaron—39, playing his 20th year in the National League and earning $200,000 a season—ended the season with 713 home runs. He hit 40 for the year, the 40th coming in the next-to-last game.

Ruth was a folk hero of old, and he was white. Aaron, in the minds of some older people, was an interloper, and he is black. Critics downgraded Aaron because he had 3,000 more at-bats than did Ruth. Aaron received much hate mail, including death threats. But he remained quiet and soft-spoken, his dignity unshaken.

The Pitchers. When the Mets won the World Series in 1969, two of their pitchers were Tom Seaver and Nolan Ryan. Seaver was their best pitcher in 1973, with a 19-10 won-lost record, a league-leading earned-run average of 2.08, and 251 strikeouts in 290 innings. Ryan, who never attained stardom with the

Mets, had been traded to the California Angels, and his 1973 record was astounding.

His 383 strikeouts (in 326 innings) broke by 1 the modern major-league record set by Sandy Koufax in 1965. His won-lost record was 21-16. He pitched no-hit, no-run games against Kansas City and Detroit and two one-hitters. His earned-run average was 2.87. Alas, his salary was a reported $45,000 (Seaver earned $140,000).

Ryan was one of 12 American League pitchers who won 20 or more games. The only National League 20-game winner was Ron Bryant of the San Francisco Giants, whose 24 victories tied him with Wilbur Wood of the Chicago White Sox as the top winners in the major leagues. There were five no-hit games during the season—two by Ryan and one each by Steve Busby of the Kansas City Royals, Jim Bibby of the Texas Rangers, and Phil Niekro of the Braves. Mike Marshall of the Montreal Expos set a major-league record by relieving in 92 games.

Designated Hitters. The American League, trying to enliven the offense, started a three-year experiment with a designated-hitter rule in 1973. The National League declined to use the rule. The rule allowed a designated player to bat for the pitcher throughout the game, and the pitcher could stay in the game. It prolonged the careers of such veteran players as Tony Oliva and Tommy Davis, who could still hit but were physically unable to play in

221

the field every day. The designated hitter helped the American League raise its batting average and score more runs. It also helped the American League set a league attendance record of more than 13.4 million and the major leagues set a record of more than 30.1 million. After the season, the league made the rule permanent.

The Managers. The season started with four new managers – Danny Ozark at Philadelphia, Whitey Herzog at Texas, Jack McKeon at Kansas City, and Bobby Winkles at California. In a six-day span in September, Detroit fired Billy Martin, Texas fired Herzog, and Texas signed Martin. Pittsburgh fired Bill Virdon in September and named Danny Murtaugh to replace him. After the season, Preston Gomez replaced Leo Durocher at Houston, Darrell Johnson succeeded Eddie Kasko at Boston, and Don Zimmer was fired at San Diego, which owner C. Arnholt Smith tried unsuccessfully to sell to Washington, D.C., and Los Angeles groups. See SPORTS.

Hall of Fame. Six men were elected to the Hall of Fame – pitcher Warren Spahn in the regular voting, outfielder Roberto Clemente on a special ballot, outfielder Monte Irvin by the Negro Leagues committee, and first baseman George (Highpockets) Kelly, pitcher Mickey Welch, and umpire Billy Evans by the veterans committee. The five-year waiting period was waived for Clemente, who died in a plane crash the previous New Year's Eve at the age of 38. Frank Litsky

Coach John Wooden smiles happily after his UCLA Bruins beat Notre Dame 82-63 in January for their 61st straight win, an NCAA record.

BASKETBALL. The University of California, Los Angeles (UCLA), dominated college basketball in the 1972-1973 season, just as it had done for a decade. The New York Knickerbockers and Indiana Pacers won professional championships. And all-star teams of college players helped regain international prestige for the United States by beating Russia's national team.

For the seventh straight year and the ninth time in 10 years, UCLA won the National Collegiate Athletic Association (NCAA) championship tourney in March. UCLA finished the regular season unbeaten in 26 games. North Carolina State, 27-0, was the only other major team with a perfect record. UCLA then won four straight games in the NCAA championships, including an 87-66 victory over Memphis State in the final on March 26 in St. Louis. In that game, Bill Walton, the UCLA center, sank 21 of 22 shots from the floor and scored 44 points, a record for a championship game.

UCLA String at 75. The Bruins finished the season with a winning streak of 75 games, going back to the 1970-1971 season. In midseason, UCLA had broken the record winning streak of 60 games set in 1956 by the University of San Francisco. More impressive, because the opposition was so strong, was its streak of 36 victories in NCAA tournaments.

The 6-foot 11-inch Walton was Player of the Year for the second straight year. He was an excellent scorer, rebounder, and blocker of enemy shots, and triggered UCLA's fast break.

Walton was a unanimous all-America choice. Others named to many teams were David Thompson of North Carolina State, Ernie DiGregorio of Providence, Ed Ratleff of Long Beach (Calif.) State, Doug Collins of Illinois State, Jim Brewer of Minnesota, and Dwight Lamar of Southwestern Louisiana.

International Revenge. Russia sent a national team to the United States in April to play an all-star team of collegians. The Americans, coached by Bob Cousy and sparked by DiGregorio, won four of the six games. Every game was marred by deliberate fouling, a practice encouraged by international rules.

Another team of college all-stars went to Moscow for the World University Games. This team, led by Thompson, defeated the Russians, 75-67, in the final on August 24, a happy victory because the Soviet team included some of the players who beat the United States in the controversial 1972 Olympic Games final.

The Professionals. The New York Knickerbockers finished second in the Atlantic Division, then won their second National Basketball Association (NBA) title in four years. The Boston Celtics led the Atlantic Division with a 68-14 won-lost record, best in the 17-team league. The Baltimore Bullets, Milwaukee Bucks, and Los Angeles Lakers won the other division championships. In the play-offs, the

Knickerbockers swept through Baltimore (4 games to 1), Boston (4-3), and Los Angeles (4-1), a tribute to the team play and defense taught by coach William (Red) Holzman.

As Dave DeBusschere, one of the Knickerbocker stars, explained it: "There is more to the game of basketball than coaching or manipulating players, and this man has it. It's difficult to describe except to say that he blends his coaching with every ingredient of life itself."

The Philadelphia 76ers found little success. In January and February, they lost 20 consecutive games, a pro record. Coach Roy Rubin, a newcomer to the pros, was fired after the ninth loss of that streak.

Dave Cowens, Boston's tireless center, was named Player of the Year. Nate Archibald of the Kansas City-Omaha Royals led the league in scoring (34 points per game) and assists (11.4 per game). In the American Basketball Association (ABA), Billy Cunningham of the Carolina Cougars was the Most Valuable Player and Julius Erving of the Virginia Squires the scoring leader (31.9 points per game).

The Carolina Cougars and Utah Stars won the ABA's division titles, but were eliminated before the play-off finals. The Indiana Pacers became champions by defeating the Kentucky Colonels, 4 games to 3, in the finals.

Although attendance rose 5.2 per cent to 5,905 per game, the 10-team ABA again lost money and continued to press for a merger with the NBA. However, NBA club owners refused to give up the option clause, which binds a player to his team year after year. The NBA Players Association had blocked any merger that required an option clause, and the ABA was willing to eliminate the clause.

Wilt Chamberlain quit the Los Angeles Lakers of the NBA on September 26 to become player-coach of the ABA's San Diego Conquistadors. Chamberlain, the NBA's all-time scoring leader, signed for an estimated $600,000 a year for three years. The option clause in his Lakers contract bound him to the Lakers for another year. A court allowed Chamberlain to coach the Conquistadors, but barred him from playing for them for one year.

Julius Erving, at 23, was perhaps the game's most exciting and most unhappy player. He left the University of Massachusetts in his junior year in 1970 to sign with the Virginia Squires of the ABA for $500,000 for four years. After an outstanding rookie season, he signed a five-year contract with the Atlanta Hawks of the NBA for $1 million for five years. Then the Milwaukee Bucks gained his NBA draft rights, and the three teams fought over him.

A judge sent him back to Virginia. In July, 1973, the New York Nets acquired him in a $4-million deal. They gave Virginia $750,000 and the draft rights to a player. They gave Atlanta $425,000. They gave Erving $350,000 a year for eight years. Frank Litsky

Final Standings in Major League Basketball

National Basketball Association

Eastern Conference

Atlantic Division	W.	L.	Pct.
Boston	68	14	.829
New York	57	25	.695
Buffalo	21	61	.256
Philadelphia	9	73	.110

Central Division			
Baltimore	52	30	.634
Atlanta	46	36	.561
Houston	33	49	.402
Cleveland	32	50	.390

Western Conference

Midwest Division			
Milwaukee	60	22	.732
Chicago	51	31	.622
Detroit	40	42	.488
K.C.-Omaha	36	46	.439

Pacific Division			
Los Angeles	60	22	.732
Golden State	47	35	.573
Phoenix	38	44	.463
Seattle	26	56	.317
Portland	21	61	.256

Leading Scorers	G.	FG.	FT.	Pts.	Avg.
Nate Archibald, K.C.-Omaha	80	1,028	663	2,719	34.0
Kareem Abdul-Jabbar, Milw.	76	982	328	2,292	30.2
Spencer Haywood, Seattle	77	889	473	2,251	29.2
Lou Hudson, Atlanta	75	816	397	2,029	27.1
Pete Maravich, Atlanta	79	789	485	2,063	26.1

American Basketball Association

Eastern Division	W.	L.	Pct.
Carolina	57	27	.679
Kentucky	56	28	.667
Virginia	42	42	.500
New York	30	54	.357
Memphis	24	60	.286

Western Division			
Utah	56	28	.667
Indiana	51	33	.607
Denver	47	37	.560
San Diego	30	54	.357
Dallas	28	56	.333

Leading Scorers	G.	FG.	FT.	Pts.	Avg.
Julius Erving, Virginia	71	889	475	2,268	31.9
George McGinnis, Indiana	82	860	517	2,261	27.5
Dan Issel, Kentucky	84	899	485	2,292	27.2
Billy Cunningham, Carolina	84	757	472	2,028	24.1
Ralph Simpson, Denver	81	727	421	1,890	23.3

College Champions

Conference	School
Atlantic Coast	North Carolina State
Big Eight	Kansas State
Big Ten	Indiana
Ivy League	Pennsylvania
Missouri Valley	Memphis State
Ohio Valley	Austin Peay
Pacific-8	UCLA
Southeastern	Kentucky
Southwest	Texas Tech
Western Athletic	Arizona State

BEAME, ABRAHAM DAVID (1906-   ), was elected mayor of New York City on Nov. 6, 1973. Campaigning as an expert on city government, he won handily over three opponents in the general election. He had won the Democratic nomination in a run-off primary in June.

Beame was born in London, England, to parents who had fled from Poland. He was brought to New York City as an infant, and grew up in the city's slums, where he earned the nickname "Spunky." He became a naturalized U.S. citizen in 1914.

Beame earned an accounting degree from City College of New York in 1928, and took a job as an accounting teacher. Meanwhile, he worked for the Democratic organization in Brooklyn. That, plus his accounting background, won him an appointment as assistant city budget director in 1946. In 1961, running on the same ticket with Mayor Robert Wagner, he won a four-year term as city comptroller. In 1965, Beame won the Democratic mayoral nomination, but lost the election to John V. Lindsay, then a Republican. In 1969, Beame won a second term as city comptroller.

The diminutive Beame—he is 5 feet 2 inches tall—lives with his wife Mary in a three-room apartment in Brooklyn. He has two sons—Bernard, who is a television producer, and Edmond, who is an economics professor at McMaster University in Hamilton, Canada.   Kathryn Sederberg

BELGIUM. After two months of political conflict, the three main parties formed a coalition government on Jan. 25, 1973. It was led by Edmond Leburton, Belgium's first Socialist prime minister since 1958 (see LEBURTON, EDMOND). The three-party coalition included Liberals (34 seats), Socialists (61 seats), and Social Christians (67 seats). The number of ministers in Parliament was increased to 36 to satisfy both Dutch- and French-speaking elements in all three parties. In October, it was cut to 29.

The government immediately promised to make more money available for private schools. As a concession to the Flemings, it promised to restrict the size of Brussels (a bilingual enclave in Flemish territory) to its present 19 communes. Both of these are explosive issues that helped to defeat the previous government. After a debate on the new government's program on February 2, the coalition was given a vote of confidence by 133 to 53.

Financial Scandals rocked the government in May, and threatened its future. The first concerned a project to build a joint Belgian-Iranian oil refinery at Lannaye, near Liège. Legislators were angered when they discovered that Belgians owned only three $25 shares in the $150,000 project. The remainder of the stock was owned by foreigners. The government won a confidence vote on May 9 after Leburton promised to correct this imbalance. The second scandal concerned charges that the state-run tele-

phone office lost millions of dollars of public funds to construction companies and other firms by awarding contracts without taking bids. The wife and son of a state secretary were found to own an interest in one firm. The secretary resigned on June 5.

One of Prime Minister Leburton's first acts was to set up a joint, all-party commission of both the Senate and Chamber, the two houses of Parliament, to deal with community problems. The group will prepare the way for greater regionalization.

Economic and Social Problems. Prices of food and services rose rapidly, and the government's budget was designed to counteract inflation. Finance Minister Willy Claes imposed a modified freeze on prices and required advance notice of all price increases. Government spending was cut. By June 1, however, increases had been permitted in many sectors of industry, including one on gasoline.

Contraceptives were legalized in Belgium on August 8, but a ban on advertising them remained in effect. Medical students went on a hunger strike for four days to protest the arrest of a doctor, Willy Peers, for performing an abortion on a young, mentally defective rape victim. Peers was freed while the government sought a formula for changes in abortion laws that would be acceptable to a majority of Belgians.   Kenneth Brown

See also EUROPE (Facts in Brief Table).

BHUTAN. See ASIA.

BIOCHEMISTRY. The chemical analysis or synthesis of three complex compounds important in biology and medicine highlighted developments in 1973. Researchers synthesized human parathyroid hormone, a double helical deoxyribonucleic acid (DNA) molecule, and vitamin B_{12}.

Human Parathyroid Hormone. The parathyroid hormone is a protein that regulates the level of calcium in the blood plasma of man and higher animals. In the body, the molecule is first synthesized in the parathyroid gland as a prohormone, a long chain of 106 amino acids that are chemically linked together. This prohormone is rapidly converted into a storage or glandular form of the hormone that contains 84 amino acids. It appears that the hormone is then further fragmented in the body. Compounds having only the first 34 amino acids of the cattle hormone and the first 30 of the pig hormone have been synthesized and they can alter the blood calcium and phosphorous levels in experimental animals.

Biochemists had found the sequences of all the 84 amino acids along the parathyroid hormone molecules from both beef cattle and pigs, two species where parathyroid gland samples are readily available. The two sequences are not identical.

In December, 1972, H. Bryan Brewer, Jr., Thomas Fairwell, and Rosemary Ronan of the National Institutes of Health in Bethesda, Md., and Glen W. Sizemore and Claude D. Arnaud of the Mayo Medi-

Mayo Clinic biochemists Glen W. Sizemore, left, and Claude D. Arnaud were successful in analyzing and synthesizing of extracts of human parathyroid gland.

cal School and Clinic, Rochester, Minn., reported that they had isolated and analyzed parathyroid hormone from human parathyroid tumors. Their work was made possible by an international cooperative effort involving more than 150 laboratories.

The Brewer report describes the sequence of the first 34 amino acids in the human hormone. The first in the chain is serine, as in the pig hormone, but unlike the cattle hormone, in which it is alanine. The molecule contains two methionines, as does the cattle species, in contrast to the single methionine in the pig hormone. Unlike both the cattle and pig species, the human hormone has asparagine at position 16, glutamine at 22, lysine at 28, and leucine at 30. Using these data, chemists can now synthesize enough of the human hormone to make investigative studies.

DNA Gene for Alanine. Har Gobind Khorana and his collaborators at the Massachusetts Institute of Technology published a series of 13 papers in December, 1972, describing their total synthesis of a double helical DNA molecule. The molecule contains 77 subunits, or nucleotides, in exactly the sequence that codes for the structure of transfer ribonucleic acid (RNA) for the amino acid alanine. In the cell, this transfer RNA attaches to an alanine molecule and transfers it to a ribosome, where the amino acid is incorporated into a growing protein.

Khorana had previously devised purely chemical methods for synthesizing polynucleotides, but these procedures are strictly limited to smaller molecules. For the 77-nucleotide project, he combined chemical and enzymic procedures, using a DNA-connecting enzyme, DNA ligase, discovered in 1967. The first step involved the chemical synthesis of 15 polynucleotide segments that range in size from 5 to 20 nucleotide units. These were joined together to make three larger fragments of the structure, using the ligase enzyme. The fragments were then combined, again using the ligase, to form the complete double-helical structure.

This monumental accomplishment opens the way to a definitive study of the structure-function relationship in DNA molecules. Biochemists can, for example, make such structural variations as purine or pyrimidine base substitutions, and delete or add individual nucleotides. At the March, 1973, meeting of the American Chemical Society in Chicago, Khorana and his co-workers reported on another application of these methods to a genetic unit, the DNA that synthesizes the precursor to the so-called tyrosine suppressor.

Vitamin B_{12}, also known as cyanocobalamine, was first isolated in 1948 and is the largest and most complex vitamin yet discovered. It is required for normal blood-cell formation, for the maintenance of nervous tissue, and for growth. It also participates in a number of metabolic reactions. Lack of B_{12} causes pernicious anemia, a severe and eventually fatal anemia in which the red blood cells are not properly formed.

Pernicious anemia is generally caused by the absence of a "gastric intrinsic factor," a sugar-containing protein needed to absorb the vitamin from the intestine. Thus doctors can control the anemia by injecting the vitamin, by administering the intrinsic factor orally, or by a combination of both.

After 25 years, the vitamin has now been chemically synthesized. This was announced jointly by chemists Robert B. Woodward of Harvard University and Albert Eschenmoser of the Eidgenosische Technische Hochschule, Zurich, Switzerland, in January, 1973. Their synthesis required the combined efforts of 99 workers from 19 countries during an 11-year period.

Cyanocobalamine is the only known vitamin to contain a metal ion, in this case cobalt. The cobalt is surrounded by a "corrin" ring consisting of four nitrogen-containing five-membered rings joined by three carbon-containing bridges. Interestingly, the corrin ring is chemically similar to, but not identical with, the dihydroporphyrin ring of chlorophyll, the green pigment responsible for photosynthesis in plants. It was synthesized by Woodward in 1960.

The final steps of the new synthesis begin with beta-corrnorsterone, so named by Woodward because it is the cornerstone of the final steps of the synthetic process. It was synthesized in 37 different steps. A further 14 steps led to the complete synthesis of vitamin B_{12}.   Earl A. Evans, Jr.

BIOLOGY. Donald D. Brown, an embryologist at the Carnegie Institution of Washington, received the 1973 U.S. Steel Foundation Award of $5,000 for his work on gene isolation. This presentation marked the coming of age of an important field of experimental biology.

Brown and his colleagues succeeded in isolating and purifying two genes from the total genetic material of two related amphibians, the African clawed toads *Xenopus laevis* and *Xenopus mulleri*. The isolated genes are those that dictate the structures of two of the three ribonucleic acid (RNA) components of the ribosomes, the cell units in which tissue proteins are synthesized. Genes in all animals are composed of double helical deoxyribonucleic acid (DNA) molecules, but because DNA molecules have very similar chemical and physical laboratory properties, they are difficult to separate.

Isolating a Gene. The researchers used two techniques in the isolation procedure. The first of these, known as hybridization, depends on the fact that a DNA molecule will bind, very precisely all along its length, to a strand of DNA or RNA that is "complementary" in terms of its matching sequence of nucleotide units.

The researchers separate the double-stranded DNA molecule of the whole gene into its two complementary strands. DNA strands are then fixed on a piece of filter paper and treated with a solution of RNA from the toad ribosomes that has been labeled with radioactive atoms. The labeled RNA molecules find and bind to those spots where the DNA is complementary. The RNA that does not bind is then washed away. By measuring the amount of radioactivity that remains, the researchers can determine how much of the DNA nucleotide sequence matches the RNA sequence and is, therefore, that portion of the gene coding for the ribosomal RNA.

The second technique Brown and his colleagues used takes advantage of the fact that the ribosomal DNA gene has unusually high numbers of heavier nucleotide units. Because of this, it can be separated from the bulk of the DNA by its difference in density in a high-speed centrifuge.

The combined results using these techniques, together with electron-microscopic and chemical analyses, give a detailed picture of the DNA that codes for RNA components of the ribosome.

Scotophobin. A molecular basis for learning, intelligence, and memory has been debated for many years. There was considerable excitement in 1968 when Georges Ungar, L. Galvan, and R. H. Clark of Baylor College of Medicine in Houston first reported experiments in which an avoidance of dark places was induced in mice solely by treating them with extracts of brain tissue taken from rats that had been trained to fear the dark. The Baylor scientists automatically recorded the time the mice spent in the dark and light areas during tests. For example, of

a total test period of 180 seconds, the mice first averaged 130 seconds in the darkened area, but only 52 seconds there after getting the brain extract.

The controversy continued in 1973 after the scientific periodical *Nature* published a paper by Ungar, D. M. Desiderio, and W. Parr. The paper had first been received by *Nature* in February, 1971, and a later revised version was received in October, 1971. In the report, published in July, 1972, the investigators describe how they isolated an active substance they named "scotophobin." Ungar and his coworkers assigned it a tentative structure as a proteinlike molecule made of 15 amino acids, called a pentadecapeptide. In view of their uncertainty as to the precise structure, they synthesized three pentadecapeptides. They reported that one had biological and chemical properties identical to those of the naturally occurring material.

The reason for the long delay is apparent from an extended commentary by Walter Stewart of the National Institutes of Health in Bethesda, Md., which follows the Ungar paper. Stewart had been asked by *Nature* to referee, or judge, the article and during the interval of 15 months between receipt and publication he corresponded with the Baylor group. However, there were still substantial disagreements between the authors and Stewart.   Earl A. Evans, Jr.

BIRTHS. See Census, U.S.; Population, World.

BLINDNESS. See Handicapped.

BOATING. Recreational boating in the United States continued its uninterrupted growth in 1973. Industry sources estimated that there were 9.4 million boats in use, up from 9.2 million in 1972. About 5.5-million of these were outboards, up from 5.4 million.

The 47 million recreational boaters spent $4.2 billion for new and used boats, motors, accessories, fuel, insurance, docking, maintenance, repairs, storage, and club memberships. The National Association of Engine and Boat Manufacturers estimated that there were 4,620 marinas and 1,310 yacht clubs.

In competitive boating, the Johnson and Evinrude divisions of Outboard Marine Corporation successfully introduced the world's first outboard motors powered by rotary combustion. Each Wankel all-aluminum engine uses four rotors, one stacked on another.

Powerboats. Bob Magoon, a 37-year-old eye surgeon from Miami Beach, Fla., won the American Power Boat Association's national inboard championship series for the fifth time. He also captured the blue-ribbon race, the Hennessy Grand Prix, on July 18 at Point Pleasant, N.J., for the third time in four years. His boat was a 36-foot Cigarette hull powered by two 600-horsepower Kiekhaefer Aeromarine engines.

The largest and fastest powerboats were the unlimited hydroplanes, which are powered by airplane engines. The most successful in 1973 were *Miss*

The Brazilian yacht *Saga* fights its way through heavy seas to win the second race of the Admiral's Cup series off the Isle of Wight.

Budweiser, driven by Dean Chenoweth of Xenia, Ohio, and *Pay 'N' Pak*, driven by Mickey Remund of Palm Desert, Calif.

Yacht Racing. The major ocean races in 1973 were from Cape Town, South Africa, to Rio de Janeiro, Brazil (3,500 miles), and the transpacific race from Los Angeles to Honolulu (2,225 miles).

Stormy, a 43-foot ketch registered from the Seychelles, finished the Cape Town-to-Rio race on February 3 and became overall winner after handicaps had been computed. It was owned and sailed by Kees Bruynzeel, a 72-year-old Dutch millionaire with a heart condition. He sailed with a nurse, a cardiac-care unit, and, for use if the worst came, a weighted burial bag.

Chutzpah, a 35-foot sloop, started the transpacific race on July 4 and finished on July 17 as handicap winner. Skipper Stuart Cowan built the sloop just for this race. The day after reaching port, he offered the boat for sale.

Munequita, a mass-produced Ranger-37, owned by Jack Valley and sailed by Gerald (Click) Schreck, both of New Orleans, won the prestigious Southern Ocean Racing Conference series. *La Forza del Destino*, a 51-foot aluminum sloop owned and sailed by Norman Raben of Sunapee, N.H., won the Northern Ocean Racing Trophy, the Marblehead-to-Halifax race, and the Stamford-Block Island-Stamford race for the Vineyard Trophy.   Frank Litsky

BOLIVIA. President Hugo Banzer Suarez was forced to name two new Cabinets in 1973. On both occasions, once on April 23 and again on September 7, he acted to end discord between the Nationalist Revolutionary Movement and the right wing Bolivian Socialist Falange, the civilian political parties that, together with a military group, constituted the coalition government. In August, and again in late September, the Banzer regime announced it had smashed plots by subversives to overthrow the government. Earlier, on May 29, Banzer had assumed supreme command of the armed forces following the murder by the Bolivian police of former Interior Minister Colonel Andres Selich Chop, who had been detained May 14 as an alleged plotter against the regime.

Labor Problems. The president also faced challenges from the labor force during the year. On March 1, tin miners at the Siglo Veinte and Catavi installations called a successful 48-hour strike demanding a wage adjustment to compensate for an earlier devaluation of the peso. Bank and insurance agency employees walked off their jobs on April 24 over wages. A government commission subsequently resolved the conflict. Privately owned newspapers and radio stations went on a two-day strike in August to protest alleged police brutality during a raid on an independent newspaper, *Nueva Jornada*.

Inflation was rampant, with living costs climbing 31.9 per cent between October, 1972, and March,

1973. The government banned all beef and coffee exports in an attempt to curb serious shortages throughout the nation. To protect itself against exchange losses due to an international monetary crisis, Bolivia's Central Bank converted a considerable portion of its holdings from U.S. dollars to German Deutsche marks.

The Inter-American Development Bank approved a $46.5-million loan to enable Bolivia to raise its oil refining capacity from 21,000 barrels per day to 41,500 by 1978. Total cost of the program was estimated at $58 million. Meanwhile, the government opened the country's resources to private oil and gas exploration firms for the first time since 1969. Union Oil of California and Occidental Petroleum were each awarded tracts of 2.5 million acres, in partnership with the state-owned oil entity. The government also began to pay the U.S.-owned Gulf Oil Corporation $78.6 million over a 20-year period in compensation for the 1969 seizure of properties.

To better protect its tin marketing, Bolivia began expanding the Vinto smelter to raise its refining capacity from the present level of around 6,500 tons a year to 20,000 by 1976. It also made arrangements to continue processing from 8,000 to 10,000 tons of its tin annually in Britain.   Mary Webster Soper

See also LATIN AMERICA (Facts in Brief Table).

BOOKS. See CANADIAN LITERATURE; LITERATURE; LITERATURE FOR CHILDREN; POETRY.

BOSTON. Racial problems plagued Boston throughout 1973. On March 2, a federal judge found that the Boston School Committee deliberately discriminated against minority children by maintaining two largely segregated school systems. Boston therefore could lose $8 million annually in federal school aid.

Racial discrimination charges were also leveled against the Boston fire department. On January 24, the U.S. Department of Justice filed suit, charging the department with discriminatory hiring practices. Of 2,100 Boston firemen, only 16 were black and 3 had Spanish surnames. The government charged that job qualification tests were, in some areas, unrelated to job requirements.

Racial tensions between blacks and whites heightened in October after two macabre murders occurred in Boston's Columbia Point area and adjacent Roxbury. On October 2, a white woman was killed when a gang of black youths forced her to douse herself with gasoline. They then set her afire. On October 4, an elderly man was attacked while fishing. He was stoned and stabbed to death with his own knife. Boston Mayor Kevin White denied the murders were racial incidents, calling them "isolated insanity."

On October 11, police evacuated two schools near the Columbia Point housing project because of threats of violence between gangs of black and white youths. Most residents of the low-income project are black or Spanish-speaking.

Major Fires. Flames fanned by a 50 mile-per-hour wind devastated a 30-block area of Chelsea, a Boston suburb, on October 14. At least 3,000 residents fled the area and more than 1,000 persons were left homeless. Damage was estimated at $500 million.

Fires also hit the Boston subway system early in the year. In January, a blaze caused 400 subway riders to flee on foot down a subway tunnel. Another fire in the same tunnel on February 6 killed 1 person and injured 87 others.

The John Hancock Mutual Life Insurance Company decided to replace all the glass window panels in its new 60-story headquarters building in Boston. The panels began to break mysteriously in mid-1972, and by September, 1973, a total of 3,112 had been damaged.

Cost of Living. A U.S. Department of Labor survey released on June 15 named Boston the third-most-expensive U.S. metropolitan area in which to live. According to the report, an average family of four in Boston would need an annual income of $13,572 to live in "moderate comfort." Living costs rose 4.9 per cent between April, 1972, and April, 1973.

The U.S. Bureau of the Census recalculated the population of the Boston area, using newly developed definitions of metropolitan areas. The Boston metropolitan area had an estimated population of 3,417,000 persons.   James M. Banovetz

BOTANY. John Heslop-Harrison and his colleagues at the Royal Botanic Gardens in Kew, England, announced in May, 1973, that they had found a way to remove the surface proteins from plant pollen grains. Such surface proteins allow other plants of the same species to recognize their species-specific pollen so that fertilization can occur. If the pollen is from another species of plant and therefore incompatible, the plant it lands on releases a substance that prevents fertilization.

The discovery of a way to remove the proteins opens new possibilities for plant breeders. Now they may be able to produce crosses between two previously incompatible plants by removing the surface proteins from the pollen grains. They may also be able to prevent fertilization between two plants of the same species by using inhibitory protein substances from another species of plant. Thus, breeders may ensure only the growth of hybrid plants.

Nitrogen Fixation. The presence of nitrogen-fixing bacteria (*Rhizobium*) on the roots of legume plants is a well-known example of symbiosis, the association of two unlike organisms for mutual benefit. Legume plants profit from the ready supply of nitrates, often lacking in cultivated land, and the bacteria are provided with a hospitable surrounding of water and minerals. Many plants that do not have such a symbiotic arrangement must be given large quantities of nitrogen fertilizer to grow well.

Several researchers are trying to produce cereal grain plants that can harbor *Rhizobium*, and thus fix nitrogen for themselves without the addition of nitrogen fertilizers. At the University of Nottingham in England, Edward Cocking, M. R. Davey, and Eileen Bush have isolated *Rhizobium*-containing cells from soybeans (legumes) in the hope that they can fuse the isolated cells with nonlegume plants and thus confer the nitrogen-fixing ability on the nonlegumes.

Botanist M. J. Trinick of Western Australia's Division of Land Resources Management in Wembly has discovered a *Rhizobium* that naturally infects some nonleguminous plants. He hopes to develop a mutant of the *Rhizobium* that lives in cereal plants. John Postgate, a botanist in Sussex, England, is attempting a more difficult approach. He hopes to transfer the nitrogen-fixing genes directly from the bacteria to the plant cells.

Cotton. Charles A. Beasley of the University of California, Riverside, showed in March that hormones can be used to artificially regulate the growth of unfertilized cotton ovules. He removed young ovules from the ovaries of cotton flowers and floated them in a glucose liquid. The ovules to which he added no hormone-growth substances shriveled and turned brown within two weeks. But when he added growth hormones, the ovules grew, remained white, and produced cotton fibers.   Barbara N. Benson

BOTSWANA. See AFRICA.

BOWLING. Don McCune, a 36-year-old right-hander from Munster, Ind., and Millie Martorella, a 26-year-old left-hander from Rochester, N.Y., gained major bowling honors in 1973.

McCune won six tournaments on the Professional Bowlers Association (PBA) yearlong tour – in Winston-Salem, N.C., and Milwaukee in February; in Downey, Fresno, and Redwood City, Calif., in June and July; and in Tokyo in September. He finished the year with $69,000 in winnings.

McCune also won the classic singles division of the Bowlers Journal Classic with 1,263 pins for five games, a 252 average. He finished fourth in the Tournament of Champions, ninth in the PBA national championship, and among the leaders in many other tournaments.

One reason for McCune's success was a discovery he made in 1972 that he could get better control of his plastic ball if he soaked it in a chemical solvent to soften the shell. He and many other pros treated their bowling balls this way until the PBA outlawed the practice in October, 1973. The PBA said that the softened ball gave the bowler an unfair advantage because it provided a better hook (the softening procedure did not work with hard rubber balls). In addition, the PBA said, the solvent was highly flammable and thus dangerous.

The PBA Tour consisted of 13 tournaments in the winter, 13 in the summer, and 7 in the fall, with purses totaling $2 million. The winners included Mike McGrath of El Cerrito, Calif., in the United States Open; Earl Anthony of Tacoma, Wash., in the PBA championship; and Dave Soutar of Kansas City in the American Bowling Congress Masters tournament.

Jim Godman of Lorain, Ohio, won the year's richest tournament ($125,000) and largest first-place purse ($25,000) in the Tournament of Champions in March in Akron, Ohio. Godman also won the $100,000 Brunswick World Open in Chicago.

The All-America Team named by the *National Bowlers Journal* consisted of McCune, Godman, McGrath, Anthony, Barry Asher of Costa Mesa, Calif., and Dick Ritger of Hartford, Wis. The women's All-America comprised Martorella; Dottie Fothergill of North Attleboro, Mass.; Patty Costello of New Carrollton, Md.; Judy Cook of Grandview, Mo.; Lorrie Koch of Carpentersville, Ill.; and Barbara Renner of Cleveland.

Martorella won the women's United States Open in Garden City, N.Y., averaging 212 for 24 games, and she and Fothergill captured the Women's International Bowling Congress (WIBC) doubles title. Fothergill, a 28-year-old left-hander, also won the WIBC Queens tournament for the second straight year. Renner, in her professional debut, won the richest women's tournament ever, the $55,000 Rick Case Honda Classic on April 28 in Akron.   Frank Litsky

BOXING. Joe Frazier of Philadelphia and Muhammad Ali of Cherry Hill, N.J., who had dominated heavyweight boxing for years, tumbled from their lofty perches in 1973. Frazier lost the world championship to George Foreman of Hayward, Calif., and Ali, the champion before Frazier, suffered the ignominy of a defeat and broken jaw in one fight.

In March, 1971, Frazier outpointed Ali in a bruising 15-round title bout that grossed $20 million and gave each fighter a guaranteed purse of $2.5 million. Since then, negotiations had gone on for a return bout that would have guaranteed each $3 million. By the time they signed, the fight had lost much of its attractiveness and the purses were smaller.

On Jan. 22, 1973, Frazier met the 6-foot 3-inch Foreman in Kingston, Jamaica. Foreman, a 3-to-1 underdog, floored Frazier three times in the first round and three in the second before the referee stopped the bout. The defeat was Frazier's first in 30 professional bouts. The victory was Foreman's 38th in 38 pro bouts. Frazier, his belly thick and his reactions slow, refused to back away from his opponent because, he said, "My pride wouldn't let me."

The 24-year-old Foreman showed no rush to defend. When he did, his opponent was Joe (King) Roman, a lightly regarded Puerto Rican. On September 1 in Tokyo, Foreman floored Roman three times before the fight was mercifully stopped in the first round.

Ali's Downfall came on March 31 against Ken Norton, a 5-to-1 underdog, in San Diego, Calif. Norton, helped by a hypnotist who convinced him he could win, broke Ali's jaw and won a split decision. Ali had trained lightly, and he was sluggish at 221 pounds. He won a split decision over Norton in a return bout on September 10 in Inglewood, Calif.

The 29-year-old Frazier and the 31-year-old Ali finally signed for a bout on Jan. 28, 1974, in New York City, each to receive at least $850,000. But, as Dave Anderson wrote in *The New York Times*, things would never be the same again.

"More and more," he wrote, "it appears that Ali and Frazier destroyed each other, physically and emotionally, in their brutal epic. Their bodies haven't been the same since. And their spirits never again will soar, as they did before their $20-million extravaganza."

Foreman was one of five boxers who enjoyed worldwide recognition as champions. The World Boxing Association and the World Boxing Council recognized separate champions in the six lightest classes.

Antonio Cervantes of Colombia (junior-welterweight) won four title bouts, three by knockouts, and Roberto Duran of Panama (lightweight) won three by knockouts.
Frank Litsky

BOY SCOUTS. See YOUTH ORGANIZATIONS.
BOYS' CLUBS. See YOUTH ORGANIZATIONS.

World Champion Boxers

Division	Champion	Country	Year Won
Heavyweight	George Foreman	U.S.A.	1973
Light-heavyweight	Bob Foster	U.S.A.	1968
Middleweight	Carlos Monzon	Argentina	1970
Junior-middleweight	Koichi Wajima	Japan	1971
Welterweight	Jose Napoles	Mexico	1971
Junior-welterweight (disputed)	Antonio Cervantes	Colombia	1972
	Bruno Arcari	Italy	1970
Lightweight (disputed)	Roberto Duran	Panama	1972
	Rodolfo Gonzalez	U.S.A.	1972
Junior-lightweight (disputed)	Ricardo Arredondo	Mexico	1971
	Ben Villaflor	Philippines	1972
Featherweight (disputed)	Ernesto Marcel	Panama	1972
	Eder Jofre	Brazil	1973
Bantamweight (disputed)	Romeo Anaya	Mexico	1973
	Arnold Taylor	South Africa	1973
Flyweight (disputed)	Chartchai Chionoi	Thailand	1972
	Betulio Gonzalez	Venezuela	1973

New heavyweight champion George Foreman turns his back on the fallen Joe Frazier after the referee stopped their Kingston, Jamaica, bout.

BRADLEY, THOMAS (1917-   ), a City Council member and former police officer, was elected the first black mayor of Los Angeles on May 29, 1973. He defeated incumbent Samuel Yorty by about 100,000 votes to become mayor of the third largest city in the United States.

Bradley lost to Yorty in a similar run-off election in 1969. Bradley said his 1973 victory proved that people will judge a candidate "on merit instead of race or creed." Unlike other major U.S. cities, such as Newark, N.J., and Gary, Ind., in which predominantly black populations have elected black mayors, Los Angeles has a black population of less than 20 per cent.

Bradley was born Dec. 29, 1917, on a cotton plantation in Calvert, Tex. His sharecropper parents moved the family to Los Angeles when Bradley was 7. After excelling in football and track in high school, Bradley won an athletic scholarship to the University of California at Los Angeles in 1936. He received a bachelor's degree in 1940, then earned a law degree in 1956 from Southwestern University School of Law in Los Angeles.

Bradley joined the Los Angeles police force in 1940, and worked as a detective, a juvenile officer, and in police-community relations. He retired in 1961 as a lieutenant. He was elected to the City Council in 1963, 1967, and 1971. Bradley married the former Ethel Arnold in 1940.
Jacquelyn Heath

BRANDO, MARLON (1924-   ), won the 1973 Academy of Motion Picture Arts and Sciences Award for best actor for his portrayal of Don Vito Corleone, the Mafioso, in *The Godfather*. But he refused to accept the Oscar in protest against the movie industry's treatment of the American Indian. Brando also won an Oscar in 1954, for a role in *On the Waterfront*.

Brando is known for his support of activities in behalf of racial minorities and many unpopular causes. He marched against segregation in the South in the early 1960s and quietly supported Indian protest movements. He has sought socially and politically significant movie roles, such as those in *The Ugly American* and *Burn!*

Brando was born in Omaha, Nebr., on April 3, 1924, and grew up in Evanston, Ill. At 19, he went to New York City and studied acting with Stella Adler. His first Broadway role was in *I Remember Mama*, in 1944. He quickly became a star and a legend as Stanley Kowalski in the play and movie version of *A Streetcar Named Desire* (1947 and 1951) and revolutionized American acting with his naturalistic, mumbling, improvised style. Some of his best roles were Zapata in *Viva Zapata!* (1952), Mark Antony in *Julius Caesar* (1953), and Fletcher Christian in *Mutiny on the Bounty* (1961). In 1973, he created a sensation as Paul in *Last Tango in Paris*, an X-rated movie.   Lillian Zahrt

See also MOTION PICTURES.

BRAZIL. The ruling military regime headed by President Emílio Garrastazú Médici, after nine years in power, gave no indication in 1973 that it was ready to reinstate civilian rule. Despite rumblings of discontent among those Brazilians who wanted a return to political democracy, the regime, on March 31, named retired General Ernesto Geisel as its presidential candidate for elections scheduled for January, 1974.

On September 10, Ulysses Guimaraes was nominated as a presidential candidate by the Brazilian Democratic Movement (MDB), the only officially tolerated opposition party. The MDB would participate in the elections, according to Guimaraes, despite "knowing they are a great farce organized by the government." The MDB leader also charged that the Médici government ruled by means of illegal arrests, violence, and censorship.

Violence and Unrest. All three charges were based on events that occurred during the year. Police "death squads," whose members considered themselves "honest lawmen interested in protecting society by getting rid of irredeemable criminals," continued to operate in the larger Brazilian cities. On March 25, the bullet-riddled bodies of two men, marked with death squad identifying tags, were found in Rio de Janeiro suburbs. The bodies of two similarly identified men were found in neighboring Rio de Janeiro state on March 28. Five more victims were found in June. Altogether, there have been at least 1,300 such murders in Brazil over the past decade.

Roman Catholic priests repeatedly denounced the government for using "repression and torture against dissidents and political prisoners." In May, 10 bishops and 3 archbishops published a 30-page document charging that "economic and governmental institutions in Brazil were devoted only to oppression and injustice." The regime contributed to the general dissatisfaction in June by reaffirming its right to censor publications without consulting the courts. It acted after overruling a federal appeals court decision that *Opiniao*, a much-censored news magazine, could publish without submitting to federal police scrutiny.

Economic Growth. Despite these undercurrents of unrest, the Médici government continued to focus its attention on Brazil's remarkable economic growth by sustaining a high development rate at the partial expense of strict monetary stability. A 10 per cent growth rate was expected for the year against nearly 10.4 per cent in 1972. The economy prospered in practically every sector except agriculture, though there were exceptions even in that area. The January-May production of most industrial goods was up substantially over the same period in 1972. The output of cement, steel, pig iron, and motor vehicles, for example, increased by 12.2, 11.5, 11.3, and 12 per cent, respectively. The 1974 national industrial product growth objective (about $13 billion) was expected to be surpassed in 1973 ($13.5 billion).

Meanwhile, Brazil became the first Latin American country to host a congress of the International Chamber of Commerce, attended by some 2,000 businessmen from all continents, in Rio de Janeiro from May 19 to 26. And from September 14 to 23, the government sponsored Latin America's first International Aerospace Show in São Paulo.

The 1973 balance of payments was expected to show a surplus of over $1 billion – down from the $2.4 billion of 1972 but still an impressive figure. Foreign monetary reserves swelled from $4.18 billion in December, 1972, to $6.34 billion in August and were expected to reach $8 billion by the end of the year. This was about 80 per cent of the nation's total foreign debt. Meanwhile, in an effort to keep the new cruzeiro's external value in line with the decline in the monetary unit's domestic purchasing power, Brazil devalued its currency from time to time throughout the year.

Agriculture expanded in 1973 by only an estimated 5.4 per cent, versus a targeted 9.2 per cent. Inclement weather, plant disease, and fewer plantings due to government efforts to keep prices down plagued farmers. The 1972-1973 coffee crop was expected to reach only 16 million bags, and the 1973-1974 harvest may be only 13 million, due to rust and frosts. However, higher world prices earned the country $1.2 billion in the 1972-1973 season – the highest since the 1960-1961 crop.   Mary Webster Soper

See also LATIN AMERICA (Facts in Brief Table).

BRENNAN, PETER JOSEPH (1918-), a New York union leader, was sworn in as secretary of labor on Feb. 2, 1973, by President Richard M. Nixon. He replaced James D. Hodgson and is the first union leader to head the Department of Labor since 1953.

A registered Democrat, Brennan has supported Republican candidates on various issues. He has supported Governor Nelson A. Rockefeller of New York since 1966. In 1968, he was active in Labor Leaders for Nixon. In 1970, he earned the nickname "Mr. Hardhat" by organizing a march in Manhattan, in which 100,000 construction workers rallied in support of the President's Vietnam War policy.

Brennan was born on May 24, 1918, in the Hell's Kitchen section of New York City. After graduation from high school in 1936, he became an apprentice in the painter's union. He became a master painter in 1944. Brennan served on a submarine in 1944 and 1945. In 1947, he became business agent of his local union.

Brennan was elected president of the New York City Building and Construction Trades Council in 1957, and president of the state council in 1958. He also served as vice-president of the New York state American Federation of Labor and Council of Industrial Organizations (AFL-CIO).

Brennan and his wife, the former Josephine Brickley, have three children.   Jacquelyn Heath

BRIDGE. See BUILDING AND CONSTRUCTION.

BRIDGE, CONTRACT. Italy handily won the Bermuda Bowl, emblematic of the world contract bridge championship, at Guarujá, Brazil, on May 27, 1973. They triumphed by the unusually wide margin of 128 international match points over the Dallas Aces, defending Bermuda Bowl champions from the United States. The Aces had previously lost to Italy in the 1972 World Bridge Team Olympiad, which replaces Bermuda Bowl competition in Olympic years.

For Giorgio Belladonna and Pietro Forquet, it was their 14th world championship and for Benito Garozzo, his 11th. Other team members were Benito Bianchi and alternates Giuseppe Garabello and Vito Pittala.

The Aces regained the Harold A. Vanderbilt knockout team championship at the American Contract Bridge League (A.C.B.L.) spring national championships in St. Louis in March. Team members were Bob Wolff, Bob Hamman, Bob Goldman, and Mark Blumenthal, all of Dallas, and Mike Lawrence of Los Angeles.

The A.C.B.L. summer national championships, which ended in Washington, D.C., on August 1, attracted the largest field in tournament history – 16,044 tables – breaking the old record by 1,533 tables. Winners of the Spingold knockout team title were Bud Reinhold of Highland Park, Ill.; Bill Eisenberg, Eddie Kantar, and Richard Katz, all of Los Angeles; and Larry Cohen of Chicago.   Theodore M. O'Leary

BRINEGAR, CLAUDE STOUT (1926-), a California oil company executive, was sworn in as U.S. secretary of transportation on Feb. 2, 1973. He succeeded John A. Volpe, who became ambassador to Italy.

Brinegar was born on Dec. 16, 1926, in Rockport, Calif. He graduated from high school in San Francisco in 1944, and served for two years in the Army Air Force in Japan and Korea. He received his B.A. degree in economics in 1950, an M.S. in mathematical statistics in 1951, and a Ph.D. in economic research in 1954 from Stanford University.

Brinegar joined Union Oil Company of California in 1953 as an economic analyst. In 1965, he was elected vice-president for economics and corporate planning. He also managed the merger between Union Oil Company and Pure Oil Company in 1965, and became president of the Pure Oil division. From 1968 to 1973, he served as senior vice-president, a member of the board of directors and the executive committee of Union Oil Company, and president of the Union 76 division.

Brinegar and his wife, the former Elva Jackson, have three children.   Jacquelyn Heath

BRITISH COLUMBIA. See CANADA.

BRITISH COMMONWEALTH OF NATIONS. See AUSTRALIA; CANADA; GREAT BRITAIN; and articles on other countries of the Commonwealth.

BRITISH HONDURAS. See LATIN AMERICA.

BUILDING AND CONSTRUCTION. Spending in the United States reached an all-time high of $136.4-billion in 1973, 10 per cent more than 1972's $123.8 billion. The U.S. Bureau of the Census attributed 7 or 8 per cent of the increase to inflation, especially in the rising cost of new housing, which in actual volume was lower than in 1972. The bureau's forecast for 1974 spending is $143 billion, only a 5 per cent increase over 1973.

At a meeting in Washington, D.C., in September, Federal Reserve Board Chairman Arthur Burns came under attack from homebuilders and financiers for the Phase 4 restrictive monetary policy that they said threatens to send homebuilding into a nose dive. Burns conceded that housing would bear a disproportionate burden of the government's tight-money policy, but he blamed homebuilders themselves, in part, for the strict anti-inflation measures. He said a too-liberal supply of mortgage money in recent years has led to overbuilding. As a result, there were twice as many unsold houses on the market in 1972 as there were in 1971.

Construction industry labor costs during the 12-month period that ended Sept. 1, 1973, were held to their smallest annual gain since 1967, according to *Engineering News-Record* (*ENR*) magazine's Building Cost Index. *ENR* gave major credit for winding down wage inflation to the recently formed Construction Industry Stabilization Committee for approving a 5.4 per cent wage raise for the first year – a considerable drop from the peak gain of 13 per cent set in the year ending in September, 1971.

Although the Phase 3½ freeze on prices and wages kept the rising cost of materials under control during the summer, September saw a rapid rise in the price of materials as well as alarming shortages of some materials. Heading the list of scarce materials was cement, and lumber and certain types of steel and other metals were also in short supply.

Codes and Specifications. Engineers attending a joint meeting of the American Society of Civil Engineers and the Structural Engineers Association of Northern California in July called for a building code supplement that would make it possible to predict building failures in earthquakes. Seismologist John A. Blume of San Francisco said a technique he developed to analyze the seismic design of buildings might serve as a basis for a supplement.

In October, New York City announced that it had been forced to revise its building codes to permit the use of plastic pipe and plastic-sheathed electric cable. Otherwise, it faced the loss of $77.5 million in federal funds. Several other cities, including Los Angeles and San Francisco, were forced to yield to a stipulation of the Department of Housing and Urban Development that cities cannot erect code barriers against the use of any material.

New Buildings. The long-delayed opera house in Sydney, Australia, opened October 20 – nine years behind schedule. Final cost was $132 million more than the original estimate of $8 million. Its sail-shaped roof is made of precast, post-tensioned segmental arch ribs joined in spherical folded plates.

In Toronto, Canada, construction has begun on a 1,805-foot-high post-tensioned concrete needle that will be the world's tallest free-standing structure. The $2-million tower will be the centerpiece of a $1-billion redevelopment project between Toronto and the harbor.

Bridges. Plans were announced in June for the proposed Interstate 410 bridge crossing the Mississippi River south of New Orleans. The design recommended will be the longest cable-stayed span in the world, as well as the most economical structure for the crossing. A main span of 2,100 feet will make a midriver pier unnecessary. Trusses will stiffen the deck structure, which must span about 280 feet between stays; a truss 34 feet deep was selected for the task. The United States first cable-stayed bridge was completed in 1972 over Sitka Harbor in Alaska.

The last members of a record U.S. cantilever truss bridge were bolted into place over the Delaware River between Chester, Pa., and Bridgeport, N.J., in June. The $118-million Commodore John J. Barry Bridge has a 1,644-foot main span, the longest cantilever truss span in the United States and the third longest in the world. The 1,800-foot main span of the Quebec Bridge is the longest.

The dam at the mouth of Germany's Eider River, put into operation in 1973, is the largest example of hydraulic architecture in Europe.

The new suspension bridge over the Bosporus was formally dedicated in October, providing the first permanent highway link between Europe and Asia. The 3,540-foot suspension span, built by a British-German consortium at a cost of $33 million, is the fourth longest in the world.

On March 16, Queen Elizabeth II of Great Britain opened a new London Bridge, the third in almost 1,000 years. The second bridge, unable to sustain modern traffic, was pulled down, shipped piece by piece to the United States, and rebuilt in Arizona. The present bridge was under construction for five years. It is 860 feet long and has three spans, six traffic lanes, and two broad pedestrian walkways.

Dams. The $135-million Dworshak Dam, a U.S. Army Corps of Engineers project in Idaho, was completed in the midsummer of 1973. The 719-foot-high dam, third highest in the United States, is part of the Columbia-Snake River multipurpose program. Its reservoir, extending 53 miles upstream, can store up to 3.5 million acre-feet of water.

A saving of $9 million was achieved on Colorado's Crystal Dam by changing its design from earth-fill to a double curvature, thin concrete arch. The lowest bid for the earth-fill dam was $31.7 million, almost $11 million more than the engineers had estimated. The dam, a Bureau of Reclamation project, was also redesigned to be compatible with its surroundings. A $1.5-million contract for the diversion and foundation tunnels was completed in 1973. The dam will have a crest length of 620 feet, and will be the thinnest dam of its type in the world, 10 feet thick at the crest and 29.7 feet at the thickest point of its arch.

Tunnels. Designs were completed late in 1973 for the parallel Interstate 70 tunnel through the Continental Divide west of Denver. The tunnel will be a companion lane to the Dwight D. Eisenhower Tunnel, an 8,148-foot, two-lane tunnel, which was completed in March, 1973, at a cost of $109 million. By mid-1973, the Eisenhower Tunnel had already carried traffic in excess of 1975 projections, and the need for a companion tunnel proved urgent. State highway engineers said the new project will cost considerably less than the Eisenhower Tunnel, because the ventilation buildings and ducts for both tunnels were completed under the original contract. The tunnels, which pierce the Rocky Mountains at an elevation of 11,000 feet, are the highest vehicular tunnels in the world. They will save 11 miles of tortuous mountain driving through passes.

After almost two centuries of studies and false starts, British and French officials agreed in September on the route and financing for a two-track bored rail tunnel under the English Channel that will cost $2 billion. The tunnel will run from Cheriton, near Dover, England, to a point near Calais, France. Completion is expected by 1980.   Mary E. Jessup

The first bridge connecting Europe and Asia was completed across the Bosporus in October, at an estimated cost of $33 million.

BULGARIA continued to make mild reforms in domestic economic policy in 1973, but showed signs of uneasiness about its relations with Russia. The Soviet Union's growing friendliness with Yugoslavia caused misgivings among some Bulgarian leaders. Rumors of an anti-Russian army coup in June proved unfounded. But Angel Tsanev, minister of the interior until April, was dismissed from the Communist Party's Politburo and Central Committee in July, allegedly because he opposed Russian policies.

Russia's Presidium Chairman Nikolai V. Podgorny visited Sofia in July, and party General Secretary Leonid I. Brezhnev was there in October, apparently to allay Bulgarian fears of a Russian sellout to Yugoslavia.

Bulgaria's own relations with Yugoslavia improved after Stane Dolanc, secretary of the Yugoslav Community Party's Executive Committee, visited Sofia in February. But a new quarrel flared up in July over Yugoslav press references to the Macedonian minority in Bulgaria. In September, Macedonian-language books were confiscated from the Yugoslav pavilion at the Plovdiv (Bulgaria) Trade Fair. But the squabbling stopped after Brezhnev visited Bulgaria and Russia's Premier Aleksei N. Kosygin visited Yugoslavia in September. However, a scheduled visit to Sofia by West German Foreign Minister Walter Scheel was canceled in August. He had been expected to work out a series of agreements leading to the signing of a diplomatic accord between the two countries.

Relations with Greece took another step forward in April with the signing of an agreement on Bulgaria's use of Greece's Salonika Bay port for its exports and imports. In May, Bulgarian Foreign Minister Petar Mladenov visited Athens and signed cultural-exchange and consular agreements.

Western Pacts. Prime Minister Pierre Messmer of France visited Bulgaria in July and signed a 10-year agreement on industrial and economic cooperation. Bulgaria signed a 10-year economic cooperation agreement with Austria in June, and in October, Todor Zhivkov, Bulgaria's first secretary and chairman of the State Council, visited Austria. The Bulgarian ministry of agriculture signed an agreement in June with the U.S. Can Corporation providing for the installation of can-making equipment.

A new top-level commission on living standards was set up in February. Its chairman stated that the domestic market should have priority, and called for radical improvements in the supply, choice, and quality of consumer goods. The government announced substantial price reductions on a variety of consumer goods in May. Wages in Bulgaria increased 6.5 per cent over the 1972 figure, and the supply of consumer goods grew by 7.4 per cent. But the government discouraged hopes of radical liberalization at home arising from East-West contacts.   Chris Cviic

See also EUROPE (Facts in Brief Table).

BURMA. This once-affluent nation continued its economic decline under Chairman U Ne Win and his "Burmese Way to Socialism" in 1973. Rangoon, once a bustling port, crumbled through inattention and general economic stagnation, and Burma, once a major rice exporter, now faced domestic rice shortages. But there were some signs that the government was beginning to shift from its policy of isolation to get the economy moving. Despite its deep suspicion of all foreign capital, leaders began talks with some 50 foreign oil companies regarding concessions to be given them to look for oil.

The nation began its own oil exploration with the aid of a $20-million loan from Japan, but little of value had been located by the end of the year. Other mining concessions were also considered. Burma's mineral potential in tin, tungsten, silver, zinc, lead, diamonds, copper, and nickel could be a big export earner for the country.

Ne Win visited Indonesia to see how that country used foreign capital while retaining control over its own resources. The shift in policy was partly stimulated by the chronic problem of insurgency, which is growing more and more intensive.

The Insurgents comprise several minority groups who intensely dislike the majority of Burmese. Their enmity originated in World War II, when some 30 Burmese leaders – including Ne Win – supported the Japanese as liberators.

The insurgents are in the Shan states, where the Communists seem to be in control, and among the Karen people along the border with Thailand. The Karens have attracted some support from dissident Burmese, and they are now well supplied with arms and ammunition, most of it coming from black markets in Thailand.

Rebel Revenue. The Thais, in turn, purchase black-market U.S. supplies from Laos and Cambodia, where the army units often sell American military aid. Bangkok, Thailand, is the focal point for such purchases. The rebels have their own system of raising revenue to pay for the arms. They maintain their own border customs posts and tax the smugglers. They also operate their own mines and sell the ore on the black market. In fact, most commodity goods found in Burma today are smuggled in from Thailand.

The insurgents have also found another source of income in mortgaging Burma's oil and mineral resources to foreign backers on the assumption that they will eventually overthrow the Ne Win government. In a sense, both the rebels and Ne Win are bidding for foreign aid in their struggle against each other. The outcome is uncertain.   John N. Stalker

See also ASIA (Facts in Brief Table).

BURUNDI. See AFRICA.

BUS. See TRANSIT; TRANSPORTATION.

BUSINESS. See ECONOMICS; LABOR; MANUFACTURING; Section One, FOCUS ON THE ECONOMY.

CABINET, U.S. There was a turnover of all but two Cabinet members in 1973. As a result, President Richard M. Nixon has named more Cabinet appointees since he first took office than any other U.S. President. In the wake of the Watergate scandal, two former Cabinet members – Maurice H. Stans, secretary of commerce from 1969 to 1972; and John N. Mitchell, U.S. attorney general from 1969 to 1972 – were indicted for securities fraud. See WATERGATE.

The Attorney General's Office suffered the most from the 1973 Cabinet shakeup. On April 30, Attorney General Richard G. Kleindienst, Mitchell's successor, resigned because of his close personal association with some of those involved in Watergate. He was replaced on May 25 by Elliot L. Richardson, secretary of defense. See RICHARDSON, ELLIOT LEE.

Richardson then appointed a special prosecutor, Archibald Cox, to investigate the Watergate case (see COX, ARCHIBALD). Although Cox had been guaranteed complete independence, President Nixon ordered him fired after he subpoenaed White House papers and tape recordings. Rather than fire Cox, Richardson resigned on October 20. He was immediately replaced by Robert H. Bork as acting attorney general. Then, Senator William B. Saxbe (R., Ohio) was confirmed by the Senate as new attorney general on December 17. See SAXBE, WILLIAM B.

Other Shifts. Richardson served as secretary of defense from January 29 until he resigned to become attorney general. James R. Schlesinger, former director of the Central Intelligence Agency, took over as defense secretary on June 28. Secretary of State William P. Rogers resigned as of September 3, and President Nixon's chief foreign-policy adviser, Henry A. Kissinger, succeeded Rogers on September 22.

Four other new Cabinet members were confirmed: Frederick B. Dent, as secretary of commerce on January 18; Peter J. Brennan, as secretary of labor on January 31; Caspar W. Weinberger, as secretary of health, education, and welfare on February 8; and James T. Lynn as secretary of housing and urban development on January 31.

Super Cabinet Dropped. President Nixon announced in January that he was creating three super-departments to be run by three Cabinet members. He chose Secretary of Agriculture Earl L. Butz as counsel for natural resources, Weinberger for human resources, and Lynn for community development. Congress, which had refused to approve his plan to cut down the number of Cabinet posts, saw this as a move to by-pass congressional authority. Mr. Nixon abandoned the plan in May, after the emerging Watergate story forced his top aides to resign and weakened his Administration.   Darlene R. Stille

CALIFORNIA. See LOS ANGELES-LONG BEACH; SAN FRANCISCO; STATE GOVERNMENT.

CAMBODIA. See KHMER.

CAMEROON. See AFRICA.

CAMP FIRE GIRLS. See YOUTH ORGANIZATIONS.

CANADA

The world crisis in oil supplies dominated the thinking of Canadians, as it did Americans, throughout much of 1973. The two peoples share a continent whose civilization is based on an ever-increasing use of energy, and their sources of energy were in danger. Compounding the problem of rising oil and natural gas prices was the Middle East War, which threatened essential oil shipments to North America. For Canada and the United States, the oil shortage tested their traditionally good relations. A close interdependence in energy supplies along the border had to be reconciled with divergent national interests that were starkly revealed by the energy crisis.

Domestically, 1973 was a quiet year for Canadians. Prime Minister Pierre Elliott Trudeau's minority administration held power with the support of the New Democratic Party (NDP), a linkage that led the government to give a high priority to economic and welfare legislation. Quebec voters decisively endorsed the continuance of a united Canada on October 29 by rejecting the separatist Parti Québécois.

The Energy Crisis. Canada's position among the world's oil producers is a special one. It is not a large oil producer, accounting for only 2.5 per cent of the world's output and proven reserves, but it exports oil to the United States and imports it for some domestic markets. Thus, the country is vulnerable to scarcities in world supply and is immediately affected by changes in overseas prices. From 1961 until early in 1973, the Canadian energy policy had been to serve domestic needs between the Pacific coast and the Quebec border with oil and gas from Alberta, the largest producing province. The needs of Quebec and the Atlantic Provinces were met with imported oil, mainly from Venezuela and the Middle East. Total Canadian crude oil production had climbed to about 2 million barrels a day in 1973, with more than half going to the United States. Eastern Canada imported about 900,000 barrels a day.

During the 1950s and 1960s, Canada had been anxious to sell oil to the United States. But American import quotas limited Canadian sales. After the United States energy shortage became apparent, the controls were relaxed by the Nixon Administration. United States refineries in the Pacific Northwest and the Midwest called for more and more Canadian oil. In 1972, Canadian oil exports to the United States averaged 956,000 barrels a day; by March, 1973, over 1.2 million were moving daily to

Prime Minister Pierre Elliott Trudeau and his wife Margaret, right, welcome Queen Elizabeth II and Prince Philip on a summer visit to Canada.

The Ministry of Canada
In order of precedence

Pierre Elliott Trudeau, prime minister
Paul Joseph James Martin, leader of the government in the senate
Mitchell Sharp, secretary of state for external affairs
Allan Joseph MacEachen, president of the queen's privy council
Charles Mills Drury, president of the treasury board
Jean Marchand, minister of transport
John Napier Turner, minister of finance
Jean Chrétien, minister of Indian affairs and northern development
Donald Stovel Macdonald, minister of energy, mines, and resources
John Carr Munro, minister of labor
Gérard Pelletier, minister of communications
Jack Davis, minister of the environment and fisheries
Jean-Eudes Dubé, minister of public works
Stanley Ronald Basford, minister of state for urban affairs
Donald Campbell Jamieson, minister of regional economic expansion
Robert Knight Andras, minister of manpower and immigration
James Armstrong Richardson, minister of national defense
Otto Emil Lang, minister of justice and attorney general of Canada
Herb Gray, minister of consumer and corporate affairs
Robert Stanbury, minister of national revenue
Jean-Pierre Goyer, minister of supply and services
Alastair William Gillespie, minister of industry, trade, and commerce
Stanley Haidasz, minister of state
Eugene Whelan, minister of agriculture
Warren Allmand, solicitor general of Canada
Hugh Faulkner, secretary of state of Canada
André Ouellet, postmaster general
Daniel J. MacDonald, minister of veterans affairs
Marc Lalonde, minister of national health and welfare
Jeanne Sauvé, minister of state for science and technology

Premiers of Canadian Provinces

Province	Premier
Alberta	Peter Lougheed
British Columbia	David Barrett
Manitoba	Edward R. Schreyer
New Brunswick	Richard B. Hatfield
Newfoundland	Frank Moores
Nova Scotia	Gerald A. Regan
Ontario	William G. Davis
Prince Edward Island	Alexander B. Campbell
Quebec	J. Robert Bourassa
Saskatchewan	Allan Blakeney

Commissioners of Territories

Northwest Territories	Stuart M. Hodgson
Yukon Territory	James Smith

American refineries. In addition, gasoline exports from Canada were 50 times greater than in 1972. As oil prices rose, there was corresponding pressure on Canadian fuel prices.

That was the situation the Canadian government faced in early 1973. On February 27, it announced that crude oil requests by U.S. refineries would have to be cut back 3.7 per cent in March. Existing contracts would be honored, but additional sales would be monitored to ensure that only oil that Canada did not need was exported.

Petroleum Controls. On June 15, the Canadian government placed strict controls on gasoline and heating oil exports. All sales abroad had to be approved by the National Energy Board. But the crude oil controls slowed down the flow of exports to the United States only slightly; for 1973, the daily export average was 1.15 million barrels.

On September 13, Donald S. Macdonald, minister of energy, mines, and resources, announced that the government would impose an export tax of 40 cents a gallon on Canadian oil going to the United States beginning in October. This was part of a plan to keep the price of oil down for Canadian consumers. Noting that oil prices in Ontario, tied to the Chicago market, had risen 30 per cent since January, Macdonald said that the export tax would bring the price of Canadian oil in the United States into line with the average American refinery price. In addition, the government asked Canadian oil companies to maintain a freeze on Canadian prices until the end of January, 1974. The freeze was later extended to the end of the winter.

The oil industry, claiming that it was being denied the market value for its product, protested the tax. So did the Alberta government and the United States, both of which claimed that they had not been consulted in the decision. A note from the U.S. State Department on September 14 said the news of a two-price structure for Canadian oil "comes as a surprise and most certainly is not welcome information."

In introducing a two-price system for Canadian oil, the Trudeau Government served notice that it was abandoning the 1961 national energy policy. It was prepared to approve an oil pipeline from Toronto to Montreal to carry Alberta oil east to Quebec refineries. Although security of supply in eastern Canada was the main reason for the change of policy, in the long run it would mean less Alberta crude would be available to supply the United States Midwest.

Arab Cutbacks. The Arab states' attack on Israel in October made the difficult oil situation in North America worse. Although Canada remained neutral in the conflict, the Arab states threatened to reduce or even ban oil exports to Canada. At the same time, Venezuela, which supplies about 54 per cent of Canada's imported oil, drastically raised oil prices.

On November 1, the government again tried to correct the worsening supply-price situation in petroleum. Effective in December, the export tax on oil going to the United States was raised to $1.90 a barrel, while the domestic price freeze was relaxed in certain respects because of the higher cost of foreign oil. A national pricing system was to be established in February, 1974, with prices based on international crude prices paid by Montreal refineries. This would standardize oil and gasoline prices throughout Canada.

The export tax and partial price freeze were attempts to carry out several aims at once. The highest priority of the Canadian government was clearly to protect the fuel and energy needs of its own people. The export tax would allow Canada to gain the higher prices prevailing internationally for its crude oil exports. It would have been politically unacceptable to have allowed U.S. refineries to buy oil from Alberta at lower prices than eastern Canadian refineries were paying for imported oil. The alternative, to raise wellhead prices in Alberta to U.S. levels, would have given the oil companies large windfall profits the government was not prepared to permit. Part of the proceeds of the export tax – almost $2 million a day – will be given to Alberta in compensation for the loss of oil royalties. Some will be used for research into the technology of recovering oil from the vast tar sands of the Athabaska district in northern Alberta.

As the Middle East restrictions on oil exports began to bite into the supply flowing to North America, the Canadian government made it clear that it would not halt exports to the United States because of Arab pressure. However, Canada would ensure that its own needs were met before exporting to the United States. The crisis showed that the United States could not look to Canada for a long-term solution to its massive shortage in petroleum supplies. Canada had been providing about 7 per cent of the United States oil needs; it was unlikely that this amount could be increased in the future. See ENERGY.

Domestic Politics remained unstable in 1973. The Liberals had emerged from the general election of Oct. 30, 1972, holding 109 seats in the 264-seat House of Commons, while the rival Progressive Conservative Party held 107. The socialist NDP, with 31 seats, held a balance of power in Parliament. The Trudeau Government's aim was to defer an election until it could implement a new legislative program that might win back the support of a majority of the Canadian people. The NDP tried to force the government to enact progressive economic and social welfare legislation. Although the Liberals built a working relationship with the NDP, the prospects for the Trudeau Government's survival were still uncertain at the end of the year.

The most critical test of strength between the Liberals and the Conservatives in Parliament centered around a proposal by Finance Minister John N. Turner to reduce the income tax on corporations to encourage more investment and create more jobs.

The NDP condemned the plan as unwarranted favoritism toward corporations. When Turner introduced legislation to reduce the tax rate on corporation profits from 49 to 40 per cent, he skillfully linked it to a proposal by Robert L. Stanfield, the Conservative leader, that the reduction be for one year only. Turner promised a report on the tax changes after April 1, 1974. Parliament could then decide whether to continue the tax reduction. As a result, the Conservatives supported the bill, and it passed the crucial second reading on June 20 by a vote of 194 to 30, and went into effect for the 1973-1974 fiscal year.

The Cost of Living, which showed its steepest rise since 1951, kept the Trudeau Government on the defensive. By October, the consumer price index had risen 8.7 per cent over the previous 12 months. Grocery prices were 16.7 per cent higher for the year, and they rose 3.2 per cent in August alone.

The government refused to seek wage and price controls in spite of Conservative demands. Instead, it enacted lower tax rates to benefit wage earners, food subsidies to head off unjustifiably large price increases, and controls on exports of scarce commodities.

Finance Minister Turner's budget, presented on February 19, estimated federal revenues at $18 billion for the fiscal year ending March 31, 1974, with a deficit of $975 million on the year's operations. The budget included a 5 per cent cut in personal income tax as well as increases in personal exemptions. It also outlined a scheme to link exemptions with price changes. Federal old-age pensions were increased to $100 a month, effective in April, and placed on a sliding scale so that they would rise with prices. Family allowances were raised to $12 a child from an average of $7.21 in September, 1972, and were to reach $20 by January, 1974. Faced with a large deficit in the unemployment insurance fund, the government was obliged to increase the rates of contribution by employees and employers by 40 per cent.

Strict export controls were placed on oilseeds and vegetable-oil production in June in an attempt to seal off the Canadian market in foodstuffs from the demands of the United States. The same thing was done for beef in August, and, at the same time, the tariff on American beef coming into Canada was temporarily removed. By September, Canadian cattlemen had managed to have the tariff reinstituted. A Food Price Review Board, created in April, monitored food prices and notified the government when it felt prices should be held in line through subsidy or direct restraint. Subsidies later stabilized the prices of bread and milk.

Parliament adjourned on July 27, but it was recalled in a little more than a month to deal with a walkout of 56,000 railway workers that brought the national rail system to a halt. At a 12-hour session, ending on September 1, the House of Commons endorsed a bill ordering the railwaymen back to work and providing minimum wage increases for them while their claims were handled through arbitration.

On October 15, Parliament met again for the last phase of the 1973 session. It renewed the suspension of capital punishment, in effect since 1967, for another five years in all cases except for convicted killers of police and prison guards.

Strict controls on foreign investment were passed by the Senate in December and put into law. The bill, which goes into effect in 1974, requires the government to screen foreign take-overs of Canadian companies with assets exceeding $250,000 or annual sales over $3 million. The House of Commons had approved the program in late November.

Federal Spending in Canada
Estimated Budget for Fiscal 1974*

	Millions of dollars
Health and welfare	5,105
Public debt	2,581
Economic development and support	2,436
Defense	2,134
Fiscal transfer payments to provinces	1,462
Transportation and communications	1,411
General government services	953
Internal overhead expenses	808
Education assistance	621
Culture and recreation	455
Foreign affairs	427
Total	18,393

*April 1, 1973, to March 31, 1974

Spending Since 1968

Billions of dollars

Fiscal Year
1968-'69 '69-'70 '70-'71 '71-'72 '72-'73 '73-'74
Est. Est.

Source: Treasury Board of Canada

Satisfying the West. Ottawa's relations with the western provinces were explored at the Western Economic Opportunities Conference in Calgary from July 24 to 26. Thirteen federal Cabinet ministers, headed by Prime Minister Trudeau, met with the premiers of the four western provinces to consider how national economic policies could more effectively meet the needs of the West. The western premiers believe that many of Ottawa's policies primarily benefit industrialized central Canada and inhibit the growth of secondary industry west of the Great Lakes.

Prime Minister Trudeau promised a thorough review of railroad freight rates. The provinces are to receive more information on the finances of the railway companies. The western premiers charged that freight rates discriminate against the West. Pending the outcome of the review, rates will be frozen for 18 months.

The federal ministers promised to propose banking legislation to allow provincial governments to own shares in federally chartered banks. This concession represented a victory for Premier David Barrett of British Columbia, who wants his province to have more influence over the policies of the private Bank of British Columbia. Ottawa also promised to set up regional offices for federal departments that carry out extensive activities in the West.

Foreign Affairs. Following the January cease-fire in Vietnam, Canada accepted membership on a new four-power Commission of Control and Supervision. Six days later, a military and civilian force of 290 men was on duty in Vietnam. Canada's original 60-day commitment was lengthened following a visit to Vietnam by Mitchell Sharp, secretary of state for external affairs. Sharp was disappointed by the failure of the Geneva Conference to set up a separate political authority to which the commission could report, and the inability of the commission members to agree among themselves on the impartiality and public disclosure of its reports caused Canada to withdraw. Sharp announced the government's decision to withdraw the Canadian contingent on May 29, and all Canadians had left by July 31. See ASIA.

The Arab-Israeli war brought a second call for Canadian services as a peacekeeper. Canada was asked to supply men to transport food and supplies and provide other accommodations for the United Nations (UN) emergency force sent to the Suez Canal area after the October 22 cease-fire. Poland shared these duties. By November 19, there were 480 Canadians serving with the 2,000-member UN force, with 600 more to come.

Canada renewed its joint air defense agreement with the United States for two years. The short renewal was designed to give time for thought about the long-term needs of North American defense, where changing technology was rapidly altering the military environment.

Prime Minister Trudeau flew to China in October,

his first visit there since diplomatic relations were established in 1970. He discussed the general international situation with Premier Chou En-lai. They signed a number of bilateral agreements, the most important one calling for the exchange of consuls. The two countries also agreed to give each other most-favored-nation status in trade relations. Trudeau also met with Chairman Mao Tse-tung.

The Commonwealth Meeting was held in Ottawa from August 2 to 10. About 700 delegates, representing the 32 independent nations in the Commonwealth, discussed world political developments, administrative procedures, and common problems, such as the impact of multinational enterprises. The meeting, probably the largest international conference ever held in Canada, was only the third time the Commonwealth Conference had met outside Britain. Queen Elizabeth II, as head of the Commonwealth, spent six days at the conference. Twenty-two heads of state, along with such leaders as Prime Ministers Edward Heath of Britain and Edward Gough Whitlam of Australia, were there. The conference took a stand against nuclear testing in the atmosphere at the insistence of the South Pacific members, who opposed the tests conducted by France on Mururoa Atoll later in August. See FRANCE.

The Canadian Economy in 1973 outperformed the record growth rates of 1972. Expansion in the last quarter of 1972 and the first of 1973 came to almost 3 per cent a quarter after allowance for inflation. It was a pace that clearly could not be maintained. Real growth dropped to 0.9 per cent in the second quarter, suggesting a real domestic product increase of 7 per cent for the year, the greatest gain in any year since 1966. The total value of Canadian goods and services was expected by economists to reach $116 billion in 1973.

A major reason for the expansion was strong consumer spending for automobiles and household goods. Business investment and government spending were also at high levels. The world shortage of raw materials and foodstuffs benefited Canada, which sent a large volume of exports to Europe and Japan. The United States continued as Canada's best customer, with automotive vehicles and parts flowing across the border in both directions. Canada harvested 628 million bushels of wheat by the end of the crop year, with all but 90 million bushels sold abroad. Exports in the first nine months totaled $17.8 billion, while imports came to $16.7 billion.

Employment increased drastically. In October, there were 8.8 million employed, and the seasonally adjusted jobless rate was 5.8 per cent. Almost 500,000 more workers were employed in October than a year before. Almost all men aged 25 to 64, the key group in the labor force, were employed, and

Quebec Prime Minister J. Robert Bourassa watches his wife vote in the provincial election in October. Bourassa's Liberals won 55 per cent of the vote.

there were shortages of skilled labor in some trades and in some regions.

The Provinces

Alberta. The two-price structure for the province's natural gas adopted in November, 1972, allowing Albertans to pay less than consumers outside the province, precipitated a stormy controversy in 1973 with Ontario, which uses almost half of Alberta's gas. In September, Premier Peter Lougheed announced the formation of the Alberta Energy Company, a quasi-crown corporation, to mobilize investment for such projects as the exploitation of the Athabaska tar sands.

British Columbia, under its first socialist government, embarked upon several ventures in public ownership. In March, the NDP government purchased an ailing paper mill at Ocean Falls from Crown Zellerbach Canada, Limited, which had planned to close the mill. The next month, the government purchased a 79 per cent interest in the Canadian Cellulose Company, which has pulp mills at Prince Rupert and Castlegar. The government also announced that in March, 1974, it would begin to operate, on a cost basis, a compulsory automobile insurance plan for the province's 1 million drivers. The state company would also provide general insurance. Stock prices of British Columbia-based companies tumbled in December after Premier Barrett announced that all tax concessions for corporations in the province would be canceled by year-end. Barrett did not elaborate on his intentions, leaving observers unsure of the impact of his announcement.

Manitoba voters gave a substantial vote of confidence to Premier Edward R. Schreyer and his NDP government on June 28. In office four years, the NDP increased its standing in the legislature from 29 to 31 seats. The Conservatives won 21 seats, a gain of 1, and the Liberals won 5 seats. There were four judicial recounts and in three constituencies, the returning official had to cast the deciding vote to break a tie.

New Brunswick was hit by the worst floods in 50 years along 100 miles of the St. John River on April 28 and 29. The floodwaters inundated over 10,000 acres of good farmland and forced 1,458 people in the Fredericton area to flee their homes. Public damage, mainly to roads, totaled over $4 million, and private claimants received $3.2 million from a federal-provincial fund. The flooding, which began on the upper waters of the river in Maine and moved downstream into New Brunswick, led to renewed demands for more effective flood control in the international river basin.

Newfoundland. The luxury liner *Queen Elizabeth II* brought 1,100 guests to the opening of a new oil refinery at the little village of Come-by-Chance on October 9. The trip was the brainchild of New York oilman John Shaheen, who originally constructed the $198-million deepwater refinery to serve the eastern

United States. The refinery, which can process 100,000 barrels of oil daily, is the first of a chain of three to be built in Canada's Atlantic Provinces. The federal government assisted the project by building a $23-million wharf for supertankers. Shaheen later announced that the refinery's output would be earmarked for local use.

Nova Scotia. Premier Gerald A. Regan's Liberal government picked up an additional seat in the legislature on June 5 by winning a by-election in Guysborough. The victory gave the party 25 seats in the assembly, compared with 19 for the Conservatives and 2 for the NDP. A controversial measure to license denturists, defeated on two previous occasions, passed on March 16. Other measures introduced were a bill to establish a board to approve the transfer of land holdings and a scheme to impose a special tax on nonresidents who acquire land. The measures resulted from the outcry against the steady acquisition of Nova Scotia's coastal property by private individuals, many of them nonresidents.

Ontario. The Progressive Conservative administration of William G. Davis came under heavy fire in 1973. The new treasurer, John White, in presenting his first budget on April 12, announced an increase in the provincial sales tax from 5 to 7 per cent and proposed to apply it to the consumption of energy. A storm of protest that followed caused the government to abandon the unpopular energy tax.

Later, a select committee of the legislature spent several months examining the circumstances in which the contract for a $45-million Toronto headquarters building for the Ontario Hydro-Electric Power Commission was awarded to a company belonging to a friend of the prime minister. Davis and his government were cleared of any impropriety, but the committee criticized the Hydro commissioners for neglecting their responsibilities in overseeing the construction contract arrangements. On March 15, the government lost two by-elections in the Toronto area, though it still controlled 76 of the 117 seats in the legislature.

Prince Edward Island celebrated the 100th anniversary of its accession to Confederation in 1973, with ceremonies inaugurated on New Year's Eve of 1972 by Governor General Roland Michener. On July 1, Canada's national holiday, Queen Elizabeth II was in the island province to provide a focal point for the festivities. The provincial budget of $125.2 million embodied a small surplus in spite of a reduction in the real property tax rate. More aid was promised to the ailing fishing industry.

Quebec residents gave an overwhelming vote of confidence to Prime Minister J. Robert Bourassa and his Liberal administration in an election on October 29. The Liberals won 55 per cent of the popular vote to gain an unprecedented 102 seats in the 110-seat legislature. The Parti Québécois, campaigning for independence for Quebec, won only 6 seats, 1 less

Mounties Still "Get Their Man"

One hundred years ago, the Royal Canadian Mounted Police was organized because crime was rampant on Canada's western plains. The Mounties soon brought law and order to the region and won fame for their exploits. Books and motion pictures later glamorized the intrepid lawmen in scarlet tunics, wide-brimmed hats, and high boots who searched for wrongdoers on horseback and dog sled.

Today, they seldom wear their distinctive red uniforms and the thundering hoofbeats no longer echo across the plains. But the Mounties, now using the most modern methods of law enforcement, continue to battle lawlessness throughout Canada.

Prime Minister John A. Macdonald founded the North-West Mounted Police in 1873 to suppress frontier whiskey traffic, calm Indian unrest, and stamp out general lawlessness in the newly acquired Canadian Northwest. The armed force, which combined military and police duties, was modeled after the Irish Constabulary. The first troop of 150 men set out from Ottawa in October, 1873, and traveled as far west as Lower Fort Garry, near Winnipeg, where it trained during the winter. The next spring, the force, now up to 300 men, moved on to the Northwest Territories.

The Mounties soon gained a reputation far exceeding their small numbers. During the first five years of patrolling the plains, not a single member of the force lost his life by human violence. To the settlers, they were guides and protectors; to the Indians, the red coats symbolized friendly authority. The bond of trust Mounties forged with the Indians led to the successful negotiation of the Blackfoot Treaty of 1877, which gave Canada 50,000 square miles of tribal land.

In 1904, King Edward VII bestowed the prefix "Royal" on the force. The name was changed again in 1920, to the Royal Canadian Mounted Police (RCMP), when the force absorbed the Dominion Police and assumed responsibility for enforcing Dominion statutes throughout Canada. Headquarters were moved from Regina to Ottawa.

Today, the force numbers about 14,000, including more than 2,000 civilian members. In addition to enforcing federal laws throughout Canada, they also serve as the provincial police force for all provinces except Ontario and Quebec, and provide police service for 162 Canadian towns. The RCMP's jurisdiction stretches from the Atlantic Ocean to the Pacific and from the North Pole to the United States border, an area of about 3.85 million square miles.

Over the years, the force has retained its semimilitary structure, while gradually shedding many of the trappings. The wide-brimmed hats and the red tunics were phased out of regular service in 1966. They are now worn only by the guards at Parliament Hill in Ottawa and for special ceremonial occasions, such as the 1973 visit to Canada by Queen Elizabeth II. Nor are horses and sled dogs used on regular duty. Today, Mounties travel by automobile and airplane, ship and snowmobile, and, occasionally, by snowshoes.

Today's Mountie deals with every kind of police work, including drunk and disorderly cases, murder, counterfeiting, national security, and traffic offenses. He reports on migratory birds, fur-bearing animals, and out-of-season hunting. He patrols the Arctic and enforces regulations governing Eskimos and Indians. He helps to enforce customs, excise tax, and immigration laws. He checks naturalization papers and passports, and investigates applicants for government positions. On occasion, he has been called upon to deliver mail, emergency medicines, and even babies.

In an average year, the force investigates nearly 1 million offenses, including about 300,000 criminal code offenses and more than 400,000 driving offenses.

Aiding the force in conducting criminal investigations are five crime-detection laboratories (in Vancouver, Edmonton, Regina, Ottawa, and Sackville). They are equipped with such modern scientific equipment as electron microscopes, microfilmed fingerprint files, and infrared spectrophotometers. With sophisticated tools, the Mounties strive to maintain their reputation: "They always get their man."   Kathryn Sederberg

Patrolling in 1878

David Lewis, leader of the New Democratic Party, uses a bullhorn in
an attempt to calm striking railway workers outside Parliament in Ottawa.

than in 1970, and its founder-leader, René Lévesque, was defeated. However, the party's popular vote climbed from 23 to 30 per cent. The Union Nationale Party, long dominant in Quebec politics, was wiped out in the election, and the Créditiste Party dropped from 12 to 2 seats.

Saskatchewan, the third western province under a socialist NDP administration, moved more strongly to public ownership of economic enterprises in 1973. In March, Premier Allan Blakeney's government purchased a 45 per cent interest in Intercontinental Packers, Limited, a meat-packing plant, and added to its holdings in Interprovincial Steel and Pipe Corporation. In both cases, government intervention headed off attempts by outside interests to gain ownership. The provincial budget, reported on February 9, forecast a modest surplus, though personal and corporate income taxes had to be increased. Grants were made to allow the property tax for education to be reduced to homeowners.

Facts in Brief: Population: 22,984,000. Government: Governor General Roland Michener; Prime Minister Pierre Elliott Trudeau. Monetary unit: Canadian dollar. Foreign Trade: exports, $21,025,-000,000; imports, $20,599,000,000.   David M. L. Farr

See also CANADIAN LIBRARY ASSOCIATION (CLA); CANADIAN LITERATURE; MICHENER, ROLAND; TRUDEAU, PIERRE ELLIOTT; Section One, FOCUS ON THE WORLD.

CANADIAN LIBRARY ASSOCIATION (CLA) held its 28th annual conference in Sackville, New Brunswick, from June 16 to 22, 1973. More than 1,000 persons attended. The central conference theme was the Canadian librarian today. The conference replaced the constitution and bylaws adopted in 1946 with legislation designed to develop "opportunities for future change." It added the chairman of the CLA's divisions to the board of directors. To the council, it added the presidents or delegates of the affiliated library associations of the Atlantic Provinces, Alberta, British Columbia, Manitoba, Ontario, Quebec, and Saskatchewan.

CLA received a grant of $27,000 from the Canadian International Development Agency to assist the Working Group for Developing Countries of the International Federation of Library Associations. It also received a bequest of $500,000 from the Mary Allen estate; the income will be used for special projects under CLA Council direction. A donation of $1,000 from the Canadian Library Exhibitors' Association was assigned to the Gurdial Pannu loan fund for students.

Medals and Awards. The Book of the Year for Children Medal was awarded to Ruth Nichols for *The Marrow of the World* (English) and to Simone Bussières for *Le Petit Sapin qui a poussé sur une étoile* (French). The Amelia Frances Howard-Gibbon Medal for illustrations was awarded to Jacques de

Roussan for *Au dè la du soleil: Beyond the Sun* (bilingual). The Merit Award of the Canadian Library Trustees Association went to Eileen Burns of the Halifax Memorial Public Library Board. The Order of Canada awarded a Medal of Service to Jessie Beaumont Mifflen for her leadership in developing regional library service in Newfoundland. The fifth Howard V. Phalin-World Book Graduate Scholarship in Library Science was awarded by a CLA standing committee to Alixe Hambleton, Supervisor of School Libraries, Toronto Board of Education. The scholarship was sponsored by World Book–Childcraft of Canada, Limited.

Publications. *Canadian Reference Sources; a Selective Guide*, edited by Dorothy E. Ryder, provides information about some 1,200 Canadian items based largely on the collection of the National Library of Canada. *Canadian Materials 1971*, selected by the Canadian Materials Committee of the Canadian School Library Association, is an annotated list of print and nonprint materials issued in 1971 for elementary and secondary school resource centers. *Notable Children's Books*, compiled by Sheila Egoff and Alvine Bélisle for an exhibition arranged by the National Library of Canada, is an annotated catalog with illustrations. *Research Collections in Canadian Libraries–I, Universities*, parts 3, 4, and 5, analyzes university collections in British Columbia, Ontario, and Quebec.   Elizabeth Homer Morton

CANADIAN LITERATURE reflected the centennial celebration in 1973 of the Royal Canadian Mounted Police as well as a heightened interest in the creative arts. *Maintain the Right; the Early History of the North West Mounted Police, 1873-1900* by Ronald Atkin; *Mountie: a Golden Treasury of Those Early Years*, a picture book compiled by Dean Charters; and *100 Years in the RCMP Saddle! Or, Stop the Musical Ride, I Want Off*, cartoons by Frank Spalding, depict the contribution of this unique police force. *Valiant Men*, edited by John Swettenham, records in one volume for the first time the stories of all the Canadians who have won the Victoria Cross "For Valor" and the George Cross "For Gallantry."

Literature. *Survival: A Thematic Guide to Canadian Literature* by Margaret Atwood has been described as "compulsive and essential reading" for all interested in Canada. *The Oxford Anthology of Canadian Literature*, edited by Robert Weaver and William Toye, spans three centuries and presents 80 writers. *Wilderness Writers* by James Polk deals with natural history and the storytelling of Ernest Thompson Seton, Charles G. D. Roberts, and Archie Belaney (Grey Owl).

Drama. *Encounter: Canadian Drama in Four Media* by Eugene Benson includes eight plays for stage, radio, television, and film. *Four Canadian Playwrights* by Mavor Moore attempts "to serve up play, playwright, literary criticism, and a partial history of Canadian drama." *Love and Whisky* by Betty Lee is

the story of the Dominion Drama Festival from 1931 to 1971.

Fiction. *Surfacing* by Margaret Atwood provides fine descriptions of northern Quebec woods and lakes and probes the emotions of the characters through a stream-of-consciousness technique. *The Manticore* by Robertson Davies continues probing the psychological problems of the Staunton family begun in his earlier novel, *Fifth Business*. *The Marrow of the World* by Ruth Nichols is a fantasy for teen-agers with remarkable descriptions of the Muskoka-Georgian Bay countryside. Interest in the work of novelists resulted in the two-volume *Conversations with Canadian Novelists*, 20 interviews compiled by Donald Cameron.

Poetry. *Collected Poems: The Two Seasons* by Dorothy Livesay; *The Dance Is One* by F. R. Scott; *Happy Enough Poems 1935-1972* by George Johnston; *Driving Home: Poems New and Selected* by Miriam Waddington; and *Selected Poems* by Ralph Gustafson are new works by established poets.

The Fine Arts. *Creative Canada*, volumes 1 and 2, initiates a biographical dictionary of 20th century creative and performing artists. Painting: *Contemporary Canadian Painting* by William Withrow; *Four Decades: The Canadian Group of Painters and Their Contemporaries 1930-1970* by Paul Duval. Sculpture: *The Girls: A Biography of Frances Loring & Florence Wyle* by sculptor Rebecca Sisler and *Sculpture of the Eskimo* by George Swinton. Architecture: *The Barn* by Eric Arthur and Dudley Witney.

Biography. *Mike: The Memoirs of the Right Honourable Lester B. Pearson, Volume 1, 1897-1948* recounts his boyhood and early diplomatic days. *Stanfield* by Geoffrey Stevens, describes the life of the Conservative Party leader. *Bush Pilot with a Briefcase* by Donald Keith is the story of Grant McConachie, who eventually became president of Canadian Pacific Airlines. *The Things That Are Caesar's: The Memoirs of a Canadian Public Servant* (1938-1970) is by Arnold Heeney, twice Canada's ambassador to the United States.

North. *The Arctic Imperative: An Overview of the Energy Crisis* by Richard Rohmer raises issues about northern development. *Tundra: Selections from the Great Accounts of Arctic Land Voyages* by Farley Mowat pleads for reclaiming barren areas that once supported animal life. *One Woman's Arctic* by Sheila Burnford describes visits to northern Baffin Island.

Governor-General's Literary Awards for books published in 1972 went to Robertson Davies for *The Manticore* (English fiction); Dennis Lee for *Civil Elegies and Other Poems*; John Newlove for *Lies* (English poetry); Jean Hamelin and Yves Roby for *Histoire économique du Québec 1851-1896* (French nonfiction); Antonine Maillet for *Don l'orignal* (French fiction); and Gilles Hénault for *Signaux pour les voyants* (French poetry).

Stephen Leacock Memorial Award for humor went to Don Bell for his book *Saturday Night at the Bagel Factory*.   Elizabeth Homer Morton

CARRERO BLANCO, LUIS (1903-1973), president of Spain, was killed on December 20 by assassins who tunneled under a Madrid street and set off an explosion under his car. He had been appointed president on June 8, 1973, by General Francisco Franco, who retained the duties of chief of state and commander of the armed forces. The new president named a new Cabinet on June 11, strengthening the right wing political faction. The new Cabinet was expected to hew closely to Franco's policies, though its conservative composition marked a turn away from the centrist-technocratic government Franco put in in 1970. It was reshuffled after Carrero Blanco's death.

Carrero Blanco was born in the north of Spain in Santoña, a town on the coast of the Bay of Biscay. He had served in government posts since the end of the Spanish Civil War in 1939. He had been Franco's closest crony and top subordinate for many years, and shared many of Franco's political views. As vice-president since 1969, Carrero Blanco handled most routine government matters.

Carrero Blanco served as the chief adviser in preparing Prince Juan Carlos for the Spanish throne. He was an admiral in the Spanish Navy and had written several books on naval history. The prince, grandson of King Alfonso XIII, who was deposed in 1931, is to become king and chief of state when Franco dies or retires.   Kathryn Sederberg

CELEBRATIONS and anniversaries observed in 1973 included the following:
Boston Tea Party Bicentennial. The U.S. Postal Service issued a block of four postage stamps on July 4, 1973, that depict the Boston Tea Party in 1773.

British Monarchy Millennial. Great Britain marked the 1,000th anniversary of the British monarchy from May to September, 1973, in the historic town of Bath. The festival, called "Monarchy 1000," commemorated the first coronation of a monarch of all England, King Edgar, in Bath Abbey on May 22, 973.

Cable Car Centennial. San Francisco observed the 100th anniversary of its 6-ton rolling landmark, the cable car. A commemorative medallion was issued. The cable car, invented by Andrew S. Hallidie, was first used on Aug. 1, 1873.

Copernicus Quinquecentennial. Many nations honored Nicolaus Copernicus, the Polish astronomer who was born on Feb. 19, 1473. See Close-Up.

Enrico Caruso Centennial. New York City's Metropolitan Opera celebrated Enrico Caruso's 100th birthday on February 25 with a display of the Italian tenor's memorabilia and a special matinée performance of *Aïda*, which Caruso popularized. Caruso was born in Naples in 1873 and died there in 1921. A commemorative 12-record set of Caruso recordings made between 1904 and 1920 was reissued.

Israel's 25th Anniversary. On May 14, 1948, David Ben-Gurion read a hastily prepared statement declaring the birth of the state of Israel. In 1973, Israel commemorated its 25th national birthday, and at the same time observed the 1,900th anniversary of the fall of Masada. In A.D. 73, 960 besieged Jews made their last stand against the Romans at this craggy citadel overlooking the Dead Sea. They destroyed their property and killed themselves rather than surrender to the Romans and become slaves. A memorial sight and sound presentation was coupled with the swearing in of new armored corps cadets at Masada on March 27. Surviving heroes of the 1948 Arab-Israeli War participated in a torchlight ceremony at Jerusalem's Wailing Wall at sundown on May 6. Military and industrial progress keynoted many of the festivities, including a military parade on May 7 in Jerusalem and an industrial progress exhibit in Tel Aviv-Yafo from May 28 to June 23. See MIDDLE EAST (Close-Up).

Marquette-Joliet Expedition Tercentennial. Seven men – clad in canvas knickers, moccasins, homespun blouses, and knit caps – paddled two birchbark canoes from St. Ignace, Mich., to Helena, Ark., and back to Green Bay, Wis., from May 17 to Sept. 19, 1973. They retraced the journey down Lake Michigan and the Fox, Wisconsin, Mississippi, Illinois, and Des Plaines rivers by two Frenchmen, Father Jacques Marquette and Louis Joliet in 1673, which opened the Mississippi River system for exploration. Other events commemorating this historic journey included the Chicago Lakefront Festival from August 11 to 19 and a nine-state celebration held under the St. Louis Gateway Arch from July 4 to 12.

Molière Tercentennial. France observed the 300th anniversary of the death of Molière, its greatest writer of comedy, in 1973. The government issued a commemorative medallion in gold, silver, and bronze, and state-subsidized cultural centers presented Molière productions throughout France.

Oxford Union Sesquicentennial. Oxford Union, the famed British orators' union, celebrated its 150th anniversary on March 2, 1973, with a five-hour banquet complete with speakers. Some of the union's more famous members attended, including Great Britain's Prime Minister Edward Heath and former Prime Minister Harold Macmillan. Oxford Union was founded in 1823 as a debating society in Oxford University's Christ Church College.

Penny Postal Card Centennial. On May 12, 1873, the U.S. Post Office issued a postal card bearing a brown, 1-cent stamp. The U.S. Postal Service celebrated the 100th birthday of the penny postal card in 1973 by issuing a replica with a 6-cent stamp.

Prince Edward Island Centennial. Canada's smallest province entered the Dominion of Canada on July 1, 1873. The centennial celebration included regattas, film festivals, and a state visit by Queen Elizabeth II and Prince Philip from June 29 through July 4.

Copernicus – After Five Centuries

Scientists and scholars in 1973 celebrated the 500th anniversary of Nicolaus Copernicus' birth. An economist, linguist, physician, and humanist, Copernicus is best known as an astronomer. He was the first scientist to demonstrate that the sun was the center of the solar system, not the earth, that the earth and other planets moved around the sun.

His theories formed the basis for modern astronomy. They led to Galileo's discoveries with the telescope, the planetary laws of the German astronomer Johannes Kepler, and Sir Isaac Newton's theory of gravitation. Until Copernicus, the conventional wisdom of the day was Claudius Ptolemy's theory of 1,400 years earlier. It said, with the confidence men place in their own senses, that the earth stood motionless at the center of creation. The sun, moon, and all the stars whirled around it.

Copernicus was born Niklas Koppernigk in Thorn (now Toruń), Poland, on Feb. 19, 1473, according to the Julian calendar then in use. By today's Gregorian calendar, the 500th anniversary of his birth fell on March 4, 1973. In Latin, the language of scholars five centuries ago, his name was Nicolaus Copernicus.

Circumstance smiled on Copernicus. The son of a prosperous merchant who died in 1483, Copernicus was reared by an uncle, who was a distinguished statesman at the Polish royal court and a high-ranking churchman. Copernicus grew up during the late Renaissance flush of intellectual freedom. The professor in Bologna, Italy, from whom Copernicus learned Greek openly told students, "The hereafter is an old wives' tale." Yet he was not persecuted. Leonardo da Vinci, one of Copernicus' contemporaries, urged men to analyze, experiment, and reason, to consider new problems and seek new answers.

Copernicus studied at the Jagiellonian University in Kraków from 1491 to 1495 and in Bologna from 1496 to 1500. His uncle secured a position for him as canon of the cathedral chapter of Frauenburg (now Frombork), Poland.

With chapter approval, Copernicus went to the University of Padua in Italy to study medicine for two years. He concluded his long formal education at Ferrara in 1503, earning a doctor's degree in canon law. That fall, he became secretary and physician to his uncle, then a bishop.

Copernicus began his astronomical observations while he was a student. He outlined the essentials of his theory in *Nicolaus Copernicus' Commentary on the Hypothesis of the Movement of the Celestial Orbs.* The book was completed in late 1508, but it was circulated only privately. He saw that the awesome complexity of Ptolemaic astronomy was unneeded if men would only accept the earth's motion around the sun.

"In the midst of all this sits Sun enthroned," Copernicus wrote. "He is rightly called the Lamp, the Mind, the Ruler of the Universe."

But others were not easily convinced. This removed the earth – and man – from the center of creation.

People in his area knew of, but did not understand, Copernican ideas of a sun-centered universe. By one story, a carnival clown dancing in the street whirled a pig's bladder at the end of a string and screeched: "I am the sun; see how the earth is dancing around me and worship me."

Copernicus had virtually completed his major work, *Concerning the Revolutions of the Celestial Spheres,* by 1520 or 1530. But it was not published, perhaps because no printer was available. Or perhaps the growing attempt to erase heresy stifled any impulse to publish controversial views. Later, a young professor from Wittenberg, Germany, source of the Lutheran Reformation, persuaded Copernicus to put the finishing touches on it and it was published in 1543. Reportedly, the first copy reached him on May 24, the day he died.

An anonymous introduction was added noting that astronomical theories are only mathematical tools to predict heavenly phenomena. Their "truth" was unimportant. This, too, may have been to protect the book from the Inquisition. Yet the Reformation, as such, was not anxious to guard Copernicus. Martin Luther himself scoffed, "The fool would overturn all astronomy."   Ed Nelson

Copernicus

Young environmentalists and a Jesuit priest celebrated the anniversary of the 1673 Marquette-Joliet discoveries by repeating the historic trip.

Rachmaninoff Centennial. The world honored the 100th anniversary of the birth of Sergei Rachmaninoff with performances of the works of the famed composer, pianist, and conductor. Rachmaninoff was born in Oneg, Russia, on April 1, 1873, and studied at the Moscow Conservatory before leaving Russia in 1917.

250th Anniversary of Adam Smith. Smith, a Scottish economist, wrote *An Inquiry into the Nature and Causes of the Wealth of Nations*, a book considered the cornerstone of capitalism. In June, scholars met for two days in Kirkcaldy, Scotland – Smith's birthplace – to discuss the book and its relevance today. The symposium began on June 6, the 250th anniversary of Smith's baptism; his actual date of birth is not known.

Swedish Royal Opera Bicentennial. On Jan. 18, 1973, the Swedish Royal Opera presented a new opera, *Tintomara*, in observance of its 200th anniversary. The opera, composed by Lars Johan Werle, is based on the last days of King Gustavus III, who was shot in the back at a midnight masquerade in the Stockholm Opera House on March 16, 1792.

150th Anniversary of the Texas Rangers. The Texas Rangers say they are North America's oldest law-enforcement agency. On August 4, 82 rangers celebrated the organization's 150th anniversary by dedicating a new Texas Ranger Hall of Fame along the Brazos River near Waco, Tex.   Jacquelyn Heath

CENSUS, U.S. In 1973, the U.S. Bureau of the Census completed reporting the results of the 1970 U.S. Census of Population and Housing. The 1970 count produced about 4 billion individual items of data, which filled more than 200,000 pages of tables and text in more than 2,000 publications. In April, the bureau estimated that the 1970 census had overlooked 5.3 million Americans. However, bureau officials noted that the estimated percentage of uncounted persons is smaller than in previous censuses.

Birth Expectations. The decline in birth expectations among young wives announced in 1972 was confirmed by a census survey in June, 1973 – 70 per cent of wives, aged 18 to 24, expected to have a maximum of two children. This came to an average of 2.3 children per wife. In 1965, young wives expected to have 3.1 children; and in 1967, 2.9. For the population to replace itself from generation to generation, there should be an average of 2.1 births per woman.

The 1973 survey showed that the U.S. population could be on the way to reaching replacement level fertility. But the popular concept known as zero population growth is not dependent only on achieving replacement level fertility. Because of immigration, which has been about 400,000 a year, women would have to have fewer than an average of 2.1 children for the population to stop growing. Actual zero growth would not occur until this rate had been maintained for some 70 years.

248

The sharp drop in fertility and birth expectations was reflected in projections of what the U.S. population will be by the year 2000. The latest projections range from 251 million to 300 million, down from earlier projections of from 271 million to 322 million.

Population Growth. The United States started 1973 with an estimated population of 209,717,000, a gain of 1,628,000 during 1972. This was the smallest increase since 1945. There were 3,256,000 births, more than a million below the peak 1957 figure. Based on these 1972 figures, the birth rate (the number of births per 1,000 persons) dropped to 15.6, the lowest in U.S. history.

A Census Bureau study, released in September, showed that population growth in the nation's metropolitan areas has slowed down since the 1970 census. Population estimates of the country's 263 metropolitan areas indicated that the largest – those with populations of 2 million or more – grew only 0.8 per cent between 1970 and 1972. Metropolitan areas as a whole grew 2.2 per cent. This was a marked decline from the 1960 to 1970 growth rate for these areas of 16.6 per cent.

As of December 31, the U.S. population, including the armed forces overseas, was estimated at 211.7-million, an increase of 1.5 million.   Vincent P. Barabba

CENTRAL AFRICAN REPUBLIC. See AFRICA.
CEYLON. See SRI LANKA.
CHAD. See AFRICA.

CHEMICAL INDUSTRY enjoyed its second consecutive year of excellent growth in 1973. Existing U.S. facilities were used to capacity. For example, plants making polyethylene, polyvinyl chloride, phthalic anhydride, and titanium dioxide were running flat out. This was also true for those making benzene, sulfur, chlorine, caustic soda, and phosphate fertilizers. New domestic plant and equipment expenditures increased by about 29 per cent, to a record $4.45 billion, up from $3.45 billion in 1972.

Despite a general upswing in prices, however, a sudden surge in costs of raw materials and fuels threatened earnings. To offset or retard the rise in commodity costs, the U.S. government sold large quantities of metals and other materials from the nation's strategic stockpile. These anti-inflation measures decreed by the government lowered prices. Yet booming exports contributed to domestic shortages because foreign buyers offered higher prices. Shortages were expected to continue for several years until new manufacturing plants begin operating.

The second devaluation of the U.S. dollar in February also served to increase chemical exports. A record of more than $5 billion in exports was estimated in 1973. But, since most exported items contain some imported components, the devaluation did not benefit the U.S. balance of trade as much as expected.

The first U.S. shipment of chemicals to mainland China since 1949 left Houston in mid-January in a deal arranged by Sobin Chemicals. Another first in the expanding trade relations with China was the licensing of its one-step acrylonitrile process by Standard Oil of Ohio in May. Three complete ammonia plants were sold to China by M. W. Kellogg of Houston, who will supply engineering, materials, and equipment.

Production Increases. Synthetic fiber production gained over 10 per cent in 1973 to more than $5-billion, after a gain of almost 25 per cent in 1972. More than $400 million worth of synthetic organic dyes and other coloring materials were produced, along with about $500 million worth of other textile chemicals, such as finishes and detergents.

It was a bumper year for agricultural chemicals after the Nixon Administration in early January urged farmers to increase plantings of wheat, soybeans, feed grains, and rice. Large volume exports to Russia and other new overseas markets were a factor. The Fertilizer Institute estimated farmers used about 46 million tons, an 8 to 10 per cent increase over the 42 million in 1972. Exports increased total fertilizer sales to more than 60 million tons.

Energy Crisis. Electric power shortages and natural gas curtailments caused temporary cutbacks in chemical production. Petrochemical producers in Arkansas, Louisiana, Oklahoma, and Texas bore the brunt of natural gas curtailment. While the U.S. demand for natural gas is growing at the rate of 5.8 per cent per year, the deficit for 1973 totaled 3.4 trillion cubic feet.

In July, President Richard M. Nixon called for an immediate increase in federal energy research and development for the fiscal year. He also asked for an intensified five-year, $10-billion program beginning in fiscal 1975.

Environmental Issues. The Council on Environmental Quality reported in September that air pollution continued to decrease; water pollution, though not significantly improved, showed no worsening.

At year's end, House and Senate conferees were working on the final version of legislation to control toxic substances. Under this legislation, new and existing hazardous chemicals must be tested, and their use and distribution will be controlled. Industrial emission standards for mercury, asbestos, and beryllium were adopted by the Environmental Protection Agency in April. Emission standards will be prepared in 1974 for arsenic, cadmium, and lead.

The Food and Drug Administration (FDA) extended interim regulations limiting the daily adult intake of saccharin to 1 gram, pending completion of a two-year study by the National Academy of Sciences. At about the same time, G. D. Searle applied to the FDA for permission to market a new low-calorie, artificial sweetener.   Edward Abrams

CHEMISTRY. Sulfur monoxide molecules were discovered in August, 1973, by an analysis of the spectrum of energy from the constellation Orion. The work was done by Harvard astronomers Carl A. Gottlieb and John A. Ball. Sulfur monoxide thus becomes the 22nd molecule to be identified in interstellar space, and the 5th molecule detected that contains sulfur. The discovery, the astronomers claim, may help scientists to determine how much oxygen there is in interstellar space.

Origin of Life. Most chemists believe that the first molecules of living matter were formed after the earth was formed. According to the commonly accepted theory, these molecules evolved from the components of the earth's early atmosphere under the influence of natural lightning. An alternative view was presented in 1973 by Gustav Arrhenius of the University of California, San Diego. He proposed that the organic building blocks of terrestrial life already existed in the solar system before the earth was formed. Arrhenius suggested that this organic matter could have been formed on the surface of interstellar dust particles from hydrogen, water, ammonia, formaldehyde, cyanoacetylene, and other known interstellar vapors under the bombardment of cosmic rays. The clustering together of these organic-coated dust particles, the first stage in the process of planet formation, could have occurred after they were electrically charged by the cosmic ray bombardment.

In support of his views, Arrhenius noted that radio telescopes have recorded over 20 types of molecules in interstellar space that either are found in living matter or could be related to primitive life. He also pointed out that dust particles brought back from the moon are electrically charged and stick together. Support for Arrhenius' concept came from experiments by Edward Anders and Ryochi Hayatsu of the University of Chicago, and Martin H. Studier of the Argonne National Laboratory near Chicago. They heated a mixture of carbon monoxide, hydrogen, and ammonia in the presence of meteoritic dust and obtained the same complex organic compounds that have been detected in meteorites.

Richard Gammon of the National Radio Observatory in Charlottesville, Va., said that Arrhenius' theory opens new possibilities for life in other parts of the universe. The idea that complex organic compounds can be formed on particles of interstellar dust, he said, "has increased the expectation of the possible evolution of life chemically similar to ours elsewhere in the Galaxy."

Tooth Decay. Metal complexes of fluoride are more effective in fighting tooth decay than is the fluoride alone, according to Nabih Kelada of the University of Michigan School of Public Health. Such complexes are formed from trace metals in drinking water that combine with natural or added fluoride. Particularly good for preventing tooth decay are complexes with iron and aluminum. They increase the resistance of the teeth to the acid produced by oral bacteria. Kelada says that up to 30 per cent of the fluorides in drinking water in some localities are in the metal-complex form. The fluorides become less effective if the concentration of trace metals in the water is decreased.

Biological Origin of Petroleum. The most popular theory about the origin of petroleum holds that oil was produced from plant material through gradual chemical changes over many millions of years. This theory is supported by the discovery, during the 1930s, of porphyrin molecules in petroleum similar to porphyrins found in chlorophyll. Wolfgang K. Seifert, a chemist with the Chevron Oil Corporation of California, reported in June, 1973, that some petroleum must also be derived from animals because he identified acids of animal origin in a 10-million-year-old California petroleum sample.

His discovery should help the basic understanding of the origin, formation, migration, accumulation, and trace composition of petroleum. Such understanding can help in predicting where and how deep to drill for oil, and how to improve fluid flow in porous media as a process of secondary oil recovery.

New atomic weight values were adopted in 1973 for nickel (58.70) and rhenium (186.207). The weights were previously 58.71 and 186.2. Alfred W. von Smolinski

See also BIOCHEMISTRY; NOBEL PRIZES.

CHESS. Speculation arose in 1973 that Bobby Fischer might retire from chess as eliminations got underway to find a challenger for his world title. After winning the world title from Boris Spassky of Russia in 1972, Fischer went into virtual seclusion. He declined an offer of $1.4 million to play Spassky or some other opponent of Fischer's choice in Las Vegas, Nev. An acquaintance of Fischer reported that for the first time in his life the world champion was not keeping abreast of current chess literature. However, Fischer's attorney, Stanley Radar, visited Paris early in September to investigate the possibilities for a Fischer-Spassky rematch.

As for Spassky, he was still being severely criticized in Russia for his loss to Fischer. The State Committee for Sport and Physical Culture charged he had "failed to display high qualities of will and morale."

Interzonal Tournaments were played in Russia and Brazil in 1973 to select candidates for a later series of matches, with the ultimate winner to play Fischer in 1975 for the world championship. In play ending on June 27 in Moscow, Russians Viktor Korchnoi and Anatoly Karpov, who tied for first, and Robert Byrne, chess editor of *The New York Times*, qualified. Karpov, 22 years old, was hailed as "the hope of the future" by Russian Chess Federation officials, still smarting from Fischer's decisive victory over Spassky, which ended Russian chess dominance.

The winner in the other interzonal tournament, which ended August 17 in Petrópolis, Brazil, was Henrique Mecking of Brazil. Lajos Portisch of Hungary and Russia's Lev Polugaievski and Efim Geller tied for second place. Elimination matches to produce a challenger for Fischer will continue in 1974.

U. S. Championships. Byrne had won the United States Chess Championship play-offs in Chicago on February 10 when eight-time champion Samuel Reshevsky of Spring Valley, N.Y., agreed to a draw in his second game with Byrne, thus assuring Byrne's victory. The play-offs resulted from a three-way tie for first in United States Chess Championship play in April, 1972. The play-offs had been delayed 10 months.

Norman Weinstein of Allston, Mass., won the United States Open Chess Championship in Chicago on August 25. The tournament ended in a five-way tie for first place, but Weinstein was named winner on the basis of having played the strongest competitors. Noting that Weinstein is 22 years old and the other top finishers were all under 30, Frank Skoff, president of the United States Chess Federation, said, "The results prove that chess is a young man's game. This is only the beginning of a youth movement in chess begun by Bobby Fischer." John Grefe of Berkeley, Calif., and Lubomir Kavalek of Washington, D.C., tied for the U.S. Chess championship in El Paso, Tex., September 28.   Theodore M. O'Leary

CHICAGO. Corruption in government was a prime issue in Chicago in 1973. On February 19, a former Democratic governor of Illinois, Otto J. Kerner, was convicted of conspiracy, fraud, perjury, bribery, and income tax evasion. At the time of his conviction, Kerner was a Federal Appeals Court judge. His former state revenue director Theodore J. Isaacs was also convicted.

On March 7, Edward J. Barrett, Cook County clerk and long-time political associate of Chicago Mayor Richard J. Daley, was convicted of taking $180,000 in kickbacks from a voting-machine manufacturing company. Chicago Aldermen Joseph Potempa and Casimir J. Staszuk and ex-Aldermen Fred D. Hubbard and Joseph Jambrone were convicted or sentenced for crimes involving corruption.

Police Department Scandals also surfaced in 1973. On August 23, a former district police commander and 13 policemen were indicted on charges of taking payoffs from tavern owners. Then, on October 5, police captain Clarence E. Braasch and 18 other policemen were convicted of similar charges, and later in the month, 5 more officers pleaded guilty to the same offense. In the wake of these revelations, pressures for the removal of police superintendent James B. Conlisk, Jr., mounted. Conlisk resigned on October 10. Deputy superintendent James M. Rochford took over as acting superintendent.

Downtown Development. A plan for the development of downtown Chicago was released on May 14 by the Chicago Central Area Committee. The scheme, which could cost as much as $20 billion, called for building middle-income housing on 650 acres of obsolete railroad yards. The plan also recommended above-grade-level pedestrian "sky streets" lined with stores, extended public transit facilities, and expansion of open-space areas.

Mass Transit problems worsened in 1973. Threatened with having to make service reductions early in the year, the Chicago Transit Authority (CTA) sought state aid. Although the Illinois legislature passed a bill subsidizing the CTA through June 30, the measure was vetoed by the governor. But, the legislature overrode the veto on March 27 and made plans to establish a six-county Regional Transit Authority (RTA).

The legislature passed a bill in late June authorizing the authority, but the governor again vetoed it in a dispute over financing. In November, state leaders finally reached an agreement, and the legislature approved establishing the RTA. A referendum on the proposal was scheduled for March, 1974.

The Chicago area moved past Los Angeles to again become the nation's second largest urban area. According to a U.S. Bureau of the Census report issued in September, Chicago's estimated population rose to 7,084,700 in 1972.   James M. Banovetz

In September, musicians striking for higher pay forced the Chicago Symphony to cancel opening performances of the concert season.

CHILD WELFARE. Day care for children of working mothers continued to be a problem in 1973. About 5.6 million U.S. children under the age of 6 have working mothers, according to the Department of Labor. But in most cases, the mother is left to her own usually inadequate resources to find safe and constructive care for her children.

As a partial corrective to the sometimes unhealthy, unsafe provisions that many working mothers are compelled to use for their children, the U.S. Department of Health, Education, and Welfare in 1973 sent a pamphlet, "Guides for Day-Care Licensing," to the governors of all states and recommended that the states enforce standards equal or superior to these minimal recommendations.

New programs for day care of children of employees reported by the Bell System and other industries possibly reflect the fact that women have recently organized to force unions to make day care a contract issue. The first conference sponsored by organized labor to discuss the child-care crisis was held in Chicago in late 1972.

The Brookings Institution study of federal spending, *Setting National Priorities: The 1974 Budget*, said, "Day care for children of working mothers is a new addition to the list of goods and services considered sufficiently 'essential' to warrant public concern and financing." Similarly, the 1973 mental health platform of the American Orthopsychiatric Association, which speaks for professionals in all areas of mental health, gave highest priority to a study of the mental health aspects of day care and the improvement of America's day-care services.

In recent years, Congress has passed two child-care bills, but both were vetoed by President Richard M. Nixon. Senator Walter F. Mondale (D., Minn.), chairman of the Senate Special Subcommittee on Children and Youth, held hearings in 1973 on the child-care problem.

Residential Care Scandals. The poor quality and scarcity of residential care for dependent and disturbed children in many parts of the United States was emphasized by a 1973 scandal in Illinois. It was discovered that almost 1,000 children, wards of the state, had been sent in recent years to private institutions in Texas, many set up or expanded hurriedly to take in Illinois support payments. There, with what was termed inadequate supervision by authorities from Illinois and Texas, many of the children had been grossly mistreated or exploited. Practically none of them appeared to have received any semblance of the "treatment for emotional disturbance" that had been promised.

A study published by the Illinois Department of Children and Family Services reported the unfortunate conditions in the Texas institutions and also criticized existing Illinois private and volunteer agencies for their refusal to accept difficult and problem children. The inadequacy of the public

institutions was only briefly mentioned. By December, all but 82 of the children had been returned to Illinois from the Texas institutions. Many of these had reportedly asked to remain. Earlier, 44 more Illinois children were flown home from Oregon institutions after a similar investigation.

Child abuse continued to be a major problem. The Senate passed a bill in 1973 calling for a national child-abuse research program after hearings had revealed the extent of the problem. A similar House bill was referred to the Education and Labor Committee, but hearings were deferred until 1974.

New Family Styles. Some young Americans are rearing children in life styles that differ from the traditional nuclear family – in communes, in unmarried voluntary families, and in single-parent families. A 1973 report based on interviews with young parents bringing up 50 children in these "counter-culture" settings described many instances of close relationship between parents and children. In many cases the father was present at birth and shared equally in child care. In some, the mother carried the infant everywhere in a backpack. Natural childbirth, home delivery, breast-feeding, and open discussion of pregnancy and childbirth were noted. Although much more serious evaluation and study is needed, the report indicated that de-emphasizing achievement may create the opportunity for more closeness within the family.   Frances A. Mullen

CHILDERS, ERSKINE HAMILTON (1905-   ), was sworn in as president of Ireland on June 25, 1973. He defeated Thomas O'Higgins, coalition candidate of the *Fine Gael* (Gaelic People) and Labour parties, in the presidential election on May 30. He is a member of the *Fianna Fáil* (Soldiers of Destiny) Party, which had governed for 16 years until its defeat in the general election on February 28. See IRELAND.

Childers is the second Protestant president in Irish history. He was born in London of an American mother and an Irish father, who was executed in 1922 for his work on behalf of Irish independence. Childers attended English private schools and took honors in history at Trinity College in Cambridge.

Before entering politics, Childers managed a Paris travel agency and was advertising manager for a Dublin newspaper. He became a naturalized Irish citizen in 1938 and was elected to Ireland's Parliament that same year. He has held various Cabinet posts, and served as deputy prime minister and minister of health from 1969 until he was elected president. His duties are largely ceremonial and non-political.

Childers has four children by his first wife, who died in 1950. He married Rita Dudley in 1952. They have one daughter.   Kathryn Sederberg

CHILDREN'S BOOKS. See LITERATURE FOR CHILDREN.

CHILE. President Salvador Allende Gossens, the first freely elected Marxist chief of state in the Western Hemisphere, was deposed in a violent military coup d'état on Sept. 11, 1973. He reportedly committed suicide rather than surrender. The military proclaimed their action a mission that liberated Chile "from the Marxist yoke." A four-man military junta, headed by General Augusto Pinochet Ugarte, took control and declared a state of siege. Congress was recessed, but Chileans were told that their economic and social accomplishments would not suffer.

The Coup followed weeks of crippling nationwide strikes as well as political and economic chaos. During that time, growing groups of workers, businessmen, and professionals joined in demands that Allende halt his attempts to bring Socialism to the country, and resign. Allende had sought to achieve his Socialist aims via the democratic system, but he had no solid electoral mandate, and many said that his coalition Marxist government violated both the letter and the spirit of the Constitution and disregarded the courts. In addition, the government was split internally.

Leaders of the armed forces, siding with the anti-Marxist opposition, had issued an ultimatum to the president, early on the morning of September 11, to step down by noon "in the face of the extremely grave economic, social, and moral crisis that is destroying the country." Allende had refused. Thus, paradoxically, in a movement that Karl Marx would hardly have credited, the middle classes (which make up over half of Chile's 9 million people) proved a vigorous mass force – supporting their demands with mass action. They opposed Allende's Socialist measures, particularly farm expropriation and factory nationalization. They suffered from abuse and threats of violence, from inflation (over 300 per cent in a year), and from shortages of all kinds. It was this surfeit of troubles that brought about the coup.

In the weeks that followed, Chile slowly began returning to normal, with truckers, small businessmen, public-transport workers, and members of various professional groups returning to their jobs. As of October 6, the official death toll since the day of the coup was given at 513. Some 7,000 suspected leftists, including foreigners – many of them left wing exiles – were arrested. There were highly publicized incidents of book burning. And the junta placed a ban on all Marxist political parties, which had commanded 43.39 per cent of the vote in the March 4 congressional elections. It also said it would soon announce a new constitution giving the armed forces a role in future legislative bodies. The junta also outlawed right wing extremist groups, and ordered the removal of all mayors and city councilmen.

Attacks by Chilean air force jets set the presidential palace afire during a revolt that ousted President Salvador Allende Gossens.

Junta's Changes. In the four weeks following the coup, the junta abolished Chile's largest labor organization, the 800,000-member Central Workers Confederation, which was controlled mainly by the Communist and Socialist parties. It also announced a temporary wage freeze, thereby dashing the hopes of millions of workers to whom the Allende regime had promised substantial raises on October 1. In addition, the junta placed most of the state-controlled factories and businesses back in the hands of the executives who had operated them before.

The new regime instituted sweeping changes to restore a free-market economy. It began dismantling agencies that controlled food and prices while simultaneously promising to restore illegally expropriated land to its former owners. It also established fairly realistic exchange rates, considering the inflation the nation had experienced. There were indications, too, that the regime would start repaying the foreign debt, variously quoted at from $3 billion to $4 billion.

Copper, the country's principal export, received special attention. The new regime said "the door is open" for negotiations on compensation for United States copper holdings seized by Allende. The junta added, however, that the mines will remain in government hands and that Chile will "maintain sovereignty over its natural resources."   Mary Webster Soper

See also LATIN AMERICA (Facts in Brief Table).

CHINA, NATIONALIST. See TAIWAN.

CHINA, PEOPLE'S REPUBLIC OF. In a year of surprises, the most startling in 1973 came in late August. The man who rose at the 10th Communist Party Congress to report on changes in the party constitution was not an aged revolutionary stalwart but a young unknown. Only six years earlier, Wang Hung-wen was a "rebel" textile worker in Shanghai. Now, looking almost boyish for all his 38 years, he sat on Chairman Mao Tse-tung's right. He was obviously being presented as Mao's heir-designate.

The congress also heard some bitter denunciations of Russia, its leaders, and its "socio-imperialist" policies. Even more time was given to attacks on Mao's previous political heir, Marshal Lin Piao, who was reported killed in a 1971 plane crash in Outer Mongolia. Lin was accused of having tried to murder Mao and, having failed, seeking to become "a defector to the Soviet revisionists."

But, for its dramatic impact, nothing matched the emergence of Wang as the third man in the Chinese hierarchy, after Mao and Premier Chou En-lai. In presenting him, the aged leaders seemed to be telling the nation that youth was at last taking its place at the top, and that the difficult problem of political succession had been solved. The communiqué from the congress underlined this with, "Our party is flourishing and has no lack of successors."

Washed up by the storm of the Cultural Revolution of the late 1960s, Wang had little government experience and no real power base. Early in 1967, during the tense struggle for power in Shanghai, he was put on the city's pro-Mao Revolutionary Committee. He soon became one of its vice-chairmen, as well as political commissar of the Shanghai garrison. In 1969, he was made a member of the party's Central Committee, and three years later he was moved to Peking to labor on changes in the party constitution, made necessary by the fall of Lin Piao. But he was a young amateur in the company of old pros. The old leaders soon were joined by returning old revolutionaries who had gone through all the harsh tests of the civil war and who were purged and humiliated as Mao's opponents during the Cultural Revolution, 1966 to 1969.

The most notable returnee was Teng Hsiao-ping, who, as the party's general secretary, was one of the seven national rulers prior to 1966. Vilified during the Cultural Revolution, he reappeared early in 1973 as a deputy premier – clearly to take some of the enormous workload off Chou's shoulders. He was reinstalled on the Central Committee in August. He was an old-timer, once again on his way up. And, with the other "rehabilitated" purgees, he was likely to support Chou En-lai, who remained dominant in governing China. Despite young Wang's rise, 1973 – like 1972 – was still the year of 74-year-old Chou.

Strange Happenings. Despite the seeming end to the search for a new heir, the time of indecision between an ending reign and a new one appeared to continue. There were signs of a continued debate on education, economic priorities, the division of power, and the course of the revolution, and what to do about the young. The radicals appeared to be quarreling with policies endorsed by Chou En-lai. There also seemed to be disagreement on how often new Cultural Revolutions should occur, how severe such upheavals should be, and how soon the next one should come.

In August, the party's organ, *People's Daily*, unaccountably denounced the ancient philosopher Confucius. One of his main transgressions, the article said, was "calling back into office those who have retired into obscurity" to support his own reactionary rule. In the Northeast, a radio station controlled by a powerful regional boss deplored Peking's decision to revive tight academic standards at the universities, as well as to relax the reins on the Muses.

But while some voices cried for more revolutionary fervor, Peking was toying with the idea of buying Charlie Chaplin films; Western symphony orchestras came to play Bach and Beethoven; and huge crowds turned out to watch a team of 300-pound sumo wrestlers from Japan. Skirts were more in evidence, and poker was allowed to return to favor as a pastime.

The old Mao badges had all but vanished; the Mao quotations that once covered every wall became relatively scarce; and radiobroadcasts began

Wang Hung-wen, left, a 38-year-old unknown, took a leadership
position next to Mao Tse-tung, center, and Chou En-lai, right, in August.

to drop the once-mandatory references to him as "the great leader of the Chinese people."

But bellicose undertones also filled the airwaves. Premier Chou urged the nation to prepare for a surprise attack by Russia. Foreign visitors to Peking were now readily shown the intricate system of air-raid tunnels under the capital. Still relatively primitive, they were designed to allow 4 million people to get out into the countryside if and when the enemy struck. And in late September, many broadcasts were dedicated to the 15th anniversary of the revival by Chairman Mao of the People's Militia during the Great Leap Forward. The militia was told that its duty, in case of invasion, was to help defend the cities, the nation's nerve centers. But there were signs that the military and the radicals regarded the militia as a huge paramilitary force controlled by the party and ready for use in the next political upheaval.

The Domestic Scene saw the continued revival of the Communist Party, all but shattered during the turmoil of the Cultural Revolution. The 10th Congress reported the party had 28 million members. There were also nationwide efforts to rebuild the other mass organizations that disbanded during the Cultural Revolution – trade unions, the Communist Youth League, the women's league, and the federation of poor and middle-class peasants.

These moves were part of an attempt by Mao and Chou to correct the change in the balance of political power that occurred during the Cultural Revolution. During Mao's struggle for power from 1965 to 1968, the military establishment and, to a lesser degree, the Red Guards, proved to be Mao's most effective allies. With the party machine wrecked, it was the soldiers who took over the administration of the government – as ministers in Peking, as chairmen of the new Revolutionary Committees, and as Mao propagandists. The high point of military ascendancy came when Lin Piao's name was written into the party constitution as Mao's successor.

But even before Lin's fall, the party began to reassert its former authority. The provincial Revolutionary Committees were still run mainly by army men in 1973, but there was an unmistakable trend in favor of the party civilians.

Industrial managers and experts also continued to regain their authority. Material incentives, damned as a bourgeois idea during the Cultural Revolution, were again being offered to the workers to ensure higher output or better quality. In the countryside, the peasants were urged to add to their lean income with "sideline occupations," such as making fish nets or weaving baskets in their spare time.

Examinations Revived. After two years of experimentation, some of the educational reforms advocated by Mao were quietly abandoned. Medical school terms, at first reduced to two years, were extended to three and a half. Similar changes were made in science and engineering courses. Schools placed more stress on academic subjects, and the examinations – one of the main targets of Red Guard fire during the Cultural Revolution – were reintroduced. In December, the first group of the new students graduated from the universities.

The transfer of high school graduates and unneeded civil servants from the cities to the countryside continued in 1973. At times, these newcomers received a cool welcome from commune members, and the Peking press appealed to them to allow the young newcomers to earn enough to avert hardship. Reports indicated a drift back to the cities.

The Economy enjoyed another good year. Foreign experts estimated that China's industry was still growing at about 10 per cent per year. This progress came despite drought in the North and floods in the South in both 1972 and 1973.

Western estimates put the harvest at about 240-million tons, about the same as in 1972. During the summer, Peking took sharp jabs at foot-dragging farm officials, and appealed to the public to eat more sparingly. Crying, "Cut off the tail of private ownership," commune zealots tried to restrict the peasants' use of their tiny private plots to raise pigs and chickens, only to be given an official tongue-lashing.

To ensure adequate food stocks in coastal cities and to build up reserves, China bought grain on the world markets. It purchased some 1.2 million tons of wheat from the United States before June, and, in July, another half-million tons of U.S. grain was bought for delivery in 1973. In all, China bought more than 5 millions tons of grain from the United States, Canada, and Australia during the year. Additional contracts were signed with Canada and Australia to provide wheat in 1974, 1975, and 1976.

Foreign Trade. Purchases of grain, cotton, tobacco, electronic gear, and Boeing 707s for China's expanding international airlines brought U.S. sales to Peking to the surprising total of from $800 million to $900 million for the year. Teams representing the largest U.S. oil companies visited China at Peking's invitation to discuss the development of the country's offshore oil and gas resources.

But the trade with the United States was only a fraction of that with Japan, which was reaching toward $2 billion for the year, in a spectacular jump over the total for 1972. China's sales to Japan included a million tons of oil (out of an estimated national production of 30 million tons in 1973). Japan's two biggest steel companies agreed to build rolling mills in China that would add at least 3 million tons to China's steel output, which was estimated in 1973 at just above 20 million tons.

Feud and Détente. The feud with Russia continued in 1973. So did the détente with the United States, begun with the visit of the U. S. table tennis team to China in 1971. The United States and China exchanged "liaison offices," which, in all but name, were top-rank embassies.

The first U.S. envoy to the People's Republic of China, 75-year-old David K. E. Bruce, arrived in Peking on May 14. China's first emissary to the United States, Huang Chen, arrived in Washington, D.C., on May 29, and opened his offices at the Mayflower Hotel.

The exchange of envoys was only one sign of the new understanding. Henry A. Kissinger visited Peking from February 15 to 19, when he was still President Richard M. Nixon's special assistant for national security affairs. He came once more in November, after he had become U. S. secretary of state. U.S. scholars, doctors, bankers, musicians, and table tennis players also traveled to Peking. In turn, Chinese physicists, editors, and jugglers toured the United States – and the Chinese journalists had complimentary things to say about capitalist America on their return home.

One more by-product of the détente was the release in March of John Downey, a Central Intelligence Agency agent. Downey spent 20 years in Chinese prisons after he was shot down in 1952 while on an intelligence mission. Mark Gayn

See also Asia (Facts in Brief Table).

CHRONOLOGY. See pages 8 through 14.

CHURCHES. See Eastern Orthodox Churches; Jews; Protestant; Religion; Roman Catholic.

Posters in China now stress the importance of exports. A caption with this one says, "Keep the Country in Heart and the Whole World in Mind!"

CITY governments in the United States enjoyed the first benefits of the new federal revenue-sharing plan in 1973. Many cities gave high priority to reducing local taxes, particularly property taxes, when they received the extra money. The general revenue-sharing program allocated $20.1 billion in federal funds to be paid to local governments between December, 1972, and December, 1976. Local governments may use the funds for any public-service programs other than education.

Revenue-Sharing Survey. The revenue-sharing office conducted a survey in April, 1973, of how local governments were using the funds. The survey covered 770 communities. According to the survey report, released on June 19, 72 per cent of all local governments and 82 per cent of all cities over 25,000 population gave capital expenditures, such as improving streets and buying new fire equipment, top priority in the use of the funds. The second priority was public safety – including law enforcement and fire protection – followed by environmental protection and recreation. Social-service programs were given the lowest priority.

Forty per cent of all local governments and 63 per cent of all cities over 25,000 reported using general revenue-sharing funds to avoid tax-rate increases. Another 8 per cent of local governments planned to lower taxes, and 17 per cent said their tax increases would be smaller as a result of revenue sharing.

Since there was no assurance that revenue sharing would be continued beyond 1976, local governments were reluctant to use the funds to start new programs. If revenue sharing is allowed to expire, any new programs would have to be financed from local taxes after 1976.

Urban-Aid Cutbacks. Almost as soon as the cities began receiving general revenue-sharing funds, the federal government started reducing other programs designed to alleviate urban problems. The first cutback came on January 8, when President Richard M. Nixon ordered a freeze on new federal commitments for subsidized housing (see HOUSING). In his January 29 budget message to Congress, the President also called for cutbacks in seven urban-aid programs, including job training, urban renewal, Model Cities, and summer employment programs.

The President proposed replacing these federal-aid programs with four special revenue-sharing plans. Funds earmarked for education, law enforcement, manpower training, and community development would be given to local governments, and local officials would decide how to use the money. The Administration proposals were introduced in Congress as the Better Communities Bill of 1974.

Mr. Nixon requested $110 million for a program to help local governments improve administrative and planning skills. He also recommended that money from the federal Highway Trust Fund be used for urban mass transit.

Mayors Protest. The National League of Cities and the U.S. Conference of Mayors issued a joint statement on February 3, charging that the Administration had broken its promise not to use revenue sharing as an excuse for eliminating other federal-aid programs. The statement pointed out that mayors, county officials, and governors had agreed to support the revenue-sharing program after the Administration assured them that revenue sharing would not be a substitute for ongoing federal programs.

Dempsey J. Travis, head of the nation's largest black-owned mortgage company and president of the United Mortgage Bankers of America, predicted that 50 per cent of black architects would be forced to close shop and 80 per cent of all black construction companies would go bankrupt by the end of 1974 if the urban programs were not restored. San Francisco Mayor Joseph Alioto charged that the cities had become an "orphan" under the Nixon Administration. Many urban leaders protested that budget cuts would affect minorities and poor people the most.

Administration Optimism. President Nixon, however, took a different view of the cities' situation. In a radio address to the nation on March 4, Mr. Nixon stated that the cities no longer faced financial catastrophe. He noted that the business world has begun investing in downtown areas, the crime rate has been

Riders on the New York City subway view the work of young graffiti "artists." Cleanup crews could not keep pace with the vandals.

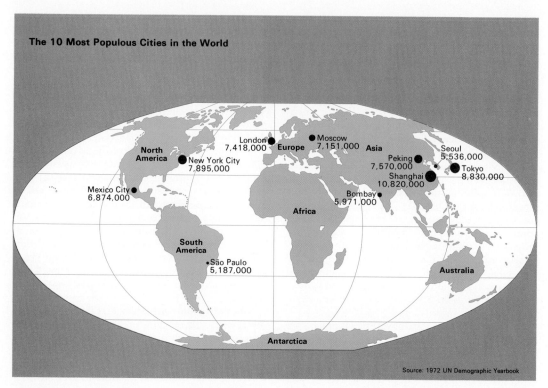

The 10 Most Populous Cities in the World

London 7,418,000 · Europe · Moscow 7,151,000 · Asia

North America · New York City 7,895,000

Peking 7,570,000 · Seoul 5,536,000

Shanghai 10,820,000 · Tokyo 8,830,000

Mexico City 6,874,000

Bombay 5,971,000

Africa

South America

São Paulo 5,187,000

Australia

Antarctica

Source: 1972 UN Demographic Yearbook

reduced in more than half the major cities, the air has been made cleaner, and the amount of substandard housing has been reduced.

The President defended his budget cuts for urban aid and criticized the old federal programs as extravagant, ineffective, and outmoded. The new special revenue-sharing proposal, Mr. Nixon said, "means giving the lead role back to grass-roots government. The time has come," he said, "to reject the patronizing notion that federal planners . . . can guide your lives better than you can."

San Francisco Conference. While most mayors agreed that local governments should have more control over solving urban problems, they still feared a loss of federal funds, particularly during the transition period from federal urban programs to special block grants. At the U.S. Conference of Mayors' meeting in San Francisco in June, the mayors endorsed the principle of the Administration's special revenue-sharing plan. However, they voted for major revisions, such as federal supervision to be sure that funds were used for slum clearance and low-income housing. They also sought assurance that federal funding for cities would not be reduced as more communities were added to the revenue-sharing list.

The U.S. mayors met again in October for the opening of the late President Lyndon B. Johnson's papers on urban affairs. During a symposium at the Johnson Library in Austin, Tex., the mayors com-

pared the attitudes of Mr. Johnson and Mr. Nixon toward city problems. None of the mayors agreed with Mr. Nixon that the urban crisis is over.

Black Influence in local politics increased rapidly. According to the Joint Center for Policy Studies, there were 92 black mayors in the United States after the November elections.

In November, Maynard Jackson became the first black mayor of a major Southern city when he was elected mayor of Atlanta. Jackson, who had been vice-mayor, remarked, "Anyone looking for the civil rights movement in the streets is fooling himself. Politics is the civil rights movement of the seventies."

Several other major cities elected black mayors in 1973. Thomas Bradley was elected mayor in Los Angeles; Coleman A. Young, in Detroit; James H. McGee, in Dayton, Ohio; and Clarence E. Lightner, in Raleigh, N.C. The voters in Miami elected a mayor of Puerto Rican descent, Maurice Ferre. See BRADLEY, THOMAS; DETROIT; LOS ANGELES.

In February, the newly organized Southern Black Mayors Conference met for the first time in Fayette, Miss. The group of 25 black Southern mayors was organized mainly by Fayette Mayor Charles Evers.

Rising City Payrolls. On August 15, the U.S. Bureau of the Census reported that the number of city government employees had increased by 17 per cent between 1967 and 1972. At the same time, municipal payrolls increased by 67 per cent.

The movement toward unionization of city workers and efforts to raise their pay to the level of pay in private industry accounted for much of the increase. The American Federation of State, County, and Municipal Employees reported a gain of 200,000 new members between 1967 and 1972.

Public Transportation was a major urban concern, especially with the nation's emerging energy crisis. On September 5, Seattle began offering free rides on transit routes through its downtown business district. Seattle is giving the idea a one-year trial, and officials hope it will cut downtown auto traffic and reduce air pollution by about 20 per cent.

The federal government agreed to help Boston and San Francisco put 230 ultramodern streetcars into operation within two years. Boston will receive 150 of the new cars, built by the Boeing aircraft firm.

In the Chicago area, a Regional Transit Authority was created to ease the financial burden of operating public transportation. And San Francisco's Bay Area Rapid Transit system continued to be plagued by technical troubles. See SAN FRANCISCO.

Pollution Control. The Environmental Protection Agency (EPA) issued a broad set of regulations in June that would drastically affect traffic in U.S. cities. So that urban areas would meet clean-air guidelines by 1977, the EPA called for a ban on street parking in Boston's central business district and on all parking in downtown Minneapolis. The agency proposed bus lanes on streets in Philadelphia and Pittsburgh and suggested gasoline rationing in the Los Angeles area.

The only city to have its own clean-air plan approved by the EPA was New York. The plan called for exclusive bus lanes, reduced taxi cruising, limited parking facilities, and more bridge tolls. New York City also planned to forbid daytime truck deliveries.

It became apparent during the year that several major cities might not be able to meet the federal government's 1977 deadline for municipal waste treatment. The plan requires secondary treatment of all sewage. St. Louis officials were almost certain that city would not meet the deadline because federal funds that were to be used for planning and constructing the treatment facilities had been impounded. Five other cities – Atlanta, Cleveland, Los Angeles, New York, and San Francisco – feared they might not have secondary treatment facilities ready by 1977.

Changes in the definition of "standard metropolitan statistical area" (SMSA), by which U.S. urban areas are outlined, were ordered on April 27 by the Office of Management and Budget. The changes added to, subtracted from, or merged various densely populated areas. As a result, 26 new areas were designated as SMSA's, 12 existing SMSA's were merged into 6 new ones, and several other SMSA's were expanded.   James M. Banovetz

See also ELECTIONS.

CIVIL RIGHTS. "Lockheed gets bailed out, the railroads get bailed out, it's socialism for the rich, and rugged individualism for the poor," declared Bishop John Adams of the Texas Episcopal District of the African Methodist Episcopal Church. As many black leaders did in 1973, Bishop Adams was protesting the Nixon Administration's budget cuts for social programs, the dismantling of the Office of Economic Opportunity, and President Richard M. Nixon's impoundment of welfare funds.

Another target of their ire was revenue sharing, which siphons funds from the predominantly black inner cities to the white suburbs, and substitutes local control for federal control of social programs. Historically, the best black gains have been obtained through the federal government. Indicative of less responsive local attitudes was a finding by the National Commission of Fire Prevention and Control, which cited "outrageous racial discrimination" in local fire departments.

Still another object of contention was the 1970 census. The National Urban League declared that the census missed nearly 2 million blacks, costing the black community the equivalent of five congressmen. Leading black Republicans criticized their party for making blacks feel unwelcome.

Politics, however, also afforded significant successes for blacks in 1973. A record number of blacks – 1,144 – were elected to public office in the South. Blacks also won elections for mayor in the country's third largest city, Los Angeles, and in Atlanta, Ga. See BRADLEY, THOMAS.

Major Rulings. Major court decisions advanced a long-standing concern of black civil rights – school desegregation. The Supreme Court of the United States ruled in June that Denver must revise its school boundaries, which confined minority children to a few schools, and use busing to desegregate its entire school system. The court upheld a decision by a federal appeals court that required black children from Detroit to be bused to the suburbs and white suburban children to be brought to Detroit to achieve racial balance. Nevertheless, the extent to which the courts will go in requiring school desegregation remains unclear. In May, the Supreme Court invalidated a school desegregation plan for Richmond, Va., that would have joined white suburbs with the heavily black city population.

Prodded by the Federal Equal Employment Opportunity Commission, the mammoth American Telephone and Telegraph Company agreed in January to pay $15 million in back wages to blacks, women, and others against whom it had discriminated in job assignments and promotions. The commission also began investigating charges of job discrimination against General Motors, Ford, General Electric, and Sears, Roebuck and the unions of those industries. Bethlehem Steel was ordered to make sweeping changes in its seniority system.

Seaman Apprentice Anneliese Knapp, 21, attends to traditional sailor's chores on U.S.S. *Sanctuary*, first Navy ship to integrate women into crew.

For Newsmen and the news media, 1973 was a tumultuous year. They deemed their liberties imperiled by legislation advocated by Clay T. Whitehead, director of President Nixon's Office of Telecommunications Policy. This legislation would hold individual television stations responsible for "consistent bias" of programming – including that provided by the networks. Stations failing to correct imbalances, Whitehead said, would "be held fully accountable at license-renewal time." Vociferous opposition stalled the legislation.

The Nixon Administration was at least partly successful, however, in pressing for a thorough examination of news shows and commentators of the Public Broadcasting Service, the country's noncommercial television network. Congress, responding to the Supreme Court's suggestion that it determine the extent that the confidentiality of newsmen's sources should be protected, struggled inconclusively with the proposed legislation.

Women's Rights. Anne Armstrong, cochairman of the Republican National Committee, became the first woman counselor to a President, and was accorded Cabinet status. In Houston, the first national women's political convention in a century was held. After bitter debate on February 9, the National Women's Political Caucus elected officers, raised funds, and wrote a Constitution. The Supreme Court dealt with a most controversial issue of wo-

men's politics when it legalized abortions, ruling that the termination of an unwanted pregnancy is properly the decision of a woman and her doctor.

On August 27, at Seneca Falls, N.Y., 20 women were named to the newly established Women's Hall of Fame, located on the site of the first Women's Rights Convention, which was held 125 years ago. The group included former Senator Margaret Chase Smith, singer Marian Anderson, actress Helen Hayes, and pediatrician Helen Brooke Taussig.

In Other Decisions, the Supreme Court declared unconstitutional several New York state programs providing financial assistance to Roman Catholic and other private schools. However, in another decision, finding that education is not a right guaranteed by the Constitution, the court declined to interfere with the system of local property taxation, often criticized as a distorted base for school financing. In addition, the court handed down guidelines on obscenity that will enable the states to ban publications, plays, and motion pictures that are offensive by local standards, even if acceptable elsewhere (see MOTION PICTURES). A federal district court dismissed all charges against Pentagon Papers defendants Daniel Ellsberg and Anthony Russo, holding that governmental misconduct precluded a fair jury trial. See ELLSBERG, DANIEL.

A nightmarish travesty of law enforcement occurred in Collinsville, Ill., on April 23, when federal narcotics agents, brandishing shotguns and acting without search warrants, ransacked the wrong houses in raids on suspected dope dens. On August 24, 12 agents involved in the raid were indicted.

At Wounded Knee, S. Dak., a prolonged confrontation between armed Indians and federal agents focused attention on the status of Indian treaties and the need for reservation reforms. See INDIAN, AMERICAN (Close-Up).

In Other Countries. Democratic rights and liberties were trampled in some places by violence and emerging dictatorial regimes. In Chile, the government of Salvador Allende Gossens was overthrown in a bloody coup and succeeded by a military junta in September. Argentina restored a former dictator, Juan Perón, to power in September, and his foes recalled the ruthless suppression of dissent and the corruption of his earlier reign.

The growing American-Russian détente was confronted by a moral issue raised by novelist Alexander Solzhenitsyn, who warned that coexistence without wars is not enough "on this tightly knit earth," and that participating nations, including Russia, must observe democratic freedoms. Russian acts against intellectual dissidents and its hampering of Jewish emigration prompted members of Congress to demand better Russian observance of freedom as a precondition to economic agreements. Louis W. Koenig

See also articles on individual countries; COURTS AND LAWS.

CLEVELAND. Republican Ralph J. Perk won re-election as mayor of Cleveland on Nov. 6, 1973. He defeated his Democratic opponent, city council clerk Mercedes Cotner, by a 2-to-1 margin.

Perk's re-election was assured after he defeated Democratic candidate James Carney, a millionaire real estate developer, in the city's nonpartisan primary in May. Carney then dropped out of the race and was replaced on the ballot by Cotner.

Cotner carried all the city's black wards, while Perk carried the white ones. However, Perk won an overall 28 per cent of the city's black vote. Only 46 per cent of the eligible voters went to the polls.

School Strike. Most of Cleveland's 140,000 public school students missed five days of classes when school custodial and maintenance workers went on strike on January 31. The workers were mainly seeking $500-a-year pay increases. The schools were forced to close because there was no heat in unattended buildings and because many teachers honored the picket lines.

The strike ended on February 5, when both sides reached partial agreement on a contract that provided no pay raise but did add paid holidays and set a maximum 63-hour workweek. The question of wage increases was deferred until the school board could eliminate the school system's $2-million deficit.

Crime Rate Down. Cleveland reported a decrease in the rate of serious crimes during the first quarter of 1973. The national decline in the crime rate was 1 per cent; the reduction in Cleveland was 19.4 per cent, according to statistics released in June by the Federal Bureau of Investigation.

Mayor Perk was acquitted of assault and battery charges on September 12, after a judge ruled that the prosecution had failed to prove that an assault had occurred. The assault charge had been filed against the mayor in July by a policeman who had an argument with Perk in a City Hall corridor.

Living Costs. A U.S. Department of Labor report released on June 15 listed Cleveland as having the 10th highest cost of living among the nation's 25 largest cities. According to the report, an average family of four would require an annual budget of $11,872 to live in "moderate comfort." Cleveland living costs rose only moderately, however—5.2 per cent between May, 1972, and May, 1973.

Changes ordered on April 27 by the U.S. Office of Management and Budget in the definition used to determine the boundaries and population of metropolitan areas brought no significant changes in the Cleveland metropolitan area's population of about 2 million persons. But the area slipped from the 12th largest urban area to 14th, because the Dallas-Fort Worth area was expanded and a new metropolitan area, Nassau-Suffolk, was created near New York City.   James M. Banovetz

CLOTHING. See FASHION.

COAL. See MINES AND MINING.

COIN COLLECTING. The number of coin collectors swelled rapidly in 1973 as more persons seeking a hedge against inflation entered the field. Partly as a consequence of this influx, the prices of rare coins soared. With the price of gold doubling by midyear, prices of gold coins rose even more rapidly. By July, the United States double eagle gold piece, which had brought $85 to $90 late in 1972, was selling for about $200.

Other examples of rising rare-coin prices included a 1787 George Clinton cent, listed in some standard coin guide books at $2,000. It brought $34,000 at an auction in New York City on April 1. At the same auction, a 1616 Sommer Islands (Bermuda) shilling sold for $10,000, and a Sommer Islands sixpence brought $28,000. Both had been priced in coin guides at under $2,000. On March 30, an 1847 Mexican silver eight-real coin with a catalog price of $25 sold for $550.

Certification Service. The American Numismatic Association (ANA) moved vigorously against the counterfeiting of rare coins. Its newly created certification service tested more than 100 coins a week with such sophisticated devices as electron microscopes and probes, specific gravity scales, and X rays. For coins found genuine, the ANA issued a printed certificate and photographs of the obverse and reverse sides of the coin. A copy of each certificate is kept on file at the association's headquarters in Washington, D.C.

Bicentennial Issues. Many coin collectors pressured the federal government, largely through appeals to the U.S. Congress, after the Department of the Treasury and the Bureau of the Mint indicated they would limit their commemoration of the American bicentennial to the issuance of Eisenhower dollars and Kennedy half dollars whose reverse sides would present Revolutionary War themes. Many collectors asserted that all six U.S. coins should have special issues. In mid-September, the House of Representatives passed legislation, similar to that enacted earlier by the Senate, adding quarters to the coins that will have special designs on their reverse side. The coins will be issued from July 4, 1975, until the treasury sets a cutoff date.

Collectors also protested a measure that would have given Eisenhower College in Seneca Falls, N.Y., $1 from the $10 price of each proof 40 per cent silver Eisenhower dollar sold. The House of Representatives killed the measure in August.

Of the more than 2 million Carson City silver dollars that the United States government put up for bids on Nov. 1, 1972, only about 700,000 had been sold at the minimum bid price of $30 by Feb. 1, 1973. Some coin dealers criticized the sale as "government hucksterism," contending that flooding the market with the dollars would diminish their value as an investment. Auctioning of the coins continued in 1973.   Theodore M. O'Leary

COLOMBIA. Labor difficulties, subversive activities, and political maneuverings were major concerns in 1973. A general transport strike on October 1 in Bogotá and four other cities led to riots protesting the high cost of living and the government's economic policies.

Subversive activities were a disruptive force during the year. In October, the government announced that two of the nation's three left wing guerrilla groups, the Castroite National Liberation Front and the Maoist People's Liberation, had been almost totally destroyed. The Communist Colombian Revolutionary Armed Forces, however, remained active, notably in an area southwest of Bogotá.

Meanwhile, political campaigning began in anticipation of the presidential elections scheduled for 1974. Among the candidates was Maria Eugenia Rojas de Morena Díaz, who was chosen as the candidate of the opposition National Popular Alliance. Her father, former President Gustavo Rojas Pinilla, had renounced the nomination earlier. Mrs. De Morena's candidacy was expected to pose a serious challenge to the other two major presidential aspirants, Álvaro Gomez Hurtado of the Conservative Party and Alfonso Lopez Michelson of the Liberal Party. Mary Webster Soper

See also LATIN AMERICA (Facts in Brief Table).

COLORADO. See STATE GOVERNMENT.

COMMON MARKET. See EUROPE.

COMMUNICATIONS. Politically, as well as operationally, global satellite communications service came of age in 1973. Since the *Early Bird* communications satellite began offering commercial service across the Atlantic Ocean on June 28, 1965, the global satellite system had grown by the end of 1973 to 2,657 satellite communications pathways linking 82 antennas at 67 stations in 50 countries.

The definitive arrangements governing the International Telecommunications Satellite Consortium (Intelsat) went into effect on Feb. 12, 1973, replacing interim arrangements that had guided the organization since its beginning. The organization has grown from 14 member countries in 1964 to the present 83 members. More than 90 countries, territories, and possessions lease satellite services on a full-time basis from Intelsat, allowing nearly a billion people to see an important event on television as it happens.

The fifth satellite in the *Intelsat 4* series was launched from Cape Kennedy, Fla. (renamed Cape Canaveral on October 9), on August 23, 10 years after *Syncom*, the world's first synchronous satellite, became operational. Each of the 3,100-pound *Intelsat 4*'s can handle an average of 5,000 two-way telephone calls or 12 simultaneous color television programs. They operate in synchronous orbits over the Atlantic, Pacific, and Indian oceans, effectively linking most of the world's population.

Domestic Communications. While international service via satellite continued to grow, the impact of space technology also was felt within countries. On January 11, Canadian Minister of Communications Gerard Pelletier inaugurated the new Telesat Canada satellite system with a call between Ottawa and Resolute, 600 miles inside the Arctic Circle, on the northern tip of Baffin Island. Telesat Canada now has two *Anik* (Eskimo for brother) satellites in orbit. Each satellite has 12 high-capacity microwave channels for color television. Or, any channel can carry as many as 960 one-way telephone calls.

The United States took several long strides toward the start of domestic satellite service. On January 4, the Western Union Telegraph Company received the first Federal Communications Commission (FCC) authorization to build a satellite system. The company said its $70-million Westar project will be ready to operate in 1974. On September 13, the FCC gave the go-ahead for additional domestic systems to the American Telephone & Telegraph Company; GTE Satellite Corporation, a subsidiary of General Telephone and Electronics Corporation; Hughes Aircraft Company's National Satellite Services; the American Satellite Corporation; and RCA Global Communications and RCA Alaska Communications.

Russia put two more of its *Molniya* satellites in orbit in 1973, one on February 8 and the other on August 29. Since the first launch in 1965, Russia has orbited 25 of these satellites, which operate in random, rather than synchronous, orbits.

Cable Systems. Four United States international carriers and 16 Western European countries agreed to share the ownership of the sixth transatlantic submarine cable. When completed in 1976, the $145-million cable will be the largest yet, with a capacity of 4,000 voice grade circuits.

Plans also moved forward on a new submarine cable system between the U.S. mainland and the island of Okinawa, via Hawaii and Guam. The first submarine cable system directly linking South America and Europe went into service in May, with the completion of a 2,700-mile leg between Recife, Brazil, and the Canary Islands, where it connects with existing cables to Spain. Among other cable projects, construction was started on the CANTAT-II link between Great Britain and Canada, and service began on a submarine facility between the U.S. mainland and the Bahamas.

The FCC reported that U.S. industry revenues from overseas telecommunications (excluding the satellite operations of the Communications Satellite Corporation) totaled $628.6 million in 1972, an increase of 13.2 per cent over 1971. Telephone carriers reported $370 million in revenues, and record (non-voice) carriers, $258.6 million. Thomas M. Malia

See also TELEPHONE.

CONGO (BRAZZAVILLE). See AFRICA.

CONGO (KINSHASA). See ZAIRE.

CONGRESS OF THE UNITED STATES.

The balance of power shifted toward Congress in 1973, away from a presidency weakened by continuing scandals. Although President Richard M. Nixon successfully vetoed eight bills, he suffered the most severe legislative defeat of his five years in office in November when his veto of the War Powers Act limiting his warmaking power was overridden. At year's end, the House Judiciary Committee was considering his impeachment, and the Senate Watergate committee was investigating corruption at the highest levels of the Nixon Administration.

The First Session of the 93rd Congress convened on January 3. In the Senate, there were 56 Democrats, 42 Republicans, 1 Conservative, and 1 Independent. In the House of Representatives, there were 240 Democrats, 192 Republicans, and 3 vacant seats.

Mike J. Mansfield (D., Mont.) continued to serve as majority leader in the Senate, and Robert C. Byrd (D., W. Va.) was Democratic whip. Hugh D. Scott, Jr. (R., Pa.), continued as minority leader, with Robert P. Griffin (R., Mich.) as minority whip.

In the House, Carl B. Albert (D., Okla.) was re-elected as speaker of the House. Thomas P. O'Neill, Jr. (D., Mass.), became majority leader, replacing Hale Boggs (D., La.), lost since an Alaskan plane crash in October, 1972 (see O'NEILL, THOMAS P.). Boggs's seat was declared vacant on January 3. John J. McFall (D., Calif.) became majority whip. Gerald R. Ford (R., Mich.) retained his post as minority leader until December, when he became Vice-President of the United States (see FORD, GERALD R.). Leslie C. Arends (R., Ill.) was minority whip.

On January 6, a joint session of Congress witnessed the official counting of the Electoral College vote to verify the result of the Nov. 7, 1972, election. Mr. Nixon received 520 electoral votes; his Democratic opponent, George S. McGovern, received 17; and Libertarian Party candidate John Hospers received 1 vote.

The Budget. The President's budget message to Congress on January 29 outlined a $268.7-billion budget for fiscal 1974 (July 1, 1973, to June 30, 1974). Defense spending was scheduled to increase $4.6 billion to a total of $79 billion. But by making more than 100 cutbacks in government programs and terminating some of them altogether, the Administration planned to cut the deficit for fiscal 1974 to $12.7 billion. On April 4 and again on May 10, the Senate approved a spending ceiling of $268 billion on the 1974 budget, $700 million less than the President had requested. The House passed a $268.7-billion limit on July 25. Both bills contained provisions to limit the President's power to impound funds.

On July 26, the White House announced that the federal deficit for fiscal 1973 was $14.4 billion, $10.4-

Chief Justice Warren Burger, left, swears in former Congressman Gerald Ford as the 40th Vice-President of the United States on December 6.

billion less than the Department of the Treasury had forecast. A gain in tax receipts because of inflation, plus the Administration's spending limit of $250 billion set in 1972 and subsequent impounding of funds, made the decrease possible.

Impounded Funds. On March 9, the President's chief domestic adviser, John D. Ehrlichman, declared that Mr. Nixon would veto 15 bills totaling $9-billion, and if necessary would continue to impound funds already appropriated by Congress in order to stay below the spending limit. Otherwise, Ehrlichman warned, individual taxpayers might face a 9 per cent increase in personal income taxes.

On February 2, Roy L. Ash, director of the Office of Management and Budget, reported that $8.7 billion in appropriated federal funds had already been impounded. However, congressional leaders estimated that the President had impounded from $12-billion to $15 billion in congressionally appropriated funds. Various federal courts ordered the Administration to release impounded funds, but the Supreme Court of the United States refused the Administration's request to expedite a ruling on the constitutionality of impounding funds.

State of the Union Messages. On February 2, President Nixon announced that he would deliver a series of State of the Union messages in written form instead of the single traditional message delivered to Congress in person. He then presented the first message, declaring that government spending must be cut back to slow inflation.

On February 15, the President delivered a second State of the Union message, calling for the passage of nine environmental protection bills, which the 92nd Congress had failed to pass. He also suggested that money from the Highway Trust Fund be used for mass transit needs, and he proposed a gradual phase-out of direct crop-subsidy payments to farmers.

In his third State of the Union message, Mr. Nixon defended planned cuts in domestic and social-welfare programs; in his fourth, he announced he was abandoning plans for a guaranteed minimum family income. The President's urban message was the fifth in the series; in the sixth, the President dealt with crime issues and suggested that the death penalty be restored for certain crimes. See CITY; HOUSING.

On September 10, the President sent Congress a seventh State of the Union message, resubmitting more than 50 legislative proposals on which Congress had failed to act. In this lengthy statement, he warned Congress against making any cuts in his defense budget or increases in his domestic budget.

In his annual State of the World message to Congress on May 3, Mr. Nixon proposed that 1973 be called the "year of Europe," and discussed his concern with "shaping a durable peace." See EUROPE.

Restricting Presidential Power. Congress and the President were in continual conflict throughout the year. On May 10, the House of Representatives voted 219 to 188 to ban the use of defense funds for continued U.S. bombing in Khmer (formerly named Cambodia). The next day, White House Press Secretary Ronald L. Ziegler announced that the bombing would continue despite the House action. On May 31, the Senate also voted, 63 to 19, to cut off all funds for bombing Khmer.

The President and Congress finally reached a compromise. On June 30, Congress passed a measure, included in an appropriations bill for federal agencies, that cut off funds for military action in Indochina as of August 15. The President signed the bill on July 1.

As U.S. involvement in Vietnam diminished, Congress was anxious to regain some of its warmaking powers. The House passed the War Powers Act on October 12, which limited the President's warmaking powers. The vote was 238 in favor to 123 opposed. The Senate had voted 75 to 20 to approve the bill on October 10. Although the President vetoed the bill on October 24, Congress overrode his veto on November 7. The House mustered a vote of 284 to 135, 4 more than the two-thirds vote necessary; the Senate vote was 75 to 18, 13 more votes than necessary.

According to the terms of the act, the President must report to Congress within 48 hours after committing U.S. troops to foreign combat or "substantially" increasing the number of U.S. combat troops in a foreign country. He must explain to Congress the reason for the action, and its expected scope. After 60 days, the President must end the hostilities unless Congress has specifically authorized the troop commitment. The 60-day deadline may be extended 30 days to assure the safe withdrawal of U.S. troops. However, Congress could force an immediate withdrawal at any time by passing a concurrent resolution not subject to the President's veto.

Emergency Energy Bills. In November, Congress began to cooperate with the President in dealing with the petroleum shortage and the consequent energy crisis. On November 13, Congress authorized construction of the Alaska pipeline, which will carry oil about 790 miles from the northern slope of Alaska at Prudhoe Bay to the port of Valdez. The President signed the measure on November 16. On November 14, Congress completed action on a bill requiring the President to allocate crude oil and refined petroleum products, including gasoline. The President signed the act on November 27.

Congress adjourned on December 22, however, without passing the National Energy Emergency Act, giving the President broad powers to enforce conservation measures, including rationing of gas and fuel oil to meet the energy crisis. Congress did pass a bill putting nationwide daylight-saving time into effect in January, 1974.

Economy-Related Measures. Congress passed an extension of the Economic Stabilization Bill, giving the President power to set wage and price ceilings, just before the act expired on April 30. A four-year Emergency Farm Loan Program was passed by Congress and signed by the President on May 20. The new program ended farm subsidies and set up a system for providing cash payments to farmers if prices fall below so-called "target" levels. These minimum prices were set by a law signed on August 13.

Other economy-related measures passed by Congress in 1973 included: a bill funding the operations of the Economic Development Agency at $430 million for one more year, signed by the President on June 19; a bill ratifying the Administration's 10 per cent devaluation of the dollar and raising the official price of gold from $38 an ounce to $42.22 an ounce, signed on September 21; and a bill requiring federal agencies to limit the interest rates they charge on time deposits of less than $100,000, signed on October 15. See ECONOMICS.

Social Welfare Legislation. Congress voted a 5.9 per cent cost-of-living increase in social security benefits effective in July, 1974. It was signed into law by

Public sessions of the special Senate committee investigating the Watergate scandal were on nationwide television.

Members of the United States House

The House of Representatives of the second session of the 93rd Congress consists of 243 Democrats, 188 Republicans, and 1 Independent (not including representatives from the District of Columbia, Puerto Rico, Guam, and the Virgin Islands), with 3 seats vacant, compared with 240 Democrats and 192 Republicans, with 3 seats vacant, for the first session of the 93rd Congress. This table shows congressional districts, legislator, and party affiliation. Asterisk (*) denotes those who served in the 92nd Congress; dagger (†) denotes "at large."

Alabama

1. Jack Edwards, R.*
2. William L. Dickinson, R.*
3. William Nichols, D.*
4. Tom Bevill, D.*
5. Robert E. Jones, D.*
6. John H. Buchanan, Jr., R.*
7. Walter Flowers, D.*

Alaska

† Don Young, R.

Arizona

1. John J. Rhodes, R.*
2. Morris K. Udall, D.*
3. Sam Steiger, R.*
4. John B. Conlan, R.

Arkansas

1. Bill Alexander, D.*
2. Wilbur D. Mills, D.*
3. J. P. Hammerschmidt, R.*
4. Ray Thornton, D.

California

1. Don H. Clausen, R.*
2. Harold T. Johnson, D.*
3. John E. Moss, D.*
4. Robert L. Leggett, D.*
5. Phillip Burton, D.*
6. William S. Mailliard, R.*
7. Ronald V. Dellums, D.*
8. Fortney H. Stark, D.
9. Don Edwards, D.*
10. Charles S. Gubser, R.*
11. Leo J. Ryan, D.
12. Burt L. Talcott, R.*
13. Vacant
14. Jerome R. Waldie, D.*
15. John J. McFall, D.*
16. B. F. Sisk, D.*
17. Paul N. McCloskey, Jr., I.*
18. Robert B. Mathias, R.*
19. Chet Holifield, D.*
20. Carlos J. Moorhead, R.
21. Augustus F. Hawkins, D.*
22. James C. Corman, D.*
23. Del M. Clawson, R.*
24. John H. Rousselot, R.*
25. Charles E. Wiggins, R.*
26. Thomas M. Rees, D.*
27. Barry M. Goldwater, Jr., R.*
28. Alphonzo Bell, R.*
29. George E. Danielson, D.*
30. Edward R. Roybal, D.*
31. Charles H. Wilson, D.*
32. Craig Hosmer, R.*
33. Jerry L. Pettis, R.*
34. Richard T. Hanna, D.*
35. Glenn M. Anderson, D.*
36. William Ketchum, R.
37. Yvonne B. Burke, D.

38. George E. Brown, Jr., D.
39. Andrew J. Hinshaw, R.
40. Bob Wilson, R.*
41. Lionel Van Deerlin, D.*
42. Clair W. Burgener, R.
43. Victor V. Veysey, R.*

Colorado

1. Patricia Schroeder, D.
2. Donald G. Brotzman, R.*
3. Frank E. Evans, D.*
4. James P. Johnson, R.
5. William L. Armstrong, R.

Connecticut

1. William R. Cotter, D.*
2. Robert H. Steele, R.*
3. Robert N. Giaimo, D.*
4. Stewart B. McKinney, R.*
5. Ronald A. Sarasin, R.
6. Ella T. Grasso, D.*

Delaware

† Pierre S. du Pont IV, R.*

Florida

1. Robert L. F. Sikes, D.*
2. Don Fuqua, D.*
3. Charles E. Bennett, D.*
4. William V. Chappell, Jr., D.*
5. Bill Gunter, D.
6. C. W. Young, R.*
7. Sam M. Gibbons, D.*
8. James A. Haley, D.*
9. Louis Frey, Jr., R.*
10. L. A. Bafalis, R.
11. Paul G. Rogers, D.*
12. J. Herbert Burke, R.*
13. William Lehman, D.
14. Claude D. Pepper, D.*
15. Dante B. Fascell, D.*

Georgia

1. Ronald Ginn, D.
2. Dawson Mathis, D.*
3. Jack T. Brinkley, D.*
4. Ben B. Blackburn, R.*
5. Andrew Young, D.
6. John J. Flynt, Jr., D.*
7. John W. Davis, D.*
8. Williamson S. Stuckey, Jr., D.*
9. Phillip M. Landrum, D.*
10. Robert G. Stephens, Jr., D.*

Hawaii

1. Spark M. Matsunaga, D.*
2. Patsy T. Mink, D.*

Idaho

1. Steven D. Symms, R.
2. Orval Hansen, R.*

Illinois

1. Ralph H. Metcalfe, D.*
2. Morgan F. Murphy, D.*
3. Robert P. Hanrahan, R.
4. Edward J. Derwinski, R.*
5. John C. Kluczynski, D.*
6. Harold R. Collier, R.*
7. Cardiss Collins, D.
8. Dan Rostenkowski, D.*
9. Sidney R. Yates, D.*
10. Samuel H. Young, R.
11. Frank Annunzio, D.*
12. Philip M. Crane, R.*
13. Robert McClory, R.*
14. John N. Erlenborn, R.*
15. Leslie C. Arends, R.*
16. John B. Anderson, R.*
17. George M. O'Brien, R.
18. Robert H. Michel, R.*
19. Thomas F. Railsback, R.*
20. Paul Findley, R.*
21. Edward R. Madigan, R.
22. George E. Shipley, D.*
23. Charles Melvin Price, D.*
24. Kenneth J. Gray, D.*

Indiana

1. Ray J. Madden, D.*
2. Earl F. Landgrebe, R.*
3. John Brademas, D.*
4. J. Edward Roush, D.*
5. Elwood H. Hillis, R.*
6. William G. Bray, R.*
7. John T. Myers, R.*
8. Roger H. Zion, R.*
9. Lee H. Hamilton, D.*
10. David W. Dennis, R.*
11. William H. Hudnut III, R.

Iowa

1. Edward Mezvinsky, D.
2. John C. Culver, D.*
3. H. R. Gross, R.*
4. Neal Smith, D.*
5. William J. Scherle, R.*
6. Wiley Mayne, R.*

Kansas

1. Keith G. Sebelius, R.*
2. William R. Roy, D.*
3. Larry Winn, Jr., R.*
4. Garner E. Shriver, R.*
5. Joe Skubitz, R.*

Kentucky

1. Frank A. Stubblefield, D.*
2. William H. Natcher, D.*
3. Romano L. Mazzoli, D.*
4. Marion Gene Snyder, R.*
5. Tim Lee Carter, R.*
6. John B. Breckinridge, D.
7. Carl D. Perkins, D.*

Louisiana

1. F. Edward Hébert, D.*
2. Lindy Boggs, D.
3. David C. Treen, R.
4. Joe D. Waggoner, Jr., D.*
5. Otto E. Passman, D.*
6. John R. Rarick, D.*
7. John B. Breaux, D.*
8. Gillis W. Long, D.

Maine

1. Peter N. Kyros, D.*
2. William S. Cohen, R.

Maryland

1. Robert E. Bauman, R.
2. Clarence D. Long, D.*
3. Paul S. Sarbanes, D.*
4. Marjorie S. Holt, R.
5. Lawrence J. Hogan, R.*
6. Goodloe E. Byron, D.*
7. Parren J. Mitchell, D.*
8. Gilbert Gude, R.*

Massachusetts

1. Silvio O. Conte, R.*
2. Edward P. Boland, D.*
3. Harold D. Donohue, D.*
4. Robert F. Drinan, D.*
5. Paul W. Cronin, R.
6. Michael J. Harrington, D.*
7. Torbert H. Macdonald, D.*
8. Thomas P. O'Neill, Jr., D.*
9. John J. Moakley, D.
10. Margaret M. Heckler, R.*
11. James A. Burke, D.*
12. Gerry E. Studds, D.

Michigan

1. John Conyers, Jr., D.*
2. Marvin L. Esch, R.*
3. Garry Brown, R.*
4. Edward Hutchinson, R.*
5. Vacant
6. Charles E. Chamberlain, R.*
7. Donald W. Riegle, Jr., R.*
8. James Harvey, R.*
9. Guy Vander Jagt, R.*
10. Elford A. Cederberg, R.*
11. Philip E. Ruppe, R.*
12. James G. O'Hara, D.*
13. Charles C. Diggs, Jr., D.*
14. Lucien N. Nedzi, D.*
15. William D. Ford, D.*
16. John D. Dingell, D.*
17. Martha W. Griffiths, D.*
18. Robert J. Huber, R.
19. William S. Broomfield, R.*

Minnesota

1. Albert H. Quie, R.*
2. Ancher Nelsen, R.*
3. Bill Frenzel, R.*
4. Joseph E. Karth, D.*
5. Donald M. Fraser, D.*
6. John M. Zwach, R.*
7. Bob Bergland, D.*
8. John A. Blatnik, D.*

Mississippi

1. Jamie L. Whitten, D.*
2. David R. Bowen, D.
3. G. V. Montgomery, D.*
4. Thad Cochran, R.
5. Trent Lott, R.

Missouri

1. William L. Clay, D.*
2. James W. Symington, D.*
3. Leonor K. Sullivan, D.*
4. William J. Randall, D.*
5. Richard Bolling, D.*
6. Jerry Litton, D.
7. Gene Taylor, R.
8. Richard H. Ichord, D.*
9. William L. Hungate, D.*
10. Bill D. Burlison, D.*

Montana

1. Richard G. Shoup, R.*
2. John Melcher, D.*

Nebraska

1. Charles Thone, R.*
2. John Y. McCollister, R.*
3. David T. Martin, R.*

Nevada

† David Towell, R.

New Hampshire

1. Louis C. Wyman, R.*
2. James C. Cleveland, R.*

New Jersey

1. John E. Hunt, R.*
2. Charles W. Sandman, Jr., R.*
3. James J. Howard, D.*
4. Frank Thompson, Jr., D.*
5. Peter H. B. Frelinghuysen, R.*
6. Edwin B. Forsythe, R.*
7. William B. Widnall, R.*
8. Robert A. Roe, D.*
9. Henry Helstoski, D.*
10. Peter W. Rodino, Jr., D.*
11. Joseph G. Minish, D.*
12. Matthew J. Rinaldo, R.
13. Joseph J. Maraziti, R.
14. Dominick V. Daniels, D.*
15. Edward J. Patten, D.*

New Mexico

1. Manuel Lujan, Jr., R.*
2. Harold L. Runnels, D.*

New York

1. Otis G. Pike, D.*
2. James R. Grover, Jr., R.*
3. Angelo D. Roncallo, R.
4. Norman F. Lent, R.*
5. John W. Wydler, R.*
6. Lester L. Wolff, D.*
7. Joseph P. Addabbo, D.*
8. Benjamin S. Rosenthal, D.*
9. James J. Delaney, D.*
10. Mario Biaggi, D.*
11. Frank J. Brasco, D.*
12. Shirley Chisholm, D.*
13. Bertram L. Podell, D.*
14. John J. Rooney, D.*
15. Hugh L. Carey, D.*
16. Elizabeth Holtzman, D.
17. John M. Murphy, D.*
18. Edward I. Koch, D.*
19. Charles B. Rangel, D.*
20. Bella S. Abzug, D.*
21. Herman Badillo, D.*
22. Jonathan B. Bingham, D.*
23. Peter A. Peyser, R.*
24. Ogden R. Reid, D.*
25. Hamilton Fish, Jr., R.*
26. Benjamin A. Gilman, R.
27. Howard W. Robison, R.*
28. Samuel S. Stratton, D.*
29. Carleton J. King, R.*
30. Robert C. McEwen, R.*
31. Donald Mitchell, R.
32. James M. Hanley, D.*
33. William F. Walsh, R.
34. Frank Horton, R.*
35. Barber B. Conable, Jr., R.*
36. Henry P. Smith III, R.*
37. Thaddeus J. Dulski, D.*
38. Jack F. Kemp, R.*
39. James F. Hastings, R.*

North Carolina

1. Walter B. Jones, D.*
2. L. H. Fountain, D.*
3. David N. Henderson, D.*
4. Ike F. Andrews, D.
5. Wilmer D. Mizell, R.*
6. L. Richardson Preyer, D.*
7. Charles G. Rose III, D.
8. Earl B. Ruth, R.*
9. James G. Martin, R.
10. James T. Broyhill, R.*
11. Roy A. Taylor, D.*

North Dakota

† Mark Andrews, R.*

Ohio

1. William J. Keating, R.*
2. Donald D. Clancy, R.*
3. Charles W. Whalen, Jr., R.*
4. Tennyson Guyer, R.
5. Delbert L. Latta, R.*
6. William H. Harsha, R.*
7. Clarence J. Brown, R.*
8. Walter E. Powell, R.*
9. Thomas L. Ashley, D.*
10. Clarence E. Miller, R.*
11. J. William Stanton, R.*
12. Samuel L. Devine, R.*
13. Charles A. Mosher, R.*
14. John F. Seiberling, D.*
15. Chalmers P. Wylie, R.*
16. Ralph S. Regula, R.
17. John M. Ashbrook, R.*
18. Wayne L. Hays, D.*
19. Charles J. Carney, D.*
20. James V. Stanton, D.*
21. Louis Stokes, D.*
22. Charles A. Vanik, D.*
23. William E. Minshall, R.*

Oklahoma

1. James R. Jones, D.
2. Clem R. McSpadden, D.
3. Carl B. Albert, D.*
4. Tom Steed, D.*
5. John Jarman, D.*
6. John N. Happy Camp, R.*

Oregon

1. Wendell Wyatt, R.*
2. Al Ullman, D.*
3. Edith Green, D.*
4. John Dellenback, R.*

Pennsylvania

1. William A. Barrett, D.*
2. Robert N. C. Nix, D.*
3. William J. Green, D.*
4. Joshua Eilberg, D.*
5. John H. Ware III, R.*
6. Gus Yatron, D.*
7. Lawrence, G. Williams, R.*
8. Edward G. Biester, Jr., R.*
9. E. G. Shuster, R.
10. Joseph M. McDade, R.*
11. Daniel J. Flood, D.*
12. Vacant
13. Lawrence Coughlin, R.*
14. William S. Moorhead, D.*
15. Fred B. Rooney, D.*
16. Edwin D. Eshleman, R.*
17. Herman T. Schneebeli, R.*
18. H. John Heinz III, R.*
19. George A. Goodling, R.*
20. Joseph M. Gaydos, D.*
21. John H. Dent, D.*
22. Thomas E. Morgan, D.*
23. Albert W. Johnson, R.*
24. Joseph P. Vigorito, D.*
25. Frank M. Clark, D.*

Rhode Island

1. Fernand J. St. Germain, D.*
2. Robert O. Tiernan, D.*

South Carolina

1. Mendel J. Davis, D.*
2. Floyd D. Spence, R.*
3. W. J. Bryan Dorn, D.*
4. James R. Mann, D.*
5. Thomas S. Gettys, D.*
6. Edward L. Young, R.

South Dakota

1. Frank E. Denholm, D.*
2. James Abdnor, R.

Tennessee

1. James H. Quillen, R.*
2. John J. Duncan, R.*
3. LaMar Baker, R.*
4. Joe L. Evins, D.*
5. Richard H. Fulton, D.*
6. Robin L. Beard, Jr., R.
7. Ed Jones, D.*
8. Dan H. Kuykendall, R.*

Texas

1. Wright Patman, D.*
2. Charles Wilson, D.
3. James M. Collins, R.*
4. Ray Roberts, D.*
5. Alan Steelman, R.
6. Olin E. Teague, D.*
7. Bill Archer, R.*
8. Bob Eckhardt, D.*
9. Jack Brooks, D.*
10. J. J. Pickle, D.*
11. W. R. Poage, D.*
12. James C. Wright, Jr., D.*
13. Robert D. Price, R.*
14. John Young, D.*
15. Eligio de la Garza, D.*
16. Richard C. White, D.*
17. Omar Burleson, D.*
18. Barbara C. Jordan, D.
19. George H. Mahon, D.*
20. Henry B. Gonzalez, D.*
21. O. C. Fisher, D.*
22. Robert R. Casey, D.*
23. Abraham Kazen, Jr., D.*
24. Dale Milford, D.

Utah

1. K. Gunn McKay, D.*
2. D. Wayne Owens, D.

Vermont

† Richard W. Mallary, R.*

Virginia

1. Thomas N. Downing, D.*
2. G. William Whitehurst, R.*
3. David E. Satterfield III, D.*
4. Robert W. Daniel, Jr., R.
5. W. C. Daniel, D.*
6. M. Caldwell Butler, R.
7. J. Kenneth Robinson, R.*
8. Stanford E. Parris, R.
9. William C. Wampler, R.*
10. Joel T. Broyhill, R.*

Washington

1. Joel Pritchard, R.
2. Lloyd Meeds, D.*
3. Julia Butler Hansen, D.*
4. Mike McCormack, D.*
5. Thomas S. Foley, D.*
6. Floyd V. Hicks, D.*
7. Brock Adams, D.*

West Virginia

1. Robert H. Mollohan, D.*
2. Harley O. Staggers, D.*
3. John M. Slack, D.*
4. Ken Hechler, D.*

Wisconsin

1. Les Aspin, D.*
2. Robert W. Kastenmeier, D.*
3. Vernon W. Thomson, R.*
4. Clement J. Zablocki, D.*
5. Henry S. Reuss, D.*
6. William A. Steiger, R.*
7. David R. Obey, D.*
8. Harold V. Froehlich, R.
9. Glenn R. Davis, R.*

Wyoming

† Teno Roncalio, D.*

Nonvoting Representatives

District of Columbia

Walter E. Fauntroy, D.*

Guam

Antonio Won Pat, D.

Puerto Rico

Jaime Benitez, D.

Virgin Islands

Ron de Lugo, D.

Members of the United States Senate

The Senate of the second session of the 93rd Congress consists of 57 Democrats, 41 Republicans, 1 Independent, and 1 Conservative, compared with 54 Democrats, 44 Republicans, 1 Independent, and 1 Conservative for the first session of the 93rd Congress. Senators shown starting their term in 1973 were elected for the first time in the Nov. 7, 1972, elections. Those shown ending their current terms in 1979 were re-elected to the Senate in the same balloting. The second date in each listing shows when the term of a previously elected senator expires. For organization purposes, the one Independent will line up with Democrats, the one Conservative with Republicans.

State	Term	State	Term	State	Term
Alabama		**Louisiana**		**Ohio**	
John J. Sparkman, D.	1946—1979	Russell B. Long, D.	1948—1975	Robert Taft, Jr., R.	1971—1977
James B. Allen, D.	1969—1975	J. Bennett Johnston, Jr., D.	1973—1979	Howard M. Metzenbaum, D.*	1974—1975
Alaska		**Maine**		**Oklahoma**	
Theodore F. Stevens, R.	1968—1979	Edmund S. Muskie, D.	1959—1977	Henry L. Bellmon, R.	1969—1975
Mike Gravel, D.	1969—1975	William D. Hathaway, D.	1973—1979	Dewey F. Bartlett, R.	1973—1979
Arizona		**Maryland**		**Oregon**	
Paul J. Fannin, R.	1965—1977	Charles McC. Mathias, Jr., R.	1969—1975	Mark O. Hatfield, R.	1967—1979
Barry Goldwater, R.	1969—1975	J. Glenn Beall, Jr., R.	1971—1977	Robert W. Packwood, R.	1969—1975
Arkansas		**Massachusetts**		**Pennsylvania**	
John L. McClellan, D.	1943—1979	Edward M. Kennedy, D.	1962—1977	Hugh D. Scott, Jr., R.	1959—1977
J. William Fulbright, D.	1945—1975	Edward W. Brooke, R.	1967—1979	Richard S. Schweiker, R.	1969—1975
California		**Michigan**		**Rhode Island**	
Alan Cranston, D.	1969—1975	Philip A. Hart, D.	1959—1977	John O. Pastore, D.	1950—1977
John V. Tunney, D.	1971—1977	Robert P. Griffin, R.	1966—1979	Claiborne Pell, D.	1961—1979
Colorado		**Minnesota**		**South Carolina**	
Peter H. Dominick, R.	1963—1975	Walter F. Mondale, D.	1964—1979	Strom Thurmond, R.	1956—1979
Floyd K. Haskell, D.	1973—1979	Hubert H. Humphrey, D.	1971—1977	Ernest F. Hollings, D.	1966—1975
Connecticut		**Mississippi**		**South Dakota**	
Abraham A. Ribicoff, D.	1963—1975	James O. Eastland, D.	1943—1979	George S. McGovern, D.	1963—1975
Lowell P. Weicker, Jr., R.	1971—1977	John Cornelius Stennis, D.	1947—1977	James G. Abourezk, D.	1973—1979
Delaware		**Missouri**		**Tennessee**	
William V. Roth, Jr., R.	1971—1977	Stuart Symington, D.	1953—1977	Howard H. Baker, Jr., R.	1967—1977
Joseph R. Biden, Jr., D.	1973—1979	Thomas Francis Eagleton, D.	1968—1975	William E. Brock III, R.	1971—1979
Florida		**Montana**		**Texas**	
Edward J. Gurney, R.	1969—1975	Mike J. Mansfield, D.	1953—1977	John G. Tower, R.	1961—1979
Lawton Chiles, D.	1971—1977	Lee Metcalf, D.	1961—1979	Lloyd M. Bentsen, Jr., D.	1971—1977
Georgia		**Nebraska**		**Utah**	
Herman E. Talmadge, D.	1957—1975	Roman Lee Hruska, R.	1954—1977	Wallace F. Bennett, R.	1951—1975
Sam A. Nunn, Jr., D.	1973—1979	Carl T. Curtis, R.	1955—1979	Frank E. Moss, D.	1959—1977
Hawaii		**Nevada**		**Vermont**	
Hiram L. Fong, R.	1959—1977	Alan Bible, D.	1954—1975	George D. Aiken, R.	1941—1975
Daniel Ken Inouye, D.	1963—1975	Howard W. Cannon, D.	1959—1977	Robert T. Stafford, R.	1971—1977
Idaho		**New Hampshire**		**Virginia**	
Frank Church, D.	1957—1975	Norris Cotton, R.	1954—1975	Harry F. Byrd, Jr., Ind.	1965—1977
James A. McClure, R.	1973—1979	Thomas J. McIntyre, D.	1962—1979	William L. Scott, R.	1973—1979
Illinois		**New Jersey**		**Washington**	
Charles H. Percy, R.	1967—1979	Clifford P. Case, R.	1955—1979	Warren G. Magnuson, D.	1944—1975
Adlai E. Stevenson III, D.	1970—1975	Harrison A. Williams, Jr., D.	1959—1977	Henry M. Jackson, D.	1953—1977
Indiana		**New Mexico**		**West Virginia**	
Vance Hartke, D.	1959—1977	Joseph M. Montoya, D.	1964—1977	Jennings Randolph, D.	1958—1979
Birch Bayh, D.	1963—1975	Pete V. Domenici, R.	1973—1979	Robert C. Byrd, D.	1959—1977
Iowa		**New York**		**Wisconsin**	
Harold E. Hughes, D.	1969—1975	Jacob K. Javits, R.	1957—1975	William Proxmire, D.	1957—1977
Richard Clark, D.	1973—1979	James L. Buckley, Cons.	1971—1977	Gaylord A. Nelson, D.	1963—1975
Kansas		**North Carolina**		**Wyoming**	
James B. Pearson, R.	1962—1979	Sam J. Ervin, Jr., D.	1954—1975	Gale W. McGee, D.	1959—1977
Robert J. Dole, R.	1969—1975	Jesse A. Helms, R.	1973—1979	Clifford P. Hansen, R.	1967—1979
Kentucky		**North Dakota**			
Marlow W. Cook, R.	1968—1975	Milton R. Young, D.	1945—1975	*In January, 1974, replaced William B. Saxbe, who became U.S. Attorney General.	
Walter Huddleston, D.	1973—1979	Quentin N. Burdick, D.	1960—1977		

the President on July 1. Then, in December, because of continuing inflation, Congress voted an 11 per cent increase in social security that superseded the 5.9 per cent rise. See SOCIAL SECURITY.

On June 5, Congress passed a $1.27-billion health-services bill, which included grants for hospital construction, regional medical programs, community mental health centers, and medical-training programs. President Nixon signed the bill on June 19, even though it exceeded his budget and contained programs he had planned to phase out.

On November 8, the President signed a bill increasing federal aid for school lunch programs by 25 per cent. A bill providing $1.55 billion in aid for the handicapped was signed on September 26.

Other Measures passed by the first session:

- The Federal Law Enforcement Administration was extended for three years.

- A ban was passed on local television blackouts of sports events that are sold out 72 hours in advance.

- $110 million was appropriated over a two-year period for the Corporation for Public Broadcasting.

- $310 million a year for two years was appropriated for airport development, and airport head taxes were banned.

- A highway bill was passed, permitting the use of highway funds to finance mass transportation.

Presidential Vetoes. In 1973, President Nixon vetoed eight bills in addition to the War Powers Act because he regarded them as either inflationary or restricting the constitutional prerogatives of the President. On March 27, he vetoed a $2.6-billion bill for aid to handicapped persons. A $120-million measure to restore water and sewer grants in rural areas was vetoed on April 5. The President vetoed a bill requiring Senate confirmation of appointees to the posts of director and deputy director of the Office of Management and Budget on May 18, and on June 27, he vetoed a supplemental appropriations bill with a provision to cut off funds for bombing in Khmer. Mr. Nixon vetoed a bill providing $185 million in emergency health-service grants on August 1. A bill expanding the Small Business Administration's disaster loan program was vetoed on September 22. On September 26, Mr. Nixon vetoed a bill raising the minimum hourly wage from $1.60 to $2.20 as of July, 1974. Finally, Mr. Nixon vetoed a bill providing operating funds for the United States Information Agency on October 23, because it required the agency to turn over any confidential material requested by Congress.

Congressional Hearings. On February 7, the Senate voted 70 to 0 to establish a committee composed of four Democrats and three Republicans to probe the Watergate affair. The Senate Select Committee on Presidential Campaign Activities, popularly known as the Watergate committee, opened its televised hearings in May, focusing national attention on corruption at the highest levels of government.

The committee was chaired by Senator Sam J. Ervin, Jr. (D., N.C.). See WATERGATE.

The Senate Armed Services Committee heard testimony in July and August about the falsification of records on the secret bombing of Khmer. On July 12, the House government operations subcommittee began looking into federal expenditures on the President's private residences at Key Biscayne, Fla., and San Clemente, Calif. And on October 30, the House Judiciary Committee opened hearings into possible grounds for impeaching President Nixon.

On December 18, the General Accounting Office (GAO), after reviewing federal funds spent on Mr. Nixon's private homes, asked for tighter congressional control on such expenditures. The GAO reported that $1.4 million had been spent, largely for security, and asked Congress to limit the number of presidential homes that could be protected at federal expense.

Congress carefully investigated the qualifications of Ford to be Vice-President, replacing Spiro T. Agnew. Final action on Ford's confirmation by both houses was completed on December 6, and he was sworn in the same day.   Carol L. Thompson

See also AGNEW, SPIRO THEODORE; NIXON, RICHARD MILHOUS; PRESIDENT OF THE UNITED STATES; Section One, FOCUS ON THE NATION.

CONNECTICUT. See STATE GOVERNMENT.

Carl B. Albert of Oklahoma continued as speaker of the House, and Thomas P. O'Neill, Jr., of Massachusetts, right, became majority leader.

CONSERVATION

CONSERVATION. The energy crisis in 1973 posed severe problems for U.S. conservationists. The nation suffered a fuel-oil shortage in the winter of 1972-1973, reduced gasoline supplies in the summer of 1973, and a grave fuel shortage in the winter of 1973-1974. Some Americans were quick to blame environmental groups for the shortages because of their opposition to efforts to develop energy sources they believed might threaten the environment. Secretary of Agriculture Earl L. Butz, for instance, said in February, "The first people to have their power shut off should be those who blocked the Alaska pipeline."

The full extent of the backlash against the environmental movement was demonstrated on November 13, when Congress approved legislation to allow construction of a $4-billion, 789-mile oil pipeline across Alaska. The bill also banned lawsuits against the pipeline based on environmental grounds. Spokesmen for the Environmental Defense Fund and the Sierra Club, two of the conservation groups that had blocked the pipeline for more than three years, said they would challenge the action on constitutional grounds. "We question the legality of a law that says a court can't review a law," they said. The pipeline would carry oil from Alaska's North Slope to the ice-free port of Valdez on Alaska's southern coast, from where it can be shipped to ports on the Pacific Coast. Conservationists contended that construction of the Alaska pipeline would endanger the environment.

Conservation spokesmen also asked early in the year if cutting back on energy demand might not be a key to solving the crisis. By fall, the Office of Energy Conservation in the Department of the Interior had launched a campaign to save energy by such measures as lowering thermostats and turning off unused lights. In November, this effort was stepped up when President Richard M. Nixon asked for and received emergency powers to curb the use of fuels and electricity. On November 25, he rationed heating oil, effective January 1, by reducing shipments to homes by 15 per cent, to business and commercial establishments 25 per cent, and those to industrial users 10 per cent. He also cut back gasoline deliveries to gas stations and asked Congress to approve other emergency measures, including a Sunday prohibition of gasoline sales.

Conservation Organizations. Environmental groups successfully fought off demands by Western wool growers early in the year that the ban on the use of poisons to kill coyotes on public lands be revoked. The ban was ordered by the President in February, 1972, in response to conservationist claims that poisoned baits kill other animals and birds as well as predators. Citing losses of $50.3 million worth of sheep a year, the sheepmen launched an energetic campaign to revoke the poison ban. In a telegram to the President on January 19, a total of 40 conservation and environmental organizations reiterated support for the ban. The message, representing almost all major groups, was a rare showing of unity among hunting and antihunting spokesmen. In September, Interior Department officials told Congress that predators can be controlled without resorting to poisoning.

Parks and Recreation. Ronald H. Walker, a White House aide who was named director of the National Park Service in December, 1972, launched a reorganization of the agency in September, 1973. The move, designed to bolster management of the service's 298 park and recreation areas, ultimately will shift 100 positions from Washington, D.C., to field locations.

Conservation spokesmen who had greeted Walker's appointment with a "wait and see" attitude because of his inexperience in park management supported the action. Walker pointed out that 211.6-million visits were recorded in national parks in 1972, up 98 per cent from 1964, while the number of permanent park employees increased by only 21 per cent, to 7,074.

The National Park Service, the Forest Service, and other federal agencies operating campgrounds stopped charging fees for camping in August. The action stemmed from new legislation banning fees for camping unless flush toilets, showers, and other facilities were available.

The National Park Service decided in September

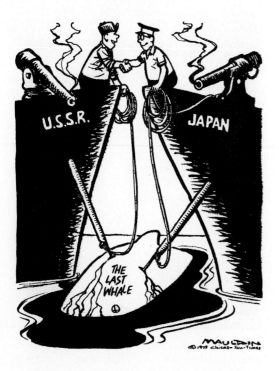

"What shall we hunt next, comrade—porpoises?"

Union Camp Corporation donated 49,000 acres of Dismal Swamp in Virginia as a federal wildlife refuge, thus saving a wilderness area from destruction.

to halt its effort to control beach erosion at Cape Hatteras National Seashore in North Carolina and at other barrier islands it manages. The service said it had spent $21 million since the 1930s fighting the sea by constructing huge dunes along the shoreline, but had now concluded that the money was wasted. Residents and motel operators in these areas protested that the government's action threatened millions of dollars in private seashore investments.

Wildlife. The first treaty to control trade in endangered species was signed by representatives of 80 nations on March 3 in Washington, D.C. The agreement bars international commerce in 375 species, including 5 of the great whales and most of the world's spotted cats. The treaty does not become effective until ratified by 10 nations. Because of this, Russell E. Train, head of the U.S. delegation, warned that the agreement might be used by unscrupulous persons as a "shopping list" for quick profits on pelts of rare animals.

With the rich wildlife heritage of Africa increasingly endangered by hunting and loss of habitat, Tanzania on September 8 banned the shooting or capture of wild animals. The action followed similar bans on elephant hunting by Kenya and Ivory Coast.

Water Resources. Spring floods that began in early March on the Mississippi River ravaged millions of acres of farmlands along its 1,400-mile watershed. The floods caused damage estimated at more than $400 million and killed 20 persons. The river reached a history-making crest of 43.3 feet, 13.3 feet above flood stage, at St. Louis on April 28.

In late July, the Bureau of Reclamation reduced the Colorado River's flow through the Grand Canyon by cutting the volume of water released from Glen Canyon Dam. Conservationists charged the action prevented raft trips through the canyon and threatened further inundation of Rainbow Bridge National Monument.

The National Water Commission on June 16 recommended a switch in financial support for the nation's water projects from the taxpayer to those who benefit from them. On August 16, more than 100 members of Congress sent a letter to President Nixon voicing alarm at the commission's proposal that flood-control projects be supported by local financing. The commission, created by Congress in 1968, said "the public bears too large a burden of the cost of many water programs."

Under an agreement between Mexico and the United States, approved August 30, the United States will spend $115 million on water projects to decrease the salinity of Colorado River water that flows into Mexico. The projects include the world's largest desalting plant, near Yuma, Ariz.   Andrew L. Newman

See also ENVIRONMENT.

CONSTITUTION, UNITED STATES. See UNITED STATES CONSTITUTION.

CONSUMER AFFAIRS. For American consumers, 1973 was a traumatic year. Living costs broke all records, resulting in an unprecedented nationwide boycott of meat. This was followed by scattered shortages of important food and fuel products. By December, the food industry was closing the gaps in supply channels, but shortages of gasoline and heating fuels were growing rapidly, and the prices for most products and services were still rising rapidly.

All was relatively calm on January 11 when President Richard M. Nixon announced Phase 3, which was essentially a shift from mandatory to voluntary price controls. But before long, food prices shot upward faster than before the first price freeze nearly 18 months earlier. Prices that farmers received in January soared 16.9 per cent over those of December, 1972. Retail food prices rose 2.3 per cent in January, according to the Bureau of Labor Statistics. This was equivalent to an annual increase of 27.6 per cent. It was the biggest monthly jump in food prices since the government began keeping such records in 1952. Another record was set in February, with a 2.4 per cent increase, mostly at the meat counter. The meat price index rose 13 per cent in three months. Much of the increase came in raw farm products, which were exempt from price controls.

Meat Boycott. Public reaction to the record food price increases was strong and widespread. The idea for a nationwide meat boycott apparently started almost simultaneously among housewives in Los Angeles and Vernon, Conn. Soon, members of Congress were helping to publicize efforts to plan the boycott for the first week in April.

Well before the boycott, many persons stopped buying meat or ate less of it. By mid-March, industry sources reported that buyers for food chains were purchasing an average of 3.5 per cent less beef. Three days before the boycott, President Nixon froze prices of beef, lamb, and pork at peak levels. According to news reports, sales of meat during the boycott dropped to about half their normal levels in many localities throughout the nation.

But the effect on prices was minimal as cattlemen, knowing in advance of the boycott plans, withheld enough animals from slaughter to offset the drop in demand. Thus they prevented meat prices from falling more than a small amount, and other prices continued to climb at a record pace. Reacting to the general public's frustration, many in Congress began pushing for legislation to lower prices and to extend presidential authority for imposing further price and wage controls. However, a plan to freeze prices as of March 16 was defeated 258 to 147 in the House. On June 4, the Senate Democratic Caucus put further pressure on the White House by declaring Phase 3 "an unmitigated failure" and pledging to pass a 90-day freeze.

Nine days later, President Nixon imposed a 60-day freeze on most prices, and froze beef prices for 90

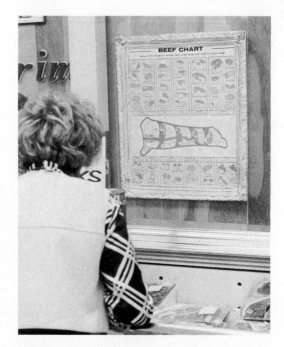

Charts identifying names of meat cuts went into national use as part of the new Uniform Retail Meat Identity Standards program to aid consumers.

days. In August, when the freeze ended and Phase 4 began with selective controls, prices again moved upward. A noticeable exception was beef; consumer demand had dropped so much that retail prices actually dipped after the freeze ended.

Increasing shortages of gasoline, fuel oil, and other products long taken for granted added to consumer problems in the fall. In November, President Nixon proposed allocation of home heating oil, cuts in gasoline deliveries, lower speed limits, and other measures to save fuel. See ENERGY.

Consumer Organizations. Although price protestors could not claim much success with their actions, the meat boycott marked a turning point in consumer activities. Traditional consumer organizations took a back seat as a new wave of aroused citizens, mostly well-educated and comparatively affluent housewives, organized and ran the boycott. One result was the launching in April of a new national consumer force, the National Consumer Congress (NCC). Its main purpose was to continue actively to resist price increases. Within a few months, the organization claimed to have more than 50 branches throughout the United States.

The boycott and the emergence of NCC symbolized not only a shift away from traditional consumer groups, but also a return to the grass-roots level of organization and activity. The shifting winds caught the six-year-old Consumer Federation of America

(CFA) at a time when its future looked bleakest, mainly because of dwindling financial support. At its annual meeting in September, a long-embittered minority of consumer citizen groups succeeded in restructuring the organization into 10 regional segments. This immediately led to the resignation of executive director Erma Angevine. She felt the CFA could not survive long in 10 parts with its limited finances, which come mostly from national labor unions. Only 44 of approximately 180 CFA member groups were citizen organizations.

As the year ended, numerous consumer leaders were meeting to explore the possibilities of a merger of NCC and CFA member organizations to strengthen state and local activities without weakening the consumer movement on the national scene.

Federal Activity fell off from the pace of earlier years. A year that started with high hopes for congressional approval of at least two long-sought bills – one calling for no-fault auto insurance and the other for a powerful new federal consumer protection agency – ended with no real progress. Although consumer issues continued to be aired frequently and sometimes loudly, including the Senate's first real investigation of life insurance, 1973 proved to be the leanest legislatively in the Ralph Nader era.

The scandals surrounding the Watergate affair were part of the reason. In the Senate, the preoccupation of Sam J. Ervin, Jr. (D., N.C.) as head of the Watergate special investigating committee left him no time to consider the consumer agency bill that languished for most of the year in his Committee on Government Operations.

The focus of legislative activity showed a decided shift to the states. Of most interest to state legislatures were antifraud laws, no-fault auto insurance, food labeling, food safety, and credit practices.

One bright spot on the federal scene, in the opinion of consumer advocates, was the Senate's rejection on June 13 of Robert H. Morris, President Nixon's choice for a vacancy on the Federal Power Commission. Morris' nomination was defeated because of objections to his ties to the oil industry. His law firm had represented an oil company for 15 years.

Winds of change were also felt in the executive branch of the federal government. The most conspicuous development was the transfer of the Office of Consumer Affairs (OCA) from the White House to the Department of Health, Education, and Welfare. OCA director Virginia Knauer retained a small office in the New Executive Office Building.

At the same time, the number of consumer offices at federal, state, and local levels increased. For the first time, all 50 states had at least one such office, with a total of 91 state consumer offices. At the county level, the number of such offices grew from 37 to 46, and at the city level from 27 to 36. An informal survey by the *National Journal*, however, concluded that, "The consumer voice still is largely unheard in the policy-making process of the federal government."

Nevertheless, regulatory action continued unabated. The Federal Trade Commission (FTC) won an important legal decision when the U.S. Court of Appeals in June confirmed its authority to issue trade regulation rules. The case involved proposals requiring that gasoline octane ratings be posted at pumps to inform motorists about gasoline quality. The decision meant that the FTC could continue to issue such rules with the force of law rather than pursue each case individually after a problem arises.

Business Responses. More companies set up consumer offices to smooth relations with customers and launch company policies and programs that consumer advocates demanded. Following the lead of the appliance manufacturers' Major Appliance Consumer Action Panel, several other business groups established similar programs to handle customer complaints.

The Chamber of Commerce responded to consumer challenges along more traditional lines. In November, it announced a program to "increase public understanding of the American economic system and to answer attacks on the private sector." It set up a Committee on Business Overview "to probe actions and influences that form the public's opinion of business and to exercise leadership in improving the private sector's stature."   Arthur E. Rowse

COSGRAVE, LIAM (1920-   ), took office as prime minister of Ireland on March 14, 1973, heading a coalition government composed of members of his own *Fine Gael* (Gaelic People) Party and the Irish Labour Party. The coalition victory in the February 28 general election ended 16 years of unbroken rule by the *Fianna Fáil* (Soldiers of Destiny) Party. The election was fought primarily on domestic issues, such as taxes, inflation, and housing. Cosgrave said his government would give first priority to economic problems. See IRELAND.

Cosgrave was born in Dublin in 1920, the eldest son of William T. Cosgrave, who served as the first president of the executive council that governed the Irish Free State from 1922 to 1932. He attended Christian Brothers schools in Dublin and Castleknock College in County Dublin.

He was called to the bar in 1943 and that same year was elected to the Dublin County legislature, where he served until 1948. He has been a member of the Irish Parliament since 1948. He has held various parliamentary posts and was minister for external affairs from 1954 to 1957. In 1956, he served as chairman of the first Irish delegation to the United Nations.

Cosgrave is a mild-mannered country gentleman who raises horses for fox-hunting on a farm outside Dublin. He and his wife Vera have two sons and a daughter.   Kathryn Sederberg

COSTA RICA. See LATIN AMERICA.

COURTS AND LAWS. Fallout from Watergate and other governmental scandals kept the spotlight on the nation's courts in 1973. In Washington, D.C., Chief U.S. District Judge John J. Sirica had a full year of Watergate-related matters. It started with the trial of the original seven burglary conspirators, continued with indictments of related individuals, and culminated with the subsequent mystery over missing and inaudible tapes. See WATERGATE.

Scandal also reached into the judiciary itself. Otto Kerner, a judge on the U.S. 7th Circuit Court of Appeals, was convicted on February 19 on 17 counts of conspiracy, fraud, perjury, bribery, and income tax evasion in connection with the purchase and sale of race-track stock while he was governor of Illinois. A codefendant, former state revenue director Theodore J. Isaacs, also was convicted.

Dropped Charges. The federal government continued its unsuccessful record of prosecutions against members of the political left. On March 26, following a mistrial, the Department of Justice dropped all indictments against the Seattle Seven, charged with inciting a riot there in 1970. No reason was given.

On May 11, Judge William M. Byrne dismissed charges of espionage, theft, and conspiracy against Pentagon Papers defendants Daniel Ellsberg and Anthony J. Russo, Jr., in Los Angeles. Byrne cited government misconduct: "Bizarre events have incurably infected the prosecution of this case," he ruled. "The totality of the circumstances . . . offend a sense of justice." See ELLSBERG, DANIEL.

On August 31, a Gainesville, Fla., jury acquitted seven members of the Vietnam Veterans Against the War on charges of conspiring to disrupt the 1972 Republican National Convention in Miami Beach. On November 4, the government dropped conspiracy charges against the Detroit Thirteen, accused of plotting a bomb campaign in Flint, Mich., in 1968.

Following the Detroit action, *The Washington Post* reported that the Justice Department had failed to convict 79 of 80 major leftist conspiracy defendants since 1968. The exception was the prison letter-smuggling conviction of Roman Catholic priest Philip F. Berrigan in 1972. Then, in December, David Dellinger, Abbie Hoffman, Jerry Rubin, and defense attorney William M. Kunstler were found guilty of contempt of court during the 1968 Chicago Seven conspiracy trial.

New Court Proposal. A report issued by a distinguished committee of lawyers and law professors recommending appointment of a National Court of Appeals–a buffer court to screen cases for the Supreme Court of the United States–encountered rough opposition. Former Chief Justice Earl Warren led opposition to the report.   David C. Beckwith

See also SUPREME COURT OF THE UNITED STATES.

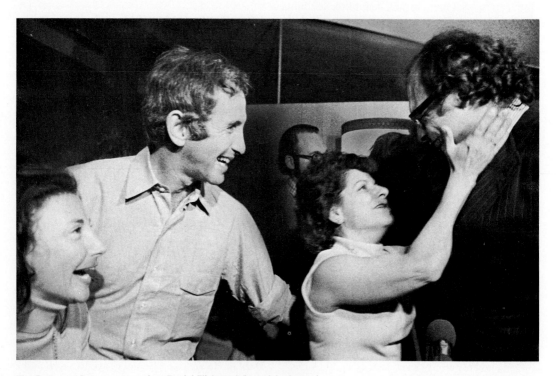

The Pentagon Papers case against Daniel Ellsberg, left, and Anthony J. Russo, Jr., right, was dropped in May because of government misconduct.

COX, ARCHIBALD (1912-   ), a professor of law at Harvard University and former U.S. solicitor general, was named as special U.S. prosecutor in the Watergate case in May, 1973. He was discharged by President Richard M. Nixon on October 20, after a disagreement over the handling of taped presidential conversations sought by a court in the case (see WATERGATE). Cox, a Democrat, had been offered the prosecuting assignment shortly after he ended a speech in Berkeley, Calif., on the importance of faith in government, and later said, "How could I refuse the job, having made a speech like that?"

Cox was born in Plainfield, N.J., and attended Harvard University. He served with the National Defense Mediation Board during World War II, and left government service to join the Harvard faculty in 1945. A specialist in labor legislation, Cox was an adviser to John F. Kennedy during the 1960 presidential campaign against Mr. Nixon, and Kennedy appointed him solicitor general in 1961. He resigned to return to Harvard in 1965. His Harvard law students included U.S. Attorney General Elliot Richardson, who named Cox to the Watergate post, and Senate Watergate committee counsel Samuel Dash.

In 1968, Cox headed a panel that investigated the causes of student riots at Columbia University, and in 1969 he mediated similar disturbances at Harvard. He married Phyllis Ames in 1937, and they have three children.   Foster Stockwell

Clarence M. Kelley, facing camera, was sworn in as chief of the Federal Bureau of Investigation in a ceremony in Kansas City, Mo., on July 9.

CRIME. Reports of white-collar crime, especially misdeeds by public officials, dominated domestic news headlines in 1973, but statistics revealed that street crime in the United States, which declined in 1972, rose only slightly in 1973. According to the Federal Bureau of Investigation (FBI), which compiles an index of serious crimes from reports by local police authorities, incidents of seven major crimes declined by 2 per cent in 1972, but rose 1 per cent above the 1972 level in the first nine months of 1973.

The increase came mostly in such property crimes as burglaries and auto thefts, which comprise the bulk of index offenses. Officials reported a 1973 rise of 5 per cent in murders, 8 per cent in forcible rapes, 5 per cent in aggravated assaults, 3 per cent in burglaries, and 1 per cent in auto thefts. There was no change in robberies or larcenies. Despite the increase, the number of serious crimes fell in 71 large cities throughout the country.

Mass Murders again provoked widespread concern. On February 5, a judge in Fairfield, Calif., sentenced Juan V. Corona, 38, to 25 consecutive life terms in prison for the 1971 slayings of 25 itinerant farmworkers.

The specter of that heinous series of murders was eclipsed in August, however, when two Houston youths led law-enforcement officials to the bodies of 27 teen-age boys reportedly killed by a friend, Dean Allan Corll, 33. The two informants said they helped procure the victims, mostly hitchhikers and runaways, for Corll, who would sexually abuse, torture, and finally kill and bury them. Elmer Wayne Henley, 17, said that he wrested a pistol away from Corll and killed him on August 7, after Corll threatened to kill him. Henley and his companion, David Owen Brooks, 18, were later indicted in the multiple murders, the largest number in U.S. history.

Seven persons, five of them children, were shot to death in January in a Washington, D.C., house. The killers were not apprehended. In Santa Cruz, Calif., Herbert W. Mullin, 26, was convicted on August 19 of killing 10 persons in February. He received a life prison term with no chance of parole.

Other Offenses. A Dallas police officer, Darryl L. Cain, was given a five-year sentence for murder with malice in the July 24 death of a 12-year-old robbery suspect. The boy, who was handcuffed, was being questioned in Cain's police cruiser when Cain shot him with a supposedly empty gun. Former United Mine Workers Union (UMW) President W. A. (Tony) Boyle was charged on September 6 with ordering the 1969 murder of UMW insurgent Joseph A. Yablonski, his wife, and daughter, in Pennsylvania. U.S. Senator John C. Stennis (D., Miss.), 71, was badly wounded by three youths during a robbery attempt on January 30.   David C. Beckwith

See also COURTS AND LAWS; SUPREME COURT OF THE UNITED STATES; WATERGATE.

CUBA. On July 26, 1973, Cuba celebrated the 20th anniversary of the revolution that brought Premier Fidel Castro to power. Delegations from the Communist world plus Communists or leftists from the United States and Latin American countries attended ceremonies held in Havana's Revolutionary Plaza.

The Cuba-Miami airlift that had brought almost 261,000 Cuban refugees to the United States since 1965 ended on April 6. Expenses had been borne entirely by the United States government. On February 15, Cuba, the United States, and Canada signed agreements to discourage hijacking and prosecute those who attempt it. Under the accord, the three countries will not provide haven for air or sea hijackers.

Some Rationing Ends. A gradual economic upturn permitted an end to the rationing of some consumer goods, such as cigarettes, gasoline, and plastic footwear. Furthermore, certain rations were increased, especially those on foods, liquor, leather footwear, and clothing. But the important sugar harvest fell short of expectations, totaling an estimated 4.75 million to 5.4 million tons during the 1972-1973 season. Limiting the output were derailments, reportedly due to sabotage on the tracks that carry the crops to the mills. Worker absenteeism, mechanical breakdowns at the mills, and torrential rains were also important factors.

Cubans celebrate the 20th anniversary of their revolution with a parade in Havana. Rebel leader Ché Guevara's face dominates the scene.

Foreign Affairs. Argentina and Cuba signed a treaty in late August providing for the purchase of $1.2 billion in Argentine goods over the next six years. Included were tractors and other farm machinery, trucks, railway material, and diesel motors.

The five new economic agreements that Premier Castro had signed with Russia in December, 1972, began to take effect in 1973. They involved an extended deferral of debt payments owed Russia; new credits to cover Cuba's 1973, 1974, and 1975 trade deficits; an accord on trade exchanges; a $330-million credit for the island's capital development over the next three years; and a Soviet pledge to pay more for Cuban sugar. The agreements also provided for Soviet aid to modernize Havana and Santiago ports and the railway system, and for Russian assistance in Cuba's transport, textile, and oil industries. Russia was also to build a new nickel plant that will double the national output over the next three years. Later reports, however, said Russia was considering a cut in its contributions to Cuba's oil-exploration program after 1975 unless the present large-scale effort produces significant new discoveries soon. Cuba also signed major new economic agreements during the year with Poland and Czechoslovakia. Each pact called for significant increases in credit as well as such other forms of aid as technicians and agricultural experts.   Mary Webster Soper

See also LATIN AMERICA (Facts in Brief Table).

CYPRUS. Civil war threatened in 1973 as the conflict intensified between Archbishop Makarios III, Cyprus' president, and General George Grivas, the underground leader. Grivas' guerrilla forces pressed the cause of *enosis* (union with Greece) by bombings and raids on police and radio stations. On July 27, they kidnaped Christos Vakis, the minister of justice. Grivas was unable to force Makarios to agree to any demands, however, and Vakis was freed August 26. Greek President George Papadopoulos publicly urged Grivas on August 24 to end his armed campaign, but Grivas vowed to go on fighting. Makarios survived uninjured after an October 7 attempt to blow up his car.

Archbishop Makarios won his battle against the three bishops of the Greek Orthodox Church of Cyprus who tried to oust him from the presidency and unfrock him. Instead, the bishops were deposed and unfrocked on July 14. Makarios, re-elected unopposed in February for a third five-year term, said on September 2 that he would not run again.

Greek and Turkish Cypriots made progress in their search for ways to administer the island republic. An agreement between Cyprus and the European Community, giving Cypriot produce preferential access to European markets, took effect June 1. Estimated cost to the island economy of a severe drought was more than $50 million.   George Scott

See also MIDDLE EAST (Facts in Brief Table).

CZECHOSLOVAKIA improved diplomatic and trade relations with several Western countries and with Romania and Yugoslavia in 1973. But the government maintained its hard-line political stance at home.

A treaty normalizing relations with West Germany was initialed on June 20, but a dispute over the status of West Berlin delayed its signing until December 20. United States Secretary of State William P. Rogers visited Czechoslovakia in July and signed a consular agreement that was expected to boost trade and travel between the two countries. And in September, talks opened on compensating the United States for property that was nationalized in Czechoslovakia after World War II.

Within Europe. President Nicolae Ceausescu of Romania, who had criticized the 1968 Russian-led invasion of Czechoslovakia, paid an "unofficial" visit to Prague in March. In the same month, President Josip Broz Tito of Yugoslavia referred to the problems arising from the 1968 invasion as having been "overcome." Czechoslovak Communist Party First Secretary Gustav Husak then visited Yugoslavia in October, and Yugoslav Prime Minister Djemal Bijedic visited Prague in December.

Czechoslovakia's relations with Austria deteriorated sharply after Czechoslovak jets shot down two Austrian sports planes that had strayed over Czechoslovak territory in July and August. Four Austrians lost their lives in those two incidents.

Domestic Events. President Ludvik Svoboda granted a partial amnesty in February for some political offenders, including an estimated 50,000 persons who fled after the 1968 Soviet invasion. In March, the government allowed the appointment of four Roman Catholic bishops, the first since the early 1950s. And Minister of Culture Miloslav Bruzek's conciliatory speech in March about "misled" members of the intelligentsia was seen as the tentative beginning of a more liberal policy. But in April, the Federal Assembly passed a number of repressive laws allowing "protective surveillance" of persons under suspended sentences. They also raised the maximum prison term for serious political offenses to 25 years. Maximum terms had been 15 years.

The Economy continued to improve, helped by a record grain harvest of 8.8 million tons. Industrial production improved, too, but delays in capital investment projects and rapidly rising industrial costs posed serious problems, especially in the automobile industry. Unlike some other East European countries, Czechoslovakia did not encourage direct capital investment from the West. Yet, imports from Western countries registered a dramatic 20 per cent increase, with West Germany continuing to be Czechoslovakia's main trading partner.   Chris Cviic

See also EUROPE (Facts in Brief Table).

DAHOMEY. See AFRICA.

DAIRYING. See AGRICULTURE.

DALLAS-FORT WORTH. The world's biggest airfield, the new Dallas-Fort Worth Regional Airport, was dedicated on Sept. 22, 1973. Three days of celebrations began with the arrival on September 20 of the British-French *Concorde* supersonic transport, making its first flight to the United States. Ambassadors from nearly 50 nations attended the dedication ceremonies.

The $700-million facility was built on 17,500 acres of land midway between Dallas and Fort Worth. The first stage of the airport's construction was completed in October; subsequent stages are scheduled for completion in 1985 and 2001.

The airport was designed to meet every known airport problem. Its runway system was planned to be tripled in capacity eventually and is expected to easily handle peak loads well into the next century. A 4½-mile buffer zone at the end of each runway separates the airport from residential areas, minimizing the airport noise problem. Terminal buildings are connected by a 10-lane superhighway and a 13-mile guideway for automatic, electric-powered vehicles.

On March 14, voters in 17 Texas counties defeated a $150-million bond issue for the Trinity River Project, a plan to construct a 384-mile canal that would link Dallas-Fort Worth and the Gulf of Mexico. The proposed facility would have cost a total of $1.6-billion and would have been built by the U.S. Corps of Engineers. Although it would have created an inland port for Dallas-Fort Worth, the idea was opposed by environmentalists.

Summer Riot. A march through downtown Dallas by a group of Mexican Americans erupted in violence on July 28, and 10 policemen were hurt, 12 demonstrators were arrested, and stores in the area were damaged extensively. The march was staged to protest the shooting by a policeman of a 12-year-old Mexican American boy who had been arrested in connection with a burglary (see CRIME).

Dallas police chief Frank Dyson, regarded as a liberal law-enforcement official, was criticized for his handling of the disturbance. The Dallas Police Association alleged that police officers were restrained from breaking up the demonstration. As a result, Dyson announced on October 17 that he was resigning, effective December 1.

New Metropolitan Area. As a result of the U.S. Office of Management and Budget's redefinition of the boundaries of metropolitan areas, Dallas in 1973 became the largest metropolitan area in Texas and the 12th largest in the United States. Combined with Fort Worth into a new metropolitan area, it has a population of 2,377,979.

The cost of living in the Dallas area increased 4.8 per cent between March, 1972, and March, 1973. A U.S. Department of Labor report issued on June 15 showed that a family of four would need $10,422 a year to live in "moderate comfort." James M. Banovetz

DAM. See BUILDING AND CONSTRUCTION.

DANCING

Dancing continued to move upward and outward across the United States in 1973 with the aid of government subsidies, but one major private sponsor, the New York City Center, was forced to retrench because of the prevailing economic squeeze. Of City Center's three dance companies, the Joffrey Ballet was most severely hit. On February 23, it received word that the City Center was cutting its yearly budget by 80 per cent, from $380,000 to $75,000. Because the Joffrey relies heavily on City Center support, this cut threatened the third largest U.S. ballet group with virtual extinction. The immediate result was that the Joffrey shortened its usual six-week fall season in New York to four weeks and initially tabled plans for 1974. In the fall, it announced a four-week spring season at the City Center theater, but dance observers wondered if the company would survive its financial crisis.

Ironically, 1973 was one of the Joffrey's most successful years artistically. Twyla Tharp's *Deuce Coupe*, which the Joffrey and Tharp's dance company premièred in Chicago in February, was a smash hit. It was subsequently danced before sold-out houses in New York City and Washington, D.C., and on the West Coast. *Deuce Coupe* is set to the Beach Boys'

rock songs and deals with such themes as social maturation and the juxtaposition between classical ballet and the social dancing of the 1960s. It was notable for its totally original approach to rock dancing and for its half-funny and half-sad, half-nostalgic and half-satiric tone. Tharp is a young, avante-garde choreographer, and the fact that her idiosyncratic style could be absorbed by establishment ballet with such aplomb was a breakthrough for each "side."

Robert Joffrey's *Remembrances*, which premièred on October 12, was his first ballet since the multimedia *Astarte* in 1967, in which the cast appeared both on film and on stage. Important new productions of older ballets were the Picasso-Satie-Cocteau *Parade*, originally produced by Sergei Diaghilev in

1917, and Frederick Ashton's *The Dream*, first performed by the Joffrey in August at the Wolf Trap Farm festival near Vienna, Va.

American Ballet Theatre (ABT) revived Agnes de Mille's farcical *Three Virgins and a Devil*, Eugene Loring's *Billy the Kid*, and Antony Tudor's psychological *Undertow*. The one major première was Peter Darrell's full-length *Tales of Hoffmann* on July 12 during ABT's stay at the New York State Theater.

Former Kirov ballerina Natalia Makarova was no longer dancing regularly with the company, and choreographer and soloist Michael Smuin moved to the San Francisco Ballet to become its associate artistic director. Several ABT dancers followed Smuin to California. Perhaps as a result of these losses, several young soloists appeared with greater frequency in leading roles during the company's seasons at the Kennedy Center in Washington, D.C., and in New York, Houston, Denver, and other cities.

The New York City Ballet offset the expenses of its historic Stravinsky Festival in June, 1972, by offering no new ballets at the State Theater during the winter season, which ended on Feb. 18, 1973. But the spring season saw two new ones: George Balanchine's *Cortège Hongrois* on May 17, in tribute to the September 1 retirement of prima ballerina Melissa Hayden; and Jerome Robbins' *An Evening's Waltzes* on May 24. Neither was a great success. On September 10, the company flew to Berlin, where 15 Balanchine ballets were filmed for television. The six-week project was the most ambitious effort undertaken so far to permanently record dance.

The Martha Graham Dance Company, after several near-dormant years, sprang to life again with new works by Graham, *Mendicants of Evening* and *Myth of a Voyage*, and a revival of her full-length classic, *Clytemnestra*. They were presented in May at the Alvin Theater on Broadway. All that was missing was Graham the dancer, who officially retired from the stage after several years of indecision.

Despite the death of José Limón on Dec. 2, 1972, the José Limón Dance Company had a busy year under the temporary direction of Daniel Lewis, a senior member of the company. Ruth Currier, a former soloist with Limón, became director in the summer. The high point was a month's tour of Russia, ending March 21, followed by a European tour. The Limón group is only the second American modern dance group to have performed in Russia.

Another unusual American-European contact occurred in November, when the staid Paris Opera Ballet presented a series of performances of *Paris Collage* by Merce Cunningham, the United States original "bad boy" choreographer. The Cunning-

Rudolf Nureyev and Veronica Tennant danced Tchaikovsky's *Sleeping Beauty* during a U.S. tour by the National Ballet of Canada in 1973.

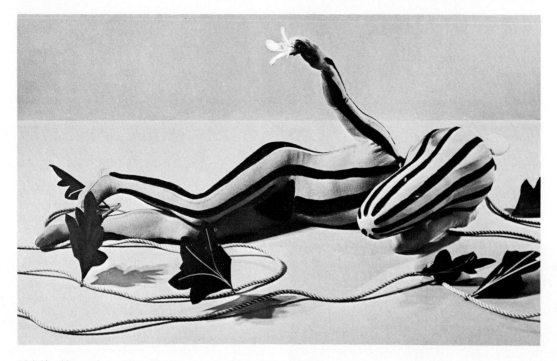

Erick Hawkins performs "Squash," his solo role of a bashful vegetable.
A comic masterpiece, it closes his eight-part classic, *8 Clear Places.*

ham company itself toured college campuses in the East and Midwest, offering what it calls "Events," collages of Cunningham's ballets. Its leading dancer of many years, the beautiful Carolyn Brown, retired.

Paul Taylor and his group offered that rarity of rarities, a full-length modern dance. Premièred on October 16 at the Walnut Theater in Philadelphia, *American Genesis* places Biblical stories in several periods of American history, as seen through Taylor's uniquely sardonic eye. A new modern dance troupe was formed – the Agnes de Mille Heritage Dance Theater, stressing American folk tradition. Its first performances were April 26 to April 29 at the North Carolina School of the Arts, and it began a national tour in October under the Sol Hurok management.

The Shenyang Acrobatic Troupe from the People's Republic of China was the most exotic of the foreign troupes visiting the United States. Although its stay was brief, from Dec. 18, 1972, to Jan. 11, 1973, it made a lasting impression by elevating mere acrobatics to a sophisticated aesthetic level. The troupe also performed in Canada and Mexico.

The National Ballet of Canada resumed a transcontinental tour in Seattle on February 5. With guest artist Rudolf Nureyev dancing at almost every performance in the classics as well as Limón's *The Moor's Pavane*, the company drew big audiences in small cities, some of which had never hosted a ballet company before. Erik Bruhn, the former *premier* of the *premier danseurs*, joined the Canadian ensemble as resident producer and adviser.

A contingent of Moscow's Bolshoi Ballet performed at the Metropolitan Opera House in New York City from June 26 to July 22 and then in Philadelphia, Wolf Trap Farm, Chicago, and St. Louis. Most of the stars were not on tour, however, and no full productions were offered. So humdrum was the programming that the most interest was generated by the Dance Academy, made up mostly of teen-age students of the Bolshoi's ballet school. Programs devoted exclusively to the school allowed a rare and treasured glimpse of its fledgling dancers.

The Stuttgart Ballet appeared at the Metropolitan from May 15 to June 3 and then in Washington, D.C., and Philadelphia. During the company's flight back to Europe on June 26, John Cranko, 45, died in his sleep. His death deprived the Stuttgart of its chief choreographer, director, and moving force.

Two dance pioneers died: Feodor Lopukhov on January 28 at age 86, and Mary Wigman, also 86, on September 19. Lopukhov was a major figure in the Russian avant-garde movement during the 1920s. When artistic experimentation fell into disfavor, he remained in Russia to nurture classical tradition. Wigman, a German, was Europe's only exponent of the modern dance during the 1920s and 1930s. She also exerted great influence on American modern dancers of the same period.   Nancy Goldner

DEATHS OF NOTABLE PERSONS in 1973 included those listed below. An asterisk (*) indicates the person is the subject of a biography in THE WORLD BOOK ENCYCLOPEDIA. Those listed were Americans unless otherwise indicated.

*Aiken, Conrad P. (1889-Aug. 17), a prolific poet who was also an essayist, novelist, and short-story writer. He won the Pulitzer Prize for poetry in 1930.

Allen, Leo E. (1898-Jan. 19), a conservative Republican congressman from Illinois. He served 28 years in the House of Representatives and was chairman of the House Rules Committee for two terms.

*Allende Gossens, Salvador (1908-Sept. 11), the president of Chile and the first freely elected Marxist president in the Western Hemisphere. He was deposed in a violent military coup, and military authorities said he committed suicide.

Ancerl, Karel (1908-July 3), conductor of the Toronto Symphony Orchestra since 1968. He had directed the Czechoslovak Philharmonic in his native Czechoslovakia for 17 years.

Arriba y Castro, Benjamin Cardinal (1886-March 8), retired archbishop of the Mediterranean diocese of Tarragona and Spain's oldest cardinal.

*Auden, W. H. (1907-Sept. 28), called the foremost poet of his generation. Wystan Hugh Auden was born in Great Britain but moved to the United States in 1939 and became an American citizen in 1946. Nevertheless, he was proposed for the title of poet laureate of England. Auden won the Pulitzer Prize for poetry in 1948.

*Balchen, Bernt (1899-Oct. 17), pioneer Norwegian-American aviator. On Nov. 29, 1929, he piloted the first airplane over the South Pole.

*Batista y Zaldívar, Fulgencio (1901-Aug. 6), the former Cuban army sergeant who became dictator of Cuba in 1933. He had lived in exile in Portugal after being deposed by Fidel Castro in 1959.

*Behrman, S. N. (1893-Sept. 9), a leading Broadway playwright for nearly 40 years, specializing in sophisticated comedy. His last published work was a memoir, *People in a Diary* (1972).

*Bemis, Samuel Flagg (1891-Sept. 26), leading authority on the diplomatic history of the United States. He had retired from Yale University in 1960 as a professor of diplomatic history and inter-American relations. Bemis won Pulitzer prizes in 1927 and 1950.

*Ben-Gurion, David (1886-Dec. 6), Israel's first prime minister, often called the architect of Israeli independence. He became a Zionist leader in 1919.

*Benton, William B. (1900-March 18), a founder of the Benton and Bowles advertising agency, assistant secretary of state from 1945 to 1947, vice-president of the University of Chicago, U.S. senator from Connecticut from 1949 to 1953, publisher of the *Encyclopaedia Britannica*, and a member of the executive board of the United Nations Educational, Scientific, and Cultural Organization.

Blackmer, Sidney (1898-Oct. 6), stage and movie actor and a founder of the Actors Equity Association.

Bonnet, Georges (1889-June 18), foreign minister of France in 1938, and an architect of the Munich agreement with Adolf Hitler that precipitated World War II.

*Bontemps, Arna (1902-June 4), author of several plays and more than 25 novels, anthologies, children's books, and histories on black life. He was writer in residence at Fisk University, Nashville, Tenn.

*Bowen, Elizabeth D. C. (1899-Feb. 22), British novelist who dealt with problems of personal relationships in the modern world. She also wrote criticism and short stories.

W. H. Auden, called the foremost poet of his time.

David Ben-Gurion was Israel's first premier.

Pearl S. Buck, China expert and author.

Pablo Casals, world-renowned cellist.

Bowles, Jane (1917-May 4), novelist and dramatist who had been living in Tangier, Morocco.She became widely known with the publication of *The Collected Works of Jane Bowles* in 1967. It won high praise.

Brookeborough, Lord (1888-Aug. 18), BASIL STANLAKE BROOKE, prime minister of Northern Ireland for 20 years until 1963. He opposed reunion with Éire.

*Browder, Earl (1891-June 27), general secretary of the Communist Party of the United States in the 1930s and early 1940s, but expelled from the party in 1946.

*Buck, Pearl S. (1892-March 6), novelist and author of more than 85 books. Most of them dealt with the lives of the Chinese, for whom she developed an enduring affection. She received both the Pulitzer (1932) and Nobel (1938) prizes for literature.

Buck, Tim (1891-March 11), a founder of the Canadian Communist Party in 1919 and its leader from 1929 until 1972. He gave up active party leadership in 1962.

Burnett, Whit (1899-April 22), founder and editor of *Story* magazine in 1931. The magazine published the works of many writers who later became famous, such as William Faulkner and Truman Capote.

Butts, Wally (1905-Dec. 17), former University of Georgia football coach who won a sensational libel suit against the Curtis Publishing Company in 1963. He had been accused of "fixing" a football game.

Calwell, Arthur (1896-July 8), the leader of Australia's Federal Parliamentary Labor Party from 1960 to 1967.

Warrior Against Poverty

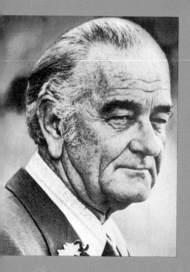

Lyndon B. Johnson
(1908-1973)

Lyndon Baines Johnson, the 36th President of the United States, was a man of many paradoxes. He was arrogant, driving, and pugnacious. He also was intimidating. But to many, Mr. Johnson could be both conciliatory and persuasive, and at the zenith of his career, he enjoyed a loyal following in both political parties.

Mr. Johnson's public career officially began in 1931, when he went to Washington, D.C., as a congressional secretary. But the move that launched his rise to the White House came in 1960. At the Democratic Party convention in San Francisco, John F. Kennedy picked Mr. Johnson as his vice-presidential running mate. Kennedy was moved by political considerations: Lyndon B. Johnson was a dangerous rival to be placated; his presence on the ticket would all but guarantee that the state of Texas would return to the Democratic column. Mr. Johnson, because of almost 24 years in Congress, would be immensely useful in pushing the proposed Kennedy legislative program through that body. There was no one more popular in Texas—and the South—than Lyndon Johnson, and no more experienced or adroit politician in Congress. After all, he had served his first senatorial term back in 1937, and he was Senate majority leader.

But there was more to LBJ—as Mr. Johnson came to be known—than political skill; there was statesmanship rooted in experience both in Texas and in Washington, D.C. Born in the worn-out hill country of west Texas, Lyndon Johnson never got Texas out of his system, or the Pedernales River country, either. His father was a farmer and teacher who had served in the state legislature; his mother was a schoolteacher. LBJ followed both into politics and teaching, but only the first with passion. Yet Mr. Johnson's brief experience with teaching gave him a permanent interest in education, and eventually he was to contribute more to the expansion of educational opportunities to all young people than any other President.

In 1931, Mr. Johnson leaped at the chance to serve as secretary to his congressional representative in Washington; while there he studied law at Georgetown University Law School. In 1935, President Franklin D. Roosevelt—Lyndon Johnson's model and hero—appointed him director of the youth administration for Texas, launching him on a public career.

During the 1950s—he was a senator by now—he worked well with President Dwight D. Eisenhower. Simultaneously, he proved himself equally adept at consolidating the various factions of his own amorphous party. By 1960, Mr. Johnson had deservedly won a national reputation for political skill, and for statesmanship, too, and emerged as a leading contender for the Democratic presidential nomination. He accepted the vice-presidential nomination only grudgingly.

President Kennedy had called on the nation to advance with him into a "New Frontier" of social and economic experimentation, but in his thousand days of office the youthful President had been unable to win support from Congress for his program. Then came Nov. 22, 1963, and Mr. Kennedy's assassination in Dallas, Tex. Lyndon Johnson, outwardly serene, took over the Kennedy program. He not only elaborated on it, he also renamed it—The Great Society.

Not since the early days of the New Deal had there been such a whirlwind of reform legislation. President Johnson signed into law a historic Civil Rights Act that not only forbade discrimination in public places, but also strengthened the voting rights of blacks. He went even further. Working hand-in-glove with a largely cooperative Congress, he greatly increased federal aid to schools and colleges, declared "War on Poverty," and fought it with energy and effectiveness. He inaugurated special projects such as the domestic Peace Corps, Operation Head Start, and Upward Bound and provided vast sums of money for urban rehabilitation and for rescuing the Appalachian Mountain region from poverty and decay.

Mr. Johnson, like most men, had his own particular Achilles' heel. Knowledgeable and astute in the domestic arena, he was out of his depth in foreign affairs. Here, too, he adopted what he assumed were Kennedy policies. President Kennedy had inherited them from his predecessor, Dwight D. Eisenhower, who had allowed himself to be drawn into guerrilla warfare in Southeast Asia. When President Kennedy died, there were some 15,000 American troops in Vietnam.

Mr. Johnson launched his presidency in the shadow of Vietnam—a shadow that lengthened steadily until it darkened the whole of his Administration. In the 1964 campaign against Republican presidential candidate Barry M. Goldwater, Mr. Johnson declared that he had no intention of sending American soldiers to fight Asia's wars. But once in office, he permitted himself to be sucked deeply into the Vietnamese morass.

To counter an alleged attack on an American destroyer in the Gulf of Tonkin by North Vietnamese gunboats, Mr. Johnson asked for and obtained authority to take any measures he thought necessary; he responded by launching a full-scale aerial bombardment of North Vietnam.

By 1968, Mr. Johnson had built an American army of 550,000 in South Vietnam and had assembled a great naval force in Vietnam waters. He had ordered a heavier tonnage of bombs dropped on Vietnam than the United States had dropped in the European and Asian theaters combined in World War II. This reckless and futile onslaught brought limitless death and devastation, but not victory. It cost the United States some 55,000 deaths and about 300,000 casualties, and it divided the American people more deeply than any crisis since the Civil War and Reconstruction. By 1968, that division threatened the unity of the Democratic Party and the harmony of the nation. In a rare act of statesmanship, on March 31, 1968, Mr. Johnson announced, in a television address, an end to the bombing; then he added, almost as an afterthought: "I shall not seek and I will not accept another term as your President."

In January, 1969, a war-weary Lyndon Baines Johnson retired to his ranch on the Pedernales River. When he died, on Jan. 22, 1973, Mr. Johnson left behind a heritage of progressive domestic legislation, and confusion and tragedy in the global arena.　　　Henry Steele Commager

*Carey, James B. (1911-Sept. 11), president of the United Electrical Workers from 1936 to 1941, and of the International Union of Electrical, Radio, and Machine Workers from 1949 to 1965.

*Casals, Pablo (1876-Oct. 22), renowned cellist and conductor. Casals left his native Spain in 1939 after the Spanish Civil War in protest against the rule of Francisco Franco. He lived in France and Puerto Rico.

Cento, Ferdinand Cardinal (1883-Jan. 13), a leading Italian diplomat of the Roman Catholic Church for more than 30 years.

Chandler, Norman (1899-Oct. 20), former publisher of the *Los Angeles Times*. He retired in 1960 in favor of his son, but continued to direct the parent company.

Chaney, Lon, Jr. (1906-July 12), who played many "monster" roles in motion pictures. His greatest critical success was as Lennie in the film *Of Mice and Men*.

*Chase, Mary Ellen (1887-July 28), Smith College professor emeritus of English literature and author of novels, biographies, histories, and essays.

Cicognani, Amleto Cardinal (1883-Dec. 17), dean of the Vatican's Sacred College of Cardinals. An Italian, he served in Washington, D.C., for 25 years as apostolic delegate and personal representative of three popes.

Clift, David H. (1907-Oct. 12), chief administrative officer of the American Library Association from 1951 until his retirement in 1972.

Condon, Eddie (1905-Aug. 4), a great jazz guitarist, who pioneered in "Chicago-style" jazz.

*Coward, Sir Noel P. (1899-March 26), British actor, playwright, composer, lyricist, and director for half a century. He wrote 27 productions and 281 songs, though he was unable to read music. He was knighted in 1970.

Cranko, John (1927-June 26), British choreographer and director of the Stuttgart Ballet company since 1961.

Creasey, John (1908-June 9), author of 560 detective and mystery novels under his own name and 28 pen names. He averaged 12 books published each year.

Croce, Jim (1943-Sept. 20), rock music singer and composer.

Darin, Bobby (1936-Dec. 20), popular singer whose biggest hits were "Mack the Knife" and "Splish Splash."

Dodd, Charles H. (1884-Sept. 22), considered one of the world's leading experts on the New Testament. He directed the panel of 30 scholars who translated *The New English Bible* between 1946 and 1970.

Dori, Yakov (1899-Jan. 29), last commander of the Haganah and the first Israeli chief of staff. The Haganah was the Jewish underground military group during the British mandate of Palestine.

Drew, George (1894-Jan. 4), national leader of Canada's Progressive Conservative Party from 1948 to 1956 and former prime minister of Ontario. He became mayor of his native city, Guelph, Ont., at 31.

Dunn, Michael (1935-Aug. 29), 3-foot 10-inch television and motion-picture actor. His real name was Gary N. Miller.

Eaton, John D. (1909-Aug. 4), one of Canada's largest merchandisers and wealthiest men. He headed T. Eaton and Company, Limited, a retail empire.

Eisendrath, Maurice N. (1902-Nov. 9), president of the Union of American Hebrew Congregations. He was slated to become head of the World Union for Progressive Judaism.

Elisofon, Eliot (1911-April 17), photojournalist and documentary-film cameraman as well as a writer and painter. He specialized in primitive art.

Fadden, Sir Arthur W. (1895-Aug. 21), Australia's acting prime minister briefly in 1941 and treasurer

William B. Benton
was a U.S. senator.

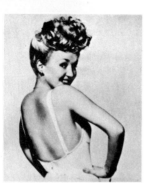

Betty Grable, dancer,
movie star, and pin-up girl.

David Lawrence, a
magazine publisher.

Frank Leahy, football coach at
the University of Notre Dame.

from 1949 to 1958. He was leader of the Australian Country Party from 1941 to 1958.

*Ford, John (1895-Aug. 31), renowned motion picture director and the only one cited four times by the New York Film Critics. He won four Oscars for feature films and one for a World War II documentary.

Fraske, Fredrak (1872-June 18), the last surviving veteran of the Indian wars, who served with the 17th Infantry.

*Frisch, Ragnar (1895-Jan. 31), Norwegian economist who shared the first Nobel Prize given for economic science, in 1969, for his part in developing a way to analyze economic processes.

Gillette, Guy M. (1879-March 2), a Republican U.S. senator from Iowa from 1936 to 1954, who helped to draft the United Nations Charter.

Ginott, Haim (1922-Nov. 4), child psychologist who focused on teaching parents to enter children's worlds with a language of compassion and understanding.

Grable, Betty (1916-July 2), star of many successful movie musicals during the 1940s and a World War II pin-up girl. Her last film, How to Be Very, Very Popular, was released in 1955.

Gustaf VI Adolf (1882-Sept. 15), king of Sweden and one of the least pretentious monarchs. He never wore a crown or held a scepter, and he rejected a coronation ceremony as a waste of money.

Hammond, Laurens (1895-July 1), inventor of the electric organ. He retired as chairman of the Hammond Electric Organ Company in 1960.

Harvey, Laurence (1928-Nov. 25), Lithuanian-born actor in stage, motion-picture, and television productions. He was a Shakespearean actor in Britain before coming to the United States in 1959.

Hawkins, Jack (1910-July 18), distinctive British motion-picture and stage actor. He appeared in about 60 films in the United States and Great Britain.

Hayakawa, Sessue (1890-Nov. 23), Japanese motion-picture actor nominated for an Academy Award for his work in Bridge on the River Kwai in 1957.

Heard, William T. Cardinal (1884-Sept. 16), a convert to Roman Catholicism who became one of the leading church experts on canon law.

Hess, Walter R. (1881-Aug. 12), Swiss physiologist who shared the Nobel Prize for physiology and medicine in 1949.

Horenstein, Jascha (1899-April 12), Russian-born orchestra conductor who became a United States citizen but was best known from recordings of performances conducted in Europe.

Howell, Charles R. (1904-July 5), Democratic U.S. congressman from New Jersey from 1949 to 1955.

*Inge, William M. (1913-June 10), prizewinning playwright who wrote Come Back, Little Sheba; Bus Stop; The Dark at the Top of the Stairs; and Picnic.

*Inönü, Ismet (1884-Dec. 25), the first premier of modern Turkey in 1923 and the nation's elder statesman.

*Johnson, Lyndon B. (1908-Jan. 22), 36th President of the United States. See Close-Up.

*Jones, Eli Stanley (1884-Jan. 25), United Methodist clergyman and author of 28 religious books. He was a missionary for more than 60 years.

Katz, Louis S. (1897-April 2), pioneer medical researcher into the cause of hardening of the arteries. He had been on the staff at Michael Reese Medical Center, Chicago, since 1930.

Kelly, Walt (1913-Oct. 18), creator of the nationally syndicated, satirical cartoon strip "Pogo."

Kertesz, Istvan (1929-April 17), music director of the Cologne (West Germany) Opera and frequently a guest conductor in the United States.

Klemperer, Otto (1885-July 6), conductor called a master of the German musical repertory. He became a successful conductor in Germany, but fled Nazi persecution in the 1930s and built another career, climaxed by 14 years conducting the London Philharmonic.

Kletzki, Paul (1900-March 5), Polish-born conductor, music director of the Dallas Symphony from 1958 to 1961 and the Suisse Romande Orchestra in Geneva, Switzerland, from 1967 to 1970.

Knutson, Kent S. (1924-March 12), president of the American Lutheran Church.

*Konev, Ivan S. (1897-May, 1973), celebrated Russian tactician and commander of tank troops during World War II. He was made a marshal of the Soviet Union in 1944. In 1961, he became commander of 20 Russian divisions in East Germany.

Kredel, Fritz (1900-June 10), German-born illustrator and woodcut artist. He illustrated about 160 books.

*Krupa, Gene (1909-Oct. 16), the first jazz drummer to become a solo artist. He made his first record on Dec. 9, 1927, and later played with the Benny Goodman orchestra.

Kuiper, Gerard P. (1905-Dec. 23), Netherlands-born astronomer who played a key role in the early United States space program.

Larraona, Arcadio Maria Cardinal (1887-May 7), Spanish-born and one of the leading experts on church law in the Roman Catholic Church's Sacred College of Cardinals.

Lawrence, David (1888-Feb. 11), founder and editor of the magazine U.S. News & World Report and a nationally syndicated newspaper columnist.

Layden, Elmer (1903-June 30), 160-pound fullback of the famous Notre Dame "Four Horsemen" backfield in 1924. He was football coach at Notre Dame from 1934 to 1940, when the school won 47 games, lost 13, and tied 3.

Leahy, Frank (1908-June 21), Notre Dame football coach from 1940 to 1954. His teams there won 87 games, lost 11, and tied 9, and won four national championships.

Lee, Bruce (1941-June 30), Chinese-American actor who starred in movies featuring karate, kung-fu, and other martial arts. He was born in San Francisco.

Lee, Harold B. (1899-Dec. 26), for 17 months president of the Church of Jesus Christ of Latter-day Saints.

Lefebvre, Joseph Cardinal (1892-April 2), president of the French Episcopal Conference and a former member of the Vatican Congregation for the Doctrine of the Faith.

Lienart, Achille Cardinal (1884-Feb. 15), Bishop of Lille, France, who championed progressive movements in the Roman Catholic Church.

*__Lipchitz, Jacques__ (1891-May 26), among the leading sculptors of the 20th century. He was born in Poland, lived and studied in France, and became an American citizen in 1957.

Lopez Contreras, Eleazar (1883-Jan. 2), president of Venezuela from 1935 to 1941.

MacMillan, Sir Ernest C. (1893-May 6), composer-conductor who directed the Toronto Symphony Orchestra from 1931 to 1956.

Magnani, Anna (1908-Sept. 26), Italian motion picture actress who won an Oscar in 1955 for her performance in *The Rose Tattoo.*

Manstein, Erich von (1887-June 10), bold German military strategist of World War II. He planned the armored thrust through southern Belgium that overwhelmed France's Maginot Line in 1940.

*__Marcel, Gabriel__ (1889-Oct. 8), one of the leaders of Christian existentialist philosophy in France. He was also a playwright, literary and music critic, composer, and accomplished pianist.

*__Maritain, Jacques__ (1882-April 28), renowned French philosopher who molded a philosophy of worldliness that led to Vatican Council II. He taught at the universities of Toronto, Chicago, Columbia, and Notre Dame, and wrote more than 50 books.

McInnis, Edgar W. (1899-Sept. 29), Canadian historian and former delegate to the United Nations. He was twice winner of the Governor General's Award for his writings.

McKernan, Ron (1945-March 8), harmonica playing blues singer with the Grateful Dead rock group.

*__Meigs, Cornelia L.__ (1884-Sept. 10), author of historical books for children.

*__Melchior, Lauritz L. H.__ (1890-March 18), Danish operatic tenor who sang with the Metropolitan Opera Company from 1926 to 1950.

Millionshchikov, Mikhail D. (1913-May 27), vice-president of the Soviet Academy of Sciences.

Mills, William O. (1925-May 24), Republican congressman from Maryland.

Mislimov, Shirali (1805?-Sept. 2), Russian peasant said to be the world's oldest man.

Mitford, Nancy (1904-June 30), British satiric novelist, essayist, and historian.

Monroe, Vaughn (1912-May 20), popular singer and bandleader during the 1940s and early 1950s, perhaps best known for "Racing with the Moon," which he composed.

Mott, Charles S. (1875-Feb. 18), businessman who guided General Motors Corregation in its early years.

Naish, J. Carrol (1900-Jan. 27), Irish-American movie actor who played in more than 150 films.

Jacques Maritain, a noted Roman Catholic philosopher.

Jeannette Rankin had two terms in Congress.

Eddie Rickenbacker, World War I ace and aviation pioneer.

Winthrop Rockefeller, a former governor.

Neill, Alexander S. (1883-Sept. 23), Scottish educational philosopher who founded England's famous Summerhill private school based on his theories of self-discipline by children.

*__Neruda, Pablo__ (1904-Sept. 23), Nobel laureate for literature in 1971. A Chilean Communist, he was active in politics and had served as ambassador to France.

Nolde, William B. (1929-Jan. 28), U.S. Army colonel who was the last American to die in the Vietnam War.

*__Nurmi, Paavo J.__ (1897-Oct. 2), Finnish long-distance runner of the 1920s. He won 9 gold medals in the Olympic Games of 1920, 1924, and 1928.

*__O'Brien, Robert C.__ (1922-March 5), whose real name was Robert L. Conly, winner of the Newbery Medal in 1972 for his book *Mrs. Frisby and the Rats of NIMH.*

Offenhauser, Fred (1888-Aug. 17), responsible for the four-cylinder engine used in most racing cars for many years in the Indianapolis 500-mile race.

Ory, Edward (Kid) (1886-Jan. 23), Dixieland jazz trombonist who included "Muskrat Ramble" among his compositions.

Pauli, Hertha (1909-Feb. 9), biographer and author of children's books.

Paxinou, Katina (1904-Feb. 22), Greek stage and motion-picture actress who won an Oscar for her 1943 role as Pilar in *For Whom the Bell Tolls.*

Peterson, David (1850?-May 31), former slave believed to be the oldest U.S. citizen. An 1866 government record indicated he was born on Nov. 22, 1850.

DEATHS OF NOTABLE PERSONS

Louis St. Laurent,
Canadian statesman.

Willie (the Lion) Smith was
a jazz pianist and composer.

Edward J. Steichen,
photographic artist.

Walter Ulbricht had been East
Germany's Communist leader.

*Picasso, Pablo (1881-April 8), Spanish artist and the most influential painter of the 20th century. He was also a sculptor and ceramist. See VISUAL ARTS (Close-Up).

Price, Margaret W. (1910-March 21), national president of the Girl Scouts of the U.S.A. from 1963 to 1969.

*Rankin, Jeannette (1880-May 18), women's rights militant, staunch pacifist, and the only member of Congress to vote against U.S. entry into two world wars. She served as a Republican congresswoman from Montana from 1917 to 1919 and from 1941 to 1943.

*Rickenbacker, Edward V. (Eddie) (1890-July 23), ace U.S. fighter pilot in World War I and retired board chairman of Eastern Air Lines.

Robinson, Edward G. (1893-Jan. 27), motion-picture actor, known particularly for gangster roles.

*Rockefeller, Winthrop (1912-Feb. 22), who served two terms as Arkansas governor, from 1966 to 1971. He was a grandson of oilman John D. Rockefeller.

Ryan, Robert (1913-July 11), rugged stage and motion-picture actor. He appeared in about 90 films.

Said, Mohammed M. (1881-Nov. 1), anti-Communist former premier of Iran. He rejected the 1944 Russian proposal for exploitation of Iran's oil.

*St. Laurent, Louis S. (1882-July 25), prime minister of Canada from 1948 to 1957. In 1949, he negotiated the entry of Newfoundland, then a British colony, as Canada's 10th province.

Sanderson, Ivan (1911-Feb. 19), Scottish-born author and naturalist.

Sands, Diana (1934-Sept. 21), stage and screen actress who won an Outer Circle Critics' Award for her work in *Raisin in the Sun* in 1959.

Santos, Rufino Cardinal (1908-Sept. 3), conservative archbishop of Manila and the first Filipino to become a cardinal of the Roman Catholic Church.

Saund, Dalip S. (1899-April 23), the first native of India to serve in the U.S. Congress. He served as a Democrat from California in the House of Representatives from 1957 to 1963.

Saylor, John P. (1908-Oct. 28), Republican congressman from Pennsylvania and a long-time conservationist and environmentalist who authored the Wilderness Act.

Schmidt-Isserstedt, Hans (1900-May 28), chief of the Hamburg (West Germany) Radio Symphony Orchestra.

Senanayake, Dudley S. (1911-April 12), three times prime minister of Ceylon (now called Sri Lanka).

Smith, Willie (1893-April 18), flamboyant jazz pianist and composer. He customarily performed wearing a red vest and a derby.

Steichen, Edward J. (1879-March 25), photographer who transformed his medium into an art. A dedicated humanist, he sought to "explain man to himself."

Stern, Gladys Bertha (1890-Sept. 19), British novelist and playwright. She customarily identified herself simply as G. B. Stern.

Szigeti, Joseph (1892-Feb. 19), Hungarian concert violinist who guarded the classic tradition, yet pioneered in introducing contemporary music.

Thatcher, Maurice H. (1870-Jan. 6), the oldest surviving former member of Congress, served as a Republican from Kentucky in the House of Representatives from 1923 to 1933.

*Tolkien, J. R. R. (1892-Sept. 2), linguist, scholar, and author of the huge, best-selling trilogy *The Lord of the Rings*, published from 1954 to 1956. It was called a fantasy on the war between good and evil though the South African-born author denied it was allegorical.

Tourel, Jennie (1910-Nov. 23), opera mezzo-soprano and concert singer. She sang professionally for more than 40 years.

Trudeau, Grace (1890-Jan. 16), the mother of Canada's Prime Minister Pierre E. Trudeau.

*Ulbricht, Walter (1893-Aug. 1), veteran Communist leader of East Germany from 1950 to 1971. He was known as the architect of the Berlin Wall sealing East Germany from the West.

*Virtanen, Artturi I. (1895-Nov. 11), Finnish winner of the 1945 Nobel Prize for chemistry for his work on the preservation of fodder crops.

*Waksman, Selman A. (1888-Aug. 16), the principal discoverer of streptomycin, for which he was awarded the Nobel Prize in physiology and medicine in 1952.

Warren, Fuller (1905-Sept. 23), governor of Florida from 1949 to 1953.

Watkins, Arthur V. (1886-Sept. 1), former U.S. senator from Utah.

*White, Paul Dudley (1886-Oct. 31), Boston heart specialist who was President Dwight D. Eisenhower's White House physician.

Wilson, Mitchell (1913-Feb. 26), novelist and science writer. He produced 10 novels and 3 nonfiction works.

Young, Chic (1901-March 14), cartoonist and creator of the comic strip "Blondie."

Ziegler, Karl (1898-Aug. 12), German chemist who devised a commercially feasible way to make polyethylene plastics. He shared the 1963 Nobel Prize in chemistry.   Ed Nelson

DELAWARE. See STATE GOVERNMENT.

DEMOCRATIC PARTY. The Democrats in 1973 began to settle some of the feuds that divided the party during the 1972 presidential election. In April, Senator Hubert H. Humphrey of Minnesota addressed the party's charter commission and urged party unity. It would be useless for a Democrat to run for any office, he said, "unless we make up our minds to pull ourselves together and start acting like a party instead of a back-alley brawling outfit."

The Unity Problem. Robert S. Strauss, chairman of the Democratic National Committee, said in February that Senator George S. McGovern of South Dakota was still the main obstacle to party unity. Strauss cited a January speech by McGovern at Oxford University in England, in which McGovern, the unsuccessful Democratic candidate in the 1972 presidential election, accused the Democrats of being a party without "principle or programs."

On July 4, Senator Edward M. Kennedy of Massachusetts made an unusual appearance, speaking with Governor George C. Wallace of Alabama at an Independence Day celebration in Decatur, Ala. Kennedy denounced the scandal-ridden Administration of President Richard M. Nixon and pointed up similarities between himself and Wallace. Kennedy said that, although they had different political opinions, both he and Wallace fought against those "who used the people's power to strike at the rights

of the people." Some political observers viewed Kennedy as the one man who could unite the party factions, and speculated that Kennedy's Alabama speech might be the beginning of a bid for the 1976 Democratic presidential nomination.

Plans for 1974 Convention. On July 22, by a narrow vote of 52 to 50, the charter commission approved a plan to limit the purpose of the off-year 1974 party convention to approving a new party charter. Under the reform rules adopted in 1972, the Democrats must hold a national convention midway between presidential election years. The commission also recommended a new plan for apportioning convention delegates, based partly on population and partly on Democratic strength in a state. It also suggested holding the midterm convention late in 1974, after the November elections.

Conservative commission members believe that the convention should give top priority to adopting a new charter and restructuring the party. However, liberals viewed this as a way to side-step potentially divisive, but important, issues. Democrats held differing opinions as to whether such conventions would further divide or serve to unite the party.

Quotas Abolished. The Delegate Selection Commission, chaired by Barbara Mikulski, a Baltimore city councilwoman, met in Washington, D.C., on October 27 and agreed to drop the controversial

Governor George C. Wallace, left, confers with Senator Edward M. Kennedy as they share the podium at a July 4 celebration in Alabama.

quota system for selecting delegates. The quota system, used for the 1972 convention in an attempt to ensure fair representation of minorities, women, and youth, resulted in the exclusion of many prominent regular Democrats, such as Mayor Richard J. Daley of Chicago.

According to the new guidelines, the party will seek women and minority delegates "as indicated by their presence in the Democratic electorate." The quota system had provided a strict formula for representation of women and minorities in accord with their percentage of a state's population. Under the new guidelines, a delegation cannot be challenged at the national convention for not including enough women and minority delegates.

Election Victories. In the off-year elections on November 6, the Democrats won the New Jersey governorship from the Republicans. They also won elections in many of the major cities.

In New Jersey, Democrat Brendan T. Byrne, a former judge, soundly defeated Republican Congressman Charles W. Sandman, Jr., by winning 67.6 per cent of the votes in the race for governor. As a result, the Democrats held the governorships of 32 states; the Republicans held 18.

The principal disappointment of the Democrats in the 1973 elections was that Henry E. Howell, a Democrat running as an independent, failed to win election as governor of Virginia. Howell, a Democratic lieutenant governor, was narrowly defeated by Mills E. Godwin, Jr. Formerly a Democrat, Godwin became a Republican for the 1973 race.

In contests for mayor, Democrats running on either partisan or nonpartisan tickets were successful in Atlanta; Buffalo, N.Y.; Dayton, Ohio; Detroit; Los Angeles; Louisville, Ky.; Miami; New York City; Pittsburgh; Raleigh, N.C., and Seattle.

In New York City, City Controller Abraham D. Beame, a Democrat, won 57 per cent of the vote in a four-man race to replace retiring Mayor John V. Lindsay, a former Republican who had become a Democrat. In Minneapolis, Mayor Charles S. Stenvig, a former policeman running for a third term as an independent, was defeated by Albert Hofstede, a candidate of the Democratic-Farmer-Labor Party.

The one major city that the Republicans retained was Cleveland, where Mayor Ralph J. Perk won an easy victory over Mercedes M. Cotner, the Democratic city council clerk. She entered the mayoral race as a replacement candidate on the ballot in the last two weeks of the campaign.

Party Telethon. An eight-hour fund-raising telethon was held in September on the National Broadcasting Company network. Viewers pledged $5.3-million to help pay off the national party's debt, mainly left over from the 1968 campaign, and to aid state Democratic organizations. After expenses, the party netted about $3 million.   William McGaffin

See also ELECTIONS; REPUBLICAN PARTY.

DENMARK. The first year as a member of the European Community (Common Market) brought increased inflation and labor trouble in 1973. Prime Minister Anker H. Jørgensen and his minority Social Democratic government fell on November 8 after a tie vote on 1974 income tax rates. In December 4 elections, Social Democrats won 46 seats, but could not form a minority government with 11 parties in the field. A new Progress Party under Mogens Glistrup emerged, after an anti-income-tax campaign, to win 26 seats.

Poul Hartling, a former foreign minister, was named on December 17 to form a Liberal Party minority government. The party held only 22 seats, and the government would have the slimmest parliamentary base in Danish history. The year ended with the Danish political crisis still unresolved.

Consumer Prices rose 7.7 per cent in the first six months of the year. On February 1, about 10,000 persons marched on parliament to protest food prices, and the Jørgensen government barely survived a censure motion on its handling of Common Market agricultural trade negotiations.

Mass Strike. Employers' refusal to hike cost-of-living wage adjustments 17½ cents an hour, on top of sick pay and other benefits, led to a strike in March. Some 260,000 workers, about a tenth of the labor force, were idled; about half of them struck and the rest were locked out. Those who continued to work had trouble reaching their jobs. Panic buying of cigarettes, gasoline, and heating oil developed, and some Danes began to hoard quantities of canned food and meat.

The government refused on March 21 to order state arbitrators to end the stoppage, but two days later, Prime Minister Jørgensen reversed his policy. Employers and unions accepted arbitrators' terms on April 19: a 7.5 per cent raise, equal pay for women, and a 40-hour workweek by 1975. Cost-of-living raises were agreed to, but only after the government agreed to investigate them.

Worker Participation. Government plans to introduce "economic democracy" in 1974 were held back by the strikes. A central fund would be financed by gradually increasing, compulsory, employers' contributions. Two-thirds would be reinvested in contributing firms and one-third as the fund directors chose. Workers would be given share certificates on the central fund, withdrawable after seven years. The plan would give the fund 35 per cent of the total share capital of all Danish companies by 1986 and 50 per cent a few years later. Many businessmen attacked the program, charging that the central fund would become too strong a factor in Denmark's economy.

On February 14, the government and opposition agreed on a new defense structure that cuts conscription from 12 to 9 months.   Kenneth Brown

See also EUROPE (Facts in Brief Table).

DENT, FREDERICK BAILY (1922-   ), a South Carolina textile manufacturer, was sworn in as U.S. secretary of commerce on Feb. 2, 1973. A leader in introducing new technology and products in the textile industry, Dent has traveled extensively in the United States and abroad studying trade developments, and served as a member of the International Business Advisory Committee of the Department of Commerce.

Dent was born on Aug. 17, 1922, in Cape May, N.J., and grew up in Greenwich, Conn. He attended St. Paul's preparatory school in Concord, N.H., and received his A.B. degree from Yale University in 1943. He entered World War II service in 1943 as an ensign in the U.S. Naval Reserve, and was serving as a lieutenant (j.g.) when released to inactive duty in 1946.

Dent became the fourth generation of his family to enter the textile industry when he joined Joshua L. Baily and Company, Inc., of New York City in 1946 as a salesman. In 1947, he joined Mayfair Mills, the family firm in Arcadia, S.C. He became president of the company in 1958.

In 1967, Dent served as president of the American Textile Manufacturers Institute. He was named "Man of the Year" by the New York Board of Trade textile section in 1971.

Dent and his wife, the former Mildred Carrington Harrison, have five children.   Jacquelyn Heath

DENTISTRY. While the Congress of the United States was deferring efforts to act on a national health insurance program in 1973, the dental profession continued to focus attention on the growing demand for dental insurance.

A major breakthrough was scored in September when the United Automobile Workers agreed on a new contract with Chrysler Corporation that provided a comprehensive dental-care program for 117,000 employees and their dependents. The Chrysler terms may set a pattern for all major industries for the expanded coverage of health-care benefits including dental treatment.

Nutrition Is Important. Dental scientists label table sugar (sucrose) an "arch criminal" in causing tooth decay. The presence of candy- and soft-drink-vending machines in schools is vigorously opposed by the dental profession. Thus, when the Child Nutrition Education Act underwent congressional scrutiny in April, 1973, the American Dental Association (ADA) strongly supported it. The measure calls for regulating the sale of foods that compete with the national school lunch program. The bill also would institute a wide-ranging program of nutrition education for schoolchildren.

Aid for Cleft Palates. A new bone-grafting technique, successfully tested in animals, may benefit cleft palate patients. In experiments, bone grafts were taken from a monkey's hipbone and implanted in a surgically created cleft in the animal's upper jaw. The grafts formed new bone in the jaw and aided complete healing of the defect. The findings were reported in April by Philip J. Boyne of the University of California, Los Angeles, school of dentistry.

Patients with bony cleft defects of the jaw ridges usually must wear a dental appliance to close the defect, Boyne said. Sometimes the appliance is bulky and interferes with normal mouth function. "If the defect could be properly grafted with bone and the teeth realigned orthodontically into the grafted area, the patient could have a complete dental arch and a normal occlusion without the necessity of having a dental prosthesis," he suggested.

Identifying "Battered Children." Nearly half of all reported cases of child abuse involve injuries to the face and mouth, while injuries to other parts of the body are less frequent, reported Knud Danielsen, a doctor, of Fuglebjerg, Denmark, in June. Many oral injuries result from beatings and gagging, when adults try to silence screaming children, and from brutal insertion of spoons or other eating utensils in attempts to force-feed children. In suspected cases, the dentist's ability to document and estimate the age at which injuries were inflicted may provide valuable legal evidence. And, by being aware of the "battered child syndrome," dentists can help in the early detection of such crimes, Danielsen contended.   Lou Joseph

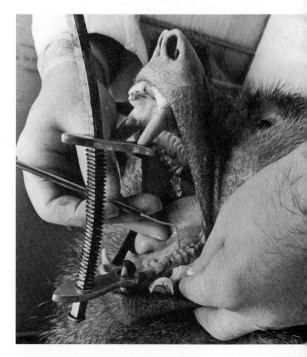

A breakthrough in dentistry was scored when a plastic tooth implanted in a baboon "took root" six months after it had been inserted.

DETROIT

DETROIT. Coleman A. Young was elected the first black mayor of Detroit when he defeated former police commissioner John F. Nichols on Nov. 6, 1973. Young, a state senator, won 51.6 per cent of the vote.

In the September 11 primary, Nichols had defeated five mayoral candidates, including Young, who finished second. Then, on September 21, Mayor Roman S. Gribbs, who had decided not to seek a second term, fired Nichols from his job as police commissioner. Gribbs asserted that he wanted to separate the police department from politics. In his campaign, Young promised to disband a controversial plainclothes crime unit set up by Nichols, put more policemen on the street, and set up mini police stations in 50 neighborhoods. Crime and police brutality were major campaign issues.

Detroit voters also approved a new city charter in the November election. The new charter gives the mayor more control over city operations, creates the post of ombudsman, and replaces the police commissioner with a five-member civilian police commission.

Teachers' Strike. Detroit's 270,000-pupil school system was hit by a teachers' strike on September 3, the city's first since 1967. The city's 10,500 teachers were seeking a 9.7 per cent pay increase.

The union ignored a back-to-work court order and was fined $11,000 per day, starting September 27. Three union officers were also fined $1,000 a day. In addition, the school board demanded that the union pay $100,000 per day in administrative costs lost due to the strike. However, that demand was dropped in an effort to end the strike. The teachers voted on October 15 to accept compromise terms and leave pay and class-size issues to binding arbitration, but they refused to return to work while the board insisted on payment of the $100,000-a-day penalty. The schools reopened on October 19.

Living-Cost Increase. Detroit's cost of living rose 6 per cent between June, 1972, and June, 1973. A U.S. Department of Labor report released on June 15 rated the city 17th on the list of the nation's 25 most expensive metropolitan areas in which to live. The report noted that an average family of four in Detroit would need an annual budget of $11,502 to live in "moderate comfort."

The population of the Detroit metropolitan area was increased as a result of the redefinition of metropolitan area boundaries ordered by the U.S. Office of Management and Budget. According to a report released by the U.S. Bureau of the Census in September, Detroit's population was estimated at 4,488,900 persons as of July, 1972.

Construction began in September on a $500-million project to renovate Detroit's downtown area. The project will include a 70-story hotel, apartments, and commercial buildings. James M. Banovetz

DICTIONARY. See Section Six, DICTIONARY SUPPLEMENT.

DIPLOMATIC CORPS. See U.S. GOVERNMENT.

DISASTERS. Raging floodwaters devastated 11-million acres along 1,400 miles of the Mississippi River and its tributaries in March and April, 1973. The widespread flooding was caused by unusually heavy winter and spring rains (see WEATHER). In St. Louis, the Mississippi crested at 43.3 feet on April 25, flooding the downtown area and causing thousands of residents to flee their homes. Farther south, the floods prevented farmers from planting their crops.

Floodwaters caused more than $300 million damage in Arkansas, Illinois, Iowa, Kentucky, Louisiana, Mississippi, Missouri, Ohio, Tennessee, and Wisconsin. As a result of the floods, 11 persons died and about 35,000 were left homeless.

Other major disasters in 1973 included the following:

Aircraft Crashes

Jan. 22—Kano, Nigeria. An Egyptian Boeing 707 crashed while attempting to land, killing 180 persons. It was the worst air disaster in history.

Jan. 29—Northern Cyprus. An Egyptian airliner crashed in a mountainous area, killing 38 passengers and crew members.

Feb. 19—Prague, Czechoslovakia. A Russian jet caught fire during a landing attempt, killing 66 of the 99 persons aboard.

Feb. 28—Near Stettin, Poland. A Polish Air Force plane crashed, killing 15 persons, including Polish and Czechoslovak government officials and high-ranking military officers.

March 3—Moscow. All 25 persons aboard a Bulgarian turboprop were killed during a landing attempt.

March 5—Near Nantes, France. Two Spanish airliners collided during an air traffic controllers strike. One plane crashed, killing all 68 persons aboard. The other landed safely.

March 8—Silver City, N.C. Fourteen persons, including 11 members of the U.S. Army's Golden Knights parachute team, were killed when their plane crashed en route to an air show in Kansas.

March 19—South Vietnam. All 58 persons aboard were killed when an Air Vietnam passenger plane crashed about 150 miles northeast of Saigon.

May 31—New Delhi, India. An Indian Airlines jet crashed while landing, killing 48 of the 65 persons aboard.

April 10—Near Basel, Switzerland. A chartered British airliner struck a hillside while trying to land in a heavy snowstorm, killing 104 persons.

April 12—Sunnyvale, Calif. A National Aeronautics and Space Administration research jet collided with a Navy patrol plane, killing 16 persons.

April 30—Yemen (Aden). A plane crash 300 miles north of Aden killed 25 Yemeni diplomats.

May 25—Southern Siberia. A Russian airliner carrying 40 persons crashed near the Chinese border, apparently during an attempted hijacking. There were no survivors.

May 31—New Delhi, India. Forty-six persons died when a Boeing 737 burst into flames and crashed while approaching the airport.

June 1—São Luís, Brazil. A Brazilian jetliner crashed while attempting to land, killing all 23 persons aboard.

June 3—Paris. The Russian TU-144 supersonic jetliner exploded and crashed during a demonstration flight at the Paris International Air Show, killing the plane's six crew members. Seven residents of a nearby village were killed by falling wreckage.

June 20—Near Puerto Vallarta, Mexico. A Mexican DC-9 crashed into a mountain, killing all 27 persons aboard.

July 6—Off the Canary Islands. A Spanish DC-8 crashed into the sea, killing all 10 crew members. There were no passengers aboard.

July 11—Paris. A Brazilian jet on a flight from Rio de Janeiro caught fire and crashed while attempting an emergency landing at Orly Airport. Of the 134 persons aboard, 122 were killed.

July 22—Off Tahiti. A Pan American World Airways Boeing 707 plunged into the sea shortly after take-off, killing 78 persons. One passenger survived.

July 23—Near St. Louis. An Ozark Air Lines turbojet crashed in a severe thunderstorm, killing 36 of the 44 persons aboard.

July 31—Boston. A DC-9 jetliner crashed and burned while landing at fogged-in Logan International Airport. Only 1 of the 89 persons aboard survived.

Aug. 13—La Coruña, Spain. All 86 passengers and crew members were killed when a landing Spanish jetliner struck treetops, exploded, and crashed.

Aug. 27—Bogotá, Colombia. A Lockheed Electra crashed after take-off, killing all 40 persons aboard.

Aug. 28—Near Madrid, Spain. Twenty-four persons, including wives and children of U.S. airmen, were killed when a U.S. military cargo plane crashed and exploded.

Sept. 11—Near Titograd, Yugoslavia. All 36 passengers and 6 crew members were killed when a Yugoslav airliner crashed into a mountaintop.

Oct. 13—Moscow. A Russian airliner crashed while attempting to land, killing 28 persons.

Dec. 22—Near Tangier, Morocco. A jet crashed while attempting to land, killing all 105 persons aboard.

Bus and Truck Crashes

Jan. 29—Near Córdoba, Argentina. A bus fell into a ravine, killing 11 persons and injuring 25 others.

March 7—Near Fort Stockton, Tex. Fifteen persons were killed when a bus collided head-on with a truck on a narrow bridge.

March 12—Antofagasta, Chile. A head-on collision between two buses killed 45 persons.

March 19—Barrie, Canada. A collision involving a bus, a truck, and 30 automobiles killed 11 persons and injured 43 others.

May 2—Near Salvador, Brazil. A bus accident killed 39 persons.

May 4—Near Dacca, Bangladesh. Fifty-two persons drowned when a bus plunged into the Bansi River.

June 7—Near Baguio, Philippines. A bus plunged into a river, killing 15 persons.

June 8—Pakistan. Eleven persons were killed when their vehicle plunged off a curving, mountain road into the Indus River.

June 22—Near Rio de Janeiro. A bus skidded off the road and into a river, killing 23 persons.

July 7—Near Delhi, India. Officials reported that 78 persons were killed in a bus accident.

July 18—Near Vizille, France. Forty-six persons died when a bus ran off the road and plunged into a river.

July 21—Northeastern Iran. A bus went off the road and plunged into a river, killing 48 persons.

Aug. 15—Patrocínio, Brazil. A bus skidded off the road and fell down an embankment, killing 16 persons.

Sept. 16—Southwestern Turkey. Twenty-one farm-workers were killed when the truck in which they were riding overturned.

Sept. 26—The Snowy Mountains, Australia. At least 15 persons were killed when a sightseeing bus plunged

A Brazilian jetliner smolders in a field near Paris' Orly Airport after it crashed and burned on July 11, killing 122 persons.

Smoke pouring from gas storage tank on Staten Island, N.Y., kept rescuers from reaching 40 workmen killed by a February 10 explosion and fire.

over the Tumut Pond Dam, part of the Snowy Mountains hydroelectric scheme.

Nov. 3—Near Sacramento, Calif. A charter bus crashed into a concrete abutment on the freeway, killing 13 persons and injuring 31 others.

Nov. 20—San Nicolas, Mexico. A bus carrying a group of religious pilgrims rolled down a ravine, killing 15 persons.

Earthquakes

Jan. 30—Western Mexico. An earthquake following the eruption of Colima Volcano killed 33 persons along the Pacific Coast.

March 17—The Philippines. An earthquake killed 13 persons on Luzon Island and injured more than 100.

April 14—Guanacaste Province, Costa Rica. An earthquake centered near the Nicaraguan border killed 16 persons.

Aug. 28—Central Mexico. More than 500 persons were killed by an earthquake that struck a wide area south and east of Mexico City.

Explosions and Fires

Jan. 29—Pleasantville, N.J. A fire in a rest home killed 10 elderly residents.

Feb. 2—Eagle Grove, Iowa. An explosion and fire, apparently touched off by a gas leak, destroyed a restaurant and a hardware store, killing 13 persons.

Feb. 6—Paris. Twenty-one persons, most of them students, were killed by a fire that raged through a high school. A 14-year-old boy was charged with arson.

Feb. 10—Staten Island, N.Y. An explosion and fire ripped through a natural gas storage tank, killing 40 workmen. The men had been sealing cracks in the tank's plastic lining when special insulating material apparently caught fire.

March 10—Neufmesnil, France. Ten children were killed when fire swept through their family home near the Belgian border.

June 24—New Orleans. Fire in a crowded bar killed 33 persons. Police suspected arson.

Aug. 2—Isle of Man, Great Britain. Fifty-one persons were killed by a fire that destroyed a resort complex.

Aug. 5—Saudi Arabia. An explosion at an oil refinery 50 miles west of Bahrain killed 15 persons.

Sept. 1—Copenhagen, Denmark. A fire in an old hotel killed 35 tourists.

Sept. 13—Philadelphia. Fire swept through a three-story nursing home, killing 11 patients.

Sept. 16—Imphal, India. Fifteen persons were killed by an explosion in a house where firecrackers were being manufactured.

Sept. 29—Hoboken, N.J. A blaze that spread through four old tenements killed 10 persons.

Nov. 15—Los Angeles. A blaze in an old apartment building killed 24 persons and injured 52 others.

Nov. 29—Kumamoto, Japan. Fire swept through a crowded department store, killing 107 persons.

Dec. 11—Zaragoza, Spain. Fire in a small furniture factory killed 25 workers.

Floods

Jan. 31—Buenos Aires, Argentina. More than 20 persons were killed by flooding that followed a sudden severe thunderstorm.

March 29—Eastern Algeria. Floods caused by torrential rains killed about 20 persons.

March 31—Western Tunisia. An estimated 86 persons were killed and 53,000 left homeless by week long heavy rains and floods.

March-April—United States. Flooding of the Mississippi River and its tributaries killed 11 persons, left some 35,000 homeless, and caused more than $300-million property damage.

July 9—Around Lake Chapala, Mexico. At least 30 persons were killed by a flash flood.

Aug. 12-Sept. 4—Pakistan. The Indus River overflowed its banks, causing devastating floods in Punjab and Sind provinces. About 290 persons were killed and 155,000 left homeless.

Aug. 25—Mexico City. Some 100 persons were killed during flooding caused by torrential rains.

Oct. 19—Southern Spain. Heavy rains caused severe flooding and mudslides. At least 190 persons were killed and an estimated 300 were missing, buried under tons of debris or swept out to sea by the floods.

Hurricanes, Tornadoes, and Storms

Jan. 1-2—Messina, Sicily. Torrential rains and landslides killed 10 persons and left hundreds homeless. Three other persons were killed by the storms in southern Italy.

Jan. 10—San Justo, Argentina. A tornado tore up buildings, killing about 50 persons and injuring 300 others.

Jan. 17—Coast of Portugal and Spain. A storm with winds of almost 80 mph killed at least 19 persons.

April 3—Western Europe. At least 10 persons were killed by a hurricane that struck parts of England, Belgium, the Netherlands, and West Germany.

April 12—Central Bangladesh. A severe storm left about 200 persons dead, 15,000 injured, and 10,000 homeless. A second storm on April 17 killed an estimated 700 persons.

April 26—Quito, Ecuador. Mudslides caused by torrential rains killed about 25 persons and left 2,000 homeless.

May 26-27—Southern and Central United States. A series of tornadoes, storms, and floods killed 24 persons: 8 in Alabama, 3 in Arkansas, 1 in Mississippi, 1 in Florida, 1 in Georgia, and 10 in North Carolina.

June 16—Indonesia. Officials reported that a series of storms in April killed 1,650 persons on the islands of Flores and Palue.

Nov. 10-11—South Vietnam. A typhoon struck four coastal provinces in the northern part of the country, killing at least 60 persons and leaving 30,000 homeless.

Nov. 24—Philippines. Officials reported that 54 persons were killed during a typhoon and flood.

Mine Disasters

Feb. 8—Near Johannesburg, South Africa. Officials reported that fire in a gold mine killed 26 miners.

March 19—Bihar State, India. A series of methane gas explosions in a coal mine killed at least 47 miners.

May 5—Near Seoul, South Korea. Eighteen miners were killed when carts carrying them to work in coal pits overturned.

Sept. 7—Northern Thailand. A mineral mine collapsed after torrential rains, killing about 50 persons.

Shipwrecks

Jan. 9—Off Vancouver Island. An African freighter, the *Dona Anita*, carrying 42 crew members, sank in stormy seas. No survivors were found.

Jan. 25—Off Seoul, South Korea. A ferryboat ran aground and sank, killing at least 13 persons.

Feb. 5—Near Dacca, Bangladesh. At least 25 persons drowned when a passenger boat sank about 80 miles south of Dacca.

Feb. 22—Burma. A passenger ferry collided with a Japanese freighter in the Rangoon River, killing about 200 persons.

March 22—Off New Jersey Coast. The Norwegian freighter *Norse Varient* sank about 130 miles southeast

of Cape May, N.J. Only 1 of the 30 crewmen was saved. Another Norwegian vessel that sailed from Norfolk, Va., two hours after the *Norse Varient* and carried 32 crew members, disappeared in the same area. At the time, a storm was raging, with winds up to 85 miles per hour.

May 5—Near Dacca, Bangladesh. Two passenger-carrying riverboats collided and one sank, killing about 250 persons.

May 18—Off Indonesia. A Portuguese freighter sank during a storm, killing 23 persons.

May 19—Off Rhode Island. A fishing boat with 28 persons aboard sank in the Atlantic Ocean. Twelve persons were killed and five others were missing and presumed dead.

June 2—New York Harbor. A U.S. cargo ship rammed a Belgian tanker, setting off an explosion and fire. Seven crew members were killed, the captain of the U.S. vessel died of a heart attack, and eight other persons were missing.

June 16—Bay of Bengal. A motor launch carrying a wedding party capsized during a storm. Twenty-two persons were killed and nine others were missing.

July 9—Coast of Bangladesh. An overloaded motor launch capsized, and about 200 persons drowned.

July 16—Off the Philippines. A passenger ship sank about 120 miles southeast of Manila. Three persons were known dead and 35 others missing.

Aug. 7—Off South Africa. A South African trawler collided with a tanker and sank in the Atlantic Ocean. The trawler's 14 crew members were killed.

Oct. 28—Punta Indio Canal, Argentina. Twenty-four persons were missing and presumed dead after two ships collided in the narrow channel.

Dec. 20—Off British Columbia. The bodies of 27 crewmen were found floating in debris from the sunken freighter, *Oriental Monarch*.

Dec. 24—Off Ecuador. A ferryboat capsized and sank, killing at least 142 persons.

Dec. 27—Off Borneo. At least 38 persons drowned when a passenger boat sank.

Train Wrecks

Jan. 30—Near Kecskemét, Hungary. A train struck a bus at a railroad crossing, killing 24 persons.

Feb. 2—Medjez-Sfa, Algeria. About 35 persons were killed when a passenger train derailed.

Feb. 2—Near Rio de Janeiro. Seventeen persons were killed when a passenger train went off the tracks.

March 16—Central Cuba. One car of a passenger train fell off a bridge into a river, killing 24 persons and injuring 31 others.

Dec. 19—London. A commuter train derailed, struck an embankment, and overturned, killing at least 14 persons and injuring 53 others.

Other Disasters

Feb. 8—Alameda, Calif. A Navy jet on a training flight crashed into a three-story apartment building. Ten persons were killed in the resulting explosion and fire.

Mar. 2—Bailey's Crossroads, Va. A 26-story building under construction collapsed when a huge crane on the upper floor toppled, killing 14 workers.

June 21—São Paulo, Brazil. A 12-vehicle chain-reaction collision on a foggy superhighway between São Paulo and Rio de Janeiro killed 16 persons and injured 18 others.

Dec. 29—Northern India. Officials reported that 321 persons living in rural areas died of exposure as temperatures fell 50° below normal during a cold wave lasting two weeks.

Darlene R. Stille

DOMINICAN REPUBLIC. See LATIN AMERICA.

DRUGS

DRUGS. A wide variety of drugs, addictive and non-addictive as well as prescriptive and nonprescriptive, came under investigation and attack in 1973 by the Food and Drug Administration (FDA) and other U.S. regulatory agencies. With the approval of the Supreme Court of the United States, the FDA announced plans in April to demand proof of effectiveness for some 40,000 prescriptive drugs, some marketed for up to 35 years.

Rockefeller Plan. On September 1, the nation's most stringent narcotics-control law went into effect in New York state. The law, drafted by Governor Nelson A. Rockefeller and passed by the New York State Legislature in May, contains what are believed to be the harshest narcotics penalties in the country. Mandatory minimum jail sentences are required for most persons convicted of trafficking in drugs. Offenders must remain on parole for the rest of their lives after serving their sentences, except those who agree to become confidential police informers and those who are first offenders in soft-drug cases (the less-addictive narcotics). Although police officials criticized the plan as unworkable, statistics disclosed that there were only one-fourth as many felony drug arrests made in New York City in September as in an average month of 1972.

Methaqualons. Beginning in June, methaqualons were placed under the United States new Controlled Substances Law, along with such commonly abused prescription drugs as morphine, methadone, and the amphetamines. Methaqualons are produced by five manufacturers and sold under the trade names of Quaalude, Sopor, Parest, Optimil, and Somnafac. The drug, which was originally sold as a sleeping pill and advertised as having fewer addictive characteristics than the barbiturates, causes a kind of drunken euphoria. In 1973, it was found to have replaced heroin and methadone as the leading drug in use on college campuses. The U.S. Bureau of Narcotics and Dangerous Drugs (BNDD) has now condemned it as extremely dangerous and even more addictive than heroin.

Under pressure from the BNDD, U.S. drug companies cut their production of amphetamines more than 80 per cent in 1972. Authorities consider this a possible reason for the growing use of alcohol in high schools and on college campuses. In April, the National Council on Alcoholism told a congressional committee that alcohol is the nation's primary drug problem, with 12 million acknowledged alcoholics and another 9 million who have various alcohol-related problems.

Nonprescriptive Drugs. In March, the Federal Trade Commission (FTC) charged the makers of 10 leading aspirin products with false and misleading advertising in asserting that their products were more effective than plain aspirin. The FTC proposed that the makers of Bufferin, Excedrin, Excedrin PM, Anacin, Arthritis Pain Formula, Bayer Aspirin, Bayer Children's Aspirin, Cope, Vanquish, and Midol not be allowed to advertise the products for two years unless they devote 25 per cent of their advertising expenses to corrective ads. By the end of the year, the issue had not yet been resolved by the courts.

Controversial new proposals by the FDA for stricter regulation of vitamin and mineral use were released in January, after a 10-year investigation. The study included two years of formal hearings, during which representatives of medicine, science, industry, and the general public expressed their views. The FDA's proposed labeling regulations were based upon medical research said to have proved that prolonged massive doses of certain vitamins – particularly A and D – can cause irreparable bone and tissue damage.

Quicker Overdose Diagnosis. Faster treatment for drug-overdosed patients should soon be possible through a new computer analysis system that quickly identifies, from a blood sample, the drug that has been taken. The system, developed at the Massachusetts Institute of Technology (MIT), can reduce waiting time for analysis from two days to two hours. This increases chances of survival through quicker treatment for an unconscious patient. The system was outlined by Klaus Biemann, professor of chemistry at MIT, at the annual meeting of the American Chemical Society in Chicago, in September.   Mary E. Jessup

EARTHQUAKES. See DISASTERS.

"When kids do it, it's called drug abuse."

EASTERN ORTHODOX CHURCHES of Greece and Cyprus were in a state of chronic crisis throughout 1973. The crisis in Greece was formally provoked by the opposition of Dimitrios I, Patriarch of Constantinople, to the termination of his nominal jurisdiction over 10 dioceses in northern Greece. In reality, however, it reflected the deep opposition of most of the Greek bishops to the Primate Archbishop Ieronymos, who was appointed head of the church in Greece in 1967 by the ruling military junta. The Assembly of Bishops overruled Archbishop Ieronymos on May 10 by electing a new Synod that is controlled by opponents of the Archbishop, and Ieronymos resigned in December.

The crisis in Cyprus originated on March 8, when the three other bishops of the Greek Orthodox Church of Cyprus ordered the official deposition of Archbishop Makarios III. They charged that his episcopal functions and his office as president of Cyprus were incompatible.

Ecumenical Affairs. Three Orthodox churches— the Ecumenical Patriarchate, the Church of Russia, and the Orthodox Church in America—criticized the World Council of Churches in August for deviating from the original goals of the ecumenical movement.

On September 16, Patriarch Pimen of Moscow, head of the Church of Russia, visited World Council of Churches headquarters in Geneva, Switzerland, and rejected Western charges of persecutions and religious limitations in Russia. His declaration, and the opposition of the Orthodox Churches in Eastern Europe to any statement of ecumenical solidarity with victims of religious persecutions in the Communist world, provoked a marked uneasiness among World Council members.

U.S. Leadership. On February 10, an American-born Orthodox clergyman was elevated to the Episcopacy of the Orthodox Church in America. Joseph (Swaiko), under the name of Herman, Bishop of Wilkes-Barre, was appointed vicar bishop of the Diocese of Philadelphia and Pennsylvania.

On May 13, the Synod of Bishops of the Orthodox Church in America elected a new bishop for the oldest Orthodox Diocese of Sitka and Alaska. Bishop Gregory (Afonsky) is a native of Kiev, Russia.

The long court litigation between two factions of the Serbian Church in America was settled on Dec. 28, 1972. Involved were a faction under the jurisdiction of the Serbian Patriarchate, and an independent group that opposed the Patriarchate because he allegedly submitted to the Communists. A Lake County, Illinois, court ruled in favor of Bishop Firmilian (Ocokoljich), head of the Patriarchal faction that sought possession of the Serbian ecclesiastical properties in this country. The court, however, declared illegal the decision of the Patriarchate to divide the American Diocese of the Serbian Church into three dioceses without the previous consent of the dioceses themselves.   Alexander Schmemann

ECONOMICS. Descriptions of the United States economy in 1973 ranged from poor to excellent, and any of the descriptions might fit, depending on which aspect of the economy was considered. In the midst of prosperity, material shortages began to appear, and skyrocketing prices shocked consumers. The nation's economic troubles were magnified when the Arab nations cut oil shipments to the United States and other industrialized nations after the Arab-Israeli war in October.

But the U.S. economy's performance rated as excellent when compared to those of many other industrialized countries. Inflation was not confined to the United States; it was a worldwide problem. Americans were surprised to learn that prices rose more during the year in such countries as France, Great Britain, Italy, and Japan. And the Arab oil cutback harmed others more than the United States. Great Britain was in a state of national emergency at the end of the year, and many feared that a prolonged Arab oil boycott might trigger a worldwide recession, or worse.

Energy Shortages. The outbreak of fighting between Israel and the Arab nations in October led to an Arab oil boycott of the United States and the Netherlands and cutbacks in supplies to other nations that threatened to cause an acute shortage of energy. As the year ended, the Arab nations announced that they would ease the oil curbs for Europe and Japan, but not for the United States or the Netherlands. The Arabs said they would increase the oil flow to Europe and Japan by 10 per cent in January, 1974, leaving production still 15 per cent below what it was in September. At the same time, the Persian Gulf nations announced that they were more than doubling the price of crude oil, to $11.65 a barrel, starting January 1, 1974. In 1970, the cost was $1.80 a barrel. Venezuela and Bolivia also announced they would raise oil prices in January.

Some observers predicted that the current energy crisis only foreshadowed a general scarcity that might last for several years. Even if Middle Eastern crude oil supplies were again to become freely available, it will take time for the U.S. to build the new refineries needed to meet current demands. The energy shortage could last even longer if it proves necessary to develop new sources of oil, such as shale or tar sands. In the meantime, U.S. citizens could look forward to slower speed limits, cooler homes, higher gasoline prices, and perhaps even fuel rationing. See Section Two, How Can We Solve the Energy Crisis?

There was the further discouraging prospect that the energy shortage might create a mild recession. Even before the energy pinch, economists had been predicting that the real rate of growth in the U.S. economy would slow from the 5 per cent level of 1973 to less than 2 per cent in 1974. With the added element of the Arab oil boycott, most economists were predicting a drop in the gross national product of 1 to 2 per cent and an unemployment rate of more than 6 per cent. Unhappily, these discouraging possibilities would probably be accompanied by still further price increases as costs continued to rise.

By December, several industries were already feeling the pinch. The major automobile manufacturers announced price increases and cut back on the production of standard-sized models in favor of smaller cars that use less gasoline. Commercial airlines were forced to reduce their flight schedules and lay off personnel. Other industries, such as plastics manufacturing, petrochemicals, construction, and trucking, were also affected, and repercussions were spreading into every sector of the economy. See AUTOMOBILE; AVIATION; CHEMICAL INDUSTRY; MANUFACTURING.

The effects were even more severe abroad. Great Britain found itself facing a total economic collapse, but only partly because of the oil cutbacks. Britain also was confronted with a massive slowdown by coal miners, railwaymen, and electrical workers. Although most British power plants use coal, the country was forced to cut back sharply in energy use. To conserve coal and oil supplies, most industries and businesses were ordered on a three-day workweek, to begin Jan. 1, 1974. See GREAT BRITAIN.

Japan, which gets about 90 per cent of its oil from Arab sources, also was hard hit, both by the production cutbacks and by higher prices for what oil it was able to buy. The oil cutback also threatened to worsen Japan's inflation rate, one of the highest in the industrial world. See JAPAN.

Economic Indicators. The note of uncertainty in November and December tended to obscure the very real economic progress that the United States made during the year. The U.S. gross national product set another record in 1973 as the production of goods and services reached $1.288 trillion, up by 11.5 per cent from the previous high of $1.155 trillion in 1972. However, inflation pushed prices up by 5.5 per cent, so that the real rate of growth came to only about 6 per cent.

Per capita disposable income, measured in real purchasing power, was up by almost 4.5 per cent to $4,150 in current dollars (the equivalent of $2,890 in 1958 dollars). Corporate profits were up to $73 billion after taxes, an increase of almost 33 per cent over 1972 levels. But investors found that prices of the stocks of these corporations had fallen much lower by December than they were at the beginning of the year. See STOCKS AND BONDS.

Farm income rose to $25.5 billion, up by almost 30 per cent from 1972. Wholesale farm prices were nearly 50 per cent higher at year-end than they had been at the end of 1972. And, for the first time in 20 years, farm prices were above parity, which meant that what the farmer received for what he sold would buy more of other products than it did in 1915. See AGRICULTURE.

The Labor Force. More than 84 million people were employed in 1973, more than ever before. How-

ever, the number of unemployed workers remained discouragingly high. The unemployment rate averaged about 4.8 per cent through most of the year, except for a brief dip to 4.5 per cent in October. Unemployment went back up to 4.9 per cent in December. Yet, this marked an improvement from 1972, when unemployment averaged 4.8 million, more than 5.5 per cent of the civilian labor force.

The disappointing failure of unemployment to drop further in 1973 was due to an unusually large number of workers entering the labor force, slightly more than 2 million. Yet, more than 2.5 million new jobs were added during the year, so the economy more than kept pace with the increasing number of workers.

The high employment figure, including rising numbers of women, somewhat offset the bite that inflation took out of the average weekly paycheck. With an increasing number of families having more than one wage earner, family purchasing power can continue to rise even if real income per worker declines.

Industrial Production continued to climb rapidly at the start of the year and more slowly thereafter. The Federal Reserve index reached 126.6 in December (1967 = 100), about 4.5 per cent above the 1972 level. Domestic production of automobiles rose 3.7 per cent to nearly 10 million units, and almost all other sectors of the economy made substantial, though less spectacular, gains.

One exception was housing, which dropped off about 20 per cent from the records set in 1972. Primarily responsible for this decline were the high interest rates that resulted from a strong demand for money, coupled with the Federal Reserve Board policy of restraining the money supply in an effort to curb inflation. By the end of the year, housing starts had dropped even faster than analysts had predicted, to the lowest level since 1970. And a sharp drop in building permits indicated that further declines were ahead. The energy crisis caused shortages of petroleum-derived building materials and of diesel fuel needed to run heavy construction equipment, adding to the industry's woes. See HOUSING.

Phases 2, 3, and 4. With the introduction of Phase 3 on January 11, the mandatory wage and price controls of Phase 2 ended. Under Phase 3, the United States shifted into a period of voluntary compliance with federal standards, with the goal of reducing inflation to 2.5 per cent or less by the end of 1973. The wage-price standards were the same as under Phase 2, but they were to be achieved by voluntary industry action, rather than by government controls. The Pay Board and Price Commission were abolished, but the Cost of Living Council absorbed some of their duties.

During the next five months, prices soared on a broad front. On June 13, President Richard M. Nixon ordered a 60-day freeze on almost all consumer prices while the Administration prepared new wage-price policies. Zooming food prices were the most im-

Selected Key Economic Indicators

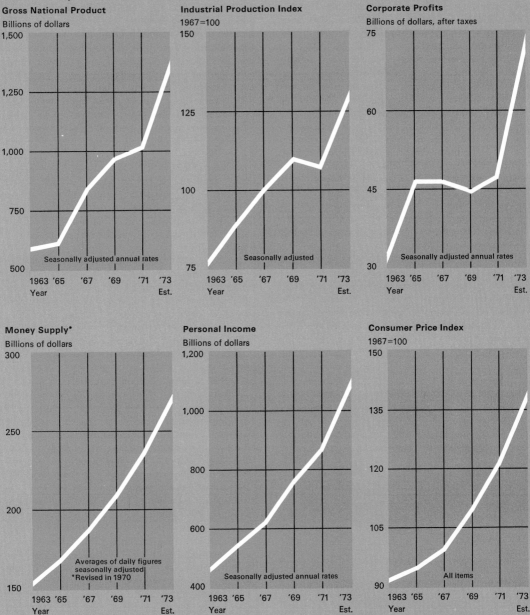

Gross National Product

Billions of dollars

Seasonally adjusted annual rates

Year — Est.

Industrial Production Index

1967=100

Seasonally adjusted

Year — Est.

Corporate Profits

Billions of dollars, after taxes

Seasonally adjusted annual rates

Year — Est.

Money Supply*

Billions of dollars

Averages of daily figures seasonally adjusted
*Revised in 1970

Year — Est.

Personal Income

Billions of dollars

Seasonally adjusted annual rates

Year — Est.

Consumer Price Index

1967=100

All items

Year — Est.

The most comprehensive measure of the nation's total output of goods and services is the *Gross National Product* (GNP). The GNP represents the dollar value in current prices of all goods and services plus the estimated value of certain imputed outputs, such as the rental value of owner-occupied dwellings. *Industrial Production Index* is a monthly measure of the physical output of manufacturing, mining, and utility industries. *Corporate Profits* are quarterly profit samplings from major industries. *Money Supply* measures the total amount of money in the economy in coin, currency, and demand deposits. *Personal Income* is current income received by persons (including nonprofit institutions and private trust funds) before personal taxes. *Consumer Price Index* (CPI) is a monthly measure of changes in the prices of goods and services consumed by urban families and individuals. CPI includes about 300 goods and services. All 1973 figures are *Year Book* estimates.

portant factor in the rising prices; they rose nearly 10 per cent during the first five months of the year.

Phase 4 went into effect on July 18, and imposed a system of controls similar to those of Phase 2. The price freeze remained in effect until August 12 for industrial and service industries. Price restrictions on health care and food, except for beef, were lifted immediately – and food prices soared again. The beef controls continued until September 12. Under the new system, most price increases were limited to reflect increases in costs. Profit-margin restrictions continued, as did the 5.5 per cent wage-increase guideline. The Administration promised "an early end" to controls, but they were still in force at year-end.

Consumer Attitudes. In the face of the year's economic uncertainties, it was not surprising that consumer confidence was at a low ebb as the year drew to a close. The University of Michigan Survey of Consumer Opinion revealed that its index was at its lowest point since World War II.

On the brighter side, however, business spending for plants and equipment was expected to reach record levels again in 1974. Such plans indicated both the underlying strength of the U.S. economy and the tremendous needs for more capital equipment if the United States is to achieve its goals of a better environment, an end to inflation, and a steadily rising level of living.

Meat price freeze led farmers to kill thousands of baby chicks in June. Soaring feed costs made it cheaper to kill them than raise them.

International Performance. Compared with that of most other industrial nations, the U.S. economic performance was excellent. While consumer prices jumped 8 per cent in the United States, they rose 14.6 per cent in Japan, 11.3 per cent in Italy, 9.3 per cent in Great Britain, and 7.9 per cent in France. Among the major industrial nations, only West Germany had a significantly slower rate of inflation, 6.4 per cent. Only Japan, with a 12 per cent growth rate, showed a significantly greater rate of growth in industrial production than the United States.

The remarkably high rates of inflation throughout the industrial world in 1973 may have occurred, at least in part, because all the nations were experiencing unusually prosperous economic conditions, at least during the first half of the year. World trade shot up by nearly 30 per cent during the first six months. While price increases accounted for about half of that growth, the result in real terms was still impressive.

However, all of the European nations and Japan are vitally dependent on Middle Eastern oil. Any prolonged cutback by the Arab states might produce a global depression. It is this possibility that provokes major concern about the course of the world economy in 1974. Even the easing of the Arab oil cutbacks at the end of the year did not completely erase the worry. European countries were left with the problem of managing sharply higher prices, and energy-conservation measures remained in effect.

At no other time since World War II have the major industrial countries all found themselves in the same phase of the business cycle. In general, the United States and the other industrial countries, excluding Russia, have been in opposite phases. When the U.S. economy was booming, there was a tendency toward recession abroad, and vice versa. The net effect was to soften the movement toward recession in one spot, while dampening inflation pressures in the other. When the United States was prosperous, American consumers would buy more goods from other countries, thus tending to prevent severe recession abroad. In a similar way, purchases from the United States by others would prevent severe downturns in the U.S. economy.

If all countries found themselves caught in the grip of an economic downturn as a result of a prolonged energy shortage of crisis proportions abroad, most economists would simply refuse to predict the consequences. Even in this contingency, no one expects a return to the conditions of the early 1930s, but the United States could expect a far deeper recession than any that has occurred since World War II.

Russian Growth. Developments in the world's economic balance followed familiar patterns. According to official statistics, Russia's economic growth continued, but there was a continuing reliance on agricultural products and modern technology imported from abroad. Negotiations continued with

American companies for the construction and initial operation of modern plants. See RUSSIA.

Latin America. In Chile, the political confrontation between President Salvador Allende Gossens' Marxist regime and non-Marxist elements, which resulted in Allende's overthrow on September 11, brought the Chilean economy to the brink of disaster. Prices rose more than 250 per cent and industrial production declined sharply. At the end of the year, there were some intimations that the new military regime might invite some American companies back to help restore the foundering economy, though not as owners. The decline in copper production was especially serious. Copper has been the major Chilean export for many years, and it financed the country's import of enough food to feed its population. See CHILE.

Elsewhere in Latin America, inflation was brought under reasonable control, with the exception of Argentina, where prices rose by 80 per cent. The rate of inflation in Brazil dropped to 13 per cent, less than 25 per cent of that experienced only a few years ago. Brazil appeared to be on the way to ultimately becoming one of the great industrial nations of the world. See ARGENTINA; BRAZIL.

Canada's Economy. Canada's economic performance was one of the brightest anywhere. Economic growth outstripped the records set in 1972, and the country's total output for the year was estimated at $116 billion, a gain in real domestic product of 7 per cent. Fueling the expansion was strong consumer spending for automobiles and household goods. Business investment and government spending were also at high levels. The cost of living, however, had its steepest rise since 1951, and the consumer price index went up nearly 9 per cent. Canada also benefited from the worldwide shortage of raw materials and foodstuffs. The United States was Canada's best customer, but a large volume of exports also went to Europe and Japan.

Canada is also in a better position than most countries to cope with the oil shortage. Canada produces enough oil to satisfy its own needs; the main problem is getting it from the oil fields of the West to the seaboard provinces of the East. In December, the Canadian government announced plans to extend the country's major pipeline from Toronto to Montreal, the largest Canadian city. See CANADA.

World Trade Patterns. Devaluation of the U.S. dollar in February, 1973, had its hoped-for impact on U.S. exports. United States shipments abroad rose by nearly $1.8 billion per month over 1972 levels as the United States became a relatively cheap source of goods and raw materials for the rest of the world. At the same time, the United States raised its level of imports by less than $1.2 billion per month. The net result was one of the most dramatic single-year turnarounds in history in the current account of the U.S. balance of payments, which measures the inter-

"We've come a long way since Phase One."

national flow of goods and services. In 1972, the U.S. current account deficit was over $8 billion. In 1973, this was turned into a surplus of almost $1 billion. On the current trade account, measuring the difference between merchandise exports and imports, the United States moved from a $6-billion deficit in 1972 to a small surplus in 1973.

There were no major shifts in worldwide trade patterns. The developed countries continued to carry on about 80 per cent of the total. Canada again was the largest U.S. customer, with nearly twice as much in purchases from the United States as Japan. West Germany and Great Britain followed, and Mexico supplanted Italy as the fifth largest customer of the United States. The same five countries, in the same order, were the principal suppliers of goods to the United States.

United States exports again demonstrated the preeminence of the country as the breadbasket of the world. Meat and food products, primarily grains, were the leading U.S. exports in dollar volume, followed by crude materials, of which agricultural products made up a substantial part. Manufactured goods and chemicals were the next most important American exports. United States purchases were primarily manufactured goods and machinery, with crude oil rising from seventh to fifth in dollar purchases.

Fighting Inflation. As 1973 drew to a close, the most pressing problem for the United States was that of bringing down the rate of inflation without bringing the economy to a point of collapse. The problem was complicated by the energy shortages that will inevitably push prices up in early 1974, and probably will provide upward pressure on costs for the next several years.

One thing, however, appears to be clear. The U.S. money supply must be strictly controlled so that it cannot again initiate such inflationary pressures as affected the economy in 1972 and 1973. It has become apparent that creation of money has a generally delayed effect on the economy, known as a lag, and undue increases in the money supply will probably show up in higher prices about six months later. If money supplies are allowed to increase at a steady rate of between 6 per cent and 7 per cent a year, it is likely that increased output would prevent prices from rising by more than 2 or 3 per cent–in the absence of any unusual circumstances. This was the rate of money expansion in the United States for most of 1973. Unhappily, from the standpoint of the ordinary citizen, whatever success the monetary policy was having or might have had in controlling inflation was obscured by the steep increase in food costs. It will continue to be obscured by the effects of energy shortages in 1974.

In 1972 and 1973, a sharp rise in the demand for food–concentrated on the U.S. market–caused a rapid increase in prices because agricultural output could not expand fast enough to meet the increased demands. Demand became sharper in 1973 when bad weather, droughts, and crop failures interfered with food production throughout the world. Thus, while all consumer prices in the United States rose by about 8 per cent, food prices rose more than 20 per cent. By the end of the year, the consumer price index was rising at an annual rate of 9.6 per cent. Had the price of food remained constant, inflation would have been reduced by more than a full percentage point. Unquestionably, energy prices will show a similar effect in 1974. Under these conditions, price controls and rationing appear attractive, but may only lead to further shortages and ultimately even greater inflation.

Environmental Concerns. A second major problem facing the United States is to reconcile the dual goals of a greatly improved environment and a continually rising level of living. An improved environment may improve the level of living, or at least the quality of life. What most people mean by a rising level of living, however, is more steak and less macaroni and cheese for dinner. This is especially true of those who live in or close to poverty. It is even more true of the hundreds of millions of people who live in the less-developed countries of the world where hunger is never far distant. The aspirations of these people for an "American" standard of living are not to be dismissed by pleas for a cleaner and better environment. This is not to say that environmental

goals should be abandoned in favor of an all-out push for more production. Rather, it is necessary to realize that improving the environment takes resources and that there is a trade-off between cleaner air and water and increased output.

In 1973, American business spent a record-breaking $100 billion on new plants and equipment. About half of this was financed, directly or indirectly, through the savings of individual Americans, which amounted to $52 billion. Almost all of the balance came from the retained profits of business. Probably no more than 5 per cent of the total was invested to meet environmental requirements. That amount will have to double in the next 10 years, if the United States is to meet the standards already set.

Avoiding Depression. A third problem of deep concern to all Americans is whether the country can avoid a depression. The oil boycott holds the only definitive answer. Assuming that the rest of the world does not continue to suffer major cutbacks in oil, regardless of what may happen to the United States, it appears that recession–and not depression –will probably result. The underlying strong demand for American goods will prevent the sort of severe economic downturn that occurred in the Great Depression of the 1930s. Warren W. Shearer

See also articles on individual countries; Banks and Banking; Energy; Labor; Money; Section One, Focus on The Economy.

ECUADOR. The Galapagos Islands, named after the giant 500-pound land turtles found there, became Ecuador's 20th province on Feb. 18, 1973. The 15-island group, which was discovered in 1535 and annexed by the republic in 1832, was used as a base for U.S. troops guarding the Panama Canal in World War II. In 1959, the government set aside the Galapagos as a national park.

The nation's domestic and international situations remained tranquil during the year. To spur industrial development, Ecuador offered tax incentives it hoped would lead to the expansion of existing companies and to the establishment of new ventures. It also encouraged the expansion of local food production, including the creation of a national fishing agency that would modernize the industry. The government also announced plans for an $11-million tuna port and a $20-million to $30-million fishing complex, with a capacity of 60,000 tons per year.

Petroleum replaced bananas as the nation's prime foreign-exchange earner in 1973. Exports of two other traditional commodities, coffee and sugar, also did exceptionally well.

On August 6, the U.S.-owned Texaco-Gulf Corporation signed a new 20-year concession contract giving Ecuador close to 80 per cent of the gross profits of the group's petroleum exports versus 60 per cent under the previous agreement. Mary Webster Soper

See also Latin America (Facts in Brief Table).

EDUCATION in the United States faced the dire consequences of inflation and public apathy in 1973. Taxpayers, troubled by the high cost of living, resisted demands for educational expenditures. Across the nation, voters turned down more than half of all school bond issues. Even school lunch programs felt the pinch: At the beginning of the 1973-1974 school year, some 800,000 children had been dropped from the lists of reduced-price or free meals because the federal subsidy of $1 billion had not kept up with rising food costs.

For the first time in 28 years, the total enrollment in American schools and colleges, which had been growing steadily, showed an actual decline – of about 400,000. The reversal of the upward trend was caused by the drop in elementary school enrollment, estimated at 1.7 per cent. Within five years, the no-growth phenomenon could therefore be expected to affect the high schools. In about 10 years, college enrollments could be expected to sag. Even in the 1973-1974 academic year there were an estimated 600,000 vacant places on the nation's campuses, though not at the high-prestige institutions. But this was attributed to overexpansion on the campus, not to declining enrollments.

In contrast to the deepening financial crisis, the mood in the schools and on the campuses was peaceful and quiet. Even the controversy over busing, a dominant one in 1972, seemed to have subsided in most school districts. Teachers' strikes prevented some schools from opening on time, affecting an estimated 800,000 pupils. But the total number of stoppages was below that of previous years, and the mood was less militant.

Teachers and Enrollment. There were 2.8 million teachers at all levels in U.S. schools, including about 660,000 college faculty members. A substantial surplus of teachers continued in virtually all fields of study. The National Education Association reported a 1973-1974 supply of 234,550 newly graduated teachers, but an actual demand for only 111,300.

The average teacher's salary for the 1972-1973 school year was $10,643, about 4.2 per cent above the average for the previous year. Average salaries ranged from Mississippi's $6,924 to Alaska's $14,491. New York was the only other state to reach an average above $12,000.

In higher education, the American Association of University Professors reported that faculty salaries had risen 5 per cent during the 1972 academic year, slightly faster than the cost of living. The Graduate Center of the City University of New York led the field with salaries of $30,303.

According to the American Council on Education, 64.7 per cent of the nation's faculty members held tenured positions in 1972-1973. This compared with 46.7 per cent five years earlier. The proportion of black college teachers increased only from 2.2 per cent to 2.9 per cent during the same period, and that

of women from 19.1 per cent to 20 per cent. Among all college faculties, 39.7 per cent of the men and 19.9 per cent of the women held doctoral degrees.

The total enrollment in public and private institutions declined to 58.9 million in 1973-1974. The elementary grades (kindergarten through grade 8) enrolled 35.1 million, with 31.3 million in public schools. High schools (grades 9 through 12) enrolled 16.8 million, with 15.5 million in public schools, about 200,000 over the previous year's total.

The 1974 high school graduating class is expected to total slightly more than 3.1 million, the largest class in the history of American public education. An estimated 958,000 bachelor's degrees, 263,000 master's degrees, and 38,000 doctorates will be conferred during the academic year.

The number of school systems continued to decline. At the latest count, there were 19,200 districts, compared with 40,500 in 1960. During the same period, the number of one-teacher schools dropped from 20,200 to only 2,000.

College Admissions. In sharp contrast to the 1960s, much of the pressure seemed gone from the college admission scene. Most colleges reported ample space for qualified applicants. A survey by the National Science Foundation said first-year science enrollments dropped about 3 per cent. The decline has affected all areas except the social sciences. Engi-

Although teacher strikes in 1973 prevented some schools from opening on time, the total number of stoppages was below that of previous years.

Boston's Highland Park Free School typifies the growing movement toward
schools free from usual rules of organization, curriculum, and behavior.

neering led the decline with 5 per cent. At the same time, the number of graduate students with federal subsidy dropped by 10 per cent.

Language Study appeared to be losing popularity. The Modern Language Association reported the sharpest decline in college foreign-language enrollments in recent decades, a drop of more than 10 per cent. Virtually all languages were affected, but French and German were hit hardest. Enrollment in French dropped 19 per cent and in German, 13.3 per cent. Latin declined by 12.3 per cent. Only the minimal enrollments in the so-called exotic languages, such as Chinese, Japanese, Hebrew, and classical Greek, showed gains. Greek gained 22 per cent.

Fewer college freshmen sought to study education, engineering, or science. The American Council on Education surveyed 188,900 freshmen and found a six-year trend continuing. Preferences for preprofessional studies, including both medicine and law, continued to grow, as did those for farming and forestry. Freshmen also described themselves as increasingly conservative. Those who identified themselves as "liberal" or "far left" diminished, while those calling themselves "middle of the road," "conservative," or "far right" increased.

Expenditures for Education at all levels in 1973-1974 were estimated by the United States Office of Education at $96.7 billion, compared with $89.4 billion the previous year. About $10.5 billion will be for construction and the rest for operations. Elementary and secondary education will require $61.5 billion. The total for the nonpublic sector is estimated at $17 billion. Altogether, American education expenditures represent just under 8 per cent of the gross national product.

Unions. The two largest U.S. teacher organizations–the National Education Association with 1.4 million members and the American Federation of Teachers (AFT) with 375,000 members–moved closer to a merger. The AFT is affiliated with the American Federation of Labor and Congress of Industrial Organizations (AFL-CIO). Only the question whether a merger would require all members of both groups to join the AFL-CIO appeared to stand in the way. But both organizations' 1973 national conventions agreed to begin merger talks. A statewide merger in New York created the United Teachers of New York, with more than 200,000 members. In December, the AFT executive council asked its president to resign in what appeared to be a dispute over handling of merger negotiations.

Integration. The U.S. Commission on Civil Rights said a survey of 10 school districts in the South and North showed that integration contributed to better educational achievements. The report said the gains may have come from "the shock of desegregation." It was described as a shock that "caused school officials to take a new and hard look at their educational program and, in some cases, realize that it was outdated and inadequate."

Controversy over school busing appeared to subside. Only two years after school buses were burned in Pontiac, Mich., schools in that district opened without incident. Similarly, Alexandria, Va., elementary schools initiated a district-wide busing schedule without apparent opposition. Court action on two of the most sweeping busing plans was indecisive. In May, the Supreme Court of the United States upheld a lower court ruling that a plan to merge predominantly black inner-city schools with white suburban schools in Richmond, Va., was unconstitutional. In June, a federal appeals court upheld a busing plan that would integrate inner-city and suburban schools in Detroit.

But President Richard M. Nixon continued to oppose busing. In his message to Congress on September 10, he said: "I continue to believe that busing is an unsatisfactory remedy for the inequities and inequalities of educational opportunity that exist in our country. . . ." The President said he would work with the Congress in "an effort to enact legislation which will end involuntary busing for purposes of racial balance. . . ."

Negro Colleges. The Office of Education disclosed that federal aid to predominantly black colleges had increased from $108 million in 1969 to $242 million in 1972. There are 114 such institutions, most of them in the South. They enroll almost 250,000 students, about one-third of all black undergraduates.

Women's Colleges. As coeducation continued to be the favored pattern, the number of single-sex colleges declined steadily. Since 1960, the number of women's colleges dropped from 300 to 146. At that rate, there will be fewer than 100 such institutions in operation by 1980. All-male colleges followed a similar trend; their number declined from 261 to only 101 in 1973.

The Carnegie Commission on Higher Education reported that annual salaries of women faculty members averaged between $1,500 and $2,000 less than those paid to men in comparable jobs. Nearly half of more than 500 job-bias complaints before the courts involved sex discrimination.

Catholic Education. Rising costs and declining enrollments forced about 300 Roman Catholic schools to close in 1973. Enrollment in the more than 10,000 remaining Roman Catholic parochial schools has dropped from a peak of 5.6 million in 1965 to 3.8 million in 1973. Moreover, the Supreme Court ruled that federal-aid provisions in New York, Pennsylvania, and Rhode Island violated the constitutional requirement of church-state separation.

Education Surveys. The most extensive international study of student achievements was made public by the International Association for the Evaluation of Educational Achievement in Stockholm, Sweden. The survey, which assessed the work

of 258,000 students and 50,000 teachers in 22 nations, found that the top 10 per cent of American high school seniors scored better in reading comprehension than similar groups in all the other countries checked. This conclusion was regarded by experts as proof that a mass-education system does no harm to gifted students.

The 1970 census showed that the level of education in the United States has been rising sharply. Eight of ten persons between the ages of 20 and 21 were found to have at least a high school education, while only 40 per cent of those between 55 and 64 had completed their secondary schooling. Taking the native-born population as a whole, 57 per cent of whites, 31 per cent of blacks, 33 per cent of American Indians, and 56 per cent of Americans of other races had completed high school.

The Carnegie commission, which warned in 1971 that most of the nation's colleges and universities were in serious financial difficulty or heading toward it, reported in 1973 that, as a result of greater economy and efficiency, fees for food, housing, and other services had not increased substantially. The annual rise in costs per student had dropped from nearly 4 per cent ahead of the rate of inflation during the period from 1966 to 1970 to only 0.5 per cent ahead in the period from 1969 to 1973.   Fred M. Hechinger

See also Section One, FOCUS ON EDUCATION.

Plight of Catholic Schools

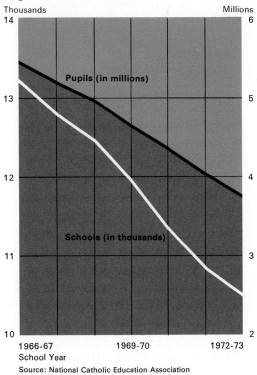

Source: National Catholic Education Association

EGYPT resumed its war with Israel on Oct. 6, 1973, attacking Israeli positions on the east bank of the Suez Canal. After a cease-fire halted the bloody fighting on October 22, Egypt and Israel signed a formal truce agreement, opening the way for the most serious Middle East peace effort in 24 years. Egypt shuffled its military leadership after the fighting and also resumed diplomatic relations with the United States after a six-year lapse. For details on the fighting and its aftermath, see MIDDLE EAST.

The assault on Israel served to unify an Egyptian society that, until then, seemed in danger of falling apart because of internal stresses. Student riots closed Cairo universities in January and March. Student complaints centered around lack of job opportunities, poor housing, and government interference in student activities. About 95 student leaders were arrested. In February, 64 journalists and literary figures were expelled from the Arab Socialist Union, Egypt's only legal political organization, on charges of inciting the students and other antistate activities. Mass trials of 100 alleged subversives began on September 15.

In an effort to allay criticism and prepare Egypt for the long-promised confrontation with Israel, President Anwar al-Sadat made significant changes in the government. On March 26, he named himself prime minister; on March 28, he appointed himself military governor general of Egypt. The office of president was reorganized in April to give senior officers and advisers greater responsibility for foreign affairs. Some 1,600 political prisoners were released on July 23, anniversary of the 1952 revolution. Former President Mohammed Naguib, under house arrest for 17 years, was among those freed.

Union with Libya. Egypt also came under heavy pressure from Libyan President Muammar Muhammad al-Qadhaafi to complete the union the two countries had scheduled for September 1. But Egypt recognized serious differences with the Libyan leader and preferred union in stages. The strain was illustrated by Qadhaafi's unannounced visit to Egypt in late June and the halting near the Egyptian border of a 3,000-member Libyan "Unity Caravan" that demanded immediate unification. On August 29, the two countries agreed to start forming joint institutions and common leadership on September 1. But Qadhaafi closed Libya's Embassy in Cairo on December 1.

Economic Gains. Political instability and the war overshadowed some positive economic developments. In March, phosphate deposits estimated at a billion tons were discovered near Abu Tartur in the Western Desert. A major oil find in the Gulf of Suez was reported in July. In August, the Tanta refinery in the Nile Delta began operations.   William Spencer

See also MIDDLE EAST (Facts in Brief Table).

President Anwar al-Sadat, right, postponed the September, 1973, union of Egypt and Libya despite pressure from Libya's Muammar Muhammad al-Qadhaafi.

ELECTIONS. The 1973 off-year elections produced a mixed bag of victories for Democratic candidates. They won the New Jersey governorship from the Republicans on November 6. They did well in most of the major municipal races, including New York City, and they cut into Republican strongholds in the New York and Connecticut suburbs.

It was a good year as well for black candidates. Atlanta, Ga.; Detroit; Los Angeles; and Raleigh, N.C., elected black mayors for the first time. The incumbent black mayor in Dayton, Ohio, was re-elected. The Republicans retained the Virginia governorship, elected a lieutenant governor, and retained the Cleveland mayoralty.

Whether the poor Republican showing only a year after President Richard M. Nixon's landslide victory could be ascribed to the Watergate scandal was difficult to assess. The President had suffered a sharp drop in the public-opinion polls and did no campaigning. Instead, he worked to restore his credibility.

Outwardly, Watergate was not an issue in most of the election races, and the rival party chairmen discounted it as a factor in the election results. "We're not taking great comfort from the results," Republican National Chairman George Bush said, "but I continue to maintain that Watergate does not appear to have been a determining factor in any of these races." Democratic National Chairman Robert S. Strauss agreed: "I don't read any national signifi-

Election winners, clockwise from top left, are Coleman Young, Detroit's first black mayor; Maynard Jackson, Atlanta's first black mayor; Abraham D. Beame, New York City's first Jewish mayor; Thomas Bradley, first black mayor of Los Angeles; and Mills E. Godwin, Jr., once Democratic governor of Virginia, re-elected as a Republican.

cance into this, but I think it shows we're on the right track here in trying to put the party back together."

Political analysts concluded that the Republicans did not discuss Watergate during the campaign because it was too embarrassing. The Democrats did not bring it up because they did not have to; they believed it would have more impact on the voters if they did not try to exploit it as a specific issue.

It appeared that voters had Watergate on their minds. Disenchantment could have accounted for the generally light turnout. Voter apathy, on the other hand, usually occurs in the first year of elections after a presidential campaign. Those who did vote may have responded to Watergate, but other factors often seemed equally plausible.

Governors' Races. In New Jersey, internal Republican disputes and scandals in the administration of outgoing Republican Governor William T. Cahill helped Democrat Brendan T. Byrne, 49, a former judge and political newcomer, win the governorship. His opponent, Representative Charles W. Sandman Jr., 52, was a conservative Republican. Sandman defeated Cahill for the Republican nomination in a June primary, but he could not unite the party. Byrne swept into office by a margin of more than 2 to 1 over Sandman. The Democrats also took control of both houses of the state legislature.

In Virginia, Republican Mills E. Godwin, Jr., narrowly defeated Independent Henry E. Howell for governor. Godwin, who had been a conservative

Democrat until this race, had served a previous term as governor from 1966 to 1970. He was the first Virginian in more than a century to be elected governor for a second time. Howell, a Democrat serving as lieutenant governor, is a liberal-populist who chose to run for governor as an Independent in an attempt to form a new coalition in the South. Republican Chairman Bush thought that Godwin's victory indicated a continuing trend in the South toward party realignment and a swing to the Republicans. Democratic Chairman Strauss disagreed. He said that he thought Howell would have won if he had run as a Democrat because he would have picked up votes from "traditional Democrats who had voted for Godwin in the past."

In the contest for lieutenant governor of Virginia, Republican State Senator John N. Dalton won an easy victory over Democratic State Senator J. Harry Michael and Independent Flora Crater.

Mayoralty Contests. In the Cleveland mayoralty race, Republican Ralph J. Perk easily won re-election to a second term over Democrat Mercedes Cotner, the city council clerk, who became a candidate after the original nominee withdrew.

In New York City, Democrat Abraham D. Beame, the 67-year-old city comptroller, became the city's first Jewish mayor when he won 57 per cent of the vote in a four-man race. He succeeded John V. Lindsay, former Republican who turned Independent, then became a Democrat. Lindsay did not run again for the office he first won in 1965. See BEAME, ABRAHAM D.

The successful black candidates:
▪ In Atlanta, Vice-Mayor Maynard Jackson defeated incumbent Mayor Sam Massell on October 16. Both are Democrats.
▪ In Detroit, State Senator Coleman Young, a liberal Democrat, won in a nonpartisan race with former Police Commissioner John Nichols.
▪ In Los Angeles, on May 29, Thomas Bradley, a city councilman and former policeman, was elected mayor over his fellow Democrat, incumbent Mayor Sam Yorty, seeking a fourth term. See BRADLEY, THOMAS.
▪ In Raleigh, N.C., City Councilman Clarence E. Lightner won a nonpartisan race against G. Wesley Williams, director of the Raleigh Merchants Bureau.
▪ In Dayton, Ohio, Mayor James H. McGee, a lawyer and business executive, won a second term by defeating Edward L. Fanning.

There were two major municipal upsets. Minneapolis Mayor Charles S. Stenvig, a former policeman running for a third term as an Independent, was defeated by Albert Hofstede, 33, candidate of the Democratic-Farmer-Labor Party. In Philadelphia, Republican District Attorney Arlen Specter lost to Democrat F. Emmett Fitzpatrick. Specter had been considered a strong future candidate for the U.S. Senate or the Pennsylvania governorship.

Other Significant Results. Pittsburgh Mayor Peter R. Flaherty, a self-styled political maverick, won a second term with the support of both the Democrats and Republicans. In Louisville, Ky., Democrat Harvey Sloane, 37, a millionaire newcomer to politics, won the mayoralty over Republican C. J. Hyde, former police chief. In Buffalo, N.Y., Democratic Mayor Stanley M. Makowski won a 3-to-1 victory over Republican Stewart M. Levy. Seattle Mayor Wes Uhlman, a Democrat, won re-election in a contest with a Chinese immigrant's son, Liem Eng Tuai.

Two potential 1976 Republican presidential contenders, Governor Nelson A. Rockefeller of New York and Governor Ronald Reagan of California, both suffered minor defeats. New York state voters rejected a $3.5-billion transportation bond issue that Rockefeller had urged. Californians rejected Reagan's proposal for a constitutional ceiling on state taxes and spending. Analysts doubted the defeats hurt either man's presidential chances.

Reagan's defeat, however, was a plus for Bob Moretti, speaker of the California Assembly, who led the drive against the proposal. Moretti, who will seek the Democratic nomination for governor, gained identity with the voters.   William McGaffin

See also DEMOCRATIC PARTY; REPUBLICAN PARTY; STATE GOVERNMENT.

ELECTRIC POWER. See ENERGY.

ELECTRONICS spread into new and broader areas of everyday use in 1973. The technology now has wide applications in automobiles, photography, and music.

The most advanced electronic camera, for example, the SX-70, was introduced in January by the Polaroid Corporation of Cambridge, Mass. This camera uses about 400 transistors, packaged on 7 integrated circuits (IC's), to control lens aperture, focusing, shutter speed, motor drive, and flash.

Electronics is also being used in home appliances. The Frigidaire division of General Motors (GM) in Dayton, Ohio, built computer logic into a line of ranges to control temperature and timing. And in music, some Hammond electronic organs use metal-oxide-semiconductor (MOS) IC's to produce a full range of sounds.

On Automobiles. Although required by federal regulations to install IC-controlled seat-belt interlocks in 1974 cars, the automobile industry began looking seriously to electronics to do even more. In addition to IC-controlled ignition, fuel injection, skid control, and turn signals, some cars will carry semiconductor pressure sensors for emission control. Moreover, the Cadillac division of GM installed an infrared thermal monitor on some models that will check the operation of the engine's valve seats, a precursor of the electronically monitored car of the future.

In Los Angeles, a Data General Corporation Nova

model 1220 minicomputer flashes information on freeway traffic conditions to motorists. In nearby Lawndale, Calif., the Atlantic Richfield Oil Company built a computerized gas station. On the Ohio Turnpike, Digital Equipment Corporation minicomputers began handling tolls automatically. In Cleveland and Philadelphia, computers are used to monitor masses of complex information for the Cleveland Illuminating Company and the Philadelphia Electric Company, respectively. Built because both cities experienced massive blackouts in the 1960s, the systems handle information gathering and monitor power and light distribution, and they can warn console operators of blackouts. And the railroad industry found a new use for computers: Railroad cars in Alexandria, Va., are now weighed on a computerized scale built by Sands Measurement Corporation of Dallas.

Laser Technology also began to come fully into its own. Lasers are now being used in vehicle control, in metalworking, and in the airline industry.

The Bendix Corporation of Southfield, Mich., has made an experimental laser system that was being tested by the U.S. Bureau of Mines in 1973. The system positions and guides mine vehicles running on tracks. Another developing Bendix system sorts airline baggage. A specially coded label is applied to the baggage and the beam of a gas laser "reads" the label to sort and route the baggage. The Caterpillar Tractor Company of East Peoria, Ill., uses lasers in its manufacturing division to machine, cut, weld, and heat-treat metals.

Solid State Technology. Several advancements had an impact on the semiconductor industry in 1973. For example, Fairchild Camera & Instrument Corporation of Mountain View, Calif., has successfully used an MOS IC called a charge-coupled device (CCD) commercially. The CCD replaces the bulky vidicon tube used in television cameras; it can sense and transmit images, using less power than the tube.

Several semiconductor companies have manufactured a new type of computer logic called integrated-injection logic (IIL). IIL allows information to be packed into the smallest area yet on a "chip," and thus allows that information to be retrieved faster than with other types of logic. IIL may replace these other types, which include transistor-transistor logic, diode-transistor logic, and emitter-coupled logic. Manufacturers of IIL hope that the new logic will bring sophisticated computers within reach of all businesses. Presently, computers of this nature cost many thousands of dollars and require many consoles of air-controlled computing banks. So far, however, there is only one IIL product. It is a random access memory that holds 256 bits of information.

Semiconductor makers realize the great potential of IIL however, and are working quickly. Other products should emerge soon.   Marilyn J. Offenheiser

ELLSBERG, DANIEL (1931-   ), the central figure in the Pentagon Papers trial, was freed of espionage, theft, and conspiracy charges in Los Angeles on May 11, 1973. U.S. District Judge William Matthew Byrne, Jr., ended the case because of what he termed gross government misconduct. Ellsberg and Anthony Russo were indicted in 1971 for making copies of a secret 47-volume government study of the Vietnam War and releasing it to newspapers. Ellsberg copied the report while working for the Rand Corporation in Santa Monica, Calif., in 1969. He said he released it because the American people had a right to know about the actions of their government.

Judge Byrne dismissed the trial after 89 days because of "improper government conduct, shielded so long from public view" that it offended "a sense of justice." The judge was referring to a number of violations of procedure, including an illegal break-in at the office of Ellsberg's psychiatrist.

Ellsberg was born in Chicago and studied at Harvard University and Cambridge University in England. He received M.S. and Ph.D. degrees in economics from Harvard. He spent four years in the U.S. Marines.   Foster Stockwell

See also WATERGATE.

EL SALVADOR. See LATIN AMERICA.

EMPLOYMENT. See ECONOMICS; EDUCATION; LABOR; SOCIAL SECURITY; SOCIAL WELFARE.

ENERGY. The American dream of an endless supply of low-cost energy came to a sudden, shocking end in 1973. There had been portents that a crisis was brewing. The first hint of trouble came during the summer with the closing of gasoline stations and a warning of heating oil shortages. The crisis blossomed quickly in October when Arab countries stopped selling oil to the United States and other nations.

The crisis developed because the U.S. could no longer produce enough oil to meet its energy needs. It must import 6 million of the more than 17 million barrels it consumes each day. About one-third of those imports comes from Arab countries.

In a nationwide address on November 7, President Richard M. Nixon described the energy shortage as the most serious the nation has faced since World War II. He proposed voluntary and congressional action to conserve energy. He urged citizens to lower furnace thermostats, to drive more slowly, and to use public transportation or car pools more. He also asked Congress for authority to suspend environmental standards so that industries can use more high-sulfur coal. In a similar address on November 25, he rationed heating oil, effective January 1, by reducing shipments to businesses and industry. On December 10, House and Senate conferees agreed on legislation that would return the nation to Daylight Saving Time on January 6. Mr. Nixon had asked for this measure under the assumption that it would cut energy consumption from 1 to 1.5 per cent.

"No gas" signs proclaimed dealer protests of price ceilings on gasoline in September. By year's end, fuel shortage brought signs back.

The Return to Coal reverses a recent trend. Utilities and many other industries have been converting their boilers to use oil in order to meet stiffened environmental standards. The nation has enough coal to supply its energy needs for many years, though most of it contains too much sulfur to meet current environmental standards. But the swing back to coal promised to be far from simple. Space must be provided for coal storage, boilers must be fitted with grates and equipment for ash removal, and many boilers now rated for oil firing must be rerated.

Worse yet, coal suppliers are hard pressed to meet the growing demand. Some were unable to accept orders. Then there is also the perennial problem of sulfur content. Ample evidence indicated that there would have to be a gradual weakening of environmental restrictions, at least temporarily.

Electric Utility Sales followed the economic boom in spite of raw energy shortages. Total sales went up 9 per cent to more than 1.7 trillion kilowatt-hours (kwh) during the year. But with emphasis on energy conservation, the growth rate retrenched during November and December.

Biggest factor in the 1973 upturn of kwh sales was industrial consumption, which climbed more than 10 per cent. One major factor in this growth is water- and air-pollution control equipment; an estimated 7 per cent of industrial electricity usage in 1973 was for pollution control.

Despite growing sales, the electric utility industry had only a modest year in terms of revenue, profit, and output:

	1972	1973	% gain
	(in millions)		
Total capability (kw)	395.5	437.6	10.6
Utilities generation (kwh)	1,747,000	1,870,000	7.0
Utilities sales (kwh)	1,578,000	1,688,000	7.0
Utilities revenue*	$24,000	$27,000	12.3

*For investor-owned companies

Electric Heating of homes has become an increasingly important factor, accounting for about 16 per cent of residential electricity sales. If fuel were available, most electric utilities could supply twice as much heat as they do today without calling for capacity additions. And with the increased concern over availability of heating oil and natural gas, residential electric heat installations are running close to 1 million a year. Residential sales per average customer rose from 7,700 kwh in 1972 to over 8,100 kwh in 1973.

How Long Will Crisis Last? This question was repeated on many fronts. Coal suppliers asked it, seeking reassurance before undertaking the expensive task of reopening closed mines. Many engineers and scientists predicted the crisis will get worse unless the nation:

- Relaxes some environmental standards.
- Accepts the urgency of developing nuclear power.
- Begins major research and development programs.

Energy conservation became a national theme in 1973. Washington lawmakers, fuel suppliers, electric utilities, and industrial users pressed hard on the energy-conservation theme with some interesting results. Major gasoline companies urged the public to slow down when they drive and gave other tips on consuming less fuel; so did heating oil and natural gas producers. Electric utilities joined the drive with campaigns on how to use appliances and electric home heating economically. President Nixon sought to double government spending on energy research and named Colorado's Governor John Love to serve as the top energy coordinator. Love resigned in December when William Simon was named to head the new Federal Energy Administration.

Advanced Energy Concepts got some share of attention. The International Solar Energy Conference, held in Paris, gave fresh impetus to power captured directly from sunlight. The conference stressed how solar energy was rapidly finding new applications, not as a result of technological advances alone, but, perhaps more importantly, because of a variety of economic, environmental, and social forces. As the limits on traditional fuels and their environmental consequences became more apparent, solar energy stood out as an inexhaustible source if it can be harnessed economically. James J. O'Connor

See also Section Two, How Can We Solve the Energy Crisis?

ENGINEERING. See Building and Construction.

ENVIRONMENT. The United States commitment to progress in cleaning up its environment was severely tested in 1973. The costs – in dollars and personal sacrifices – of the effort to clean up the nation's air and water in the face of a severe energy shortage created a backlash against environmental programs.

Russell E. Train, who was confirmed as administrator of the Environmental Protection Agency (EPA) on September 10, recognized this fact when he appeared before a Senate committee. He promised there would be no slackening in the commitment to clean air and water.

"The environment and quality of life issue is the major issue ahead for the remainder of the century," he said. "There is a short-term danger that the public, being faced finally with the real costs of protecting the environment, will face these costs before the real benefits from the environmental cleanup become evident. There is also a tendency to use the energy issue as an excuse for relaxing our environmental efforts."

Environment Report. Train's summary of the "second generation" of environmental problems was underlined by the fourth annual report of the Council on Environmental Quality, issued September 17. The council estimated that the nation must spend $274.2 billion on environmental cleanup in the next 10 years. The report, which is the primary annual assessment of the state of the nation's environment,

pared more than $1 billion from the council's previous estimate of the cost of pollution controls in the next decade. The report also stressed that the outlay would be more than offset by savings in public health and property damage. In forwarding the 500-page report to Congress, President Richard M. Nixon cited it as demonstrating "our considerable progress in arresting environmental decay."

Air Pollution. On July 30, the EPA granted automobile manufacturers a one-year delay, until the 1977 model year, on meeting limits on auto nitrogen oxide emissions. On April 11, the agency granted a similar delay, until the 1976 model year, on exhaust-emission standards for hydrocarbons and carbon monoxide. The Clean Air Act of 1970 permitted the year's delay if the goals were determined to be unreachable. The Public Interest Research Group, affiliated with consumer advocate Ralph Nader, attacked the postponement as "the final installment on emission standard concessions" to auto manufacturers and "their environmental blackmail."

The Supreme Court of the United States, by a 4-to-4 vote on June 11, affirmed a lower court decision that EPA must not permit deterioration of air quality in any part of any state. The Sierra Club, a national conservation organization, had brought the suit to prevent "significant deterioration" of air quality in areas where the air is cleaner than federal standards

To restore polluted Lake Palic in Yugoslavia, workmen drained it and then scraped a 5-foot layer of foul-smelling muck from the lake bottom.

ENVIRONMENT

Pollution in the Atlantic Ocean

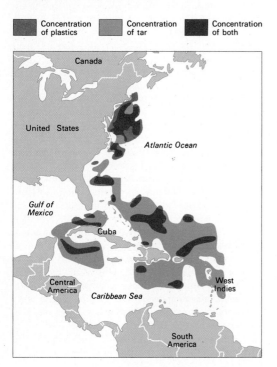

Concentration of plastics

Concentration of tar

Concentration of both

require. The organization hailed the court decision as the greatest environmental law victory ever achieved. At hearings in August on proposals to meet the court ruling, EPA spokesmen contended that, "Adequate technology is simply not yet available to permit completely pollution-free growth."

Water Pollution. In a series of actions in August and September, the EPA set effluent standards for the 28 major categories of American industry that discharge material into bodies of water. The actions were taken to implement the tough Federal Water Pollution Control Act of 1972. Some industrial groups – including large animal feed lots, phosphate plants, and cement plants – were told to aim for zero waste-water discharge by 1983. The effluent standards form the basis for issuing waste-water discharge permits to industries. These permits are the primary means through which federal-state programs control water pollution.

The new EPA regulations also require that those discharging waste water into federally aided municipal treatment systems must pay a share of the system's construction cost.

Solid Wastes. The EPA budget for recycling and reducing solid wastes was slashed from $30 million to $5.8 million. President Nixon defended the cut, saying that reducing solid waste is "a local not a national problem." The action eliminated a planned EPA program of subsidies and incentives to spur recycling.

An Oregon law, which became effective in October, 1972, outlawed pull-tab openers on beer cans and required a 5-cent deposit on all beverage containers. An EPA survey showed that the law reduced bottle and can litter by 81 per cent. A similar law became effective in Vermont in July.

The Supreme Court rejected on July 18 a suit by environmental groups to get a reduction in rail rates for "recyclable" goods. However, in what was viewed as a victory for the environmental law movement, the court ruled that a broad category of persons has the right to sue in matters affecting the environment.

Land Protection. On June 21, the Senate approved a bill that authorized the Department of the Interior to distribute $1 billion in grants to the states over an eight-year period for the development of land-use programs. The legislation is aimed at preventing unplanned land development and urban sprawl, especially in areas of environmental concern. A "sanctions" amendment that would have withheld some federal funds from states that did not carry out land-use planning was defeated.

Legislation regulating the strip mining of coal was approved by the Senate on October 9. Designed to prevent the type of land scars left by strip mining in West Virginia, the legislation requires a strip miner to restore a hillside to its original contour after coal has been removed. The legislation was supported by conservation groups, but was opposed in its key provisions by the coal and power industries.

On November 14, a Senate vote of 80 to 5 approved construction of the controversial trans-Alaska oil pipeline. The House had approved the construction by a vote of 361 to 14 the day before. The approved bill contained a section barring court review of the environmental impact of the project. Spokesmen for environmental groups that had blocked passage of the bill in past years claimed this section was unconstitutional. Many congressmen who approved the bill claimed they did so primarily because of the oil shortage in the United States. The new pipeline should ultimately carry 2 million barrels of low-sulfur crude oil a day.

World Environment Day was observed in countries throughout the world on June 5. The observance was in accord with a resolution of the United Nations Stockholm Conference on the Human Environment in June, 1972. In proclaiming the day's importance in the United States, President Nixon said the flight of the *Skylab 1* astronauts was a fresh reminder that all mankind is "bound together by the finite resources of one small planet."

The United Nations Environmental Program, established in December, 1972, to coordinate international environmental activities authorized by the Stockholm conference, established a new headquarters in Nairobi, Kenya, in October. The 17-nation Council of Europe rejected a proposal for collaboration by European countries in fighting pollution in March. Delegates said their governments were unwilling to commit large sums to international environmental efforts.

At a 91-nation conference in Geneva, Switzerland, on August 21, the United States proposed that an international tribunal settle disputes over use of the oceans. The conference was a prelude to the major 140-nation Law of the Sea Conference planned for Santiago, Chile, in April, 1974. Interest in the U.S. proposal has been heightened by ambitious plans by the United States and others to recover large amounts of scarce minerals from the seabeds.

Pesticides. An EPA study of endrin, a pesticide increasingly used to kill pests that attack cotton crops, found that the insecticide kills or debilitates birds, fish, and some domesticated animals. Two related insecticides, aldrin and dieldrin, have also been cited as environmental hazards by the EPA. Appeals by pesticide manufacturers have delayed expected bans.

Pressure increased in the Northwest to restore the use of DDT when the tussock moth attacked 700,000 acres of woodland. Early in 1973, the EPA rejected a Forest Service request to permit use of the banned pesticide against the moth infestation, but Secretary of Agriculture Earl L. Butz said in August that he would work to get the ban lifted as an emergency measure. Andrew L. Newman

See also CONSERVATION.

EQUATORIAL GUINEA. See AFRICA.

ERVIN, SAMUEL JAMES, JR. (1896-   ), Democratic U.S. senator from North Carolina, headed the Senate Committee on Presidential Campaign Activities that conducted the Watergate hearings in 1973 (see WATERGATE). A folksy man who often quotes from the Bible and various North Carolina sages to make a point, Ervin is respected in the Senate for his fairness and his knowledge of the U.S. Constitution.

Sam Ervin was born in Morganton, N.C., in the foothills of the Appalachian Mountains. An infantryman in World War I, he was wounded twice and was cited for gallantry in action twice. After getting a law degree at Harvard Law School in 1922, he practiced in Morganton with his father. He served as a judge in the Burke County criminal court and the state superior court, then was elected to Congress in 1946. He went to the state supreme court in 1948.

Ervin went to the Senate in 1954, when he was named to complete the term of Clyde R. Hoey, and served on the committee that considered censure charges against the late Senator Joseph R. McCarthy. Ervin opposed civil rights legislation during the 1950s. More recently, he has warned against the invasion of privacy involved in federal wiretapping. In December, he announced he would not seek re-election to the Senate in 1974.

Ervin married Margaret Bruce Bell in 1924. They have three children. Foster Stockwell

ETHIOPIA. A disastrous drought brought famine and death to a remote province in northern Ethiopia in 1973. A survey published on September 16 by the United Nations Children's Fund reported that over a 12-month period, between 50,000 and 100,000 Ethiopians had died of starvation in Wallo Province. The report added that an estimated 670,000 persons were in dire need of assistance.

The government immediately began an investigation to ascertain why the magnitude of the catastrophe had been kept secret. A report from a minor official in the province had reached the government in March, and an emergency session was immediately called to set up a relief committee. But the governor general of the province had apparently attempted to deal with the problem behind the scenes rather than publicize the event, and had reassured the government that the situation was under control.

Boundary Area Dispute. A long-simmering disagreement involving the Ethiopia-Somalia border flared into open dispute in 1973. The area in question lies in the Ogaden region in southern Ethiopia and encompasses about one-third of Ethiopia's territory. Because most of the inhabitants are Somalis, Somalia has claimed the area. The Ethiopians, however, disputed the Somalis' claim. Complicating the issue was the fact that prospectors had discovered potential oil resources in the disputed area. The quarrel was temporarily resolved on May 29 when the Organization of African Unity, holding its annual summit conference in Addis Ababa, set up a committee composed of eight heads of African states to mediate the long-standing problem.

On September 21, the government denied a report that members of the Eritrean Liberation Front had attempted to hijack a jetliner that was carrying Emperor Haile Selassie I to Milan, Italy. It also denied a report that during the flight a grandson of the emperor had tried to persuade him to abdicate.

International Relations. French President Georges Pompidou visited Addis Ababa on January 17 as part of a five-day tour. During his stay, he conferred with the emperor and reaffirmed close ties between the two countries. Diplomatic ties between Ethiopia and the Democratic Republic of (East) Germany were formally established on February 1.

Ethiopia was represented at a meeting attended by representatives of more than 40 African, Caribbean, and Pacific developing nations that met with the Council of Ministers of the European Community in Brussels, Belgium, on July 25 and 26. The representatives discussed preliminary details of their future relationship with the community. Earlier in the year, the World Bank approved a $5-million loan to Ethiopia. It would be used to help finance a project designed to improve slaughtering and marketing facilities for Ethiopia's livestock industry. Paul C. Tullier

See also AFRICA (Facts in Brief Table); Section One, FOCUS ON THE WORLD.

EUROPE

The European Community (EC or Common Market) faced three major problems when Great Britain, Denmark, and Ireland became its seventh, eighth, and ninth members on Jan. 1, 1973. Two were the continuing currency crisis and rampant inflation. The third was external relations, particularly with the United States.

In what President Richard M. Nixon had called the "Year of Europe," it was not until September that members agreed on an approach to outstanding problems that would justify the President meeting with its leaders. A Nixon trip was tentatively set for later in the year, but was finally put off to 1974. Moves toward an East-West détente in Europe included progress on plans for full-scale conferences on security and cooperation in Europe and on the general reduction of military forces there.

U.S. Relations. In October, relations with the United States reached their lowest ebb in years. America's partners in the North Atlantic Treaty Organization (NATO) were caught without warning when U.S. military forces were placed on an alert as an aftermath of the Arab-Israeli war. More bitterness followed over the supply of U.S. arms to Israel for use in fighting the Arabs, reportedly from stocks in Europe.

Arab oil sanctions hit all European countries. Sunday driving was banned in eight, and many governments imposed speed limits in efforts to conserve gasoline.

A complete Arab embargo on oil for the Netherlands threatened to disrupt the unity of the European Community. The Dutch appealed for solidarity and joint action to solve the problem. But any nation that supplied the Dutch with oil faced the danger that its own supplies from Arab sources would be cut off. In December, the bitterness spread at NATO's annual ministerial meeting. As the year drew to an end, the EC had not resolved the dilemma.

In March, representatives of the United States asked for talks on trade, monetary, and defense questions. A Europe-America Conference in Amsterdam from March 26 to 28 was sponsored by the International Europe Movement. Most of the 350-odd delegates had made or influenced their governments' policy toward North Atlantic nations since World War II. Eugene Rostow, leader of the 70 American delegates, said Western Europe and the United States had become "so interdependent and fused economically" as to require common management. The conference ended indecisively after George Ball, a former

U.S. undersecretary of state, warned of the growing danger of "American Gaullism," a term he used to describe a tendency toward unilateral action.

President Nixon met French President Georges Pompidou in Reykjavík, Iceland, on May 31 and decided to pursue a series of negotiations on outstanding problems with the possibility of a "grand summit" later in the year. The political approach of the Europeans to this summit occupied Common Market members through most of the summer. Marked differences arose between West Germany and France. Prospects for the meeting rose after a Common Market foreign ministers' meeting in Copenhagen, Denmark, on September 10, at which three working papers were drafted. They included a definition of "European identity" and a list of 10 topics for summit discussion.

Financial Crises. A huge inflow of American dollars caused an international currency crisis. The action reduced confidence in the dollar's value and brought emergency measures. On February 6, the West German Federal Bank had to use $1.2 billion on foreign exchange markets to keep the dollar above its lowest fixed rate of 3.150 Deutsche marks. Another $1.8 billion was used on February 9. François-Xavier Ortoli, president of the European Commission, a Common Market executive body, said in Luxembourg on February 13 that a "virtually permanent currency crisis" made reform of the international monetary system necessary and urgent. A 10 per cent devaluation of the U.S. dollar on February 13 led the market's finance ministers to speed up their timetable for economic and monetary union, but the crisis continued.

Beginning on March 4, the foreign exchange markets of all Common Market countries closed to give the experts time to find a solution. On March 16, finance ministers of 14 nations, including the United States, agreed in Paris on a currency system based on floating, rather than fixed, rates of exchange to ensure "orderly exchange markets." Exchanges reopened on March 19.

Revaluation of the Deutsche mark on June 29, the fifth since the signing of the Treaty of Rome in 1957, worsened the situation. The value of the dollar and the British pound sterling continued to slide in July.

Battling Inflation. Virtually every European country took measures to combat inflation. The Organization for Economic Cooperation and Development (OECD) said there was a risk of "too strong an expansion" of demand. The only exception was Italy, where economic growth had only recently resumed. The OECD regarded inflation as the most serious problem confronting member countries and predicted it would last "for some time."

On July 27, the Common Market's Commission,

Russia's party leader Leonid Brezhnev visited Chancellor and Mrs. Willy Brandt in Bonn in May and President Georges Pompidou in Paris in June.

The enlarged European Community's Commission,
an executive body, opened its first foreign
ministers meeting in Belgium on January 15.

part of its executive branch, said food prices continued to show the sharpest consumer-price advances. It also said the upsurge in import prices stimulated inflation. The commission also pointed to "deterioration" in the Common Market's balance of trade, particularly in Great Britain and Italy. Only West Germany and the Netherlands showed improvements in the balance of trade.

Food Prices. The market's Common Agricultural Policy provoked dissension for most of the year. After a 30-hour meeting ending on January 24, Britain gained some respite for cereal, sugar, and bacon prices. After Italian and British demands for a price freeze on all products except beef, farm price increases averaging 2.76 per cent were proposed on March 21. The Common Market farmers' organization rejected the commission's proposal and asked for a 7.5 per cent increase. On April 6, the European Parliament asked the commission to reconsider.

To break the deadlock, the commission evolved a complicated price formula. It allowed more costly milk and beef in France and Italy than in other member countries. Member countries could subsidize butter, and price increases for sugar and cereals were to be limited to 1 per cent.

World Relations. Ministers and delegates from 41 developing nations in Africa, the Caribbean, and the Pacific went to Brussels on July 25 for a conference on their future relations with the Common Market.

The Caribbean group was disappointed because the EC offer to help developing nations lacked "dynamism and innovation," and the African states ruled out any question of reciprocity. The two sides met again on October 17 and worked out favorable arrangements for imports that would be coming from developing countries.

Mediterranean countries – Tunisia, Morocco, Spain, and Israel – were equally disappointed on August 9 with the Common Market's limited trading offer. The market sought a trade agreement that would protect Italian and French farmers who specialize in Mediterranean-type crops. It would also encourage industrial exports to the nonmember Mediterranean countries. Negotiations were adjourned until the end of the year.

On August 27, Secretary-General Nikolai Fadeyev of the Russian-led Council for Mutual Economic Assistance asked the market for a meeting to discuss possible cooperation. The market's policy-making Council of Ministers promised to consider the idea.

Troop Cuts. Exploratory talks began in Vienna, Austria, on January 31 between 12 NATO countries and 7 Warsaw Pact countries on reducing military forces in Central Europe. The NATO nations held that more Warsaw Pact troops should be withdrawn for two reasons: More of them were present in Central Europe; and, after any agreement, U.S. troops would presumably recross the Atlantic while Russian home bases were nearer. France opposed the idea of Western troop cuts, and did not participate in the talks.

On November 22, NATO presented the Soviet bloc with a proposal for a two-phase program. Under it, the superpowers would make the first cuts. Then a common ceiling would be set for all forces, both NATO and Warsaw Pact forces, in Europe. Russia was still considering the proposal as the year came to an end.

Observers said the latest proposal contained the same figures that NATO officials in Brussels complained about on September 14. They had objected then that American sources had leaked a Western plan for the phased reduction of NATO and Warsaw Pact military forces to about 700,000 each, a 20 per cent cut by the Warsaw Pact and 10 per cent by NATO.

Security Conference. Malta's insistence on the inclusion of five Mediterranean Arab countries as full participants in the 35-nation Conference on Security and Cooperation in Europe blocked agreement on June 6 after six months of preparatory talks in Helsinki, Finland. But two days later, Malta gave in to pressure from other delegates. Ultimately, in keeping with a compromise proposed by Spain, the five and Israel were allowed to speak, but not to take part in the conference.

Regional Aid. The European Community was pledged to set up a regional development fund by

Facts in Brief on the European Countries

Country	Population	Government	Monetary Unit*	Foreign Trade (million U.S. $) Exports	Imports
Albania	2,432,000	Communist Party First Secretary Enver Hoxha; Premier Mehmet Shehu; People's Assembly Presidium Chairman Haxhi Lleshi	lek (4.15 = $1)	60	100
Austria	7,568,000	President Franz Jonas; Chancellor Bruno Kreisky	schilling (17 = $1)	3,883	5,216
Belgium	9,845,000	King Baudouin I; Prime Minister Edmond Leburton	franc (38.6 = $1)	16,081 (includes Luxembourg)	15,606
Bulgaria	8,721,000	Communist Party First Secretary & State Council Chairman Todor Zhivkov; Premier Stanko Todorov	lev (1.65 = $1)	2,603	2,548
Czechoslovakia	14,719,000	Communist Party First Secretary Gustav Husak; President Ludvik Svoboda; Premier Lubomir Strougal	koruna (12.5 = $1)	5,124	4,662
Denmark	5,078,000	Queen Margrethe II; Prime Minister Poul Hartling	krone (5.7 = $1)	4,412	5,069
Finland	4,740,000	President Urho Kekkonen; Prime Minister Kalevi Sorsa	markka (3.9 = $1)	2,947	3,198
France	52,656,000	President Georges Pompidou; Prime Minister Pierre Messmer	franc (4.1 = $1)	26,052	26,754
Germany (East)	17,002,000	Communist Party First Secretary Erich Honecker; State Council Chairman Willi Stoph; Prime Minister Horst Sindermann	mark (1.84 = $1)	6,184	5,905
Germany (West)	62,687,000	President Gustav Heinemann; Chancellor Willy Brandt	Deutsche mark (2.67 = $1)	46,208	39,763
Great Britain	56,113,000	Queen Elizabeth II; Prime Minister Edward Heath	pound (1 = $2.58)	24,344	27,860
Greece	8,958,000	President Phaidon Gizikis; Prime Minister Adamandios Androutsopoulos	drachma (30 = $1)	871	2,346
Hungary	10,485,000	Communist Party First Secretary Janos Kadar; President Pál Losonczi; Premier Jenö Fock	forint (24.9 = $1)	3,292	3,154
Iceland	226,000	President Kristján Eldjárn; Prime Minister Olafur Johannesson	króna (93 = $1)	191	233
Ireland	3,106,000	President Erskine Hamilton Childers; Prime Minister Liam Cosgrave	pound (1 = $2.56)	1,611	2,102
Italy	55,332,000	President Giovanni Leone; Prime Minister Mariano Rumor	lira (591 = $1)	18,548	19,282
Liechtenstein	21,000	Prince Francis Joseph II	Swiss franc	no statistics available	
Luxembourg	348,000	Grand Duke Jean; President & Prime Minister Pierre Werner	franc (38.6 = $1)	16,081 (includes Belgium)	15,606
Malta	318,000	Governor General Sir Anthony Mamo; Prime Minister Dom Mintoff	pound (1 = $2.73)	67	174
Monaco	25,000	Prince Rainier III	French franc	no statistics available	
Netherlands	13,675,000	Queen Juliana; Prime Minister Johannes Martin den Uyl	guilder (2.53 = $1)	16,826	16,985
Norway	3,999,000	King Olav V; Prime Minister Trygve Bratteli	krone (5.4 = $1)	3,251	4,332
Poland	33,541,000	Communist Party First Secretary Edward Gierek; State Council Chairman Henryk Jablonski; Premier Piotr Jaroszewicz	zloty (33.2 = $1)	4,932	5,335
Portugal	8,599,000	President Américo Deus Rodrigues Thomaz; Prime Minister Marcello Caetano	escudo (23.1 = $1)	1,287	2,183
Romania	21,153,000	Communist Party General Secretary & State Council President Nicolae Ceausescu; Prime Minister Ion Gheorghe Maurer	leu (14.4 = $1)	2,101	2,103
Russia	253,039,000	Communist Party General Secretary Leonid I. Brezhnev; Premier Aleksei N. Kosygin; Supreme Soviet Presidium Chairman Nikolai V. Podgorny	ruble (1 = $1.38)	15,361	16,047
San Marino	18,000	2 regents appointed by Grand Council every 6 months	Italian lira	no statistics available	
Spain	35,286,000	Chief of State (El Caudillo) Francisco Franco; President Carlos Arias Navarro	peseta (58.16 = $1)	3,803	6,755
Sweden	8,301,000	King Carl XVI Gustaf; Prime Minister Olof Palme	krona (4.1 = $1)	8,749	8,062
Switzerland	6,576,000	President Ernst Brugger	franc (2.96 = $1)	6,828	8,470
Turkey	38,942,000	President Fahri Koruturk; Prime Minister Naim Talu	lira (14 = $1)	885	1,058
Yugoslavia	21,173,000	President Josip Broz Tito; Prime Minister Djemal Bijedic	dinar (17 = $1)	2,237	3,233

*Exchange rates as of Nov. 1, 1973

the end of 1973 to reduce the gap between its advanced and underdeveloped regions. The 1974 budget provided $1 billion for this fund.

In a "social action program" published on April 20, the commission suggested that assembly lines should be abolished in EC nations because of their psychological damage to workers. It also proposed setting up a European vocational training center by mid-1974 and greater protection for migrant and women workers and the handicapped. The commission called for an examination of minimum wages and equal pay for men and women.

Parliamentary Reforms designed to make the European Parliament more democratic and to encourage it to act were proposed by Britain, and agreed to in Strasbourg, France, on January 17. The commission proposed on June 13 that the Parliament be given more influence on policies and a voice in how Common Market funds are spent.

The Cod War delayed introduction of a free-trade agreement between Iceland and the Common Market. The dispute began when Iceland extended fishing limits from 12 nautical miles from its coast to 50 miles. Incidents, mainly involving British trawlers, continued through the spring and summer.

Negotiators for Britain and Iceland agreed on October 16 on a compromise that they proposed to their governments. It was accepted on November 13. Fewer small British trawlers are allowed to fish around Iceland. Factory and freezer trawlers are excluded.

Other Action. The 55th ministerial session of the North Atlantic Council opened in Copenhagen on June 14. The delegates decided that their 15 governments should examine their relationships in the light of the profound changes taking place in every field of international activity. No time limit was set. NATO formed its second permanent international force on May 11. Called the Standing Naval Force, Channel, it was inaugurated at Ostend, Belgium.

In Vienna, ministers of 17 European nations called on March 30 for international laws to protect Europe from pollution. The Common Market drew up a wide-ranging two-year program on April 12 to improve the environment.

After five years of fruitless discussion, the nine Common Market countries approved a four-year, $160-million nuclear research program on February 6. On August 1, science ministers of 11 West European countries inaugurated an $875-million European space research program. It was to include development of a satellite launcher, a manned space satellite, and a marine satellite.

The all-male electorate of the tiny principality of Liechtenstein again rejected a proposal to allow women to vote. The vote on February 11 was 2,128 to 1,675.　　　　　　　　　　Kenneth Brown

See also EUROPE (Facts in Brief Table).

EXPLOSIONS. See DISASTERS.

FAIRS AND EXPOSITIONS. More than 4,000 international conventions and 600 international trade fairs were held from Afghanistan to Zaire in 1973. They ranged from general exhibitions to highly specialized fairs designed to attract buyers of specific products. One, as large as similar combined fairs held in Paris, Brussels, and Milan, was held in Hanover, West Germany, in April. There, producers and buyers met in 26 exhibit halls covering 957 square yards of space and housing 5,500 exhibits.

The U.S. Department of Commerce sponsored more than 150 trade fairs in the United States, and opened a trade center in Teheran, Iran, on November 5. It is the 14th in a worldwide chain of U.S. export-promotion centers.

Cooperation with Russians. In an effort to overcome the shortage of basic facilities that plague American executives trying to do business in Russia, the Soviet Chamber of Commerce and Industry and the Occidental Petroleum Corporation, a U.S. firm, announced plans on September 18 for a $110-million trade center in Moscow. The center is to be completed in 1977.

Under a cultural-exchange agreement between Russia and the United States, a yearlong, traveling outdoor-recreation exhibition opened in Moscow on May 21. It was to travel to five other Russian cities, some of which had never before had an American exhibition. Under the agreement, a similar Russian youth program will tour the United States.

The 30th International Air and Space Show made Paris the world's most important meeting place for the aeronautical and space world from May 24 to June 3. Some 580 exhibits from 17 nations were spread over 485,000 square feet of exhibit space. For the first time, Russia and the United States cooperated in jointly displaying a full-scale mock-up of the Apollo command module and the Soyuz spacecraft, docked together in a special pavilion.

Expo '74, in Spokane, Wash., the only major international exposition in the United States during its bicentennial decade, will open on May 4, 1974. It is expected to attract more than 4.8 million visitors during its six-month run. "Celebrating Tomorrow's Fresh, New Environment," Expo '74 is intended to stimulate a greater understanding of our environmental problems and their solutions. The $11.5-million U.S. pavilion will incorporate waterfalls, pools, and a garden courtyard overlooking the Spokane River and will remain as a permanent addition to the riverfront park.

U.S. Bicentennial. The United States will celebrate its 200th birthday in a far more modest manner than was originally anticipated. A shifting mood, widespread lack of interest, partisan politics, and inaction resulted in a considerable scaling down of the nation's plans to commemorate its bicentennial. There will be no grand federal expositions, parks, new buildings, or monuments. Instead, each state

Huge rings of steel, fashioned for every kind
of tunnel design, were among the exhibits at
the 1973 Hanover Trade Fair in West Germany.

and town, with limited federal assistance, will commemorate the nation's anniversary as it sees fit.

Plans that got underway in 1973 include the assembly of a frontier ranch in Lubbock, Tex., and a traveling heritage exhibition in California. Boston will refurbish its historic "Freedom Trail," and New Jersey plans to build a "Liberty Park" on a 45-acre waterfront site in Jersey City.

The only national project thus far to receive unanimous approval from the U.S. Bicentennial Commission is the American Bicentennial Fleet, Incorporated, which will consist of 100 steel barges that will carry the pavilions of major national corporations and states. These barges will cruise the waterways, rivers, the Great Lakes, the Gulf of Mexico, and both coasts from April 1, 1975, to Oct. 2, 1977.

A record $50 million in business was transacted at the fifth annual Discover America Pow Wow and Travel Mart, held in Tucson, Ariz., in September. Nearly 300 foreign tour operators from 46 countries met in a total of 8,000 one-to-one meetings with sales representatives from 587 airlines, hotels, motels, sightseeing companies, and a number of tourist attractions.   Lynn Beaumont

FARM MACHINERY. See MANUFACTURING.

FASHION

FASHION. The key to fashion in 1973 was the knitting needle, as the sweater became the number-one look on both sides of the Atlantic and Pacific. Sweaters turned up in sportive yarns by day; they lit up the nights with metallic threads.

There were sweater coats, sweater dresses, sweater suits—even sweater sweaters. Many of them were trimmed with fur, especially fox. Floor-length sweaters came with or without sparkle, the most luxurious being to-the-ankle cashmere shifts or one-shoulder sweaters trembling with sequins, rhinestones, or bugle beads. Sweater sweaters were longer, looser, and more rugged. The chunky, shawl-collared, belted cardigan—often in a brown-and-white Ecuadorean motif—replaced 1972's shrink

Fashions in 1973 echoed the roaring 1920s with designs reminiscent of flappers, sheiks, and what was known as the Gatsby look.

tops with the young blue-jeans crowd. Bulky Shaker knits, Irish fishermen's pullovers, and ribbed-tweed oversweaters were favored by sports-minded women of means. Cable-knit white tennis sweaters, inspired by a forthcoming film, *The Great Gatsby*, were the rage with men and women of all ages.

Everyone was in the sweater act in 1973: the high-fashion houses on Seventh Avenue, Rue Saint Honoré, and Via Veneto, as well as the workshops in Taiwan, Hong Kong, and Tokyo. Sales promotion exalted the sweater's warmth in view of the energy crisis, but the more immediate reason for its popularity was that it fit the mood of the moment. This was away from the revolutionarily new, and more toward the tried and true. Even the most innovative designers played it safe by offering fluid, functional, flattering clothes in familiar shapes: classic shirtwaists, the perennial pants suits, and sweaters. Hemlines settled in the vicinity of the knee.

Although some sprinklings of the midi reappeared in late-season collections, designers hastened to explain that they intended them only for a few fashion mavericks or as attention-getters in shop windows. Designers understood that women were not about to discard last year's garments, but were again building up wardrobes and looking for versatile purchases. Collecting season-crossing clothes was part of the new sentiment that outfits had to work harder and longer for a woman—be able to change with the simple addition of a shirt, pants, or a prized jewel.

Designers were also painfully aware in 1973 that the fashion dollar had to compete with the high cost of food. Furthermore, the fashion industry was plagued by its own raw materials crises. Shortages in cotton, wool, pelts – heavily bought up by Japan and Europe – made it difficult to keep garment price tags within reasonable limits. By the end of the year, there were indications of a synthetics squeeze as well. Such fabric and leather substitutes as polyvinyl chloride, a petrochemical derivative, grew scarce because of the oil shortage. Nylon was up; the cost of vinyl rose 30 per cent in the last quarter of 1973.

Simplification was the motto of the year and it took shape through the elimination of gew-gaws and the "layered" look. Silhouettes were starker, more minimal, conforming to what used to be called "good taste." Tight, high armholes of the last decade gave way to dropped shoulders and deep sleeves.

Proponents of this trend were Italy's Missoni, England's Jean Muir, and American avant-gardists Stephen Burrows, Scott Barrie, and Jon Kloss. Their dresses, which flowed with new ease, wafted and whirled in georgette, charmeuse, pongee, crepe de Chine, and jersey. They had yoked bodices, long torsos, shirred waists, blouson tops, and pleated or gathered skirts. The short black cocktail dress, strip-strapped "slip dress," and strapless tube were evening news. Neatly tailored suits, toppers, unlined clutch coats, balmacaans – as well as reversible haberdashery – had simplicity, practicality, and comfort.

Fabrics followed suit in flannels, tweeds, plaids, checks, and stripes in subdued color ranges – rust, peach, tangerine, and copper or forest green, loden green, pistachio, and celery. Black and white, camel and beige, in combinations or alone, prevailed.

Unmonumental Accessories were the norm: golden chains, gold-button earrings, rhinestone clips; oblong cashmere scarves or russet challis squares; shoes unburdened by platforms – high-heeled pumps, laced walking shoes, sandals, ghillies, T-straps, oxfords, newest in oxblood, dark green, or brandy-brown kid.

Perhaps the biggest change in the look of a fashionable woman was her shorter hair: a polished, shoulder-length page boy or a close crop with upturned bangs framing the face. Shorter hair prompted a yen for hats – tennis brims for summer, the shallow-crowned, tilted cloche for chillier weather. A chic evening conceit was the little black veiled hat, often accompanied by boas in fur or feathers.

Menswear was agreeable rather than aggressive. Sedate and urbane styling in inconspicuous colors led the trend in everything from suits and jackets to sweaters and sportswear. Flannels, often with chalky stripes and plaids, Shetlands, camel's hair, nubby tweeds, and muted plaids, expressed the new gentleness and gentlemanliness. News-making addenda were contrasting trim – particularly piping –

on blazers and suits, as well as bow ties and vests that matched or contrasted with jacket or trousers.

The big outerwear message was the new widened collar on polo coats, balmacaans, swanky raglans, and wrap-arounds. Pea jackets, baseball jackets, and varsity-type jackets went where the action was.

Fashion Events. The Coty American Fashion Critics' Awards on October 17 included Winnies to Stephen Burrows and Calvin Klein. Oscar de la Renta was voted into the Hall of Fame. A special award for "fashion at a price" went to 26-year-old Clovis Ruffin. Honored for accessories were: Don Kline, millinery; Judith Leiber, handbags; Michael Moreaux of Debaux and Celia Sebiri, jewelry; Beth Levine and Joe Famolare, shoes.

Menswear winners: a Winnie to Dimitri; a return award to Ralph Lauren of Polo; a special award to Don Robbie of Pierre Cardin, U.S.A.; a creative retailing award to Kackie Rogers, Roland Meledandri, and Berny Schwarz of Eric Ross.

A historic first took place at the Versailles Palace in France on November 29 when the cream of French and American couture presented a glittering joint fashion show. Sought-after invitations were awarded to five American designers: Bill Blass, Stephen Burrows, Halston, Anne Klein, and Oscar de la Renta. The five French couturiers were Marc Bohan of Dior, Pierre Cardin, Givenchy, Yves Saint Laurent, and Ungaro. *Kathryn Zahony Livingston*

FINLAND. Parliament was recalled on Sept. 3, 1973, a week early. Its first aims were to deal with a deteriorating labor situation and resolve differences with the European Community (Common Market). An agreement with the Common Market for free trade in industrial goods was initialed in July, 1972, but Foreign Minister Ahti Karjalainen was unable to get parliamentary approval. The Social Democrats offered to support it only if a package of "protective" economic laws was enacted first. These called for permanent powers to allow the government to maintain price and rent controls and prevent "distortion" of trade. One feature was a system of compulsory counter-cyclical deposits by companies during boom periods to counteract an unnatural boom. Another was a levy on corporate "windfall" profits, such as devaluation might provide.

The proposed new laws were opposed by Conservatives and Communists, but the agreement was ratified, 141 votes to 36, November 16.

Labor Problems. Collective bargaining on labor contracts, which run out in 1974, was held up until the fate of the economic laws was known. Inflation rose from a rate of 7 per cent in 1972 to 10 per cent in 1973, and unions lost control of militant labor groups.

From January to September, strikes cost more than 2 million working days. The breakdown of collective bargaining resulted in a chaotic free-for-all. Industrial workers won an increase averaging about

13 per cent, but with the 10 per cent growth in the cost of living, the gain was small, especially since bigger income tax payments were called for.

Funding Squeeze. Shortage of equipment, brought on by inflation and rising costs, hampered the training of the Finnish armed forces, according to the Finnish *Armed Forces Review*. It reported that soldiers had to shout "bang" instead of firing weapons because of a shortage of ammunition. It said the navy had to cancel half its planned maneuvers because of lack of money, and 13 of the 15 air force planes were inactive and awaiting servicing. It called the authorized $225 million inadequate.

Diplomatic representatives were exchanged on January 7 with East and West Germany. On March 12, Finland opened negotiations with the Council for Mutual Economic Assistance, the trade group of Communist Europe, on a cooperation agreement. Such an agreement would be the first between that body and a capitalist country. The outcome depended on passing of the new economic laws.

Parliament passed a bill on January 18 extending President Urho Kekkonen's term of office from 1974 to 1978. He first took office in 1956. Observers said the bill showed Finland's dedication to Kekkonen's long-standing policy of strict neutrality. Kenneth Brown

See also Europe (Facts in Brief Table).

FIRES. See DISASTERS.

FISHING. Conflicts over fishing rights increased in 1973 between commercial and sport fishermen. In October, 1972, Connecticut had limited commercial fishing on its waters in Long Island Sound by banning fishing with nets within 2 miles of shore. The action came after sport fishermen protested that large hauls of menhaden taken by commercial bunker boats reduced opportunities to fish for the bluefish that feed on the menhaden. On July 12, 1973, commercial fishermen won a temporary restraining order against the Connecticut law and began operating within a half mile of shore. Sport fishermen then harassed commercial trawlers by preventing them from retrieving their nets, and the court redrew the fishing limit lines on July 28 along a course that came closer to satisfying both sides.

Disputes between commercial seiners and sport fishermen at Cape Hatteras National Seashore in North Carolina led to new fishing rules there. The Outer Banks of the seashore provide some of the nation's greatest fishing for striped bass and other species. On July 8, the National Park Service restricted commercial fishing permits to residents.

More than 550 anglers aboard 138 boats took part in one of the largest big-game fishing tourneys ever, on August 4 and 5 in the northeastern Gulf of Mexico. Fishermen caught a total of 33 trophy fish, including billfish, dolphin, and wahoo. Andrew L. Newman

Ice fishing is a popular winter pastime on many of Finland's lakes. Perch and pike are among the chief targets of these patient sportsmen.

FISHING INDUSTRY. Intensified international fishing disputes and problems were underlined in 1973. Robert M. White, administrator of the U.S. National Oceanic and Atmospheric Administration, warned on May 11 that the world is nearing the limit of its fishery possibilities.

Peru's anchovy catch dropped from 10 million tons a year to about 2 million tons when a shift in equatorial currents warmed waters off Peru's Pacific coast and killed plankton, the major food source for anchovies. The reduced anchovy catch had worldwide repercussions, because Peru's anchovies normally contribute 70 per cent of the world's fish meal, a prime source of protein. Fish meal, which sold for $157 a ton in 1970, climbed to $500 a ton in 1973, setting off a chain reaction. Substitutes, such as soybeans, skyrocketed in price, and the prices of chicken and pork were pushed up. With more than 4,000 anchovy boats and their 22,000 crewmen idled, Peru nationalized its fishing industry on May 7. Anchovy stocks are not expected to reach levels that would permit renewed harvesting until after several more spawning periods.

The Cod War. Icelandic patrol boats and British frigates clashed in May and June in disputed fishing waters off the coast of Iceland. Concerned about depletion of valuable fishing stocks, Iceland extended its fishing zone from 12 miles to 50 miles in 1972. This denied British fishermen access to waters from which they took 208,000 tons of fish in 1971. In negotiations with Iceland, the British agreed to limit their catch to 145,000 tons. On October 2, the British agreed to withdraw their ships from the disputed area. See ICELAND.

Conservation Efforts. The International Whaling Commission, at its annual meeting in London in June, failed to enact the 10-year moratorium on killing whales sought by the United States and many world conservationists. Japan and Russia, who harvest about 85 per cent of the whale catch, blocked the three-fourths vote required to pass the moratorium.

Spokesmen for the American tuna fleet told a congressional panel in August that they cannot meet a 1974 deadline for halting the killing of porpoises accidentally trapped in their nets. Despite intensive efforts, which have reduced porpoise deaths per ton of yellowfin tuna from 5.4 in 1968 to 1.35 in 1973, the tuna operators said they need more time to devise better methods of protecting the porpoises.

United States commercial fishermen caught 4.7-billion pounds of fish and shellfish in 1972. This is a 6 per cent decline from the 5 billion pounds caught in 1971, but still 5 per cent above the annual average for the previous five years. The 1972 catch was worth about $704 million. The world fish catch in 1972 was about 143 billion pounds.   Andrew L. Newman

FLOODS. See DISASTERS.

FLORIDA. See STATE GOVERNMENT.

FLOWER. See GARDENING.

FOOD. The U.S. Food and Drug Administration (FDA) issued new regulations in 1973 to protect and aid consumers. Sweeping changes, some mandatory and others voluntary, were made in the labels that go on food products. Many food packagers were required to disclose the nutritional components of their products on the labels. They were also permitted to indicate on their packages the cholesterol and fat content of the foods being marketed. The FDA also discouraged excessive health claims sometimes made for food products.

Over the next two years, most of the nation's food packages are expected to be relabeled to provide details, including their content of calories, carbohydrates, fats, proteins, minerals, and vitamins.

Meanwhile, the National Live Stock and Meat Board issued a standard identification and labeling system for meat cuts and placed copies in shops to eliminate the confusion produced by regional and misleading names. Instructions for cooking the different cuts of meat were posted, along with the identification charts.

Food additives used to increase weight gains in farm animals, such as the hormone diethylstilbestrol (DES), were banned by the FDA. Experiments indicated that the additives may cause cancer in some animals, and small amounts of the additives are known to persist in meat from animals slaughtered and sold for human consumption.

The FDA invited the public to participate in a safety review of 533 foods. In addition, a basic program of consumer education was advocated that would help the shopper to read and understand the universal product code, open dating, and unit pricing, and the special vocabularies that are used in various food fields.

Food Prices. Government controls on food prices, especially beef, generally led to better distribution of available supplies but also to localized shortages and to temporary disruption of the industry. Foreign purchases of U.S. beef and poultry, especially by the Japanese, helped push meat prices to new highs in the United States.

Heavy purchases of U.S. food grains by Russia and other nations drained American stocks and raised prices for the U.S. consumer. Unfavorable conditions in the Pacific Ocean off Peru and in other Pacific fishing grounds cut heavily into the catch of anchovies and fish meal. In some American cities, consumers reacted to the price hikes triggered by all these conditions by staging boycotts or by forming consumer cooperatives to buy and distribute foods.

Frozen Foods. The hottest news in the American food market was the sharp increase in the sale and consumption of frozen convenience foods. The smaller, busier, and richer American families turned more eagerly than ever to frozen foods and dinners. Especially popular sellers were frozen vegetables that can be heated and eaten, mainly green beans

Thousands of angry shoppers staged a nationwide meat boycott in the United States in March and April to protest rising food prices.

and broccoli. Staggering quantities of potato products, especially frozen French fries, were sold. This increase in the consumption of vegetables was probably due to the shortages and high prices of meats. Frozen juices, cakes, and ethnic foods also set new sales records during the year.

But not all new frozen items won ready acceptance. Of the 12,912 new frozen products offered during 1973, only 3,972 remained permanently on sale in supermarket freezers. Indications were that frozen meat cuts had the brightest future. Frozen cuts can be marketed for about 8 per cent less in price than fresh meats, and they can be delivered to the consumer in more convenient portions and in less-deteriorated condition.

Food Trends underwent a few marked changes. Meat consumption generally declined, while the sale of frozen vegetables increased by about 6 per cent and fresh vegetables remained stable. But the average American still ate about 112.5 pounds of beef during 1973 (114.8 in 1972), 2.7 pounds of lamb (3.4), 41.6 pounds of chicken (42.9), and 9.1 pounds of turkey (8.9). In addition, he ate about 63.4 pounds of pork and 12.3 pounds of fish, slightly more than in 1972. The average per capita consumption of eggs declined by two dozen, from 318 to 294. Consumption of fresh, canned, and frozen fruits and juices increased by 2, 0.5, and 1 pound, respectively.

Per capita consumption of cheese increased slightly, from 13.2 to 13.9 pounds. Milk consumption declined, and butter continued to lose ground to margarine, 4.7 pounds of butter to 11.3 pounds of margarine per person. Potatoes declined, probably because of shortages and higher prices, from 120.9 pounds to just over 116 pounds. Beer, wine, and soft drink sales continued to rise, while the consumption of coffee continued to decline. Grocery store sales for the year were more than $100 billion, a record.

New Products. Most new products in 1973 came in frozen packages: bakery items, entrees, snacks, and concentrated juice drinks. Frozen cupcakes, apple fritters, and soft German pretzels vied for space in freezers with frozen oysters on the half shell with or without mornay sauce. Frozen bread mix came in a box that expands automatically in a heated oven to become a bread pan of the right size for the final loaf. Many supermarkets introduced a telephone service for ordering fresh-baked items, and more stores than ever before set up counters for specialty cheeses, seafoods, and party goodies.

Some grocery chains opened departments for natural, organic, and health foods in their stores; others began to invest in shops to sell these popular foods. The common American ice cream cone, once available everywhere, was once again becoming a popular treat for young people. The available variety of ice cream flavors was limited only by the imagination of the new purveyors.

Alma Lach

FOOTBALL. The Miami Dolphins and the Minnesota Vikings, both solid, experienced, and battle-tested, were professional football's most successful teams in 1973. But their exploits were overshadowed by the heroics of O. J. Simpson of the Buffalo Bills, who established himself, statistically at least, as history's outstanding runner.

In college football, the University of Notre Dame, coached by Ara Parseghian, upset Alabama in a memorable Sugar Bowl game and became national champion. Ohio State and Michigan, which had aspired to that honor, wound up instead in a bitter dispute over which team should represent the Big Ten conference in the Rose Bowl. Ohio State won the vote and the game.

Pro Play-Offs. The National Football League's (NFL) 26 teams played 14-game schedules from mid-September to mid-December. The six division winners and two wild-card teams advanced to the play-offs.

In the American Football Conference (AFC), the Dolphins easily defeated the Cincinnati Bengals, 34 to 16, and the Oakland Raiders beat the Pittsburgh Steelers, 33 to 14, in the first round. In the championship game, the Dolphins whipped the Raiders, 27 to 10, running for 266 yards against the AFC's top defense. In the National Football Conference's (NFC) first round, the Vikings stopped the Washington Redskins, 27 to 20, and the Dallas Cowboys eliminated the Los Angeles Rams, 27 to 16, but lost their

Standings in National Football Conference

Eastern Division	W.	L.	T.	Pc.
Dallas	10	4	0	.714
Washington	10	4	0	.714
Philadelphia	5	8	1	.393
St. Louis	4	9	1	.321
New York Giants	2	11	1	.179

Central Division	W.	L.	T.	Pc.
Minnesota	12	2	0	.857
Detroit	6	7	1	.464
Green Bay	5	7	2	.429
Chicago	3	11	0	.214

Western Division	W.	L.	T.	Pc.
Los Angeles	12	2	0	.857
Atlanta	9	5	0	.643
San Francisco	5	9	0	.357
New Orleans	5	9	0	.357

Standings in American Football Conference

Eastern Division	W.	L.	T.	Pc.
Miami	12	2	0	.857
Buffalo	9	5	0	.643
New England	5	9	0	.357
New York Jets	4	10	0	.286
Baltimore	4	10	0	.286

Central Division	W.	L.	T.	Pc.
Cincinnati	10	4	0	.714
Pittsburgh	10	4	0	.714
Cleveland	7	5	2	.571
Houston	1	13	0	.071

Western Division	W.	L.	T.	Pc.
Oakland	9	4	1	.679
Denver	7	5	2	.571
Kansas City	7	5	2	.571
San Diego	2	11	1	.179

National Conference Individual Statistics

Scoring	TDs.	E.P.	F.G.	Pts.
Ray, L.A.	0	40	30	130
Mike-Mayer, Atl.	0	34	26	112
Dempsey, Phil.	0	34	24	106
Gossett, S.F.	0	26	26	104

Passing	Att.	Comp.	Pct.	Yds.	TDs.
Staubach, Dallas	286	179	62.6	2,428	23
Tarkenton, Minn.	274	169	61.7	2,113	15
Hadl, L.A.	258	135	52.3	2,008	22
Gabriel, Phil.	460	270	58.7	3,219	23

Receiving	No. Caught	Total Yds.	Avg. Gain	TDs.
Carmichael, Phil.	67	1,116	16.7	9
Taylor, Wash.	59	801	13.6	7
Young, Phil.	55	854	15.5	6
Tucker, N.Y. Giants	50	681	13.6	5

Rushing	Att.	Yds.	Avg. Gain	TDs.
Brockington, G.B.	265	1,144	4.3	3
Hill, Dallas	273	1,142	4.2	6
McCutcheon, L.A.	210	1,097	5.2	2
Hampton, Atl.	263	997	3.8	4

Punting	No.	Yds.	Avg.	Longest
Wittum, S.F.	79	3,455	43.7	62
H. Weaver, Det.	54	2,333	43.2	66
Widby, G.B.	56	2,414	43.1	60
James, Atl.	63	2,682	42.6	72

Punt Returns	No.	Yds.	Avg.	TDs.
Taylor, S.F.	15	207	13.8	0
Stevens, N.O.	17	171	10.1	0
Bertelsen, L.A.	26	259	10.0	0
Brown, Atl.	40	360	9.0	0

American Conference Individual Statistics

Scoring	TDs.	E.P.	F.G.	Pts.
Gerela, Pittsburgh	0	36	29	123
Yepremian, Miami	0	38	25	113
Turner, Denver	0	40	22	106
Blanda, Oakland	0	31	23	100

Passing	Att.	Comp.	Pct.	Yds.	TDs.
Stabler, Oakland	260	163	62.7	1,997	14
Griese, Miami	218	116	53.2	1,422	17
Anderson, Cin.	329	179	54.4	2,428	18
Johnson, Denver	346	184	53.2	2,465	20

Receiving	No. Caught	Total Yds.	Avg. Gain	TDs.
Willis, Houston	57	371	6.5	1
Podolak, K.C.	55	445	8.1	0
Rucker, N.E.	53	743	14.0	3
Biletnikoff, Oak.	48	660	13.8	4

Rushing	Att.	Yds.	Avg. Gain	TDs.
Simpson, Buffalo	332	2,003	6.0	12
Csonka, Miami	219	1,003	4.6	5
E. Johnson, Cin.	195	997	5.1	4
Clark, Cin.	254	988	3.9	8

Punting	No.	Yds.	Avg.	Longest
Wilson, K.C.	80	3,642	45.5	68
Guy, Oakland	69	3,127	45.3	72
Van Heusen, Denver	69	3,114	45.1	78
Seiple, Miami	48	2,031	42.3	57

Punt Returns	No.	Yds.	Avg.	TDs.
Smith, S.D.	27	352	13.0	2
Thompson, Denver	30	366	12.2	0
Scott, Miami	22	266	12.1	0
Pruitt, Cleveland	16	180	11.3	0

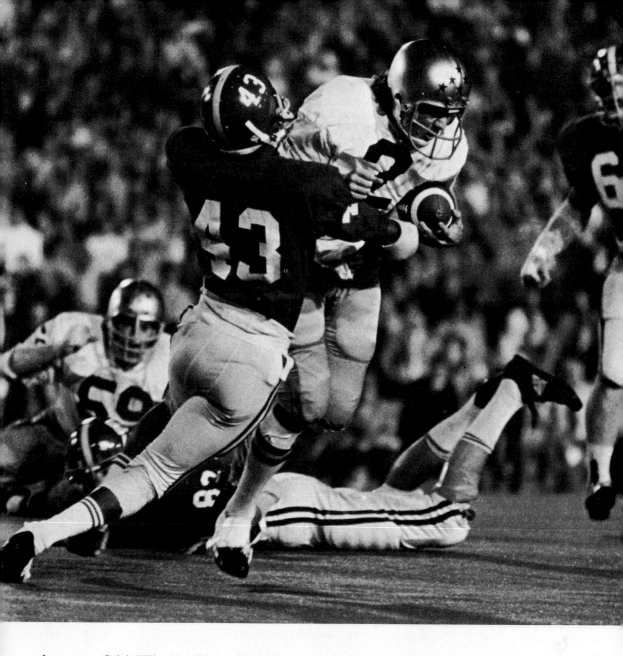

Quarterback Tom Clements of Notre Dame tries
to elude Alabama's Tyrone King during the
thrilling Irish Sugar Bowl victory, 24 to 23.

best runner, Calvin Hill, with a dislocated left elbow.
The Vikings then beat the Cowboys, 27 to 10, in the
conference final.

But in the Super Bowl game on Jan. 13, 1974, in
Houston's Rice Stadium, the Dolphins decisively
whipped the Vikings, 24 to 7. Fullback Larry Csonka
gained a record 145 yards in 33 carries as Miami won
its second straight Super Bowl.

The Dolphins, who climaxed a 1972 season of 17
consecutive victories by beating the Redskins, 14 to
7, in the previous Super Bowl on Jan. 14, 1973, won
their 1973 opener before losing to the Raiders, 12 to
7, on four field goals.

The best record in 1973 belonged to the Dolphins,
Vikings, and Rams, the surprise team of the year.

Each team had 12 victories and 2 defeats. The Dolphins used a strong running game. The Vikings were
led by quarterback Fran Tarkenton and rookie runner Chuck Foreman. The Rams were led by new
coach Chuck Knox and new offensive stars in John
Hadl, Harold Jackson, and Lawrence McCutcheon.

When Tommy Prothro failed to produce a winning
team in 1972, the Rams fired him and turned to
Knox, the offensive line coach for the Detroit Lions
and, before that, the New York Jets. Knox was in-

tense, patient, and organized. He also benefited from good trades.

Before the season, the Rams traded their sore-armed quarterback, Roman Gabriel, to the Philadelphia Eagles for Jackson, Tony Baker, and three draft choices, and they acquired Hadl from the San Diego Chargers to replace Gabriel. Hadl, in his words, "never played better." Jackson led the league by catching 13 touchdown passes. McCutcheon set a Rams record of 1,097 yards rushing.

Gabriel helped the Eagles win five games under their new coach, Mike McCormack. The New Orleans Saints won five games for their new coach, John North. The New England Patriots won five games for their new coach, Chuck Fairbanks. The Atlanta Falcons won nine games and seemed headed for the play-offs until they lost two of their last three games. The Buffalo Bills won nine games, a tribute to Simpson and a newly found offensive line.

Simpson's Success. For his first four years as a pro, Simpson had been widely acclaimed as perhaps the game's finest runner, and he gained big yardage despite inexperienced blockers. In 1973, the Bills' offensive line matured, and Simpson was off and running.

In the first game of the season, he ran for 250 yards, an NFL record, against the Patriots. He entered the season's final game, against the Jets, needing 61 yards to break Jim Brown's 1963 record of 1,863 yards rushing in one season. Simpson had those 61 yards before the first period ended, and he finished the game with 200 yards and a season total of 2,003. He also set NFL records for most rushes in one game (39) and one season (332), and he helped the Bills set an NFL record of 3,088 yards rushing in one season. At 26, Simpson had become a legend.

There were disappointing teams, too. The Houston Oilers posted a 1-13 record for the second straight year, and general manager Sid Gillman returned to coaching, replacing Bill Peterson in midseason. The New York Giants, winner of all 6 preseason games, finished the regular season 2-11-1, and coach Alex Webster quit. Coach Harland Svare resigned in favor of Ron Waller during the San Diego Chargers' 2-11-1 season. The Jets played most of the season without injured quarterback Joe Namath, and coach Wilbur (Weeb) Ewbank retired at 66 after a 4-10 season. He was succeeded by Charlie Winner, his son-in-law.

TV Blackout. For years, the NFL had promoted its product by televising road games but never home games. In 1973, that policy was changed by the Congress. Three days before the season opened, the Congress decreed that any game sold out 72 hours in advance could not be "blacked out" in the city in which it was being played.

The NFL was furious. How could it give away its product, it asked, and then try to sell it? It feared that many season ticketholders would stay home in bad weather, and fail to renew their tickets next year.

1973 College Conference Champions

Conference	School
Atlantic Coast	North Carolina State
Big Eight	Oklahoma
Big Sky	Boise State
Big Ten	Michigan-Ohio State (tie)
Ivy League	Dartmouth
Mid-American	Miami (Ohio)
Missouri Valley	Tulsa-North Texas State (tie)
Ohio Valley	Western Kentucky
Pacific Eight	Southern California
Southeastern	Alabama
Southern	East Carolina
Southwest	Texas
Western Athletic	Arizona-Arizona State (tie)
Yankee	Connecticut

The Bowl Games

Bowl	Winner	Loser
Astro-Bluebonnet	Houston 47	Tulane 7
Cotton	Nebraska 19	Texas 3
Fiesta	Arizona State 28	Pittsburgh 7
Gator	Texas Tech 28	Tennessee 19
Liberty	North Carolina State 31	Kansas 18
Orange	Penn State 16	Louisiana State 9
Rose	Ohio State 42	Southern California 21
Sugar	Notre Dame 24	Alabama 23
Sun	Missouri 34	Auburn 17

All-America Team (as picked by UPI)

Offense
Ends—Lynn Swann, Southern California; Dave Casper, Notre Dame.
Tackles—John Hicks, Ohio State; Daryl White, Nebraska.
Guards—Buddy Brown, Alabama; Bill Yoest, North Carolina State.
Center—Bill Wyman, Texas.
Quarterback—David Jaynes, Kansas.
Running Backs—John Cappelletti, Penn State; Roosevelt Leaks, Texas; Archie Griffin, Ohio State.

Defense
Ends—Van DeCree, Ohio State; Roger Stillwell, Stanford.
Tackles—John Dutton, Nebraska; Randy Crowder, Penn State.
Middle Guard—Lucious Selmon, Oklahoma.
Linebackers—Randy Gradishar, Ohio State; Richard Wood, Southern California.
Defensive Backs—Mike Townsend, Notre Dame; Artimus Parker, Southern California; Dave Brown, Michigan; Randy Rhino, Georgia Tech.

The first fear was borne out. More than a million seats, or 10 per cent of the total sold to season ticketholders, went unused during the year. On the last day of the season, the holders of 35,793 seats in Kansas City stayed home rather than brave 20-degree cold. The game was televised locally.

Other Problems. The NFL faced other problems –dullness, player relations, drugs, and a challenge from a new league. The excitement that had made pro football so successful started to wane. A 1972 rules change, which started all plays closer to the middle of the field rather than the sidelines, was intended to help the passing game by impairing zone defenses. Instead, it led to more running, and to more field goals (the kicker now had a better angle). Scoring decreased, touchdowns decreased, and most teams adopted a no-risk offense.

The NFL worried not only about play but also about players. Its four-year contract with the National Football League Players Association, governing all working conditions except individual salaries, expired after the 1973 season. The players association was militant, and it was angry at Commissioner Alvin (Pete) Rozelle for his indefinite suspension of Lance Rentzel, the Rams' wide receiver, for possession of drugs. Rentzel had been on probation after a conviction for indecent exposure. A greater drug problem existed in the reputed wide use by players of amphetamines before games. George Burman, a veteran reserve center for the Redskins, said that one-third of the Redskins used that drug.

New League. A fresh challenge faced the NFL with the formation of the World Football League (WFL). It planned to start play in 1974 with from 8 to 12 teams, including one in Honolulu. Each team would play 20 games on weekday nights from June to November. The WFL planned six rules changes, including: (1) two-point conversion attempts would be optional; (2) kickoffs would be made from the 30-yard line rather than the 40 to promote runbacks; and (3) long, unsuccessful field-goal attempts would be returned to the line of scrimmage.

The new league, if it got off the ground, was not expected to spirit away many NFL players at first. But it posed a threat to the nine-team Canadian Football League (CFL) because it seemed likely to compete with the CFL for players.

Canadian Football. The CFL continued to fight to keep solvent, and it worried that the NFL and WFL would expand into Canada. However, it bid against the NFL for a few blue-ribbon players, and it enjoyed occasional success. Its 1973 prize was Johnny Rodgers, the Nebraska back, Heisman Trophy winner, and number-one draft choice of the San Diego Chargers of the NFL. Rodgers signed with the Montreal Alouettes and became a wide receiver and CFL rookie of the year. In the Grey Cup championship game, the Ottawa Rough Riders defeated the Edmonton Eskimos, 22 to 18, on November 25 in Toronto.

College Champion. When the regular season ended, the major teams with the best record were Alabama (11-0), Penn State (11-0), Notre Dame (10-0), Miami of Ohio (10-0), Oklahoma (10-0-1), Michigan (10-0-1), and Ohio State (9-0-1). United Press International's board of coaches, voting before the bowl games, named Alabama as national champion. The National Football Foundation said it would recognize the winner of the Notre Dame-Alabama Sugar Bowl game in New Orleans on New Year's Eve as national champion. The Associated Press delayed its vote until after the bowl games.

Alabama was a 7-point favorite in the Sugar Bowl, but Notre Dame won, 24 to 23. With three minutes left, Notre Dame was backed up to its 2-yard line, with third down and 8 yards to go for a first down. On the next play, quarterback Tom Clements completed a 35-yard pass to tight end Robin Weber to get out of danger.

The Associated Press poll of writers then named Notre Dame as national champion, with Ohio State second, Oklahoma third, Alabama fourth, Penn State fifth, and Michigan sixth. Penn State defeated Louisiana State, 16 to 9, in the Orange Bowl in Miami and Ohio State whipped Southern California, 42 to 21, in the Rose Bowl in Pasadena, Calif., both on Jan. 1, 1974. Oklahoma was banned from bowl games as part of a two-year probation assessed by the National Collegiate Athletic Association for recruiting violations.

Ohio State and Michigan, both undefeated and untied to that point, met November 24 in Ann Arbor, Mich., to decide the Big Ten champion and Rose Bowl representative. When they played a 10-to-10 tie, the Big Ten athletic directors had to choose a bowl team. By a 6-4 vote, they picked Ohio State. Michigan coach Glenn (Bo) Schembechler charged that "petty jealousies were involved" and accused Big Ten commissioner Wayne Duke of influencing the directors' vote.

John Cappelletti, Penn State running back, won the Heisman Trophy as the nation's outstanding college player. Frank Litsky

FORD, GERALD RUDOLPH (1913-   ), was confirmed by Congress and sworn into office as the 40th Vice-President of the United States on Dec. 6, 1973. Ford, a Republican congressman from Michigan and minority leader in the U.S. House of Representatives, replaced Spiro T. Agnew, who resigned on October 10. See AGNEW, SPIRO T.

President Richard M. Nixon named Ford as Agnew's successor on October 12. It was the first time in U.S. history that a Vice-President had been replaced in midterm. Political analysts considered the nomination of a noncontroversial figure such as Ford to be a wise decision, and most congressmen immediately expressed their approval.

Ford was born on July 14, 1913, in Omaha, Nebr. His name was originally Leslie King, but his parents divorced when he was 2 years old and his mother married a Grand Rapids, Mich., paint manufacturer who adopted the boy and renamed him after himself.

Ford earned his bachelor's degree in 1935 at the University of Michigan, where he was a star football player. He received his law degree in 1941 from Yale University, then practiced law in Grand Rapids. During World War II, he served as an officer in the Navy. Ford was elected to Congress in 1948, winning 60.5 per cent of the vote, and became House minority leader in 1965.

Ford married Elizabeth Bloomer in 1948. They have four children. Darlene R. Stille

FOREST AND FOREST PRODUCTS. Soaring demand and the end of price controls resulted in skyrocketing prices for lumber and plywood products in the United States in the first half of 1973. To increase the domestic supply of wood products and thus help restrain prices, the Nixon Administration on May 29 directed the National Forest Service to increase sales of timber from its lands by 10 per cent in 1973 and 1974.

The accelerated cutting will increase the amount of timber sold annually from national forests to about 11.8 billion board feet. The Administration also announced in May that Japan had voluntarily agreed to reduce imports of logs from the United States by 8 per cent.

On September 24, a presidential panel recommended increases of from 50 to 100 per cent in logging on federal lands. The report also approved clear-cutting, the controversial practice of logging all the trees in a selected area.

The worst forest fires in 20 years ravaged 200,000 acres in California, Oregon, Washington, Idaho, and western Montana in August. Damage estimates exceeded $100 million. However, spokesmen for lumber companies said they could salvage up to 90 per cent of the wood if they could remove it before insects infested the burned trees.   Andrew L. Newman

FORMOSA. See Taiwan.

FOSSE, BOB (1927-   ), became the first person ever to win three major show-business honors in the United States in one year. In 1973, he won an Oscar for his direction of the motion picture *Cabaret;* two Tonys for directing and choreographing *Pippin,* a Broadway musical; and three television Emmy awards for producing, directing, and choreographing "Singer Presents Liza with a 'Z,' " starring Liza Minnelli.

Fosse was born in Chicago on June 23, 1927. He went to dancing school, and started dancing in vaudeville and burlesque shows at the age of 13. Later, he studied acting in New York City, was a chorus dancer in national tours of Broadway shows, and made his Broadway debut in 1950 in the revue *Dance Me a Song.* He then danced and sang in three Hollywood musicals: *Affairs of Dobie Gillis, Kiss Me Kate,* and *Give a Girl a Break.* Returning to Broadway, he choreographed dances for *The Pajama Game* in 1954 and *Damn Yankees* in 1955. He won his first Tony awards with them and began his collaboration with *Damn Yankees* star Gwen Verdon, who became his wife in 1960. Then came a string of hits, including *My Sister Eileen, Bells Are Ringing,* and film versions of *The Pajama Game* and *Damn Yankees.*   Lillian Zahrt

FOUR-H CLUBS. See Youth Organizations.

FUTURE FARMERS OF AMERICA (FFA). See Youth Organizations.

Timber is loaded at Tacoma, Wash., for shipment to Japan. Such exports led to U.S. lumber shortages, and Japan agreed in May to limit imports.

FRANCE

FRANCE. The Gaullist coalition lost about 100 seats in legislative elections in March, 1973, but held its absolute majority in the National Assembly. Gaullist parties won 294 of the 490 seats, defeating the Socialists and Communists in the most hotly contested election since the Fifth Republic was established in 1958. Foreign Minister Maurice Schumann was among those who lost Assembly seats as a result of the election.

More than 80 per cent of the eligible voters cast ballots in the two-day election, held March 4 and 11. The losses of the Gaullist party, the Union of Democrats for the Republic, will force it to depend more on its allies, the Independent Republicans and the Center for Democracy and Progress.

Reform Program. Trade unions announced plans to fight for social advances promised during the March election. These included full pensions at age 60, a 40-hour workweek, more opportunities for women, and salary increases in all areas. The Communist-dominated labor union, the Confederation Genéralé du Travail (CGT), demanded, "Settle the social program, or it will be the action of the workers which will settle the matter."

President Georges Pompidou interpreted the elec-

Saudi Arabia's King Faisal, arriving in Paris to discuss Middle East oil cutbacks, is met at Orly Airport by President Georges Pompidou, right.

tion results for his Council of Ministers on March 14. France, he said, had expressed the desire that "stability and renewal, continuity and change, be reconciled." Pompidou reappointed Pierre Messmer prime minister on March 28. Edgar Faure, twice prime minister under the Fourth Republic, was elected president of the National Assembly on April 2. Faure is an author and scholar.

Nuclear Tests. France conducted five nuclear tests in July and August on Mururoa Atoll in the South Pacific Ocean in defiance of the International Court of Justice and protests at home and overseas. Australian Minister of Justice Lionel Murphy went to Paris on April 18 to ask France to cancel the tests. He was told that France "will not renounce the necessary steps to perfect her nuclear defense weapon."

New Zealand, similarly rebuffed, took the matter to the International Court of Justice at The Hague. The government answered on May 16 that France did not recognize the competence of the International Court to rule on the tests, because they were "concerned with France's national defense." When the court, on June 23, ordered France not to carry out the tests, France again refused to be bound by the ruling. Trade union action in other countries in the first week of July included a boycott of French goods, transport, and communications.

French cardinals and bishops found themselves pitted against generals and admirals over the issue. The navy chief of staff told the clergy to "render unto Caesar the things which are Caesar's. . . ." He said it was the clerics' business "to preach the faith and to dispense charity."

Labor Trouble. Most serious of many strikes in France during the year was one by air-traffic controllers that began on February 20. The armed services took over flight and radar control during the strike. The midair crash of two Spanish planes over western France on March 5, which killed 68, was blamed on improper control. British European Airways and 30 other airlines then canceled flights to France, and the French Airline Pilots Association called on its members not to fly. The strike ended on March 19.

A wildcat strike by 373 immigrant workers at the Renault automobile factory at Billancourt on March 29 caused 7,000 others to be laid off. The plant was closed on April 17, but work resumed on April 23.

When a watch factory near Besançon was closed because of bankruptcy on August 15, the 1,280 workers seized 60,000 watches "to guarantee our wages." Sympathy demonstrations were held in many centers, and police guarded the factory. There were no radio or television programs on August 23, when all the staff, including journalists, stopped work for 24 hours in sympathy.

Student Unrest. In anti-Vietnam War riots in Paris in January, 700 young people, most of them students, were arrested. Thousands of students marched again on March 21, against a law that virtually ended draft deferments for college students. Authorities said 70 to 80 per cent of the nation's 152,000 high school students joined the strike. On April 2 and 19, the students continued their protests, and the laws were eased on April 29.

Foreign Affairs. Russian Communist Party leader Leonid I. Brezhnev held talks with Pompidou in Paris on January 11 and 12. They failed to resolve their differences on the reduction of military forces in Europe. Pompidou also met in Paris with British Prime Minister Edward Heath on May 21 and with U.S. President Richard M. Nixon in Reykjavík, Iceland, on May 30 and 31. Pompidou went to Russia in June and to China in September.

Common Market. Enlargement of the European Community (Common Market) on January 1 led to arguments between France and West Germany on agricultural and regional policies. France demanded higher prices for milk and beef and more "regionalization." Inflation continued steadily, but Pompidou said it was better than an economic slowdown. In November, controls were applied to retail food profits. Thousands of Paris produce shops closed in protest.   Kenneth Brown

See also EUROPE (Facts in Brief Table).

GABON. See AFRICA.

GAMBIA. See AFRICA.

Traffic control at the port of Le Havre gets a radar system presenting televised images. It uses a technique borrowed from aviation radar.

GAMES, MODELS, AND TOYS. Inventors and manufacturers rushed games derived from the Watergate scandal to market in 1973. "The Watergate Game" (the last person to stay out of jail is declared the winner) sold out its first printing of 10,000 in four days.

Howard Mercer, a former Los Angeles disk jockey, and Joe Sugarman, a Chicago advertising man, invented the "Watergate Scandal Game," described as "a game of cover-up and deception for the whole family." The object of the "Watergate Caper Game" was to gain investigative points by indicting and convicting various officials.

The Public Action Coalition on Toys was formed in February in New York City. The coalition wants the toy industry to allow consumer advisory groups to "preview (not censor) toy advertising and packaging and to accept stricter policing of toy safety standards." The coalition was denied booth space at the 1973 National Toy Fair. Randolph Barton, vice-president of the Toy Manufacturers of America (TMA), said the toy industry viewed the coalition as pushing an idea whose time had not yet arrived.

Production Up. Figures compiled by the TMA showed that the 1972 wholesale value of toys manufactured in the United States reached $2.6-billion, a 12 per cent increase over 1971. The TMA forecast a 10 per cent increase in 1973.

A trend toward safer toys was evidenced by the popularity of soft, cuddly, stuffed toys. These included pandas, toy cars made of synthetic foam that are silent and won't scratch furniture or hurt children, and "the friendly football," which doesn't hurt if it hits you.

Sales rose for table football, basketball, and hockey games but languished for baseball games. "We used to manufacture two baseball games," said Barton, executive vice-president of Parker Brothers. "Now we have none and it's the same throughout the industry."

With the United States out of the war in Vietnam, some of the public pressure against war toys eased, but the trend in toy guns was still away from military and toward Western types. Toy airports in realistic detail and models of the supersonic transport airplanes gained in popularity.

Model Making. Bucky Servaites of Kettering, Ohio, regained his grand national championship at the 42nd annual National Model Airplane Championships in Chicago and Oshkosh, Wis., in August. Servaites also won the national open championship. The senior national championship went to Brian Pardue of Greensboro, N.C., and the junior national championship was won by Bruce Pailet of Brookfield, Glen Head, N.Y. The Dixie Whiz Kids were winners of the national team championship, and the Chicago Aeronuts were the year's club team champions.   Theodore M. O'Leary

GARDENING. Soaring food prices in the United States during 1973 brought about a resurgence of interest in vegetable and fruit gardening. There also were signs that plant patenting will increase because of changes in the law governing it during the year.

Under the old law, only plants reproduced by asexual means such as grafting, rooting, or cuttings could be patented. The new provisions mean that plants normally propagated by seeds may also be protected. Patents grant the originator of a new plant the right to control its production and sale completely for 17 years.

All-America Plants of 1973 included two flowers and a vegetable. "Peter Pan Scarlet" zinnia, an early, large-flowered dwarf, won a silver medal. Winners of bronze medals were "Happy Face" marigold with double, golden flowers on 26-inch stems, and "Aristocrat" hybrid zucchini squash, an early bearer of spoilage-resistant fruits.

All-America roses included "Perfume Delight," a fragrant, bright-pink hybrid tea; and two floribundas, the white "Bon-Bon" and the pink-orange "Bahia." All-America gladioli were "Big Daddy," a creamy-peach 7-footer; "Mexicali Rose," a silvery-edged, rose-pink flower; and "Brightside," a red-edged, yellow flower.

Other noteworthy plants introduced included "Lakemont" and "Suffolk Red," two seedless grapes; "Rippled Velvet," a hardy, hybrid tea rose; and "Jumbo," a 2-pound apple.

Awards. In Swarthmore, Pa., the celebrated Arthur Hoyt Scott medal and $1,000 gift were awarded to George H. M. Lawrence, director emeritus of Carnegie-Mellon University's Hunt Library in Pittsburgh.

Boston's Massachusetts Horticultural Society presented the following awards: Thomas Roland Medal to George L. Slate of Geneva, N.Y., for the development of many small fruits and lilies; Jackson Dawson Medal to David Leach for his work with rhododendrons; Gold Medals to Henry T. Skinner for his development of the U.S. National Arboretum and to John E. Voight, director, for development of the Milwaukee County Park System. The Ecology Award went to Paul Brooks of Boston, a writer, editor, and promoter of conservation.

The Liberty Hyde Bailey Medal, highest award of the American Horticultural Society, went to Louis C. Chadwick, professor emeritus of Ohio State University, Columbus, and the Pennsylvania Horticultural Society's Distinguished Achievement Medal went to Henry T. Skinner. The American Society for Horticultural Science presented the Gourley Award to Cecil Stushnoff of the University of Minnesota for his work on cold hardiness. Its Distinguished Teaching Award went to Steve Fazio of the University of Arizona.   Edwin F. Steffek

GAS AND GASOLINE. See ENERGY; PETROLEUM AND GAS.

GEOLOGY. Helgafell volcano erupted on Jan. 23, 1973, and opened a mile-long gash near the town of Vestmannaeyjar on Iceland's island of Heimaey. After two weeks, the volcanic cone had grown 700 feet high, and in three months, lava increased the island's eastern area by more than half a square mile. Lava and ash from the volcano nearly engulfed the town and threatened to block the harbor. Over 100 homes were destroyed or damaged.

Volcanic eruptions are common in the region because Iceland and its adjacent islands lie on the Mid-Atlantic Ridge, most of which is under the ocean. Molten rock bubbles to the surface along this ridge, and it is an area subject to earthquakes and various underground movements that occur beneath the ocean floor

On April 5, the snow-capped Hudson volcano in Chile exploded in a gigantic fireball that killed 2 persons and more than 1,000 animals. Debris from the 7,500-foot-high volcano, dormant for almost two years, fell over a 25-mile area in the Huemules Valley, a thinly populated cattle-raising region about 900 miles south of Santiago. The volcano last erupted in August, 1971, killing 15 persons.

California Earthquake. A rolling earthquake shook the southern California coast on February 21. Office buildings trembled and swayed in downtown Los Angeles, windows were shattered, and plaster was cracked in thousands of homes and office buildings along the coast. There were few serious injuries, however, and no reported deaths.

Seismologists at the California Institute of Technology measured the intensity of the quake at 5.75 on the Richter scale. The last major earthquake to hit southern California occurred on Feb. 9, 1971, when a minor earth fault snapped at the foot of the San Gabriel Mountains on the northwest rim of the San Fernando Valley, killing 62 persons.

Oldest Pterosaur Tracks. Fossil footprints made by pterosaurs were found in July on a slab of Navajo sandstone near Moab, Utah. The prints were discovered by Jim Ottinger, a guide, and geologist William Lee Stokes of the University of Utah. Stokes said that these are the oldest known traces of this peculiar reptile.

Pterosaurs were winged lizards that lived during the Mesozoic Era, from 150 million to 65 million years ago. They had long beaks, and claws on each wing, which were leathery membranes. Their wingspread ranged from less than 1 foot to nearly 30 feet.

North Carolina Glacier? In February, 1973, James O. Berkland and Loren A. Raymond of Appalachian State University in Boone, N.C., announced evidence of prehistoric glaciers on Grandfather Mountain in western North Carolina. The apparent glaciation tracks were in the form of polished bedrock,

A new volcanic island has been added to the Iwo Jima chain in the Pacific Ocean. Japanese seismologists first noted the volcano's rumbling in May.

grooves, striations, and gouge marks in the bedrock found at an elevation of 4,450 feet. Prior to this discovery, few geologists believed that continental glacial ice occurred south of northern Pennsylvania, the most southerly known advance of the glaciers.

As glacial ice advances over a region, it scours, plucks, and plows the bedrock and soil over which it slides. This material becomes embedded in the base of the glacier and is carried along, scraping on the bedrock beneath. This process produced the polished, scratched, grooved, and gouged bedrock surface found on Grandfather Mountain, the two scientists believed.

In early 1974, however, Raymond said that "we goofed." He and Berkland, he said, had found that the grooves actually were caused by cables used in logging operations in the area during World War I. The new finding does not disprove the idea that glaciers once existed in North Carolina, Raymond said. "Though it takes away what we thought was the best evidence of glaciation, it doesn't alter our view," he said. He noted that skeletal traces of some animals now confined to northern regions have been found as far south as Florida, and that there is proof of there having been adequate precipitation for glaciation in the area.

Oldest Rocks. In July, geologist E. V. Sobotovich of the Institute of Geochemistry and Mineral Physics of the Ukrainian Academy of Sciences found 4-billion-year-old rocks in Antarctica, the oldest rocks on earth. They are more than 200 million years older than the rocks found in Greenland in 1971 by L. P. Black of the University of Oxford, England.

Diamonds. Evidence is accumulating that diamonds are formed deep in the earth and forced to the surface by rocketlike eruptions. Diamonds are a form of carbon that solidifies in pressures that are comparable to those 90 miles below the earth's surface. They are usually found in subsurface "pipes," columns of fragments of rock a few hundred feet in diameter.

According to a new theory developed by Thomas R. McGetchin of the Massachusetts Institute of Technology, a combination of gases in their fluid form, under extremely high pressure in the earth's upper mantle, triggers eruptions in the pipelike columns. When the pressure becomes great enough, the material begins forcing its way up through the crust.

Geodynamics Project. A six-year program to study the motions of the interior of the earth was designed in 1973. Known as the International Geodynamic Project, the 52-nation effort will begin in 1974. New techniques are being developed as part of the project to chart internal structures of the earth by means of sound and to record the subtle warping of the terrain that reveals activity far below. The project has its roots in the recent accumulation of evidence that the earth's surface constitutes a mosaic of gigantic moving plates.   Thomas X. Grasso

GEORGIA. See STATE GOVERNMENT.

GERMANY, DEMOCRATIC REPUBLIC OF (EAST), opened its windows to the non-Communist world in 1973. East Berlin established diplomatic relations with numerous countries during the year, among them Argentina, Denmark, Ethiopia, Finland, France, Great Britain, Iceland, Japan, Luxembourg, Mexico, the Netherlands, Spain, and Switzerland. The government also began talks in August about establishing formal relations with the United States.

East Germany also ratified the good-will treaty it had signed with West Germany in December, 1972. This pact paved the way for closer East-West relations. On September 18, both East and West Germany were admitted to the United Nations (UN).

In applying for UN membership, East Germany had pledged to "contribute to strengthening European and international security and promote worldwide cooperation on the basis of the principles of sovereign equality of states." The question of war reparations was raised by some countries as the price East Germany should pay for worldwide recognition in its 24th year. The Americans, Dutch, Finns, and Israelis were all said to be considering claims for war reparations or the nationalization of industrial assets after World War II.

The Divided City of Berlin continued as a stumbling block to further rapprochement, however. Its West sector was still under four-power control. On August 13, the 12th anniversary of the wall that divides Berlin, Kurt Neubauer, West Berlin's acting burgomaster (mayor), denounced the wall as a "barbarous monster." But the East Germans replied that fortified borders with the West were still needed.

Frontier traffic was particularly heavy. Almost 4,440,000 West Germans visited East Germany between January 1 and August 8. In the same period, 933,719 East Germans visited West Germany.

The Economy. National income rose by 5.4 per cent, with a 6 per cent growth in manufacturing. Nearly all enterprises fulfilled their plan targets. The 1973 plan, calling for consumer goods production to grow by 7 per cent and investment goods by 5 per cent, was a radical reversal of traditional priorities in East Germany. Observers felt the decision to emphasize consumer goods was designed to avoid unrest by raising the standard of living. Growth of 13 per cent in investment was to extend automation and help to overcome labor shortages.

Foreign Trade. Under the Council for Mutual Economic Assistance, the East European trade pact also called COMECON, plans went ahead for joint chemical and automobile production with Czechoslovakia, Hungary, and Poland.

East Germany's head of state, Walter Ulbricht, 80, died on August 1. Regarded as the creator of East Germany, Ulbricht was general secretary of the ruling Socialist Unity Party from 1950 to 1971. Kenneth Brown

See also EUROPE (Facts in Brief Table).

West Berlin children peer through a hole torn in the Berlin Wall by irate West Berliners after East German guards fired on fleeing refugees.

GERMANY, FEDERAL REPUBLIC OF (WEST).

Chancellor Willy Brandt had a difficult year in 1973. His administration fought inflation, a wave of un-official strikes, and an attack on the Deutsche mark. A Brandt announcement on January 18 suggested a switch in diplomatic emphasis, stressing Western European unity and the European Community (Common Market) goals.

After West Germany had absorbed a billion un-wanted U.S. dollars in January, the Cabinet imposed foreign-exchange controls. Speculators disposed of dollars in exchange for Deutsche marks as the dol-lar's value went down. In March, the mark was re-valued by 3 per cent, but a further revaluation of 5.5 per cent was considered necessary on June 29 after the dollar exchange rate sank to 2.473 Deutsche marks. Finance Minister Helmut Schmidt said the anti-inflation program was threatened by enforced purchases of other currencies.

Rising Inflation. West Germany had its highest inflation rate in 20 years – 7.5 per cent. On February 18, the government increased taxes on the rich, on motorists, and on commerce. A state bond issue was floated, aimed at soaking up liquid capital that de-veloped, in part, from speculation during the inter-national monetary crisis. These measures were not enough. On May 9, a second anti-inflation package of money, credit, and public spending policies was instituted to take $5.89 billion out of the economy.

Economics Minister Hans Friderichs appealed to employers and trade unions to show restraint in price increases and wage demands. By August 9, the infla-tion rate had dropped to 7.2 per cent, but a wave of unofficial strikes brought a new threat.

The strikes began in the industrial state of North Rhine-Westphalia, with workers demanding raises beyond those already negotiated to combat rising prices. Brandt intervened in an August 27 broadcast appealing to business and unions for industrial peace.

The strikes spread to the states of Hesse and Schleswig-Holstein, and closed Cologne's huge Ford automobile plant. Most strikers returned to work at the end of August, but new outbreaks came when new wage talks between engineering employers and trade unions broke down on September 5.

Foreign Policy. In Paris on January 22, at a cere-mony to mark the 10th anniversary of the Franco-German friendship treaty, Brandt said, "The com-munity of peace which we founded together means that European union will become a force for peace." But during the year, differences between the two countries led to growing strain. They disagreed on the Common Market's agricultural policy, troop re-ductions in Europe, and relations between the mar-ket and the United States. The French charged that Germany was drifting to neutralism; the more con-servative opposition parties in West Germany held similar views. The Bonn government denied there was a rift, and on September 13 Brandt told the Bundestag (parliament) that the North Atlantic Treaty Organization and the Common Market remained the bases of his policy.

Russian Communist Party leader Leonid I. Brezhnev visited Bonn in May for three days of talks. He and Chancellor Brandt agreed that the four-power pact on Berlin must be strictly applied as an "essential prerequisite" for peace in central Europe.

Two brief ceremonies in Bonn on June 20 concluded the bilateral phase of West Germany's détente policy with Eastern Europe. Instruments ratifying the general relations treaty with East Germany were exchanged and a nonaggression pact with Czechoslovakia was initialed. The Czechoslovak agreement became possible when the two governments agreed that the 1938 Munich agreement by which Hitler took the Sudetenland from Czechoslovakia was void.

The state government of Bavaria asked the constitutional court whether the treaty with East Germany was in keeping with the "basic law." The court ruled on July 31 that it was. West Germany was admitted to the United Nations on September 18.

Opposition leader Rainer Barzel resigned on May 9, to be succeeded by Karl Carstens. The Cabinet approved a draft bill to change the divorce laws and improve the rights of women.   Kenneth Brown

See also EUROPE (Facts in Brief Table).

GHANA. The military government of Ghana appeared to gain confidence in 1973. On January 13, the first anniversary of the coup that deposed former Prime Minister Kofi A. Busia, the government released 67 political prisoners. Several of the prisoners had been ministers in Busia's Progressive Party. But about 200 other party members remained in jail.

Former supporters of the late President Kwame Nkrumah, who was overthrown in 1966, appeared to gain influence. Nkrumah's finance minister was reportedly advising Chairman Ignatius Kutu Acheampong, head of the ruling National Redemption Council. In August, five persons were arrested and charged with plotting to overthrow the military government. Two were former ministers in Nkrumah's government.

In March, Ghana reportedly asked the World Bank to reschedule its entire $300-million debt. Also, Ghana refused to reconsider its repudiation of a $94-million debt owed to Great Britain.

On March 28, Ghana announced that it was extending its territorial waters limit from 12 to 30 miles, so that the government could control the continental shelf and possible oil deposits there. Ghana also reserved a 100-mile fishing zone.   John Storm Roberts

See also AFRICA (Facts in Brief Table).

GIRL SCOUTS. See YOUTH ORGANIZATIONS.
GIRLS' CLUBS. See YOUTH ORGANIZATIONS.

West German Chancellor Willy Brandt, center, passes concentration-camp mural in Jerusalem's Yad Vashem memorial to Jewish victims of Nazis.

GOLF. Jack Nicklaus and Tom Weiskopf, both from Columbus, Ohio, and former students at Ohio State University, were the most successful professional golfers in 1973. Nicklaus won seven tournaments and, at the age of 33, became the all-time leader in winning major championships. Weiskopf, in an 11-week span from May to July, won 5 of the 8 tournaments he played.

Nicklaus captured the Professional Golfers' Association (PGA) championship, Tournament of Champions, Bing Crosby Pro-Amateur, Atlanta Golf Classic, Greater New Orleans Open, the Ohio-Kings Island Open, and the Walt Disney World Classic. The PGA victory was his 14th in major tournaments (3 PGA's, 3 United States Opens, 2 British Opens, 4 Masters, and 2 United States Amateurs). Bobby Jones held the previous record of 13. As Weiskopf said, "Jack's the greatest player who ever played the game." He is also the richest. His 1973 earnings of $308,362, the most on the tour, raised his career total to $2,012,068.

The 30-year-old Weiskopf had the best streak in tournament competition since Byron Nelson won 11 tournaments in a row in 1945. In order, Weiskopf was first in the Colonial National Invitation, second in the Atlanta Golf Classic, first in the Kemper Open and the Philadelphia Golf Classic, third in the United States Open, fifth in the American Golf Classic, and first in the British Open and the Canadian Open. In those eight tournaments, he won $185,605, averaged 68.9 strokes per round, and was 77 under par.

Nicklaus, Weiskopf, and Bruce Crampton, an Australian with a precision game, led the money-winners. Crampton won the Phoenix, Tucson, and Houston opens and the American Golf Classic. Lee Trevino passed another milestone in May, when he finished second in the Danny Thomas-Memphis Classic. The $16,188 prize pushed his career earnings over the $1-million mark.

Major Tournaments. In the four major tournaments, Johnny Miller of San Francisco won the U.S. Open by a stroke at Oakmont, Pa., in June; Nicklaus took the PGA championship by four strokes in August in Cleveland; Weiskopf captured the British Open by three strokes in July at Troon, Scotland; and Tommy Aaron won by a stroke over J. C. Snead in the Masters in April in Augusta, Ga.

Miller won the U.S. Open by shooting a record 63 on the final round. He also tied for second with Neil Coles of Great Britain in the British Open, and won the World Cup individual competition in November at Marbella, Spain. At the age of 26, Miller is tall, handsome, and mod.

The year's largest purse was offered in the $500,000 World Open tournament, which was played over two November weekends in Pinehurst, N.C. Miller Barber won the tournament's record first prize of $100,000.

The PGA tour of 47 tournaments carried purses totaling more than $8.6 million, a rise of $1.2 million over 1972. For the first time, the Ladies Professional Golf Association (LPGA) tour of 34 tournaments was worth more than $1 million, and it included four $100,000 tournaments.

The Women's Tour. Kathy Whitworth of Richardson, Tex., won seven tournaments and, with $85,209, led the women's tour in earnings for the eighth time in nine years. Susie Maxwell Berning of Incline Village, Nev., won the women's United States Open and a $6,000 prize in July in Rochester, N.Y. It was her second straight U.S. Open victory and third in six years. Her five-stroke margin was achieved with a sidesaddle putting style and a putter her husband bought for $5 in an Oklahoma City pawnshop three months earlier.

Mary Mills of Laurel, Miss., won the LPGA title in June at Sutton, Mass. She shot a 288 to capture the $5,250 first prize.

A U.S. District Court judge in Atlanta ruled in June that the LPGA had violated antitrust laws in the Jane Blalock case. The LPGA suspended Blalock, of Portsmouth, N.H., in May, 1972, for a year on charges that she cheated. But the judge ruled that Blalock was entitled to the $43,800 in prize money she won in LPGA tournaments while she was under suspension. *Frank Litsky*

GOVERNORS, U.S. See STATE GOVERNMENT.

Tom Weiskopf caresses the trophy he received after winning the Canadian Open in July.
He won five tournaments in an 11-week span.

GREAT BRITAIN

On Nov. 13, 1973 – the day before millions of Britons celebrated the wedding of Princess Anne – the Government proclaimed a state of national emergency. A record October trade deficit of $769 million and an impending crisis caused by overtime bans imposed by power-station engineers and coal miners and uncertainty about oil shipments from the Middle East forced the action. The Government drastically curbed credit and ordered cuts in the use of electricity. The Bank of England hoisted its minimum lending rate to an all-time high of 13 per cent, which meant that other interest rates would go up to from 14 to 18 per cent.

This tough action by Chancellor of the Exchequer Anthony Barber saved the pound sterling from collapse. But gloom swept the stock exchange; share prices fell to their lowest level in over two years.

A three-day workweek was imposed on "nonessential industries," beginning December 31, by restricting their electricity. Shops could stay open longer, but without electricity.

The state of emergency, the fifth since the Conservatives took office in June, 1970, gave the Government wide powers to maintain essential services. Floodlights and advertising signs were switched off, and heating by electricity was almost totally banned. Coupons had already been printed, awaiting a Government decision to ration gasoline. The British people, who had begun 1973 with a spending spree, prepared for another winter of power cuts and economic crises. The Government dug in to resist union challenges to its counter-inflation policy, which began in November, 1972, with a freeze on wages, prices, rents, and stock dividends.

Strikes Protest Controls. Under the second phase, which started on April 1, a Pay Board and a Price Commission were set up. The board restricted individual wage increases to about $650 a year. The only price raises allowed were those caused by unavoidable cost increases.

More than 1½ million union workers staged a day of protest on May 1. No national newspapers appeared, and much of the country's production and transportation was halted. During the first four months of the year, strikes in support of wage claims cut gas supplies, postponed operations in hospitals

Royal panoply and sacred tradition mingled at rites uniting Princess Anne and Captain Mark Phillips in London's Westminster Abbey.

An IRA bomb exploded, killed 1 person,
injured 216, and wrecked the Old Bailey,
London's central criminal court, on March 8.

and sent patients home, slowed government work, closed schools, and severely disrupted the railroads. But the Government refused any concessions. Nevertheless, by October, pay raises had averaged nearly 8 per cent and retail prices had gone up by more than 7 per cent since the freeze began.

A third phase of the fight against inflation set a 7 per cent norm for pay raises, but allowed exceptions, especially for less pleasant jobs. The firemen were first through the gap, citing "unsocial hours" and forcing a 19 per cent raise after an unofficial strike in Glasgow. The coal miners led the race to exploit this breach, and other unions followed closely.

The new flexibility of the Phase-Three pay code also ended a 14-week strike by 156 electricians at Chrysler Corporation's Coventry plant in June. The workers were awarded a 14.5 per cent raise. The strike was the largest and most damaging since the American-owned company entered the British automobile industry. Chrysler counted a production loss of 37,000 cars valued at about $90 million. But the whole British car industry suffered from strikes, which had caused a total loss of 400,000 cars by the time the London Motor Show opened on October 17. In what was by far the industry's worst year for strikes, imports of foreign cars took more than 30 per cent of the British market, another record.

The unions also persisted in their opposition to the Industrial Relations Act. However, only the Engi-

neering Workers' Union, the nation's second biggest, continued to refuse to recognize the National Industrial Relations Court (NIRC). For refusing to be represented before the court, the union was fined $193,000, bringing the total cost of its opposition to NIRC over the past few years to $351,000. More than 250,000 engineering workers joined a one-day strike on November 5 to protest against the fine; Britain's national newspapers were shut down again.

Public Support Falters. At the end of the first year of the Government's anti-inflation policy, opinion polls showed that public support was waning, a large majority thinking the policy neither fair nor likely to be effective. The Government itself had displaced the unions as the chief culprit for the country's economic troubles.

Growing discontent was reflected in the Conservative Government's loss of three supposedly impregnable seats to the Liberals in parliamentary by-elections. On July 26, bookseller David Austick turned a Conservative majority of 12,064 in the Yorkshire seat of Ripon into a Liberal majority of 946. And gourmet and television personality Clement Freud, grandson of Sigmund, won an Isle of Ely seat that the Conservatives had won by 9,606 in 1970. At Berwick-upon-Tweed, on the Scottish border, Liberal university lecturer Alan Beith won by 57, overturning a Conservative majority of 7,145.

Parliamentary Affairs. The by-election at Berwick was caused by the resignation of Lord Lambton, a member of Parliament since 1951 and a junior defense minister. Lambton, 50, resigned on May 21 after admitting "a casual acquaintance" with a call girl, Norma Levy, "and one or two of her friends." It was later revealed that Mrs. Levy's husband had sold compromising photographs and a tape recording of Lambton to a Sunday newspaper. Lambton was also charged with drug offenses. The resignation of Earl Jellicoe, 55, Lord Privy Seal, leader of the House of Lords, and a member of the Cabinet, was announced on May 24. Jellicoe also admitted "some casual affairs" with call girls.

Prime Minister Edward Heath asked the Security Commission to find out if national security had been endangered by Lambton, Jellicoe, and the Levys. The commission reported on July 12 that there had been no security leaks. It also virtually exonerated Jellicoe of risking security. The commission considered, however, that Lambton's use of drugs constituted a "significant danger" that he might unintentionally divulge classified information. The two resignations necessitated a Government reshuffle, and Lord Windlesham, 41, took over from Jellicoe.

The Labour Party. Despite the voters' dissatisfaction with the Conservative Government, the major opposition party took hard knocks at the polls, too. It lost two parliamentary seats at by-elections. At Lincoln, Dick Taverne had resigned his seat in 1972 after being disowned by the local Labour Party for

Thirty-two members of the Commonwealth of Nations held their meeting in Ottawa, Canada, in August. Twenty-three heads of government attended.

voting with the Government for British entry into the European Community (Common Market). Taverne fought the by-election on March 1 as an independent Democratic Labour candidate and routed the official Labour candidate, boosting his own majority from 4,750 in 1970 to 13,191.

On November 8, Margo Macdonald, of Glasgow, won for the Scottish Nationalists a seat considered to be one of Labour's safest. During her campaign, she hammered on the theme that Scotland should control the vast revenues from the oil and gas finds off its north and east coasts. Cautious estimates put the 1980 production of oil found under Scottish waters at 2 million barrels a day, enough to meet up to 80 per cent of the predicted British demand. Expectations of more big discoveries brought comfort to the Scottish Nationalists.

Foreign Affairs. Public disenchantment with the Common Market, as reflected in the opinion polls, deepened throughout the year. The Government blamed the steep rises in world commodity prices for much of the inflation at home. But many Britons saw the Common Market as the cause and demanded reform of its agricultural policy.

British and French foreign ministers signed a treaty on November 17 giving the diplomatic go-ahead to an auto-rail tunnel under the English Channel. A final decision on the project, estimated to cost $1.2 billion, rested on the results of test borings.

The cod war between Iceland and Britain ended on November 13 when the two nations signed a two-year agreement on fishing rights. The dispute started on Sept. 1, 1972, when Iceland extended fishing limits along its coasts from 12 miles to 50. British trawlers continued to fish within the 50-mile limit, however, despite harassment from Icelandic gunboats. Talks between the two governments failed.

When a diplomatic breach between the two countries seemed certain, Heath invited Iceland's Prime Minister Olafur Johannesson to London. Their talks brought an agreement allowing British trawlers inside the 50-mile area, but it reduced their numbers and their annual catch.

IRA Violence hit London on March 8, the day of the border plebiscite in Northern Ireland. Bombs planted in parked cars by the Irish Republican Army exploded, killing 1 person and injuring 216. On December 10, British spokesmen joined with representatives of the Irish Republic, as well as Protestants and Roman Catholic leaders of Northern Ireland, in adopting an agreement that cleared the way for the first Protestant-Catholic coalition in Northern Ireland's history.

The Royal Wedding. Princess Anne, daughter of Queen Elizabeth II and the Duke of Edinburgh and fourth in line to the throne, married Captain Mark Phillips of the Queen's Dragoon Guards in Westminster Abbey on November 14. The wedding was seen on television by an estimated 500-million people throughout the world. The couple flew to Barbados, where they boarded the royal yacht, *Britannia*, for a honeymoon cruise. Captain Phillips won a gold medal in equestrian events at the 1972 Olympics. In September, Anne went to Kiev, Russia, to defend the European Three-Day Event equestrian title she won in 1971, but she withdrew after a hard fall.

Federal Government Rejected. After deliberating a possible transfer of power within the United Kingdom for 4½ years, the Royal Commission on the Constitution issued a divided report on October 31. The commission completely rejected establishing separate, sovereign parliaments for Scotland and Wales and a federal system of government. Instead, a majority of members proposed schemes that would maintain the political and economic entity of the country. It recommended Scottish and Welsh legislatures elected by proportional representation.

For England, the Royal Commission suggested regional advisory councils, with most members elected by local authorities. A minority report recommended a uniform system of elected assemblies, giving Scotland, Wales, and five English regions executive power. The minority also wanted the Westminster Parliament radically reformed and the party political system changed.　　　George Scott

See also EUROPE (Facts in Brief Table).

GREECE struggled with political turmoil throughout 1973. On June 1, the monarchy of King Constantine II was abolished and the nation was transformed into a "presidential parliamentary republic." The authoritarian regime held a referendum in July in which the voters ratified the change. Prime Minister George Papadopoulos, who had led the governing junta since 1967, became provisional president and the referendum confirmed him.

But troubles quickly beset the new republic and overturned it. In February, student violence increased. The strife was in reaction to a law passed February 12, threatening student agitators with the loss of their draft deferments. On February 21, about 2,000 students barricaded themselves in the Athens University law school.

In May, the Papadopoulos regime said it had foiled a plot to seize the fleet and overturn the government. Nearly three dozen officers were rounded up. Exiled King Constantine was blamed, and his $15,000 monthly allowance was stopped.

Government Changes. After the republic was proclaimed, Papadopoulos called for the referendum. It was made clear, however, that voter rejection of the new constitution would not end the republic. The proposals would simply be offered again later. Papadopoulos was the only candidate for the presidency in the July 29 voting.

Greek President George Papadopoulos took his oath of office in mid-August, *above*; but in November, Phaidon Gizikis took over, *right*.

Taking office formally on August 19, he announced a broad political amnesty. He soon promised "impeccable" general elections for 1974. Military officers were removed from the government and a civilian Cabinet, under historian and political leader Spyros Markezinis, was installed. The ousted military appeared indignant and resentful.

During the tension, students occupied major campuses in November, demanding more academic freedom. They held Athens Polytechnic University for four days until martial law, which had been lifted, was reimposed on November 17.

The Coup. About 3 A.M., on Sunday, November 25, military units moved into Athens and set up roadblocks. About 5 A.M., tanks and ships surrounded Papadopoulos' seaside villa about 26 miles away. At 8 A.M., a 24-hour curfew was announced over the Greek radio, and the take-over was proclaimed.

Lieutenant General Phaidon Gizikis, whom Papadopoulos had failed to oust in October, was sworn in as the new president. Adamandios Androutsopoulos, an American-educated economist and lawyer, became prime minister. Brigadier Dimitrios Ioannidis, chief of the military police, appeared to be the strong man behind the coup.   Kenneth Brown

See also EUROPE (Facts in Brief Table); PAPADOPOULOS, GEORGE.

GUATEMALA. See LATIN AMERICA.

GUINEA. See AFRICA.

GUSTAF, CARL XVI (1946-   ), became king of Sweden after his grandfather, King Gustaf VI Adolf, died on Sept. 14, 1973. He was officially crowned four days later. Carl Gustaf's father and former heir to the throne, Crown Prince Gustaf Adolf, was killed in a plane crash in 1947.

Carl Gustaf was born on April 30, 1946. He received his early education from tutors at the royal court and at a private boarding school near Stockholm. He attended the army and air force cadet schools, served in the Swedish Navy, and was commissioned a naval officer in 1968.

The crown prince then concentrated on learning about affairs of state. He studied economics, history, political science, and sociology at the University of Uppsala and Stockholm University. He also spent a month at the United Nations in New York City and studied private banking practices in London. In addition, he observed how the Swedish government ministries, Parliament, and the courts function, and studied the Swedish press, church, and business communities.

Since he was 25 years old, the new king has performed some state duties. He received the credentials of foreign ambassadors and acted as regent when his grandfather was out of the country. The new Swedish king is a bachelor. He is also an avid outdoorsman who enjoys hunting and fishing.   Darlene R. Stille

GUYANA. See LATIN AMERICA.

HAITI. On Feb. 11, 1973, Haitians voted for the first time in nearly 12 years. They elected 58 representatives to the Legislative Chamber from about 300 candidates, most of them openly committed to the Duvalier government. Supporters of President Jean-Claude Duvalier won all of the seats.

In an effort to end hoarding, President Duvalier announced in March that he had cut rice, beans, and corn prices by from 40 to 50 per cent. Duvalier also halted construction work on a free port and resort project underway on the Isle de la Tortue because, he claimed, the U.S. development company handling the operation "wanted to exploit the island."

U.S. Embargo Ends. After an 11-year embargo, the United States placed Haiti back on its list of countries qualified for U.S. military sales and foreign credits. Most U.S. aid had been suspended in 1962 because of the misuse of U.S. funds by the late President François Duvalier. On April 16, shortly after the embargo was ended, Haitian Foreign Minister Adrien Raymond reported that the U.S. Agency for International Development had approved a $3.5-million loan to Haiti for road maintenance. In August, the Inter-American Development Bank approved a $22.2-million loan to help build a highway between Léogâne and Les Cayes.

French Planning and Housing Minister Olivier Guichard visited the republic in July. On his return to Paris, he announced that France would give Haiti $1.25 million in aid in 1973 and more in 1974. The two nations had signed a 10-year scientific, cultural, and economic agreement in June.

Explosions in a munitions depot in the basement of the presidential palace started a five-hour fire that seriously damaged the building and forced the evacuation of President Duvalier and his family on July 23. Later in the day, President Duvalier made a nationwide radio broadcast to dispel rumors of an attempted coup. The fire, he said, had been accidental. On September 12, about 20 guerrillas landed on the northern coast, followed on September 13 by another 60 dissidents. The government announced, however, that the invaders had been repulsed by a coast guard cutter after an intense shoot-out.

U.S. Envoy Kidnaped. Three armed Haitians seized U.S. Ambassador Clinton E. Knox in Port-au-Prince on January 23, and demanded $70,000 in ransom, the release of 12 Haitian prisoners, and safe conduct to Mexico. The kidnapers, two men and a woman, were linked to exiled groups opposed to the Duvalier government. After all-night negotiations, the government released the prisoners in exchange for the safe return of the ambassador. He was freed, unharmed, the following day, and the 3 kidnapers and 12 freed prisoners were flown to Mexico. However, they were refused asylum by the Mexican government and were eventually flown to Chile. Ambassador Knox resigned on March 13.   Paul C. Tullier

See also LATIN AMERICA (Facts in Brief Table).

HANDICAPPED. The National Advisory Committee on Handicapped Children issued a call to action early in 1973, urging U.S. schools, state and national agencies, and others to initiate comprehensive programs for all handicapped children as quickly as possible. As a guide, the committee recommended the following:

- Reaffirm the right of all handicapped children to an appropriate, tax-supported education.
- Recognize the need for sufficient federal funds to finance education programs for handicapped children, and have such funds clearly identified and earmarked for this purpose.
- Extend the federal Education of the Handicapped Children Act to include all handicapped children.
- Call for a White House Conference on the Handicapped to be held not later than 1976.
- Strive for equal educational opportunities, unbiased testing and assessment, and placement of handicapped children in all types of educational facilities, and include handicapped adults – and parents or guardians of handicapped children – in all advisory groups.

The Handicapped in Head Start. The Office of Child Development and the Bureau of Education for the Handicapped in the U.S. Office of Education authorized funds for three experimental projects to demonstrate ways to serve handicapped children in

A new sounding device can convert printed directions on a metallic plaque into "spoken" directions for a blind person.

Head Start school programs. Techniques developed in the experimental projects will be used by other Head Start programs. One early result indicates that handicapped children benefit most by learning with other children rather than by being in a special group. The wide range of Head Start services will be tailored to meet the special needs and unique capabilities of handicapped children.

Outdoor Facilities. A drive to create a more usable and comfortable outdoor environment for the handicapped was initiated in 1973. The U.S. Department of Housing and Urban Development (HUD) awarded a $107,000 contract to the American Society of Landscape Architects Foundation, of McLean, Va., to seek ways to reduce some existing hardships. Under the terms of the contract, the foundation will:

- Develop a comprehensive guidebook on how outdoor facilities and layouts can be made more usable for the handicapped.
- Undertake a census of disabled persons who cannot use outdoor facilities.
- Identify existing outdoor facilities that present problems and those that can be altered to suit the needs of the handicapped.

The foundation will also review the HUD minimum property standards and recommend improvements to enlarge their scope to accommodate the handicapped.

Aid to the Blind Programs. A study released in 1973 showed that about 1 in 4 visually handicapped persons in the federally assisted aid to the blind programs can now get around without the help of another person, a dog, or such devices as canes, crutches, or walkers.

Meanwhile, speakers at an international conference sponsored by the International Cerebral Palsy Society emphasized the importance of enabling the handicapped to live normal lives. "Handicapped persons must be able to function as normal human beings within the urban system," Panayiotis Psomopoulos of Athens, Greece, told more than 400 persons attending the conference in New York City in October.

The Library of Congress, Division for the Blind and Physically Handicapped, Washington, D.C. 20542, has published two helpful "talking books." The first explains social security rules and benefits for the blind and disabled. The second is a guide to the use and benefits of Medicare.

A Training Manual to prepare the mentally retarded as housekeeping-management assistants has been developed at the Rehabilitation Research and Training Center in Mental Retardation at Texas Tech University in Lubbock. Its lessons include how to do laundry and maintain floors and bedrooms. Its aim is to help the mentally retarded person understand the working world and to develop pride in whatever he does. Joseph P. Anderson

HARNESS RACING. See HORSE RACING.

HAWAII. See STATE GOVERNMENT.

HEALTH AND DISEASE. Smallpox, once a feared killer, was near extinction in the world in 1973. Only six countries (Bangladesh, Ethiopia, India, Nepal, Pakistan, and Sudan) were listed by the World Health Organization as nations in which the disease was found regularly.

According to Alexander D. Langmuir, former director of the epidemiology program at the U.S. Center for Disease Control in Atlanta, Ga., two or three years of reasonable stability in international relations could bring the complete eradication of smallpox. While eradication efforts continued, Langmuir suggested that the best course for smallpox-free nations was surveillance and selective vaccination. The last reported case in the United States occurred in 1949. However, smallpox, cholera, and other dread diseases were reported on the increase in Asia and Africa. The World Health Organization said on August 30 that 3,400 persons had died of cholera in 20 African and Asian countries. An outbreak of cholera in August killed about 25 persons in Italy.

Tick Fever. Victims of Colorado tick fever may be hazardous blood donors, according to the National Institute of Allergy and Infectious Diseases (NIAID). In August, investigators at the institute's Rocky Mountain Laboratory reported that they had detected the virus of Colorado tick fever in a patient's blood nearly four months after he had recovered from the disease.

"Involvement of the red blood cell system and persistent shedding of virus add a new dimension to Colorado tick fever as a health problem," NIAID officials said. "Although recipients of blood transfusions in the Rocky Mountain area are at greatest risk, Colorado tick fever also poses a threat in other parts of the United States."

Drugs. Researchers at the University of Southern California, in Los Angeles, have linked heroin addiction to intervertebral disk space infection, thus adding to the growing list of hazards faced by heroin users. As with so many other heroin-related problems (hepatitis, bacterial endocarditis, infectious arthritis), the infection results from using contaminated needles to inject the drug. The study was conducted from July, 1969, to October, 1972, on 25 heroin users who were treated for intervertebral disk space infection at the Los Angeles County-University of Southern California Medical Center.

According to Michael J. Patzakis, assistant professor of orthopedic surgery at the university, "It is hard to pick up the diagnosis early, and in our group, we had some complications and one death." He suggested that intervertebral disk space infection should be suspected in all addicts who complain of neck and back pains. Treatment for the disorder includes antibiotic therapy and bed rest for from 3 to 12 months.

Allergies. Solomon E. Barr, clinical professor of medicine at George Washington University in Washington, D.C., has singled out the need for prompt

Rome citizens, fearful of an outbreak of cholera, line up in the courtyard of a health clinic to receive free immunization shots.

emergency treatment for persons who are allergic to insect stings. Barr spoke before the allergy section of the American Medical Association's 122nd annual convention in New York City in June. He said that out of 191 patients studied, only 1 in 3 could identify the offending insect with any degree of certainty. Yellow jackets (47 per cent) and honeybees (27 per cent) led the list of the identified insects.

A Washington, D.C., investigator told the same allergy section that cockroaches may be partially to blame for the development of respiratory allergic diseases. Nick Chehreh, associate professor of pediatrics and director of the allergy clinics at Howard University College of Medicine, said that many allergic people react to breathing house dust, which is a breakdown product of everything within the home. "In houses with a prevalence of cockroaches, it is logical to assume that dust might include breakdown products from cockroaches."

Chehreh and two colleagues worked at Freedman's and District of Columbia General Hospitals with 95 children from 8 months to 13 years of age. Parents of many of the children had reported that cockroaches were a continuing problem in their homes. The researchers took skin tests with cockroach extract on 70 of the youngsters who had a history of such allergic illnesses as bronchial asthma, allergic rhinitis, and atopic dermatitis. The extract produced reactions in 21 of the children.　　　Richard P. Davies

HERNÁNDEZ COLÓN, RAFAEL (1936-   ), became governor of Puerto Rico on Jan. 2, 1973. He
defeated Governor Luis A. Ferré of the New Progressive Party by an overwhelming margin of 93,000
votes. During the campaign, he accused the Ferré
Administration of not doing enough to alleviate such
social ills as unemployment and drug abuse.

Hernández Colón was born in Ponce, Puerto Rico,
the son of a distinguished lawyer who later served on
Puerto Rico's Supreme Court. He attended Johns
Hopkins University in Baltimore, Md., and received
his law degree in 1959 from the University of Puerto
Rico. While a student, he wrote a thesis on the political ties between Puerto Rico and the United States
that attracted the attention of Luis Muñoz Marín,
then the governor. Muñoz Marín appointed Hernández Colón to the public service commission. He
served as attorney general for two years, then was
elected to the Senate in 1968. Hernández became
head of the Popular Democratic Party in 1969.

Hernández favors commonwealth status for Puerto
Rico. He has argued that political and economic ruin
would result from either statehood or independence.
However, if forced to choose between the latter two,
he prefers independence.

Hernández Colón married Lila Mayoral Wirsh-
ing in 1959. They have four children.   Foster Stockwell

HIGHWAY. See BUILDING AND CONSTRUCTION;
TRANSPORTATION.

Mitchell Mehdy proudly holds one of nine
known surviving copies of the first Superman
comic book. He paid $1,800 to get it.

HOBBIES. An anonymous New York collector paid
$27,500 on May 8, 1973, for a letter written by
George Washington. It was the highest price ever
paid at auction for a Washington letter. The letter,
sold by the auction house of Sotheby Parke Bernet,
was addressed to Governor William Livingston of
New Jersey on June 12, 1783. It was one of 13 letters
Washington sent to state governors when he resigned
as commander of the Continental Army.

A 49-word autobiography of Abraham Lincoln,
handwritten while he was still a member of the
United States House of Representatives, was purchased by Maury A. Bromsen, a Boston rare book
dealer, for $16,000 on June 8 at an auction in Phila-
delphia. Lincoln had received a request in 1858 for
an autobiographical sketch from Charles Lanman,
who was compiling a "Biographical Dictionary of
the American Congress." Lincoln penned the information on the bottom of the letter and returned it.

Other 1973 transactions related to politics included
$2,400 for a letter written in 1946 by President Harry
S. Truman, $1,300 for a piano Mr. Truman once
played, and $950 for six letters written by James
McCord, Jr., the convicted Watergate burglar.

Expensive Cars. A 1940 Mercedes-Benz model
77OK that Adolf Hitler once used as a parade car
was sold at auction in Scottsdale, Ariz., on January 6
for $153,000. Tom Barnett of Scottsdale sold the car
to Earl Clark of Lancaster, Pa.

A Japanese cavalry sword made in 1603 brought a
record price of $70,000 on May 31 from Sam Some-
ya, a London gallery owner. The sword had been
consigned to auction by an anonymous British
colonel. Altogether, 396 Japanese swords, fittings,
and armor brought $407,000 at the auction.

Items of the Old West. John Bianchi of Teme-
cula, Calif., paid $20,000 on September 19 for a
45-caliber Colt six-shooter purportedly carried by
lawman Wyatt Earp while tracking down outlaw
Curly Bill Brocius. The revolver was one of a group
of Old West items that brought more than $500,000
at a three-day auction at the Sotheby Parke Bernet
galleries in Los Angeles.

Collecting children's books became more popular.
On June 5, a representative of the Toronto Public
Library paid $1,800 for an early edition of *Mother
Goose* at an auction in New York City. The price was
three times what had been expected.

And, in a related area, Mitchell Mehdy, an 18-
year-old Sacramento, Calif., high school student, on
May 14 bought one of only nine known surviving
copies of the first Superman comic book, issued in
1938. To get it, he paid $1,800 to Theodore Holstein,
also of Sacramento. Calling his purchase "the ultimate comic book," Mehdy said he wouldn't part
with it for less than $10,000.   Theodore M. O'Leary

See also COIN COLLECTING; GAMES, MODELS, AND
TOYS; STAMP COLLECTING.

HOCKEY. The World Hockey Association (WHA), a new major league of 12 teams, started play in the 1972-1973 season and survived. It created grave concern among officials and owners in the established National Hockey League (NHL) and sent player salaries rocketing as the two leagues fought for talent.

On the ice, the Montreal Canadiens won the Stanley Cup, emblematic of NHL supremacy. The New England Whalers, playing in Boston, became the first WHA champions.

The odds were stacked against the WHA, because 6 of its 12 teams played in cities with NHL teams. Some played in old arenas. Attendance averaged 5,298, and every team lost money, but "a lot less than anyone had expected," said a league official.

Realizing it needed well-known players to survive, the WHA raided the opposition. It signed 68 NHL players, including Bobby Hull, Derek Sanderson, J. C. Tremblay, Gerry Cheevers, Bernie Parent, and John McKenzie. Sanderson and Parent later returned to the NHL. The Winnipeg Jets of the WHA signed Hull for $1.7 million to be player-coach for five years and a coach or executive for the next five, and gave him a $1-million bonus for signing.

The NHL, afraid the courts would nullify its reserve clause, went to court to prevent Hull from playing for any team except the NHL Chicago Black Hawks. An Illinois court kept Hull sidelined for 15 games until a United States District Court judge in Philadelphia ruled that the NHL could not use the

Standings in National Hockey League

East Division

	W.	L.	T.	Points
Montreal	52	10	16	120
Boston	51	22	5	107
N.Y. Rangers	47	23	8	102
Buffalo	37	27	14	88
Detroit	37	29	12	86
Toronto	27	41	10	64
N.Y. Islanders	12	60	6	30

West Division

	W.	L.	T.	Points
Chicago	42	27	9	93
Philadelphia	37	30	11	85
Minnesota	37	30	11	85
St. Louis	32	34	12	76
Pittsburgh	32	37	9	73
Los Angeles	31	36	11	73
Atlanta	25	38	15	65
California	16	46	16	48

Scoring Leaders

	Games	Goals	Assists	Points
Phil Esposito, Boston	78	55	75	130
Bobby Clarke, Philadelphia	78	37	67	104
Bobby Orr, Boston	63	29	72	101
Rick MacLeish, Philadelphia	78	50	50	100
Jacques Lemaire, Montreal	77	44	51	95
Jean Ratelle, N.Y. Rangers	78	41	53	94
Mickey Redmond, Detroit	76	52	41	93
John Bucyk, Boston	78	40	53	93
Frank Mahovlich, Montreal	78	38	55	93
Jim Pappin, Chicago	76	41	51	92

Leading Goalies

	Games	Goals against	Avg.
Ken Dryden, Montreal	54	119	2.26
Wayne Thomas, Montreal	10	23	2.37
Michel Plasse, Montreal	17	40	2.58
Montreal Totals	78	184	2.36
Peter McDuffe, N.Y. Rangers	1	1	1.00
Gilles Villemure, N.Y. Rangers	34	78	2.29
Ed Giacomin, N.Y. Rangers	43	125	2.91
N.Y. Rangers Totals	78	208	2.67
Dave Dryden, Buffalo	37	89	2.65
Roger Crozier, Buffalo	49	121	2.76
Rocky Farr, Buffalo	1	3	6.21
Buffalo Totals	78	219	2.81

Awards

Calder Trophy (best rookie)—Steve Vickers, N.Y. Rangers
Hart Trophy (most valuable player)—Bobby Clarke, Philadelphia
Lady Byng Trophy (sportsmanship)—Gil Perreault, Buffalo
Norris Trophy (best defenseman)—Bobby Orr, Boston
Ross Trophy (leading scorer)—Phil Esposito, Boston
Smythe Trophy (most valuable in Stanley Cup play)—
Yvan Cournoyer, Montreal
Vezina Trophy (leading goalie)—Ken Dryden, Montreal
Masterton Trophy (perseverance, dedication to hockey)—
Lowell McDonald, Pittsburgh

Standings in World Hockey Association

East Division

	W.	L.	T.	Points
New England	46	30	2	94
Cleveland	43	32	3	89
Philadelphia	38	40	0	76
Ottawa	35	39	4	74
Quebec	33	40	5	71
New York	33	43	2	68

West Division

	W.	L.	T.	Points
Winnipeg	43	31	4	90
Houston	39	35	4	82
Los Angeles	37	35	6	80
Alberta	38	37	3	79
Minnesota	38	37	3	79
Chicago	26	50	2	54

Scoring Leaders

	Games	Goals	Assists	Points
Andre La Croix, Philadelphia	78	50	74	124
Ron Ward, New York	77	51	67	118
Danny Lawson, Philadelphia	78	61	45	106
Tom Webster, New England	77	53	50	103
Bobby Hull, Winnipeg	63	51	52	103
Norm Beaudin, Winnipeg	78	38	65	103
Chris Bordeleau, Winnipeg	78	47	54	101
Terry Caffery, New England	74	39	61	100
Gordon Labossiere, Houston	77	36	60	96
Wayne Carleton, Ottawa	75	42	49	91

Leading Goalies

	Games	Goals against	Avg.
Gilles Gratton, Ottawa	51	187	3.71
Les Binkley, Ottawa	30	106	3.72
Frank Blum, Ottawa	2	3	6.42
Ottawa Totals	78	296	3.74
Danny Sullivan, Philadelphia	1	3	3.00
Bernie Parent, Philadelphia	63	220	3.61
Yves Archambault, Philadelphia	6	17	3.92
Tom Cottringer, Philadelphia	2	8	3.93
Marcel Paille, Philadelphia	15	49	4.81
Philadelphia Totals	78	297	3.78
Serge Aubry, Quebec	52	182	3.59
Jacques Lemelin, Quebec	9	29	4.00
Richard Brodeur, Quebec	24	102	4.75
Quebec Totals	78	313	3.94

Awards

Gary L. Davidson Trophy (most valuable player)—
Bobby Hull, Winnipeg
W. D. (Bill) Hunter Trophy (leading scorer)—
Andre La Croix, Philadelphia
Lou Kaplan Award (best rookie)—Terry Caffery, New England
Ben Hatskin Trophy (leading goalie)—Gerry Cheevers, Cleveland
Dennis A. Murphy Award (best defenseman)—J. C. Tremblay,
Quebec
Howard Baldwin Award (coach of the year)—Jack Kelley,
New England

Montreal Canadiens captain Henri Richard holds the Stanley Cup after Canadiens beat Chicago Black Hawks for National Hockey League title.

NHL officials insisted that the talks were completely unofficial.

Meanwhile, both leagues planned expansion. The NHL, which had only 6 teams as recently as the 1967-1968 season, played the 1972-1973 season with 16 teams, including new ones in Long Island, N.Y., and Atlanta, Ga. It planned to expand to 18 by adding teams in Kansas City and Washington, D.C., in 1974-1975 and to 20 in 1976-1977, when it would split its present two divisions into four. The WHA moved three teams–Philadelphia to Vancouver, Ottawa to Toronto, and New York to Cherry Hill, N.J. It sold a 1974-1975 franchise for $2 million (an NHL franchise cost $6 million).

The Stanley Cup. The Canadiens and Black Hawks won the NHL division titles and reached the Stanley Cup play-off finals. The Canadiens won, 4 games to 2, and became Stanley Cup champions for the second time in 3 years, fourth time in 6 years, sixth time in 9 years, and eleventh time in 17 years. In September, Ken Dryden, their $80,000-a-year goalie, quit hockey to become a $7,000-a-year law clerk.

Phil Esposito of the Boston Bruins led the NHL in goals (55), assists (75), and points (130). Bobby Clarke of Philadelphia, second in scoring, won the Hart Trophy as Most Valuable Player.   Frank Litsky

HOME FURNISHINGS. See INTERIOR DESIGN.

HONDURAS. See LATIN AMERICA.

reserve clause to bar players from jumping. Hull went on to become the Most Valuable Player and major box-office attraction of the new league.

The NHL teams responded by giving higher salaries to stars and fringe players alike. After the season, they lost such players as Pat Stapleton, Ralph Backstrom, Marc Tardif, Mike Walton, Rejean Houle, and Rick Smith to the WHA. But they foiled WHA bids for such stars as Stan Mikita and Henri Richard by paying each at least $100,000 a year.

One defection that embittered the NHL was that of Gordie Howe, its all-time scoring leader, who had retired in 1971 after 25 years with the Detroit Red Wings. In June, 1973, he signed with the Houston Aeros of the WHA for $1 million to play for one year plus one game (the first in a new arena) and then be a club executive for three years. His sons–Marty, 19, and Mark, 18–had just signed with Houston, each for $100,000 a year for four years.

The NHL was angry, because, to protect amateur hockey in Canada, its teams no longer sign teen-age amateur players. The NHL threatened to change that policy unless the WHA adopted it. Meanwhile, the NHL concentrated on the draft of amateur players, and all 16 clubs signed their first-round choices.

Merger and Expansion. Four NHL and three WHA club owners held secret merger talks in March. Later, under pressure from its players' association and a $48-million antitrust suit filed by the WHA,

HORSE RACING. Secretariat dominated thoroughbred racing in North America during 1973 and became a popular public favorite while winning 9 of 12 races, including the elusive Triple Crown. The Meadow Stable 3-year-old became the first since Citation in 1948 to win the Kentucky Derby, Belmont, and Preakness. And he set track records in the first two and possibly also in the Preakness, where accuracy of the timing equipment was disputed.

Syndicated for stud purposes for a record $6.08-million, Secretariat returned from a unique Horse-of-the-Year 2-year-old campaign, in which he had 7 wins in 9 races and earned $456,404, to win his first two 1973 starts. But he was third in the Wood Memorial, raising doubts about his ability to win his next race, the Derby, much less the Triple Crown. However, he beat Sham by 2½ lengths in the Kentucky Derby, won the Preakness by an identical margin over the same rival, then brilliantly ran off to take the 1½-mile Belmont by 31 lengths.

His Other Victories. After winning the Arlington Invitational in Chicago, Secretariat met older horses for the first time in the Whitney at Saratoga in August and was defeated by a 4-year-old, Onion. A soon-discovered virus infection was the reason, and Secretariat recovered quickly to meet the best older horses in a new, commercially sponsored race, the $250,000 Marlboro Cup in September. He won, defeating stablemate Riva Ridge, the 1972 Kentucky

Secretariat's 31-length victory in the Belmont Stakes earned him the Triple Crown and recognition by some as the greatest horse of all time.

Derby winner, in world-record time of 1 minute 45⅖ seconds for 1⅛ miles.

The son of Bold Ruler and Somethingroyal was runner-up to Prove Out in the classic Woodward in September. In his first race on grass, Secretariat set a new course record in the Man o' War at Belmont in October, then ended his racing by winning the Canadian International Championship at Woodbine on October 28, bringing his career earnings to $1,316,808, fourth highest in racing history.

A 3-year-old filly, Desert Vixen, won seven consecutive stakes, among them the Alabama. Against the best older fillies in the 1⅛-mile Beldame at Belmont Park, Desert Vixen equaled the world record of 1:46⅕, which was surpassed one race later by Secretariat in the Marlboro Cup.

Canadian jockey Sandy Hawley rode his 500th winner of the year on December 15 at Laurel Race Course in Maryland. He broke a 20-year mark of 485 set by Bill Shoemaker.

Harness Racing. Flirth won the Hambletonian trotting classic, and the Little Brown Jug in pacing went to Melvin's Woe. Sir Dalrae, a 4-year-old pacer, won 19 of 22 starts, including 14 in a row, and was named Harness Horse of the Year by the U.S. Trotting Association.

Quarter Horse Racing. A 2-year-old colt, Time to Thinkrich, won the All-American Quarter Horse Futurity at Ruidoso Downs, N. Mex.   Jane Goldstein

Major U.S. Horse Races of 1973

Race	Winner	Value to Winner
Alabama Stakes	Desert Vixen	$34,620
Belmont Stakes	Secretariat	90,120
Brooklyn Handicap	Riva Ridge	67,200
Coaching Club American Oaks	Magazine	70,200
Hollywood Derby	Amen II	90,000
Hollywood Gold Cup	Kennedy Road	90,000
Jockey Club Gold Cup	Prove Out	66,060
Kentucky Derby	Secretariat	155,050
Man o' War Stakes	Secretariat	68,160
Marlboro Cup Handicap	Secretariat	150,000
Preakness Stakes	Secretariat	129,900
Santa Anita Derby	Sham	79,400
Santa Anita Handicap	Cougar II	105,000
Suburban Handicap	Key to the Mint	65,700
United Nations Handicap	Tentam	75,000
Washington, D.C., Int'l.	Dahlia	100,000
Woodward Stakes	Prove Out	64,920

Major U.S. Harness Races of 1973

Race	Winner	Value to Winner
Cane Futurity Pace	Smog	$50,621
Hambletonian	Flirth	72,355
Kentucky Futurity	Arnie Almahurst	25,669
Little Brown Jug	Melvin's Woe	44,400
Messenger Pace	Valiant Bret	61,366
Roosevelt International	Delmonica Hanover	75,000
Yonkers Futurity	Tamerlane	46,621

HOSPITAL. Cost containment and rising prices combined to influence the present and future abilities of U.S. hospitals to provide high-quality health care in 1973. The Nixon Administration's Economic Stabilization Program (ESP) was partly responsible for reducing the rate of increase in average daily service charges from 8 per cent in 1971 to 5.4 per cent in 1972, but it produced some inequities. ESP disallowed significant price increases by hospitals but left unchecked the price increases of hospital suppliers. As a consequence, hospitals were forced to borrow from funds reserved for future expansion in order to finance their daily operations. Congress supported a one-year extension of the Hill-Burton Act, which provides funds for hospital construction, and 11 other federal health programs.

The American Hospital Association (AHA) adopted a "Patients Bill of Rights," which included such issues as informed consent and the right to refuse treatment. They also registered 7,061 hospitals with 1.5 million beds in 1972. The hospitals reported 33.26 million inpatient and 219 million outpatient admissions in 1972, representing 1.8 and 9.7 per cent increases, respectively, over 1971. They had 2.67 million full-time employees. Community hospital costs rose 13.8 per cent in 1972 to $105.09 per day, and expenditures for all hospitals rose 13.4 per cent to $32.7 billion. Madison B. Brown

HOUSING. Near disaster hit the U.S. housing industry in 1973. Sharp increases in mortgage rates, caused by government efforts to fight inflation, combined with rapidly increasing construction costs to severely cut the rate of new housing starts.

Federal Housing Freeze. On January 8, President Richard M. Nixon ordered a freeze on new federal commitments for subsidized housing. The freeze affected public housing, rent supplements, mortgage-interest subsidies, and home-ownership assistance.

George Romney, then secretary of housing and urban development, said the government hoped to find better ways of meeting the nation's housing problems and wanted to encourage state and local governments to assume greater responsibility for housing programs, using federal revenue-sharing funds. President Nixon made no provision for federal-housing subsidies in his fiscal 1974 (July 1, 1973, to June 30, 1974) budget proposal.

Sharp Building Declines. In April, 25 per cent fewer home building permits were issued than in December, 1972. By September, 1973, housing starts had dropped to a seasonally adjusted annual rate of 2.05 million units from the record 2.36 million units started in 1972.

Chief cause of the building decline was a shortage of money for home mortgages. Spurred by the Federal Reserve Board's efforts to curb inflation, annual

Hospital Costs

Daily Hospital Costs per Patient (Inpatient Only)

Less than $55 $56 to $74 $75 to $94   More than $95

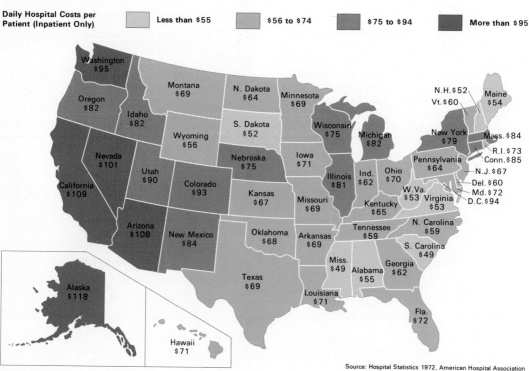

Source: Hospital Statistics 1972, American Hospital Association

"Crunch"

crease the payments as their income increased. And finally, Mr. Nixon proposed that, in the future, direct housing allowances be paid directly to poor people.

Rent Control. To prevent unfair rent increases in the face of a growing shortage of housing, many states and cities enacted rent-control measures. The New Jersey State Supreme Court, in April, upheld the right of municipalities to regulate rents in that state. Montgomery County, Maryland, limited rent increases to 7.5 per cent annually, and landlords in northern Virginia cooled demands for local rent control by promising to hold increases to 6 per cent. Massachusetts started rent control in the Boston area, and voters in Berkeley, Calif., approved a rent-control law after builders cut back on construction.

Urban Homesteading emerged as a new concept for solving part of the housing problems of inner cities. To institute a homesteading plan, a city acquires abandoned houses and sells them to poor families for a small fee, such as $1. The purchasers in turn must live in their new dwellings for a stipulated minimum period of time and make enough repairs to bring the home into compliance with building codes. The concept was tried in Baltimore; Philadelphia; Wilmington, Del.; and Norfolk, Va.

Condominium housing continued to increase in popularity. The number of units rose from 235,000 in 1972 to 420,000 in 1973.   James M. Banovetz

interest rates for home mortgages rose sharply, reaching from 9 to 9.5 per cent. Usury laws in some states set the maximum interest rate on home mortgages at 8 per cent or less, further complicating home financing problems. As a result, banks and many savings and loan associations stopped making home-mortgage loans.

Meanwhile, construction costs steadily increased. *U.S. News and World Report* magazine noted that a typical new house had increased in price from $25,400 in 1968 to $34,100 in 1973.

Easing the Crisis. President Nixon announced on September 19 that his Administration would pump $5.5 billion into the nation's housing industry. He directed the Federal Home Loan Bank Board to cover an additional $2.5 billion in future loan commitments of savings and loan associations. He also ordered the Government National Mortgage Association to provide up to $3 billion to subsidize private investors' interest rates for Federal Housing Administration (FHA) mortgages.

In a message to Congress on the same day, the President proposed relaxing down-payment requirements on FHA loans. He also suggested that the first 3.5 per cent of interest earned by financial institutions on home mortgages be tax-free, as an incentive to investors. The President favored flexible repayment terms for FHA loans so that young couples could start with small monthly payments and in-

Condominiums continued to grow in popularity. The number of these owned-apartments in the U.S. increased by 185,000 units during 1973.

349

HOUSTON. The bodies of 27 murder victims, all teen-age boys, were uncovered in August, 1973, in the Houston area. The mass killing was the largest in United States history. The murders came to light when 17-year-old Elmer Wayne Henley summoned Houston police on August 7 and told them he had killed the alleged leader of a homicide ring, 33-year-old Dean Allan Corll, whom he said had tried to molest and kill him. Henley told police about a number of murders Corll had committed. Police said he later admitted participating in the killings, and implicated another teen-ager, 18-year-old David Owen Brooks. Henley and Brooks were indicted on August 14 for their part in the slayings.

On December 4, Fred Hofheinz, son of Houston Astros owner Roy Hofheinz, was elected mayor, replacing Louie Welch. Hofheinz captured 95 per cent of the black vote to narrowly defeat City Councilman Dick Gottlieb. A promised shakeup in city government began the next day, when the police chief and the city attorney resigned.

Public Transit. In March, the Houston City Council approved a mass-transportation plan, calling for construction of a rapid-transit system and highway express lanes reserved for buses. Mayor Louie Welch proposed an exhaust-emissions tax to subsidize mass transit. Annual fees would range from $5 for small cars to $20 for trucks.

In February, construction began on a $200-million medical center in Houston. The complex will include a 26-story professional building, housing for senior citizens, and a hotel for the families of patients.

Population Change. The population of the Houston metropolitan area increased to almost 2 million persons as a result of a redefinition of metropolitan area boundaries. However, the Houston area fell in rank from the 13th to the 16th largest U.S. urban center.

A U.S. Department of Labor report released on June 15 showed that Houston was one of the nation's least expensive large cities in which to live. According to the report, an average family of four could live in Houston in "moderate comfort" on an annual budget of $10,270. Living costs in the Houston area increased only 4.6 per cent between April, 1972, and April, 1973.

Houston hosted two events of importance to women. The first convention of the National Women's Political Caucus was held there from February 9 to 11. Then, on September 21, women's tennis champion Billie Jean King beat Bobby Riggs in the Astrodome, winning the $100,000 match in three straight sets. See TENNIS.

Houston public-school teachers walked off their jobs in August demanding higher pay. However, they returned to work after only a day's absence.

On February 20, the Manned Spacecraft Center near Houston was renamed the Lyndon B. Johnson Space Center.   James M. Banovetz

HUNGARY increased its trade with the West impressively in 1973, but it imposed stronger economic controls at home. The economic measures were coupled with mildly tighter political controls.

By midyear, Hungary had a $40-million foreign-trade surplus. Total exports were 20 per cent higher than they had been in the corresponding period in 1972. Of that amount, the exports to Western nations were 31 per cent higher.

Industrial output increased 7 per cent and labor productivity 5.3 per cent. The best results were in the chemical industry (14.3 per cent) and light industry (12.1 per cent). About 1.3 million industrial and building workers received pay raises of from 6 to 8 per cent in March, costing the economy $100 million. In June, a new, top-level, state planning committee chaired by Deputy Premier György Lázár was set up "to strengthen central control over the Hungarian economy."

In Domestic Politics, the government placed new stress on ideological orthodoxy. On May 15, a leading sociologist and former premier, Andras Hegedüs, was expelled from his university post, together with two other leading "revisionist" philosophers. An ultraleftist poet, Miklos Haraszti, was arrested on May 22 for alleged incitement, but his trial was postponed indefinitely. Strong international criticism seemed to be a factor in the delay.

Foreign Relations. Hungary settled its differences with Russia over future Soviet supplies of oil, gas, and other raw materials. But the Hungarian government was embarrassed at preparatory talks in Vienna on mutual force reductions by Russia's insistence that Hungary be excluded from any cuts unless Italy was included.

Party leader Janos Kadar visited Yugoslavia in July. The two countries announced that they would build an oil pipeline to carry Middle Eastern oil from the Adriatic Sea to Hungary and Czechoslovakia. Also in July, Hungary announced that more than 300 miles of highways would be built between 1974 and 1985 to stimulate tourism and trade. The project will cost an estimated $1 billion.

On March 6, Hungary agreed to pay the United States government $18.9 million in settlement of claims arising out of its nationalization of U.S. property in Hungary after 1948. In return, the United States agreed to release between $150,000 and $175,000 in Hungarian accounts held in the United States. The Nixon Administration also promised that it would advocate most-favored-nation status for Hungary's exports to the United States. In June, Hungary set up its first joint venture with a Canadian firm, Bowmar of Canada, for the manufacture and development of minicomputers. On September 9, Hungary became the sixth Communist country to join the General Agreement on Tariffs and Trade.   Chris Cviic

See also EUROPE (Facts in Brief Table).

HUNTING. Sportsmen and some conservation groups battled in 1973 against attempts to ban hunting entirely or to limit hunting opportunities. Antihunting tactics included increased posting of farmlands against hunting, and the purchase by non-hunters of limited licenses for duck blinds.

In answer, many of the 18 million hunters in the United States began a campaign to show that hunters are closely linked to wildlife conservation efforts. The National Shooting Sports Foundation, a trade-supported association, argued that hunters have been "at the head of every significant conservation program implemented in this country."

High meat prices moved a growing number of people to shoot deer out of season. West Virginia, New York, Pennsylvania, Michigan, Wisconsin, and Colorado were among states that reported increased deer poaching.

Drought caused poor production of ducks in 1973, and fall flights were down by as much as 30 per cent. The largest decreases occurred in the Mississippi and Central flyways. Tightened regulations banned the hunting of canvasbacks and redheads entirely in the Atlantic flyway and in high-harvest areas of the Central and Mississippi flyways. The U.S. Department of the Interior is expected to require the use of steel shot instead of lead shot on the Atlantic flyway in 1974, and on all flyways in 1975. Lead shot poisons waterfowl when swallowed. Andrew L. Newman

ICE SKATING. The United States, which made a strong showing in speed skating in the 1972 Winter Olympics, did even better in 1973 as Sheila Young of Detroit and Bill Lanigan of New York City won world championships. Karen Magnussen of Canada was the only North American to win a world title in figure skating.

Speed Skating. Four world-championship competitions–men's and women's all-around and men's and women's sprint–were held in February in Deventer, the Netherlands; Stromsund, Sweden; and Oslo, Norway. The 22-year-old Young was the outstanding skater of that series. In the sprints, she won three races and placed second in the fourth and easily became overall champion. In the all-around championships, she won the 500-meter title. Earlier, she set a world record of 41.8 seconds to win the 500-meter title in January in Davos, Switzerland.

In August, she won the world sprint championship in bicycle racing, a sport many speed skaters use to keep in condition.

Lanigan, 25, was a surprise winner of the world 500-meter title for men, because he had retired briefly after the 1972 Olympics. "I was tired of riding a hundred miles a day on a bicycle, going skating for three hours a day, six days a week," he said. After winning the world title in February he quit again, saying, "I can't work and skate, too, so I guess I'll have to retire."

The overall world champions, in addition to Young, were Goeran Claesson of Sweden (men's all-around), Antje Keulen-Deelstra of the Netherlands (women's all-around), Valeri Muratov of Russia (men's sprint), and Ard Schenk of the Netherlands (the new European professional circuit).

Figure Skating. Magnussen, a 20-year-old psychology student from Vancouver, British Columbia, won the women's world title on March 1 in Bratislava, Czechoslovakia. Janet Lynn, 19, of Rockford, Ill., finished second. A month earlier, Lynn had won her fifth straight United States championship.

Ondrej Nepela, performing in his hometown, took the men's world title for the third consecutive year, then retired to study civil law. Gordon McKellen of Lake Placid, N.Y., the U.S. champion, finished seventh.

After the world championships, Magnussen signed a three-year contract with the Ice Capades for more than $100,000 a year. Lynn signed a three-year contract with the Ice Follies worth $1,455,000.

A new scoring system helped such gifted free skaters as Magnussen and Lynn. In 1973, a rules change made compulsory figures and free skating worth 40 per cent each and a new classification of designated free maneuvers worth 20 per cent in the scoring. Frank Litsky

See also MAGNUSSEN, KAREN.

Karen Magnussen of Canada won the women's world figure-skating title in Czechoslovakia on March 1; then she became a professional.

ICELAND. The Helgafell volcano on Heimaey Island, dormant for thousands of years, erupted without warning on Jan. 23, 1973. The eruption opened a fissure almost 1½ miles long, nearly cutting the island in half. Thousands of tons of burning lava flowed, cutting a 2-mile-long swath to the sea. Red-hot stones and fiery ashes rained down on Vestmannaeyjar, the island's only town.

Authorities immediately assembled a fleet of fishing boats, coastal vessels, and coast guard cutters and began evacuating about 5,000 island residents. No injuries were reported, but most of the homes on the island were either badly damaged or completely destroyed. Only a few firemen, policemen, and rescue workers remained behind to salvage what they could.

Deep-drifting ashes, almost rooftop high, nearly smothered a town on Iceland's Heimaey Island during a volcanic eruption in 1973.

The lava flow did not cease until July 7, according to teams of geologists on the scene. The government immediately began studying how soon the town of Vestmannaeyjar could be rehabilitated. See GEOLOGY.

Fishing Controversy. A long-running dispute over fishing rights between Iceland and Great Britain ended on October 2 when the British government yielded to an Icelandic ultimatum and withdrew its naval frigates from the disputed fishing waters.

The dispute arose late in 1972, when Iceland announced it was extending its territorial waters from 12 to 50 nautical miles from the shoreline. It also prohibited foreign fishing within the new limit.

The decision was hotly protested by the British, whose fishermen had long operated in the waters off Iceland. In the ensuing months, the nets of 68 British trawlers were cut, 13 collisions occurred between Icelandic gunboats and British trawlers, and Icelandic gunboats fired at British vessels, including frigates that the British government had assigned to protect its fishermen. On May 24, demonstrators stoned the British Embassy in Reykjavík. Iceland threatened to break diplomatic relations and indicated it might even withdraw from the North Atlantic Treaty Organization unless some solution was forthcoming.

On October 12, the two governments finally agreed to an interim two-year settlement whereby the British would limit the number and size of British trawlers working in Icelandic waters and confine them to special areas designated by the Icelanders.

In November, the United States and Iceland began talks on Iceland's demands that the American air base in Keflavík be closed within two years. Iceland also insisted that U.S. civilians replace military men at the base in the interim period.　Paul C. Tullier

See also EUROPE (Facts in Brief Table).

IDAHO. See STATE GOVERNMENT.

ILLINOIS. See CHICAGO; STATE GOVERNMENT.

IMMIGRATION AND EMIGRATION. The U.S. House of Representatives passed two measures in 1973 dealing with immigration problems in the Western Hemisphere. However, both measures needed Senate approval.

The first measure, approved on May 3, would penalize U.S. employers who knowingly hire illegal aliens. It provided for the U.S. attorney general to warn the employer after the first offense. After a second violation, the employer would be fined $500 for each alien he knowingly hired. A third violation would bring a year in prison or a $1,000 fine or both for each alien hired.

The other legislation, passed on September 26, would restrict immigration from Western Hemisphere countries – which is limited to an annual total of 120,000 – to the same 20,000 per-country limit in force in the Eastern Hemisphere. The bill also provided that Cubans in the United States would no longer be charged against the 120,000 ceiling when they become permanent residents. The large numbers of Cubans and Mexicans admitted under the present system have caused a two-year wait for visas in other parts of Latin America.

In fiscal 1973, 400,063 immigrants were admitted to the United States, compared with 384,685 in 1972. During the same period, 120,740 aliens became citizens and 16,842 were deported.　William McGaffin

INCOME TAX. See TAXATION.

INDIA. "There has never been a more depressing period in the 25 years of independence than the one we are going through now." This comment, in a leading Indian newspaper, seemed to reflect the country's mood in 1973. The elation and sense of unity and purpose produced by the victory over Pakistan in 1971 had evaporated. Opinion polls showed Prime Minister Indira Gandhi still popular, but with much of her authority clearly eroded. The country was restless, violence was on the rise, and the economy was stagnant.

The main cause of distress was the failure of the monsoon rains in 1972. Much of India lay parched, with crops withering, drinking water scarce, and cattle dying. By mid-1973 some 200 million people were living on lean rations.

The government's relief effort was massive. It put millions to work, building roads or crushing rock at more than 100,000 projects. The pay was minimal, but it was meant to provide the people with enough food to survive.

Riots. But all this was not enough. The daily ration of food shrank from 12 ounces for each adult to 7 and less. Beginning in April, there were food riots; and later, peasants in need of seed for sowing turned to violence. The black market was rampant.

The opposition blamed Mrs. Gandhi for failing to avert hoarding and for delaying purchases abroad. But the harshest criticism was aimed at the nationalization of the wholesale grain trade, allegedly begun without proper preparations. Mrs. Gandhi answered that the move was made to ensure a fair ration for the poor. After the summer wheat harvest, the opposition parties openly urged farmers to withhold their grain from the state. Still, with the purchase of nearly 3 million tons of wheat in the United States, Canada, and elsewhere, and a Russian loan of another 2 million tons, India managed to get through the months before the new harvest in November.

Mrs. Gandhi had to cope with other problems as well. Her Congress Party machine was sputtering, and the national government had to take over the governing of some key states, including the most populous, Uttar Pradesh. In April, Mrs. Gandhi brought opposition wrath on herself by naming liberal Ajit Nath Ray as chief justice of the Supreme Court over the heads of three senior justices.

Foreign Relations. Relations with the United States improved slowly after the angry months of 1971 when Washington openly sided with Pakistan against India. Talks were afoot to settle India's debt of $3 billion worth of rupees incurred in buying surplus food from the United States in the 1960s. A proposal to cut the number of U.S. scholars allowed to work in India was dropped after protests. Harsh denunciations of "American imperialism" became fewer.

But if the distrust of the United States persisted, India's relations with Russia grew warmer. The climax came in late November with a visit by the Russian leader, Leonid I. Brezhnev. The agreements signed during the four-day talks provided for vastly increased aid over the next 15 years, with the Russian-assisted projects ranging from a huge new refinery to a subway in Calcutta. The two sides also agreed to dovetail their economic planning. But while Mrs. Gandhi made sure huge crowds turned out to cheer the guest, she also resisted his persuasions to join in an Asian security system likely to be turned against China.

The monsoon rains were good in 1973. Foreign aid reached nearly $1 billion. But the happiest omen was the settlement of the prisoner of war dispute between Pakistan and India.

On August 28, the two countries agreed on a complicated three-way exchange. India would release the 90,000 Pakistani prisoners it had been holding since the 1971 war–all but the 195 whom Bangladesh wished to put on trial for war crimes. In return, Pakistan would accept a "substantial number"– probably 25,000 to 30,000–of the 200,000 Biharis (non-Bengali) in Bangladesh who chose to go to Pakistan. Finally, Pakistan would allow 150,000 to 200,000 Bengali to leave for Bangladesh. Once the massive migration is ended in 1974, a long step will have been made toward peace and stability. Mark Gayn

See also ASIA (Facts in Brief Table); BANGLADESH.

INDIAN, AMERICAN. Armed militant members of the American Indian Movement (AIM) seized the historic hamlet of Wounded Knee, S. Dak., on the Oglala Sioux Pine Ridge Reservation and held it for more than two months in 1973. The tiny village is near Wounded Knee Creek, where Indians and white men fought their last big battle on Dec. 29, 1890. See Close-Up.

The militants seized the village on the night of February 27. They demanded the ouster of Richard Wilson as president of the Oglala Sioux tribal council and vowed to stay until the United States Senate held hearings on 371 United States-Indian treaties and investigated Wilson's administration.

Government agents surrounded the village, but they avoided any direct attack on the Indians. However, sporadic gunfire resulted in the death of two Indians and injuries to a U.S. marshal, a Federal Bureau of Investigation agent, and a dozen Indians. The occupation ended on May 8 after an agreement by which White House representatives went to the reservation to discuss grievances with Indian leaders.

The government law-enforcement effort cost an estimated $5 million. The village suffered massive damage, which D. Kent Frizzell, solicitor of the Department of the Interior, described as "wanton." The trading post, the Roman Catholic church, and other buildings were destroyed.

Russell Means, left, and D. Kent Frizzell represented the Indians and the government, respectively, in talks to end the occupation of Wounded Knee.

Return to Wounded Knee

Militant members of the American Indian Movement (AIM) seized a symbolic spot when they occupied Wounded Knee, S. Dak., and held it against federal agents from Feb. 27 to May 8, 1973. At Wounded Knee (now a tiny village on the Pine Ridge Sioux Reservation), the Indians suffered their final defeat in 1890 in the fight for control of the Great Plains. So the area has become symbolic of the fate of native Americans.

The matter of Indian lands and broken treaties lies behind both the 1890 Battle of Wounded Knee and the 1973 occupation. From the time of the earliest European settlers, white men steadily pushed the Indians westward. Time after time, they promised the Indians territory, only to seize the land later and drive the Indians out.

By the 1860s, they had pushed west to the land of the Sioux in what is now western Minnesota, North and South Dakota, Montana, and Wyoming. The Sioux chief, Red Cloud, knowing that white men had ruined other Indian hunting grounds, went on the warpath to keep the whites out.

The U.S. government made peace in 1868, and the treaty acknowledged that the Sioux owned the land between the Black Hills of South Dakota and the Bighorn Mountains of Montana. No white man was supposed to enter this area.

But in 1874, gold was discovered in the Black Hills, and the government tried to buy the land. The Indians refused to sell. When fighting broke out between white invaders and the Indians, the government decided to confine the Indians to reservations.

Led by such famous Sioux chiefs as Sitting Bull and Crazy Horse, the Indians fiercely resisted. They won their greatest victory in 1876 by defeating Colonel George A. Custer in the Battle of the Little Bighorn. But after "Custer's Last Stand," the Army pursued them relentlessly, and by 1877, most of the Sioux had been confined to reservations.

Life on the reservations was devastating to a people accustomed to roaming freely. The great buffalo herds had been slaughtered by white men, and to keep from starving, many Indians depended on government food rations.

In the late 1880s, the Indians turned to the Ghost Dance, a new religion that prophesied that the dead Indians and buffalo would come back to life and the white man would be driven from the land. Fearing another uprising, government officials sent troops to disarm the reservation Indians in 1890.

A band of Indians, camped on Wounded Knee Creek on the Pine Ridge Reservation, were surrounded by soldiers, and surrendered. The soldiers began ransacking lodges in search of weapons. One Indian, enraged at this indignity, shot at a soldier. The troops immediately opened fire, and, in the massacre that followed, killed at least 146 men, women, and children. The Indian Wars were over.

With the Indians totally subdued, the government began regulating almost every aspect of their lives. Their religions were outlawed. Their children were sent to government boarding schools.

Caught between two cultures, their own and the white man's, the Indians were unable to function in either. Poverty and unemployment became the norm on the reservations, and alcoholism and suicide rates soared far beyond the national averages. Furthermore, the government agency set up to administer to their needs, the Bureau of Indian Affairs (BIA), only seemed to add to their problems.

From this setting, there arose in the mid-1960s a new Indian militancy that led to such actions as the occupation of Wounded Knee.

AIM leaders of the 1973 uprising demanded a U.S. Senate investigation of the BIA and a review of the 371 treaties between the United States and Indian nations.

While all Indians do not agree with these aggressive tactics, they do agree that Indians have a right to self-determination, that Indians themselves—not the BIA—should make the social and economic decisions affecting their lives. And most Indians are deeply suspicious of the federal government. To them, the words Red Cloud spoke a century ago still hold true today: "The white man has made many promises but he only kept one. He promised to take our land, and he took it."

Darlene R. Stille

Slain Indians were buried in mass grave after 1890 Wounded Knee massacre.

Russell C. Means, an AIM leader, called the agreement that ended the occupation, "A small victory, a preliminary victory, in our war with the United States over treaty rights." Means and more than 200 others have been indicted and face trial on such charges as conspiracy, riot, and arson stemming from the Wounded Knee take-over.

The federal government moved to reorganize the Bureau of Indian Affairs (BIA) and make other changes. President Richard M. Nixon, in his seventh State of the Union message to Congress, on September 10, urged action to establish an Indian Trust Counsel Authority, to raise the status of the Indian commissioner to assistant secretary, to provide credit and financing for Indian economic development, and to allow Indians to assume control of federal programs. Most of this legislation had been before Congress since 1970.

Dissatisfaction was not limited to the Sioux or Wounded Knee. At a national conference on the organization of the BIA in Denver, on September 14, Peter MacDonald, president of the Navajo Nation, urged the dismantling of the bureau so that it could "never again exercise total control over activities of tribal governments."

New Commissioner. Morris Thompson, 34, of Juneau, Alaska, was appointed commissioner of Indian affairs on October 30. An Athabascan Indian, Thompson is the youngest commissioner in history. He succeeded Louis R. Bruce who resigned on Dec. 8, 1972, shortly after AIM forces occupied BIA headquarters in Washington, D.C., in November, 1972.

President Nixon signed legislation on August 16 authorizing the United States to acquire for up to $70 million the productive timberlands belonging to the "remaining members" of the Klamath tribe of Oregon. The 473 members of the tribe who originally voted not to divide their holdings under the Klamath Termination Act of 1954, would receive about $120,000 each for the land. The 136,000-acre tract was expected to become part of the Winema National Forest.

U.S. Census Reports issued in July showed an Indian population of 792,730 in 1970, a startling 51.4 per cent increase since 1960. This compares with a national growth rate of 13 per cent.

Nearly half of the Indians live in urban areas, about 28 per cent on 115 major reservations, and the rest on smaller reservations and in rural areas. Their annual median income is $5,832, as compared with a national average of $9,590. The census figures also showed that urban Indians have higher incomes and are better educated than reservation Indians. In Los Angeles, the median yearly income of Indian families was $8,342; on the Navajo Reservation, the largest Indian reservation, the median family income was $3,084.　　　　　　　Andrew L. Newman

INDIANA. See STATE GOVERNMENT.

INDONESIA. President Suharto's government continued to drive ahead with its economic reconstruction of the country in 1973, and its policies obviously bore fruit. Several world trends accelerated this modernization of Indonesia.

The Organization of Petroleum Exporting Countries increased the price of Indonesia's sulfur-free oil, and the government took advantage of the Arab cutback in Middle East production by increasing its oil price in October. Oil production was also stepped up to almost 2 million barrels per day. This accounted for a major hike in export earnings, which were expected to reach $2.5 billion for the year.

The Economy. The government's stability continued to attract large-scale foreign investment. About $300 million in private funds from the United States, Europe, and Japan gave promise of new economic enterprises and much-needed employment. Public investment in the form of credits for more economic development and expansion accounted for another $800 million.

Yet there were weak spots in this buoyant expansion. Most of these centered around unemployment on the island of Java, which contains 70 per cent of the population of Indonesia. Many of the landless peasants of Java have crowded into the cities looking for jobs that do not exist. They can find only seasonal work or the most menial jobs. Efforts have been

Indonesia's President Suharto, left, and Prime Minister Edward Gough Whitlam of Australia discussed regional cooperation in February.

made to restrict peasant entry into Djakarta, but this has only caused them to crowd other cities. Hopes that the new miracle rices might encourage the peasants to stay on the farmland have proved fruitless. Introduction of the rice has been slow, and it requires extensive fertilizing, which many farmers cannot afford.

Rice Production. Indonesia produced more than 14 million tons of rice in 1973, but still had to import about 1 million tons. The government began a small public-works program for the rural areas that was expected to provide the peasants with additional work. The government also hoped to encourage and help unemployed Javanese to move to other, more sparsely populated islands, such as Halmahera and Kalibantan. It was estimated that about 50,000 migrate each year, but the numbers must be greatly increased before crowded conditions on Java can be alleviated.

President Suharto was cautious in his conduct of foreign affairs, preferring to play a role in the Association of Southeast Asian Nations rather than to attempt any large moves on his own. He politely rebuffed an Australian bid for inclusion in a general Asian Pacific regional organization that would include China. Relations with China were guarded, reflecting hostility to China's role in support of the overthrown Sukarno government.   John N. Stalker

See also ASIA (Facts in Brief Table).

INSURANCE. Eight states—Arkansas, Colorado, Hawaii, Kansas, Nevada, New York, Texas, and Utah—enacted no-fault automobile insurance laws in 1973. The new laws, under which victims of accidents are reimbursed for their net medical and wage losses by their own insurance companies, were to become effective in seven of the states in early 1974. Texas started its system on Aug. 27, 1973. No-fault laws also became effective in 1973 in Connecticut, Maryland, Michigan, and New Jersey. The laws, like others enacted earlier, vary as to compulsion to buy coverage, the extent of benefits, and the right to bring lawsuits.

No-fault laws were also considered by 21 other state legislatures in 1973. The governors of New Mexico and Illinois vetoed no-fault bills passed by the state legislatures. In Michigan, an association of lawyers started court action in September to test the constitutionality of the no-fault law, but they failed to win an injunction sought to bar the law from becoming effective on October 3. Also in September, the Florida Supreme Court heard arguments on the constitutionality of the Florida law, which has been in effect since 1971. In July, the court had declared the basic property-protection provision of the Florida law unconstitutional. The provision had exempted auto property damage of up to $550 from lawsuits.

A federal no-fault bill was referred to the Senate Judiciary Committee for further consideration, with the understanding that its findings be reported by Feb. 15, 1974.

Insurance Availability. In October, Massachusetts and North Carolina enacted new laws that require all automobile insurers in the two states to accept without question any motorist entitled to coverage. For the purpose of equitable distribution of loss only, risks that are considered unusual may be reinsured in a pool facility supported by all the auto insurers. A somewhat different version of the system became effective in Florida on October 1.

The concept is vigorously supported by Federal Insurance Administrator George K. Bernstein, who calls it Full Insurance Availability. He favors its application to all personal lines of insurance so that assigned risk plans, by which insurance companies group together to minimize unusual risks, can be discarded. A bill that closely follows the Bernstein proposal was drafted in New York in mid-1973 for legislative consideration in 1974.

Workmen's Compensation. By the end of 1973, various state legislatures had passed more than 200 laws designed to reform state workmen's compensation systems. The new laws were part of a conscious effort to comply with recommendations made in a 1972 report to Congress and President Richard M. Nixon by the National Commission on State Workmen's Compensation Laws. The 1973 scoreboard showed 46 states with unlimited medical coverage, 44 states with coverage for all occupational diseases, and 40 states making coverage mandatory.

However, Senators Harrison A. Williams (D., N.J.) and Jacob K. Javits (R., N.Y.) considered the record not good enough and introduced a bill to establish strict minimum federal standards. If passed, the bill would require states to adopt the federal standards by Jan. 1, 1975. Their proposal is strongly opposed by the private insurance business and by many state officials who see it as a threat to traditional state regulation.

A Major Scandal hit the insurance industry in April when Equity Funding Corporation of America, which has headquarters in Century City, Calif., was accused of engaging in a multimillion-dollar fraud involving at least 56,000 bogus life insurance policies, forged bonds and death certificates, and $210 million in nonexistent assets. The plan was intended to inflate the company's financial status, thus boosting the price of its stock. Although Equity Funding filed for bankruptcy on April 5, federal and state investigations of the parent company and its various life insurance affiliates are continuing.

Prepaid Legal Insurance. In August, President Nixon signed into law an amendment to the Taft-Hartley Act to permit collective bargaining by unions to obtain legal services insurance as a fringe benefit. Several insurance companies indicated they would be willing to underwrite the coverage on either a group or individual basis.   Emanuel Levy

INTERIOR DESIGN. The Americana-country look was the favorite design theme in 1973. Its comfortable styling and motifs of ecology and American history appealed to all ages. Animals, insects, plants, and outdoor scenes were featured in designs. Brown was the most popular color, along with greens and other natural and earth tones. The combination of red, white, and blue was also popular.

Colonial and Early American furniture stylings were part of the mood. Cheerful prints covered chairs and sofas that were fully skirted. Patchwork-quilt patterns were offered everywhere in coordinated wallpaper and drapery fabrics. Quilt patterns adorned print carpets and flooring materials. The most popular design for curtains, tablecloths, draperies, and wallpaper was gingham checks.

Completing the Americana mood were accessories, clocks, lamps, and lighting selections with motifs from nature and American heritage. Countless reproductions of grandfather clocks, patriotic symbols, and Indian pottery, crafts, and arts appeared.

Chinese Furnishings. American retailers and designers visited China and imported furnishings after the United States renewed contacts with the People's Republic of China. Oriental design was a strong influence. Several manufacturers offered such accent selections as an *armoire* (cupboard or closet) in Chinese Chippendale style with pagoda design crown. Indoor and outdoor furnishings teamed rattan with tortoise-shell finish and split bamboo. Chinese jars and vases were reproduced in lamp bases. The Chinese oil lamp from clipper-ship times was also reproduced.

Mediterranean/Spanish stylings continued to dominate sales of bedroom and dining room furnishings. The trade newspaper *Home Furnishings Daily* reported in September that a survey of retailers indicated that 62 per cent considered Mediterranean the leading bedroom style and 33.8 per cent regarded it as the most popular dining room selection.

New Products. The year's most exciting new product was ready-to-assemble furniture, sold for decades by mail order. Manufacturers dubbed it K-D because the furniture can be knocked down for packing, storage, or shipping. Available in many styles, K-D offerings included curved-arm rockers with curved legs and padded seats, colorful plastic desks with matching chairs, butcher-block tables with folding chairs for either dining or game table use, and lounge chairs with padded seats and backs.

Among the new K-D products were wall systems that offer a variety of storage and display capabilities. The systems were produced in wood, wood and metal, all metal, chrome and glass, chrome and plastic, and plastic and metal. The systems can be assembled with interlocking devices to obtain the needed size. Free-standing or attached to walls, the systems provide shelves and storage space as well as surfaces for desks, food and beverage bars, and housing for audio and visual equipment.

Wood shortages made plastics even more important as a raw material for furniture. Plastics were used as components for dressers, chests, and cabinets, and for decorative panels on drawers.

Another new product was fire-resistant vinyl upholstery material with a soft leather look. The new covering meets federal flammability specifications and can self-extinguish within two seconds.

A report by Seidman & Seidman, a Grand Rapids, Mich., accounting firm, predicted that shipments of wood and upholstered furniture would break all records in 1973. They projected total shipments at $7.25 billion, a 24 per cent increase over 1972. The predictions were based on increased personal income and home construction, and consumer optimism.

The furniture-warehouse type of store grew in popularity. The largest such operation, Levitz, Inc., operated 54 stores in the United States in 1973 and planned to open more. More than 25 home furnishings retail sales organizations sell furniture in warehouses. Customers carry their selections home immediately upon purchase.

Industry Awards included the National Home Fashions League Trailblazer Award to Mary Kraft, director, home building and decorating department, *Good Housekeeping* magazine. Furniture designer Leonard Eisen received the "Polymer Man of the Year" award from the Society of the Plastics Industry. Helen C. Schubert

INTERNATIONAL LIVE STOCK EXPOSITION.

Michelle Gropper, 13, of Grinnell, Iowa, showed Cuddles, the 1,425-pound crossbred Simmental-Angus steer that won the 1973 grand championship at the 74th International Live Stock Exposition. The event was held in Chicago from November 19 to 25.

Another 13-year-old girl, Peggy Rodibaugh of Rensselaer, Ind., showed the best barrow (hog). Her champion, a 200-pound Chester White-Hampshire crossbreed, brought a high bid of $14.25 a pound at auction. James Heggemeier of Kirkland, Ill., showed the champion wether lamb, a Suffolk.

Michelle's steer was also named champion of the junior (21 and under) competition, where reserve went to Jeff Hibbs, 15, of Albion, Iowa. The reserves in the open show included a 1,435-pound Maine-Anjou-Angus crossbreed owned by Don and Duane Hilbert of LuVerne, Iowa, and Garrett and Lee DeJong of Kennebec, S.Dak.

Winning in the hog trucklot (10 head) competition were Chester White-Hampshire-Duroc crossbreeds belonging to the whole Rodibaugh family. In the junior lamb competition, the champion was a Suffolk-Hampshire crossbreed belonging to Jeff Granger, 16, of Lake Charles, La.

International directors voted on November 23 to keep the annual show in Chicago. They acted after city and state officials assured them of financial aid to continue the show. Morris E. Rogers

Michelle Gropper poses with her grand champion steer Cuddles and the trophies it won at the 1973 International Live Stock Exposition in Chicago.

INTERNATIONAL TRADE AND FINANCE. Despite uncertainty, occasional crises in the international monetary system, and currency-exchange rates that fluctuated daily, world trade showed explosive growth in 1973. By the second quarter, total world imports had surpassed an annual rate of $500-billion, an amazing 31 per cent above the same period in 1972.

Because the figures are in U.S. dollars, they are partly inflated by the several devaluations of the dollar's exchange rate against most of the other main currencies since 1971. In addition, part of the huge trade increase simply reflects higher prices due to inflation. But the International Monetary Fund (IMF) reported that "even after corrections have been made for these influences, there remains considerable growth in trade volume, surpassing the average annual rate of increase over the past three years."

The boom in trade reflected the surging, prosperous economies of all the industrial countries. The year brought rare simultaneous booms in the United States, Europe, and Japan. There was a disadvantage, in the form of rapid inflation throughout the world. However, employment and production were high everywhere. The year's growth in trade also supplied strong evidence that floating currency-exchange rates do not disrupt trade, as had been feared.

Exchange Rates. Another of the monetary crises that have afflicted the world periodically since 1967 erupted early in February. These crises, involving massive flows of funds from one currency into another, occurred because currency-exchange rates did not reflect the economic realities of each country. Above all, the U.S. dollar was badly overvalued in relation to nearly all the other major currencies except the Canadian dollar. The February crisis produced a 10 per cent devaluation of the dollar against European currencies, the second since 1971.

The quick dollar devaluation did not settle the currency markets, however, and the finance ministers of the leading countries, meeting in Paris in March, decided on a bold experiment. Nine European countries, most of them members of the European Community (Common Market), agreed to lock their exchange rates together and then float jointly against the dollar in daily trading. Floating allows exchange rates to move with market supply and demand, with no regular intervention by government central banks to hold the rate at any particular level. The jointly floating group used central bank intervention to keep their currencies at the agreed exchange rates among themselves, but they let the whole "snake," as it was called, move up or down against the dollar without intervention. Great Britain, Italy, and Switzerland remained outside the joint float and let their currencies float independently.

Nervous markets in June and early July sent the dollar plunging to levels that nearly all economic ex-

The International Monetary Fund and the World
Bank met in Africa for the first time in September,
in the Kenyatta Conference Center in Nairobi, Kenya.

perts regarded as too low. This, it was thought, appeared to be caused partially by the emerging Watergate scandal in the United States. In early July, the European central banks and the U.S. Federal Reserve System agreed to intervene in the dollar market from time to time to prevent disorderly conditions. Although actual intervention was never great, the dollar quickly steadied and then rose gradually. Against the German Deutsche mark, for example, it rose 13 per cent over the July low by year-end.

U.S. Trade Balance. The fundamental reason for the improvement in the value of the dollar was the radical improvement in the U.S. balance of trade and the overall balance of international payments, which was the original objective of the change in currency-exchange rates. The large devaluation of the dollar began to work as intended – imports cost more to Americans and American goods less to foreigners – and the enormous U.S. trade deficit (imports over exports) of $6.3 billion in 1972 was transformed into a small surplus in 1973.

New Monetary System. As the world moved toward better overall balance than had prevailed for many years, and as floating exchange rates became more familiar and exchange markets calmer, 20 nations designated by the IMF continued to seek a more permanent monetary system. The old system had collapsed in 1971 when President Richard M. Nixon decided to suspend convertibility between the dollar and gold. The Committee of 20 agreed early in its deliberations that the new system, like the old, should be based on fixed exchange rates, but that rates should be changed more frequently than in the past, and that individual countries be allowed to float under agreed rules. At the annual IMF meeting in Nairobi, Kenya, in September, the committee set a deadline of July 31, 1974, for resolving the outstanding issues.

Meanwhile, the temporary floating system appeared to be working fairly well. In the United States, in particular, a rising chorus of voices advocated that a permanent solution to the international monetary problems be based on a general floating system – with occasional intervention by central banks – instead of fixed rates. Japan and most European nations, however, continued to advocate a return to "stable but adjustable" exchange rates.

Trade Negotiations. Preliminary steps were taken in 1973 for major new trade negotiations, aimed essentially at lowering tariffs and other trade barriers. A keystone of the negotiations was to be new U.S. trade legislation. In April, President Nixon submitted the Trade Reform Act to Congress. It gave him new authority to negotiate reductions in U.S. tariffs and other barriers, such as import quotas, and authority to curb imports in certain cases. Although the bill finally passed the House on December 11, it was held up for two months by controversy over a section that would ease trade with Russia.

"Remember the rules, boys.
Floating only—no swimming."

IRAN experienced a year of internal stability and continued economic development in 1973. Shah Mohammed Reza Pahlavi pursued a vigorous foreign policy and a military preparedness program designed to make Iran a major factor in regional affairs.

In February, the U.S. Department of Defense made the biggest single arms deal it had ever arranged. In it, Iran contracted for from $2 billion to $3 billion in arms. The purchase included primarily fighter aircraft but also tanks and other sophisticated equipment. Border clashes with Iraq and anti-Shah broadcasts from secret radio stations on Iraqi territory, along with subversion by the Front for the Liberation of the Arab Gulf, underscored Iranian concern.

The Shah exchanged state visits with Pakistani Prime Minister Zulfikar Ali Bhutto and Saudi Arabia's King Faisal. He visited Romania in June and signed a cooperation agreement. Also in June, he signed an agreement with King Mohammed Zahir Shah of Afghanistan for distribution of waters from the Helmand River, which serves both countries. It would permit irrigation of Iran's parched Sistan Province adjoining Afghanistan. The Afghan military government agreed to honor the pact following the overthrow of Zahir in July. See AFGHANISTAN.

Reforms Planned. The fifth five-year plan started on March 21. It is described as an effort to close the

As part of the new era of friendliness between the United States and Russia, President Nixon had asked Congress to give Russia "most favored nation" status, which would permit Russian goods to be charged the same relatively low tariffs as goods from non-Communist countries. He also asked that the U.S. Export-Import Bank be allowed to extend credits to help finance shipments of machinery and other capital goods from the United States to Russia. Both moves became snarled, however, when the House made them contingent upon Russia adopting a free emigration policy, especially for Jews seeking to go to Israel. Fearing that such curbs might damage U.S.-Russian cooperation in the Middle East peace negotiations, the President asked the House in October to postpone consideration of the entire trade bill. He changed his mind in early December. Final resolution of the issue will depend on what action the Senate takes in 1974.

The Less-Developed Countries benefited in 1973 from sharply higher prices for primary products, both for their farm products and such nonfarm goods as metals. While problems of poverty and development continued to be enormous, at least their foreign trade was in better shape, and they were able to borrow record sums in markets abroad. Edwin L. Dale, Jr.

See also ECONOMICS; Section One, FOCUS ON THE ECONOMY.

IOWA. See STATE GOVERNMENT.

Shah Mohammed Reza Pahlavi of Iran, on an arms-buying trip to the United States, tries out the cockpit of a new Navy jet fighter for size.

gap between rich and poor with agricultural and social reforms, and will cost $32 billion. An annual growth rate of 11 per cent and an increase in per capita income from $481 to $851 were projected. The record $7-billion 1973 budget increased expenditures by 24 per cent, with 28 per cent of the total earmarked for defense, apart from the U.S. arms deal.

Attaining the plan's objectives and continuing economic growth remained tied to oil exports. On May 24, Iran reached agreement with a consortium of Western oil companies to end the 25-year 1954 concession ahead of schedule. Ownership of consortium assets was transferred to the National Iranian Oil Company (NIOC) in return for a 20-year commitment from NIOC for oil exports to consortium markets overseas. NIOC also reached an agreement with Ashland Oil Company to market Iranian oil directly in the United States in the first such deal for a Middle Eastern oil-producing country.

Foreign Investors were attracted by Iran's economic health. In March, the World Bank loaned $82 million for telecommunications, including construction of a second earth satellite terminal in Teheran. A consortium of U.S. banks loaned $250-million for industrial projects in July.

The Russian-built Isfahan steel mill began production on March 16.   William Spencer

See also MIDDLE EAST (Facts in Brief Table).

IRAQ. The Ba'ath Party regime of President Ahmad Hasan al-Bakr was nearly ousted in 1973. While Bakr was in Bulgaria, Ba'athist leaders led by Colonel Nazem Kazzar, the head of internal security, attempted a coup on June 30, with the help of army units. The plotters seized the defense and interior ministers, but the plan to seize Bakr at the Baghdad airport on his return misfired when the president's plane was delayed. Loyal troops then surrounded the airport. Kazzar and his supporters fled toward the Iranian border with their captives, but were captured. Kazzar was executed. Defense Minister Hammad Shihab was killed during the chase.

A wave of arrests followed, with some 35 persons sentenced to death or prison terms. The plot appeared to involve officials higher than Kazzar in the regime. The attempted coup provided clear evidence of the existence of army disloyalty and of factional hatreds within the Ba'ath Party.

Deal with Communists. In an effort to broaden its base of popular support, the regime formed a National Front with the Iraq Communist Party on July 14, the 15th anniversary of the 1958 revolution that ended the monarchy. It also resumed peace talks with the rebellious Kurdish minority. A "Charter of National Action," issued on August 26, listed 16 members: 8 Ba'athists, 3 Communists, 3 Kurds, and 2 independents. The Kurdish Democratic Party re-

Iraq's Revolutionary Command Council marched in the funeral procession for Defense Minister Hammad Shihab, killed in an attempted coup in June.

fused to become a member of the front, however.

At the same time, amendments to the provisional Constitution increased the authority of the president, delegated greater legislative powers to the Cabinet, and reinstated a 1970 law providing for a 100-member National Assembly. The assembly would be appointed by the ruling Revolutionary Command Council from the Ba'ath membership, National Front groups, and trade unions. President Bakr also became premier and commander in chief of the armed forces. He was given the power to appoint or dismiss every other government official.

Kurdish reluctance to enter the National Front stemmed from continued delays in implementing the 1970 agreement providing regional autonomy for the Kurds. On August 19, Kurdish leader Mustafa Barzani set conditions for Kurdish support. They included government jobs and free elections.

Oil Agreement. Settlement of the 10-year dispute between the government and the Iraq Petroleum Company (IPC) in February cleared the way for resumption of oil production. The settlement nationalized IPC assets in return for free deliveries of 15-million tons of oil, worth $288 million, to IPC at eastern Mediterranean ports. The company also agreed to pay Iraq $338.4 million in back royalties. As a result, Iraqi oil began flowing again to Syrian and Lebanese refineries on March 19. William Spencer

See also MIDDLE EAST (Facts in Brief Table).

Liam Cosgrave, new prime minister of Ireland, is congratulated by his daughter, Mary, on the results of the February 28 general election.

IRELAND. A coalition of the *Fine Gael* (Gaelic People) and Labour parties defeated the *Fianna Fáil* (Soldiers of Destiny) in the general election on Feb. 28, 1973. The Fianna Fáil had held power since 1957. Liam Cosgrave, 52, leader of Fine Gael, became prime minister, and quickly showed he was at least as determined as his predecessor, Jack Lynch, to work for understanding with Great Britain over Ireland. See COSGRAVE, LIAM.

On September 17, Edward Heath became the first British prime minister to visit Dublin since Ireland won independence in 1921. Heath and Cosgrave agreed to cooperate and to seek a Council of Ireland that would represent both the republic and Northern Ireland. It was agreed to on December 10 by Great Britain, Ireland, and Northern Ireland.

The conciliation process had been set back briefly in August when two brothers, jailed in Dublin for bank robbery, claimed they had been working for British intelligence. The British government admitted recruiting them to gather information about the Irish Republican Army (IRA). Dublin stiffly described British intelligence activities in Ireland as "unacceptable and counterproductive." But the row cooled when it was revealed that Lynch, then prime minister, was told on January 3 of Britain's connection with the case.

Tough Policy. A tough anti-IRA policy was pursued throughout the year. Lynch had refused to release Sean Mac Stiofain, Provisional IRA chief of staff who was jailed for six months. Rory O'Brady, Provisional *Sinn Fein* (Ourselves Alone) society president, was sentenced to six months in prison on January 11. He was one of many IRA men convicted on the uncorroborated testimony of a senior police officer. Such convictions were possible under special legislation that became effective in December, 1972.

On March 28, the Irish Navy seized a small Cyprus-registered ship, the *Claudia*, as it tried to rendezvous with a launch off the Waterford coast of Ireland. The ship was carrying some 5 tons of Libyan arms for the provisional IRA. Six Irishmen were arrested, including Joe Cahill, a former commander of the provisional IRA in Belfast. Cahill was sentenced to three years in prison on May 21.

Ireland joined the European Community (Common Market) on January 1. Inflation ran higher than in any other Common Market country, but membership brought economic benefits, including a saving on agricultural subsidies. On May 16, Finance Minister Richie Ryan introduced a record $2.6-billion budget, with increased welfare payments.

On May 30, Erskine H. Childers, 67 and a former deputy prime minister, was elected president. He succeeded Eamon de Valera, 91, who retired after 14 years. See CHILDERS, ERSKINE H.　George Scott

See also EUROPE (Facts in Brief Table); NORTHERN IRELAND.

ISRAEL. The fourth round of the Arab-Israeli war erupted on Oct. 6, 1973, ending 10 months of relative calm along Israel's borders and in occupied Arab territories. When a cease-fire ended the fighting on October 22, neither side could claim a decisive advantage. For details on the fighting and its aftermath, see MIDDLE EAST.

Until the outbreak of war, Israel observed its 25th anniversary year under circumstances favoring orderly development and concentration on internal affairs (see MIDDLE EAST [Close-Up]). The Palestinian guerrilla movement was virtually neutralized as a threat to internal stability when three top leaders in Gaza were killed in March. An Israeli commando raid on April 10 on Beirut further reduced Palestinian leadership.

Israel took several positive steps to improve relations with its Arab population. On May 24, Mapai, the majority Labor Party, approved membership for Arabs. A campaign by Histadrut, the Israeli Labor Confederation, added 8,000 Arab members to its rolls. The first Histadrut-sponsored Arab trade unions, a printing cooperative and a building society, were established in East Jerusalem.

Occupied Areas were quiet except for a brief protest strike by Arab shopkeepers in Jerusalem to mark the sixth anniversary of the 1967 war on June 5. The government decided Arab families in East Jerusalem could claim compensation for property abandoned during their flight from the 1948 fighting. Families of victims on a Libyan airliner shot down by Israeli jets on February 21 were paid $30,000 each.

On April 10, biophysicist Ephraim Katchalsky, the majority Mapai candidate, was elected president by 66 to 41. In accord with government policy, he changed his name to Katzir. See KATZIR, EPHRAIM.

Of the other elections scheduled for 1973, those held for Histadrut leadership on September 11 brought a turnout of only 6.5 per cent of the 1.2-million eligible voters. In Knesset (parliament) elections on December 31, Mapai remained the leading party, but lost ground to a hard-line rightist coalition, Likud. The results were expected to make Middle East negotiations more difficult.

The Economy. Early in the year, public interest focused less on politics than on inflation. Doctors, truckers, teachers, civil servants, and even garbagemen struck for higher wages and fringe benefits. On June 24, the government imposed a three-month price freeze in an effort to stabilize the cost of living.

Israel's second oil refinery opened in June at Ashdod. Its production of 4.2 million tons annually from the Sinai fields would make the country self-sufficient in oil. Former Premier David Ben-Gurion died on December 1. William Spencer

See also MIDDLE EAST (Facts in Brief Table).

Israel celebrated its 25th anniversary with a parade of military power in May in Jerusalem. That power had to be put to use in the October war.

ITALY ended 1973 with a new center-left government, its 35th government since World War II. Christian Democrat Mariano Rumor became prime minister in July and pledged to combat inflation and industrial unrest and defend the lira. Giulio Andreotti's centrist coalitition, which excluded the Socialists, lasted less than a year. He resigned on June 12 in the face of labor unrest, a currency crisis, and dwindling support from Liberals and Republicans.

Rumor welded together Roman Catholics and Socialists in a new government announced on July 8, but the powerful left wing trade unions withheld support. Parliament delayed approval until July 20.

Domestic Problems. On January 12, some 14 million Italians went on strike for social reforms and more help for the underdeveloped south. A second general strike on February 27 was followed by a stoppage of customs men and a three-week strike of postal, telephone, and telegraph workers that ended on May 6. Charges that "reactionary businessmen" were gaining control of leading newspapers for political ends led to a journalists' 24-hour "day of silence" strike on June 5.

After a three-day strike by bakers sent the cost of some bread up to $1.75 a pound, more than 10 times the normal price, bread riots broke out in Naples, where vast numbers of poor and unemployed look on bread as their staple food. Women erected blazing barricades and tore up paving stones on July 19. The shortage was overcome with an influx of 235,000 tons of wheat from the Common Market.

On July 24, the new government froze most manufacturers' and retail prices, mainly of foods and other necessities. Later, police began arresting grocers and bakers found violating controls. Forty-eight Turin bakeries were closed for five days for price-freeze violations. Working-class rents were also frozen.

Prison riots broke out on July 27. Rampaging prisoners caused $1.67 million in damage to Rome's Queen of Heaven prison. Trouble in jails in Milan, Naples, Trieste, and four other cities was resolved only when Minister of Justice Mario Zagari promised prison and penal-code reforms.

Measures to protect the lira included tighter control on imports payments and a curb on bank borrowing. In his first budget, Rumor estimated a 1973 deficit of $14.7 billion. Industrial production rose 10.2 per cent in the year ending in June.

Other Events. A referendum on the 1970 divorce legalization was postponed by the Council of State until 1974. On April 13, the Senate approved an internationally financed $550-million project to save Venice from sinking into its lagoon. About 25 people died in a cholera outbreak in late August. Outlets for raw sewage into the Bay of Naples were blamed for contaminating mussel beds.   Kenneth Brown

See also EUROPE (Facts in Brief Table).

IVORY COAST. See AFRICA.

JAMAICA. See WEST INDIES.

JAPAN. Foreign relations made much of the news in Japan in 1973. Prime Minister Kakuei Tanaka paid official visits to Washington, D.C., Moscow, Paris, Bonn, and London during the summer and early fall. He and the host governments were primarily concerned with mutual economic problems, but they also discussed other issues.

The prime minister conferred with President Richard M. Nixon on July 31 and August 1. At the end of the meeting, they announced their satisfaction with the improved trade balance between the two countries and their hopes regarding the global trend toward détente. They also looked to coordinated efforts to ensure a stable supply of energy sources, including oil supplies, for both countries. They approved Japanese participation in building a uranium-enrichment plant in the United States. Tanaka announced a Japanese grant of $10 million to major American universities for Japanese studies, and Mr. Nixon pledged U.S. support for a permanent seat for Japan in the United Nations Security Council. The close ties with the United States were a problem after the outbreak of war in the Middle East. Japan, which imports about 90 per cent of its oil from that area, was badly hurt by the Arab oil boycott.

Relations with Russia. The prime minister's October visit in Moscow was not too successful. It failed to produce agreement on the most difficult problem in Japanese-Russian relations, the return to Japan of Kunishiri, Etorofu, Habomai, and Shikotan, four islands lying northeast of Hokkaido that were occupied by Russian forces at the end of World War II. This territorial impasse is the principal barrier to a formal peace treaty, although the two nations have had normal relations since 1956. However, the two governments agreed to promote economic cooperation and to sign contracts on economic matters. Other agreements between Japan and Russia related to scientific and technical cooperation, collaborative research on the peaceful uses of atomic energy, and preliminary cooperative efforts in environmental protection. Russian Communist Party leader Leonid I. Brezhnev and Tanaka also agreed that the United States could become involved in joint Japanese-Russian projects.

In Paris, London, and Bonn, just prior to his Moscow visit, the prime minister's talks centered on increased cooperation between Japan and Western Europe, particularly in economic affairs. He invited Queen Elizabeth II to visit Japan in 1975 and President Georges Pompidou to visit in 1974. In addition, he arranged for a showing of Leonardo da Vinci's *Mona Lisa* in Japan in 1974.

Relations with China. In late March, Japan and the People's Republic of China exchanged ambassadors for the first time. Even in the absence of a formal trade agreement, Japanese-Chinese trade in the January to June period reached $1.05 billion, 72 per cent more than for the same 1972 period. Exports to China totaled $565.5 million and the imports totaled $488.6 million.

Although formal relations between Japan and the Nationalist Government in Taiwan were broken off in 1972, trade between them also rose sharply in 1973. Taiwanese officials estimated that it might total $2 billion for the year.

A difficult problem in Japanese-Korean relations arose with the abduction to Seoul of Kim Dae Jung, a South Korean opposition leader, from his Tokyo hotel on August 8. He was taken to Seoul and finally released in late October. Japanese officials asserted that the Korean Central Intelligence Agency was involved in the Tokyo incident, a violation of Japan's sovereignty. At first, Korea refused to cooperate in an investigation, but early in November, Prime Minister Kim Jong Pil went to Tokyo and formally apologized.

Financial Reserves. Japan's external reserves totaled $14 billion at the end of September after reaching a record high of $19 billion in February. It was estimated that United States-Japanese trade would close the year just under $2 billion in Japan's favor, less than half of what it was in 1972. Severe and unexpected limitations imposed by President Nixon in July on U.S. exports of soybeans, a major source of protein for Japanese diets, shocked the Japanese. Japan and Canada have become each other's second-best trading partners, being outranked only by the United States in both cases.

Japan's gross national product in the fiscal year ending March 31 reached $321.1 billion, an 11.5 per cent increase over the preceding year. The per capita income topped $3,000 for the first time, at $3,022. Consumers continued to be plagued by rising prices with the consumer price index in October up 12 per cent from 1972. A contributing factor was the international rise in the price of Japan's imports. The value of the yen continued to rise, reaching 266 per $1 in October as compared with 308 in February. In December, the Cabinet decided on an "austerity" budget for 1974.

The Environment. In an unprecedented statement, Emperor Hirohito expressed hope in September that land development, greatly intensified in recent years, would "go hand in hand with environmental protection." The government is also considering plans to limit Japan's steelmaking capacity at about 140 million metric tons, in part because of pollution problems. Production in 1973 was estimated at 120 million metric tons.

Japan started the first year of a five-year plan to improve its defense capabilities in 1973. Its Self Defense Forces are designed to defend the nation in a localized war. The five-year plan will cost a total of $15 billion.   John M. Maki

See also ASIA (Facts in Brief Table).

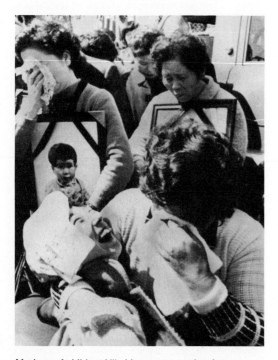

Mothers of children killed by mercury poisoning weep after a Japanese court found a chemical firm guilty of polluting fish the victims ate.

JEWS. The war between Israel and the Arab countries, which began in October, 1973, was the major issue that captured the attention of Jewish communities throughout the world. Massive fund-raising and other relief efforts were made. However, U.S. Jews dealt with numerous other issues relating to group survival and assimilation.

The question of marriages between Jews and Gentiles came into sharp focus with the National Jewish Population Study report that the rate of intermarriage had risen to a high of 48.1 per cent between 1966 and 1972. Responding to this problem at its June convention, the Central Conference of American Rabbis (Reform) adopted an unprecedented policy opposing the sanctioning of mixed marriages by its members.

In the United States. Christian-Jewish relations were also the subject of concern. The Christian evangelical Key 73 program, launched on Christmas Day, 1972, caused some fears about possible Christian proselytization efforts in the Jewish community. The unrelated activities of missionary groups, the most prominent of which was the San Francisco-based "Jews for Jesus," added to these fears. However, the National Jewish Community Relations Advisory Council, programmatic coordinator of 34 Jewish organizations, concluded at its June convention that fears about "the aggressive missionizing content" of Key 73 had abated. Likewise, they

A group of Russian Jews protests outside the ministry of internal affairs in Moscow against government refusal to grant visas to Israel.

confined within 3 miles of their homes and were denied permission to emigrate. The condition of the 350-member Iraqi Jewish community also deteriorated. A series of government-ordered executions was reported.

The economic and political upheavals in Chile adversely affected the Jewish community there. By August, about 5,000 Chilean Jews had emigrated to Brazil, Ecuador, and Costa Rica. Most left because of financial reverses experienced under Marxist President Salvador Allende Gossens. Shortly after Allende's fall, on September 11, there were signs of anti-Semitism, and the future of the remaining 28,000 Chilean Jews was uncertain.

During late 1972 and 1973, the Jewish community lost four major figures. Rabbi Abraham Joshua Heschel of the Jewish Theological Seminary (Conservative), one of the leading authorities on Jewish mysticism, died on Dec. 23, 1972, at the age of 65. Jacques Lipchitz, the noted sculptor and artist, died at 81 on May 26. Rabbi Joseph Henkin, a prominent Orthodox scholar of Jewish religious law, *halakha*, died on August 11, at the age of 93. Rabbi Maurice N. Eisendrath, President of the Union of Hebrew Congregations, died November 9, at the age of 71.

The Jewish population for 1971 (the most recent year for which figures were available) was 14,236,000 as opposed to 13,950,000 in 1970. Of that total 50 per cent lived in the Americas.   Judah Graubart

adjudged the missionary efforts of the "Jews for Jesus" as largely unsuccessful.

The role of women in American Judaism received increased attention. An unprecedented conference of 450 Jewish feminists under the auspices of the North American Jewish Students Network was held in New York City in February. On August 15, the Conservative movement accorded women equal rights with men in the synagogue.

American Jews of North African and Spanish descent, known as Sephardic Jews, moved to establish themselves as a distinct element of the American Jewish community. The founding convention of the American Sephardic Federation was held on February 25 in New York City. Professor Daniel Elazar of Temple University was elected the federation's president.

In Other Countries. The status of the Russian Jewish community remained a major concern. Jews in other countries protested against the exit visa tax imposed on Jews emigrating from Russia to Israel. Legislation reinforcing this protest was introduced in both houses of U.S. Congress. The legislation intended to deny Russia a most-favored-nation tariff status until the exit tax was rescinded. Within Russia, although some Jews were allowed to leave, the arrest and trial of Jews continued.

In Syria, the 4,350-member Jewish community continued to live under harsh conditions. Jews were

JORDAN resumed diplomatic relations with Egypt and Syria in September, 1973. This marked the return of King Hussein I to favor with other Arab nations. Jordan had been isolated for three years after Hussein suppressed the Palestinian guerrillas in 1970 and proposed a binational Arab-Israeli state in 1972.

Hussein's restoration to favor followed his taking a strong stand against the proposal by President Habib Bourguiba of Tunisia for meetings with Israeli representatives. Hussein shared the view of his former Arab rivals. Jordan broke diplomatic relations with Tunisia on July 17 after Bourguiba suggested that Jordan be returned to the Palestinians as part of an overall Arab-Israeli peace settlement.

Jordan joined the war against Israel in October, sending troops into the fighting in Syria. See MIDDLE EAST.

Immediately after the announcement, Jordan and Tunisia resumed diplomatic relations. And on October 18, Kuwait announced it would resume paying its $46-million annual subsidy to Jordan.

Hussein's first concrete step toward reconciliation involved releasing political prisoners. A number of Palestinians jailed since 1970 were freed on September 19. A general amnesty was proclaimed for the remaining 750 Palestinians still in prison.

New Cabinet. Prime Minister Ahmad al-Lawzi resigned for health reasons in May. He was replaced by Zayd Rifai, formerly ambassador to London.

Rifai's new Cabinet included 11 ministers serving for the first time. Half of the 20 members were of Palestinian origin as the king sought to strike a balance between his traditional supporters and young Palestinian technocrats. A new post, that of minister of occupied territories affairs, was added to the Cabinet.

For much of the year, Jordan's economic progress was slow in the absence of Libyan and Kuwaiti financial subsidies. They had been suspended in 1971 after Jordan suppressed the Palestinian guerrillas.

Development Project. A hopeful sign was the beginning of work on the eastern Jordan Valley agricultural project, the major element in the 1973-to-1976 development plan. The project will eventually irrigate and develop 20,000 acres in the valley.

The United States loaned Jordan $10 million in February for construction of the Zarqa Dam, part of the same project. In August, $25 million in other aid followed Hussein's visit to the United States. More backing for the Jordan Valley project, a total of $104 million, came from the World Bank and West Germany. Kuwait granted Jordan $8.5 million through its Fund for Arab Economic Development, and the World Bank approved a second loan of $8.7-million for Amman's water system.   William Spencer

See also MIDDLE EAST (Facts in Brief Table).

JUNIOR ACHIEVEMENT (JA). See YOUTH ORGANIZATIONS.

KANSAS. See STATE GOVERNMENT.

KATZIR, EPHRAIM (1916-   ), a Russian-born molecular biologist, was elected president of Israel by the Knesset, or parliament, on April 10, 1973. The youngest president in Israel's 25 years as a nation at 57, he was sworn into the largely ceremonial post on May 24, 1973. As Ephraim Katchalsky, he had been among Israel's best-known scientists. Immediately after the parliamentary action, he changed his name to Katzir in accord with a government policy that calls for all state officials to have Hebrew names.

Katzir was born in Kiev, Russia, on May 16, 1916. His family emigrated to Palestine in 1922. During Israel's war of independence in 1948, the noted scientist headed the science corps of Haganah, the Jewish underground organization. After Israel was established, he became chief science adviser to the new nation's defense ministry.

In 1949, Katzir joined the newly created Weizmann Institute of Science at Rehovot, Israel, and became head of the biophysics department. He is also a founder of the Israel Academy of Sciences and Humanities. His older brother, Aharon Katchalsky, head of Weizmann Institute's polymer research department, was killed by terrorists in a Tel Aviv airport massacre on May 30, 1972.

Katzir planned to continue his research during his service as president. He is married to the former Nina Gotlieb. They have two children.   Ed Nelson

KELLEY, CLARENCE MARION (1911-   ), was sworn in as director of the Federal Bureau of Investigation (FBI) on July 9, 1973, in Kansas City, Mo., his hometown. Kelley was nominated for the post after L. Patrick Gray III, acting FBI director since May 3, 1972, withdrew his name when it became obvious he would not be confirmed by the U.S. Senate.

Kelley has spent his entire career in law enforcement. From 1940 to 1961, he was with the FBI as a special agent in Memphis, Tenn., except for three years of service in the U.S. Navy during World War II. He served as police chief in Kansas City from 1961 until his appointment as FBI director. He is a strong advocate of modern technological assistance for the police, and pioneered in using computers to provide instant access to files. He also originated the first 24-hour helicopter patrol used in an American city.

Born in Kansas City in 1911, Kelley graduated from the University of Kansas in 1936 and the University of Kansas City Law School, now part of the University of Missouri, in 1940. Politically nonpartisan, he headed the security advisory board for the national conventions of both major political parties in 1972.

Kelley and his wife, Ruby, have two grown children and two grandchildren. He has been a Sunday school teacher and deacon of the Country Club Christian Church in Kansas City.   Kathryn Sederberg

KENTUCKY. See STATE GOVERNMENT.

KENYA celebrated the 10th anniversary of its independence from Great Britain in 1973, and two events occurred that enhanced Kenya's international prestige. The United Nations Human Environment Program headquarters opened in September in Nairobi, the capital, and the International Monetary Fund (IMF) met there in October. Kenya waived its ban on contact with white southern African governments and allowed the Portuguese and South African delegations to attend the IMF meeting. However, the South African minister's speech was boycotted by Asian and African finance ministers.

Political critics continued to charge that Kenya's prosperity benefits only a few and that too much economic power is concentrated in the hands of Asian and European minorities. There were also charges of rampant tribalism favoring the largest ethnic group, the Kikuyu.

Noncitizen Minorities. Kenya continued its measured withdrawal of noncitizen Asian and European work permits, recalling 418 in January. An estimated 2,000 persons, including dependent women and children, were forced to leave Kenya because of this. One of Kenya's most pressing problems was the presence of noncitizen Asians who had been expelled from Uganda in 1972 and barred from settling in Britain.

British Home Secretary Robert Carr warned the East African Commonwealth countries in January that Britain could not accept another mass wave of

Asian immigrants. There were an estimated 35,000 Asians with British citizenship living in Kenya. Nevertheless, Kenya's commerce minister announced in April that the government intended to continue its plan to Africanize the economy.

However, President Jomo Kenyatta, in a speech in June, reaffirmed minority rights. And there were rumors in October that Kenya had agreed to accept the entire British quota of Asian immigrants from Commonwealth countries.

In February, Swahili was declared Kenya's national language. However, English remained the language of international communication.

Dispute with Uganda. Reports circulated in February that officials of the East African Railways Corporation had disappeared while working in Uganda. Kenya's newspapers charged that some officials had been murdered by Ugandan soldiers and that others had fled the country.

Ugandan officials blamed Kenyans of the Luo tribe who work on the railroad in Uganda for circulating the accusations and threatened to expel some of them. All the Luos then threatened to leave. The dispute was finally settled, and Uganda guaranteed the safety of all Kenyans living there. See UGANDA.

Kenya instituted the death penalty for armed robbery in April. John Storm Roberts

See also AFRICA (Facts in Brief Table).

KHMER. The so-called cease-fire and armistice in Vietnam brought no peace to this war-torn nation in 1973. Instead, the Vietnamese peace meant an increase in the fighting in the Republic of Khmer, formerly known as Cambodia.

Three major elements were involved. Most of the government forces, nominally under the control of President Lon Nol, were clustered around the capital city of Phnom Penh. These forces were badly organized and badly led. North Vietnamese units, coming back from South Vietnam, moved into sanctuaries along the border in Khmer. The North Vietnamese forces gave some support to a Khmer group opposing Lon Nol, the Khmer Rouges.

During the spring and summer, the rebel forces appeared to have gained the upper hand. They cut off Phnom Penh from the provinces and snapped a vital river link with the south. It looked as though the Lon Nol government would soon fall.

Government Shakeup. Two factors combined to save the government. Lon Nol gave in to the needs of the moment and brought the able Sisowath Sirik Matak and In Tam back into the government in April. They are two of his leading political opponents, but both had worked with Lon Nol in the past. They set about the task of reorganizing the army and the government, as well as trying to solve the problems caused by the tide of refugees that flooded into

Khmer Rouge rebels turn in their weapons, including some U.S. rifles, to troops loyal to the government. Communist forces surrendered in January.

the capital. In Tam resigned to return to private life in December, and Foreign Minister Long Boret was named to replace him. The second factor was heavy U.S. bombing during the late spring and early summer, which dispersed rebel troops threatening to take the city.

The cutoff of U.S. bombing on August 15, imposed by the U.S. Congress, raised doubts about whether government forces could continue to hold out against the rebels. In a surprising move, however, government troops regrouped and even retook the all-important port town of Kompong Cham in October. Monsoon rains halted further large-scale military operations until the end of the year.

Prince Sihanouk. The situation was further complicated by the diplomatic maneuvering of the big powers in relation to deposed Prince Norodom Sihanouk, now living in Peking, China. During the year, Sihanouk issued a series of statements indicating a host of contradictory possibilities. He said, among other things, that the rebels would win easily, that he would return soon to take over the government, that the North Vietnamese would assist him, and finally, that he despaired of ever being able to return. That there were diplomatic talks by the big powers over the disposition of Khmer was obvious. As the year ended, no settlement between the opponents had been reached.   John N. Stalker

See also Asia (Facts in Brief Table).

KING, BILLIE JEAN (1943-   ), won her fifth Wimbledon singles tennis championship in England in July, 1973, and became a hero in the women's rights movement when she defeated 55-year-old "male chauvinist" Bobby Riggs on September 20. The match, billed as the "Battle of the Sexes," was played in the Houston Astrodome, and it paid King $100,000 in prize money. Earlier in the year, she won her fifth Wimbledon singles championship in England. See Tennis.

Billie Jean Moffitt King was born in Long Beach, Calif., on Nov. 22, 1943. She began playing tennis seriously when she was 11 years old. Although she briefly attended college, she spent most of her earlier years training for a professional tennis career. She won her first Wimbledon championship, in doubles, in 1961. She has won nine doubles and three mixed doubles titles at Wimbledon in addition to her five singles championships. She has also won the U.S. Open title three times.

An outspoken advocate of increased prize money for women tennis players, King helped organize the all-woman Virginia Slims circuit in 1970. In 1971, she became the first female athlete to win more than $100,000 in one year. In 1973, King organized the professional Women's Tennis Association.

She married Larry King, a lawyer, in 1965. He acts as her agent and manages her investments in tennis camps and equipment.   Darlene R. Stille

KIWANIS INTERNATIONAL took pride in 1973 in the fact that new clubs were being established at a record rate. In the 1971-1972 administrative year, 265 new clubs were approved in the 40 Kiwanis nations, the most since 1922, when 273 new clubs were formed. During the current administrative year, Kiwanis built 221 new clubs in the United States and Canada, 28 in Kiwanis International Europe, and 14 in the remaining international extension nations.

The 10th anniversary of the 1963 Kiwanis European Mission – "to open Europe to Kiwanis extension" – was marked in 1973. The 1963 Mission granted charters to Basel, Switzerland; Vienna, Austria; Brussels, Belgium; Oslo, Norway; and Reykjavík, Iceland. Kiwanis International Europe now has 159 clubs in 12 nations.

The rapid growth of Kiwanis Clubs, especially in other parts of the world, received the attention of the Kiwanis World Secretariat, which was created to coordinate the policies and programs of Kiwanis International and Kiwanis International Europe. At a meeting in June, 1973, the secretariat gave new club building top priority, with special attention to expanding Kiwanis Europe and helping other overseas areas form clubs.

The 58th annual convention was held in Montreal, Canada, in June. William M. Eagles of Chesterfield, Va., was elected president and Roy W. Davis of Chicago, president-elect.   Joseph P. Anderson

KORBUT, OLGA (1955-   ), Russian gymnast, was named female athlete of the year by the Associated Press in January, 1973. She was the first athlete from a Communist country to win this distinction from the U.S. news wire service.

The tiny gymnast won three gold medals and one silver medal at the 1972 Olympic Games in Munich, West Germany. The graceful, daring performance of this 4-foot 11-inch, 84-pound girl captivated the spectators and made her one of the most popular athletes in the games. Since then, an International Gymnastics Federation commission has suggested some of her feats, such as a double backward somersault on the balance beam, be barred as too dangerous.

Olga Korbut was born in Grodno, a city near the Polish border. Her father is an industrial engineer; her mother, a cook. She has two sisters and a brother.

At school, a physical education teacher discovered her outstanding athletic ability and sent her to a school where she received special sports instruction in addition to her regular schooling. In 1969, she entered Russia's national gymnastic championships, demonstrating for the first time her difficult backward somersault on the balance beam. Although she was the smallest and youngest contestant, she won fifth place. She also won a gold medal for horse vaulting in Russia's national title meet in 1970, and in 1972, before her Olympic victories, she won several top awards in Russian competitions.   Darlene R. Stille

KOREA, NORTH. President Kim Il-song brought North Korea into a more active world role in 1973. By decision of the Korean Workers' Party, the Communist Party that runs the country under Kim, the North Korean Parliament adopted a new Constitution on Dec. 27, 1972. It created a strong presidency, which Kim assumed after being premier for 24 years, thus enhancing his near-dictatorial control.

Unification talks with South Korea made no significant progress. On April 6, the North Koreans charged in a letter to the U.S. Congress that the U.S. government was discouraging the talks. North Korea shifted emphasis from the talks to attempts to end its virtual isolation from non-Communist countries. About 10 nations established commercial or diplomatic relations. With admission to the World Health Organization on May 17, North Korea began to achieve a status comparable to that of South Korea.

When South Korea, in reaction, proposed on June 23 that both join the United Nations (UN) separately, Kim called for confederation and one UN membership. The South rejected this. A UN debate in November postponed a choice between the two positions. North Korea broke off direct unification talks, accusing South Korea's chief delegate, Lee Hu-rak, with involvement in the kidnaping of Kim Dae-jung, which he denied (see KOREA, SOUTH). Lee resigned on December 3.   Henry S. Bradsher

See also ASIA (Facts in Brief Table).

KOREA, SOUTH. Kim Dae-jung, the 1971 presidential candidate who nearly defeated President Chung Hee Park, was kidnaped on Aug. 8, 1973, from a hotel in Tokyo, Japan. This followed Kim's criticism abroad of Park's 1972 constitutional changes to increase his personal control. Kim was released on August 13 near his home in Seoul, Korea, and then was placed under virtual house arrest until October 26, when he emerged to say he was quitting politics for a while. The kidnaping caused strong protests abroad, particularly in Japan. It was widely blamed on the Korean Central Intelligence Agency, although this agency denied it.

After some hesitation, Japanese Prime Minister Kakuei Tanaka announced on September 7 that Japan would not restrict its aid and trade as a result of the incident. The United States also did not react, though the Korean agency reportedly had harassed Korean exiles in the United States as well.

Internal Affairs. Domestic protests to the kidnaping and to tight government control grew, despite arrests of students, Protestant clergymen, and other protest leaders. Beginning in October, students at a number of universities and colleges defied threats of severe penalties to launch a series of demonstrations demanding free speech, other liberties, and release of those arrested. In an effort to quell the trouble, Prime Minister Kim Jong Pil accepted responsibility for public unrest and reshuffled his Cabinet on

December 3. Lee Hu-rak resigned as head of the Central Intelligence Agency, which demonstrators accused of secret police oppression.

Per capita income rose to $302 a year in 1972 as a planned economic boom continued. A goal of doubling this purchasing power by 1981 was based on more industrialization. Greater attention was being paid to agricultural modernization in order to reduce the need for imported food.

With North Korea emerging from isolation and direct North-South talks on unification stalemated, South Korea dropped efforts to block the North's general acceptance as a parallel regime. The United Nations (UN) decided on November 28 to postpone a decision on Korean membership, to dissolve the UN Commission for the Unification and Rehabilitation of Korea, and to leave untouched the UN military command, under which U.S. troops remained in South Korea.

In security talks, held in Seoul on September 12 and 13, U.S. Deputy Defense Secretary William P. Clements, Jr., reassured South Korea of "the continued readiness and determination of the United States to render prompt and effective assistance" if the South were attacked. Clements said the United States had no present plans to reduce its troops in South Korea.   Henry S. Bradsher

See also ASIA (Facts in Brief Table).

Over 200 students of Seoul National University were arrested when they defied martial law and demonstrated for the return of civil rights.

KORUTURK, FAHRI (1903-   ), became Turkey's sixth president on April 6, 1973, ending a month-long struggle between the nation's parliamentary and military leaders. Parliament elected Koruturk after 15 ballots, giving him 47 votes more than the necessary simple majority of 318. See TURKEY.

Koruturk's selection as president was considered a compromise between the military and parliamentary leaders. When he took the oath of office, Koruturk said he would try to carry out his task "with the cooperation of constitutional institutions." The remark was called acknowledgment of the armed forces' consent to his election.

Koruturk was born in Istanbul. After completing elementary school, he entered the Naval School in 1916. He was an admiral and commander of Turkish naval forces when he retired from the navy in 1960. He had also served as naval attaché in Rome, Berlin, and Stockholm.

After leaving the navy, he joined the Turkish foreign service. For four years, Koruturk served as ambassador to Russia, but he was relieved at his own request. In 1968, President Cevdet Sunay chose Koruturk as one of the 15 senators who are appointed by the president. He was described as an impartial, honest, courageous military man.

President Koruturk was married in 1948. His family includes two sons and one daughter. He speaks English, German, and Italian.   Ed Nelson

KUWAIT. A long-simmering border dispute with Iraq produced clashes and an abortive occupation of a Kuwaiti post by Iraqi troops in March, 1973. This issue and the approach of another Arab-Israeli war stimulated a new government policy of excessive military spending. In June, the Supreme Defense Council placed orders for $1.5 billion worth of military hardware—including tanks, Crusader aircraft, and the Hawk missile system—from the United States. British naval vessels were also ordered. Universal conscription began, making 18 months of military service compulsory for males from 18 to 30.

Apart from military preparedness, Kuwait continued to use its oil revenue to support the Arab cause. It loaned $13 million to Sudan for a sugar refinery and an equal amount to Egypt for development of Mediterranean offshore natural gas fields in Abū Qīr Bay.

Despite a 3.8 per cent drop in oil production, Kuwait continued to prosper. The 25 per cent participation agreement with the Western-owned Kuwait Oil Company would have brought Kuwait $100 million per year. The National Assembly refused to ratify the agreement, however. In December, it reportedly won a 60 per cent share of the nation's largest oil concern. Kuwait cut off oil shipments to the United States on October 21 because of U.S. support for Israel.   William Spencer

See also MIDDLE EAST (Facts in Brief Table).

LABOR. Another year of controls, marked by the implementation of Phases 3 and 4, saw the standard for wage increases in the United States remain at the familiar 5.5 per cent in 1973. Wage increases resulting from collective bargaining were generally within stabilization guidelines, but the prices workers had to pay, especially for food, rose substantially. On the bright side, the unemployment picture improved, and more workers than ever had jobs. They also lost less time due to work stoppages, as strike idleness fell to a nine-year low.

Prices, as measured by the Bureau of Labor Statistics' (BLS) Consumer Price Index (CPI) rose 7.4 per cent in the 12 months ending September 30. This rise, which occurred despite the imposition of a 60-day price freeze on June 13, reversed the encouraging trend of the previous two years. After the CPI rose 5.9 per cent (a 20-year high) in 1970, anti-inflation efforts kept the rates down to 4.3 per cent in 1971 and 3.3 per cent in 1972.

The unemployment rate finally sank below 5 per cent in June, to 4.8 per cent. By October, it had dropped to 4.5 per cent, the lowest since April, 1970; unemployment had averaged 5.9 per cent in 1971 and 5.6 per cent in 1972. Total employment reached 85.7 million, an impressive 3.2-million increase since October, 1972.

Real earnings, however, were disappointing. In the 12-month period ending September 30, a 6.7 per cent increase in average hourly earnings was more than offset by the 7.4 per cent rise in the CPI, resulting in a 0.9 per cent decline in real average weekly earnings. Real weekly spendable earnings declined 2.3 per cent.

BLS preliminary estimates given in the table below show some of the major employment changes that occurred in 1973:

	1972	1973*
	(in thousands)	
Total labor force	**88,991**	**90,708**
Armed forces	2,449	2,340
Civilian employment	86,542	88,368
Unemployment	4,840	4,328
Unemployment rate	5.6%	4.9%
Change in real average weekly earnings		
(Private nonfarm sector)	4.3%	−2.3%†
Increase in output per man-hour		
(Private nonfarm sector)	4.2%	2.7%‡

*January-September average, seasonally adjusted
  except for armed forces data.
†For 12-month period ending Sept. 30, 1973.
‡Compared to third quarter of 1972.

Collective Bargaining affected some 4.7 million unionized workers in 1973, a substantial rise over the 2.8 million whose contracts expired or were subject to reopening in 1972. BLS figures for the first nine months showed an average increase in wages of 5.5 per cent over the life of settlements affecting 1,000 or more workers. This compares with an average increase of 6.4 per cent in 1972, and 8.1 per cent in 1971. First-year wage adjustments also declined, averaging 6 per cent, as opposed to 7.3 per cent in 1972 and 11.6 per cent in 1971.

The moderate negotiated wage increases in the face of a re-escalation of prices could be attributed in part to the 5.5 per cent wage stabilization guideline, as well as the protection afforded by automatic cost-of-living provisions. In 1973, 4.1 million workers were covered by escalator clauses, which provide automatic increases when prices rise.

Auto Settlements. A three-year agreement at the Chrysler Corporation was reached on September 17, three days after workers went on strike. The settlement, covering 115,000 members of the United Auto Workers (UAW), was a prime example of the emphasis on nonwage items. Workers gained and management lost historic "rights" over overtime scheduling. Auto workers won the right to refuse to work more than nine hours a day or more than two consecutive Saturdays, and to decline Sunday work. The limits did not apply, however, during the car-model changeover period. The UAW also gained the "30-and-out" retirement goal as part of a five-year pension agreement. Beginning in March, 1974, workers could retire at a guaranteed $550 a month after 30 years of service, regardless of age. The sum was to rise to $700 a month by 1978. Previously, an auto worker's $500 monthly pension, attained after 30 years, was reduced by 8 per cent for each year he was under age 56. Normal pensions were also liberalized, rising to $11 a month for each year of service by 1978. Wages were not completely forgotten, with a 3 per cent plus 12 cents increase the first year, and 3 per cent hikes in both the second and third years.

The Ford Motor Company pact reached on October 26 for 185,000 auto workers generally followed the Chrysler terms. However, Ford production workers were subject to two hours of daily involuntary overtime, compared to only one hour at Chrysler. In November, a similar settlement was negotiated for 400,000 auto workers at General Motors Corporation.

Farm implement settlements followed patterns set in the auto round. A contract negotiated on September 30 at Deere and Company for 23,000 UAW members allowed workers to retire after 30 years regardless of age (with a minimum pension of $625 a month), but provided an option not included in the auto pacts. If a worker chooses to continue working after 30 years of service, he will receive 1 to 4 weeks supplemental vacation, depending on his age. The Deere contract also provided workers with 24 hours' notice of an overtime assignment. Similar settlements were concluded for 40,500 UAW members at International Harvester on November 2 and at the Caterpillar Tractor Company on November 21.

Electrical Equipment agreements were reached in June at General Electric (GE) Company and Westinghouse Electric Corporation. The 37-month GE settlement covered 140,000 workers, and in-

Militant workers took over a Chrysler stamping plant to emphasize demands for better working conditions, a major item in contract talks.

creased wages by from 67 to 88 cents an hour over the term of the contract, depending on CPI changes. The pact liberalized both normal pension and early retirement benefits. The accord at Westinghouse, for 75,000 workers, generally followed the GE pattern.

The Teamsters Union and Trucking Employers, Incorporated, negotiated a 33-month settlement for 400,000 drivers and 1,200 trucking companies on June 28. Wages were increased by 35 cents an hour, effective immediately, with additional 30 cent hikes in 1974 and 1975. Truckers will also get from 8 to 11 cents an hour in cost-of-living boosts in both the second and third years. In December, the Teamsters announced they would reopen contract talks in 1974 to seek higher wages to offset pay losses resulting from the petroleum shortage.

Railroad Bargaining was concluded without the turmoil evident in previous rounds. An 18-month settlement affecting 500,000 members of 15 unions was reached with the nation's major railroads on March 13, well in advance of the June 30 contract expirations. The settlement provided a 4 per cent wage hike on Jan. 1, 1974. It also increased workers' net income by up to $42.75 a month on Oct. 1, 1973. The railroads assumed part of the employees' contributions to the Railroad Retirement System.

The Steelworkers' Union reached an experimental negotiating agreement with a committee bargaining for 10 major steel producers. Ratified by the

Steelworkers Basic Steel Conference on March 29, the historic agreement was designed to avert a strike threat until 1977 and consequently eliminate stockpiling by strike-anxious steel customers. It provided for binding arbitration of unresolved issues arising in the upcoming 1974 negotiations, and prohibited either strikes or lockouts. The parties agreed to begin bargaining by Feb. 1, 1974, for renewal of contracts that expire on August 1. Unresolved issues would be submitted to a five-member arbitration panel that would render a decision by July 10, three weeks before the contracts expire. The pact also guaranteed a 3 per cent wage hike on August 1 of 1974, 1975, and 1976 as a minimum "floor" that could be augmented in the 1974 bargaining. Steelworkers also will receive a $150 bonus on Aug. 1, 1974, for their contribution "to stability of steel operations."

In a similar vein, major aluminum companies agreed to start negotiations three months earlier with the Steelworkers' and Aluminum Workers' unions over contracts expiring May 31, 1974. Talks began Nov. 27, 1973. If settlements were not reached by Feb. 1, 1974, disputed issues were to be submitted to the presidents of the unions and companies for possible arbitration. The aluminum approach, however, did not specifically prohibit strikes.

Farmworkers received encouragement and financial support from the AFL-CIO in their jurisdic-

Cesar Chavez of the United Farm Workers, left, confers with AFL-CIO President George Meany at a union meeting in Washington, D.C., in May.

tional dispute with the Teamsters for control of California's grape and lettuce fields. In January, Cesar Chavez' embattled United Farm Workers saw the Teamsters renegotiate the remainder of five-year contracts the Teamsters had reached in 1970 for 30,000 field-workers employed by lettuce growers. In April, the Teamsters replaced the Farm Workers in the grape fields of California's Coachella Valley.

To aid the Farm Workers in their struggle, the AFL-CIO in May established a $1.6-million fund to pay strike benefits. On August 21, after meeting with AFL-CIO President George Meany, Teamsters' President Frank E. Fitzsimmons repudiated the Teamsters' grape pacts, but he reversed himself on November 7. In late October, the Teamsters' Executive Council rejected a compromise solution in which the Farm Workers would have represented field hands, and the Teamsters those workers employed in canneries and warehouses.

The AFL-CIO Convention. Growing disenchantment with President Richard M. Nixon's Administration came into focus in August when Meany announced that the President and Secretary of Labor Peter J. Brennan would not be invited to the federation's convention. At the convention, held from October 18 to 23 in Bal Harbour, Fla., the delegates approved an unprecedented resolution calling for the President's resignation because of the "constitutional crisis" brought about by the firing of Special Prosecutor Archibald Cox and the resignations of Attorney General Elliot L. Richardson and Deputy Attorney General William D. Ruckelshaus. The resolution called on the House of Representatives to impeach the President if he did not resign.

W. A. (Tony) Boyle, former United Mine Workers' president, was arrested on September 6 in connection with the 1969 slayings of union insurgent Joseph A. (Jock) Yablonski, his wife, and daughter. The arrest followed Boyle's indictment by a federal grand jury in Pittsburgh on charges of conspiracy to deprive Yablonski of his right to participate in union affairs. Meanwhile, the state of Pennsylvania filed a murder warrant against Boyle. On November 9, Boyle, who was confined to a wheelchair, was ordered removed to Pittsburgh, where he was scheduled to be arraigned on Feb. 25, 1974. A Washington County grand jury also indicted Boyle for murder in December. In a separate case, Boyle lost an appeal to the U.S. Supreme Court and was sentenced to three years in prison and fined $130,000 for illegally contributing union funds to political candidates.

Job Discrimination. Women employees joined racial minority groups in fighting job discrimination. In a landmark antibias agreement concluded in January, the American Telephone and Telegraph Company (AT&T) agreed to pay $15 million in back wages to victims of sex and racial discrimination. The giant utility also agreed to establish new promotion and wage policies for women and minori-

Strike Activity Nose-Dives

Man-days lost (millions)

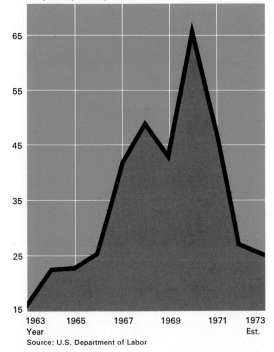

Source: U.S. Department of Labor

ties, at an estimated cost of $23 million the first year. The agreement introduced the concept of "delayed restitution," with AT&T agreeing to reimburse workers who "missed" wage hikes because they felt the company did not encourage applications for promotion. Women also won back pay when job discrimination suits were settled at PPG Industries, Incorporated, in Pittsburgh, and at a GE plant in Fort Wayne, Ind. See CIVIL RIGHTS.

Major Strikes. In early November, New York City suffered simultaneous walkouts by firemen, hospital workers, and members of the Newspaper Guild at the *New York Daily News.* The first strike in the 108-year history of the New York City Fire Department ended after 5½ hours when the Firefighters Union signed an accord with the city calling for binding arbitration of disputed salary contract issues. The Drug and Hospital Workers Union struck 48 voluntary hospitals and nursing homes over the Federal Cost of Living Council's delay in approving a deferred 7.5 per cent wage increase that was due on July 1. The strike ended after a week when the hospital workers accepted the council's recommendation of a 6 per cent wage increase. The newspaper strike ended after two days when the guild accepted a *Daily News* contract offer. Leon Bornstein

See also Section One, FOCUS ON THE ECONOMY; Section Two, BLUE-COLLAR BLUES, WHITE-COLLAR WOES; Section Three, ECONOMICS.

LAOS. An uneasy peace came at last in 1973 to the tiny landlocked country, which has suffered immense wartime deprivation and destruction since 1960. It began in February, when Prime Minister Souvanna Phouma and his rightist group of advisers in the capital city of Vientiane accepted a cease-fire agreement with the Communist Pathet Lao. The agreement left two-thirds of the countryside in Pathet Lao hands, while two-thirds of the population remained under the control of Vientiane. It also imposed a coalition government that gave half the ministry posts to the Pathet Lao and half to the Vientiane government, and ended U.S. bombing of Pathet Lao positions.

Both Sides Stall. Supporters of the Vientiane regime, however, were prone to reject the compromise. For seven months, it appeared that the agreement would not be implemented. Both sides seemed to stall, even though they were prodded to accept the terms by outside supporters. Right wing government supporters even attempted a coup in August to overthrow the Vientiane government. The uprising was quickly suppressed, and U.S. advisers pressed for acceptance of the settlement.

It was clear that North Vietnam was also pressuring the Pathet Lao to accept the cease-fire. North Vietnam did not want the Laotian hostilities to endanger its peace talks with the United States.

The rightists made one last military effort against the Pathet Lao when they tried to recapture Saravane in August. Their troops were badly beaten. After that, it was only a matter of time and haggling until the agreement was implemented. The accord was finally signed by both sides in September.

The signing ceremony, on September 14, took place in the dining room of Prime Minister Souvanna Phouma's residence on the outskirts of Vientiane. It was preceded, on September 12, by the initialing of the agreement by representatives of both sides.

Souvanna Phouma was to remain as prime minister, and his supporters would control five ministries in the new provisional government, including defense, interior, and finance. But the agreement provided that the Council of Ministers must act unanimously, so major decisions could easily be stalled by the Pathet Lao. The agreement also called for the withdrawal of all foreign troops within 60 days. But it did not provide any way to enforce such withdrawals.

It was a grudging, uneasy peace at best, with few guarantees for the future. But Laotians were too exhausted to continue the conflict. The provisional government was faced with a staggering reconstruction program. About one-fourth of the Laotians had abandoned their homes during the war, and an estimated 800,000 refugees were crowded in and around Vientiane. While the agreement called for helping refugees return to their villages if they wished, neither side appeared to be doing much to make this either possible or desirable. John N. Stalker

See also ASIA (Facts in Brief Table).

LATIN AMERICA

Three major political events roiled the Latin American continent in 1973. In Argentina, former dictator Juan Domingo Perón staged an amazing comeback; a violent military coup rocked Chile; and democracy received a severe setback in Uruguay. The Chilean revolt left only four South American nations – Argentina, Colombia, Venezuela, and Guyana – under civilian governments. See ARGENTINA; CHILE; COLOMBIA; URUGUAY; VENEZUELA.

On the economic front, soaring world prices for regional Latin American commodities brought greater earnings, but this was a mixed blessing. Several countries were forced to curtail certain exports to help avoid unpopular shortages and higher domestic prices. Latin Americans also had to buy grains, steel, and oil abroad at the prevailing higher prices, thus adding to their foreign debts.

U.S. Policy. On May 12, U.S. Secretary of State William P. Rogers began a two-week visit to Latin America to discuss ways to develop better relations. He told various Latin American leaders that the days of American "paternalism" are over. He promised "new forms of cooperation," and later said the United States "welcomes positive nationalism that is in no way antagonistic to the United States or other nations of the hemisphere, but is a serious and determined drive to make things better."

On October 5, Secretary of State Henry A. Kissinger, who succeeded Rogers in August, called on the republics to join with the United States in a "new dialogue" that would re-examine the structure and assumptions of the hemispheric alliance: "We in the United States . . . do not believe that any institution or any treaty arrangement is beyond examination." Here, he apparently was referring to the Organization of American States (OAS), whose value, in view of world changes, has been challenged in recent years both in the United States and in Latin America. It was Kissinger's first policy statement on the area, and was meant to signal a major effort by the Nixon Administration to take a fresh approach to the problems of the Western Hemisphere.

The OAS had set up a special committee in April to study its charter in depth and to propose changes. Subsequently, the committee analyzed the "philosophy, instruments, structure, and functioning" of the

Chilean soldiers round up suspected government supporters outside the national palace during a coup d'état that toppled President Allende.

operation, and drew up recommendations for reforms deemed necessary to make the OAS "respond adequately to the new political, economic, social, and cultural situations in all the member states, and to hemisphere and world conditions." For the first time in OAS history, the expression "recognition of the plurality of political, economic, and social systems" joined the time-honored principles of the inter-American system: juridical equality of the states, self-determination, and nonintervention. The committee was to present a general report on its work to the various governments by the end of the year.

Banking Reforms Weighed. The Inter-American Development Bank (IDB) was deluged during the year with renewed calls to revamp its operations. Apart from suggestions that the United States was using the multilateral institution to settle its bilateral disputes, the lesser-developed republics expressed the view that bank funds for development uses did not flow fast enough. There was also the complex question of how to attract nonregional bank members and thus secure more capital, without the IDB losing its hemispheric image. It was expected, however, that by early 1974 the stage would be set for an expanded bank and that the IDB might subsequently become about $1 billion richer.

Venezuela agreed on February 13 to join the Andean Common Market, which includes Bolivia,

Kidnapings of U.S. citizens plagued Latin America in 1973. Here, security guards check cars at a Ford plant in Pacheco, Argentina.

Chile, Colombia, Ecuador, and Peru. As the year ended, only minor formalities remained before the republic became a full member. The newly enlarged group will have a combined gross national product of about $33 billion, a total population of about 70-million, a combined import market of some $5 billion, and well over half of Latin America's known petroleum reserves, which, in 1973, were estimated at about 3.8 billion metric tons. In June, the Andean Common Market had established its first formal tie with a nonhemispheric country with the creation of a mixed Spanish-Andean Commission headquartered in Madrid, Spain.

Early in 1973, the Andean group put into effect a new list reducing tariffs on 2,370 items. Progress toward integrating the various national economies continued, as the group neared agreement on such issues as industrial development, transportation facilities, agriculture, and standardized fiscal, monetary, and commercial policies. Colombia and Venezuela, meanwhile, agreed to consolidate their merchant marine fleets, and to settle border and territorial waters disputes involving the Gulf of Venezuela, which is thought to be rich in oil deposits. The greatly strengthened and enthusiastic Andean Common Market contrasted vividly with the almost lifeless Latin American Free Trade Association, whose member nations fear that any discussion of trade among themselves might lead inadvertently to more sensitive political issues.

Agricultural Ups and Downs. Financial reserves of the Central American Monetary Council's five member nations – Costa Rica, El Salvador, Guatemala, Honduras, and Nicaragua – hit a record high of $550 million in May, an increase of $200 million within a year. The gain reflected the substantially improved trade position of all the republics as the result of more favorable prices for traditional agricultural exports, which include bananas, cacao, and coffee. In the spring, however, the entire Central American isthmus suffered its worst drought in 50 years, causing over $100 million in damage and affecting the production of basic grains and other farm products. In many areas, water and electricity were rationed.

Meanwhile, the U.S. Agency for International Development approved a $40-million loan to the Central American Economic Integration Bank to help finance the development of roads and promote tourism. Costa Rica and Honduras signed a treaty restoring their trade links, which had been broken off in January, 1971. El Salvador and Honduras held peace talks in September in an effort to settle soon the issues involved in renewing diplomatic and trade relations, which were disrupted after the 1969 "soccer" war.

Other Developments. On April 26, Brazil and Paraguay signed an agreement covering the construction of the 10.7-million-kilowatt (kw) Itaipu

After the return to Argentina of Juan Perón, banner-waving youths marched near his home in Buenos Aires, demanding that he assume the presidency.

hydroelectric project on the Paraná River. Construction costs were estimated at $2 billion. The facility, when completed, will be the world's largest. The two nations will divide the power produced by the project, with Paraguay expected to sell any surplus to Brazil.

Argentina protested the scheme, arguing that the accompanying 720-foot-high, 4,600-foot-long dam would create a reservoir of about 515 square miles and could very well wreck the viability of its own hydroelectric projects farther downriver at Corpus and Apipe-Yacireta. Despite this potential problem, Argentina reached a final agreement with Paraguay to proceed with the building of the 3.3- to 3.5-million-kw Apipe-Yacireta hydroelectric power station. Costs were estimated at about $1 billion.

Central America

Costa Rica. Daniel Oduber, president of the Senate, resigned in May to campaign as presidential candidate of the ruling National Liberation Party in the 1974 elections. An unprecedented six candidates will seek the presidency following the failure of Costa Rica's five opposition parties to unite behind a single candidate to oppose Oduber.

On May 23, political pressures forced President José Figueres Ferrer to explain on nationwide television and radio his dealings with Robert A. Vesco, an American citizen who had taken refuge in San Jose. Vesco, who has large investments in Costa Rica, is charged by the U.S. Securities and Exchange Commission with looting four mutual funds and also faces charges of conspiracy to commit fraud and obstruct justice. Figueres maintained that large sums of money deposited in his New York City bank account by Vesco-controlled companies were intended for cultural and scientific ventures in Costa Rica and elsewhere. Vesco subsequently left Costa Rica for the Bahamas.

El Salvador. A prolonged drought in Central America during the early part of the year had an adverse effect on Salvadoran coffee production. Some estimates indicated that crop yields would be from 30 to 40 per cent less than in the previous year. The drought also brought in its wake shortages of beans, rice, and maize. Heavy rainfall in June, though it came too late to alter the crop situation, did help to avert a potentially severe shortage of electricity.

Guatemala. The school system was seriously disrupted in May by a strike involving about 2,000 teachers who demanded a 50 per cent wage increase. The government broke the strike by dismissing 50 teachers. President Carlos Arana Osorio maintained the strike was a cover-up concealing a Communist plan to overthrow the government. About 3,000 peasants seized a large plot of land outside the hamlet of Palo Verde, near Jalapa, on May 26. In a battle between the peasants and government troops who were sent to expel the squatters, 17 persons were

Facts in Brief on Latin American Political Units

Country	Population	Government	Monetary Unit*	Foreign Trade (million U.S. $) Exports	Imports
Argentina	24,628,000	President Juan D. Perón; Vice-President Maria Estela (Isabel) Martinez Perón	peso (5=$1)	1,867	1,977
Bahamas	212,000	Governor General Sir Milo B. Butler; Prime Minister Lynden O. Pindling	dollar (1=$1)	90	338
Barbados	240,000	Governor General Sir Arleigh Winston Scott; Prime Minister Errol W. Barrow	East Caribbean dollar (1.93=$1)	38	130
Belize	135,000	Governor General Richard Neil Posnett; Premier George Price	dollar (1.6=$1)	19	35
Bolivia	5,468,000	President Hugo Banzer Suarez	peso (20=$1)	212	171
Brazil	103,648,000	President Emílio Garrastazú Médici	cruzeiro (6.12=$1)	3,991	4,783
Chile	9,375,000	President (of military junta) General Augusto Pinochet Ugarte	escudo (350=$1)	962	980
Colombia	23,930,000	President Misael Pastrana Borrero	peso (23.6=$1)	586	836
Costa Rica	1,963,000	President José Figueres Ferrer	colón (6.62=$1)	282	374
Cuba	9,268 000	President Osvaldo Dorticos Torrado; Premier Fidel Castro	peso (1=$1.21)	1,043	1,300
Dominican Rep.	4,576,000	President Joaquín Balaguer	peso (1=$1)	347	321
Ecuador	6,961,000	President Guillermo Rodríguez Lara	sucre (25=$1)	311	327
El Salvador	4,098,000	President Arturo Armando Molina Barraza	colón (2.5=$1)	278	277
Guatemala	5,861,000	President Carlos Arana Osorio	quetzal (1=$1)	300	324
Guyana	788,000	President Raymond Arthur Chung; Prime Minister L.F.S. Burnham	dollar (2=$1)	149	134
Haiti	5,274,000	President Jean-Claude Duvalier	gourde (5=$1)	47	60
Honduras	2,951,000	President Oswaldo López Areliano	lempira (2=$1)	196	193
Jamaica	1,978,000	Governor General Florizel Glasspole; Prime Minister Michael Norman Manley	dollar (1=$1.10)	379	621
Mexico	55,867,000	President Luis Echeverría Alvárez	peso (12.49=$1)	1,825	2,935
Nicaragua	2,290,000	3-member National Governing Council (Roberto Martinez Lacayo, Alfonso Lovo Cordero, Edmundo Paguaga-Irias)	córdoba (7.03=$1)	237	229
Panama	1,615,000	Supreme Revolutionary Leader Omar Torrijos Herrera; President Demetrio B. Lakas	balboa (1=$1)	127	439
Paraguay	2,706,000	President Alfredo Stroessner	guaraní (126=$1)	86	70
Peru	15,359,000	President Juan Velasco Alvarado; Prime Minister Edgardo Mercado Jarrín	sol (38.7=$1)	943	790
Puerto Rico	2,712,000	Governor Rafael Hernández Colón	dollar (U.S.)	1,974	3,108
Trinidad and Tobago	1,074,000	Governor General Sir Ellis Clarke; Prime Minister Eric Eustace Williams	dollar (1.87=$1)	555	751
Uruguay	3,027,000	President Juan María Bordaberry Arocena	peso (911=$1)	197	187
Venezuela	11,979,000	President Carlos Andrés Peréz	bolívar (4.3=$1)	3,155	2,301

*Exchange rates as of Nov. 1, 1973

killed and an undetermined number were wounded.

Inflation soared early in the year. By May, consumer prices were a staggering 14.6 per cent above their level at the start of 1973, primarily because of a shortage of such basics as corn and beans and higher import costs. Meat exports were limited to 40.15 million pounds, so that Guatemalans would have a reasonable amount reserved for home consumption.

Honduras remained under the rule of Armed Forces Commander General Oswaldo López Arellano. He had been installed as chief of state for the five remaining years of President Ramón Ernesto Cruz's term in December, 1972, following the ouster of Cruz. Previously, López had overthrown the government in 1963, and had served as chief of state until

Cruz was elected in 1971. The main reason for the take-over in 1972 was the failure of a bipartisan agreement that had been inspired by López before the 1971 campaigning began. Under its terms, power was to be shared by the two major parties, the Nationalists and the Liberals. But friction had quickly developed between the two groups over the division of power, and conditions had become chaotic.

Nicaragua. The aftereffects of an earthquake that shattered Managua in late December, 1972, continued to be felt in 1973. About 80 per cent of the capital's buildings had been destroyed and those still standing were unsafe.

In January, General Anastasio Somoza Debayle asserted Managua would be rebuilt, with its commercial center located about 6 miles from its previous site. Subsequently, millions of dollars in aid for earthquake victims as well as rebuilding projects flowed in from abroad. The International Monetary Fund estimated it would take about $430 million, or 40 per cent of the nation's 1972 gross national product, to replace physical assets destroyed by the quake. To support these efforts, the government introduced a 10 per cent levy on principal exports.

Caribbean Islands

Dominican Republic. Gun battles involving left wing guerrillas and political killings in which left wingers were assassinated by members of a right wing "death squad" plagued the government of President Joáquin Balaguer. One of the most serious of these offenses occurred on February 17, when rebel leader Colonel Francisco Caamano Deno was killed by an army patrol just two weeks after his clandestine landing with a group of well-armed guerrillas. The rebel leader's demise strengthened the political position of President Balaguer, whose plan to run for a third term in 1974 was bitterly opposed by the Dominican Revolutionary Party.

Hundreds of students staged antigovernment disturbances in Santo Domingo on June 1. They were demanding more funds be allocated to the Autonomous University of Santo Domingo. Mary Webster Soper

LAW. See CIVIL RIGHTS; COURTS AND LAWS; CRIME; SUPREME COURT OF THE UNITED STATES.

LEBANON struggled through one political crisis after another in 1973, even before the Arab-Israeli war resumed in the Middle East (see MIDDLE EAST). The problems were rooted in the Palestinian guerrillas' campaign of terror against Israel from Lebanon, and the Israeli responses.

The first crisis followed an April 10 Israeli commando raid on Beirut. Three top guerrilla leaders were killed by the raiders. Prime Minister Saeb Salaam resigned to protest the army's failure to act against the raiders. Kamal Junblat, parliamentary leader of the Druse sect, accused the government of collusion in the raid. Violent demonstrations took place during funeral services for the slain guerrillas. Order was finally restored on April 25. President Suleiman Franjieh named a Sunni Moslem leader, Amin al-Hafez, as Salaam's successor.

Civil War. But sectarian rivalries and a civil war that broke out in May between the guerrillas and the army made Hafez's task all but impossible. The fighting, concentrated in Beirut and in Palestinian refugee camps, claimed heavy casualties before a truce was arranged on May 17.

Hafez resigned on June 14. As his main reason, he cited lack of support for his plan to include nonpolitical technocrats in his Cabinet. The civil war, he said, was secondary. Moslems in parliament and the Cabinet joined against his government, considering it too weak to guarantee a Moslem share of the power with

President Franjieh, a Maronite Catholic. After lengthy negotiations, the president named Sunni deputy Takieddin Solh as the year's third prime minister. A compromise "Cabinet of all Lebanon" then won a vote of confidence in parliament.

Booming Commerce. Lebanon's growth as a banking and financial center was hardly affected by the recurrent political crises. The banking system reached the unusual state of over-liquidity, a condition partly solved by loans in Lebanese currency to India, Algeria, and the World Bank.

On March 6, Lebanon reached an agreement with Iraq on ownership of the Tripoli refinery and other assets of the nationalized Iraq Petroleum Company. The agreement, good for 15 years, enabled the refinery to resume oil production after a nine-month break. Lebanon would receive royalties of 11 cents per barrel of oil shipped through Tripoli, and was guaranteed 40 per cent of Iraqi oil production.

The Lebanese-Syrian border reopened on August 17. It had been closed for three months by Syria to protest the Lebanese Army's antiguerrilla campaign. The closure cost Lebanon $130 million in transit trade and exports to Asian countries. Lebanon also promised to provide working permits and better wages for the 100,000 Syrians working in Lebanon. Their status had been a bone of contention between the two neighbors for some time. William Spencer

See also MIDDLE EAST (Facts in Brief Table).

LEBURTON, EDMOND (1915-   ), became prime minister of Belgium on Jan. 26, 1973, heading a new coalition Cabinet of three political parties. Leburton's success in forming the coalition ended a 63-day government crisis that began with the resignation of Prime Minister Gaston Eyskens' Cabinet in November, 1972. The new coalition included the Social Christian Party, the smaller Liberal Party, and Leburton's own Socialist Party. See BELGIUM.

Edmond Leburton was born on April 18, 1915. He received a degree in political and social science from Liège University. He started his career in public service in 1936, when he was 21, as principal controller of labor. Leburton was commandant of the Secret Army and was active in various underground resistance groups while Belgium was occupied by German troops during World War II. In 1947, he was mayor of Waremme. Since then, he has held several Cabinet offices, including minister of economic affairs.

In early 1971, while he was minister of economic affairs, Leburton was elected the Walloon, or French-speaking, co-president of the Socialist Party. The party had decided it would have one Walloon and one Flemish, or Dutch-speaking, co-president because of the strong tensions between the two cultural groups. Ed Nelson

LESOTHO. See AFRICA.

LIBERIA. See AFRICA.

LIBRARY. Cutbacks in federal aid programs for libraries in 1973 were only partially offset by money from the federal revenue-sharing program. Among the organizations hardest hit by the cutbacks were state libraries and regional and state networks. In Minnesota, for example, libraries lost more than $1-million in service and construction funds.

Library Grants. The Atlanta (Ga.) School of Library Service received a $165,000 grant from the Andrew W. Mellon Foundation. It will support a three-year fellowship program to prepare students for careers as academic librarians in predominantly black institutions. The Folger Shakespeare Library in Washington, D.C., was awarded $98,609 by the National Endowment for the Humanities. The grant will help support the central library.

National Library Week. President Richard M. Nixon, in acknowledging the start of National Library Week on April 8, asked all Americans to support libraries generously and to make the fullest possible use of the rich treasures they possess. He said that "it is imperative that we intensify our efforts to provide every American with a truly equal opportunity to realize the full potential of his abilities." National Library Week had as its 1973 dual themes: "Get Ahead . . . Read" and "Widen Your World."

New Libraries. Northwestern State University of Louisiana opened the new $3-million Eugene P. Watson Memorial Library. The new $460,000 San Carlos Branch Library of the San Diego, Calif., Library System was opened, and the Peabody Museum of Harvard University broke ground for a new $1.6-million library in honor of the late Alfred M. Tozzer. The Woonsocket, R.I., Public Library broke ground for a $900,000 library building.

Construction of the pyramid-shaped John F. Kennedy Library is scheduled to begin in 1974. The $27-million complex will be built on the banks of the Charles River, adjoining the Harvard University campus in Cambridge, Mass. It will house the papers and memorabilia of the late President. Voters in Florida served by the Miami-Dade Library System approved a $34.7-million bond issue to build a new central library building, 4 new regional libraries, and 14 others.

New Studies of public library funding, regional lending library resource centers, and continuing education have been contracted by the National Commission on Libraries and Information Science. The results will be used to draft formal recommendations for nationwide library service.

The 39th session of the International Federation of Library Associations was held in Grenoble, France, from August 25 to September 1. Its theme was "Universal Bibliographic Control."   Robert J. Shaw

See also AMERICAN LIBRARY ASSOCIATION.

The new $24-million Boston Public Library wing, right, provides 170,000 square feet of public space, and it can house more than 600,000 volumes.

LIBYA. President Muammar Muhammad al-Qad-haafi was active on many fronts in 1973, both in shaping Libyan foreign policy and as the architect of Libya's "cultural revolution," a program of internal reforms designed to purge Libyan culture of all "subversive" foreign elements. Qadhaafi's major effort in foreign policy was the merger of Libya and Egypt.

According to an agreement reached in August, 1972, the two countries were to be united as of Sept. 1, 1973. But as the various joint committees grappled with legislative and policy guidelines, the Egyptians increasingly began to favor a gradual merger.

The September 1 deadline passed with no clear timetable for union. However, Egypt and Libya issued a declaration on August 30, setting up a 100-member Constituent Assembly to draw up a draft constitution and nominate a president.

But relations worsened dramatically in October after Egypt accepted the cease-fire that halted the war with Israel. Qadhaafi denounced the cease-fire and charged that Egypt's military strategy was leading to the destruction of Arab military power. Libya closed its embassy in Cairo on December 1.

Cultural Revolution. On April 15, Qadhaafi announced a code of "revolutionary action" that would replace all existing secular laws with Moslem religious law, provide weapons for the people, purge the country of political dissidents, and set up "people's committees" to carry out the cultural revolution.

People's committees took control of Libyan radio and television stations, schools and universities, hospitals, businesses, industries, financial instititions, and government departments. A campaign was underway to remove foreign-language books from libraries. Libya limited the number of foreigners entering the country by demanding that all passports and airline tickets be written in Arabic. However, the government began to have second thoughts about the revolution after mass dismissals of provincial and local administrators by the people's committees in July and August. The Revolution Command Council halted registration of all people's committees as of September 1.

Oil Companies Nationalized. Throughout the year, Libya demonstrated its determination to control its oil assets and to use them to put pressure on Western governments supporting Israel. On June 11, Libya nationalized the Bunker Hunt Company's assets in the Sarir Desert oil field. On August 13, Libya took over 51 per cent ownership of Occidental Petroleum's assets in return for a $135-million payment. On September 1, the fourth anniversary of the revolution, all other oil companies operating in Libya were nationalized on the same 51 per cent basis. Libya was among the Arab nations that instituted an oil boycott of countries deemed pro-Israel during the October Arab-Israeli war. William Spencer

See also AFRICA (Facts in Brief Table).

LIECHTENSTEIN. See EUROPE.

LIONS INTERNATIONAL passed an unusually significant milestone in 1973. It became the first world service club organization to attain a membership of 1 million men. On March 1, it reported 1,011,067 members in 26,222 clubs in 148 countries and geographic areas.

The first Canadian Lions Club with an exclusively deaf membership was chartered on March 2. The Metro Toronto Deaf Lions Club, with an initial membership of 24 was sponsored by the Scarborough Eglenton Ontario Lions Club. More than 500 persons attended the charter night ceremonies including several men who are deaf or hard of hearing. These men expressed interest in joining the new club.

The 56th Lions International Convention was held in Miami Beach, Fla., in June. Tris Coffin of Rosemere, Canada, was elected president. Lions attending the convention discussed and analyzed two important Lion services: work for the blind and work for the deaf. New approaches to sight and hearing programs that Lions clubs can carry out were discussed and analyzed.

The sight seminar discussed such subjects as eye banks, research, employment, and examination and detection clinics for glaucoma and diabetes. The hearing seminar discussed research, bone banks, detection programs, services for those suffering partial auditory loss, rehabilitation, and employment problems of the deaf. Joseph P. Anderson

LITERATURE. Despite soaring prices and unsettled conditions, the American reader and the book-publishing industry that feeds his appetite showed no signs of slowing down in 1973. The novel and the nonfiction book at $6.95 and up appeared here to stay, and illustrated or gift books at $19.95 and up were a commonplace commodity in the booming Christmas market. Those critics and readers given to wondering periodically whether the novel is dying as an art form got a resounding "no" as an answer. Established authors and newcomers created an unusual number of fine novels and short stories.

On May 27, Russia began adherence to the Universal Copyright Convention. Members of the convention agree to grant copyright privileges to the authors of other member nations.

The Novels. Innovation and experiment was the order of the day. Some of the most talked-about novels were marked by an unconventional approach or attempts at unusual comic or satirical effects. By far the most ambitious of these efforts was Thomas Pynchon's *Gravity's Rainbow*, a huge, puzzling but impressive tale about a secret rocket-building conspiracy in London during World War II. With this and two other widely praised novels, *V* and *The Crying of Lot 49*, Pynchon seemed to be staking his claim to the literary eminence once enjoyed by William Faulkner.

Two other well-regarded novelists who came up with unconventional stories were Kurt Vonnegut,

Pianist Arthur Rubinstein, right, contracted in 1941 to write his life story for publisher Alfred Knopf, left. It finally appeared in 1973.

Jr., and Philip Roth. Vonnegut's *Breakfast of Champions* was a comic, surrealistic account of a Midwestern car dealer, while Roth's *The Great American Novel* was a satirical story of a mythical baseball league.

Thomas Berger took the satirical approach, with special inspiration from the Women's Liberation Movement, in *Regiment of Women*, a novel about the take-over of the United States by the female sex. There was satire also in J. P. Donleavy's *A Fairy Tale of New York*, which is a kind of moralistic fable of city life.

One of the year's more impressive performances came in Thomas McGuane's *Ninety-Two in the Shade*, a novel with a Key West background by a writer who frankly conceded he works in the Hemingway tradition. Two other novelists to turn in impressive work were Joyce Carol Oates, who continued her taut and dramatic explorations of modern love and marriage in *Do With Me What You Will*, and Gore Vidal, whose *Burr* was a fictionalized biography of the first U.S. Vice-President to be indicted.

Among other established novelists to publish during the year were the veteran Thornton Wilder, whose *Theophilus North* was a deftly done society tale with a Newport, R.I., background; Allen Drury, whose *Come Nineveh, Come Tyre* envisioned a Washington dictatorship; William Humphrey, whose *Proud Flesh* concerned a Texas matriarch; and Wil-

frid Sheed, whose *People Will Always Be Kind* was a fine novel about an Irish politician.

Other well-known novelists who published well-reviewed books were Mark Harris, with *Killing Everybody;* Wright Morris, *A Life;* Irwin Shaw, *Evening in Byzantium;* Richard G. Stern, *Other Men's Daughters;* and Peter DeVries, *Forever Panting.*

The year's other offerings included C. L. Sulzberger's *The Tooth Merchant*, Robert Sobel's *For Want of a Nail . . . If Burgoyne Had Won at Saratoga*, and Arthur C. Clarke's *Rendezvous with Rama.*

Among the first novels that impressed the critics were Robert Early's *The Jealous Ear*, about a boy growing up in the modern South; Johanna Davis' *Life Signs*, about a troubled young mother who is undergoing psychoanalysis; and Paul Reb's short and comic *Confessions of a Future Scotsman*. In a class by itself was the late John Berryman's autobiographical *Recovery*, dealing with the battle against alcoholism that ultimately brought about the poet's suicide.

Books from Abroad. The most important new novel from abroad was English novelist Graham Greene's *The Honorary Consul*, a serious and philosophical narrative. New novels by three other English authors were well received. They are Iris Murdoch's *The Black Prince*, Doris Lessing's *The Summer Before the Dark*, and Anthony Powell's *Temporary Kings*, the 11th in his projected sequence of novels about English upper-class life under the series title

"A Dance to the Music of Time." Others well received in the United States include Günter Grass's *From the Diary of a Snail;* Heinrich Böll's *Group Portrait with Lady*, a story of Nazi Germany; and Alice Munro's *Lives of Girls and Women*, about a childhood in Canada.

Short Stories. Several writers best known for their novels offered impressive short stories in 1973. Among them were Vladimir Nabokov, with *A Russian Beauty and Other Stories;* Isaac Bashevis Singer, with *A Crown of Feathers;* John Cheever, with *The World of Apples;* Bernard Malamud, with *Rembrandt's Hat;* and Stanley Elkin, with *Searches & Seizures*. Judith Rascoe's *Yours, and Mine* was an impressive first collection of short stories.

There were also several collections of merit from abroad, notably a group of macabre tales by John Collier in *The John Collier Reader;* the late E. M. Forster's tales of homosexuality in *The Life to Come and Other Stories;* the Italian writer Alberto Moravia's *Bought and Sold*, 34 short stories about women, told in the first person; and Julio Cortazar's *All Fires, the Fire and Other Stories*, an impressive group of tales by an Argentine increasingly well regarded in America.

Biography and Autobiography. The lives of literary men again dominated biographies. One of the year's best was A. L. Rowse's *Shakespeare the Man*, a sequel to his *William Shakespeare*, which concentrated more on Shakespeare's literary work than on his private life. Peter Quennell's *Samuel Johnson: His Friends and Enemies*, portrayed Johnson at the peak of his powers.

Two major French literary figures were the subjects of notable biographical studies in V. S. Pritchett's *Balzac* and Francis Steegmuller's *Flaubert in Egypt*, which examined an Egyptian interlude in the life of the young Flaubert.

H. G. Wells has fascinated many biographers, but perhaps none has portrayed him better and in more depth than Norman and Jeanne MacKenzie, whose *H. G. Wells* was one of the year's best biographies. Two other English literary figures who set tongues wagging in their times were V. Sackville-West and Harold Nicolson, whose son Nigel Nicolson published the literary shocker of the year in *Portrait of a Marriage; V. Sackville-West and Harold Nicolson*. The son's gossipy memoir deals frankly with his parents' unorthodox sex lives, including his mother's love affair with Virginia Woolf.

Four other famous writers, each deceased, were the subjects of noteworthy biographical studies. They were Ann Charters' *Kerouac*, a portrait of the one-time hero of the "Beat" writers; Finis Farr's *O'Hara*, about John O'Hara; Donald Day's *Malcolm Lowry*, a sympathetic biography of the alcoholic author of *Under the Volcano;* and Michael Fabre's *The Lonely Quest of Richard Wright*, a detailed and perceptive portrait of that black novelist as he struggled for recognition in a predominantly white literary world.

The playwright Lillian Hellman contributed a series of reminiscences about her contemporaries in an autobiographical memoir, *Pentimento: A Book of Portraits*.

Private lives of six Presidents and their families were explored in *Upstairs at the White House* by J. B. West, retired chief usher at the White House, writing in collaboration with Mary Lynn Kotz. Ishbel Ross offered a sympathetic portrait of another White House occupant who has been often misunderstood in *The President's Wife: Mary Todd Lincoln*. Elliott Roosevelt lifted eyebrows and left himself open to widespread criticism in revealing marital difficulties of his parents, Eleanor and Franklin D. Roosevelt, in *An Untold Story: The Roosevelts of Hyde Park*.

Among the year's outstanding works about statesmen and world leaders were Robert Payne's *The Life and Death of Adolf Hitler;* Forrest C. Pogue's *George C. Marshall: Organizer of Victory*, the fourth and final volume in a major biography; Brian Urquhart's *Hammarskjöld*, a study of Dag Hammarskjöld's seven years as secretary-general of the United Nations; and Antonia Fraser's heavily researched, highly readable *Cromwell: The Lord Protector*, which most critics considered the definitive work.

One of the year's more absorbing autobiographies was the piano virtuoso Arthur Rubinstein's *My Young Years*. Peter Reich's *A Book of Dreams* was a compelling account by the son of the controversial psychiatrist and biophysicist Wilhelm Reich. Anne Morrow Lindbergh offered an intimate and moving memoir in *Hour of Gold, Hour of Lead*, drawn from her letters and diaries from 1929 to 1932.

But the year's most controversial biography was *Marilyn*, written by Norman Mailer and with pictures by some of the world's foremost photographers. Some critics used such words as "exploitation," "abysmal," "impertinent," and "travesty" to describe the book, which is about the late motion-picture star Marilyn Monroe. Others said it was "compulsively readable," "brilliantly realized," and "a giant banana split."

History, Politics, Public Affairs. In a year that saw President Richard M. Nixon and his Administration engulfed by scandal, there was an outpouring of books of contemporary political interest. Two that seemed to have some permanent importance examined the institution of the presidency and the manner in which presidential power has been exercised. Emmet John Hughes, in *The Living Presidency*, examined the human side of the institution. Arthur M. Schlesinger, Jr., in *The Imperial Presidency*, offered a historical study of the domination of foreign affairs by the presidency and the increasing efforts of Presidents to similarly dominate domestic affairs.

It also seemed an especially appropriate time for the appearance of historian Daniel J. Boorstin's *The Americans: The Democratic Experience*, third and final volume of a trilogy. Three other political books that were of special interest were Stefan Kanfer's *A Journal of the Plague Years*, about the blacklisting of show-business personalities during the anti-Communist hysteria of the 1940s and 1950s; Philip M. Stern's *The Rape of the Taxpayer*, which called for reforms in the tax system and the closing of loopholes; and James Trager's *Amber Waves of Grain*, the story of how Russian trade officials almost cornered the U.S. wheat market in an extraordinary coup in 1972.

A top nonfiction best seller of the year was Alistair Cooke's *America*. The 400-page words-and-picture book by the British-born television personality had sold more than 170,000 copies at $15 in the first eight weeks following publication. An urbane and witty book, it also struck some warm and upbeat notes about Cooke's adopted country.

An old historical debate was revived in two books about the discovery of the North Pole–Dennis Rawlins' *Peary at the North Pole: Fact or Fiction*, which favored the explorer Peary's claim, and Hugh Eames's *Winner Lose All: Dr. Cook and the Theft of the North Pole*, which, while favoring Cook, remained an inconclusive brief. Conor Cruse O'Brien, an Irishman well known in the United States, offered a lucid and informative discussion of the contemporary problems of Ireland as well as a plea for reconciliation in *States of Ireland*.

The reopening of American contacts with China brought a number of books from visitors to that country. Two of the best were Emmett Dedmon's *China Journal*, which included an extensive interview with Chou En-lai by the editorial director of the *Chicago Daily News* and the *Chicago Sun-Times*, and *To Peking and Beyond: A Report on the New Asia*, by Harrison Salisbury, an associate editor of *The New York Times*.

Contemporary Problems also concerned many other writers. Jessica Mitford attacked American penal policies in *Kind and Usual Punishment*. Joseph Wambaugh, a Los Angeles policeman, published *The Onion Field*, a notable "factual novel" that dealt with the killing of a policeman. Peter Davies, a New York insurance broker, stimulated a new inquiry into the killing of four Kent State University students by Ohio National Guardsmen in 1970, with his book *The Truth About Kent State*.

The problems of the "senior citizen" were examined in Sharon Curtin's penetrating social study, *Nobody Ever Died of Old Age*. And one of the year's most widely read books, Jane Howard's *A Different Woman*, focused on the role of the new "liberated" woman in American life.

Letters, Essays, and Criticism. The death of W. H. Auden in September lent a special interest to the publication of *Forewords and Afterwords*, a collection of the poet's literary journalism that included essays on Poe and Shakespeare. *The Devils and Canon Barham*, a final collection of essays and reviews by the late Edmund Wilson, fittingly climaxed that eminent critic's literary career. The recent revival of interest in the work of the novelist John Dos Passos received new stimulation with the publication of *The Fourteenth Chronicle: Letters and Diaries of John Dos Passos*, edited by Townsend Ludington.

Lord Byron's biographer, Leslie A. Marchand, published the initial volumes of *Byron's Letters and Journals*, the first of which was subtitled *In My Hot Youth* and the second *Famous in My Time*. Another series of literary letters of great interest was Franz Kafka's *Letters to Felice*, written to a girl who was twice his fiancée but never his bride.

Two contemporary novelists who published prose collections of interest during the year were Truman Capote, with *The Dogs Bark: Private Places and Public People*, and Vladimir Nabokov, whose *Strong Opinions* included letters, interviews, and articles.

One of the year's best works of criticism was Polish playwright Jan Kott's *The Eating of the Gods*, in which Kott, a teacher at the State University of New York, offered an interpretation of the hero in Greek tragedy. A much-needed exploration of the richness of modern Latin American literature was offered by Rita Guilbert in *Seven Voices*, a series of interviews with leading figures in that field.   Van Allen Bradley

See also LITERATURE FOR CHILDREN; NOBEL PRIZES; POETRY.

LITERATURE, CANADIAN. See CANADIAN LIBRARY ASSOCIATION; CANADIAN LITERATURE.

Author Norman Mailer, left, looks at pictures from his book *Marilyn* with Milton Greene, a photographer who took many of them.

LITERATURE FOR CHILDREN.

A new children's literary magazine, *Cricket*, was launched in 1973. Only time will tell whether it will become the milestone in children's literature that *St. Nicholas*, the magazine that inspired it, was. However, it is the first literary magazine for children to be published since the demise of its illustrious predecessor in 1940. Many in the field noted with appreciation the reissue of several classics by Arthur Rackham, the British illustrator of children's books. The trend toward paperbacks continued, and many of the older classics, both for the picture-book-age child and his older counterpart, came out with the identical internal format of hard-cover editions.

Here are some of the outstanding books published in 1973:

Picture Books

The Church Cat Abroad, by Graham Oakley (published by Atheneum). A picture book with a real plot, wonderful full-color pictures, adventure, and humor. Not many like this come along any year. Ages 5 to 10.

The Star-Spangled Banner, illustrated by Peter Spier (Doubleday). A book the entire family will enjoy, this has big, beautiful illustrations as a setting for the words of the national anthem, including some scenes as Francis Scott Key himself might have seen them. The book shows 115 flags and gives a description of events leading up to the composition of the title poem. Up to age 12.

Izzard, by Lonzo Anderson, illustrated by Adrienne Anderson (Scribners). This is the unusual story of a native Virgin Islands boy and his pet lizard. The charming full-color illustrations make this an attractive, distinctive book. Ages 5 to 9.

The Princess and the Giants, by Zilpha Keatley Snyder, illustrated by Beatrice Darwin (Atheneum). While the text explains the wonderful imaginary adventures of a princess, the pictures show what the little girl who imagines herself the princess is actually doing. This delightful and humorous picture book should be especially appealing to girls in the first, second, and third grades. Ages 5 to 8.

Don't You Remember? by Lucille Clifton, illustrated by Evaline Ness (Dutton). Four-year-old Desire Mary Tate remembered everything everybody told her they would let her do "someday," but to her it seemed that day would never come. The attractive illustrations show a lively and appealing black girl and her family. Ages 4 to 7.

Calf, Goodnight, by Nancy Jewell, pictures by Leonard Weisgard (Harper & Row). A simple, gentle picture book showing a calf as it meets various creatures on its way to the barn on the first night of its life. The lovely nighttime pictures are soft and tranquil. Up to age 6.

Tim Mouse and the Major, by Judy Brook (Lothrop, Lee, and Shepard). Charming water-color illustrations show mice marching busily to and fro when they find themselves unwillingly recruited by a wooden soldier; Tim Mouse eventually figures out a solution to their problem, however, and they return to their old leisurely way of life. Ages 5 to 8.

The Wind's Child, by Mark Taylor, illustrated by Erik Blegvad (Atheneum). Highly poetic text and pictures tell a story of a small black kitten that finds a home and an owner. The concern with the sound and feel of words is apparent, and there are appropriate mood-creating pen-and-ink drawings. Ages 5 to 8.

An Eskimo girl's courage and the will to survive in a potentially alien world are explored in *Julie of the Wolves*. Publisher: Harper & Row.

Paddington's Garden, by Michael Bond, illustrated by Fred Banbery (Random House). A pleasant little adventure of that delightful bear Paddington, this book has attractive full-color pictures on every page and a simple story, so that even a 3- or 4-year-old might be able to make an early acquaintance with a bear everyone should know. Ages 4 to 8.

The Clay Pot Boy, by Cynthia Jameson, pictures by Arnold Lobel (Coward, McCann and Geoghegan). Based on a Russian version of the gingerbread boy tale, this has the repetitive appeal of the original, plus a satisfactory ending and illustrations. Ages 5 to 8.

Little Toot on the Mississippi, by Hardie Gramatky (Putnam). Little Toot, the popular tugboat, finds a way to rescue animals marooned in a flood and to make the old river steamboats useful again. Full-color illustrations have the animation and verve one associates with Little Toot. Ages 5 to 8.

For the Beginning Reader

The Bear's Almanac, by Stan and Jan Berenstain (Random House). This book shows the humor and delightfully lively drawing style that have made the Berenstain's cartoons so popular with all ages. It takes one on a quick exploration of the year, supplying information about months, seasonal activities, and weather.

Mine's the Best, by Crosby Bonsall (Harper & Row). Two little boys with identical balloons have an argument; the quietly humorous pictures show the contest they engage in and the amusing background action they never even notice.

Pippa Mouse, by Betty Boegehold, illustrated by Cyndy Szekeres (Knopf). Six simple little tales are enhanced by soft drawings that endow the small animals shown with personality and make them irresistibly appealing.

Music, People, and Places

Birthdays of Freedom from Early Man to July 4, 1776, by Genevieve Foster (Scribners). Illustrations on every page and a fast-moving text make this a fascinating journey through the ages. It offers the reader a bird's-eye view of the history of the world during the period of time covered. Ages 8 and up.

St. George and the Dragon; A Mummer's Play, by John Langstaff, illustrated by David Gentleman (Atheneum). An unusual Christmas play based on very old traditional ones, this has descriptions of characters, songs, costumes, and a simple sword dance. Unusual woodcuts provide the amateur performer with additional costuming and characterization suggestions. Ages 8 and up.

Eye Winker, Tom Tinker, Chin Chopper: A Collection of Musical Finger Plays, by Tom Glazer, illustrations by Ron Himler (Doubleday). This should be useful and fun for anyone who wishes to teach children to sing and act out these well-known songs, chosen for their special appeal to children. Melody, piano, and guitar accompaniments are given. Up to age 10.

A Rainbow of Sound: The Instruments of the Orchestra and Their Music, by Herbert Kupferberg, photographs by Morris Warmen (Scribners). This book describes the tonal character of various orchestral instruments, and gives a little of the history and unique personality of each. Ages 10 and up.

Five Famous Operas and Their Backgrounds, by Helen L. Kaufmann and Henry Simon (Doubleday). This fascinating account of *Don Giovanni, Fidelio, Aïda, Boris Godunov*, and *Carmen* tells the story of each opera, gives the background of its composition, composer, and early performances, and also lists musical highlights within it. Ages 12 and up.

Talking Drums of Africa, by Christine Price (Scribners). Using language more poetic and suggestive than informative, the author tells how the Ashanti and Yoruba tribes of Africa make and use drums. Its picture-book format includes bold woodcutlike illustrations. Ages 5 to 9.

In Africa, by Marc and Evelyne Bernheim (Atheneum). Beautiful and informative photographs show the children of different sections of Africa and describe the homes, schools, people, and occupations of each area. Ages 4 to 8.

Science, Animals, and Skills

Kids Camping, by Aileen Paul, illustrated by John DeLulio (Doubleday). This guidebook gives complete information on what to take, where to go, how to erect a tent, menus to try, and where to write for more detailed information. The book is helpful not only for children, but also for adults just starting to camp. Ages 10 and up.

Writing with Light; A Basic Workshop in Photography, by Paul Clement Czaja (Doubleday). Starting with suggestions about *really* seeing, this book goes on to suggest interesting activities that explain what photography is, how to make pictures without a camera, how to make a camera from a ball, and how to use a camera and develop film. Interesting and thorough, it has many instructive photographs. Ages 10 and up.

1 Pinch of Sunshine; 1/2 Cup of Rain; Natural Food Recipes for Young People, by Ruth Cavin, illustrated by Frances Gruse Scott (Atheneum). These recipes – some simple and unusual – should lure a young cook into useful kitchen experiments the whole family can enjoy. Ages 10 and up.

City Rocks, City Blocks, and the Moon, by Edward Gallob (Scribners). An introduction to geology as one can discover it in looking at the construction materials found in any city, this offers an unusual and interesting approach and is well illustrated by photographs. Ages 8 and up.

The Buffy-Porson: A Car You Can Build and Drive, by Peter and Mike Stevenson (Scribners). A father-and-son combination tells – and shows in excellent photographs and drawings – how a boy can build this handsome downhill racer (with only the occasional help of an older person). An appendix gives

A Japanese lady chases a dumpling through a hole and discovers a strange exotic world. *The Funny Little Woman*. Publisher: E. P. Dutton & Co., Inc.

Text © 1972 by Arlene Mosel.
Illustration © 1972 by Blair Lent.

lumber and hardware requirements. Ages 10 to 14.

The Chess Book: To Start You on Your Way to Being a Great Chess Player, by Jane Sarnoff and Reynolds Ruffin; consultant: Bruce Pandolfini, U.S. Chess Master (Scribners). A beginner's book explaining chess moves, terms, and notation, this suggests simple strategy, gives the Scholar's Mate in detail, and has little bits of chess history sprinkled among the full-color, picture-book type of illustrations. Ages 10 and up.

Defensive Football, by Dick Anderson and Nick Buoniconti, edited by Bill Bondurant (Atheneum). Written by two leading players of the Miami Dolphins, this book explains the duties of each defensive player in clear, interesting text and informative photographs. Ages 10 and up.

Wheels for Kids, by John Gabriel Navarra, photographs by Celeste Scala Navarra (Doubleday). Large, clear photographs and explicit information in the text describe the parts of motorbikes and the skills required to ride them safely. Ages 10 and up.

Mockingbird Trio, by Arlene Thomas (Scribners). This fascinating and informative book tells of the rescue of three baby mockingbirds by a member of the bird-saving corps of the Audubon Society, and gives many interesting facts about mockingbirds in general and these birds in particular. Ages 8 and up.

Animals That Frighten People; Fact Versus Myth, by Dorothy E. Shuttlesworth (Dutton). The book has photographs and information on wolves, big cats, bears, gorillas, spiders, and scorpions, as well as some other creatures usually considered fearsome. It tells how the animal came by its reputation, if it deserves it, and how to deal with the creature wisely. Ages 8 and up.

Biography of a Bald Eagle, by Lydia Rosier (Putnam). In text and illustrations, the author shows this magnificent bird as it raises its family and finds man sometimes an enemy and sometimes a protector. Ages 7 to 10.

The Story of Sea Otters, by William Weber Johnson (Random House). Filled with photographs of these delightfully appealing animals, this book tells something of the life history of this once-feared-extinct creature, lists its enemies, and tells how man can help protect the ecosystem of which it is a vital part. Ages 9 to 12.

Fiction

The Dark Is Rising, by Susan Cooper, illustrated by Alan E. Cober (Atheneum). A compelling fantasy in which one follows young Will Stanton through the highly exciting and sometimes terrifying adventures that start on his 11th birthday, when he finds he is one of the "old ones" who join forces in the age-old fight against evil – "the Dark." Ages 9 to 14.

The Court of the Stone Children, by Eleanor Cameron (Dutton). An engrossing story of Nina, who is attracted to a young girl she meets in a museum and who then becomes involved in the solution of a 150-year-old mystery. The reader is irresistibly drawn into an atmosphere of prophetic dreams, unseen visitors, and the challenges of understanding time. Ages 10 and up.

The Home Run Trick, by Scott Corbett, illustrated by Paul Goldone (Atlantic Little Brown). A baseball book with a different twist: Two sandlot teams try to *lose* a game to avoid being challenged by a visiting girls' team. There is humor galore, realistic boys and baseball, plus a touch of chemistry magic to turn the trick. Ages 8 to 12.

Master Cornhill, by Eloise Jarvis McGraw (Atheneum). Full of adventure and excitement, this account of the year of the plague and the Great Fire of London in 1666 is seen through the eyes of a very appealing boy almost 12 years old as he makes friends, finds a family to belong to, and begins to make his way in life. Ages 10 to 14.

The Ghost of Thomas Kempe, by Penelope Lively, illustrated by Antony Maitland (Dutton). James had always managed to get into enough trouble by himself, but when a discontented ghost started embroiling him in even more difficulties, James had to find a way to stop him. Ages 8 to 12.

The Coat-Hanger Christmas Tree, by Eleanor Ester, illustrated by Susanne Suba (Atheneum). Marianna and Kenny long for a Christmas tree, but their mother, who likes being different, never let them have one. After several attempts, Marianna solves the problem in an unusual way. The author invests the story with a simple realism. Ages 9 to 12.

Away Went the Balloons, by Carolyn Haywood (Morrow). Blue Bell School had a Balloon Day when each child released a balloon tagged with the child's name, address, and a request for a letter. This book has eight stories of the adventures of the balloons of first-graders and shows the simplicity and everyday interest this author is noted for. Ages 6 to 10.

The Preposterous Adventures of Swimmer, by Alexander Key (Westminster). The adventures of a runaway, trained otter that has learned to talk are given appeal by the personality of Swimmer himself and the feeling conveyed of the animals' intercommunication with their native surroundings.

Awards in 1973 included:

American Library Association Children's Services Division Awards: The *Newbery Medal* for "the most distinguished contribution to American literature for children" was awarded to Jean Craighead George for *Julie of the Wolves* (Harper), illustrated by John Schoenherr. The *Caldecott Medal* for "the most distinguished American picture book for children" was presented to Arlene Mosel for *The Funny Little Woman* (Dutton), illustrated by Blair Lent. The *Mildred L. Batchelder Award* for "a book considered to be the most outstanding of those books originally published in a foreign country and subsequently translated and published in the United States" was given to a publisher, Morrow, for *Pulga*, by S. R. van Iterson, translated from the Dutch by Alexander and Alison Gode.

British Book Awards: The *Carnegie Medal* for "the most outstanding book of the year" went to Richard Adams for *Watership Down*. The *Kate Greenaway Medal* "for the most distinguished work in the illustration of a children's book" was presented to Jan Pienkowski for his superbly produced *The Kingdom Under the Sea*.   Lynn de Grummond Delaune

LIVESTOCK. See AGRICULTURE; INTERNATIONAL LIVE STOCK EXPOSITION.

LOS ANGELES—LONG BEACH. City councilman Thomas Bradley became the first black mayor of Los Angeles on May 30, 1973. He defeated incumbent Mayor Sam Yorty by winning 56 per cent of the vote. Only 18 per cent of the population is black.

Bradley, a retired Los Angeles policeman, had served on the City Council since 1963. He was defeated by a narrow margin when he ran for mayor against Yorty four years earlier. Bradley was sworn into office as mayor on July 1 by former U.S. Chief Justice Earl Warren. Shortly after his victory, Bradley promised auto-clogged Los Angeles a rapid-transit system. See BRADLEY, THOMAS.

Smog and Traffic. An emergency smog plan went into effect on July 26 during the year's worst smog attack in the Los Angeles-Long Beach area. Acting for the first time under authority granted in the 1970 Clean Air Act, the Environmental Protection Agency (EPA) asked all federal agencies to close down and urged limited automobile use. California Governor Ronald Reagan ordered state agencies in the area to use state vehicles only in emergencies. About 100,000 persons were affected by the EPA action.

On January 15, William D. Ruckelshaus, then EPA administrator, proposed gasoline rationing for southern California during the May-to-October smog season. Ruckelshaus called for up to an 80 per cent reduction in motor-vehicle travel, citing gas rationing as one of several transportation controls that would be needed by 1975 to meet air-quality goals in the Los Angeles area. But many state and local officials thought gas rationing would be unworkable.

Los Angeles failed to present a clean-air plan to the federal agency by the February 15 deadline, so, in March, the EPA held hearings on traffic control. It issued its own clean-air guidelines for Los Angeles on June 15. The plan included limitations on gasoline sales, a ban on new parking facilities, and a 20 per cent cutback in the number of existing parking places.

Population Changes. The Los Angeles-Long Beach metropolitan area fell from second to third place behind New York and Chicago in population. According to a U.S. Bureau of the Census report released on September 25, the area fell in population from 7,042,000 persons to 6,999,600 between 1970 and 1972, while the Chicago area increased to 7,085,000.

Living costs in the Los Angeles area rose 5.7 per cent between June, 1972, and June, 1973. According to a U.S. Department of Labor report released on June 15, Los Angeles-Long Beach ranked 15th among the nation's 25 most expensive urban areas. A family of four would need $11,534 a year to live in "moderate comfort" in the area. James M. Banovetz

LOUISIANA. See NEW ORLEANS; STATE GOV'T.

LUMBER. See FOREST AND FOREST PRODUCTS.

LUXEMBOURG. Against British opposition, the Grand Duchy on June 25, 1973, won the right to be the center for the European Community (Common Market) monetary cooperation fund. The fund could become the central bank of the European economic and monetary union that is expected to develop from the Common Market. The six original members agreed in 1965 that Luxembourg should have prior claim on financial institutions if this did not impair efficiency. Great Britain had wanted the fund center to be located at the market's headquarters in Brussels.

On April 15, France and West Germany urged changes in Luxembourg's tax and banking laws to prevent a "tax haven" from developing. Funds were being sent to Luxembourg to evade French or German taxes. Prime Minister Pierre Werner resisted these demands. By the end of March, 60 banks had been established in Luxembourg. Three years earlier, there had been only 32.

Industrial output grew steadily in 1973, with metal processing and chemicals leading the way. Failure by the government to grant equal pay to women led the European Commission on July 25 to threaten to take the Grand Duchy to the Common Market's Court of Justice. The difference in the hourly pay rates of men and women – 46 per cent – is the highest in the Common Market. Kenneth Brown

See also EUROPE (Facts in Brief Table).

LYNN, JAMES THOMAS (1927-), was sworn in as U.S. secretary of housing and urban development on Feb. 2, 1973, succeeding George W. Romney. At 45, he became the youngest member of President Richard M. Nixon's Cabinet. Lynn had previously served the Nixon Administration as general counsel in the Department of Commerce from 1969 to 1971, and as undersecretary of commerce from 1971 to 1973.

Lynn was born on April 27, 1927, in Cleveland, and attended public schools there. During 1945 and 1946, he served in the U.S. Navy. He received his B.A. degree in political science and economics from Western Reserve University (now Case Western Reserve University) in Cleveland in 1948. In 1951, he graduated magna cum laude from Harvard Law School, where he served as an officer of the *Harvard Law Review.*

Lynn entered private law practice in 1951 with Jones, Day, Cockley, and Reavis, a prominent Cleveland law firm. He became a partner in the firm in 1960. While in Cleveland, Lynn was active in civic affairs. He was a member of the Cleveland World Trade Association and the Greater Cleveland Growth Association, and was active in mental-retardation programs carried on by the Cleveland Welfare Federation.

Lynn and his wife, the former Joan Miller, have three children. Jacquelyn Heath

MAGAZINE. The U.S. industry experienced a year of growth and prosperity in 1973, despite some problems. Advertising revenues continued to rise each month, and new titles were at an all-time high. According to the Publishers Information Bureau, magazines received a record high of more than $1.3-billion in advertising revenue in 1973, and Americans bought about 5.5. billion copies of consumer magazines.

The average magazine reader spent 83 minutes reading one issue of a magazine, and there were 3.6 adult readers per average issue. At that rate, the average magazine issue provided about five hours of adult reading time.

There were serious problems, however. Publishers struggled to have increased postal rates phased in over a 10- instead of 5-year period. The industry was also confronted with the Phase 4 price-freeze regulations, as well as worsening paper shortages.

New Magazines entered the scene, despite the problems. In the first eight months of the year, 118 new magazine titles were announced. Among them was the first news magazine launched in 40 years, *New Times,* published by George A. Hirsch, former publisher of *New York* magazine. Steve Gelman, former articles editor of *Life* magazine, is editor. The *New Times* goal is to write about the news, not report the news, featuring by-lined articles that entertain as well as inform. The new biweekly appeared in October and cost 60 cents an issue.

In September, Triangle Publications introduced *Good Food,* which is sold mainly at supermarket check-out counters. The magazine is designed to increase the readers' knowledge of food and drink and to make creating menus more enjoyable. *Homelife,* a new television-programming guide, was introduced by In-Store Publications, Incorporated, in the New York metropolitan area. Plans call for further expansion later. This publication, sold in supermarkets for 5 cents, combines television listings with ideas connected with the home environment.

Johnson Publishing Company brought out *Ebony Jr!* in May. It is a fun and learning magazine designed to boost the reading skills of black children while entertaining and informing them in the areas of literature, science, history, and general knowledge. *Cricket,* a new literary magazine for children, made its debut in September. Published monthly during the school year by the Open Court Publishing Company in La Salle, Ill., it is written for 6- to 10-year-olds.

Other new titles included *Photo World,* which began publication in June with emphasis on the art rather than the mechanics of photography. *Players,* the first all-black Playboy-type men's magazine, was launched in the fall by Players International Publications. It is designed to appeal to the young black audience. *Chicagoan,* published by Jon and Abra Anderson, former columnists for the *Chicago Daily News,* bowed in September.

Among the many magazines that made their debuts in 1973 are *Cricket* and *Ebony Jr.!*, two highly acclaimed publications for youthful readers.

***Saturday Review* Merges.** One of the big events in the magazine industry was the merger of *The Saturday Review*, which ceased publication in April, with Norman Cousins' *World* magazine, which first appeared in 1972. The first edition of *Saturday Review/World*, a biweekly, premièred on September 11 at 60 cents a copy.

David J. Mahoney, chairman and president of Norton Simon, Incorporated, announced that *McCall's*, the century-old women's magazine with a circulation of 7.5 million a month, was sold to Jay A. Pritzker, chairman, president, and chief executive officer of the Hyatt International Corporation.

Magazine Milestones. *Outdoor Life*, a Popular Science Publishing Company, Incorporated, magazine, celebrated its 75th year with its January 1 issue. *Time* magazine, which began publication in March, 1923, celebrated its 50th anniversary. *Sunset* magazine, which began publication in 1898, celebrated its 75th year with its May issue. The October issue of *Esquire* magazine marked its 40th anniversary. According to the publisher, Arnold Gingrich, that issue was the largest American consumer magazine ever printed. It had a total of 564 pages.

Norman Cousins, editor of *Saturday Review/World*, was honored by the magazine industry with the Henry Johnson Fisher Award as Publisher of the Year. The award was presented to him by the Magazine Publishers Association.   Gloria R. Dixon

MAGNUSSEN, KAREN (1952-   ), figure skater from Vancouver, Canada, won the world women's figure skating championship at the World Games in Bratislava, Czechoslovakia, in March, 1973. The title is the latest in a long string of championships for Magnussen, who has been skating since she was 7. She won her first national title – the Canadian junior women's championship – in 1965 at the age of 12. One year later, she placed fourth in the senior women's competition and went on to win the senior women's title in 1968, 1970, and 1971.

Her 1970 Canadian title climaxed a dramatic comeback after she suffered stress fractures in both legs that forced her to withdraw from the world championships in 1969. The fractures relegated her to the sidelines for nearly a year amid predictions that her career was over. However, after taking the 1970 Canadian title, she went on to become North American champion in 1971 and won a silver medal in the 1972 Olympic Games. She won three gold medals in the 1973 World Games in Bratislava. In May, she gave up her amateur status to sign a three-year contract with the Ice Capades.

A vivacious blonde, Magnussen is the eldest of three girls. She lives in Vancouver and attends Simon Fraser University there.   Kathryn Sederberg

MAINE. See STATE GOVERNMENT.

MALAGASY REPUBLIC. See AFRICA.

MALAWI. See AFRICA.

MALAYSIA. The government of Prime Minister Abdul Razak staged a series of circuitous maneuvers in 1973 that were largely designed to keep it in power. But it did little to bolster a declining economy and other sources of political unrest.

The majority Alliance Party formed a coalition with the nationalistic and highly racist Party Islam, led by Dato Mohammed Asri. The Dato and his fellow sultans represent conservative Moslem elements who want to extend Malay control to the country's economic and cultural spheres. They are opposed to the Chinese who comprise half the population.

Malays already dominate the government as well as the army, and control the educational system. There is only token political opposition in the Malaysian Parliament, and the Chinese are unable to play any effective role in government. Yet the Chinese continue to be the key factor in the economic life of the country, and without them, Malaysia's economy would only continue to decline.

In March, Malaysia withdrew from the Asian and Pacific Council because it said the group had done nothing. The council, formed in 1966, binds Japan, Australia, New Zealand, Thailand, Taiwan, South Korea, the Philippines, and South Vietnam to social and economic cooperation, but China has called it an anti-Communist bloc.

There were signs during the year that Chinese investors and businessmen were shifting their assets out of Malaysia, or waiting to see how the trends in the Malaysian economy and politics would continue before risking additional private investment. The investment rates projected in the second National Development Plan were woefully undersubscribed. Unemployment was increasing.

Chinese Coalition. Faced with this kind of highly discriminatory government, Chinese political and business leaders began efforts to form a new Chinese coalition political movement. They made some progress, but the new coalition was promptly assailed by Malay politicians as being a racist, political, and economic club directed against them. Chinese leaders have traditionally been sensitive to such charges, though such sensitivity may have been dulled in the last few years. Their coalition movement was not confined to Malaysia proper, but also was fostered in the states of Sabah and Sarawak, on Borneo.

Racism, then, continued to dog this potentially affluent nation, with prejudice on both sides being exploited by irresponsible political elements. There was the real possibility of another series of communal riots. None occurred during 1973, but tensions were rising. There were signs that such outbreaks might well occur in 1974. If they do, the struggle will be far more protracted and violent than previous outbreaks, such as the one that occurred in 1971.   John N. Stalker

See also ASIA (Facts in Brief Table).
MALDIVES. See ASIA.
MALI. See AFRICA.

MALTA pledged at the nonaligned nations' conference on Sept. 3, 1973, in Algiers to end Great Britain's use of the island's military base when the current lease runs out in 1979. On August 28, Prime Minister Dom Mintoff outlined a seven-year development plan to secure "self-reliance and self-determination." Main goals include phasing out the base, modernizing the dry docks, mobilizing resources for economic growth, and developing such backup facilities as roads, housing, and modern social services. On March 16, Mintoff was booed when he proposed tough measures to reduce losses in the dry docks, Malta's biggest industry. They were estimated at more than $38 million since 1968. Even after Mintoff's proposals were modified, the dockworkers had to accept longer hours and lower pay.

On March 24, Finance Minister Joseph Abela announced a record budget of $138.4 million. He promised bigger old-age pensions and social benefits, pay raises for dry-dock workers and other government employees, but no extra taxes.

British tourism headed for a new high. Mintoff demanded, with little success, more aid from the British Commonwealth and the Common Market. In June, the United States granted Malta a $5-million loan, and Libya provided equipment for Malta's armed forces.   George Scott

See also EUROPE (Facts in Brief Table).
MANITOBA. See CANADA.

MANUFACTURING. United States industry may well remember 1973 as a year of crisis. Buoyed by the surge in nearly all categories of durable and nondurable goods, manufacturing mirrored the strength of the entire economy as the year started. By midyear, however, there were signs of a strain. By the third quarter, shortages began to surface in almost every industry. By year-end, it seemed the country could be heading for a recession or a depression due to the serious materials shortages, especially in fuel.

Industrial Production continued strong in spite of this. In the third quarter, production rose at an annual rate of 6.7 per cent, topping the very healthy 5.5 per cent gain of the second quarter. The Federal Reserve Board (Fed) indicated that production in September had bounced back from a slight decline in August to a seasonally adjusted 127.5 per cent of the 1967 average, 8.3 per cent above 1972.

The Fed also reported a sharp rise in plant utilization – to 96.3 per cent of capacity in the third quarter, up from the second quarter's 94.5 per cent. Industries operating at or near capacity included steel, wood pulp, paper, paperboard, and man-made fibers. This one indicator was dramatic proof of the extent of the 1973 boom. In the third quarter of 1972, industry was using 83 per cent of its total capacity, and that had been a substantial rise from the 75.5 per cent in 1971.

The big gains in industrial production early in the

third quarter were offset by a sharp drop in new factory orders for September, the last month of the quarter. New orders slumped $1.19 billion, or 1.6 per cent, to a seasonally adjusted $74.9 billion. Department of Commerce figures indicated that the important durable goods sector declined for the third month in a row. September durable goods orders fell $583 million, to an adjusted $42.1 billion, still well above the 1972 figure of $36.8 billion.

The pace of factory shipments also fell off in September, for the second straight month. September shipments slowed by 0.3 per cent, to a seasonally adjusted $72.8 billion, down from August's $73 billion. Order backlogs remained high, climbing 2 per cent in September to an adjusted $109.4 billion.

Capital Spending and Productivity. Capital spending reflected the torrid pace of the boom. Investment for new plants and equipment was estimated at $98 billion, topping 1972's record $89 billion.

For the 12-month period that ended September 30, manufacturing productivity rose 5 per cent over the previous fiscal year. More important, manufacturing productivity in the third quarter increased at an annual rate of 6.8 per cent, compared with a 3.8 per cent increase in the second quarter. Actual output in the third quarter rose at a 6.9 per cent adjusted annual rate, while work hours increased at only a 0.1 per cent annual rate. In the second quarter, output rose at a 7.7 per cent annual rate, but work hours rose at a 3.8 per cent rate. Finally, unit labor costs in the third quarter rose at an annual adjusted rate of just 2.2 per cent, against a 4.2 per cent climb in the previous quarter.

Employment. Unemployment in October fell to only 4.5 per cent of the work force, the lowest point in 3½ years. The drop came after a four-month period during which unemployment had remained unchanged at 4.8 per cent. Manufacturing, where employment had been faltering, added 105,000 new jobs, for an adjusted total of about 20 million workers. Factory payrolls expanded strongly in such durable goods industries as autos, machinery, metals, and electric gear. However, the manufacturing workweek in October declined to a seasonally adjusted average of 40.6 hours, compared with 40.8 hours in September. Overtime fell off to 3.7 hours a week, from 3.8 hours. These figures often signal trends of future labor demands.

Material Shortages. Beginning with the second quarter, shortages became a way of life for U.S. industry. The most publicized shortage was that of fuel. But the petrochemical shortage caused shortages in manufacturing that most consumers were unaware of, and probably would not feel until 1974.

Plastics were a good example. The petrochemical industry supplies feedstocks for plastic resins, but plastics did not have priority to receive refined crude oil. Allocations to the plastics industry were reduced sharply. Western plastics producers were particularly

hard hit. Faced with higher freight rates and shipping costs, many raw materials producers concentrated on increasing their business with the materials-hungry East. By the end of August, the supply of many plastic feedstocks to the West had been cut back by as much as 50 per cent.

The materials shortages severely affected delivery and production schedules. The National Association of Purchasing Management reported in September that a wait of from 40 to 50 weeks for delivery was not uncommon. The association listed aluminum, copper, steel, zinc, forgings, castings, motors, corn syrup, fuels, lumber and lumber products, bearings, paper and paper products, cotton, and chemicals as items in short supply.

As the year drew to a close, shortages began to affect employment. Firestone Synthetic Fibers Company, for example, laid off 450 workers by December 31 because a petrochemical used to make nylon was in short supply, forcing a cut in nylon production.

New Technology. The growing influence of federal regulatory agencies on the development of new technologies and machinery increased the cost of new developments. In one such case, the National Acme Division of Acme-Cleveland Corporation introduced screw machines 10 decibels quieter than the 90 decibels required by the government. But the cost of the machines was increased by 10 per cent.

Two manufacturers combined to produce a metal-stamping machine that could make presses safe enough for the Occupational Safety and Health Act (OSHA). The system, developed by Union Special Machine Company of Chicago, keeps employees from injuring themselves while loading power presses. It meets one of OSHA's toughest regulations – that a worker must not be able to put his hands between the jaws of a poised power press. To produce the system, Union teamed with Danly Machine Corporation, an established press builder and die maker. Their 1973 package, called NHIDA (no hands in the die area), sells for about $4,000 and will enable most presses to comply with OSHA.

Xerox achieved a breakthrough with the 6500 color copier, the first copier to make full-color copies on plain unsensitized paper or on transparent material for projection on a screen. The unit can deliver a seven-color copy in 33 seconds, with additional copies from the original made every 18 seconds.

Bell Telephone Laboratories used a laser beam to melt a glass rod so that it could be drawn into a fiber. Bell claimed the carbon dioxide laser beam was a highly controllable and clean source of heat, far superior to conventional heaters that put minute impurities in glass. Bell anticipated that glass fibers made by this laser technique could transmit light beams carrying telephone messages, data, and computer information.

Machine Tools. Orders for the first nine months of 1973 totaled $1.9 billion, larger than for any previ-

Demand for heavy machinery boomed in 1973. In Rockford, Ill., the Ingersoll Milling Machine Company made this $1.5-million stub borer, largest ever built.

ous year except 1966, and 101.6 per cent ahead of 1972. Orders for September alone were $231.5 million, a 25 per cent gain over August, and almost 66 per cent ahead of September, 1972.

Electrical Manufacturing. The National Association of Electrical Manufacturers estimated 1973 shipments at $58.9 billion, an increase of nearly 13 per cent over the $52.2 billion shipped in 1972. Industrial equipment shipments increased by 12.5 per cent, to $8.4 billion. Consumer electric products totaled $13.3 billion, a 15 per cent increase. And electronics and communications equipment totaled $19 billion, a rise of 12.5 per cent.

Rubber Manufacturers claimed record shipments in many categories, but the Rubber Manufacturers Association declined to make predictions for 1974 because of many unpredictable factors, "such as driving restrictions, materials shortages, and other effects of the energy shortage."

The association estimated 1973 automobile tire shipments at 204 million units, up 5 per cent over 1972. Bus and truck tires also achieved record levels. Some 37.2 million units were shipped, compared with 33 million in 1972.

Total rubber consumption was at a record level of 3.1 million tons, a 6 per cent gain over 1972. Synthetic rubber accounted for 78 per cent of the total.

Paper and Paperboard production was expected to reach 65.2 million tons in 1973, according to the American Paper Institute. But this high volume was still not enough to prevent a tight supply situation in the United States.

The shortage occurred, in part, because most capital investment over the past few years had gone to correct environmental problems and not to increase capacity. In addition, the high cost of making existing facilities conform to new environmental standards was the principal reason for the closing of 30 mills.

In wastepaper, the demand for recycling was so great throughout the world that U.S. supplies were running very low at year-end. Prices skyrocketed. Old newspapers were bringing $40 to $50 a ton at U.S. mills, and corrugated wastepaper $60 to $70 a ton. Two factors combined to force the wastepaper shortage and send prices upward. The first was work stoppages at Canadian mills and railroads. The second was strong foreign demands that siphoned off U.S. supplies. In November and December, the shortage worsened because old-paper drives and normal wastepaper collections fell off. George J. Berkwitt

MARINE CORPS, U.S. See NATIONAL DEFENSE.

MARYLAND. See BALTIMORE; STATE GOV'T.

MASSACHUSETTS. See BOSTON; STATE GOV'T.

MAURITANIA. See AFRICA.

MAURITIUS. See AFRICA.

MEDICAID. See SOCIAL WELFARE.

MEDICARE. See SOCIAL WELFARE.

MEDICINE. Harvard University medical school researchers said in June, 1973, that it may soon be possible to use specific antibodies to diagnose and treat some cancers. In diagnosis, antibodies grown in animals can be radioactively labeled and injected into human patients. Investigators can then trace the antibody as it moves through the human system to see if it identifies a cancer or tumor growth. Labeled or unlabeled antibodies can be used in therapy by injecting them into a patient's abdomen.

Stanley E. Order, associate professor of radiation therapy at the Joint Center for Radiation Therapy in Boston, has purified and used antibodies grown in rabbits against two human antigens associated with Hodgkin's disease. One of these, called F (fast-migrating) antigen, occurs in Hodgkin's tumors, and the other is called S (slow-migrating) antigen.

Specific antiserum against both F and S antigens is produced by inoculating rabbits with a soluble extract of Hodgkin's tumor tissue. The antiserum is then produced in a highly purified state, Order told the American Cancer Society's Seminar for Science Writers in Nogales, Ariz.

Bernard Laski, a Toronto pediatrician, theorized that some infectious viral diseases may furnish protection against leukemia. He reported that a boy at Toronto's Hospital for Sick Children lived 15 years after he had been diagnosed as having the disease.

Six months after the initial diagnosis of leukemia, the youth contracted measles. There was then an unexpected turn of events. The leukemia appeared to go into remission, and the boy, after a course of drug therapy, was discharged from the hospital.

About 10 years later, the boy's health was essentially normal. But four years after that, he developed complications from unrelated encephalitis and died. Physicians noted, however, that an autopsy showed no trace of leukemia.

"I don't think we can say that the drug therapy we gave in those days [the late 1950s] could be responsible for the apparent cure of this boy's leukemia," Laski observed. "It's conceivable that the measles virus 'turned off' the [leukemic] process...."

Radioactive phosphorus and a Geiger counter were used to determine if a hard-to-get-at lesion in the back of the eye is malignant. The tests were conducted under the direction of Richard S. Ruiz, director of the opthalmology program at the University of Texas Medical School in Houston.

Before the radioactive examination, the patient drinks a liquid containing the radioactive phosphorus. Two or more days later, an incision is made in his *conjunctiva* (eyeball membrane), the eye is rolled over, and a Geiger counter probe is maneuvered directly over the lesion. "Radioactive phosphorus is rapidly assimilated by malignant tissue," Ruiz says.

Nobel Prize-winner Dennis Gabor, discoverer of holography, uses ultrasonic energy and laser beams to make holographic pictures of internal organs.

"If the count is twice as high over the suspicious region as in the normal area, we consider it to be cancerous."

The Heart. A rechargeable cardiac pacemaker—small, electrically stable, and warranted for 10 years—was developed in 1973 by investigators at the Johns Hopkins University Applied Physics Laboratory. The patient can recharge the pacemaker's cadmium battery.

The rechargeable power cell is the unit's most significant feature. But its developers, cardiologist Kenneth B. Lewis and physicist Robert E. Fischell, also point to other features that should prolong the pacemaker's operation. Cardiac leads—so prone to failure—have always been a source of pacemaker trouble. The Johns Hopkins unit's lead consists of two sets of coaxial wire coils, one inside the other. One will work if the other breaks.

The new pacemaker is virtually insensitive to electromagnetic interference, according to its developers. This means that patients should have few difficulties around microwave ovens or airport weapons detectors. In addition, the model is designed to be unaffected by external noise.

Probucol Trials. A cholesterol-reducing drug, probucol, scored well in clinical trials. William B. Parsons, Jr., research director at the Jackson Clinic Foundation in Madison, Wis., reported that the drug is "remarkably nontoxic in animals," and no toxic side effects had been reported.

The drug has not aggravated diseases commonly present in hypercholesterolemic patients, Parsons said. He expressed the hope that "if longer experience continues to confirm its efficacy, lack of side effects, and safety, probucol should become an important agent in the treatment of hypercholesterolemia."

Eyes and Light. Contrary to popular opinion, too much lighting may be harmful to the eyes. No one can verify that hypothesis, but at least one researcher suggests that physicians should consider the possibility that some forms of corneal degeneration may be related to the cumulative effects of a well-lighted lifetime, including hours devoted to television watching.

Mark O. M. Tso, research associate at the Armed Forces Institute of Pathology and assistant professor of ophthalmology at George Washington University Medical Center in Washington, D.C., told a science writers' seminar in Los Angeles that work with 24 rhesus monkeys suggests the possibility that low-intensity light (bright household light) causes at least temporary eye degeneration.

In humans, he told the seminar, it may be that some individuals have a genetically determined predisposition to *photic maculopathy* (light-caused corneal degeneration), through either greater susceptibility to damage or less ability to regenerate after degeneration.   Richard P. Davies

See also HEALTH AND DISEASE.

MEMORIALS dedicated or announced in 1973 include the following:

Chamizal National Memorial. A 55-acre park at El Paso, Tex., was dedicated on November 17 by U.S. Secretary of the Interior Rogers C. B. Morton. It became a part of the U.S. National Park System. With Mexico's companion Chamizal Park across the Rio Grande at Juárez, it commemorates the spirit of international friendship between the two countries marked by the 1963 Chamizal agreement that settled a 99-year boundary dispute. In that year, the Rio Grande, which had often shifted course, was diverted into a new, concrete-lined channel that became the boundary between the two countries. The new park includes a visitors center with a museum and a 506-seat auditorium. The auditorium is used for theatrical productions from both nations in Spanish and English. The first production, Shakespeare's *Romeo and Juliet*, was performed on November 21.

Ross Memorial. Edmund G. Ross, the U.S. senator credited with saving the impeached President Andrew Johnson more than 100 years earlier, was given recognition at the Johnson National Historic Site in Greeneville, Tenn. A plaque was placed there honoring Ross, a Kansas Republican who was appointed to the Senate a year after the Civil War ended. Ross was a strong Radical and earnest opponent of President Johnson's Reconstruction stand. At the height of the battle, with Johnson trying to grant amnesty to Confederates and the Congress trying to disenfranchise them, Johnson was impeached by the House of Representatives and tried by the Senate. Despite strong pressure from his colleagues, Ross voted for acquittal, and the Senate vote fell one vote short of the two-thirds majority needed to remove Johnson from office. Ross's vote ruined his political career, but it saved President Johnson from dismissal.

Tuskegee Memorial. Legislation to create the Tuskegee Institute National Historic Site at Tuskegee, Ala., was introduced in Congress in October. The site would be a memorial to Negro educator Booker T. Washington, who founded Tuskegee Institute as a vocational and normal school in 1881. Washington was a former slave and a largely self-educated scholar. The first students made the bricks and helped construct the first campus buildings. George Washington Carver went to Tuskegee in 1896, and his agricultural experiments there developed products from peanuts, pecans, soybeans, and sweet potatoes. His work encouraged Southern farmers to plant new crops to help restore soils exhausted by the one-crop cotton system. Under the proposed legislation, the historic site would consist of four sections: The Oaks, Washington's home; the Carver laboratory; a 50-acre historic district at the center of Tuskegee Institute's campus; and Grey Columns, an antebellum mansion that stands immediately adjacent to the campus.   Foster Stockwell

MENTAL HEALTH. Community mental health centers and the widespread use of psychotropic drugs – drugs that affect the mental process – have combined to drastically cut the rate of admissions to state mental hospitals in the United States in recent years. But some people are still committed. Most of those committed are patients who have previously been hospitalized for mental illness, according to a 1973 study by four California psychiatrists.

The investigators, all associated with the Department of Psychiatry at the University of California, Davis, and the Sacramento County Mental Health Service, compared recent statistics in their own area with figures from the Colorado Psychiatric Hospital in Denver. The records of about 2,700 patients were studied. The findings indicate that the patient who has already been hospitalized is often a more likely candidate for treatment in a state facility than for treatment in his own community health center.

Schizophrenia. Physicians in Tel Aviv, Israel, reported in 1973 that the drug propranolol, commonly used in treating heart disorders, has successfully alleviated some manifestations of schizophrenia. Abraham Atsmon, an Israeli physician, reported in March that the drug's efficacy was discovered "quite by accident." He and a psychiatrist colleague noted improvement in a mental patient who had been given the drug for a heart abnormality. This led to a study of 42 patients, most of whom benefited from the agent. Several cases of acute schizophrenia responded to high doses of propranolol, and so did manic-depressive patients and persons suffering post-childbirth psychosis and agitated depression.

Atsmon warned, however, that the results are preliminary, and that the treatment requires constant in-hospital patient observation. "It is a potentially dangerous treatment because of the high doses of the drug," he said. Nevertheless, the Israeli investigators said that propranolol did not produce such unpopular side effects as loss of memory, loss of libido, or a host of other generalized symptoms that often accompany high doses of other drugs.

Tranquilizers. In a related development, researchers reported that physicians have far more faith in tranquilizers than do patients. Pharmacologist I. T. Borda of the University of Western Ontario, London, Canada, described the findings of a drug study at the 1973 meeting of the American Society for Clinical Pharmacology and Therapeutics, held in New Orleans in March.

The study, begun in 1966, was based on records of more than 15,000 patients in 10 hospitals. Tranquilizers, such as diazepam and phenothiazine derivatives, yielded "good" results according to 65.6 per cent of the physicians, but only 21.3 per cent of the patients reported feeling better because of the drugs. Furthermore, adverse reactions – notably drowsiness and disorientation – were reported in from 8.6 per cent to 18.1 per cent of the patients . Richard P. Davies

MEXICO. President Luis Echeverría Alvárez continued his efforts to improve the nation's political system in 1973. At his urging, a number of reforms in the election laws were approved by the Congress in January. They included awarding free television and radio time to all contesting parties and reducing the minimum age for election to the Senate from 35 to 30. The minimum age in the Chamber of Deputies was lowered from 30 to 21. Other provisions in the bill, which affected the old proportional representation laws, made it possible to award more seats in the lower house to small opposition groups. The opposition parties, however, charged that the reforms were only token ones and that President Echeverría's ruling Institutional Revolutionary Party (PRI) still controlled the presidency and all 60 seats in the Senate. They repeated their charges when, in general elections held July 1, the PRI won 189 out of 194 elective seats in the Chamber of Deputies, 7 state governorships, and 87 mayoral races.

Foreign Relations. Relations with the United States continued to improve, despite some objections over the stringent American antismuggling policies along the U.S.-Mexico border. On August 30, the United States formally agreed to build a multimillion dollar desalting plant in Arizona to remove salt from the Colorado River. This would end a decades-old complaint that farming in the Mexicali Valley in Baja California was all but curtailed by the salinity of the lower Colorado's water.

Between March 29 and April 26, President Echeverría visited six countries on three continents to expand economic and political ties. In addition to going to Canada, Great Britain, Belgium, and France, he paid calls on leaders in Russia and China.

Civil Disturbances continued to plague the government. On March 30, students demanding a regional university in Torreón seized the public transportation system and blocked the principal roads leading to the city. In May, 4 students were killed and about 20 persons wounded in a shoot-out between police and students at the Autonomous University of Puebla. Guerrillas were also active throughout the year. On April 6, three policemen were shot to death in a clash with guerrillas that occurred near Acapulco. Police arrested 10 guerrillas and seized a large cache of arms in March in Guerrero. In May, left-wing guerrillas, known as the People's Revolutionary Armed Forces, kidnaped U.S. Consul General Terrance G. Leonhardy in Guadalajara. He was freed unharmed after the Mexican government agreed to guerrilla demands that 30 alleged political prisoners be released and allowed to go to Cuba.

The Domestic Economy was troubled by inflation, rising foreign debts, and a chronic trade deficit of over $1 billion. About 9.6 million of a working-age force totaling about 24 million persons were without jobs. This, combined with a 3.3 per cent annual increase in population, compounded the problems of

An earthquake that struck Orizaba, Mexico, in August took a heavy toll. President Luis Echeverría Alvárez, foreground, views the damage.

unemployment, housing, living standards, and social unrest.

Living costs, which rose about 11 per cent in the first eight months of the year, spurred labor demands for a 33 per cent hike in salaries as well as a 5-day, 40-hour workweek. In the first week of October, workers in hundreds of firms walked off their jobs to back up demands for an immediate, 20 per cent across-the-board wage hike for employees not covered by the 18 per cent average minimum pay increase announced on September 13. Management was forced to relent, and minimum wage scales were raised in December to cover the years 1974 and 1975.

The workers received firm government support, principally through President Echeverría who, on September 1, repeated his backing for collective bargaining and for labor's right to strike. Several days earlier, he had authorized pay increases of from 12 to 15 per cent for public employees. The president was determined to curb inflation, but not at the expense of the workers. Here, he had some success in persuading firms to absorb cost increases. The private sector on September 1 agreed not to raise prices of goods of "necessary consumption" until March 31, 1974, unless overall production cost increases exceed 5 per cent. Mary Webster Soper

See also LATIN AMERICA (Facts in Brief Table); and Section Two, MEXICO: THE SURGING SPIRIT OF NATIONALISM.

MICHENER, ROLAND, served his final year as governor general of Canada in 1973. He had been the queen's representative in Canada since 1967. It was announced on October 5 that Jules Leger, a career diplomat, would succeed Michener in the vice-regal post in January, 1974. Michener's term had been extended twice.

Queen Elizabeth II of Great Britain stayed at Government House from July 31 to August 4 during the Commonwealth meeting. On August 9, the governor general hosted a large garden party at Rideau Hall for delegations to the Commonwealth meeting. From August 17 to September 15, he took up his customary residence at the Citadel, the historic vice-regal seat overlooking Quebec City. On July 19, the Micheners welcomed Princess Alexandra when she arrived to take part in celebrations commemorating the 200th anniversary of the first Scottish immigrants to Pictou County in Nova Scotia.

On January 4, the governor general read the speech from the throne to open the 29th Parliament. Later official duties included receiving 27 ambassadors and high commissioners who arrived to take up diplomatic posts in Canada. The governor general also presided at investitures for the new Order of Military Merit and the Order of Canada. In addition, he presented awards for journalism, literature, and acts of bravery. David M. L. Farr

MICHIGAN. See DETROIT; STATE GOVERNMENT.

MIDDLE EAST

The fourth Arab-Israeli war in 26 years broke out with dramatic suddenness on Oct. 6, 1973, abruptly ending three years of relative peace. When a frail cease-fire ended fighting on October 22, the results were inconclusive. Both sides had gained and lost territory.

In contrast to Israel's relatively one-sided victory in the 1967 war, the Arabs this time exacted a heavy toll in Israeli men and equipment. And for the first time, they used their oil supplies as a political weapon against countries that traditionally had supported Israel. As peace talks began in Geneva, Switzerland, in December, Israel was more isolated than ever before.

The Attack came simultaneously on two fronts, with Egyptian and Syrian forces striking into territory occupied by Israel since 1967. Egypt crossed the Suez Canal into the Sinai Peninsula southwest of Israel; Syria attacked in the Golan Heights, on the northeast. The attack came on Yom Kippur, the Jews' holiest festival. The feast day delayed mobilization, and Israeli forces could not regain the initiative for several days.

Other Arab nations quickly joined Egypt and Syria. Iraq sent ground and air units. Tunisia and Kuwait sent troops to the Sinai. Algerian planes were in action there. Morocco and Jordan sent troops to the Syrian front. Sudan and Saudi Arabia also sent troops. Lebanon opened its entire Israeli border to the Palestinian guerrillas, and some Israeli settlements were shelled. The guerrillas were not a major direct factor, however. An Israeli commando raid on Beirut in April had cut into their leadership.

Quick Triumphs. In their initial assault, the Egyptians quickly overran Israel's fortified Bar-Lev line along the east bank of the Suez Canal, and they moved about 8 miles into Sinai. Syrian forces captured Mount Hermon, but an Israeli counterattack drove them back. Supported by heavy air raids, Israeli forces drove to within 25 miles of Damascus. On October 15, Israeli armor crossed to the west bank of the Suez Canal between two Egyptian armies and encircled one of them on October 23.

The Cease-Fire, proposed by the United Nations (UN) Security Council, was accepted by Egypt and Israel on October 22. It called on the combatants to halt the fighting within 12 hours and hold their positions. On October 25, the Security Council voted to establish a UN Emergency Force – using troops from smaller nations – to ensure the cease-fire. Israel and Egypt finally signed a cease-fire agreement on November 11 in a tent beside a dusty road near Suez city, at the head of the Gulf of Suez. It was only informally accepted by Syria. Iraq and Libya also assailed the cease-fire, and violations became common.

Tolls High. The war was costly to both sides, but particularly to Israel. On November 6, Israeli officials listed casualties at 1,854 killed, about 4,800 wounded, and 450 missing, high in proportion to the nation's population. Arab casualties were estimated at nearly 18,000, plus an estimated 2,000 Syrian civilians killed in Israeli air raids. Equipment losses were enormous on both sides. An estimated 1,800 tanks and more than 200 airplanes were destroyed,

Israeli tanks speed across the Sinai Desert toward Suez. Some of the bloodiest tank battles ever fought erupted in the Sinai in 1973.

but massive Russian and U.S. airlifts to their respective "clients" restored the prewar military balance.

The conflict marked a dramatic change in the balance of political power in the region. The impressive Arab military performance was a key in this shift.

Arab forces fought not only bravely, but skillfully, with sophisticated equipment, attesting to their mastery of Russian technical training. Egyptian surface-to-air missiles, launched from west of the canal, protected advancing Arab armies from Israeli air attacks and took a heavy toll of Israeli tanks. The Egyptians also demonstrated technical competence in using radar to spot approaching Israeli jets, and television cameras to pinpoint the targets before they were shot down by guided rockets.

Psychological Lift. The Arabs' ability to meet Israeli forces on equal terms gave them an enormous psychological lift, despite the faulty coordination that eventually let Israel outmaneuver Arab armies. Egypt's acceptance of the cease-fire caused considerable resentment – in Egypt as well as in Syria and other Arab countries. Syria, which had not accepted the formal cease-fire, boycotted the Geneva peace talks. The Iraqi brigades that fought on the northern front went home in a huff.

The restoration of Arab self-respect was accompanied by rare evidence of Arab unity. But King Hussein I of Jordan, though he sent troops to Syria, refused to open a third front against Israel because of the absence of air protection for his army. Some Arab

Egyptian and Israeli representatives sign the cease-fire agreement on November 11 in a roadside tent at Kilometer 101, near the city of Suez.

leaders, notably Libya's President Muammar Muhammad al-Qadhaafi, warned that the invasion might eventually lead to the destruction of Arab armies and end any chance of liberating "the sacred soil" of Palestine.

Egypt's Role. Developing a viable Arab unity had been largely the work of Egypt's President Anwar al-Sadat. He sent Foreign Minister Hafez Ismail to the United States in February, 1973, to seek new peace initiatives. When that trip produced only increased American military aid to Israel, Sadat named himself commander in chief and began quiet preparations for war. His efforts to unite all elements in the Arab cause were helped by a U.S. veto in July of a UN resolution condemning Israel for raids against Palestinian guerrillas in Lebanon and Syria. Sadat took another major step in August when he and King Faisal of Saudi Arabia reached an agreement. Egypt delayed its projected federation with Libya and resumed relations with Jordan. In return, Faisal committed $600 million to aid Egypt after the projected war. He also agreed to coordinate a campaign to reduce Arab oil shipments to the United States and other countries. The Arabs planned to use an oil boycott to pressure these countries to withhold aid from Israel. When relations with Jordan reopened in September, the ring around Israel was complete.

Frail Unity. How long the Arabs would remain united was difficult to estimate. Interpretations among them as to the usefulness of "the oil weapon" varied widely. Enormous internal pressures to resume the war were felt by Sadat and other leaders. But 15 Arab chiefs of state met in Algeria in November and widened the oil embargo to include Portugal, Rhodesia, and South Africa, and they gave conditional approval to "political efforts" for a Middle Eastern peace. Libya and Iraq did not attend.

Initially, Arab oil exports to the United States and Western Europe had been cut by 60 per cent, from 1.75 million barrels a day to 1 million. Thereafter, a selective policy was followed. All shipments to the United States and the Netherlands were banned. The reduced supplies to Great Britain and Western European countries continued until Christmas Day, when the Arabs eased restrictions on them. Arab oil provides only 6 per cent of U.S. domestic needs, but the ban, along with increasing energy demands, accelerated a U.S. "energy crisis."

Fragile Cease-Fire. Equal uncertainty clouded efforts to convert the shaky cease-fire into a permanent peace settlement. The November 11 cease-fire signing ceremony underscored the fact that the war had altered forever the structure of Middle Eastern relations. Israeli and Egyptian officers met face to face in a tent beside the hot, dusty Cairo-Suez road to sign a six-point agreement. It was the first direct contact between the Arabs and Israelis since the establishment of Israel. Direct negotiations had been a long-

Israel: 25 Years Under Arab Siege

Israel's flag

Israel celebrated its 25th anniversary as an independent nation on May 14, 1973. It was one of history's sharper ironies that—five months later—a nation born in the turmoil of a war for survival should find itself again fighting for its life.

The intervening years were equally turbulent. Twice, war erupted between Israelis and Arabs—in 1956 and again in 1967. And neither conflict brought true peace. Repeatedly, the Arabs, particularly Palestinian guerrillas, have made Israel the target of terrorist attacks at home and abroad. For example, a two-year "war of attrition" by Egypt, Syria, and Jordan-based Palestinian guerrillas ended in August, 1970. Israel thus found it necessary to devote more human effort and more of its gross national product to defense than any other nation.

Despite this unremitting pressure, Israel has made remarkable economic, cultural, and scientific strides. It expanded agricultural and industrial output by introducing modern production methods, achieving a sixfold increase in gross national product between 1952 and 1970. During that same period, its annual rate of growth averaged 9 per cent, an unparalleled accomplishment in that it was accompanied by a nearly equivalent population growth. When the state was established in 1948, it had 650,000 Jews and 150,000 non-Jews. The 1972 census showed 3,164,000 people in Israel; 83 per cent are Jews, the remainder are Moslems, Christian Arabs, Druses, Circassians, and others. The proportion of Jews in the population grew only slightly—from just over 80 per cent to 83 per cent.

Israel has created a technology capable of supporting an advanced industrial economy. It has a modern telecommunications network, extensive highways and harbor facilities, and electric power plants. It can produce more than 75 per cent of the arms and ammunition it needs.

These are proud achievements. But Israel is aware of its drawbacks, many deriving from the nation's unique security burden.

One is a chronic deficit in the balance of payments—$1.075 million in 1972—attributed to massive imports of warplanes and armor, mainly from the United States. The deficit has been balanced by generous loans and grants from Jews abroad, friendly foreign governments, and international institutions. Government economists hope that the trade balance will level off in the early 1980s.

Complicated social problems have been nurtured by the diverse cultural and ethnic backgrounds of the Jewish immigrants who poured into Israel after independence. More than half of the newcomers came from relatively backward Arab countries. In time, a "cultural gap" was detected by local sociologists—and described in the Hebrew press as "the second Israel."

Overlaying these social problems is a constant controversy over religion. Only 20 per cent of Israel's Jews are Orthodox adherents of Judaism. But party politics, combined with the legacy of the *Milliyet* (community) system of religious autonomy bequeathed to Palestine by the Ottoman Turks, have provided a "status quo" arrangement that often jars the non-Orthodox majority's personal values.

In deference to the Orthodox, the law does not permit civil marriage or public transport during the Sabbath (except in the port city of Haifa and in Arab sectors). The state also supports separate Orthodox Jewish religious schools.

Contributing to this and other problems is Israel's lack of a constitution. A draft was prepared soon after statehood, but the Orthodox blocked it. They argued that Israel's laws must derive from the *Torah*, the first five books of the Bible. The issue has been left in abeyance ever since.

Israelis are optimistic about their future. They expect the population to reach 4 million by 1981 and 5 million by 1992. If Israel continues to control areas occupied in June, 1967—the Golan Heights, the West Bank of the Jordan, the Gaza Strip, and the Sinai Peninsula, which have an Arab and Druse population of 1 million—the ratio of Jews and non-Jews in Israel will be radically upset.

However, the Israelis' philosophy is akin to American pragmatism. They believe in their ability to tackle this problem if it arises.   Jay Bushinsky

Facts in Brief on the Middle East Countries

Country	Population	Government	Monetary Unit*	Foreign Trade (million U.S. $) Exports	Imports
Bahrain	240,000	Amir Isa bin Salman Al Khalifa; Prime Minister Khalifa bin Salman Al Khalifa	dinar (1=$2.53)	72	266
Cyprus	658,000	President Archbishop Makarios III	pound (1=$2.90)	135	319
Egypt	36,754,000	President & Prime Minister Anwar al-Sadat	pound (1=$2.56)	825	874
Iran	32,545,000	Shah Mohammed Reza Pahlavi; Prime Minister Amir Abbas Hoveyda	rial (68.17=$1)	2,964	2,410
Iraq	10,716,000	President Ahmad Hasan al-Bakr	dinar (1=$3.37)	1,180	711
Israel	3,309,000	President Ephraim Katzir; Prime Minister Golda Meir	pound (4.2=$1)	1,101	1,922
Jordan	2,634,000	King Hussein I; Prime Minister Zayd Rifai	dinar (1=$3.10)	48	267
Kuwait	1,100,000	Emir Sabah al-Salim al-Sabah; Prime Minister Jabir al-Ahmad al-Sabah	dinar (1=$3.38)	2,761	658
Lebanon	3,303,000	President Suleiman Franjieh; Prime Minister Takieddin Solh	pound (2.4=$1)	256	677
Oman	741,000	Sultan & Prime Minister Qabus bin Said	Saidi rial (1=$2.86)	130	74
Qatar	94,000	Amir & Prime Minister Khalifa bin Hamad Al-Thani	riyal (3.9=$1)	25	15
Saudi Arabia	8,628,000	King & Prime Minister Faisal	riyal (3.73=$1)	3,844	806
Sudan	17,476,000	President Sayed Gaafar Mohamed Nimeiri	pound (1=$2.87)	357	353
Syria	7,111,000	President Hafiz al-Asad; Prime Minister Mahmud al-Ayyubi	pound (4.3=$1)	287	539
Turkey	38,942,000	President Fahri Koruturk; Prime Minister Naim Talu	lira (14=$1)	885	1,058
United Arab Emirates	215,000	President Zayid bin Sultan al-Nuhayan; Prime Minister Maktum ibn Rashid al-Maktum al-Falasa	Bahrain dinar & Qatar riyal	no statistics available	
Yemen (Aden)	1,612,000	Presidential Council Chairman Salim Ali Rubayya; Prime Minister Ali Nasir Hassani	dinar (1=$2.89)	118	150
Yemen (Ṣan'ā')	6,391,000	Republican Council Chairman Abdul Rahman Iryani; Prime Minister Abdullah al-Hajri	rial (4.5=$1)	7	41

*Exchange rates as of Nov. 1, 1973

standing Israeli demand; at last the two sides had met. The agreement was negotiated by U.S. Secretary of State Henry A. Kissinger with Russian support. It provided for strict observance of the earlier cease-fire, for provisioning of the surrounded Egyptian III Corps, for UN control of all checkpoints, and for an exchange of prisoners. Both sides would also return to the positions they held on October 22.

But, other than the prisoner exchange, the two sides interpreted the agreement's provisions differently. Two weeks of daily meetings failed to produce joint action on the withdrawal lines or even their location. The talks were broken off and renewed fighting became a distinct possibility. Israel also accused Egypt of blockading the Bab el Mandeb strait at the southern entrance to the Red Sea, thus denying the use of an international waterway to shipping bound for the Israeli port of Elat. Egypt charged that Israel encircled the III Corps after the October 22 cease-fire. Seemingly, only the presence of the UN Emergency Force, commanded by Finnish Major General Ensio Siilasvuo, kept them from fighting. Syria, meanwhile, refused to exchange prisoners or even provide a list of the Israeli prisoners it held.

Isolated Victors. Israel emerged as the war's "victor," in the sense that it had successfully defended its own territory, and taken more, but the Israelis were left more isolated than ever. Britain, France, and other European countries openly criticized Israel for making no meaningful concessions and refusing to withdraw from occupied Arab lands.

By the year's end, some 25 African states had broken diplomatic relations with Israel. They included such long-standing allies as Ethiopia, Gambia, and Togo, recipients of substantial Israeli technical and financial aid. As Israel prepared for national elections on December 31 and entered the peace conference in Geneva, Switzerland, its future status in the Middle East seemed increasingly precarious.

The death on November 20 of former Prime Minister David Ben-Gurion, 87, architect of Israel's independence, symbolized his country's new loneliness. Internally, Israel began investigations into what some Israelis saw as its military unpreparedness, its inefficient conduct of the war, and its lack of a clear-cut political policy.

And, as 1973 neared its end, terrorists claiming to be "proud Palestinian Arabs" reminded the world again of Middle Eastern volatility. On December 17, they killed 31 persons in a fire bomb attack on a Pan American Airways jet at the Rome airport. They then hijacked another jet and flew to Athens, Greece, where they killed a hostage. They finally surrendered in Kuwait and released 12 hostages. Guerrilla organizations and both Arab and non-Arab political leaders condemned the hijacking.   William Spencer

See also ISRAEL and articles on the Arab countries.

MINNELLI, LIZA (1946-   ), won the 1973 Academy of Motion Picture Arts and Sciences Award for best actress for her portrayal of Sally Bowles, the nightclub performer in *Cabaret*. She was nominated for an Oscar in 1969 for her first starring role in *The Sterile Cuckoo*.

With *Cabaret* and her popular nightclub performances, Minnelli has proven she is far more than merely Judy Garland's daughter. She was born on March 12, 1946, in Hollywood, the only child of Judy Garland's marriage to movie director Vincente Minnelli. When she was 2½, she made her movie debut in one of her mother's films. At 7, she danced at the Palace Theatre in New York City while her mother sang "Swanee," and at 16, she starred in a high school production of *The Diary of Anne Frank*.

Her first big break came in 1963, when she landed the third lead in an off-Broadway revival of *Best Foot Forward*. By 1965, Minnelli had become Broadway's youngest Tony Award winner as best actress in *Flora, the Red Menace*. That same year she made her nightclub debut at the Shoreham Hotel in Washington, D.C., and a few months later took her act to the Plaza Hotel in New York City.

In addition to the movies *Charlie Bubbles* (1968) and *Tell Me That You Love Me, Junie Moon* (1970), she has recorded several albums: *Liza, Liza* (1964), *It Amazes Me* (1965), *There Is a Time* (1967), *Liza Minnelli* (1968), and *The Singer* (1973).   Lillian Zahrt

MINES AND MINING. The U.S. Geological Survey predicted in 1973 that demand for minerals will eventually lead to severe shortages unless the nation stops wasting its resources and seeks better ways of finding and using low-grade ores. The survey released a 722-page study in May that covers coal, oil, natural gas, and all the industrially important metals. It is the first overall survey of the nation's mineral use and resources in 21 years.

The report notes that the United States produces about 9 per cent of the world's zinc, but uses three times that amount. It says that at the time of the study, the United States imported 29 per cent of the oil and gas it needed, about 33 per cent of its iron ore, and 87 per cent of its aluminum. Copper was still in ample supply, and imports accounted for only a small percentage of the 2 million tons used in the United States each year. However, at current rates of consumption, it is estimated that the nation's known resources would be used up in 45 years.

In terms of quantities used, iron, aluminum, copper, and zinc are, in that order, the most important industrial metals. The report notes that the United States has no known reserves of manganese, the fifth most important metal, which is indispensable to the production of steel and has other essential industrial uses.

Paradoxically, in April, President Richard M. Nixon announced plans to sell about $6 billion of the $6.7 billion worth of critical materials in the government's stockpile. The President said a major aim of the massive sale, which includes hundreds of tons of silver and other metals, is to curb rising prices.

Coal Comeback. One of the nation's largest producers of electricity, the American Electric Power System, said in April that coal can and should be the nation's primary source of energy for producing power. The energy shortage during the winter of 1972 and the crisis of 1973, spawned by fuel oil shortages, was followed by increased coal production. The *Keystone News Bulletin*, a McGraw-Hill publication, placed the total output of coal in 1972 at 590-million tons, and predicted that the industry could produce another 40 million tons in 1973.

Despite restrictive legislation and protests from environmentalists, most of the needed coal is expected to come ultimately from the West. Some 70 per cent of the nation's coal reserves lie west of the Mississippi River, with 44 per cent of it in North Dakota, Montana, and Wyoming. A major advantage of these deposits is that they lie close to the earth's surface and can be recovered with cheap strip-mining techniques. Also, their sulfur content is low enough to meet the air-pollution-control standards of the cities. The Senate, however, has passed a bill setting strict controls over strip mining, including a provision that land be restored to its "original contours." A similar bill is pending in the House.

Mine Safety. In May, the U.S. Department of the Interior transferred mine safety and inspection powers from the Bureau of Mines to a new federal Mining Enforcement and Safety Administration. The Bureau of Mines had been criticized as being too deeply concerned with promoting the interests of the mineral companies to enforce federal safety regulations vigorously. Donald P. Schlick was named acting director of the new safety organization in July, after several months of union protest. The union contended that Schlick, formerly assistant director for coal-mine safety in the Bureau of Mines, had failed in that post and was unfitted for the new one.

Gold Rush. The spectacular rise in the price of gold, which reached a high of $133 an ounce at times in 1973, aroused new interest in gold mining. The largest U.S. producer, the Homestake Mining Company in the Black Hills of South Dakota, started scouting the West in February for other productive properties. Nevada, with five major working mines, and Alaska, with two, will each have two more within a year. The biggest rush, however, was to Colorado, which has the nation's largest reserves. The Cripple Creek Mine, located in the shadow of Pike's Peak and the site of the last and greatest gold rush, is back in operation. Developers say it has the largest known deposit of gold in the Western world. Unlike the famous California mother lode, it has not been mined out, though it has already produced almost $1 billion in gold.   Mary E. Jessup

MINNEAPOLIS-ST. PAUL. The law-and-order mayor of Minneapolis, Charles S. Stenvig, lost his bid for re-election on Nov. 6, 1973. Instead, the voters chose Albert J. Hofstede, a liberal Democrat. The Democrats also won 11 of 13 City Council seats. The election was the first in which candidates were allowed to run with political party affiliation.

On June 12, voters approved an amendment to the Minneapolis city charter, requiring a referendum before any capital project costing $15 million or more could be approved. However, plans for financing a new concert hall and park in downtown Minneapolis were approved before the amendment was passed. The $16.8-million complex will include an extension of the Nicolet Avenue pedestrian mall.

Schools and Housing. Area taxpayers received relief in 1973, while educational opportunities between school districts were equalized as a result of a new policy on state aid to public schools. The plan raised the state share of local school costs from 43 per cent to 70 per cent. This permitted local districts to provide tax relief for property owners, and equalized expenditures per pupil among the school districts.

Minneapolis schools implemented a court-ordered desegregation plan when classes began in September. Although the plan, which relies on busing between neighborhoods, had no strong supporters among the 10 candidates for two school-board posts in the November elections, the posts were won by liberal candidates.

After 49 summer seasons, the Twin Cities' famed Excelsior Amusement Park finally shut down on September 16. The park's 17-acre lakeshore site reportedly will be used for a housing development.

The Twin Cities Metropolitan Council, in spite of a closely divided vote, in September reaffirmed its support for an areawide housing and redevelopment authority. Both support and opposition to the proposal centered on the role the authority would play in sponsoring and locating public-housing projects.

Population Change. In 1973, the Minneapolis-St. Paul metropolitan area increased in size from 5 counties to 10, including 1 county in neighboring Wisconsin. This resulted from a federal redefinition of the boundaries of metropolitan areas. The change boosted Minneapolis-St. Paul from 17th to 15th place among U.S. metropolitan areas.

Living costs in the area rose 5.3 per cent between April, 1972, and April, 1973. U.S. Department of Labor statistics released on June 15 showed that a family of four would require an annual budget of $11,767 to live in moderate comfort. Minneapolis-St. Paul ranked 12th among the 25 most expensive urban areas in terms of living costs. James M. Banovetz

MINNESOTA. See MINNEAPOLIS-ST. PAUL; STATE GOVERNMENT.

MISSISSIPPI. See STATE GOVERNMENT.

MISSOURI. See ST. LOUIS; STATE GOVERNMENT.

MONACO. See EUROPE.

MONEY. The U.S. money supply, defined as currency and coin plus checking accounts held by the public, rose at an annual rate of about 5 per cent in 1973. That was less than the 6 per cent annual increase since 1967, and well under the 8.3 per cent in 1972. These growth rates were well above the average annual increase of 2.9 per cent from 1957 to 1967.

The annual growth in the U.S. money supply rose to 8 per cent in 1968, then dropped to 3 per cent in 1969, anticipating the 1970 recession. Such events historically are the basis of the so-called monetarist hypothesis, which predicts that changes in monetary growth will be followed by changes in total spending. This, in turn, affects output and jobs in the short run before prices and wages adjust. In the long run, after markets have adjusted, it affects the price level. The principal exponent of the monetarist view is Milton Friedman of the University of Chicago. Other influential monetarists include economists at the Federal Reserve Bank of St. Louis and First National City Bank of New York City.

Monetary Growth in 1973 peaked in midyear and then fell off very sharply in the second half. Monetarists generally associate this type of change with a forthcoming recession. In contrast, from 1970 to 1973, the money supply showed a nearly 7 per cent annual growth rate. Monetarists believe this kind of growth eventually brings further economic expansion and inflation. And, indeed, there was accelerated economic activity and inflation in the United States through 1973. By the end of the year, the money supply was climbing again.

It is far from certain that every change in monetary growth rates will be followed by a corresponding change in total spending. For example, the monetary growth rate slowed in the last half of 1971 – a consequence of the international financial turmoil after devaluation of the dollar. Yet the economy speeded up in 1972, contrary to the monetarist hypothesis which would have predicted an economic turndown. Despite such failures of the theory from time to time, many people in business and government were carefully watching monetary growth rates as a possible harbinger of future events.

Spending Increased more rapidly than the money supply early in 1973. Total spending increased at a 12.5 per cent annual rate in the first half of the year, more than double the rate of increase in the money stock. This lent support to a belief that the burst of spending in the first half could not continue indefinitely without the money supply expanding. The annual rate of demand deposit turnover at banks in 233 U.S. metropolitan areas was up a whopping 18 per cent over 1972. At least part of the more intensive use of money was attributable to high interest and inflation rates. This made holding noninterest-bearing money balances doubly expensive.

Currency. The $20 bill continued to be the most popular in terms of dollar value. It accounted for

The Zoom in Credit Card Spending

Amount owed (billions of dollars)

Source: Federal Reserve Board

$22.4 billion, or about 33 per cent, of the currency in circulation in June.

U.S. Money Stock, September, 1973

Currency in Circulation	Amount
Federal reserve notes	$60,011,000,000
Treasury currency	
Dollar coins	718,000,000
Fractional coin	6,879,000,000
U.S. notes	320,000,000
Monies in process of retirement	289,000,000
Total currency in circulation	68,217,000,000
Less currency held by banks	8,117,000,000
Currency held by public	60,100,000,000
Demand deposits	201,800,000,000
Total money stock	261,900,000,000

Source: Federal Reserve Board

Commercial bank deposits with Federal Reserve Banks totaled about $33 billion at the end of June. Added to the $68 billion of government-issued currency and coin in circulation at that time, this comprised a "monetary base" of $101 billion. The monetary base represents money issued by the federal government and Federal Reserve System, and is often analyzed as a primary determining factor of trends in monetary growth. The base, adjusted for required reserve changes, increased at an annual rate of more than 7 per cent in 1973. By the end of August, currency in circulation totaled about $68.4 billion, the highest amount to date. William G. Dewald

MONGOLIA. See ASIA.

MONTANA. See STATE GOVERNMENT.

MOROCCO sent armor and infantry units to fight on the Syrian front during the Arab-Israeli war in October, 1973. Some 500 Moroccans were reported killed or missing in the fighting (for details on the war and its aftermath, see MIDDLE EAST). At home, Morocco continued to experience internal unrest, but there were no direct attempts to overthrow King Hassan II comparable to the bloody efforts of 1971 and 1972.

The 11 air force men sentenced to death for a 1972 attempt on the king's life were executed on January 13. The executions were widely resented because of the date—the eve of Aid el Kebir, a great Moslem religious holiday. One Moroccan compared it to carrying out executions on Christmas Eve in a Christian country. In Libya, which calls Hassan a feudal despot, the government radio warned that the executions would "sow the seeds of a growing revolution." Hassan countered by beaming a Moroccan radio program, the "Voice of Truth," to Libya.

Coup Attempt Reported. Moroccan security forces said they thwarted a planned military uprising in March in the Atlas Mountains. Leaders of the opposition National Union of Popular Forces were arrested on March 21 on charges of planning an uprising in the cities. The government claimed they organized a subversive movement financed, trained, and armed by Libya. After a series of trials, 16 defendants were sentenced to death in August and 7 received long prison sentences. However, 72 others were acquitted of all charges.

The king on March 7 ordered all foreign-owned farmland nationalized in stages, with cereals cropland taken first. French proprietors owned 400,000 acres of the 617,000 acres taken, but the expropriated area also included the U.S. government's Voice of America radio station and the high-frequency radio relay station at Tangier, owned by RCA Global Communications, Incorporated.

Because of reaction to the trials and periodic student and trade-union strikes, Hassan imposed press censorship in April and banned public assemblies. But, on August 19, he personally led army and student volunteers to harvest 34,000 acres of cereals in the Berrechid area near the Atlantic coast.

The Economy. Political unrest and the increasing take-over of farms and foreign-owned businesses did not seriously affect the flow of foreign aid to Morocco. The five-year plan inaugurated June 7 envisages an annual growth rate of 7.5 per cent and investments of $6 billion, 40 per cent from abroad. The World Bank granted $48 million for agriculture and small businesses in May. West Germany loaned $20 million for dam construction and farm credits in January. The Investment Code issued July 31 would encourage tourism, crafts, and export firms, and require 50 per cent Moroccan ownership as a means of generating public confidence in the economy. William Spencer

See also MIDDLE EAST (Facts in Brief Table).

MOTION PICTURES

MOTION PICTURES. The most significant event in motion pictures in 1973 was not a film but a decision by the Supreme Court of the United States. Ruling on five obscenity cases, a five-member majority, speaking through Chief Justice Warren E. Burger, handed down a set of guidelines on obscenity on June 22. They declared that community standards rather than national standards should prevail in defining obscenity, that states may ban works considered offensive by local standards, and that "redeeming social value" could no longer serve as a defense as it had done since a 1966 Supreme Court decision.

The ruling affected books, magazines, and plays, as well as motion pictures, and was viewed by some people not only as the groundwork for chaos in the various industries, but also as a moralistic and even hypocritical pronouncement in a nation besieged by the corruption surrounding the Watergate scandal. Almost immediately, the Association of American Publishers and the American Civil Liberties Union joined forces with the Motion Picture Association of America to petition the court for a rehearing on these cases and to assist litigants in arrests and convictions that might flow from the court's decision.

The most crucial concern underlying this strong and swift reaction was that the new ruling would be used to suppress major works of art, not merely hard-core pornography. The worst fears of these professional groups were soon realized. On July 2, the Georgia Supreme Court upheld a local obscenity conviction against an Albany, Ga., theater manager for exhibiting the film, *Carnal Knowledge*. The film, judged as "appealing to prurient interest," was an R-rated major release from a large and respectable film company, Avco Embassy. It was directed by one of America's most successful film artists (Mike Nichols), scripted by a highly regarded satirist (Jules Feiffer), and won an Academy Award nomination for actress Ann-Margret.

The Specter of Censorship also threatened to shadow films with political content. In April, George Stevens, Jr., director of the American Film Institute (AFI), removed *State of Siege*, Greek-born director Costa Gavras' French-language political thriller, from the opening program of the AFI's new theater in Washington, D.C.'s Kennedy Center for the Performing Arts. A fictionalized account of the 1970 kidnaping and murder of a U.S. Agency for International Development police adviser by Uruguayan revolutionaries, the film is a powerful and passionate indictment of U.S. policy in Latin America. Seeing in the film "a rationalization of assassination," Stevens regarded its showing at the Kennedy Center as "inappropriate." But others in the film community saw his decision as reflecting a fear of offending the government and consequently of losing a portion of AFI's federal funding. The AFI, established in 1965 under the National Endowment for the Arts, is supported in part by government funds. Since *State of Siege* was promptly shown in theaters throughout the country, the issue of censorship became largely academic. However, the case raised the question of how government subsidies for the arts affect freedom of artistic expression.

Last Tango. In keeping with the year's characteristic tone of controversy was its most important film. Italian director Bernardo Bertolocchi's French production, *Last Tango in Paris*, starring newcomer Maria Schneider and veteran actor Marlon Brando, stimulated many a legal battle about its right to be shown. In *Last Tango*, Brando portrays a bitter, middle-aged man involved in a savage relationship with an amoral 20-year-old girl. He and Schneider play out erotic scenes of unprecedented daring and violence for a general-release film.

Critic Pauline Kael declared that *Last Tango* had "altered the face of an art form" and that the date of its first showing at the New York Film Festival, Oct. 14, 1972, was "a landmark in movie history." Released to the general public in January, 1973, *Last Tango* garnered raves from other critics significantly less intense, but raves nonetheless. And even those not convinced of the film's magnificence still admitted to its importance.

Leading Money-Makers. *Last Tango* captured considerable attention from the media and was one

American Graffiti takes a nostalgic look at American youth in the 1950s. Motion-picture critics praised the film for its authenticity.

of 1973's top-grossing films. Still, its estimated $25-million domestic gross was a good deal less than the approximately $80 million brought in by the year's commercial winner, *The Poseidon Adventure*. An old-fashioned yarn filled with special effects, it shows us an assortment of Hollywood stereotypes—the courageous priest, the fat Jewish mother, and the mischievous little boy—trying to escape from an overturned ship.

The critical response to *The Poseidon Adventure* was overwhelmingly negative. It also was to the year's other two largest money-makers, *The Getaway*, and *Live and Let Die*. *The Getaway* is a caper film with director Sam Peckinpah's characteristic flair for vividly chromatic shoot-outs and with criminals that get away with their crimes, as is the prevailing mode. *Live and Let Die* is a James Bond opus starring Roger Moore.

The critics—or at least the powerful Eastern establishment—evidently exerted little influence on the moviegoing public's choices in 1973. And as *The Getaway* and *Live and Let Die* suggest, and as the continued commercial health of blood-and-guts black films made clear, sex may have been getting the headlines in 1973, but violence was still in control at the box office. Further evidence for its drawing power lay in the startling financial success of a string of low-budget martial arts imports, all featuring Kung Fu carnage. An early 1973 release, for example, *Five Fingers of Death*, brought in $10 million in six months, while a late release, *Enter the Dragon*, earned $6 million at the box office in six weeks.

By July, 1973 promised to be a fairly depressing year for American film—both as industry and art. Box-office receipts were down 11 per cent and not a single artistically important film had been released, except, perhaps, for Jerry Schatzberg's *Scarecrow*, which won acclaim at the Cannes Film Festival for Gene Hackman and Al Pacino (also impressive in 1973 in the title role of *Serpico*), and Peter Bogdanovich's paean to 1930s movies, *Paper Moon*.

New Films, Directors. In late summer, however, the tide began to turn in the realm of art. There was considerable disagreement as to the ultimate quality of 28-year-old John Milius' blood-soaked biography of *Dillinger;* of 33-year-old Ralph Bakshi's often vulgar, consistently brutal, but technically brilliant X-rated animated feature, *Heavy Traffic;* and of 27-year-old James William Guercio's magnificently photographed *Electra Glide in Blue*. However, by the time *American Graffiti*, 28-year-old George Lucas' nostalgic glance at youth in the early 1950s, and *Bang the Drum Slowly*, 34-year-old John Hancock's tragicomic tale of a dying baseball player, opened, it became clear not only that there was an extraordinary cluster of gifted young directors on the American movie scene, but also that American film was indeed alive and well. These feelings were dramatically confirmed by the New York Film Festival

The Iceman Cometh, with Fredric March and Lee Marvin, was one of eight plays filmed for showing in movie houses by the American Film Theatre.

showings of 29-year-old Terence Mallick's 1950s fable about a boy and girl who romantically turn to murder in *Badlands* and 30-year-old Martin Scorsese's moving depiction of life in New York's Little Italy, *Mean Streets*. The latter film starred Robert De Niro, who also appeared in *Bang the Drum Slowly* and was widely considered 1973's up-and-coming actor.

Significantly, the two most lauded of these films, *Mean Streets* and *Badlands*, were the work of directors who had been educated to their art, Mallick by the AFI school in Beverly Hills, Scorsese by New York University's School of the Arts. It seemed, then, that film study was making its mark in creation as well as in scholarship.

While the emergence of these new directors made 1973 seem a forward-looking year, it was in other ways backward-looking. Both Warner Brothers and the Disney studios celebrated their 50th anniversaries, and giant retrospectives were launched at the Kennedy Center, at Lincoln Center, and at the Museum of Modern Art in New York City. Nostalgia ran high. But so, too, did a sense of seriousness. History was affirming the growth and accomplishment of film, as were these prestigious institutions its importance as art. Joy Gould Boyum

See also AWARDS AND PRIZES; BRANDO, MARLON; FOSSE, BOB; MINNELLI, LIZA.

MOZAMBIQUE. See AFRICA.

MUSEUMS

MUSEUMS in the United States wrestled with three ethical problems in 1973. By purchasing specimens from unverified sources, museums in the past had inadvertently encouraged illicit traffic in objects looted from archaeological sites or native tribes. Strong policies supporting a United Nations Educational, Scientific, and Cultural Organization convention to prevent the unscientific collection and illegal export of cultural property were adopted by the American Association of Museums (AAM), the Association of Art Museum Directors, and several museums. These included the Arizona State Museum, the Brooklyn Museum, the Field Museum of Natural History, and the Smithsonian Institution.

American Indians questioned the right of museums to possess and display collections they considered their racial heritage. Museum officials and Indian advisers studied ways to assure continued preservation and better use of these treasured objects.

Many persons criticized museums, particularly the Metropolitan Museum of Art in New York City, for selling or trading specimens for more desirable ones. In consultation with museum officials, the New York state attorney general developed guidelines to safeguard the public interest.

Expansion. As museum visits in the United States swelled to an estimated 700 million, more space for museum services became necessary. Along the Mall

Museum-goers study a 2,500-year-old Greek vase, which, critics charged, was bought under odd circumstances by the Metropolitan Museum of Art.

in Washington, D.C., construction began on the National Air and Space Museum, continued on the National Gallery of Art extension, and neared completion on the Joseph H. Hirshhorn Museum.

The Virginia Museum of Fine Arts began building a $6.2-million wing in Richmond. In San Francisco, the California Academy of Sciences received a $1-million gift to build facilities for preserving and exhibiting its anthropology collections. The National Infantry Museum prepared to move its collections into a large building being erected for it at Fort Benning, Ga. Old Sturbridge Village, Mass., invested more than $1.6 million in a Learning Resource Center that is being constructed to serve visiting school classes.

Education. The Chicago Museum of Science and Industry offered free science-related dramatic performances to school classes visiting the museum. The plays, supported by a National Science Foundation grant, were staged by the Goodman Theatre of The Art Institute of Chicago. The American Museum of Natural History in New York City used live performers along with exhibits and other media in its new People Center. This facility provided programs to help visitors understand the value of differences among cultures. The Field Museum of Natural History in Chicago combined exhibitions, films, lectures, and publications into a major coordinated program on man and his environment.   Ralph H. Lewis

MUSIC, CLASSICAL. A touch of the turmoil that later enveloped the nation's political scene was experienced musically during January, 1973, festivities marking President Richard M. Nixon's second inauguration. The National Symphony Orchestra, historically the performing group at inaugural concerts, was slighted in favor of the Philadelphia Orchestra. About half of the Philadelphians supported a petition condemning the bombing of North Vietnam, an issue at the time.

Composer Vincent Persichetti had been asked to compose a work for narrator and orchestra based on Lincoln's second inaugural address ("With malice toward none, with charity for all"). He did so. But the White House then dropped his composition from the program, reportedly because the Lincoln text with its references to war might embarrass the President.

In its place, guests at the concert on January 19 heard actor Charlton Heston recite portions of the Declaration of Independence with the Roger Wagner Chorale humming an accompaniment. The Persichetti work premièred in St. Louis a week later with William Warfield as narrator.

On the same evening as the inaugural concert, the National Cathedral in Washington, D.C., offered conductor Leonard Bernstein, an orchestra comprised of National Symphony players, a chorus, and soloists in a "Concert for Peace." They performed

Haydn's *Mass in Time of War*, written in 1796 during Napoleon's conflict with Austria.

The President asked the Philadelphians to be the first American orchestra to tour the People's Republic of China. They did in September. Their repertory included a Chinese work, the *Yellow River Concerto*.

Architecture joined music in a dramatic splash when the Sydney Opera House and companion concert hall opened in September. The Australians had lavished close to $150 million on this spectacular music center of billowing, sky-sweeping shells. Prokofiev's *War and Peace*, based on the Tolstoy novel, was the opening opera. Soprano Birgit Nilsson and the Sydney Symphony inaugurated the concert hall.

Financial Woes. While Australia spent money on its architectural wonder, several U.S. musical aggregations wondered where to get money to operate. The Metropolitan Opera's new general manager, Schuyler Chapin, said his company was broke, living on credit from persons of good will, and burdened with a deficit of $8 million.

The New York City Opera was also besieged by financial woes. Its orchestra was on strike for three weeks in the fall before a contract settlement could be reached. Before those musicians returned to work in October, members of the New York Philharmonic walked out to begin a lengthy strike. They wanted pay similar to that just won by Chicago Symphony players after a dispute that delayed the Chicago opening by three weeks.

Welcome because of the increasing importance of Gustav Mahler's music was a scholarly, 982-page volume-one of Henry-Louis de La Grange's study of the composer. Concert schedules in 1973 included Mahler's Second Symphony, the "Resurrection" (in Buffalo, Philadelphia, Washington, D.C.); the Third (Chicago, Detroit, Los Angeles, St. Louis); Sixth (Chicago, Los Angeles); Eighth, "Symphony of a Thousand" (Cincinnati); Ninth (San Francisco); Tenth (Philadelphia, Pittsburgh); and *Das Lied von der Erde* (Baltimore).

A flurry of publishing honored the late George Gershwin on the 75th anniversary of his birth in September. Other anniversaries were noted – composers John Cage at age 60 and Roy Harris at 75, impresario Sol Hurok for 60 years of service to music and 85 years of living. The late Sergei Rachmaninoff, Enrico Caruso, and Feodor Chaliapin were lauded on the 100th anniversaries of their birth.

Opera Favorites Maria Callas and Giuseppe di Stefano returned from vocal retirement in a duo concert in Hamburg, West Germany, on October 25. Callas also shifted her talents to a new activity in April when she successfully directed Verdi's *I Vespri Siciliani* to open the new opera house in Turin, Italy.

Among major new appointments were those of Rolf Liebermann of the Hamburg Opera as administrator for the Paris Opera, Rafael Kubelik as music director of the Metropolitan Opera, and Seiji Ozawa

as music director of the Boston Symphony (in addition to his leadership of the San Francisco Symphony). Riccardo Muti was named principal conductor of London's New Philharmonia Orchestra (succeeding the late Otto Klemperer); Carlo Maria Giulini became chief conductor of the Vienna Symphony; and James Levine, music director of Chicago's Ravinia Festival.

Unusual Musical Events. The controversial director Maurice Bejart offered a new production of Verdi's *La Traviata* in Brussels, in March. In it, the heroine, Violetta, dies not once but three times – at the beginning, before act three when suddenly she is carried in a coffin, and at the end, as is normal.

In March and April, Carol Neblett became the best unclothed opera singer of the year in two much-debated productions. The New York City Opera revived Monteverdi's *The Coronation of Poppea*. Its stage director had the beautiful soprano take a bath sans clothes behind a see-through screen of feathers. Then she followed the libretto more explicitly than usual when she performed Jules Massenet's *Thaïs* in New Orleans. She disrobed during a scene in which she is to shock and change a saintly priest.

The Santa Fe Chamber Music Festival moved in June to Window Rock, Ariz., capital of the Navajo Nation, to perform under the unusual rock formation called the "hole in the sky." At about the same time, the New York Philharmonic put rugs and cushions where seats usually are and played a week of "Rug Concerts" to enthusiastic young audiences. Soprano Eleanor Steber's answer was an October "Towel Concert" at New York City's Continental Baths.

Soprano Beverly Sills completed her trilogy of English royalty at the New York City Opera with Donizetti's *Anna Bolena* in October. Earlier she had sung Elizabeth in that composer's *Roberto Devereux* and the title role in his *Maria Stuarda*.

The nation's orchestras seemed drawn to more contemporary composers. The most popular were Igor Stravinsky and Aaron Copland, but repertories flowered with the works of the French composer Olivier Messiaen and the Pole Krzyztof Penderecki. Messiaen music was heard in Cleveland (*Turangalila*), Los Angeles (*Oiseaux Exotiques*), Minneapolis-St. Paul (*Celestial City*), Pittsburgh (*L'Ascension*), and St. Louis (*Les Offrandes oubliées*). Penderecki's *St. Luke's Passion* was done in Cincinnati, Philadelphia, and Washington, D.C., and his *Polymorphia* in New Orleans and San Francisco.

World Premières included Ross Lee Finney's *Symphony No. 4* (Baltimore), James Drew's *West Indian Lights* (Boston), William Karlins' *Concert Music No. 5* (Chicago), Claus Adam's *Cello Concerto* (Cincinnati), Elie Siegmeister's *Symphony No. 4* (Cleveland), Alberto Ginastera's *Milena* (Denver), Fisher Tull's *Trumpet Concerto* (Houston), Ginastera's *Piano Concerto No. 2* (Indianapolis), Arne Nordheim's

411

The Metropolitan Opera gave Berlioz's *The Trojans* its first staged production in New York City on October 22, the Met's 90th birthday.

Greening for Orchestra (Los Angeles), Walter Piston's *Fantasy for Violin and Orchestra* (Milwaukee), Leonardo Balada's *Steel Symphony* (Pittsburgh), David Sheinfeld's *Time Warp* (San Francisco), Leroy Ostransky's *Songs for Julia* (Seattle), Louis Ballard's *Devil's Promenade* (Tulsa), and Marvin David Levy's *Masada*, commemorating the 25th anniversary of the founding of Israel (Washington, D.C.).

Concert versions of opera continued to be popular with orchestras: Mozart's *Impresario* (Cleveland), Rossini's *Le Comte Ory* (Cincinnati), Puccini's *Madama Butterfly* (Indianapolis), Johann Strauss' *Die Fledermaus* (Denver), Stravinsky's *Le Rossignol* (New York), Carl Orff's *Carmina Burana* (Houston and New Orleans), and the third act of Wagner's *Die Götterdämmerung* (Chicago).

Unusual Programming was featured by many U.S. opera companies. Rochester's "Opera Under the Stars" did Ralph Vaughan Williams' *Poisoned Kiss.* Houston's Spring Festival featured Stravinsky's *Soldier's Tale.* Frederick Delius' *Village Romeo and Juliet* was produced in St. Paul by the New York City Opera.

Other out-of-the ordinary productions included Benjamin Britten's *Turn of the Screw* by the Hartford Theater Association; his *Rape of Lucretia* at Chautauqua, N.Y.; Marco da Gagliano's *La Dafne* at the Caramoor Festival in Katonah, N.Y.; Donizetti's *Rita* by the Baltimore Opera; Kurt Weill's *Rise and*

Fall of the City of Mahagonny in Boston and Colorado Springs; Leoš Janáček's *Jenufa* in Louisville, Ky.; Donizetti's *Maria Stuarda* in Chicago; and Berlioz' *The Trojans* at the Metropolitan.

Among the most talked about opera premières was Gian Carlo Menotti's *Tamu-Tamu* (*The Guests*). It was commissioned by and performed for the Ninth International Congress of Anthropological and Ethnological Sciences in Chicago in September. The work is a fantasy involving a Western "have" couple invaded in their suburban home by a "have not" family of Indonesian refugees from a bitter war. The result is emotional and tragic.

Benjamin Britten's *Death in Venice*, based on the Thomas Mann story, garnered considerable praise following its June première at Great Britain's Aldeburgh Festival. Another transfer from literature to music was *Transformations*, Conrad Susa's musical theater piece developed from 11 poems by Pulitzer Prize-winning poet Anne Sexton. It was premièred by the Minnesota Opera in May.

Other new operas included Günther Lüder's *Under Milk Wood* (Hamburg), Salvatore Sciarrino's *Amor e Psiche* (Milan), Isan Yun's *Geisterliebe* (Nuremberg), Carl Orff's *De Temporum Fine Comoedia* (Salzburg), Leif Söderström's *Tintomara* (Stockholm, to celebrate the 200th anniversary of the Royal Opera), Felix Werder's *The Affair* (Sydney), and Josef Tal's *Masada 967* (Tel Aviv).

Peter P. Jacobi

MUSIC, POPULAR. More than ever, popular music, especially rock, established itself in 1973 as the most widely listened-to music in history. This was reaffirmed when 600,000 rock fans converged on Watkins Glen, N.Y., in July to hear the Allman Brothers, The Grateful Dead, and The Band. This was twice the number that attended the Woodstock Festival in 1969.

Australian-born singer Helen Reddy, whose hit single "I Am Woman" became a gold (million-selling) record in December, 1972, reached new peaks of success. Her second chart-topping single, "Delta Dawn," and two albums achieved $1 million in sales.

Bette Midler, a Hawaii-born singer in her 30s, who has a wildly extrovert personality, led the trend toward nostalgia during the year. She revived "Boogie Woogie Bugle Boy of Company B," an Andrews Sisters hit in 1941, with such success that the original Andrews Sisters records were reissued.

The Pointer Sisters quartet took nostalgia in a different direction with their thrift-shop gowns, sometimes old-fashioned vocal blend, and a repertoire that encompassed pop, soul, and rhythm-and-blues, as well as a strong jazz orientation. On the strength of their unusual appearance and personality, they, like Midler, became as popular in person as on records.

Barry White, a singer, writer, and record producer, found success with a series of songs such as "I'm Gonna Love You Just a Little More, Baby" and "I've Got So Much to Give." Stevie Wonder, as well as White, seemed to transcend the black audience. He found mass appeal in several hit singles, including "Superstition" and "You Are the Sunshine of My Life." Pop-jazz singer Roberta Flack, following up her huge 1972 success, scored again with her interpretation of "Killing Me Softly with His Song." Organist Billy Preston emerged as an important pop soloist with his single "Will It Go Round in Circles?"

Reggae, the contagious rhythmic style from the West Indies, made its strongest attempt to break through in U.S. popular music circles. Johnny Nash, a singer from Houston, Tex., became the first American artist to succeed with several Reggae singles, including "I Can See Clearly Now" and "Stir It Up." Reggae was also performed in the United States by such Jamaican artists as The Wailers and Jimmy Cliff, as well as American singers Paul Simon, Art Garfunkel, and Peter Yarrow.

While two albums repackaging early hits by the Beatles leaped to the top of the charts, ex-Beatles Paul McCartney and George Harrison enjoyed individual success. McCartney scored with his album "Red Rose Speedway" and two singles, "My Love" and "High High High." Harrison did well with his LP, "Living in the Material World," out of which came the hit single "Give Me Love."

Musical Tours. Other groups in consistent popular favor were the The Allman Brothers, Chicago,

Photo from "W"

The Pointer Sisters exploded on the pop music scene in 1973 with rich, powerful voices and an exciting jazz-rock musical style all their own.

Grand Funk, War, Jethro Tull, and Led Zeppelin. Procol Harum, after recording with the Edmonton Symphony, joined forces with other symphony orchestras for successful concerts in several U.S. cities. The 5th Dimension toured Turkey and Eastern Europe as a cultural presentation under a program of the U.S. Department of State. Early in the year Eumir Deodato, a Brazilian pianist and composer, became a major force on records, first with a theme from the film *2001: A Space Odyssey* (based on Richard Strauss's *Thus Spake Zarathustra*) and later with a modernized treatment of George Gershwin's *Rhapsody in Blue.* He employed an instrumental style that embraced classical, jazz, and rock disciplines. Jim Croce, the singer heard on such recordings as "You Don't Mess Around with Jim" and "Bad, Bad Leroy Brown," was in the middle of a concert tour when he and five members of his band were killed in a plane crash in Natchitoches, La., on September 20.

The pop artists' complete domination of the music world was accentuated by estimates in the trade that their records had accounted for 66 per cent of all sales in 1972. Soul music placed second with about 14 per cent, followed by country with 10 per cent, classical with 6 per cent, and jazz with 1.5 per cent.

The Jazz Resurgence continued. Record companies discovered a new means of merchandising jazz by repackaging the best material from their catalogs and offering two records for the price of one.

The Newport Jazz Festival, held June 29-July 8 in New York City, incorporated a record number of 52 outdoor and indoor concerts in almost every area of the city. At one all-star jam session, on July 4, Singer Bowl in Flushing Meadow was officially renamed Louis Armstrong Memorial Stadium.

Japan became an increasingly important country for jazz. Miles Davis toured Japan in June for two weeks. Benny Carter and many other jazz stars also took their groups to the Orient.

The oldest living major jazz musician, ragtime pianist and composer Eubie Blake, was also one of the most widely traveled. After celebrating his 90th birthday in February, he continued to make concert and television appearances at home and abroad.

Trumpeter Freddie Hubbard, composer Duke Ellington, and vibraphonist Gary Burton received Grammy Awards for the best jazz performances of 1972. Donald Byrd, composer, trumpeter, and teacher of black history at Howard University, became a nationally important figure in jazz-rock with the success of his album "Black Byrd."

The jazz world suffered several losses. Trombonist Kid Ory, 86, died in January and drummer Gene Krupa in October. Others who died include Eddie Condon, Wilbur De Paris, Bill Harris, J. C. Higginbotham, lyricist Andy Razaf, Willie (The Lion) Smith, and Clara Ward.   Leonard Feather

Charley Pride won a Grammy Award for his album "Charley Pride Sings Heart Songs," judged best male country vocal performance.

NAMIBIA. Political discontent among the black majority of Namibia (South West Africa) increased dramatically during 1973. In 1972, the South African government, which administers the territory in defiance of United Nations (UN) resolutions for Namibian independence, had agreed with the UN on the principle of independence. However, the white minority regime moved to ensure that Namibian independence would best fit its own self-interests.

The government continued to create separate "homelands" for blacks and whites. The white homeland in Namibia would include almost all the valuable lands. The South African government also set up a multiracial advisory council to discuss the territory's future and administer Namibia under the direction of the South African government. Two black homelands, or Bantustans, were set up during the year. Ovamboland was created on May 1. The Okavango Bantustan was established on May 9.

Black Protests. There was almost total black opposition to the government's plans. The National Convention, a nonwhite political front, rejected both the council and the homeland concept. On March 6, blacks protesting the creation of the council burned a government building in Windhoek, Namibia's administrative capital. When the advisory council finally met on March 23, almost all the major nonwhite leaders boycotted the meeting. The council refused to accept the UN demand for a united and independent Namibia and refused to use the name Namibia, rather than South West Africa. Then, in April, 10 antigovernment black leaders were arrested.

Riots broke out near Windhoek on August 17 after police broke up a meeting of the youth league of the militant South West African People's Organization (SWAPO). One black was killed and 265 others arrested. Rioting by striking black workers continued for three days. Reportedly, they were responding to a SWAPO pamphlet calling for a strike until the government gave in to such demands as releasing political prisoners and granting independence.

The riots followed an August 2 election for an all-black Ovamboland Legislative Assembly. SWAPO had called for a boycott of the election, and only the conservative, progovernment Ovambo Independence Party ran candidates. Only 1,300 of 50,000 voters cast their ballots.

UN Reaction. In April, UN Secretary-General Kurt Waldheim and South African Foreign Minister Hilgard Muller discussed the Namibia question. Muller said that independence for Namibia "might not take longer than 10 years." However, African nationalists remained mistrustful of the white government.

The UN Council for Namibia issued a statement in April opposing continued dialogue with South Africa. In August, Waldheim admitted that the talks had failed up to that time.   John Storm Roberts

See also AFRICA (Facts in Brief Table).

NATIONAL DEFENSE. The United States signed peace accords officially terminating its military involvement in Vietnam on Jan. 27, 1973. The peace agreement provided for an exchange of prisoners and the withdrawal of all U.S. troops within 60 days. On May 29, the last 2,500 U.S. support troops in Vietnam were flown out to bases in Guam, Japan, and Thailand. The Military Assistance Command, Vietnam, which once controlled more than 540,000 U.S. troops, was abolished.

Beginning on February 12, the last of the 587 U.S. prisoners of war (POW's) were released by the North Vietnamese and Viet Cong. Once the prisoner exchange was completed, POW's told of the severe physical and mental torture inflicted by their captors. Several POW's reportedly died in captivity as a result of torture. See Close-Up.

American casualties in Vietnam between Jan. 1, 1961, and the final troop withdrawal included 46,104 combat deaths and 10,317 deaths from accidents or illness. A total of 303,652 Americans were wounded in action, and 1,216 were listed as missing.

Military Strength. The United States trimmed its military forces to 2,231,908 troops as of Sept. 30, 1973, the lowest level in 23 years. Elliot L. Richardson, then secretary of defense, announced the largest reduction in domestic military bases in nearly 25 years on April 16. The reductions affected 274 installations and were scheduled to eliminate 42,812 military and civilian jobs by June, 1974.

Richardson said the cutback was "commensurate with reduced force levels and training requirements resulting in large part from the end of the Vietnam conflict." He estimated that the reductions would save $3.5 billion over the next 10 years.

Six Air Force, 5 Army, and 29 Navy bases were ordered closed, including the Navy's huge complex at Newport-Quonset Point, R.I. The Navy also planned to close two shipyards, including the Boston Naval Shipyard, and naval stations at Key West, Fla., and Long Beach, Calif., and three naval air stations.

Bases the Air Force planned to close were Westover in Massachusetts, Ramey in Puerto Rico, McCoy in Florida, Laredo in Texas, Forbes in Kansas, and Hamilton in California. Army bases ordered closed included Fort Wolters, Texas; Hunter Army Airfield, Georgia; and the Charleston (S.C.) Army Depot. The Army was to decide by 1974 whether to close its basic-training base at Fort Dix, N.J., or reduce operations at all nine training centers. More military base closings were being prepared for 1974.

The military draft was halted on January 27, five months before the conscription law expired. However, the Army's all-volunteer program fell 16 per cent short of its recruiting goals for the first eight

©1973 Chicago Daily News

"Mooooo-la," said the sacred cow . . .

Return
Of the
POW's

The war in Vietnam was over for Americans, and the prisoners of war (POW's) finally came home in 1973. The nation's longest battle ended without glory in a complex suspension of hostilities. The return of the POW's was a tangible finality that the peace negotiations could never offer.

Last-minute haggling between Saigon and Hanoi delayed the repatriation. But then it was announced on February 12 that the first 115 of the 456 men held in North Vietnam were to be turned over in Hanoi, and 27 of the 120 held by the Viet Cong in South Vietnam were freed at Quan Loi, about 60 miles north of Saigon. As part of the bargain, South Vietnam released 4,000 North Vietnamese and Viet Cong POW's. The freed American POW's were immediately flown to Clark Air Base in the Philippines, then to the United States.

The prisoners' return was dampened, however, by the knowledge that more than 1,200 men were still missing and 46,104 other Americans had died in the fighting.

The average prisoner had been away from home for four years. Army Major Floyd Thompson and Navy Lieutenant Commander Everett Alvarez, Jr., had been gone for more than eight years. Thompson was captured on March 26, 1964, and Alvarez was shot down over North Vietnam on Aug. 5, 1964. During his imprisonment, his wife divorced him and remarried, and his sister became a critic of the war.

The returning prisoners were greeted warmly and emotionally, and in some cases with touches of exaggerated sentimentality. One automobile manufacturer, for example, wanted to give each POW a new car, and Baseball Commissioner Bowie Kuhn quickly offered each returnee a gold lifetime pass good at any major-league game. But President Richard M. Nixon probably expressed the opinion of most Americans when he said, "This is a time that we should not grandstand it; we should not exploit it."

No one, of course, could minimize the ordeal of the POW's. After all of them had been returned to the United States, they talked about their ordeal. Many of the men charged they had been beaten, tied, shackled, and starved until they gave their captors information on U.S. war plans or signed antiwar confessions.

To the surprise of many of them, physical torture was used to extract propaganda statements more often than military secrets. In a world where media manipulation has become almost as important as battlefield victories, the North Vietnamese pressed hard for propaganda material, and they got what they wanted more often than not.

The POW's reported that life improved significantly in the prison camps after 1969, when the United States made them the subject of a massive international lobbying campaign. Camp conditions also improved in proportion to the prospects for peace.

By the time the final prisoner was released on April 1, a total of 595 POW's had been freed by the Viet Cong and the North Vietnamese. Of these, 587 were Americans, including 24 civilians. There were also 2 each from West Germany, Thailand, Canada, and the Philippines. The Department of Defense listed 1,216 Americans missing in action or unaccounted for and 1,100 killed in action whose bodies had not been recovered.

But while many of the returned POW's moved smoothly back into military or civilian life, some found it difficult to find peace. In May, eight of the returned prisoners were charged by Air Force Colonel Theodore W. Guy with "alleged misconduct while in a North Vietnamese prison camp." The charges were dropped in July, the Department of Defense explaining it was not its policy to hold "trials for alleged propaganda statements." In the meantime, however, one of the men charged committed suicide. Charges brought by the Navy against two others were also dropped in September. Another returnee, not among those charged with misconduct, committed suicide; he just found "life not worth living" after he returned.

During the years of the Vietnam War, the world had changed and so had the attitudes of many Americans toward that war. But what was important was that the POW's were now home, and for this, everyone was glad.   Foster Stockwell

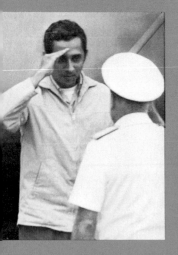

Commander Alvarez returns

months of 1973. The Army even lowered educational standards in an effort to meet quotas.

In his annual military posture report released on March 27, Admiral Thomas H. Moorer, chairman of the Joint Chiefs of Staff, repeated his 1972 warning that "the military power of the United States, when compared to other nations in the world, has clearly peaked and is now declining.

"We no longer have that substantial strategic superiority which, in the past, provided us with such a clear-cut margin of overall military power so that we could, with confidence, ensure the protection of our interests and those of our allies worldwide. Accordingly, we must plan our national security programs with greater precision . . . ."

Defense Budget. Despite a steady decline in U.S. troop strength, the ending of U.S. involvement in the Vietnam War, and the Nixon Administration's efforts to achieve détente with Russia and China, defense spending continued to rise. In 1973, it approached the World War II peak of $79.8 billion. Rising defense costs were attributed to pay increases, inflation, and continued cost overruns in developing and manufacturing new weapons systems.

The Department of Defense submitted a fiscal 1974 (July 1, 1973, to June 30, 1974) budget request of $79 billion, $4.2 billion more than the previous year. The budget would support 13 Army and 3 Marine divisions, 21 Air Force tactical wings, 17 Navy and Marine air wings, and a Navy fleet of 523 vessels. An estimated $7.4 billion was slated for strategic forces. The Navy was scheduled to receive the largest share of the budget, $26.4 billion; the Air Force, $24.6 billion; and the Army, $21.2 billion.

The Navy requested $1.7 billion for the Trident missile-submarine program, $657 million for a nuclear-powered aircraft carrier, $591 million for DD-963 destroyers, and $633 million for the F-14 Tomcat jet fighter. Because of cost overruns and production problems, the F-14 contractor threatened to halt production, but the Navy agreed to rewrite the contract. The first 134 planes would be built at the original price of $16.8 million each, but the price for the rest would be renegotiated annually.

The Air Force asked for $1.1 billion for the F-15 Eagle jet fighter and $474 million for the B-1 strategic bomber. However, both projects had severe technical problems. Because there were problems with the F-15 engine, the Air Force cut back its first production order from 77 to 39 planes. Difficulties with the B-1 bomber prototype forced the Air Force to delay the first test flight from April, 1974, to June, 1974. The Air Force also asked for $142 million for the A-10 battlefield support plane.

The Army requested $52 million for an advance attack helicopter and $49 million to begin development of the XM-1 tank. The Army also requested $194 million for the SAM-D missile and $109 million for a new utility helicopter.

SALT Agreement. The United States and Russia continued their efforts throughout 1973 to lessen the chances for nuclear confrontation, and sought further arms control accords to supplement the strategic arms limitation treaty (SALT) signed on May 26, 1972. The two superpowers signed a declaration of principles on June 20, 1973, pledging that both sides would begin "urgent consultations" whenever relations between them or another country "appear to involve the risk of nuclear conflict." Both sides also agreed to accelerate the second round of SALT talks and complete a new arms treaty by the end of 1974.

Richardson supported efforts to achieve this détente in his March 27 report to Congress. But he also urged the continued development of several weapons systems to strengthen the U.S. bargaining position at the SALT talks. The priority defense project for 1973 was the Trident missile submarine. At a total cost of $12.7 billion, Trident would be the most expensive weapons system in history.

The 10 Trident submarines would carry 24 missiles with multiple warheads and a 4,000-mile range. Richardson urged that Trident development be speeded so the system could be operational in 1978. He also urged continued development of the B-1 strategic bomber, the "site defense" advance antiballistic missile system, a submarine-launched cruise missile, an airborne warning and control system, and more accurate nuclear warheads.

Command Changes. Melvin R. Laird resigned as secretary of defense in January and was replaced by Richardson, former secretary of health, education, and welfare. On April 30, however, Richardson was named attorney general. He was replaced by James R. Schlesinger, former director of the Central Intelligence Agency.

John S. Foster, Jr., resigned as director of defense research and engineering and was replaced on August 27 by Robert N. Parker. Howard H. Callaway became secretary of the Army on May 15, replacing Robert F. Froehlke. John L. McLucas, undersecretary of the Air Force, became secretary of the Air Force on July 19, replacing Robert C. Seamans, Jr. General John D. Ryan retired as Air Force chief of staff and was replaced by General George S. Brown on August 1.

General Alexander M. Haig, Jr., who became Army vice-chief of staff on January 4, resigned on June 6 to become White House chief of staff. He was succeeded by General Frederick C. Weyland, the last commander of U.S. forces in Vietnam.

Jeanne Holm, the first woman Air Force general, was promoted from brigadier general to major general. Daniel James, Jr., became the highest ranking black officer on May 21, when he was promoted to Air Force lieutenant general.   Thomas M. DeFrank

NATIONALIST CHINA. See TAIWAN.

NAVY, U.S. See NATIONAL DEFENSE.

NEBRASKA. See STATE GOVERNMENT.

NEPAL. A fire that destroyed the national secretariat in Katmandu on July 9, 1973, may indirectly have led to the resignation of Prime Minister Kirti Nidhi Bista and his 27-month-old government. Although no specific reason was given for Bista's resignation, it was assumed that his move followed acceptance of moral responsibility for the fire that destroyed the historic site. King Birendra Bir Bikram Shah Deva appointed Nagendra Prashad Rijal, chairman of the National Assembly, to replace Bista.

Hundreds of Nepalese students trying to march through the center of Katmandu on August 16 were dispersed by the police. Dozens of students were arrested, and Tribhuvan University canceled its annual convocation because of the unrest. The students were on strike for reforms in the nation's administrative system and university educational policies.

A Nepalese airliner carrying 15 passengers and a crew of 3 was hijacked on June 10 while en route from Birātnagar to Katmandu. The three armed hijackers, all Nepalese, forced the plane to land at Forbesganj, India, and they escaped in a waiting jeep. They reportedly had stolen about $400,000 from the Nepalese state bank.

On April 12, Queen Kanti Rajya Laxmi Devi Shah, the 66-year-old grandmother of the king, died in Katmandu. She was the eldest of two wives of the late King Tribhubana.   Paul C. Tullier

See also Asia (Facts in Brief Table).

NETHERLANDS. Dutch support for Israel in the Middle East war in October resulted in a complete Arab boycott of petroleum exports to the Netherlands, which promised to have a severe effect on the economy. Earlier in the year, after five months without a government, a compromise coalition of 10 ministers from the left and 6 from the center was sworn in on May 11, 1973. They were led by Johannes M. den Uyl as prime minister. The government's main task was to fight inflation, and its first step was to cut the salaries of all ministers and secretaries of state by 10 per cent. Drastic defense budget cuts were promised for 1974. In his first policy statement, Den Uyl called for the development of strong, democratically controlled European institutions. "The decision on direct elections to the European Parliament cannot be postponed any longer," he said. He promised that the new government would combat racial discrimination and colonialism.

A 5 per cent revaluation of the guilder, announced on September 15, was the major measure of an anti-inflation package. The European Community (Common Market) Commission expressed regret that the Dutch had not consulted the community "in the spirit of the community's moves toward economic and monetary union."

In its September 18 budget, the government allocated $300 million to create new jobs in redevelopment areas. Agriculture was to be compensated for the revaluation, with more tax incentives for small businessmen, farmers, and fishermen.

Industrial Unrest. Unions struck in the spring for flat, across-the-board pay raises of "cents, not per cent." In a series of short strikes, up to 40,000 workers a day stayed out in heavy metal, textiles, pulp, ceramic, and shipbuilding industries. After six weeks of disruption, unions threatened a national strike at Easter, and beer and milk supplies were in doubt. All the strikes were suspended on April 17.

Queen's Jubilee. Queen Juliana celebrated 25 years on the throne on September 6. A nationwide collection was distributed to needy children in Holland and developing countries to observe the date.

At the state opening of Parliament on September 18, the queen said the government wanted to work toward changes in the Common Market. The Dutch seek an organization that "is more concerned with the welfare of its citizens, has greater powers and a truly democratic structure which will direct its attention to the needs of the third world."   Kenneth Brown

See also Europe (Facts in Brief Table).

NEVADA. See State Government.

NEW BRUNSWICK. See Canada.

NEW GUINEA. See Pacific Islands.

NEW HAMPSHIRE. See State Government.

NEW JERSEY. See Newark; State Government.

NEW MEXICO. See State Government.

Urged by a draftees' union, the Netherlands government ruled soldiers could wear long hair if they kept it in nets for maneuvers.

NEW ORLEANS. A heavily armed sniper, positioned in a downtown Howard Johnson motel, killed 6 persons and wounded 15 others on Jan. 7, 1973. About 500 policemen exchanged gunfire throughout the day and night with the sniper. The following day, police hovering in a helicopter over the 18-story motel shot and killed him. They then stormed the motel rooftop, but no other snipers could be found. The dead man was Mark J. Essex, a 23-year-old black from Emporia, Kans., who had reportedly been embittered by the racial discrimination he encountered while in the U.S. Navy.

A dispute broke out about whether more than one sniper had been involved in the shootings. Police disclosed evidence on January 11 indicating that there had been at least one other gunman. A police officer had surprised two men in a hallway of the motel during the shoot-out. One of the men shot him.

Garrison Trial. New Orleans' controversial district attorney, Jim C. Garrison, stood trial during August and September on charges of conspiracy to obstruct law enforcement by taking bribes to protect illegal pinball gambling in New Orleans. Federal prosecutors produced recordings of conversations during which Garrison allegedly was offered, and accepted, bribes.

The government's key witness was Pershing O. Gervais, a former Garrison aide and bail bondsman. Gervais had agreed to be a government informer after the Internal Revenue Service (IRS) found evidence that he had evaded taxes. Gervais testified that he had delivered payoffs to Garrison and had helped IRS agents secretly tape Garrison's conversations.

Garrison pleaded innocent, fired his attorney, and argued his own defense. The government prosecutors thought they had an airtight case, but Garrison was acquitted by the jury on September 27.

In December, Garrison lost the district attorney slot in the Democratic primary to Harry Tucker. Garrison charged his opponent with vote fraud.

Floods and Fires. New Orleans was threatened with inundation in early April as the swollen Mississippi River rose still higher after heavy rain. For the first time since 1950, the U.S. Army Corps of Engineers opened the Bonnet Carré spillway. This diverted water from the Mississippi into Lake Pontchartrain to prevent flooding of the city itself. Environmentalists were concerned that the diversion of fresh water into the salt-water lake would adversely affect oysters, crabs, and shrimp in the lake.

Thirty-three persons were killed and 15 injured on June 24 when fire swept through a cocktail lounge in New Orleans' French Quarter. In October, Raymond Wallender, a 32-year-old transient, confessed to police in Sacramento, Calif., that he had set the fire. Wallender later retracted his story and, on November 1, waived extradition and agreed to return to Louisiana for trial.   James M. Banovetz

NEW YORK. See NEW YORK CITY; STATE GOV'T.

New Orleans District Attorney Jim Garrison, accompanied by his wife, waves to supporters after a jury acquitted him of bribery charges.

NEW YORK CITY. City Controller Abraham D. Beame was elected mayor of New York City on Nov. 6, 1973, succeeding John V. Lindsay. Beame, a Democrat, soundly defeated Republican State Senator John Marchi, Democratic Congressman Mario Biaggi, and Democratic State Assemblyman Albert Blumenthal. Biaggi ran as the Conservative Party candidate; Blumenthal, as the Liberal Party nominee. Lindsay had announced in March that he would not run for re-election. See BEAME, ABRAHAM D.

Firemen Strike. On November 6, New York City firemen went on strike for the first time in the fire department's history. The walkout, which lasted only five hours, was in defiance of both a court order and a state law against strikes by public employees. The firemen agreed to submit their demands to binding arbitration.

Railway workers staged a 63-day strike against the Port Authority Trans-Hudson Railroad. The strike, which ended on May 2, affected about 95,000 riders.

On November 5, 30,000 nonmedical hospital workers went on strike. The walkout, which lasted a week, affected 48 hospitals and nursing homes in the New York City area. Hospitals cut back on services, including emergency aid. The strikers were protesting the federal Cost of Living Council's failure to act on a 7.5 per cent wage increase that was to have taken effect in July. They settled for either a 6.1 per cent or a $9-a-week increase, whichever was greater.

Offering a new weapon against crime, television cameras look down on New York City's Times Square and relay the view to police monitors.

The World Trade Center was dedicated on April 4. The 1,350-foot-high twin towers form the second tallest building in the world, surpassed only by Chicago's Sears Tower. See ARCHITECTURE (Close-Up).

The New York Yankees baseball club was sold in January by its Columbia Broadcasting System owners to a 10-man syndicate for $10 million. Yankee Stadium was closed at the end of the 1973 baseball season for modernization, and the Yankees will play in Shea Stadium for two years.

Population Change. The New York metropolitan area suffered a decline in its population because of the broadened definition of metropolitan areas adopted by the U.S. Office of Management and Budget. The lost population was allocated to a new metropolitan area composed of Nassau and Suffolk counties on Long Island. According to an estimate released by the U.S. Bureau of the Census in September, the New York metropolitan area has a population of 9,943,800 persons.

New York was ranked as the nation's fourth most expensive urban area in which to live according to figures released on June 15 by the Department of Labor. A family of four would require an annual income of $13,179 to live in "moderate comfort."

In August, Welfare Island was renamed Franklin D. Roosevelt Island in honor of the late Democratic President. James M. Banovetz

NEW ZEALAND. French-sponsored nuclear tests in the South Pacific were a grave concern to New Zealand in 1973. On May 9, New Zealand joined Australia in asking the International Court of Justice at The Hague, to ban the tests. Their immediate concern was possible fallout from the tests France planned to carry out over Mururoa Atoll in June. Despite the court's request that the tests be suspended and such protest measures as stationing the New Zealand frigate *Otago* about 12 miles off the atoll, France carried out the tests. See AUSTRALIA; PACIFIC ISLANDS.

Inflation continued to plague the nation. On May 25, the government froze prices on a wide variety of products including food, clothing, and footwear. But the move failed to halt the inflationary trend. On August 12, the government again imposed a price as well as wage freeze. The government said the new anti-inflationary measure was designed to prevent "widespread industrial unrest" as well as "the collapse of the government's stabilization policy." In yet another move to halt the inflationary trend, the government devalued its dollar by 10 per cent on September 9, making the new exchange rate 1.478 U.S. dollars to 1 New Zealand dollar. One result of the action was immediately apparent on the New Zealand Stock Exchange, where the market experienced a 40-point drop in share prices.

Defense Policies. On May 12, the government announced that the New Zealand Army had begun an exchange system in collaboration with the U.S. Army in order that each could learn the other's infantry training methods. Units of each army would train for a month in the other nation.

Prime Minister Norman E. Kirk announced on June 16 that New Zealand would gradually reduce its military role in the Southeast Asia Treaty Organization. The alliance, he said, had originally been conceived as "a move to contain China," but China's new and friendlier role in international relations made such a position no longer tenable. Chinese envoy Pei Tsien-chang, meanwhile, had arrived in Wellington on May 10 to serve as China's ambassador to New Zealand.

Domestic Crisis. Late in January, a controversy over a proposed visit by an all-white South African Rugby team known as the Springboks almost reached crisis proportions. At the core of the controversy was South Africa's racial policy. Its all-white team had been chosen in segregated trials rather than in trials open to all races. The 30-nation Supreme Council for Sport in Africa announced it would boycott New Zealand's annual Commonwealth Games in Christchurch in 1974 if the team was allowed to make the tour, and Prime Minister Kirk feared that other Commonwealth nations would also decide to boycott the event. On April 10, Kirk asked the New Zealand Rugby Union to withdraw its invitation, and the union complied. Paul C. Tullier

See also ASIA (Facts in Brief Table).

NEWARK City Council President Louis M. Turco pleaded guilty on Oct. 9, 1973, to charges of failing to file an income tax return in 1970 and filing a false tax return in 1969. Turco, who had been considered a possible mayoral candidate, had been indicted by a grand jury on April 4 on federal charges of income tax evasion and mail fraud. The government charged that Turco, a lawyer, had defrauded nine clients and that he had sent false medical reports to five insurance companies.

U.S. Secretary of Labor Peter J. Brennan announced on April 17 that he had asked Mayor Kenneth A. Gibson to remove three of his appointees in Newark's Public Employment Program. Brennan also requested the return of more than $1 million in federal job funds, which the Labor Department claimed were misused. The U.S. government charged Manpower Director Harry Wheeler, Assistant Business Administrator Elton Hill, and Director of the Public Employment Program Alvin Moore with failure to follow guidelines contained in the Emergency Employment Act. Mayor Gibson agreed only to study Brennan's recommendations.

Serious crimes in Newark dropped 12 per cent during the first quarter of 1973, according to Federal Bureau of Investigation crime statistics.

Floating City. In August, the Newark Housing Authority presented a $2.5-billion plan, called Gateway 2000, for rejuvenating Newark. The elaborate project calls for a 1½-mile-long "floating city" to be constructed over existing buildings.

Major corporations are expected to finance the project, which will take 20 years to complete and will include hotels, housing, schools, stores, and recreational facilities. The plan also calls for a rapid-transit system, because motor vehicles will not be permitted in the complex.

Two huge new passenger terminals opened at the Newark International Airport in August and September. A third terminal was planned for 1976.

In February, about 200 white demonstrators attempted to halt construction on the controversial $6.4-million, black-owned Kawaida Towers highrise apartments. The project was funded by a 48-year loan from the New Jersey Housing Financing Agency to a black nationalist group. The apartment complex, being built in Newark's largely white North Ward, was strongly opposed by white residents of the area, who filed suit in April in state and federal courts to block construction of the project.

Population Change. The population of the Newark metropolitan area was increased as a result of new definitions of standard metropolitan statistical areas put into effect by the U.S. Office of Management and Budget. According to a September report from the U.S. Bureau of the Census, the population of the Newark urban area was estimated at 2,082,000 as of July, 1972. James M. Banovetz

NEWFOUNDLAND. See CANADA.

NEWSPAPERS in the United States got a sizable lift in 1973 from their performance in reporting the Watergate scandals. Their credibility increased measurably as a result of deft digging to expose the scandals. At the same time, the press was demanding a "shield law" against being subpoenaed to testify concerning corrupt politicians, the drug traffic, and other forms of criminality.

Shield Laws. As state and local grand juries joined with federal juries in demanding that more and more reporters face the choice of disclosing confidential news sources or going to jail, it became evident that press freedom needed shoring up.

The clamor for shield laws started when the Supreme Court of the United States ruled on June 29, 1972, that the First Amendment to the Constitution does not protect newsmen from grand jury subpoenas. Many media observers believed that a shield might be more difficult to obtain because Watergate left the impression that the press needs no protection.

Newsprint Shortage. In July, when the coverage of Watergate, President Richard M. Nixon, and Vice-President Spiro T. Agnew was eating up tons of newsprint, a shortage that had been developing for two years suddenly hit publishers. It forced newspapers throughout the country to conserve newsprint by cutting back on news and advertising space, eliminating features, limiting press runs, and even

Reporters Bob Woodward, left, and Carl Bernstein helped the *Washington Post* win a Pulitzer Prize for its Watergate exposés.

dropping some editions. The major cause of the shortage was strikes against Canadian mill owners and railroads. The shortage appeared to slacken somewhat toward year's end, but a dwindling supply still was in prospect for at least 1974.

The Newsprint Information Committee in November estimated newspaper production loss at 500,000 tons. Smaller papers were hardest hit. Canada supplies 7 million tons of newsprint, about two-thirds of the U.S. supply. The balance comes from U.S. mills. Most Canadian mills had increased newsprint price to $200 a ton by January, 1974, a new high. Publishers dealing with Canadian mills would subsequently have to pay the increases. United States mills increases would be subject to approval of the Cost of Living Council.

Daily newspapers in the United States increased total circulation by almost 300,000 in 1972 and posted a new record-high daily-circulation figure of 62,510,242. The number of daily newspapers increased from 1,749 in 1971 to 1,761 in 1972 in spite of the loss and merger of three large metropolitan newspapers in Boston, Newark, and Washington, D.C. Group newspaper acquisitions of independent papers continued at an accelerated rate. Gerald B. Healey

See also Section Two, THE RISE AND FALTER OF THE FREE PRESS.

NICARAGUA. See LATIN AMERICA.

NIGER. See AFRICA.

NIGERIA clearly emerged as the leading nation of black Africa in 1973. Yakubu Gowon, head of the federal military government, was appointed chairman of the Organization of African Unity. In June, Gowon became the first leader of an African Commonwealth of Nations country to make an official state visit to Great Britain.

Oil and Trade. Phillips Petroleum Company announced on January 31 that it had found a sizable low-sulfur oil deposit in the Niger River Delta. On June 11, Nigeria acquired 35 per cent of Shell-British Petroleum's holdings in Nigeria; the government reportedly agreed to pay $500 million. By June, Nigeria's oil production had reached 2 million barrels a day. As of October 1, Nigeria raised the price of its crude oil from $4.29 to $8.31 per barrel.

Britain bought 10 per cent of its oil from Nigeria, and, in general, Nigeria's trade with Britain grew more important. According to figures released in 1973, Nigeria exported $385 million worth of goods to Britain in 1972 and imported $455 million.

African Leadership Role. Nigeria used its growing trade position to lobby for a sterner British stand against the minority white regimes in southern Africa. Nigeria also tried to influence black African relations with the European Community (Common Market), encouraging other West African nations to be cautious of proposed relations with the Common Market. Nigeria hosted talks among 40 developing nations of

Africa and the Caribbean and Pacific areas from July 9 to 11, and, at the July Common Market meeting in Brussels, these nations took the position that poorer nations would need to receive special trade privileges.

President Mathieu Kerekou of Dahomey visited Nigeria in April to discuss establishing economic ties. Dahomey had decided to forego full membership in the new French-speaking West African Economic Community, which was created in part to offset the economic power of English-speaking Nigeria.

Youth Corps. In July, the government began drafting university graduates under 30 years of age to serve in the new National Youth Service Corps. The corps was created to help develop rural areas by building bridges, roads, schools, and medical clinics.

However, many students opposed the program, and the first draft touched off riots at the University of Lagos in July. The students demanded that government leaders, who had been accused of corruption and affluent living, make public their financial assets and begin setting a national example.

Despite Nigeria's growing prosperity, individual poverty was a major problem, and unemployment remained high. The government opened the Nigerian Bank for Industry and Commerce in October as part of a plan to involve more Nigerians in the development of the economy. John Storm Roberts

See also AFRICA (Facts in Brief Table).

NIXON, RICHARD MILHOUS. The first year of his second term was disastrous for President Richard M. Nixon. When the year began, the President basked in the afterglow of a landslide electoral victory. In his words, "peace with honor" had been achieved in Vietnam, and he regarded the 1972 election as a broad mandate for his policies.

But by the year's end, he was worn and defensive. In the shadow of the Watergate scandal, trusted members of his staff had resigned or were dismissed. Two former Cabinet members were indicted for conspiracy to defraud the government. Vice-President Spiro T. Agnew resigned and pleaded "no contest" to charges of tax evasion (see AGNEW, SPIRO THEODORE). The Department of Justice was shaken by the resignations of top officials. Mr. Nixon's popularity fell to record lows. See WATERGATE.

Secluded President. As the story of the scandals unfolded, Mr. Nixon first sought seclusion, spending a great deal of time either at Camp David in the Maryland mountains, at his home in San Clemente, Calif., or at Key Biscayne, Fla.

Although his top aides resigned after being implicated in Watergate, his new staff sheltered him, much as the old staff had. General Alexander M. Haig, Jr., was named on May 4 as the President's new chief of staff after H. R. Haldeman resigned on April 30. Haig shielded the President from day-to-day contact with all but a small group of aides.

The President and Mrs. Nixon stroll across the lawn of their Florida home with their daughters and sons-in-law on Easter morning.

Federal expenditures to maintain Camp David more than quadrupled since Mr. Nixon took office.

The financing of the President's San Clemente estate also came under scrutiny. On May 25, a White House statement revealed that the estate is controlled by an investment firm formed by the President's friend, industrialist Robert H. Abplanalp. Another friend, C. G. (Bebe) Rebozo, was a principal financial backer of the San Clemente estate.

Mr. Nixon's original net investment was $374,514. He spent a total of $811,728 in payments, taxes, and improvements on San Clemente and Key Biscayne.

In October, Rebozo told the Senate Watergate Committee he had accepted $100,000 in cash for Mr. Nixon from millionaire Howard Hughes. Rebozo declared the money was placed in a safety deposit box, never used, and was returned early in 1973.

Tax Problems. With an annual salary of $200,000, the President paid only $792.81 in federal income taxes for 1970 and $878.03 for 1971. Mr. Nixon's low tax payments were due largely to a $570,000 tax deduction he claimed for giving his vice-presidential papers to the National Archives. However, some tax experts questioned the legality of this transaction. Taxes on the sale of Florida property owned by the President and his daughter Tricia Nixon Cox were also investigated. See TAXATION.   Carol L. Thompson

See also CONGRESS; PRESIDENT OF THE UNITED STATES; Section One, FOCUS ON THE NATION.

Operation Candor. In response to pressure, largely from Republican congressional leaders, Mr. Nixon began a series of public appearances in October–"Operation Candor"–designed to regain the public's confidence. He met with Republican and some Democratic senators and congressmen and spoke to a meeting of Republican governors. He allowed himself to be interviewed by newspaper editors attending a meeting in Disney World in Florida. He denied that he was implicated in any scandals and declared that he would not resign.

He seemed tense and nervous in his public appearances. But aside from a bout of viral pneumonia that hospitalized him for a week in July, the President's health was good.

In a news conference on October 26, Mr. Nixon lashed out at the media for "hysterical distortion" of the news, and intimated he had "no respect" for the television networks. Angered at the growing demands for his resignation or impeachment, President Nixon blamed the media for biased reporting.

Personal Finances. On July 12, the House government operations subcommittee began looking into the federal funds that were spent on the President's homes. On August 6, the Nixon Administration reported that about $10 million in federal funds was spent for improvements to Mr. Nixon's personal properties in California and Florida, and to the five houses occupied over the years by his daughters.

NOBEL PRIZES in literature, peace, economics, and science were presented in 1973.

Literature Prize was awarded to Patrick White, an Australian novelist and author of short stories and plays. White was born in London, England, on May 28, 1912, while his Australian parents were there on a vacation. He grew up in Sydney, attended college in England, and was an intelligence officer for the British Royal Air Force in the Middle East during World War II. His first novel, *Happy Valley*, which is set in the snow country of New South Wales, was published in 1939 in London. Among his other novels are *The Aunt's Story* (1948), *The Tree of Man* (1955), *Voss* (1957), *Riders in the Chariot* (1961), *The Vivisector* (1970), and *The Eye of the Storm* (1973).

Peace Prize was given jointly to U.S. Secretary of State Henry A. Kissinger and North Vietnamese negotiator Le Duc Tho for negotiating the Vietnam cease-fire agreement. The accord, the Nobel committee said, "brought a wave of joy and hope for peace over the entire world." Kissinger, 50, is the 16th American and the fifth secretary of state to receive the Nobel Peace Prize. Tho, 62, is the first Vietnamese awarded the prize. However, he refused to accept it, charging on October 23 that "peace has not yet really been established in South Vietnam."

Economic Science Prize was awarded to Wassily Leontief, 67, Russian-born director of Harvard University's Economic Research Project. The Nobel committee praised him as the "sole and unchallenged creator of the input-output technique," a method effective in analyzing sudden changes in an economy. The committee noted that the technique would help planners to determine what would happen economically in the event of sudden peace, disarmament, or military mobilization. Leontief has also applied his method to studying residuals of the production system—smoke, water pollution, and scrap.

Chemistry Prize was given to Ernst Otto Fischer, 55, of the Technical University in Munich, West Germany, and Geoffrey Wilkinson, 52, of the University of London. They were cited for their independent contributions to the field of organometallics, specifically for explaining "sandwich" molecules. In such molecules, two symmetrical rings of hydrocarbon molecules make a sandwich around a metal. The rings may lie parallel to each other, or in staggered or eclipsed configurations. The first sandwich molecule, called ferrocene, was discovered in 1951, partly by Wilkinson. Because ferrocene is exceedingly heat-stable, it had been thought to consist of two symmetrical carbon rings joined together by iron until Fischer and Wilkinson determined its structure.

Physics Prize was shared by Ivar Giaever, 44, of the General Electric Company in Schenectady, N.Y., and Leo Esaki, 48, of the International Business Machines Company in Yorktown Heights, N.Y., and Brian D. Josephson, 33, of Cambridge University in England. Giaever and Esaki were cited for their work with semiconductors and superconductors, and Josephson for his theoretical predictions of the properties of a supercurrent passing through a tunnel barrier. This tunneling effect, called the "Josephson effect," is a phenomenon that permits particles to go where classical physics says they cannot. They tunnel through potential barriers instead of going around them.

Physiology and Medicine Prize was shared by three behavioral science pioneers, Karl von Frish, 86, who is living in retirement in Munich; Konrad Lorenz, 69, of the Max Planck Institute for Behavioral Physiology at Seewiesen, West Germany; and Nikolas Tinbergen, 66, professor of animal behavior in the Department of Zoology at Oxford University, England. Tinbergen's brother Jan was a co-winner of the economics prize in 1969. At a time when studies of learning in animals were generally conducted in the laboratory, thereby posing problems largely irrelevant to natural biology, these scientists, working with insects, fish, and birds, discovered both learned and innate patterns in their natural behavior. At one stroke they explained some of the most remarkable examples of elaborate behavior patterns known to science. Foster Stockwell

NORTH ATLANTIC TREATY ORGANIZATION (NATO). See EUROPE.

NORTH CAROLINA. See STATE GOVERNMENT.

NORTH DAKOTA. See STATE GOVERNMENT.

NORTHERN IRELAND voters chose overwhelmingly—591,820 to 6,463—on March 8, 1973, to remain part of the United Kingdom rather than unite with the Irish Republic. About 90 per cent of the Protestants voted, but Roman Catholic and Republican parties urged their supporters to boycott the referendum, and only about 1 per cent of the Catholics voted.

William Whitelaw, Britain's secretary of state for Northern Ireland, followed the plebiscite with constitutional proposals that were swiftly passed by the British Parliament. The legislation provided that Ulster would remain a part of Great Britain as long as the majority wished. It established a Northern Ireland Assembly to replace Stormont, the Ulster Parliament dissolved in 1972. Just after Whitelaw's transfer to Britain's employment ministry, British, Irish, and moderate Ulster leaders met in December. Agreements they reached let the British government activate Northern Ireland's new Constitution.

Its new Constitution still gave Northern Ireland more self-government than any other part of Great Britain, but less power than before. Britain would keep ultimate control over police, security, and law and order. Discrimination over jobs and housing was outlawed and a charter of human rights protected individuals. Direct rule from London was extended on March 28 for another year. Elections were held on May 30 for the 26 new district councils under a system of proportional representation. Traditional sectarian voting patterns were apparent.

The New Assembly. The same voting system, designed to ensure fair representation for the Roman Catholic minority, was applied to the Assembly elections on June 28. Protestant candidates won heavily, but the Unionist Party, which had ruled for 51 years at Stormont, was splintered by disagreements over the new Constitution. Alliance, the one party dedicated to ending Protestant-Catholic divisions, won only 8 seats.

Talks Held. After what was called Ulster's "last-chance election," Whitelaw had to persuade Brian Faulkner, the Unionist leader, to share power with Catholics. The Constitution said the executive power must no longer be based on one party drawing its power from only one section of a divided community. Extremist Unionists sought to make the new Assembly unworkable but Faulkner, despite obstructions, successfully negotiated an agreement with the wary Catholics that led to the formation of an executive body (cabinet). The Unionists, however, rejected Faulkner's plan and on Jan. 7, 1974, he resigned his party post.

Violence by both republican and loyalist extremists, including torture and mutilation, erupted throughout the year. On October 31, a hijacked helicopter lifted three republican militants to freedom from a Dublin jail yard. George Scott

See also EUROPE (Facts in Brief Table).

Northern Ireland voted in March to remain in the United Kingdom, as Belfast poster shows. But Republican forces boycotted the election.

NORWAY. A close-fought general election on Sept. 10, 1973, brought Norway's Labor Party back into control—but in a potentially unstable political situation. Labor actually lost 12 seats in the Storting (parliament). It could govern only with the support of the Socialist Election Alliance, a coalition of left-wing Socialists, Labor dissidents, and Communists. Labor and the alliance both rejected a coalition, but their working agreement added 16 seats to Labor's 62 to provide a Socialist majority of 1 seat. Labor leader Trygve Bratteli took over as prime minister from Lars Korvald of the Christian People's Party after parliament opened on October 10, because the non-Socialists had only 77 seats.

Exports Boom. Norway had little reason to regret the 1972 referendum that kept it out of the European Community (Common Market). World demand for Norwegian raw materials was high. In the first six months of 1973, total exports rose by 17.5 per cent. Those to market countries increased 20 per cent. Neither Great Britain nor Denmark, who joined the market on Jan. 1, 1973, experienced such a boom.

Norway bargained with the Common Market for a favorable trade agreement, which became effective on July 1. It allows Norway to move in step on tariff changes with other countries still in the European Free Trade Association. Arrangements cover wood and paper, fish products, and aluminum. In his speech opening the new parliament, King Olav V ex-pressed strong support for European cooperation. He pledged to work for a treaty to give coastal states sea-bed exploitation rights up to 200 miles offshore.

Rocket Deal. The Korvald government was attacked on June 6 for its handling of a planned deal to buy a French-built rocket and also get better Common Market arrangements. Parliament's foreign relations committee criticized government silence on the deal. Only the imminence of the September elections saved the government. Norway reportedly considered an $82-million deal for the Crotale, a ground-to-air rocket for airfield defense. As a condition for buying it, Norway asked an annual import quota of 250,000 to 300,000 tons of aluminum to the Common Market with gradually lowered tariffs. No contract was signed, and the quota was fixed at 190,000 tons.

Rising Inflation. Growth rate of the economy slowed to about 4 per cent and inflation continued despite a price freeze introduced in 1972. Spring pay raises and cost-of-living guarantees accented the trend. The prospect of improving the balance of payments by exploiting North Sea gas and oil discoveries was promising.

The 1974 budget, introduced on October 11, included small income tax concessions and old-age pension increases, higher taxes on gasoline, and increased telephone charges.   Kenneth Brown

See also EUROPE (Facts in Brief Table).

NOVA SCOTIA. See CANADA.

OCEAN. The United States deep-sea drilling project completed its sixth year in 1973, exploring the sea floor beneath Antarctic and western Pacific waters. Meanwhile, the U.S.-Russian Joint Commission on Scientific and Technical Cooperation announced on March 21 that Russian scientists would take part in the planning and execution of future explorations.

During its search in the Antarctic, the drill ship *Glomar Challenger* brought up cores showing that Australia began drifting away from Antarctica about 50 million years ago. The samples also indicate that glaciation began on Antarctica about 20 million years ago. Drilling along a track between New Zealand and Guam provided core samples containing evidence that the marginal basins along this track originated when separated by the Australian and Pacific plates some 160 to 180 million years ago. A record recovery of sediment cores from a single site was achieved on this leg of the 1973 operations.

Drilling along other legs confirmed the geologic youth of the Philippine Sea (60 million years old) and suggested that major climatic changes occurred in the region of the Sea of Japan during the past million years. Drills also brought up rock as old as late Jurassic (120 million years old) on the southwest bank of the Shatsky Rise, a geologic feature in the northwest Pacific Basin between Japan and Midway Island. This region is now believed to be the oldest portion of the Pacific crust.

Rescuers open the hatch of the minisub *Pisces III* to free two men who had been trapped for 76 hours on the Atlantic seabed off Cork, Ireland.

Environmental Experiment. Scientists with the Environmental Quality Program of the International Decade of Ocean Exploration (IDOE) began a five-year Controlled Ecosystem Pollution Experiment (CEPEX) to understand how chemical pollutants affect the stability of marine biological populations. To contain the natural populations for investigation, scientists plan to use large, flexible, plastic cylinders installed vertically in the water, open to the atmosphere at the top and closed at the bottom.

Feasibility experiments were conducted during the summer with four quarter-scale prototype cylinders in Saanich Inlet, Georgia. One cylinder was subjected to engineering tests, and the other three were reserved for biological studies. Zooplankton, phytoplankton, and bacteria counts in the first cylinder maintained themselves at the same level as those outside the enclosure. Other tests were begun to determine stability of the populations in the other two cylinders installed later. If the populations are maintained in all three enclosures, investigators will add a heavy-metal pollutant to one enclosure and examine the response of the organisms within the polluted enclosure.

The United States and Russia signed an agreement for oceanographic cooperation on June 19. The pact calls for global investigations of the oceans as well as intercalibration and standardization of oceanographic instrumentation and methods.

Undersea Tragedy. Two men died in what began as a routine undersea mission off Key West, Fla., on June 17. The minisub *Johnson-Sea Link* was scouting the hulk of a World War II destroyer that had been scuttled by the Navy to create an artificial reef to attract sea life for study by oceanographers. The underwater craft was trapped in the debris surrounding the sunken destroyer. Two of the four trapped men aboard died of carbon dioxide poisoning before the *Johnson-Sea Link* was finally freed and returned to the surface. One of the victims was Clayton Link, son of the minisub's creator, millionaire inventor Edwin A. Link. The other was Albert D. Stover, a veteran diver and submarine safety expert. The pilot, Archibald (Jock) Menzies, and ichthyologist Robert Meek survived.

In another midget-submarine incident, Britons Roger Mallinson and Roger Chapman were trapped for three days in the *Pisces III* off the coast of Southern Ireland. But they were rescued on September 1, just 90 minutes before their air supply ran out. The sub sank during the laying of a transatlantic cable in 1,325 feet of water.

Experts C. J. Delucchi and D. L. Rodocker tried unsuccessfully in August to salvage about $2 million in cash and valuables from the sunken Italian liner, *Andrea Doria*.   Arthur E. Alexiou

OHIO. See CLEVELAND; STATE GOVERNMENT.

OKLAHOMA. See STATE GOVERNMENT.

OLD AGE. Congress raised U.S. social security benefits again in 1973 to keep them abreast of the rising cost of living. At the same time, controversy flared over how much the federal government spends on the elderly.

The controversy followed President Richard M. Nixon's Message on Aging in March, when he said, "Overall federal spending for the elderly in fiscal 1973 will be $50 billion." He did not remind the Congress that $48.5 billion of this is for social security and health programs, which are paid for almost entirely from payroll contributions made to government trust funds. They are therefore similar to insurance funds for which the individuals pay personally. The U.S. Senate Subcommittee on Aging commented: "A close analysis of discretionary-type spending [such as housing programs for the elderly or manpower efforts for older workers] – as opposed to trust fund outlays – will reveal that aged Americans have not been given preferential treatment. Quite the contrary, they have oftentimes been overlooked or ignored by federal programs."

Expanded Services. A major expansion of services for the elderly was enacted in September, when the federal government released $100 million to pay for a nutrition program for the elderly. This provides low-cost hot meals at least five days a week for persons 60 years or older who live with their spouses. State and local agencies are operating the program, and providing transportation where necessary. Participants pay part of the cost of the meals.

Militancy among the elderly showed itself in the activities of a loosely organized group known as the Gray Panthers. Organized in a growing number of communities and led by women, the Gray Panthers worked to influence local and state governments, social agencies, and business concerns to provide better services for elderly people.

Employment. The Age Discrimination in Employment Act of 1967, intended to protect workers in their middle years and below age 65 from discriminatory employment and retirement practices, has proven ineffective, according to the Special Committee on Aging of the U.S. Senate. This committee issued a working paper in September, designed to stimulate the U.S. Department of Labor to enforce the act more strictly. At the same time, the National Council on the Aging, a private organization, in cooperation with the Chicago Association of Commerce and Industry and the Chicago Federation of Labor, held a symposium in Chicago on the employment of the over-40 worker. They heard reports from a two-year experiment in Portland, Me., that provided a flexible employment program, which has proven satisfactory to both employers and older workers. The methods used were developed by Leon F. Koyl, industrial physician with The De Havilland Aircraft of Canada, Ltd.   Robert J. Havighurst

See also SOCIAL SECURITY.

OLYMPIC GAMES. The prestige of the Olympic movement suffered in 1973. The International Olympic Committee (IOC), which had awarded the 1976 Summer Games to Montreal and the Winter Games to Denver, watched financial worries develop in both cities. Montreal resolved its problems and kept the Summer Games. Denver lost the Winter Games when Colorado voters refused to finance them, citing economical and ecological reasons.

The United States Olympic Committee (USOC) nominated Salt Lake City as host, but Salt Lake City withdrew three weeks later because of lack of money. The USOC then nominated Lake Placid, N.Y., but the IOC, angry and embarrassed by the American failures, chose Innsbruck, Austria.

The IOC, fearing that the Olympics had become too large, trimmed 10 events from the program in October. Starting with the 1976 games, the competition will be reduced in track and field, swimming, canoeing, shooting, and cycling. In addition, the number of competitors per country will be reduced in swimming, cycling, gymnastics, fencing, and archery.

Meanwhile, the USOC, Amateur Athletic Union, and National Collegiate Athletic Association opposed an omnibus sports bill that provided for a national sports board, a national sports foundation, and federal expenditures of up to $50 million annually to develop amateur sports.   Frank Litsky

OMAN. The government of Sultan Qabus bin Said, Oman's prime minister, tried vigorously but failed in 1973 to end the eight-year rebellion in Dhofar Province. The war originally was waged by tribesmen resisting the sultan's father. It developed wider implications, however, when the rebels organized as the Front for the Liberation of the Occupied Arabian Gulf (FLOAG), dedicated to the overthrow of all "reactionary" rulers in favor of Socialist regimes.

Supplied with arms from neighboring Yemen (Aden), they extended their operations into northern Oman. Seventy-seven persons were arrested in Muscat, the capital, on January 19, on charges of plotting a coup. After a three-day trial, 10 were executed on June 20 and 56 received long jail terms. All were said to be FLOAG members.

Development proceeded rapidly, as the sultan acted on his promise to bring Oman into the 20th century. The first radio station began broadcasts from Wattayah on March 30, linking Oman to the rest of the world. A national bank opened in Muscat on March 9, and internal air service began on April 6. Oil production, the basis of the economy, reached an annual figure of 106.2 million barrels. A new oil strike, estimated at 60,000 barrels daily, was made in Ghaba district. On September 21, the sultan dedicated the first two of eight deepwater tanker berths at Port Qabus.   William Spencer

See also MIDDLE EAST (Facts in Brief Table).

O'NEILL, THOMAS P., JR., (1912-   ), a Democratic congressman from Massachusetts, was elected majority leader of the U.S. House of Representatives on Jan. 2, 1973. He replaced Hale Boggs (D., La.), who disappeared while on a flight over Alaska in October, 1972.

O'Neill was born in Cambridge, Mass., on Dec. 9, 1912, and graduated from Boston College in 1936. When he was 21 years old and still a student, he ran for a seat on the Boston City Council, but lost by a narrow margin. It is the only election he has lost in more than 40 years in politics.

O'Neill was elected to the Massachusetts House of Representatives in 1936. He served as a state representative until 1952. In 1947 and 1948, he was state House minority leader and was the first Democratic speaker of the state House from 1948 to 1952.

In November, 1952, O'Neill was elected to the U.S. House of Representatives. He served for 18 years on the House rules committee and is an authority on parliamentary procedures. He opposed the Vietnam War and is regarded as a liberal Democrat. O'Neill became the House majority whip in 1971, and served until his election as majority leader.

O'Neill married Mildred Anne Miller in June, 1941. They have five children.   Darlene R. Stille

ONTARIO. See CANADA.

OPERA. See MUSIC, CLASSICAL.

OREGON. See STATE GOVERNMENT.

The International Court of Justice ordered France to delay its South Pacific nuclear tests, but Paris ignored the injunction.

PACIFIC ISLANDS. Three major developments dominated the news in the thousands of islands dotting the vast Pacific during 1973. The first concerned the swelling protest aroused by the French nuclear tests held over Mururoa Atoll in July. The second was Australia's granting of full independence to Papua New Guinea. The third was the breakdown in negotiations between the United States and Micronesia over the islands' future political status.

Bitter Reactions. For some years, the French had used the Society Islands as a major nuclear testing ground. Criticism had been widespread but for the most part ineffectual. Tests held in 1973, however, provoked reactions that went beyond mere criticism.

When the French announced their new test series in January, the governments of New Zealand and Australia spearheaded a movement to halt the tests. Prime Ministers Norman E. Kirk of New Zealand and Edward Gough Whitlam of Australia repeatedly lodged antitest protests in Paris without results. Finally, they were forced to take their case to the International Court of Justice in The Hague, the Netherlands. France denied the court's jurisdiction.

Nevertheless, the court called on France to avoid conducting any tests that would produce radiation fallout on the two protesting nations, including the Cook Islands, a dependency of New Zealand.

In French Polynesia, some 5,000 Tahitians marched in protest in Papeete. Official protests were also lodged by Japan, Chile, Ecuador, and Peru. International trade unions also joined in opposing the tests, instituting boycotts against French shipping and French products in Australia, New Zealand, Singapore, and elsewhere in the Pacific area.

France stubbornly proceeded, however. The tests were held on July 21 and 29. France withdrew from the Mururoa Atoll area on August 1.

Independence Moves. Papua New Guinea became an independent nation on December 1, with Australia reserving the right to handle defense and foreign affairs. This was a major advance for the estimated 2.7 million persons who occupy the rugged islands north of Australia. Yet independence might also prove to be a mixed blessing for the new nation, primarily because of the diversity of its people, primitive tribalism, and regional rivalries.

Some critics held that the territories had been inadequately prepared for self-government, and they blamed Australia, which had been administering the territory under a United Nations (UN) trusteeship. But there were also divisive forces at work within the new nation itself. The largely untutored tribesmen in the New Guinea highlands, fearful of domination by the better educated lowlanders, were bitterly opposed to independence. The people of Bougainville, too, had a strong secessionist movement underway.

Continuing United States efforts to work out a

new relationship with Micronesia ran into major stumbling blocks during the year. Talks had been going on since 1969 between representatives of the United States and Micronesia, an area of scattered islands and islets that is administered by the American government under a UN trusteeship. Their main purpose was to establish the future political status of the islands and their 110,000 inhabitants.

The United States, pulling back its military forces from Asia, wanted to ensure that it could maintain its defense bases in the islands. They advocated a policy of long-term "free association" under which the Micronesians would be self-governing except in defense and foreign affairs. But the Micronesians seemed divided. Some agreed to this type of association because it would give them greater freedom and continued financial support from the United States. Others, however, held different views, and some islands, notably the Marshalls and the Marianas, sought separate commonwealth or territorial status.

Talks were suspended in November because of a major stumbling block: U.S. financial support. Micronesians of five districts, excluding the Marianas, jointly asked for from $90 million to $100 million as part of their annual support. The United States, however, offered $45 million. By year's end, many disappointed Micronesians had begun to consider total independence.   Paul C. Tullier

PAINTING. See Visual Arts.

PAKISTAN. Emotion ran high on April 10, 1973, when the National Assembly approved a new Constitution. There were cheers and shouts. Members of the ruling Pakistan People's Party embraced and kissed the opposition members in the Assembly, even though the latter nearly prevented passage of the bill with seven last-minute changes. Under their pressure, the new charter made all laws subject to possible referral to a special Islamic Council that would decide if they were repugnant to Islam.

The man who pushed the Constitution through, President Zulfikar Ali Bhutto, jubilantly called it "democratic, federal, and Islamic." With the Constitution approved, Bhutto gave up the presidency in August to become prime minister, with wide powers under the new Constitution.

POW's Come Home. Passage of the new Constitution was one of two encouraging events in 1973. The other was an agreement with India in late September to begin an exchange of people trapped during the Indo-Pakistani war of December, 1971. On September 28, the first group, 842 men and women, most of them civil servants and their dependents, crossed the 6-foot-wide neutral strip into Pakistan. In subsequent weeks, they were followed by many of the 93,000 Pakistanis held in prisoner of war camps in India. In return, thousands of Bengali civil servants were moved from Pakistan to Bangladesh, which, until 1971, was Pakistan's own east wing.

Disastrous Floods. The year began well. With a high world demand – and prices – for raw cotton and textiles, Pakistan expected its exports to reach $800-million (compared to $520 million in 1972).

But this was before the country's five main rivers, swollen with water from the melting snow from the Himalaya and heavy rains in Kashmir, roared down the length of Pakistan. Floodwaters swept aside dikes, washed away villages and stored grain, cut roads and railways, and destroyed standing crops.

Civil Unrest remained the main political problem. Two provinces, Baluchistan and the North-West Frontier, continued to press their separatist claims. In the North-West Frontier, troops were ambushed, and tribal chiefs were murdered. Bhutto fired the governor of Baluchistan in February for separatist activities, and had him put under arrest in August.

While the relations with India seemed to be improving, Bhutto continued to budget an extraordinary 7 per cent of the gross national product for military needs. When Bhutto visited Washington, D.C., on September 18, his plea for U.S. arms shipments was turned down. Bhutto himself remained the man for all seasons, maneuvering adroitly to hold together what was left of Pakistan after the 1971 war.   Mark Gayn

See also Asia (Facts in Brief Table).

Flood victims in Pakistan's Punjab region rush for relief supplies dropped by helicopter. The region was devastated by heavy floods in August.

PANAMA. The United Nations (UN) Security Council, at Panama's invitation, met in Panama City from March 15 to 21, 1973. General Omar Torrijos Herrera, the republic's strongman, hoped the special regional session would apply new pressure on the United States, which he accused of perpetuating a blatantly colonial situation by refusing to surrender its control over the Canal Zone.

Over the years, the two nations had held intermittent but fruitless talks, seeking to replace the 1903 treaty that gave the United States control over the 553-square-mile zone "in perpetuity." The United States, which vetoed a proposed UN resolution calling for an agreement abrogating the treaty, argued that the negotiations were bilateral and continuing.

Panama sought to raise its real economic growth rate from the 6.9 per cent to which it had fallen in 1972 to the average 8 per cent it had achieved in other years, and to reduce unemployment in urban areas, where it hovered around 9 per cent. Public investment for 1973, meanwhile, was budgeted at $229-million, up 32 per cent from the previous year. Panama allocated $16 million to expand its fishing industry. The World Bank approved a $4.7-million loan to support a five-year, $13.5-million livestock-development project. The republic also borrowed $115 million abroad to help fund its foreign debts and finance new programs.   Mary Webster Soper

See also LATIN AMERICA (Facts in Brief Table).

PAPADOPOULOS, GEORGE (1919-   ), became president of Greece in 1973, then was ousted in a military coup on November 26 (see GREECE). On June 1, he announced a decree that ended the monarchy of King Constantine II, made the country a "presidential parliamentary democracy," and made him provisional president. His appointment was approved in a July 29 referendum in which he was the only candidate. He became prime minister soon after he led an army officers' coup in April, 1967.

Panayotis Kanelopoulos, Greece's last elected prime minister, called Papadopoulos the "self-appointed president of a nonexistent democracy." Papadopoulos argued, however, that Greece, even under the junta, was a democracy. "Liberty and freedom do not mean anarchy," he said. "We forbid nothing except anarchy."

George Papadopoulos was born the son of a village schoolmaster on the Peloponnesus, Greece's southern peninsula. He graduated from the War Academy just before the 1940 attack by Italy. He served in that war and also against the Communist guerrillas in the late 1940s. He was a professional soldier until 1967.

In December, 1967, Papadopoulos retired from the army as a brigadier. He then became minister of defense and prime minister.

Papadopoulos married Nekee Vassiliadis in 1941. They have two children.   Ed Nelson

PARAGUAY. President Alfredo Stroessner and his Colorado Party were overwhelmingly continued in power in elections held Feb. 11, 1973. Stroessner's inauguration on August 15 marked the start of his fifth consecutive presidential term. The opposition Democratic Liberal Party had been barred from taking part in the elections on Stroessner's orders because it was considered a leftist organization.

Despite his arbitrary methods against any leftist influence, Stroessner enjoyed a good deal of popularity, which derived, for the most part, from a strengthening economy. Unfortunately, the factors that were helping to boost Paraguay's foreign-exchange earnings were also causing more inflation at home. With world meat prices rising, Paraguayan beef exports rose considerably in the first six months of the year, and, conversely, meat became more expensive for Paraguayans. At the end of June, because of this situation, the government suspended the slaughter of cattle for export for the balance of 1973.

The Economy. Exports were exceptionally high in the first six months, climbing to $73.93 million for an overall 83 per cent increase over the January-June period in 1972. Imports also rose sharply, up 51.4 per cent to $48.79 million. But the country recorded an impressive trade surplus of $25.14 million, compared with $8.16 million for the same period in 1972 and one of $16.35 million for all of 1972. Gold and foreign-exchange reserves also bounded upward, reaching a record $56.3 million on July 31, compared with $31.5 million at the start of the year and $26.7 million on July 31, 1972.

Paraguay closed its borders with Argentina for two days at midnight on August 17 because of the presence on the Argentine side of what the Stroessner regime considered subversive elements and terrorists. On the other hand, the regime's five-year conflict with the Roman Catholic Church appeared to be easing. Bishops, who have assailed the government's treatment of peasant farmers and political prisoners, indicated that official attitudes seemed to have softened, which could benefit the rural society.

Meantime, the bulk of the population remained poor. Many of the people were living outside the economy. Over the years, lack of work in Paraguay has sent an estimated one-third of the total population to Argentina and other countries in search of jobs. The exodus, uncontrolled and uncounted, seemed to be at a high tide in 1973. Within Paraguay, some 100,000 persons were unemployed, while another 25,000 were only marginally employed in such activities as sidewalk vending and shining shoes.

Paraguay, meanwhile, anticipated that the proposed construction of the massive $2-billion Itaipu hydroelectric project and the $1-billion Apipe-Yacireta power station, both on the Paraná River, would help lure industry to the poor, basically agricultural country.   Mary Webster Soper

See also LATIN AMERICA (Facts in Brief Table).

PARENTS AND TEACHERS, NATIONAL CONGRESS OF (PTA). Delegates to the 1973 national convention, held in St. Louis in May, voted two to one against court-ordered school busing. Their action must be approved by the 31 state assemblies to become an official PTA position, however.

The PTA expanded its National PTA Smoking and Alcohol Education Project. The project is funded by agencies of the U.S. Department of Health, Education, and Welfare. The PTA gave funds in 17 states to support project goals.

American Education Week, sponsored in part by the National PTA, was observed October 21 to 27 with the theme "Get Involved." PTA members were urged to: Give teachers and school officials a chance to interpret educational objectives and methods to the public and to describe school needs and problems; encourage parents to help determine educational needs, and encourage public support for adequate school financing; and evaluate school programs in order to provide the best possible education for all children.

Elected at the National PTA Convention in St. Louis were: Mrs. Lillie E. Herndon, Columbia, S.C.; president; Mrs. Walter G. Kimmel, Rock Island, Ill., first vice-president; and Dudley E. Flood, Raleigh, N.C., second vice-president.   Joseph P. Anderson

PENNSYLVANIA. See PHILADELPHIA; STATE GOVERNMENT.

PERÓN, JUAN DOMINGO (1895-   ), was re-elected president of Argentina on Sept. 23, 1973. Elected as his vice-president was his 42-year-old second wife, Maria Estela (Isabel) Martinez de Perón. See ARGENTINA.

The 77-year-old leader had served as president of Argentina from 1946 to 1955. However, intense opposition to his regime, notably among the military leaders, forced his resignation. Following his ouster, he led a wandering life. Perón went first to Panama, on to Venezuela, and then to the Dominican Republic. He eventually settled in Spain, where he set up permanent residence in an exclusive suburb outside of Madrid. It was there that he met and married Isabel Martinez, a cabaret dancer, in 1961. She has frequently been compared to Eva, Perón's first wife, who died of cancer at 33 after virtually co-governing the country for six years with her husband.

During his sojourn in Spain, Perón formed the Justicialist Liberation Front, an Argentine political organ that provided a convenient listening post on Argentine affairs. It was the front's influence, too, that helped pave the way for Perón's return and eventual election to office.

Late in November, Perón suffered what was officially described as "recrudescence of bronchitis," but some government sources characterized it as a mild heart attack. He was ordered by his physicians to rest for 45 days before resuming work. Paul C. Tullier

PERSONALITIES OF 1973. Americans named U.S. Secretary of State Henry A. Kissinger as the man they most admired in 1973, according to the Gallup Poll. Others in the top 10, in order, were: evangelist Billy Graham, President Richard M. Nixon, who led the list the previous four years, Senator Edward M. Kennedy (D., Mass.), Vice-President Gerald R. Ford, Governor George C. Wallace of Alabama, Ralph Nader, Senator Henry M. Jackson (D., Wash.), Pope Paul VI, and Senator Barry Goldwater (R., Ariz.).

Dropped from the 1972 list were the late President Harry S. Truman, former Vice-President Spiro T. Agnew, Senator George S. McGovern (D., S. Dak.), and West German Chancellor Willy Brandt.

The most admired woman was Israeli Prime Minister Golda Meir, who last topped the list in 1971. She was followed by Mrs. Nixon, who was 1972's most-admired woman. The others were, in order: Mrs. Joseph (Rose) Kennedy, U.S. Representative Shirley Chisholm (D., N.Y.), Indian Prime Minister Indira Gandhi, Mrs. Dwight D. (Mamie) Eisenhower, Mrs. Lyndon B. (Lady Bird) Johnson, Mrs. Aristotle (Jacqueline Kennedy) Onassis, Queen Elizabeth II of Great Britain, and Mrs. Robert (Ethel) Kennedy and former Maine Senator Margaret Chase Smith (tied for 10th). Dropped from the list was Mrs. Martin Luther (Coretta) King.

Duke Ellington wears a French Legion of Honor medal, honoring his jazz contributions, as he performs at the Newport Jazz Festival in July.

431

Brezhnev, Leonid I., general secretary of the Russian Communist Party, confessed in May that he cheats on a device that is supposed to help him cut down smoking. He showed West German magazine editors a cigarette case with a time lock designed to control his smoking. But if it doesn't open soon enough, Brezhnev confessed that he carries a reserve pack.

Brundage, Avery, 85, former president of the International Olympic Committee, nearly postponed his June wedding to German Princess Mariann Reuss, 37, because of a gray, cloudy sky. "We want only sunshine over this marriage," the bridegroom declared. The ceremony proceeded when the skies over Garmisch-Partenkirchen, Germany, cleared 15 minutes later.

Bucher, Commander Lloyd M., captain of the intelligence ship *Pueblo* captured by North Korea in January, 1968, retired from the U.S. Navy in June after 21 years of service. Commander Bucher and his crew spent 11 months in a North Korean prison after their capture. Bucher said he planned to become a free-lance writer, but would not write about the *Pueblo* incident. "It's been written to death," he said.

Dietrich, Marlene, revealed in June that a bit of penicillin culture developed by the late Sir Alexander Fleming is among her treasures. "When I saw how his discovery saved the lives of soldiers who had lain in the mud for days, I had to see him with my own eyes," the actress said. "A meeting was arranged–a dinner party. I cooked. We became very close friends." In a postscript not likely to win her any feminist friends, she added: "Men are better than women. I fancy myself as probably having more of a male brain. I am not easily distracted."

Douglas, William O., celebrated his 34th anniversary as a member of the Supreme Court of the United States in April. Only three men had served on the court longer:

Humorist Clement Freud, a grandson of Sigmund, won a Liberal Party seat in the British House of Commons and may liven Parliament's debates.

Baburnich, Chip, a student at Rend Lake College, near Mount Vernon, Ill., became the new lemon-eating champion of the world in June. While witnesses looked on with clenched teeth, Baburnich ate three lemons in 100 seconds, beating the old record of 162.

Bernhard, Prince, of the Netherlands, purchased 37,000 acres of land near Lake Nakuru in Kenya in August. He bought the land for $519,000 on behalf of the World Wildlife Fund, of which he is president. The purchase will be used to triple the size of Nakuru National Park, home of 2 million flamingos and many other types of birds.

Bishop, Granville, of Redding, Calif., was arrested in May on a charge of firing 17 rifle shots into his television set after the San Francisco Giants lost a televised baseball game to the Houston Astros. "Didn't you ever want to shoot your TV?" the frustrated Bishop asked arresting officers.

Skating champion Janet Lynn happily turned professional on June 19 when she signed a three-year, $1,455,000 Ice Follies contract.

The year's interesting roles included Jonathan Livingston Seagull as a film star and Walter Cronkite as king of a Dartmouth College ball.

John Marshall, Stephen J. Field, and Hugo L. Black. By year's end, Douglas had served longer than any other justice. On the anniversary, Chief Justice Warren E. Burger described Douglas as "a strong, articulate individualist, willing to blaze new trails, whether in the majority or in dissent, but also willing to tread ancient paths of the law."

Doyle, Warren, 23, of Shelton, Conn., set a new Appalachian Trail walking record in August. He completed the 2,000-mile wilderness walk from Georgia to Maine in 66½ days, averaging about 30 miles a day. Doyle wore out four pairs of boots and became ill twice.

Ellington, Duke, jazz pianist, received the French Legion of Honor, France's highest honor, in July. It was the first time that the award had been given to a jazz musician. Jacques Kosciusko-Morizet, the French ambassador to the United States, described Ellington as the creator of music "which has become classic in the history of jazz." Then Ellington sat down at the piano and played a new tune that he named "Yanie," in honor of the ambassador's wife.

Farmer, Bertha Rosenthal, 83, achieved a lifelong goal in September when she enrolled at Baruch College in New York City. Ever since she received her high school diploma in 1907, Mrs. Farmer had vowed that someday she would go to college. But she first had to work as a typist and bookkeeper to help support her widowed mother. Later she worked as a self-taught typesetter in the printing business owned by her husband, Anthony, who died in 1940.

Fegion, Johnnie Lee, of Stockton, Calif., filed suit for divorce after 28 years of marriage on the grounds that her husband "chases girls." Mrs. Fegion is 100 years old; her husband, Solomon, is 103.

Figueres Ferrer, José, president of Costa Rica, has little patience with formalities. Learning there was no

"Maybe I'll cry tomorrow," Willie Mays said in announcing his retirement after 22 years as one of baseball's greatest superstars.

car available to take him to San José from his home 4 miles away, Figueres walked to a highway bus stop. When no bus came along, he hitchhiked and finally caught a ride. "It's characteristic of him," said a government spokesman.

Fries, Jim, 30, of Hayward, Calif., decided about three years ago that life as a fat man was not for him. "Fat people have to be jolly," he explained, "everybody expects it. But jolly we are not. It's misery. It's lonely." So he lost 406 pounds. The 587-pound Fries went on a diet of one TV dinner a day. Later he underwent intestinal by-pass surgery. After 30 difficult months, Fries is "tremendously happy" at 181 pounds because he can tie his own shoes and "sit down and have a lap."

Gilbert, Annette, 9, of Salt Lake City, Utah, wants to "operate on and check people," but she can't find anyone willing to let her practice her medical skills. She wrote to John Dixon, dean of the University of Utah College of Medicine, and complained that she can't find anyone who will let her use the stethoscope her grandmother gave her for Christmas. "What is a stethoscope for, if there's nobody to use it on?" she asked plaintively. Dixon suggested it might help if Annette didn't mention that she likes to operate a lot. "At least, it seems to work that way in my practice," he told her.

Gray, Hanna Holborn, 42, dean of the College of Arts and Sciences at Northwestern University in Evanston, Ill., will become provost of Yale University in New Haven, Conn., in July, 1974. She becomes the university's chief educational and financial officer and a possible successor to the presidency, now held by Kingman Brewster, Jr. She has taught at Bryn Mawr, Harvard, and the University of Chicago, where her husband, Charles, is a professor of English history.

Hershey, General Lewis B., the oldest U.S. army man on active duty, retired with a 17-gun salute on March 27. General Hershey, 79, headed the U.S. Selective Service from 1941 to 1970, then served as a manpower adviser to President Richard M. Nixon. During the period that he headed the Selective Service, 14.6 million men were drafted and 18,321 were imprisoned for draft evasion. General Hershey was never drafted himself. He enlisted as a private in the Indiana National Guard in 1911.

Hickson, Charles, of Pascagoula, Miss., touched off a rash of Unidentified Flying Object sightings in October when he and Calvin Parker reported encountering strange visitors while fishing at dusk from an old pier outside of town. They said a strange blue light floated across the water toward them. Parker fainted, but Hickson stayed conscious to report that a cigar-shaped spaceship disgorged three creatures with pointy ears and crab-claw hands who examined the two fishermen, then flew off.

Hughes, Senator Harold E., announced in September that he would leave the U.S. Senate to take up religious work when his term expires in 1975. The Iowa Democrat, a reformed alcoholic and former governor, will work with groups that sponsor prayer breakfast meetings throughout the United States. Hughes said, "I have long believed that government will change for the better only when people change for the better in their hearts. Rightly or wrongly, I believe I can move people through a spiritual approach more effectively than I have been able to achieve through the political approach."

Magro, Antonio Carlos, of São Paulo, Brazil, was shocked when he went to the civil registry office in September to obtain a marriage permit and was told he was dead. Police showed him a death certificate signed by his father and a doctor stating that he had died at the age of 2. Magro was eventually issued a marriage permit. Meanwhile, police investigating the false death

Troy Hofmann frolics in the 1 million bottle caps collected by Normal, Ill., pupils just to see what a million of anything looks like.

certificate ran into difficulty because both Magro's father and the doctor are dead—or so their death certificates say.

Mays, Willie, 42, center fielder for the New York Mets baseball team, retired from playing at the end of the 1973 season. Mays entered the National League in 1951 with the old New York Giants. He went to San Francisco with the Giants in 1958 and returned to New York in 1972 when he was traded to the Mets. He has a lifetime total of 660 homers and was the National League home-run king three times.

Merrill, Robert, sang his 500th performance—the role of the Count di Luna in Verdi's *Il Trovatore*—at the Metropolitan Opera in New York City on March 5. The 53-year-old baritone is the only current Met principal to have sung 500 performances. Merrill credits his longevity to conserving energy. "Vocally, there is no reason why you cannot sing for 30 or 40 years," he said.

"I have a theory of not spreading myself too thin, of doing fewer roles but more often, so people will remember me for a role."

Murphy, Ethel, of Horsham, England, paid $3,700 to hire a local taxi to take her on a 12,000-mile trip across Europe, the Middle East, and Asia, then by boat to Australia. "When you're going this far, it's silly to rush it by jet and see nothing," she said. "Going by car is the only civilized way of doing it."

Nordwall, Adam, a Chippewa Indian also known as Lucky Eagle, pulled a switch in September when he stepped off a plane in Rome, Italy, and claimed possession of the country in the name of the American Indian people. Nordwall, who teaches sociology at California State College, Hayward, made his claim "by right of discovery," in the same way Christopher Columbus claimed America. "What right did Columbus have to discover America when it had already been inhabited for thousands of years?" he said. "The same right that I have to come now to Italy and proclaim the discovery of your country."

Pelosi, James J., 21, of West Hempstead, N.Y., was graduated from the U.S. Military Academy at West Point in June, more than a year and a half after he was officially "silenced" by his fellow cadets. Pelosi had roomed and eaten alone since November, 1971, and cadets had talked to him only on official business. The "silence" was imposed by a cadet honor committee after Pelosi was accused of answering a quiz question after the allotted time, a charge he denied. Several months after Pelosi's graduation, the honor committee ended the "silence" as a punishment.

Pohlman, Florence Dianna, of La Jolla, Calif., was sworn in as the first female chaplain in the United States armed forces in July. Lieutenant Pohlman was ordained a Presbyterian minister one week before being sworn in as a Navy chaplain. After eight weeks of training at Newport, R.I., she went to the Naval Training Center in Orlando, Fla.

Reese, Mason, 7, a red-haired, freckle-faced cherub, became television's newest celebrity in 1973. His appearances in commercials won him a Clio advertising award for best male salesman on television. That achievement brought a flood of talk-show invitations and, in September, he made his debut as a children's news correspondent on New York City's WNBC-TV. He is a self-proclaimed gourmand, but his mother watches his diet carefully because he has a tendency toward pudginess.

Simenon, Georges, creator of the French detective, Inspector Maigret, announced in January that he would write no more novels. The 70-year-old author complained he was becoming "a slave of my characters—the typewriter will go." Simenon, one of the world's best-selling living authors, wrote more than 200 books, including about 80 detective stories featuring Maigret. About 50 million copies of his books have been published in 40 languages.

Simpson, Robert H., of Sacramento, Calif., celebrated his 93rd birthday on July 8 with his 234th arrest. He was arrested under an antipicketing law that was passed several years ago just to keep him away. Simpson has been picketing the State Capitol in Sacramento for 10 years. The original cause of his picketing has long since been forgotten, but in recent years, he has been protesting the Simpson Law, as the antipicketing measure is known. He also advocates freedom of speech and the impeachment of California Governor Ronald Reagan.

Spencer, Scott, 12, of New Castle, Del., claimed the world's pogo stick hopping record in August with 20,007 hops, achieved over a span of 3 hours 13 minutes. Why did Scott do it? "I always wanted to hold a world's record," he explained.

Strndgaard, Leif, of Sweden, fell 100 feet to the bottom of a mine in June, got up, dusted himself off, and walked away unhurt. A large case of dynamite cushioned his fall.

Tanner, Ray, of Edmonton, Canada, thanks a note he put in a bottle for his rescue in August after drifting for 11 days on an isolated Canadian lake. Tanner was on a fishing trip when his motorboat ran out of gas 60 miles west of Yellowknife in the Northwest Territories. The bottle carrying his note floated 5 miles before it was found by 9-year-old Mary Ann Madsen.

Tiburzi, Bonnie, 24, became the first woman to join the flight crew of a major U.S. airline when she received her silver wings in June as a first officer for American Airlines. After three years of training, she will become a copilot, qualified to fly passenger jetliners. Emily Howell was the first woman to break the sex barrier on commercial U.S. airlines when she began flying a feeder run for Frontier Airlines in 1972.

Williams, Nancy, 17, startled visitors to the Indianapolis Zoo in June. She spent the day in an animal's cage to study people's reactions. Over her head was the sign: "Modern man, *homo sapiens*." She said that most adults just laughed at her, but small children stared in wonder or ran away in fear.

Willis, Dorsie W., 87, of Minneapolis, was honorably discharged from the U.S. Army on February 11, and Major General DeWitt Smith, Jr. officially apologized to him in public for a mistake made 66 years earlier. President Theodore Roosevelt gave dishonorable discharges to Willis and 168 other black soldiers in 1906 for failing to volunteer information about a 10-minute shooting spree in Texas. Later evidence showed that the soldiers knew nothing about the incident, but the official record was not corrected until 1973. Willis is the only living member of the group.   Kathryn Sederberg

PERU. The all-important fish meal and fish oil industry was in dire straits in 1973. A continuing ecological disaster related to changes in Pacific Ocean currents has reduced the once-abundant schools of anchovies off Peru's shores almost to the vanishing point. Until 1972, the processed anchovy catch produced 40 per cent of the nation's foreign-currency income annually.

On May 8, the military regime of Juan Velasco Alvarado expropriated the fishing industry, once one of the world's largest. By creating a state monopoly, the government hoped to solve an economic crisis created because of the huge amounts of money privately owned fishing and processing companies owed to state banks. The government further justified the take-over by declaring that fishing, as a "natural resource," should be under state control. The explanation caused alarm in many privately owned Peruvian industries, particularly mining, which was mostly in the hands of U.S.-based corporations. There was concern that the government might be moving toward state control of mining and possibly oil resources.

Labor Problems arose frequently during the year. A law stabilizing retirement benefits for Peruvian workmen set off a series of crippling strikes in July and August. The law required that all male workers retire at 60 and all female workers at 55. It was the government's contention that the measure would end discrimination between blue-collar and white-collar workers. About 40,000 workers, who could retire after completing 25 years of service regardless of age under the old law, vigorously protested the new law. Other strikes included an 18-day walkout by 3,000 workers at the state steel complex in Chimbote in May and June, and a general strike in Pucallpa in June to support a teachers' walkout.

Economic Development. Peru made plans to install industrial complexes across the nation over the next 18 years. The scheme, to cost an estimated $1.3 billion, assigns specific industries to different regions to tie up with the location of natural resources and existing industrial installations. An automotive complex that will assemble vehicles and also manufacture such basic parts as engines, transmission systems, gear boxes, and axles is to be built in Trujillo on the northern coast. It will turn out tractors, trucks, buses, and cars. Also in the north, work started in October on a $34.2-million light-engineering plant in Chimbote. It will produce transmission towers, metal bridges, and gantries. In the far south, a heavy engineering complex in Arequipa will turn out specialized machinery and tools required in mining, hydroelectric plants, irrigation, and industry. And also in the far south, a $40-million metallurgical engineering complex in the Ilo-Tacna region will produce specialized copper products. Mary Webster Soper

See also LATIN AMERICA (Facts in Brief Table).

PET. A campaign took shape in 1973 to reduce the risks of shipping pets, particularly dogs, by air. Animal lovers, breeders, humane societies, and government officials complained of inadequate air supply, extreme temperatures in baggage compartments, careless handling of the cages by airline employees, and neglect of the animals after they were removed from the airplanes. The airlines responded that, compared to the number of pets transported, the number killed or injured is minuscule. Bruce Gebhardt, director of cargo sales and service for United Air Lines, said that cats are better air travelers than dogs.

Best in Show. Ch. Acadia Command Performance, a white standard poodle owned by Jo Ann Sering of Portland, Ore., and Ed Jenner of Richmond, Ill., was named best-in-show at the Westminster Kennel Club dog show in New York City on February 13. It was the 11th best-in-show title for the poodle, which won over 3,026 competitors. Many of the crowd of 10,000 booed the award, believing that the winner had not gaited properly. Best-in-show honors at the International Kennel Club show in Chicago on March 31 and April 1 went to Ch. Pin Money Pedlar, a West Highland white terrier owned by Mrs. B. G. Grame of Indianapolis. It was the 28th best-in-show for the terrier. This show drew 3,095 entries.

Ch. Acadia Command Performance, a standard poodle, poses proudly after winning best-in-show at the Westminster Kennel Club show in February.

Breed Standings. Registration figures released in March by the American Kennel Club showed that poodles were the most popular breed of dog in the United States for the 13th consecutive year. Then, in order, came German shepherds, beagles, dachshunds, Irish setters, miniature schnauzers, Saint Bernards, Labrador retrievers, collies, and Doberman pinschers. Dobermans were the only newcomers to the top 10, replacing Pekingese.

The Ken-L Ration Dog Hero of the year gold medal was awarded to Budweiser, a 14-month-old Saint Bernard owned by Mr. and Mrs. B. M. Carter of John's Island, S.C. Budweiser made two trips into the Carters' burning house on Oct. 20, 1972, to pull two of the Carters' grandchildren to safety.

Cats. Joelwyn the Wild One III of Nile, a ruddy Abyssinian male owned by Maureen Nottingham of Sunland, Calif., received the *Cats* magazine 1973 All-America award as *Cat of the Year*. Second best *Cat of the Year* was Mer-C's Contessa, a chinchilla Persian female owned by Mr. and Mrs. Eugene Coutre of Cranston, R.I. Third best *Cat of the Year* was Shawnee Tammey, a cream Persian male owned by Isabel Roberts of Clyde, N.Y. *Best Kitten* was Mac-Dot's Heather, a blue-cream Persian female owned by Dorothy A. MacDonald of Santa Monica, Calif. *Best Alter* was Francine Little Princess, Jr., of McGarvey, a white Persian spay, owned by Rose Marie McGarvey of Philadelphia. Theodore M. O'Leary

The world's largest offshore storage tank, which holds 1 million barrels of oil, is towed from Stavanger, Norway, to North Sea oil fields.

PETROLEUM AND GAS. Shortages of fuel oil and gas caused constant concern throughout the world in 1973. Concern mounted in November when Arab oil-producing nations cut off oil shipments to the United States and the Netherlands because they supported Israel in the Middle East war. The Arabs also cut production 25 per cent to prevent other Western countries from exporting surpluses.

The United States imported more than 1 million barrels of oil a day from the Arab nations, about 6 per cent of its daily consumption of 17.4 million barrels. Another million barrels of Arab oil came to the United States after processing in other countries. The United States also had expected the Middle East to supply the additional oil needed to meet growing American energy needs – projected at up to 20 million barrels a day in 1974. Because of this, the cuts had an immediate impact on the United States.

A mandatory fuel allocation program went into effect on December 27, covering gasoline, crude oil, heating oil, diesel fuel, aviation fuel, residual fuel, propane and butane gas, and other petroleum products. Although gasoline rationing remained under consideration, it was ruled out before 1974.

World Shortages. Energy experts, meeting in Paris in March, forecast a decade of growing dependence for oil on the Middle East and Africa, which hold two-thirds of the world's proven oil reserves. Their report was adopted by the oil com-

mittee of the Organization for Economic Cooperation and Development (OECD), which includes the United States, Canada, the European Community countries, and Japan. It predicts that the world demand for oil by 1980 will be more than half again as great as in 1970, and 70 per cent of it will be consumed in the 20 OECD countries. Less than one-third of this growth can be filled from these countries' own resources.

The OECD foresees a rise in U.S. oil imports from 22 per cent of supply in 1970 to an annual 40 per cent, or 1.2 billion tons, by 1980.

In April, Russia began pumping oil into a new 1,250-mile pipeline that is carrying supplies from western Siberia to Al'met'yevsk in central Russia, where it links up with pipelines to Eastern Europe. Despite this new supply, Russia reported a decline in its net export of petroleum for the first time since World War II. Although Russia is the world's second largest oil producer, it has been importing some oil and gas from the Middle East to help Arab countries that have had marketing problems since they nationalized Western oil properties.

Natural Gas. President Richard M. Nixon said efforts to increase domestic fuel production should focus on several areas. Natural gas, he noted, is America's premium fuel. Because it is clean-burning, it has the least detrimental effect on the environment. Currently, it accounts for 32 per cent of the nation's

energy supply, 20 per cent over consumption in 1966. However, the nation's sources of natural gas have decreased by 20 per cent during this period.

Easing the problem somewhat, Russia signed a multimillion-dollar natural gas deal with three Houston concerns in June. The agreement was similar to a $10-billion, 25-year gas deal arranged earlier with a three-company West Coast group. Algeria, which has one of the world's largest reserves of natural gas, agreed in March to let American concerns take more than 3 trillion feet of natural gas a year. And 29 natural gas companies made plans for a joint search for natural gas along the Atlantic Coast.

New Oil Sources. New undersea supplies of oil were also being sought. In April, the U.S. Geological Survey disclosed that potentially rich oil-bearing deposits have been found on the continental shelf off Long Island and New Jersey. To obtain drilling rights to 104 sections of offshore territory south of Texas and Louisiana, oil companies offered a record $6.2 billion in bids in June. Also, American contractors joined the British in installing huge offshore rigs in the North Sea, where oil reserves are expected to produce as much as 4 million barrels a day by 1980. And, in November, Congress authorized construction to begin on the long-delayed pipeline from Alaska's North Slope. Mary E. Jessup

See also ENERGY; Section Two, How CAN WE SOLVE THE ENERGY CRISIS?

PHILADELPHIA endured one of the longest public school strikes in U.S. history in 1973. Philadelphia teachers went on strike on January 8 and returned to work on February 27. Approximately 260 of the city's 285 schools remained open on at least a part-time basis during the strike, even though about 9,500 of the city's 13,000 teachers stayed off their jobs.

Police arrested 317 picketing teachers on February 16 for refusing to move from school doorways. A week earlier, two officers of the Philadelphia Federation of Teachers were jailed on charges of contempt for disobeying a court-ordered injunction against the strike.

Union Fined. The court also fined the union $116,000 and assessed it an additional $10,000 for every day the strike continued. On February 20, school board president William Ross, a professional labor leader, resigned.

The final settlement called for 4 per cent to 7 per cent salary increases, with starting pay eventually being raised to $10,000. In addition, class size was limited to 33 students. Mayor Frank L. Rizzo estimated the agreement would cost the city $99.5-million over the next four years.

Money Problems. To help prevent financial disaster in the city, Mayor Rizzo's administration began working on a unique plan to raise millions of dollars by soliciting contributions, primarily from local businesses. The city was hurt financially when the state supreme court declared in September that the city's $3 per person tax on departing airline passengers was unconstitutional.

Philadelphia '76, Incorporated, the group organized to prepare plans for Philadelphia's bicentennial observance in 1976, also experienced financial problems. The group threatened to disband after Jan. 1, 1974, if the federal government did not allocate a promised $100 million to finance bicentennial programs and projects.

On October 5, the Atomic Energy Commission (AEC) barred construction of a nuclear power plant on a Delaware River island 11 miles from Philadelphia, because the proposed plant was too close to a major metropolitan area. This was the first time the AEC had taken such action.

Cost of Living. Philadelphians experienced a 6.5 per cent increase in their cost of living between June, 1972, and June, 1973. A U.S. Department of Labor survey released on June 15 ranked the area 11th among the nation's 25 most expensive urban areas. The survey also reported that an average family of four would need an annual budget of $11,825 to live in "moderate comfort" in Philadelphia.

Mayor Rizzo, a conservative Democrat, suffered a serious setback in Philadelphia's November elections. Republicans he backed for re-election as district attorney and city controller were defeated by Democratic candidates.   James M. Banovetz

PHILIPPINES. A national referendum held from Jan. 10 to 15, 1973, officially gave 94 per cent approval to a new Constitution. Original plans for a secret plebiscite were abandoned when opposition to the Constitution arose; instead, public voting in village meetings was adopted. The Constitution, which President Ferdinand E. Marcos put into effect by decree on January 17, ended the U.S.-type presidential system. It was one of several changes that followed Marcos' declaration of martial law in late 1972.

The new Constitution provides for a figurehead president, a strong prime minister, and a one-house Parliament with six-year terms for its members. General elections were postponed for at least seven years, however, with an interim government to continue in office. Another public vote held July 27 reportedly gave 91 per cent approval to Marcos remaining in office indefinitely as head of a martial-law regime.

Marcos Foe Arrested. Marcos was challenged, however, by Senator Benigno S. Aquino, Jr., the most prominent person arrested under martial law. The senator, who had been expected to seek the presidency in 1973 under the old system, was put on trial August 27 on charges of murder, subversion, and illegal possession of arms. He refused to defend himself, calling the trial "a mockery" and accusing Marcos of being "a tyrant." Marcos halted the trial

for further investigation, but Aquino also refused to cooperate with the investigation.

On Mindanao and in the Sulu Archipelago of the southern Philippines, conflict between Moslem residents and Christian settlers from other parts of the country, which had smouldered for years, flared up into guerrilla warfare. The main reason for the trouble was the regime's effort to collect weapons now in private hands. The Moslems feared they would be left defenseless against further land encroachments. On September 24, Defense Secretary Juan Ponce Enrile claimed that the crisis had passed. He said 3,560 insurgents had been killed in the preceding 12 months, while government casualties were 271 killed and 32 missing. Fighting was continuing on some islands, however.

Rice Shortage. During the year, a serious shortage of rice developed in the Philippines, where the "miracle" varieties of high-yield new rice had been developed. In May, a 1960 law to nationalize the rice and corn industries was repealed in an effort to attract foreign investment to increase productivity. A failure of local capital to invest in many irrigation and fertilizer projects was blamed for part of the shortage. On August 8, President Marcos placed rice and corn stocks under military control to ensure even distribution.   Henry S. Bradsher

See also ASIA (Facts in Brief Table).

Rebel leader Usham Ambihal, left, headed one of many Moslem bands waging an intensified guerrilla war in the Philippines during 1973.

PHOTOGRAPHY

PHOTOGRAPHY lost two giants in 1973. One, Edward Steichen, changed the kind of pictures we make. The other, Joseph Ehrenreich, changed the kind of cameras we use. Steichen, a painter-turned-photographer, raised photography to an art form with his own work, then created the "Family of Man" exhibit that set the standard for photo exhibits. Ehrenreich, a New York City retailer-turned-importer, convinced the American photographer that the Japanese single-lens reflex was a worthy successor to the German range-finder camera. His import, the Nikon, tumbled even the mighty Leica from its dominance.

New Cameras. Leitz, in its effort to recapture the market, announced a new Japanese-made Leica in 1973. Designed in West Germany, but produced essentially by Minolta in Osaka, Japan, the new camera is similar to the Leica M5 but smaller, lighter, and less costly.

On the 50th anniversary of home movies, Kodak added sound to its 8mm film. Its new Ektasound movie cameras have a plug-in microphone and use film with a magnetic recording stripe. The companion Ektasound projectors accept both the sound-striped film and the older silent Super-8 film.

The completely automated, pocket-sized, waste-free Polaroid SX-70 Land instant-color camera announced in 1972 finally became available at dealers,

as stubborn manufacturing problems were solved. The Topcon, a professional-caliber Japanese 35mm single-lens reflex, is now distributed by Paillard, importers of the prestigious Bolex movie and Hasselblad still cameras. Canon of Japan set up its own U.S. distribution agency for its cameras, formerly distributed by Bell & Howell. At the same time, Bell & Howell introduced its own FD35, made by Canon. The FD35 accepts all the Canon FD lenses.

Suits Against Kodak. German and Japanese camera makers increased their close collaboration, but major manufacturers in the United States were falling out. Bell & Howell, GAF, and Berkey filed separate antitrust suits against Eastman Kodak. Bell & Howell asked the court to order Kodak to give advance notice of new film developments or else divest itself of its camera and projector business. GAF asked the court to dissolve Kodak into 10 separate corporations. The actions were filed after Kodak placed on the market, all in one day and with no prior notice, a completely new film size, 110, in a patented cassette that would fit no existing cameras; a full line of Pocket Instamatic cameras to take that film; and the machinery for processing that film.

Laserphoto. Efforts to produce dry photographic prints outside the instant-picture field received a boost from a new photo transmission system devel-

The new Polaroid SX-70 Land camera ejects a developing picture just 1.5 seconds after the button is pushed. Pictures develop outside the camera.

oped by William F. Schreiber of the Massachusetts Institute of Technology, working with the Associated Press (AP). A laser in the receiver, responding to the originals from a laser "reader" in the transmitter, traces out an image somewhat the way the electron beam does in television. The new AP process uses a roll of dry silver paper; the print comes out of the receiver through a heated roller processor.

The older AP wirephoto system uses telephone lines for transmission, but the Laserphoto transmits its impulses over the faster, more stable, and less expensive new American Telephone and Telegraph Company computer network. The new AP system also provides for computer storage of photographs and electronic retouching on a cathode-ray tube.

X-Ray Inspections. X-ray inspection of hand luggage during airport antihijack surveillance was causing serious film spoilage for travelers and processing laboratories. The machines used at many airports in the United States were considered safe because their image-intensifier and image-holding circuits used a minute X-ray pulse. Other machines, particularly in overseas airports, however, were exposing luggage to massive doses and fogging film. To protect their film, travelers were sealing it in newly available bags lined with lead and barium.

The Smithsonian Institution in Washington, D.C., without fanfare, opened an exciting new Hall of Photography in April.   Rus Arnold

PHYSICS. Two independent experiments on weak interactions caused great excitement among physicists in 1973. The experiments tend generally to support recent theoretical conclusions about the basic forces of nature.

Theory of Weak Interaction. The force known as "weak interaction" is one of the most pervasive in nature. It apparently acts on every known form of matter. It is called weak because it is a trillion times weaker than the interaction that holds protons and neutrons together to form atomic nuclei, and a billion times weaker than the interaction that causes electric and magnetic phenomena.

Almost all of the weak interactions that are experimentally observed can be explained by the conserved vector current (CVC) theory, developed during the past two decades. The CVC theory describes the weak force as an interaction among currents of charged particles. This interaction mathematically is analogous to electromagnetic currents.

In spite of its successes, however, many theorists have been dissatisfied with the CVC theory, because while it correctly describes the weak interaction to a first approximation, it is not adequate with better approximations. In the past, this feature of CVC has been patched up in ways that are largely arbitrary. The theory must then fail to describe phenomena in the realm of the high-energy collisions being explored by the latest particle accelerators.

Theoretical Models. Some theorists have developed possible models of the weak interaction in which good high-energy behavior is built into the model right from the beginning. Their task has then been to discover if such models can be brought into accord with experimental findings, and if so, what new phenomena might be predicted with the models. These new theories of weak interactions technically are called "renormalizable gauge theories."

Steven Weinberg of Harvard University is one physicist whose work in this field has been especially prominent. In 1967, he proposed a theory in which the weak and electromagnetic interactions could be considered as two aspects of a single force. For the next four years, he and other theorists struggled to understand the implications of some of the mathematical operations in this theory as it relates to the high-energy behavior of the weak interaction. Then, in 1971, Weinberg announced that his theoretical approach appeared to meet the important requirements of a renormalizable gauge theory. The natural way in which weak and electromagnetic interactions were unified caused considerable interest among physicists.

Neutral Currents. Physicists can study the weak interaction at high energies by producing beams of neutrinos (tiny, electrically neutral particles) in high-energy accelerators, and observing their reactions as they collide with atomic nuclei. In such collisions, the neutrino normally loses its identity and an electrically charged particle emerges in its place. This is called a "charged current" reaction, and is accounted for by the CVC theory. For many years, physicists have also searched for neutral currents, the reactions in which the neutrino scatters without losing its identity. These reactions do not occur according to CVC theory, but are required by renormalizable gauge theories like that of Weinberg.

In August, 1973, a group of physicists from seven European laboratories announced the results of an experiment on neutrino interactions using the giant bubble chamber Gargamelle at the European Center for Nuclear Research in Geneva, Switzerland. In this bubble chamber, charged reaction products left trails of tiny bubbles that were photographed and measured. More than 160 reactions that might be neutral current events were observed.

At about the same time, physicists from four U.S. laboratories announced a similar result from an experiment using a neutrino beam at the National Accelerator Laboratory near Chicago.

Weinberg emphasizes that much remains to be done – both theoretically and experimentally – to build a complete theory that unifies the weak and the electromagnetic interactions. He is, nevertheless, optimistic about the new theories, and suspects that, eventually, strong as well as weak electromagnetic interactions might be successfully described within a common theoretical model.   Thomas O. White

PITTSBURGH. Mayor Peter R. Flaherty, a Democrat, easily won election to a second four-year term on Nov. 6, 1973. He had won both the Republican and Democratic Party primaries on May 15, and his only opposition in the November 6 election came from a Socialist candidate, Paul LeBlanc, who drew so little attention that the county election center decided against counting his vote returns.

In the Republican primary, Flaherty defeated Democrat Thomas A. Livingston, who had been endorsed by the Republican Party when no Republican entered the race. In the Democratic primary, Flaherty defeated Councilman Richard S. Caliguiri, who had received the endorsement of the city's Democratic Party, both major newspapers, the policemen and firemen, and most labor unions.

Anti-Administration Suit. Pittsburgh joined Philadelphia and the Commonwealth of Pennsylvania on June 9 in a court challenge of President Richard M. Nixon's impoundment of federal education funds. Their suit charged that the President had no authority to impound the funds, since Congress had clearly appropriated the money for educational purposes. In December, a federal judge ordered the Department of Health, Education, and Welfare to release the impounded $20 million that had been slated for educational programs.

The Supreme Court of the United States, on June 21, upheld Pittsburgh's ordinance prohibiting newspapers from listing help-wanted advertising according to sex.

Cost of Living in the Pittsburgh area increased 5.2 per cent between April, 1972, and April, 1973. According to U.S. Department of Labor reports, the city's cost of living has increased 31.2 per cent since 1967. A labor department report issued on June 15 noted that an average family of four would need an annual budget of $11,189 to live in "moderate comfort." This was the lowest figure reported for major cities in the Northeastern United States.

Pittsburgh dropped out of the list of the nation's 10 largest metropolitan areas in 1973, after the U.S. Office of Management and Budget redefined the boundaries of metropolitan areas. Pittsburgh's population of 2,401,245 was essentially unaffected by the change, but two newly defined metropolitan areas, Dallas-Fort Worth and Nassau-Suffolk, N.Y., moved ahead of it in size.

Federal Bureau of Investigation statistics revealed that Pittsburgh's crime rate fell during the first quarter of 1973. The Pittsburgh crime rate declined 15.9 per cent during that period, compared with a national decline of only 1 per cent.

Pittsburgh renamed a park near Three Rivers Stadium the Roberto Clemente Memorial Park. The change honored the late baseball star, who died in a plane crash in 1972 while on his way to aid earthquake victims in Nicaragua.   James M. Banovetz

PLASTICS. See Chemical Industry.

POETRY. Two famous poets died in September, 1973. Pablo Neruda of Chile, one of the great poets of all time, died at 69 on September 23, and W. H. Auden, a master of English poetry, died at 66 on September 28.

Neruda won the Nobel Prize in 1971 for his poems. He was a mystic of the earth in all its diversity – its rocks, ants, Andes, oceans, poets, banana trees, strip mines, taxis, taxes, history books, and camels. "Sometimes the sea is so good, I applaud it," he once said ecstatically.

Few poets ever began with such promise and appreciation as Auden did in the 1930s, and yet few proved to be as disappointing as they grew older. However, such poems as his *Musée des Beaux Arts* (1940), *Lay Your Sleeping Head, My Love* (1940), and *In Praise of Limestone* (1951) will be read as long as people remember English.

American Poetry recorded a somewhat tame year. No poets had outstanding volumes published, although much decent, occasionally excellent work was written, published, and recited in public.

The most exciting and important event, in fact, was *The American Poetry Review*, edited by Stephen Berg, David Bonanno, Stephen Parker, and Rhoda Schwartz, in Philadelphia. Its several issues presented good work by established as well as younger and often unknown poets. It also featured unusually excellent fresh translations of classics such as Rainer M. Rilke's *Duino Elegies* (1923), translated by A. Poulin, Jr., and works by important poets largely unknown on the American poetry scene, such as those of the Greek Yannis Ritsos. The *Review* also published the finest piece of criticism in recent years: Robert Coles's essay "James Wright: One of Those Messengers." It is distinguished for its brilliant compassion for human deprivation, suffering, and longing, as well as its appreciation for the beauty that can appear, even amid such unpromising conditions. Other critical studies, ranging from extended treatment of both popular and neglected poets, to good, earthy, literary gossip, are usually of a high order and always worth reading.

A. R. Ammons' *Collected Poems* earned the National Book Award for poetry. Considered a leader of what one critic has called the New Transcendentalism, Ammons writes verse that is philosophical, quiet, and often tends to the bland. The Pulitizer Prize for 1973 was awarded to Maxine Kumin for *Up Country*. Her gift is to wrestle poetry from such everyday subjects as the death of a favorite dog, moving, or remembering some episode of one's youth.

Among Established Poets, William S. Merwin's *Writings to an Unfinished Accompaniment* contains some of the haunted, proud verse that has earned him a reputation as one of the best poets in the country. John Logan, another superb artist, published tender, wounded, often very moving lyrics in *Anonymous*

Lover. Other poets who had books published during 1973 included Wendell Barry, Daniel Berrigan, the late Paul Blackburn, Turner Cassity, Hayden Carruth, Larry Eigner, Clayton Eshleman, Irving Feldman, Donald Finkel, Gene Frumkin, Barbara Guest, Edwin Honig, Lawrence Lieberman, Thomas McGrath, Eve Merriam, Joyce Carol Oates, May Sarton, James Wright, and Louis Zukovsky.

Among the younger poets, Andrei Codrescu's *The History of the Growth of Heaven* presented fierce, witty, often stunningly magical verses. Terry Stokes's *Crimes of Passion* had memorable, hard poems about love and its catastrophes; and Charles Wright presented good, intelligent poems in *Hard Freight.*

Important books of translations appeared. *The Poems of St. John of the Cross*, rendered by Willis Barnstone; *Yval Goll*, by Galway Kinnell; Neruda's *The Captain's Verses*, by Donald D. Walsh; Vladimir Mayakovsky, put into Scottish by Edwin Morgan under the title *Wi' the Haill Voice; C. P. Cavafy*, by Edmund Keeley and Philip Sherrard; the Russian *Akhmatov*, by Stanley Kunitz and Max Hayward; and *Lorca and Jimeniz*, by Robert Bly. Other poets who appeared in new English translations were Paul Eluard, Miguel Hernandez, Martial, Octavio Paz, Lucio Piccolo, Francis Ponge, Valery, and Villon.

Outstanding Anthologies included: W. S. Merwin's *Asian Figures*, containing proverbs, short poems, and riddles from many Asian countries; *Zen Poems of China and Japan: The Crane's Bill*, edited by Lucien Stryke and others; *The Orchid Boat: Women Poets of China*, edited by Kenneth Rexroth and Ling Chung; and *East German Poetry*, edited by Michael Hamburger.

Two books of criticism were widely appreciated: Harry Levin's *The Wasteland from Ur to Echt*, and Jerome J. McGann's *Swinburne: An Experiment in Criticism.*

Other notable events included: The presentation of the Bollingen Prize to James Merrill; the $10,000 Fellowship of the Academy of American Poets to W. D. Snodgrass; the appointment of Daniel Hoffman as consultant in poetry to the Library of Congress; the death in August of Conrad Aiken; and the 19th Annual Poetry Day reading on November 17 sponsored by *Poetry* magazine, at which John Ashbery read fine verses in a mediocre way, and John Hollander recited poor poems in an impressive, theatrical manner.

Distinguished series of readings continued to enrich the poetry scene during the year. Among them was the series presented by the Academy of American Poets in New York City. This included a good evening in January, "A Quiet Requiem for Ezra Pound," with readings by Leon Edel, Robert Lowell, Robert MacGregor, and Robert Fitzgerald. Another, at the Poetry Center, Young Men's and Young Women's Hebrew Associations in New York City, included the Discovery Program.   Paul Carroll

POLAND posted some impressive economic results and maintained its drive for closer economic relations with the West in 1973. In domestic politics, it remained cautiously reformist.

Industrial production in the first half of the year increased 12 per cent over the same period in 1972. Wages increased 11 per cent. Imports were up 28 per cent, but those from the West were up 60 per cent. Exports increased 15 per cent. Communist Party leader Edward Gierek complained in October that the 6 per cent growth in labor productivity was still too slow, and that labor discipline in general was a serious problem.

West German Talks. Poland's trade deficit with its largest Western partner, West Germany, increased from $67 million in the first half of 1972 to $209 million in the second half of 1973. In October, during a visit to Warsaw by German Foreign Minister Walter Scheel, the two countries discussed cheap credits by West Germany to help Poland reduce this large trade deficit. The Poles demanded more than $1 billion, but the Germans offered only a third that much.

The two countries also disagreed over how many ethnic Germans Poland would allow to emigrate to West Germany. Germany claimed that 283,000 wanted to leave, but that figure was disputed by the Poles. It was agreed that negotiations should be continued and that party leader Gierek would visit West Germany in 1974.

Thanks to American credits, Polish-American trade jumped from $90 million in the first half of 1972 to $197 million in the first half of 1973. The Chase Manhattan Bank granted Poland a $40-million credit in March.

Church Relations. Julius Cardinal Döpfner, Roman Catholic Archbishop of Munich and chairman of the German Episcopal Conference, visited Poland in October at the invitation of the Polish bishops. Relations between the Polish government and the Roman Catholic Church deteriorated in 1973 because of disagreements over the place of religious instruction in the new educational system. The government blueprint for educational reform was presented to the Sejm, Poland's parliament, in October. On October 24, the bishops issued a statement protesting "limitations on religious freedom imposed by local government bodies."

At a special party conference in October, Gierek announced that a purge to rid the party of undesirable elements would be carried out before the next party congress in 1976. He also announced that the price freeze on essential foodstuffs, introduced in 1971, would be extended another year. However, two leading newspapers, the party daily *Trybuna Ludu* and the weekly *Polityka*, were freed from government censorship in March.   Chris Cviic

See also EUROPE (Facts in Brief Table).

POLLUTION. See ENVIRONMENT.

POPULATION, WORLD

POPULATION, WORLD. United Nations (UN) estimates showed on Dec. 31, 1973, that the world population had reached nearly 3.9 billion. This represented a gain of more than 77 million for the year—the largest on record. UN experts also anticipated that "the decade of the 1970s may show a higher rate of world population growth than has ever been experienced in the history of man."

The UN General Assembly designated 1974 as "Population Year." Secretary-General Kurt Waldheim expressed the hope that the "first intergovernmental meeting ever to be held on population" and the other activities of the Population Year "will rank among the great events of the 1970s and will bring us appreciably closer to the time when the world can say the demographic problems facing us will be understood, and actions to solve them are underway."

Two Sectors. World population can be divided into two distinct sectors. The "developed" sector, comprising the industrial nations of North America, Europe, and Japan, has a population of about 1.2-billion and is increasing by 1 per cent a year. The "developing" sector, embracing most of the rest of the world, has a population of 2.7 billion and is increasing at the rate of 2.5 per cent a year.

U.S. Births Decline. With the exception of 1969 and 1970, fertility in the United States has been declining every year since 1957. The estimated number of births in 1973 – 3.2 million – was more than a million fewer than the 1947 peak of 4.3 million and the lowest number since the mid-1940s, when the nation's population was just over 140 million. The remarkable shift in fertility that has taken place in the past 16 years leads the trend throughout the developed world.

Nobody knows how long the downward trend will continue; and the only prediction that can be made is that the present trend will change, one way or the other. That it could move up is a real possibility. There are about 10 million more women 15 to 44 years of age today than there were in 1960, toward the end of the baby boom, when 1.25 million more births occurred than in 1973.

In a controversial decision handed down on January 22, the Supreme Court of the United States ruled that, during the first three months of pregnancy, the decision to have an abortion is the sole concern of the woman and her doctor. The decision made most state abortion laws unconstitutional, and aroused heated opposition. Recourse to legalized abortion has increased rapidly in the United States. By mid-1973, 24 states and the District of Columbia reported 480,259 legal abortions. Of these, 79 per cent were from two states; New York had 55 per cent and California 24 per cent.

Robert C. Cook

See also CENSUS, U.S.

Carrying 370 baby pictures, symbolizing daily increase in Britain's population, London marchers focus on the perils of overpopulation.

PORTUGAL. Charges of Portuguese atrocities in East Africa triggered a worldwide reaction in 1973. *The Times* of London published charges by Adrian Hastings, a Roman Catholic priest, that Portuguese forces fighting Mozambique Liberation Front (FRE-LIMO) guerrillas had massacred "several hundred people" in a village in December, 1972.

Portugal said the charges, published on July 10, 1973, had "the obvious aim of starting a scandal" just before Prime Minister Marcello Caetano's arrival in London on July 16. The commander of Portuguese forces in Mozambique said his units spent 10 days urging residents to go to safe areas before they began operations. Those who did not, he said, must have been FRELIMO sympathizers.

On the eve of Caetano's visit, more than 5,000 London demonstrators marched on Portugal's embassy. When the prime minister returned to Lisbon, 40,000 Portuguese demonstrated against the "odious offensive" in London.

On August 19, the ministry of defense in Lisbon said there had been no massacre, though it admitted isolated "retaliatory acts." On October 10, 700 Roman Catholics called on Pope Paul VI to condemn Portuguese behavior in Africa.

Parliamentary Elections. The political opposition was allowed to meet for the first time in four years in April. Various political groups, from monarchists to Communists, held meetings in a small-town movie theater for a week. Delegates from all parts of the country agreed on outspoken appeals for an end to warfare in Africa. Strict censorship, however, prevented news of the action from reaching most of the Portuguese people. Sixty-five opposition candidates campaigned for seats in the 150-member National Assembly.

In effect, the opposition was prohibited from discussing the fighting in the African territories. The regime had declared Angola, Guinea-Bissau, and Mozambique "overseas provinces" rather than colonies of Portugal. Independence movements there were thus subversive, and opponents of the war were accused of aiding subversion. And gatherings of more than 21 people were illegal unless they had been specifically authorized.

Four days before the October 28 balloting, the 65 withdrew, charging restrictions made the elections a "farce." According to a September 12 decree, they would lose political rights for five years by refusing to follow the electoral process to its conclusion. Some said they had no such rights, anyway. Official candidates won all 150 seats.

In Geneva, Switzerland, on August 27, the World Council of Churches set up a $500,000, five-year program to help deserters and draft dodgers evading service with Portuguese forces in Africa. An estimated 100,000 Portuguese fall into this category and cannot go home.   Kenneth Brown

See also Europe (Facts in Brief Table).

POSTAL SERVICE, U.S. In its second year of operation, which ended June 30, 1973, the Postal Service received a congressional subsidy of $1.4 billion and suffered a net loss of about $20 million.

Postmaster General Elmer T. Klassen estimated that there would also be a deficit for fiscal 1974 of $352 million, since new rates would not go into effect until six months after a wage increase for postal workers. By the end of fiscal 1975, he anticipated the increased revenue should enable the Postal Service to meet its expected expenses of about $12 billion.

Klassen asked the Postal Rate Commission on Sept. 25, 1972, to approve an across-the-board increase in postal rates. The new rates were scheduled to go into effect temporarily March 2, 1974. They would not be permanent until approved by the commission and the board of governors of the Postal Service. The last increase in first-class and airmail rates was in 1971.

The New Rates would boost first-class postage to 10 cents an ounce and airmail to 13 cents. Postal cards would rise to 8 cents, and airmail cards to 11 cents. Among the increases is a 38.6 per cent average rise on second-class material, mainly newspapers and magazines. The third-class bulk-mail rate used for direct-mail advertising would rise from 4.8 to 6.1 cents for the first 250,000 pieces mailed in a year, and from 5 to 6.3 cents for all mail above that volume.

Pants legs were up almost as high as postal rates when relaxed dress rules permitted shorts for U.S. mailmen beginning April 1.

Klassen estimated that the new rates would bring in about $2.1 billion a year. Most of the money would finance the wage increase of 14 per cent over two years that went into effect for 600,000 union postal employees in July. If the new rates were not approved by the Postal Rate Commission, the Postal Service would seek equivalent funds from Congress, he said. The service is required by law to keep its budget balanced.

New delivery standards announced by Klassen included a commitment to deliver overnight 95 per cent of the airmail destined for cities within a radius of 600 miles, and for selected cities regardless of their distance.

Improvements in Service in 1973 included a nationwide stamps-by-mail program. Under this program, small stamp orders may be placed by mail and paid by check. As another convenience for customers, the maximum denomination of money orders was increased from $100 to $300.

A contract for rapid rail delivery of parcel post and other bulk mail to the West and Midwest was granted to the Overland Mail, an all-mail train. This was reported to cut as much as 48 hours off the normal time for bulk mail from the Midwest to California.

The Postal Service handled 89.7 billion pieces of mail in fiscal 1973 compared with 87.2 billion in fiscal 1972. It employed 683,670 persons and operated 31,686 post offices.   William McGaffin

POVERTY. For the first time in history, the 122-member World Bank held its joint annual meeting with the International Monetary Fund in Africa – in Nairobi, Kenya, in September. The conference was attended by 3,000 delegates and observers from 126 nations.

The site of the meeting emphasized the interest of the more affluent nations in helping underdeveloped countries to aid their poor. It also encouraged a more realistic appraisal of the factors that create poverty and of who the "poor" really are.

Recent studies show that most of the people of underdeveloped nations are farmers. Discussions at the conference brought out the following suggestions on how to help such farmers: Teach them how to use the latest growing techniques. Make money available to them for seeds and fertilizer. Develop cooperative marketing organizations, and help them develop financial and psychological independence. Reduce the flow of the unemployed to cities, and locate small-scale industry in rural areas. Introduce rural improvement programs to expand agricultural output, assure water and other facilities, and get better credit for small farmers. Improvements in education facilities and opportunities, health, and family planning are also needed.

In support of these principles, Robert S. McNamara, World Bank president, announced a five-year, $22-billion lending program for underdeveloped countries. It will stress help for nearly 800-million persons living in rural areas that have been by-passed by economic growth. The program represents a 40 per cent rise in World Bank financing over the outlay in the last five years.

U.S. Poor Defined. As of September, 1973, an American family of four in an urban area is considered "poor" by government standards if annual family income is $4,200 or less in the continental United States, $4,850 in Hawaii, or $5,250 in Alaska. For farm families, the standard is slightly lower – $3,575, $4,125, or $4,475, respectively.

According to the U.S. Department of Labor, the new "poverty" levels are about $193 higher than those for 1972. The figures are guidelines used to help determine eligibility for manpower-training and job-placement programs.

Nutrition Program. Secretary Caspar W. Weinberger of the Department of Health, Education, and Welfare (HEW) announced in August that $100-million for the Nutrition Program for the Elderly would be released to the states. Projects funded under this program will provide low-cost hot meals at least five days a week for persons 60 years of age or older and their spouses.

Although the program places priority on the eligibility of low-income and minority persons, it also includes those who lack the skills and knowledge to select and prepare nourishing and well-balanced meals, are unable to shop and cook for themselves, or feel so rejected and lonely that they will not prepare and eat a meal alone.

The nutrition program provides transportation for participants to reach meal sites and also provides "outreach services" to find persons most in need of the program. It also offers supportive social services, including information and referral, health and welfare counseling, consumer and nutrition education, and opportunities for recreation and volunteer services. The program will provide at least 200,000 meals per day by March 31, 1974.

The Demise of OEO. The Nixon Administration recommended sweeping reforms in the nation's social welfare programs. President Richard M. Nixon proposed four principles to govern the nation's human resources policy for the 1970s:

▪ Government at all levels should seek to support and nurture, rather than limit, the diversity and freedom of choice that are the hallmark of the American system.

▪ The federal government should concentrate more on providing incentives and opening opportunities and less on delivering direct services.

▪ Rather than stifling initiative by trying to direct everything from Washington, D.C., federal efforts should encourage state and local governments to make those decisions and supply those services for which their closeness to the people best qualifies them. The federal government should also encourage private citizens and groups to learn how to help solve social problems.

- All federal policy must be fiscally responsible.

As a major point of the proposal, the Administration decided to discontinue the Office of Economic Opportunity (OEO) and transfer its essential activities to other departments and agencies. The Administration believes existing departments can serve the poor effectively while eradicating much duplication of services. Mr. Nixon appointed Howard Phillips, formerly associate director in charge of the OEO Office of Program Review, as acting director of the OEO on January 31. Phillips began his new assignment by announcing that almost all current program objectives would continue to receive at least as much federal money as in fiscal 1973, thus enabling some agencies to be funded through the 1973 calendar year. He also said he would transfer all OEO programs to other departments and agencies and terminate their federal funding on June 30.

Meanwhile, the union of government employees in OEO brought suit in a federal court to stop what they termed "the illegal termination" of OEO. On April 11, 1973, the Federal District Court in Washington, D.C., ruled in favor of the union, stopping Phillips from using funds appropriated by Congress for fiscal 1973 to abolish OEO.

Several members of the Senate filed suit in the same federal court against Phillips on grounds that he was named OEO acting director, but was not confirmed by the Senate as required by statute. The judge ruled on June 11 that Phillips was, indeed, serving illegally.

The President then withdrew Phillips' name and nominated Alvin J. Arnett, who was serving as assistant director of OEO. Arnett was confirmed as OEO director on September 15.

Status of OEO Programs. On Jan. 29, 1973, the President submitted his proposed budget for fiscal 1974 to Congress. It transfers all but two OEO programs to other federal departments or to a new status. Those programs dealing with American Indians, health affairs, and research development go to HEW. Those dealing with migrant workers go to the Department of Labor, and some research and development functions go to the Department of Housing and Urban Development.

OEO's legal services program is to be transferred to a separate corporation, and its economic development programs are to be shifted to the Office of Minority Business Enterprise in the Department of Commerce. These two transfers require special legislation to be passed.

That leaves only OEO headquarters in Washington, D.C., 10 regional offices, and the Community Action programs operated by the regional offices. The budget requests no funds for OEO or Community Action.

On July 6, the President formally approved the transfer of these program functions to the other departments of the executive branch. Congressional approval of funds budgeted for these departments to accommodate the transferred OEO programs has been completed in some cases.

Parks and the Peace Corps. A cooperative agreement between the National Park Service and ACTION, an agency that handles Peace Corps and certain domestic programs, will enable the Peace Corps to provide developing nations with volunteers qualified in planning and managing national parks, nature reserves, and recreation areas.

The agreement provides for the development of assignments overseas, the recruitment and selection of qualified volunteers, and the provision of training, including on-the-job training, for Peace Corps members. In addition, a limited number of National Park Service employees will be given leaves of absence in order to fill assignments as Peace Corps volunteers.

The new program is in response to a growing number of requests for technical assistance in the development of parks, conservation areas, and recreational facilities. Among the nations that have made such requests are British Honduras, Colombia, Costa Rica, Ecuador, Ghana, Iran, Kenya, and Tunisia. Volunteers will serve for two years. Their living and international travel costs will be paid by the Peace Corps.   Joseph P. Anderson

Another U.S. withdrawal

PRESIDENT OF THE UNITED STATES

For Richard Milhous Nixon, 1973 was a year of stark contrasts and grave constitutional questions. As the year began, the President entered his second term after a sweeping victory in the 1972 presidential election. He was inaugurated on January 20.

Interpreting his victory as a broad mandate from the American people, the President moved to reorganize the executive branch of government by executive decree. He set a limit on federal spending and impounded federal funds already appropriated by Congress in order to stay within this limit. He also ordered the bombing of Khmer (formerly Cambodia) to continue after the Vietnam cease-fire agreement, despite growing congressional opposition and legislative efforts to cut off funds for military action in Khmer.

By the end of the year, however, the President faced a grave crisis of confidence. His Vice-President had resigned and pleaded "no contest" to charges of income tax evasion (see AGNEW, SPIRO THEODORE).

His original White House staff was gone. His Administration had been rocked by scandals stemming from his re-election committee's questionable activities during the 1972 campaign. There was growing public pressure for the President to resign, and a congressional committee began studying the possibility of impeachment.

Shadows of Watergate. The break-in at the Democratic Party's national headquarters in the Watergate apartment complex in Washington, D.C., in June, 1972, had not attracted much attention outside of Washington. In January and February, when the seven men who broke into the Watergate were tried and sentenced, public attention was focused on the end of the war in Vietnam, the homecoming of

U.S. prisoners, and rising food costs. But when the U.S. Senate committee investigating the break-in began to hear testimony in March about possible involvement of high Administration officials, public attention shifted to Watergate.

In the months that followed, the President's top aides in the White House, former members of his Cabinet, and his personal friends were implicated in Watergate and related scandals. Reluctantly, the President admitted White House involvement in April. In October, he reluctantly began to surrender relevant confidential tape recordings and documents in response to a court order and congressional and public pressure. But his earlier claims of executive privilege, his insistence on the integrity of his associates, the firing in October of special Watergate prosecutor Archibald Cox, and the resignation of Attorney General Elliot L. Richardson severely damaged the President's credibility. Still, Mr. Nixon maintained that he had known nothing about the break-in or the cover-up, although he accepted ultimate responsibility for the actions of his subordinates. See Cox, ARCHIBALD; RICHARDSON, ELLIOT L.; WATERGATE.

Other Scandals also diminished public confidence in the President. On April 27, U.S. District Court Judge William M. Byrne, Jr., released a Department of Justice memorandum disclosing that two of the convicted Watergate burglars had also been involved in a burglary connected with the so-called Pentagon Papers case. At the time, Daniel Ellsberg and Anthony J. Russo, Jr., were being tried before Judge Byrne in Los Angeles on charges that in 1971 they had stolen and made public highly classified papers dealing with the Vietnam War.

Former presidential assistant John D. Ehrlichman disclosed on May 1 that the President had ordered a secret White House investigation that led to the burglary of Ellsberg's psychiatrist's office in Los Angeles. The next day, Judge Byrne stated that he had met Ehrlichman twice during the Ellsberg trial. They discussed the possibility that Byrne might be offered the post of Federal Bureau of Investigation director. This created speculation about possible government bribery for a verdict of guilty. On May 11, Judge Byrne dismissed all charges against Ellsberg and Russo because of "improper government conduct," and these events cast further doubt on the integrity of the President. See ELLSBERG, DANIEL.

On May 10, a federal grand jury indicted President Nixon's friend and former Attorney General John N. Mitchell, former Secretary of Commerce Maurice H. Stans, former New Jersey State Senator Harry L. Sears, and financier Robert L. Vesco on charges of conspiracy to defraud the government and obstruct justice. Mitchell and Stans were also charged with perjury. The Securities and Exchange Commission chairman, G. Bradford Cook, resigned when he became implicated in the Vesco case.

Still other scandals were possible. There were charges that dairy interests and the giant International Telephone and Telegraph Corporation (ITT) unlawfully and secretly paid large sums of money to the Committee to Re-Elect the President (CRP). Allegedly, they were seeking favors from the Administration. Extortionlike solicitations by CRP workers of illegal and secret campaign contributions from large corporations and unions also came under investigation, and several companies admitted they had illegally donated money to the President.

Grave Constitutional Questions were raised in 1973 by the President's handling of the scandals rocking his Administration, the problem of national security and secret bombing, and the impounding of federal funds appropriated by Congress.

As the Senate Watergate committee and special Watergate prosecutor Cox drew closer to key White House figures in their investigation, the President relied on the doctrine of executive privilege to justify his refusal to allow White House personnel to testify and to surrender relevant documents and tapes.

"The manner in which the President personally exercises his assigned executive powers is not subject to questioning by another branch of government," he declared on March 12. Executive privilege, he said, extended to his present and former staff. On July 7, he formally notified the Senate Watergate committee that he considered it his "constitutional responsibility to decline to appear personally under any circumstances before your committee or to grant access to presidential papers." In October, the President yielded to a court order, upheld by an appellate court, and released the tapes and documents. So the broader issue of the scope of the doctrine of executive privilege (which is not mentioned in the Constitution) was not tested in the Supreme Court of the United States. However, the President then revealed that two pertinent tapes had never been made and that 18½ crucial minutes of one had been erased.

Unauthorized and sometimes illegal wiretapping for national security reasons also posed legal and constitutional questions. On May 22, the President explained that "a special program of wiretaps" had been set up in 1969 in order to prevent leaks of classified information. Fewer than 20 taps were ordered, and all had been discontinued by February, 1971. Members of the National Security Council, the Department of Defense, foreign policy adviser Henry A. Kissinger's staff, and some news correspondents had been targets of wiretapping.

President Nixon confers with his two new top aides, Alexander Haig, left, and Melvin Laird, who replaced John D. Ehrlichman and H. R. Haldeman.

Ehrlichman cited national security as justification for the project, authorized by the President, that eventually led burglars into the office of Ellsberg's psychiatrist. All the activities of the so-called "plumbers" unit, set up in the White House to stop leaks of information, were regarded by some critics as unconstitutional exercises of presidential power.

Relations with Congress were very troubled. The President consistently vetoed measures that he regarded as inflationary. In addition, he impounded funds already appropriated by Congress to hold federal expenditures to the $250-billion limit he had set in 1972. On February 1, the director of the Office of Management and Budget declared that the President could withhold funds appropriated by Congress under his constitutional duty to "take care that the laws be faithfully executed," because he had to make sure that the legal limit on the national debt was not exceeded.

By early October, about 40 lawsuits were pending, trying to force the Administration to release the funds. On October 9, the Supreme Court refused an Administration request to expedite a ruling on the constitutionality of impounding funds. However, in December, a federal judge ordered the Department of Health, Education, and Welfare (HEW) to release $20 million of impounded funds for state educational programs, and HEW then released more than $1-billion for various programs.

The President also clashed with Congress early in the year over the continued bombing of Khmer. This prompted a congressional move to limit the President's warmaking powers. On June 29, the President promised Congress that he would halt the bombing of Khmer by August 15. If further U.S. air support was needed by Khmer, he pledged to seek congressional approval.

Congress acted quickly to approve Representative Gerald R. Ford (R., Mich.) as the new Vice-President. Ford was nominated on October 12 and confirmed on December 6. See CONGRESS OF THE UNITED STATES; FORD, GERALD R.

Because of continuing inflation, the nation moved from Phase 2 of the President's economic stabilization program to Phase 3 on January 11. A 60-day price freeze went into effect on June 13, and Phase 4 began on August 13. See ECONOMICS.

Foreign Policy. President Nixon's most popular move in 1973 was winding down U.S. participation in the war in Indochina. On January 23, the President announced an agreement had been reached with North Vietnam on a cease-fire. The agreement was signed on January 27 (see ASIA). On April 2 and 3, he met with South Vietnamese President Nguyen Van Thieu at San Clemente, Calif., and pledged economic aid to South Vietnam.

The return of U.S. prisoners of war from Southeast Asia began on February 12 and the last prisoner was released on April 1. That same day, the remaining U.S. ground combat forces left South Vietnam, but 7,200 civilian employees of the defense department remained. See NATIONAL DEFENSE (Close-Up).

However, the bombing of Khmer cast a cloud over the President's success in Vietnam. A new headquarters was established in Thailand for the U.S. Seventh Air Force, and U.S. B-52s continued to bomb Communist positions in Khmer.

Then, on July 17, a defense department spokesman revealed that, acting on the President's orders, U.S. B-52s had made more than 3,500 secret bombing raids over Khmer in a 14-month period that began in March, 1969. Highly classified reports had been falsified in 1969 and 1970 to conceal the facts.

On August 20, President Nixon defended ordering the secret bombing of Khmer as "absolutely necessary" to save U.S. lives and bring peace to Indochina. The Administration denied falsifying records but admitted that there had been "separate reporting procedures" to conceal the raids. Congressional and other critics of the President charged that the secret bombing was unconstitutional.

On May 30, the President met in Reykjavík, Iceland, with Icelandic leaders, and the following day he conferred there with French President Georges Pompidou. But Mr. Nixon did not visit Europe in the fall of 1973 as he had planned. See EUROPE.

President Nixon entertained Soviet Communist Party General Secretary Leonid I. Brezhnev in June. On June 19, he and Brezhnev signed four treaties involving agriculture, oceanography, culture, and transportation. On June 21, they pledged to work for nuclear arms control.

The United States did not formally recognize China in 1973. However, on March 15, the President named retired Ambassador David K. E. Bruce to head the United States liaison office in Peking.

Middle East Crisis. The President's hopes for a lasting détente with Russia were shaken in October by the possibility that Russia might interfere in the Arab-Israeli war. On October 25, President Nixon ordered a worldwide military alert for U.S. armed forces, the first such alert since President Lyndon B. Johnson alerted all troops the day President John F. Kennedy was assassinated in 1963. At a news conference the next day, Mr. Nixon described his action as a "precautionary alert." The United States and Russia then agreed to cooperate on a cease-fire in the Middle East, and the alert was discontinued on October 31. See MIDDLE EAST.

An energy shortage developed into a crisis in October when Arab nations shut off oil deliveries to the United States because of its support for Israel. The President called upon all Americans to conserve fuel, and asked Congress for new controls. See ENERGY.   Carol L. Thompson

See also NIXON, RICHARD MILHOUS; REPUBLICAN PARTY; Section One, FOCUS ON THE WORLD.

PRINCE EDWARD ISLAND. See CANADA.

PRISON. The U.S. National Advisory Commission on Criminal Justice Standards and Goals issued a 636-page report on Oct. 15, 1973, calling for substantial changes in corrections procedures in U.S. prisons. The recommendations, endorsed by the U.S. Department of Justice, were only the latest addition to a growing demand for prison reform, additional financing, and revised procedures for treating various types of criminal offenders.

Large-scale action to overhaul corrections, however, was not generally forthcoming. The fiscal 1974 federal budget for prison construction was reduced to $14.8 million from 1973's $42 million. State officials, with few exceptions, continued to resist the spending necessary to bring correctional facilities and personnel training in line with modern penal theory.

Statistics released during the year indicated that about 224,000 prisoners were housed in state and federal institutions on a typical day, slightly more than one-tenth of 1 per cent of the national population. Of this total, approximately 22,500 were lodged in 35 federal correctional institutions, while 201,500 more were held in 550 major adult and juvenile state facilities. Only two of the federal penitentiaries– McNeil Island, Wash., opened in 1865, and Leavenworth, Kans. (1895)–were more than 75 years old.

Disturbances. Among more than 45 major prison disturbances reported in 1973, the two most severe occurred in Pennsylvania and Oklahoma. The warden and deputy warden of Holmesburg Prison, a Philadelphia detention facility for prisoners awaiting trial and sentencing, were stabbed to death by inmates on May 31. Some 800 rebellious prisoners almost totally demolished the Oklahoma State Penitentiary at McAlester after seizing 21 hostages and setting the prison ablaze on July 27. By the time national guardsmen gained complete control on August 3, rioters had caused an estimated $20-million damage, and four inmates were dead, all apparently victims of fellow prisoners.

Legal Actions. On February 1, U.S. District Judge Robert Merhige, Jr., ordered the Virginia director of corrections to pay $21,265 out of his own pocket to three prisoners adjudged to have received "cruel and unusual punishment" at the state penitentiary in Richmond. On November 23, the inmates dropped their claim for damages after state officials promised full compliance with Merhige's orders for reform in prison procedures. In Florida, U.S. District Judge Charles Scott ruled on January 5 that a prisoner may not be placed in solitary confinement or deprived of any of his already credited "good time" unless he has first been given a hearing in the presence of his counsel.
David C. Beckwith

PRIZES. See AWARDS AND PRIZES; CANADIAN LIBRARY ASSOCIATION; CANADIAN LITERATURE; NOBEL PRIZES; PULITZER PRIZES.

PROTESTANT. The World Council of Churches quietly celebrated its 25th anniversary on Aug. 26, 1973. Founded in Amsterdam in 1948, this early postwar flowering of Protestant and Eastern Orthodox unity efforts seemed at first to be a kind of spiritual United Nations. It prospered through the 1950s and much of the 1960s, but has recently run into difficulties. The trend has been away from large ecumenical organizational activities.

At ceremonies in its Geneva, Switzerland, headquarters, General Secretary Philip A. Potter spoke realistically about the problems ahead. He noted "decreasing commitment" in the United States and a "loss of concern for the church life" in Western Europe. Inflation and a decline in support combined to crimp the World Council's activities. Yet it remained the largest forum ever organized for Protestant churches. Among its other activities in 1973, one of its agencies sponsored a consultation on "Salvation Today." The program, held in Bangkok, Thailand, revealed the degrees of disagreement that now exist concerning Christian mission.

In the United States, institutionalized Protestant unity movements have also failed to regain the prominence they held a decade ago. The Consultation on Church Union (COCU), which would possibly lead to the union of nine participating churches, regrouped after a year of losses. The United Presbyterian Church, meeting in Omaha, Nebr., in May,

Inmates burned Oklahoma state prison buildings in a week of rioting that started July 27. Four died, and damage was set at $20 million.

Jacob A. O. Preus was re-elected president of the Lutheran Church—Missouri Synod in July after a bitter convention fight in New Orleans.

Protestant churches, as well as among Catholics. At the beginning of the century, many of these had organized into denominations that upper-class Americans dismissed as "holy rollers," because they often revealed highly emotional tendencies. But beginning in 1960, the more established churches also reported large numbers of people who were "moved by the Spirit" in new ways.

For some, the change was represented chiefly in intensified prayer life and devotion. Others accented spiritual healing. But the most noticeable—and often the most sought-after—experience was glossolalia, a form of unrepressed and ecstatic speaking. Denominations as historically remote from such enthusiasm as the Lutherans found thousands attracted to charismatic conferences.

Evangelist Problems. The Protestant right wing also had difficulties. Carl McIntire lost his license to broadcast through his station WXUR in Media, Pa. This was the hub of a network of hundreds of radio stations that broadcast McIntire's antiliberal messages. McIntire retaliated by starting to broadcast from a boat offshore, in an attempt to circumvent Federal Communications Commission regulations. The station went off the air after one day of broadcasting because of complaints that it was interfering with the reception of another station.

Akron, Ohio, evangelist Rex Hubbard, a highly successful religious entrepreneur whose Cathedral of Tomorrow was supported by various secular businesses, was found to be in deep financial trouble. The U.S. Securities and Exchange Commission stepped in and asked a federal court to appoint a receiver.

The best-known evangelist, Billy Graham, had a mixed year. He drew the largest crowds of his career in Korea. In South Africa, he mentioned that he thought castration would be a good punishment for rapists, and he argued for restoration of capital punishment. While many Protestants cheered the latter appeal, he was forced to modify the former.

The Watergate scandal produced many critics of Graham. He was attacked for his identification with President Richard M. Nixon, whose informal chaplain Graham had long been. Although conservatives had often cheered the spiritual tone and the law-and-order character of the Nixon Administration, many of them found it advisable to dissociate themselves from the White House in the wake of the scandal.

Protestant overtones showed up in many of the political expressions of the year, most notably in the Bible-quoting of Senator Sam Ervin (D., N.C.), who chaired a committee to investigate election scandals of 1972. Senator Mark Hatfield (R., Ore.), a generally liberal politician but a theological conservative, took the occasion of a Washington prayer breakfast to criticize contemporary attempts to use the name of God for partisan political causes. Senator Harold Hughes (D., Iowa) surprised supporters by announcing that he would not seek a new term, but

voted itself back into COCU after surprising other churches by withdrawing in 1972. But the trend was still away from formal union and toward cooperative activities on looser terms.

Key 73. Among the conservatives, evangelism and Pentecostalism were the major news-making accents. The year was to have found its focus in a venture called Key 73. This evangelistic outreach had been designed several years earlier by evangelicals, but as time passed, it came to attract and encompass more moderately liberal Protestant groups and many Roman Catholics. Combining the use of mass media, Bible distribution, rallies, crusades, worship, and, most of all, attempts to gain new members, Key 73 was the most broadly based and ambitious program of its kind in U.S. church history.

Many partisans and most observers came to see, however, that in its pursuit of the original goals, the effort was largely a failure. Most Americans seemed unaware of Key 73. Had it not been for Jewish complaints against the tendency of some evangelicals to use the cause to convert Jews, national publicity would have been very slight. It failed to attract funds, and mass-media efforts were unsuccessful. Many moderates believed the more fundamentalistic groups were using the campaign to compete more than to cooperate, so they withdrew.

More media excitement was generated by the continuing, if not increased, presence of charismatics in

would go into full-time religious work. He argued that America's spiritual crisis went deeper than its political crisis.

Denominational News revealed the stresses of the time. Most troubled were two conservative churches. The Presbyterian Church in the United States, a largely Southern group, experienced a schism as 260 member churches voted on May 19 to form a new denomination. In December, they became a new denomination, the National Presbyterian Church. The dissidents claimed that the parent denomination was drifting toward liberalism and ecumenism.

In the Lutheran Church–Missouri Synod, the elected leadership moved further to the theological right, but the synod's moderate slight minority did not leave. Jacob A. O. Preus was elected to head the synod for a second term at a convention in New Orleans, in July. His election in 1969 had signaled a take-over by forces opposed to the prevailing faculty theological position at the denomination's seminary in St. Louis. The president of the seminary, John H. Tietjen, and the faculty majority were condemned by a delegate majority that varied from 56 per cent to 60 per cent on various issues.

Preus was given new and virtually absolute doctrinal authority, and the majority voted in one of his own doctrinal statements as a kind of test or touchstone for synodical doctrine. The moderates organized after the New Orleans convention and announced their determination to continue to witness and work for their position.

In December, the Mormon church named Spencer W. Kimball as their 12th president. An apostle for 30 years, he has been one of the church's most traveled and energetic leaders.

Social Concerns. Protestants were a less-visible force in social action than they had been in the mid-1960s. United States Supreme Court decisions on abortion and pornography evoked divided reactions among them. The disarray of black religious forces was visible in the troubles of Martin Luther King, Jr.'s, Southern Christian Leadership Conference. King's successor, Ralph Abernathy, resigned the presidency of the financially depressed and dispirited organization in July, but was prevailed upon to give the cause a second effort.

A number of denominations were asked to support amnesty for draft evaders and exiles, but most failed to do so. Others refused to condemn Watergate-type politics, though many individual churchmen spoke out critically. Women's rights remained an issue. The United Church of Christ voted at its June convention to supplement or remove masculine pronouns from its constitution. The Indian take-over of the village of Wounded Knee, S. Dak., and the inter-Indian tensions revealed there, tended to confuse Protestant churches that had set out to make the Indian cause their own.   Martin E. Marty

See also RELIGION.

PSYCHOLOGY. Psychologists Duane Rumbaugh and Timothy Gill of the Yerkes Primate Center in Orange Park, Fla., reported in 1973 how they trained a young chimpanzee named Lana to read. For this purpose, they constructed an artificial language called Yerkish. Each word in the language is represented by a geometric symbol composed from nine elements used singly or in combination. They painted these symbols on keys that Lana could press in specific sequences. Every time she pressed a key, a computer-controlled system projected the corresponding symbol on a screen directly above her keyboard.

During her six months of training, Lana learned to watch the projected symbols and to reject incorrect sequences before completion by pressing an erase key. Later tests showed that Lana could successfully complete Yerkish sequences of words to form meaningful sentences and erase nonsense word sequences. Lana scored 100 per cent on sentence completion, and better than 90 per cent on nonsense sequences.

Theory of Learning. Psychologists have two different theories of learning, one based on principles of classical conditioning developed by Russian physiologist Ivan Pavlov and his followers and the other based on instrumental conditioning principles developed primarily by psychologists Edward Thorndike, John B. Watson, Clark Hull, and B. F. Skinner. While it is possible to use whichever principles are

Trying to overcome fear of dogs, New York City psychologists project pictures of friendly and angry dogs while patients try to relax.

more appropriate to a given situation, this is not very satisfactory.

Proof of the usefulness of Pavlovian principles in explaining aspects of learned responses that cannot be explained by instrumental principles was shown in 1973 by experiments of two Canadian psychologists, Herbert M. Jenkins and Bruce R. Moore. For the experiments, they used pigeons, which they put into cages where there was a lighted disk and some grain. The pigeons could see the grain but could not get it until they pecked, or put some pressure, on the disk. Almost all pigeons spontaneously began to peck at the disk. Since the birds had never before been given grain for pecking at the disk, their somewhat automatic response was called "auto-shaping."

To test the hypothesis that the pigeons pecked the disk because pecking is the normal response when grain is present, the psychologists also used a lighted disk and water. Under these conditions, the birds gently pressed the disk with the same head movements they would normally use for drinking, and they did not peck it. These results indicate that a simple response such as pressing a lighted disk is not neutral, as the instrumental conditioning theory suggests, but is related to the nature of the reward. The results were entirely predictable, however, by the principles of Pavlovian conditioning.   Robert W. Goy

PUBLISHING. See CANADIAN LITERATURE; LITERATURE; MAGAZINES; NEWSPAPER; POETRY.

PUERTO RICO. Rafael Hernández Colón, the nation's fourth elected governor, was sworn into office on Jan. 2, 1973. Hernández Colón's Popular Democratic Party had swept the Nov. 7, 1972, elections to win control of both houses of the legislature. The rival Puerto Rican Independence Party held only three seats, one in the Senate and two in the lower house. See HERNÁNDEZ COLÓN, RAFAEL.

The new governor mapped an ambitious program for his first term in office. It included reform of an inefficient electoral law, sweeping tax changes, setting priorities for a universal health system, and an expanded industrialization program. On January 13, six women were named to Cabinet posts that ranged from secretary of education to director of economic opportunities. One of Hernández Colón's principal goals was to discourage Puerto Ricans from leaving the island to seek employment elsewhere. On June 21, he swore in a newly formed council of 27 Puerto Ricans to look after the interests of émigrés in the United States.

A long-standing controversy over the U.S. Navy's use of Culebra Island for gunnery practice appeared near an end in 1973. On May 24, U.S. Secretary of Defense Elliot L. Richardson ordered gunnery and air-bombardment training shifted to Desecheo and Monito, two small islands off Puerto Rico's west coast, by mid-1975.   Paul C. Tullier

See also LATIN AMERICA (Facts in Brief Table).

PULITZER PRIZES in journalism, letters, and music were announced in New York City on May 7, 1973. The following awards were made:

Journalism

Public Service. A gold medal to the *Washington Post* for its investigation of the Watergate affair, which began with an attempt to bug the Democratic National Headquarters in June, 1972 (see WATERGATE). The *Post*'s investigation was carried out mainly by Carl Bernstein, 29, and Bob Woodward, 30. As their disclosures developed the Watergate case into a major political scandal of national proportions, the *Post* backed them up with strong editorials, many of them written by Roger Wilkins, and editorial cartoons drawn by the two-time Pulitzer Prize winner, Herbert A. Block (Herblock).

General Local Reporting. $1,000 to the *Chicago Tribune* for its work in uncovering law violations in Chicago's primary election of March 21, 1972. The *Tribune* task force, under the command of investigative reporter George Bliss, accumulated documented evidence of more than 1,700 cases of ghost voting, forgery, and other election frauds. As a result, a federal grand jury returned 75 indictments, and a succession of guilty pleas and convictions followed in the wake of the prosecutions.

Special Local Reporting. $1,000 to the Sun Newspapers of Omaha, Nebr., a chain of seven weeklies, for revealing that the charitable institution known as Boys Town, a home for orphans near Omaha, had a net worth of at least $209 million.

National Reporting. $1,000 to Robert Boyd, 45, and Clark Hoyt, 30, of the Knight Newspapers for disclosing that Senator Thomas F. Eagleton (D., Mo.), the Democratic nominee for Vice-President, had a history of psychiatric treatment. In July, 1972, Hoyt was assigned to investigate an anonymous tip that Senator Eagleton had had psychiatric therapy. Hoyt and Boyd later submitted a two-page memorandum to Senator George S. McGovern's staff to inform the Democratic presidential nominee before the article was published. Hoyt joined Knight Newspapers in 1968 and two years later was assigned to the Washington bureau. Boyd has been chief of the Washington bureau since 1967.

International Reporting. $1,000 to Max Frankel, 43, of *The New York Times* for his coverage of President Richard M. Nixon's trip to China in February, 1972. While in China, Frankel filed 35,000 words in eight days. It was probably his most remarkable assignment in a long and distinguished career as a national and foreign correspondent. On Jan. 1, 1973, he was named Sunday editor of the *Times*.

Editorial Writing. $1,000 to Roger B. Linscott, 53, associate editor of the *Berkshire Eagle*, Pittsfield, Mass., for 10 editorials that influenced community affairs. Of the 10, he is particularly proud of one in which "we rather wildly endorsed McGovern for President," largely on the grounds of "the crooked

Nixon Administration." Linscott graduated from Harvard University in 1941 and joined the *Eagle* staff in 1948.

Spot News Photography. $1,000 to Huynh Cong (Nick) Ut, 22, of the Associated Press (AP), for his June 8, 1972, photograph, "Terror of War," which showed a naked 9-year-old Vietnamese girl fleeing a napalm bombing. Ut took the photo along Route 1 after the South Vietnamese Air Force dropped napalm on its own people by mistake. Ut joined the AP bureau in Saigon in 1965 after his brother, also an AP photographer, was killed in combat.

Feature Photography. $1,000 to Brian Lanker, 25, of the *Topeka* (Kans.) *Capital-Journal* for "The Moment of Life," one picture in a sequence of photos on natural childbirth that appeared in the *Capital-Journal* on Feb. 2, 1972. Lanker joined the newspaper's staff in 1969 and in 1971 was named National Press Photographer of the Year.

Distinguished Commentary. $1,000 to David S. Broder, 44, a political reporter and columnist for the *Washington Post* since 1966. He received an M.A. degree in political science from the University of Chicago in 1951 and a fellowship from the Harvard University Institute of Politics in 1969. In a 1972 poll of political correspondents, Broder was chosen as the most respected political writer in the nation.

Distinguished Criticism. $1,000 to Ronald Powers, 31, of the *Chicago Sun-Times*, who writes a six-day-a-week column of radio and television criticism. After graduating from the University of Missouri in 1963, Powers worked as a sportswriter and suburban news reporter for the *St. Louis Post-Dispatch*. He joined the *Sun-Times* in 1968 and became its radio and television critic in June, 1969.

Letters

Biography. Special citation to James T. Flexner, 65, historian, for *George Washington*, a four-volume biography that took 12 years to write. The last volume was published in 1972. Flexner graduated magna cum laude from Harvard College in 1929 and was a reporter for the *New York Herald Tribune* for the next two years. He then turned to historical studies and in 36 years produced nearly 20 books.

Drama. $1,000 to Jason Miller, 34, for *That Championship Season*, a play that opened at Broadway's Booth Theatre on Sept. 14, 1972. Miller was born in Scranton, Pa., and began his career as an actor. His play *Nobody Hears a Broken Drum* was produced off-Broadway in 1970.

Fiction. $1,000 to Eudora Welty for *The Optimist's Daughter*. A novelist, essayist, and short-story writer, Welty received a B.A. degree from the University of Wisconsin in 1929. Her first novel, *A Curtain of Green*, was published in 1941.

General Nonfiction. $1,000 to Frances Fitz-Gerald, 32, a free-lance journalist who spent more than a year in Vietnam, and Robert M. Coles, 43, a psychiatrist on the staffs of Massachusetts General Hospital and the Harvard Medical School. Fitz-Gerald was cited for *Fire in the Lake: The Vietnamese and the Americans*, which also won a National Book Award in 1973. Educated at Foxcroft School and Radcliffe College, FitzGerald studied Vietnamese history, sociology, and culture at Yale University. Coles was honored for Volumes 2 and 3 of *Children in Crisis*, a study of Southern rural poor. Coles studied at Harvard, Columbia University, and the University of Chicago.

History. $1,000 to Michael Kammen, 35, a professor of history at Cornell University, for *People of Paradox: An Inquiry Concerning the Origin of American Civilization*. Kammen graduated from George Washington University and received a Ph.D. degree from Harvard. He is the author of four other books.

Poetry. $1,000 to Maxine W. Kumin, 47, who teaches English at Tufts University in Medford, Mass., for *Up Country*, her fourth collection of poems. Kumin received an M.A. degree from Radcliffe College in 1948.

Music. $1,000 to Elliott Carter, 65, composer, for *String Quartet No. 3*. Carter also won a Pulitzer Prize in 1960 for his *String Quartet No. 2*. He received an M.A. degree from Harvard University in 1932 and taught mathematics, Greek, and music at St. John's College, Annapolis, Md. He now teaches composition at the Juilliard School of Music in New York City.
Lillian Zahrt

QATAR. The continued demand for Middle Eastern oil and the absence of internal unrest allowed Qatar to concentrate on economic development in 1973. Sheik Khalifa bin Hamad Al-Thani marked his first anniversary in power on February 22 by opening the Qatar Fertilizer Company, largest single industry in the state. It can produce 430,000 tons a year at full capacity. He also dedicated the 124-room Gulf Hotel in Doha, which was built to attract both tourists and businessmen.

Increased oil revenues seemed assured with the signing of a participation agreement with Shell Oil Company in January. Under the agreement, Qatari ownership in all phases of Shell operations will grow from 25 per cent in 1973 to 51 per cent in 1982. Qatar signed a similar agreement in February with Qatar Petroleum Company, the other major Western-owned oil company.

Qatar was one of 10 Arab states whose oil ministers met in Kuwait on September 4 to map a common policy on the use of oil resources as a diplomatic weapon against Israel. In October, Qatar joined other Middle Eastern nations in cutting off oil exports to the United States and other nations because of their support of Israel.
William Spencer

See also MIDDLE EAST (Facts in Brief Table).
QUEBEC. See CANADA.
RACING. See AUTOMOBILE RACING; BOATING; HORSE RACING; SWIMMING; TRACK AND FIELD.

RADIO. The controversial sex-oriented talk show – U.S. radio's most imitated new format in 1972 – was a major problem for the industry in 1973. By February, Congress and the Federal Communications Commission (FCC) had received an unprecedented amount of mail from outraged listeners protesting the obscene nature of so-called "topless radio." On March 22, the FCC voted to hold a closed-door inquiry to determine whether any broadcasters were violating the statute banning obscenity and profanity.

At the same time, the National Association of Broadcasters (NAB) Radio Code Board directed the NAB Code Authority to monitor both sex-talk shows and rock disk-jockey programs (for questionable lyrics). In April, the FCC fined station WGLD-FM of Oak Park, Ill., $2,000 for airing two allegedly obscene "Femme Forum" broadcasts.

Meanwhile, the original sex-talk jockey, Bill Ballance of station KGBS in Los Angeles, whose "Feminine Forum" was described in March by Senator Marlow W. Cook (R., Ky.) as "the nation's first X-rated radio show," adopted a modified format. His new show still featured phone calls from women listeners, but the conversations were less clinical. Other stations throughout the United States performed similar clean-up operations.

"Pirate" Radio. The problem of license renewals was as troublesome for radio as it was for television broadcasters (see TELEVISION). Station WXUR-AM-FM of Media, Pa., went off the air in July, the first station ever refused a license renewal by the FCC because of fairness-doctrine violations. Fundamentalist preacher Carl McIntire, owner of WXUR, resumed broadcasting on September 19 from a "pirate" radio ship 12 miles off the New Jersey coast in the Atlantic Ocean. But a federal restraining order quickly put him off the air the next day.

Payola Probe. Broadcasters also were haunted by the specter of a new payola scandal. In late spring, charges that the recording industry was using cash and drugs to buy air play for their new disks were under investigation by the Department of Justice, a federal grand jury, a Senate copyright committee, and Senator James L. Buckley (Cons., N.Y.).

Nostalgia was a strong programming influence in both local and network radio. More and more stations were playing old hit records, many dating back to the rock-and-roll era of the 1950s. Radio serials from the 1930s and 1940s continued to be popular.

Black Radio. After more than a year's delay, the National Black Network (NBN) began broadcasting over 41 affiliate stations on July 1. The new network joined the NAB in September and NBN president Eugene D. Jackson became the first black member of NAB's Radio Board. Mutual Broadcasting's Mutual Black Network, with 73 affiliates, celebrated its first anniversary in May.   June Bundy Csida

RAILROAD. U.S. railroads set records in both ton-miles and revenue in 1973, but net earnings and return-on-investment showed only a small increase. A 9 per cent increase in freight traffic resulted in a new high of 847 billion ton-miles.

Grain shipments and a generally strong economy were key factors in producing the record ton-miles. However, there was a slight decline in the coal shipments that normally account for 25 per cent of the industry's total tonnage. Grain shipments, spurred by record exports, increased 31.5 per cent over 1972.

Traffic growth and two freight-rate increases totaling 4.9 per cent pushed rail operating revenues up 9 per cent to $14.6 billion. However, spiraling operating costs, particularly for fuel, caused earnings to show only a modest increase over 1972's $492.5 million. The rate of return on net investment was 3 per cent compared with 2.9 per cent in 1972. Twenty-two railroads operated in the red.

Pending Legislation. Congress postponed consideration of most pending rail legislation to focus its attention on critical rail problems in the Northeast that threatened complete collapse in rail service. Six railroads were in receivership and facing shut-downs – Penn Central, Boston & Maine, Erie-Lackawanna, Reading, Central Railroad of New Jersey, and Lehigh Valley.

The House of Representatives and the Senate passed varying versions of a reorganization plan,

Ben Grauer left his NBC microphone in July after 43 years as a radio announcer. He will continue to work, for the Voice of America.

Amtrak's new French turbotrains began service between Chicago and
St. Louis on October 1, after ceremonies in Chicago's Union Station.

and a conference committee met to resolve the differences in December. The bill, as finally passed, would restructure seven railroads – the six northeastern lines and the Ann Arbor (Mich.) Railroad – into one federally backed private corporation. The act provides $1.5 billion in government-guaranteed loans to plan and finance a 17-state rail network, operating on less trackage than is now used. It also makes available more than $500 million in federal funds for interim operating expenses and compensation for displaced workers. President Richard M. Nixon signed the bill on Jan. 2, 1974.

Passenger Travel. Lured by solid, if uneven, improvements in the quality of passenger trains, the American public reversed its long retreat from the rails in 1973. Amtrak estimated that it carried more than 18 million passengers in 1973, compared with 16.4 million in 1972 and about 15 million in 1971.

Amtrak's success in attracting passengers was somewhat diminished, however, by continuing high losses. It calculated its losses at $124 million during fiscal 1973 ($340,000 a day), and forecast a loss of $95.6 million during fiscal 1974 ($262,000 a day).

President Richard M. Nixon on November 3 signed a bill to increase funding and independence for Amtrak. The measure authorizes Amtrak to spend $154.3 million – $107.3 million in new funding, and $47 million left over from the fiscal year that ended on June 30, 1973. Kenneth E. Schaefle

RAY, DIXY LEE (1914-   ), a marine biologist, became the first woman to head the Atomic Energy Commission (AEC) on Feb. 6, 1973. She replaced James R. Schlesinger, who resigned to take over the Central Intelligence Agency and, later in the year, became secretary of defense (see SCHLESINGER, JAMES R.). Ray was appointed an AEC commissioner in August, 1972.

Dixy Lee Ray was born in Tacoma, Wash., on Sept. 3, 1914. She received a master's degree from Mills College, Oakland, Calif., in 1938 and a doctorate in biology from Stanford University in 1945. Meanwhile, she taught in Oakland public schools from 1938 to 1942.

In 1945, she joined the faculty of the University of Washington. At the time of her appointment to the AEC, she was associate professor of zoology at the university and director of the Pacific Science Center in Seattle.

She has also served on the Committee on Public Understanding of Science of the American Association for the Advancement of Science and on the President's Task Force on Oceanography. She won the William Clapp Award in marine biology in 1959 and, in 1971, was made an honorary member of a Kwakiutl Indian tribe.

Ray brought a new informality to her AEC post. Not fond of city life, she lives in a mobile home 15 miles from AEC headquarters. Darlene R. Stille

RECORDINGS. Further progress was made in 1973 in quadraphonic (four-channel) sound systems, which use four speakers instead of two as with stereo. There were still two rival methods of recording, discrete and matrix, and American record companies were slow in lining up behind either system. Still, quadraphonic business made up 20 per cent of all electronic equipment sales, with a value of $100 million. It was expected that, during 1974, the four-channel equipment would account for 50 per cent of all audio sales. Elvis Presley's album "Aloha Hawaii" became the first long-playing disk in quadraphonic sound to reach $1 million in sales.

The federal government began to take action against the proliferating bootleggers of tape recordings. For the first time, the Federal Bureau of Investigation staged a series of raids on these illegal operators. In one raid in New Jersey, 50 agents seized a half-million dollars' worth of tape-duplicating equipment and 5,000 allegedly bootlegged tapes.

Sales Increase. Total sales of all prerecorded music on records and tapes for 1972 reached a reported $1.92 billion, up $180 million from 1971. Of these, record-album sales reached $1.2 billion and single-disk sales totaled $180 million.

Payola Probe. As a result of widespread charges that *payola* (bribery) was rampant in the record industry, the federal government began investigations in several cities. Drugs and sex allegedly have been used to buy influence with disk jockeys and as presents for recording artists.

In the midst of this development, Clive J. Davis, president of Columbia Broadcasting System Records, was fired amid allegations that he had misused $94,000 in company funds. In September, Mike Curb, head of Metro-Goldwyn-Mayer (MGM) Records, resigned. He had been guiding MGM toward a middle-of-the-road type of music.

"Lady Sings the Blues," starring Diana Ross, led the sales of a large number of successful motion-picture sound-track albums. Other popular sound-track albums included "Jesus Christ Superstar," "Live and Let Die," "Cabaret," and "Godspell."

Television actress Vicki Lawrence emerged as a vocalist with her single hit "The Night the Lights Went Out in Georgia." A single called "Monster Mash," by Bobby Pickett and the Crypt Kickers, was released for the third time and again became a hit.

Classical and Semiclassical. Ragtime, a music born at the turn of the century, finally became seriously accepted as a classical form. At one point, three of the four top-selling albums in classical circles featured the compositions of ragtime pioneer Scott Joplin (1868-1917). Other classical works that found a large audience included a version of Bizet's *Carmen*, conducted by Leonard Bernstein with singers Marilyn Horne and James McCracken.   Leonard Feather

RED CROSS workers in the Philippines and in 31 U.S. military hospitals aided Operation Homecoming in 1973 in the United States. They provided essential services to U.S. prisoners of war (POW) when they were released from POW camps in Southeast Asia. Red Cross chapters at home also assisted the returnees and their families.

The withdrawal of U.S. servicemen from South Vietnam brought to an end one of the biggest American Red Cross service programs for combat forces since World War II. The first Red Cross personnel went to South Vietnam in February, 1962. The last staff members to leave Vietnam were with the American Red Cross Southeast Asia Regional Office, in Saigon, which moved to Bangkok, Thailand.

The American Red Cross National Convention was held in June in New Orleans. During the four-day gathering, delegates focused their attention on such ways to improve community services as broadening the organization's activities in safety and nursing.

E. Roland Harriman resigned as chairman of the American National Red Cross after serving in that post since 1950. He was succeeded by Frank Stanton, vice-chairman of the Columbia Broadcasting System, on April 1. The International Committee elected Eric Martin, former rector of the University of Geneva, Switzerland, as its new president. He succeeds Marcel Naville.   Joseph P. Anderson

Roberta Flack's two Grammy Awards included the year's best record, "The First Time Ever I Saw Your Face." It, in turn, won a Best Song award.

U.S. Church Membership Reported for Bodies with 150,000 or More Members*

African Methodist Episcopal Church	1,166,301
African Methodist Episcopal Zion Church	940,000
American Baptist Association	955,900
American Baptist Churches in the U.S.A.	1,484,393
The American Lutheran Church	2,492,355
Armenian Church of America, Diocese of the (Including Diocese of California)	372,000
Assemblies of God	1,099,606
Baptist Missionary Association of America	199,640
Christian Church (Disciples of Christ)	1,352,211
Christian Churches and Churches of Christ	1,036,460
Christian Methodist Episcopal Church	466,718
Christian Reformed Church	287,114
Church of God (Anderson, Ind.)	155,920
Church of God (Cleveland, Tenn.)	297,103
The Church of God in Christ	425,000
The Church of God in Christ, International	501,000
The Church of Jesus Christ of Latter-day Saints	2,185,810
Church of the Brethren	179,686
Church of the Nazarene	404,732
Churches of Christ	2,400,000
Conservative Baptist Association of America	300,000
The Episcopal Church	3,062,734
Free Will Baptists	203,000
General Association of Regular Baptist Churches	214,000
Greek Orthodox Archdiocese of North and South America	1,950,000
International General Assembly of Spiritualists	164,072
Jehovah's Witnesses	431,179
Jewish Congregations	6,115,000
Lutheran Church in America	3,034,366
The Lutheran Church—Missouri Synod	2,781,297
National Baptist Convention of America	2,668,799
National Baptist Convention, U.S.A., Inc.	5,500,000
National Primitive Baptist Convention, Inc.	1,645,000
Orthodox Church in America	1,000,000
Polish National Catholic Church of America	282,411
Presbyterian Church in the U.S.	946,536
Progressive National Baptist Convention, Inc.	521,692
Reformed Church in America	372,681
Reorganized Church of Jesus Christ of Latter Day Saints	179,763
The Roman Catholic Church	48,460,427
The Salvation Army	358,626
Seventh-day Adventists	449,188
Southern Baptist Convention	12,065,333
Unitarian-Universalist Association	265,408
United Church of Christ	1,895,016
The United Methodist Church	10,334,521
United Pentecostal Church, International	250,000
The United Presbyterian Church in the U.S.A.	2,908,958
Wisconsin Evangelical Lutheran Synod	385,077

*Majority of figures are for the years 1972 and 1973.
Source: National Council of Churches, *Yearbook of American and Canadian Churches* for 1974.

RELIGION. The end of direct U.S. military involvement in Vietnam occasioned a fresh look at the human cost and spiritual devastation in Indochina. It also permitted Americans to become more aware of the state of religion elsewhere in Asia.

The World Council of Churches announced a $5-million fund appeal to begin reconstruction and reconciliation in Indochina. While such appeals would result chiefly in increased contact with the Christian minority in Southeast Asia, there was a new consciousness of the suffering of Buddhists and others.

In India, a strong trend toward religious change was noted among the untouchables, a caste of almost 100 million persons whose past was rooted in Hinduism. Many of these victims of class distinction were turning to Buddhism. In March, for example, 2,500 of them trekked to New Delhi to embrace Buddhism, a classless religion that offers immediate benefits to all believers. More than 2 million untouchables were said to have taken vows symbolizing the move from Hinduism to Buddhism.

Indian Prime Minister Indira Gandhi, in a friendly interreligious gesture, praised Christian missionaries in India, thanking them in particular for their educational work. She took pleasure in noting that "every major religion in the world lived and flourished" in India, and that four of them—Hinduism, Buddhism, Sikhism, and Jainism—originated there. A national Indian council for research into Jainism was established during the year. It marked the 2,500th anniversary of the *nirvana* (salvation) of Jainism's founder, Bhagwan Vardhamana Mahavira, who led a revolt against the spiritualism and the caste system of Hinduism.

Thaw in China? Also in Asia, there were signs that Roman Catholicism was making tentative moves of friendliness toward China's Mao Tse-tung. A Vatican paper, *Fides*, noted "Christian reflections" in Mao's thoughts, and praised the People's Republic of China for its search for justice and for improving the life of the poor. But if there were traces of a thaw there, nothing similar was occurring in China's closest European partner. Albania, in 1967, had become the first self-proclaimed atheist state, one which forbade every form of religious practice. The Vatican acknowledged that few traces of the church remained there in 1973.

In Russia, the continued restrictions on emigration of Jews and the reports of increased Christian growth kept religion in the news. For the first time in years, there were accounts of "revivalist" stirrings among the Christian young in Russia. The prestigious dissenter, author, and Nobel Prize-winner Alexander I. Solzhenitsyn repeatedly praised the Christian past and presence in his nation.

Among Non-Christian faiths in the United States, Black Muslims made news, in part because of their sectarian tensions. Orthodox Black Muslims and the newer sectarians often engaged in violent confronta-

The Dalai Lama of Tibet, now exiled in India, officiated when more than 2,500 Hindu untouchables embraced the Bhuddist faith in New Delhi.

tions. In January, a mass slaying in Washington, D.C., was blamed on one such feud. The Black Muslims still prevailed statistically among the factions and seemed to be growing.

Americans continued to show interest in many Eastern forms of religion, from popular attention to the transcendental meditation associated with the Maharishi Maheṣh Yogi and the visiting "Perfect Master," the 15-year-old guru Maharaj Ji, to more traditional forms. The posthumous publication of *The Asian Journal of Thomas Merton* described earlier serious encounters between a Roman Catholic monk and Buddhist leaders.

Religion in every form remained noticeable and noteworthy. *The Living Bible* and *Jonathan Livingston Seagull*, the latter a more or less spiritual tale of striving, topped the nonfiction and fiction best-seller lists. It was announced that religious book sales had climbed to $9 million in 1972.

Evidence that religious groups were still capable of stirring controversy showed in California, where they successfully forced the state board of education to revise biology textbooks so that evolution would be presented as just one theory, not as fact. A more frivolous sign of continued religious interest was the proliferation of plans for "Bible Land" amusement parks in Ohio, Florida, and Alabama. Martin E. Marty

See also EASTERN ORTHODOX CHURCHES; JEWS; PROTESTANT; ROMAN CATHOLIC CHURCH.

REPUBLICAN PARTY. Republicans won two major contests in the 1973 off-year elections. They elected a Republican governor in Virginia and re-elected a Republican mayor in Cleveland on November 6. However, the party lost the New Jersey governorship, and failed to dislodge the Democrats from their control of a number of major cities.

Virginia voters elected Mills E. Godwin, Jr., to succeed retiring Governor Linwood Holton. Godwin defeated Lieutenant Governor Henry E. Howell, Jr., a liberal Democrat running as an Independent. Godwin, a conservative Democrat, switched to the Republican Party for the 1973 race.

Republican National Chairman George Bush saw the Virginia election as indicating a continuing trend in the South toward the Republican Party. But Democratic National Chairman Robert S. Strauss said Howell would have won if he had run as a Democrat.

In the Cleveland election, Republican Mayor Ralph J. Perk easily won a second term over Democrat Mercedes M. Cotner. Cotner, the city council clerk, entered the campaign in its last two weeks.

In other races, it was a generally bad year for Republicans, and the poor showing at the polls represented a setback for President Richard M. Nixon's dream of establishing a lasting new majority of Republicans. Whether the Watergate scandal, which was very much on the voters' minds, had anything to

John B. Connally, former treasury secretary
in the Nixon Administration, switched from
the Democratic to the Republican Party in May.

do with the Republican losses was a subject for debate. Mr. Nixon, busy trying to clear his name, took no part in the campaign. See WATERGATE.

Republican Losses. In New Jersey, Congressman Charles W. Sandman, Jr., a conservative Republican, lost the contest for governor to Democrat Brendan T. Byrne, a former judge and county prosecutor. As a result of this loss, Republicans controlled only 18 state governorships while the Democrats controlled 32 governorships.

The Republicans also lost major city elections. In New York, Republican State Senator John J. Marchi of Staten Island came in second in a four-man race for mayor. He ran a strong law-and-order campaign, but Democrat Abraham D. Beame won the election to succeed John V. Lindsay.

In Louisville, Ky., Republican C. J. Hyde, former police chief, was defeated for mayor by Democrat Harvey Sloane, a millionaire physician and political newcomer. In Buffalo, N.Y., Republican Stewart M. Levy failed to unseat Democratic Mayor Stanley M. Makowski. In Seattle, Republican City Council President Liem Eng Tuai lost a nonpartisan contest to overturn Democratic Mayor Wes Uhlman.

The Agnew Resignation. In addition to the Watergate scandal, the Republicans were shaken by the resignation of Vice-President Spiro T. Agnew on October 10. Agnew pleaded "no contest" to a charge of federal income tax evasion rather than face charges

of accepting bribes when he was governor of Maryland. He was sentenced to three years of unsupervised probation and a $10,000 fine. See AGNEW, SPIRO THEODORE.

House Republican leader Gerald R. Ford of Michigan was chosen by President Nixon on October 12 to succeed Agnew. He was confirmed by the Senate on December 6. See FORD, GERALD R.

Until his resignation, Agnew was considered a top contender for the Republican presidential nomination in 1976. His political downfall created a gap in the Republican Party's leadership, and his successor, Ford, vowed he would not seek the presidency.

Republican Hopefuls. Two of the most prominent Republican governors in the nation, Nelson A. Rockefeller of New York (who resigned as governor in December) and Ronald Reagan of California, were considered to be in the running for the 1976 presidential nomination. Two other possible candidates for 1976 were former Democratic Governor John B. Connally of Texas and Senator Charles H. Percy of Illinois. Connally, who had served as secretary of the treasury in the Nixon Administration, switched parties and became a Republican on May 2. Percy announced that he had hired a polling organization to sound out his prospects.

A new Republican star came into prominence in Chicago in 1973 – the U.S. Attorney for the Northern District of Illinois, James R. Thompson. He was being discussed as a possible Republican candidate for mayor of Chicago in 1975. He achieved sudden fame in 1973 by prosecuting some of Democratic Mayor Richard J. Daley's top associates. See CHICAGO.

As they looked ahead to the 1974 races, some Republicans were concerned about the effect of Watergate. Congressman John B. Anderson of Illinois, chairman of the House Republican Conference, announced in November that he would not run for the Senate in 1974 against Democratic Senator Adlai E. Stevenson III. Anderson said that a major factor in his decision was the "specter of Watergate."

Bush, who replaced Kansas Senator Robert J. Dole as chairman of the Republican Party in January, announced in November that he would not run for governor of Texas in 1974. Watergate was not a factor in his decision, Bush said.

The Watergate Scandal hurt Republican fund-raising efforts. The party expected to raise $2 million from a $1,000-a-plate dinner in Washington, D.C., in May. However, they took in only $750,000.

In July, the Republican National Committee said contributions had fallen so low that they face a $1-million deficit. Reportedly, Bush agreed to a 10 per cent cut in his $42,500-a-year salary.

Congressman Donald W. Riegle, Jr., of New York switched to the Democratic Party in February. In March, Congressman Paul N. McCloskey, Jr., of California became an Independent.   William McGaffin

See also DEMOCRATIC PARTY; ELECTIONS.

RETAILING sales were substantially better in the United States in all categories in 1973, but profits were not proportionately improved for many retailers because of higher overhead and Phase 4 restrictions. Total U.S. retail sales set new records, with an estimated volume of nearly $488 billion. Fear of continuous price increases spurred sales of "big ticket" items. Such durables as building materials, hardware, automobiles, television sets, and appliances scored the most impressive sales gains.

The Middle East crisis and the fuel shortage began to dampen buying psychology in November. Even so, December sales approached $50 billion, for the best Christmas business in history. There were finally signs of softening demand, however, indicating a slowing of the pace that recorded 13 per cent sales increases nationwide for the first 10 months.

Moreover, rising costs of food and other necessities tended to reduce the discretionary purchasing power of many families. Merchants received strong responses to special sales, but they found that supplies of goods available for special pricing were often limited; manufacturers were confronted with worldwide shortages of cotton, wool, polyester, and other fibers as well as some metals. The shoplifting epidemic was probably stimulated further by rising prices.

Catalog Showrooms continued to mushroom as retailing's latest phenomenon, though there were indications of saturation in some areas. For some of the big general-merchandise discount chains, 1973 was a year of reckoning. Several were forced to retrench because of serious financial difficulties. One large New England chain closed. The country's oldest department store, Gladdings, founded in Providence, R.I., in 1766, sadly announced its closing.

Retailers' Convention. "Look Out, Here Comes Tomorrow" was the theme of the National Retail Merchants Association (NRMA) annual convention in New York City in January, 1973. NRMA has been warning its members to be alert to ever-faster socioeconomic changes with dramatic impact on retailing. New life styles have already altered many facets of merchandising and promotion; stores are responding to growing interest in crafts, natural foods, and more casual living. Increasing numbers of stores are turning to computer technology with point-of-sale systems to learn inventory details, rates of sale, and customer preferences more quickly.

Simpson-Sears in Toronto, Canada, began experimenting successfully with customers placing orders directly to computers by touch-tone telephones, following catalog reference numbers. Some knowledgeable observers believe this in-home buying technique may be sufficiently perfected and accepted for widespread use by the end of the 1970s.   Joseph R. Rowen

RHODE ISLAND. See STATE GOVERNMENT.

Checkout counter scanner, triggered by a special symbol on groceries, sends data on sales to a computer, which updates the store's inventory.

RHODESIA. Hope for a settlement with Great Britain over the 1965 Rhodesian declaration of independence collapsed in 1973. Rhodesian Prime Minister Ian D. Smith said in June that there could be no agreement on Britain's requirement for black majority rule in Rhodesia "as long as Britain maintains the fiction that she can influence events here." Smith also warned the African National Council, a black antigovernment group, not to count on their British "fairy godmother."

On January 9, Rhodesia closed its border with Zambia, charging that African nationalist guerrillas were attacking Rhodesia from bases in Zambia. Rhodesia later reopened the border, but Zambia permanently closed its side and rerouted its valuable copper shipments through Tanzania. See ZAMBIA.

A Guerrilla War that began in December, 1972, escalated in 1973. Guerrillas repeatedly raided white farms, and the government was forced to admit that local Africans were aiding them. In January, the government gave white officials near the Mozambique border emergency powers to levy collective fines against black communities suspected of aiding the guerrillas. Also, blacks who failed to report the presence of guerrillas could be sentenced to 20 years in prison. Churches, schools, and other public places were closed in February, and the government reportedly sent air force jets to attack guerrilla bases.

Government troops sealed off several rural areas during the year, and the government warned that guerrilla activity could spread to towns. Thousands of blacks living in areas where there was terrorist activity were forced to leave their homes and resettle elsewhere. An estimated 2,000 African refugees from Rhodesia began arriving in Zambia in August. They told of atrocities committed by Rhodesian troops in the sealed-off areas. There were also reports that the blacks being held for questioning were tortured.

Niesewand Affair. The government stirred up international protest after arresting a Rhodesian free-lance journalist, Peter Niesewand, in February. Niesewand was secretly tried, reportedly for writing about military actions against guerrillas based in Mozambique. On April 6, he was convicted of violating the official secrets act and was sentenced to two years in prison.

On May 1, the Rhodesian Appeals Court, after reviewing the case in secret, overturned the conviction. However, the government refused to release Niesewand. This brought strong international criticism, especially from Britain. On May 3, Niesewand was released and forced to leave Rhodesia.

Black Areas. In March, the Rhodesian government announced plans to establish all-black tribal areas similar to the black homelands, or Bantustans, in South Africa. The African National Council and other critics denounced the move as a step toward total separation of the races.   John Storm Roberts

See also AFRICA (Facts in Brief Table).

RICHARDSON, ELLIOT LEE (1920-   ), served as U.S. attorney general from May 23 to Oct. 20, 1973. He replaced Richard G. Kleindienst, who was forced to resign because of the Watergate investigation. Richardson resigned rather than obey President Richard M. Nixon's order to fire Watergate prosecutor Archibald Cox. See WATERGATE.

As attorney general, Richardson was serving in his third post in the Nixon Cabinet. He became attorney general four months after President Nixon appointed him secretary of defense on Jan. 4, 1973. He had previously served as secretary of health, education, and welfare from 1970 to 1973, and as undersecretary of state from January, 1969, to June, 1970.

Richardson was born on July 20, 1920, in Boston. He received his A.B. degree in philosophy from Harvard University in 1941, and graduated from Harvard Law School in 1947. During World War II, he served in the Army from 1942 to 1945. He worked as a law clerk for U.S. Appeals Court Judge Learned Hand in 1947 and 1948, and for Supreme Court Justice Felix Frankfurter in 1948 and 1949.

President Dwight D. Eisenhower appointed Richardson assistant secretary of health, education, and welfare in 1956. In 1964, he was elected lieutenant governor of Massachusetts, and in 1966, was elected state attorney general.   Jacquelyn Heath

ROADS AND HIGHWAYS. See TRANSPORTATION.

ROMAN CATHOLIC CHURCH. Tensions decreased within the worldwide Catholic community in 1973, reflecting the gradual but not enthusiastic consolidation of reforms inspired by Vatican Council II. The more progressive members of the church concentrated on broad discussions of basic issues rather than confrontations with church officials. Conservative zealots, however, attracted considerable attention, and the Pentecostal movement made substantial gains.

On the international scene, the Vatican met with no violent opposition, but became painfully aware of trouble brewing in Latin America and in the Middle East. On January 15, Pope Paul VI met with Prime Minister Golda Meir of Israel. Rumors that Mrs. Meir had been coldly received were contradicted by favorable reports from Vatican diplomats and Israeli officials.

On April 9, President Nguyen Van Thieu of South Vietnam had an audience with Pope Paul, despite violent protests in Rome from antiwar radicals. *L'Osservatore Romano,* the Vatican daily newspaper, said that the pope had discussed a possible truce in Vietnam and the problem of political prisoners in the South as well as in the North.

Despite Episcopal condemnations, violence continued in Ireland. On August 7, the Catholic bishops and the Irish Council of Churches announced the formation of a joint Catholic-Protestant working

Pope Paul VI greets Prime Minister Golda Meir of Israel at the Vatican.
January visit was the first between a pope and an Israeli prime minister.

group to attempt to end this tragedy. Many Catholic leaders in Northern Ireland warned the Provisional Wing of the Irish Republican Army that civil war would surely erupt if the terrorist bombings did not cease. Augustinian Professor Gabriel Daly of the Irish School of Economics declared, however, on August 9, that the more frequent the clerical condemnations became, the more they were interpreted as "political" rather than "religious" and thus lost their effectiveness.

U.S. Developments. On the American scene, the Administrative Committee of American Bishops on February 16 rejected as "erroneous, unjust, and immoral" a Supreme Court of the United States decision that a woman has almost unlimited access to abortion during the first six months of pregnancy (see SUPREME COURT OF THE UNITED STATES). Humberto Cardinal Medeiros of Boston urged the 2-million Catholics under his jurisdiction, on May 31, to support legislation designed to protect hospital personnel who do not want to become involved in abortions, sterilization, or contraceptive services. This plea reflected the national pro-life, anti-abortion crusade flourishing in Catholic circles.

Due to rising costs and recent legal decisions, 1973 was a crisis year for Catholic schools. In a series of rulings on June 25, the Supreme Court declared invalid several forms of state and federal aid to non-public schools, and to tuition-paying parents of non-public-school children. Many Catholic elementary and high schools closed their doors. The Administrative Committee of American Bishops called for a constitutional amendment that would allow prayers and religious instruction in public schools and other public institutions.

When Jesuit Father Robert Drinan of Massachusetts ran for and won a seat in the U.S. House of Representatives in 1970, many conservative Catholics objected to "a priest in politics." There was surprisingly little criticism, however, when he became the first congressman to introduce a resolution, on July 31, 1973, calling for the impeachment of President Richard M. Nixon.

Papal Pronouncements. The growth of the Pentecostal movement in Catholic circles continued to draw notice. On June 14, Pope Paul urged Catholics interested in charismatic forms of worship to make sure they were "on the right road" and to refrain from dividing the charismatic from the institutional elements in the church.

The Vatican Congregation for the Clergy, in a letter dated March 21, created a storm of protest by ruling that confession for children about to receive their first Holy Communion should not be deferred until they reach the age of 9 or 10. Pastoral experiments permitting first communicants to postpone confession for psychological and other reasons had been in progress in the United States, but the Vatican stated they must be terminated. Another congregation, that of the Doctrine of the Faith, issued a document on June 24 reaffirming the infallibility of the church and the truth of dogmatic formulas. Swiss theologian Hans Kung, generally presumed to be the target of this pronouncement because of his book *Infallible: An Inquiry* (1971), protested that the congregation was passing public judgment on him before trial.

On January 11, the American Bishops Committee issued a text called *Basic Teachings for Catholic Religious Education*. Its language, however, could easily be misinterpreted, and Father Raymond Brown, the only American member of the Pontifical Biblical Commission in Rome, charged on April 23 that archconservatives are misusing the text "to turn the clock back on genuine theological progress." He was speaking to the National Education Association (NEA) in New Orleans.

A few innovative seminaries had to slow down their reforms in 1973, and in mid-January, the American Jesuits announced plans to close Woodstock College in New York City. The school has been a center of controversy for its radical innovations in life styles.

Clerical celibacy, folk masses, and women's liberation were discussed at Catholic conventions, but somewhat apathetically. However, the influential Joint Committee of Organizations Concerned with the Status of Women in the Church declared on July 23 that the church's refusal to ordain women is an injustice "which should not be allowed to exist."

Labor Issues. Many church leaders supported the strike and boycott in California led by Cesar E. Chavez of the United Farm Workers' Union (UFWU). The action began on April 15 and was directed against certain table-grape growers and segments of the Teamsters Union, which, the UFWU charged, was out to destroy them.

Bishop Joseph Donnelly of Hartford, Conn., one of the bishops who joined the UFWU picket line, addressed the farmworkers on September 24, saying, "I want order and decency in American agriculture, and without a strong labor movement that will not come." Dorothy Day, a founder of the Catholic Worker movement, was arrested August 1 in Fresno, Calif., for taking part in the UFWU picketing. In another labor dispute, Bishop Sidney Metzger of El Paso, Tex., joined by the bishops of New Mexico and Arizona, assisted in the boycott of Farah products and in the effort to unionize Farah plants. This company manufactures slacks and other clothing.

The Ecumenical Movement, except at top official levels, failed to arouse much interest in Catholic circles in 1973. A joint international Anglican-Roman Catholic Commission, which met in Canterbury, England, from August 28 to September 6, agreed on the fundamental ideas of priesthood and ordained ministry. Canon William Purdy of the

Vatican Unity Secretariat, however, warned against hasty optimism about Anglican-Roman Catholic reunion. In December, the commission announced that they had reached "basic agreement" on the nature of the priesthood and the ministry of laymen.

Among the prelates named to the College of Cardinals by Pope Paul on February 2 were Archbishops Humberto Medeiros of Boston, Timothy Manning of Los Angeles, and Luis Aponte Martinez of San Juan, Puerto Rico. The pope also announced, on February 19, that a synod of the world's bishops would be held at the Vatican in October, 1974, to discuss "Evangelization," and that a Holy Year (dedicated to reconciliation) would be held in 1975.

Membership. The *Official Catholic Directory* for 1973, which gives the figures for 1972, reported that the number of Catholics in the United States increased by 69,437. The directory revealed an overall percentage decrease in Catholic population from 23.3 per cent to 23.1 per cent, with a total membership of 48,460,427 in the 50 states. There was a decrease of Catholic school children from 3,105,417 to 2,814,029 in 1972. Converts dropped by 5,087 to 73,925. The total of seminarians was 21,780 as against 22,963 the previous year; the total number of priests, 56,969, as against the previous 57,421; and the total number of sisters, 143,054, down from 146,914.

John B. Sheerin

See also RELIGION.

ROMANIA, trying to raise its standard of living while maintaining its independence, continued its policy of balancing carefully between East and West in 1973. Marshal Andrei Grechko, Russia's minister of defense, visited Romania in April, but President Nicolae Ceausescu emphasized in his May 1 speech that Romania would remain the master of its own destiny.

Romania continued its independent stand at the European Security Conferences in Helsinki and Geneva, speaking up for the rights of smaller nations against the superpowers. It also objected to various proposals for mutual troop reductions in meetings preparing for the Vienna conference that opened on October 30. Romania's independent position in the Communist bloc was underlined by the visits to Peking of General Ion Gheorghe, military chief of staff, in June, and Emil Bodnaras, senior Politburo member, in September.

Internal Affairs. Work was resumed on the Cernavoda-Constanta Canal, which will provide a short cut to the Black Sea for shipping on the Danube River. Work had been suspended in 1953.

Three new governmental bodies were set up in March. The Supreme Council for Economic and Social Development was established to supervise overall economic policy. A council for economic and social organization and a higher financial control court were set up to reduce the power of the bureaucracy and to eliminate corruption. By June, administrative and managerial personnel in the economic ministries had been reduced by one-third, and the industrial associations from 5,400 to 3,600.

Western Ties. On June 4, Romania became the first Soviet-bloc country to join the European Community's generalized preference scheme for developing nations. This allows Romania's industrial products and some of its food products free entry into community countries.

President Ceausescu signed industrial, economic cooperation, and shipping agreements when he visited Italy in May. He signed economic, technological, cultural cooperation, and consular agreements in West Germany in June. He toured eight Latin American countries in August. On December 5, in Washington, D.C., he and President Richard M. Nixon signed a joint statement pledging "the continued development of friendly relations." They also committed the two countries to economic, industrial, and technical cooperation.

The first joint Romanian-U.S. venture was announced in April by the Control Data Corporation of Minneapolis and the Romanian industrial group for the joint manufacture of computer equipment. Control Data will have a 45 per cent interest in the Bucharest firm, and the Romanian government will guarantee the U.S. firm's investment.   Chris Cviic

See also EUROPE (Facts in Brief Table).

ROTARY INTERNATIONAL defined "senior active" memberships more clearly in 1973. The change became effective on January 1. Senior active status is automatic for any Rotarian who has been an active member for 15 years, or is 60 or older and an active member for 10 years, or is 65 and an active member for 5 years, or serves as an officer of Rotary International. Past service members and former Rotarians are also eligible for senior active membership.

The number of young people committed to Rotary throughout the world continued to grow. As of June 30, Interact (for pre-university students) added 195 new clubs, including new groups in Wales and Sierra Leone. Rotaract (for 18- to 28-year-olds) added 269 new clubs, including new groups in the Cayman Islands and Northern Ireland. Interact had an estimated membership of 69,104 in 3,107 clubs in 70 countries. Rotaract had an estimated 32,960 members in 1,648 clubs in 59 countries. As of June 25, there were 736,750 Rotarians in 15,703 clubs in 15 countries and regions. In September, the Rotary Foundation appropriated $4,172,000 for Rotary educational awards in 1974-1975.

Rotary International held its 64th annual convention in Lausanne, Switzerland, in May. William C. Carter of London assumed the presidency of Rotary International on July 1.   Joseph P. Anderson

ROWING. See SPORTS.

RUBBER. See MANUFACTURING.

RUSSIA expanded its trading and technological links with the United States and other advanced Western countries in 1973. But diplomatic relations with the United States cooled after the Middle East war broke out in October. In that war, Russia gave its backing to the Arab states, while the United States backed Israel (see MIDDLE EAST). At home, Russia continued to suppress all forms of dissent vigorously. There was a growing sensitivity toward Western criticism, however, and an apparent readiness to meet it to a degree.

Communist Party chief Leonid I. Brezhnev visited the United States from June 16 to 25, another step in the process of steadily improving relations between the two superpowers. Important accords on a variety of subjects were signed during the visit.

These included agreements on preventing nuclear war, on the basic principles of negotiation for limiting strategic offensive weapons, and on setting up a U.S. commercial center in Moscow and a Soviet trading mission in the United States. The two nations also agreed to cooperate in the peaceful uses of atomic energy; in agricultural, transport, cultural, and scientific exchanges; and in the study of the world's oceans.

Nuclear War Pact. The most generally acclaimed decision, signed on June 22, was to limit offensive strategic armaments by 1974, if at all possible.

Workmen adjust machinery in the new repair and instrument plant of the Kama Auto Works, a new Russian truck-manufacturing project.

Russian men buy gifts for their ladies and do the housework on March 8, Women's Day in Russia, when Soviet women are hailed as men's equals.

Article 4 of the agreement calls for the two nations to consult each other when the risk of nuclear war involves either one. But this article provoked serious misgivings among America's Western allies. And the announcement on August 17 by United States Secretary of Defense James R. Schlesinger that Russia had successfully tested the so-called multiple independent re-entry vehicles (MIRV's), which the United States has had available since 1970, created misgivings in the United States. The Russian success appeared to shift the balance of power and made prospects for the strategic arms limitation talks more difficult. On September 12 and October 8, Russia conducted underground nuclear tests powerful enough to cause a number of small earthquakes in neighboring Finland and damage Finland's seismographic instruments.

During the Arab-Israeli war in October, Russia and the United States kept in close touch, and U.S. Secretary of State Henry A. Kissinger visited Moscow for talks with Brezhnev and other Russian leaders from October 20 to 22. But when President Richard M. Nixon ordered a worldwide alert of U.S. forces on October 25, the Russian press criticized his action as an attempt to draw attention away from new aspects of the Watergate scandal.

Industrial Agreements. On April 12, Deputy Foreign Trade Minister Nikolai Komarov and Armand Hammer, president of Occidental Petro-

leum Corporation signed a 20-year, $8-billion agreement in Moscow. The agreement calls for Occidental and the Bechtel Corporation of San Francisco to help in building a large mineral fertilizer complex at Kuybysev in central Russia. The complex will produce 4 million tons of ammonia and 1-million tons of urea yearly. Occidental also is to deliver large quantities of superphosphoric acid, used in producing the fertilizer. Russia and Occidental will also build a pipeline to carry the liquid ammonia to two huge seaports, one to be built on the Black Sea near Odessa and the other at Nakhodka on Russia's far eastern coast. In return, Russia will give Occidental Petroleum supplies of ammonia and urea from the Kuybysev plant, and also potash.

On September 18, Occidental Petroleum also signed a $110-million agreement to build an American trade center in Moscow by 1977. Other important deals include a five-year cooperation agreement with Monsanto Chemicals for computer applications in its chemical industry and to develop products for rubber-industry compounds; and a 10-year, $500-million agreement with Control Data Corporation to produce computer components in Russia. Ten Russian cosmonauts started their training in the United States on July 8 for the 1975 U.S.-Soviet link-up in space.

However, strong congressional opposition spearheaded by Senator Henry Jackson (D., Wash.) led to the shelving of President Nixon's April request to grant Russian exports so-called most-favored-nation status until Russia allows free emigration to all Jews and anybody else wishing to leave Russia. Perhaps to appease critics in the West, Russia continued to allow limited emigration of Russian Jews even after the outbreak of the Middle East war. The result was that about the same number (31,000) emigrated in 1973 as in 1972.

A Record Harvest of 215 million tons of grain reduced Russia's dependence on imports of Western grain and improved the outlook for Russian exports and for home consumption. Good crops were also reported in sugar beets, potatoes, and sunflower seeds. This good harvest strengthened the position of Dmitri Polyansky, who took over as minister of agriculture on February 3.

Russia's industrial production increased by 7 per cent in the first half of 1973 (planned target 5.8 per cent), and labor productivity grew by 5.4 per cent. Chemical and petrochemical industries increased their output 10 per cent, and engineering and metalworking industries 12 per cent. But the output in food-processing and light industries grew by only 3 per cent, while crude oil, gas, and electric power were below the increases envisaged for 1973 in the revised five-year plan.

On April 3, the government announced a major reorganization affecting some 50,000 industrial enterprises. Under the new scheme, enterprises dealing with the same products are being grouped in giant production associations, each with its own budget and research and development organization. These bodies are modeled on American corporations. They will no longer be under the industrial ministry directorates, but the ministry will retain overall control. Some industries will have an intermediate group of "industrial associations" between the ministries and the "production associations." *Pravda* reported on September 12 that the new scheme was being implemented very slowly and indicated that bureaucrats in various ministries were resisting it.

Brezhnev's Travels. Party chief Brezhnev visited West Germany from May 18 to 22 and signed agreements on economic, industrial, and technological cooperation as well as a protocol on West Germany's Lufthansa Airline's flights over Siberia to Japan. This visit was preceded by short stopovers in Warsaw and East Berlin.

On his return from the United States in June, Brezhnev met with President Georges Pompidou in France. Disputes over the status of West Berlin in West Germany's negotiations with Russia's East European allies caused some tension between Bonn and Moscow. Foreign Minister Walter Scheel of West Germany went to Moscow in November to sort out the Berlin problem and also to obtain more Russian gas and oil. The natural gas pipeline linking West Germany and Russia went into operation on October 10.

European Relations. In Eastern Europe, Russia continued to consolidate its treaties with other Warsaw Pact countries to counter alleged Western ideological subversion. Russia also held several conferences in Eastern Europe to discuss ways of countering that "danger."

At the European Security Conference meetings in Helsinki in July and in Geneva in September, Russia opposed Western demands for a free flow of men and ideas between the East and the West. But on the eve of the Geneva session in September, jamming of Western radio broadcasts beamed to Russia stopped suddenly.

On December 18, the Soviet Union held a three-day conference in Moscow attended by ranking party officials from its inner circle of allies. Participants included representatives from the seven Warsaw Pact powers as well as Cuba and Mongolia. The sessions dealt primarily with ideological and organizational questions and were presumably called to prepare for a world Communist meeting at some future date.

The decision to join the Universal Copyright Convention on May 27 and the sudden ratification of the

About 3,000 delegates from 144 countries, many wearing national costumes, attended the World Congress of Peace Forces held in Moscow in October, 1973.

Russian physicist Andrei D. Sakharov received repeated official reprimands in 1973 for his outspoken criticism of Soviet Union policies.

human rights covenants that Russia had signed in 1968 represented an attempt to forestall Western demands for liberal changes within Russia itself as part and parcel of the diplomatic and military détente. Premier Aleksei N. Kosygin's visit to Yugoslavia in September was another step in improving Russian-bloc relations.

On September 20, the government announced the formation of a state copyright agency that would serve as a clearing house for the publication abroad of works by Soviet writers and of foreign works in the Soviet Union. Boris Pankin, a former editor of *Komsomolskaya Pravda*, the Young Communist League newspaper, was named to head the new All-Union Copyright Agency. He was chosen at a meeting of 14 unions representing writers, artists, composers, journalists, scientists, filmmakers, and others.

In discussing his new position, Pankin pointed out that since 1917, Russia had published translations of the works of writers from 101 countries, including 1,200 authors from Socialist countries, 520 French authors, 470 German, 320 American, some 300 British, 130 Italian, and about 500 authors from Asian and African countries.

Russia and China. There was no improvement in relations with the People's Republic of China. Russia accused China of setting up a "second front" against Russia in Asia. On August 15, Brezhnev charged China with "rabid anti-Sovietism and subversive action against Socialist countries." But he proposed a security pact for Asia, with China and Russia among its signers. In a speech in Tashkent on September 24, he disclosed that Russia had offered China a nonaggression pact in June, but that China "did not even deign to reply to this completely concrete proposal."

Relations with Japan did not significantly improve, either. Premier Kakuei Tanaka visited Moscow in October, but Russia refused to return the four northernmost Kuril Islands, which Russian troops had occupied in 1945.

Domestic Affairs. The Soviet Communist Party's Central Committee passed a resolution in April approving "the work done by the Politburo for a lasting peace," thus endorsing the Brezhnev foreign-policy line. Pyotr Shelest, former boss of the Ukraine, and Gennady Voronov were dropped from the Politburo and replaced by chief Yuri Andropov of the KGB (secret police), Foreign Minister Andrei Gromyko, and Defense Minister Marshal Andrei Grechko.

Suppression of dissidents continued with unabated vigor. In May, historian Andrei Amalrik was rearrested after serving a three-year sentence for alleged anti-Soviet propaganda. In August, he was secretly sentenced to another three years in prison. Novelist Alexander Solzhenitsyn and physicist Andrei D. Sakharov were harassed, but at liberty. However, their charges that human improvements were designed to aid relations with the West infuriated the Russian leadership and led to an organized campaign of abuse against them. On August 28, it was revealed that 40 members of the Soviet Academy of Sciences had urged Sakharov to stop his public criticism of the Kremlin's domestic and foreign policies. That same day, Sakharov and other Soviet dissidents appealed to United Nations Secretary General Kurt Waldheim for help in dissuading Moscow from using compulsory psychiatric hospitalization to punish critics of the government. Sakharov sent his appeal via a telephone message to the International League for the Rights of Man, a nongovernmental organization in New York City.

In September, Pyotr Yakir and Victor Krasin, who had been arrested in 1972 for "anti-Soviet propaganda," were each sentenced to three years in prison to be followed by three years of exile. But both were released in October. Western delegates to a world psychiatric conference held in Tiflis and Erevan in October were invited to visit the dissident General Pyotr Grigorenko, who was arrested in 1970. Grigorenko had championed the exiled Crimean Tartars, who have not been allowed to return to their Black Sea homeland from Soviet Central Asia. Two psychiatrists accepted the invitation and one of them reported that Grigorenko would be released shortly.   Chris Cviic

See also EUROPE (Facts in Brief Table).

RWANDA. See AFRICA.

SAFETY might benefit from the lower speed limits and other measures caused by the 1973 energy crisis, the National Safety Council said in December. If fuel conservation and other measures become widespread, there could be as many as 14,000 fewer deaths per year from motor-vehicle accidents in the United States, the council estimated.

The failure of most of the driving public to use safety belts and harnesses—now on nearly all passenger cars—costs about 14,000 lives annually, the council said. Legal safety standards effective with 1974 model cars required seat belts interlocked with ignition circuits so the cars cannot start unless belts are in use.

Accidental Deaths and Death Rates

| | 1972 | | 1973† | |
	Number	Rate††	Number	Rate††
Motor Vehicle	56,600	27.1	56,800	27.2
Work	14,100	6.8	14,100	6.7
Home	27,000	12.9	26,500	12.6
Public	23,500	11.3	24,000	11.5
Total*	117,000	56.6	117,000	56.8

†For 12-month period up to Oct. 1, 1973.
††Deaths per 100,000 population.
*The total does not equal the sum of the four classes because *Motor Vehicle* includes some deaths also included in *Work* and *Home*.

Source: National Safety Council estimates

Laws requiring the use of the belts were reported under consideration in 34 states, and bills were introduced in 21 state legislatures. In midsummer, Puerto Rico passed a mandatory-use bill to take effect on Jan. 1, 1974.

Controversy over airbag systems for U.S. cars was expected to continue in 1974, though the bags became available in some cars. They inflate automatically on impact to protect the car's occupants. The system's proponents said it needed no more "real world" tests. Reports of accidents involving vehicles equipped with airbags seemed to support their claim.

Safety Recalls. More than 5.6 million motor vehicles were recalled by manufacturers because of safety-related defects during 1973. More than 12-million have been called back since the safety-recall law was signed in late 1966. Less than half of the cars four years old or older are actually brought back to dealers, the safety council said.

Bicycle Safety grew in importance during 1973, with more than 71 million estimated in use in the United States and more than 14 million produced each year. Bicycles were cited on September 9 as the most hazardous product on the market by the new U.S. Consumer Product Safety Commission.

The agency said its data showed bicycles were involved in some 372,000 injuries requiring hospital emergency-room treatment annually. The safety council said there were about 1,100 bicycle fatalities in 1973, about the same as in 1972 and 29 per cent over 1971's toll.

An experimental automobile, testing the effectiveness of airbags in protecting passengers, crashes into a barrier at 50 miles per hour.

Local laws for bicycle safety varied, but some requirements were slowly becoming standard. They included requirements for reflectors, nonslip pedals, and brakes able to stop the bicycle in 15 feet from 15 miles per hour.

Work Safety. In a major safety report, the U.S. Bureau of Mines on February 12 blamed "pedestrian" mine-safety practices and "obviously deficient" federal regulations for the Sunshine mine disaster in May, 1972. An underground fire in the Kellogg, Ida., silver mine killed 91 miners by asphyxiation. At least 18 failures to follow good practice were cited; many of the failures were not covered by "mandatory" regulations, nor even by "advisory" rules.

In February, the Department of Labor released the first data it has collected on occupational injuries and illnesses under the 1970 Occupational Safety and Health Act. It showed nearly 4,300 work-related deaths in the six months it covered.

Howard Pyle, president of the National Safety Council since 1959, retired and was succeeded in October by Vincent L. Tofany, former New York State motor vehicles commissioner. Douglas W. Toms, head of the National Highway Traffic Safety Administration, was replaced by James B. Gregory, a former oil company official. Gregory assumed the post on August 3.   Vincent L. Tofany

SAILING. See BOATING.

472

ST. LOUIS voters elected a new mayor, former City Controller John H. Poelker, in April, 1973. He succeeded Alfonzo J. Cervantes, who had held the office for eight years. Poelker and Cervantes fought a hotly contested battle for the Democratic Party nomination in the March primary, with Poelker winning a narrow victory. Poelker then defeated Joseph L. Badaracco, a Republican and president of the Board of Aldermen, in the general election.

Teachers' Strike. St. Louis public-school teachers went on strike on January 22 for the first time in the city's history. Two teachers' organizations, the St. Louis Teachers Association and the St. Louis Teachers Union, voted to strike in defiance of a temporary court injunction. The teachers were seeking an immediate pay increase.

The board of education at first tried to keep the city's schools open for its 103,000 pupils, because only three-fourths of the schoolteachers were members of the striking organizations. On the second day of the strike, however, the board ordered all schools closed. The strike ended after the teachers voted on February 18 to accept a $1,000 salary increase paid over an 18-month period.

New Train Service. Amtrak, the nation's passenger rail service, began running turbotrains between St. Louis and Chicago on October 1. The new trains, leased from a French rail-equipment manufacturer, seat 294 passengers and are capable of traveling 125

miles per hour (mph). Amtrak held speeds down to 79 mph, however, until signaling systems could be improved. The new trains make two round trips a day between Chicago and St. Louis.

The Cost of Living in the St. Louis area went up 5.1 per cent between June, 1972, and June, 1973. According to a U.S. Department of Labor report issued on June 15, an average family of four would require an annual budget of $11,258 to live in "moderate comfort" in the area. The report listed St. Louis as the least expensive of the 25 large U.S. urban areas where living costs were highest.

Changes instituted by the U.S. Office of Budget and Management in defining metropolitan area boundaries resulted in a slight increase in the population of the St. Louis area. According to a report released by the U.S. Bureau of the Census in September, the estimated population of St. Louis was 2,410,163 persons as of July, 1972.

On August 24, St. Louis and the U.S. Department of Housing and Urban Development agreed to demolish the Pruitt-Igoe low-income housing project. A 1972 effort to save the project by creating open spaces failed.

Almost all of the U.S. Army's records on servicemen who either retired or were discharged between 1912 and the early 1960s were destroyed in a fire on July 12 at the giant U.S. Military Records Center in suburban Overland.

James M. Banovetz

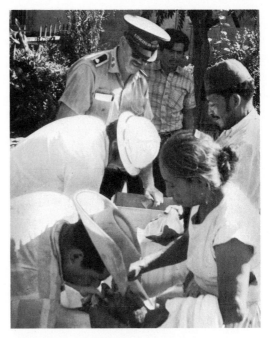

Salvation Army workers man food-distribution center in Nicaragua for victims of earthquake that devastated Managua in late December, 1972.

SALVATION ARMY. A significant highlight in 1973 was the observance of "National Family Week" from May 28 to June 5 and the Salvation Army's concentration on Family Focus 1973. In keeping with this theme, guidelines were suggested by the Army on how to achieve a successful family life. The guidelines say that a family should endeavor to eat at least one meal a day together, share the household work, make time for family fun, and pray together.

The Salvation Army is one of six national voluntary youth-serving organizations that received grants totaling $512,174 to develop Education for Parenthood programs for teen-age boys and girls. The other organizations receiving grants are Boys' Clubs of America, Boy Scouts of America, Girl Scouts of the U.S.A., National Federation of Settlements and Neighborhood Centers, and Save the Children Federation (Appalachian Program).

Education for Parenthood is designed to prepare adolescents for parenthood by teaching them about child development and the role of parents. The first phase of the program concentrates on the development and improvement of parenthood education courses within the schools.

In the second phase, the national voluntary organizations will develop and put into practice their own programs outside the school system to prepare teenagers for parenthood.

Joseph P. Anderson

SAN FRANCISCO-OAKLAND. Mayor Joseph L. Alioto of San Francisco broadened his efforts in 1973 to lure local travelers from private autos to public transit. San Francisco reduced Golden Gate Bridge tolls for passengers in carpools. In addition, the city used toll revenues to subsidize the operation of 188 buses and to create a fleet of four commuter boats. The four boats, on order at a cost of $4.2 million each, are capable of hauling 2,500 passengers across the bay within 30 minutes.

BART System. Although still plagued by technical troubles, most of the Bay Area Rapid Transit (BART) system went into operation in 1973. The east San Francisco Bay section was completed on May 22 with the opening of a line between Oakland and suburbs in Contra Costa County. The San Francisco section opened on November 3 between the downtown financial district and Daly City.

However, the state would not allow opening of the BART tunnel under San Francisco Bay, which connects the San Francisco and Oakland sections of the transit system. Until computer problems in detecting the exact location of trains are worked out, state authorities considered operation of the total system to be too dangerous.

Local Politics. Mayor Alioto announced on October 2 that he would run for governor of California in 1974. Alioto declared himself vindicated of charges that he once had ties with the Mafia.

In Oakland, Black Panther leader Bobby Seale became a serious candidate for mayor, after finishing second in the April 17 election. None of the nine candidates won a clear majority, so a run-off election was set. Seale campaigned in shopping centers wearing tweed suits and talking about peaceful reform. However, his efforts failed to unseat incumbent Mayor John H. Reading, who won the run-off election on May 15.

On January 18, vandals in Oakland opened valves on five tanks of reclaimed auto engine oil, releasing 200,000 gallons into San Francisco Bay. At least 280 birds were killed as a result of the contamination, which threatened a wide stretch of the bay's eastern shore. Over 200 military and civilian workers were used in the $500,000 cleanup operation.

Alcatraz, the former federal prison built on an island in San Francisco Bay, opened to the public for the first time on November 1. The National Park Service, which took over management of Alcatraz on April 1, began conducting guided tours.

The cost of living rose 5.3 per cent in the San Francisco-Oakland area between June, 1972, and June, 1973. An average family of four would need $12,324 to live in "moderate comfort," according to a U.S. Department of Labor survey released on June 15.   James M. Banovetz

SAN MARINO. See EUROPE.

SASKATCHEWAN. See CANADA.

SAUDI ARABIA cut off all oil shipments to the United States and the Netherlands on Oct. 20, 1973. By this action, King Faisal confirmed Saudi Arabian support for the Arab cause against Israel and demonstrated his determination to play a role in the Middle East commensurate with the nation's wealth. See MIDDLE EAST.

The threat of subversion against existing regimes in Arabia caused King Faisal to work for improved relations with Iran and Ethiopia as well as the Persian Gulf states. Cooperative defense agreements signed with Yemen (Şan'ā'), Kuwait, Bahrain, Oman, and Qatar guaranteed them Saudi support in the event of an attack by Yemen (Aden).

To bolster its military arsenal for such an eventuality, Saudi Arabia agreed to pay Great Britain $600 million for an air defense system and purchased jet aircraft and naval attack craft from France and the United States.

The 1972 formula giving Saudi Arabia 25 per cent of Western-developed oil operations ensured more revenue. The share would grow to 51 per cent by 1982, but Saudi officials indicated they may demand an immediate 51 per cent of the Arabian American Oil Company. Even without that change, nearly all the nation's $7.8-billion annual budget—70 per cent above the previous one—would have been paid for by oil revenue.   William Spencer

See also MIDDLE EAST (Facts in Brief Table).

SAXBE, WILLIAM BART (1916-   ), Republican senator from Ohio, was confirmed as U.S. attorney general by the Senate on Dec. 17, 1973. He succeeded Elliot L. Richardson, who resigned October 20 (see RICHARDSON, ELLIOT L.). Saxbe, elected to the Senate in 1968, had indicated that he would not seek re-election.

Although an outspoken critic of President Richard M. Nixon on Watergate and the Vietnam War, Saxbe supported the President on many other issues and campaigned for the Nixon-Agnew ticket in 1972. Saxbe expressed confidence that the President was not implicated in the Watergate scandal.

Born in Mechanicsburg, Ohio, Saxbe received his law degree from Ohio State University in 1948. A year earlier, he had been elected to the Ohio House of Representatives, where he served until 1955. He also served from 1957 to 1958, and from 1963 to 1968, as Ohio attorney general. In that post, he was regarded as a tough crime fighter and made his office responsible for criminal investigations.

Saxbe classifies himself as a hard-liner on law enforcement, and advocates capital punishment as a deterrent to crime. Law and order was an important theme in his 1968 Senate campaign, but at the same time he defended the rights of protestors. He also has called for gun controls and has long been a civil rights advocate. In his spare time, he likes to fish and hunt quail.   Kathryn Sederberg

SCHLAFLY, PHYLLIS (1924-   ), author, lecturer, and politician, was a leader in 1973 in efforts to defeat the Equal Rights Amendment (ERA) to the United States Constitution. The amendment would guarantee equal rights for women. She helped organize anti-ERA groups in several states and directed letter-writing campaigns urging legislators to vote against their state ratification of the amendment. She also publishes a conservative newsletter, *The Phyllis Schlafly Report.*

Phyllis Stewart Schlafly was born in St. Louis. She received an A.B. degree from Washington University in 1944 and an M.A. from Radcliffe College in 1945.

She entered politics during the 1950s, serving as a delegate to the Republican National Conventions in 1956, 1964, and 1968. She was first vice-president of the National Federation of Republican Women from 1965 to 1967. She ran unsuccessfully for Congress in 1970.

Mrs. Schlafly wrote *A Choice Not an Echo* (1964) in support of Senator Barry Goldwater's (R., Ariz.) bid for the presidency. Since 1962 she has aired conservative viewpoints as a radio commentator on various programs. She married John F. Schlafly, a lawyer, in 1949. They have six children and live in Alton, Ill.   Paul C. Tullier

SCHOOL. See CIVIL RIGHTS; EDUCATION; Section One, FOCUS ON EDUCATION.

SCIENCE AND RESEARCH. The search for new sources of energy became a major research priority in 1973. Shortages of gasoline and fuel oil, made worse by the Middle East war, brought home forcibly the limits of the world's fossil fuel supply. On November 7, President Richard M. Nixon announced a $10-billion crash energy-research program and promised he would request more funds from Congress for energy research in the near future.

Researchers began seeking new methods to use the sun's radiant energy, to drill into the earth's core and capture its internal heat, and to harness fusion – the conversion of hydrogen into helium. Of the three, fusion appeared the most promising, and the Atomic Energy Commission announced that commercial fusion reactors might be operating by the 1990s.

The liquid-metal fast breeder reactor, which had been the Nixon Administration's major hope for new sources of commercial energy, encountered some trouble. In the reactor, a fission process converts the plentiful uranium 238 isotope along with plutonium into energy and more plutonium. The Administration had argued that the fast breeder was necessary because the world's supply of uranium 235, which fuels conventional reactors, was limited. Environmentalists, however, maintained that the fast breeder would generate immense stockpiles of hazardous radioactive material. They won a significant victory when a federal appeals court ruled on April 28 that the government must file an environmental impact statement for the entire project. See ENERGY.

Proscience. A poll of the American public conducted by the Gallup Poll found little evidence of any antiscience feelings. The pollsters said that 54 per cent of those questioned believed that science did more good than harm, while only 7 per cent held the opposite view. With the same optimism, the public also expressed the belief that science would eventually solve society's problems. In a prestige list of professions, the participants rated scientists second, only slightly behind physicians.

Federal Action. While scientists could take heart that reports of a popular dissatisfaction with science had proven unfounded, they had less cause for celebration of their treatment by the federal government. Apart from funds for military and energy research, and cancer and heart disease studies, President Nixon's budget called for either the same or less federal spending for most areas of research.

The President also abolished the executive Office of Science and Technology, the agency that advised the government in scientific matters. It was established in the wake of the first Russian satellite launching of 1957. The head of that office, Edward E. David, Jr., resigned on January 3 and his post – personal science adviser to the President – was abolished. That function was transferred to the director of the National Science Foundation, H. Guyford Stever, but he was to report to the President's economic adviser,

Secretary of the Treasury George P. Shultz, not to the President himself. Many scientists believed that they had thus lost a primary voice in government.

The Nixon Administration also moved to eliminate training grants – the primary form of support for postgraduate and postdoctoral researchers. But a protest from thousands of scientists, including nine Nobel winners, forced a reconsideration of this Administration proposal.

Science Indicators. A National Science Foundation report, *Science Indicators, 1972*, was sent to Congress by the President on September 5. It represented the first results of an effort to develop indicators of the state of the nation's science enterprise. According to the report, such indicators are needed to provide an early warning of trends and events that might reduce the ability of U.S. science and technology to meet the nation's needs.

The report showed that the percentage of the U.S. gross national product spent on research and development has been declining for several years. There has been a steady decline since 1967, when an estimated 3 per cent of the gross national product was devoted to research and development efforts. By 1971, this had dropped to 2.6 per cent. In the period from the early 1960s to the early 1970s, Great Britain and France also reduced research and development, while Russia, Japan, and West Germany increased theirs. The United States reduction is the most marked, while Russia and Japan have had the largest increases. By 1971, the figure for Russia had climbed to 3 per cent from about 2.3 per cent in 1963, while Japan's had risen from 1.4 per cent to about 1.8 per cent.

New Projects. A joint commission set up to facilitate United States-Russian scientific cooperation held its first meetings in March and formulated plans for a joint Apollo-Soyuz docking in space in 1975. It also discussed cooperation in energy, computer, and agricultural research. However, the entire project was threatened when the U.S. National Academy of Sciences sent a sharp note to the Soviet Academy to protest what it called the "harassment" of Andrei D. Sakharov, a noted Russian physicist who had openly criticized some of his government's policies.

Project Cyclops, a study funded by the National Aeronautics and Space Administration (NASA), concluded that, "We now have the technological capability of making an effective search for extraterrestrial life." The study recommended a $600-million-per-year program to begin the search. In view of the budget cuts suffered by NASA, however, life in outer space may have to wait much longer before it might be found. Robert J. Bazell

See also the various science articles.

SCULPTURE. See VISUAL ARTS.
SENEGAL. See AFRICA.
SERVICE CLUBS. See KIWANIS INTERNATIONAL; LIONS INTERNATIONAL; ROTARY INTERNATIONAL.

SHIP AND SHIPPING. Most United States ocean shipping companies had a good year in 1973, thanks to a strong domestic economy, expanding world trade, the absence of labor disputes, and a more favorable regulatory climate. However, the industry continued to suffer from overcapacity on North Atlantic and Pacific trade routes, rising fuel costs, predatory rate cutting on established trade routes by third parties, and the maritime policies of other countries favoring their own vessels.

As the year ended, some experts feared that the international shipment of grain and other freight could drop by 20 per cent in 1974 if the fuel shortage continued. To conserve fuel, shipping lines began operating their vessels at slower speeds. As a result of the fuel shortage, the Federal Maritime Commission was working out a ranking system for cargo that gave first priority to oil shipments to the United States.

U.S. Shipbuilding. The dollar volume of orders for commercial shipping in private shipyards was estimated at $3.5 billion, more than $400 million over 1972 and $2.4 billion more than in 1971. The total dollar volume of both merchant and naval shipbuilding, for ships of 1,000 gross dead weight tons or more, in United States yards was about $6 billion compared with $5.7 billion at the end of 1972.

The largest merchant ship ever built in a U.S. shipyard, the 1,094-foot, 230,000-ton tanker *Brooklyn*, was launched on June 30. The $80-million supertanker can carry 1.5 million barrels of oil.

The United States shipbuilding boom was aided by the Merchant Marine Act of 1970, which, for the first time in history, extended shipbuilding and operating subsidies to tankers and liquid natural gas (LNG) carriers. Also, until October, 1973, it was assumed that the United States would rely increasingly on oil imports from the Middle East to meet its energy needs. Of the 93 merchant ships under construction in American yards on October 31, 50 were oil tankers and 9 were LNG carriers.

Late in the year, however, the Arab embargo on oil shipments caused shipbuilders to worry whether there would be enough energy available to maintain construction schedules, and whether shipping companies would continue to order vessels if they could not obtain fuel to operate them.

World Shipbuilding. According to Lloyd's Register of Shipping, there were 2,157 merchant ships under construction throughout the world on Sept. 30, 1973, a 9 per cent increase over the same date in 1972. Shipbuilding orders, including those under construction, increased to 4,678 from 3,612 in 1972.

Gross tonnage of vessels on order increased to 114.3 million tons, the highest figure ever recorded. This was a 44 per cent increase from the 78.9 million in September, 1972.   Kenneth E. Schaefle

SHOOTING. See HUNTING; SPORTS.

SHORTER, FRANK (1948-   ), a long-distance runner, was awarded the Amateur Athletic Union's Sullivan Award in 1973. The award is given annually to the best American amateur athlete. Shorter won the 1972 Olympic Games marathon race in Munich, the first American to do so since 1908. He also holds the U.S. 2-mile indoor and U.S. 10,000-meter outdoor records.

Shorter was born in Middletown, N.Y., the second of 10 children of Samuel Shorter. His family later moved to Taos, N. Mex., when his father decided to give up a sizable medical practice to work in a mission clinic on an Indian reservation. Shorter attended Yale University and then the medical school at the University of New Mexico, but dropped out to work in 1969. He enrolled in the University of Florida Law School in 1971.

Track experts are amazed at Shorter's unique ability to pace himself almost perfectly. If he decides to run for an hour at a "6-minute pace" (a mile in 6 minutes), he will finish within 300 feet of the 10-mile distance after 60 minutes. He says he can "feel" his time for a quarter mile within half a second. He is in constant training since, as he defines it, "running is 98 per cent training and only 2 per cent competition."   Foster Stockwell

SIERRA LEONE. See AFRICA.
SIKKIM. See ASIA.
SINGAPORE. See ASIA.

U.S. Shipbuilding Soars

■ Number of ships under construction
■ Total weight (millions of tons)
■ Value in dollars

3.4 bil.

3.6

1.5

800 mil.

93

387 mil.

45 0.5

63

*1963   *1968   1973
*End of year   Oct.

Source: Shipbuilders Council of America

SIRICA, JOHN J. (1904-   ), chief judge of the U.S. District Court for the District of Columbia, played a leading role in breaking open the Watergate case in 1973. Sirica was not satisfied that the seven defendants charged with breaking into Democratic Party headquarters in the Watergate Hotel in Washington, D.C., in 1972 told the whole truth at their trial. So he "provisionally" sentenced the men to maximum prison terms and recommended that they cooperate fully with a federal grand jury and with the Senate committee set up to investigate the Watergate case. Shortly afterward, defendant James W. McCord, Jr., told his story to the Senate committee and implicated high Administration officials.

Later in the year, Sirica presided over the legal battle between the White House and Archibald Cox, the special Watergate prosecutor who had subpoenaed presidential tape recordings. Sirica ordered the President to turn over the tapes and then appointed a panel of technical experts to determine whether they had been altered. He also probed the reasons two tapes turned up missing. See WATERGATE.

Sirica was born in Waterbury, Conn., on March 19, 1904. He earned his law degree from Georgetown University law school in 1926. He practiced law and was active in Republican politics until 1957, when President Dwight D. Eisenhower appointed him a federal judge. He became chief judge of the district court in 1971. Darlene R. Stille

SKIING. Gustavo Thoeni of Italy and Annemarie Proell of Austria won the World Cup championships in 1973 for the third consecutive year. American skiers did poorly again.

The World Cup series consists of 24 races for men – 8 special slalom, 8 giant slalom, and 8 downhill – and 24 similar races for women. The competition, from December 1972, to March, 1973, was held in Europe, the United States, Canada, and Japan.

The 19-year-old Proell set three notable records. She won all 8 women's downhill races, becoming the first skier, male or female, to sweep one discipline. In all, she won 11 races during the year for a career total of 27, the most ever by any skier. And her series total of 297 points was the highest ever posted.

Thoeni, a 22-year-old customs guard, captured the men's title in a close battle with David Zwilling of Austria, 166 points to 151. Austria easily won the Nations Cup for the best overall score, combining men's and women's results.

The United States finished sixth in the combined standing, sixth in men's, and fourth in women's. The skiing Cochrans captured the highest American series placings. Bob Cochran finished 8th among the men, and his sisters Marilyn and Barbara were 8th and 21st, respectively, among the women. Marilyn won a special slalom at Chamonix, France, and a giant slalom at Naeba, Japan. Bob took first place in the giant slalom and second in the special slalom at

South Lake Tahoe, Nev., in the season's last meet.

Bob Cochran also won the United States and National Collegiate Athletic Association downhill titles, and sister Lindy captured the women's national championship in special slalom. The Cochrans – Marilyn, Barbara, Bob, and Lindy – are the children of Gordon (Mickey) Cochran of Richmond, Vt., who was named national coach for the 1973-1974 season.

Two Americans excelled in Nordic events. Martha Rockwell of Putney, Vt., won three United States and two North American titles in cross-country. Jerry Martin of Minneapolis captured the United States and North American jumping championships.

The Professionals. Jean-Claude Killy of France, winner of three gold medals in the 1968 Winter Olympics, returned to competitive skiing after a four-year retirement and became world professional champion.

The 14 professional meets pitted two skiers simultaneously on identical adjacent courses in special slalom and giant slalom races. There were $400,000 in purses, including a $40,000 bonus for the winner. Killy fell twice in his first meet and earned $750. Six weeks later, he finally won a race. When the 4½-month circuit ended, he had won the title and $68,625, including bonus money.

Why did Killy return at age 29? Said Killy, "If there's money to be won, I'm interested." Frank Litsky

Gustavo Thoeni, 22-year-old customs guard from Italy, won an unprecedented third straight World Cup skiing championship.

SOCCER. The North American Soccer League enjoyed the most successful season in its seven-year history in 1973. Its nine professional teams – seven in the United States and two in Canada – averaged 6,290 spectators per game and the champion Philadelphia Atoms 11,382, both records. Commissioner Phil Woosnam said the league hoped to expand to 32 teams eventually.

Philadelphia defeated the Dallas Tornado, 2-0, in the play-off final on August 25 in Dallas. The Atoms, created in February, had a local owner and a local coach, and most of the players were Americans. The league's scoring champion and Rookie of the Year was Kyle Rote, Jr., of Dallas, son of a one-time New York Giants football star.

Los Angeles Maccabee won the United States Open title, Ajax of Amsterdam the European Cup, Liverpool the European Union Cup and the English League first division, AC Milan of Italy the European Cup Winners Cup, Glasgow Celtic the Scottish League first division (for the eighth straight year), and Glasgow Rangers the Scottish Cup.

Sunderland scored an astounding upset by defeating Leeds, 1-0, in the English Football Association Cup final on May 5 in Wembley Stadium. Sunderland, a second-division team, was 250-1 in pretournament betting. In the richest player transaction in soccer history, AC Milan sold Pierino Prati to Roma of Italy for $1,036,665.   Frank Litsky

SOCIAL SECURITY benefits in the United States were increased 11 per cent in 1973. Under the provisions of a new law passed by Congress on December 21, the amount of a person's annual income subject to social security tax was raised from $10,800 to $13,200 effective Jan. 1, 1974. Increases for recipients of social security payments will occur in two stages, in April and July, 1974. The maximum payment to a recipient would be $304 as of July; the minimum, $93.80. See OLD AGE; SOCIAL WELFARE.

Raise Earnings Limit. Effective on Jan. 1, 1974, the annual earnings limit for social security beneficiaries under 72 years of age will increase from $2,100 to $2,400. For earnings in excess of this amount, $1 in benefits will be withheld for each $2 of earnings. This is expected to provide an additional $200 million in benefits for 1.5 million elderly and disabled persons in 1974.

Aid for Aged, Blind, and Disabled. Under 1972 legislation, the federal government takes over from the states the public-assistance programs for the needy, aged, blind, and disabled on Jan. 1, 1974. The 1972 legislation assured recipients at least $130 a month for individuals and $195 a month for couples. But 1973 legislation raised these levels, effective Jan. 1, 1974, from $130 to $140 for individuals and from $195 to $210 for couples. As of July, individuals will receive another increase of $6 and couples, $9. In addition, the first $20 of monthly income from

any source will not be considered in determining eligibility under the program. By July, the average elderly person will have a minimum income of $186 a month for individuals and $310 a month for couples. To ensure that recipients will not lose any income when the federal program takes over, states will be required to make up the difference between existing payments, if higher, and the federal income.

Essential Persons Covered. The 1973 social security legislation extends eligibility to so-called essential persons who are not yet 65 years old. An estimated 125,000 persons, mostly wives, will now receive additional federal payments. The legislation also requires that preference in hiring under the new Supplemental Security Income Program be given to present state and local employees who will be displaced when the new program takes over.

Social Security Numbers and Records. Under new regulations proposed by Department of Health, Education, and Welfare Secretary Caspar W. Weinberger, applicants for social security numbers must submit evidence to establish identity, age, citizenship, and alien status. Beginning in 1973, all numbers are being issued from the Baltimore, Md., headquarters because of their increasing importance.

Robert M. Ball resigned as commissioner for social security in January. He was succeeded by James B. Cardwell, department controller.   Joseph P. Anderson

Social Security Increases

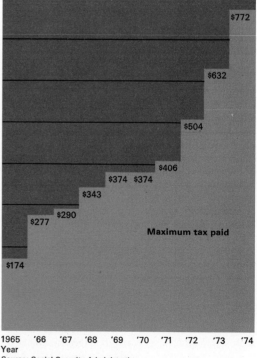

1965   '66   '67   '68   '69   '70   '71   '72   '73   '74
Year
Source: Social Security Administration

SOCIAL WELFARE rolls were reduced in 1973 for the first time in seven years. At the same time, the growth in U.S. welfare costs slowed significantly.

Department of Health, Education, and Welfare figures showed that 14.8 million persons were receiving public assistance as of June 30. This was down by 249,000 persons, or 1.7 per cent, from the previous year. Federal-state welfare programs cost $19.4 billion in 1973, an increase of $1.1 billion, or 6 per cent, over 1972. In that year, spending had increased by 17.4 per cent and the number of recipients exceeded 15 million.

The last time the nation's social welfare caseload decreased was in 1967, when a net loss of about 100,000 recipients decreased the total by 1.2 per cent to 7.7 million persons. In 1968, the rolls showed an increase to 9.1 million, and in 1972 to 15.1 million.

Most of the 1973 reduction in caseload took place among the elderly, who were removed from welfare rolls when they began receiving higher social security benefits, and among those persons on general assistance. The old age assistance caseload dropped 180,000, or 8.9 per cent, to 1.8 million persons. The number on general assistance fell 136,000, or 15.3 per cent, to 760,000.

The 10.9 million recipients of Aid to Families with Dependent Children in 1973 represented a decrease of only about 5,000 persons. This was a marked change over 1972, however, when the caseload had mushroomed 6.8 per cent, or nearly 700,000 persons. The aid to the blind caseload decreased 4.1 per cent to 77,900, and aid to the permanently and totally disabled rose 6.6 per cent to 1.2 million.

For the fiscal year ending on June 30, cash payments to federal welfare recipients totaled $10.5 billion, an increase of 2.3 per cent. However, Medicaid expenditures rose by 14.2 per cent, to $8.8 billion.

Supplementary Security. A major change in the income-maintenance programs of the nation will take place on Jan. 1, 1974. The old age assistance, aid to the blind, and aid to the permanently and totally disabled programs will end. They will be replaced by the Supplementary Security Income (SSI) Program. This new federal program will be administered by the Social Security Administration (SSA), even though the funds will come from different sources.

The existing welfare programs are federal-state programs. Since the new program is federal, the usual variations that characterize all federal-state programs—such as ineligibility provisions, level of payment, and method of administration—will be replaced with a single standard of payment and uniform national eligibility standards.

To obtain the data on which informed estimates can be made on how many aged, blind, and disabled are eligible for the new welfare payments, the SSA made a survey of 400,000 persons in large metropolitan areas and 88,000 in a nationwide sample.

Officials believe more persons will receive aid because the payments ($140 per month for an individual and $195 for a couple) are above those paid in some states, and the resource level of $1,500 is above that allowed in several state welfare programs. Relatives' responsibility is largely eliminated, and the minimum age of 18 is removed from the disabled program, thus including disabled children who are not now eligible.

Medicare and Medicaid. On July 1, the 1973 amendments to social security legislation raised the premium for the supplementary medical insurance part of Medicare to $6.30 a month and changed the annual deductible charge from $50 to $60. A Medicare beneficiary became responsible for the first $84 of his hospital bill, an increase of $12 over the present amount. The legislation also protects those eligible for Medicaid against loss of this service when SSI takes over in January, 1974. In addition, it guaranteed, until June, 1975, continued eligibility for Medicaid services to men and women of limited income who would otherwise have lost their eligibility because of social security increases.

The 17th International Conference on Social Welfare will be held from July 17 to 20, 1974, in Nairobi, Kenya. The theme of the conference is Development and Participation–Operational Implications for Social Welfare.   Joseph P. Anderson

SOMALIA. See AFRICA.

SOUTH AFRICA, REPUBLIC OF. Black politics assumed greater importance in white-ruled South Africa in 1973. The focus of black activity shifted from the exiled guerrilla groups to black workers and the leaders of black homelands, or Bantustans. The Bantustan leaders warned repeatedly that violence would result if blacks did not get some political rights. Meanwhile, two new homelands, Gazankulu and Venda, became officially self-governing in 1973.

Africa Workers' Strike. A series of massive strikes defied laws forbidding black workers to strike. Black workers make up 80 per cent of South Africa's labor force, but many were earning less than $15 a week. Among mine workers, whites on the average earned $475 a month; blacks, $30. The all-white Trade Union Council urged union representation for blacks. It warned that the African workers' movement was "fast developing into an avalanche," because the blacks could not live on their wages.

In February, about 34,000 striking blacks shut down more than 100 companies in an industrial area near Durban. They were joined by 16,000 Durban city employees. More than 700,000 black workers won pay increases as a result of 160 strikes from January through March throughout South Africa. By May, the strikes had spread to the textile industry in Johannesburg.

On May 22, the government proposed black workers' committees be set up within companies. If a committee or a government labor officer could not settle a grievance in 30 days, the blacks could strike.

The first black trade union, representing about 200 metalworkers, was founded in June. However, the government did not recognize the black union, so it had no power to negotiate contracts.

Mine Workers Killed. During the strikes, there were few arrests, and relatively little police violence. But, on September 11, police shot and killed 11 mine workers rioting at the Western Deep Levels mine in Carletonville. Relatively high-paid black machine operators were angered because their wages were not raised when the lowest-paid black workers received a 46 per cent increase. Prime Minister Balthazar Johannes Vorster claimed the police were acting in self-defense, but the incident stirred international protest.

In April, proposals for the final Bantustan borders were announced. The plan would allot 14 per cent of South Africa's land to blacks, much of it in small fragments. Black leaders warned that there would be a "blood bath" if this plan, which would displace 364,000 blacks, went into effect.   John Storm Roberts

See also AFRICA (Facts in Brief Table).

SOUTH AMERICA. See LATIN AMERICA and articles on Latin American countries.

SOUTH CAROLINA. See STATE GOVERNMENT.

SOUTH DAKOTA. See STATE GOVERNMENT.

SOUTH WEST AFRICA (NAMIBIA). See AFRICA.

SPACE EXPLORATION. Man began to live in space in 1973. Instead of short journeys to explore specific areas or to test equipment and maneuvers, astronauts lived and worked in space on a routine basis for months at a time. They proved that man can successfully carry out a strenuous program of scheduled and emergency tasks on a spacecraft.

On May 14, the National Aeronautics and Space Administration (NASA) used a Saturn 5 rocket to launch an 86-foot-long, 85-ton cluster of modules known as the *Skylab* space station. About one minute after lift-off, a thin aluminum meteoroid and heat shield was ripped off the station by aerodynamic pressure. This, in turn, caused one of two winglike solar panels to be torn away and the other to jam in a partly open position. The solar panels were needed to generate electricity for the station. Within the shielding, inside temperatures rose dangerously.

After a 10-day delay, the crew–Charles Conrad, Jr., Joseph P. Kerwin, and Paul J. Weitz–lifted off from Cape Kennedy, Fla., in a modified Apollo spacecraft on May 25 and docked with the disabled station on May 26. The next day, they erected a parasol-like sunshade in place of the lost shield, and temperatures eventually dropped to a comfortable level. On the 13th day of the mission, Conrad and Kerwin went outside the station and succeeded in fully extending the partly opened solar panel, solving the electric power problem.

The crew completed 80 per cent of their mission objectives, including taking 30,000 pictures of the sun and collecting data on 182 Earth resources sites in 31 states and 9 countries. They splashed down in the Pacific Ocean on June 22, after a mission of 28 days.

Alan L. Bean, Owen K. Garriott, and Jack R. Lousma left Cape Kennedy on July 28 aboard a Saturn IB and became the second crew to man the *Skylab* station. For the first week and a half in space, they were plagued with motion sickness and equipment failures. The astronauts gradually overcame their illness and completed several repair tasks, including erection of a second sunshade. With planned objectives exceeded by 150 per cent, this was the most successful space mission to date. When the crew returned on September 25, after spending 59 days 11 hours in space, they had 37,000 photographs and data filling 17 miles of magnetic tape. Their work also provided the most detailed information ever obtained on the sun's structure and activity.

Because the second crew readapted so quickly to earth's gravity, NASA considered extending the third crew's stay in *Skylab* from 59 to 84 days. The *Skylab 3* crew, Gerald P. Carr, Edward G. Gibson, and William R. Pogue was launched on November 16.

Joint Space Venture. Both the United States and Russia named flight crews for the joint Apollo-Soyuz Test Project (ASTP), which is scheduled for launching in July of 1975. Prime crewmen for the United States are Thomas P. Stafford, Donald K. Slayton, and Vance D. Brand. Alexei A. Leonov and Valery N. Kubasov make up the prime *Soyuz* crew, which will link up with the *Apollo* craft.

NASA selected 17 scientific and space experiments to be conducted on the ASTP. Four are in astronomy and space physics, five are in the life sciences, and eight are space-applications experiments.

Cosmonauts assigned to the ASTP visited the Johnson Space Center near Houston in July, and astronauts assigned to the joint flight went to Star City, near Moscow, in November. These were the first of several training sessions that are to be conducted in both countries.

In July, Konstantin D. Bushuyev, Russian technical director for ASTP, said that his country would make several test flights in *Soyuz* craft modified specifically for the joint mission. On September 29, Vasily G. Lazarev and Oleg G. Makarov completed a two-day space flight believed to be such a mission. It was the first venture into space by cosmonauts since three of them died during the return to earth of the *Soyuz 11* mission in June, 1971. The success of *Soyuz 12* showed that the Russians have solved the problem of a leaky hatch, which was blamed for the deaths. It also assuaged growing concern about the Russians' ability to participate in the joint flight after a 2½-year series of failures in their manned space program. On December 18, Russia launched a *Soyuz* spacecraft containing two cosmonauts into Earth orbit. The

Three teams of astronauts lived and worked in the *Skylab* space station, *above*, in 1973. Scientist Owen K. Garriott deployed particle collection equipment, *above right*, during *Skylab 2* extravehicular activity. Arabella, a spider, went on the *Skylab 1* mission in one of the experiments suggested by high school students. Garriott works at the *Skylab 2* telescope mount console, *below right*, where solar observations were made. On the *Skylab 1* mission, *below*, Charles Conrad, Jr., gave fellow astronaut Paul J. Weitz a haircut.

cosmonauts began a series of studies of the Sun, other stars, and methods of forecasting weather and natural calamities. The day after the *Soyuz* launch, the Russians launched a single rocket that carried eight unmanned *Cosmos* satellites, *Cosmos 617-624*, into Earth orbit.

Space Women. In September, NASA began testing 12 Air Force nurses with the aim of developing physical requirements for women passengers on the space shuttle. The shuttle is expected to carry nonastronauts, such as scientists and technicians, on space missions in the 1980s. The women were tested at Ames Research Center in California to determine their tolerance to weightlessness and increased gravity forces experienced during re-entry. Similar studies were conducted on men in 1972.

The orbiter part of the shuttle, which will land on Earth like an airplane, contains a compartment for up to six passengers. The passengers could eat and sleep in the orbiter and carry out their experiments in a separate laboratory module known as a spacelab. Each spacelab could be equipped for a particular research or engineering activity, flown on a 7- to 30-day mission, then replaced with a different type of lab when the orbiter returned to Earth.

European Participation. In September, NASA administrator James C. Fletcher signed an agreement with nine European countries calling for the European Space Research Organization (ESRO) to design and build a spacelab flight unit for the shuttle system. Costing from $300 million to $400 million, the ESRO spacelab represents a major step in cost sharing between the United States and European countries. This could lead to joint programs involving U.S. and European scientists and astronauts. Belgium, Denmark, France, West Germany, Italy, the Netherlands, Spain, Switzerland, and the United Kingdom signed the agreement.

NASA also began studies of a space tug. This craft would be an additional stage of the shuttle that would extend its range to high Earth orbits, or send payloads on planetary missions.

The Planets. Continuing their exploration of the planets, Russia launched four spacecraft toward Mars in July and August. Ronald Z. Sagdeyev, chief of the Soviet Space Research Institute, said that one or more of these craft would land on Mars to test soil and rocks and try to transmit television images from the surface. Reports suggested that the caravan consisted of two Mars landers and two orbiters, all scheduled to reach the planet before mid-March, 1974.

About the time the Russian craft are exploring Mars, history's first two-planet flight will provide a close-up look at Venus and Mercury. The United States launched *Mariner 10* on November 3. The spacecraft was to fly by Venus in February, and use that planet's gravity field to propel it to Mercury. If successful, *Mariner 10* would make history's first approach to Mercury in March, 1974.

The United States added a second automated spacecraft, *Pioneer 11*, to its caravan to Jupiter in April. This craft is expected to complete its 620-million-mile journey to the giant planet in December, 1974, one year after *Pioneer 10* took the first close-up pictures of the planet.

In June, NASA placed *Explorer 49* in lunar orbit to monitor radio noise in our Galaxy and beyond. The Moon shielded its antennas from static generated on Earth. In addition to *Explorer 49*, more than 40 spacecraft continued to record and transmit scientific data on the solar system, the universe beyond, and the Earth. These included Earth Resources Technology Satellite-1, which completed a year in orbit in July, far exceeding its expected lifetime of 90 days.

Budget Problems. NASA marked its 15th anniversary on October 1. Gone are the spectacular and dramatic manned missions to the Moon, and the mid-1960s' budgets exceeding $5 billion. In October, Congress was considering a fiscal 1974 budget of $3.6 billion, as compared with $3.2 billion in 1973.

Budget cuts have stemmed from declining public interest and the belief by many that the funds could be better spent on improving conditions on Earth. This has led NASA to emphasize the benefits of studying the Earth from space, and the jobs and products that emerge from the technology the space program has developed.   William J. Cromie

SPAIN. General Francisco Franco, 80, went into semiretirement on June 9, 1973, after ruling Spain for nearly 34 years. He turned over the daily chores of government to Admiral Luis Carrero Blanco, vice-president since 1967 (see CARRERO BLANCO, LUIS). Carrero Blanco was sworn in as president of the Cabinet. His new Cabinet reduced the influence of the Roman Catholic organization Opus Dei. Franco was freed from routine government tasks and making policy decisions. He continued as the nation's chief of state and as commander in chief of its armed forces. Carrero Blanco died December 20 when his car was blown up as he left a church. On December 29, Franco named Carlos Arias Navarro, Spain's security chief, to Carrero Blanco's post.

On the economic scene, Spain sought to have its preferential trade agreement with the European Community (Common Market) adapted to apply to the new market members—Great Britain, Iceland, and Denmark. On October 1, Spain also demanded compensation for losses in farm-product exports caused by enlarging the market. Britain's market entry meant tariff increases for Spain on agricultural products. The market promised Spain a free trade zone by 1977 for industrial goods, and by 1980 for agriculture. Spain branded these proposals unrealistic because they involved the removal of duties on 80 per cent of industrial imports in three years.

Police in Madrid threatened mutiny on May 2

A mysterious explosion in December ended the brief term of Luis Carrero Blanco, here being sworn in as president of Spain on June 9, 1973.

after a sub-inspector was assassinated on May Day. The police blamed the death on strict orders not to make use of their firearms in demonstrations. At a demonstration near Barcelona on April 3, police had killed one construction worker and badly wounded another. After the May Day incident, police leaders said they would refuse to break up another leftist demonstration unarmed. On May 4, the government said police in the future would be "authorized to use every available means" to deal with any act that "might disrupt order."

Church Support for the government weakened steadily during the year. On January 20, Spain's 83 Roman Catholic bishops voted a carefully worded bid to separate the church from state affairs, though not from its financial support. Only 20 voted No.

In March, the archbishop of Pamplona in northern Spain's Basque country made use of a privilege the hierarchy had sought to give up. Sermons attacking Spain's political leaders and supporting Basque militants brought the arrest of 11 priests, but the archbishop invoked special church rights to prevent their civil prosecution. In Barcelona, 113 antigovernment leaders – 2 of them priests – were arrested October 28 at an "illegal" meeting in a church parish house. In their support, the archbishop of Barcelona said that freedom of assembly and association were natural rights.
Kenneth Brown

See also EUROPE (Facts in Brief Table).

SPORTS. Expansion moves in 1973 were felt most strongly in hockey. The 16-team National Hockey League (NHL) said it would expand to 20 teams in 1976. Kansas City and Washington, D.C., have been awarded 1974-1975 franchises, and two more teams will be created for 1976. Meanwhile, the NHL, which had been playing in two divisions, announced a four-division plan starting in the 1974-1975 season.

The World Hockey Association (WHA), which started play in 1972, had 12 teams for 1973-1974 and awarded 1974-1975 franchises to Phoenix, Indianapolis, and Cincinnati. But when financing for a new arena fell through, the Cincinnati franchise needed a new home. See HOCKEY.

Gary Davidson, president of the WHA and a founder of the American Basketball Association (ABA), was a creator of the World Team Tennis League, which planned to start play in 1974 with 16 teams in the United States. Tennis has never had league competition, and national and international officials feared that league players would by-pass traditional tournaments. Davidson resigned his WHA post in October after announcing organization of the World Football League, which planned to start play in 1974 with week-night games in the summer. The 26-team National Football League (NFL), which expected to expand to 32 teams in the 1980s, had no immediate expansion plans. See FOOTBALL.

The two major leagues in baseball and the two in professional basketball stood pat in numbers, though franchises were moved. In basketball, Dallas moved to San Antonio in the ABA (see BASKETBALL). In hockey, Ottawa shifted to Toronto, Philadelphia to Vancouver, and New York to Cherry Hill, N.J., in the WHA.

San Diego Sale. The most protracted struggle involved baseball's San Diego Padres, unsuccessful both artistically and financially. The franchise was sold in August to a Washington, D.C., group that planned to move it to Washington. However, the city of San Diego filed damage suits totaling $84 million against the National League, and the league insisted that the new owners guarantee protection against such damages if the Padres were moved.

That deal was canceled after the San Diego owners announced that the Washington group did not meet these terms. On December 29, the club was sold to a Los Angeles group that included racetrack operator Marjorie Everett, composer Burt Bacharach, and others. This group announced it would keep the team in San Diego. However, the sale was rejected by the league's other club owners.

The most expensive franchise sale of the year established a value of $20 million for the New Orleans Saints of the NFL. The purchase price for the San Diego Padres was $12 million, and the New York Yankees, once the most valuable franchise in baseball, were sold for $10 million in cash. The

Hang gliding became a new craze in 1973.
All you need to participate is a kite, a
wind, and enough nerve to jump off a cliff.

Kansas City-Omaha Kings of the NBA were sold for $5.1 million, the Kentucky Colonels of the ABA for $2 million, and the Philadelphia Blazers of the WHA for $1.9 million.

Among the Winners in 1973 sports competition were:

Curling. Sweden surprisingly won the world championship by upsetting Canada, 6-5, in an extra-end final in March in Regina, Saskatchewan. Canada had won the 5 previous titles and 41 consecutive matches in world championships. The United States champions from Winchester, Mass., tied for fifth place among the 10 nations.

Fencing. Russia won team honors and two of the eight titles in the world championships in July at Göteborg, Sweden. Brooke Makler of Philadelphia, nationally ranked in foil and épée, gained the épée quarterfinals of the world championships. No other American survived the second round in any weapon.

Handball. Terry Muck of St. Paul, Minn., won the U.S. Handball Association's (USHA) four-wall championship and the YMCA national title. Fred Lewis of Miami Beach, Fla., the USHA 1972 champion, captured the Canadian Open title. Muck and Lewis later joined the first professional handball circuit.

Rowing. U.S. crews made their best showing in a decade at the Henley Royal Regatta in July in England, winning four finals. Among the champions were the Harvard junior varsity (Ladies' Challenge Plate) and

the Princeton lightweights (Thames Challenge Cup). Wisconsin, the Intercollegiate Rowing Association champion, lost to Northeastern University of Boston in the Henley semifinals.

Shooting. Major Lones Wigger of Columbus, Ga., the 1972 Olympic champion in free rifle, won the small-bore prone and small-bore position titles in the national championships in Camp Perry, Ohio, and the same titles in the international championships at Mexico City. His double at Camp Perry was the first since he won the same two events in 1963.

Weight Lifting. Russia dominated the world championships in September in Havana, Cuba, and its 320-pound super heavyweight, Vassili Alexeev, retained his title. Dan Cantore of San Francisco finished seventh among lightweights, the best performance by an American.

Wrestling. Russia dominated the world champion-

ships in September in Teheran, Iran, winning 6 of the 10 titles in free-style, 5 of 10 in Greco-Roman, and 9 of 10 in sambo (which combines wrestling with judo). In free-style, Lloyd Keaser of Quantico, Va., was first in the 149.5-pound class, and Ben Peterson of Comstock, Wis., placed third in the 198-pound class.

Other Champions. *Archery*, world champions: men, Viktor Sidoruk, Russia; women, Linda Myers, York, Pa. U.S. champions: men, Darrell Pace, Reading, Ohio; women, Doreen Wilber, Jefferson, Iowa. *Badminton*, U.S. champions: men, Sture Johnsson, Sweden; women, Eva Twedberg, Sweden. *Biathlon*, U.S. champion: Dennis Donahue, Worcester, Vt. *Billiards*, world pocket champion: Lou Butera, Reseda, Calif. *Bobsledding*, world champions: four-man, Switzerland (Rene Stadler, driver); two-man, West Germany (Wolfgang Zimmerer, driver). *Canoeing*, U.S. champions: men's canoe (500 meters), Andy Toro, Newport Beach, Calif.; men's kayak (500 meters), Phil Rogoseski, Alexandria, Va.; women's kayak (500 meters), Marcia Smoke, Niles, Mich. *Casting*, U.S. all-around champion: Steve Rajeff, San Francisco. *Court tennis*, U.S. open champion: Eugene Scott, New York City. *Cross-country*, U.S. champions: A.A.U., Frank Shorter, Florida Track Club; National Collegiate Athletic Association (NCAA), Steve Prefontaine, Oregon. *Cycling*, world champions: men's sprint, Daniel Morelon, France; women's sprint, Sheila Young, Detroit; men's pro road, Felice Gimondi, Italy; women's road, Nicole van den Broeck, Belgium. *Field hockey*, U.S. champion: Aer Lingus, Ireland. *Gymnastics*, U.S. Gymnastics Federation all-around champions: men, Marshall Avener, University Park, Pa.; women, Joan Moore Rice, Philadelphia. A.A.U. all-around champions: men, tie between Yoshi Hayasaki, Champaign, Ill., and Yoshiaki Takei, Statesboro, Ga.; women, Joan Rice. *Horseshoe pitching*, U.S. champion: Elmer Hohl, Wellesley, Ont., Canada. *Karate*, All-American Open champion: Albert Cheeks, Silver Springs, Md. *Lacrosse*, U.S. champions: NCAA, Maryland; club, Long Island Athletic Club. *Luge* (tobogganing), world champions: men, Hans Rinn, East Germany; women, M. Schumann, East Germany. *Modern pentathlon*, world champion: Pavel Lednev, Russia. *Motorcycling*, U.S. grand national champion: Ken Roberts, Woodside, Calif. *Paddleball*, U.S. champion: Steve Keeley, San Diego, Calif. *Parachuting*, U.S. overall champions: men, Chuck Collingswood, U.S. Army; women, Gloria Porter, Maple Valley, Wash. *Polo*, U.S. champions: open, Oak Brook, Ill.; 20 goal, Houston. *Racquetball*, U.S. champion: Charlie Brumfield, San Diego, Calif. *Racquets*, world champion: Howard Angus, England. *Rodeo*, U.S. all-around champion, Larry Mahan, Dallas. *Roller skating*, world champion: men, Randy Dayney, East Meadow, N.Y.; women, Sigrid Mullenback, West Germany. *Softball*, U.S. fast-pitch champions: men, Clearwater (Fla.) Bombers; women, Raybestos Brakettes, Stratford, Conn. *Squash racquets*, U.S. champions: men, Victor Niederhoffer, New York City; women, Gretchen Spruance, Greenville, Del. *Squash tennis*, U.S. Open champion: Pedro Bacallao, New York City. *Table tennis*, world champions: men, Hsi En-ting, China; women, Hu Yu-lan, China. *Team handball*, U.S. champion: Adelphi, Garden City, N.Y. *Trampoline*, U.S. champions: men, Mason Kauffman, Ann Arbor, Mich.; women, Alexandra Nicholson, Rockford, Ill. *Volleyball*, U.S. Volleyball Association champions: men, Chuck's Steak House, Santa Monica, Calif.; women, E Pluribus Unum, Houston. *Water polo*, world champion: Hungary; A.A.U. champion, Concord (Calif.) Aquatic Club. *Water skiing*, world champions: men George Athans, Canada; women, Lisa St. John, Fall River Mills, Calif.   Frank Litsky

See also OLYMPIC GAMES.

SRI LANKA. Prime Minister Sirimavo Bandaranaike's government muddled through another disastrous economic year in 1973. Soaring world prices and mismanagement of the country's economy were the major causes of trouble.

During the year, the government raised flour, sugar, and kerosene prices, and placed a tax on medicine, which had been free. But this hardly sufficed. Rising world grain prices, delays in rice imports, and a 15 per cent drop in local rice production forced a 50 per cent hike in the price of rationed rice. Even this was not enough, however, and the government introduced more stringent measures in October.

Basic foods were put on wartime rationing. Free rice rations were cut by 75 per cent and sugar rations by 25 per cent, and strict controls were placed on flour prices. To cushion the effect, low-paid government workers were given a 10 per cent wage hike. Agriculture was put under the control of political officers.

Middle Class Unhappy. The measures affected the middle class most, and resulted in a steady exodus of intellectuals and professionals from the country. The government tried to stem the tide of this "brain drain" by forcing those who wanted to leave to sign bonds obligating them to send back up to 10 per cent of their earnings. It justified the move on the grounds that the intellectuals had received a free education in Sri Lanka.

Unrest. Debt took a third of all export earnings, and import prices continued to rise, as did the population. In addition, promises of more jobs and cheaper living costs to the newly educated youth were not fulfilled. These unemployed graduates had been the backbone of the Maoist rebellion in April, 1971. They were a dangerous opposition force for the government to reckon with in 1973. To counter this threat, the government allocated much of its revenue to the armed forces.

Armed Forces Strengthened. Prior to the 1971 revolt, defense took only 6 per cent of the national budget, but in 1973 it was given 13 per cent. The armed forces were equipped with new weapons from Russia, China, and the United States, all of which were expensive and used up much of the needed foreign exchange.

Some members of the government warned that strengthening the armed forces might lead to a military coup backed by the dissident middle class. But the government appeared to be counting on the fact that the death in April of Dudley Senanayake, long-time leader of the United National Party, would disorganize the opposition. J. R. Jayawardena, Senanayake's successor, had yet to prove that he could lead an effective parliamentary opposition. If he cannot, the possibility of a normal change in government is lessened, and the likelihood of armed revolt from either the left or the right is enhanced.   John N. Stalker

See also Asia (Facts in Brief Table).

STAMP COLLECTING. The United States Postal Service created a Stamps Department in August, 1973, consolidating all its stamp activities. The department will select stamp designs, develop and promote philatelic products, produce and distribute new stamps, and promote philatelic education. Gordon C. Morison, who had been director of the division of philately, was named head of the new department.

Some stamp collectors approved the move, hoping it would end the secondary role of philatelic affairs in the Postal Service. Others said they feared that the new department would emphasize salesmanship rather than service to collectors. Early in the year, Morison estimated that sales of special-issue stamps to collectors netted about $20 million annually to the Postal Service.

Black-Blotted Issue. For only the second time, a United States stamp issue was *black blotted* (censured) by the American Philatelic Society. It was the 10-stamp Postal People issue of April. The society termed it an "excessive extended" issue. The issue was also the first in the United States to carry printed matter (postal statistics, such as the fact that about 27 billion U.S. stamps are sold annually) under the adhesive on the backs of the stamps. This also irritated some collectors, since they had to purchase two sets of the stamps to display both sides.

The celebrated 1918 U.S. 24-cent inverted airmail

Australia is trying to ease its transition to the metric system by issuing cartoon-style postage stamps that help explain the change.

stamp brought a record price of $37,000. It was sold at auction in New York City on January 9 by the Robert A. Siegel Galleries to Irwin Wienberg, a Wilkes-Barre, Pa., collector.

Early Canadian stamps were among the most sought after in 1973. These stamps are scarce because of the low population of Canada in earlier days and because most of the stamps produced were used on mail and not saved by collectors. A large Queen Victoria 5-cent Canadian, with a catalog listing of $125, sold for $1,500 at an auction in Toronto.

In accordance with tradition, stamps honoring two deceased U.S. Presidents, Harry S. Truman and Lyndon B. Johnson, were issued by the Postal Service May 8 and August 27, respectively. About 328,000 first-day sales of the Truman stamp were made in his hometown of Independence, Mo.

To mark the 1976 U.S. bicentennial, the Postal Service issued four stamps during the year under the title, "The Rise of the Spirit of Independence."

Favorite Stamps. Polls taken by two stamp periodicals showed that the favorite 1972 U.S. stamp was the 8-cent Wild Life Conservation block of four.

Bhutan, a Himalayan kingdom that issues novel stamps for collectors, produced two oddities: A rose stamp, placed on sale in six denominations, had been treated to emit the fragrance of a rose; and seven "talking stamps" produced native folk songs when played on a phonograph.   Theodore M. O'Leary

Women lobbyists, protesting the Equal Rights Amendment, distribute home-baked goodies to members of Illinois' General Assembly in January.

STATE GOVERNMENT. The continuing impact of revenue sharing and a near 10 per cent increase in tax collections left most states with surpluses in state funds at the close of fiscal 1973. The states collected $66.2 billion in taxes in 1973, more than $6 billion over the previous year's receipts.

A surplus of more than $850 million in California resulted in a reassessment and a subsequent rollback of a 1 per cent increase in the state's sales tax, enacted in December, 1972. Alaska's surplus of $642 million, attributable mostly to the $900-million North Slope oil-lease sale in 1969, was the second highest surplus. Other surpluses were more modest, though welcome.

Most of the state reductions were made on real property taxes, personal income taxes, and income tax exemptions. Direct property tax relief for all types of homeowners was provided in Arizona, Georgia, Indiana, Michigan, Minnesota, Ohio, Oregon, Vermont, and Wisconsin.

Delaware raised the personal income tax by 10 per cent, the only state to do so during the year. Montana made permanent a 10 per cent surcharge on personal income taxes. State income tax reductions or exemptions were instituted in Arkansas, California, Idaho, Iowa, Michigan, Mississippi, Nebraska, New York, Ohio, Utah, and Wisconsin.

A controversial California tax referendum backed by Governor Ronald Reagan would have permanently reduced personal income tax rates by 7.5 per

cent and would have limited state spending to a declining percentage of personal income. It was defeated at the polls on November 6. Colorado was the only state to raise its cigarette tax. Connecticut's tax of 21 cents per pack of cigarettes remains the highest in the nation. Motor fuel taxes were raised in Arkansas, Delaware, Michigan, and Mississippi.

Governmental Ethics. The reverberations of Watergate spread quickly. More than half of the states passed new laws or strengthened existing legislation dealing with open meetings and records, conflict of interest, financial disclosure, lobbyist registration and regulation, and campaign financing. Disclosure of financial interests that might conflict with public interests were required in Alabama, California, Maryland, Montana, Ohio, and Wisconsin. Campaign financial reporting requirements were strengthened in California, Florida, Hawaii, Iowa, Nebraska, New Jersey, and Texas.

Campaign spending was limited by new laws in Hawaii, Nevada, and Wyoming. The governors of Illinois, Michigan, and Missouri adopted codes of ethics for executive branch officials and employees. Rhode Island voters approved a constitutional amendment in November requiring disclosure of election-campaign contributions and expenditures by candidates for top state offices.

Comprehensive legislation calling for open committee meetings as well as legislative assembly ses-

Selected Statistics on State Governments

State	Resident Population(a)	Governor	Legislature(b) Senate (D.)	(R.)	House (D.)	(R.)	State tax rev. (c)	Tax rev. per cap. (d)	Public school enroll-ment 1972-73 (e)	Pub. school expenditures per pupil in aver. daily attendance 1972-73(f)
Alabama	3,539	George C. Wallace (D.)	35	0	104	2	$931	$263	783	$590
Alaska	330	William A. Egan (D.)	9	11	20	19(g)	109	330	85	1,473
Arizona	2,058	Jack Williams (R.)	12	18	22	38	682	331	542	1,110
Arkansas	2,037	Dale Bumpers (D.)	34	1	99	1	523	257	459	652
California	20,601	Ronald Reagan (R.)	20	19(h)	49	31	7,324	355	4,570	1,000
Colorado	2,437	John D. Vanderhoof (R.)	13	22	28	37	667	274	578	955
Connecticut	3,076	Thomas J. Meskill (R.)	13	23	58	93	1,122	365	674	1,241
Delaware	576	Sherman W. Tribbitt (D.)	10	11	20	21	287	497	134	1,162
Florida	7,678	Reubin O'D. Askew (D.)	25	14(g)	77	43	2,488	324	1,437	902
Georgia	4,786	Jimmy Carter (D.)	48	8	151	29	1,358	284	1,084	782
Hawaii	832	John A. Burns (D.)	17	8	35	16	433	520	180	1,046
Idaho	770	Cecil D. Andrus (D.)	12	23	19	51	225	292	185	772
Illinois	11,236	Dan Walker (D.)	29	30	88	89	3,676	327	2,388	1,144
Indiana	5,316	Otis R. Bowen (R.)	21	29	27	73	1,190	224	1,220	878
Iowa	2,904	Robert D. Ray (R.)	22	28	44	56	854	294	649	1,058
Kansas	2,279	Robert B. Docking (D.)	13	27	45	80	610	268	492	919
Kentucky	3,342	Wendell H. Ford (D.)	29	9	80	20	1,015	304	715	693
Louisiana	3,764	Edwin W. Edwards (D.)	38	1	101	4	1,166	310	847	927
Maine	1,028	Kenneth M. Curtis (D.)	13	19	71	79(h)	304	295	247	840
Maryland	4,070	Marvin Mandel (D.)	33	10	121	21	1,456	358	921	1,188
Massachusetts	5,818	Francis W. Sargent (R.)	32	8	184	51(i)	2,652	353	1,190	1,102
Michigan	9,044	William G. Milliken (R.)	19	19	60	50	3,520	390	2,193	1,183
Minnesota	3,897	Wendell R. Anderson (D.)	38	28(g)	78	56	1,638	420	911	1,146
Mississippi	2,281	William L. Waller (D.)	50	2	119	2(g)	661	290	526	689
Missouri	4,757	Christopher S. Bond (R.)	21	13	97	65(h)	1,190	250	1,030	881
Montana	721	Thomas L. Judge (D.)	27	23	54	46	187	260	172	943
Nebraska	1,542	J. James Exon (D.)	49(j)		(Unicameral)		375	243	328	735
Nevada	548	Mike O'Callaghan (D.)	14	6	25	15	203	371	132	971
New Hampshire	791	Meldrim Thomson, Jr. (R.)	10	14	137	263	156	197	168	892
New Jersey	7,361	Brendan T. Byrne (D.)	29	10(g)	66	14	1,919	261	1,514	1,352
New Mexico	1,106	Bruce King (D.)	30	12	51	19	387	350	289	829
New York	18,265	Malcolm Wilson (R.)	23	37	67	83	8,170	447	3,511	1,584
North Carolina	5,273	James E. Holshouser, Jr. (R.)	35	15	85	35	1,657	314	1,159	802
North Dakota	640	Arthur A. Link (D.)	11	40	26	76	180	281	142	855
Ohio	10,731	John J. Gilligan (D.)	16	17	58	41	2,676	249	2,416	945
Oklahoma	2,663	David Hall (D.)	38	10	74	27	695	261	614	704
Oregon	2,225	Tom McCall (R.)	18	12	33	27	596	268	478	1,004
Pennsylvania	11,902	Milton J. Shapp (D.)	26	24	94	107(k)	4,367	367	2,368	1,177
Rhode Island	973	Phillip W. Noel (D.)	37	13	73	27	317	326	190	1,116
South Carolina	2,726	John C. West (D.)	43	3	103	21	825	303	640	751
South Dakota	685	Richard F. Kneip (D.)	18	17	35	35	151	221	162	833
Tennessee	4,126	Winfield Dunn (R.)	19	13(g)	51	48	1,006	244	892	730
Texas	11,794	Dolph Briscoe (D.)	28	3	132	17(h)	2,819	239	2,694	1,044
Utah	1,157	Calvin L. Rampton (D.)	13	16	31	44	359	311	305	739
Vermont	464	Thomas P. Salmon (D.)	7	23	58	91(g)	175	378	113	1,211
Virginia	4,811	Mills E. Godwin, Jr. (R.)	34	6	65	20(l)	1,400	291	1,069	920
Washington	3,429	Daniel J. Evans (R.)	30	19	57	41	1,287	375	791	929
West Virginia	1,794	Arch A. Moore, Jr. (R.)	24	10	57	43	568	317	414	749
Wisconsin	4,569	Patrick J. Lucey (D.)	15	18	62	37	1,868	409	995	1,134
Wyoming	353	Stanley K. Hathaway (R.)	13	17	17	44(g)	105	298	86	960
District of Columbia	746								140	1,327

(a) Numbers in thousands, provisional estimate as of July 1, 1973 (Bureau of the Census)
(b) As of Dec. 31, 1973
(c) 1973 preliminary figures in millions (Bureau of the Census)
(d) 1973 preliminary figures in dollars (*Tax Collections in 1973*)
(e) Numbers in thousands 1972-73 (National Education Association, *Estimates of School Statistics, 1972-73*)
(f) Numbers in dollars, 1972-73 (National Education Association, *Estimates of School Statistics, 1972-73*)
(g) 1 Independent
(h) 1 Vacancy
(i) 3 Vacancies, 2 Independents
(j) Nonpartisan
(k) 2 Vacancies
(l) 15 Independents

sions was passed in 10 more states. A large majority of states now have laws or regulations requiring open meetings and open records.

Iowa, Maine, Massachusetts, Rhode Island, and Utah passed laws that permit citizens to direct $1 of their state income taxes to local and state political parties. The states continued to conform to the Supreme Court of the United States voting requirements by reducing the residency period to 30 days or less.

Off-Year Elections. State Democratic parties increased their legislative majorities in Kentucky and Virginia. Democrats increased their majority in the New Jersey House of Representatives to 5 to 1 and gained control of the Senate by a 3 to 1 ratio. The Republican Party previously held a 22 to 18 margin in the New Jersey Senate. Democrat Brendan T. Byrne was elected governor in New Jersey by a near 700,000-vote majority. Mills Godwin, Jr., was elected as a Republican governor in Virginia. He had previously served a gubernatorial term as a Democrat. See ELECTIONS.

For the second time in four years, Kentucky voters rejected annual legislative sessions. Annual sessions also failed in Texas, as did a proposal to increase legislative pay from $4,800 to $15,000. A proposal that would have increased a Rhode Island legislator's pay to $2,000 a year was rebuffed. In the state of Washington, where legislators had increased their pay from $3,600 to $10,560 by 1975, voters substantially approved an initiative measure voiding the pay hike and limiting legislators to a 5.5 per cent increase, or about $200 per year. Salaries of other elected officials and judges were also restricted by the measure.

Energy and Environment. State officials acted to deal with the related issues of environment and energy. Connecticut created a commission to regulate petroleum prices and to bring civil actions against unfair oil-distribution practices. Connecticut, Florida, and New York were among states suing major U.S. oil companies for alleged violations of antitrust laws. Alabama and Mississippi joined in a compact that would authorize an offshore facility for petroleum loading and unloading. The Oregon and Washington legislatures enacted special laws to curtail the use of electric energy. At least 16 states lowered their speed limits, and many governors were empowered to take decisive action in the energy crisis.

In a special session, the Maryland legislature passed the first state "Emergency Powers–Energy Crisis" legislation. It gave the governor extensive power to meet the energy crisis, but also provided that regulations promulgated by the governor must be reviewed by a special legislative committee. If the committee fails to act within five days after the orders are submitted, they become effective.

Florida, Massachusetts, New Hampshire, New Jersey, and Rhode Island temporarily relaxed pollution standards to allow the use of fuel oil and coal with higher sulfur content. The energy crisis also stimulated more interest in public-transportation systems. Seven states acted to bolster finances for mass transit. These were Arkansas, California, Colorado, Connecticut, Massachusetts, Tennessee, and Washington.

The states forged ahead with environmental protection measures, however, with nearly all of the 49 states that met during the year acting on some form of environmental legislation. Nearly three-fifths of them passed new water-pollution-control laws. Bonds for sewage-treatment plants were approved in 7 states, and solid-waste-management laws were enacted in 16. Comprehensive statewide land-use planning legislation was approved for Oregon and Colorado. Previously, Hawaii was the only state with such land-use legislation.

Arkansas, Connecticut, Florida, Minnesota, Montana, and New Hampshire joined the states with laws regulating the location of new power plants. Minnesota, Montana, and North Dakota regulated strip mining and land reclamation.

Government Reorganization. Kentucky and South Dakota reorganized state government services by consolidating several agencies into a relatively few departments or agencies that report directly to the governor. Kentucky's reorganization was carried out under executive orders of Governor Wendell H. Ford, but the plan must have the 1974 General Assembly's approval before becoming final. Piecemeal forms of executive and legislative reorganization were carried out in more than 30 other states.

Legislative pay raises were approved in 13 states. Pay increases for executive officials were passed in 16 states, and for judicial officers in 11.

Constitutional commissions were working late in the year in Louisiana and Texas. The Texas legislature was to convene in January, 1974, as a constitutional convention to act on the Texas commission's work.

Reapportionment. For most states, a new U.S. Supreme Court decision in the Virginia case of *Mahan v. Howell*, which eased numerical equality standards for state legislative redistricting purposes, came too late. House districts were redrawn in 11 states during the year, and Senate districts in 10. On November 28, the California Supreme Court ordered a special master reapportionment plan into effect immediately, thus ending a three-year struggle over state legislative district boundaries. The master plan also reapportioned California's congressional seats. On December 4, North Dakota voters rejected a legislative reapportionment plan passed by the legislature and a proposal to establish a reapportionment commission to redistrict the state into single-member legislative districts. The state's reapportionment was thus thrust back into the hands of a federal court.

Health and Welfare. The U.S. Supreme Court's abortion ruling on January 22 came early enough in the year to permit several legislatures to act on the

Six state governors testified on proposed domestic budget cuts during
U.S. Senate subcommittee hearings in Washington, D.C., in February.

subject. At least 13 states enacted abortion laws, but the legislation in 4 states was restrictive in terms of the time during which an abortion may be performed. States with new abortion laws are Georgia, Idaho, Illinois, Indiana, Minnesota, Nebraska, Nevada, North Carolina, North Dakota, Rhode Island, South Dakota, Tennessee, and Utah. A federal court voided Utah's law in September, and Rhode Island's law forbidding any abortion not necessary to save a woman's life is now being contested in court. Legislation allowing doctors, hospitals, and other medical personnel to refuse to perform abortions on conscientious grounds was passed in 18 states. See SUPREME COURT OF THE UNITED STATES.

Hospital rates were regulated in Connecticut and Washington, while Nevada became the first state to license the practice of acupuncture. Changes in welfare systems were also enacted in 11 states.

Crime and Law Enforcement. At the end of the year, 21 states had re-enacted death-penalty laws. Most of these contain careful review procedures before the death penalty can be administered, and most of them conform to the U.S. Supreme Court's requirements for specificity. Others, however, are flexible. A compromise between the governor and the legislature in Illinois resulted in a law that contains a provision for "mercy" in certain situations. States that now have death-penalty laws are Arizona, Arkansas, California, Connecticut, Florida, Georgia,

Idaho, Illinois, Indiana, Louisiana, Montana, Nebraska, Nevada, New Mexico, Ohio, Oklahoma, Rhode Island, Tennessee, Texas, Utah, and Wyoming. In Massachusetts, the governor vetoed a death-penalty bill.

Rights and Regulations. The state legislatures of eight more states ratified the amendment to the U.S. Constitution guaranteeing equal rights for women. This brings the total to 30. Nebraska's ratification, however, is in doubt because the legislature later acted to rescind its ratification. Ratification by 38 states is required before the amendment becomes effective. Several states passed new laws prohibiting discrimination based on sex in employment practices, and New Mexico voters approved a constitutional amendment to that effect.

Gambling Laws. Voters in Maine, Ohio, and Rhode Island authorized state lotteries in the November elections, and the Illinois legislature enacted similar legislation in November. The states with lotteries already authorized or in operation are Connecticut, Maine, Maryland, Massachusetts, Michigan, New Hampshire, New Jersey, New York, Ohio, Pennsylvania, and South Dakota.

Five more states authorized bingo operations by certain charitable or nonprofit organizations. They were Iowa, Oklahoma, South Dakota, Virginia, and Washington.   Ralph Wayne Derickson

See also ELECTIONS.

STEEL INDUSTRY. The American steel industry produced 150.2 million tons of steel in 1973, 13 per cent more than the 132.8 million tons produced in 1972. This was enough to move the United States ahead of Russia, which produced 144.1 million tons, an increase of 4 per cent. Russia had been the world's top steel producer in 1971 and 1972. Total world-wide steel production in 1973 was 765.4 million tons, up 10 per cent over 1972. Spokesmen for the American Iron and Steel Institute said world output would probably rise again in 1974.

The Nixon Administration's decision to place strict export controls on scrap iron, one of the major materials required in steel production, contributed to the improved U.S. showing. The new controls, enacted in early July, prohibit acceptance of new orders of more than 500 tons of scrap.

Bargaining Agreement. The possibility of a steel strike in 1974 was probably averted in March, when 10 major steel companies agreed to a new bargaining procedure with the United Steelworkers of America, whose present labor contract expires Aug. 1, 1974. Under the new procedure, unresolved issues, including wages, will be submitted to arbitration. Steelworkers will get a minimum wage increase of 3 per cent a year for three years, plus cost-of-living increases and incentive wage payments provided in the present contract.

In September, the Cost of Living Council authorized the steel industry to make a two-stage, $400-million-a-year increase in prices for sheet and strip steel. Steel companies were allowed to increase prices by an average of $4.50 a ton on October 1, and by another $4.50 a ton on Jan. 1, 1974. In December, steel producers applied for additional price hikes, averaging 5.3 per cent, but the council postponed a decision until January, 1974. However, steelmakers were allowed to pass along higher costs for scrap.

Global Demand. Despite increased steel production in the United States in 1973, engineers and builders said that a serious shortage of reinforcing bars, metal decking, and bar joists was delaying the completion of some projects and the start of others. A worldwide shortage of steel, together with the devaluation of the U.S. dollar, substantially reduced imports, thus compounding the problem.

William T. Hogan, professor of economics at Fordham University in New York City and an expert on steel-industry economics, wrote in the June issue of *Iron and Steel Engineer* that if world steel production is to meet world demand, it would have to reach 1-billion net tons by 1980. This is 50 per cent more than the 1972 world output of 692.4 million net tons. None of the large U.S. companies has announced a major capital expansion program, he wrote, though Japan, Great Britain, and West Germany have. In February, Russia announced the start of production at its largest blast furnace, in Lipetsk, with an annual capacity of 2.2 million metric tons.   Mary E. Jessup

STOCKS AND BONDS. Despite record corporate profits due to high production output and rising prices, investors remained inordinately cautious in 1973. Stock prices reached peaks in January, with most averages at all-time highs. Prices drifted down through August in the face of revelations about the Watergate scandal, renewed inflation, devaluation in February, and tight money. Prices advanced in September and October close to the January highs, but the energy crisis sent prices tumbling again. The Dow Jones industrial average closed the year at 850.56, down nearly 170 points from the level at which it closed 1972, and more than 200 points below the record 1051.7 closing average on January 11. Trading volume totaled 4,053,066,600 shares on the New York Stock Exchange (NYSE) and 759,844,265 shares on the American Stock Exchange.

James J. Needham, chairman of the NYSE, challenged the so-called third market in a number of statements. The third market, trading in listed stocks off the exchanges, permitted institutional investors to avoid disclosing stock transactions, as well as undercut established commissions. The exchanges have a fixed rate system except for transactions larger than $300,000, which, under Securities and Exchange Commission rules since 1971, must be negotiated. The industry was concerned that new communication technology might make it possible for

Stocks Plunge in 1973

New York Stock Exchange composite averages

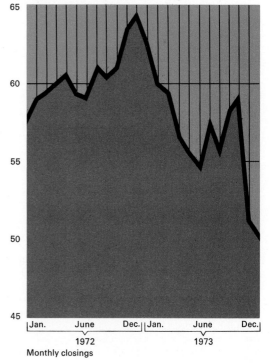

Monthly closings

even small investors to trade away from the exchanges. Reflecting such problems, as well as poor profits performance by brokerage houses, NYSE memberships sold at the lowest price since the recession of 1958.

Despite relatively low stock prices and the highest borrowing costs in a century, corporations financed record capital expansion in 1973. Unsurpassed corporate profits, coupled with Nixon Administration curbs on dividends, permitted companies to generate substantial funds internally, avoiding much of the problem.

Mutual Funds had more redemptions than sales again in 1973. The market value of their assets, which had peaked at nearly $60 billion at the end of 1972, fell to $48 billion by mid-1973 before turning up. Part of the problem stemmed from discouraged small investors who had suffered losses in the book value of their holdings. But perhaps the most important factor was growing investor awareness of the high commissions and fees charged by most mutual funds.

Gaining rapid market recognition, at the expense of mutual funds, were plans by major corporations to allow dividends to be reinvested automatically in the company's stock. Also, major banks introduced plans that allowed customers to arrange for automatic monthly purchases of listed stocks. Merrill Lynch, Pierce, Fenner & Smith, the world's largest brokerage house, set up a mutual fund that has only a 6.5 per cent sales charge compared with the typical 8.5 per cent. The new vehicle, named the Lionel D. Edie Capital Fund, attracted $233 million from 38,000 investors–the second largest mutual fund sale in history.

Equity Funding. The NYSE halted trading on March 27 in Equity Funding Corporation of America, a financial services firm headquartered in Century City, Calif. It had been a popular holding for large institutional investors. The company subsequently filed bankruptcy proceedings. Investigators discovered that over two-thirds of the insurance policies written by a key subsidiary were phonies that had been sold to reinsurers for cash. Twenty-two company officials were indicted in Los Angeles in November. All pleaded not guilty. A hearing on pretrial motions was scheduled for Feb. 18, 1974.

The IBM Ruling. Shares of International Business Machines (IBM), another popular institutional holding, dropped $26 on September 17 at the news that IBM had been ordered to pay rival Telex Corporation a record $352.5 million in a triple damage antitrust suit. Telex, in turn, was found to have violated IBM copyrights and trade secrets, and was ordered to pay $21.6 million to IBM. Then, in a surprising reversal, Federal District Judge A. Sherman Christensen of Tulsa, Okla., conceded that he had made a substantial error in assessing damages against IBM. An amended judgment on November 10 reduced the award to Telex by $93 million.   William G. Dewald

SUDAN remained relatively calm in 1973 as President Sayed Gaafar Mohamed Nimeiri's government concentrated on internal problems. Top priority was given to restoring the southern region, which had been ravaged by civil war. Government officials reported in March that 6,000 former rebels had joined the Southern Command military forces and that a million refugees had returned to their villages from the bush or neighboring countries.

There was some internal unrest. In September, all schools in the capital, including Khartoum University, were closed because of student demonstrations. The students were protesting military control of the government. Six unions, including the railway workers, then went on strike to protest police brutality against the students. The government declared a four-day state of emergency, and 1,500 persons were arrested. Nimeiri blamed the disorders on both Communist and right wing Moslem factions. Although most of those arrested were released without being charged, the university remained under military control when it reopened on September 9.

Americans Killed. On March 1 and 2, eight Arab guerrillas belonging to the Black September movement seized the Saudi Arabian Embassy in Khartoum, the capital of Sudan, and executed two U.S. diplomats–Ambassador Cleo A. Noel, Jr., and Chargé d'Affaires George C. Moore–and a Belgian.

Palestinian terrorist stands watch on balcony after his group seized Saudi Arabian Embassy in Khartoum, Sudan. Three diplomats were killed.

The guerrillas later surrendered to Sudanese forces and were charged with murder. The Palestinian Liberation Organization denied any connection with the guerrilla action, and the Sudanese accused Libya's President Muammar Muhammad al-Qadhaafi of having instigated the attack.

New Constitution. On April 12, the president approved Sudan's first permanent Constitution since its independence in 1956. The new Constitution confirmed regional autonomy for the southern region, which had been granted as part of the 1972 peace settlement between the government and the predominantly non-Moslem rebels. Religious freedom for all Sudanese citizens was guaranteed, even though Islam is the religion of the majority.

The Constitution also stipulated that the ruling Sudan Socialist Union would be the country's only legal political organization. Another provision prohibited detention of prisoners without trial. As a consequence, a former premier, Sadiq al-Mahdi, and members of the Sudan Communist Party, imprisoned since 1971 for their part in trying to overthrow President Nimeiri, were released.

The Constitution also established a National People's Assembly of 250 members as Sudan's supreme legislative body. Elections were set for 225 members of the Assembly in February, 1974. The remaining members would be appointed.   William Spencer

See also AFRICA (Facts in Brief Table).

Movers haul "adult" material from a Cincinnati store after a Supreme Court ruling that local courts may apply local standards on pornography.

SUPREME COURT OF THE UNITED STATES.
Virtually all state anti-abortion laws were declared unconstitutional by the Supreme Court in a historic decision on Jan. 22, 1973. In other important decisions during the year, the court issued new guidelines on obscenity, and it refused to declare that the local property-tax method of financing public schools discriminates unconstitutionally against poor areas.

An analysis prepared by *The New York Times* in July revealed that the four justices appointed by President Richard M. Nixon – Warren E. Burger, Harry A. Blackmun, Lewis F. Powell, and William H. Rehnquist – voted as a unit on 70 per cent of the cases decided in the court's 1972-1973 term. Justice Byron R. White joined them in 101 out of 107 decisions, forming the nucleus of a court majority.

Abortion Ruling. Justice Blackmun wrote the court's decision in the main abortion case, *Roe v. Wade.* The expectant mother, he stated, enjoys a "right of privacy" under the due process clause of the 14th Amendment that entitles her and her doctor to decide whether she should have an abortion during the first three months of pregnancy. In later stages of pregnancy, the state's interest in the health of the woman and in potential human life allow it to regulate abortions, Blackmun wrote, but only "in ways that are reasonably related to maternal health." Only after the fetus is viable – presumably after six months of pregnancy – could the state legally forbid abortion.

Justices White and Rehnquist dissented vigorously.

New Obscenity Guidelines. The court had previously ruled that a constitutional right of privacy allowed individuals to possess obscene materials in their own homes. However, it refused to extend that right to include the freedom to buy obscene material, sell it, advertise it, display it in theaters, import it, or transport it on public carriers. The decisions came in a series of eight cases decided on June 21 and June 25. All the decisions were 5 to 4 votes with White joining the four Nixon appointees in the majority.

The court implied that in determining whether material was "patently offensive," and therefore illegal, trial courts could apply state or local standards rather than more vague "national standards." Chief Justice Burger, speaking for the court, specifically struck down a 1966 ruling that held that a suspect work would have to be "utterly without redeeming social value" to be subject to prosecution. In the new ruling, Chief Justice Burger wrote that if, "taken as a whole, [the work] lacks serious literary, artistic, political, or scientific value," then it can be judged as obscene.

In a dissenting opinion, Justice William J. Brennan, Jr., who had authored previous court rulings on obscenity, predicted that the new ruling would create substantial danger to First Amendment rights. He also said it would burden the high court with repeated demands for clarification on individual cases.

493

In December, the court agreed to hear in 1974 a case from Georgia involving the attempted suppression of the "R" rated, but critically acclaimed motion picture, *Carnal Knowledge*.

School Cases. Two major questions on equality in public schools were at least partly resolved in 1973. On June 21, in *Keyes v. (Denver) School District No. 1*, the court ruled 8 to 1 that if unofficial racial segregation results from deliberate actions by school authorities, then desegregation must follow.

Although the case was initially viewed as its first major confrontation with *de facto* (in fact) segregation, rather than *de jure* (by law), the court opinions tended to view the two categories of racial separation in much the same way. Justice Powell noted that pure *de facto* segregation rarely occurs on its own. The condition must ordinarily be perpetuated, even if not created, by official acts of school administrators.

The Supreme Court decided 5 to 4 on March 21, in *San Antonio Independent School District v. Rodriguez*, that the local property-tax system for school financing did not violate the equal protection clause of the 14th Amendment. The local property-tax system of financing public school education had been under wholesale attack ever since the California Supreme Court ruled in 1971 that it unjustly discriminated against children living in poorer school districts.

The plaintiffs argued that the wide variation in funds available for educating students in different school districts amounted to irrational, invidious discrimination. However, the high court concluded that the situation, while regrettable, might well have "no perfect solution."

Press Freedom. In a 5 to 4 decision, the court ruled on June 21, in *Pittsburgh Press Company v. Pittsburgh Commission on Human Relations*, that the human relations commission could constitutionally order a newspaper to stop printing sex-segregated help-wanted advertisements. In a strong dissent, Justice Potter Stewart said the ruling marked the first time in U.S. history that the court allowed a governmental body to "tell a newspaper in advance what it can print and what it cannot."

On May 29, the court held 7 to 2 that neither the First Amendment nor the "fairness doctrine" of the Federal Communications Act required broadcasters to accept controversial paid political announcements.

In another important case, the court held on June 21, 5 to 4, that in a federal civil suit, a jury of only six persons satisfies the Seventh Amendment's guarantee of "trial by jury." On June 11, by a 7 to 2 decision, the court declared unconstitutional a Connecticut statute that permanently relegated out-of-state students at the state university to nonresident status and, therefore, higher tuition. David C. Beckwith

See also COURTS AND LAWS.

SURGERY. See MEDICINE.

SWAZILAND. See AFRICA.

SWEDEN. A political crisis resulted from a dead heat in the Sept. 16, 1973, elections. The Social Democrats, who have ruled for 40 years, and their allies, the Communists, held 175 seats in parliament. So did the coalition of three non-Socialist parties. Prime Minister Olof Palme, defying demands to resign, said he could run the government "by lottery," a device used before in parliament. A tie vote on a key question is decided by drawing lots from an urn. If the result goes against the governing party, parliament is dissolved and new elections are held. Such crucial votes are rare in Sweden.

King Dies. King Gustaf VI Adolf, 90, died on September 15. His death heralded the end of the monarchy as a political factor. The new king, 27-year-old Carl XVI Gustaf, will have only symbolic and ceremonial functions when constitutional reform takes effect, probably on Jan. 1, 1975. On his accession on September 19, the bachelor king said his royal motto would be "For Sweden–with the times." Many Swedes believed he might be the nation's last king. See GUSTAF, CARL XVI.

The need for better relations with the United States, strained by Sweden's antagonism to U.S. bombing in Indochina and its help for U.S. deserters, was stressed by Foreign Minister Krister Wickman on March 21. "It is especially important to preserve the means of high-level dialogue," he said. Follow-

Carl XVI Gustaf, Sweden's newly crowned king, accepts the plaudits of the crowd from the balcony of the royal palace in Stockholm.

Rosemarie Kother of East Germany set a world record in the women's 200-meter butterfly at the world swimming championships in Belgrade.

ing Sweden's criticism in December, 1972, President Richard M. Nixon had indicated Sweden's new ambassador would not be welcome in Washington for the time being. The third-ranking diplomat was left in charge of the U.S. Embassy in Stockholm. United States Secretary of State William P. Rogers accused Sweden of prolonging the Vietnam War by its attitude.

An unusual program calling for government stock purchases took effect as 1973 ended. Financed by the $1.4- trillion state pension fund, the government can purchase up to 5 per cent of selected industries. On July 18, Palme said he favored greater representation for workers on boards of directors, even less unemployment (down to 2 per cent in 1973), and general economic improvement.

Relations with Russia. Premier Aleksei N. Kosygin visited Stockholm in April, and confirmed that Sweden will buy natural gas from Russia. He predicted that Swedish-Soviet trade will rise substantially. Wickman rebuked Russia on September 6 for "persecuting Soviet dissidents."

Exports Boom. Merchandise exports increased by 30 per cent in the first half of 1973 over the comparable period in 1972. Inflation remained a problem, and the government responded to housewives' pressure by freezing prices charged for meat and dairy products.   Kenneth Brown

See also EUROPE (Facts in Brief Table).

SWIMMING. America's traditional dominance of swimming was shaken in 1973. The American men retained supremacy, but the East German women, never a factor before, became the best in the world.

Previously, the best swimmers met only once every four years, in the Olympic Games. In 1973, the first world aquatic championships were staged in Belgrade, Yugoslavia, in September. The East German women won 10 of 14 events and broke 7 world records. They were uniformly tall and strong; their strength probably came from weight lifting.

The pride of the East Germans was 14-year-old Kornelia Ender, who won four gold medals (two in relays) in the world championships. During the year, she broke three world records – in free-style, butterfly, and individual medley – a total of seven times and shared two relay records. As a child, she was fragile and suffered hip problems. "Swimming should help cure your pains," her physician said, so she started swimming at the age of 5.

U.S. Winners. American women won only 3 world titles. American men took 8 gold, 8 silver, and 3 bronze medals in 15 events. The only East German man to win was Roland Matthes, who captured both backstroke races and extended his domination in that stroke to six years.

The most successful American men at Belgrade were Jim Montgomery of Madison, Wis.; John Hencken of Santa Clara, Calif.; Robin Backhaus of

Redlands, Calif.; and Rick DeMont of San Rafael, Calif.

Montgomery won the 100-meter and 200-meter free-styles and swam on all three winning relay teams. Hencken was first and second and set a world record, then broke it the same day, in the 100-meter breast stroke. Backhaus finished first and third in the two butterfly races.

DeMont's Comeback. DeMont won the 400-meter free-style in the world-record time of 3 minutes 58.19 seconds, the first time anyone had bettered 4 minutes. DeMont, stripped of a gold medal in the 1972 Olympics because his asthma medicine contained a forbidden drug, was taking different medication.

DeMont finished second in the world 1,500-meter free-style to Stephen Holland of Australia. The 15-year-old Holland, swimming high in the water, set a world record of 15 minutes 31.85 seconds and en route established a record of 8 minutes 16.27 seconds for 800 meters.

Keena Rothhammer, a free-styler from Santa Clara, Calif., and Melissa Belote, a backstroker from Springfield, Va., took one gold and one silver medal each in world-championship individual races. Bruce Robertson of Canada won the 100-meter butterfly. Phil Boggs, an Air Force lieutenant, swept the 3-meter springboard diving titles in the world and U.S. indoor and outdoor championships. Frank Litsky

SWITZERLAND decided to float the franc without a fixed exchange rate on Jan. 24, 1973, after withdrawing support for the U.S. dollar in international markets. The move followed Italy's adoption of a two-tier foreign-exchange system to defend the lira, which forced the Swiss to provide $200 million to support its currency.

The Swiss move was tied up with a fight against inflation. Cost of living rose at an annual rate of 8 per cent during 1973, the highest since World War II. A tight labor market worsened the situation.

Beginning in January, immigration controls were relaxed for Italian laborers, and seasonal workers were allowed to apply for annual residence status provided they had worked in Switzerland for 45 months. By March 21, there were 1,032,285 foreigners living in Switzerland, almost one-sixth of the population. Of this number, 596,000 were working.

In January, a special economics unit was created to oversee prices, wages, and profits. On June 1, it ordered cancellation of a gasoline price boost. Eleven oil companies appealed to the Supreme Court, but the order was upheld on August 21.

Revised Constitution. The government announced on September 6 the creation of a commission to revise the country's Constitution. Minister of Justice and Police Kurt Furgler said the commission would have a draft Constitution ready early in 1974.

The government also named a consultative committee to examine the possibility of Switzerland joining the United Nations.

Industrial Boom. Fears that revaluation of the Swiss franc would hurt foreign trade were unfounded. In the first six months of 1973, exports rose by 13.4 per cent and imports, 11 per cent. Exports are vital, as Swiss industries sell about 70 per cent of their production abroad – in the case of watches, 99 per cent.

Labor unions campaigned for workers' participation in management, and a referendum on the issue will be held in 1974. The government is lukewarm to the idea, favoring "appropriate" worker participation "compatible with sound management."

Religious Freedom. In a national referendum on May 20, the Swiss people agreed to repeal two articles in the federal Constitution under which the Roman Catholic Society of Jesus has been forbidden in Switzerland for 125 years. Sixteen of the country's 22 cantons favored lifting the ban. Only 39.7 per cent of the eligible voters cast ballots. The referendum also ended a ban on new monasteries in Switzerland.

Mutual Aid. The United States and Switzerland signed a treaty on May 25 on mutual assistance in criminal matters. It was aimed at numbered bank accounts and the "upper echelon" of organized crime. Swiss banks will open their books to inspection if there is reasonable suspicion of involvement by international organized crime.   Kenneth Brown

See also EUROPE (Facts in Brief Table).

SYRIA. Representative government moved a step closer to reality on March 13, 1973, when voters approved the nation's first permanent Constitution since 1961. The new document replaced the provisional Constitution of 1964, which was issued after the Ba'ath Party seized power.

Syria joined Egypt in attacking Israel in October and lost some territory in the Golan Heights, but it refused to attend initial peace talks. For details on the war and its aftermath, see MIDDLE EAST.

The new Constitution was approved by 97.6 per cent of the voters. Nearly 89 per cent of the electorate cast ballots in the referendum, the government said. Legislative power is vested in a National Assembly with 186 members who are elected for four-year terms. Workers and peasants were to comprise half its members. The president is limited to a seven-year term, but he can appoint and discharge ministers, and his veto cannot be overridden.

Before it was submitted to the voters, the Constitution aroused some opposition, primarily on religious grounds. The majority Sunni Moslem community protested the absence of a clause naming Islam as the state religion. A compromise formula was adopted, requiring the president to be a Moslem; otherwise, religious freedom is guaranteed.

National Elections were held on May 25 to form the National Assembly. They were the first national elections since 1961, when the country seceded from the short-lived United Arab Republic. The results were not surprising. The Ba'ath Party won 122 of the 186 seats. The National Progressive Front, made up of the Communists and three small Arab Socialist parties, won 18. Five women were among the successful candidates.

The poor voter turnout illustrated the regime's problems. Only about 51 per cent of those eligible cast ballots, and a one-day extension of the elections was needed to ensure a majority. The regime's main support comes from the minority Alawis, an unorthodox Islamic sect representing less than a tenth of the population.

Assassination Attempt. The depth of anti-Alawi feeling was demonstrated in July when Sunni army officers tried to assassinate President Hafiz al-Asad, an Alawi Moslem, during an inspection tour of military installations. The president's car was riddled with bullets, but he escaped with slight wounds. A purge of the officer corps followed, with an estimated 300 arrests and 42 executions.

The principal economic event was the inauguration on July 5 of a huge new dam across the Euphrates River. Built at a cost of $336 million with Russian financial and technical help, the dam will create an artificial lake 50 miles long and will double Syria's electric power output. William Spencer

See also MIDDLE EAST (Facts in Brief Table).

TAIWAN. The future of Taiwan's position in Asia was partly resolved in 1973 through a series of carefully worded statements by the big powers. First, there was the U.S. acknowledgment in February that Taiwan was traditionally part of China, though no date was set for its reincorporation with the mainland. See CHINA, PEOPLE'S REPUBLIC OF.

Other governments were less cautious. Australia quickly recognized the People's Republic of China and transferred Chinese Nationalist holdings to Peking. Japan, following the same line after Prime Minister Kakuei Tanaka's 1972 visit to Peking, began to sever its ties with Taiwan. The Japanese suspended further credits to Taiwan.

Trade Continues Strong. Despite these setbacks, trade and investment did not suffer as much as many in Taiwan had expected. Trade continued at a brisk pace, about $5 billion for the year. European and American investments continued to be heavy, with the United States financing a $300-million power plant formerly projected by the Japanese. Further, there was a significant move toward greater Taiwanization of all political institutions. In elections held at the end of 1972 for the two legislative bodies, only 15 Nationalists from the mainland were among the 89 candidates elected. The rest were Taiwan-born.

The 85-year-old President Chiang was ill for much of the year with pneumonia, which he contracted in

A huge dam, reaching almost 3 miles across the Euphrates River in Syria, began filling its reservoir on July 5. Its construction took five years.

1972, and his governmental duties were assumed by his son. In July, Chiang was reported to be "on the way to full recovery," though he was still confined to a hospital at the time.

Peking's Attitude appeared to be one of patience with the problem. After the February joint communiqué by U.S. Secretary of State Henry A. Kissinger and Chinese Premier Chou En-lai, the Chinese staged a carefully prepared series of meetings and pronouncements in the Taiwan Room of the Great Hall of the People, in Peking. These March 1 statements were timed to coincide with the 26th anniversary of the Taiwanese uprising against the Nationalists. In effect, Peking both warned and cajoled the Taiwanese on the grounds that they had no alternative to accommodation with Peking. Underlying the message was the fact that the United States had begun to withdraw its support of Taiwan.

Peking pointedly reminded Taiwan that no one will replace the United States influence in Taiwan, a reference to both Japan and Russia. The Chinese then promised a general amnesty for all patriots regardless of past wrongdoing, and urged the Taiwanese to send special envoys to Peking, pledging both safety and secrecy for any such emissaries. Peking also made it clear that independence was out of the question, that Taiwan must become an integral part of China. John N. Stalker

See also ASIA (Facts in Brief Table).

TALU, NAIM (1919-   ), was named prime minister of Turkey on April 12, 1973, by President Fahri Koruturk. He formed a coalition government composed of 13 ministers from the Justice Party, 8 from the Republican Reliance Party, and 3 Independents. His government was to serve until a permanent one could be named after the elections scheduled for October. The returns, however, failed to give any of the competing parties a majority, and the government remained in a quasi-caretaker status. See TURKEY.

Naim Talu was born July 22, 1919, in Istanbul. He studied economics at Istanbul University. After completing his military service, Talu joined the Central Bank of Turkey in 1946. He became assistant director of the bank's Ankara branch in 1955, director of its exchange department in 1958, and assistant director-general in 1962. In 1967, Talu became director-general of the Central Bank. That year he also became chairman of the Banks Association of Turkey, and, in 1967 and 1968, he served as chairman of Turkey's Foreign Investment Encouragement Committee.

Appointed minister of commerce, Talu served as a nonpolitical technical expert in the Cabinets of Nihat Erim and his successor, Ferit Melen. Talu had been minister of commerce since December, 1971.

Talu was married to Gevher Erdogan in 1946 and is the father of two daughters. His leisure interests include sailing and tennis. Ed Nelson

TANZANIA. Relations between Tanzania and Uganda were again strained in 1973. In March, Uganda accused Tanzania of preparing an invasion. Tanzania denied the allegation, and a Somali fact-finding team announced it found no evidence of hostile intent on Tanzania's part.

Tanzania arrested 48 Ugandans on espionage charges in March. Uganda denied that they were spies and charged that, since most of the Ugandans arrested worked for the East African Community, Tanzania was trying to destroy that organization.

Tanzania's President Julius K. Nyerere and Uganda's President Idi Amin Dada met during the 10th anniversary conference of the Organization of African Unity in May. Emperor Haile Selassie I of Ethiopia mediated the dispute between Amin and Nyerere, a supporter of Uganda's former President Apollo Milton Obote, whom Amin overthrew in a 1971 coup. Relations between the two nations improved somewhat after the meeting, and in July, they began negotiations on the compensation Uganda would pay the families of 24 Tanzanians murdered in Uganda over the previous two years.

Border Violence between Tanzania and Burundi sputtered between March and July. In March, Burundi troops attacked two Tanzanian villages containing many Hutu (Bahutu) refugees, who had fled from tribal strife in Burundi. The troops killed about 75 persons. Hutu raiders entered Burundi from both Tanzania and Rwanda in May, killing about 50 persons. In July, Tanzanian troops crossed the Burundi border and killed 10 soldiers. However, the countries settled a border dispute on July 22, and Burundi accepted responsibility for killing 10 Tanzanians in a June border raid. See AFRICA.

In January, Tanzania accused Portugal of bombing a Tanzanian village near the Mozambique border. Allegedly, Portugal suspected guerrillas were hiding in the village. Portugal denied the accusation.

Political Trials. Authorities on the island of Zanzibar tried 81 persons in May, including 18 being held on the mainland, for their involvement in the 1972 assassination of Sheik Abeid A. Karume, Zanzibar's former ruler. President Nyerere refused to turn over the 18 held on the mainland because defendants are denied counsel in Zanzibar, and the judges are political appointees with no legal training. Nine of the defendants pleaded guilty to treason and were sentenced to death.

Tanzam Railroad. Work on the Tanzanian section of the Chinese-built Tanzania-Zambia railroad was finished on August 27, two years ahead of schedule. In January, Tanzania's finance minister announced that Zambian copper would be transported through Tanzania to the seaport at Dar es Salaam by trucks and the Tanzam Railroad. Zambia had permanently cut off copper shipments through Rhodesia. See ZAMBIA. John Storm Roberts

See also AFRICA (Facts in Brief Table).

Hutu refugees arrive at a railroad station in Tanzania after fleeing
from bloody tribal warfare that has killed thousands in Burundi.

TAXATION. President Richard M. Nixon, the
United States most prominent taxpayer, disclosed
information about his personal income tax on Dec.
8, 1973. In this unprecedented action, the President
revealed that he paid personal federal income taxes
of $792.81 in 1970; $878.03 in 1971; and $4,298.17
in 1973. Averaged over the three-year period, the
President and Mrs. Nixon paid approximately what
an average family with an income of $25,000 a year
would pay. But the President's total adjusted gross
income averaged $280,556 a year between 1969 and
1972.

Mr. Nixon claimed a tax deduction of $570,000 for
the "charitable donation" of his vice-presidential
papers to the National Archives. This saved him
$235,000 in income taxes. Whether the gift was
properly recorded and therefore deductible was one
question raised by the President's disclosure. But the
larger issue raised by the disclosure was the advisa-
bility of the President's seeking every tax advantage.

Responding to the charges that he had not paid
enough federal income taxes, the President declared
that a Congressional Joint Committee on Internal
Revenue Taxation chaired by Congressman Wilbur
D. Mills (D., Ark.) and Senator Russell B. Long
(D., La.) would go over his tax returns for the past
four years. If the committee decided he had not paid
his full taxes, the President would accept its decision
and pay whatever additional sum it sought. The

President also revealed that he and his wife had paid
no state income taxes in California during his presidency, even though he is legally a resident of that
state.

Taxes and Budget. In his budget message to Congress on January 29, President Nixon outlined a
$268.7-billion budget for fiscal 1974 (July 1, 1973,
to June 30, 1974). The planned federal deficit would
be $12.7 billion.

In order to keep federal spending down, the President had ordered cutbacks in many government programs. In addition, according to estimates by congressional leaders, he impounded some $12 billion to
$15 billion in congressionally appropriated funds to
keep federal spending within the $250-billion spend-
ing limit the Administration had set for fiscal 1973.
Presidential aide John D. Ehrlichman warned on
March 9 that if the President's spending ceiling was
not enforced, individual taxpayers might face a 9 per
cent increase in their personal income taxes. On
July 26, the White House revealed that the federal
deficit for fiscal 1973 was $14.4 billion, $10.4 billion
less than the amount that the Department of the
Treasury had forecast.

No tax rise was proposed in 1973, but on September 13, Melvin R. Laird, counselor to the President,
told a news conference that a tax increase on personal
income was being considered to fight inflation. On
September 23, however, Laird declared that no tax

499

rise was being planned for 1973 and that his September 13 statement was aimed at stimulating "open discussion" of tax policies

Tax Revenue Increase. Because of inflation, there was an unexpected gain in tax receipts, with the government collecting $17 billion more in fiscal 1973 than had been planned. At the same time, the White House had kept federal spending at $246.6 billion, below the ceiling set by the Administration. Spending for social-service grants to the states fell $831-million short of the official estimate, because states had not been as active in using federal funds as the Administration had anticipated.

The government collected a total of $237.8 billion in federal taxes in fiscal 1973. Of this, $177.2 billion came from individual and employment taxes; $39-billion from taxes on corporations; $4.34 billion from estate taxes; $636.9 million from taxes on gifts; and $16.6 billion from excise and other taxes.

Social Security Taxes. On December 21, Congress approved an 11 per cent increase in social security benefits to take effect in two stages. President Nixon signed the bill on Jan. 3, 1974. The first benefit increase was scheduled for April, 1974, and the second for July.

To finance the increase, the maximum wage base for social security taxes was raised from $10,800 in 1973 to $13,200 in 1974. This increased the maximum annual social security tax from $631.80 to $772.80, but there was no increase in the rate of taxation. The 11 per cent increase superseded a 5.9 per cent increase voted by Congress in June. See SOCIAL SECURITY.

State and Local Taxes. State tax collections in fiscal 1973 totaled $67.9 billion, 13.5 per cent higher than the $59.9 billion collected in fiscal 1972. In fiscal 1973, local tax collections totaled $51.8 billion, about 23.7 per cent less than state tax revenue collected during the same period.

New York and California again collected more tax revenue than any other states. Eight states accounted for more than half the total state tax revenue collected in the United States – New York, California, Pennsylvania, Illinois, Michigan, Texas, Ohio, and Florida.

Five states collected tax revenue of $400 or more per capita in fiscal 1973; 9 states collected per capita revenue of $350 to $399; 12 states, $300-349; 18 states, $250-$299; 6 states, less than $250.

Forty-four states collected individual income taxes; 45 states collected sales and gross receipts taxes. The six greatest sources of state tax revenue in fiscal 1973 were: general sales and gross receipts taxes ($19.7 billion); individual income taxes ($15.6-billion); motor fuel taxes ($8.0 billion); corporate income taxes ($5.4 billion); tobacco taxes ($3.1-billion); alcohol taxes ($1.8 billion). Carol L. Thompson

TELEPHONE. Investigations of the settlement of a 1971 antitrust case against International Telephone and Telegraph Corporation (ITT) multiplied in 1973. At issue was ITT's acquisition of the Hartford Fire Insurance Company. An out-of-court settlement with the U.S. Department of Justice in 1971 permitted ITT to retain Hartford, provided the corporation divested itself of several other companies. But when the settlement was linked to a proposed ITT contribution to finance the 1972 Republican convention, the Senate launched a full-scale investigation into ITT ties to the White House.

The House of Representatives initiated its own probe in 1973. In June, Special Watergate Prosecutor Archibald Cox also began looking into the ITT case in connection with possible charges connected with the Watergate investigation. In August, a grand jury began studying allegations of criminal actions by government and ITT officials. The White House continued to deny any connection between the antitrust settlement and the ITT convention contribution. White House officials also denied that they had pressured the Justice Department to drop charges.

In June, a Senate subcommittee on multinational corporations concluded that ITT had overstepped the bounds of responsible corporate behavior by seeking to interfere in the 1970 Chile election. Although such action was not illegal, the subcommittee proposed legislation to make it illegal in the future.

"Watching the Watcher"

The Dyna T-A-C portable telephone, which uses FM radio frequencies to relay signals, may be in operation in New York by 1976.

Revenues, Investments. The Federal Communications Commission authorized rate increases in November, 1972, for the American Telephone and Telegraph Company that would produce an additional $145 million a year in interstate revenues. Even with this increase, the company said, overall interstate rates would still be lower than they were in 1953.

The U.S. Department of Commerce said that gross capital investment of the nation's domestic telephone and telegraph industries would top $100-billion by the end of 1973. Domestic telephone revenues were estimated at more than $27 billion, up 13 per cent. International revenues were put at $597 million, 27 per cent higher than in 1972.

New Services. Telephone service took on a new look with more and more companies seeking to interconnect their equipment with the telephone networks to provide specialized communications services. In a number of countries – notably the United States, Great Britain, and Canada – government and industry were examining the implications for the future that such services portend. One forecast was that this market will account for $3 billion within the next decade for companies that make equipment that can be used with standard telephone equipment. The Bell System estimated that such services could cause a potential annual loss of $250 million in interstate revenues by 1976.   Thomas M. Malia

TELEVISION. Live broadcasts of the Watergate hearings provided the most dramatic and suspenseful fare in the United States in 1973. Viewers spent an estimated 1.6 billion home-hours watching Watergate proceedings on the three major networks, plus an additional 400 million hours viewing taped replays on public television at night. The networks logged more than 319 hours of marathon daytime coverage during the initial 37-day run (May 17 to August 7) of the congressional investigation.

All three networks carried the first five days of the hearings. On June 5, they adopted a daily rotation plan, the first in network history. By taking turns, the networks curtailed coverage costs (well over $7-million in lost revenue) and, at least partly, appeased irate soap-opera and game-show fans.

Watergate was a windfall for public television stations, which carried the National Public Affairs Center's (NPACT) full-text taping of the hearings on a delayed basis in prime evening time. According to NPACT officials, public TV outlets throughout the United States received more than $1 million in contributions from grateful Watergate viewers.

The long-time rift between broadcasters and the Nixon Administration was deepened by television's all-out coverage of the Watergate hearings and related events. On October 27, President Richard M. Nixon bitterly assailed television's commentary on Watergate as "outrageous, vicious, distorted reporting." However, some industry observers believed the Administration's Watergate problems and Vice-President Spiro T. Agnew's resignation in October might ultimately result in less intimidation of broadcasters by the executive branch. See Section One, Focus on The Arts.

The Licensing Problem. Most worrisome for broadcasters in 1973 was the problem of license renewals. In January, the White House Office of Telecommunications Policy (OTP) submitted a bill to Congress designed to amend TV station license-renewal provisions of the Communications Act of 1934. The bill, in effect, would have made the nation's network-affiliated local stations responsible for network news content. However, OTP conceded in June that the Administration's license bill was dead.

The House Communications Subcommittee approved a compromise licensing bill on October 9. The bill, still to be voted on by the full Commerce Committee, would extend a broadcaster's license period from three to four years. It would also allow the Federal Communications Commission (FCC) to award an existing station to a license challenger if the latter demonstrated a clear superiority.

Minorities and other citizen groups filed numerous license challenges, but only a handful were pending before the FCC in the fall. Some broadcasters made conciliatory gestures to protesting citizen groups by establishing employment and promotion

"The Waltons" brought viewers a warm, if often sugary, view of family life in Virginia during the years of the Great Depression of the 1930s.

quotas and increasing special-interest programming. According to a 1973 study by the United Church of Christ's Office of Communications, 78 per cent of all new full-time employees at 584 stations polled were from minorities. Discrimination against women, though, was still widespread both in hiring and promotion.

The Year's Programming. "An American Family" was the most talked-about documentary of 1973. Edited down from 300 hours of filming during a seven-month period, the cinéma vérité series made instant "stars" of the Louds, a troubled Santa Barbara, Calif., family. The $1.2-million-plus package was underwritten by the Ford Foundation and the Corporation for Public Broadcasting (CPB).

The surprise TV hit of the year was "The Waltons," a wholesome drama about rural family life during the Great Depression. The series won six Emmys. The top Emmy winner (seven) was "The Julie Andrews Show," which was canceled in the fall. Also dropped were such old favorites as "Mission Impossible," "Laugh-In," Doris Day, Bill Cosby, and the comparatively new "Bridget Loves Bernie."

More than half of the new fall shows spotlighted

law-and-order heroes, including two black private eyes—James McEachin as "Tenafly" and Richard Roundtree as "Shaft." None of the new series scored high in early rating reports. "All in the Family" was consistently number one throughout the year. Also maintaining positions on the top 10 list were "Sanford and Son," "Maude," "Hawaii Five O," "The Mary Tyler Moore Show," and "Columbo."

Among the year's stand-out programs were *The Sins of the Fathers*, a poignant documentary about abandoned American-Vietnamese children; a syndicated program "Black Omnibus," the first regular commercial all-black entertainment series; and the carnival-like Billie Jean King-Bobby Riggs tennis match, watched by an estimated 72-million persons.

Two remarkable dramas—Eugene O'Neill's *Long Day's Journey into Night* starring Sir Laurence Olivier, and Joseph Papp's three-hour version of *Much Ado About Nothing*—won high critical praise, but low, low ratings.

A second Papp production, *Sticks and Bones*, was postponed in March because 69 Columbia Broadcasting System (CBS–TV) affiliates refused to schedule it. The controversial antiwar drama, about the suicide of a blind Vietnam veteran, was blacked out by 94 stations when it finally was aired on August 17.

The networks did yeoman duty on an unusual number of historic news events. These included the return of the Vietnam POW's, the presidential inauguration, the continuous crisis-upon-crisis state of Watergate, Agnew's surprise resignation, the death of former President Lyndon B. Johnson, the Arab-Israeli war, and the lengthy journey of *Skylab*, the first flying television station capable of transmitting color pictures both live and on tape.

Sexy Television. Although the trend toward more permissive "adult" programming continued, there were signs of a growing backlash. Citizen complaints to the FCC about "obscene" broadcast material were 15 times greater in number than in 1972. In March, the FCC announced a closed-door investigation to determine if any station or cable television systems had aired "obscene, indecent, or profane material." One of the FCC's targets was KVVU-TV, Henderson, Nev. At the beginning of the year, the station was televising X-rated movies late at night but it discontinued the practice after viewers threatened to boycott KVVU-TV advertisers. In April, the National Association of Broadcasters (NAB) launched a campaign to clean up "tasteless and vulgar program content, whether explicit or by sexually oriented innuendo." See RADIO.

Labor Troubles. The industry was plagued by a strike by members of the Writers Guild of America that lasted from April 12 until early July. As a result of the strike, some fall season premières had to be

Brothers Kevin (with guitar) and Grant Loud (at piano) are filmed in their Santa Barbara, Calif., home for television series "An American Family."

Law enforcement dominated television screens in 1973. Clifton Davis, left, and George Maharis starred in an episode on NBC-TV's "Police Story."

delayed until late October and new shows were introduced over several weeks, rather than being concentrated in one seven-day period.

On the Pacific Coast, members of the International Alliance of Theatrical Stage Employees Stagehands local 33 staged a 22-day strike against all three networks and their owned and operated stations in late October. The dispute centered on pay issues.

It was a troubled year for public television. A power struggle developed over control of the national network between the CPB and the Public Broadcasting System (PBS), a network of some 230 public television stations. In April, Thomas B. Curtis resigned as CPB chairman, claiming the Nixon Administration pressured certain CPB members to minimize news broadcasts of national affairs on public TV. His successor was James R. Killian, Jr. CPB and PBS resolved their differences in May. The pact guaranteed PBS the right to schedule network programs other than those funded by CPB.

After a two-year debate, KTTV, Los Angeles, acceded in October to demands by a citizens' coalition group led by the National Association for Better Broadcasting and Action for Children's Television. The station agreed to drop 42 "excessively violent" cartoons and to preface telecasts of 81 "live" series with a "Caution to Parents." June Bundy Csida

See also AWARDS AND PRIZES (Arts Awards).

TENNESSEE. See STATE GOVERNMENT.

TENNIS experienced a momentous year throughout the world in 1973. The Association of Tennis Professionals (ATP), whose members included most of the important male players, boycotted the All-England championships at Wimbledon, the world's most prestigious tournament, in June. Women professionals were almost barred from Wimbledon competition because of a power struggle similar to the men's. World Team Tennis, a new group with franchises in 16 major cities in the United States, was formed in May, despite opposition from international officials and the ATP.

Hustling Bobby Riggs. With all this, the broadest impact on the sport was made by bandy-legged Bobby Riggs, once a United States and Wimbledon champion, who had become a confessed tennis and golf "hustler," one who made all kinds of outrageous bets with opponents and inevitably won. His 1973 hustles proved to be huge financial successes.

Riggs fashioned his coup by seizing the role as the nation's leading male chauvinist. He described himself as "a 55-year-old player with one foot in the grave." Even so, he said, he could beat the best women players. He challenged Margaret Court of Australia, probably the best player among the women, to a special challenge match. After surprising Court with a Mother's Day bouquet of roses, Riggs beat her, 6-2, 6-1, on May 13 in Ramona, Calif.

Men and women had never played publicly like this before, and even though Riggs made only $12,500 (plus his inevitable side bets) from the match, he knew bigger days were ahead. They were. He next played Billie Jean King, a Women's Liberation spokeswoman, on September 20 in the Houston Astrodome. This time, the purse was $100,000, winner take all, and each player was assured at least $100,000 from ancillary rights.

The King-Riggs match took on a circus atmosphere. United States television rights sold for more than $700,000, and an estimated 48 million watched on television. In the Astrodome, 30,492 watched in person, paying up to $100 for the best seats. King was ill the week before the match, but she beat Riggs easily, 6-4, 6-3, 6-3. See KING, BILLIE JEAN.

Player Discord. King and most other players on the Virginia Slims women's professional circuit felt the United States Lawn Tennis Association (USLTA) was stifling them, and the International Lawn Tennis Federation (ILTF), which supported the USLTA, almost suspended the women.

Among male pros, 82 members and supporters of the ATP refused to play at Wimbledon. Ostensibly, the dispute centered on Yugoslavia's suspension, upheld by the ILTF, of Nikki Pilic for failing to play in a Davis Cup series. Pilic, an ATP member, said he had never agreed to play. Actually, the players felt that the conservative ILTF was giving them little control of their tournaments.

By year's end, the men and women pros had

THAILAND, one of the oldest and most stable nations in Asia, ousted its military dictator in 1973. Violent student demonstrations forced Field Marshal Thanom Kittikachorn to resign on October 14. Kittikachorn, his son-in-law Marshal Praphas Charsathien, and his son, Colonel Narong Kittikachorn, had steadily enriched themselves at the expense of the country ever since they took over in a military coup in 1971. King Phumiphon Aduldet named Sanya Thammasak prime minister. Two groups, aided by a courageous press, brought the regime to an end. These were the labor unions and practically all the university students in Bangkok.

In April, a Thai Army helicopter crashed not far from Bangkok, killing six high-ranking military police officials and injuring five others. The Thai press revealed that the officials were on an illegal hunting expedition in a government game preserve. The government said the party was on a "secret mission," but their story was exposed when it was revealed that movie starlets were participating in the outing.

Beatings Arouse Students. The exposé was followed in June by a large student demonstration protesting the expulsion of nine students for the publication of a satire about the government. The students were aroused when government thugs beat up the student leaders. As a result of the demonstrations, the government was forced to make concessions to the students, and the rector of the university resigned.

In the past, this would have ended the protest. But in October, the government arrested 13 students for distributing pamphlets urging the adoption of a constitution. They were charged with various crimes, including the treasonable charge of communism. No evidence was produced to prove the case. Crowds of protestors then grew at Thammasat University. On October 11, some 200,000 people demanded the release of the students. The government ordered troops to disband the protestors, but on the following day, 400,000 marched in the streets, and their leaders secured an audience with the king. An uneasy truce was concluded between the protestors and the government.

Army Fires on Crowd. The next day, the truce broke down, and the army began to fire on the crowds. More than 200 persons were killed, and an estimated 1,000 were wounded. That night, King Phumiphon Aduldet appeared on television to announce the resignation of Marshal Thanom and the appointment of Professor Sanya Thammasak, the rector of Thammasat University, as prime minister.

Marshal Praphas and Colonel Narong fled to Taiwan, and Marshal Thanom found refuge in the United States. A new constitution was promised in six months, and Thailand returned to civilian government. On December 16, the king dissolved the National Assembly to pave the way for the election of a new legislature on December 19.   John N. Stalker

See also ASIA (Facts in Brief Table).

"Sorry, old man." Billie Jean King consoles male chauvinist Bobby Riggs after beating him decisively in the Houston Astrodome.

reached separate peace agreements with the tennis establishment. All were concerned about the new team tennis league, which already had signed King, Evonne Goolagong, Ken Rosewall, and John Newcombe of Australia, and others. The league's May-to-July schedule conflicted with many major European tournaments. The new league had franchises in Boston, Chicago, Cincinnati, Denver, Detroit, Houston, Los Angeles, Minneapolis-St. Paul, New York City, Philadelphia, Phoenix, Pittsburgh, St. Louis, San Diego, San Francisco, and Toronto.

The Year's Winners. The most successful player was Margaret Court, who won her 5th U.S., 5th French, and 11th Australian championships and 14 of the 23 tournaments on the Virginia Slims circuit. At Wimbledon, where King won, Court lost in the semifinals. Among the men, Jan Kodes of Czechoslovakia won in the watered-down Wimbledon field and lost in the U.S. final to Newcombe. In December, Newcombe and Laver won the Davis Cup for Australia by defeating the United States, 5-0, in Cleveland.

Ilie Nastase of Romania won the French title and dominated the Grand Prix circuit. He was also one of the three ATP members who played at Wimbledon despite the boycott. The ATP fined him $5,000 and expelled him.   Frank Litsky

TEXAS. See DALLAS-FORT WORTH; HOUSTON; STATE GOVERNMENT.

THEATER

The theater declared its independence from Broadway in 1973, three years before America's bicentennial. Plays and musicals found near-capacity audiences on cross-country tours. Two plays that won major awards from drama critics originated off Broadway and in the regional theater. The spiraling cost of producing a play cut independent presentations in New York City, but they gave impetus to producing organizations that offered a series of plays to subscription audiences. These organizations took their cue from regional theaters that owe their success to subscription audiences.

On Broadway, groups such as the Circle in the Square, the New York Shakespeare Festival at Lincoln Center, and the New Phoenix found enthusiastic subscription audiences. Off Broadway, subscription seasons made possible new plays and revivals by the American Place, the Circle, the Chelsea Manhattan, the Negro Ensemble, and the New Repertory companies.

Touring Shows. With a moderate musical costing about half a million dollars, producers of touring shows relied on stars and/or revivals of past hits. Carol Channing starred in *Lorelei*, which opened in Oklahoma City in February and played in 17 other cities from coast to coast. It was scheduled to open in New York City in January, 1974. The show incorporates some of the songs from the 1949 musical *Gentlemen Prefer Blondes* in a framework in which an older Lorelei, still good-hearted and muddle-headed, looks back on her earlier days when diamonds were a girl's best friend. Deborah Kerr starred as a Victorian lady who helps her pregnant servant in *The Day After the Fair*, which embarked on a 19-week tour in Denver in August. Some productions, such as *Gone with the Wind*, did not include Broadway in their tours. See Section One, FOCUS ON THE ARTS.

New Playwrights looked off Broadway and beyond to get their plays produced. The Circle Theatre Company presented Lanford Wilson's *The Hot L Baltimore*. The title refers to a seedy hotel's neon sign, which has lost an "e." In the hotel lobby, the residents, who are also losers, discuss their plight. The New York Drama Critics' Circle chose it as the best American play of the year. The critics elected *The Changing Room* by Englishman David Storey as the best foreign play. It was produced at the Long Wharf Theatre in New Haven, Conn. Storey sees the changing (locker) room as a metaphor of life. Twenty-two men who work during the week, members of a semiprofessional weekend rugby team, prepare for the contest, return to the changing room during halftime, and celebrate their victory there after the game.

Glynis Johns, center, one of the stars of
A Little Night Music, won a Tony as best
actress, and the play was named best musical.

They are decent men who rush into the fray with little knowledge of their aim beyond the welcome extra money. Outstanding ensemble acting characterized this production and also that of *The River Niger*, by the Negro Ensemble Company. Through vivid characterization and dialogue, Joseph A. Walker depicts a family headed by a house painter who is also a poet. Their human and social problems reflect those of the black minority. In *When You Comin' Back, Red Ryder?* at the Eastside Playhouse, Mark Medoff depicted youth alienated from society when a cowboy-hoodlum terrorizes a Western diner.

Subscription Audiences. At the new 650-seat Joseph E. Levine Theatre, Circle in the Square subscription audiences saw a star-studded *Uncle Vanya*. The Anton Chekhov play was directed by Mike Nichols and starred George C. Scott as Dr. Astrov, Nicol Williamson as Vanya, and Julie Christie as the young wife. *The Iceman Cometh* was their impressive winter revival. The New York Shakespeare Festival offered an all-star black cast in Chekhov's *The Cherry Orchard*, with James Earl Jones, Earle Hyman, Gloria Foster, and Ellen Holly.

Papp Replaces Repertory. In March, producer Joseph Papp and his New York Shakespeare Festival were invited to take over the two theaters of the Repertory Theater of Lincoln Center. The Center's new theater company is called the New York Shakespeare Festival at Lincoln Center. Papp renamed the experimental Forum Theater the Mitzi E. Newhouse Theater and turned it into a year-round home for Shakespeare. The Vivian Beaumont Theater will emphasize new works instead of revivals of the classics. The season opened November 8 with a controversial new play by David Rabe, *Boom Boom Room*, whose main character is a go-go dancer. A new work by Hugh Leonard, *The Au Pair Man*, and three Shakespeare plays—*Troilus and Cressida*, *The Tempest*, and *Coriolanus*—were scheduled.

The Chelsea Theatre Center Manhattan offered its subscription audiences David Storey's *The Contractor* and a revival of Leonard Bernstein's musical version of Voltaire's *Candide*. The musical's delightful and inventive score matches the wry humor of the story.

Musicals were either revivals, earlier plays, or films musicalized. The best was *A Little Night Music*, based on Ingmar Bergman's film *Smiles of a Summer Night* (1955). Stephen Sondheim provided sophisticated, melodic, and witty music and lyrics for the story of love's illusions and disillusions. Set in Sweden at the turn of the century, the intrigues involve an aging lawyer, his young wife, his former mistress (Glynis Johns), and her mother (Hermione Gingold). *Seesaw* set to music William Gibson's comedy about a Jewish girl from the Bronx and a married Protestant lawyer from the Midwest. Imaginative direction and choreography by Michael Bennett and inspired film projections transformed the small play into an enjoyable musical.

Debbie Reynolds starred in *Irene*, a revival of the 1919 musical-comedy hit about a poor Irish girl who succeeds in the dress business and marries a wealthy Long Islander. President Richard M. Nixon, who saw the show in Washington, D.C., predicted it would be a hit with "out-of-towners" because he felt most Americans were tired of "all that way-out stuff" in the modern theater.

Three Broadway musicals originated in regional theaters. Based on *Raisin in the Sun*, Lorraine Hansberry's dynamic and moving play about the conflict between a man's aspirations and his integrity, *Raisin* came from Washington, D.C.'s Arena Stage. Donald McKayle's direction and choreography, and music and lyrics by Judd Woldin and Robert Brittan, contributed to the appeal of this story of a black family in Chicago in the 1950s. Christopher Plummer starred in *Cyrano*, a musical based on Edmond Rostand's play as adapted by Anthony Burgess and staged at the Tyrone Guthrie Theatre in Minneapolis. The Actors Theatre of Louisville brought in *Tricks*, Jon Jory's commedia dell' arte adaptation of Molière's *Scapin*.

Major Playwrights were involved with theater around the country. Arthur Miller accepted a post as adjunct professor at the University of Michigan, his alma mater, where he won the Hopwood drama prize in 1936. In the spring of 1974, the University Players will stage scenes from *The American Clock*, Miller's uncompleted play about the Great Depression. Tennessee Williams rewrote *Out Cry* as it toured New Haven, Chicago, Philadelphia, and Washington, D.C. In the drama, a brother and sister, actors locked in a deserted theater, play out scenes of their unhappy past. Williams' new play is *The Red Devil Battery Sign*, set in Dallas after the 1963 assassination of President John F. Kennedy.

Regional Theaters continued to encourage new plays and playwrights. David Epstein's *Darkroom* was staged at the Yale Repertory Theatre. In Chicago, the Goodman Memorial Theatre staged the American première of Brian Friel's *The Freedom of the City*. At The Mark Taper Forum in Los Angeles, 10 writers, 90 actors, and 7 directors participated in a festival of 10 new plays.

Alice Griffin

See also AWARDS AND PRIZES (Arts Awards); Section Two, THE THEATER IS ALIVE, WELL, AND LIVING ALL OVER.

TOGO. See AFRICA.

TORNADOES. See DISASTERS; WEATHER.

TOYS. See GAMES, MODELS, AND TOYS.

TRACK AND FIELD. Three athletes from the Pacific Coast Club of Long Beach, Calif. (Dwight Stones, Al Feuerbach, and Steve Smith), and three natives of Coos Bay, Ore. (Steve Prefontaine, Mac Wilkins, and Mrs. Fran Sichting), provided track and field excitement in 1973.

Stones won the bronze medal for the high jump in the 1972 Olympic Games in Munich, West Germany. He returned there July 11, 1973, to set a world record of 7 feet 6 ½ inches, the first by a high-jumper using the flop style rather than the straddle. Stones cleared 7 feet 4 ¼ inches and 7 feet 5 ⅜ inches en route to his record, and during the year had two winning jumps of 7 feet 5 inches and five others over 7 feet 4 inches. Only three other men had ever cleared 7 feet 5 inches.

Stones, 19 and exuberant, said, "I hope to jump as long as possible for my own pleasure and also for the joy of those who like and appreciate me. I would like to have it said of me sometime that I had fun and perhaps attained my limit."

Feuerbach made six of the seven longest shot-puts of the year. His best, 71 feet 7 inches on May 5 in San Jose, Calif., broke Randy Matson's world record. He also engaged in a running feud with Brian Oldfield, a 1972 Olympic teammate who had become the leading money-winner of the new professional track circuit. Feuerbach suspected that

Professional track began in 1973, and its pioneers included pole-vaulter Bob Seagren, ex-miler Marty Liquori as emcee, and promoter Mike O'Hara.

World Track and Field Records Established in 1973

Event	Holder	Country	Where made	Date	Record
Men					
100 yards	Steve Williams	U.S.A.	Fresno, Calif.	May 12	:09.1*
800 meters	Marcello Fiasconaro	Italy	Milan	June 27	1:43.7
880 yards	Rick Wohlhuter	U.S.A.	Los Angeles	May 27	1:44.6
1,000 meters	Danie Malan	S. Africa	Munich	June 24	2:16.0
2 miles	Brendan Foster	England	London	August 27	8:13.8
10,000 meters	Dave Bedford	England	London	July 14	27:31.0
120-yard high hurdles	Rod Milburn	U.S.A.	Eugene, Ore.	June 20	:13.0*
110-meter high hurdles	Rod Milburn	U.S.A.	Zurich	July 6	:13.1
	Rod Milburn	U.S.A.	Siena, Italy	July 22	:13.1*
3,000-meter steeplechase	Ben Jipcho	Kenya	Helsinki	June 27	8:14.0
2-mile relay	U. of Chicago T.C. Bach, Sparks, Paul, Wohlhuter	U.S.A.	Durham, N.C.	May 12	7:10.4
6,000-meter relay	Polhill, Walker, Dixon, Quax	New Zealand	Oslo	August 22	14:40.4
High jump	Dwight Stones	U.S.A.	Munich	July 11	7 ft. 6½ in.
Shot-put	Al Feuerbach	U.S.A.	San Jose, Calif.	May 5	71 ft. 7 in.
Javelin throw	Klaus Wolfermann	W. Germany	Leverkusen, W. Germany	May 5	308 ft. 8 in.
Women					
100 meters	Renate Stecher	E. Germany	Dresden	July 20	:10.8
200 meters	Renate Stecher	E. Germany	Dresden	July 21	:22.1
400 meters	Mona-Lisa Pursiainen	Finland	Helsinki	September 16	:51.0*
800 meters	Svetla Zlateva	Bulgaria	Athens	August 24	1:57.48
1 mile	Paola Pigni	Italy	Viareggio	August 8	4:29.5
2 miles	Francie Larrieu	U.S.A.	Hayward, Calif.	June 3	10:02.8
100-meter hurdles	Annelie Ehrhardt	E. Germany	Dresden	July 22	:12.3
400-meter hurdles	Danuta Piecyk	Poland	Warsaw	August 11	:56.7
400-meter relay	Kandarr, Stecher, Heinich, Selmigkeit	E. Germany	Potsdam	September 1	:42.6
3,200-meter relay	Zlateva, Tomova, Petrova, Yordanova	Bulgaria	Sofia	August 12	8:08.6
Shot-put	Nadezhda Chizhova	U.S.S.R.	Varna	September 29	70 ft. 4½ in.
Discus throw	Faina Melnik	U.S.S.R.	Edinburgh	September 7	227 ft. 11 in.
Javelin throw	Ruth Fuchs	E. Germany	Edinburgh	September 7	216 ft. 10 in.
Pentathlon	Burglinde Pollak	E. Germany	Bonn	September 22-23	4,932 pts.

*Equals record

Oldfield's long indoor puts, including a world indoor record of 70 feet 10½ inches, were made with an underweight shot.

Smith, with his colorful warm-up shirt and a Harpo Marx hairdo, was a crowd favorite. He was unbeaten in 11 indoor meets and made the nine highest pole vaults of the winter, including a world indoor record of 18 feet ¼ inch in Madison Square Garden in January. His best outdoor mark was 17 feet 10½ inches. In November, he turned professional.

Before a back problem cut short his European tour, Prefontaine set American records for 2 miles (8 minutes 24.6 seconds) and 5,000 meters (13 minutes 22.4 seconds). Wilkins, Prefontaine's University of Oregon teammate, won the discus throws in the Amateur Athletic Union (A.A.U.) and National Collegiate Athletic Association (NCAA) outdoor championships. He became perhaps the finest all-around thrower ever, with career bests of 212 feet 6 inches in the discus throw, 63 feet 8 inches in the shot-put, 257 feet 4 inches in the javelin throw, and 201 feet 3½ inches in the hammer throw.

Fran Sichting, at 19 America's best female sprint prospect in years, set a U.S. women's record of 23.2 seconds for 220 yards in June in Irvine, Calif. But her husband, Ted, a logger, refused to allow her to compete in Europe and she stayed home, saying, "It's track or my marriage."

Jipcho's Year. Ben Jipcho, a 30-year-old Kenyan, broke the world record for the 3,000-meter steeplechase twice, lowering it to 8 minutes 14.0 seconds. On July 2, in Stockholm, Sweden, he won the mile in 3 minutes 52.0 seconds, beating Filbert Bayi of Tanzania (3:52.6). Only Jim Ryun, who turned pro, had run faster than Jipcho or Bayi.

Rod Milburn of Southern University in Baton Rouge, La., and Dave Wottle of Bowling Green State University in Ohio, 1972 Olympic champions, had successful years. Milburn won three A.A.U. and NCAA high-hurdles championships, equaled his world record of 13.0 seconds for the 120-yard high hurdles, and set (and later tied) a world record of 13.1 seconds for the 110-meter high hurdles. Wottle won the NCAA mile in 3 minutes 57.1 seconds as the first eight finishers bettered 4 minutes, then captured many races in the United States and abroad.

Steve Williams of San Diego State University, who missed the 1972 Olympics because of injury, returned and won both the 100- and 220-yard A.A.U. sprints and tied the world record for 100 yards. He received greater pleasure by beating Valeri Borzov of Russia, winner of both Olympic sprints, in a relay in July in Minsk, Russia.

Dave Bedford of England set a world record of 27 minutes 31.0 seconds for 10,000 meters July 14 in London in the British championships. That night, he celebrated with champagne but no sleep. The next day, he finished far back in the 5,000-meter race.

Because Mary Decker of Garden Grove, Calif., was only 14, she had an earlier nightly curfew than the other women on the U.S. team that toured Europe. Perhaps the extra sleep helped, because she won the 800 meters in meets against Russia (2 minutes 2.9 seconds), Italy, and Africa. The American women won the meets against Italy and Africa and lost to Russia and West Germany; the American men lost only to the Russians.

Internationally, Renate Stecher, a 23-year-old East German, set women's world records of 10.8 seconds for 100 meters and 22.1 for 200 meters in the East German championships July 20 and 21.

Professional Track. The International Track Association (ITA) conducted 16 indoor meets in different cities from early March to early June as professional track, long a dream of many athletes, became a reality in 1973. Attendance averaged 6,000 but the New York City meet attracted 15,501.

Much of the success was due to the quality of the stars. They included Ryun, Lee Evans, Matson, Kipchoge Keino, Bob Hayes, John Carlos, Wyomia Tyus Simburg, Bob Beamon, and Bob Seagren.

Oldfield was the unexpected star as a shot-putter and sprinter. He raced a woman sprinter at 30 yards in every meet and never lost.   Frank Litsky

See also SHORTER, FRANK.

TRANSIT. Public concern about urban mass transportation intensified in the United States in 1973. Increasing traffic congestion, continuing antipollution efforts, emerging energy problems, and mounting deficits among the nation's transit systems added to transit woes.

The federal government reversed two major policies regarding the financing of urban transportation. On August 13, President Richard M. Nixon signed a $23-billion highway bill that, for the first time, permitted cities to use a share of the Federal Highway Trust Fund for nonhighway mass transit. And, on November 30, Transportation Secretary Claude S. Brinegar indicated that the Nixon Administration was considering the use of federal funds for mass transit operating subsidies.

The Highway Bill, signed in August, offered an opening wedge into the Highway Trust Fund, a wedge long sought not only by transit officials anxious to relieve congestion, but also by environmentalists anxious to ease automobile pollution.

Under the compromise three-year bill, the $6-billion Highway Trust Fund, made up of revenues from federal taxes on gasoline, tires, and truck tonnage will continue to be restricted to road use through June 30, 1974. However, beginning on July 1, 1974, $200 million will be available for municipal bus purchases. Starting on July 1, 1975, $800 million

Seattle passengers are enthusiastic about the new Magic Carpet bus service, which gives free rides within a 77-square-block downtown area.

will be available for buses, rail systems, and subways. After July 1, 1974, communities would not lose any of their highway funds when they qualified for mass-transit subsidies. Until then, communities can seek immediate relief for local transportation by substituting mass transit for highway projects. They can finance the substitution by turning back highway funds and receiving an equal amount in general revenue funds. The bill authorized $3 billion for such purposes through fiscal 1977.

Operating Subsidies. Until November, the Nixon Administration had steadfastly opposed the use of federal funds to subsidize mass transit operating costs. The Administration contended that states and localities should provide operating subsidies as part of their overall plans for dealing with traffic congestion, land use, and other urban problems. Administration officials had also argued that operating subsidies would constitute blank checks to local authorities, who could then bow to political expediency and keep transit fares low and transit salaries high while the federal government paid the difference. Consequently, federal assistance to transit had been limited solely to capital grants.

Secretary Brinegar's announcement that the Administration was considering the use of federal funds for operating subsidies was confirmed on December 26 when President Nixon told New York Governor Malcolm Wilson that he favored the flexible use of federal funds for mass transit.

More Aid Needed. Despite these two encouraging developments, there was growing concern that transit systems soon would not have enough money to meet rising operating costs. Demands for federal transit aid are expected to soar in 1974 and 1975 as previous federal grants to finance transit planning work begin to pay off.

The Urban Mass Transportation Administration's (UMTA) fiscal 1974 budget was about $1 billion, and the fiscal 1975 budget was expected to be about $2 billion. Many transit experts felt, however, that at least $3 billion would be needed in fiscal 1975 if UMTA was to continue providing financial assistance to all requests that meet requirements.

Passengers. The national decline in the use of public transportation that began after World War II slowed markedly in 1973. Preliminary American Transit Association (ATA) statistics indicated that the 25-year declining trend in passengers may have bottomed out. During the first 10 months of 1973, transit ridership decreased only 0.5 per cent from the same period in 1972. This compared with a drop of 4.1 per cent in the same 1971 and 1972 periods, and an average annual decrease of 3 per cent to 6 per cent during the last 25 years. The ATA's preliminary estimates forecast a total of 6.57 billion passengers, up slightly over the 6.567 billion passengers in 1972. Operating losses for 1973 were put at $400 million, about the same as in 1972.   Kenneth E. Schaefle

TRANSPORTATION. The U.S. transportation industry had a mixed year in 1973. The industry benefited from a strong economy and expanding foreign trade through the first three quarters of the year. Starting in the fourth quarter, however, the transport sector began to feel the effects of a slowing economy, continuing inflation, soaring fuel costs, and fuel-allocation programs. At year-end, most transportation segments were greatly concerned about the threat of a slump or recession in 1974.

Airlines, railroads, and ocean-shipping companies showed profit increases over 1972, but trucking profits declined slightly. All modes of transport reached new highs in the amount of freight carried. The airlines also set new records for passenger travel.

Given the volume of freight moved, however, the carriers had expected profits to be much higher. Profits for railroads, truckers, and ocean-shipping companies suffered from rising costs and governmental lags in approving rate increases because of wage and price controls. Airline passenger traffic grew, but it was sluggish and far below early estimates. At the same time, air carriers also experienced rising costs, and fare increases they requested did not become effective until December.

However, the year may have been a critical turning point in public recognition of the need for a more balanced transportation system. There was growing acceptance of the idea that it was necessary and desirable to have public transportation and intercity rail service as alternatives to automobile transport.

The total U.S. transportation bill for 1973 was about $252 billion, a 6.2 per cent increase over 1972, according to preliminary estimates of the Transportation Association of America (TAA). The TAA's preliminary estimates of total U.S. mainland traffic volume were:

Freight	1972	1973
(billions of intercity ton-miles)		
Rail	785.0	856.0
Truck	470.0	495.0
Pipeline	457.0	484.0
Rivers and canals	218.0	229.0
Lakes	107.0	118.0
Air	3.8	4.2
Total	2,040.8	2,186.2

Passenger		
(billions of intercity passenger-miles)		
Auto	1,129.0	1,134.6
Private air	10.0	10.5
Public commercial air	123.0	132.5
Bus	25.6	25.7
Rail	9.0	9.0
Water	4.0	4.0
Total	1,300.6	1,316.3

Department of Transportation. Claude S. Brinegar, a senior vice-president with Union Oil Company in California, became U.S. secretary of transportation on Feb. 1, 1973. He is the third person to hold the position since the Department of Transportation (DOT) was established in 1967. See BRINEGAR, CLAUDE S.

After a two-year struggle, DOT succeeded in persuading Congress to open the Highway Trust Fund to urban mass transportation projects in August. Also, contract authority for the department's Urban Mass Transportation Administration (UMTA) was increased by $3 billion to $6.1 billon through fiscal 1977. UMTA loans, grants, and contracts to cities for mass transit totaled $1 billion during fiscal 1973, and another $68 million was allocated during the first four months of fiscal 1974.

DOT helped develop legislation to deal with the Northeast railroad crisis, involving the pending bankruptcy of six major Eastern rail carriers. Legislation that would create a new rail system was approved by a Senate-House conference committee in December.

Acting through the Federal Aviation Administration, DOT instituted strict preboarding procedures for passenger airlines. As a result, there were no successful skyjackings in the United States in 1973, compared with an average of 28 a year between 1968 and 1972.

DOT also campaigned for state laws that would make the use of auto safety belts mandatory. Statistics indicated that the use of seat belts by all motorists could save from 10,000 to 15,000 American lives a year.

Kenneth E. Schaefle

See also AUTOMOBILE; AVIATION; RAILROAD; SHIP AND SHIPPING; TRANSIT; TRUCK AND TRUCKING.

TRAVEL. International tourism increased by 9 per cent in 1973, with about 215 million visits across international borders. Expenditures in destination countries, fares, and charges for private automobiles accounted for a grand total in excess of $30 billion.

Double devaluation of the dollar put the United States virtually on sale to foreign visitors in 1973. It was 30 to 40 per cent cheaper for visitors from abroad to travel in the United States, and an estimated 14.2 million of them took advantage of the bargain, an increase of 8.7 per cent over 1972. They spent a record $3.6 billion, 13 per cent more than in 1972, putting the United States in first place in dollar receipts. At the same time, some 25 million Americans who traveled abroad found that inflation increased the cost of their trips by as much as 25 per cent. American tourists spent $7 billion abroad, up 9 per cent, and increased the U.S. travel deficit by 8 per cent, or $3.5 billion.

An estimated 90 per cent of American vacation travel was by car, a stunning 200 billion miles. Reports of fuel shortages held sales of both campers and recreational vehicles at about 1972's level. Of the estimated 90 million Americans who vacationed by car in 1973, some 40.4 million went camping, and 700,000 recreational units were purchased.

There were about 700 million scheduled air passengers in 1973. Air transportation represented 75 per

Passenger ship service between Russia and the United States began on May 23 when the *Mikhail Lermontov* arrived in New York City.

cent of all intercity carrier travel and more than 90 per cent of overseas travel. Stolen and counterfeit air tickets increased, and nearly 80,000 stolen from travel agencies alone cheated the airlines out of more than $24 million. Low, advance-booking, charter air fares made it possible for Europeans to pay as little as $200 for a round trip to the United States. A similar U.S. coast-to-coast fare structure enabled people to travel from Eastern Seaboard cities to Los Angeles and San Francisco for as little as $89.50.

About 14.3 million Americans traveled to Canada, a gain of 8 per cent over 1972; some 3 million traveled to Mexico, a gain of 20 per cent; and 7.8 million went overseas, an increase of 6 per cent. The United States hosted 8.9 million visitors from Canada who remained more than 48 hours. About 1.6 million came from Mexico and 3.5 million from overseas.

The Japanese, almost overnight, ranked among the world's biggest globetrotters. An estimated 2 million of them swarmed over the Pacific, Europe, and the United States in 1973. Japan replaced Great Britain as the largest overseas producer of travel to the United States, and a record 580,000 Japanese visited the United States. They have also been acquiring and even building hotels, to serve not only their own countrymen, but also Westerners. Amsterdam, Guam, New York City, Paris, and San Francisco now have Japanese-owned-and-operated hotels. In Hawaii, Japanese interests have bought 11 properties and have 2 under construction. They also own two of the islands' golf courses and have purchased 3,000 acres of resort-development land.

Although an increasing number of foreigners visited the People's Republic of China, all but about 400 of the American visitors were sponsored by the U.S. Department of State. The average cost for a three-week tour, including air fare from New York City, was $1,600.

Israel anticipated a record number of visitors during its 25th anniversary year, but the Arab-Israeli war in October brought tourism almost to a halt. Nine-month traffic totaled about 560,000, a percentage point off the same period in 1972.

Amtrak ridership was up 11 per cent on its second birthday, May 1. The nationwide rail system's losses for fiscal 1973 were estimated at $124 million, down 18.6 per cent from fiscal 1972. Amtrak now operates more than 1,600 trains weekly over more than 24,000 miles of track serving 440 communities. It has entered the tour market and has 100 package tours available, ranging from a $24 weekend in Washington, D.C., or New York City to a $1,295, 24-day, coast-to-coast circle tour. The first two of a series of new French turbine trains began service between Chicago and St. Louis on October 1.

Hotel and motel chains, those with three or more properties, now represent 30 per cent of all rooms available in the United States. By the end of 1973, there were 5,482 units with a total of 824,810 rooms.

Holiday Inns alone built 74 new motels, bringing that company's total properties to 1,540.

The American Indian, though not classified as a tourist, is an object of tourism, and as such is beginning to cash in on the unique assets of his past. With cooperation from the Bureau of Indian Affairs and other governmental agencies, Indians have begun to build hotels, ski lodges, trading posts, campgrounds, museums, and other recreational projects. By the end of 1973, 18 Indian-owned-and-operated motels had been constructed, and some 15 other tourist facilities were in operation or planned.

The National Tourism Resources Review Commission reported to President Richard M. Nixon on June 25 on its two-year study of tourism needs. Its major recommendation was the establishment of a National Tourism Administration (NTA) that would be responsible for a single federal policy that would specifically address tourism problems in the national interest and in the interest of both the tourism industry and the consumer.

The commission also recommended that the Bureau of the Census be authorized and adequately funded to conduct an annual tourism survey. The report noted that tourism expenditures affected the general economy to the extent that for every $4 of income earned directly by tourism, another $3 was generated indirectly. Lynn Beaumont

TRINIDAD AND TOBAGO. See West Indies.

TRUCK AND TRUCKING. Despite the energy crisis and related problems of securing fuel supplies, trucks continued to handle an increasing share of the United States freight in 1973. The industry again set new records in total revenue and tons transported.

A number of factors, however, combined to reduce net profit below 1972 levels. They included the rising costs of supplies, delays in granting needed rate increases to offset the higher costs of a new labor contract that went into effect on July 1, and fuel shortages and increasing fuel costs resulting from the energy crisis.

Total trucking revenues rose to $21 billion, a 12.5 per cent increase over 1972. Net earnings were $475-million, a 7 per cent decline from the $510 million earned in 1972. Net income in 1973 was 2.5 per cent of total revenue in contrast to 2.7 per cent in 1972.

Labor Pact. On June 28, the industry and the Teamsters Union agreed to a new 33-month master freight contract for 400,000 truckdrivers providing wage and benefit increases totaling 21 per cent over the length of the contract. The wage increases went into effect on July 1, but the price freeze caused a six-week delay in the granting of rate increases needed to offset higher labor costs. Higher interest rates and increases in the cost of equipment and supplies were almost entirely absorbed by the carriers. Consequently, net earnings dropped sharply in the second half of the year.

The impact of the energy crisis more than offset the small productivity gains in 1973. Shortages of diesel fuel in some locations began to appear early in the year. The situation steadily worsened in the second half, and was compounded by rapidly rising fuel prices. Spurred by shortages and higher fuel costs, truckers pressed programs to obtain increases in productivity through greater use of twin trailers.

Trucking Protests. Wildcat highway blockades spread through several states in early December as truckers blocked traffic to protest high fuel costs and low speed limits that were set to conserve energy. Dozens of trucks were abandoned on major highways, snarling traffic for miles.

Thousands of independent truckdrivers pulled off the road on December 13 in a two-day protest against fuel shortages. They also attempted to close truck stops and cut off fuel for drivers who did not participate. Police in some industrial states estimated that truck traffic was reduced by from 70 per cent to 80 per cent.

On December 18, Teamsters President Frank E. Fitzsimmons announced plans to reopen contract talks with the trucking industry. The Teamsters sought increased wages to offset losses caused by the fuel shortage and lower speed limits. Kenneth E. Schaefle

See also AUTOMOBILE; AVIATION; ENERGY; RAILROAD; SHIP AND SHIPPING; TRANSIT; TRANSPORTATION.

TRUDEAU, PIERRE ELLIOTT, headed a minority government in Canada in 1973 following the Liberal Party's setback in the 1972 general election. Trudeau governed with the parliamentary support of the New Democratic Party, a condition that required him to move cautiously in framing legislation and dealing with the House of Commons.

At the Liberal policy convention in Ottawa on September 14 and 15, Trudeau met 1,700 delegates in an "accountability session." He defended his party leadership and praised the role of political conventions in the democratic process. He pointed out that 85 per cent of the resolutions approved at the 1970 convention have been translated into legislation. Trudeau said that Canada should stress five major areas in the future: regional development, social security, urban policy, industrial development, and transportation. With the gross national product expected to double by 1983, Canada faced a unique opportunity to better the life of its people. "It is not enough to double goods and services if it means twice as many rich people and twice as many poor, or to have twice as much industry and twice as much pollution," Trudeau said.

Trudeau and his wife, Margaret, became the parents of their second son, Alexandre Emmanuel, on December 25. Their eldest son, Justin, was also born on Christmas Day, in 1971. David M. L. Farr

See also CANADA.

TUNISIA. Former economics minister Ahmed Ben Salah escaped from prison on February 4, underlining the friction and uneasiness that continued among Tunisian leaders in 1973. Tunisia sent a token, "unofficial" force in October to fight in the Arab-Israeli war. For details on the war, see MIDDLE EAST.

Ben Salah had been sentenced in May, 1970, to 10 years' hard labor for abuse of public power and funds. He escaped to Algeria with the help of prison officials and went to Italy. In newspaper interviews, he accused President Habib Bourguiba's government of keeping the country in a state of "acute, permanent crisis." On June 21, Ben Salah was sentenced in absentia to 5½ more years in prison.

Former Prime Minister Bahi Ladgham resigned from the Central Committee of the ruling Socialist Destour Party in April to protest Bourguiba's dictatorial policies. A June 26 law barred resigned or dismissed Central Committee members from their Assembly seats, and Ladgham left public office entirely. Neither Ladgham's resignation nor Ben Salah's defection seriously weakened Bourguiba's authority.

Another Term. On April 12, Bourguiba said he was ready to run for a fourth five-year term in 1974. This statement and his apparent return to good health made the question of a successor less urgent. The National Assembly had proposed a law setting aside the Constitution to make Bourguiba president for life.

During the August 3 celebration of his 70th birthday, Bourguiba announced an amnesty for all his political opponents. Refugees were welcomed home for the rest of 1973. They included Ben Salah, who received a special pardon.

Economic Gains. The simmering political crisis did not slow Tunisia's development. Bourguiba inaugurated the fourth five-year plan on July 23. It would cost about $2.8 billion, with 20 per cent of the funds coming from foreign sources, compared with 40 per cent in the previous plan. The new plan emphasized developing light industry, tourism, and agriculture. It aimed to create 300,000 new jobs.

One report said that Tunisia's economy provides less than half of the 50,000 new jobs it needs each year. An independent study reported early in the year that about 24 per cent of Tunisian men were unemployed. Many young Tunisians have left their homeland to work in Europe.

On January 18, a major irrigation project in the Badrouna district of the Majardah Valley was launched, bringing nearly 8,000 acres of unused land under cultivation. In the far south, the poorest part of the country, Prime Minister Hedi Nouira opened the huge Ghannouche thermal power station on May 19. It has a capacity of 250 megawatts. The two projects underscored Tunisia's description by the Economic Commission for Africa as "the fastest-growing state on the continent." William Spencer

See also AFRICA (Facts in Brief Table).

TURKEY. What is normally a nonpolitical process in Turkey—the selection of a president by the Grand National Assembly—generated a crisis in March, 1973. The uneasy balance between the nation's military and its civilian leaders was underscored by efforts to choose a successor for incumbent President Cevdet Sunay, whose seven-year term ended March 28.

Deputies of the moderately leftist Republican People's Party (RPP) withheld their votes in protest against continued martial law and censorship. That left the candidate of Sunay and the Turkish Army—General Faruk Gurler, who had just resigned as chief of the general staff—unable to muster the Assembly majority he needed.

The resulting deadlock lasted from March 13, when voting began, until April 6. Senator Fahri Koruturk, a compromise candidate nominated by the three main political parties, was elected president then by a margin of 365 votes to 85. Prime Minister Ferit Melen resigned, and Minister of Commerce Naim Talu formed a temporary government to prepare for the October 14 parliamentary elections. See KORUTURK, FAHRI; TALU, NAIM.

Domestic Changes. As the campaign proceeded, martial law was lifted. Some 35 generals were retired or transferred, including those in command when the military intervened in politics in 1971. Two new right wing parties, the Democrats (a splinter of the

Justice Party) and the Islamic-Socialist National Salvation Party (NSP), emerged during the campaign.

The RPP won its first plurality with 185 of the 450 Assembly seats to 149 for the more conservative Justice Party and 49 for the NSP. Bülent Ecevit, RPP leader, was named prime minister. However, he was unable to form a new coalition Cabinet. At the end of the year, Talu's shaky caretaker government was still in office.

Economic Outlook. Although unemployment remained high at 11.3 per cent of the labor force, completion of several projects plus continued foreign aid promised an economic upturn, assuming the political crisis could be solved. Oil discoveries near Diyarbakır could increase Turkey's production by 65,000 barrels a day. On May 11, a new refinery at Aliaga, began operations.

On June 22, a land-reform bill involving some 8.2-million acres was passed by the Assembly. It would limit holdings to 250 irrigated or 500 unirrigated acres. Surplus lands would be nationalized and distributed among landless peasants on long-term 6 per cent loans.

Celebrations to mark the 50th anniversary of the founding of modern Turkey began October 29 at the tomb of Kemal Atatürk, its first president. Atatürk's successor, Ismet Inönü, died on December 25 at the age of 89.   William Spencer

See also MIDDLE EAST (Facts in Brief Table).

Retired Admiral Fahri Koruturk, a compromise candidate, was elected the sixth president of Turkey in April, after a month-long crisis.

UGANDA. Many Ugandan citizens were either killed by soldiers or mysteriously disappeared in 1973. There were rumors that President Idi Amin Dada's government had lost control of the army. Amin denounced the terrorism, but there were renewed reports in August and September of killings of prominent Ugandans.

A dossier on these killings was released on May 26 by former President Apollo Milton Obote, who was overthrown by Amin in 1971. Obote claimed that between 80,000 and 90,000 persons had been killed since Amin took over the government.

In protest against the killings, Uganda's education minister resigned in February. The foreign minister resigned on April 29 "because of the continual disappearance of innocent people without investigation."

In January, Amin had warned of pro-Obote guerrilla activity in Uganda. Twelve alleged guerrillas were publicly executed in February. However, many observers believed this was only a move to divert attention from growing lawlessness in the army.

Uganda's relations with neighboring Kenya and Tanzania were strained during the year. In February, Kenya charged that some Kenyans working on the railroad in Uganda had been killed and others had fled the country. Amin claimed that Kenyans of the Luo tribe living in Uganda were plotting against his government. However, after Kenyan trade unions demanded that the railway workers be withdrawn from Uganda, Amin guaranteed the safety of all Kenyans in Uganda (see KENYA). In March, Amin accused Tanzania of plotting an invasion. However, a Somali fact-finding team found no evidence of a Tanzanian troop build-up. See TANZANIA.

In February, Uganda warned that it would take reprisals against British citizens living in Uganda if Uganda was expelled from the Commonwealth of Nations. At the Commonwealth conference in Ottawa, Canada, in August, Uganda accused Great Britain of practicing racism and neocolonialism.

Amin sent President Richard M. Nixon several insulting notes during the year, one of which wished him "a speedy recovery from the Watergate affair." The United States recalled its ambassador in March. In October, Uganda accused the six U.S. Marines stationed at the U.S. Embassy of engaging in subversive activity and ordered them to leave the country.

Amin detained 112 U.S. Peace Corps volunteers in July when their plane landed for refueling in Uganda. Amin said he suspected them of being mercenary soldiers. However, he let them go after Zaire's President Mobutu Sese Seko assured him that they had been invited to Zaire. John Storm Roberts

See also AFRICA (Facts in Brief Table).

UNEMPLOYMENT. See ECONOMICS; LABOR.

UNION OF SOVIET SOCIALIST REPUBLICS (U.S.S.R.). See RUSSIA.

UNITED ARAB EMIRATES (UAE). The UAE took an active role in regional and Arab affairs in 1973, its second full year of independence. Resources and economic wealth among its members varied widely; only two of the seven, Abu Dhabi and Dubai, are oil producers. Nevertheless, the spin-off effects of oil revenues generated economic growth and cooperation among the five others. Abu Dhabi, largest UAE oil producer, cut off oil shipments to the United States in October because of U.S. support for Israel. For further details on the Middle East conflict and the energy crisis, see ENERGY and MIDDLE EAST.

A new UAE currency, the dirham, was introduced May 18 to facilitate transfers within member states. Its initial value was equivalent to U.S. $0.20.

New oil discoveries off Abu Musa Island and the start of shipments through a 23-mile pipeline from the Mubarraz field in June enabled Abu Dhabi to increase oil production by 38.8 per cent. Contracts were let on January 19 for construction of the $162-million Dubai dry dock. When completed in 1976, it will be the world's largest. On March 16, Abu Dhabi formed a company to exploit offshore natural gas. Japan agreed to buy 3 million tons annually.

The Supreme Council on August 3 approved the establishment of a federal supreme court and a federal censorship board for publications. William Spencer

See also MIDDLE EAST (Facts in Brief Table).

UNITED ARAB REPUBLIC (U.A.R.). See EGYPT.

UNITED NATIONS (UN). The spirit of East-West détente pervaded UN corridors with new vigor as the General Assembly opened its 28th session on Sept. 18, 1973. The Vietnam War had been declared over and a resurgence of European unity seemed imminent. Problems of environment, fluctuating currencies, inflation, the burgeoning energy crisis, the population explosion, food shortages, and untapped resources in undeveloped lands and seas offered more reason than ever before to find common avenues toward global solutions. East and West Germany were admitted to membership, and North Korea was present for the first time as an official observer. The Bahamas also was admitted to the General Assembly, bringing total membership to 135.

Newly appointed United States Secretary of State Henry Kissinger, in his maiden speech before the Assembly, declared the United States was seeking "true peace, not simply an armistice" with its former adversaries, despite the fact that he found "the world . . . uneasily suspended between old slogans and new realities."

Assembly President Leopoldo Benites of Ecuador hailed the beginning of an era of "true universality." "The trend towards integration of the world community is an irreversible process," Benites noted.

Middle East. Secretary-General Kurt Waldheim returned in September from an eight-day official tour of five Middle Eastern countries and warned, "Time is not on our side in this explosive situation." Unfortunately, he proved to be right.

Within a month after Waldheim's return, Israel and the Arabs clashed in 17 bloody days of desert and mountain fighting. The battle ended after the Security Council voted a cease-fire in the early morning hours of October 22. The United States and Russia, in a historic joint resolution, pushed through the cease-fire demand by a vote of 14 to 0. China, maintaining that the rights of the Palestinian guerrillas were being ignored because of "superpower collusion," did not participate.

The Council went on to create a new UN Emergency Force (UNEF) composed of 7,000 armed troops from 13 countries – Austria, Canada, Finland, Ghana, Indonesia, Ireland, Kenya, Nepal, Panama, Peru, Poland, Senegal, and Sweden – to act as a buffer between the Israeli and Arab soldiers. A $60-million budget was approved for its first year of duty. Major General Ensio Siilasvuo of Finland, commander of the UN Truce Supervisory Organization, was named UNEF commander. The Council, at the insistence of the United States, rejected an Arab request that a joint U.S.-Russian force be stationed in the war zone. The Council excluded all five major powers from participation in the armed UNEF, but allowed Russian personnel to join Americans as unarmed observers. See MIDDLE EAST.

Peace Negotiations. Gunnar Jarring of Sweden, who had acted as special UN mediator in the Middle

Delegates congratulate West Germany's Walter Scheel, far left, and East
Germany's Otto Winzer, far right, as their countries become UN members.

East since early 1968, retired from his diplomatic
career in 1973 and unofficially dropped his efforts at
finding a Middle East solution. The United States
and Russia will co-chair further peace talks in
Geneva.

Earlier in the year, the Arabs had mounted a special diplomatic initiative in the Security Council,
demanding Israeli withdrawal from the Arab territories they had occupied since 1967. After six weeks
of discussion and negotiation, the United States
vetoed a resolution calling for Israel's withdrawal.
U.S. Ambassador to the UN John Scali explained
that the resolution would have altered the delicate
balance of an earlier Security Council resolution
that had been the framework for Middle East negotiations up to that time.

Twice during the year, however, the United States
refrained from vetoing Security Council condemnations of Israel—once in April, after Israel attacked
Palestinian commando bases in Lebanon and killed
three Palestinian guerrilla leaders; again in August,
after Israeli fighter jets forced down an Iraqi commercial airliner to search for Palestinian guerrillas.
The Council took no action when Israeli fighters
shot down a Libyan commercial jet over the Sinai
Peninsula in February. The plane crash-landed and
burned, killing 106 persons.

Middle East Refugees. Under Arab-Soviet duress,
Secretary-General Waldheim turned down an Aus-

trian request that the UN take over the management
of a transit camp at Schönau Castle near Vienna for
Russian Jews emigrating to Israel. Palestinian guerrillas had captured hostages and demanded the
camp's closing in September. See AUSTRIA.

Meanwhile, the 1.5 million Palestinian refugees
still housed in UN Relief and Works Agency tent
camps faced severe cutbacks. The devaluation of the
U.S. dollar in February contributed to an already fat
deficit that threatened to reach $10 million by 1974,
more than 15 per cent of the total $60-million annual
budget provided to the agency by contributions.

Far East. Japan seemed ready to emerge from its
quiet political stance. It pledged $100 million toward
the new UN University in Tokyo, increased substantially its contributions to various UN agencies, and
mounted pressure for a seat as a sixth permanent
member on the Security Council.

China also mounted two major campaigns during
the session. A Chinese call for the ouster of the remaining 40,000 UN troops in South Korea—most of
them Americans—was dropped in favor of a compromise resolution calling for "greater national unity"
and a continuing dialogue between North and South
Korea. The two Koreas are expected to become UN
members in 1974.

China also campaigned to oust the representatives
of the Lon Nol government in Khmer (formerly
Cambodia) in favor of a delegation representing

517

Prince Sihanouk, now living in exile in Peking. Action was postponed after the United States and others complained that it would set "dangerous precedents."

Latin America. The United States faced another political challenge in March, when the Security Council met in Panama City to discuss ways to "strengthen peace and foster cooperation in Latin America." The United States exercised its third veto in UN history against a Panamanian resolution calling for a revision of the Canal Zone treaty. Later in the year, Cuba succeeded in getting a General Assembly hearing for Puerto Rican independence movement leaders over U.S. objections.

African Nations expressed concern over the continued colonial presence of Portugal in Mozambique, Angola, and Guinea-Bissau, formerly Portuguese Guinea. They also protested the presence of South Africa in Namibia, the former territory of South West Africa, and the white-minority regime of Ian Smith in Rhodesia.

The Security Council dispatched a special four-country mission – including representatives from Indonesia, the Sudan, Peru, and Austria – to Africa after Zambia complained in January that Rhodesia had closed its borders, thus preventing commercial travel. The mission reported that Zambia needed at least $250 million in aid to reroute 75,000 tons of the 120,000 tons of crucial copper and other materials it exports monthly. The Security Council passed a resolution March 10 asking all nations to help Zambia establish alternative trade routes.

A series of resolutions in various committees called on Great Britain to force down the Smith regime in Rhodesia and turn over the government to representatives of the black majority. Britain dismissed the resolutions as "wishful thinking," and the United States supported its viewpoint. The U.S. Senate voted in December to repeal legislation allowing the United States to import Rhodesian products, especially chrome. The UN had voted an embargo against Rhodesian trade in 1966.

The General Assembly also overwhelmingly voted to recognize the self-proclaimed independent republic of Guinea-Bissau after guerrilla leaders claimed to control three-quarters of the former Portuguese colony.

The Assembly voted October 5 to reject the credentials of the South African delegation. Assembly President Benites ruled, however, that this did not constitute expulsion from the Assembly, though it represented a "vehement condemnation" of South Africa's political policies. The Assembly also approved a resolution declaring that apartheid, the South African system of race separation, was a crime against humanity. Later in the year, the Security Council decided to cut off talks between Secretary-

A local chief checks distribution of sorghum in Upper Volta, one of six drought-stricken African countries to receive UN relief supplies.

General Waldheim and the South African government on the future of Namibia.

Disarmament Issues. Russia proposed that each of the Big Five nations cut its defense budget by 10 per cent and channel the savings to developing countries. The resolution was overwhelmingly approved by the General Assembly, but the other four major powers shunned it as "impractical."

In other disarmament moves, the Assembly approved restrictions on the use of napalm and other incendiary weapons, urged a halt to all nuclear testing, advanced plans for a World Disarmament Conference, looked for ways to ensure the Indian Ocean as a zone of peace, and declared chemical and biological weapons unacceptable.

The problem of terrorism was again deferred. African and Arab nations argued that those who committed terrorist acts in the name of "national liberation" should be exempted from sanction. The United States rejected such a proposal. However, the Assembly approved a treaty to protect diplomats that provides for the extradition and punishment of persons who kidnap, maim, or kill diplomats.

Development and Environment Issues were highlighted by a December conference on the Law of the Sea in New York City. Coastal limits, fishing rights, sharing of undersea resources, and the creation of economic zones for landlocked nations will be discussed at conferences in 1974 and 1975.

The UN's new Environment Secretariat headquarters was opened in Nairobi, Kenya, on October 2. Its executive director, Maurice Strong of Canada, announced a goal of $100 million in voluntary contributions for the new environmental fund.

Relief Operations. Waldheim announced the end of a massive two-year relief program for the 78 million people of Bangladesh. More than $1 billion in food and aid had been channeled through the UN to the people. UN membership for Bangladesh continued to be withheld, however, largely because of a threatened veto by the Chinese, who said they would block membership until 90,000 Pakistani prisoners of war were returned. Pakistan, suffering from massive floods, was promised $1.7 million from the UN's World Food Program.

Earlier in the year, the UN assisted homeless Nicaraguans after a December, 1972, earthquake. Also, six drought-stricken countries in West Africa – Chad, Niger, Mali, the Sudan, Senegal, and Upper Volta – received more than $30 million in aid and $500,000 worth of foodstuffs through the UN.

Multinational Corporations. A special UN report warned that the unwarranted influence of giant international firms on international politics and economics should be curtailed by a voluntarily imposed code of ethics. More than half of the largest multinational companies are controlled by U.S. interests.

Ironically, the report echoed the words of the late President Salvador Allende Gossens of Chile, who

Members of a United Nations peacekeeping force in the Middle East arrive in Suez, Egypt, in October to set up watch posts along the canal.

had addressed the Assembly on that subject in 1972. Allende died during a military coup in September. At a special Security Council session in September, Cuba accused the United States of complicity in Allende's overthrow. U.S. Ambassador Scali denied the allegation, and the Council adjourned without taking action.

The World Court at The Hague in the Netherlands had three major cases on its docket. Both Britain and West Germany filed complaints against Iceland's extension of its coastal limits to 50 miles. The court asked all three parties to adhere to a compromise restricting fishing intakes until a legal decision could be reached. See ICELAND.

New Zealand, Australia, and Fiji filed complaints against France, which has conducted nuclear explosion tests on Pacific atolls. All three countries charged that the tests result in dangerous fallout. France has until March, 1974, to reply to the charges. See FRANCE; PACIFIC ISLANDS.

Pakistan sought to prevent India from turning over 195 Pakistani prisoners of war and civilian internees to Bangladesh for trial on genocide charges. Private India-Pakistan talks on the issue resulted in Pakistan asking for a postponement of any court action.

Manfred Lachs of Poland was elected World Court president in February, succeeding Sir Muhammad Zafrulla Khan.   Betty Flynn

UNITED STATES, GOVERNMENT OF. There was a startling shift in the balance of power between President Richard M. Nixon and Congress in 1973. The power of the President was challenged not only by Congress and the courts, but also by the American people. Charges of widespread corruption at the highest levels of the government, the replacement of Vice-President Spiro T. Agnew, televised Senate committee hearings into Watergate and related scandals, challenges to the principle of executive privilege, and lengthy discussions of impeachment made 1973 a yearlong national civics class.

The Executive Branch. On January 5, the President revealed plans to reorganize his White House staff, headed by H. R. Haldeman. The President announced he was cutting personnel from 4,000 to 2,000.

He also established four super Cabinet posts, dealing with human resources, natural resources, community development, and economic policy. The four super Cabinet officials reported to the President through his chief domestic counselor, John D. Ehrlichman. At the same time, many former White House staffers moved into the various departments of the government as deputy secretaries.

However, the President was forced to abandon his plans after the Watergate scandal broke. Haldeman and Ehrlichman resigned in April after being impli-

cated in the Watergate affair, and the super Cabinet was dissolved. In the wake of new disclosures, top White House staffers, Cabinet members, and other high-ranking officials resigned or were shuffled from one post to another. See CABINET; WATERGATE.

General Alexander M. Haig, Jr., replaced Haldeman as White House chief of staff. Melvin R. Laird took over Ehrlichman's job, and J. Fred Buzhardt replaced John W. Dean III as special counsel to the President. Laird announced in December that he would leave the White House staff in January, 1974.

William Colby became director of the Central Intelligence Agency, replacing James R. Schlesinger, who became secretary of defense. Kansas City Police Chief Clarence M. Kelley became director of the Federal Bureau of Investigation when L. Patrick Gray III stepped down after revealing that he had destroyed Watergate evidence. Attorney General Elliot L. Richardson resigned on October 20, rather than obey Mr. Nixon's order to fire special Watergate prosecutor Archibald Cox. Although Cox was fired, public pressure forced Mr. Nixon to appoint another prosecutor, Leon Jaworski, on November 1.

The Legislative Branch. On December 6, acting for the first time under the 25th Amendment to the U.S. Constitution, Congress confirmed Congressman Gerald R. Ford (R., Mich.) as the 40th Vice-President of the United States. He succeeded Agnew, who

After years of no official U.S.-China relations, Chinese soldier stands guard outside U.S. liaison office in Peking, China, which opened in 1973.

Federal Spending and Revenue Receipts

Estimated U.S. Budget for Fiscal 1974*

	Billions of dollars
National defense	81.0
International affairs and finance†	3.8
Space research	3.1
Agriculture and rural development	5.6
Natural resources and environment	3.7
Commerce and transportation	11.6
Community development and housing	4.9
Education and manpower	10.1
Health	21.7
Income security	82.0
Veterans benefits	11.7
General government	6.0
Interest	24.7
General revenue sharing	6.0
Allowances	1.8
Undistributed deductions	−9.1
Total	$268.7

*July 1, 1973, to June 30, 1974

†Includes foreign aid

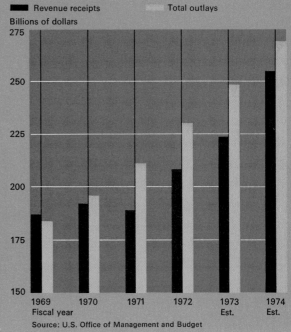

U.S. Income and Outlays

■ Revenue receipts   Total outlays

Source: U.S. Office of Management and Budget

had resigned on October 10. See AGNEW, SPIRO THEODORE; FORD, GERALD R.

Democratic majorities in both houses of Congress tried to limit presidential powers. After a great deal of congressional pressure, the President signed legislation on July 1 that provided that the bombing of Khmer (formerly Cambodia) would stop on August 15. In spite of the President's veto, Congress passed the War Powers Act on November 7, limiting the President's power to commit U.S. forces to action in foreign countries without congressional consent.

The Senate Select Committee on Presidential Campaign Activities, chaired by Senator Sam J. Ervin, Jr. (D., N.C.), held televised hearings that brought out details of political corruption, illegal campaign activities, and White House involvement in a massive obstruction of justice in the Watergate affair. In response to growing public disapproval of the President, the House of Representatives set up a committee to consider grounds for impeaching President Nixon.

Although the energy crisis grew more acute, Congress failed to pass the National Energy Emergency Act, which would have given the President unusual emergency powers to enforce energy conservation measures. However, Congress did institute year-round daylight saving time, beginning Jan. 6, 1974, to conserve energy. Congress passed a 5.9 per cent increase in Social Security benefits effective in July,

1974. However, in December, Congress raised it to 11 per cent. See SOCIAL SECURITY.

Other legislation passed by Congress included: extension of the President's authority to set wage and price controls; provision for the eventual transfer of highway trust funds to mass-transit projects; a ban on local television blackouts of sports events that are sold out 72 hours in advance; and approval of the construction of the Alaska pipeline. See CONGRESS OF THE UNITED STATES.

The Judicial Branch. On January 22, the Supreme Court ruled 7 to 2 that state laws forbidding or restricting a woman's right to an abortion in the first three months of her pregnancy are unconstitutional. On obscenity, the court took a narrower view, holding in a series of 5-to-4 decisions in June that communities may censor any book, play, film, or magazine that "appeals to the prurient interest" in sex, according to community standards.

In other important cases, the court ruled that the one-man, one-vote ruling should apply less strictly to state legislative districts than to federal congressional districts; left standing a lower court ruling that the Richmond, Va., school desegregation plan was unconstitutional; and said the local property-tax system of financing education was not unconstitutional. See COURTS AND LAWS; EDUCATION; SUPREME COURT OF THE UNITED STATES.   Carol L. Thompson

See also Section One, FOCUS ON THE NATION.

Diplomatic Corps

Official ambassadors representing the United States of America in other countries and their counterparts to the United States, as of Dec. 31, 1973.

Country	From U.S.A.	To U.S.A.
Afghanistan	Theodore L. Eliot, Jr.	Abdullah Malikyar
Argentina	Robert C. Hill	Vacant
Australia	Marshall Green	Sir Patrick Shaw*
Austria	John P. Humes	Arno Halusa
Bahamas	Ronald I. Spiers	Livingston Basil Johnson
Bahrain	William A. Stoltzfus, Jr.	Vacant
Bangladesh	Vacant	M. Hossain Ali
Barbados	Eileen R. Donovan	Valerie Theodore McComie
Belgium	Robert Strausz-Hupé	Walter Loridan
Bolivia	William Perry Stedman, Jr.	Edmundo Valencia-Ibañez
Botswana	David B. Bolen*	Amos M. Dambe
Brazil	John Hugh Crimmins	João Agusto de Araujo Castro
Bulgaria	Vacant	Christo Zdravchev
Burma	Vacant	U Lwin
Burundi	Robert L. Yost	Joseph Ndabaniwe
Cameroon	C. Robert Moore	Francois-Xavier Tchoungui
Canada	Adolph W. Schmidt	Marcel Cadieux
Central African Republic	William N. Dale	Gaston Banda-Bafiot
Chad	Edward W. Mulcahy	Lazare Massibe
Chile	David H. Popper	Walter Heitmann
Colombia	Viron P. Vaky	Douglas Botero-Boshell
Costa Rica	Vacant	Marco Antonio Lopez
Cyprus	Marshall Wright*	Zenon Rossides
Czechoslovakia	Albert W. Sherer, Jr.	Dusan Spacil
Dahomey	Robert Anderson	Tiamiou Adjibade
Denmark	Philip K. Crowe	Eyvind Bartels
Dominican Republic	Robert A. Hurwitch	S. Salvador Ortiz
Ecuador	Robert C. Brewster	Alberto Quevedo-Toro
Egypt	Hermann F. Eilts, Jr.*	Ashraf Ghorbal*
El Salvador	James F. Campbell	Vacant
Ethiopia	Vacant	Kifle Wodajo
Finland	V. John Krehbiel	Leo Tuominen
France	John N. Irwin II	Jacques Kosciusko-Morizet
Gabon	John A. McKesson III	Vincent Mavoungou
Gambia	O. Rudolph Aggrey	Vacant
Germany, West	Martin J. Hillenbrand	Berndt Von Staden
Ghana	Fred L. Hadsel	Harry Reginald Amonoo
Great Britain	Walter H. Annenberg	The Earl of Cromer
Greece	Henry J. Tasca	Vacant
Guatemala	Francis E. Meloy, Jr.	Julio Asensio-Wunderlich
Guinea	Terence A. Todman	Sadan Moussa Touré
Guyana	Max V. Krebs*	Frederick Hilborn Talbot
Haiti	Heyward Isham	René Chalmers
Honduras	Philip V. Sanchez	Roberto Galvez Barnes
Hungary	Richard F. Pedersen	Karoly Szabo
Iceland	Frederick Irving	Haraldur Kröyer
India	Daniel Patrick Moynihan	Triloki Nath Kaul
Indonesia	David D. Newsom	Sjarif Thajeb
Iran	Richard M. Helms	Ardeshir Zahedi
Ireland	John D. J. Moore	John Gerald Molloy
Israel	Kenneth B. Keating	Simcha Dinitz
Italy	John A. Volpe	Egidio Ortona
Ivory Coast	Robert S. Smith*	Timothée N'Guetta Ahoua
Jamaica	Vacant	Douglas V. Fletcher
Japan	Vacant	Takeshi Yasukawa
Jordan	Vacant	Abdullah Salah
Kenya	Anthony D. Marshall	Leonard Oliver Kibinge
Khmer Republic	Vacant	Um Sim
Korea, South	Philip C. Habib	Hahm Byung Choon*
Kuwait	William A. Stoltzfus, Jr.	Salem S. Al-Sabah
Laos	Charles S. Whitehouse	Peng Norindr
Lebanon	G. McMurtrie Godley*	Najati Kabbani
Lesotho	David B. Bolen*	Ephraim Tsepa Manare
Liberia	Melvin L. Manfull	S. Edward Peal
Libya	Vacant	Vacant
Luxembourg	Ruth Lewis Farkas	Jean Wagner
Madagascar	Joseph A. Mendenhall	Henri Raharijaona
Malawi	William C. Burdett	Robert B. Mbaya
Malaysia	Francis T. Underhill, Jr.	Mohamed Khir Johari
Mali	Ralph J. McGuire	Seydou Traoré
Malta	John I. Getz	Joseph Attard-Kingswell
Mauritania	Richard W. Murphy	Ahmedou Ould Abdallah
Mauritius	Vacant	Pierre Guy Girald Balancy
Mexico	Joseph J. Jova	José Juan de Olloqui
Morocco	Robert G. Neumann	Badreddine Senoussi
Nepal	William I. Cargo	Yadu Nath Khanal
Netherlands	Kingdon Gould, Jr.	Baron Rijnhard B. Van Lynden
New Zealand	Vacant	Lloyd White
Nicaragua	Turner B. Shelton	Guillermo Sevilla-Sacasa
Niger	Vacant	Abdoulaye Diallo
Nigeria	John E. Reinhardt	John M. Garba
Norway	Thomas R. Byrne	Søren Christian Sommerfelt
Oman	William A. Stoltzfus, Jr.	Faisal Bin Ali Al-Said
Pakistan	Henry A. Byroade	Sultan M. Khan
Panama	Robert M. Sayre	Nicolas Gonzalez-Revilla
Paraguay	George W. Landau	Miguel Solano-Lopez
Peru	Taylor G. Belcher	Fernando Berckemeyer
Philippines	William H. Sullivan	Eduardo Z. Romualdez
Poland	Richard T. Davies	Witold Trampczynski
Portugal	Stuart Nash Scott	João Hall Themido
Qatar	William A. Stoltzfus, Jr.	Abdullah Saleh Al-Mana
Romania	Harry G. Barnes, Jr.	Corneliu Bogdan
Russia	Walter J. Stoessel, Jr.	Anatoliy F. Dobrynin
Rwanda	Vacant	Fidèle Nkundabagenzi
Saudi Arabia	James E. Akins	Ibrahim Al-Sowayel
Senegal	O. Rudolph Aggrey	Andre Coulbary
Sierra Leone	Clinton L. Olson	Philip J. Palmer
Singapore	Edwin M. Cronk	Ernest Steven Monteiro
Somalia	Roger Kirk	Abdullahi Ahmed Addou
South Africa	John G. Hurd	Johan S. F. Botha
Spain	Horacio Rivero	Angel Sagaz
Sri Lanka	Christopher Van Hollen	Neville Kanakaratne
Sudan	William D. Brewer	Abdel Aziz Al Nasri Hamza
Swaziland	David B. Bolen*	James L. F. Simelane
Sweden	Vacant	Vacant
Switzerland	Shelby Davis	Felix Schnyder
Taiwan	Walter P. McConaughy	James C. H. Shen
Tanzania	W. Beverly Carter, Jr.	Paul Bomani
Thailand	William R. Kintner	Anand Panyarachun
Togo	Dwight Dickinson	Epiphane Ayi Mawussi
Trinidad & Tobago	Lloyd I. Miller	Victor McIntyre
Tunisia	Talcott W. Seelye	Slaheddine El Goulli
Turkey	William B. Macomber, Jr.	Melih Esenbel
Uganda	Vacant	Mustapha Ramathan
UAR Emirates	William A. Stoltzfus, Jr.	Vacant
Upper Volta	Vacant	Telesphore Yaguibou
Uruguay	Ernest V. Siracusa	Hector Luisi
Venezuela	Robert McClintock	Andrés Aguilar
Vietnam, South	Graham A. Martin	Tran Kim Phuong
Yemen (San'ā')	William R. Crawford, Jr.	Yahya H. Geghman
Yugoslavia	Malcolm Toon	Toma Granfil
Zaire	Sheldon B. Vance	Lombo Lo Mangamanga
Zambia	Jean M. Wilkowski	Unia G. Mwila

*Ambassador designate   Sources: U.S. Dept. of State and Congressional Record

UNITED STATES CONSTITUTION. The 25th Amendment to the U.S. Constitution, outlining the procedure for filling a vice-presidential vacancy, received its first test in 1973 when Vice-President Spiro T. Agnew resigned on October 10.

The amendment became law in February, 1967, almost two years after its approval by Congress in 1965. It is designed to deal with the possibility of presidential disability, or with a vacancy in the vice-presidency, whether due to resignation or to succession to the presidency. President Dwight D. Eisenhower's precarious health, followed by the assassination of President John F. Kennedy in 1963, spurred Congress to act on the amendment.

The amendment treats the matter simply: "Whenever there is a vacancy in the office of the Vice-President, the President shall nominate a Vice-President who shall take office upon confirmation by a majority vote of both houses of Congress." Within days after receiving Agnew's resignation, President Richard M. Nixon nominated U.S. Representative Gerald R. Ford (R., Mich.) as Agnew's successor. After a series of hearings, Ford was confirmed and sworn in on December 6. See FORD, GERALD R.

Equal Rights. Washington became the 30th state to ratify the equal rights amendment on March 22. The amendment, which prohibits discrimination on the basis of sex, needs ratification by at least eight more states by 1979 to become law. However, an attempt by Nebraska to rescind its earlier ratification left the exact total in some doubt. Other states ratifying the amendment in 1973 were Connecticut, Minnesota, New Mexico, Oregon, South Dakota, Vermont, and Wyoming.

Opposition to the amendment grew in 1973. Members of well-organized and well-financed opposition groups began appearing before state legislatures, arguing that the amendment would subject women to military draft and eliminate protective legislation enacted in previous years.

Supporters argue that the amendment would free women from restrictive labor laws and end discriminatory practices in child custody, jury selection, age of majority, establishment of legal domicile, and prison sentences, all of which are covered by laws in one or more states. Men, as well as women, would be affected by the amendment. If it is ratified, widowers would be able to receive social security benefits on the same basis as widows. Its enactment could also bring changes in alimony and child-support rulings.

School Prayer. The Senate constitutional amendments subcommittee held hearings in September on a proposed amendment that would allow voluntary prayer in public schools. The amendment, introduced by Senator Richard S. Schweiker (R., Pa.), acknowledged "the right of persons lawfully assembled in any public building to participate in voluntary prayer." Kathryn Sederberg

UPPER VOLTA. See AFRICA.

URUGUAY. The nation ceased to be one of Latin America's few remaining democracies in 1973. Following a power struggle, President Juan María Bordaberry Arocena reached an agreement on February 14 with the armed forces under which democratic institutions were preserved. But the agreement also provided for a parallel "cabinet" called the National Council of Security and Development, through which the military would gain supervisory control over the government. This council, in effect, was the real government.

A major drive against corruption, inefficiency, and left wing subversion was announced by Bordaberry. He also stressed the need for long-term reforms, economic development, greater export trade, the reduction of unemployment, and a tax reform.

Congress Abolished. Acting under intense military pressure, the president abolished Congress on June 27, thus ending constitutional rule in Uruguay for the first time in 40 years. In place of Congress, a 20-man Council of State was to be established to oversee the president's activities and to do legislative work, while Bordaberry was to rule by decree until constitutional changes could be prepared for a national plebiscite. By year-end, however, the council was still not set up, primarily because most prominent Uruguayans refused to join it.

Bordaberry declared there was a "grave deterioration" of constitutional rule and attributed the crisis to "the criminal actions of the conspiracy against the country, aligned with the complacency of political groups without national spirit." The conspiracy he referred to involved the Marxist Tupamaro guerrillas, but it also was a fact that the president and his military advisers were faced with resistance from various political parties, including the dominant Colorado Party. In addition, businessmen, factory owners, and trading organizations were unhappy.

Resistance Grows. In a protest against the abolition of Congress, a general strike was called on June 21 by the powerful Communist-led National Workers Confederation (CNT). It brought the economy to a virtual standstill. The regime then dissolved the CNT and arrested hundreds of union leaders. On July 11, the confederation called off the crippling walkout. A sharp upturn in anti-Communist sentiment became evident in September as newspapers were closed and anti-union measures were enforced.

The country devalued the peso several times during the year in an effort to keep up with the inflation rate. In the year ending on July 31, living costs soared 106 per cent. The government announced in September that no further increases in the prices of essential goods would be allowed during the rest of 1973. Mary Webster Soper

See also LATIN AMERICA (Facts in Brief Table).

UTAH. See STATE GOVERNMENT.

UTILITIES. See COMMUNICATIONS; ENERGY; PETROLEUM AND GAS; TELEPHONE.

VENEZUELA. On Dec. 9, 1973, 4.6 million voters went to the polls to choose a president from among 13 candidates representing 20 political parties. Carlos Andrés Peréz, a candidate of the Democratic Action Party, scored a landslide victory over his principal rival, Lorenzo Fernandez of the ruling Social Christian Party. President Rafael Caldera could not seek re-election because of a constitutional provision forbidding a president to serve consecutive terms.

On April 17, after eight years of fruitless negotiations, Venezuela and Colombia broke off talks over who controls the continental shelf and territorial waters in the Gulf of Venezuela. Both claimed the area, which reportedly has rich oil deposits. Colombia proposed that the dispute be taken to the International Court of Justice at The Hague. Venezuela, however, preferred negotiations between the foreign ministers, and rejected the proposal.

Discussions on another issue involving territorial boundaries began on June 29 when representatives of Venezuela and the Netherlands met in Caracas. At issue was the continental shelf between Venezuela and the island of Aruba in the Netherlands Indies. It, too, was reportedly rich in minerals.

Frequent student strikes and riots were a serious problem throughout the year. Most of the disturbances were due to overcrowded classrooms and antiquated teaching methods rather than political disaffection with the government's policies. In February, students supporting a strike by educational workers looted stores, burned a bank, and stoned several buildings in Caracas before order was restored. However, disturbances by high school and university students that erupted on May 15 and 16 in Caracas and other cities were a protest against a visit by U.S. Secretary of State William P. Rogers.

Joins Trade Group. On February 13, Venezuela formally agreed to join the Andean Common Market to become the sixth and wealthiest member of the trade group, which consists also of Bolivia, Chile, Colombia, Ecuador, and Peru. As of early October, only minor formalities remained to be completed before the republic became a full member. The Venezuelan Congress made only one important change in the entry terms: President Rafael Caldera originally asked for blanket powers for the president to approve Andean group decisions. But Congress stipulated that its approval must be obtained for any decisions that modify existing Venezuelan laws. The government also instituted a program to modernize its customs system and a program of port renovation.

The country's fiscal accounts were in good shape, due mostly to periodic price increases on Venezuelan oil exports. The cost of Venezuelan oil rose to about $8 per barrel by December 31, versus $3.12 on January 1, netting an extra $400 million in annual income. Mary Webster Soper

See also LATIN AMERICA (Facts in Brief Table).
VERMONT. See STATE GOVERNMENT.

VETERANS of the Vietnam War were increasingly concerned in 1973 over their difficulties in re-entering the mainstream of U.S. civilian life. The return of the discharged GI's was hampered by cutbacks in veterans' benefits and a lack of public interest in their problems.

Finding a job became all but impossible for the many veterans who were poorly educated and unskilled. The unemployment rate for veterans from 20 to 29 years old did decline from 8.8 per cent in 1971 to 5.7 per cent in February, 1973. This was comparable to the rate for nonveterans of the same age. But the job outlook remained very bleak, especially for the most recently discharged GI's. The U.S. Bureau of Labor Statistics reported that 308,000 Vietnam veterans could not find work during the fiscal year ending June 30. In many cities, 15 per cent of the Vietnam veterans were unemployed, and many were subsisting on welfare.

During the Vietnam War, more than 178,000 servicemen received undesirable, bad conduct, or dishonorable discharges, not infrequently on the basis of only a commander's administrative hearing. These men are denied medical and educational benefits, and are also the last hired and first fired in a tight labor market.

Most of the veterans who were discharged for drug-related offenses could not get treatment in Veterans Administration (VA) facilities. Authorities estimate that there are at least 100,000 veterans addicted to drugs. Many of them picked up their habits in the service.

GI Bill Revision. One group studying needs of veterans was a committee sponsored by the National League of Cities and the U.S. Conference of Mayors. After conducting hearings in Cleveland, Newark, and Seattle, the committee described the present GI Bill as so inadequate that nearly 57 per cent of the more than 6 million Vietnam veterans have not taken advantage of its provisions.

The committee proposed that the educational allowance should be $1,200 a year plus a subsistence payment of at least $150 a month, and that more remedial education courses should be offered GI's still in service.

The committee also urged that Congress extend the Emergency Employment Act to include veterans, that every veteran enrolled in a work-study program should be guaranteed a job, and that federal jobs should be set aside for veterans on a sharing basis. The committee also stated that all less-than-honorable discharges should be reviewed with the view that veterans with such discharges be hired without restriction.

Legislation. The first important legislation approved in 1973 was a $1.36-billion emergency supplemental appropriation measure. The money will go to public school districts serving large numbers of children of civilian or military government em-

Veterans Hot Line in Los Angeles helps solve problems for ex-servicemen. Aid ranges from tips on jobs to advice on drug problems.

VIETNAM, NORTH. The United States announced on July 18, 1973, that it had completed clearing mines from North Vietnamese waters. "Operation End Sweep," carried out over a five-month period by an 18-ship minesweeping force, was part of the peace agreement signed by the United States and North Vietnam on Jan. 27, 1973. United States officials said that between May and December, 1972, about 11,000 mines had been dropped by U.S. planes on the approaches to Haiphong and seven other ports.

In July, a North Vietnamese delegation headed by Communist Party Secretary Le Duan and Premier Pham Van Dong visited Russia seeking postwar economic aid. Russia announced it would supply Hanoi with consumer goods, transport, foodstuffs, and industrial and agricultural equipment.

In June, it was reported that the crops in five provinces south of Hanoi were in poor condition because of a six-month drought. These natural conditions, which had caused water levels in rivers and lakes in the area to drop severely, were further complicated by severe damage that U.S. bombing had caused to the irrigation system in 1972.

Australia established diplomatic relations with North Vietnam on February 26. The agreement came during a visit by a North Vietnamese trade delegation to Melbourne. Canada, France, and Great Britain also re-established ties.   John N. Stalker

See also ASIA (Facts in Brief Table).

ployees; to the Department of Health, Education, and Welfare for grants, work-study programs, and student loans; and to increase GI education and training under the 1972 Vietnam Era Readjustment Assistance Act.

On August 2, the Veterans Health Care Expansion Act of 1973 became law. It broadens the use of outpatient care, and permits veterans with service-connected disabilities to get nursing care at home. The new law holds down costs and will mean a 41 per cent reduction in federal outlays over the next five years.

Veterans Organizations. The American Legion held its 55th national convention in Honolulu from August 17 to 23. Delegates to the convention elected Robert E. L. Eaton of Chevy Chase, Md., national commander. Thomas E. Martin, 17, of Roebuck, S.C., was elected president of the 1973 American Legion Boys Nation. The Sons of the American Legion elected James Hartman, Jr., of Laurel, Md., national commander.

The American Veterans Committee held its 30th convention in Atlantic City, N.J., from June 8 to 10. Arthur S. Freeman of Chicago was elected national chairman for a two-year term.

The Veterans of Foreign Wars held its 74th annual national convention in New Orleans from August 17 to 24. Ray R. Soden of Bensenville, Ill., was elected commander in chief.   Joseph P. Anderson

VIETNAM, SOUTH. The cease-fire agreement ending the Vietnam War was signed in Paris on Jan. 27, 1973. It was a fragile peace at best, and the agreement made concessions to both sides. An International Control Commission composed of Canada, Poland, Hungary, and Indonesia was set up, but Canada withdrew on July 31 and was replaced by Iran. No coalition government was imposed on South Vietnam, and President Nguyen Van Thieu retained his office.

Fighting continued on a small scale after the cease-fire, as the Communists tried to expand their area of control and Thieu's armies attempted to keep them penned up and expand their own holdings. Fighting reached its fiercest level in November. Throughout the year, the Communists also stepped up more conventional political tactics, as did the supporters of President Thieu.

Politically, the Communists concentrated on trying to gain control of the rural villages by promising various kinds of support to get displaced villagers to return to their homes. The Communists refused an offer by the Thieu government calling for general elections in return for a withdrawal of all Communist military forces.

Thieu instituted his own political action program by scrapping the U.S. plan to hold hamlet elections and making the hamlet chiefs directly responsible to the provincial chiefs. National elections for half the

South Vietnamese wave flags to welcome their prisoners of war
who returned to Saigon after the peace negotiations were concluded.

Senate seats were held August 18, and Thieu's slate swept to an easy victory. This ensured his majority in the Senate.

The Economy. The worldwide food shortage and spiraling food prices, coupled with bad weather, drought, and floods, sharply reduced rice production in South Vietnam. The South needs about 4-million tons per year to adequately feed its 20 million people. The 1973 crop produced only about 3.3-million tons. Prices for rice on the open market jumped 60 per cent, with certain grades going up from 80 to 150 per cent.

President Thieu ordered all rice produced in the Mekong Delta to be channeled through Saigon, and he tried to fix the retail price. At first, this did not work well, and black-market prices soared. By November, however, prices had begun to steady. But this was being accomplished by milling the first crop of the year early, before it was fully ripe. In effect, President Thieu was borrowing from 1974's rice stocks. If weather and military disturbances cut deeply into the crops in 1974, Thieu's government will face a crisis. Each increase in the price of rice will undoubtedly be matched by a corresponding erosion of confidence in the Thieu government. President Thieu acknowledged this when he said, "Consider each grain of rice a bullet." John N. Stalker

See also Asia (Facts in Brief Table).

VIRGINIA. See State Government.

VISUAL ARTS enjoyed a quietly active year in 1973. There were many fine shows, yet few spectacular museum exhibitions. Radical experimental forms such as conceptual and performance art were assimilated into the mainstream and no longer caused the concern of recent years. Attempts to incorporate technology into the visual arts continued at a slow pace, and the prices in all categories of art continued to rise at public auctions.

Several shows featured academic or traditional realist art of the 1800s, testifying to the continued interest in nonmodernist art. Leon Gerome, a prime practitioner of the carefully painted, storytelling picture, was featured in large shows in the Dayton, Ohio, and Minneapolis institutes of art. The Funt collection of Lawrence Alma-Tadema, a late 19th century British artist, was shown at the Metropolitan Museum of Art in New York City. The National Collection of Fine Arts in Washington, D.C., presented another aspect of this world in the exhibition "Dusseldorf Academy and the Americans." The Winslow Homer exhibition, seen at the Whitney Museum of American Art in New York City, the Los Angeles County Museum, and The Art Institute of Chicago, was one of several held with the support of corporate business.

At the other end of the spectrum of style and attitude was The Art Institute of Chicago's large exhibition of the French impressionist Renoir. It broke attendance records in February and March and gave hope to those who wish to retain the large museum loan exhibition. "American Impressionist Painting" was displayed at the National Gallery of Art in Washington, D.C., and at the Whitney Museum. The mysterious work of the little-known Swiss artist Ferdinand Hodler was seen at the University of California Museum in Berkeley and the Guggenheim Museum in New York City.

The most closely observed show of the year was the first exhibition of Western art loaned to the United States by Russia. It comprised 41 major impressionist and postimpressionist paintings and was seen in New York City and Chicago after its March 31 to April 29 showing in Washington, D.C.

Old Master Exhibitions were few, but subtle and enthralling, with material not calculated to excite the casual viewer. The National Gallery of Art presented essentially an "in-house" exhibition of "Early Engravings." This type of exhibition, with material drawn from the museum's collections, has grown more popular because of the financial pressure placed on American museums. The Metropolitan Museum's "Early Italian Renaissance Sculpture" was another fine show of this type. In Canada, the National Gallery in Ottawa mounted a loan show from the Louvre, "Fountainbleu: Art in France, 1528-1610."

The glamorous and expensive U.S. museum acquisitions of the year included the National Gallery of Art's large Picasso masterwork from his analytical cubist period, *Femme Nue.* The Detroit Institute of Art received two major 17th century works—an altarpiece by the French artist Charles LeBrun and a heretofore unknown work by the great Italian realist Caravaggio, *Christ in the House of Mary and Martha.* The Cleveland Museum of Art acquired a 14th century Italian Gothic sculpture of the *Madonna and Child* by Andrea Pisano.

New Forms. Two attempts to solidify new interests were seen in the museum world. The Museum of Modern Art in New York City gave space for the documentation of earth and conceptual art, and for "performance" works—presentations of events and ideas as an art form, an outgrowth of the earlier "Happening." The Museum Film Society was launched during the year to supply single films or entire programs to museums that are unable to undertake such ventures alone. The program promised to spread an understanding of the larger range of film more rapidly than heretofore.

Several events revealed that the American museum was involved in a process of self-examination. After much public debate and recrimination because of alleged secrecy and disregard of the public interest in handling several *de-acquisitions* (selling or exchanging works), the Metropolitan Museum of Art presented its own guideline for future transactions: Public notice will be given for the sale or

exchange of works valued at more than $25,000, and any sale, other than to another museum, will be made at public auction.

New Attributions. Both the National Gallery of Art and the Metropolitan Museum of Art made news when they "re-attributed" many works on their gallery walls. Some 300 paintings were "downgraded" at the Metropolitan, and the more famous names—such as El Greco, Goya, Velázquez, and Rembrandt—were removed in favor of pupils or followers of the masters. Traditionally, museums have shied away from such moves because it tends to disillusion the public; yet, they are necessary if United States museums are to foster a more flexible image.

Several important archaeological museums in the United States took a firm stand against the acquisition or attribution of any property that could not be shown to be legally acquired. This was done in an effort to stop the worldwide looting of sites and the smuggling of ancient works of art.

The finest archaeological exhibition of the year was held at the Brooklyn Museum of Art to celebrate its 150th anniversary. "Art from the Age of the Sun King" was a collection of Egyptian art from the reign of Nefertiti and Akhenaton in the 1300s B.C.

Twentieth century European art was seen in several large exhibitions. They included two shows

Staff members of the National Gallery of Art in Washington, D.C., hang *Madame Matisse,* one of 41 impressionist paintings lent by Russia.

A large exhibition of the works of French impressionist Renoir at The Art Institute of Chicago drew record crowds in February and March.

honoring both the recent and retrospective works of French painter Jean Dubuffet, the whimsical and elegant exponent of naïve art, which he calls *art brut*. His works were seen at the Walker Art Center in Minneapolis and the Guggenheim Museum. The Guggenheim Museum also displayed the little-known nonrepresentational work of the Russian Kasimir Malevich, who called his geometrical art Suprematist. The Rice University Institute for the Arts in Houston presented 104 pieces from the De Menil Family collection representing 30 years' work by the great German surrealist artist Max Ernst.

Controversial Exhibitions included the Bruce Nauman retrospective at the Whitney Museum of American Art and the Eve Hesse show at the Guggenheim. Each attempts to extend or revise current concepts of artistic meaning – through the use of video, the body, or ideas alone, or through casual and unformed shapes and industrial materials. The Philadelphia Museum of Art, together with New York's Museum of Modern Art, displayed a large retrospective exhibition of Dada and conceptual works by the French painter Marcel Duchamp, father of these moves away from tradition.

Among the Americans seen was Jules Olitski, one of the foremost practitioners of "lyrical abstraction" – that is, attempts to continue the full force of the nonrepresentational paintings of the post-World War II period. Olitski, an innovator with spray painting, was honored with a retrospective at the Albright-Knox Gallery in Buffalo, N.Y. The Ellsworth Kelly exhibition at the Museum of Modern Art summed up the other point of view in United States painting of the 1960s – hard-edge precisionist brilliance, verging at times on what has come to be called Minimalism.

Auction Sales. The Norton Simon auction garnered $13 million for 354 works, including $1.4-million each for paintings by Cézanne and Manet. At other auctions, world records were set for paintings by Canaletto, $446,250, and Pieter Breughel the Younger, $393,650. Especially interesting was the fact that 219 American works sold at the October auction of Edith Halpert, the late owner of a 40-year-old New York gallery, brought $3.5 million. The greatest price ever paid for an American work – $2 million – purchased *Blue Poles*, a Jackson Pollock painting, for the Australian National Gallery in Canberra at a sale in New York City in September. Christie's of London, one of the world's important auction houses, reported a 70 per cent gain in volume of sales. All of this, of course, signifies the essential value of works of art in a time of fluctuating economies.   Joshua B. Kind

VITAL STATISTICS. See CENSUS, U.S.; POPULATION, WORLD.

WASHINGTON. See STATE GOVERNMENT.

A Titan Of the Palette

Pablo Picasso, who died at 91 on April 8, 1973, was the world's most famous living artist for more than half a century and one of the half dozen most influential in the history of Western art. The man's gifts were so prodigious that it is hard to realize how young he was when he transformed painting.

By the age of 15, he was so accomplished that there was nothing more for him to do conventionally. By the time he was 21, he had invented what has been known since as his Blue Period. This group of paintings, drawings, and etchings focused on themes of loneliness and despair. They are rendered in spare, elongated terms, gray and blue in color. The imagery is haunting and has a melancholy tenderness.

In his Rose Period, Picasso abruptly turned to stately, immobile images done in beiges, terra cottas, and earth-pinks. The forms are more robust than before. Then, about 1906, Picasso demonstrated his awareness of the bleak Spanish landscape and old Iberian sculpture.

In 1907, he had all but completed a monumental work, *Les Demoiselles d' Avignon*, a sort of ultimate salon piece, done in a highly simplified manner. Before it was completed, Picasso discovered African aboriginal art.

Its effect on him was so shattering that he redid much of *Les Demoiselles* in a fashion that reflects the overwhelming character of the African images. The result was a picture that broke decisively with traditional standards of beauty and harmony.

This new pictorial rhetoric was to be perfected in the next two years, and Picasso established his real subject matter for the rest of his long life: pictorial space.

In 1909, he made a new turn, and he and his friend Georges Braque subsequently invented Cubism, another new visual rhetoric. For the next five years, he created a series of masterpieces. These gray and beige pictures usually consist of studies of the human figure done in patchy touches of earth colors with delicately applied brush lines, mostly black. Picasso reduced the visual reality of his subject to its fundamental geometric elements of curves, cones, prisms, and spheres. The canvases explore the limits of pic-

Picasso (1881-1973)

torial space and present various views of a subject simultaneously. This heroic period, known as Analytical Cubism, established Picasso as the great and constructive revolutionary of modern Western art.

Contact with Sergei Diaghilev's Les Ballets Russes and a trip to Italy during World War I had a strong impact on Picasso. Commissions for stage decorations, which required a simplified manner, and the influence of old Italian painting led to Synthetic Cubism, in which the sharpened forms of Analytical Cubism are rendered in terms of paper cutouts. The resulting works are among Picasso's most glorious, and the two versions of *The Three Musicians*, both done late in 1921, may be the summit of his entire work. Later in the 1920s, he created his version of surrealism – strange, bonelike images set in defined spatial areas.

Suddenly, in the 1930s, Picasso produced what was to be his last innovative style and probably his most powerful. These works, mostly of the female model, are painted in rough and thick paint in brilliant and exquisite colors in forms that seemingly have melted and been distended to provide new comments about space and the forms within it. He painted the *Guernica*, his most famous work, in 1937. It is a huge polemical canvas in black, grays, and white, protesting the bombing of a Basque town during the Spanish Civil War. By 1945, Picasso had produced two more major works, *Night Fishing at Antibes* and *Charnel House*, his reaction to the horrors of Buchenwald.

Almost 30 years remained to the artist, years that are problematic for the observer. Working late at night, a lifelong habit, he produced hundreds of paintings in which he continued to record his reactions to space, women, and the works of other painters such as Eugène Delacroix or Diego Velázquez. But unless a group of unknown masterpieces remains sequestered in his studio, his great accomplishment was done by 1939.

After Picasso, no painter for generations to come can paint and not be in Picasso's debt. More important, he painted what seem to be the greatest pictures of this century and some of the most beautiful of all time. John Maxon

WASHINGTON, D.C.

WASHINGTON, D.C. Voter control over the city government came a step closer in 1973. The two houses of Congress passed separate versions of a bill that would permit local residents to elect a mayor and city council. Under the proposed new governing structure, voters would choose their governmental leaders, but Congress would continue to control the district's budget. Because the U.S. Constitution gives Congress exclusive authority to govern the district, Congress would still have the right to overturn decisions made by the mayor and the council.

The bill passed by the House of Representatives in October would also create a special federal enclave covering the Capitol, the White House, the Kennedy Center for the Performing Arts, and five military posts. The enclave would be governed by a presidentially appointed director, while the remainder of the city would govern itself under the new mayor-council format. The bill passed by the Senate did not provide for the federal enclave.

The Crime Rate. Statistics released during the year by the Federal Bureau of Investigation showed that the crime rate in Washington, D.C., fell by 27.1 per cent in 1972, compared with a national decrease of only 3 per cent.

Despite the reduction, the area was the scene of two crimes that drew national attention in 1973. On January 18, assassins invaded the national headquarters of the Hanafi Madhab Muslim sect and killed two adults and five children. Two adults were critically wounded. Then on January 30, Senator John C. Stennis (D., Miss.), head of the Senate Armed Services Committee, was shot and critically wounded after being robbed outside his home in northwest Washington.

New Theater. On April 3, the American Film Institute opened its new theater in the John F. Kennedy Center for the Performing Arts with a three-week film tribute to the masters of American cinema. The $250,000 theater, made possible by a gift from motion-picture producer Jack L. Warner, will be a national showcase for outstanding motion pictures. See MOTION PICTURES.

Plans for a new civic and convention center were released in October. The $65-million Dwight D. Eisenhower Bicentennial Civic Center will have a 300,000-square-foot exhibit hall.

Population Changes. The Office of Management and Budget redefined the boundaries of the Washington, D.C., metropolitan area, leading to a 3.1 per cent increase in population for the area. The new population of 2,998,900 persons reported by the Bureau of the Census in September did not change the area's rank as the seventh largest U.S. urban center.

Living costs in the Washington area increased 6.1 per cent between May, 1972, and May, 1973. A Department of Labor report on June 15 ranked Washington, D.C., 13th among the 25 large U.S. cities with the highest living costs.   James M. Banovetz

WATERGATE.

WATERGATE. The United States was wracked by the greatest political scandal in its history in 1973. Revelations about secret funds, spying, burglaries, and "dirty tricks" against political opponents during the 1972 election campaign led to disaster for high Administration officials and close associates of President Richard M. Nixon. The scandal spread like a cancer, infecting the Federal Bureau of Investigation (FBI), the Department of Justice, and the Central Intelligence Agency (CIA). The U.S. Senate set up a select committee, a federal grand jury was convened, and the President appointed a special prosecutor to investigate the Watergate affair. As the complex story unraveled, public opinion polls showed that President Nixon's credibility and prestige fell so low that his ability to govern was called into question.

The Break-In. The tip of the Watergate iceberg first emerged on June 17, 1972, when police arrested five rubber-gloved men with wiretapping gear in the Democratic National Committee Headquarters in the Watergate apartment and office complex in Washington, D.C.

One of those arrested was James W. McCord, Jr., a veteran of 19 years with the CIA and chief of security for the Committee to Re-Elect the President (CRP). Disturbing clues found at the scene, however, pointed to higher-level involvement in the Watergate affair. Two other men were subsequently arrested: E. Howard Hunt, a former CIA agent working as a White House consultant; and G. Gordon Liddy, a former FBI man serving as counsel to the CRP.

All seven men were brought to trial before Chief Judge John J. Sirica of the U.S. District Court in Washington, D.C. Hunt maintained he had been acting "in the best interests of the country," but he nevertheless pleaded guilty – as did three of the others – to charges of second-degree burglary, eavesdropping, and conspiracy. On January 30, Liddy and McCord likewise pleaded guilty to the same charges.

The FBI, meanwhile, had traced $100 bills found on the intruders to the Miami, Fla., bank account of Bernard L. Barker, one of the five men initially seized by the police. Further investigation showed that $114,000 in secret contributions intended for the President's campaign had passed through Barker's bank account. Judge Sirica was convinced that the full story had not been revealed during the trial. Also, *The New York Times* charged that the men had been promised large sums of money if they would plead guilty and thus block further investigation.

On March 23, McCord informed Judge Sirica that political pressure was applied to silence the defendants, and that perjury had been committed during the trial. McCord also implicated former Attorney General John N. Mitchell, counsel to the President John W. Dean III, and deputy campaign director Jeb Stuart Magruder. Sirica then imposed heavy provisional sentences, ranging from 35 to 40 years in prison. It seemed, by implication, that the sentences might be reduced if the men told all they knew. The federal grand jury that indicted the Watergate 7 in 1972 was reconvened in March, 1973, to continue the probe.

In spite of these developments, Mr. Nixon assured the nation on March 2 that Dean had conducted a thorough investigation of the affair and that no one in the White House was involved. But he refused to allow any of his staff to testify before the Senate committee set up to investigate the Watergate affair.

Some members of the press insisted that there was a conspiracy to cover up White House involvement in Watergate. There were rumors in the media, too, that the Watergate grand jury was about to indict some of the President's closest associates. Consequently, the U.S. public began to take sides, with a clamor for explanations mounting on the one hand, and accusations of bias in a news media "out to get the President" rising on the other.

White House Resignations. On April 17, the President announced he had conducted his own investigation and that there were "major developments." He also stated that his staff would be allowed to testify.

On April 30, in a dramatic attempt to settle the Watergate affair, the President dismissed Dean. He accepted the resignations of his two most trusted advisers, John D. Ehrlichman and H. R. Haldeman,

who became targets of the Watergate grand jury. Attorney General Richard G. Kleindienst also quit because, he said, close friends of his were Watergate suspects.

More of the Watergate iceberg began to emerge. On May 10, Mitchell and Maurice H. Stans, former commerce secretary and chief fund-raiser for the President's re-election campaign, were indicted for allegedly conspiring to block a fraud investigation of financier Robert L. Vesco after Vesco gave $200,000 in cash to the 1972 Nixon campaign.

Mr. Nixon selected Secretary of Defense Elliot L. Richardson to replace Kleindienst on April 30, and authorized him to appoint a special prosecutor to conduct an independent investigation of Watergate. On May 18, Richardson picked Archibald Cox, a Harvard law school professor and former U.S. solicitor general. Mr. Nixon gave Richardson "absolute authority to make all decisions bearing upon the prosecution of the Watergate case and related matters" and promised Cox "total cooperation."

Dean's Testimony. The Senate Select Committee, chaired by Senator Sam J. Ervin, Jr. (D., N.C.), began hearing public testimony on the Watergate affair May 17. On June 25, Dean testified under a limited grant of immunity from prosecution. Dean said Mr. Nixon was aware as early as Sept. 15, 1972, of efforts to keep White House officials from being

President Richard M. Nixon denies he was involved in Watergate, but John Dean testified that the President knew about the cover-up.

indicted in connection with the Watergate burglary. He also said the President had discussed executive clemency and the payment of hush money to the seven Watergate break-in defendants in March and April, 1973.

While millions watched on television, Dean described a "siege mentality" in the White House that led to the Watergate scandal. Mr. Nixon, Dean claimed, had approved a plan in July, 1970, to use wiretaps, burglary, and other forms of surveillance against citizens he considered radical or subversive. Faced with strong opposition from the late FBI director J. Edgar Hoover, Dean said, the President abandoned the plan.

Dean also made public a White House "enemies list" of 256 persons in the media, business, entertainment, politics, and the academic world. The idea, Dean said, was to "use the available federal machinery to screw our political enemies" through such government actions as tax audits.

Dean also told about efforts to use the CIA in blocking a full FBI investigation of Watergate. And Dean described how he worked secretly with the President's personal attorney, Herbert W. Kalmbach, to deliver $250,000 in cash to the original seven Watergate defendants. In addition, Dean stated that Ehrlichman and Haldeman took leading roles in the Watergate cover-up. The White House issued angry denials.

In October, Dean pleaded guilty to charges of conspiring to obstruct justice and defraud the government in matters related to Watergate.

The Plumbers. Another key witness, former Attorney General Mitchell, appeared before the committee from July 10 through 12. Mitchell admitted that he aided the Watergate cover-up to hide what he termed other "White House horrors" that might have endangered Mr. Nixon's re-election. Heading the list of horrors was a secret unit known as the "plumbers," created by the President to stop news leaks.

The unit was formed, Mitchell said, after Daniel Ellsberg turned over the top-secret Pentagon Papers to *The New York Times* and other newspapers in June, 1971. On Sept. 3, 1971, Hunt and Liddy directed a burglary of the office files of Ellsberg's psychiatrist in an effort to uncover possibly derogatory information about Ellsberg's emotional and mental health.

Mitchell maintained that Mr. Nixon knew nothing about either the Watergate break-in or the cover-up. However, he did implicate Ehrlichman and Haldeman.

In his testimony, given from July 24 to July 27, Ehrlichman claimed he was not involved in the Watergate cover-up. He disagreed with Dean's testimony, particularly about Mr. Nixon's alleged offer of executive clemency and hush money. He was under the impression, he said, that the cover-up was undertaken to hide Mitchell's role.

There were discrepancies in the testimony of, *from left*, James W. McCord, Jr., John D. Ehrlichman, H. R. Haldeman, Jeb Stuart Magruder, Maurice Stans, John N. Mitchell.

Haldeman, appearing before the committee from July 27 to August 1, also disputed Dean's testimony. He added that he had listened to tape recordings of conversations between Dean and the President. The tapes, he said, proved that Mr. Nixon was not involved in the cover-up. Alexander Butterfield, a former White House aide, had revealed in earlier testimony that conversations in the President's Oval Office and Executive Building office, and many of those in the Cabinet Room, had been taperecorded. Some White House telephone calls were also taped.

The White House Tapes. The Senate committee and special prosecutor Cox demanded that Mr. Nixon turn over specific tapes of his talks concerning Watergate with Dean, Mitchell, Haldeman, and Ehrlichman. Mr. Nixon refused, citing executive privilege, a doctrine designed to protect communications within the executive branch. A historic legal battle ensued.

On July 23, Cox issued a subpoena demanding that nine tapes be given to a grand jury investigating Watergate. The Ervin committee issued two subpoenas for five tapes and numerous documents. Judge Sirica ruled on August 29 that the President must give up the tapes for the judge's private scrutiny. His decision was upheld by an appellate court on October 12.

Saturday Night Massacre. Faced with the choice of appealing to the U.S. Supreme Court or turning over the tapes, Mr. Nixon did neither. On October 19, he directed Cox to accept an arrangement whereby Senator John C. Stennis (D., Miss.) would screen the tapes and verify a summary made up by the White House for use by the grand jury and the Senate panel. The President also demanded that Cox forego all other efforts to get evidence from the White House through court-enforced subpoenas. Cox refused.

In what became known as the "Saturday night massacre" of October 20, the President officially told Richardson to fire Cox. Richardson refused, and immediately resigned as attorney general. His deputy, William D. Ruckelshaus, also resigned. Mr. Nixon then named Solicitor General Robert H. Bork as acting attorney general, and Bork fired Cox.

Many Americans sent Congress and the White House telegrams and letters protesting the Cox firing. Friends and foes alike contended that the President had tried to place himself "above the law" by refusing to obey or appeal the court order. Some said he should resign or be impeached. Again there were charges that the news media were out "to get the President."

Suddenly, Mr. Nixon agreed on October 23 to produce the tapes. A week later, the President again startled the nation and revived impeachment talk when he said that two of the tapes covered by the subpoenas had never existed. Many Americans simply did not believe him, and the story of the missing

Guard Frank Wills, *left*, first detected the intruders in the Watergate, in background. Telephone taps, *above*, were used for spying.

tapes further undermined his credibility. His Gallup Poll approval rating plunged to 27 per cent.

Tape Erased. President Nixon's personal secretary, Rose Mary Woods, admitted to Judge Sirica on November 26 that she had erased a conversation between Mr. Nixon and Haldeman while transcribing the subpoenaed tape. According to Woods, she accidentally pushed the "record" button and kept her foot on the power pedal while reaching for a telephone on a desk several feet behind her. Woods testified that she erased only about 5 minutes of the conversation, but the tape contained an 18-minute gap. White House attorneys had no adequate explanation for the 18 minutes of humming noise.

Sirica sent most of the tapes to the Watergate grand jury. But, on December 19, he upheld Mr. Nixon's claim of executive privilege for tapes not relating to Watergate, and withheld two tapes and part of a third from the grand jury.

On December 20, the House Judiciary Committee appointed John M. Doar, a former assistant attorney general, to prepare evidence of impeachable offenses.

Related Revelations. Surrounding the probe of the burglary and cover-up was a web of other revelations. Financial dealings related to the President's purchase of homes in San Clemente, Calif., and Key Biscayne, Fla., came under scrutiny. Reports that he paid only $1,670 in income taxes on total income of over $400,000 in 1970 and 1971 also aroused criticism.

Former acting FBI director L. Patrick Gray III revealed that Kalmbach had paid $40,000 to Donald H. Segretti, a young lawyer hired by presidential appointments secretary Dwight L. Chapin to sabotage Democratic presidential primary campaigns in 1972. Chapin was forced to resign, and Segretti later pleaded guilty to sending a letter falsely accusing two Democratic senators of illicit sexual conduct. He was sentenced to six months in prison. Gray himself admitted that he had destroyed documents related to the Watergate affair and withdrew from nomination as FBI director. The resignation of Vice-President Spiro T. Agnew on October 10, after he pleaded "no contest" to an income tax evasion charge, further eroded confidence in the Nixon Administration.

At the end of the year, President Nixon was attempting to re-establish public confidence. He met personally with members of Congress and appointed a new Watergate special prosecutor, Leon Jaworski, giving him far more guarantees of independence than his predecessor. But it was still unclear whether the President, who seemed to thrive on crises, could survive the Watergate scandal.   William J. Eaton

See also Agnew, Spiro T.; Baker, Howard; Congress of the United States; Cox, Archibald; Elections; Ellsberg, Daniel; Ervin, Sam; Ford, Gerald F.; Nixon, Richard Milhous; President of the United States; Republican Party; Richardson, Elliot L.; Sirica, John J.

WEATHER was unusual throughout the United States in 1973. The winter was little like normal anywhere in the country. In early January, an ice storm caused extensive damage throughout the Southeast. Georgia reeled from a record snowfall across the state on February 9. Yet, such normally frigid states as the Dakotas, Minnesota, and Wisconsin experienced an unusually warm winter.

According to National Weather Service (NWS) records, March was the wettest month on record. Several major storms raced up the Mississippi Valley and through the Eastern states. Flooding occurred throughout the South and East, and the already swollen Great Lakes reached record highs. See DISASTERS.

Tornadoes battered many Central and Eastern states. A record 43 tornadoes were reported in January. There were also a record 240 tornadoes reported in April, making a total of 362 during the period from January through April. A barrage of 160 tornadoes touched down in a 72-hour period from May 25 to 28. By the end of November, there had been more than 1,000 tornadoes, a record number for a year. Timely warnings issued by the National Severe Storm Forecast Center in Kansas City, Mo., kept the toll of dead and injured from being as great as it might otherwise have been.

Weather Satellite. The National Aeronautics and Space Administration launched the experimental satellite *Nimbus-5* in December, 1972. It carried an infrared temperature profile radiometer to measure atmospheric temperatures at different altitudes with greater horizontal resolution than previous devices. Other instruments carried by *Nimbus-5* include a microwave spectrometer, which "sees" through thin clouds to measure temperatures in the atmosphere beneath them and at the earth's surface, and a temperature-humidity infrared radiometer, which provides cloud pictures and water vapor data.

Forecasts for Travelers were issued twice daily by the NWS beginning in May. The goal of the new service is to provide weather forecasts for distant cities in a convenient format. It also makes Canadian weather data available to U.S. citizens.

New automated forecasts of thunderstorm activity and of sleet and snow, developed by the Techniques Development Laboratory of the NWS, will help provide better forecasts. The thunderstorm forecasts give the probabilities of general thunderstorms over the continental United States, and whether those storms occurring east of the Rocky Mountains will be severe. The snow and sleet forecasts are issued twice a day to 152 stations in the United States. Both forecasts were developed using statistical data and computer models.

In February, the Coast Guard radio station at Point Reyes, Calif., began transmitting forecasts and

Lightning travels upward, then horizontally, from a television tower in a rare photograph by lightning-research scientists at Lugano, Switzerland.

warnings by Morse telegraphy, voice, and radio-facsimile. The NWS and Coast Guard program is the first designed for commercial shipping and fishing boats in the eastern North Pacific Ocean.

Acoustic Sounding. A ground-based system being developed by Stanford University for the NWS has measured the atmospheric temperature profile to an altitude of 5,000 feet. The Radio Acoustic Sounding System is based on the fact that temperature alone controls the speed of sound in the atmosphere. A short burst of sound is sent vertically upward and the return signal is monitored by radar. The speed at which the pulse travels is determined much as police radar determines the speed of a car. When the measured temperature profiles were compared with simultaneous temperature readings from both tethered balloons and radiosondes (instruments on balloons aloft), they showed excellent agreement.

Chemical Film. A harmless chemical film a few molecules thick on the ocean's surface may someday help to prevent hurricanes from gaining their destructive energy from the ocean. Scientists at the National Hurricane Research Laboratory and the Illinois Institute of Technology Research Institute began testing the effects of the film on ocean wave activity and the transfer of water vapor into the air. The tests, at a site 15 miles east of Miami, Fla., indicated a possible use of the film in choking hurricanes.　　　　　　　　　　　　　　William G. Collins

WEINBERGER, CASPAR WILLARD (1917-　　　), was sworn in as U.S. secretary of health, education, and welfare (HEW) on Feb. 12, 1973, in San Clemente, Calif. He had served as chairman of the Federal Trade Commission in 1970, as deputy director of the Office of Management and Budget (OMB) from 1970 to 1972, and as that agency's director from 1972 until his appointment to HEW.

Weinberger assumed leadership of the government's largest agency with a reputation for cutting government spending. As director of OMB, he had trimmed the 1973 federal budget from $255 billion to $250 billion. Liberal Senate Democrats opposed his confirmation in protest against the Administration's withholding of funds for social welfare programs.

Weinberger was born in San Francisco on Aug. 18, 1917. He graduated from Harvard University in 1938, and from the Harvard Law School in 1941. He served in the Army during World War II as an infantryman, and later, as a member of General Douglas MacArthur's intelligence staff.

Weinberger entered private law practice in 1947. From 1952 to 1958, he was a member of the California state legislature. In addition to his law practice, from 1959 to 1968, he wrote a twice-weekly column on state government for California newspapers. He also reviewed books for the *San Francisco Chronicle*.

Weinberger and his wife, the former Jane Dalton, have two children.　　　　　　　　　　Jacqueline Heath

WEST INDIES. Moves toward independence continued among the Caribbean Islands in 1973. On July 10, the Bahamas formally became an independent nation (see BAHAMAS). On July 30, the British government announced that it would grant Grenada, an island in the Windward group, full independence in 1974. Grenada has been an associated state in the British Commonwealth since 1967.

Tourism remained the principal industry in the islands. In Barbados, German and British investors were planning huge new tourist complexes that would send the number of hotel rooms on the island soaring from 5,000 to 18,000 within five years. Motel accommodations were also being increased on St. Vincent Island and Antigua. In Jamaica, 800 hotel rooms added in 1973 increased the total for the island to 9,800.

Self-Help Programs. Caribbean island governments, meanwhile, explored ways in which native West Indians could share more fully in the economic benefits derived from tourism. Barbadians were encouraged to participate in tourist-oriented operations through governmental offers of tax-free certificates in hotel enterprises and incentive loans of $2,500 to local businessmen. The government of St. Vincent Island launched a sweeping land-reform program intended to break up the old colonial estates. Jamaica announced a program designed to bridge the poverty gap and break down class barriers. Plans included Project Self-Help, under which financial aid on favorable terms would be supplied, and Project Land Lease, which would provide small farmers with land.

Economic Development. During the year, Kingston, Jamaica, was chosen as the site of what was optimistically believed would be the largest and most containerized port in the Western Hemisphere. It was to be built by a consortium of Japanese banks, aided by a $15-million government loan. Also in Jamaica, a foreign consortium launched a $50-million project to renovate the waterfront of Montego Bay. The Jamaican government also signed an agreement with the Moratti group of Milan, Italy, for the construction of a $350-million refinery capable of producing 250,000 barrels of oil a day. The Inter-American Development Bank on June 1 approved a $7.9-million loan to help launch the third stage of Jamaica's farm development program.

Pressures for greater United States interest in the Caribbean area grew. In September, U.S. Department of State officials, military planners, and members of Congress called for an expansion of U.S. economic and social interests.　　　　　　　Paul C. Tullier

See also LATIN AMERICA (Facts in Brief Table).

WEST VIRGINIA. See STATE GOVERNMENT.

WILDLIFE. See CONSERVATION.

WISCONSIN. See STATE GOVERNMENT.

WRESTLING. See SPORTS.

WYOMING. See STATE GOVERNMENT.

YEMEN (ADEN). The government's policy of providing support for rebel movements in the region further isolated Yemen (Aden) from its neighbors in 1973. It used the Front for the Liberation of the Occupied Arab Gulf as an avenue for the support. When that group was allegedly involved in assassinating a member of the three-man Yemen (Ṣanʻāʼ) presidential council in May, the union of the two Yemen states, agreed on in 1972, was delayed. In September, the union was postponed for a year.

Support Reduced. Ironically, the isolation of the Aden regime reduced its support from the Socialist countries. Its strongest support previously had come from China, with Russia being content to provide technical aid and advisers for agriculture and fisheries development. But China's foreign minister condemned all subversion in the area during a visit to Iran. He said China would support all legitimate governments.

The statement left doubts as to Aden's ability to continue to supply arms or provide sanctuary for rebels fighting in neighboring Oman. Oman said in January that it had arrested 39 members of the People's Front for the Liberation of Oman and the Arab Gulf and seized large caches of Chinese arms supplied by the Aden regime. The border between the two countries is not clearly defined. In June, a Latin American newsletter reported that pilots from Yemen (Aden) were being trained in Cuba to fly Russian MIG 21 jet fighter planes.

Tragedy struck the Yemen (Aden) diplomatic service in April. Twenty-five Yemeni diplomats, including Foreign Minister Mohammed Salah Aulaqi, died in an air crash north of Aden. The government declared a week of national mourning.

Economic Gains. The leftist government's radical policies and its hostility toward its neighbors made it a poor prospect for foreign investors. There were, however, a few bright spots. On March 30, a joint Aden-Kuwait company was formed to expand Aden's bunkering facilities for refueling Kuwaiti oil tankers. Refueling had been the main source of Aden's revenue before it gained independence from Great Britain in 1967.

Most foreign interest was centered on the potentially rich fishing industry. In April, Japan gave the industry two refrigerated power cruisers, and the International Development Association loaned Aden $25 million to finance the construction of storage and fish-processing plants. In May, Denmark sent experts to supervise work on the main Aden fishing port at Nakhtun.

Two locally financed industrial plants—a skin-dyeing plant and a cigarette factory to process Yemeni-grown tobacco—went into operation in June. Economic aid agreements totaling $57 million were signed in April with Poland, Czechoslovakia, and Hungary. William Spencer

See also MIDDLE EAST (Facts in Brief Table).

YEMEN (ṢANʻĀʼ). Despite early optimism, the proposed unification with neighboring Yemen (Aden) ran into trouble in 1973. The two states had agreed in November, 1972, that they would unite within a year. In February, 1973, they formed a joint Constituent Assembly, and the Ṣanʻāʼ regime formed a political group, the Yemeni Union, to promote unification. On May 1, Ṣanʻāʼ issued a national charter calling for the immediate union of the two Yemens.

However, on May 30, Sheik Mohammed Ali Othman, a member of the three-man presidential council, the highest executive authority in Ṣanʻāʼ, was assassinated in front of his home in Taʻizz. The government charged that the killers came from territory controlled by the Aden regime.

Many suspected terrorists were arrested and 30 were executed for the sheik's murder. These events, coupled with armed border clashes with Aden forces earlier in May, slowed the move toward union.

Faced with a $30-million debt, the regime turned to foreign aid for its development program. The World Bank granted loans of $10.9 million for the reclamation of 34,000 acres in the Tihama coastal plain. The move could nearly double agricultural production. Saudi Arabia provided $18.8 million for hospitals and roads in January. A second World Bank loan, $11 million, would expand primary school facilities by 80 per cent. William Spencer

See also MIDDLE EAST (Facts in Brief Table).

YOUNG MEN'S CHRISTIAN ASSOCIATION (YMCA). The national council called in May, 1973, for a greater YMCA role in dispensing the social services provided by the federal government. The action was taken by more than 600 delegates attending the national council's 46th meeting in Chicago. The delegates also approved resolutions urging the government to develop new plans and policies for such services, and to provide resources to concerned public and private agencies. They also called for greater focus on the employment and educational needs of youth, and for legislation allowing nonprofit organizations greater latitude in working for social legislation.

The council also asked the national board to develop a plan for YMCA's to work with returning veterans and to support a rehabilitation program for Indochina. It offered to act as liaison with the United States, Canada, and Sweden to bring exiled Americans home. It also issued a policy to guide local YMCA's in working with American Indians.

The national council also created a Commission on Women to ensure significant female leadership on YMCA boards and committees, and in programs. And it urged the federal government to encourage the development of local environmental policy, including land use. Belford V. Lawson of Washington, D.C., was elected president of the YMCA's national council. Joseph P. Anderson

YOUNG WOMEN'S CHRISTIAN ASSOCIATION

(YWCA). Delegates to the 1973 national convention voted to reorient YWCA programming, including classes, to open new opportunities for women in education, jobs, careers, and politics. About 2,500 delegates representing more than 8,000 local Y's attended the convention in San Diego, Calif., in March. The delegates' statement of goals also called for quality, voluntary, nonracist, and nonsexist child care to be made available to working women; and for programs that train women to be politically active.

The delegates reaffirmed the YWCA's One Imperative, a commitment to work for the elimination of racism wherever it exists and by any means necessary in order to help build a just and equitable society for women, youth, and citizens of the developing nations.

The National Teen Organization became an officially authorized national group of members of the YWCA. This group includes girls from 12 to 14 years of age. At present, there are 400,000 Y-Teen members. In addition to granting other rights and responsibilities, the delegates approved voting privileges for members who have reached the age of 15.

The delegates elected Elizabeth Steel Genne of Montclair, N.J., to serve as president for a three-year term. Winona C. Banister of Warren, N.J., and Jewel P. Graham of Yellow Springs, Ohio, were elected vice-presidents.   Joseph P. Anderson

YOUTH ORGANIZATIONS.

Six national voluntary youth-serving organizations and their affiliates were given an unusual opportunity to help in developing Education for Parenthood programs for teen-age boys and girls in 1973. These programs, designed to prepare adolescents for more effective parenthood, began with emphasis on developing and improving parenthood education courses within the schools. In the next phase, the participating organizations will offer their own approaches to preparing teen-agers for parenthood.

The six organizations participating in the project are Boy Scouts of America, Boys' Clubs of America, Girl Scouts of the United States of America, National Federation of Settlements and Neighborhood Houses, The Salvation Army, and Save the Children Federation (Appalachian Program). They received grants totaling $512,124 from the Office of Child Development of the U.S. Department of Health, Education, and Welfare. In addition to nationwide activities for teen-age boys and girls, the organizations will initiate special demonstrations that will reach more than 6-million young people over a three-year period.

Boy Scouts of America (BSA). Nearly 4 million Scouts and other concerned citizens picked up 750,-000 tons of trash from nearly 1 million acres of parks and 500,000 miles of highway on Keep America Beautiful Day, April 28, 1973. President Richard M. Nixon presented an award to the BSA for exceptional initiative for its Operation Reach program, which encourages young Americans to decide voluntarily against taking drugs.

The 1973 National Scout Jamboree was held at two locations: 25,000 boys at Farragut State Park in Idaho, August 1 to 7; and 45,000 boys at Morraine State Park in Pennsylvania, August 3 to 9.

The 63rd annual meeting of the BSA was held in Minneapolis, from May 23 to 25. Robert W. Reneker of Chicago was elected president.

Boys' Clubs of America achieved two of its major goals in 1973 when the Wheeler Boys' Club of Indianapolis became the 1,000th club, and James Manning II, of Pittsfield, Mass., was named the 1-millionth member.

A goals-oriented program, "Design for the Seventies," was developed. This program includes expanding services to meet the needs of additional boys and clubs, recruiting and training the staff to provide these services, and doubling the budget within the next 10 years to preserve high standards of service.

Gilbert Baez, 17, of the R. W. Brown Boys' Club in Philadelphia was chosen Boy of the Year.

Camp Fire Girls. To give high-school-age members a greater part in decision making, the Camp Fire Girls gave teen-age members the right to serve as voting members at the National Council meeting in 1973. The name of the second age-level group (9

Boy Scout at the National Scout Jamboree displays some of the items he is willing to trade. Such swapping has become a tradition.

to 11 years), was changed from Camp Fire Girls to Camp Fire Adventurers.

Self-awareness, decision making, and eliminating sex stereotyping are goals in new program materials. *Adventure*, for Camp Fire Adventurers, replaced the traditional *Book of the Camp Fire Girls. It's All About Me, Here I Am*, and *I Can Do Lots of Things* became the first distinctive set of materials for Camp Fire Blue Birds(6 to 8 years old).

4-H Clubs. "4-H Gets It All Together" was an apt theme as about 5 million young people of all races, incomes, and ways of life got together in the nation's largest coeducational youth program in 1973. These 4-H'ers gathered in clubs, instructional 4-H television series, day camps, special-interest courses, and special 4-H nutrition programs. Over half a million adult and teen volunteers and 3,000 paraprofessionals guided them in such projects as animal science, clothing, food and nutrition, recreation and crafts, and plant science.

Future Farmers of America (FFA) membership grew by more than 15,000 to 447,577 in 1973. The 46th national FFA convention, held in Kansas City, Mo., attracted a record 15,500 FFA members and guests. Conducted entirely by six elected student national officers, the convention included business sessions, agricultural contests, and recognition of hundreds of members for their achievements.

The highest FFA awards, Star Farmer and Star Agribusinessman of America, were presented to William A. Sparrow of Unadilla, Ga., and two agribusinessmen, Jack Rose of Elko, Nev., and Steven Redgate of Waynoka, Okla. The top chapter in the FFA's Community Improvement (Building American Communities) program was the Bloomer FFA Chapter of Bloomer, Wis.

Girl Scouts of the United States of America lowered the age limit to permit 6-year-olds to become Brownie Girl Scouts in 1973. They also worked at getting more adults to volunteer as leaders and assistant leaders. The Girl Scouts now serve 1 out of every 7 U.S. girls between the ages of 6 and 17.

Decision making by girls was given impetus in 1973. Senior Girl Scouts took part in the January and May national board and committee meetings at National Girl Scout headquarters in New York City. And an increasing number of girls sat on council boards and committees and shared in tasks formerly performed only by adults.

Girls in Nashville, Tenn., worked in partnership with adult volunteers to initiate and conduct CISUM (music spelled backwards), a highly successful music workshop for 150 Girl Scouts from throughout the nation and 6 Girl Guides from overseas. Henry Romersa, national director of the National Academy of Recording Arts and Sciences, worked with the girls of Cumberland Valley Girl Scout Council to recruit the talent. Minnie Pearl, Grand Ole Opry star, was honorary chairman of the two-week July event.

During the summer, more than 7,000 girls participated in national and international events. These included exploration trips, camping, conferences, and home visits abroad, financed in part by the Juliette Low World Friendship Fund. In addition, 39 Girl Guides and Girl Scouts from abroad attended events in the United States.

New uniforms for Brownies, Juniors, and Cadettes were introduced in 1973. In tune with the times, each uniform features mix-and-match separates, jumper, skirt, pants, top, and shorts, to allow each girl to choose her own individual look while still being in an approved uniform.

Girls Clubs of America membership continued to increase in 1973. By year's end, there were more than 150,000 girls in more than 220 club centers. The National Conference, held in Dallas from April 8 to 11, attracted more than 500 representatives. Nearly 100 teen-age girls, some of whom had won grants and awards for excellence in scholarship, citizenship, and sewing fashions attended.

Junior Achievement continued its opinion survey of young people in 1973. The survey indicates that, contrary to widespread reports, the American business system has broad public support and credibility. The poll was conducted at the 30th National Junior Achievers Conference, which was held from August 12 to 17 on the campus of Indiana University in Bloomington.   Joseph P. Anderson

YUGOSLAVIA expanded its political and economic links with the Russian bloc in 1973 while maintaining its independent position in Europe. At home, it continued the restrictive political policies that began with the purges in Croatia in December, 1971.

Visits by Czechoslovak foreign minister Bohuslav Chnoupek in March and Communist Party leader Gustav Husak in October completed the normalization of relations between the two countries. Relations had been strained by the 1968 Russian-led invasion of Czechoslovakia and removal of the reform-minded Czechoslovak leadership. Yugoslavia's President Josip Broz Tito declared in March that problems arising from the 1968 invasion had been "overcome."

Oil Pipeline. Polish party leader Edward Gierek visited Yugoslavia in June, followed by Hungary's leader, Janos Kadar, in July. During Kadar's visit, it was announced that Hungary and Yugoslavia would build a 300-mile oil pipeline from the port of Bakar on Yugoslavia's Adriatic coast to Szazhalombatta in Hungary, where it would connect with the so-called Friendship Line to Czechoslovakia. The pipeline is to supply Hungary and Czechoslovakia with 5-million tons each of Middle Eastern oil annually.

Russian Premier Aleksei N. Kosygin visited Yugoslavia in September. He discussed political relations and the implementation of Russia's $1.3-billion loan to Yugoslavia, whose first $540-million installment had been agreed on in September, 1972. A Russian naval squadron visited Yugoslav naval ports at the same time.

In Domestic Affairs, purges of allegedly nationalist, liberal, and technocratic groups continued, especially in Serbia. The main targets there were the party itself, the universities, and writers and film makers.

At a special party conference held on May 10 and 11, tough Slovene leader Stane Dolanc was re-elected secretary of the Communist Party's executive bureau. In June, General Ivan Miskovic, President Tito's closest security adviser, was quietly removed because of his demand for greater powers for the political police. On July 9, Mitja Ribicic, another Slovene leader and former federal premier, became the federal vice-president.

The Economy. In March, Yugoslavia concluded a five-year nonpreferential trade agreement with the Common Market. In the first nine months of 1973, exports increased 26 per cent, but imports went up 46 per cent. In June, subsidiaries of a United States firm, Global Marine, agreed to the first joint venture for the exploration and development of Yugoslavia's offshore oil resources. In October, a $64-million loan to modernize existing enterprises in Yugoslavia was granted to Yugoslav banks by a Western consortium led by Lloyds and Bolsa International Bank of London. Chris Cviic

See also EUROPE (Facts in Brief Table).

ZAIRE. President Mobutu Sese Seko made a 10-day visit to the People's Republic of China in January, 1973, marking a major turnaround in relations between the two nations. He met with both Premier Chou En-lai and Communist Party Chairman Mao Tse-tung. Accounts in Zaire's press made it clear that Mobutu was trying to win international recognition for Zaire as one of Africa's largest and richest nations. He returned with a $100-million interest-free loan as well as agreements on economic and technical aid and on trade.

In a speech following his return, Mobutu emphasized the Chinese "miracle called work." Then, on January 30, he announced the establishment of various compulsory free-time work and cleanup projects, based on the Chinese model.

Other Foreign Affairs. Zaire broke diplomatic ties with Israel when Arab-Israeli fighting broke out in October. Mobutu visited French President Georges Pompidou and announced that Pompidou would visit Zaire in 1974.

Relations between Belgium and Zaire were strained in August after President Mobutu accused Belgium of "monetary sabotage." But the hostility apparently ended when Belgian Prime Minister Edmond Leburton visited Zaire in September. In November, Zaire nationalized all foreign agricultural companies.

Domestic Developments. Mobutu's emphasis on cultural authenticity continued. Economics and authenticity were combined when the government passed a ban on foreign beer and mineral water and European-style coats and ties. Lake Albert was renamed Lake Mobutu Sese Seko.

The government tightened press censorship in February, and tension between the government and the Roman Catholic Church continued. In May, Mobutu called for local control of churchmen, whom he said were "under remote control from abroad." Mobutu's comments followed the publication of a report written by the bishops of Zaire that was considered hostile to the government. But there was enough calm on the domestic front to permit the government to abolish the death penalty in July.

The second phase of the Inga Hydroelectric Project was started. The project will eventually harness the Zaire (Congo) River and produce 30,000 megawatts of power when it is completed early in the 2000s.

During the year, Zaire returned assets to a Belgian mining company that had been nationalized in 1970. Apparently, this was the first time an African nation had returned foreign assets after a takeover.

Zaire received European and U.S. loans for expansion of its air-transport facilities. The government awarded a contract worth almost $100 million to a British firm for airport construction. John Storm Roberts

See also AFRICA (Facts in Brief Table).

In keeping with President Mobutu's campaign to eliminate colonial influences, citizens of Zaire return to authentic African dress.

ZAMBIA. The changeover to a one-party political system was Zambia's main governmental concern in 1973. The new system had been decided on in December, 1972. President Kenneth D. Kaunda officially signed Zambia's new Constitution into being on Aug. 25, 1973.

The new Constitution provides for a prime minister, appointed by the president, to run the government. The members of Parliament are elected. Zambia's first general election under the new system was held on December 5.

Internal Politics. During the year, a great deal of political activity was aimed at bringing leaders of the former opposition parties into the ruling United National Independence Party (UNIP). Founder of the banned opposition United Progressive Party, Simon Kapwepwe, a former ally of Kaunda, was released from detention in January. He had been arrested in February, 1972. However, Kapwepwe refused to join the UNIP. Another major opposition leader, Harry Nkumbula, rejoined the UNIP on June 27.

The UNIP made great effort to bring the opposition into its ranks because of a growing threat of political instability. There was increased friction between ethnic factions and widespread rumors that the Zambian Army might be getting out of control.

Border Closing. On January 9, Rhodesia closed its border with Zambia, allowing only copper shipments to pass through. The Rhodesian government claimed the border was closed because Zambia was harboring African nationalists who made guerrilla raids into Rhodesia. Two days later, Zambia retaliated by stopping its copper exports and ordering Zambian banks to halt foreign-exchange transactions with the white-minority governments of both Rhodesia and South Africa.

Zambia began rerouting its exports overland through Mozambique and Tanzania. Kaunda intended to find routes that would permanently bypass Rhodesia. Since Rhodesian railways stood to lose all Zambian freight, Rhodesia announced it was reopening its border on February 3. Zambia, however, refused to open its side.

The effect of the border closing on Zambia's export trade was eased by a rise in world copper prices in May. The increase was caused, in part, by Zambia's reduced copper ore exports. According to United Nations estimates, the rerouting of its exports cost Zambia $124 million. The nation also faced shortages of imported goods that would normally enter the country through Rhodesia.

There were several incidents of violence along the Rhodesian-Zambian border during the year. Land-mine explosions on the Zambian side reportedly killed six persons in January. One of the most serious incidents occurred on May 15, when a Zambian soldier shot across the Zambezi River and killed two Canadian tourists in Rhodesia.   John Storm Roberts

See also AFRICA (Facts in Brief Table).

ZOOLOGY. Scientists have known for several years that the salmon's sense of smell guides it back to its birthplace when spawning time comes. But it was not until 1973 that they identified the odor that attracts them. Now, David J. Solomon, a zoologist with the British Ministry of Agriculture, Fisheries, and Food, has found that a chemical given off by young salmon that have never left the river attracts the older salmon.

Solomon discovered that salmon, after their 18-month stay in the ocean, swam only to rivers containing young salmon. He also found that some rivers that had no salmon in them could be turned into spawning grounds for the older salmon by placing newly hatched salmon there.

Solomon believes that a chemical called pheromone, given off by the young salmon, attracts the older salmon. They are so sensitive to this substance that only one gram per day of pheromone in a river is enough to attract them.

Water Birds. The glare of reflected sunlight from the surface of a body of water usually makes it difficult for fish-eating birds to see. Some birds are known to hold out their wings to shadow the water surface so they can see into the water better. However, the fish dive deeper when they become aware of shadows.

J.R. Krebs and B. Partridge of the University of British Columbia in Vancouver, Canada, have now found that the great blue heron lessens the effects of the glare by tilting its long neck and head to one side. Observers found that the birds always tilted their heads toward the sun, and more so if the water was cloudy and thus more reflective.

At first, the zoologists thought that the birds tilted their heads to get into a better diving position. But they found that the birds strike wherever they see fish, not just on the tilted side. Thus, it was clear that the tilted head overcame the sun's glare.

Rat Perception. Research by Justin M. Joffe and his colleagues at the University of Vermont showed that a rat develops more normal emotions if it sees the consequences of its actions as it grows up, but becomes abnormal if it does not. They put newborn rats in experimental cages that contained special training levers. One group could control its living conditions by pressing the levers, which supplied food, water, and light. The others were in cages where living conditions were controlled by the lever-pressing of the first group. The two groups were exposed to the same living conditions, the only difference being that the one group could assess the relationship between its actions and living conditions.

After 60 days, the rats that could see the consequences of their actions were found to be emotionally normal, but the others were emotionally disturbed. Researchers judged the difference by measuring defecation frequency, a widely accepted test procedure in such rat studies. Frequency increases under emotional stress.   Barbara N. Benson

Paddiwack, a 13-week-old polar bear cub, relaxes with his mother, Sally, at the London Zoo. He is the third cub successfully reared at the zoo.

ZOOS AND AQUARIUMS. Increasing concern for the survival and welfare of wild animals stimulated new construction work in many zoos and aquariums in 1973. Major construction projects included the Metropolitan Toronto Zoo, in Canada; the state zoos in Mankato, Minn., and Raleigh, N.C.; and a large zoo at Columbia, S.C. A Sea World complex was also opened near Orlando, Fla.

Among the new exhibits that were opened during the year are an Andean animal display scene at the Oklahoma City Zoo; grottoes and dens for carnivores at the Louisville (Ky.) Zoo; a twlight zoo section at the Highland Park Zoological Gardens in Pittsburgh; an African veld canyon exhibit at the San Diego Zoo; and a house for great apes at the Stuttgart Zoo in West Germany. The Steinhart Aquarium in San Francisco unveiled a tidal pool and a doughnut-shaped 120,000-gallon tank for schools of tuna, mackerel, and dogfish sharks. The Vancouver Aquarium in Canada placed three sea otters in a new 20,000-gallon display pool.

Endangered Species. Most zoos persevered in their breeding programs for rare and endangered species. Of special interest were the births of five white rhinoceroses at the San Diego Zoo and hatchings of golden eagles at the Topeka (Kans.) Zoo for the second year in a row. Bald eagles were raised at the National Zoo in Washington, D.C.; and at the Crandon Park Zoo in Miami, Fla.; and 11 American crocodiles were hatched at the Atlanta (Ga.) Zoo. Second-generation cheetahs were born at Whipsnade Park, in Bedfordshire, England, and two bongos (a rare antelope) were born at the Frankfurt Zoo in West Germany.

A significant achievement was the first successful artificial insemination of a great ape. The baby female chimpanzee fathered in this way was born on July 15 at the Toledo (Ohio) Zoo.

New Regulations. Delegates from 80 nations assembled in Washington, D.C., in February to draft a comprehensive international agreement regulating trade in endangered species of plants and animals. Before the agreement goes into effect, it must be ratified by the participating governments. The U.S. Marine Mammal Protection Act became effective at the beginning of 1973. It regulates capture of several species of whales, seals, and sea lions.

Late in the year, the U.S. Department of Agriculture modified its embargo on exotic birds, allowing some to be imported under strict quarantine rules. The embargo was originally imposed to reduce the danger to poultry from Newcastle disease.

The American Association of Zoological Parks and Aquariums endorsed a computerized census system for all zoo animals in the United States and Canada. The system will help zoos keep accurate records on endangered species, and will promote pairing in breeding programs.　　　George B. Rabb

Section Five

World Book Supplement

In its function of keeping WORLD BOOK owners up to date, THE WORLD BOOK YEAR BOOK herewith offers significant new articles from the 1974 edition of THE WORLD BOOK ENCYCLOPEDIA. These articles should be indexed in THE WORLD BOOK ENCYCLOPEDIA by means of THE YEAR BOOK cross-reference tabs.

Planes Waiting to Take Off from an Airport Runway   Travelers Purchasing Tickets in the Terminal

George Hall   WORLD BOOK photo

AIRPORT

A Major Airport handles hundreds of airplanes and thousands of passengers daily. Travelers and their friends crowd the bustling terminal. Behind the scenes, workers service planes and perform countless other jobs to ensure safe, comfortable flights.

AIRPORT is a place where airplanes and other aircraft land and take off. Airplanes have become the chief means of long-distance travel—and so airports have become highly important transportation terminals. Every day at the world's busiest airports, more than 1,000 planes land and take off and over 50,000 passengers arrive and depart.

Big-city airports are busy, exciting places. Overhead, planes circle the field, waiting their turn to land. On the ground, one jet plane after another takes off. Automobiles, buses, and taxis pull up to the passenger terminal to pick up or drop off travelers and their friends and relatives. Thousands of people jam the terminal building. Most of them are travelers, such as business executives, government officials, and vacationists. Many others are airport and airline employees. Crowds of visitors often gather at airports to greet championship sports teams, politicians, and movie stars and other celebrities. Families and friends come to meet students home for the holidays, servicemen returning from training, and relatives arriving for a visit.

Airports differ in many ways from other transportation terminals, such as bus or train stations. Two important differences are in the amount of land required and the location of that land. An airport needs much more land to handle the same number of passengers as a bus or train station. A large bus station may cover about 3 acres of land, and a large railroad station about

J. Larry Donoghue, the contributor of this article, is President of Ralph H. Burke, Inc., a firm that planned Chicago-O'Hare International Airport and many other U.S. airports.

9 acres. But even small airfields, such as the grass runways farmers use for light airplanes, require about 4 acres. Medium-sized city airports need from 500 to 1,500 acres. The largest airport in the United States, Dallas-Fort Worth Regional Airport, occupies about 17,500 acres, an area larger than Manhattan Island. The airport began handling passengers in 1973, but all its facilities will not be completed until the year 2000.

Because they require so much land, most airports have been built on the edge of town. As a result, many airports have poor connections with public transportation. Most bus and train stations, on the other hand, are in town, convenient to public transportation.

The United States has about 12,000 civilian airports and more than 190,000 civilian aircraft. Over 11,000 U.S. airports handle mostly small private planes and *charter planes*, which may be hired for special flights. Fewer than 1,000 U.S. airports can handle aircraft large enough for 20 or more passengers. Of these airports, about 530 serve *scheduled airlines*, which operate planes over certain routes on a timetable. Canada has almost 1,500 civilian airports and more than 11,000 civilian aircraft. About 50 Canadian airports handle large jets.

Cities or public corporations own most large airports, and individuals or private groups own most small ones. In the United States, the Federal Aviation Administration (FAA) licenses aircraft and sets airport safety standards. It directs federal aid programs to develop publicly owned airports. The FAA also supervises airport security programs to prevent airliner hijacking attempts. The Canadian Ministry of Transport licenses airports and aircraft in Canada.

Workers Loading Food for Passengers' Meals

Customs Officials Inspecting International Passengers

Travelers Claiming Baggage After a Flight

WORLD BOOK photos

Air Traffic Controllers Directing Aircraft Movements

AIRPORT / *Kinds of Airports*

The FAA classifies U.S. civilian airports in two categories: (1) air carrier airports and (2) general aviation airports. Military air bases make up a third classification.

Air Carrier Airports serve planes of scheduled airlines. In addition, they may serve such small aircraft as business, charter, or private planes. All major civilian airports in the United States are air carrier airports.

An air carrier airport may serve regional, trunk, or international airlines—or a combination of these types. *Regional airlines* limit their service to one area within the United States, such as the South or the Great Lakes region. *Trunk airlines* serve larger areas within the nation. Most trunk airlines include routes that connect major cities on the Atlantic and Pacific coasts or on the northern and southern borders of the nation. *International airlines* provide flights to and from foreign cities. Most airports that handle international flights have the word *international* in their name. International airports serve foreign as well as U.S. international airlines.

General Aviation Airports serve all types of aircraft except scheduled airline planes. They serve business, charter, and private aircraft as well as scheduled *air taxis*, which carry passengers between small towns and to and from air carrier airports. General aviation airports also handle small aircraft used for aerial surveys, crop-dusting, and flight instruction. Airports that handle only specialized aircraft, such as helicopters or seaplanes, also fall into the general aviation category.

The FAA classifies all general aviation airports—except those that serve only specialized aircraft—in four groups. The classifications are based on the size of the planes the airports can handle. *Basic utility airports* serve single-engine and some small twin-engine, propeller-driven planes. *General utility airports* can handle slightly heavier propeller aircraft. *Basic transport airports* can accommodate small jet airplanes. *General transport airports* are large enough to handle four-engine jets, such as the McDonnell Douglas DC-8, which can carry up to 240 passengers.

Special classifications of general aviation airports include heliports and seaplane bases.

Heliports are areas where helicopters land and take off. A heliport may be on land, the flat roof of a building, or the deck of a ship. Even a bay or other body of water may serve as a heliport for helicopters equipped with *pontoons* (floats).

Seaplane Bases are used by seaplanes and amphibians. *Amphibians* are aircraft that can land and take off on water or land. Seaplane bases may be on bays, lakes, or rivers. Most seaplane bases have on-shore facilities to service the aircraft.

Military Air Bases are airports operated by the armed forces. In addition, some military units, such as the U.S. Air National Guard, rent facilities at commercial airports. The United States has more than 200 military air bases. These bases range in size from small fields for light planes to huge airports for heavy jet bombers. Canada has about 40 military air bases, including several Royal Canadian Mounted Police bases. See AIR BASE.

OVERVIEW OF AN AIRPORT

Major airports, such as Kansas City (Mo.) International, diagrammed at the right, have passenger terminals, hangars, and cargo terminals for major airlines. *General aviation* facilities serve small aircraft. *Clear zones* at the ends of runways give planes space to rise or descend. A close-up view, *below*, shows the ring-shaped design of the passenger terminals. Passengers park within the ring, enter the terminal at the gate marked for their flight, and walk only a short distance to a plane.

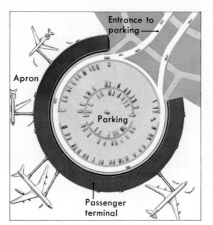

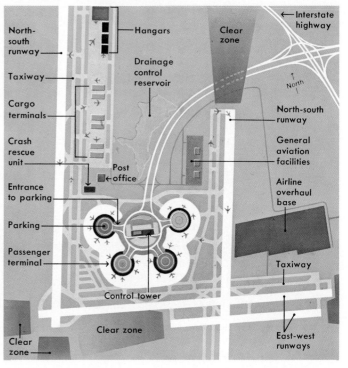

An airport's facilities depend on its size and the kinds of aircraft it serves. This section deals chiefly with the facilities provided by most large air carrier airports.

The Terminal Building. Passengers begin and end their flights at the terminal building. At the various airlines' ticket counters, departing passengers purchase or have their tickets checked. They also have their baggage checked. Loudspeakers, TV sets, and lighted boards announce flight arrivals and departures. Waiting rooms provide seats for travelers and their friends. Passengers board and leave aircraft from terminal areas called *gates.* Arriving passengers pick up their luggage at a baggage claim area.

The terminals of major airports resemble small cities. Restaurants serve meals day and night. Shops sell books, clothing, gifts, and other items. Some terminals include a bank, chapel, and hotel. The terminal building may also have an observation deck, from which people can watch take-offs, landings, and other operations.

Many terminal activities go on behind the scenes. Most large air carrier airports in the United States have a National Weather Service station. It gives airlines general information on weather conditions throughout

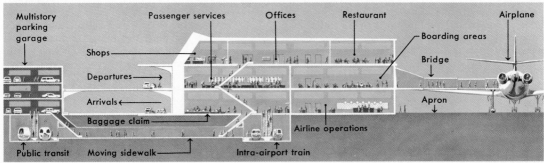

WORLD BOOK diagrams by Einbecker-Butler & Associates

The Terminal Area of many airports has three main levels that handle a variety of activities. An additional underground level may provide links with mass transportation and intra-airport trains.

the country as well as around the world. The station also supplies weather information to pilots who do not fly airline planes. Most airlines also maintain their own weather bureaus to check weather conditions for specific flights. Each airline has a *briefing room*, where pilots receive flight information. The briefing room includes a *dispatch office*, which handles communications with the airline's ticket counter and with its airplanes, both on the ground and in flight. The airport manager, who oversees the operation of the airport, also has an office in the terminal building.

Some large airports have several buildings that form a terminal group. Passengers may check in at one building. Workers may handle mail and other cargo in another. In still another building, customs, public health, and immigration officials may check passengers arriving on international flights.

Hangars are used to store and repair aircraft. Most airlines have their own hangars. Some hangars can hold several large jets at one time. Most airports locate hangars far enough from the terminal building to avoid interference with aircraft traffic on the ground.

The Control Tower is the airport's nerve center. In the tower, *air traffic controllers* use radar, radio, signal lights, and other equipment to direct air traffic near the airport as well as movements of aircraft on the ground. Control towers at major airports may handle almost 190 landings and take-offs an hour during peak periods. Most airports have control towers on top of the terminal. Large windows enclose the tower and give the controllers a clear view of the airport grounds and of landings and take-offs. Some airports have a separate control tower building.

Runways must be long enough and wide enough to handle the largest planes using the airport. They must be as level as possible and should provide good drainage. In the United States, the FAA sets minimum runway lengths for different types of aircraft.

Many small airports use only strips of mowed grass, called *landing strips*. Some of these strips are only 2,000 to 2,500 feet long. Large airports have paved runways. These runways may be as long as 13,000 to 14,000 feet to handle the biggest planes. All runways must have a *clear zone* at each end to give aircraft space to rise or descend. Some large airplanes require a clear zone 2,700 feet long. They thus need a total runway and clear zone length of nearly 4 miles.

Lines painted down the center and sides and across the ends of runways guide pilots in the air and on the ground. Numbers painted on each end of a runway tell pilots the compass direction in which the runway is laid out. For example, 18 and 36 indicate a north-south runway. The 18 (an abbreviation for 180°) appears on the north end of the runway, and the 36 (360°) appears on the south end. Most airports lay out runways in at least two directions so planes can take off and land as nearly as possible into the wind.

At night and other periods of low visibility, white lights outline each runway, and green lights mark the beginning of a runway. Red and white approach lights indicate the spot just before a landing plane should touch down on the runway.

Loading Aprons and Taxiways. The aircraft parking area at the terminal gates is called a *loading apron*. While an airplane is on the apron, workers refuel it and load baggage, cargo, and meals for the passengers. The crew and passengers board airplanes on the loading apron. A small airport may be able to service only 1 or 2 aircraft on the apron at one time. But large airports may service as many as 100 planes at once.

Taxiways are lanes aircraft use to taxi from the apron to the runways and from the runways to the hangars. Many large airports have double taxiways so aircraft can move to and from the runways and hangars at the same time. At night, blue lights mark taxiways, and red lights mark any barriers or other dangers.

Ground Transportation and Parking. Large airports provide driveways alongside the terminal buildings where airport *limousines* (special buses), motel station wagons, private cars, and taxis can pick up and drop off passengers. Some airports also have links with subways or other mass transportation systems.

Most airports maintain parking lots, where passengers, visitors, and employees may leave their automobiles. Several airports have replaced their parking lots with multistory parking garages. These garages take up much less land to hold as many cars as parking lots hold. In addition, they may be located nearer to the terminal than parking lots, thus reducing the distance people must walk to and from their cars.

——— WORLD'S 25 BUSIEST AIRPORTS ———

Airport	Passenger Departures and Arrivals*	Aircraft Take-Offs and Landings*
1. Chicago-O'Hare International	30,100,000	565,826
2. Los Angeles International	20,300,000	373,870
3. John F. Kennedy International (New York City)	20,200,000	309,725
4. Hartsfield (Atlanta)	18,200,000	387,775
5. Heathrow (London)	16,200,000	249,391
6. San Francisco International	14,100,000	297,323
7. La Guardia (New York City)	12,700,000	287,192
8. Miami International	11,200,000	233,958
9. Orly (Paris)	10,900,000	183,478
10. Tokyo International	10,700,000	170,366
11. Love Field (Dallas)	10,400,000	270,573
12. Washington National (District of Columbia)	10,400,000	222,739
13. Frankfurt	10,000,000	183,738
14. Logan International (Boston)	9,600,000	213,594
15. Osaka International	9,200,000	157,212
16. Fiumicino and Ciampino (Rome)	7,500,000	171,582
17. Stapleton International (Denver)	7,200,000	184,720
18. Detroit International	7,100,000	177,254
19. Kastrup (Copenhagen)	7,000,000	152,776
20. Philadelphia International	6,900,000	191,197
21. Honolulu International	6,800,000	118,935
22. Toronto International	6,200,000	126,245
23. Newark	6,100,000	166,080
24. Palma de Mallorca, Spain	6,100,000	74,962
25. Tempelhof Central (West Berlin)	6,100,000	88,104

*Includes only commercial airline traffic in 1971. Excludes airports of China, Russia, and a few other countries that do not belong to the International Civil Aviation Organization (ICAO).
Sources: *Digest of Statistics No. 162, Airport Traffic, 1971,* International Civil Aviation Organization; ICAO estimates.

WORLD BOOK photo   WORLD BOOK photo

Cargo Handling is a major airport activity. Many airlines have special cargo planes like the one above. Workers pack small cargo items in containers shaped to fit the airplane's interior. They load the cargo through the plane's wide door.

Refueling is one of the important activities carried out while a plane stands outside the terminal between flights.

The airport manager and the management staff oversee the operation of the entire airport. They are responsible for all facilities owned by the airport. The staff directs airport police and firemen. The staff also manages the maintenance teams, which care for airport buildings, check and replace airport lights, and operate snow removal and grass-mowing equipment. The management staff coordinates the activities of airline and airport workers to ensure safe, efficient operation of the airport.

Airline Passenger Services. Airlines employ the largest number of workers at most commercial airports, and most of their employees work in the terminal building. Ticket counter employees sell flight tickets, check in passengers who already have tickets, and provide information about the times and gates for flight arrivals and departures. Most regional and trunk airlines have computer systems that quickly print tickets and check for vacancies on flights.

Ticket counter workers also check in passengers' baggage. Baggage handlers see that all baggage is loaded on the correct flight. Handlers at the destination airports unload the bags and transport them to the baggage claim area.

Other airline workers include an airline station manager, who oversees passenger services, and reservations clerks, who keep records of flight reservations. The airline dispatch staff maintains contact with planes in the air and with other airports serving the airline.

STACKING PLANES IN A HOLDING PATTERN — Planes waiting to land may be stacked in an oval-shaped *holding pattern* around a radio beacon several miles from the airport. Several planes, at levels 1,000 feet apart, may descend through the pattern at the same time. A protected zone, which no planes may enter, surrounds the holding pattern.

WORLD BOOK diagram by Einbecker-Butler & Associates

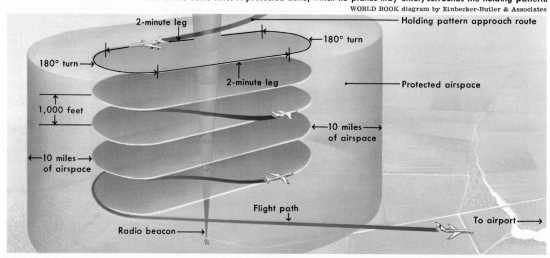

Air Carrier Airport is an airport that serves planes of scheduled airlines. Air carrier airports may also serve other types of aircraft, such as business, charter, or private planes.

Cargo is all freight, except baggage, carried by an airplane.

Closed In means an airport is closed to air traffic because of bad weather.

Control Tower is a glass-enclosed booth equipped with radar, radio, lights, and other navigation aids for directing aircraft movements on the ground and in the air. *Air traffic controllers* work in the tower.

Gate is the entryway passengers use when boarding or leaving planes. Each airliner is assigned a *gate position* for loading or unloading passengers.

General Aviation Airport is an airport that does not serve scheduled airline planes. General aviation airports serve mostly air taxis and business, charter, and private planes.

General Aviation Traffic is all air traffic except scheduled airline flights.

Loading Apron is the paved area around the terminal where aircraft are serviced, passengers board and leave planes, and baggage and cargo are loaded and unloaded.

Taxiway is a paved lane aircraft use to move between the apron, hangars, and runways. Aircraft follow a *taxi route* to reach a take-off point or parking area.

Terminal is the main airport building for passenger services. It also houses offices of airline employees and the airport management staff.

Cargo Handling. Most airports use the term *cargo* for mail and all other freight carried by aircraft except baggage. The number of tons of cargo processed by airports is growing almost twice as fast as the number of passengers.

Small airports handle cargo with passenger baggage at the passenger terminal. Larger airports have one or more separate terminals for cargo processing. Trucks bring the cargo from the city to the airport, where it is sorted for various flights. Postal workers sort mail. Carts, towed by small vehicles called *tugs*, then carry the cargo to the apron, where workers load it into the airplanes.

Most air cargo has a value of over $10 per pound and a density of under 10 pounds per cubic foot. Typical air cargoes include electronic goods and machinery parts. Banks and other financial firms transport checks, stocks, and bonds by air. Much air cargo also includes items that spoil rapidly, such as fresh flowers, fruits, and vegetables.

Small Aircraft Services. Air carrier airports must provide many services for small planes not operated by scheduled airlines. In the United States, these planes account for 10 per cent of the traffic at large air carrier airports and about 90 per cent of the flights at small air carrier airports. A *Fixed Base Operator* (FBO) provides small aircraft with such services as flight maps and other flight information, fuel, and hangars.

Air Traffic Control. In the control tower, the air traffic controllers guide aircraft as they land, take off, and taxi. The controllers see that the traffic keeps moving smoothly, rapidly, and safely. They must have good eyesight, speak clearly over the radio, and be able to think quickly. The controllers must also be able to remain calm during periods of heavy air traffic. Their job becomes especially difficult when fog or other weather conditions reduce visibility. In such situations, the controllers must rely entirely on radar to locate and guide aircraft in flight.

The control tower has several types of electronic all-weather landing equipment to help bring planes down safely. Most commercial airports use an electronic aid called an *Instrument Landing System* (ILS). The ILS sends radio signals from the runway to receivers on an airplane. The airplane receivers show the pilot whether the plane is to the left, right, above, below, or

MAKING INSTRUMENT LANDINGS

The *Instrument Landing System* (ILS) transmits four radio signals to receivers on a landing plane. A vertical *localizer beam* guides the plane to the runway. A *glide-slope beam* shows the angle on which the plane should descend. Two *marker beacons* indicate the distance to the runway.

WORLD BOOK diagram by Einbecker-Butler & Associates

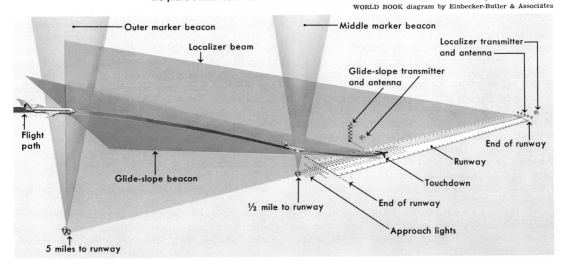

Outer marker beacon — Middle marker beacon

Localizer beam

Localizer transmitter and antenna

Glide-slope transmitter and antenna

Flight path

Glide-slope beacon

End of runway

Runway

Touchdown

½ mile to runway

End of runway

Approach lights

5 miles to runway

WORLD BOOK photo   WORLD BOOK photo

Security Checks at Airports help prevent hijacking of planes. Passengers walk through a device that detects metal weapons. Another machine uses X rays to check for weapons in any luggage that passengers carry aboard the plane.

Major Aircraft Repairs, such as the work done on this engine, are performed in hangars located some distance from the terminal.

directly on the correct approach path to the airport.

Other navigation aids include *Precision Approach Radar* (PAR) and *Airport Surveillance Radar* (ASR). PAR guides planes to safe landings during fog or other conditions that reduce visibility. ASR gives traffic controllers a view of all aircraft activity within 50 miles of the airport. This information helps the controllers prevent midair collisions by choosing the safest route for pilots to follow to and from the airport.

Engineers are developing a *Microwave Landing System* (MLS), which will land a plane from the ground by electronically operating the plane's automatic pilot system. The MLS will locate the aircraft several miles from the airport and fly it to a safe landing, while the pilot has his hands off the controls. The FAA expects the MLS to begin replacing the ILS in the United States in 1978.

Watching the Weather. The National Weather Service stations keep hourly records of the extent of cloud cover, the amount of rain or snow, and the height of the *bases* (lower edges) of the clouds. They also record hourly the humidity, temperature, and visibility.

To determine general visibility, the stations observe whether large objects near the airport can be seen. If objects one mile from the Weather Service station cannot be seen, the station uses certain instruments to test for visibility. A device called a *transmissometer*, located at some point on a runway, sends a beam of light to a nearby photoelectric cell. The cell measures the amount of light it receives. If visibility is poor due to fog, rain, or snow, the light received is much dimmer than the light transmitted. After measuring the light, the photoelectric cell sends a signal to a recording instrument in the weather station. This instrument, called a *Runway Visual Range* (RVR) indicator, registers the estimated visibility at the end of the runway. Pilots use the RVR reading, given in hundreds of feet, as a gauge of visibility.

Airport Security became a serious problem during the late 1960's and early 1970's because of many airliner hijacking attempts. In 1973, all air carrier airports in the United States began to follow certain security regulations set up by the FAA. Under these regulations, airline employees must inspect all baggage that passengers carry onto the plane. They look for weapons or a bomb that a person who intends to hijack a plane might be carrying. The passengers themselves must also be electronically searched before entering the aircraft. At some airports, they walk through a device that detects knives, guns, and other metal weapons. At airports that have no walk-through machines, airline officials use a hand-held device to check each passenger. In addition, airports must station local police officers at boarding gates in case a possible hijacker is discovered or other problems arise.

Other Operations. Some airline employees work in the hangars. There, mechanics repair planes and stockroom employees keep records of spare parts needed for repairs. Many airline employees work in the apron area. Some direct aircraft into parking spaces. Mechanics check the engines and other equipment to be sure each aircraft is working properly. Some employees clean the interior of airplanes between flights. After all the work has been completed properly, an airline employee in the dispatch office notifies the flight crew that the plane is ready to leave.

Some airlines have their own flight kitchens to prepare food for passengers. Dietitians plan the menus, chefs do the cooking, and food handlers transport the meals to waiting aircraft.

The federal government also employs workers at U.S. airports. At many airports, FAA employees maintain electronic navigation aids and other equipment in the control tower. Other federal employees include postal workers and, at international airports, public health, immigration, and customs officers.

In the late 1920's, the United States had about 1,000 airports. Today, the country has about 12,000. Many airport problems have developed because airport planners did not foresee this rapid growth in air travel. Many major airports suffer from overcrowded highway connections that make it difficult for passengers to get to and from the airport. Major airports also suffer from heavy air traffic, which causes delays in take-offs and landings. Although the FAA limits the number of take-offs and landings at some major airports during peak hours, air traffic remains heavy. Many airports need more room for ground traffic and for facilities for jumbo jets, such as the Boeing 747. But they have no space for expansion. They also lack adequate space for the heavy passenger and baggage loads carried by jumbo jets.

Residents in many airport areas complain of noise and air pollution caused by jets. The FAA and the Environmental Protection Agency (EPA) set limits for aircraft noise. The Airports and Airway Development Act, passed by Congress in 1970, offers federal funds for airport construction that includes measures to limit pollution.

Planning and Building a Major Airport may cost as much as $500 million. After a city decides to build a major airport, it hires a firm that specializes in airport planning. The airport planners begin by choosing a location that airplane passengers can reach easily. The site should have good drainage and be far enough from other airports to avoid interference with existing air traffic. The planners must also foresee changes and problems in future transportation so the airport will remain practical for many years.

The airport planners prepare a report called a *master plan* that shows how the fully developed airport will look in 20 to 30 years. The master plan shows the amount of land needed and the number, size, and location of the various facilities. Most cities construct the

facilities in stages, using the master plan as a guide. Each facility is put into operation as soon as possible after it is completed. An airport with several terminals, for example, may open each one on a different date. It takes about 7 to 10 years before a large airport can begin to handle passengers.

Airports of the Future will attempt to relieve some major airport problems. Many airports will occupy larger land areas to serve jumbo jets and to absorb the noise of take-offs and landings. Communities with limited land may construct airports on landfill or floating structures in lakes or oceans. Many cities are planning links with public transportation systems to make ground travel easier to and from airports.

Some large airports already have moving sidewalks and miniature trains to transport passengers inside the terminals. In the future, more airports will have such devices. Other airports, including those being built in Kansas City, Mo., and Dallas-Fort Worth, will eliminate long distances within the terminals. These airports will have a series of terminals shaped like rings or horseshoes. Passengers will enter a terminal at the gate marked for their flight and walk only about 75 feet through the building to their aircraft. J. LARRY DONOGHUE

Related Articles. See the *Transportation* section in the various city, country, state, and province articles. See also the following articles:

Airline	Airplane	Federal Aviation
Airmail and Air	Aviation	Administration
Parcel Post		Radar

Outline

I. Kinds of Airports
    A. Air Carrier Airports   C. Military Air Bases
    B. General Aviation Airports

II. Airport Facilities
    A. The Terminal Building E. Loading Aprons
    B. Hangars   and Taxiways
    C. The Control Tower F. Ground Transporta-
    D. Runways   tion and Parking

III. Airport Operations
    A. Airline Passenger Services E. Watching the
    B. Cargo Handling   Weather
    C. Small Aircraft Services F. Airport Security
    D. Air Traffic Control   G. Other Operations

IV. Airport Development
    A. Planning and Building a Major Airport
    B. Airports of the Future

Questions

What security regulations must U.S. air carrier airports follow to prevent hijacking attempts?

What things are shown in an airport master plan?

What do the numbers painted on runways mean?

How do air carrier airports differ from general aviation airports?

What are some of the activities that go on behind the scenes in an airport terminal?

What is the job of the airport management staff?

What are some of the navigation aids used by air traffic controllers?

Who employs the largest number of workers at most commercial airports?

What are some of the responsibilities of the FAA?

What is the largest airport in the United States?

Ron Church, Tom Stack & Assoc.

Planes Create Noise and Air Pollution when they fly low over communities near the airport. Residents in many of these areas complain about problems caused by the aircraft.

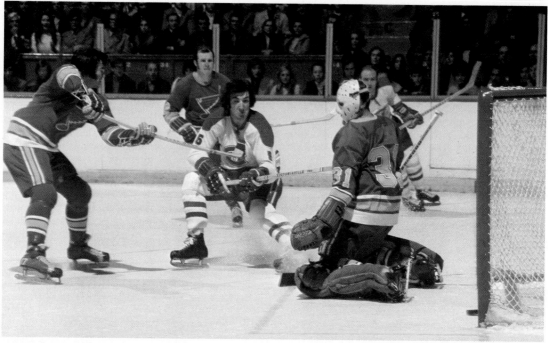

Canada Wide from Pictorial Parade

Hockey's Fast, Rough Action makes it one of the most exciting sports. A high point in the action occurs when one team drives the puck into the opposing team's goal, *above*.

HOCKEY

HOCKEY, or ICE HOCKEY, is a fast, exciting sport played by two six-man teams on an ice-covered rink. All the players wear skates. The players flash up and down the rink, slamming a hard rubber disk called a *puck* along the ice with long wooden sticks. They try to score points by hitting the puck into a *goal cage*, or *net*.

Hockey has swifter action than almost any other sport. The players streak across the ice at speeds up to 20 miles per hour (mph) or more. Their powerful swings at the puck often send it traveling faster than 100 mph. A goalkeeper on each team defends his team's net. He must often make lightning slides across the front of the net on his knees, stomach, or back to block shots of the puck. A puck that enters the net scores a *goal* (point) for the other side. The side that scores the most goals wins the game. To keep the action fast, hockey has an unusual rule. It is the only major sport that allows players to be substituted while play is in progress. Hockey's exciting action sometimes includes fights among players, though fighting is against the rules.

The game of hockey began in Canada in the mid-1800's. By the early 1900's, it had become Canada's national sport. Since then, hockey has become popular in

Gordie Howe, the contributor of this article, plays with the Houston Aeros and formerly played with the Detroit Red Wings. He is the author of Hockey: Here's Howe *(paperback title,* Let's Play Hockey*).*

many other countries, especially Czechoslovakia, Russia, Sweden, and the United States. In the United States and Canada, millions of fans go to professional contests each year, and millions more watch them on television. Hockey is also a popular amateur sport in the two countries. Hundreds of thousands of amateur players take part in community, high school, and college contests.

HOCKEY TERMS

Face-Off occurs when an official drops the puck between the sticks of two opposing players, who try to hit it to one of their teammates or in the direction of their opponents' goal.

Hat Trick occurs when a player scores three goals in one game.

Icing the Puck is a violation that occurs when a defending player shoots the puck from his team's half of the ice across the opponents' goal line. Icing is not called if the offending team has fewer players on the ice than the other team or if the puck enters the net. In games without a centerline, icing occurs when the puck is shot across both blue lines and the opposing team's goal line.

Offside is a violation that occurs (1) when any attacking player crosses the blue line into the opposing team's defending zone ahead of the puck; and (2) when a player passes the puck from his defending zone to a teammate beyond the centerline.

Power Play occurs when a team sends all its players except the goalkeeper in a drive against the opposing team's goal while one or two of the opposing players are in the penalty box.

Hockey rules differ somewhat between professional and amateur groups. This section deals mainly with the rules followed by professional leagues in the United States and Canada. There are two major leagues—the National Hockey League (NHL) and the World Hockey Association (WHA)—and several minor leagues. Most amateur teams in the United States and Canada have nearly the same rules that professional leagues have. But U.S. high school and college teams follow a special set of amateur rules, as do most teams in international competition. This section notes the chief differences between the professional rules and various amateur rules.

The Rink. The standard hockey rink measures 200 feet by 85 feet. The corners are rounded. A 40- to 48-inch-high white wooden fence—called the *boards*—surrounds the rink. Most indoor rinks consist of two layers of artificial ice. The bottom layer is painted white, with various red and blue markings. A thin layer of clear ice covers the painted layer.

A red *goal line* extends across each end of the rink, 10 feet from the boards. A goal cage stands in the middle of each goal line. The cage consists mainly of heavy netting supported by two metal *goal posts*, which are joined across the top by a metal *crossbar*. The opening at the front of the cage measures 4 feet high by 6 feet wide. Players aim the puck at this opening to score goals. An 8-foot by 4-foot area, called a *goal crease*, is outlined in red in front of each cage. No player may deliberately enter the opposing team's crease unless he is going after the puck.

Two blue lines divide the area between the goal lines into two 60-foot end zones and a center zone, which is also 60 feet long on most rinks. The end zone that a

team defends is that team's *defending zone*. The opposite end zone is the team's *attacking zone*. Actually, one team's defending zone serves as the other team's attacking zone. The center zone is called the *neutral zone*. In all hockey games, except U.S. high school and college games, the rink also has a red *centerline*. It divides the neutral zone—and the rink—in half. Most outdoor rinks have the zone boundaries marked on the boards rather than on the ice.

Colored *face-off spots* mark the places on the ice where officials hold *face-offs*. In a face-off, an official drops the puck between the sticks of two opposing players, who try to hit it to a teammate or in the direction of the opponents' goal. Face-offs are used to begin each game and to resume play after a game has been stopped for any reason. The neutral zone has four red face-off spots, and each end zone has two. Each end zone face-off spot is surrounded by a red circle. Only an official and two opposing players may stand inside a circle during a face-off. A blue face-off spot and circle are at the center of the rink.

Most hockey rinks have a *players' bench* for each team and a *penalty bench*, or *penalty box*, where players must stay temporarily if they break the rules. The benches are behind the sideboards. Every rink has two or more clocks to keep track of the playing time and the time players serve in the penalty box. Most indoor rinks also have a red light behind each goal that is flashed on when a puck enters the net and scores.

Playing Time. Most hockey games are played in three 20-minute periods separated by two 10- or 15-minute intermissions. The periods last less than 20 minutes in some amateur games. Only actual playing time

A STANDARD HOCKEY RINK

Almost all professional and many amateur rinks are laid out like the one below. Other rinks differ in certain ways. In some amateur rinks, for example, the blue lines are less than 60 feet from the goal lines. But they still divide the area between the goals into three equal zones. In U.S. high school and college hockey, the rink does not have a centerline.

WORLD BOOK diagram

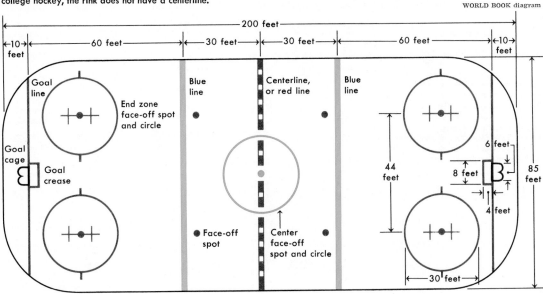

Kolbrener-Portnoy Photography

Fighting for Control of the Puck often sends players slamming into the wooden boards that surround a hockey rink. Fans seated close to the rink watch the game through shatterproof glass.

is counted in a hockey game. The clock is stopped when play stops. Time outs are not allowed, and so play is normally stopped only when a team scores a goal or a rule is broken. An official's whistle stops play in most cases.

In the NHL, a game ends after three periods of play even if the score is tied. In the WHA and most other leagues—and in NHL play-off games—a game tied at the end of three periods continues into *sudden-death overtime*. The first team to score in the overtime wins.

The Starting Lineup consists of the goalkeeper, or *goalie*; three *forwards*; and two *defensemen*. The goalie has the most demanding job on the team. He is the last defense against a score by the opposing team, and the least mistake on his part may cost his team a goal. He

almost always remains in or near the goal crease. The goalie is the only player allowed to catch the puck or pick it up with his hands.

The main job of the forwards is to score goals. But they must also help defend their team's goal. Each forward has an assigned position—*center, left wing,* or *right wing*—which together make up the *forward line.* The center usually leads his team's attack and takes part in most face-offs. His starting position is in the middle of the forward line. But during play, he chases the puck wherever it goes. The left wing generally patrols the side of the rink to the left of the center. The right wing patrols the right side. But the wings skate into each other's territory when the play requires.

The defensemen's main job is to guard their team's defending zone and so keep the opposing team from scoring. But defensemen also sometimes lead the attack and score goals. They normally cover the part of the rink between their team's forward line and their goal. The *left defenseman* generally covers the left half of the rink, and the *right defenseman* covers the right half. But like the wings, they skate into each other's territory when necessary. The sections on *Offensive Play* and *Defensive Play* describe the players' duties in more detail.

Players may be substituted anytime during a game, but play is never stopped to make substitutions. Coaches usually change the entire forward line and both defensemen about every 2 minutes during professional games. The starting goalie usually plays the entire game.

A team often has to play *short-handed*—that is, with fewer players on the ice than the opposing team has. This situation occurs when one or two players on a team are in the penalty box.

Equipment. Hockey players need a puck, skates, and sticks. The puck is a hard, black rubber disk 1 inch thick and 3 inches in diameter. It weighs from 5½ to 6 ounces. Hockey skates have strong, heavy shoes designed for both support and protection. The blades are made of hard steel and are *rockered* (curved) along the

HOCKEY EQUIPMENT

Skates and a stick are part of every hockey player's equipment. Every player also wears special protective equipment, as shown in these drawings. The left-hand drawing shows a goalie's equipment. It is specially designed to protect him against bulletlike shots of the puck. The right-hand drawing shows the equipment of the other players.

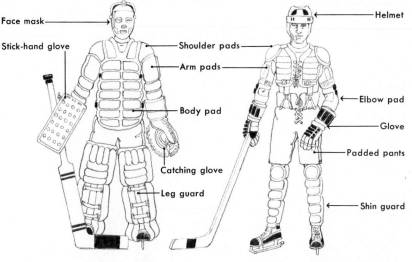

Face mask

Stick-hand glove

Shoulder pads

Arm pads

Body pad

Catching glove

Leg guard

Helmet

Elbow pad

Glove

Padded pants

Shin guard

WORLD BOOK diagram by James Buckley

bottom. A player can turn and make other maneuvers more easily with rockered blades than with flat ones. Each player uses an L-shaped wooden stick. The *shaft* (handle) may be no more than 55 inches long. Except on goalies' sticks, the *blade* must be no more than $12\frac{1}{2}$ inches long and 3 inches wide. The blade of a goalie's stick may be up to $15\frac{1}{2}$ inches long and $3\frac{1}{2}$ inches wide.

A player's uniform consists mainly of knee-length pants, a sweater, and long socks. Under his uniform, each player wears shoulder pads, elbow pads, a special supporter, a garter belt, and shin guards. The pants are padded to protect a player's kidneys and thighs. Each player also wears heavily padded gloves with long cuffs to protect the wrists. Nearly all amateur players must wear a protective helmet. Players in professional games do not have to wear a helmet, but they may if they so choose.

A goalie wears extra-thick protective padding under his uniform, including special pads to protect his arms and the front of his body. A thick, 10-inch-wide leather pad shields the front of each leg from above the knee to below the ankle. These pads help him block shots at the net. One of a goalie's gloves has a large pad on the back, which he uses, along with his stick, to bat away lightning shots of the puck. His other glove resembles a first baseman's mitt with a long cuff. He uses this glove to catch pucks and toss them away from the net. Goalies must wear a protective face mask in most amateur play. Almost all professional goalies also wear one, though the rules do not require it.

Hockey Skills. Hockey requires a variety of skills. They include (1) skating, (2) stickhandling, (3) passing, (4) shooting, and (5) checking. Hockey has few standard plays, and so players must also have the skill to develop plays as the action progresses.

Skating is the most important hockey skill. A player must be able to turn sharply, skate backwards, and perform many other maneuvers—all at top speed. His skating must be so automatic that he can make any maneuver without taking his attention from the game.

Stickhandling is the use of the stick to control the puck. In the most common form of stickhandling, a player moves the puck first with one side of the blade and then with the other as he skates. He makes some sweeps of the stick wide and some narrow. In this way, he keeps his opponents guessing as to his next move and also makes it difficult for them to steal the puck.

Passing is the means by which a player who has possession of the puck transfers it to a teammate. In most cases, a player uses his stick to propel the puck toward a receiver. Such passes are either *flat passes* or *flip passes*. To make a flat pass, the passer sends the puck traveling along the surface of the ice. To make a flip pass, he causes it to rise off the ice to avoid interception by an opponent. Sometimes, a passer simply leaves the puck behind him where a teammate can quickly get it. Such a pass is called a *drop pass*.

Shooting is the skill needed to drive the puck into the net and so score goals. As in passing, a player propels the puck with his stick. Most shots are either *wrist shots* or *slap shots*. In a wrist shot, the blade does not leave the ice. The player uses strong wrist action to propel

Kolbrener-Portnoy Photography

A Face-Off starts play again after a game has been stopped for any reason. An official drops the puck between two opposing players, who try to hit it to a teammate or into scoring position.

the puck. For a slap shot, the player raises his stick in a backswing and brings it down against the puck with great force. Slap shots are more powerful but less accurate than wrist shots.

Checking is the chief means a player uses to get the puck away from an opponent. There are two main types of checks: *stick checks* and *body checks*. For a stick check, a player uses his stick to hook or poke the puck away from an opponent's stick. In a body check, a player bumps against an opponent with his hip or shoulder to try to block his progress or throw him off balance. Both stick checking and body checking are allowed only against a player in control of the puck or the last player to control it. In professional and most amateur play, body checks may be made anywhere on the ice. But in U.S. high school and college hockey, they are allowed only in the defending and neutral zones.

A goalie needs a special set of skills. To block shots at the net, he must be able to move nearly every part of his body and all his equipment quickly, surely, and almost automatically.

Playing the Game. Each period begins with a face-off at the center face-off spot. A face-off also starts play again after it has been stopped for any reason. These face-offs are held at various face-off spots, depending on the reason for stopping play. The team that gains possession of the puck as a result of the face-off tries to move it into scoring position. During play, the puck must be kept moving. If the puck is hit out of the rink, frozen between opposing players, or is otherwise temporarily out of play, an official blows his whistle for a face-off.

A player may *carry* (move) the puck along the ice, pass it to a teammate, or shoot it at the goal. But the rules limit these plays in certain ways. One extremely important rule states that no player of an attacking team may be in the attacking zone ahead of the puck. One member of the team must carry or shoot the puck

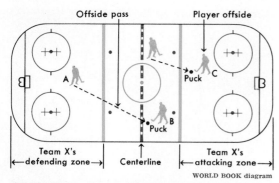

Offside pass   Player offside

A

Puck C

B
Puck

Team X's
←—defending zone—→   ↑Centerline   Team X's
←—attacking zone—→

WORLD BOOK diagram

Offside Plays rank among the most common hockey violations. There are two types of offsides, illustrated above by players on Team X. An *offside pass* violation occurs when a player (A) hits the puck from his defending zone to a teammate (B) across the center-line. A *player offside* violation occurs when a player (C) enters his team's attacking zone ahead of the puck.

across the attacking blue line before any other player on the team crosses the line. For violations of this rule, an official signals the offending team *offside* and conducts a face-off in the neutral zone.

A player may pass to a teammate anywhere in the same zone. He may also pass from his defending zone to a teammate in his team's half of the neutral zone. If the pass is received in the opposing team's half of the neutral zone, an official signals the pass offside and conducts a face-off where the play began. In WHA games, a player may pass from the defending zone to any spot in the neutral zone. But the pass receiver must not cross the centerline ahead of the puck. In games played without a centerline, a player may pass from his defending zone to a teammate anywhere in the neutral zone.

Offensive Play centers on the attack, or *rush*, against the opposing team's goal. An attacking team moves the puck down the ice until one player is in position to carry or shoot it across the defending team's blue line. If he carries the puck across, his teammates rush in after him to receive a pass. If he shoots the puck across the line, he and as many of his teammates as possible rush in after it to keep control.

Once the attackers control the puck in the opposing team's end zone, the attacking defensemen station themselves as *point men* at opposite ends of their opponents' blue line. Their main job is to keep the puck in the attacking zone. The center tries for shots at the goal or passes the puck to a wing in better scoring position. The center and one of the wings go after any shot that misses the goal or is batted away by the goalie and try to score it on the *rebound*. If the opposing team gets the puck, the attackers quickly begin checking to regain control. Checking an opponent who controls the puck in his defending zone is called *fore-checking*. Throughout an attack, one wing must always play far enough back to go after an opponent who breaks into the neutral zone with the puck.

The most spectacular offensive play is the *power play*. It occurs when one team is short-handed. The other team sends all its players except the goalie into the attacking zone in an all-out drive to score.

Defensive Play is designed to break up attacks. At the start of an attack, both defensemen begin skating rapidly toward their defending zone. They skate backward to keep close watch on the attackers and use their sticks to prevent a pass or a shot at the goal. Each defending wing guards the attacking wing on his side of the ice. After the puck crosses the defending team's blue line, one defenseman positions himself in front of the goalie. The other defenseman guards the puck carrier. The defending center goes after the puck. Each defending wing guards the attacking defenseman stationed on his side of the ice as a point man. All the defending players must check strongly. Their chief aim is to get control of the puck and carry or pass it out of their end zone. Checking to break up an attack is called *back-checking*. To defend themselves against power plays, most professional teams send in substitutes called *penalty killers*. These players are expert at back-checking and keeping control of the puck.

An illegal defensive play called *icing the puck*, or *icing*, occurs when a defending player shoots the puck from his team's half of the ice across the opponents' goal line. But for icing to occur, a player on the other team must touch the puck after it crosses the goal line. In games played without a centerline, icing occurs when a player shoots the puck from his defending zone across both blue lines and the opponents' goal line. The penalty for icing is a face-off in the offending team's end zone. There are two major exceptions to the icing rule. If an iced puck enters the net, it counts as a score. In addition, a short-handed team may ice the puck as a defensive play.

Violations and Penalties. Offside plays and icing account for most violations of the rules. For these violations, the offending team risks losing the puck in the resulting face-off. For more serious violations, players receive penalties ranging from 2 minutes in the penalty box to removal from the game. But a team must always have at least four men on the ice. If a third player is penalized while two of his teammates are in the penalty box, a substitute may replace him on the ice. The third player's penalty time does not begin until one of the first two penalized players has served his penalty. But this player may not return to the ice until play is stopped for some reason. When he returns, the substitute must leave the ice. A teammate may serve a goalie's penalties in most cases.

Hockey has five main kinds of penalties: (1) minor penalties, (2) major penalties, (3) misconduct penalties, (4) match penalties, and (5) penalty shots.

Minor Penalties are given for such violations as holding or tripping an opponent or hooking him with a stick. They bring 2 minutes in the penalty box. The team must play short-handed until the penalty is served or until the other side scores a goal.

Major Penalties are given mainly for fighting and bring 5 minutes in the penalty box. The penalized team must play short-handed, and the entire penalty must be served. But if a player on each team receives a major penalty at the same time, substitutes may replace both players on the ice.

Misconduct Penalties are given chiefly for improper

behavior toward an official. A misconduct penalty brings 10 minutes in the penalty box, but a substitute may replace the penalized player. A *game misconduct penalty* is given chiefly for more serious offenses against officials. In the NHL, it is also awarded against the first player to join a fight between two other players. The offending player is removed for the rest of the game, but a substitute may replace him.

Match Penalties are given for deliberately injuring or attempting to injure an opponent. The offending player is removed for the rest of the game. But a substitute may replace him after 5 or 10 minutes, depending on the seriousness of the offense.

Penalty Shots are free shots at the opposing team's goal defended only by the goalie. They are chiefly awarded against a defending team when an attacking player with a clear shot at the goal is pulled down from behind and so prevented from taking the shot.

The Officials. The chief officials are the *referee* and two *linesmen*. They wear skates and are stationed on the ice. The referee supervises the entire game and decides all penalties. The linesmen call offside and icing violations and conduct most face-offs.

All other officials work off the ice. The *game timekeeper* keeps track of actual playing time. He stops the official clock when a penalty or face-off is called and starts it again when play resumes. The *penalty timekeeper* keeps track of the time a player serves in the penalty box. The *official scorer* records the goals scored, the names of the scorers, and the players who score *assists*—that is, passes or other plays that contribute to goals. Two *goal judges*, one behind each goal cage off the ice, carefully watch shots at the goal. They turn on the red goal light to show that a puck has entered the net and scored. The *statistician* records team and individual performances.

HOCKEY PENALTY SIGNALS

Signals for penalties stop play at once. If the penalty is against the defending team, the official signals a *delayed call* and stops play when the other team loses possession of the puck.

WORLD BOOK photos

Holding

Charging

Icing the puck

Slashing

Cross-checking

Boarding

Interference

High-sticking

Tripping

Hooking

Misconduct

Delayed call of penalty

Professional Leagues. The United States and Canada have two major professional hockey leagues—the National Hockey League (NHL) and the World Hockey Association (WHA). There are also several minor professional leagues. Almost all the minor-league teams are in U.S. cities. Most are associated with a particular major-league team to provide playing experience and training for the major-league team's beginning players.

The regular hockey season lasts from October to early April. In the NHL, the four top teams in each division engage in postseason play-offs. The finalists play for the Stanley Cup, professional hockey's most famous award. The NHL also makes annual awards to players. The awards include the Art Ross Trophy to the leading scorer; the Hart Memorial Trophy to the player judged most valuable to his team; and the Vezina Trophy to the goalie or goalies on the team that had the fewest goals scored against it. The WHA holds postseason play-offs similar to those of the NHL. The finalists compete for the Avco World Trophy, named after a commercial television sponsor.

NATIONAL HOCKEY LEAGUE*

East Division	West Division
Boston Bruins	Atlanta Flames
Buffalo Sabres	California Golden Seals
Detroit Red Wings	Chicago Black Hawks
Montreal Canadiens	Los Angeles Kings
New York Islanders	Minnesota North Stars
New York Rangers	Philadelphia Flyers
Toronto Maple Leafs	Pittsburgh Penguins
Vancouver Canucks	St. Louis Blues

*A Kansas City and a Washington, D.C., team, added to the NHL in 1973, were to start play in the fall of 1974.

WORLD HOCKEY ASSOCIATION

East Division	West Division
Chicago Cougars	Edmonton Oilers
Cleveland Crusaders	Houston Aeros
New England Whalers	Los Angeles Sharks
New York Golden Blades	Minnesota Fighting Saints
Quebec Nordiques	Vancouver Blazers
Toronto Toros	Winnipeg Jets

NATIONAL HOCKEY LEAGUE CHAMPIONS

Season	Finished First	Won Stanley Cup	Season	Finished First	Won Stanley Cup
1917-1918	Toronto Arenas	Toronto Arenas	1948-1949	Detroit Red Wings	Toronto Maple Leafs
1918-1919	Montreal Canadiens	No winner*	1949-1950	Detroit Red Wings	Detroit Red Wings
1919-1920	Ottawa Senators	Ottawa Senators	1950-1951	Detroit Red Wings	Toronto Maple Leafs
1920-1921	Ottawa Senators	Ottawa Senators	1951-1952	Detroit Red Wings	Detroit Red Wings
1921-1922	Toronto St. Pats	Toronto St. Pats	1952-1953	Detroit Red Wings	Montreal Canadiens
1922-1923	Ottawa Senators	Ottawa Senators	1953-1954	Detroit Red Wings	Detroit Red Wings
1923-1924	Montreal Canadiens	Montreal Canadiens	1954-1955	Detroit Red Wings	Detroit Red Wings
1924-1925	Montreal Canadiens	Victoria Cougars†	1955-1956	Montreal Canadiens	Montreal Canadiens
1925-1926	Montreal Maroons	Montreal Maroons	1956-1957	Detroit Red Wings	Montreal Canadiens
1926-1927	Ottawa Senators	Ottawa Senators	1957-1958	Montreal Canadiens	Montreal Canadiens
1927-1928	New York Rangers	New York Rangers	1958-1959	Montreal Canadiens	Montreal Canadiens
1928-1929	Boston Bruins	Boston Bruins	1959-1960	Montreal Canadiens	Montreal Canadiens
1929-1930	Boston Bruins	Montreal Canadiens	1960-1961	Montreal Canadiens	Chicago Black Hawks
1930-1931	Montreal Canadiens	Montreal Canadiens	1961-1962	Montreal Canadiens	Toronto Maple Leafs
1931-1932	New York Rangers	Toronto Maple Leafs	1962-1963	Toronto Maple Leafs	Toronto Maple Leafs
1932-1933	Toronto Maple Leafs	New York Rangers	1963-1964	Montreal Canadiens	Toronto Maple Leafs
1933-1934	Detroit Red Wings	Chicago Black Hawks	1964-1965	Detroit Red Wings	Montreal Canadiens
1934-1935	Toronto Maple Leafs	Montreal Canadiens	1965-1966	Montreal Canadiens	Montreal Canadiens
1935-1936	Detroit Red Wings	Detroit Red Wings	1966-1967	Chicago Black Hawks	Toronto Maple Leafs
1936-1937	Detroit Red Wings	Detroit Red Wings	1967-1968	Montreal Canadiens (E)**	
1937-1938	Toronto Maple Leafs	Chicago Black Hawks		Philadelphia Flyers (W)**	Montreal Canadiens
1938-1939	Boston Bruins	Boston Bruins	1968-1969	Montreal Canadiens (E)**	
1939-1940	Boston Bruins	New York Rangers		St. Louis Blues (W)**	Montreal Canadiens
1940-1941	Boston Bruins	Boston Bruins	1969-1970	Chicago Black Hawks (E)**	
1941-1942	New York Rangers	Toronto Maple Leafs		St. Louis Blues (W)**	Boston Bruins
1942-1943	Detroit Red Wings	Detroit Red Wings	1970-1971	Boston Bruins (E)**	
1943-1944	Montreal Canadiens	Montreal Canadiens		Chicago Black Hawks (W)**	Montreal Canadiens
1944-1945	Montreal Canadiens	Toronto Maple Leafs	1971-1972	Boston Bruins (E)**	
1945-1946	Montreal Canadiens	Montreal Canadiens		Chicago Black Hawks (W)**	Boston Bruins
1946-1947	Montreal Canadiens	Toronto Maple Leafs	1972-1973	Montreal Canadiens (E)**	
1947-1948	Toronto Maple Leafs	Toronto Maple Leafs		Chicago Black Hawks (W)**	Montreal Canadiens

*Play-off between Montreal Canadiens and Seattle Metropolitans not finished because of influenza epidemic in Seattle.
†Member, Pacific Coast League.   **(E) East Division, (W) West Division.

WORLD HOCKEY ASSOCIATION CHAMPIONS

Season	Finished First	Won Avco World Trophy
1972-1973	New England Whalers (E)*	
	Winnipeg Jets (W)*	New England Whalers

*(E) East Division, (W) West Division.

For many years, the United States and Canada had the only professional hockey teams. In 1973, a small professional league was started in Europe. It consists of four teams—two from Sweden and one each from Great Britain and West Germany. The league was scheduled to start play in the fall of 1973.

Amateur Organization. There are three main types of amateur hockey competition. They are (1) U.S. and Canadian amateur competition, excluding U.S. high school and college play; (2) international competition; and (3) U.S. high school and college competition. Each type is organized differently and has different rules.

The Amateur Hockey Association of the United States (AHAUS) regulates U.S. amateur play. In Canada, the Canadian Amateur Hockey Association (CAHA) is the controlling group. The rules of both groups resemble the professional rules. The AHAUS and the CAHA set up local organizations, hold tournaments, and establish amateur classifications by age groups. The main classifications are *mite* (ages 7 and 8); *squirt* (ages 9 and 10); *pee wee* (ages 11 and 12); *bantam* (ages 13 and 14); *midget* (ages 15 and 16); *juvenile* (ages 17 and 18); *junior* (any age up to age 20, depending on

individual skill); and *senior* (over age 20). Teams in each classification compete against one another.

International, or *world amateur*, hockey is regulated by the International Ice Hockey Federation (IIHF), which has its headquarters in London. Amateur hockey organizations from about 30 countries belong to the IIHF. They include the AHAUS and the CAHA. Players on teams registered with IIHF members are called *registered amateurs*. Canada has about 600,000 registered amateurs. The United States has about 250,000.

Each year, outstanding amateur teams from a number of countries compete for the world amateur championship. Until 1972, every fourth world competition was held as part of the Winter Olympics (see OLYMPIC GAMES [table: Ice Hockey Winners]). In 1972, the world and Olympic championships were held separately. The IIHF establishes the rules for these contests. Most IIHF members have adopted IIHF rules.

The National Collegiate Athletic Association (NCAA) sets up the rules for U.S. college hockey and holds annual college championship matches. Most U.S. high school teams follow NCAA rules. Canadian high school and college teams follow CAHA rules.

HOCKEY / History of Hockey

Beginnings. Hockey developed in Canada. According to the CAHA, British soldiers in Kingston, Ont., and Halifax, N.S., played the first games, about 1855. The idea for ice hockey probably came from the older game of field hockey. In field hockey, the players use curved sticks to hit a rubber ball through a goal at each end of a playing field (see FIELD HOCKEY).

In the 1870's, a group of students at McGill University in Montreal drew up the first formal ice hockey rules. The rules substituted a puck for the earlier rubber ball and set the number of players on a team at nine. The McGill rules were widely distributed during the

1880's. Hockey teams began to spring up in many parts of Canada. By 1893, the game was so popular that the governor general, Lord Stanley of Preston, donated a silver bowl to be awarded annually to Canada's champion hockey team. In 1894, a Montreal team won the first Stanley Cup match. The first hockey games in the United States were probably played about 1895 at Yale University and Johns Hopkins University.

Professional Hockey. The first professional hockey team was organized at Houghton, Mich., in 1903. Most of the players were Canadians. Hockey's first professional league, the International Pro Hockey League,

McCord Museum of McGill University, Montreal

Early Hockey Games, like this 1893 match in Montreal, featured unmarked rinks. The action was slower and less rough than in today's games, and so players needed little protective equipment.

was started in 1904. It included teams from both Canada and the United States. Several other professional leagues were started soon after 1904.

The NHL was formed in Montreal in 1917 from an earlier professional league, the National Hockey Association. The original NHL teams were the Montreal Canadiens, Montreal Wanderers, Ottawa Senators, and Toronto Arenas. Six-man teams, first introduced in 1904, became the rule in the newly organized NHL.

In 1924, the Boston Bruins became the first U.S. team to join the NHL. A team each from Chicago, Detroit, and Pittsburgh and two teams from New York City joined in 1925 and 1926. The Pittsburgh team and one New York City team later dropped out. By 1942, the NHL consisted of the Boston Bruins, Chicago Black Hawks, Detroit Red Wings, Montreal Canadiens, New York Rangers, and Toronto Maple Leafs. This membership remained unchanged until 1967.

Famous Players and All-Star Teams. The early hockey stars were almost all Canadians, as are most professional stars today. They included such colorful players as Newsy Lalonde, Joe Malone, Lester Patrick, and Cyclone Taylor. Hockey grew more popular after U.S. teams joined the NHL. Hockey fans of the late 1920's and early 1930's flocked to see such stars as forwards Bill Cook and Howie Morenz; defensemen King Clancy, Lionel Conacher, Ching Johnson, and Eddie Shore; and goalies Chuck Gardiner and George Hainsworth. Clancy, Cook, Gardiner, Johnson, Morenz, and Shore were named to the first annual NHL hockey All-Star teams. Hockey writers and broadcasters began the tradition of naming players to a first and second All-Star team just after the 1930-1931 season.

The NHL held its first annual All-Star Game in 1947. The All-Star team for this game was selected from the first and second All-Star teams of the preceding season. It included such players as forwards Doug Bentley and his brother Max, Ted Lindsay, Maurice Richard, and Milt Schmidt; defensemen Ken Reardon and Jack Stewart; and goalies Frank Brimsek and Bill Durnan. This team met the Toronto Maple Leafs, the 1947 Stanley Cup winners. The game was won by the All-Stars.

Today, writers and broadcasters choose a first and second All-Star team from NHL divisions. A team of selected West All-Stars meets a team of selected East All-Stars for the All-Star Game. Since 1947, the games have featured such forwards as Jean Beliveau, Phil Esposito, Bernie Geoffrion, Gordie Howe, Bobby Hull, and Stan Mikita. Defensemen have included Doug Harvey, Bobby Orr, and Pierre Pilote. Among the goalies have been Tony Esposito, Ed Giacomin, Glenn Hall, Jacques Plante, and Terry Sawchuk.

The Hockey Hall of Fame opened in Toronto in 1961. It honors former players, referees, and other persons who helped develop and promote the sport.

Amateur Development. The IIHF was founded in 1908. The first world championship was held in 1920 as part of the Olympic Games and marked the beginning of Olympic hockey competition. Canadian teams won most world and Olympic championships until the 1950's, when strong Russian teams began a long string of victories. Because the best Canadian players are professionals, Canada withdrew from world amateur and

Olympic competition in 1970. The United States has won two world titles—the first in 1933 and the second in 1960 as part of the Winter Olympics.

The CAHA was founded in 1914 and began organizing Canadian amateur hockey on a national basis. The AHAUS was founded in 1937 and by the early 1950's had organized U.S. amateur hockey nationally. The NCAA started its annual tournaments in 1948.

For many years, U.S. amateur hockey was limited largely to the northernmost states. Since the 1940's, many communities have built indoor rinks so that hockey can be played in any weather. Today, hockey is played in almost every state and has become one of the most popular U.S. amateur sports.

Recent Developments. The NHL began a major expansion in 1967, when it added six more teams and set up an East and West division. By 1972, four more teams had joined the NHL. In 1973, a team from Kansas City and one from Washington, D.C., joined the league. Both teams were scheduled to start play in the fall of 1974. The WHA was organized in 1971 and began its first season of play in the fall of 1972.

During the 1960's, Canada tried to arrange a hockey match between the best Canadian and Russian players. Russia turned down the offer because almost all of Canada's top players are professionals. The Russians, on the other hand, take pride in their amateur standing. But in 1972, Russia let a championship Russian team meet a team of Canada's top professionals for an eight-game tournament. The Canadian team won four games and tied one to capture the series.　　GORDIE HOWE

HOCKEY / Study Aids

Related Articles in WORLD BOOK include:

Outline

I. **How to Play Hockey**
   A. The Rink
   B. Playing Time
   C. The Starting Lineup
   D. Equipment
   E. Hockey Skills
   F. Playing the Game
   G. Offensive Play
   H. Defensive Play
   I. Violations and
      Penalties
   J. The Officials

II. **Organized Hockey**
   A. Professional Leagues　B. Amateur Organization

III. **History**

Questions

What are the only times that play is normally stopped during most hockey games?

Which player on a hockey team is the only one allowed to catch the puck?

What organizations regulate U.S., Canadian, and world amateur hockey?

What are the names of the three zones into which a hockey rink is divided?

Who drew up the first hockey rules? When?

What are the five main kinds of hockey penalties?

When was the NHL formed?

What are *stick checks? Body checks?*

When may players be substituted during a hockey game?

What are *point men?* What is their main job?

El Pueblo De Los Angeles, Inc.

Mexican Americans in Los Angeles take part in *Las Posadas,* a Mexican tradition. This Christmastime ceremony represents the journey of Joseph and Mary to Bethlehem.

MEXICAN AMERICANS are Americans of Mexican descent. The approximately 5 million Mexican Americans make up one of the largest minority groups in the United States. Mexican Americans live throughout the nation, but about 70 per cent of them live in California and Texas. Many Mexican Americans use Spanish as their main language, though most speak both Spanish and English.

Americans of Mexican descent generally use four terms to refer to themselves: Chicano, La Raza, mestizo, or Mexican American. The term *Chicano* is a short form of *Mexicano,* the Spanish word for *Mexican. La Raza* means *the people* or *one's people* in Spanish. Mexican Americans use this term to identify their cultural ties with other Spanish-speaking people. *Mestizo* is a Spanish word for people of mixed white and American Indian ancestry. *Mexican American* is the term most commonly used to distinguish members of this ethnic group from those of other U.S. ethnic groups.

Most Mexican Americans are mestizos by descent. They trace their heritage to Indian groups that built great civilizations in the region of Mexico long before Spanish explorers arrived during the 1500's. Some Mexican Americans have ancestors who lived in the West before it became part of the United States in the 1800's. Many more are descendants of people who moved from Mexico to the United States after 1900.

The ancestors of today's Mexican Americans had a strong influence on early American history. They helped establish Los Angeles and several other settlements that became major U.S. cities. They also taught important methods of farming, mining, and ranching to Americans who settled in the West. Between the late 1800's and the mid-1900's, most Mexican Americans worked on farms. Today, most of them live in cities.

Like most other minority groups, Mexican Americans suffer discrimination in education, housing, and jobs. Difficulty with the English language also has slowed their progress in obtaining a good education and neces-

sary job skills. But more and more Mexican Americans are overcoming the problem of prejudice and are slowly gaining positions of high responsibility in all areas of American life.

The Mexican-American Heritage

The Olmec Indians established the first major Mexican civilization. Their culture flourished along the southern Gulf Coast from about 1200 B.C. to 100 B.C. During the next 1,300 years, the Maya, Toltec, and Zapotec Indians built rich and powerful empires in the region of Mexico. See MAYA; OLMEC INDIANS; TOLTEC INDIANS; ZAPOTEC INDIANS.

The Aztecs ruled the last great Indian civilization of Mexico. They borrowed much of their culture from the earlier civilizations. Beginning about A.D. 1200, the Aztecs built large cities and developed well-organized governments. In 1521, an army led by the Spanish adventurer Hernando Cortes conquered the Aztec empire for Spain. See AZTEC.

During the next 300 years, Spain extended its rule over the region that now includes California and the southwestern United States. The Spaniards and Indians learned much from each other. The Indians introduced the Spaniards to new foods and medicines and helped them adapt to the desert and the climate. The Spaniards taught the Indians to ride horses and to raise cattle and sheep. Roman Catholic missionaries from Spain taught Christianity to the Indians. Many Spanish men took Indian women as mates. Their descendants became the first mestizos of Mexico.

During the 1600's and 1700's, the Spaniards and Mexicans established many missions and other communities that later became important cities in the United States. In 1610, they founded Santa Fe in what is now New Mexico. Mexicans also helped establish Albuquerque, Los Angeles, San Antonio, and Tucson.

In the late 1700's and early 1800's, the Mexicans became increasingly displeased with Spanish rule. Miguel Hidalgo y Costilla, a Mexican priest, led a revolt against the Spaniards in 1810. This uprising was put down, but it started Mexico's struggle for independence. Mexico won its freedom from Spain in 1821.

During the 1820's, Mexico allowed many Americans to settle in what is now Texas. Dissatisfaction with Mexican rule led the Americans and some Mexican Texans to revolt in 1835. The next year, the Texans defeated Mexican forces in the Battle of San Jacinto and established the Republic of Texas. See TEXAS (History).

Mexico refused to recognize Texas' independence, and the conflict over Texas became a chief cause of the Mexican War (1846-1848). By the Treaty of Guadalupe Hidalgo, the United States gained most of the land that is now Arizona, California, Colorado, Nevada, New Mexico, Utah, and Wyoming. Mexico recognized Texas. See MEXICAN WAR; MEXICO (History).

The Meeting of Two Cultures

New Relationships. More than 75,000 Spanish-speaking persons lived in the areas that the United States acquired from Mexico during the mid-1800's. Most of these people became U.S. citizens. After the discovery of gold in California in 1848, settlers from the

MEXICAN AMERICANS

eastern United States poured into the West. They soon outnumbered the Mexican Americans in every area except New Mexico.

In California, Mexican Americans taught the newcomers important mining techniques. One such technique was how to use the gold-mining pan. Another was the use of mercury to separate silver from ore. Mexican Americans also showed their new countrymen how to tame wild horses, brand cattle, and irrigate the land.

Nevertheless, the two groups of Americans usually did not get along together. Racial and religious differences became chief sources of conflict. The newcomers were white, and most of them were Protestants. Most Mexican Americans were mestizos and Roman Catholics. The two groups also spoke different languages and had different customs. Many white newcomers regarded Mexican Americans as Mexicans and "foreigners."

Many Mexican Americans suffered as a result of laws dealing with the registration of property and the collection of property taxes. They spoke little or no English, and they did not understand the laws. Many did not see why they should register or pay taxes on land that their families had occupied for generations. Their land titles became worthless because they failed either to register the titles or to pay the new taxes. Other Mexican Americans had their land records burned or stolen. Many fought to keep their property, and thousands were murdered.

The courts offered little justice to Mexican Americans. Most courts prohibited the use of Spanish, which gave English-speaking Americans a great advantage.

Gradually, most Mexican Americans became tenants or workers on land that belonged to English-speaking Americans. The two groups lived apart in the towns and cities, and each had its own schools, stores, and places of entertainment. The Mexican Americans called their sections *barrios*, the Spanish word for *neighborhoods*.

The Growing Minority. The Mexican-American population began to grow rapidly during the early 1900's. Thousands of Mexicans fled the violence of the Mexican Revolution of 1910 and moved to the United States. Many were recruited by American railroads, mining companies, and farm owners. Others sought jobs that appeared after the United States entered World War I in 1917. Between 1910 and 1930, more than 600,000 Mexicans settled in the United States.

Throughout the early 1900's, Mexican Americans suffered discrimination in jobs and wages and lived in run-down housing. To fight these conditions, they organized labor unions and took part in strikes to obtain higher wages and better working conditions. Mexican Americans also formed civic groups to deal with their problems. In 1929, the major groups merged to form the League of United Latin American Citizens.

During the Great Depression of the 1930's, the number of people of Mexican descent in the United States declined. As a result of mass unemployment, thousands of Mexican immigrants were either deported or pressured to return to Mexico by U.S. government officials. A large number of these immigrants had lived in the United States for more than 10 years. Many of their children had been born there and were U.S. citizens.

MEXICAN AMERICANS IN THE UNITED STATES

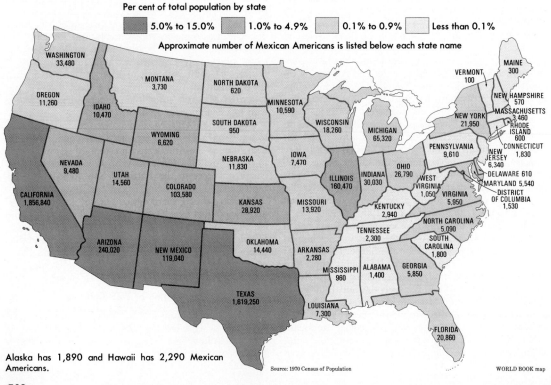

Per cent of total population by state

5.0% to 15.0%   1.0% to 4.9%   0.1% to 0.9%   Less than 0.1%

Approximate number of Mexican Americans is listed below each state name

WASHINGTON 33,480
OREGON 11,260
MONTANA 3,730
IDAHO 10,470
NORTH DAKOTA 620
MINNESOTA 10,590
MAINE 300
VERMONT 100
NEW HAMPSHIRE 570
MASSACHUSETTS 3,460
RHODE ISLAND 600
WYOMING 6,620
SOUTH DAKOTA 950
WISCONSIN 18,260
MICHIGAN 65,320
NEW YORK 21,950
PENNSYLVANIA 9,610
CONNECTICUT 1,830
NEW JERSEY 6,340
NEVADA 9,480
UTAH 14,560
NEBRASKA 11,830
IOWA 7,470
OHIO 26,790
INDIANA 30,030
WEST VIRGINIA 1,050
DELAWARE 610
MARYLAND 5,540
CALIFORNIA 1,856,840
COLORADO 103,580
ILLINOIS 160,470
VIRGINIA 5,950
DISTRICT OF COLUMBIA 1,530
KANSAS 28,920
MISSOURI 13,920
KENTUCKY 2,940
NORTH CAROLINA 5,090
ARIZONA 240,020
NEW MEXICO 119,040
OKLAHOMA 14,440
ARKANSAS 2,280
TENNESSEE 2,300
SOUTH CAROLINA 1,800
MISSISSIPPI 960
ALABAMA 1,400
GEORGIA 5,850
TEXAS 1,619,250
LOUISIANA 7,300
FLORIDA 20,860

Alaska has 1,890 and Hawaii has 2,290 Mexican Americans.

Source: 1970 Census of Population

WORLD BOOK map

Thousands of Mexicans came to the United States to work during World War II (1939-1945). Many were *braceros*, farmworkers who had been issued temporary work permits by the federal government. Many others entered the United States illegally. These workers found jobs throughout the country.

Hundreds of thousands of Mexican Americans served in the U.S. armed forces during World War II. After the war, many Mexican-American veterans still faced discrimination. As a result, many of them helped form national organizations to deal with the urgent needs of Mexican Americans. These groups included the American G.I. Forum, the Community Services Organization, and the Mexican American Political Association.

Expanding Influence. During the 1960's, four Mexican Americans won election to Congress and became champions of civil rights. They were Senator Joseph Montoya of New Mexico and Representatives Eligio de la Garza and Henry B. Gonzales of Texas and Edward R. Roybal of California.

President Lyndon B. Johnson appointed several Mexican Americans to high government posts in the 1960's. For example, Vicente T. Ximenes became chairman of the President's Cabinet Committee on Mexican-American Affairs. Johnson made Hector P. García a member of the U.S. delegation to the United Nations and appointed Raul H. Castro U.S. ambassador to El Salvador. Other Mexican Americans who won distinction during this period included civil rights leaders Lupe Anguiano and Dolores Huerta, entertainer Vikki Carr, writer Tomas Rivera, golfer Lee Trevino, and playwright Luis Valdez. In addition, several Mexican-American theater companies won recognition. The best-known theater groups were Centro Cultural in San Diego and Teatro Campesino in Fresno, Calif.

Foods of Mexican origin also became increasingly popular in many parts of the United States during the 1960's. These foods included *chile con carne*, *enchiladas*, *tacos*, and *tamales*. See MEXICO (Food).

The Chicano Movement. In spite of the success of a growing number of Mexican Americans, many others became increasingly resentful about their unsolved problems. Such feelings found expression in the Chicano, or "brown power," movement. In Mexico, *Chicano* is a mocking slang expression for a clumsy person. Mexican Americans used the term in jest during the 1950's when referring to one another. But in the 1960's, many young Mexican Americans gave the term a positive meaning that suggested racial and cultural pride.

One of the earliest Mexican-American spokesmen to reflect this new pride was Cesar Chavez, a labor union leader who began to organize California grape pickers in 1962. California grape growers refused to accept his union. So in the mid-1960's, Chavez called a strike against the growers and organized a nationwide boycott of grapes. These measures ended in 1970, when the growers recognized Chavez' union.

In 1965, another Chicano leader, Rodolfo Gonzales, founded the Crusade for Justice in Denver. This group worked to provide social services and to develop job opportunities for Mexican Americans. In 1970, José Angel Gutiérrez helped establish La Raza Unida, a political party based in Texas. Gutiérrez won election to the school board of Crystal City, Tex., that same year and later became the board's president.

Mexican Americans Today

Most of the approximately 5 million Mexican Americans still live in the West. California has about 1,856,000 Mexican Americans, more than any other state. About 80 per cent of all Mexican Americans live in cities.

Customs and Holidays. Most Mexican Americans observe several customs and holidays of Mexico in addition to those of the United States. For example, many Mexican Americans celebrate a Mexican Christmastime ceremony called *Las Posadas*. This celebration features a series of marches that symbolize the journey of Joseph and Mary to Bethlehem.

Some Mexican Americans observe such Mexican holidays as *Cinco de Mayo* (May 5) and Guadalupe Day, on December 12. Cinco de Mayo honors a Mexican army's victory over an invading French force at Puebla, Mexico, in 1862. Guadalupe Day is Mexico's most important religious holiday.

Continuing Problems. Some Mexican Americans live in fine homes in cities or suburbs. They have good-paying jobs in business, government, the professions, and all other occupations. But most Mexican Americans lack work skills and have low-paying and low-prestige jobs. They live in crowded, run-down barrios—chiefly because they cannot afford better housing. Large numbers of Mexican Americans still work on farms. Most of these are migrant laborers. They move from one area to another, depending on where there are crops to be harvested. They generally receive low wages, and live under substandard conditions in unsanitary camps.

Mexican Americans have completed fewer years of school than most other ethnic groups in the United States. Largely because of this condition, they earn much less than most other U.S. ethnic groups. Many Mexican-American youths who enter school speak only Spanish. Many have difficulty understanding English, the language commonly used for instruction. This handicap greatly slows their progress. Many Mexican-American students also suffer from racial prejudice among teachers, a lack of Spanish-speaking teachers, and little attention to Mexican-American affairs. These conditions lead to a high rate of failure and cause many Mexican Americans to quit school. Racial prejudice makes it difficult even for educated Mexican Americans to find good jobs and housing.

Some Mexican Americans support the use of violence to draw public attention to their problems. Many others, however, reject such action as distasteful to the Mexican-American tradition of respectful conduct, hard work, and persistence.

Recent Developments. During the early 1970's, La Raza Unida candidates won election to school and municipal agencies in several Texas communities. A number of school systems responded to Chicano pressures by hiring more Spanish-speaking teachers and adding Mexican-American studies.

In 1971, President Richard M. Nixon appointed Romana A. Bañuelos as treasurer of the United States. She became the first Mexican-American woman to hold such a high government post. DELUVINA HERNÁNDEZ

Sports Events

The Olympic Games; Eiji Miyazawa, Black Star

"Sesame Street"; Children's Television Workshop

Learning and Fun for Children

Walter Cronkite; CBS

The Latest News

"The Flip Wilson Show"; NBC

Comedy

Television is sometimes called "the device that brings the world into the home." TV provides millions of home viewers with a wide variety of entertainment, information, and special events. The pictures on this and the following page show some examples of television's far-reaching coverage.

TELEVISION

TELEVISION, or TV, is one of man's most important means of communication. It brings pictures and sounds from around the world into millions of homes. A person with a television set can sit in his house and watch the President make a speech or visit a foreign country. He can see a war being fought and watch statesmen try to bring about peace. Through television, home viewers can see and learn about people, places, and things in faraway lands. TV even takes its viewers out of this world. It brings them coverage of America's astronauts as the astronauts explore outer space.

In addition to all these things, television brings its viewers a steady stream of programs that are designed to entertain. In fact, TV provides many more entertainment programs than any other kind. The programs include action-packed dramas; light comedies; soap operas; sporting events; cartoon, quiz, and variety shows; and motion pictures.

More than 60 million homes in the United States—or 96 per cent of all the country's homes—have at least one television set. On the average, a television set is in use in each home for about 6 hours each day. Thus, television has an important influence on how people

The contributors of this article are Sig Mickelson, Professor of Journalism at Northwestern University and author of The Electric Mirror; *and Herbert Zettl, Professor of Broadcast Communication Arts at San Francisco State University and author of* Television Production Handbook.

spend their time, as well as on what they see and learn.

Because of its great popularity, television has become a major way to reach people with advertising messages. Most television stations carry hundreds of commercials each day. In 1972, more than $4 billion was spent on television advertising in the United States. The use of television advertising has greatly changed the process of getting elected to public office in the United States. Before TV, candidates relied chiefly on public appearances to urge people to vote for them. Today, most candidates for high office reach many more people through television commercials than they reach in person.

The name *television* comes from the Greek word *tele*, meaning *far*, and the Latin word *videre*, meaning *to see*. Thus, *television* means *to see far*. Most pictures and sounds received by a television set are beamed from a television station on electronic signals called *electromagnetic waves*. The television set changes these waves back into pictures and sounds.

Many scientists contributed to the development of television, and no one person can be called its inventor. Experiments leading to the invention of TV began in the 1800's, but progress was slow. Television as we know it today was not developed until the 1920's, and it had little importance in communication until the late 1940's. But during one 10-year period—the 1950's— it became part of most households in the United States. Since then, television has gained importance in most other countries. In addition, many organizations, including businesses, hospitals, and schools, now use television for their own special purposes.

Astronaut Aldrin reaches the moon; NASA

Space Exploration

The Watergate Investigation; Fred Ward, Black Star

Government Hearings

"The Waltons"; CBS

Family Drama

TELEVISION / Television in the Home

More than 60 million homes in the United States—or 96 per cent of the total—have at least one television set. About two-thirds of all American homes have two or more TV's. Altogether, there are about 93 million sets in the United States. On the average, a television set is in use in each home for about 6 hours a day.

About three-fourths of the more than 900 television stations that broadcast in the United States are *commercial stations*. The rest are *public stations*. Commercial stations are those that sell advertising time to pay for their operating costs and to make a profit. Public stations are nonprofit organizations that rely on business, government, and public contributions to pay for their operating costs. The programming of commercial and public stations differs greatly.

Commercial Television. Commercial television stations broadcast many more entertainment programs than any other kind. These shows include light dramas called *situation comedies;* action-packed dramas about cowboys, detectives, doctors, and lawyers; variety shows featuring comedians, dancers, and singers; and movies, including some made expressly for television. They also include daytime quiz shows and *soap operas* (melodramatic plays), and cartoons and other children's shows.

Another kind of commercial television program is the *documentary*. A documentary is a dramatic, but nonfictional, presentation of information. Some television documentaries entertain as well as inform. These include travel programs about people, animals, and things in faraway places. TV also presents documentaries with

little entertainment content, such as studies of alcoholism, drug abuse, poverty, and racial prejudice.

Commercial television stations broadcast many *discussion*, or *talk*, shows. On these shows, a host interviews people from many walks of life—including athletes, authors, movie and television stars, and politicians.

Commercial television stations cover almost every kind of sports event—from baseball and football to table tennis and skydiving. Every four years, TV brings its viewers the colorful Olympic Games—often from halfway around the world.

All commercial stations broadcast brief summaries of local, national, and international news every day. Also, stations often interrupt their regular program schedules to present extended coverage of special events, such as space shots, political conventions, and important presidential activities.

Advertising makes up an important part of commercial television. Television commercials appear between and during most programs. The vast majority of the commercials urge viewers to buy some kind of product —from dog food and hair spray, to cars and insurance policies. At election time, many political candidates buy advertising time on television to ask people to vote for them. A small percentage of TV advertising provides a *public service*. Public service ads include messages that tell people to drive carefully and follow other safety rules. They also include announcements about local community activities.

Commercial television attracts huge audiences.

Often, more than 50 million persons tune into a top entertainment show or sporting event. About 50 million persons watch a television newscast daily. Thus, it must be assumed that large numbers of people like what commercial television offers. Even so, many persons criticize its coverage. They say that commercial TV shows too many programs designed only to entertain, and not enough programs that inform, educate, or provide cultural enrichment. The critics also claim that much of the entertainment is of poor quality because it aims at the largest possible audience. They criticize television newscasts for being too brief to provide the real meaning of news stories.

The persons responsible for deciding what appears on commercial television disagree with these criticisms. They point out that commercial TV can stay in business only by selling much advertising time at high prices. To do this, the programs must attract large numbers of viewers. Statistics show that many more people watch popular shows and brief news reports than watch more sophisticated shows and in-depth news reports.

Public Television. Because public television stations do not rely on advertising to stay in business, they do not have to attract huge audiences. Their programming focuses chiefly on educational and cultural subjects.

Public stations broadcast educational programs on a wide range of subjects, from literature and physics to cooking and yoga. In some cases, viewers can earn college credits by passing tests based on what the programs teach. Some educational programs on public TV take much the same form as classroom instruction. But others use a more entertaining approach. Examples include "Sesame Street" and "The Electric Company," two lively, yet educational, children's shows.

Public television stations offer many programs that combine entertainment and cultural enrichment. They telecast such things as plays by leading dramatists, ballets and symphonies, and surveys of man's art and history. Such shows draw up to 2 million viewers. This is a small number by commercial TV standards, but much larger than ever attended a theater or concert hall.

Public television stations do not carry regular newscasts. But they often present in-depth discussions of news events. For example, leading journalists and others who deal closely with current events hold long discussions of news developments on public TV.

TELEVISION / *Specialized Uses*

Television has many uses other than broadcasting to the home. Schools, businesses, hospitals, and many other organizations use TV for special purposes.

Most of TV's specialized uses involve *closed-circuit television*. That is, the signals are sent—by way of wires—to only certain television sets. Broadcasting, on the other hand, is a form of *open-circuit television*. This means the signals can be received by all sets within the area the signals can reach.

Schools. Many classrooms have TV sets that receive specially prepared lessons by way of closed-circuit television. In addition, some schools show open-circuit broadcasts of special events—such as space shots and the President's inauguration.

Businesses and Hospitals make extensive use of television. Many companies instruct new employees and conduct nationwide sales meetings through prerecorded television programs. Sometimes, television cameras are placed in hospital operating rooms. The cameras send close-up pictures of actual operations to medical students. The illustration in this section shows one of the many other medical uses of television.

Security and Surveillance. Many banks focus TV cameras on customers so that guards can watch for attempted robberies. Television cameras in jails make it possible for one guard to watch many prisoners at once. United States and Russian satellites equipped with TV cameras circle the earth. The cameras can detect such military operations as troop build-ups and shifts. Satellite cameras also take pictures of weather patterns that help weathermen make forecasts.

Video Cassettes rank among the newest developments in closed-circuit television. A video cassette is a videotaped program inside a book-sized container. The user slips the container into a slot in a playback machine. The machine transmits the program to the user's television receiver or receivers. Many businesses and some schools already use video-cassette television. Home use of this device has begun on a small scale. Home users can buy prerecorded programs of their choice and play them on a TV set in their homes.

A Surgeon Uses Television in diagnosing heart disease, *below*. He injects dye into a patient's arteries and follows its course on television screens. A stoppage may indicate a blocked artery.

WORLD BOOK photo

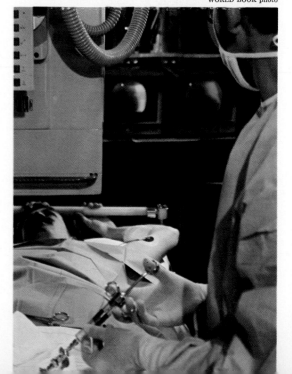

A Television Production involves achieving an appearance of naturalness amid much activity. Viewers of "The Tonight Show" see Johnny Carson and Ed McMahon chatting in a relaxed atmosphere, above. But off camera, many production workers are doing vital jobs that require split-second timing.

The *production* (putting together) of a television program is an extremely complicated process. A program requires careful planning, much preparation, and the combined efforts of many workers with artistic and technical skills.

Most television productions take place in television studios. But TV production companies also create shows in movie studios, on city streets, in stadiums, in deserts and jungles, and even under water. Broadcasters telecast some programs *live* (as they happen). But most TV programs—including almost all entertainment shows—are prerecorded, and then telecast at a later time. The recording may be done on videotape or on film.

Many prerecorded programs are produced from beginning to end, in the manner of a stage play. But television production companies also use the *piecemeal approach* of the motion-picture industry. In this approach, each scene is recorded separately, and *spliced* (connected together) later.

The first two parts of this section—*Planning and Preparation* and *Putting a Show on the Air*—trace the development of an entertainment program produced

All the photographs in this section were taken for WORLD BOOK *at the production facilities of "The Tonight Show Starring Johnny Carson" by John Hamilton, Globe Photos.*

straight through in a television studio and recorded on videotape. But much of the information under these headings applies to all TV productions. The last part of this section describes the differences involved in other production methods.

Planning and Preparation

The planning of television shows begins in the programming department of the networks and stations that broadcast programs. Members of these departments decide what programs their companies will telecast. Networks and stations produce many programs themselves. Independent producers create others, and sell them to networks and stations. In either case, once a programming department approves an idea for a program, a *producer* takes full responsibility for its production.

The Producer usually begins his work by obtaining a script and choosing a director. Sometimes—especially for uncomplicated shows—the producer writes the script himself. He may also serve as his own director—in which case he is called a *producer-director*. But more often, the producer assigns the script-writing job to a professional writer or team of writers, and the directing job to a professional director. The producer and director select the *talent* (actors, actresses, or other people who will appear on the show). The producer also chooses the production specialists needed to produce the show. These persons may include an art director, a costume designer, and a composer. In addition, the producer works closely with the director throughout the production process.

Writers prepare the scripts for television programs. A television script is a written account of what is to be said and done during the program. The amount of detail a script contains varies, depending on the program. A talk show script, for example, may include only the host's opening remarks, some of the key questions to ask his guests, and directions for any special acts that may take place during the show. During most of the show, the host and his guests carry on *adlibbed* (unplanned) conversations. A script for a television drama, on the other hand, includes every word to be spoken by the actors and actresses. It also describes the actions they are to perform.

The Director. As soon as the writers complete the script, the director reads it and tries to visualize how he can translate it into an actual television program. He gets ideas about how the characters should speak, move, and generally behave. He decides what camera shots will be needed to create the effects he visualizes. Sometimes, the director has an artist prepare a *storyboard* (a series of drawings) that shows how key parts of the program will look.

Production Specialists. The producer and director call on many production specialists to help prepare for the program. An *art director* and artists and craftsmen who work with him design and build the show's scenery. A *costume designer* creates or obtains costumes needed for the production. A *property manager*, or *prop man*, gets special items called *props* for the show. These items include furniture, vases of flowers, and guns. Specialists in technical work also play a key role in the production

process. They advise the producer and director on what kinds of cameras, microphones, and lights will be needed. A *production manager*, or *production coordinator*, sees to it that all the required equipment is available when needed.

Talent is a technical term for all the persons who appear on television programs. A talent may be a *performer*, or an *actor* or *actress*. A talent who appears as himself on television is a performer. A talent who plays someone else is an actor or actress. Television performers include newscasters, sports announcers, and talk show hosts. The people who play roles in TV dramas and situation comedies are actors and actresses.

Selection of talent ranks among the key steps in the planning of a television program. The producer and director do this important job. If a talent is a big star, he may get television roles because of his fame and proven ability. But usually, a talent must *audition* (try out) for the parts he wants to play. During an audition, the director and producer may ask the talent to *take a screen test* (perform in front of a camera).

A talent who earns a job gets a script so he can study his lines. An actor or actress may have less than a week to learn the lines for a one-hour drama. Those who perform on TV's daily soap operas have only a few hours each day to memorize their lines.

Some television productions make use of *cue cards* to help the talent with their lines. A cue card is a large piece of cardboard or similar material with writing on it. The writing may be a key word or phrase, or an entire passage from a script. An off-camera stagehand holds the card up so the talent can see it.

The *Teleprompter* is another aid sometimes used in television productions. A Teleprompter is a mechanical device that contains a roll of paper with words from a script printed on it. The roll moves continuously,

Planning for a TV Program begins long before the telecast. For example, the "Tonight Show" producer, *at desk above,* and his assistants schedule guest appearances weeks in advance.

Production Preparations may include setting up a *Teleprompter,* a device that shows parts of a script. The Teleprompter above shows lines of a commercial Ed McMahon will read.

Rehearsals are the practice sessions of TV productions. During dress rehearsal for a "Tonight Show" comedy routine, *left*, the director (*holding script*) goes over the skit with Carson and other cast members. At right, guest singer James Brown runs through his songs with members of the band.

giving the talent a line-by-line view of the script. Television performers who deliver commercials, news stories, and speeches often use a Teleprompter.

Composers and Musicians. Most television programs include music. A producer and director may decide they need an original musical composition for their show. If so, the producer hires a composer. The composer meets with the producer and director to discuss the theme, mood, and *climaxes* (dramatic high points) of the program. The composer bases his composition on what he learns about the show. Often, producers and directors decide to use existing music for their programs. To do so, they must get permission from the holder of the copyright on the music, and pay him a fee.

The producer hires musicians and a conductor to perform the music. For prerecorded shows, the musicians often record the music after the actual program is produced. Then, technicians combine the music with the rest of the program.

Rehearsals are practice sessions for television shows. Most TV productions require at least one rehearsal. Complicated productions often require many more.

During a rehearsal, the talent—under the director's guidance—practice their lines and their actions. The director also directs the actions of the cameraman and other off-camera workers.

Rehearsal for a dramatic production may begin with a *script reading*. Then, the director may call for a *dry run* (rehearsal without equipment or costumes). Many dry runs take place in a *rehearsal room*. This room has lines on the floor that indicate where such things as doors, chairs, and tables will be during the actual production. A director may watch a dry run through a *director's viewfinder*. This device resembles the viewfinder on a still camera. It enables the director to get an idea of how scenes will appear on television.

Finally, the director calls for a *dress rehearsal*, or *camera rehearsal*, in the studio. The goal of a dress rehearsal is to achieve a performance that is the same as the final production will be. In fact, directors sometimes record both the dress rehearsal and the actual production. In reviewing both recordings, the director may decide that parts of the dress rehearsal came out better than the actual production. He may then substitute the parts of the dress rehearsal he likes for the corresponding parts of the actual production.

Television rehearsals stress the importance of split-second timing. A theater drama may run as much as five minutes more than its planned time. But a television show must be timed exactly. A show cannot run even a few seconds past its planned time, because that time is set aside for the next program.

Putting a Show on the Air

When the time comes to tape a program, everything needed for the process is brought together in a television studio. Workmen put the scenery and props in place in the studio. Other workmen put floodlights and spotlights in place. Technicians turn these lights off and on and brighten and dim them during the production to achieve the desired effect for various scenes. Often, a single televised scene requires as many as 20 different lighting instruments. One or more microphones are put in place. Workmen bring television cameras—usually at least two and sometimes four or five—into the studio. The persons responsible for the technical parts of the show's production get ready in the *control room*. This room lies off to the side of the place where the telecast occurs.

Some studios have rows of seats, very much like a theater. Visitors can come to these *audience areas* and watch shows being produced.

Putting a Show on the Air requires the skills of many behind-the-scenes workers. A "Tonight Show" audio engineer controls the program's sounds at an audio console, *left*. Monitors, *right*, show all the scenes the studio cameras are photographing. The director decides which scenes go on the air.

Before the show begins, makeup men apply makeup to the talent who will appear on the show. Makeup helps people look natural on camera. The talent put on special costumes, if the show calls for such costumes. Finally, they come into the studio and perform the production before the cameras.

The Cameras used to *shoot* (photograph) the production are big, heavy instruments. They are mounted on devices that have wheels so the cameramen can move them around the studio to change the direction of their shots. Many cameras can be lowered and raised mechanically to change the vertical angles. In addition, all broadcast cameras have a lens that allows the cameraman to vary televised scenes without moving the camera. This device is called a *zoom lens*. By pressing a button or turning a handle, the cameraman causes adjustments in the lens. These adjustments enable the cameraman to gradually change a scene from a close-up of a talent's face to a long-range view of an entire scene. *Zooming* (moving in and out on scenes) is a widely used television production technique.

A broadcasting camera also has a *viewfinder* (tiny television set) on it. The viewfinder shows the cameraman the exact scene his camera is photographing.

Microphones. Most studio TV productions involve the use of one or more *boom microphones*. A boom microphone is attached to a *boom* (long metal arm). A worker called the *boom operator* uses mechanical devices to move the microphone above and in front of the person speaking. For dramatic productions, it is essential that the microphone be kept out of camera view. Imagine a dramatic scene in which an actor lies exhausted in a hot desert, crying for help. If suddenly the boom microphone that hangs above him dropped into camera view, the scene would look ridiculous. Sometimes, television makes use of *hidden microphones*—either in addition to,

or in place of, boom microphones. Such microphones may be hidden in or behind scenery or props.

Talk shows and other nondramatic productions may use boom microphones. But they also use microphones that viewers can see. These include *desk microphones*, which stand on desks or tables in front of performers; and *hand microphones*, which performers hold. Another kind of microphone, the *lavalier*, is hung around a performer's neck or attached to his clothing. It may be in camera view, or hidden in the clothing.

The Control Room. During a television program, scenes from each of the studio's cameras will appear on the viewer's screen. Pictures from other video sources, including filmed commercials and slides that show titles, will also be seen. The job of determining which scenes appear when is done in the control room. A program may also include sounds from several sources. Technicians in the *audio control* section of the control room regulate the program's sounds. In addition, engineers operate equipment that keeps up the quality of the pictures and sounds.

The control room has several *monitors* (television sets). Each monitor shows the scenes from a different camera or other video source. The director watches the monitors when choosing which scenes to put on the air. The picture that is on the air at any given time appears on a monitor called the *master*, or *line*, *monitor*.

An important piece of equipment in the control room is the *switcher*. This instrument has many buttons, including buttons for controlling each studio camera and each other picture source. On command from the director, a technician called the *technical director* (T.D.) presses buttons to change the televised scene. If the director wants the scene being photographed by camera number 1 to be shown, he tells the technical director to press the button for camera number 1. To change to camera number 2, the T.D. presses button number 2, and so on. This switching process goes on throughout the program. But it is done so smoothly that viewers hardly realize it is happening.

The switcher also has levers. By moving levers in various ways, the T.D. can combine scenes from two or more cameras or other video sources. Such combinations are called *special effects*. They include the *dissolve*, the *super*, the *wipe*, and *matting*, or *keying*.

The *dissolve* is a gradual change from one picture to another in which the two pictures overlap briefly. A dissolve can take place slowly or rapidly, depending on how fast the T.D. moves the levers. Directors use the dissolve to move smoothly from scene to scene and, sometimes, to indicate a passage of time.

The *super*, or *superimposition*, is the blending together of two scenes. Television often uses this device to show dream scenes. One camera shows a close-up of the face of the sleeping person, and the other shows the scene about which the person is dreaming.

A *wipe* is a special effect in which one picture seems to push another picture off the screen. A wipe that is stopped halfway is called a *split screen*. TV productions use the split-screen technique to show scenes from two different locations at the same time. Other common wipes include the *circle* and the *diamond*, in which the second picture appears on the screen as an expanding circle or diamond.

The *matting*, or *keying*, technique is used to show titles and other objects over a scene. The letters of the titles come from a title card, title slide, or electronic letter-making machine. The picture on which the letters appear comes from a studio camera, or film or tape.

The switcher also enables television broadcasters to *cut* (switch instantly) from the program to filmed commercials, and back again.

The sound inputs of a television program are controlled by an instrument called an *audio console*. An *audio engineer* operates this instrument. He pushes buttons and moves levers to choose and mix together various audio inputs. For example, a scene of two persons sitting in an automobile might require the audio engineer to mix the sounds of the persons' conversation with recorded sounds of the automobile engine, outside traffic, and mood music. The audio engineer also controls the volume of sounds.

Taping the Program. The program produced in the studio and control room is immediately recorded on a videotape machine. This machine stands in or near a special part of the television studio called *master control*. The director reviews the finished tape, and tape editors correct any major errors in it. Then, the tape is stored until the time the program is scheduled for broadcasting. For technical information on videotape, see *Videotape Recording* later in this article.

Master Control is the electronic nerve center of a television station. Much of the electronic equipment that helps create television pictures is located there. A program goes from master control by cable or microwave to the transmitter. Then, the transmitter sends it on its way to the viewers. Master control also has equipment for switching from program to program. The pro-

grams include those that originate at the station, at network headquarters, and at remote locations.

Other Production Methods

A television production can differ from the method just described in four chief ways. (1) Television producers put some programs together piecemeal rather than straight through. (2) They create many programs with film cameras rather than with TV cameras. (3) They telecast many programs live instead of recording them first. (4) They create programs in locations away from studios. Such programs are called *remote telecasts*.

The Piecemeal Approach involves recording a program on videotape or film scene-by-scene with *stopdowns* (stops) between scenes. Each recorded scene is called a *take*. After each take, the director can play back the tape or film and judge its merits. If he likes the take, he goes on to another one. If he does not like it, he can call for a *retake* (shoot the scene over again). The piecemeal approach also allows directors to shoot scenes out of order. If, for example, the first and last scenes of a TV play happen in the same location, the director may shoot them one right after the other. Upon completion, film or tape editors splice all the scenes together in their proper order to create a continuous story.

Filming Television Programs. Film cameras can be carried around and operated more easily than can television cameras. As a result, many television producers use film cameras to create programs that take place at several locations. For example, television news programs, which report on widely scattered events, use film cameras. Programs shot at faraway locations usually use film. In addition, motion-picture studios create many entertainment programs with film cameras (see MOTION PICTURE [How a Motion Picture Is Made]).

After cameramen film a program, broadcasters telecast it from a telecine unit. For technical information, see *Telecine* later in this article.

Live Telecasts include coverage of political conventions, speeches by the President, and sports events. The part of newscasts in which the announcers speak are also live. But most of the news scenes shown on these programs come from film or videotape recordings.

Broadcasters usually videotape live programs at the same time as they telecast them. This allows them to rerun all or parts of a show at a later time. For example, videotaped highlights of a live telecast of a speech by the President are often shown later on newscasts. Videotapes of live sports events allow sportscasters to rerun and analyze key plays immediately after they happen. This process is called *instant replay*.

Remote Telecasts. Almost all remote telecasts are broadcast live. They include telecasts of sports events and political conventions. Producers of these programs use regular-sized television cameras. But they also use cameras small enough to be carried around. These *hand-held cameras* help TV crews cover the huge area of a sports field or convention hall. Broadcasters park a *remote truck* near the place of the telecast. This truck contains control room and master control equipment needed to create TV signals. The signals travel by microwave or wire from the truck to the transmitter.

The enormous public interest in TV programs in the United States has created a huge television industry in a short time. In 1946, there were only six television stations in the United States. Today, the country has more than 900 stations. In 1962, sponsors spent less than $1½-billion to advertise on TV. Ten years later, the figure had jumped to more than $4 billion—an increase of about 300 per cent.

The number of television stations and the money spent on commercials account for only part of television's impact on the American economy. The manufacture and sales of television sets and broadcasting equipment became big businesses because of the rise of television. In addition, broadcasting, manufacturing, and sales created thousands of new jobs.

The National Networks. About 80 per cent of all commercial television stations in the United States are *affiliates* of one of three national networks. That is, they agree to carry programs provided by the networks. The national television networks are those of the American Broadcasting Companies (ABC), the Columbia Broadcasting System (CBS), and the National Broadcasting Company (NBC). The networks create some of their programs and buy others from independent producers.

An affiliate agrees to carry about 7½ hours of a network's programs daily. The network pays the affiliate for carrying the programs. Sponsors, in turn, pay the networks for showing their commercials on the stations.

A network's success depends on its ability to select programs that attract large audiences. The bigger a program's audience, the more money sponsors will pay for the right to show commercials on it. For top-rated shows, sponsors pay from about $75,000 to $200,000 for one minute of commercial time.

The persons who choose a network's programs know that certain shows, such as championship sports contests and appearances by famous entertainers, will usually attract huge audiences. But they choose most programs on the basis of their own intuition, or "educated guesses."

After a network program goes on the air, the network and sponsors keep close watch on its *ratings*. Ratings are the results of surveys that supposedly show how many people watch various programs. The Nielsen Survey, conducted by the A. C. Nielsen Company, ranks as the most important survey. The company arrives at its ratings by determining what programs 1,200 American families watch. The viewing habits of these families supposedly reflect the habits of the entire nation. Networks usually cancel programs that get low ratings. They sometimes do so after only a few showings.

Local Commercial Stations. About 700 local commercial stations operate in the United States. About 80 per cent of them are affiliates of the three national networks. The rest operate independently.

An affiliate's agreement to carry about 7½ hours of network programs daily usually includes about 2½ hours each of morning, afternoon, and nighttime programs. Affiliates can, and often do, present more than 7½ hours of network programs. But, in 1971 the Federal Communications Commission (FCC)—which regulates broadcasting in the United States—limited the amount of network programming affiliates can carry during *prime time*. Prime time extends from 6 P.M. to 10 P.M. in the Central and Mountain time zones and from 7 P.M. to 11 P.M. elsewhere. The FCC ruled that local stations in the nation's 50 largest television markets cannot broadcast more than 3 hours of network programs during prime time. This ruling was designed to force the stations to offer a wider variety of prime-time programs—especially programs of local interest.

The nonnetwork programs of affiliates and the programs of independent stations come from several sources. The stations fill some of their time with shows they produce themselves, especially local newscasts. They also telecast interview, discussion, and other kinds of programs of local interest. Both affiliates and independent stations show programs produced by organizations called *syndicates*, films from motion-picture distributors, and reruns of old network shows. The local stations sell commercial time to advertisers to pay for the cost of their programs and to make a profit.

Public Stations. Over 200 public television stations operate in the United States. They create many of the programs they show and buy programs from independent producers. Often, a program created by one public station is carried by many other stations. An agency called Public Broadcasting Service (PBS) serves as a distributor of locally produced public programs.

Public stations are nonprofit organizations, but they need money to cover their production and operating costs. The largest part of a station's funds come from viewer contributions. A viewer who contributes to a public television station becomes a member of the station. Businesses and foundations also help support public television. Local and state taxes help support many public stations. In addition, stations get funds from the Corporation for Public Broadcasting (CPB).

CPB, created by Congress in 1967, gets most of its funds from the federal government. CPB encourages public stations to serve the needs of their local communities through grants for programming and technical facilities. It also finances the production of programs

NUMBER OF TELEVISION SETS IN USE

Millions of television sets

World*
1969:
251,000,000

United States
1971:
93,000,000

1950:
11,000,000

1950:
6,000,000

Year: 1950 1955 1960 1965 1970 1975 1980

*Excluding China for most years

Sources: *Statistical Yearbook*, various years, UN and UNESCO; *World Communications*, UNESCO

distributed by PBS and sets policies for a national public broadcasting service.

Cable Television Systems bring television to the home by means of cables rather than through the air. These systems rank among the fastest-growing parts of the television industry.

Cable television began in the early 1950's. Originally, its only purpose was to bring network and local station programs to places that either cannot receive TV signals through the air, or can receive them only with much interference. Such places include mountain valleys, extremely hilly regions, and areas with heavy concentrations of tall buildings, such as New York City.

Today, businessmen operate more than 2,800 cable television systems in the United States. Some systems provide TV to over 50,000 homes. Others serve fewer than 100 homes. Altogether, cable television serves more than 6 million homes in about 5,300 communities.

Improved reception of regular television programs still ranks as the main purpose of cable television. But since the 1960's, people have begun to use it for other purposes. A single cable system can carry as many as 60 TV signals. Thus, a cable system can provide homes with regular television programs and still have the capacity to serve other purposes.

In many communities, channels are set aside for coverage of local community activities. Such activities include city council and school board meetings, community and neighborhood news, and local plays and concerts. In 1972, the Federal Communications Commission ruled that operators of cable systems in the 100 biggest television markets had to set aside a channel for *public access*. This means they must provide a channel for use by anyone who wants to put his own TV show on the air. Such broadcasts now take place on a small scale. Minority-group members have appeared on public access cable TV to discuss their problems, and civic groups have used it to promote community improvements.

Cable television has great economic potential despite the high cost of installing cable systems. Many operators charge an installation fee. Subscribers to all cable systems pay a monthly service charge, which averages $5 nationwide. An operator can also create his own programming and sell advertising time to sponsors. In addition, some cable operators now use their systems for *pay-television*.

Pay-Television. Ever since television broadcasting began, there have been businessmen who wanted to set up *pay-television systems*. Under such a system, the viewer pays a fee to see certain programs in his home. The Federal Communications Commission has consistently opposed attempts to make programs that are part of *free* (regular) television part of pay-TV systems. But promoters of pay-TV believe it is possible to gain subscribers by offering programs that are not available on free TV, such as first-run motion pictures, live telecasts of theater plays, and certain sporting events.

In the past, attempts to establish pay-TV systems met with little success. However, since the late 1960's, pay-TV promoters have made some progress in selling program packages to subscribers of cable television systems. In addition, promoters continue to work to estab-

— LEADING COUNTRIES IN NUMBER OF TV SETS —		
Country	Number of Sets	Sets Per 1,000 Persons
United States	93,000,000	449
Russia	39,300,000	160
Japan	23,281,000	222
West Germany	17,673,000	299
Great Britain	16,569,000	298
France	11,655,000	227
Italy	10,344,000	191
Canada	7,610,000	349
Brazil	6,500,000	68
Poland	4,709,000	144

Source: *Statistical Yearbook, 1972,* UN

lish successful pay systems that use the airwaves for broadcasting programs.

Related Industries. The spectacular growth of television broadcasting caused a similar growth in other industries. In 1946, manufacturers in the United States turned out only 56,000 television sets, and the American people spent about $1 million for sets. Today, manufacturers produce more than 14 million sets a year, and people spend more than $3 billion yearly on sets. Set sales have improved the business of many retail stores, including radio and phonograph shops, department stores, and appliance stores. Also, TV repair shops have sprung up throughout the country.

Television broadcasting requires much expensive equipment, including cameras, control boards, and transmitters. The manufacture of such equipment has become a multimillion-dollar industry.

The huge demand for television commercials has created a boom in the advertising industry. About 15 per cent of all the money now spent on advertising in the United States goes to television commercials. Many advertising agencies now devote most or all of their time to creating TV commercials.

Careers in Television. The television industry has opened up thousands of job opportunities in a variety of fields. The broadcasting industry needs such workers as writers, producers, directors, cameramen, engineers, electronic technicians, stagehands, lighting specialists, graphic artists, and set designers to help produce television shows. Actors, actresses, and performers are needed to appear in them. TV news departments provide a variety of jobs for journalists. TV broadcasting also creates jobs for specialists in management, market research, and advertising.

The television industry also employs workers in technical fields outside of broadcasting. Scientists and engineers are needed to design television equipment. Factory workers manufacture television sets and other TV equipment. Repairmen service home receivers.

Almost all careers in television require special training. Many colleges and universities have departments that train students in most nontechnical broadcasting careers. Journalism schools teach courses in broadcast, as well as printed-media, journalism. Technological institutes and engineering departments of colleges offer training in technical areas of television. Information on television careers is available from the National Association of Broadcasters, 1771 N Street NW, Washington, D.C. 20036.

A person looking directly at a scene sees the entire view all at once. But television cannot send a picture of an entire scene all at once. It can send only one tiny part of the picture, followed by another tiny part, until it has sent the complete picture. A television camera divides a picture into several hundred thousand tiny parts by a process called *scanning*. As the camera scans the picture, it creates electronic signals from each part of the picture.

A television set uses these signals in re-creating the picture on its screen. The scanning process puts the picture back together again piece by piece. A person looking at the screen of a TV set does not realize this is happening. The scanning process works so quickly that the viewer sees only a complete picture.

Sending television pictures and sounds involves three basic steps. (1) The light and sound waves from the scene being televised must be changed into electronic signals. (2) These signals must be transmitted to the television receiver. (3) The receiver must unscramble the signals and change them back into copies of the light and sound waves that came from the original scene.

Creating Television Signals

A television signal begins when light from the scene being televised enters a television camera. The camera changes the light into electronic signals. At the same time, a microphone picks up the sounds from the scene and changes them into electronic signals. Television engineers call the signals from a camera *video* and the signals from a microphone *audio*.

This section describes how a TV camera creates video signals. It also explains how video signals are produced by *telecine* (television film) and videotape. TV audio signals are created in the same way as radio signals. For information on this process, see RADIO.

The video signals broadcast by most television stations are *compatible color signals*. These signals produce a color picture when received on a color set. The same signals also produce a black-and-white picture on a black-and-white set.

Color television uses the three *primary colors of light*—

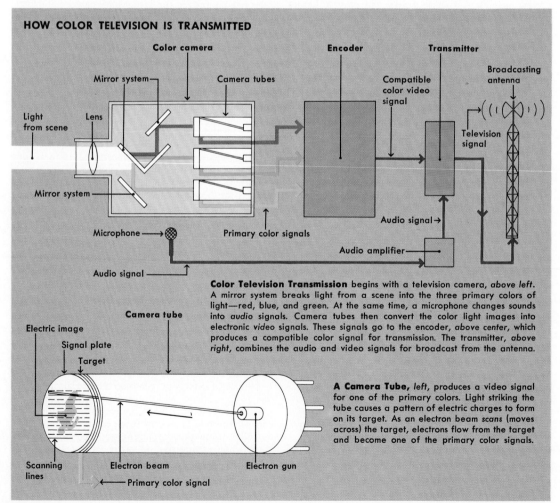

HOW COLOR TELEVISION IS TRANSMITTED

Color camera · Encoder · Transmitter

Mirror system · Camera tubes · Broadcasting antenna

Compatible color video signal

Light from scene · Lens

Television signal

Mirror system

Audio signal →

Microphone → · Primary color signals

Audio amplifier

Audio signal

Color Television Transmission begins with a television camera, *above left*. A mirror system breaks light from a scene into the three primary colors of light—red, blue, and green. At the same time, a microphone changes sounds into *audio* signals. Camera tubes then convert the color light images into electronic *video* signals. These signals go to the encoder, *above center*, which produces a compatible color signal for transmission. The transmitter, *above right*, combines the audio and video signals for broadcast from the antenna.

Camera tube

Electric image

Signal plate

Target

A Camera Tube, *left*, produces a video signal for one of the primary colors. Light striking the tube causes a pattern of electric charges to form on its target. As an electron beam *scans* (moves across) the target, electrons flow from the target and become one of the primary color signals.

Scanning lines · Electron beam · Electron gun

Primary color signal

red, blue, and green—to produce full-color pictures. The proper mixture of these three colors can produce any color of light. For example, a mixture of red and green light produces yellow light. Equal amounts of red, blue, and green light produce white light. See COLOR.

The Television Camera. In producing a compatible color signal, the TV camera must: (1) capture the image of the scene being telecast; (2) create video signals from the image; and (3) encode the color signals for transmission. To perform these tasks, a television camera uses a lens, a system of mirrors, camera tubes, and complex electronic circuits. All the electronic circuits used by the camera are not inside it. They would make the camera too bulky and heavy. Instead, many of the camera circuits are located elsewhere in the TV station and connected to it by wires.

Capturing the Image. The lens gathers the *image* (picture) of the scene in front of the camera. Like the lenses in other cameras and the human eye, the TV lens *focuses* (collects and bends) the light from the scene to form a sharp image. This image contains all the colors of the scene. But to produce color signals, the camera must split the full-color image into three separate images—one for each primary color.

The camera uses two *dichroic mirrors* to split the image into the primary colors. The first mirror reflects the blue image and allows red and green light to pass through it. The second mirror reflects the red image, leaving only the green image. Other mirrors within the camera reflect each of the images to a separate camera tube.

Creating the Video Signals. A camera tube changes the light image into video signals. A black-and-white camera has only one camera tube. Color cameras have at least three such tubes—one for each primary color. These tubes create a separate video signal for each primary color. Some color cameras have a fourth tube that produces a black-and-white signal. The tubes in most color cameras are *Plumbicon tubes,* an improved version of a tube called the *vidicon.* For simplicity, this section describes the working of one vidicon tube.

A vidicon tube has a glass *faceplate* at its front end.

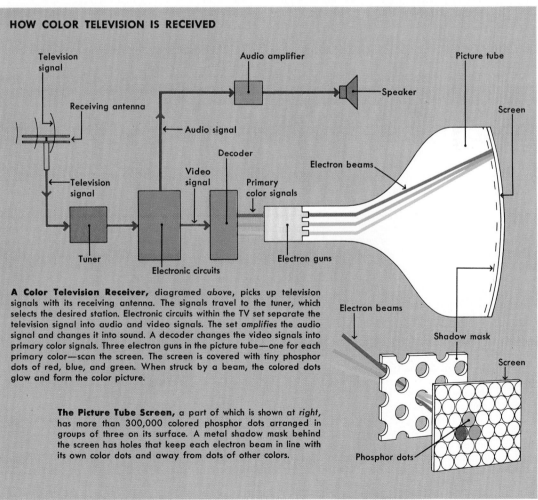

HOW COLOR TELEVISION IS RECEIVED

A Color Television Receiver, diagramed *above,* picks up television signals with its receiving antenna. The signals travel to the tuner, which selects the desired station. Electronic circuits within the TV set separate the television signal into audio and video signals. The set *amplifies* the audio signal and changes it into sound. A decoder changes the video signals into primary color signals. Three electron guns in the picture tube—one for each primary color—scan the screen. The screen is covered with tiny phosphor dots of red, blue, and green. When struck by a beam, the colored dots glow and form the color picture.

The Picture Tube Screen, a part of which is shown at *right,* has more than 300,000 colored phosphor dots arranged in groups of three on its surface. A metal shadow mask behind the screen has holes that keep each electron beam in line with its own color dots and away from dots of other colors.

WORLD BOOK diagram by Mas Nakagawa

In back of the faceplate is a transparent coating called the *signal plate*. A second plate, called the *target*, lies behind the signal plate. The target consists of a layer of *photoconductive material* that conducts electricity when exposed to light. At the rear of the tube is a device called an *electron gun*.

Light from the image reaches the target after passing through the faceplate and the signal plate. The light causes negatively charged particles called *electrons* in the photoconductive material to move toward the signal plate. This movement leaves the back of the target with a positive electric charge. The strength of the positive charge on any area of the target corresponds to the brightness of the light shining on that area. The brighter the light, the higher the positive charge. The camera tube thus changes the light image gathered by the lens into an identical electric image of positive charges on the back of the target.

The electron gun shoots a beam of electrons across the back of the target. The beam moves across the target in an orderly pattern called a *scanning pattern*. As the beam moves across the target, it strikes areas with different amounts of positive charge. Areas of the target that have the strongest charge attract the most electrons from the beam. This occurs because particles of unlike electric charge attract each other. Other areas of the target attract fewer electrons. The electrons from the beam move through the target and cause an electric current to flow in the signal plate. The voltage of this current changes from moment to moment, depending on whether the beam is striking a bright or dim part of the image. This changing voltage is the video signal from that camera tube.

The electron gun scans the target much as a person reads—from left to right, top to bottom. But unlike the way a person reads, the electron beam skips every other line on the target. After the beam scans the top line, it quickly snaps back to the left. Then, it scans the third line, fifth line, and so on. When the beam reaches the bottom of the target, it snaps back and then scans line two, line four, line six, and so on.

The scanning pattern of TV cameras in the United States is made up of 525 lines ($262\frac{1}{2}$ odd-numbered and $262\frac{1}{2}$ even-numbered lines). The beam completes the scanning of one *field* each time it scans $262\frac{1}{2}$ lines. Two fields make up a complete television picture, called a *frame*. The electron beam moves with such extreme speed that it scans a line in $\frac{1}{15,750}$ of a second and produces 30 complete frames in a second. This speed is fast enough so the television picture does not flicker and it shows moving objects smoothly.

Each of the three vidicon tubes converts its particular primary color to a video signal by means of the scanning process. Wires carry the signals to electronic circuits in the camera that *amplify* (strengthen) them. The three signals then go to the *encoder*.

Encoding the Color Signals. At the encoder, the three video signals are combined with other signals to produce a compatible color signal. The first step in this process involves combining the three video signals into two color-coded signals and a black-and-white signal. The two color-coded signals are called *chrominance*

signals and the black-and-white signal is called a *luminance signal*. A circuit in the encoder, called the *matrix*, performs this function.

Another circuit in the encoder, the *adder*, combines the chrominance and luminance signals and, in the process, adds a *color burst* and a *synchronization signal*. The color burst enables a color TV set to separate the color information in the chrominance signals. This information, along with the luminance signal, produces a full-color picture on the TV screen. The synchronization signal locks the receiving set into the same scanning pattern as that used by the camera.

Telecine (pronounced *TEHL ih SIHN ee*) is motion-picture or still film shown on television. A TV station uses a combination of a film projector and a small television camera to create a video signal from telecine. The projector is aimed directly at the television camera, which converts the light images into a video signal by the method just described. A typical telecine unit has two motion-picture projectors and one or two slide projectors set up around one camera. The projectors and camera together are often called a *film chain*.

Videotape Recording stores television pictures and sounds as magnetic impulses on tape. Unlike film, which must be developed before showing, a videotape can be played over the air immediately.

The videotape recorders used by television stations record the video signals crosswise in the center of a 2-inch-wide strip of magnetic tape. Sound and control signals are recorded along the edge of the tape.

Transmitting Television Signals

Most television signals are broadcast through the air. Engineers at a television station use a device called a transmitter to produce a TV signal from separate audio and video signals. The signal is then carried by wire to an antenna and broadcast. The signal is called an *electromagnetic wave*. Such waves can travel through the air at the speed of light, about 186,282 miles per second. But the signal can be received clearly only up to a distance of about 150 miles. To send TV signals farther, other means of transmitting must be used. These include coaxial cable, microwaves, and satellites.

Broadcasting. Before a television signal is broadcast, the transmitter boosts its *frequency* (rate of vibration). A television signal needs a high frequency in order to carry the picture information through the air. The transmitter then amplifies the signal so it has enough power to reach a large area.

The transmitter increases the frequency of both the video and audio signals by a process called *modulation*. High-frequency electromagnetic waves, called *carrier waves*, are first generated by the transmitter. The transmitter uses the video signal to vary the *amplitude* (strength) of the carrier waves to produce the video part of the TV signal. This process is called *amplitude modulation* (AM). The video signal is then amplified to a power of 1,000 to 100,000 watts.

The transmitter uses the audio signals to modulate another carrier wave, which becomes the audio part of the television signal. This process, called *frequency modulation* (FM), shifts the frequency of this carrier wave slightly. The transmitter then combines the modulated video and audio carrier waves to form the television signal.

A wire called the *transmission line* carries the television signal to the transmitting antenna, which releases the signal into the air. Television stations erect their antennas on high buildings or towers so the signal can reach as far as possible. The maximum range of most TV signals is between 75 and 150 miles, depending on the antenna design and transmitting power.

Television stations in the same area transmit on different frequencies so their signals do not interfere with one another. The group of frequencies over which one station broadcasts is known as a *channel*.

A total of 68 channels are available for television broadcasting in the United States. These channels are divided into two groups. Channels numbered 2 through 13 are called *very high frequency* (VHF) channels. VHF refers to signals with a frequency between either *54 megahertz* (54,000,000 vibrations per second) and 72 megahertz, 76 and 88 megahertz, or 174 and 216 megahertz. Channels numbered 14 through 69 are called *ultrahigh frequency* (UHF) channels. UHF signals have a frequency between 470 and 809 megahertz.

Coaxial Cable is used to carry television signals for long distances or to areas that have difficulty receiving signals. The television networks often send programs to their affiliated stations throughout the country through coaxial cables. The affiliates then broadcast the programs to their viewers. Cable television systems use coaxial cables to carry signals to the homes of persons who subscribe to the service.

Microwaves are electromagnetic waves, similar to television signals. Tall relay towers spaced about 30 miles apart across the country carry programs from the networks to affiliate stations on these waves. Equipment in a tower automatically receives, amplifies, and then retransmits the microwave signal to the next tower. The affiliate stations must change the microwave signals back into TV signals before they can be received by an ordinary television set.

Satellites carry television signals between stations where cables or microwave towers cannot be built. For example, satellites relay signals across oceans and connect stations on different continents. Satellites work like relay towers in space. They receive coded television signals from a special earth station, amplify them, and send them on to another earth station. The two stations may be thousands of miles apart.

Receiving Television Signals

The television signal from a transmitter is fed into a home television set through a *receiving antenna* or *aerial*. The set uses the signal to make copies of the pictures and sounds from the televised scene. In reproducing the television program, a TV set uses a tuner, amplifiers and separators, and a picture tube.

Receiving Antenna. A good antenna collects a strong enough television signal for the receiver to produce a picture. The type of antenna needed depends on the distance between the receiver and the transmitting antenna. A simple *dipole* (rabbit ear) antenna collects

enough signal within a few miles of the transmitter. At greater distances, a more elaborate antenna mounted on the roof may be necessary. The best reception results when the antenna is pointed toward the desired station. Some antennas can be rotated by remote control to align them with widely separated TV stations.

Tuner. Signals from the antenna are fed into the set's tuner. The tuner selects only the signal from the station the viewer wants to receive. It shuts out all others. Most TV sets have two tuning knobs. One knob selects the VHF channels, 2 through 13, and the other knob selects the UHF channels, 14 through 69.

Amplifiers and Separators. From the tuner, the television signal goes to a group of complicated electronic circuits in the set. These circuits amplify the signal and separate the audio and video portions of it. The audio signals are changed into sound waves by the speaker. The video signals go to the *picture tube*, or *kinescope*, where they re-create the picture.

A color set has circuits that use the color burst to separate the video signal into the two chrominance signals and the luminance signal. Another group of circuits, called the *decoder* or *matrix*, transforms these signals into red, blue, and green signals that duplicate the signals from the three camera tubes. These signals then go to the picture tube.

The Picture Tube transforms the video signals into patterns of light that duplicate the scene in front of the camera. One end of the picture tube is rectangular and nearly flat. This end forms the screen of the TV set, where the picture appears. Inside the set, the picture tube tapers to a narrow neck. The neck of a color picture tube holds three electron guns—one each for the red, blue, and green signals. A black-and-white tube has only one electron gun.

Each electron gun in a color picture tube shoots a separate beam of electrons at the screen. Each beam scans the screen just as the beam in each camera tube scanned its target. The synchronization signal, which is a part of the video signal, ensures that the picture tube's scanning pattern follows exactly the pattern used by the camera. The beams must be in step with each other in order to produce a picture.

The screen of most color tubes is coated with more than 300,000 tiny phosphor dots. The dots are grouped in triangular arrangements of three dots each—one red, one blue, and one green. These dots glow with their respective color when struck by an electron beam. A metal plate perforated with thousands of tiny holes lies about one-half inch behind the screen of a color tube. It is called the *shadow mask*. Its holes keep the beams from hitting any color dots but their own.

The amount of light given off by the dots depends on the strength of the beam at the instant it strikes them. Since the strength of the beam is controlled by the video signal from the camera, the dots are bright where the scene is bright and dark where it is dark. When the set shows a color program, the three colored dots blend together in the viewer's mind to produce all the colors in the original scene (see EYE [How We See]). The dots produce only differing amounts of white light when showing a black-and-white program.

Television ranks as one of the major influences on life in the United States. Some people even call it the most important single influence of all. The *Television Industry* section of this article discusses TV's enormous impact on the American economy. This section deals with some of television's many effects on people and on *institutions* (established parts of society).

Effects on Learning. Home television contributes greatly to what its viewers learn. It provides, on a small scale, *formal* or "classroom" *instruction*. For example, on certain TV programs teachers instruct viewers in such things as foreign languages, literature, mathematics, and science. But television is much more important for the *informal learning* it provides through its noninstructional programs. The term *informal learning* refers to all the things a person learns through the new experiences he has.

No communication system has ever provided so many people with as wide a range of new experiences as television does. Without leaving their homes, television viewers can watch political figures perform important functions, and see how people of far-off lands look and live. Television takes viewers to deserts, jungles, and the ocean floor, and shows the kinds of animals and plants that live there. A TV viewer can see how a famous actor performs the role of Hamlet, and get an idea of how top comedians draw laughter. Television shows its viewers what real-life tragedy is like, as when it covers the victims of war, natural disasters, and poverty. It also captures moments of great triumph, such as when man first set foot on the moon. The total effect of television's many offerings has been an enrichment of the public's experience far beyond what was possible before the age of television.

Not all of television's effects on learning are generally accepted as "good," however. For example, many television entertainment programs show scenes of extreme violence. Large numbers of people believe these scenes may cause viewers—especially children—to act violently themselves. In 1969, a research group sponsored by the United States government studied TV's effect on children. The researchers suggested that television violence might influence children who have violent tendencies to act violently. They also said they could reach no definite conclusion about the effect of TV violence on the vast majority of children.

Effects on Material Expectations. Television programs and commercials often show people who lead more glamorous lives and have more material possessions than most viewers. Many social scientists believe such episodes raise the *material expectations* of viewers. That is, they cause viewers to wish they were better off materially. Such a desire can be helpful. For example, it can cause a person to work harder so he can afford more of the things he wants. But social scientists believe raised material expectations can also be harmful. The expectations can cause a person to become so dissatisfied with his life that unhappiness results.

Some sociologists believe that television's effect on material expectations even contributes to violence. They say that violent acts of poor minority-group members may be partly, and indirectly, caused by tele-

vision. These people—the theory says—continually see on television how much better off other people are in comparison to them. This may stir up anger in the viewers, and thus contribute to violent behavior.

Effects on Institutions. Television has brought about major changes in several American institutions. These institutions include politics, the motion-picture and radio industries, and professional sports. TV's effect on advertising, another institution, is discussed earlier in this article.

Politics. Every election year, thousands of political candidates use television in their campaigns. They buy commercial time to urge voters to support them. They also appear on interviews to answer questions about their views. Many candidates now reach more voters through a single television appearance than through all the in-person campaigning they do.

Television has led to a unique kind of political campaigning—the *spot announcement*. Spot announcements are political messages that last from 10 to 90 seconds. These brief messages rank as the most widely used form of political advertising on television. They contrast sharply with the long political speeches that are typical of traditional, in-person campaigning.

Television does much to promote interest in politics and political issues. But political advertising on TV also draws criticism. Critics say spot announcements are too short to allow candidates to discuss issues. Instead, candidates use the time to present oversimplified statements to win support or attack their opponents. Critics also claim that, because television time is so expensive, TV campaigning gives unfair advantage to the candidates with the most money. Another complaint about television campaigning is that it leads to the "selling" of candidates through advertising methods similar to those used to sell products.

Motion Pictures and Radio. From the 1920's through the 1940's, motion pictures and radio ranked as the chief forms of entertainment for millions of Americans. Large numbers of people went to the movies at least once a week. They listened to comedies, dramas, and other entertainment programs on the radio almost every night. The rise of television in the 1950's caused a sharp decline in motion-picture attendance. Ever since, the motion-picture industry has faced economic problems (see MOTION PICTURE [Postwar American Movies; Motion Pictures Today]). Radio entertainment changed completely after TV became part of American life. Almost every radio entertainment program went off the air. Recorded music replaced these shows as the chief kind of radio entertainment (see RADIO [History]).

Professional Sports have long attracted millions of spectators yearly. But many more millions now watch the events on television. Television networks and stations pay team owners large amounts of money for the right to televise games. These funds, in turn, help owners pay the high salaries of today's professional athletes. Television also helps increase the popularity of sports. For example, professional football had a limited following when its games began appearing on TV in the 1950's. But largely because of television, professional football's popularity has soared.

The Federal Communications Commission (FCC) regulates television—and also radio—broadcasting in the United States. An agency of the federal government, the FCC issues broadcasting licenses to stations and assigns frequencies the stations must broadcast on. These regulations are needed to maintain order in the airwaves. If anyone who wanted to were allowed to broadcast and use any frequency, signals would interfere with each other and make broadcasting impossible.

The FCC also regulates broadcasting in other ways. It cannot censor programs, but it sets standards for broadcasters. The FCC has the power to take away, or refuse to renew, a station's license if the station violates the standards too much. One of the most important FCC standards requires stations to provide public services and programs designed to meet the needs of their local communities. The FCC also insists that stations present all points of view when dealing with controversial subjects. In addition, it expects stations to avoid obscenity and pornography in their programs. The FCC and another government agency, the Federal Trade Commission (FTC), evaluate truthfulness in television advertising.

Congress. The Congress of the United States can also regulate broadcasting. In 1970, it passed a law that prohibited cigarette advertising on television after Jan. 2, 1971. Congress based its decision on the government's conclusion that cigarette smoking is harmful to health. In 1973, Congress called for a change in the *blackout* policy of the National Football League (NFL). Under this policy, NFL games were not shown on television in the areas where the games were played. Congress ruled that games must also be televised locally if all the seats offered are sold out 72 hours before game time. The ruling also applies to other sports.

Broadcasters and Regulations. Broadcasters generally oppose government regulations. They say regulations that affect programming interfere with their rights to freedom of expression. The FCC and most congressmen disagree. They claim that because the airwaves are public property, the government must create regulations that serve the public's interest.

TELEVISION/*Television in Other Lands*

Television broadcasting developed more slowly in other parts of the world than it did in the United States. Throughout the 1950's, there were more television sets in the United States than in all other countries combined. But beginning about 1960, a television boom began in many nations. The U.S. still has more TV sets than any other country, but it no longer has more than all other countries combined. Today, there are about 93 million sets in the United States, and about 158 million sets elsewhere.

Every country except South Africa now has television, and that country is scheduled to get it in the mid-1970's. Television programming varies from country to country. But in all nations, the programs provide entertainment, cultural enrichment, education, news, and special events.

The government of every country regulates broadcasters in some ways. But in general, democratic governments—such as those of Australia, Canada, Great Britain, and New Zealand—allow broadcasters much freedom. Communist and other undemocratic governments tightly control broadcasting. They use TV as a tool to promote the government's beliefs and policies.

Canada. The Canadian people own about 7,600,000 television sets, or about 350 for every 1,000 persons. Only the United States—with about 450 per 1,000—has more sets per person.

The Canadian Broadcasting Company (CBC), a publicly owned corporation, operates about 100 television stations in Canada. About 300 stations are privately owned. Most Canadian people speak English, but many speak French. Therefore, some Canadian stations broadcast in English, and some in French. Most Canadians live in the southern part of the country, close to the United States. As a result, large numbers of Canada's television viewers can receive programs from U.S. stations, as well as from their own stations.

Europe. World War II and the economic problems that followed it slowed the development of television in Europe. But since the 1960's, television has grown at a rapid rate in Western Europe. Four West European nations have over 10 million sets and rank among the world's leading nations in the number of sets. They are West Germany, Great Britain, France, and Italy.

People in the Communist countries of Eastern Europe have fewer television sets and other luxury items than do people in the West. Russia, the region's most developed country, has about 39,300,000 TV sets. It ranks second to the United States in the total number of sets. But its ratio of sets to persons (about 160 to every 1,000) is lower than in most Western nations. Poland is the only other Eastern European nation that ranks among the world's leaders in TV sets.

Asia. Japan has about 23,300,000 television sets—over 50 times more than any other Asian nation. Japan ranks third, after the U.S. and Russia, in total number of sets. Television is still a small industry in much of Asia. But it is growing rapidly in some countries, including Israel, Kuwait, and South Korea.

Africa has fewer television sets than any other continent except Antarctica. In Egypt, the African nation with the most TV's, there are only about 15 sets for every 1,000 persons. Most African nations have fewer than 5 sets per 1,000 persons.

Australia and New Zealand have thriving television industries. In each country, there are more than 225 TV sets per 1,000 persons, a high figure by world standards. But the countries have small populations, and neither ranks among the leaders in total sets.

Latin America. Television is more widespread in Latin America than in Africa and much of Asia. But Latin America lags behind Europe and North America. Brazil has more television sets than any other Latin-American country. Argentina and Mexico rank next.

Early Development. Many scientists contributed to the development of television, and no one person can be called its inventor. Television became possible in the 1800's, when man learned how to send communication signals through the air in the form of electromagnetic waves. This process is called *radio communication*. For details on its development, see RADIO (History).

The first radio operators sent code signals through the air. By the early 1900's, operators could transmit words. Meanwhile, many scientists had conducted experiments involving the transmission of pictures. As early as 1884, Paul Gottlieb Nipkow of Germany had invented a scanning device that sent pictures short distances. His system worked mechanically, rather than electronically as television does. In 1922, Philo T. Farnsworth of the United States developed an electronic scanning system. He was then 16 years old.

Vladimir K. Zworykin probably made the most important contributions to television as we know it today. In 1923, this Russian-born American scientist invented the *iconoscope* and the *kinescope*. The iconoscope was the first television camera tube suitable for broadcasting. The kinescope is the picture tube used in television receivers. Zworykin demonstrated the first completely electronic, practical television system in 1929.

The Start of Broadcasting. Many experimental telecasts took place during the late 1920's and the 1930's. The British Broadcasting Corporation (BBC) in Great Britain, and CBS and NBC in the United States were leaders in experimental telecasts. World War II and the economic problems that followed the war caused Great Britain to abandon television experiments. The United States moved far ahead of the rest of the world in television broadcasting.

The first American telecasts on anything like a regular basis began in July, 1936. The Radio Corporation of America (now RCA Corporation), which owns NBC, installed television receivers in 150 homes in the New York City area. NBC's New York station began broadcasting programs to these homes. A cartoon of Felix the

---

IMPORTANT DATES IN TELEVISION

1800's Man learned how to send communication signals through the air as electromagnetic waves.

1929 Vladimir K. Zworykin demonstrated the first practical television system.

1936 NBC made the first regular telecasts in the U.S.

1946 A television boom began. It resulted in making television part of most American homes by 1960.

1951 The first coast-to-coast telecast showed President Harry S. Truman opening the Japanese Peace Treaty Conference in San Francisco.

1953 Color telecasts began.

1954 Television covered the Army-McCarthy hearings.

1960 Presidential candidates John F. Kennedy and Richard M. Nixon debated on TV before a nationwide audience.

1965 Television programs were relayed between the United States and Europe by way of *Early Bird*, the first commercial communications satellite.

1967 Congress established the Corporation for Public Broadcasting to help finance public TV stations.

1969 TV viewers saw man's first landing on the moon.

1973 Television covered the Watergate hearings.

Cat was its first program. The United States entered World War II in 1941. Television broadcasting was suspended until after the war ended in 1945.

The Television Boom. The national networks—all based in New York City—resumed broadcasting shortly after the war. At first, their telecasts reached only the Eastern Seaboard between Boston and Washington, D.C. But by 1951, they extended coast-to-coast. TV stations sprang up throughout the country to telecast the network shows and local programs. TV programs changed greatly from prewar days. Elaborate entertainment, news, special events, and sports contests replaced the simple, largely experimental, prewar shows.

The American people became fascinated with the idea of having so wide a range of visual events available in their homes. The demand for TV sets became enormous. In 1945, there were probably fewer than 10,000

RCA

An Experimental Telecast of the late 1920's showed a statue of the comic strip character Felix the Cat.

Culver

Milton Berle became the first big TV star. His zany comedy show drew a huge audience during the early 1950's.

Wide World

Professional Wrestlers, including Gorgeous George (*being thrown*), ranked among the favorite television performers of the 1950's.

Wide World

TV Coverage of the Army-McCarthy Hearings of 1954 brought a major event of American history into millions of homes. The dramatic hearings included charges by U.S. Senator Joseph R. McCarthy, *center above*, that the Army was "coddling Communists."

vision's appeal. In 1951, TV broadcast the Kefauver hearings, in which U.S. Senator Estes Kefauver and his Senate committee questioned alleged mobsters about organized crime. In 1954, television covered the famous Army-McCarthy hearings. Viewers watched spellbound as Senator Joseph R. McCarthy accused the United States Army of "coddling Communists," and the Army charged McCarthy's staff with "improper conduct." The hearings reached a dramatic high point when Joseph Welch, a soft-spoken lawyer for the Army, and the outspoken McCarthy clashed in an emotion-filled argument (see McCARTHY, JOSEPH R.).

The 1960's opened with a milestone of television broadcasting. During the summer and fall of 1960, presidential candidates John F. Kennedy and Richard M. Nixon faced each other and the nation in a series of television debates. It marked the only time presidential candidates have debated on television. Many persons believe the debates made an important contribution to Kennedy's victory in the 1960 election.

Popular entertainment remained the major part of television's coverage during the 1960's. But TV also reflected the turmoil that marked American life. President Kennedy was assassinated on Nov. 22, 1963. Two days later, millions of viewers witnessed one of the most startling scenes ever shown on television. In full view of TV cameras, Jack Ruby shot and killed accused Kennedy assassin Lee Harvey Oswald as policemen were taking Oswald from one jail to another.

From the mid-1960's on, television regularly brought viewers battle scenes from the Vietnam War. The conflict was sometimes called "the first war to be fought on television." TV viewers also watched war protesters demonstrate—sometimes violently—and witnessed bitter debates over America's war policy. Civil rights protests by blacks and other minority groups also became part of television coverage. Violence also sometimes accompanied these protests.

Technological Advances made during the 1950's and 1960's helped improve the physical quality of tele-

sets in the country. This figure soared to about 6 million in 1950, and to almost 60 million by 1960. In TV's early days, people who had no set often visited friends who had one just to watch television. Also, many stores placed television sets in windows, and crowds gathered on the sidewalk to watch programs.

Early Programs. Milton Berle became the first television entertainer to attract a huge, nationwide audience. His show, "The Texaco Star Theater," was filled with zany comedy routines. It ran from 1948 to 1956, and often attracted 80 per cent of the total television audience. "I Love Lucy," starring Lucille Ball, went on the air in 1951. This early situation comedy also attracted a huge following. Other highly popular early entertainment programs included Ed Sullivan's variety show, "The Toast of the Town"; professional wrestling matches; and quiz shows that offered prizes of thousands of dollars. A major scandal hit television in 1959, when it was learned that quiz show producers had helped some contestants answer questions.

Coverage of special events did much to widen tele-

CBS

"The $64,000 Question" was one of several TV quiz shows of the 1950's that offered huge prizes.

UPI

Vietnam War Scenes appeared often on TV in the 1960's. They brought the horrors of war into millions of homes.

CBS

"All in the Family," starring Carroll O'Connor, *left*, became a hit show of the 1970's. It combines comedy with treatment of controversial topics.

casts. In TV's early days, most screens measured 7 or 10 inches diagonally. Today, 21- and 25-inch screens are common. Improvements in broadcasting and receiving equipment provide much clearer television pictures than were available in the past. In early days, all programs were telecast in black and white. Color telecasting began in 1953, and today most programs are telecast in color. More than half of all American households now have a color set. These developments made television easier to watch and more realistic.

Technological advances also resulted in production methods that benefited viewers. At first, most telecasts were live productions or programs made from film. The film took time to develop. Also, the equipment and techniques used to film programs produced pictures and sounds of poor quality. Videotaping of programs began in the mid-1950's, and became a major production method. Videotapes are produced instantly, and result in almost no loss of quality. They allow broadcasters flexibility in program scheduling, and make possible such viewing aids as instant replays of sports events. Later, scientists developed equipment and techniques that enabled broadcasters to produce filmed shows with almost no loss of quality.

Early Bird, the first commercial communications satellite, was launched in 1965. Satellites made worldwide television broadcasting possible. As a result, view- ers could see events such as the Olympic Games from Asia and Europe and President Nixon's 1972 visits to China and Russia as they happened.

Television Today continues to be a source of entertainment more than anything else. But it also carries on its role of providing coverage of important events. For example, in 1973 networks canceled many regular programs to cover the Watergate hearings—a U.S. Senate investigation of charges of illegal campaign practices during the 1972 election (see WATERGATE).

Through the years, television broadcasters generally avoided controversial themes, such as abortion, alcoholism, divorce, drug abuse, political satire, racial prejudice, and sex. They feared that such themes would result in a loss of viewers. However, beginning in the late 1960's, broadcasters found that they could deal with controversial themes and still attract large audiences. The comedy show "Laugh-In" included many jokes about sex and much political satire. But it became the top-rated show of the late 1960's. "All in the Family," a situation comedy that satirizes prejudice, gained top ratings in the early 1970's. "The Waltons," a drama that deals with many moral and ethical problems, also gained a large audience in the 1970's. The success of such programs has led broadcasters to include a wider range of topics in their entertainment programs than before.

SIG MICKELSON and HERBERT ZETTL

TELEVISION / *Study Aids*

Related Articles in WORLD BOOK include:

BIOGRAPHIES

EQUIPMENT AND PHYSICAL PRINCIPLES

OTHER RELATED ARTICLES

Outline

Questions

What is the role of electromagnetic waves in television?
How does television affect our lives?
What is a dissolve? A super? A wipe?
How did Vladimir K. Zworykin contribute to the development of television?
Who was the first major television entertainer?
What career opportunities are available in television?
What are the methods of transmitting TV programs?
What are some criticisms of television?
What is a video cassette?
How much do advertisers spend on television yearly?

Reading and Study Guide

See *Television* in the RESEARCH GUIDE/INDEX, Volume 22, for a *Reading and Study Guide*.

Section Six

Dictionary
Supplement

This section lists important words to be included in the 1974
edition of THE WORLD BOOK DICTIONARY. This dictionary, first
published by Field Enterprises Educational Corporation in 1963, keeps
abreast of our living language with a program of continuous editorial
revision. The following supplement has been prepared under the
direction of the editors of THE WORLD BOOK ENCYCLOPEDIA and
Clarence L. Barnhart, editor in chief of THE WORLD BOOK DICTIONARY.
It is presented as a service to owners of the dictionary and as an
informative feature to subscribers of THE WORLD BOOK YEAR BOOK.

A

acid rock, rock 'n' roll music with sound and lyrics suggestive of psychedelic experiences: ... *kids who have grown tired of the predictable blast-furnace intensity of acid rock* (Time). [< *acid* (LSD)]

acid trip, *Slang.* a hallucinatory experience that results from taking acid (LSD): *He sometimes receives telephone calls from kids on bad acid trips thinking of suicide* (New York Times).

age·ism (ā′jiz əm), *n.* discrimination against old or elderly people, especially in employment and housing: *The youngsters applauded his* [*Richard Nixon's*] *denunciation of "the insidious bigotry of age-ism"* (Time).

AIM (no periods), American Indian Movement.

application satellite, any earth satellite designed for some practical use on earth, such as a weather satellite, a communications satellite, or a navigational satellite: *France had refused to support an expensive European programme for the development of applications satellites to be used for navigation, meteorology, and air traffic control* (John Newell).

ar·col·o·gy (är kol′ə jē), *n., pl.* **-gies.** a planned city housed entirely within a single structure of enormous size: *There are arcologies for sea, shore or plain, for populations the size of Sarasota (30,000), Atlanta (400,000) or Dallas (1,000,000)* (Estie Stoll). [(coined by Paolo Soleri, an American architect) < *arc*(hitectural) (ec)*ology*]

artificial intelligence, 1. the ability of certain electronic devices to obey spoken commands, show recognition of simple objects, and carry out tasks such as assembling objects in various ways. **2.** the programming of such devices or the means by which such devices operate.

B

bar·i·at·rics (bar′ē at′riks), *n.* the medical treatment of overweight people. [< Greek *báros* weight + English *-iatrics* (as in *geriatrics, pediatrics*)]

bi·o·feed·back (bī′ō fēd′bak), *n.* a method of monitoring and learning to control changes in one's own body by the use of such electronic instruments as electrocardiographs and electroencephalographs: *"Biofeedback," or voluntary control of internal states, already has been used in many laboratories to enable individuals to alter brain waves, blood pressure, blood flow, heart rate, and muscle tensions* (Samuel Moffat).

Black English, any of various Negro dialects of English, especially as spoken in the United States: *"Black English" is ... remarkably rich in nuances* (Time).

bod·y·suit (bod′ē süt′), *n.* a tight-fitting, one-piece garment covering the trunk of the body.

C

cat·e·chol·a·mine (kat′ə chōl′ə-mēn, -kōl′-), *n.* any of a class of hormones, such as adrenalin, that acts upon the nerve cells: *Stress liberates certain hormones called catecholamines into the human bloodstream which will promptly raise the blood pressure* (Science News Letter). [< *catechol* + *amine*]

chair·per·son (chãr′pér′sən), *n.* *U.S.* a person who presides at a meeting; chairman or chairwoman: *Joseph E. Trimble of Oklahoma* [*was*] *chairperson of the symposium* (Science News).

cin·e·ma·theque (sin′ə mə tek′), *n.* a theater showing experimental or unconventional motion pictures. [< French *cinémathèque* (literally) film collection, film cabinet; see DISCOTHÈQUE]

con·scious·ness-rais·ing (kon′shəs nis-rā′zing), *n.* a method of making people more aware of their potentials, especially their ability to bring about changes or reforms: *The S.D.S. saw students as in need of education. "Consciousness-raising," they called it* (New York Times Magazine).

crash pad, 3. *U.S. Slang.* a place where one may sleep or lodge free or without invitation: *There were a series of hostels, or "crash pads," along our route, where it was even possible to get free meals* (Bill Sertl).

D

de·crim·i·nal·i·za·tion (dē krim′ə nə lə zā′shən), *n.* a decriminalizing; legalization: ... *an eventual decriminalization of marijuana* (Science News).

de·rail·leur (dē rā′lər); *French* dä-rä yér′), *n.* a device on a bicycle which moves the chain from one gear to another: *There are dozens of varieties, makes, and models of derailleurs in use today* (Lawrence Teeman). [< French *dérailleur* < *dérailler*; see DERAILMENT]

dis·e·con·o·my (dis′i kon′ə mē), *n., pl.* **-mies.** something that is economically harmful, inefficient, or unprofitable; misuse of the economy: *The old stock example of a diseconomy ... was the factory pouring out smoke and grime to the detriment of the family washing on the line* (Sunday Times).

dys·to·pi·a (dis tō′pē ə), *n.* the opposite of a utopia; a place or condition that is bad or imperfect: *It may be that only a vision of Utopia can combat the dystopia of contemporary life* (Time). [< *dys-* + (u)*topia*]

E

Earth Day, a day in April set aside by environmentalists to dramatize the need for pollution control. The first Earth Day in the U.S. was April 22, 1970.

ego trip, *Informal.* something done mainly to show off or boost one's self-esteem: *Like most records of rock musicians ... it's a harmless, if superfluous, ego trip* (New Yorker). *There is much more ... in this primary than these "ego trips" by diverse political personalities* (New York Times).

energy crisis, a critical shortage in the supply of energy-producing fuels such as gas, oil, and coal, due to their increased consumption, the depletion of natural resources, a decline in coal mining and in oil and gas exploration, and other economic factors.

en·gi·neered food (en′jə nird′), food made from vegetable or synthetic substances to supplement or replace existing foods, such as meat, milk, and eggs, that are too expensive, scarce, or not sufficiently nutritious; fabricated food: *The development of distinctly new types of foods, often designated as engineered or fabricated foods, was stimulated by the school lunch program* (Howard P. Milleville).

eth·nic (eth′nik), —*n.* a member of a racial, cultural, or national minority: *All sports are now saturated with ethnics* (Harper's). *The new populism finds romance in the "ethnics"—Poles, Czechs, Hungarians, Italians, and even Irishmen* (Time).

Eu·ro·bond (yur′ō bond′), *n.* a bond issued by an American or other non-European corporation for sale in European countries: *Issued abroad by both U.S. and foreign companies and usually payable in dollars, Eurobonds are used to tap the $60 billion in American money that is sloshing around Europe* (Time).

F

fab·ri·cat·ed food (fab′rə kā′tid), engineered food.

fi·do or **FI·DO** (fī′dō), *n., pl.* **-dos** or **-DOS.** a coin minted with an error or defect. [< *f*(reaks), *i*(rregulars), *d*(efects), *o*(ddities); coined by Edward V. Wallace, an American numismatist]

frag (frag), *v.,* **fragged, frag·ging,** *n.* *U.S. Army Slang.* —*v.t., v.i.* to kill or injure (one's superior officer or a fellow soldier), especially by using a fragmentation grenade. —*n.* a fragmentation grenade: *When MPs were called in to quell the riot at Camp Baxter, they found ... sequestered about the camp stocks of frags* (Saturday Review).

free school, a privately operated school in which traditional methods of teaching are discarded in favor of the open classroom and other experimental forms of education: *In hundreds of tiny private "free" schools ... the fixed rows of desks and the fixed weekly lessons have been abandoned* (Time).

G

GDP (no periods) or **G.D.P.,** gross domestic product.

Gi·ro or **gi·ro²** (ji′rō, zhir′ō), *n.* a postoffice service in Great Britain and various European countries, which provides subscribers with a computerized system of money transfer similar to a checking account. [< German *Giro* <

Italian *giro* circulation, ultimately < Greek *gŷros* circle]

gross domestic product, *Economics.* the gross national product minus the net payments on foreign investments: *In 1971 the combined gross domestic product (GDP) of the less developed countries grew at the rate of 6.9%* (Irving S. Friedman).

group·ie (grü′pē), *n. Slang.* **1.** a teen-age girl who is a fan of rock 'n' roll singing groups and follows them wherever they perform. **2.** a teen-age fan who follows any celebrity wherever he appears: *Flocks of pretty chess groupies gathered for a glimpse of him* [Bobby Fischer] *outside the Presidente Hotel.*

H

human growth hormone, a synthetic form of the pituitary hormone somatotropin, which regulates growth of the human body. It was first synthesized in 1970. *The creation of the synthetic "human growth hormone" (H.G.H.) was the work of Dr. Choh Hao Li and Dr. Donald Yamashiro, of the hormonal research laboratory of the University of California* (London Times).

I

im·pound (im pound′), *v.t.* **4.** to seize or hold back, especially by legal means: *The Administration moved to impound the funds of discontinued government programs.*

incomes policy, a government policy designed to combat the inflationary spiral by various means short of full controls on wages and prices: *An "incomes policy" ... might involve presidential persuasion to hold down wages and prices, the establishment of industry-composed wage guidelines, or the publicizing of statistics that point up exceedingly high wage or price increases* (Norman Thompson).

information science, the study of the means by which information is collected, processed, and transmitted through computers and other automatic equipment: *Information science ... is concerned with devising means for providing more efficient access to documents and improving the dissemination of information* (Harold Borko).

ISBN (no periods), **1.** International Standard Book Number (a system for numbering newly published books, widely adopted by publishers to facilitate their ordering, mailing, etc.) **2.** a number in this system.

J

job action, *U.S.* an action by workers, such as a refusal to do a certain type of work, taken to express a grievance or to enforce a demand: *The Uniformed Fire Officers Association yesterday voted a* "*job action*"—*the refusal to perform nonfire-fighting duties—to back up demands for more manpower* (New York Times).

K

KREEP or **kreep** (krēp), *n.* a yellow-brown glassy mineral found on the moon: *Another Apollo 12 find of general agreement was that of an exotic component called KREEP by some—for high content of potassium, rare earth elements and phosphorus—found in ... material dated about 4.5 billion years old* (Science News). [< *K* (symbol for potassium) + *R*(ar)*E-E*(arth) + *P*(hosphorus)]

L

laun·der (lôn′dər, län′-), *v.t.* **2.** to rid of any taint; make seem innocent, legitimate, or acceptable: [*He*] *developed the world network of couriers ... that allows the underworld to take profits from illegal enterprises, to send them halfway around the world and then have the money come back laundered clean to be invested in legitimate business* (Atlantic).

letter bomb, a letter whose envelope or contents hold an explosive material designed to detonate on being opened and kill the person opening it, used especially by terrorists: *All the letter bombs received in the London and Paris embassies had been posted in Amsterdam* (London Times).

Local Group or **local group,** a cluster of galaxies that appear to be bound together by gravity, including the Milky Way, the Magellanic Clouds, the spiral nebula in Andromeda, and some smaller associated galaxies: *Our own galaxy is a member of the "local group," an association of about 20 galaxies, only one of which, the Andromeda galaxy, has a mass comparable to that of ours* (Scientific American).

lunar rover, a vehicle for exploratory travel on the moon's surface: *Apollo 15 was first of three missions to transport heavier payloads than the earlier flights and to carry an electric-powered vehicle resembling a golf cart, called Lunar Rover* (William Hines).

M

Maf·fe·i galaxy (mä fā′ē), either of two large galaxies which are part of the Local Group, discovered in 1971. One is an elliptical and the other a spiral galaxy; they are about 3 million light-years away from earth. *The Maffei galaxies, obscured by the Milky Way dust, appear as small, diffuse patches* (Hyron Spinrad). [< Paolo *Maffei*, an Italian astrophysicist who first called attention to the galaxies in 1968]

meg·a·vi·ta·min (meg′ə vī′tə-min), *adj.* of or based on the use of very large doses of vitamins to control disease: *Megavitamin treatment for schizophrenia* (Science News). *It is my opinion that in the course of time it will be found possible to control hundreds of diseases by megavitamin therapy* (Linus Pauling).

meson factory, any of a class of particle accelerators designed to produce intense beams of mesons with which to probe the nuclei of atoms: *A new generation of machines, called meson factories, should yield a sharper dimension in the study of what goes on in atomic nuclei* (Science News).

microwave oven, an oven for baking food with heat produced by microwaves: *Microwave ovens take 50 per cent more power than conventional ovens ... A five-pound roast can be cooked in a microwave oven in one-fifth the time required by a conventional oven and with one-half the energy* (Saturday Review).

min·i·com·put·er (min′ē kəm-pyü′tər), *n.* a small, low-cost, general-purpose computer that can be used alone or linked to a larger computer or computers: *Minicomputers are now available with power equivalent to the fastest commercial third-generation computers.*

mod·em (mod′əm, mō′dəm), *n.* a device used in telecommunication to convert digital signals to analogue form and vice versa: *Modems ... adapt alphanumeric information (letters and numerals) for transmission over standard voice channels* (Scientific American). [blend of *mod*(ulator) and *dem*(odulator)]

N

Na·der·ism (nā′də riz əm), *n.* the championing of consumerism, or consumer protection, especially by investigating and exposing practices detrimental to consumers in large companies and organizations: *The emergence of a sort of British hybrid of Naderism is apparent in the way Rio Tinto-Zinc and other major United Kingdom companies are the target of increasingly strident criticism* (London Times). [< Ralph *Nader*, born 1934, an American lawyer and champion of consumerism + *-ism*]

neu·ro·trans·mit·ter (nur′ō-trans mit′ər, nyur′-; -tranz-), *n.* a chemical substance that transmits impulses between nerve cells: *Norepinephrine is a neurotransmitter, a substance responsible for carrying a signal across the gap between two neurons. Neurons that use norepinephrine as a neurotransmitter have a role in the control of mood, learning, blood pressure, heart rate, blood sugar, and glandular function* (Science News).

NOW (no periods), National Organization for Women (a Women's Liberation group founded in 1966).

Pronunciation Key: h**a**t, **āge, c<u>a</u>re, f<u>ä</u>r; l**e**t, **ē**qual, t**ė**rm; **i**t, **ī**ce; h**o**t, **ō**pen, **ô**rder; **oi**l, **ou**t; c**u**p, p**u̇**t, r**ü**le, **ū**se; **ch**ild; lo**ng**; **th**in; **т**н**e**n; **zh**, measure; **ə** represents **a** in about, **e** in taken, **i** in pencil, **o** in lemon, **u** in circus.

585

O

open admission, *U.S.* the admission of any high school graduate to a college or university, regardless of his grades or academic standing: *In recent years pressure for open admission—particularly for disadvantaged nonwhite urban youths—has been increasing* (Fred M. Hechinger).

open classroom, *U.S.* a classroom, especially at the elementary level, in which the activities are completely informal and the teacher's function is to guide or advise rather than to give formal instruction: *An open classroom means ... that learning is not dependent at every level on the presence of a teacher* (Ned O'Gorman).

open university, *U.S.* a college or university without regular classroom instruction. Students receive instruction through mailed assignments, tape recordings, television, independent study, and periodic guidance and testing sessions at designated locations.

O·von·ic or **o·von·ic** (ō von'ik), *adj.* of or based upon the property shown by certain glasses of switching from a state of high electrical resistance to one of low resistance upon the application of a particular voltage to the glass: *Ovonic devices, Ovonic switches.* [< Stanford R. *Ov*(shinsky), an American inventor, who discovered the Ovonic property + (electr)*onic*]

O·von·ics or **o·von·ics** (ō von'iks), *n.* the use or application of Ovonic devices.

P

par·ton (pär'ton), *n. Nuclear Physics.* a hypothetical part or constituent of a proton or neutron: *It takes very high energy even to get evidence of the individuality of partons, let alone to pull them apart* (Science News). [(coined by Richard P. Feynman, an American physicist) < *part* + *-on*, as in *proton, nucleon*]

phar·ma·co·ge·net·ics (fär'mə-kō jə net'iks), *n.* the study of the interaction of drugs and the genetic makeup of the persons using them: *Pharmacogenetics ... showed that the fate of a drug in the body, or even the nature and extent of its therapeutic effect, depends in certain cases upon a discrete genetic trait* (Sumner M. Kalman).

play·group (plā'grüp'), *n.* an informal type of nursery school organized privately, often by working parents, at a home or in a neighborhood church or other establishment: *As more and more playgroups open each year, parents are beginning to invest in the tougher, more imaginative toys* (London Times).

port·a·ble 2. having to do with or designating a pension plan under which a worker's contributions and privileges are carried over from one job or employer to another: *a portable pension plan or legislation.*

Pro·vo (prō'vō), *n., pl.* **-vos.** a member of an extreme militant faction of the Irish Republican Army (IRA), active chiefly in Northern Ireland. [shortened form of *Provisional*, part of the name of this faction]

psy·cho·ger·i·at·rics (sī'kō jer'ē-at'riks), *n.* the study of the psychological problems and mental illnesses of old age: *In the expanding field of psychogeriatrics these drugs will ... help to replace the present fear of death with the possibility of educating patients into the acceptance of their own forthcoming end* (New Scientist).

Q

quad·ra·phon·ic (kwod'rə fon'-ik), *adj.* of or having to do with sound transmission or reproduction using four different channels: *Your car will, in addition to ordinary stereo, have equipment for the playing of quadraphonic cartridges* (London Times).

R

re·leas·ing factor (ri lē'sing), a substance that triggers the release of hormones from an endocrine gland: *There appears to be a chemically distinct releasing factor for each of the six anterior pituitary hormones* (New Scientist).

ro·bot·ics (rō bot'iks), *n.* the science or technology that deals with robots: *There has been some excellent progress in robotics—the study of computer-controlled robots ... programmed to "see" (some things), to "hear," and even to "speak" (some sounds)* (Alan L. Perlis).

S

Saturday night special, *U.S.* a kind of inexpensive, widely sold, handgun: *A Senate subcommittee on juvenile delinquency voted ... a proposal that would outlaw the public sale of "Saturday night specials," cheap and ubiquitous pistols* (Time).

Sky·lab (skī'lab'), *n.* the first earth-orbiting space station of the United States, launched in 1973: *Skylab ... carries scientific experiments in the fields of astronomy, space physics, biology, oceanography, water management, agriculture, forestry, geology, geography, and ecology* (R.P. Abramson). [< *Sky* + *lab*(oratory)]

smack[4] (smak), *n. U.S. Slang.* heroin. [origin uncertain]

stag·fla·tion (stag flā'shən), *n. Economics.* a condition of continuous inflation combined with a stagnant rate of business and industrial expansion: *Inflation in West Germany, driving up prices by an average 6% annually, was turning into "stagflation"* (Andreas Dorpalen).

street value, the cost of a product in illegal trafficking or on the black market: *the street value of heroin, the street value of bootleg cigarettes.*

T

tax shelter, an investment, depletion allowance, or other means used by a person or company to reduce or avoid liability to income tax: *Other Administration proposals chip away at ... such tax shelters as farm losses and certain trust income* (Time).

to·ka·mak (tō'kə mak), *n.* a device for producing controlled thermonuclear power, in which highly ionized gas is confined in an endless tube by magnetic fields generated by electric currents flowing through the gas: *Medium-density plasma containers with a toroidal geometry include the stellarators, originally developed at the Princeton Plasma Physics Laboratory, and the tokamaks, originally developed at the I.V. Kurchatov Institute of Atomic Energy near Moscow* (Scientific American). [< Russian *tokamak*]

to·tal *U.S. Slang,* to wreck beyond repair; destroy totally: *The car was totaled in the crash.* **2.** *U.S. Slang.* to be totally destroyed: *The car almost totaled in the crash.*

U

ul·tra·fiche (ul'trə fēsh'), *n., pl.* **-fich·es, -fiche** (-fēsh'), a strip of microfilm containing extremely reduced images of printed matter: *Ultrafiches of the photochromi microimage process store up to 4,000 pages on a 4 in. by 6 in. film and provide complete industrial data compilations on a pocket scale* (London Times). [< *ultra-* + (*micro*) *fiche*]

V

val·ue-ad·ded tax (val'yü ad'id), a form of national sales tax that is levied on the increase in value or price of a product at every stage in its manufacture and distribution. The cost of the tax is added to the final price and is eventually paid by the consumer. *Many European countries have a value-added tax, a kind of national sales levy that pounds up prices on everything from shoelaces to plumbing repairs* (Time). *Abbr.:* VAT (no periods).

VAT (no periods), value-added tax.

vision phone, *Especially British.* videophone.

W

wind[2]**—wind down,** *Informal.* **a.** to reduce by degrees; bring or come gradually to an end: *to wind down space exploration. Now ... the war is supposed to be "winding down"* (New York Times). **b.** to relax; unwind: *to wind down tensions.*

Z

zeit·ge·ber (tsīt'gā'bər), *n., pl.* **-ber** or **-bers.** *Biology.* any time indicator, such as light, dark, or temperature, that influences the workings of the biological clock: *Light is considered by many researchers to be the most critical external timer or zeitgeber* (Joan Lynn Arehart). [< German *Zeitgeber* (literally) time giver]

Section Seven

Index

How to Use the Index

This index covers the contents of the 1972, 1973, and 1974 editions of
THE WORLD BOOK YEAR BOOK.

Each index entry is followed by the edition year (in *italics*) and the page
numbers, as:
  BURMA, *74–235, 73–247, 72–255*

This means that information about Burma begins on the pages indicated
for each of the editions.

An index entry that is the title of an article appearing in THE YEAR BOOK is
printed in capital letters, as: **AUTOMOBILE.** An entry that is not an article
title, but a subject discussed in an article of some other title, is printed: **Pollution.**

The various "See" and "See also" cross references in the index list are to
other entries within the index. Clue words or phrases are used when two or
more references to the same subject appear in the same edition of THE YEAR
BOOK. These make it easy to locate the material on the page, since they refer to
an article title or article subsection in which the reference appears, as:
  Nutrition: dentistry, *74–289*; food, *74–321*

The indication *"il."* means that the reference is to an illustration only. An index
entry in capital letters followed by *"WBE"* refers to a new or revised WORLD BOOK
ENCYCLOPEDIA article that is printed in the supplement section, as:
  MEXICAN AMERICANS, *WBE, 74–561*

A

M

INDEX

Washington, D.C., 72-552. See also **CIVIL RIGHTS; Protests; Terrorism.**
Virginia: elections, 72-335; Republican Party, 72-494; state government, 74-488, 73-512
Virtanen, Artturi I., 74-286
Virus: chemistry, 73-261; medicine, 73-415, 72-426
VISTA, 73-469, 72-476
VISUAL ARTS, 74-526, 73-547, 72-549; *Close-Up,* 74-529; motion pictures, 73-424
VITAL STATISTICS, 72-551; population, 72-475. See also **CENSUS.**
Vitamins: biochemistry, 74-225, 73-238; drugs, 74-304; food, 73-341
Volcano: geology, 74-331, *il.,* 72-364; Iceland, 74-352; space exploration, 72-510
Volkov, Vladimir N., 72-314
Volleyball, 74-485, 73-509, 72-517
Von Békésy, Georg, 73-299
Von Braun, Wernher, 73-506
Vorster, Balthazar Johannes, 74-480
Australia, 74-206
Voting: elections, 73-320, 72-333; Europe, 74-316, 72-348; Haiti, 74-341; U.S. Constitution, 72-543; women, 73-151. See also **ELECTIONS.**

W

Wages: agriculture, 74-189; Austria, 74-207; automobile, 74-208; economy, 73-29, 311; Great Britain, 74-336; labor, 74-372, 73-387, 72-401; Luxembourg, 74-391; Mexico, 74-399; Poland, 74-443; postal service, 74-446; South Africa, 74-479. See also **LABOR.**
Wailing Wall, *il.,* 73-382
Waksman, Selman A., 74-286
WALDHEIM, KURT, 73-550; United Nations, 73-539, 72-541
WALLACE, GEORGE CORLEY, 73-550, 72-552; American Party, 73-205, 72-211; Democratic Party, 73-300; elections, 73-321; Republican Party, 73-483
Walters, Jack, 72-384
Walther, David (Salt), 74-209
Walton, Bill, 74-222
Wang Hung-wen, 74-254
Wankel engine, 74-208, 73-223; boating, 74-226
War: Asia, 73-218; Cambodia, 72-256; India, 72-385; Korea, South, 72-405; Laos, 72-405; national defense, 72-446; Pakistan, 72-459; religion, 72-493. See also **ARMED FORCES OF THE WORLD; NATIONAL DEFENSE; Vietnam War.**
War Power Act: Congress, 74-263
WARNER, JOHN W., 73-550
Warren, Constance, 72-314
Warren, Fuller, 74-286
Warsaw Pact: armed forces, 73-212, 72-217; Europe, 74-314, 73-336, 72-346; Hungary, 73-369; Russia, 74-469
Washington (state): Jackson, Henry M., 72-395; state government, 74-488, 73-512, 72-519
Washington, Booker T., 74-397
WASHINGTON, D.C., 74-530, 73-550, 72-552; architecture, 74-195, 72-215; building, 72-252; Fauntroy, Walter E., 72-352; memorials, 72-429; music, 72-440; state government, 74-488
Waste disposal: Chicago, 72-279; city, 74-259; environment, 72-341
Water: Afghanistan, 72-199; China, 72-66; conservation, 74-271, 72-299; weather, 74-552
Water pollution: consumer affairs, 73-283; environment, 74-310, 73-327, 72-341; Girl Scouts, 72-556; ocean, 73-443
Water Pollution Control Act, Federal, 74-310
Water polo, 74-485, 73-509
Water skiing, 74-485, 73-509, 72-517
Watergate: Baker, Howard Henry, Jr., 74-216; Cabinet, U.S., 74-235; Congress, 74-269; consumer affairs, 74-273; courts and laws, 74-274; Democratic Party, 73-301; elections, 74-304; Ervin, Samuel James, Jr., 74-311; games, 74-330; international trade, 74-360; newspapers, 74-421; Nixon, Richard M., 74-422; President of the U.S., 74-449; Protestant, 74-453; Republican Party, 74-461, 73-484; Richardson, Elliot L., 74-464; Sirica, John J., 74-477; state government, 74-487; television, 74-501; U.S. government, 74-520
Waterways: environment, 72-341; Malaysia, 73-408
Watkins, Arthur V., 74-286

Weapons. See **ARMED FORCES; Guided missiles; NATIONAL DEFENSE.**
WEATHER, 74-535, 73-551, 72-552; agriculture, 74-189; disasters, 72-320; space exploration, 72-513
WEBER, JOSEPH, 72-553
Webster, Margaret, 73-299
Webster, Sir David, 72-314
Weddings: Canada, *il.,* 72-258; Nixon, Richard M., 72-454
Weeks, Sinclair, 73-299
Weight lifting, 74-484; Olympic Games, 73-450; sports, 73-508, 72-517
WEINBERGER, CASPAR W., 74-536; Cabinet, 74-235; education, 73-248; poverty, 74-446; President of the U.S., 73-474
Weiskopf, Tom, 74-335
Weitz, Paul J., 74-202; space exploration, 74-480
Welch, Mickey, 74-222
Welfare. See **CHILD WELFARE; SOCIAL WELFARE.**
Wellington, Duke of, Gerald Wellesley, 73-299
Welty, Eudora, 73-397
Werner, Pierre, 74-391
West African Economic Community: Africa, 74-180, 73-198; Dahomey, 73-289
West Germany. See **GERMANY, WEST.**
WEST INDIES, 74-536, 73-552, 72-554
West Virginia, 74-488, 73-512
Western Union Telegraph Company, 74-262
Westminster Kennel Club, 74-436
Westwood, Jean: Democratic Party, 73-301
Whaling: fishing industry, 73-340; ocean, 73-444
Whaling Commission, International, 74-321
Wheat: agriculture, 74-186, 72-206; Argentina, 74-196; *Special Report,* 72-60
Wheat, Zack, 73-299
White, Kevin H.: Boston, 72-248; elections, 72-334
White, Patrick, 74-423
White, Paul Dudley, 74-286
White House "plumbers," 74-451, 532
White House tapes, 74-533; Sirica, John J., 74-477
Whitehead, Clay T., 72-528; civil rights, 74-260
Whitelaw, William: Northern Ireland, 74-424
WHITLAM, EDWARD GOUGH, *il.,* 74-356, 73-553; Australia, 74-205, 73-219; Canada, 74-241; Pacific Islands, 74-428
Whitworth, Kathy, 74-335
Wigman, Mary, 74-280
Wildlife, 73-282; conservation, 74-270, 72-299; hunting and fishing, 74-351, 73-369, 72-384; zoology, 72-557; zoos, 74-542
Williams, Dick, 74-220
Williams, Ralph Vaughan, 73-258
Williams, Randy, 73-528
Williams, Tennessee, 72-533
Willis, Edwin E., 73-299
Wilson, Edmund, 73-299
Wilson, (James) Harold, 72-370
Wilson, Mitchell, 74-286
Wilson, Richard, 74-354
Winchell, Walter, 73-299
Windsor, Edward, Duke of: deaths, 73-294; Great Britain, 73-359
Wine, 73-343, 72-514
Winter sports, 72-517. See also **Bobsledding; Curling; HOCKEY; ICE SKATING; SKIING.**
Wiretapping: courts and laws, 73-285, 72-288; President of the U.S., 74-450
Wisconsin: conservation, 72-298; hunting and fishing, 72-384; state government, 74-488, 73-512, 72-519
Women: advertising, *il.,* 72-199; child welfare, 74-252, 72-280; civil rights, 74-260, 72-287; Congress, 72-296; courts and laws, 72-302; education, 74-303, 72-332; Europe, 74-316, 72-348; fashion, 74-318; golf, 74-335; Houston, 74-350; Ireland, 72-393; Jews, 74-367; King, Billie Jean, 74-370; labor, 74-374; Luxembourg, 74-391; Latting, Patience, 72-410; Norway, 72-457; Protestant, 74-454, 72-484; Roman Catholic, 74-466, 72-497; space exploration, 74-482; Spain, 73-507; state government, 74-490, 73-511; Switzerland, 72-525; tennis, 74-504, 73-525; U.S. Constitution, 73-541; visual arts, 72-551; *WBE,* 73-580
Women's Hall of Fame, 74-260
WOMEN'S LIBERATION MOVEMENT: *Special Report,* 73-151; architecture, 74-193; civil rights, 74-260; Steinem, Gloria, 73-515
Women's Political Caucus, National, 74-260
Wooden, John, *il.,* 74-222
Woodhull, Victoria Claflin, 73-152
Worden, Alred M.: astronauts, 72-223; space exploration, 73-506, 72-510

World Bank, 74-446, 73-468
World Book-Childcraft of Canada, Limited, 74-245
World Book Dictionary, 74-583, 73-603, 72-601
World Book Encyclopedia: supplement, 74-543, 73-559, 72-559
World Council of Churches: Africa, 72-201; ecumenism, 73-172; Potter, Philip A., 73-468; Protestant, 74-452, 73-475; religion, 74-460, 73-482; Roman Catholic, 73-487
World Court, 74-519, 73-541, 72-543
World Environment Day, 74-310
World Football League, 74-326
World Health Organization, 74-343, 73-309, 72-377
World Hockey Association, 74-345
World Series, 74-220, 73-233, 72-239
World Trade Center, 74-420
Wottle, Dave: Olympic Games, 73-446; track and field, 73-528
Wounded Knee: *Close-Up,* 74-355; civil rights, 74-260; Indian, American, 74-354; Protestant, 74-454
Wrestling, 74-485; Olympic Games, 73-450; sports, 73-508, 72-517
Wylie, Philip G., 72-314
Wyoming, 74-488, 73-512

X

X rays: astronomy, 74-203, 72-224; photography, 74-441
Xerox, 74-394

Y

Yablonski, Joseph A., 74-374
Yachting: boats and boating, 74-227, 73-240; Olympic Games, 73-450
Yad Vashem, *il.,* 74-334
Yahya Khan, Agha Mohammed: Asia, 72-222; Pakistan, 73-452, 72-459
Yasgur, Max, 72-466
Yellowstone National Park, 73-281
YEMEN (ADEN), 74-537, 73-553; Yemen (San'ā'), 74-537. See also **SOUTHERN YEMEN, PEOPLE'S REPUBLIC OF.**
YEMEN (SAN'Ā'), 74-537, 73-553, 72-554; Yemen (Aden), 74-537
Yevtushenko, Yevgeny, *il.,* 73-465
Yom Kippur, 74-400
Yorty, Samuel W.: Bradley, Thomas, 74-230; Democratic Party, 72-316; Los Angeles, 74-390, 72-420
Young, Chic, 74-286
Young, Coleman A., 74-290, *il.,* 305
Young, Sheila, 74-351
Young, Whitney M., Jr.: civil rights, 72-286; deaths, 72-314
YOUNG MEN'S CHRISTIAN ASSOCIATION, 74-537, 73-554, 72-555
YOUNG WOMEN'S CHRISTIAN ASSOCIATION, 74-538, 73-554, 72-555
Youth: Africa, 72-204; child welfare, 72-279; city, 72-285; elections, 72-333; motion pictures, 72-437; PTA, 72-461; Protestant, 72-483; Red Cross, 72-491; religion, 72-491; state government, 72-519; U.S. affairs, 72-26; U.S. Constitution, 72-543
YOUTH ORGANIZATIONS, 74-538, 73-554, 72-555; service clubs, 73-497; Young Men's Christian Association, 74-537, 73-554, 72-555; Young Women's Christian Association, 74-538, 73-554, 72-555
YUGOSLAVIA, 74-539, 73-556, 72-557; anthropology, 74-192; Australia, 74-206; Bulgaria, 74-234; Czechoslovakia, 74-277; Hungary, 72-383

Z

Zahir Shah, Mohammed: Afghanistan, 74-179; Iran, 74-361
ZAIRE, 74-540, 73-556; Africa, 74-180. See also **CONGO (KINSHASA).**
ZAMBIA, 74-541, 73-557, 72-557; Africa, 73-198, 72-202; Rhodesia, 74-464; South Africa, 72-509
Zero population growth: census, U.S., 74-248; population, 73-466
Ziegler, Karl, 74-286
ZOOLOGY, 74-541, 73-557, 72-557; archaeology, 72-212; conservation, 72-299
ZOOS AND AQUARIUMS, 74-542, 73-558, 72-558

Acknowledgments

The publishers acknowledge the following sources for illustrations. Credits read from left to right, top to bottom, on their respective pages. An asterisk (*) denotes illustrations created exclusively for THE YEAR BOOK. All maps, charts, and diagrams were prepared by THE YEAR BOOK staff unless otherwise noted.

3	Library of Congress; Dennis Brack, Black Star
8	Wide World
9	Wide World; *New York Daily News*
10	Wide World; Wide World; NASA
11	Pictorial Parade; Wide World
12	Wide World; S. Julienne, Sygma
13	J. P. Laffont, Sygma; Wide World; Keystone
14	Wide World
16	Jackson Zender*; Wide World
17	Boris Spremo*
18-19	Wide World
20	Pictorial Parade
21	Wide World
22	Jackson Zender*; Wide World
23	Robert Isear*
24	Wide World
25	United Press Int.
26	Wide World
28	Jackson Zender*; Wide World
29	Robert Isear*
30	Wide World
31	Keystone
32	Marshall Berman*
33	Keystone
34	Jackson Zender*; Pictorial Parade
35	Gene Trindl*
36	The University of Wisconsin
37	Sygma
38	NASA
40	Jackson Zender*; Wide World
41	Dan Budnik*
42	Gilbert Meyers*
43	Lee Balterman
44	WORLD BOOK photo*
46	Jackson Zender*; Martha Swope
47	Dan Budnik*
48	Theatre Guild
49	Richard Gray Gallery
50	Wide World
51	Pictorial Parade
52	Jackson Zender*; Wide World
53	J. R. Eyerman*
54-55	Wide World
56	WORLD BOOK photo*
58-69	José Gonzales Prieto*
70	Raúl Anguiano
71-73	José Gonzales Prieto*
77	George Hall, Woodfin Camp, Inc.
79	Standard Oil Company (Indiana)
80-81	WORLD BOOK photo*; Jerry Howard, DPI; Jon Brenneis
82	George Hall, Woodfin Camp, Inc.
83	Marvin Newman, Woodfin Camp, Inc.
85	Jon Brenneis
86-87	Dan Budnik, Woodfin Camp, Inc.; Adam Woolfitt, Woodfin Camp, Inc.; Jon Brenneis
88	Dan Budnik, Woodfin Camp, Inc.
89	Standard Oil Company (Indiana); Jon Brenneis
90	George Hall, Woodfin Camp, Inc.
94-98	Fred Leavitt*
99	Joseph Erhardt*
100	Fred Leavitt*
101	Marshall Berman*
102-105	Joseph Erhardt*
106-119	Bill Charmatz*
120-121	Stoll Thrust Theatre, University of Minnesota; George E. Joseph; Marshall Berman*; Marshall Berman*; M. L. Carlebach from Nancy Palmer; Marshall Berman*; Hank Kranzler, American Conservatory Theater; Marshall Berman*; Marshall Berman*
123	Culver Pictures; NBC-TV
124	Zodiac; Bert Andrews
126	Hank Kranzler, American Conservatory Theater
127	Marshall Berman*
128	Harold Whyte
129	Marshall Berman*
130	George E. Joseph; Marshall Berman*; M. L. Carlebach from Nancy Palmer; Charles Warren, Smoky Mountain Passion Play Assoc.
131	V. Kersh*
132-134	Marshall Berman*
136	Rus Arnold*; Marshall Berman*; Marshall Berman*; Marshall Berman*; Jim Richardson*; Marshall Berman*
139	Wide World
140	Rus Arnold*
141	Marshall Berman*
144-145	Jim Richardson*
147-150	Marshall Berman*
153-164	Alan E. Cober*
168-170	Historical Pictures Service
171	Culver Pictures
172	Bettmann Archive
173	Historical Pictures Service
174	Remington Rand; Culver Pictures Service; Historical Pictures Service
175	Historical Pictures Service
178	Wide World
179	Foote, Cone & Belding
181	Sygma
182	Camerapix from Keystone
185-186	Wide World
188	Stephen Gates, *Memphis Commercial Appeal*
190-193	Wide World
194	Sears, Roebuck and Company
195	Ezra Stoller © Esto
196	Liaison
198	Henri Bureau, Gamma
201	Wide World
204-206	Australian Information Service
207	William Mauldin, © 1973 *Chicago Sun-Times*
209	Wide World
211	American Airlines
212	Sygma
214	*Ladies' Home Journal*
216	Pictorial Parade
219	Robert R. McElroy, *Newsweek*
220	Wide World
222	United Press Int.
225	National Institutes of Health
227	Wide World
230	United Press Int.
233	Pictorial Parade
234	Keystone
236-237	United Press Int.
241	Wide World
243	Royal Canadian Mounted Police
244	United Press Int.
247	Historical Pictures Service
248	Gary Settle, *The New York Times*
251	Edmund Jarecki, *Chicago Daily News*
253	S. Julienne, Sygma
255	Wide World
256	Jan M. Rosen, *The New York Times*
257	William Vandivert
260-263	Wide World
264-265	J. P. Laffont, Sygma
269	United Press Int.
270	William Mauldin, © 1973 *Chicago Sun-Times*
271	Union Camp Corporation
272	Perry Riddle, *Chicago Daily News*
274	United Press Int.
275-276	Wide World
278-279	National Ballet of Canada
280	Ted Yaple, Erick Hawkins Dance Company
281	Mark Gerson; Wide World; Wide World; Wide World
282	Wide World

A Preview of 1974

January

S	M	T	W	T	F	S
		1	2	3	4	5
6	7	8	9	10	11	12
13	14	15	16	17	18	19
20	21	22	23	24	25	26
27	28	29	30	31		

1 **New Year's Day.**
6 **Epiphany,** 12th day of Christmas, celebrates visit of the Three Wise Men.
20 **Jaycee Week** through January 26, marks founding of Jaycees.
21 **World Religion Day,** emphasizes need for world religious unity.
93rd Congress convenes for second session.
23 **Chinese New Year,** begins year 4672 of the ancient Chinese calendar, the Year of the Tiger.

February

S	M	T	W	T	F	S
					1	2
3	4	5	6	7	8	9
10	11	12	13	14	15	16
17	18	19	20	21	22	23
24	25	26	27	28		

1 **National Freedom Day.**
American Heart Month through February 28.
Boy Scouts of America Anniversary Celebration through February 28.
2 **Ground-Hog Day.** Legend says six weeks of winter weather will follow if ground hog sees its shadow.
12 **Abraham Lincoln's Birthday,** observed in 26 states.
Holiday of the Three Hierarchs. Eastern Orthodox holy day, commemorating Saints Basil, Gregory, and John Chrysostom.
14 **Saint Valentine's Day,** festival of romance and affection.
15 **Susan B. Anthony Day,** commemorates the birth of the suffragist leader.
16 **National FFA Week,** through February 23, publicizing the role of Future Farmers of America in U.S. agriculture.
17 **Brotherhood Week** to February 24.
18 **George Washington's Birthday,** according to law is now legally celebrated by federal employees, the District of Columbia, and 42 states on the third Monday in February, not on the actual anniversary, the 22nd.
26 **Mardi Gras,** last celebration before Lent, observed in New Orleans and many Roman Catholic countries.

27 **Ash Wednesday,** first day of Lent, the penitential period that precedes Easter.

March

S	M	T	W	T	F	S
					1	2
3	4	5	6	7	8	9
10	11	12	13	14	15	16
17	18	19	20	21	22	23
24	25	26	27	28	29	30
31						

1 **Easter Seal Campaign** through April 14.
Red Cross Month through March 31.
World Day of Prayer.
3 **Save Your Vision Week** through March 9.
8 **Purim,** commemorates the saving of Jews through the death of the ancient Persian despot Haman.
10 **Girl Scout Week,** through March 16, marks the 62nd birthday of U.S. Girl Scouts.
17 **St. Patrick's Day,** honoring the patron saint of Ireland.
Camp Fire Girls Birthday Week, to March 23, marks 64th birthday of the organization.
20 **First Day of Spring,** 8:07 P.M., E.D.S.T.
21 **Earth Day,** opens yearlong program to replenish the earth.
31 **National Boys' Club Week** through April 6.

April

S	M	T	W	T	F	S
	1	2	3	4	5	6
7	8	9	10	11	12	13
14	15	16	17	18	19	20
21	22	23	24	25	26	27
28	29	30				

1 **April Fools' Day.**
Cancer Control Month through April 30.
7 **Palm Sunday,** marks Jesus' final entry into Jerusalem along streets festively covered with palm branches.
Holy Week, through April 3, commemorates the Crucifixion and Resurrection of Jesus Christ.
Passover, or Pesah, first day, starting the 15th day of the Hebrew month of Nisan. The eight-day festival celebrates the deliverance of the ancient Jews from bondage in Egypt.
11 **Maundy Thursday,** celebrates Christ's injunction to love each other.
12 **Good Friday,** marks the death of Jesus. It is observed as a public holiday in 17 states.
14 **Easter Sunday,** commemorating the Resurrection of Jesus Christ.
Pan American Week through April 20.

21 **National Library Week** through April 27.
26 **National Arbor Day.**
30 **Walpurgis Night,** according to legend, the night of the witches' Sabbath gathering in Germany's Harz Mountains.

May

S	M	T	W	T	F	S
			1	2	3	4
5	6	7	8	9	10	11
12	13	14	15	16	17	18
19	20	21	22	23	24	25
26	27	28	29	30	31	

1 **May Day,** observed as a festival of spring in many countries.
Law Day, U.S.A.
Mental Health Month through May 31.
5 **National Music Week** through May 12.
12 **Mother's Day.**
13 **Salvation Army Week** through May 19.
18 **Armed Forces Day.**
22 **National Maritime Day.**
23 **Ascension Day,** 40 days after Easter Sunday, commemorating the ascent of Jesus into heaven.
26 **Indianapolis 500-Mile Race** in Indianapolis, Ind.
27 **Memorial Day,** according to law, is the last Monday in May.
Shabuot, Jewish Feast of Weeks, marks the revealing of the Ten Commandments to Moses on Mt. Sinai.

June

S	M	T	W	T	F	S
						1
2	3	4	5	6	7	8
9	10	11	12	13	14	15
16	17	18	19	20	21	22
23	24	25	26	27	28	29
30						

2 **Whitsunday,** or Pentecost, the seventh Sunday after Easter, commemorating the descent of the Holy Spirit upon Jesus' 12 apostles.
3 **Stratford Festival,** drama and music, Ontario, Canada, through October 19.
6 **D-Day,** commemorates the day the Allies landed to assault the German-held continent of Europe in 1944.
9 **National Flag Week** through June 15.
14 **Flag Day,** commemorates the adoption of the Stars and Stripes in 1777 as the official U.S. flag.
15 **Queen's Official Birthday,** marked by trooping of the colors in London.
16 **Father's Day.**
21 **First Day of Summer,** 2:38 P.M., E.D.S.T.
27 **Freedom Week** through July 4.

A Preview of 1974

July

S	M	T	W	T	F	S
	1	2	3	4	5	6
7	8	9	10	11	12	13
14	15	16	17	18	19	20
21	22	23	24	25	26	27
28	29	30	31			

1 **Dominion Day** (Canada) celebrates the confederation of the provinces in 1867.
Battle of Gettysburg commemorative ceremonies in Gettysburg, Pa., through July 7.

4 **Independence Day**, marks Continental Congress's adoption of Declaration of Independence in 1776.

14 **Bastille Day** (France), commemorates popular uprising against Louis XVI in 1789 and seizure of the Bastille, the infamous French prison.
Captive Nations Week through July 20.

15 **Saint Swithin's Day.** According to legend, if it rains on this day, it will rain for 40 days.

20 **Moon Day,** the anniversary of man's first landing on the moon in 1969.

26 **Salzburg International Music and Drama Festival,** Salzburg, Austria, through August 30.

28 **Tishah B'ab,** Jewish fast day, on ninth day of Hebrew month of Ab, marking Babylonians' destruction of the First Temple in Jerusalem in 587 B.C.; Roman destruction of the Second Temple in A.D. 70; and Roman suppression of Jewish revolt in 135.

August

S	M	T	W	T	F	S
				1	2	3
4	5	6	7	8	9	10
11	12	13	14	15	16	17
18	19	20	21	22	23	24
25	26	27	28	29	30	31

14 **V-J Day** (original), marks Allied victory over Japan in 1945.

15 **Feast of the Assumption,** Roman Catholic and Eastern Orthodox holy day celebrates the ascent of the Virgin Mary into heaven.

18 **Edinburgh International Festival,** music, drama, and film, through September 7.

19 **National Aviation Day.**

26 **Women's Equality Day,** commemorating the ratification of the 19th Amendment, giving women the vote.

September

S	M	T	W	T	F	S
1	2	3	4	5	6	7
8	9	10	11	12	13	14
15	16	17	18	19	20	21
22	23	24	25	26	27	28
29	30					

2 **Labor Day** in the United States and Canada.

17 **Citizenship Day.**
Constitution Week, through September 23, commemorates the signing of the U.S. Constitution in Philadelphia, on Sept. 17, 1787.
Rosh Hashanah, or Jewish New Year, the year 5735 beginning at sunset. It falls on the first day of the Hebrew month of Tishri and lasts for two days.

18 **Ramadan** begins, the ninth month of the Moslem calendar, observed by fasting.

23 **First Day of Autumn,** 5:59 A.M., E.D.S.T.

26 **Yom Kippur,** or Day of Atonement, most solemn day in the Jewish calendar, marking the end of the period of penitence.

27 **American Indian Day,** honoring native Americans.

October

S	M	T	W	T	F	S
		1	2	3	4	5
6	7	8	9	10	11	12
13	14	15	16	17	18	19
20	21	22	23	24	25	26
27	28	29	30	31		

1 **Sukkot,** or Feast of Tabernacles, begins the nine-day Jewish observance, which originally celebrated the end of harvest season.
Harvest Moon, the full moon nearest the autumnal equinox of the sun, shines with special brilliance for several days and helps farmers in the Northern Hemisphere to get more field work done after sunset.

6 **National Employ the Physically Handicapped Week** through October 12.
National 4-H Week through October 12.
Fire Prevention Week through October 12.

9 **Leif Ericson Day,** honoring early Norse explorer of North America.

13 **National Cleaner Air Week** through October 19.
National Y-Teen Week through October 19.

14 **Thanksgiving Day,** Canada.
Columbus Day commemorates Columbus' discovery of America in 1492. Previously celebrated on October 12.

20 **American Education Week** through October 26.

28 **Veterans Day,** observed on the fourth Monday in October.

31 **Halloween,** or All Hallows' Eve.
Reformation Day, celebrated by Protestants, marks the day in 1517 when Martin Luther nailed his Ninety-Five Theses of protest to the door of a church in Wittenberg, Germany.
United Nations Children's Fund (UNICEF) Day.

November

S	M	T	W	T	F	S
					1	2
3	4	5	6	7	8	9
10	11	12	13	14	15	16
17	18	19	20	21	22	23
24	25	26	27	28	29	30

1 **All Saints' Day,** observed by the Roman Catholic Church.
Christmas Seal Campaign through December 31.

5 **Guy Fawkes Day** (Great Britain) marks the failure of a plot to blow up King James I and Parliament in 1605 with ceremonial burning of Guy Fawkes in effigy.
Election Day.

7 **Anniversary of 1917 Bolshevik Revolution,** Russia's national holiday, through November 8.

11 **National Children's Book Week** through November 17.

28 **Thanksgiving Day,** United States.

December

S	M	T	W	T	F	S
1	2	3	4	5	6	7
8	9	10	11	12	13	14
15	16	17	18	19	20	21
22	23	24	25	26	27	28
29	30	31				

1 **Advent,** first of the four Sundays in the season preceding Christmas.

2 **Pan American Health Day.**

6 **Saint Nicholas Day,** when children in parts of Europe receive gifts.

9 **Hanukkah,** or Feast of Lights, eight-day Jewish holiday beginning on the 25th day of the Hebrew month of Kislev that celebrates the Jewish defeat of the Syrian tyrant Antiochus IV in 165 B.C. and the rededication of The Temple in Jerusalem.

10 **Human Rights Week** through December 17.
Nobel Peace Prize Presentation, in Oslo, Norway.

15 **Bill of Rights Day,** marks the ratification of that document in 1791.

21 **First Day of Winter,** 1:57 A.M., E.D.S.T.

25 **Christmas.**

31 **New Year's Eve.**